Routledge Handbook of Political Management

The *Routledge Handbook of Political Management* is a comprehensive overview of the field of applied politics, encompassing political consulting, campaigns and elections, lobbying and advocacy, grassroots politics, fundraising, media and political communications, the role of the parties, political leadership, and the ethical dimensions of public life. While most chapters focus on American politics and campaigns, there also are contributions on election campaigns in Europe, the Middle East, Russia, Australia, East Asia, and Latin America. In addition to a thorough treatment of campaigns and elections, the authors discuss modern techniques, problems, and issues of advocacy, lobbying, and political persuasion, with a special emphasis throughout the volume on technology, the Internet, and online communications as political tools.

Grounded in the disciplines of political science, political communications, and political marketing, this book explores the linkages between applied politics and social science theory. Leading American and international scholars and practitioners provide an exhaustive and up-to-date treatment of the state of this emerging field. This publication is a major resource for advanced undergraduates, graduate students, and scholars of campaigns, elections, advocacy, and applied politics, as well as for political management professionals.

Dennis W. Johnson is professor of political management and former associate dean of the Graduate School of Political Management, George Washington University. He is author of *Congress Online, No Place for Amateurs*, and *The Laws that Shaped America* (forthcoming). He is editor of *2008 Presidential Election* (forthcoming) and author (with Gary Nordlinger) of *Campaigning in the Twenty-first Century* (forthcoming). He is also senior editor of the *Journal of Political Marketing* and serves on the editorial boards of the *Journal of Information Technology and Politics* and the *Journal of Public Affairs*. He is a member of the American Association of Political Consultants, the International Association of Political Consultants, and the European Association of Political Consultants.

Routledge Handbook of Political Management

Edited by
Dennis W. Johnson
The George Washington University

Routledge
Taylor & Francis Group

NEW YORK AND LONDON

First published 2009
by Routledge
711 Third Avenue, New York, NY 10017

Simultaneously published in the UK
by Routledge
2 Park Square, Milton Park, Abingdon, Oxon OX14 4RN

First issued in paperback 2012

Routledge is an imprint of the Taylor & Francis Group, an informa business

© 2009 Taylor & Francis; individual chapters, the contributors

Typeset in Bembo by
Swales & Willis Ltd, Exeter, Devon

Library of Congress Cataloging in Publication Data
Routledge handbook of political management / edited by Dennis W. Johnson.
    p. cm.
    Includes bibliographical references and index.
    1. Politics, Practical—Handbooks, manuals, etc. 2. Political consultants—Handbooks, manuals, etc.
    3. Political campaigns—Handbooks, manuals, etc. 4. Campaign management—Handbooks, manuals, etc.
    5. Elections—Handbooks, manuals, etc. I. Johnson, Dennis W.
    JF2051.R758 2008
    324.7—dc22
                                    2008008169

ISBN13: 978–0–415–96225–4 (hbk)
ISBN13: 978–0–203–89213–8 (ebk)
ISBN13: 978-0-415-52294-6 (pbk)

Contents

Part 3: Campaigns Worldwide

Part 4: Lobbying, Advocacy, and Political Persuasion

Part 5: Political Parties, Political Management, and Democracy

List of Illustrations

Figures

Tables

Permissions

Chapter 14 is an excerpt from Nicholas J. O'Shaughnessy and Stephan C. Henneberg, "The Selling of the President 2004: A Marketing Perspective," *Journal of Public Affairs* 7 (3) (August 2007): 249–68. Copyright 2007, John Wiley & Sons, Ltd. Permission to reprint was kindly granted.

"Stouthearted Men" by Sigmund Romberg and Oscar Hammerstein II.
Copyright © 1927 by Harms, Inc.
Copyright Renewed.
The Oscar Hammerstein II interest assigned to Bambalina Music Publishing Co.
(administered by Williamson Music) for the extended renewal copyright term in the USA.
International Copyright Secured. All Rights Reserved.

Introduction

Dennis W. Johnson

Political management is a growing field of study at American colleges and universities, and in institutions of higher education throughout the world. Political management is sometimes referred to as applied politics or applied political science; in the field of communications it is referred to as applied political communications; and in the disciplines of commerce and marketing it is referred to as political marketing.

Whatever the academic label, scholars and students are showing increased interest in understanding how modern sophisticated elections are carried out, how activists are using the latest tools of electronic advocacy, how corporations and non-profits are tapping into the skills and practices of political campaigners, and how throughout the world there is a growing professionalization of election campaigns.

This *Handbook* brings together forty-nine of the leading scholars and practitioners from throughout the world to discuss the growing importance of political consultants, modern campaign techniques, and the growing revolution in technology in campaigns, public policymaking, and governance.

Part 1 gives a general overview of the field of political management and looks at it from the perspective of three academic disciplines. Chapter 1 is an overview of American political consulting, from its inception in the 1930s to recent times. In this chapter, I discuss the early days of political consulting, show how the business has developed over the years, and how it has branched out from candidate elections to several other fields. In Chapter 2, Paul S. Herrnson and Colton C. Campbell survey the dimensions of present-day election campaigns in the United States. Among other things they discuss the role of political parties and group efforts in election campaigns, and analyze the effect of campaigns on election outcomes. Fritz Plasser, in Chapter 3, surveys elections globally, analyzing, among other things, the professionalization of campaigns throughout the world, the changing models of campaign practices, and the worldwide activities of campaign consultants.

In the next three chapters, political management is analyzed within the context of the theories and scholarly literature of three fields of study. Stephen C. Craig surveys the literature of political science in Chapter 4. A growing body of political science research explores the ways that campaigns shape voter behavior and election outcomes. In a related field, Lynda Lee Kaid, in Chapter 5, demonstrates how political management has had "long-standing ties" to applied political communications and to the discipline of political communications. In Chapter 6, Wojciech Cwalina, Andrzej Falkowski, and Bruce I. Newman look at the scholarly record of their field, political marketing, and show how it and political management both have similar grounding and where they differ.

The second part of the *Handbook* deals with American political campaigns and elections. In Chapter 7, David Dulio and Terri L. Towner write about the permanent campaign. Campaigning in the United States, especially for the presidency, seems to go on forever, starting well over a year before the general election, and in some cases, not even ending once the president is elected to office. Much has changed in the way campaigns are conducted, and some of biggest changes have come in the area of technology, from the early days of radio and television, to computer-assisted telephone interviewing, e-mail and YouTube videos. Stephen K. Medvic explores the evolving challenges and opportunities of the technological revolution in Chapter 8. One of the most important elements of political communication is finding the right message and breaking through the clutter of thousands of other messages that people receive each day. Brian C. Tringali in Chapter 9 outlines several of the sophisticated techniques used in modern campaigns to determine what works and what does not.

Just a generation ago, political communication was fairly straightforward: radio, the three television networks, newspapers, and print material. That was the "stone age," writes Peter Fenn in Chapter 10, which surveys how profoundly media communication has changed and what new challenges await candidates for public office. They are called "monster PACs," the new political action committees that have been created in the last decade that bring in an extraordinary amount of money and political clout. In Chapter 11, Steve Billet examines these PACs and discusses their influence and motives. Nearly thirty years after the landmark 1974 Campaign Finance Reform amendments, Congress enacted new campaign reform legislation. It was meant to cure some of the excesses in campaign spending, such as so-called soft money. But, as Anthony Gierzynski writes in Chapter 12, the new law, the Bipartisan Campaign Reform Act (BCRA), not only created needed reforms, but also led to several unintended campaign spending consequences. One of the most important evolutions—some might say revolutions—in campaign communication has been the use of the Internet and online communication. Emilienne Ireland, in Chapter 13, discusses how the Internet has developed as an indispensable communications tool, and how it is transforming the way campaigns are conducted.

The 2004 presidential election saw the use of the most sophisticated communication tools in this extraordinarily tight battle between George W. Bush and John Kerry. Nicholas J. O'Shaughnessy and Stephan Henneberg, in Chapter 14, analyze this extravagant, bitter, and expensive contest from the perspective of business marketing, the candidates as products, and the impact of advertising. Television advertising can be extraordinarily expensive, and in a presidential campaign, literally hundreds of millions of dollars are spent trying to persuade voters through this medium. In Chapter 15, Robin Kolodny and Michael Hagen examine the data of television buying and try to resolve this question: what drives the cost of political advertising? Running for office, particularly in modern times, is a difficult, complex, and often frustrating experience. Ronald A. Faucheux, who himself has been a statewide officeholder as well as a veteran political consultant, looks at the difficulties of seeking office in Chapter 16.

For years, conservatives have poured money and support into recruiting the next generation of leaders and followers, and in developing core conservative values and ideas. Kathleen Barr, in Chapter 17, argues that if Democrats and progressives are to take back power, they must have the ideas, money, and infrastructure to beat conservatives and Republicans at their own game. For nearly three decades, there has been a growing activism among Christian conservatives and others who consider themselves part of the Religious Right. They form a key bloc of strength in the Republican Party, and their values and issues have done much to shape the national agenda. Mark J. Rozell in Chapter 18 looks at the historical roots of the Religious Right and its impact today.

Part 3 looks at elections and campaigning throughout the world. Fritz Plasser and Günther Lengauer in Chapter 19 survey the importance of television advertising and television coverage of elections on a worldwide basis. Despite the rise of the Internet and other online communication, Plasser and Lengauer argue that television continues to be the "driving force" in campaigning throughout the world. Mobile telephone technology has been used in many parts of the world to advance political participation and political causes. In many ways, the United States is relatively behind the times in mobile technology. Julie Barko Germany and Justin Oberman in Chapter 20 discuss what the rest of the world can teach America in using mobile phones for political causes.

Dominic Wring in Chapter 21 looks at modern British campaigns, and the enormous influence that political consultants and marketers have had in campaigns, especially during the Margaret Thatcher and Tony Blair eras. In Chapter 22, Marco Althaus looks at modern campaign techniques in Germany. The political parties have lost some of their grip and influence, and in German elections there is a new reliance on informal networks, viral marketing and ad hoc campaigning. Dahlia Scheindlin and Israel Waismel-Manor look at how Israeli elections have been transformed and particularly look at the role and influence of American political consultants in Chapter 23. In December 2007, Vladimir Putin won overwhelming support in parliamentary elections amid widespread cries of voter fraud and government abuse. Derek S. Hutcheson in Chapter 24 looks at this election and puts it into the context of modern Russian elections and campaign techniques.

In Chapter 25, Ian Ward looks at the growing professionalization of campaigning and elections in Australia. He concludes that Australia, like other advanced democracies, is heading into a new postmodern phase, with greater reliance on consultants and a more presidential-like focus on party leaders. Louis Perron, in Chapter 26, looks at recent political campaigns in the Philippines. Often characterized as loud, boisterous affairs, Philippine campaigns are in fact a "fascinating mix of traditional patronage politics and modern high tech campaigns." In Chapter 27, Christian Schafferer surveys the growing dimensions of modern campaigning in the Asian market, with a particular focus on electioneering in Taiwan. Eduardo Robledo discusses the triumph of Vicente Fox and the defeat of the long-ruling party PRI in the 2000 elections. In Chapter 28, he discusses whether this was the result of a long transition or a sudden triumph of political marketing.

Part 4 turns to lobbying, advocacy, and political persuasion. Lobbying has long been a staple in American political life. In Chapter 29, Conor McGrath and Phil Harris give an historical analysis of how the lobbying industry was created, showing that lobbying and influence peddling have been central to American politics for a very long time. One of the newest and most promising forms of communication and advocacy comes from online resources. Brad Fitch in Chapter 30 discusses the best practices of online advocacy for associations, non-profit organizations, and corporations. One of the most important and sometimes difficult of tasks is to form and keep together a group of like-minded individuals who can be called on to voice their concerns to officeholders. In Chapter 31, Edward A. Grefe discusses the building of constituencies for advocacy in the United States and in other democracies.

Douglas Lathrop in Chapter 32 discusses the growing use of political consultants in the field of issue advocacy. He discusses how political consultants have become involved in this field, their effectiveness in affecting public policy, and the larger implications for the legislative process and governance. Military and defense spending are an extraordinary component of the US federal budget. Julius W. Hobson, Jr, in Chapter 33, uses a case study of the Crusader artillery system to see the interplay of politics, national priorities, and hardball lobbying. Marco Althaus looks at grassroots advocacy in the European Union. In Chapter 34, he writes that while still in its infancy, grassroots advocacy is changing the dynamics of European business and politics.

In Part 5, we look at political parties, political management, and democracy. Maik Bohne, Alicia Kolar Prevost, and James A. Thurber look at the interplay of political consultants and American political parties. They conclude in Chapter 35 that consultants have played an important role in keeping political parties strong, but have changed the dynamic by injecting a "fluid, non-hierarchical, and loosely-coupled network structure." One of the most important developments in recent American campaigns is identifying likely voters and get-out-the-vote (GOTV) efforts. Peter Ubertaccio in Chapter 36 argues that if both parties use network marketing techniques they may help reverse the trend of declining party organizations. In Chapter 37, Jennifer Lees-Marshment looks at the governments of Tony Blair in the UK and Helen Clark in New Zealand, and discusses how both leaders, with varying degrees of success, have used market-orientation techniques. Phil Harris, Conor McGrath, and Irene Harris reach back to Niccolo Machiavelli to discuss what they characterize as "Machiavelli marketing." In Chapter 38, they argue that political marketing, good governance, lobbying, ethics, and effective communication with the consumer are "all issues developed from an understanding of Machiavelli's thought."

Scandal, personal shortcomings, and ethical lapses are recurring themes in American campaigns and public affairs. Candice J. Nelson in Chapter 39 discusses such nefarious problems and the attempts to reform American campaigns and the legislative process. The final chapter, by Bonnie Stabile and Susan Tolchin, looks at a persistent problem in American life, the angry, cynical citizen. Using a case study of the debate over stem cell research and other biotechnologies, Chapter 40 addresses the question of how to win over a cynical public.

At the end of the book, in About the Editor and Contributors, there are short biographical statements for each of the authors and the editor. In addition, there is a comprehensive list of Resources that were cited in the forty chapters.

Part 1

The Field of Political Management

American Political Consulting

From its Inception to Today

Dennis W. Johnson

Today in the United States, political consulting is a vibrant, mature business that plays a key role in shaping and managing political campaigns. Political consultants measure public opinion, design television and web advertisements, target and identify likely voters, raise campaign funds, write blogs and maintain websites, and research the records of candidates and opponents. They use their skills and experience to develop sound messages and overarching campaign themes, to formulate and carry out campaign strategy, and above all, to help their candidate achieve victory. A very select few political consultants are household names; but the vast majority work behind the scenes, unseen and unknown to the general public. Some consultants are generalists, responsible for the overall running of a successful campaign; but the large majority of consultants are specialists who focus on a particular aspect of a campaign.

Political consultants have used their skills, experience, and techniques to move beyond candidate races, such as contests for governor, senator, or president. Consultants now reach down the electoral food chain and assist candidates at the local level of government. They work in the growing market of ballot initiatives, where issues are voted upon, rather than candidates. American consultants have branched out to candidate elections in other countries, and they have increasingly been involved in issue advocacy battles, both at the federal and the state level of policy making. In addition, corporations concerned about their image or those that find themselves engaged in a tough policy fight have turned to political consultants for assistance.

Early Years of Political Consulting

For much of the early years of US history, the political parties were the central focus of campaigns, fundraising, and organization. As Paul S. Herrnson and Colton C. Campbell write in Chapter 2, during the earlier part of the twentieth century the political party began giving way to the individual candidate. Candidates hired their own campaign managers and brought on people who could help raise money or could round up voters and get them to the polls. Very often, these campaign workers were volunteers, often friends or co-workers of the candidates. In many instances, they worked for free, or for the love of politics, or the admiration of the candidate. Some had good political instincts, had politics in their blood, and made valuable contributions.

But who would do this for a living, going from campaign to campaign, offering skills and services? Election scholars generally consider that the beginning of political consulting as a business was a husband–wife firm called Campaigns, Inc., created in the early 1930s. Clem Whitaker, a newspaper publicist, and his wife, Leone Baxter, who had worked for a local chamber of commerce, pioneered the use of campaign publicity in California elections. Whitaker and Baxter helped their clients win state-wide referenda, they developed grassroots lobbying techniques to pressure state lawmakers, and employed nasty opposition research tactics against author-activist Upton Sinclair, who was running for California governor. Later, they helped defeat California governor Earl Warren's proposal for a state-wide medical insurance plan; and in perhaps their biggest triumph, Whitaker and Baxter were hired by the American Medical Association to fight against President Harry Truman's 1948 plan for national health insurance.[1] In all, Whitaker and Baxter won seventy out of seventy-five of the campaigns for which they were hired.

Whitaker and Baxter had created a new business. They helped define messages, shape campaigns, spread the message to constituents, and influence lawmakers through grassroots pressure. They did this during nearly every election cycle, for a variety of mostly conservative clients, both individual candidates for office and corporate causes. Nevertheless, Whitaker and Baxter considered themselves in the business of public relations, not political consulting. For the most part, they had the business to themselves during the 1930s and 1940s.

Especially with the advent of television, candidates and parties turned to public relations specialists. During the 1952 presidential election, Dwight D. Eisenhower and Adlai E. Stevenson turned to New York advertising agencies to help craft their message for this new medium.[2] Professional assistance was now filtering down to other elections as well. By 1957, Alexander Heard found that forty-one public relations firms were offering campaign services.[3]

Soon, however, others not working for public relations firms would become involved in the business of politics. Joseph Napolitan, a former sports writer for a local Massachusetts newspaper turned campaign professional, was probably the first operative to be called a "political consultant." By and large, those who began to call themselves political consultants were generalists, who managed campaigns, perhaps wrote radio or television scripts, and helped formulate campaign strategy. By the late 1950s, David L. Rosenbloom found that perhaps thirty or forty professionals were managing campaigns, and like Napolitan, those who stayed with the business cycle after cycle, were the foundation of the political consulting business.[4]

A few political scientists, like Rosenbloom, began to take notice. Writing in 1956, Stanley Kelley, Jr was one of the first political scientists to recognize the importance of campaign consultants. In the 1970s, Dan Nimmo and David L. Rosenbloom discussed the first years of campaign management, followed by Larry Sabato's seminal book on the rise of political consultants in 1981.[5]

Polling for Candidates

Survey research is the key to that most important of campaign questions: what is on peoples' minds? Not surprisingly, polling research was one of the first tools sought after by political parties, candidates, and even office holders. Yet, during the 1930s and 1940s political polling and campaign predictions had fallen on tough, skeptical audiences. During the 1936 presidential election, a popular magazine, *The Literary Digest*, boldly predicted that governor Alf Landon of Kansas would readily beat incumbent president Franklin D. Roosevelt. Roosevelt overwhelmed Landon, carrying the electoral votes of forty-six out of forty-eight states in one of the most lop-sided elections in the twentieth century, and the popular magazine folded in disgrace. Pollster George Gallup, using more reliable scientific techniques, correctly predicted the Roosevelt landslide, but in 1948, like nearly every other close observer, predicted that incumbent president Harry Truman would lose to New York governor Thomas E. Dewey. Survey researchers Gallup, Archibald Crossley, and Elmo Roper all had made the mistake of stopping their polling well before the election, and missing the surge in Truman support during his fabled "whistlestop" campaign.

Despite the flaws of survey research, Franklin Roosevelt used the services of in-house pollsters Emil Hurja and Hadley Cantril. In the 1950s, Eisenhower relied indirectly on the services of the Gallup polling organization. But it wasn't until the 1960 presidential campaign that a major candidate, John F. Kennedy, employed a professional pollster, Louis Harris. Harris had become a private political pollster in the late 1950s, and helped guide the 1960 campaign of Kennedy. By 1963, exhausted from the demands of private political polling, Harris abandoned private political polling and began writing a weekly newspaper column, worked with national news organizations, and created the Harris Poll.[6] Up until this time, polling was still done through personal interviews and time-consuming number crunching; only during the late 1960s would telephone interviews become the norm, and even later would technologies such as the CATI system (computer assisted telephone interviews) and random-digit dialing be employed.

Private polling became an integral part of election campaigns during the 1960s and early 1970s, and a small number of pioneering survey researchers set up shop. On the Democratic side, William R. Hamilton (Hamilton and Staff)[7] began polling in 1964; Patrick Caddell (Cambridge Survey Research) became the pollster for the 1972 presidential campaign of George McGovern. Peter D. Hart (Hart Research) has polled for an extraordinary range of Democratic candidates. Since 1974, Hart has served as an election consultant to CBS News and has conducted polls for the *Wall Street Journal*. Hart's campaign work comes through partner Geoff Garin, who heads Garin-Hart-Yang Strategic Research Group. At one time, roughly 80–90% of all Democratic private polling business emanating from Washington was done by the firms run by Hamilton, Caddell, and Hart. Of these firms, Garin-Hart-Yang remains at the forefront of the private political polling profession.

On the Republican side, there were four early private polling firms. Richard Wirthlin (Decision/Making/Information, then the Wirthlin Group) began in 1969 and was best known as an early adviser to Ronald Reagan. Robert M. Teeter (Market Opinion Research, Detroit), worked for a wide variety of candidates and was presidential pollster for Richard Nixon, Gerald Ford, and George H. W. Bush. Arthur Finkelstein worked closely with conservative Republicans, while V. Lance Tarrance (Tarrance, Hill, Newport, and Ryan, Houston) polled for Reagan's 1984 re-election and Republican clients in the South and West.

The techniques and sophistication of polling have evolved over the years. Survey research has been supplemented by focus group analysis, by dial-meter research, and more recently by mall testing techniques and online surveys. Today, polling and survey research is at the heart of any sophisticated, professionally run campaign. By 2007, there were approximately seventy-six firms who were in private polling and research business in the United States.[8]

Media Firms

When Dwight Eisenhower ran for president in 1952, his campaign turned to the New York advertising firms of Ted Bates & Company and Batten, Barton, Durstine, and Osborn (BBDO). Another early advertising firm used in presidential campaigns was Jack Tinker and Partners. During the 1960s, however, media firms were created that specialized in political campaigns.[9] One of the first such media consultants was Tony Schwartz, working closely with general consultant Joe Napolitan. Schwartz is best known for his "Daisy" commercial for the Lyndon Johnson presidential campaign of 1964. He is also the author of a seminal book on political advertising, *The Responsive Chord*.[10] Another pioneer media consultant was Charles Guggenheim, who began working for Democratic presidential candidate Adlai Stevenson in the 1956 election, then worked for a variety of liberal candidates and causes. By the early 1970s, however, Guggenheim was out of the business, burned out by the pace and disillusioned with the direction of political advertising.

Several of the pioneer media firms began working in the late 1960s, including David Garth (David Garth Associates, New York), Marvin Chernoff (Chernoff/Silver Associates, Columbia, South Carolina), Robert Squier (Squier and Associates, Washington, D.C.), Robert Goodman (The Goodman Group, Brookland, Maryland), Douglas Bailey and John Deardourff (Bailey/Deardourff, Washington, D.C.), and Roger Ailes (New York).

A second and third generation of media firms were created in the 1970s through 2000, and by 2007, there were seventy-eight media consulting firms working in American elections.[11] One veteran media advisor, who began working in the 1980s, Peter Fenn, outlines in Chapter 10, the extraordinary changes that have occurred in the media advertising business over the past twenty-five or thirty years.

Reaching Out to Voters

The Eisenhower presidential campaign in 1952 was the first to use direct mail in an effective way, but it wasn't until 1964, during the presidential campaign of Republican Barry Goldwater, that direct mail came into its own. From the lists of activist conservatives compiled during that campaign, Richard Viguerie was able to create a list of over 12,000 donors. In 1972, the presidential campaign of George McGovern was the first Democratic campaign to compile a large list of probable donors, and to use direct mail to solicit them. Since then, creating, expanding, and maintaining lists of supporters and donors has become big business for campaigns.

Apart from Viguerie, some of the pioneer direct mail firms were Butcher-Forde Consulting (Irvine, California), known for its work with the California Proposition 13 "tax revolt" in 1978; Roger Craver of Craver, Mathews, Smith, and Company (Vienna, Virginia), a Democratic firm, working with liberal Democratic causes. Probably the best known direct mail firm was Karl Rove and Associates, thanks to Rove's later high profile role in the Bush II White House. In 2007, there were 126 firms that engaged in political direct mail.[12]

For many years, Jack Bonner (Bonner and Associates, Washington, D.C.) and Walter Clinton (the Clinton Group, Washington, D.C.), dominated the field of political telemarketing. Today, there are twenty-eight firms that specialize in telephone and direct contact services.[13] Telemarketers provide services such as voter identification and persuasion, volunteer recruitment, fundraising, mobilization of activists, get-out-the-vote (GOTV) efforts, and coordination with direct mail activities. A tactic employed by some telemarketing firms has come in for heavy criticism: the use of push-polling. Under the guise of a legitimate poll, anonymous telephone marketers feed misleading or inaccurate information to voters receiving the telephone calls. This practice has been condemned by the American Association of Political Consultants; nevertheless, it still persists in isolated races.

Beyond Candidate Campaigns

Political consultants have also worked in ballot issue and direct democracy contests. Twenty-eight states and the District of Columbia provide for some form of direct citizen involvement in ballot measures, recalls, initiatives, or referendums. Further, eighteen states allow constitutional amendments offered by citizen initiative, and twenty-two states permit statutory amendments created by citizens. In recent years, citizens campaigns have placed before state voters such issues as term limits, gambling, ban on same-sex marriages, and campaign finance reform. A wide variety of issues has been resolved by direct citizen involvement. Among them, there have been efforts to ban cockfighting in Arizona, restrict the size of hog farms in Colorado, allow medical use of marijuana in Maine, restrict bear wrestling in Michigan, and to permit dental technicians to sell false teeth directly to patients in Florida.[14] In some cases, the ballot initiatives are handled on a purely voluntary, amateur basis. This was the original intent: the essence of populism, where citizens, acting alone or as concerned groups, would roll up their sleeves and have a direct voice in government and lawmaking. But for the most part, citizen initiative and control has been far overshadowed by costly, sophisticated campaigns.

Ballot initiatives have become big business: high-stakes, high-cost operations that involve professional political consultants throughout the election process. During the 2004 election cycle, $540 million was raised to mount direct democracy contests throughout the United States; during the 2006 cycle, the total was $648.4 million.[15]

Nowhere is this more true than in California, indeed the land of milk and honey for political consulting firms. Direct democracy became a part of the California constitution during the early years of the twentieth century, in response to the push for greater populism and citizen input. But for many years, Californians did not use the initiative, referendum, or recall provisions. That all changed in 1978, when Howard Jarvis and Paul Gann offered Proposition 13, a popular and successful measure that called for property taxes to be cut in half. Jarvis and Gann called in direct mail specialists William Butcher and Arnold Forde, who built up an impressive grassroots network of anti-tax advocates. Thereafter, ballot issues proliferated in the state. By 1988, California voters were faced with forty-one ballot questions when they went to the polls. By 2000, millions of dollars were poured into California ballot issues, mostly from corporate and business interests, and increasingly from business and labor interests nationwide.

In 2003, California governor Gray Davis was booted out of office, movie actor Arnold Schwarzenegger became the chief executive, and political consultants and television stations reaped a payday of $70 million before the recall fight was over.[16] In 2005, during an off-election year, where there were no candidate elections held in California, there were nonetheless eight contentious ballot issues. Altogether, those trying to defeat and those trying to pass the ballot measures spent an astounding $417.2 million. By contrast, all 2004 presidential candidates in the primaries and general election spent a total of $880.5 million.[17] The great share of the money spent on ballot initiatives went for television advertising, direct mail, billboards and newspaper ads, and GOTV drives. Special political skills were tapped as well: law firms specializing in the ballot initiative process, petition signature firms that gathered up millions of signatures for the measures to go on the ballot, and coalition building firms that lined up celebrities and sympathetic groups.

Down Ballot Campaigns

State-wide candidates (like those for governor, US senator, state attorney general), congressional candidates, and big city mayoral candidates aren't the only office seekers who use professional consultants. Starting in the 1990s, local candidates increasingly began to use the services of political consultants. Each week, *Congressional Quarterly*'s "Campaign Insider" would publish the names of candidates and the consultants that they had hired. Here is a profile of just one week: a candidate for the Harris County (Houston, Texas) commissioner, a candidate for Florida secretary of state, a candidate for the Texas Supreme Court, and a candidate for the Norfolk County (Massachusetts) district court each hired a professional media consultant. Candidates for the California Board of Equalization, the San Francisco Superior Court, and the South Carolina Agricultural Commission all hired consultants.[18]

Consultant services, of course, cost money, and the more professional services a campaign uses, the greater the cost of running the campaign. A well-financed multi-million dollar campaign can afford a full range of survey research and focus group studies, produce television spots, maintain a first-class website, use direct mail, hire a candidate and opposition research team, telemarketers, and fundraising specialists to keep the money coming in. By contrast, a campaign that has only a

$50,000 budget may be able to hire a campaign manager, send out a piece or two of direct mail, order yard signs and bumper stickers, but nothing else. As more and more down ballot candidates seek to employ campaign consultants, there is greater pressure to raise funds to pay for those services.

Issue Advocacy

Clem Whitaker and Leone Baxter paved the way for political consultants to work in issue campaigns, particularly with their successful work with the American Medical Association and its fight against so-called "socialized medicine" (a term coined by Whitaker).

Over the years, political consultants have been recruited to assist in issue fights and causes. Ironically, the next big issue management fight dealt with the same issue fought by Whitaker and Baxter in 1948. The campaign against the 1992–1993 Clinton national health care plan was particularly successful. The plan, created by the Clinton administration with First Lady Hillary Clinton as its public face, was a complex, unwieldy 1,342-page document. There were competing Democratic and Republican plans, and nearly every health care interest had endorsed some kind of proposal.[19] But the public simply didn't understand the Clinton program. In one pointed example, when members of a focus group heard the Clinton proposal described to them, 70% approved of it; when the name "Clinton" was attached to it, that very same proposal dropped by 30–40%. Big business organizations, originally interested in some sort of reform, turned against the Clinton plan. So, too, did the health care and insurance industries. Chief among the critics was the Health Insurance Association of America, which crafted an effective $15 million issue advocacy advertising program, featuring Harry and Louise, a well-read, concerned married couple sitting in their kitchen despairing over the supposedly unintelligible Clinton plan.[20] The Health Insurance Association had brought in Ben Goddard of Goddard-Claussen/First Tuesday, a California-based political consulting firm, to craft the "Harry and Louise" ads.

Since then, issue advocacy has been an important part of the portfolio of the political consulting business. As Doug Lathrop points out in Chapter 32, issue advocacy groups have spent over $400 million in a recent two-year session of Congress trying to get their views heard. Much of that money went directly to consulting firms that conducted the polling and focus groups, crafted the media advertising, and, just like in a candidate campaign, created the overarching themes and with discipline drove home the message.

International Campaigns

American political consultants have also brought their skills and experience to campaigns throughout the world. Joseph Napolitan was one of the first such consultants when he helped engineer a re-election victory for Ferdinand Marcos in the 1969 Philippine presidential election. Since then a steady flow of American consultants have worked in a wide variety of international elections. American consultants have worked in Canada, throughout Latin America, and as far away as the island of Mauritius. They have trained candidates in image building in Austria, crafted thirty-second television spots for candidates in Colombia, conducted focus group sessions in Italy, helped build party organizations in Hungary, and developed computerized voting files in Ireland.[21] A number of the authors in this *Handbook* have discussed the reach and impact of American consultants, and I invite you to read their analyses. In Chapter 26, Louis Perron discusses some of the challenges of the Philippine election process and looks at some of the American consultants in the post-Marcos era. Further, Dahlia Scheindlin and Israel Waismel-Manor discuss the Americanization of election campaigns in Israel in Chapter 23; Eduardo

Robledo discusses consultants and the 2000 Mexican election in Chapter 28; and in his overview of campaigns worldwide, Chapter 3, Fritz Plasser discusses the impact of growing professionalization.

As the following chapters will suggest, the business of political consulting will continue to flourish and grow, not only in the United States but also throughout the world. Despite occasional outbursts from lawmakers and the public about the need for clean-running elections and reform, the ineluctable fact is that candidates want, need, and for the most part appreciate the services and expertise provided by professional political consultants. Professional consultants are indispensable players in modern, sophisticated campaigns.

Notes

1 Stanley Kelley, Jr., *Professional Public Relations and Political Power* (Baltimore, MD: Johns Hopkins University Press, 1956); Carey McWilliams, "Government by Whitaker and Baxter: The Triumph of Chrome-Plated Publicity," *The Nation*, April 14, 21, May 5, 1951; Greg Mitchell, *The Campaign of the Century: Upton Sinclair's Race for Governor of California and the Birth of Media Politics* (New York: Random House, 1992); Walt Anderson, *Campaigns: Cases in Conflict* (Pacific Palisades, Calif.: Goodyear Publishing Company, 1970), ch. 7; Jim Newton, *Justice for All: Earl Warren and the Nation He Made* (New York: Riverhead Books, 2006); Monte M. Poen, *Harry S. Truman Versus the Medical Lobby: The Genesis of Medicare* (Columbia, MO: University of Missouri Press, 1979).

2 Edwin Diamond and Stephen Bates, *The Spot: The Rise of Political Advertising on Television*, 3rd ed. (Cambridge, MA: MIT Press, 1992).

3 Alexander Heard, *The Cost of Democracy* (Chapel Hill, N.C.: University of North Carolina Press, 1960), 418.

4 Napolitan personal communication with author; David L. Rosenbloom, *The Election Men: Professional Campaign Managers and American Democracy* (New York: Quandrangle Books, 1973), 51.

5 Kelley, *Professional Public Relations and Political Power*; Dan Nimmo, *The Political Persuaders: Techniques of Modern Election Campaigns* (Englewood Cliffs, N.J.: Prentice-Hall, 1970); Rosenbloom, *The Election Men*; Larry Sabato, *The Rise of Political Consultants: New Ways of Winning Elections* (New York: Basic Books, 1981); Dennis W. Johnson, "The Business of Political Consulting," in *Campaign Warriors: Political Consultants in Elections*, ed. James A. Thurber and Candice J. Nelson (Washington, D.C.: Brookings Institution Press, 2000), 37–52.

6 David W. Moore, *The Superpollsters: How They Measure and Manipulate Public Opinion in America* (New York: Four Walls Eight Windows, 1995); Lawrence Jacobs and Robert Y. Shapiro, "Issues, Candidate Image, and Priming: The Use of Private Polls in Kennedy's 1960 Presidential Campaign," *American Political Science Review* 88 (September 1994): 527–40; On the history of the political polling business, see William Hamilton, "Political Polling: From the Beginning to the Center," in *Campaigns and Elections American Style*, ed. James A. Thurber and Candice J. Nelson (Boulder, CO: Westview Press, 1995).

7 Throughout this chapter, the original name of the political consulting firm is given; many of the firms have gone through name changes as partners leave, are added, or the firm is merged with another.

8 "Political Pages, 2006–2007," *Campaigns and Elections* (March 2007). The numbers should be used only as a rough guide. See also, Johnson, *No Place for Amateurs*, 241–7, for a listing of the leading political polling firms.

9 Diamond and Bates, *The Spot*.

10 Tony Schwartz, *The Responsive Chord* (New York: Anchor Press/Doubleday, 1973).

11 "Political Pages, 2006–2007". See also, Johnson, *No Place for Amateurs*, 247–54, for a listing of the leading media firms.

12 "Political Pages, 2006–2007". See also, Johnson, *No Place for Amateurs*, 255–60, for a listing of the leading direct mail and fundraising firms.

13 Political Pages, 2006–2007". See also, Johnson, *No Place for Amateurs*, 261–2, for a listing of the leading political telemarketing firms.

14 Johnson, *No Place for Amateurs*, 195–208. On California ballot initiatives, Peter Schrag, *Paradise Lost: California's Experience, America's Future* (New York: The New Press, 1998). John Haskell, *Direct Democracy or Representative Government: Dispelling the Populist Myth* (Boulder, CO: Westview Press, 2001); David S. Broder, *Democracy Derailed: Initiative Campaigns and the Power of Money* (New York: Harcourt, 2000);

Richard J. Ellis, *Democratic Delusions: The Initiative Process in America* (Lawrence, KS: University Press of Kansas, 2002).

15 National Institute on Money and State Politics website, www.followthemoney.org.

16 Johnson, *No Place for Amateurs*, 195.

17 Data compiled from "California 2005 Ballot Measures," National Institute on Money and State Politics website.

18 Johnson, *No Place for Amateurs*, 211.

19 Paul Starr, "What Happened to Health Care Reform?" *The American Prospect* 20 (Winter 1995): 20–31.

20 Robin Toner, "Harry and Louise and a Guy Named Ben," *New York Times*, September 30, 1994, A22. See also, Darrell West, Diane Heath, and Chris Goodwin, "Harry and Louise Go to Washington: Political Advertising and Health Care Reform," *Journal of Health Politics, Policy and Law* 21 (1996): 35–6.

21 See Dennis W. Johnson, "Perspectives on Political Consulting," *Journal of Political Marketing* 1 (1) (2002): 16–20.

2

Modern Political Campaigns in the United States

Paul S. Herrnson and Colton C. Campbell

Elections are central to the struggle for power in democracies, and political campaigns bring meaning to those struggles. Like much of our political landscape, the participants, strategies, and campaign tactics involved in elections have shifted over time. Early campaigns were inexpensive, nonpartisan, and highly personalized events geared toward persuading a small percentage of the population. By contrast, many contemporary campaigns are orchestrated events that entail large sums of money, professional campaign organizations, political parties, interest groups, volunteers, and complicated targeting and marketing strategies involving millions of voters. The one principle that has remained relatively constant is that the candidate who garners the most votes wins. This winner–takes–all principle applied to the campaigns for colonial legislatures held prior to the United States' founding, and it continues to hold true for most contemporary elections. With some exceptions, most notably the requirement that presidential candidates win a majority of the Electoral College vote, it applies to nomination contests, general elections, and run-off elections.

The Strategic Environment and Electioneering

The types of campaigns that characterize a democracy are shaped by the strategic environment in which they take place.[1] This typically includes the constitutional design of the political system, the nature of the offices candidates seek, the laws and rules governing party nominations or general elections, and the relatively enduring aspects of a nation's political culture involving citizens' attitudes toward politics, politicians, political parties, and interest groups. The strategic environment also encompasses the methods available for candidates, parties, advocacy groups, and others participants in elections used to communicate with voters. These methods have evolved over time from word of mouth and pamphlets to television advertising to Internet web sites. A final element of the strategic environment is the immediate—and very fluid—political setting. This may involve national factors such as the state of the economy, presidential popularity, and the mood of the public, as well as local factors involving the partisanship and competitiveness of the district where an election is being held, whether an incumbent is seeking reelection, and local conditions and events.

The strategic environment influences the roles of candidates, political parties, and interest groups in the campaign process.[2] The institutional design of the American political system, including the separation of powers, federalism, bicameral legislatures, and the further decentralization of state and local offices, which formally separates elections for political offices from one another, allows for wide latitude in tailoring campaigns to fit state and local traditions, political conditions, and the preference of voters. It also tends to grant those who hold elected offices independent claims to exercise political power. These institutional features enable voters to hold individual officeholders accountable for their performance in office.

The US system contrasts sharply with the party-focused campaigns that are common in parliamentary democracies, such as Great Britain, which do not spread power to as many separate different political institutions or encourage voters to hold individual candidates responsible for their entire party's performance in office. (See Chapter 21, by Dominic Wring on British campaigns.) Moreover, the United States' single-member simple-plurality elections, in which the voters in a given district cast one vote and the candidate receiving the most votes wins, also encourage independence among candidates and officeholders and give voters the motivation to make discrete assessments of individual candidates for office.

The widespread use of these single-member simple-plurality elections also discourages the formation of third parties and minimizes their prospects for success, helping to reinforce the United States' two-party system. This system differs substantially from democracies such as Italy and Germany that use proportional representation, in which parties and political groups are allocated seats in legislative bodies in proportion to their share of the vote. (See, for example, Chapter 22, by Marco Althaus on German elections.) Proportional representation lends itself to the formation of many political parties, and by tying the electoral fortunes of candidates of the same party together it encourages those candidates to practice greater teamwork in elections than do US candidates.

Of course, the nature of election constituencies also influences the conduct of campaigns. Candidates running for offices that have small districts comprising few voters, such as a city council, can run campaigns consisting primarily of grassroots activities. Door-to-door canvassing, newsletter drops, house parties (also called "meet and greets"), and yard signs typically form the core of these campaigns. Meeting with local newspaper editorial boards can also be important. Candidates for offices that have geographically large districts, such as the presidency or statewide office, must run much more complex campaigns. The same is true of House members and candidates from large cities. These campaigns require considerably more planning, money, and professional expertise. Most rely on television, radio, direct mail, and mass telephone calls for communication. Even their grassroots efforts are influenced by complex voter targeting analyses.

The rules governing the nomination process strongly influence the types of campaigns that candidates wage.[3] Candidates who must win a party nomination through a primary election, as is used to select general election candidates in most states, or a caucus, like that used in Iowa, create campaign organizations to wage their nomination campaigns. Candidates who are selected in private meetings where dues-paying party members decide among themselves who should win the party nomination do not need to assemble an organization to mount a nomination campaign. The first approach, used in the contemporary United States, results in candidates possessing general election campaign organizations that are more or less independent of party committees. The second approach, which was used in the party-centered era in the US, and remains in use in most modern industrialized democracies, produces election campaigns that are primarily conducted by party committees rather than candidates.

Campaign finance especially shapes political campaigns. Whether campaigns rely on public funds furnished by the government, funds raised by political parties, or funds that candidates must raise from individuals, interest groups, party committees, or their own resources has a tremendous impact on campaign independence from other organizations and campaign conduct. Of course, campaign finance laws can have a significant impact on whom candidates turn to for money. The Bipartisan Campaign Reform Act of 2002 and its predecessors, including the Federal Election

Campaign Act of 1971 and its amendments, regulate the flow of money in presidential and congressional elections. (See Chapter 12, by Anthony Gierzynski on financing American elections.) Among other things, they determine which individuals and organizations can legally make contributions and expenditures in federal elections and, in some cases, establish limits for these transactions. Similar effects are due to the myriad of state and local laws that govern the financing of state and local campaigns. These laws are important. Not surprisingly, candidates who rely on public funds, including some presidential candidates, invest less time and energy in raising money than those who finance their campaigns with funds raised from private sources. Indeed, the money chase in most US elections is a campaign in and of itself. This sets the United States apart from most Western democracies, where parties raise most of the campaign money or receive the lion's share of the public campaign subsidies from the government. Campaigns in those nations are generally dominated by party committees; candidates are much less in the front and center in these party-focused campaigns.

Broader societal conditions also affect the nature of political campaigns. Public attitudes toward parties, candidates, and politics more generally influence the style and tenor of campaigns. Candidate-centered campaigns typically occur in locations and eras where the citizenry are ambivalent about parties and politics. Such campaigns are often characterized by populist themes or anti-government or anti-politician rhetoric. Party-focused elections are more prevalent in places and times where voters consider political parties part of the natural order of government and society, such as the nineteenth-century United States and contemporary Europe.

Finally, technology plays a very important role in the conduct of campaigns. Campaigns are first and foremost about communicating to and mobilizing voters to show up at the polls. As technology advances the methods available for voter outreach also improve. This has several other implications for campaigning. First, those with the most ready access to the means for reaching out to voters are among the most influential in elections. Thus, wealthy candidates, political parties, and interest groups are the most likely to benefit from technological innovation. Second, innovations can alter the balance of power between different participants in the election process. For example, television, with its potential for unmediated candidate-to-voter contact, increased the degree to which campaigns focus on candidates, as opposed to parties.[4] Third, technological improvements can lead to refinements in the planning and execution of campaign strategies. The advent of direct mail, e-mail, and computerized databases, for instance, provided candidates, parties, and interest groups with opportunities to tailor their appeals to specific groups of voters. (See Chapter 8, by Stephen K. Medvic on technology and campaigning.)

Political Campaigns in Early America

The first campaigns for public office in America were markedly different from those waged in the twenty-first century, in large part because the voting population was so different. Roughly 5% of the overall population was eligible to vote in colonial times, as voting was restricted primarily to white, male, Anglo-Saxon, Protestant, landowners. Additionally, politics was a part-time enterprise: colonial and later state legislatures conducted legislative business for just a few months each year and the compensation received by most elected officials was minimal to nonexistent, barely making up the time lost at their actual professions. Given this narrow electorate and the limited direct financial pay-off for elected officials and their followers, political campaigns were highly elitist, personal, and fairly inexpensive. They more closely resembled extended semi-private conversations among society's elite than the very public communications of contemporary campaigns that intrude on the lives of virtually everyone who owns a television. Political discussions took place without the benefit of political parties, campaign commercials, rallies, or large fundraising events.

Political campaigning in the new American states was not too dissimilar. Aspirants for public office held quiet meetings and corresponded with those few individuals who were eligible to vote. Campaign conversations generally were well-reasoned discussions of the great issues of the day between candidates and voters. In short, candidates did not take to the stump, there were no organized rallies, nor did candidates or parties launch full-blown public relations campaigns. Even the presidential elections of this period did not have the massive communications, voter registration, and get-out-the-vote (GOTV) drives that typify modern elections. Electioneering entailed a small number of gentleman candidates requesting the votes and political support of others similarly situated in society.

By the early 1820s through the early 1900s, however, the elite-level principled discussions of colonial days gave way to organized rallies, speeches, parades, and other popular events designed to convey a message and mobilize the masses. Party machines fostered bonds between themselves and voters both during and between campaign seasons, with the goal of building a loyal voter base.[5] The result was the emergence of strong identification and partisan loyalties among most voters to a particular party. As such, parties became the major vehicles for virtually every facet of the campaign process: from candidate recruitment, to the nomination process, to the resources needed to communicate with the electorate, and to the party symbols and labels that gave meaning to voters and helped them choose candidates.[6]

Party-dominated campaigns eventually lost ground to candidate-focused campaigns due to one set of progressive reforms passed in the early 1900s and a later set passed in the 1960s and 1970s. Both sets of reforms sought to limit the role of the party organizations in the nomination process and general election. The people planning and conducting campaigns were no longer reliant on party loyalists, but instead on a personal team assembled by—and beholden to—the candidate, such as professional political consultants. Consequently, candidates were "marketed" not as party members, but as individuals. Candidates and their campaign managers made the strategic and tactical decisions as well as supervised the day-to-day activities of the campaign.[7] They were responsible for hiring the staff and the political consultants to carry our fundraising, research, communications, and most other campaign activities. And they used new-found survey research techniques to develop their own public images and to select the issues and themes that formed their message, as well as choose the specific forms of media—such as radio, television and direct mail—to convey that message directly into voters' living rooms. Perhaps most important, candidates, not political parties, became the central focus of fundraising appeals. Almost every candidate organization hired individuals to raise funds using appeals based on the candidate's background, experience, and stance on issues, and who had expertise in more modern techniques, such as direct mail solicitations and bundling.[8]

Political Campaigns in the Modern Era

Political campaigns in the modern era continue to revolve primarily around candidates and the staff hired to mount their campaigns.[9] Candidates are responsible for assembling their own campaign team. They and those individuals with whom they surround themselves are responsible for the conduct of their own election campaigns. According to at least one study, in the 2004 federal election cycle, presidential candidates, national party committees, general election candidates for Congress, and various interest groups spent nearly $2 billion on such professional consultant services.[10] Party organizations and some interest groups, however, have become increasingly involved in closely contested elections to assume a greater role in the candidate-centered system. While less visibly involved in localities where these contests are officially non-partisan and party labels do not appear with the candidates' names, parties and outside groups help recruit candidates and provide many, especially those running for Congress, with traditional grassroots support, such as fundraising and campaign organization, as well as communicating with and mobilizing voters. Additionally, parties and interest groups participate through independent, parallel, and coordinated campaigns designed to influence both the political agenda and the voters' behavior.[11]

Candidates and Campaign Management

Campaign management in most elections for Congress, state legislatures, local and municipal offices—or down-ballot races—is now dominated by candidate campaign organizations. Figure 2.1 depicts the level of professionalism of different campaigns, where campaign professionalism is measured by the number of major campaign activities performed by a paid campaign aide or political consultant. Ranging from 0–12, the measure includes campaign management, press relations, issue or opposition research, fundraising, polling, mass media advertising, direct mail, web site construction and maintenance, mass telephone calls, GOTV activities, legal advice, and accounting. It shows that the typical House campaign employs roughly six professionals. The number is larger for Senate campaigns, which average between eight and nine campaign professionals per candidate organization. Most of these campaigns hire such experts to manage activities that require technical expertise, such as polling and media advertising, in-depth research, or connections with sources of funds, which as the figure demonstrates, has a significant impact on the number of votes candidates receive. Presidential campaigns, not surprisingly, are off the chart in terms of campaign professionalism. In campaign activities where a typical House candidate would hire consultant or campaign aide and a Senate candidate might hire a team of consultants,

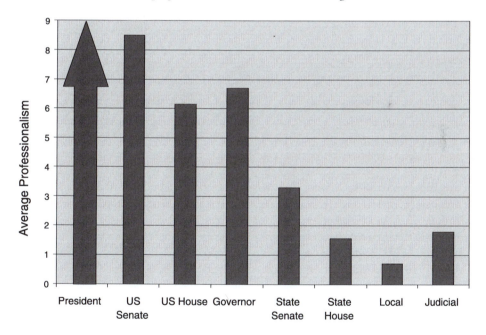

Figure 2.1. The Professionalism of Different Campaigns

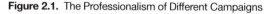

Source: Paul S. Herrnson, *The 2002 Congressional Campaign Study* (College Park, Md.: University of Maryland, 2002); and Paul S. Herrnson, *The Campaign Assessment and Candidate Outreach Project* (College Park, Md.: University of Maryland, 2001).

Notes: The figures represent the number of major campaign activities performed by a paid campaign aide or political consultant. The activities are: management, press relations, issue or opposition research, fundraising, polling, mass media advertising, direct mail, web site construction and maintenance, mass telephone calls, GOTV activities, legal advice, and accounting. The data for federal offices are from 2002; data for state and local offices are from 1997–1998.

presidential campaigns often hire a team of consultants for each state or region. Campaigns for the state legislature and for judgeships tend to hire fewer campaign professionals. However, the trend toward more sophisticated and expensive campaigns has led to more professionalized campaign organizations for elections further down the ballot.

Do such campaign organizations have a significant impact on election outcomes? If House campaigns are typical, then the answer is a resounding yes. Congressional challengers and open-seat contestants are typically helped the most by fielding a professional campaigning organization, sometimes increasing their vote share by as much as five percentage points.[12] While this may not be enough to defeat an entrenched incumbent, hiring a team of skilled campaign aides and political consultants can help a candidate raise more money, attract more media attention, and wage a more competitive campaign. In some cases, it may be critical in bringing about victory.[13]

The Role of Party and Group Efforts in Contemporary Campaign Politics

At the national level party organizations in Washington, D.C., have assumed an important role in the recruitment of congressional candidates. National party organizations, particularly the Democratic and Republican congressional and senatorial campaign committees, actively identify and encourage some candidates to run for Congress and discourage others.[14] The same is true of legislative campaign committees in many states. These party committees provide modest encouragement and advice for large numbers of politicians who wish to run for Congress, or a state legislature. They instead commit a significant amount of time courting certain candidates to run for the few seats they anticipate will be competitive. This is done through a variety of methods, including providing poll results demonstrating the person's popularity with voters or potential for winning, and promising to provide campaign contributions and assistance with fundraising, communications, and other campaign activities should the candidate win the nomination.

In primary contests where the party leaders who direct these committees believe that one candidate will be more viable in the general election than the others, these leaders and committee staff may actively discourage the others from running. Usually candidates who are ideological extremists are discouraged from running in favor of moderates. The 2006 mid-term elections provide a noteworthy example. In its successful effort to retake the House of Representatives, rather than rallying its liberal base, the Democratic Congressional Campaign Committee (DCCC) sought moderate-to-conservative candidates who could attract more traditional voters. Such de-recruitment strategies can be very effective at winnowing the field of potential candidates. However, in a few cases where they fail, and where party leaders believe one potential contender would be much stronger in the general election than another, the congressional campaign committees actively back one primary candidate.

Like political parties, many interest groups recruit candidates for public office. These include various labor unions; the Club for Growth, an anti-tax group that supports Republican candidates who favor free-market economics; the League of Conservation Voters, an environmental group that supports mainly Democrats; and EMILY'S List (whose motto is "Early Money is Like Yeast. . . . It makes the dough [i.e. money] rise"), which seeks to elect pro-choice Democratic women. Unlike political parties, however, these organizations become extremely involved in contested nomination contests, with some providing candidates with endorsements, monetary contributions, and campaign assistance during the primary season. They also supply campaigns with volunteers; air campaign advertisements on radio and television supporting one candidate (or opposing others); make similar appeals via mail, e-mail, or telephone; and mobilize their members on primary day.

Political parties and interest groups are much bolder about participating in the opposing party's nomination contests. The 2002 California gubernatorial contest provides a particularly noteworthy example. Incumbent governor Gray Davis, who faced only token opposition in his race for the Democratic nomination, spent an estimated $10 million attacking former Los Angeles mayor and moderate Richard Riordan in the Republican primary. His goal was to boost the prospects of conservative businessman Bill Simon, who Davis and most Democrats considered the less viable of the two opponents. The plan ultimately succeeded as Simon defeated Riordan by roughly 49% of the vote to 31% in the Republican primary, and Davis went on to defeat Simon by 47% to 42% in the general election. Ironically, Davis was recalled in late 2003, less than a year after being reelected.

The influence of political parties and interest groups in the conduct and management of campaigns depends primarily on the resources those organizations can bring to bear on the campaign. In the case of presidential elections, the two major-party candidates, and some minor-party contestants, have sufficient financial and personnel resources to wage substantial campaigns. Party committees and allied interest groups typically assist presidential campaigns by providing financial and organizational support, communications, and voter mobilization assistance. In return, they may ask a candidate to visit a particular locality, make an effort to boost the prospects of a candidate for lower office, or draw attention to one or more issues when making a speech. The same type of cooperation exists in most gubernatorial campaigns.

Political parties, particularly congressional, senatorial, and state legislative campaign committees in many states, assist legislative candidates with hiring campaign aides and political consultants and with management, fundraising, communications, and other aspects of campaigning requiring specialized expertise.[15] These party committees maintain lists of qualified consultants, facilitate matchmaking between consultants and candidates, and provide some campaigns with general strategic and organizational advice. They also hold training seminars for candidates, campaign aides, and political activists.

However, in a small number of elections featuring candidates in very close contests, political parties and other groups often play larger roles.[16] Party operatives take a vigorous interest in ensuring these campaigns hire staff and consultants that have the ability to wage a strong campaign. They help the campaign write a sound campaign plan, and party field-staff routinely visit campaign headquarters to provide strategic advice and to report to their party committees about the campaign's progress. In a few cases, party committees, and some interest groups, dispatch some of their personnel to work full time on a campaign as well as state legislative or congressional staff to work in the final weeks. While most candidates appreciate the support they receive from these organizations, it can stir tensions because the campaign's own aides consider themselves experts on their candidate or the local strategic environment and the party and interest group aides consider themselves as experts on campaign politics. Some candidates and campaign aides view party and interest group personnel to be outsiders and are resentful of the roles they seek to assume in the campaign. Nevertheless, even these candidates and their aides usually accept advice from these individuals because to do otherwise could result in their campaigns being cut off from large contributions and other forms of campaign assistance.

Fundraising

The roles of party committees and interest groups in fundraising have increased considerably. The parties' congressional, senatorial, and state legislative campaign committees have become especially aggressive and adept at raising and channeling campaign money to specific candidates, namely those in competitive elections. In the first quarter of 2007, for instance, the DCCC raised $19 million while the National Republican Congressional Committee (NRCC) raised $15.8 million.[17] Additionally, to boost its campaign coffers in order to protect its new majority the DCCC has implemented a new biannual dues structure that requires members to raise money specifically for the DCCC. Besides their regular party dues, House Democrats are now required to pay the DCCC either $75,000 or $100,000—depending on different factors such as committee assignments—over the course of the two-year election cycle.[18] Members can meet their individual goals any number of ways: by hosting events specifically for the DCCC, making telephone calls, e-mailing or mailing solicitations, and by meeting with certain donors.

Some party committees and interest groups assist candidates with fundraising, provide candidates with lists of potential donors and give them advice on how to solicit contributions from them. They use letters, newsletters, e-mail, briefings, and other methods to circulate favorable information about the candidates they support to other donors that fall within their sphere of influence. And some organizations, mainly party committees, ask powerful officeholders to use their political muscle to encourage donors to contribute to other candidates who are in need of funds. This so-called "buddy system" works particularly well when legislative incumbents are paired with non-incumbents who share their political views.

The new roles of party committees and interest groups in fundraising have had a number of important consequences. They have contributed to the development of a more nationalized system of campaign finance and enhanced the parties' and interest groups' abilities to influence the flow of money in that system. They have the ability to regulate the flow of contributions to individual campaigns. Indeed, a direct effect of these organizations' efforts to control the flow of money to some campaigns is that others are starved for cash and unable to compete for votes.

Communications and Voter Mobilization

Although politicians and political consultants continually refine the techniques they use to gauge the public's mood, those used in the modern era are, for the most part, the same as those used in the era that preceded it. The major difference is that political parties and, to a lesser degree, interest groups have assumed larger roles in taking the electorate's political pulse. Some of these organizations take polls to encourage prospective candidates to run for office. These same organizations also use polling data when formulating their own campaign strategies and deciding how to distribute their campaign resources. In addition, party committees and interest groups routinely disseminate the results of national surveys and other research through newsletters they send to candidates, the media, and political activists. These organizations also conduct polls in a limited number of competitive elections and share the results with the candidates in those contests in order to improve the campaigns' decision making. Party and interest group polling has increased these organizations' influence in contemporary elections.

With the exception of the introduction of Internet and satellite television uplinks, only incremental changes have taken place in the techniques campaigns use to communicate with voters. What have changed are the roles of political parties and outside groups in assisting candidates gain access to, and in some cases utilize, these techniques. In the 1980s the parties' congressional campaign committees and some state legislative committees helped candidates with communicating with voters in several ways. Some candidates received basic party issue packages that also were sent to political activists or were given the use of generic television ads and assistance in customizing them with voiceovers and text. Others benefited from more individualized assistance, including extensive issue and opposition research, help with message development, and the use of party facilities and media experts in writing, recording, editing, and disseminating television, radio, and direct mail advertisements.[19]

These organizations continue to provide generic communications assistance to many candidates, but changes in technology have made it more cost-effective for candidates and consultants to tape and edit their own campaign ads. The typical House campaign, for instance, devotes more than one-third of its budget to broadcast media advertising (see Figure 2.2). Another one-fifth is committed to direct mail, campaign literature, and other communications. The remainder is committed to staff salaries, fundraising, other forms of overhead, and research.

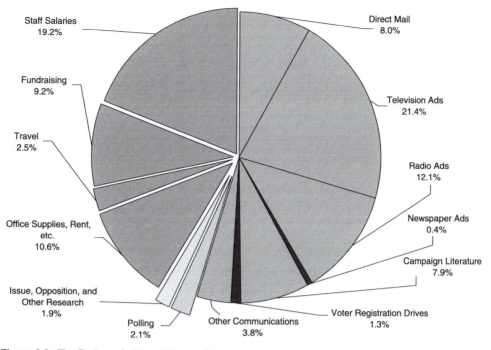

Figure 2.2. The Budget of a Typical House Campaign

Source: Paul S. Herrnson, *Congressional Elections: Campaigning at Home and in Washington,* 4th ed. (Washington, D.C.: CQ Press, 2004).

Note: Figures don't add to 100% due to rounding.

Parties continue to provide candidates with access to generic television ads, and they furnish access to satellite technology to candidates, mostly congressional incumbents, in Washington, D.C., that enables the candidates to interact in real time with their constituents. Most of the communications assistance that parties provide directly to contemporary campaigns involves furnishing candidates competing in close races with timely feedback on campaign ads. Using streaming video on the Internet, party communications staff can typically provide candidates with commentaries on their ads in a matter of hours, and sometimes even in minutes. In addition to the assistance they provide to campaign organizations, party committees (and some interest groups) also directly communicate with voters to influence the outcome of some elections.

Voter mobilization is a campaign activity that is often less candidate centered and involves substantial party and interest group involvement. The transference of funds raised by national party organizations to state and local party committees has helped local party organizations playing a greater role in these efforts. Similarly, financial and organizational improvements made by labor unions, conservative Christian groups, and other organizations have enabled them to play a larger role in mobilizing voters. The Democratic Party and labor unions had long established a coordinated voter mobilization program, which gave many Democratic candidates an advantage over Republicans, even when the former were outspent. The Republicans responded in 2002 by organizing their own nationally directed voter mobilization program, referred to as the "72 Hour Task Force." In 2004 the Republican Party took another step forward by introducing micro-targeting techniques developed in marketing research into the political arena. Micro-targeting involves creating voter files that combine previous election results with individuals' voter turnout histories, contact information, and demographic and consumer information that is correlated with political preferences.[20] These data are used to identify partisan voters, and in some cases swing voters, and target them for personalized voter contacts to get them to vote.

The Impact of Campaigns on Election Outcomes

The pressures of modern campaigns are enormous. They consume time and energy as well as intellectual and financial resources. Successful campaigns for president, and statewide, as well as many congressional and some local offices typically require the analysis of massive amounts of data on previous voting patterns, the commissioning of polls to gauge voters' views about the issues and the candidates, the formulation of a campaign strategy, and the raising and spending of campaign funds. Attracting endorsements and free media coverage is also very important. Campaigns also require strong grassroots organizations for voter registration and GOTV drives. Political parties, labor unions, some trade associations, organizations associated with the religious right, and other causes assist some candidates with voter mobilization efforts.

Nevertheless, candidates do not begin (or end) the election season as equals when it comes to performing the tasks associated with campaigning or attracting the support of the media, parties, or interest groups. The power of incumbency provides overwhelming advantages to current officeholders. Some of these advantages come into play during the campaign season; others are relevant well before a prospective challenger may even decide on whether to run.

First, merely holding office provides most incumbents with resources they can use to strengthen their visibility and ties to their constituents well before the campaign season starts.[21] Pre-election efforts at generating name recognition and constituent approval provide incumbents with significant advantages once the election begins. Members of Congress, for example, are able to call on their congressional staff to help draft speeches, conduct research, write letters to constituents, perform casework, and win funding for federal projects or favorable tax considerations for local industries—allowing the member to claim credit for all of these efforts.[22] Free mailings, unlimited telephone service to home districts, Internet web sites, and access to television and radio recording studios, interpreting services, and graphic services assist members in broadcasting their accomplishments. The news media typically give the activities of sitting officeholders a reasonable amount of free news coverage. Although most of these efforts are considered part of a legislator's job, not campaigning, they enable members of Congress to increase their popularity among constituents, which, in turn, provides tremendous benefits once the campaign season begins.[23]

Second, as many challengers know all too well, incumbents have a clear advantage in campaign funding. Political action committees (PACs) and wealthy individual donors prefer to support incumbents more than challengers because they see incumbents as solid investments.[24] In the case of House incumbents, for example, the fact that more than 90% routinely win reelection encourages campaign donors who wish to influence public policy to funnel their resources to legislators who have a near-permanent hold on power rather than those who have little chance of acquiring it. During the 2006 congressional elections, for instance, incumbent House members of both parties raised roughly three times more money than their general election challengers. PACs were particularly generous with incumbents. Those in two-party contested elections raised, on average, nearly $531,000 from PACs, as opposed to the less than $43,000 raised by House challengers.[25] Additionally, many incumbents are able to use surplus money at the end of an election to finance skeletal campaign organizations between election cycles. These campaign organizations then fend off challengers, communicate with supporters, and prepare for the next election. Despite enacting various campaign finance reforms over the years, incumbents have perpetuated an election system that works to their advantage.

Third, when involved in close races, incumbents can rely on a disproportionate share of money and manpower from their party organizations and interest groups. Local party committees often provide assistance with registering voters, GOTV drives, direct mail, and providing campaign volunteers. State party committees help with other voter mobilization activities and money. While national party committees frequently provide information about voters, issue and opposition research, assistance with campaign communications, and fundraising to most candidates in competitive elections, protecting incumbents is their number one priority. They typically distribute substantial resources to incumbents in danger of losing their seats. They also frequently make independent expenditures designed to undermine whatever headway a challenger has made in building voter support. PACs and other interest groups also marshal their resources to come to the aid of incumbents in hotly contested contests. Often taking the form of television, radio, and direct mail advertisements, this spending is usually comparative or negative in tone and intended to undermine an opponent rather than enhance the reputation of the preferred candidate.[26]

Despite their near overwhelming advantages not all members of the US House, the US Senate, state legislatures, or the occupants of other offices win reelection. The benefits of incumbency do not automatically ensure success. In some situations, the national political climate combines with the local conditions and the efforts of individual candidates to enable a challenger to unseat even the most entrenched incumbent. Newly gerrymandered districts can also cause difficulties for incumbents. They have historically been less favorable to incumbents than other districts— although the House districts drawn following the 2000 census seem to have had the opposite influence.[27] Officeholders implicated in scandal are occasionally subject to voter backlash.[28] Moreover, a strong party agenda can force incumbents to confront difficult issues, which sometimes turns them out of office in a tidal wave that washes in large numbers of the opposing party. During the 1994 elections, for example, Republicans railed against what they labeled a White House and Democratic-controlled Congress that were corrupt and out of step with voters. They offered as an alternative a national platform called the "Contract with America" and succeeded in winning control of both Houses of Congress for the first time in forty years. In 2006 the Democrats took a page from the Republican playbook by offering their "Six for '06" campaign agenda that outlined six broad legislative goals, along with a promise for a new direction on the Iraq war. Combined with their attacks on the Republican-led administration's response to Hurricane Katrina and the scandals that roiled the Republican-controlled Congress, the Democrats were able to win back both houses of Congress for the first time in twelve years. It is important to note that these instances are more the exception than the norm. In general, few challengers are able to mount the sort of campaign needed to overcome the advantages of incumbency and changes in party control of Congress have been relatively rare.

Conclusion

Political campaigns in the United States have progressed through many stages, often in response to changes in the larger strategic environment in which elections are conducted. Early in US history, before the days of mass suffrage, campaigns consisted primarily of informal caucusing among those few political elites who enjoyed the right to vote. With the rise of mass suffrage and strong party organizations, the party-centered era took hold. During this period, local party machines dominated most aspects of political campaigning, including candidate selection, recruitment, campaign strategy, and the implementation of the campaign itself. Regulatory reform and broader systemic change in society resulted in candidates becoming more self-selected and campaigns becoming more candidate centered. Political parties and interest groups responded to the candidate-centered system, finding ways to assume important supplement roles in elections. Despite this last set of changes, most elections in the United States remain candidate centered and uncompetitive. Top-of-the-ticket races, such as presidential and gubernatorial contests, may generate strong competition, but the vast majority of congressional, state legislative, and local elections usually begin and end with the incumbent enjoying a commanding lead.

Notes

The views expressed here are those of the authors and not of the National Defense University, the Department of Defense, or any other agency of the United States government.

1 Paul S. Herrnson, *Congressional Elections: Campaigning at Home and in Washington*, 4th ed. (Washington, D.C.: CQ Press, 2004).

2 Portions of this section are drawn from Paul S. Herrnson, "The Evolution of Political Campaigns," in *Guide to Political Campaigns in America*, ed. Paul S. Herrnson (Washington, D.C.: CQ Press, 2005), 19–36.

3 See Robert L. Dudley and Alan R. Gitelson, *American Elections: The Rules Matter* (New York: Longman Publishers, 2002); and Harold F. Bass, Jr., "Partisan Rules, 1946–1996," in *Partisan Approaches to Postwar American Politics*, ed. Byron E. Shafer (New York: Chatham House Publishers, 1998), 220–70.

4 See Larry Sabato, *The Rise of the Political Consultants: New Ways of Winning Elections* (New York: Basic Books, 1981).

5 A. James Reichley, *The Life of the Parties: A History of American Political Parties* (New York: The Free Press, 1992), ch. 7.

6 See John H. Aldrich, *Why Parties? The Origin and Transformation of Political Parties in America* (Chicago, IL: University of Chicago Press, 1995).

7 See David Menefee-Libey, *The Triumph of Campaign-Centered Politics* (New York: Chatham House, 2000).

8 See Robert J. Dinkin, *Campaigning in America: A History of Election Practices* (Westport, CT: Greenwood Press, 1989); Sandy L. Maisel, *Parties and Elections in America: The Electoral Process*, 3rd ed. (Lanham, MD: Rowman & Littlefield, 1999); and Dennis W. Johnson, "The Business of Political Consulting," in *Campaign Warriors: Political Consultants in Elections*, ed. James A. Thurber and Candice J. Nelson (Washington, D.C.: Brookings Institution Press, 2000), 37–52.

9 See David A. Dulio, *For Better or Worse? How Political Consultants are Changing Elections in the United States* (Albany, N.Y.: State University of New York Press, 2004).

10 Sandy Bergo, *Campaign Consultants: The Price of Democracy* (Center for Public Integrity, Washington, D.C., 2006).

11 Herrnson, *Congressional Elections*, 117–24, 157–61.

12 Stephen K. Medvic, *Political Consultants in U.S. Congressional Elections* (Columbus, OH: Ohio State University Press, 2001), 115.

13 Medvic, *Political Consultants in U.S. Congressional Elections*, 115, 129–32; Herrnson, *Congressional Elections*, 237–8; and Paul S. Herrnson, "Campaign Professionalism and Fundraising in Congressional Elections," *Journal of Politics* 54 (1992): 859–70.

14 Paul S. Herrnson, *Party Campaigning in the 1980s* (Cambridge, MA: Harvard University Press, 1988); and L. Sandy Maisel, Cherie Maestas, and Walter J. Stone, "The Party Role in Congressional Competition," in *The Parties Respond: Changes in American Parties and Campaigns*, 4th ed., ed. L. Sandy Maisel (Boulder, CO: Westview Press, 2002), 121–38.

15 Herrnson, *Congressional Elections*, 105–16; and Robin Kolodny, "Electoral Partnerships: Political Consultants and Political Parties," in *Campaign Warriors: Political Consultants in Elections*, ed. James A. Thurber and Candice J. Nelson (Washington, D.C.: Brookings Institution Press, 2000), 110–32. See also Robin Kolodny and Angela Logan, "Political Consultants and the Extension of Party Goals," *PS: Political Science and Politics* 31 (2) (1998): 155–9.

16 Herrnson, *Congressional Elections*, 96–131.

17 Lauren W. Whittington, "DCCC Fundraising Surges," *Roll Call*, April 19, 2007, http://www.rollcall.com/issues/52_111/news/18060-1.html.

18 House Democrats assign biannual dues on a sliding scale. Those in leadership owe $600,000, for instance, while rank-and-file members sitting on nonexclusive committees pay $125,000. Members of the five exclusive committees—Appropriations, Ways and Means, Energy and Commerce, Rules, and Financial Services—each owe $150,000, while the chairs of those committees are responsible for $300,000.

19 Herrnson, *Party Campaigning in the 1980s*, 46–111.

20 Matt Bai, "The Multilevel Marketing of the President," *New York Times Magazine*, April 25, 2004.

21 Roger H. Davidson, Walter J. Oleszek, and Francis E. Lee, *Congress and Its Members*, 11th ed. (Washington, D.C.: CQ Press, 2008), 70–2.

22 See Morris P. Fiorina, *Congress: Keystone of the Washington Establishment*, 2nd ed. (New Haven, CT: Yale University Press, 1989), 53–8.

23 Michael John Burton and Daniel M. Shea, *Campaign Mode: Strategic Vision in Congressional Elections* (Lanham, MD: Rowman & Littlefield, 2003), 139.

24 Herrnson, *Congressional Elections*, ch. 6; Peter L. Francia, John C. Green, Paul S. Herrnson, Lynda W. Powell, and Clyde Wilcox, *The Financiers of Congressional Elections* (New York: Columbia University Press, 2003), 99–121.

25 Herrnson, *Congressional Elections*, 171, 181.

26 Ken Goldstein and Joel Rivlin, "Political Advertising in the 2002 and 2004 Elections," University of Wisconsin at Madison, Wisconsin Advertising Project, 2002, updated February 2005, ch. 5, www.polisci.wisc.edu/tvadvertising/Analysis%20of%20the%202000%20elections.htm.

27 However, the districts drawn following the 2000 elections form an important exception to that generalization. See, e.g. Herrnson, *Congressional Elections*, 242–3.

28 See, for example, Gary C. Jacobson and Michael Dimock, "Checking Out: The Effects of Bank Overdrafts on the 1992 House Election," *American Journal of Political Science* 38 (1994): 601–24.

3

Political Consulting Worldwide

Fritz Plasser

The worldwide market for political consultancy and campaign communication is a multi-billion-dollar market. In the United States nearly $2 billion flowed through consultants in 2003–2004 federal elections. About 600 professional consultants were paid more than a combined $1.85 billion according to a review conducted by the Center of Public Integrity. Abundant spending on campaign communication and strategic advice is not confined to the United States. Total expenditures for the recent Brazilian and Mexican presidential campaigns exceeded $600 million. About 60% of that amount has been spent on campaign communication and the production of vivid television spots crafted by top media consultants and advertising agencies. In Russia the gray market in elections is at least $1 billion a year. In the Asia-Pacific region more than $1 billion is spent on campaign communication every election cycle. Even in Western Europe where expensive paid political television advertising campaigns are rare exceptions and campaigns are planned and directed by professional party managers, there are business opportunities for external political consultants. In the United Kingdom Labour and the Tories spent more than $2 million on outside consultants in 2005. About the same amount has been spent in Italy in 2006 by Forza Italia and Ulivo on strategic advice by American overseas consultants. In 2006 even in a small country such as Austria the Social Democrats spent considerable money on advice and services provided by a team of top US consultants.

Extensive spending on campaign consultancy can also be observed in developing and emerging democracies often funded by international democracy assistance programs.[1] A rough estimate of current annual total party aid worldwide—often concentrating on campaign-related aid and covering the expenditures for the services of political consultants—would be approximately $200 million.[2] The flow of campaign money in some of the least developed countries in Asia and Africa is almost surreal. The annual worldwide election market can be roughly estimated at $6 to 8 billion depending on the respective election calendar and election cycles.[3] Although the bulk of campaign spending covers expenses for paid media, buying airtime, production of television spots, print advertising, posters, organization of mass rallies and logistics, and only a fraction of the total expenditures is direct income to political consultants and their firms, the political market of 123 electoral democracies worldwide is a flourishing business for campaign professionals, pollsters, marketing experts and advertising agencies.

Until recently no systematic research on the practices of political consultants outside the United States had been carried out apart from anecdotal evidence. In the meantime there are numerous studies dealing with the ongoing internationalization of professional political consulting.[4] Starting with the worldwide proliferation of modern campaign expertise and the activities of overseas consultants, I will concentrate on country-specific consultancy practices before discussing the variety of role definitions of a worldwide sample of campaign professionals based on the Global Political Consultancy Project.[5]

Professionalization of Campaigning Worldwide

During the last decades, the style and practice of election campaigns have been modernized and professionalized according to country- and culture-specific variations.[6] A comparison of actual changes in campaign practices shows several macro-trends, which can be observed in industrial democracies as well as in democracies of economically less developed countries.[7] The first and presumably most important trend is the exclusive television-centeredness of campaign communication. Television nowadays is the primary source of news in almost all countries. Campaigns are won or lost during an intensive encounter between candidates and parties primarily fought on television. The contestants are trying to present their topics in a favorable way and to reach undecided voters with carefully defined messages and planned, camera-ready events.

The second macro-trend is the growing importance of paid television advertising with consequently increasing campaign expenditures.[8] While there were worldwide only four countries in the 1970s permitting candidates and parties the purchase of television time, it was also possible to buy television time for political advertising in sixty countries at the end of the 1990s. With the exception of Western European democracies where only six countries allow paid political television advertising with considerable limitations, paid television campaigning replaced the traditional media and forums of campaigning such as posters, print ads and mass rallies in most of the countries.

The third macro-trend is the growing importance of television debates between leading politicians. Such debates represent the culmination of election campaigns in at least fifty countries, compared to only ten countries at the end of the 1970s.[9] This in turn leads to the fourth macro-trend: the increased personalization of election campaigns. Even in countries with party-centered election systems and strong party organizations, campaigns increasingly focus upon the personality of top candidates.[10] The communication of messages requires a messenger. In media-centered democracies this means that party leaders take over the central communication tasks in front of the television cameras. Attentive observers of campaign practices in Western Europe, where the prevailing election formula is proportional representation and the decisive vote is the vote for a party, speak of a trend toward presidentialization in the sense of moving away from party-centered election campaigns to media-centered personality campaigns.[11]

The fifth macro-trend is the growing importance of professional campaign managers and external political consultants. The worldwide diffusion of American campaign techniques and the progressive professionalization of leading staff members within the party headquarters transformed election campaigning from an activity of amateurs into a highly professional enterprise.[12] Both observations point to specialists, who are either recruited from a circle of external political consultants or well-educated and qualified party staff members.

The transformation of political campaign practices during the past decades can be divided into *three* consecutive phases, which in practice, of course, are overlapping (see Table 3.1).[13] The first phase could be described as a party-dominated style of campaigning based on substantial messages, programmatic differences, a party-oriented press and the loyalties of core groups of the electorate. The second phase, starting in the 1960s, was characterized by the spread of television as the dominant medium of political communication. In order to cope with the structural requirements of a visual and scenic medium, candidates and parties had to accept the standards of a new media logic based upon the communicative abilities of the candidates, their competence of

25

Table 3.1. Modeling Changing Campaign Practices Worldwide

Phase	Traditional	Modern	Postmodern
Mode of Political Communication Systems	Party-dominated	Television-centered	Multiple channels and multi-media
Dominant Style of Political Communication	Messages along party lines	Sound bites, image and impression management	Narrow-casted, targeted micro-messages
Media	Partisan press, posters, newspaper adverts, radio broadcasts	Television broadcasts through main evening news	Television narrow-casting, targeted direct mail and e-mail campaigns
Dominant Advertising Media	Print advertisements, posters, leaflets, radio speeches and mass rallies	Nationwide television advertisements, colorful posters and magazine adverts, mass direct mailings	Targeted television advertisements, e-mail campaigns and telemarketing, web-based videos, YouTube and blogs
Campaign Coordination	Party leaders and leading party staff	Party campaign managers and external media, advertising and survey experts	Special party campaign units and more specialized political consultants
Dominant Campaign Paradigm	Organization and party logic	Television-focused media logic	Data bank-based marketing logic
Preparations	Short-term, ad hoc	Long-term campaign	Permanent campaign
Campaign Expenditures	Low budget	Increasing	Spiraling up
Electorate	Cleavage- and group-based stable voting behavior	Erosion of party-attachments and rising volatility	Issue-based and highly volatile voting behavior

Source: Plasser, *Global Political Campaigning: A Worldwide Analysis of Campaign Professionals and Their Practices* (Westport, Conn.: Praeger, 2002), 6.

self-presentation, impression management and the creation of camera-ready events.[14] With these changes a new entrepreneurial profession entered the political market place: political consultants specialized on strategic communication, image-building, the production of television spots and extensive opinion research.[15] A new style of candidate-centered politics replaced the old style of party-centered election campaigns; and since the parties did not have any experts in that field, they hired external advisors, especially advertising and marketing experts for strategic planning and management tasks.[16]

The third, still developing phase of political campaigning is characterized by a fragmentation of television channels and target groups, the intrusion of Internet and bloggers into the campaign process as well as the transformation of large-scale campaign messages into micro-messages targeted to carefully defined voter segments. The negative tone of mass media reporting becomes more intensive and reacts upon advanced techniques of news management. The increasing professional competence of public relations experts and media advisors is defining, shaping and spinning campaign news and this leads to another factor changing the practice of electioneering: the marketing-revolution of campaigns.

In confrontation with the progressive erosion of party loyalties and the growth of voter mobility the practice of selling politics has been replaced step by step by a political marketing approach.[17] Standardized campaign operations characterized by political marketing contain: careful segmentation of the electoral market, strategic positioning toward the political opponent, research-supported development of micro-messages appealing to the needs and emotions of selected groups of target voters, rigid message discipline and intensive use of focus groups.[18]

Core features of traditional campaign practices were:

- their concentration upon the personal communication with voters in form of canvassing, door-to-door contacts, party meetings and mass rallies;
- the importance of the party press, the widespread use of posters, stickers, brochures and print ads or radio speeches of party politicians and candidates to mobilize the core voters; as well as
- a party- and organization-centered approach to planning and waging election campaigns.

In comparison, professional campaign practices are based on:

- the available media formats of political television and professional techniques of news management, impression management, arranged camera-ready events and the potential of viral marketing activities;
- but equally upon political television advertising in the form of free air time or as paid television advertising campaigns replacing traditional campaign media such as posters, print ads and mass rallies by web-based videos, e-mails, direct mail-campaigns; as well as
- professional political consultants, pollsters, media, marketing and political management experts responsible for primarily candidate-centered and media-driven campaigns.[19]

Regarding the professionalization of election campaigns, the United States is considered to be a role model of campaigning in the view of European, Latin American and Asian campaign managers. Campaign techniques originally developed in the United States found worldwide acceptance.[20] In fact, American presidential election campaigns have become a political shopping mall for foreign campaign managers, a virtual political supermarket for new campaign techniques and campaign innovations, which they leave after their selective shopping tours with filled baskets. The most widespread model for the transfer of select techniques and innovations of American election campaigns is the *shopping model*, where concrete practices and methods of American election campaigns suitable for unproblematic use in the national context are imported to Europe, Latin America or Asia in modified form.[21] There would be, however, more consequences in the case of taking over the *adoption model*, where foreign campaign managers also try to accept the strategic axioms of American campaign activists and transfer the political logic of competition in American presidential campaigns to their national parliamentary campaigns. In the end this would actually lead to a transformation of the worldwide campaign styles in the direction of "global reproduction of American politics."[22]

While the *adoption model* results in a gradual standardization of election practices following the American role model of campaigns in media-centered democracies (for which no empirical evidence exists until now), the *shopping model* leads to a hybridization of the international practice of election campaigning. *Hybridization* of campaign practices stands in this context for a supplementation of country- and culture-specific campaign traditions by select components of a media- and marketing-oriented campaign style which, however, needs to be oriented in no way exclusively on the American role model.[23]

The British campaign for the general election of 2005 represents an impressive example of hybridization of European election campaigns. The Conservative Party hired two Australian campaign experts, Lynton Crosby and Mark Textor, specialists in marginal-seat campaigns (regional mobilization of target groups in highly competitive districts), as well as negative attack campaigns, who took over the planning and management of the Conservatives' campaign. At the same time the Conservatives imported software from the strategic data bank maintained by the

Republican Party in the United States during the presidential campaign of 2004. The Labour Party on the other hand relied, just like during previous general elections, on the expertise of a team of high ranking political consultants from the United States, who had given strategic and advertising advice to the Democratic presidential candidates during the American presidential elections in 2000 and 2004. Directing the campaign of the Labour Party, however, were British campaign strategists who themselves had been involved in the planning of American presidential election campaigns as foreign experts in the past years. The British example of a selective takeover of foreign expertise, which agrees with the institutional and cultural rules of the national competitive system, corresponds better with the manifold reality of European or Latin American election campaigns than the misleading idea of a global standardization of campaign practices.

Worldwide Activities of Political Consultants

American overseas consultants have played a leading role in the worldwide proliferation of professional election campaign techniques. The extremely high number of political consultancy firms within the United States, the intensifying competition for lucrative contracts, the increasing cost of overheads at the full service-companies, and the cyclic dynamics of the political consultancy business caused leading representatives during the 1980s either to switch to corporate consulting and public affairs management[24] or motivated them to look for new markets outside the United States. Pioneers of the political consulting business such as the legendary Joseph Napolitan made their first experiences as American overseas consultants during the 1960s. At the end of the 1990s more than 50% of all American top political consultants had worked as overseas consultants in around eighty countries.[25] Clearly the most important market for the services of American overseas consultants is Latin America, followed by Western Europe, East-Central and Eastern Europe, while the electoral markets of Asia and Africa have only been entered on a commercial basis by few American consultants so far.[26] Although only a small fraction of American overseas consultants can be classified as super consultants, earning more than 50% from their work overseas, a global electoral market for American political consultants has evolved, contributing to the worldwide diffusion of American campaign techniques and campaign expertise.

According to our Global Political Consultancy Survey, one-third of the interviewed party managers and consultants outside the United States have cooperated with an American consultant during the last years.[27] In the late 1990s, American consultants worked in almost all Western European countries. The situation is similar in the new democracies in East-Central Europe, where market-driven activities of American overseas consultants, combined with donor-driven activities of democracy assistance programs, have led to a sustainable influx of American campaign expertise. American consultants frequently have been involved in Latin American countries, worked in Australian campaigns, traveled to the Philippines and South Korea and temporarily left their footprints also in Russian presidential campaigns. With the notable exception of Asian countries such as Japan, Taiwan, Indonesia and India, where severe cultural and regulatory constraints represent a barrier that is only rarely overcome by US consultants[28] and francophone Africa, where French top consultants dominate the electoral markets, American consultants shaped campaign practices worldwide to a considerable degree.[29] (On Philippine elections, see Chapter 26 by Louis Perron; on Asian elections see Chapter 27 by Christian Schafferer.)

In addition to market-driven activities of prominent US consultants, campaign training seminars, trade journals and academic programs such as the high-quality curriculum of the Graduate School of Political Management (GSPM) at the George Washington University, contributed to the worldwide diffusion of American campaign expertise. In addition, democracy assistance programs of such organizations as the National Endowment for Democracy (NED), International Republican Institute (IRI), National Democratic Institute (NDI) or the US Agency for

International Development (USAID) invested hundreds of millions of dollars in campaign-related aid to emerging democracies.[30] Using the expertise and services of US consultants, but increasingly from other countries, donor-driven party aid covers fundraising, platform development, message development, polling, recruitment and training of staff and volunteers, door-to-door outreach, media relations, ad writing and placement, public speaking for candidates, and get-out-the-vote campaigns.[31] These programs also provide instructive training opportunities for domestic campaign staffers interested in state of the art techniques of political management. In addition, transnational and regional political consultancy associations have a key function in the worldwide dissemination of professional campaign know-how (see Table 3.2). These networks are platforms for exchanging experience and discussing the latest trends and innovations in international election campaigns. In the meantime there is a worldwide network of professional associations emerging, indicating the globalization and professionalization of the political consultancy business.

Although every year more than a hundred US consultants spend considerable time overseas as campaign advisors, media experts, pollsters, webmasters or guest speakers at professional conferences and party campaign manager seminars, the international demand for American political consultants actually concentrates on a few superstars of consultancy business. Largely they are former advisors of American presidential candidates or leading figures of the American political consultancy business. Celebrities in the international consultancy market are the former Clinton advisor Dick Morris, who has been involved in dozens of Latin American presidential campaigns in Mexico, Argentina, Honduras, Venezuela, Uruguay and Guyana, worked as consultant in dozens of Western and Eastern European campaigns and recently acted as campaign consultant to the Yushenko presidential campaign in the Ukraine. Also there is James Carville, who with Philip Gould and Stanley Greenberg founded in 1997 the London-based opinion polling group and transnational consulting organization GGC/NOP; Carville is also partner in the global political consultancy and strategy company Greenberg Carville Shrum. Greenberg Quinlan Rosner Research is also a pre-eminent international political consultancy firm. The team around Stanley Greenberg has been involved in campaigns in over sixty countries so far and was consulting among others in three campaigns of Tony Blair (United Kingdom), the 1998 election campaign of Gerhard Schröder (Germany), and the 1999 and 2001 campaigns of Ehud Barak (Israel). In 2006 they advised the Labour candidate Amir Peretz in Israel, the successor to Nelson Mandela in South Africa, Thabo Mbeki, several Latin American presidential candidates and were also involved in numerous West European parliamentary campaigns.

Table 3.2. Transnational and Regional Political Consultancy Associations

Platform	Founded	Members (approx.)
International Association of Political Consultants (IAPC)	1968	120
American Association of Political Consultants (AAPC)	1969	1,100[a]
Associacao Brasileira de Consultores Politicos (ABCOP)	1991	100
Association of Professional Political Consultants (APPC) (UK)	1994	35[b]
European Association of Political Consultants (EAPC)	1996	75
Asociacion Latinoamericana de Consultores Politicos (ALACOP)	1996	60
Associazione Italiana Consulenti Politici (AICP)	1999	50
Association of (Russian) Political Consulting Centers (ACPK)	2000	40[b]
German Association of Political Consulting (degepol)	2002	70
Asia Pacific Association of Political Consultants (APAPC)	2005	50
Asociacion Espanola de Consultores Politicos (AESCOP)	2007	20

Notes:

a Additionally there are about 600 corporate members.

b Only corporate membership for consulting firms.

An impressive example of the increasingly global market activities of American top consultants is VOX Global Mandate SM, a worldwide operating cooperation of three leading consulting firms headquartered in Washington D.C. and London. It offers its services to candidates, political parties and democracy movements worldwide. Top strategists of these three consulting firms have been involved in more than 500 presidential, prime minister and party election campaigns worldwide. Similarly impressive is the list of clients of Penn, Schoen and Berland (PSB), which offered polling operations and strategic advice in over seventy campaigns outside the United States. PSB offered its services to more than twenty presidential campaigns in the Far East, Latin America, Western Europe, Georgia and Ukraine. PSB also was involved in Slobodan Milosevic's overthrow in the Serbian presidential election of 2000, which may go down in history as the first poll-driven, focus-group-tested democratic revolution based on the expertise of American consultants.[32]

The heavy engagement of American overseas consultants leads increasingly to the paradox of American consultants facing each other as campaign opponents. Examples of such paradox competitions between American consultants are the parliamentary election in Israel 2006 (James Carville, Stanley Greenberg and Robert Shrum versus Arthur Finkelstein), Italy 2006 (Frank Luntz versus Stanley Greenberg), Mexico 2006 (Dick Morris versus James Carville) and the Ukraine 2006, where former Clinton's Chief of Staff John Podesta and former Clinton's Press Secretary Michael McCurry advised Yushenkov's Our Ukraine bloc, while the former campaign manager of Ronald Reagan and George H.W. Bush, Paul Manafort, advised Yanukovych's Party of Regions. The third candidate, Yulia Tymoshenko, refrained from hiring American overseas consultants and relied on the advice of prominent European consultants. (On the Israeli elections, see Chapter 23 by Dahlia Scheindlin and Israel Waismel-Manor; on Russian elections, see Chapter 24 by Derek S. Hutcheson.)

In the 2006 Ukraine presidential election as well as in the 2007 parliamentary elections, candidates and parties exclusively used the expertise of Western political consultants, while the 2004 Ukraine presidential campaign stood for a clash between two cultures of consultants: The pro-Western coalition *Nasha Ukraine* (Our Ukraine) was supported by a team of high ranking American consultants (among them PSB and Aristotle International Inc.), while the Yanukovych election group, which was preferred by the Kremlin, got support for its campaign from the elite of Russian spin doctors such as Gleb Pavlovsky, the Head of the Foundation for Effective Politics, and dozens of other leading Russian political technologists. Pavlovsky, Markov and other Russian top public relations consultants had been hired on request of the Kremlin and Russian business corporations invested about $300 million in Yanukovych's campaign. Similarly conflicting consultancy battles also took place in Georgia and in other Commonwealth of Independent States (CIS) countries, where the Kremlin tried to influence the outcome of the elections based on strategic and economic motives.

A fierce *guerra de asesores* is also fought on the heatedly contested Latin American consultancy market, where often two teams of US consultants have found themselves in opposing camps during election campaigns.[33] Since the 1980s, leading figures of the American consultancy business have been specializing on Latin American *campanas electorales*. Top consultants such as Ralph D. Murphine have been involved in sixteen Latin American presidential campaigns; others such as Gary Nordlinger focused on the subpresidential level and specialized on gubernatorial and mayoral campaigns. Super consultants such as Dick Morris, James Carville, Stanley Greenberg, Douglas Schoen and Gary Nordlinger—just to mention a few—spend considerable time in Latin America and have been involved in dozens of presidential and gubernatorial campaigns. Their competitors are not only American colleagues and domestic Latin American consultants, but with increasing frequency also top French consultants, who are trying to get a hold on the Latin American electoral market. French *conseils politiques* such as Jacques Seguela (Havas), Stephane Fouks (EURO RSGG Worldwide) and Thierry Saussez (Image et Strategie) have been involved in several presidential campaigns in Latin American countries during the past years, but also top Russian consultants such as Igor Mintusov (Niccolo M.) and Alexei P. Sitnikov (Image Kontakt) exported Russian campaign know-how to Bolivia, Chile, Nicaragua and Venezuela.

However, the fiercest competition in Latin America does not take place between overseas consultants from the United States and Europe, but between Latin American *consultores politicos*, who specialized on interregional campaign consulting. Two to three dozen Brazilian, Argentine and Venezuelan political consultants divide the Latin American consultancy market up between themselves and compete for attractive consultancy contracts. Carlos Manhanelli, the founder of the Brazilian professional association ABCOP, has been engaged in more than 200 campaigns in Brazil and other Latin American countries. The activities of the former superstar of Brazilian consultancy business, Duda Mendonca, are legendary; he helped Luiz Lula de Silva win the presidency and appeared as a highly paid and visible advisor in dozens of Latin American election campaigns until his career experienced a setback in 2005 following his involvement in the *escandalo do mensalao* (political corruption and illegal party financing). Another Brazilian super consultant is *publicitario* Nizan Guanaes (DM9, São Paulo), who was the top advisor of Fernando Cardoso in 1994 and 1998 and managed the election campaign of Jose Serra, going up against consultant Mendonca in 2002. Prominent *consultores politicos* such as Carballido, Chavarria, Hugo Haime, Felipe Noguera and Pessoa, to name only a few leading figures, have frequently been involved in presidential and gubernatorial campaigns across Latin America.[34] In the meantime Latin American election campaigns have become multinational operations in political manage-ment. In 2006 in Venezuela there were, besides the domestic advisors, also consultants from Mexico, Cuba and the US engaged in the campaign. In other campaigns there was a mix of Brazilian, Argentine, American and Russian consultancy styles, resulting in a *hibridez de estilos communicionales y technologias*, as attentive observers described the reality of consultant- and money-driven campaigns in Latin America.[35]

As mentioned before, US political consultants have no monopoly on the international elect-oral market and since the 1990s, they have seen themselves confronted with increasing competi-tion by a new generation of highly professional regional consultants, many of whom made their first professional experiences as staff members of American consultants before they founded their own companies. One example showing the spin off of American consultants' expertise is the election campaign in Israel in 2006. As in past elections Amir Peretz, the candidate of the Labour Party, relied on the know-how of Stanley Greenberg and Mark Penn and Doug Schoen, while Benjamin Netanyahu, the candidate of the Likud Bloc, used the hard-hitting advice of Arthur J. Finkelstein from New York City. But the winner, Ehud Olmert and his newly founded Kadima Party, was exclusively advised by younger Israeli consultants who had cooperated with American consultants as domestic junior partners in earlier campaigns.

While American overseas consultants operate on the highly competitive electoral markets in Latin America, French *conseils politiques* control the lucrative market in the francophone countries of Africa. Thierry Saussez (Image et Strategie), who advised Jacques Chirac, Alain Juppe, Edouard Balladur and in 2007 Nicolas Sarkoszy in France, specialized on consulting African presidential candidates, and has been involved in large-scale and highly expensive presidential campaigns in numerous countries such as the Ivory Coast, Cameroon, Togo and Congo-Brazaville.[36] Claude Marti and Bernard Rideau are also French superstar overseas consultants, and have been active, along with others, as political consultants in Burkina Faso, Gabun, Guinea Bissau, Cameroon, Madagascar, Nigeria, Senegal and Togo among others. Besides French *conseils politiques* there were also American top consultants such as Paul Manafort involved as strategic advisors in Angola, Congo, Nigeria and Somalia during the past years. With the exception of South Africa, where the African National Congress (ANC) uses American consultants along with domestic experts and the opposition party Democratic Alliance engages British and West European advisors, the African electoral market is primarily an area of business for French political consultants.

Next to the American overseas consultants, leading Latin American *consultores politicos* and French *conseils politiques*, also Russian spin doctors have established themselves on the international political consultancy market since the middle of the 1990s. They first concentrated on the neighboring CIS countries but in the meantime also have invaded overseas markets. The increased international activity of leading Russian spin doctors is a reaction to incisive changes within the domestic consulting scene as well. Since a few years ago the Russian political consulting market has been characterized by a process of concentration in the direction of large-scale firms with links to the Kremlin parties of power.[37] Today the consultancy market is already dominated by a few large multi-disciplinary corporations such as the Center of Political Research Nikkolo M. (Igor Mintusov and Ekaterina Egorova), the Foundation for Effective Politics (Gleb Pavlosky), Image-Kontakt (Alexei P. Sitnikov), Novkom and the Center of Political Technologies.

Apart from freelancing *prshchiks*, a pejorative Russian term for superficial image-handlers, the Russian elite consultants do not see themselves primarily as political consultants, but as political technologists, which can mean

> a policy analyst or political consultant; it can mean an expert in "black PR" or in containing the political environment; but it can also mean a Kremlin insider or a political provocateur. What makes political technologists a different species from the other election strategists or PR consultants is their direct or indirect connection to the Kremlin.[38]

In Vladimir Putin's managed democracy the access to the corridors of power and to state-controlled administrative resources are preconditions of successful campaigns.[39]

Following the recent incisive reforms of the Russian electoral process such as the abolishment of the direct election of half of the Duma representatives, the introduction of a party-centered list-voting system, and the nomination of provincial governors instead of their direct election, attentive observers expect a dramatic curtailment of the Russian consultancy market. In order to finance their staff and overheads between the election cycles, the remaining Russian consulting firms will appear even more often as advisors outside of Russia. Already Russian political consultants have been involved in election campaigns in Belarus, Bulgaria, Georgia, Kazakhstan, Mongolia, Poland, Serbia, Slovakia and Ukraine. Beside their operations in CIS countries and several East-Central European countries, some top Russian consultants have also been engaged in campaigns in Colombia, Mexico, Nicaragua and Venezuela. Obviously the Russian style of consultancy, preferring hard-hitting attacks, using dirty technologies, "black PR," and their expertise in influencing the electoral process through administrative resources and media structures[40] seems to correspond to a Third World-style of campaigning prevalent in fragile electoral democracies in the Latin American, Asian and African regions.

In the Asia-Pacific region mainly Australian campaign professionals appear as overseas consultants. Sydney-based firms such as Anderson & Company, the Hawker-Britten political consulting group, and Malcolm McGregor, Ian Kortlang, John Utting and Nick Straves, to name only a few leading Australian consultants, offer their services not only to Australian and New Zealand candidates but also to clients in Indonesia, Malaysia and South Korea. Recently two Australian top consultants, Lynton Crosby and Mark Textor, have been in charge as campaign managers of the British Conservatives. Similar to the African electoral market, the Asia-Pacific region represents an emerging market for international consultants. At present only a few professional political consultancy firms are operating in the market, but the recent founding of an Asia-Pacific Association of Political Consultants is a sign that the Asian consultancy market has started to move as well. (On Australian elections, see Chapter 25 by Ian Ward.)

Prominent representatives of the Asian political consultancy business, which so far has only been accessible in exceptional cases for selected American overseas consultants, are in Japan.

Takayoshi Miyagawa (Center for Political Relations Inc.), Hiroshi Miura (Ask Co.), a political consulting firm that so far advised already more than 200 Japanese candidates, and Kazuo Maeda, a professional campaign advisor in Tokyo. Political consultants who are known outside their own countries are Kim Hak-Ryang from South Korea and Wu Hsiang-hui from Taiwan. The interregional consulting networks in Asia are currently only loosely tied and election campaigns in countries such as Japan, India and Taiwan are almost exclusively supported by domestic expertise.[41]

The political consulting networks in Western Europe are comparatively also loosely tied and quite informal.[42] Few European political advisors are working outside their own countries. Interregional political consulting in Western Europe is limited to regular meetings and campaign manager seminars organized through the networks of conservative or social democratic parties and serving the mutual exchange of experiences. While American overseas consultants have been engaged in most West European countries, there exists only a handful of European political consultants who have been involved in four of five European parliamentary campaigns outside their own country. The regional fragmentation of the European consultancy markets has several causes. On the one side is the market for strategic consultancy services strongly segmented by party loyalties and the ideological background of external consultants, on the other side the professionalization of political management in Europe has taken a completely different direction than in the United States or in Latin America.

External professionalization is characteristic for the United States. Candidates hire professional, external advisors who offer their specific expertise to a candidate against payment. However, in Europe *internal* professionalization dominates.[43] Qualified staff members who are fully employed at the party headquarters meet more or less those political management and strategic tasks in parliamentary election campaigns that are fulfilled by external consultants in the United States.[44] If external communication and campaign consultants are contracted by European parties, they work in a team with internal staff experts and are tied to the programmatic party lines as well as the strategic decisions of leading official party managers. On the contrary, advisors of American candidates are obliged primarily to their candidates, which consequently leads to autonomous, party distant, exclusively candidate-centered election campaigns.[45]

In spite of the regional fragmentation and internal professionalization of the European practice of political management, the European consultancy market has started to move during the past years. A new generation of ambitious and qualified entrepreneurs founded consulting firms in Austria, Germany, France, Italy, Spain, Greece and Sweden, and media, public affairs and corporate consulting in Europe has turned into a growth industry. But in spite of the multitude of European consulting firms the degree of professionalization of the political consultancy business still differs significantly from that in the US. It is predominantly former politicians, party managers or political journalists who start a second professional career as self-employed advisors. The majority of these newly founded consulting firms specializes in media consulting, public relations, media training and coaching, and primarily uses the advantages of professional contacts and personal networks from their previous activities. Only during the last few years has a definite professional development in the direction of strategic political consulting taken place. In the meantime several European universities offer special programs and MA curricula for political management, political consultancy and public affairs management. The graduates of these programs represent the second generation of European political advisors, who are equally familiar with the techniques of American consultants in Washington, D.C., as they are with the practices of European lobbying in Brussels. Should an increased coordination and cooperation of European party alliances develop within the next few years, this could also lead to a Europeaniza-tion of national election campaigns and the formation of a genuine European consultancy market.

Professional Orientations of Political Consultants Worldwide

The worldwide proliferation of modern campaign techniques has resulted in an ongoing process of professionalization and internationalization of electioneering and campaign practices in media-centered democracies. As seen in Table 3.3, rather than an American-dominated one-way transfer we have to differentiate between several paths of diffusion of modern campaign expertise determined by country-specific institutional arrangements, regulatory frameworks, electoral laws, candidate-centered versus party-centered campaign styles and external versus internal professionalization of campaign managers, putting severe constraints on campaign and consultancy practices worldwide.

Table 3.3. Campaign Regulations and Campaign Practices in Thirty-Seven Countries

Countries	Public Funding of Campaigns	Ceiling on Campaign Expenditures	Restrictions on Political Advertising Practices	Dominant Medium of Political Advertising	Development of General Campaign Strategies	Frequent Cooperation with US Overseas Consultants
Argentina	Yes[a]	Yes[c]	No	TV-ads, Mass Rallies	Consultants	Yes
Australia	Yes	No	No	TV-ads, Direct Mail	Party staff	Yes
Austria	Yes	No	No	Print-ads, Posters	Party staff	Yes
Bolivia	Yes[a]	No	No	TV-ads, Mass Rallies	Consultants	Yes
Brazil	Yes[a]	No	Yes	TV-ads, Mass Rallies	Consultants	No
Bulgaria	Yes	Yes	No	Posters, Mass Rallies	Party staff	No
Canada	Yes	Yes	Yes	TV-ads, Direct Mail	Party staff	Yes
Chile	No	No	Yes	Posters, Print-ads	Party staff	No
Columbia	Yes[a]	Yes[c]	No	TV-ads, Mass Rallies	Consultants	Yes
Czech Rep.	Yes	No	No	Posters, Print-ads	Party staff	No
Finland	No	No	No	TV-ads, Print-ads	Party staff	No
France	Yes	Yes	Yes	Posters, TV-ads	Consultants	Yes
Germany	Yes	No	No	Posters, Print-ads	Party staff	Yes
Greece	Yes	No	No	TV-ads, Posters	Party staff	Yes
India	No	No	Yes	Mass Rallies, Posters	Party staff	No
Indonesia	Yes	Yes	Yes	Mass Rallies, Posters	Party staff	No
Israel	Yes	Yes	No	TV-ads, Posters	Consultants	Yes
Italy	Yes[a]	Yes[c]	No	TV-ads, Posters	Party staff	Yes
Japan	Yes[a]	Yes[c]	Yes	Posters, Print-ads	Party staff	No
Mexico	Yes[a]	Yes[c]	Yes	TV-ads, Mass Rallies	Consultants	Yes
Netherlands	Yes	No	No	Print-ads, Posters	Party staff	No
Norway	Yes	No	No	Print-ads, Posters	Party staff	No
Poland	Yes	Yes	No	TV-ads, Posters	Party staff	Yes
Portugal	Yes	Yes	No	Posters, Mass Rallies	Party staff	No
Romania	Yes	No	No	TV-ads, Posters	Party staff	Yes
Russia	Yes[a]	Yes	No	TV-news, Print-ads	Consultants	No
South Africa	Yes	No	Yes	Radio-ads, Mass Rallies	Party staff	Yes
South Korea	Yes[a]	Yes[c]	Yes	TV-ads, Posters	Consultants	No
Spain	Yes	No	No	Posters, Mass Rallies	Party staff	No
Sweden	Yes	No	No	Print-ads, Posters	Party staff	No
Switzerland	No	No	No	Posters, Print-ads	Party staff	No

Taiwan	Yes[a]	Yes[c]	No	TV-ads, Mass Rallies	Consultants	No
Ukraine	Yes[a]	Yes[c]	Yes	TV-ads, Mass Rallies	Consultants	Yes
United Kingdom	No	Yes	No	Print-ads, Posters	Consultants	Yes
United States	Yes[b]	Yes[d]	No	TV-ads, Direct Mail	Consultants	N/a
Uruguay	Yes[a]	No	No	TV-ads, Mass rallies	Consultants	Yes
Venezuela	No	No	No	TV-ads, Mass rallies	Consultants	Yes

Sources: Reginald Austin and Maja Tjernström, *Funding of Political Parties and Election Campaigns* (Stockholm: International IDEA, 2003); Lynda Lee Kaid and Christina Holtz-Bacha, *The Sage Handbook of Political Advertising* (Thousand Oaks, Calif.: Sage, 2006); Karl-Heinz Nassmacher, *Foundations for Democracy: Approaches to Comparative Political Finance* (Baden-Baden: Nomos, 2001); Fritz Plasser, *Global Political Campaigning: A Worldwide Analysis of Campaign Professionals and Their Practices* (Westport, Conn.: Praeger, 2002).

Notes:
a Covers only marginal proportion of total campaign expenditures.
b Public finance is optional for presidential candidates only, congressional candidates don't have access to public campaign finance.
c Frequently circumvented.

A comparison of institutional backgrounds of the electoral process in Australia, Latin America, Europe and Asia with the institutional context in which political consultants operate in the United States only offers few indicators for similarities. Political campaigns in the US are candidate-centered, strongly influenced by capital and media as well as highly professional, largely autonomously management and marketing operations.[46] In most countries outside the United States campaigns follow the traditional model: they are party-centered and labor-intensive, they receive free air time on television, are publicly supported and primarily planned and coordinated by party staff members.[47] Yet, candidate-centered campaign styles compared to party-centered styles represent only *one* essential differentiation. Other important context factors of the political consultancy practice include:[48]

- the electoral system (e.g. majority or plurality vote system versus proportional election system, density of the election cycle, candidate versus party elections);
- the system of party competition (e.g. number of party activists, dominant cleavages within electorate, ability of the organization to mobilize party followers, member versus voter parties);
- the legal regulations of election campaigns (e.g. public versus private campaign financing, limits on expenditures, access to television advertising, time limits for official campaigns, candidate nomination, primaries);
- the degree of professionalization of election campaigning (professional sophistication of campaign management, expertise and use of political consultants);
- the media system (e.g. public versus dual versus private media systems, differentiation of the media system, level of modernization, professional roles of journalists, autonomy of mass media, degree of media competition);
- the national political culture (e.g. homogeneous versus fragmented cultures, hierarchical versus competitive political cultures, degree of trust in the political process, political involvement, high versus low turnout cultures);
- the political communication culture (e.g. professional self-image of political journalism, closeness versus distance of the relationship between politics and media, degree of mutual dependencies); and
- the degree of modernization in society (e.g. degree of societal differentiation and segmentation, industrialized versus information society, socioeconomic mobility).

In the light of these criteria the situation of political competition differs substantially in the majority of electoral democracies worldwide from the one in the United States, a fact that consequentially is reflected in the different professional role-interpretation of political consultants. The data of the Global Political Consultancy Survey, a worldwide survey among over 600 campaign managers and political consultants from forty-five countries, which was conducted between 1998 and 2000, allow insights into the professional role definitions of political consultants and campaign managers and allow a typological differentiation of different approaches and orientations.[49]

A typology of the evaluations of success factors of a campaign resulted in two groups representing different types of strategic approaches toward a professional campaign. Consultants belonging to the first type have been classified as *Party-Driven Sellers* while the second type could be characterized as *Message-Driven Marketers*. Party-Driven Sellers concentrate on party-related success factors such as a strong and effective party organization, the programmatic policies of their respective parties and, while also stressing the importance of the candidates' personalities, they seem to be primarily party-focused. For Party-Driven Sellers the centerpiece of a campaign is the product of party-related factors. They try to sell the policy agenda of their party even when concentrating on the communicative role of their top candidates, who are regarded as party advocates, representing and communicating party positions and partisan arguments.[50]

In contrast, Message-Driven Marketers are more concerned about the strategic positioning of their candidates and developing messages that appeal to the expectations of specific target groups. Apparently, Message-Driven Marketers are more inclined to define campaigns in terms of political marketing operations, where segmentation, strategic positioning and targeting are seen as essential prerequisites of professional politics.[51]

Message-Driven Marketers concentrate more on resources such as the availability of campaign funds and tend to evaluate the role of external advisors and campaign consultants as far more important than Party-Driven Sellers. These two types of professional role definitions differ also substantially regarding their estimations of party-related campaign factors. Message-Driven Marketers seem to be more party distant, doubting the relevance of a strong party organization within the overall campaign operations.[52] Sixty percent of the political consultants interviewed in forty-five countries operate as party-centered Party-Driven Sellers, 40% correspond more with the political marketing logic of Message-Driven Marketers. Table 3.4 reveals the distribution of these two different styles of professional role definitions within select areas.

A majority of campaign professionals from seven out of ten areas worldwide are following the first type of professional role definition and can be classified as Party-Driven Sellers. Operating in

Table 3.4. Professional Campaign Styles by Areas (1) (percentage)

Campaign Professionals Classified as . . .	Party-Driven Sellers	Message-Driven Marketers
India	97	3
East Asia	84	16
Australia, New Zealand	79	21
South Africa	77	23
Western Europe	73	27
East-Central Europe	72	28
Other CIS Countries	67	33
Latin America	50	50
Russia	41	59
United States	15	85
Political Consultants Worldwide	**60**	**40**

Source: Global Political Consultancy Survey (1998–2000).

different media environments and shaped by different institutional arrangements and cultural traditions, these campaign professionals share a common point of reference: their party-focused approach toward campaign strategy. Among campaign managers from Latin America there was found at least a balanced distribution of selling versus marketing approaches. Apparently, one-half of Latin American *consultores politicos* are following a more traditional party-focused approach, while the other half seem to be influenced by the logic of *marketing politico* when reflecting about essential factors of a campaign.[53] Also a majority of Russian campaign experts prefers already a political market approach. Weak party organizations, concentration on strong leader personalities and a diffuse voter market favor a technocratic approach at the mobilization of disillusioned, largely detached voters.[54]

American political consultants come closest to the type of Message-Driven Marketers. Eighty-five out of 100 American campaign consultants interviewed could be classified as driven by strategic message development based on market segmentation and targeting operations. Comparing the composition of these types, more than 40% of respondents classified as Message-Driven Marketers are American political consultants, whereas only 5% of Party-Driven Sellers are from the United States. Data from the Global Political Consultancy Survey offer indications that the focus of modern campaign strategies also shifts toward candidate- and message-centered factors among political advisors from traditionally party-centered cultures such as Austria, Germany, Italy or Sweden.[55] This transformation seems to be especially pronounced among political consultants with strong affinity to the US role model of modern election campaigning.

Although only a minority of campaign professionals outside the United States could be classified as Message-Driven Marketers, we should be careful about concluding that party-focused approaches toward campaign strategies can be regarded as constant and resistant to advanced professionalism as represented by the American style of campaigning. While in the US emerged a division of labor between political parties and external consultants, with advantages for both sides, frequently tensions can be observed in West European campaign headquarters when party managers, fixed upon their organizations, are confronted with the strategic recommendations of party-external marketing consultants.[56]

Looking at the distinction between strategic orientations of party-internal and party-external campaign experts, we can assume that the ongoing professionalization of campaign management seems to be contradictory to party-centered styles of campaigning. Contrasting select core components of campaign strategies, we found divergent perspectives between Party-Driven Sellers and Message-Driven Marketers. Party-Driven Sellers tend to focus their campaign strategy on the national party organization and on the mobilizing force of strong party organizations, preferring a centralized and coordinated approach. Message-Driven Marketers primarily concentrate on available financial resources and on the central campaign message based on market segmentation and the expectations and emotions of target voter groups. In this case internal party managers primarily choose large-scale mobilization campaigns and personal voter contacts, while external consultants prefer targeted advertising campaigns on television, direct mail and phone banks. Finally, the American presidential campaign 2004 so far represented the most intensive mobilization campaign (ground war) as well as the so far most expensive television campaign (air war). Presidential and congressional candidates, political parties and affiliated advocacy groups combined aired 1.1 million 30-second spots, sent 5.5 billion mailings to target households, mailed 1.3 billion personal e-mail messages to target voters, made 120 million telephone calls and organized 30 million household visits by campaign volunteers during the 2004 presidential and congressional campaign season.[57]

A second cluster analysis based on evaluations of campaign experts regarding the importance of several mass media for advertising strategies resulted in *three* distinct types of orientations. Respondents belonging to the first cluster could be characterized as *Mobilizers*. While estimating the influential power of television, their communication strategies focus also on radio and on traditional forms of political advertising such as street posters and mass rallies.

The second type can be described as *Broadcasters*. This group of campaign managers is far more television centered, obviously highly attracted by the possibility of reaching a mass audience. In addition, radio and advertisement in daily newspapers are regarded as effective channels to communicate central campaign messages to target voter groups. Broadcasters also rely on traditional forms of political advertising strategies but to a significantly lesser degree than Mobilizers. Generally, Broadcasters tend to evaluate direct mail campaigns as slightly more effective than street posters and mass rallies.[58]

The third cluster seems to represent an advanced style of campaign communication. Political consultants belonging to this group can be described as *Narrowcasters*. While centered on paid television advertising campaigns as the most effective form of campaign communication, they also evaluate targeted communication forms such as direct mail as exceptionally important aspects for their advertising strategies. The Internet, as a new medium to communicate with connected voters via e-mail, banner ads and web-based videos, is seen as an enormously powerful campaign tool by Narrowcasters. Traditional advertising channels, such as print media advertising, large-scale street poster campaigns and mass rallies, seem to be regarded as outdated and as a waste of money and energy. Table 3.5 shows the area-specific distribution of these three distinct approaches to effective campaign communication.[59]

These data offer indicators for a combination of traditional and modern styles of political communication in most of the regions studied. West European political consultants differ significantly from the modus operandi of American political consultants. Two-thirds could be classified as television-concentrated, appealing to a mass public and trying to optimize the reach of their campaign messages. On the contrary, American political advisors prefer a rather *postmodern* strategic communication logic. Three out of four interviewed US political consultants could be classified as Message-Driven Marketers. Confronted with a multitude of news channels, "media clutter" and the declining effect of large-scale advertising campaigns in national networks, they focused upon segmented advertising campaigns in local cable channels, target group-oriented direct marketing activities and on the potential of the Internet and YouTube.[60]

On first sight the distribution of different political communication styles among political consultants seems to reflect the degree of modernization of the media systems in the respective regions. But with the exception of India and South Africa and the majority of African countries, where the media revolution of election campaigns only started recently, television is now almost everywhere the dominant medium. We should therefore expect that Latin American campaign

Table 3.5. Professional Campaign Styles by Areas (2) (percentage)

Campaign Professionals Classified as . . .	Mobilizers	Broadcasters	Narrowcasters
India	68	32	0
Russia	53	43	4
Other CIS Countries	50	39	11
South Africa	50	50	0
Latin America	50	45	5
East Central Europe	48	47	5
East Asia	24	73	3
Western Europe	15	74	11
Australia, New Zealand	8	64	28
United States	4	19	77
Political Consultants Worldwide	**35**	**45**	**20**

Source: Global Political Consultancy Survey (1998–2000).

managers, just like their West European and East Asian colleagues, will direct their communication strategies primarily toward television. Yet, one-half of all Latin American campaign managers interviewed has been classified as Mobilizers who continue to believe in traditional forms of campaign communication and voter mobilization. Western European political and campaign managers on the other hand see themselves mostly as Party-Driven Sellers and regard television as the core medium of strategic self-presentation and communication. Although they are recognizably influenced by the American role model and every second one had direct contacts to American political consultants during the past years, their professional self-image is oriented on the institutional rules of the game of parliamentary party-centered democracies.[61]

The data of the Global Political Consultancy Survey show that the political consultants and campaign managers outside the United States have more in common than expected. Generally the differences between the role definitions of consultants outside the United States are less pronounced than their distance to the professional style of American political consultants. American consultants prefer a marketing-oriented, party-distant campaign style while the majority of campaign experts outside the United States represents a party-centered "selling approach." In spite of observable tendencies toward Americanization there remains a substantial difference between consultancy styles and professional orientations of campaign professionals outside the United States and the professional role models of American political consultants. Their approach is unparalleled and seems to represent a unique style driven by institutional and media factors characteristic for the American electoral democracy.

Notes

1 Gerald Sussman, *Global Electioneering: Campaign Consulting, Communications and Corporate Financing* (Lanham, MD: Rowman & Littlefield, 2005).

2 Thomas Carothers, *Confronting the Weakest Link: Aiding Political Parties in New Democracies* (Washington, D.C.: Carnegie Endowment for International Peace, 2006), 86.

3 Reginald Austin and Maja Tjernstrom, eds, *Funding of Political Parties and Election Campaigns* (Stockholm: International IDEA, 2003).

4 Shaun Bowler and David M. Farrell, "The Internationalization of Campaign Consultancy," in *Campaign Warriors. Political Consultants in Elections*, ed. James A. Thurber and Candice J. Nelson (Washington, D.C.: Brookings Institution Press, 2000), 153–74; Ralph Negrine, Paolo Mancini, Chistina Holtz-Bacha, and Stylianos Papathanassopoulos, eds, *The Professionalization of Political Communication* (Chicago, IL: University of Chicago Press, 2007); Fritz Plasser, Christian Scheucher, and Christian Senft, "Is There a European Style of Political Marketing?" in *Handbook of Political Marketing*, ed. Bruce I. Newman (Thousand Oaks, CA: Sage Publications, 1999), 89–112; David M. Farrell, Robin Kolodny, and Stephen Medvic, "Parties and Campaign Professionals in a Digital Age: Political Consultants in the United States and Their Counterparts Overseas," *The Harvard International Journal of Press/Politics* 6 (4) (2001): 11–30; David M. Farrell, "Political Parties as Campaign Organizations," in *Handbook of Political Parties*, ed. Richard S. Katz and William Crotty (Thousand Oaks, CA: Sage Publications, 2006), 122–33; Sussman, *Global Electioneering*; Louis Perron, "Internationale Wahlkampfberatung," in *Handbuch Politikberatung*, ed. Svenja Falk et al. (Wiesbaden: VS Verlag, 2006).

5 Fritz Plasser with Gunda Plasser, *Global Political Campaigning: A Worldwide Analysis of Campaign Professionals and Their Practices* (Westport, CT: Praeger, 2002).

6 David Butler and Austin Ranney, eds, *Electioneering: A Comparative Study of Continuity and Change* (Oxford: Oxford University Press, 1992); David L. Swanson and Paolo Mancini, eds, *Politics, Media, and Modern Democracy: An International Study of Innovations in Electoral Campaigning and Their Consequences* (Westport, CT: Praeger, 1996); Pippa Norris, "Campaign Communications," in *Comparing Democracies 2: New Challenges in the Study of Elections and Voting*, ed. Lawrence LeDuc, Richard G. Niemi, and Pippa Norris (Thousand Oaks, CA: Sage Publications, 2002), 127–47; Darren G. Lilleker and Jennifer Lees-Marshment, eds, *Political Marketing: A Comparative Perspective* (Manchester: Manchester University Press, 2005); Negrine et al., *The Professionalization of Political Communication*; Lynda Lee Kaid and Christina Holtz-Bacha, eds, *The Sage Handbook of Political Advertising* (Thousand Oaks, CA: Sage Publications, 2006).

7 Ruediger Schmitt-Beck, "New Modes of Campaigning," in *The Oxford Handbook of Political Behavior*, ed. Russell J. Dalton and Hans-Dieter Klingemann (Oxford: Oxford University Press, 2007), 744–64.

8 Kaid and Holtz-Bacha, *The Sage Handbook of Political Advertising.*

9 Plasser, *Global Political Campaigning.*

10 Kees Aarts, Andre Blais, and Herman Schmitt, eds, *Political Leaders and Democratic Elections* (Oxford: Oxford University Press, 2007).

11 Ian McAllister, "The Personalization of Politics," in *Oxford Handbook of Political Behavior*, ed. Russell J. Dalton and Hans-Dieter Klingemann (Oxford: Oxford University Press, 2007), 571–88.

12 Dennis W. Johnson, *No Place for Amateurs: How Political Consultants are Reshaping American Democracy*, 2nd ed. (New York: Routledge, 2007).

13 Jay G. Blumler and Dennis Kavanagh, "The Third Age of Political Communication: Influences and Features," *Political Communication* 16 (3) (1999): 209–30; Pippa Norris, *A Virtuous Circle: Political Communication in Postindustrial Society* (New York: Cambridge University Press, 2000); Plasser, *Global Political Campaigning.*

14 David M. Farrell, "Political Parties in a Changing Campaign Environment," in *Handbook of Political Parties*, ed. Richard S. Katz and William J. Crotty (Thousand Oaks, CA: Sage Publications, 2006).

15 David A. Dulio, *For Better or Worse? How Political Constulants are Changing Elections in the United States* (Albany, N.Y.: State University Press of New York, 2004), 13–41.

16 Dennis W. Johnson, "Perspectives on Political Consulting," *Journal of Political Marketing* 1 (1) (2002): 7–21.

17 Lilleker and Lees-Marchment, eds, *Political Marketing.*

18 Plasser, *Global Political Campaigning.*

19 Norris, "Campaign Communications," and Johnson, *No Place for Amateurs.*

20 Plasser, "American Campaign Techniques Worldwide," *The Harvard International Journal of Press/Politics* 5 (4) (2000): 33–54.

21 Plasser, *Global Political Campaign*, 18–20.

22 Gerald Sussman and Lawrence Galizio, "The Global Reproduction of American Politics," *Political Communication* 20 (3) (2003): 309–28.

23 Plasser, *Global Political Campaigning*, 348–50.

24 Patrick Novotny, "From Polis to Agora: The Marketing of Political Consultants," *The Harvard International Journal of Press/Politics* 5 (3) (2000): 12–16.

25 Plasser, *Global Political Campaigning*, 24–5.

26 Bowler and Farrell, "The Internationalization of Campaign Consultancy," 163–5; Farrell, Kolodny, and Medvic, "Parties and Campaign Professionals," 23–5; Perron, "Internationale Wahlkampfberatung," 301–3; Plasser, *Global Political Campaigning*, 25–7; Christian Schafferer, "Is There an Asian Style of Electoral Campaigning?" in *Election Campaigning in East and Southeast Asia*, ed. Christian Schafferer (Aldershot: Ashgate, 2006).

27 Plasser, *Global Political Campaigning*, 26–8.

28 Schafferer, "Is There an Asian Style of Electoral Campaigning?"

29 Plasser, "American Campaign Techniques Worldwide."

30 Sussman, *Global Electioneering.*

31 Carothers, *Confronting the Weakest Link*, 92–4.

32 Douglas E. Schoen, *The Power of the Vote: Electing Presidents, Overthrowing Dictators, and Promoting Democracy Around the World* (New York: HarperCollins, 2007).

33 Plasser, *Global Political Campaigning*, 22–3.

34 Plasser, *Global Political Campaigning*; Roberto Espindola, "Professionalized Campaigning in Latin America," *Journal of Political Marketing* 1 (4) (2002): 65–81; Maria Belen Mende Fernandez, *Campanas Electorales: La Modernization en Latinoamerica* (Mexico City: Editorial Trillas, 2003).

35 Silvio Waisboard, "Practicas y Precios del Proselitismo Presidencial: A Puntes Sobre Medios y Campanas Electorales en America Latina y Estados Unidos." *Contribuciones* 2 (1997): 159–82 (quote); Frank Priess and Fernando Tuesta Soldevilla, eds, *Campanas Electorales y Medios de Communicacion en America Latina*, 2 vols. (Buenos Aires: Editorial Trillas, 1999).

36 Steffan I. Lindberg, *Democracy and Elections in Africa* (Princeton N.J.: Princeton University Press, 2006).

37 Derek S. Hutcheson, "How to Win Elections and Influence People: The Development of Political Consulting in Post-Communist Russia," *Journal of Political Marketing* 5 (4) (2006): 47–70.

38 Iwan Krastev, "Democracy's 'Doubles,' " *Journal of Democracy* 17 (2) (2006): 52–62.

39 Regina Smyth, *Candidate Strategies and Electoral Competition in the Russian Federation: Democracy without Foundation* (New York: Cambridge University Press, 2006).

40 Hutcheson, "How to Win Elections and Influence People," 60.

41 Christian Schafferer, *Election Campaigning in East and Southeast Asia* (Aldershot: Ashgate, 2006).

42 Perron, "Internationale Wahlkampfberatung"; Fritz Plasser, "Selbstverstaendnis Strategischer Politikber-ater," in *Handbuch Politikberatung*, ed. Svenja Falk *et al.* Wiesbaden: VS Verlag, 2006.

43 Negrine et al., *The Professionalization of Political Communication.*

44 Farrell, "Political Parties in a Changing Campaign Environment."

45 David Farrell and Paul Webb, "Political Parties as Campaign Organizations," in *Parties without Partisans: Political Change in Advanced Industrial Democracies*, ed. Russell J. Dalton and Martin Wattenberg (Oxford: Oxford University Press, 2000), 102–28.

46 Stephen K. Medvic, "Campaign Organization and Political Consultants," in *Guide to Political Campaigns in America*, ed. Paul S. Herrnson (Washington, D.C.: CQ Press, 2005), 162–75.

47 Paul Webb and Robin Kolodny, "Professional Staff in Political Parties," in *Handbook of Party Politics*, ed. R.S. Katz and W.J. Crotty (Thousand Oaks, CA: Sage Publications, 1999), 337–47.

48 Plasser, *Global Political Campaigning*, 78–80.

49 Ibid.

50 Ibid., 324–5.

51 John Philip Davies and Bruce I. Newman, eds, *Winning Elections with Political Marketing* (Binghampton, N.Y.: Haworth Press, 2006).

52 Plasser, "Parties' Diminishing Relevance for Campaign Professionals," *The Harvard International Journal of Press/Politics* 6 (4) (2001): 44–59.

53 Martinez-Pandiani, "La Irrupcion del Marketing Politico en las Campanas Electorales de America Latina," *Contributiones* XVIII (2) (2000): 69–102.

54 Smyth, *Candidate Srategies and Electoral Competition in the Russian Federation.*

55 Lars W. Nord, "Still the Middle Way: A Study of Political Communication Practices in Swedish Election Campaigns," *The Harvard International Journal of Press/Politics* 11 (1) (2006): 64–76.

56 Dulio, *For Better or For Worse?*; David A. Dulio and Candice J. Nelson, *Vital Signs: Perspectives on the Health of American Campaigning* (Washington, D.C.: Brooking Institution Press, 2005); Plasser, *Global Political Campaigning*, 326.

57 Daniel E. Bergan et al., "Grassroots Mobilization and Voter Turnout," *Public Opinion Quarterly* 69 (5) (2005): 760–77.

58 Plasser, *Global Political Campaigning*, 327.

59 Ibid.

60 Daniel M. Shea and Michael John Burton, *Campaign Craft: The Strategies, Tactics, and Art of Political Campaign Management*, 3rd ed. (Westport, CT: Praeger, 2006).

61 Plasser, *Global Political Campaigning*, 232.

4

Political Science and Political Management

Stephen C. Craig

Do campaigns really matter? There is a good bit of academic literature suggesting that they do not—or at least not as much as politicians and the media tend to think they do. It has now been more than half a century since President Franklin Roosevelt's campaign manager, James Farley, offered what is known as Farley's Law: that most elections are decided before the campaign even begins. More recently, in an analysis of presidential elections, Thomas Holbrook concluded that the *general* level of support for candidates during a campaign season is a function of national conditions (which vary primarily from one election to the next), while *fluctuations* in candidate support over the course of a single election year occur mostly in response to campaign-specific events. While Holbrook acknowledged that these events (including the so-called "convention bump," debates, blunders by one of the candidates, and so on) do have an impact, national conditions (measured in terms of *consumer sentiment* and *presidential job approval*, both factors that are in place before the general election campaign begins in earnest) ultimately matter a great deal more in determining who wins and who loses.[1]

Similarly, James Campbell conceded that *nonsystematic* campaign events (those that are idiosyncratic to a particular election, for example, Truman's relentless attacks on the "do-nothing" Republican Congress in 1948; Kennedy's strong performance in the first-ever televised presidential debates in 1960; the violent clashes between police and anti-Vietnam protesters during the 1968 Democratic national convention in Chicago; Ford's apparent misstatement about the Soviet domination of Eastern Europe in a 1976 debate), can have significant—and even decisive—effects on the outcome of an extremely close contest. Yet he argued that such events were important precisely *because* the elections in question were close.[2] In most instances, with the great majority of votes falling into place very early (because of the effects of partisan attachments, the national economy, incumbency, and selective perception and overall indifference on the part of voters) and one candidate often running clearly ahead of the other(s), nothing that happens during the campaign is likely to have more than a marginal impact.

The analyses by Holbrook and Campbell apply specifically to the top of the ticket, but there are reasons to suspect that short-term forces such as issues, candidate traits, and campaign events may have even less impact on lower-level races where voter attention is typically limited, and where factors such as partisanship and incumbency often appear to be decisive regardless of what happens or doesn't happen over the course of the campaign.[3] Overall, the conventional wisdom within the academic community has been that campaign events and the decisions made by candidates and their advisors matter relatively little, except under the most unusual of circumstances.[4] That wisdom may be changing, especially after the spectacular failure of forecasting models to predict accurately the outcome of the 2000 presidential election.[5] Nevertheless, the weight of the evidence seems to indicate that most campaigns at all levels are over, or almost over, before they even begin.

Candidates, consultants, and the political media would disagree, of course, and there is a growing amount of academic research to suggest they may be right—at least up to a point. In the present chapter, I will review some of that research and discuss how campaigns can shape election outcomes in a variety of ways, including the following:

- *persuading* voters, especially independents and others who initially are undecided or have weak preferences, to support one candidate or the other;[6]
- *activating* latent predispositions, primarily partisanship, that is, providing cues that lead Republicans and Democrats to make a choice in line with their underlying loyalties;[7]
- *educating* voters by providing information about (1) economic and other conditions for which elected officials can be held accountable (punished or rewarded); and (2) whether the issue stands of candidates are consistent with their own views and self-interests;[8] and
- *mobilizing* potential voters who, absent the stimulus (general or targeted) provided by the campaign, would otherwise be inclined to stay home on election day.[9]

While this list may not exhaust all of the possibilities, it serves as a reminder that campaigns are often about more than simply changing people's votes.[10]

In contrast, the "minimal effects" school of academic research is rooted in the fact that many citizens decide whom they are going to support before the campaign begins and remain firm in that choice throughout.[11] In the last twelve elections (1960–2004), for example, between 31 and 55% of presidential voters claim to have made a decision by the time their favored candidate entered the race, and a majority in each contest (between 54 and 70%) did so during the nominating conventions or before.[12] William G. Mayer has defined the "swing voter" as someone "who could go either way, a voter who [reflecting either ambivalence or cross-pressures] is not so solidly committed to one candidate or the other as to make all efforts at persuasion futile."[13] Based upon comparative ratings for major-party candidates on the 101-point feeling thermometer (a measurement device whereby people evaluate political objects according to how "warm" or "cold" they feel toward them), Mayer identified swing voters as those with scores ranging between −15 and +15 (that is, they rated one candidate no more than 15 "degrees" higher or lower than the other). His analysis revealed, first, that in presidential elections from 1972 to 2004, these individuals averaged a mere 23% of all voters; and, second, that although they were more likely than those with more polarized evaluations to change their preferences during the campaign, the number that actually did so was fairly small (approximately 15%).[14]

Although a campaign that captures the lion's share of these switchers has a good chance of winning, especially in a close race, there is a growing body of academic research that suggests that the other processes described above are important as well. How important? According to Michael John Burton and Daniel M. Shea, the answer to this question depends in part on who you are:

> A political scientist who is interested in the big picture of American elections . . . will tend to find that, in most elections, most of the time, campaigns just do not matter very much. A political journalist, on the other hand, looks for "news" (dramatic stories, sensational events), and will therefore seek out the hot campaign, complete with attention-grabbing characters and tragic ironies that emphasize the volatility of elections. A political practitioner, by contrast, is intimately familiar with the details of campaigns, the assumption being that the quality of the campaign is the most important factor in the outcome of the election. . . .[15]

As political scientists, Burton and Shea recognize that "[i]t is a rare campaign strategy that can elect candidates whose background, ideology, and partisanship are at odds with the people they are seeking to represent. There are half a million elective offices in the United States," and it is possible to predict with considerable accuracy "the outcome of races for the vast majority of them."[16] That said, academics are nonetheless increasingly aware that the final distribution of votes on election day, and sometimes even the identity of winner and loser, can be influenced by factors unique to the particular race in question. Those factors come in many varieties, beginning with the ebb and flow of day-to-day events that define the campaign and shape the media's coverage of it.

Campaign Events

The "minimal effects" perspective is based on the predictability of election outcomes and, to a lesser extent, of the individual voting decisions that produce them. According to Andrew Gelman and Gary King, campaigns provide voters with the information they need to cast a ballot consistent with their pre-existing attitudes and interests.[17] Since many of these attitudes and interests are known in advance, it is possible to make accurate projections about how most people will vote and which candidates are likely to be successful. This does not mean, however, that campaigns are irrelevant (for example, a candidate who chooses not to engage his or her opponent at all will surely lose), but rather that "[t]he critical thing about the campaign is its very existence."[18] When all is said and done, campaigns are about moving "basically rational partisan commitments back where they belong";[19] the strategic and tactical choices made by candidates and consultants (including variations in these choices across campaigns) simply do not matter all that much.

I will return to the informational role of campaigns later, but for now let me suggest that the argument here essentially has to do with whether the glass is half-empty or half-full. Is there a predictability to election outcomes that is rooted in the tendency for individual voters to cast their ballots based on considerations (party identification, incumbency, economic trends, presidential performance, and perhaps others) that are fixed, known in advance, and beyond the control of any campaign? Absolutely. But within these broad parameters, is it possible that campaign events and the actions of candidates have more of an impact than the "minimal effects" school would have us believe? Once again, the answer is yes. Although Holbrook found, for example, that the national economy and presidential approval were easily the most important factors influencing the outcomes of presidential elections in the late 1980s and early 1990s, his analysis revealed that the nominating conventions, presidential debates, and day-to-day campaign events played a meaningful (if usually modest) role as well.[20]

Research by Daron Shaw confirms that conventions and debates have a significant impact on presidential outcomes, as do campaign appearances,[21] television advertising (measured in terms of gross ratings points), and the occasional candidate blunder (gaffes and ill-advised comments of one sort or another) and outside event.[22] Consistent with Gelman and King's contention that campaigns serve mainly to reveal voters' "enlightened preferences," these effects tend to be larger and more durable for candidates who are doing several points better or worse in the trial-heat polls than expectations based on forecasting models;[23] they occur most often among mismatched partisans (whose initial preference was for the other party's candidate) and undecideds.[24] Campaign events also can influence election outcomes by shaping voter turnout; that is, exposure to campaigns of greater intensity (living in a presidential battleground state, for example) increases the probability of people making it to the polls on election day.[25]

Shaw's assessment of the importance of campaign advertising, especially in close races, is affirmed by Richard Johnston, Michael G. Hagen, and Kathleen Hall Jamieson, whose analysis of the 2000 presidential election led them to conclude, first, that Al Gore "won the news war" that took place during the closing days of the campaign (news coverage was largely favorable); but, second, that this advantage was more than offset by the sheer volume of televised ads on behalf of George W. Bush in pivotal battleground states. Had the Democratic nominee "saved up more resources for the last week and seriously closed the ad gap" in these states, Johnston and his colleagues believe that he probably would have been able to win an electoral majority.[26] The importance of earned media is evident in a recent study that examines voter reactions to the third debate between President Bush and John Kerry in October 2004. As one of the best opportunities for obtaining information about candidates (issue positions, rhetorical skills, ability to handle themselves under pressure), debates would seem to have great potential for shaping citizens' vote choices. Indeed, watching the Bush–Kerry debate did have an impact on viewers' evaluations of the candidates—but that impact was mediated by the particular "instant analysis," if any, to which a person was exposed (those who watched NBC News offered more favorable assessments of the president, while those who watched CNN.com gave higher marks to his Democratic opponent).[27] Numerous other studies indicate that while the overall impact is not always strong, debates sometimes have significant effects on vote intention, issue preferences, and perceptions of candidate personality.[28]

Campaign Strategy

In contemporary campaigns, one of the first decisions that candidates must make is whether to hire professional consultants. These are the men and women "who help to develop and deliver a candidate's strategy, theme, and message to the electorate," and the possibility that they might play a key role in shaping election outcomes has only recently begun to attract the attention of academic scholars.[29] Consultants themselves certainly believe that they provide essential services ("even to the point of self-deception")[30] and, increasingly, so do candidates, the media, and other political insiders. In 2004, for example,

> one of the first battles waged among contenders for the . . . Democratic [presidential] nomination was for the services of heavyweight political consultant Robert Shrum. This competition was a reflection not only of Shrum's skills but also of his reputation, that is, landing him as an advisor would automatically enhance the credibility of any candidate, especially in the eyes of journalists covering the campaign. . . .[31]

Whether because of this essentially self-fulfilling prophecy (hiring consultants makes candidates credible, hence they attract more/better press and raise more money—each of which contributes, more than anything the consultants actually do, to a better showing on election day), or because the services and strategic advice they provide help to persuade and mobilize voters on behalf of their clients, there is now some empirical evidence suggesting that candidates who hire consultants tend to fare better than those who don't.

According to Paul Herrnson, a higher degree of "professionalization" (referring to whether consultants were hired to handle fundraising, advertising, polling, and various other facets of the campaign) was associated with greater success in the 1992 congressional elections, especially among challengers and open-seat candidates.[32] Similar results were reported by Stephen Medvic for House races in 1990–1992, with pollsters appearing to have a greater impact than other types of consultants (at least among challengers).[33] There also are indications that consultants who are better known and more highly regarded by their peers tend to have the greatest success with regard to both fundraising and attracting votes.[34]

But what, one might wonder, do talented consultants *do* to achieve this level of success? Describing campaigns as communication events, Medvic offers a "theory of deliberate priming"

45

which suggests that "campaigns attempt to deliberately prime voters to utilize criteria in making voting decisions that work to the advantage of the campaign," that is, they generate messages intended to "resonate when they tap into voters' predispositions" (including their beliefs about whether one party or candidate is better suited to dealing with the issue in question); decisions about which issues and traits to emphasize, and how, are made with the advice of professional consultants, most notably pollsters and media specialists.[35] Part of this process involves identifying and then addressing the issues that are most salient to voters. As Medvic notes, however, another (and some might say more important) part involves campaigns priming voters on issues and traits that are likely to work in their favor. What we are talking about here is something called *issue ownership*, which exists when a preponderance of voters believe (based on "a history of attention, initiative, and innovation")[36] that one party or the other is better able to handle an issue or problem. Democrats, for example, are seen as better for helping the poor and protecting social security, while Republicans are usually favored on national defense and dealing with terrorism.[37]

Numerous studies have examined the issue ownership phenomenon and the extent to which it leads to campaigns in which candidates end up talking past one another, each side emphasizing its strengths and avoiding issues on which the party is seen as being relatively weak. Indeed, there appears to be a tendency in presidential, House, and Senate races for candidates to focus (in their speeches, paid ads, and other campaign communications) on issues that "belong" to their party.[38] At the same time, some studies show a fair amount of issue convergence[39] (or diversity),[40] with candidates occasionally (1) trespassing on issues typically associated with the other party (more common among those who are trailing in the polls);[41] (2) trying to "steal" an issue by giving it a particular spin (for example, Bill Clinton's support for the death penalty, which was accompanied by rhetoric that stressed crime prevention as well as punishment);[42] (3) addressing issues that are not clearly owned by either party (crime, immigration);[43] or (4) discussing other-party issues that are highly salient to voters at a given moment in time.[44]

For any of this to work, of course, campaign messages must be received by voters in something close to their intended form. In a study of 1988 US Senate elections, Jon K. Dalager found a very tenuous match between campaign themes (as identified by leading political journals) and the issues thought to have been important by citizens in their own state's Senate race.[45] Communication is a reciprocal process and, according to Dalager, it does not appear that voters always hear what the candidates are trying to say. Perhaps this is why the evidence is mixed as to whether issue ownership strategies actually help candidates to achieve their ultimate goal of electoral victory. Some studies suggest that campaign appeals are more effective when they deal with party-owned issues,[46] but others conclude that this is not necessarily the case. John Sides, for example, looked at Senate and House races in 1998, 2000, and 2002 and found that once other factors were taken into account, there was no significant relationship between how much candidates emphasized owned issues and the percentage of the vote they received.[47]

Readers will recall, by the way, that Medvic's theory of deliberate priming refers not only to issues, but also to personal traits that might work in a candidate's favor. Research suggests that issue and trait ownership tend to go together, that is, candidates own certain traits that are associated with party-owned issues. Thus, for example, "Republican Party ownership of national defense makes Republican candidates' claims of strong leadership qualities more credible; Democratic Party ownership of issues related to the social safety net makes more plausible Democrats' assertions that they feel the electorate's pain" (in other words, that they should be viewed as more compassionate and empathetic than their opponents).[48] The implication is that candidates will benefit when they are able to prime voters to give greater weight to party-owned traits when deciding whom to support and, importantly, that they will find it easier to persuade voters that they themselves possess those traits. Alternatively, data from presidential elections from 1980 to 2004 indicate that candidates actually gain the most when they score high on traits normally associated with the other side, that is, when they trespass.[49]

Moving from communications and message development to other elements of campaign strategy, the insights derived from academic research are fairly modest. A handful of studies have considered how campaigns choose to allocate scarce resources, specifically money (especially for televised ads) and time (candidate appearances). In presidential races, the unsurprising conclusion is that apart from national television buys, both parties usually concentrate their efforts in competitive battleground states; there also is a tendency for candidates to allocate more resources in response to an opponent doing the same in a particular state.[50] During the pre-nomination phase, established candidates are likely to emphasize the acquisition of delegates, while those who are less well-known (and who therefore lack the resources to compete effectively in delegate-rich primaries) focus on a smaller number of contests where success might generate support among both voters and financial contributors.[51]

A more prolific area of inquiry has to do with the decision to attack. Although not very popular among most voters (at least that's what they say when asked),[52] negative campaigning is something that occurs fairly often in campaigns at every level. Some candidates are, however, more likely to attack than others. Based primarily on data from presidential and US Senate elections, it appears that the strategic choice of "going negative" (as reflected in campaign ads, press releases, or media reports) is more likely to be made by (1) challengers;[53] (2) trailing candidates;[54] (3) those engaged in competitive races;[55] (4) candidates who have been attacked by their opponent;[56] (5) Republicans;[57] and (6) men.[58] In addition, there may be a tendency for the level of negativity to escalate as election day draws near.[59] All of this begs the question of whether negative campaigning actually works as intended, that is, does it help candidates attract votes and increase their chances of winning the election? In specific instances the answer is undoubtedly yes, but it is less clear that negative messages are more effective than positive messages on any sort of consistent basis.[60] This topic is dealt with more fully by Lynda Lee Kaid in Chapter 5, so I will not dwell on it here. I do, however, want to examine negative campaigning briefly within the context of another subject area in which political scientists have lately produced quite a bit of interesting and illuminating research: voter turnout and mobilization.

Voter Turnout and Mobilization

As noted earlier, one effect of campaigns may be to mobilize (or perhaps demobilize) potential voters and thereby shape the election outcome by determining the kinds of people who go to the polls on election day. An influential study some years ago by Stephen Ansolabehere, Shanto Iyengar, and others used both experimental data and an aggregate-level analysis of Senate campaigns to show that negativity is associated with lower turnout; the authors speculated that attack ads discourage some individuals from participating by lowering their sense of political efficacy (referring to the belief that ordinary citizens can use their votes to influence what the government does).[61] That negative campaigning is a demobilizing force quickly became the conventional wisdom, and to some extent remains the conventional wisdom[62] despite mounting evidence to the contrary. For example, Deborah Jordan Brooks' re-analysis of the same Senate races studied by Ansolabehere, Iyengar and others led her to conclude that the relationship between campaign tone and voter turnout is not statistically significant.[63] Indeed, a growing number of empirical studies suggest that negative campaigning *stimulates* turnout[64]—at least under certain circumstances,[65] and so long as the level of negativity doesn't cross over the line and degenerate into mudslinging.[66] What could account for such an effect? Paul Martin concluded that any or all of three psychological mechanisms may be involved: republican duty (negativity encourages participation by generating a perceived threat to the community); threat (attacks foster anxiety about specific candidates, hence greater interest in the election and an increased likelihood of voting); and closeness (negative messages generate turnout by signaling to citizens that the race is tight and their vote may therefore be decisive).[67]

Looking at this from the candidate's point of view, going negative provides one avenue for a campaign to manipulate the composition of the electorate and thereby enhance its prospects for electoral victory. Another and more direct approach would be to mobilize voters the old-fashioned way, through a grassroots effort that gets more of your candidate's supporters to the polls than those who are backing the opponent. As the moment of decision nears, campaigns are advised that

> everything you have done to this point is about the GOTV [get-out-the-vote] effort. Everything. You've canvassed, mailed, advertised, phoned, raised money, and delivered your message again and again and again. Why? To move voters and activate your base for support on election day. But voters get busy . . . and best intentions to vote are out the window. Now, after months of campaigning, your job, your one and only job, is to remind, remove obstacles, and motivate your [supporters] to do their civic duty.[68]

There are many aspects to grassroots mobilization, of course, including some (such as the initial canvassing of voters and identification of likely supporters) that take place well in advance of the final GOTV push. Further, some efforts to increase turnout are undertaken by individuals and groups whose motivation is primarily civic-minded, that is, their goal is to encourage people to vote regardless of which side of the partisan fence they happen to be on.

Much academic research has focused on activities of the latter type, and the consensus is that they do make a difference—not a huge difference necessarily, but a difference nonetheless. A series of field experiments by Donald P. Green and Alan S. Gerber, for example, indicated that the probability of a person's voting can be increased by appeals to his or her sense of civic duty, especially when those appeals are made face-to-face rather than by mail, phone call, or printed leaflet;[69] in fact, individuals who are mobilized to vote in one election also appear more likely to participate in future contests.[70] Looking specifically at the impact of phone calls from both professional and volunteer phone banks on young voters, David W. Nickerson found that (1) only calls made during the closing days of the campaign are effective at boosting turnout; and (2) the content of the message matters less than the manner in which it is delivered (rigid adherence to a prepared script does not appear to be effective).[71]

In one sense, the impact of partisan mobilization is clear-cut: people who are contacted (in whatever manner) by a political party or by someone representing a specific campaign tend to vote in higher numbers than those who are not.[72] There is, however, the question of whether mobilization actually increases turnout—or does it just seem that way because parties and candidates reach out to people who are expected to vote in the first place (because they are richer, better-educated, older, and have voted in the past)? Although these individuals *are* the ones most likely to be contacted in a competitive race,[73] the results of a field experiment conducted during the 2002 Michigan governor's race indicate that personal canvassing, phone calls, and door hangers all have a positive effect on turnout even with other factors (such as prior voting history) held constant.[74] In addition, there is some evidence to suggest that personal contact has a greater impact on occasional voters than on those who participate regularly.[75] Properly targeted, such activities may also help to generate votes (which, after all, are the campaign's main interest) for the sponsoring candidate or party on election day.[76] Overall, then, the academic literature leaves little doubt that mobilization activities can help to produce positive outcomes, especially in a close race.

The Education of Voters

Democratic theory has never been specific about how much information and knowledge is needed in order for individuals to be able to fulfill the obligations of effective citizenship. Most would agree, however, that at a minimum one must have a basic understanding of the policy differences that exist between candidates for office, and between the parties they represent. Without such an understanding, the public will be unable to cast its ballots wisely and, hence, unable to hold elected leaders accountable for their actions. Unfortunately, more than half a century of empirical research has left the distinct impression that "voters have a limited amount of information about politics, a limited knowledge of how government works, and a limited understanding of how governmental actions are connected to consequences of immediate concern to them."[77]

Much of the knowledge that citizens do possess concerning candidate and party differences is acquired within the context of spirited electoral competition. According to Gelman and King, the instability in public opinion polls that frequently occurs during presidential (and other) elections is a direct result of information flow; that is, as voters acquire additional information about candidates and issues, their initial preferences sometimes shift as they become better able to make choices that are consistent with their pre-existing political attitudes, beliefs, and interests.[78] Numerous studies reveal that a significant amount of learning occurs during campaigns, though it is less clear how different media (especially newspapers vs. television news vs. paid ads)[79] contribute to this learning, whether patterns of learning are similar at all levels of competition (presidential vs. statewide vs. legislative vs. local),[80] whether campaigns tend to narrow the information gap between the relatively more and less politically engaged segments of the electorate,[81] and whether the tone of a campaign (positive vs. negative) affects learning.

Given their growing interest in negative campaigning generally, it is surprising that the latter question has not received closer scrutiny by political scientists. Negative campaigning, and negative advertising in particular, is frequently defended for providing information without which it would be "much more difficult for the voters to make intelligent choices about the people they elect to public office."[82] As for whether voters learn more from positive or negative ads, however, the jury is out: some studies suggest that there is little difference between the two,[83] while others conclude that negativity promotes greater learning.[84] If the latter is true, it could be due to any of several factors, including (1) the higher issue content of negative ads;[85] (2) that negative ads heighten feelings of anxiety, thereby causing voters to seek out more information about candidates' issue stands or other attributes;[86] and (3) the tendency for people to have greater recall of negative ads;[87] and/or (4) to give greater weight to negative information than to positive information.[88]

The practical importance of all this is that information affects how people vote. In a study of presidential elections from 1972–1992, Larry Bartels found that fully informed women were consistently more likely to vote Democratic (often by a wide margin) than women who were less informed, while fully informed Protestants and Catholics were usually at least somewhat more Republican than their less-informed counterparts.[89] Focusing on policy views rather than vote choice, Scott Althaus estimated fully informed opinion by assigning the preferences of the most highly informed members of a given demographic group to all members of that group (also taking into account the influence of other demographic variables). He concluded that the average difference between actual and fully informed opinion on various issues was about seven points—not a huge number perhaps, but enough to switch a group's collective preference from one side of an issue to the other in several cases.[90] Studies such as these suggest that information about political issues helps citizens to recognize their self-interest and vote accordingly, and that campaigns play a crucial role in facilitating that process. Whether or not this is a good thing (should people vote for their own interests or for the interests of the larger community?) is a question that I will leave for others to answer.

Conclusion

Do campaigns matter? Although the conventional wisdom once was that they generally do not (except in unusual circumstances), more recent research suggests otherwise. There is little doubt that many races are decided before the campaign even begins, but scholars today have a greater appreciation for the various ways in which candidates and external events can sometimes shape the outcome on election day. Not in every contest perhaps, but certainly in those instances where the balance of both long-term (voter partisanship) and short-term forces (economic trends, incumbency, the overall mood among voters,[91] campaign resources) is relatively even. In this chapter, I have discussed four broad areas in which campaigns can make a difference: events, strategic choices, mobilization, and voter education.

These do not exhaust the possibilities, of course. One question that political scientists have addressed at length has to do with the role of money in campaigns. Common sense tells us that candidates who spend a great deal of money will probably fare better than those who spend little or none and, indeed, that is usually the case, especially for non-incumbents. While the results of academic studies are not always consistent, the basic pattern seems to go something like this: Higher levels of spending can help (1) challengers and open-seat candidates to overcome *some* of the electoral disadvantages they face (low name recognition, unfavorable district partisanship); and (2) incumbents to fend off opponents, especially experienced opponents, who are themselves well-funded (though the presence of such opponents is often a sign that the incumbent is vulnerable and that additional spending might not be effective). In addition, it appears that (3) challengers and open-seat candidates tend to spend money more efficiently than incumbents (that is, they generate more votes for each dollar spent); and (4) there is a minimum level of spending below which non-incumbents cannot be competitive, and a maximum level beyond which added spending by any candidate is likely to yield diminishing returns. Finally, when assessing the relationship between campaign spending and electoral success, one should not forget that even if money does attract votes, probable success also attracts money; in other words, because many donors prefer to maximize their investment, candidates with the most money are precisely the ones who are likely to win in the first place.[92]

Another area where scholars have just begun to scratch the surface has to do with the effects of electronic campaigning. Candidates at all levels, political parties, interest groups, and others are increasingly turning to the Internet for purposes of advertising, e-mailing campaign messages to supporters (and prospective supporters), fundraising, and mobilization.[93] What is not yet clear is the extent to which these activities have a substantial impact on individual voting decisions or election outcomes. We know, for example, that the Internet helped Howard Dean to become a credible candidate for the Democratic presidential nomination in 2004—though it was not enough to sustain his candidacy beyond the first few primaries, much less lead him to the White House. Relatively few voters use the web extensively for political purposes, and campaigns would be well-advised to employ the Internet as one tool among many in their communications arsenal.[94] Nevertheless, e-campaigning is here to stay and political scientists will be studying its effectiveness very closely in the years to come.

In sum, academic research has identified (and presumably will continue to identify) a variety of ways in which campaigns help to shape voter behavior and election outcomes. That these effects are evident mostly "at the margins" reflects the fact that, first, voters often make their decisions based on factors that are unrelated to the campaign and therefore beyond any sort of short-term manipulation; and second, many races are not competitive to begin with and there is little that any candidate or party, no matter how skilled or well-funded they may be, can do to change that basic reality. Within these parameters, however, it is clear that campaigns do matter. And, after several decades of testing models that seemed to suggest otherwise, political scientists and scholars in other academic disciplines are increasingly helping us to understand how.

Notes

1 Thomas M. Holbrook, *Do Campaigns Matter?* (Thousand Oaks, CA: Sage, 1996).

2 James E. Campbell, *The American Campaign: U.S. Presidential Campaigns and the National Vote* (College Station, TX: Texas A&M University Press, 2000).

3 For a different view, see Thomas M. Holbrook, "Do Campaigns Really Matter?" in *The Electoral Challenge: Theory Meets Practice*, ed. Stephen C. Craig (Washington, D.C.: CQ Press, 2006), 16–17; Daron R. Shaw and Brian E. Roberts, "Campaign Events, the Media and the Prospects of Victory: The 1992 and 1996 U.S. Presidential Elections," *British Journal of Political Science* 30 (2) (April 2000): 262.

4 Also see Christopher Wlezien and Robert S. Erikson, "The Timeline of Presidential Election Campaigns," *Journal of Politics* 64 (4) (November 2002): 969–93. These authors reviewed over 1,400 pre-election polls covering the period 1944–2000, and concluded that most of the observed variance from one survey to the next is due to sampling error rather than genuine attitude change on the part of voters.

5 See the symposium "Election 2000 Special: Al Gore and George Bush's Not-So-Excellent Adventure," *PS: Political Science and Politics* 34 (1) (March 2001): 8–44.

6 William G. Mayer, "The Swing Voter in American Presidential Elections," *American Politics Research* 35 (3) (May 2007): 358–88; Larry M. Bartels, "Messages Received: The Political Impact of Media Exposure," *American Political Science Review* 87 (2) (June 1993): 267–85; Gregory A. Huber and Kevin Arceneaux, "Identifying the Persuasive Effects of Presidential Advertising," *American Journal of Political Science* 51 (4) (October 2007): 957–77; Michael M. Franz and Travis N. Ridout, "Does Political Advertising Persuade?" *Political Behavior* 29 (4) (December 2007): 465–91.

7 Steven E. Finkel, "Reexamining the 'Minimal Effects' Model in Recent Presidential Campaigns," *Journal of Politics* 55 (1) (February 1993): 1–21; D. Sunshine Hillygus and Simon Jackman, "Voter Decision Making in Election 2000: Campaign Effects, Partisan Activation, and the Clinton Legacy," *American Journal of Political Science* 47 (4) (October 2003): 583–96.

8 Andrew Gelman and Gary King, "Why Are American Presidential Election Campaign Polls So Variable When Votes Are So Predictable?" *British Journal of Political Science* 23 (4) (October 1993): 409–51; Kevin Arceneaux, "Do Campaigns Help Voters Learn? A Cross-National Analysis," *British Journal of Political Science* 36 (1) (January 2006): 159–73.

9 Thomas M. Holbrook and Scott D. McClurg, "The Mobilization of Core Supporters: Campaigns, Turnout, and Electoral Composition in United States Presidential Elections," *American Journal of Political Science* 49 (4) (October 2005): 689–703; Peter W. Wielhouwer, "Grassroots Mobilization," in *The Electoral Challenge: Theory Meets Practice*, ed. Stephen C. Craig (Washington, D.C.: CQ Press, 2006), 163–82.

10 This is unlikely to happen on a wide scale since many races (1) involve matchups that are not very competitive to start with: see Holbrook, "Do Campaigns Really Matter?"; or, when they are, (2) most voters are exposed to offsetting messages from the candidates, thereby ensuring that persuasion effects will be modest: see Shanto Iyengar and Adam F. Simon, "New Perspectives and Evidence on Political Communication and Campaign Effects," *Annual Review of Psychology* 51 (2000): 149–69.

11 Paul F. Lazarsfeld, Bernard Berelson, and Hazel Gaudet, *The People's Choice: How the Voter Makes Up His Mind in a Presidential Campaign* (New York: Duell, Sloan, and Pearce, 1944); Bernard R. Berelson, Paul F. Lazarsfeld, and William N. McPhee, *Voting: A Study of Opinion Formation in a Presidential Campaign* (Chicago, IL: University of Chicago Press, 1954); Angus Campbell, Philip E. Converse, Warren E. Miller, and Donald E. Stokes, *The American Voter* (New York: John Wiley and Sons, 1960); Finkel, "Reexamining the 'Minimal Effects' Model in Recent Presidential Campaigns."

12 "Time of Presidential Election Vote Decision 1948–2004," available from the ANES Guide to Public Opinion and Electoral Behavior website, www.electionstudies.org/nesguide/toptable/tab9a_3.htm.

13 Mayer, "The Swing Voter in American Presidential Elections," 359.

14 Ibid., 362–5.

15 Michael John Burton and Daniel M. Shea, "Campaign Strategy," in *The Electoral Challenge: Theory Meets Practice*, ed. Stephen C. Craig (Washington, D.C.: CQ Press, 2006), 23.

16 Ibid., 27.

17 Gelman and King, "Why Are American Presidential Election Campaign Polls So Variable When Votes Are So Predictable?" 435. The authors are referring here specifically to presidential elections, though a similar dynamic may be evident at other levels as well.

18 Richard Johnston, Michael G. Hagen, and Kathleen Hall Jamieson, *The 2000 Presidential Election and the Foundations of Party Politics* (Cambridge: Cambridge University Press, 2004), 12.

19 Ibid.

20 Holbrook, *Do Campaigns Matter?*; also see James E. Campbell, "When Have Presidential Campaigns Decided Election Outcomes?" *American Politics Research* 29 (5) (September 2001): 437–60.

21 Appearances made later in the campaign have a greater impact than those earlier. See Jeffrey M. Jones, "Does Bringing Out the Candidate Bring Out the Votes? The Effects of Nominee Campaigning in Presidential Elections," *American Politics Quarterly* 26 (October 1998): 395–419; J. Paul Herr, "The Impact of Campaign Appearances in the 1996 Election," *Journal of Politics* 64 (August 2002): 904–13.

22 Daron R. Shaw, "The Effect of TV Ads and Candidate Appearances on Statewide Presidential Votes, 1988–96," *American Political Science Review* 93 (June 1999): 345–61; Daron R. Shaw, "A Study of Presidential Campaign Event Effects from 1952 to 1992," *Journal of Politics* 61 (May 1999): 387–422.

23 Shaw, "A Study of Presidential Campaign Event Effects from 1952 to 1992," 415.

24 Hillygus and Jackman, "Voter Decision Making in Election 2000," 591–93.

25 Jennifer Wolak, "The Consequences of Presidential Battleground Strategies for Citizen Engagement," *Political Research Quarterly* 59 (September 2006): 353–61. Also see James G. Gimpel, Karen M. Kaufmann, and Shanna Pearson-Merkowitz, "Battleground States versus Blackout States: The Behavioral Implications of Modern Presidential Campaigns," *Journal of Politics* 69 (August 2007): 786–97; David Hill and Seth C. McGee, "The Electoral College, Mobilization, and Turnout in the 2000 Presidential Election," *American Politics Research* 33 (September 2005): 700–25.

26 Johnston, Hagen, and Jamieson, *The 2000 Presidential Election and the Foundations of Party Politics*, 184.

27 Kim Fridkin Kahn, Patrick J. Kenney, Sarah Allen Gershon, Karen Shafer, and Gina Serignese Woodall, "Capturing the Power of a Campaign Event: The 2004 Presidential Debate in Tempe," *Journal of Politics* 69 (August 2007): 776–7.

28 William L. Benoit, Glenn J. Hansen, and Rebecca M. Verser, "A Meta-Analysis of the Effects of Viewing U.S. Presidential Debates," *Communication Monographs* 70 (December 2003): 335–50.

29 James A. Thurber, Candice J. Nelson, and David A. Dulio, "Portrait of Campaign Consultants," in *Campaign Warriors: Political Consultants in Elections*, ed. James A. Thurber and Candice J. Nelson (Washington, D.C.: Brookings Institution, 2000), 10–11. Also see David A. Dulio, *For Better or Worse? How Political Consultants Are Changing Elections in America* (Albany, N.Y.: State University of New York Press, 2004); Dennis W. Johnson, *No Place for Amateurs: How Political Consultants are Reshaping American Democracy*, 2nd ed. (New York: Routledge, 2007).

30 Burton and Shea, "Campaign Strategy," 33.

31 Ibid., 32.

32 Paul S. Herrnson, "Hired Guns and House Races: Campaign Professionals in House Elections," in *Campaign Warriors: Political Consultants in Elections*, ed. James A. Thurber and Candice J. Nelson (Washington, D.C.: Brookings Institution, 2000), 65–90. Consultants mattered less for incumbents, who often did not bother to mount a highly professional campaign in the absence of a serious challenge; also see Dulio, *For Better or Worse?*, 162.

33 Stephen K. Medvic, "Professionalization in Congressional Campaigns," in *Campaign Warriors: Political Consultants in Elections*, ed. James A. Thurber and Candice J. Nelson (Washington, D.C.: Brookings Institution, 2000), 91–109; Stephen K. Medvic and Silvo Lenart, "The Influence of Political Consultants in the 1992 Congressional Elections," *Legislative Studies Quarterly* 22 (February 1997): 61–77; Stephen K. Medvic, *Political Consultants in U.S. Congressional Elections* (Columbus, OH: Ohio State University Press, 2001).

34 Dulio, *For Better or Worse?*, 165. Once again, however, this may be less true for incumbents than for challengers and open-seat candidates (see note 32).

35 Stephen K. Medvic, "Understanding Campaign Strategy: 'Deliberate Priming' and the Role of Professional Political Consultants," *Journal of Political Marketing* 5 (1/2) (2006): 18–19.

36 John R. Petrocik, "Issue Ownership in Presidential Elections, with a 1980 Case Study," *American Journal of Political Science* 40 (August 1996): 826.

37 Ibid., 832; Andrew Kohut, "Midterm Match-Up: Partisan Tide vs. Safe Seats," Pew Research Center for the People and the Press, http://pewresearch.org/pubs/2/midterm-match-up-partisan-tide-vs-safe-seats.

38 Patrick J. Sellers, "Strategy and Background in Congressional Campaigns," *American Political Science Review* 92 (March 1998): 159–71; Constantine J. Spiliotes and Lynn Vavreck, "Campaign Advertising: Paritsan Convergence or Divergence?" *Journal of Politics* 64 (February 2002): 249–61; John R. Petrocik, William L. Benoit, and Glenn J. Hansen, "Issue Ownership and Presidential Campaigning, 1952–2000," *Political Science Quarterly* 118 (Winter 2003): 599–626; Holly Brasher, "Capitalizing on Contention: Issue Agendas in U.S. Senate Campaigns," *Political Communication* 20 (October 2003): 453–71; Tracy Sulkin and Jillian Evans, "Dynamics of Diffusion: Aggregate Patterns in Congressional Campaign Agendas," *American Politics Research* 34 (July 2006): 505–34.

39 Lee Sigelman and Emmett H. Buell, Jr., "Avoidance or Engagement? Issue Convergence in U.S.

Presidential Campaigns, 1960–2000," *American Journal of Political Science* 48 (October 2004): 650–61; David F. Damore, "Issue Convergence in Presidential Campaigns," *Political Behavior* 27 (March 2005): 71–97.

40 Sulkin and Evans, "Dynamics of Diffusion."

41 David F. Damore, "The Dynamics of Issue Ownership in Presidential Campaigns," *Political Research Quarterly* 57 (September 2004): 391–7; John Sides, "The Origins of Campaign Agendas," *British Journal of Political Science* 36 (July 2006): 407–36.

42 David B. Holian, "He's Stealing My Issues: Clinton's Crime Rhetoric and the Dynamics of Issue Ownership," *Political Behavior* 26 (June 2004): 95–124; John Sides, "The Consequences of Campaign Agendas," *American Politics Research* 35 (July 2007): 465–88; Sides, "The Origins of Campaign Agendas."

43 Noah Kaplan, David K. Park, and Travis N. Ridout, "Dialogue in American Political Campaigns? An Examination of Issue Convergence in Candidate Television Advertising," *American Journal of Political Science* 50 (July 2006): 724–36; Sulkin and Evans, "Dynamics of Diffusion."

44 Kaplan, Park, and Ridout, "Dialogue in American Political Campaigns?" There also is the question of whether issues are discussed at all, something that Kahn and Kenney found to be more common in competitive races; see Kim Fridkin Kahn and Patrick J. Kenney, *The Spectacle of U.S. Senate Campaigns* (Princeton, N.J.: Princeton University Press, 1999).

45 Jon K. Dalager, "Voters, Issues, and Elections: Are the Candidates' Messages Getting Through?" *Journal of Politics* 58 (May 1996): 486–515.

46 Stephen Ansolabehere and Shanto Iyengar, "Riding the Wave and Claiming Ownership over Issues: The Joint Effects of Advertising and News Coverage in Campaigns," *Public Opinion Quarterly* 58 (Fall 1994): 335–57; Adam F. Simon, *The Winning Message: Candidate Behavior, Campaign Discourse, and Democracy* (Cambridge: Cambridge University Press, 2002).

47 Sides, "The Consequences of Campaign Agendas," 482.

48 David B. Holian, "Trust the Party Line: Issue Ownership and Presidential Approval From Reagan to Clinton," *American Politics Research* 34 (November 2006): 777–802.

49 Danny Hayes, "Candidate Qualities through a Partisan Lens: A Theory of Trait Ownership," *American Journal of Political Science* 49 (October 2005): 908–23. Some interesting historical examples are provided by James N. Druckman, Lawrence R. Jacobs, and Eric Ostermeier, "Candidate Strategies to Prime Issues and Image," *Journal of Politics* 66 (November 2004): 1180–202; Lawrence R. Jacobs and Robert Y. Shapiro, "Issues, Candidate Image, and Priming: The Use of Private Polls in Kennedy's 1960 Presidential Campaign," *American Political Science Review* 88 (September 1994): 527–40.

50 Daron R. Shaw, "The Methods behind the Madness: Presidential Electoral College Strategies, 1988–1996," *Journal of Politics* 61 (November 1999): 893–913; also see Larry M. Bartels, "Resource Allocation in a Presidential Campaign," *Journal of Politics* 47 (August 1985): 928–36.

51 Paul-Henri Gurian, "Resource Allocation Strategies in Presidential Nomination Campaigns," *American Journal of Political Science* 30 (November 1986): 802–21; Paul-Henri Gurian and Audrey A. Haynes, "Campaign Strategy in Presidential Primaries, 1976–88," *American Journal of Political Science* 37 (February 1993): 335–41.

52 Although true, this statement should not be taken to mean that the public rejects all forms of negative campaigning. See Richard R. Lau and Lee Sigelman, "Effectiveness of Negative Political Advertising," in *Crowded Airwaves: Campaign Advertising in Elections*, ed. James A. Thurber, Candice J. Nelson, and David A. Dulio (Washington, D.C.: Brookings Institution, 2000), 29–32; David A. Dulio and Candice J. Nelson, *Vital Signs: Perspectives on the Health of American Campaigning* (Washington, D.C.: Brookings Institution, 2005), 123–9; Richard R. Lau and Gerald M. Pomper, *Negative Campaigning: An Analysis of U.S. Senate Elections* (Lanham, MD: Rowman & Littlefield, 2004), 12–14.

53 Kahn and Kenney, *The Spectacle of U.S. Senate Campaigns*; Jon F. Hale, Jeffrey C. Fox, and Rick Farmer, "Negative Advertisements in U.S. Senate Campaigns: The Influence of Campaign Context," *Social Science Quarterly* 77 (June 1996): 329–43. For a different perspective on this relationship, see Stergios Skaperdas and Bernard Grofman, "Modeling Negative Campaigning," *American Political Science Review* 89 (March 1995): 49–61; John Theilmann and Allen Wilhite, "Campaign Tactics and the Decision to Attack," *Journal of Politics* 60 (November 1998): 1050–62.

54 Lee Sigelman and Emmett H. Buell, Jr., "You Take the High Road and I'll Take the Low Road? The Interplay of Attack Strategies and Tactics in Presidential Campaigns," *Journal of Politics* 65 (May 2003): 518–31; David F. Damore, "Candidate Strategy and the Decision to Go Negative," *Political Research Quarterly* 55 (September 2002): 669–85.

55 Kahn and Kenney, *The Spectacle of U.S. Senate Campaigns*; Hale, Fox, and Farmer, "Negative Advertisements in U.S. Senate Campaigns."

56 Damore, "Candidate Strategy and the Decision to Go Negative"; Lau and Pomper, *Negative Campaigning*; but also see Kahn and Kenney, *The Spectacle of U.S. Senate Campaigns*.

57 Lau and Pomper, *Negative Campaigning*.

58 Kim Fridkin Kahn and Patrick J. Kenney, *No Holds Barred: Negativity in U.S. Senate Campaigns* (Upper Saddle River, N.J.: Pearson Prentice Hall, 2004); Paul S. Herrnson and Jennifer C. Lucas, "The Fairer Sex? Gender and Negative Campaigning in U.S. Elections," *American Politics Research* 34 (January 2006): 69–94.

59 Damore, "Candidate Strategy and the Decision to Go Negative." On the decision to attack in primaries, see David A.M. Peterson and Paul A. Djupe, "When Primary Campaigns Go Negative: The Determinants of Campaign Negativity," *Political Research Quarterly* 58 (March 2005): 45–54.

60 Richard R. Lau, Lee Sigelman, Caroline Heldman, and Paul Babbitt, "The Effects of Negative Political Advertisements: A Meta-Analytic Assessment," *American Political Science Review* 93 (December 1999): 851–75; Lynda Lee Kaid, "Political Advertising," in *The Electoral Challenge: Theory Meets Practice*, ed. Stephen C. Craig (Washington, D.C.: CQ Press, 2006); Lau and Pomper, *Negative Campaigning*. One reason why scholars have been unable to isolate such an effect may be that voters and academic scholars define "negativity" in different ways; see Lee Sigelman and Mark Kugler, "Why Is Research on the Effects of Negative Campaigning so Inconclusive? Understanding Citizens' Perceptions of Negativity," *Journal of Politics* 65 (February 2003): 142–60.

61 Stephen Ansolabehere, Shanto Iyengar, Adam Simon, and Nicholas Valentino, "Does Attack Advertising Demobilize the Electorate?" *American Political Science Review* 88 (December 1994): 829–38; also see Stephen Ansolabehere and Shanto Iyengar, *Going Negative: How Political Advertisements Shrink and Polarize the Electorate* (New York: Free Press, 1995).

62 Deborah Jordan Brooks, "The Resilient Voter: Moving Toward Closure in the Debate over Negative Campaigning and Turnout," *Journal of Politics* 68 (August 2006): 684–96.

63 Ibid.

64 John Geer and Richard R. Lau, "Filling in the Blanks: A New Method for Estimating Campaign Effects," *British Journal of Political Science* 36 (April 2006): 269–90; Paul Freedman, Michael Franz, and Kenneth Goldstein, "Campaign Advertising and Democratic Citizenship," *American Journal of Political Science* 48 (October 2004): 723–41; Kenneth Goldstein and Paul Freedman, "Campaign Advertising and Voter Turnout: New Evidence for a Stimulation Effect," *Journal of Politics* 64 (August 2002): 721–40; Richard R. Lau and Gerald M. Pomper, "Effects of Negative Campaigning on Turnout in U.S. Senate Elections," *Journal of Politics* 63 (August 2001): 804–19.

65 It appears that campaign ads (whether positive or negative) can sometimes produce higher turnout among specific target groups for whom the message contained in the ad is particularly salient; see Joshua D. Clinton and John S. Lapinski, " 'Targeted' Advertising and Voter Turnout: An Experimental Study of the 2000 Presidential Election," *Journal of Politics* 66 (February 2004): 69–96. To the extent that negativity does stimulate turnout, it is unclear from existing studies whether this effect is more likely to occur among highly politicized or more marginal voters. See, for example, Lau and Pomper, "Effects of Negative Campaigning on Turnout in U.S. Senate Elections"; Kim Fridkin Kahn and Patrick J. Kenney, "Do Negative Campaigns Mobilize or Suppress Turnout? Clarifying the Relationship between Negativity and Participation," *American Political Science Review* 93 (December 1999): 877–89.

66 Kahn and Kenney, "Do Negative Campaigns Mobilize or Suppress Turnout?"

67 Paul S. Martin, "Inside the Black Box of Negative Campaign Effects: Three Reasons Why Negative Campaigns Mobilize," *Political Psychology* 25 (August 2004): 545–62.

68 Catherine Shaw, *The Campaign Manager: Running and Winning Local Elections*, 3rd ed. (Boulder, CO: Westview, 2004).

69 These studies are summarized in Donald P. Green and Alan S. Gerber, *Get Out the Vote! How to Increase Voter Turnout* (Washington, D.C.: Brookings Institution, 2004). The problem with face-to-face mobilization is that it is not very cost effective. See David W. Nickerson, Ryan D. Friedrichs, and David C. King, "Partisan Mobilization Campaigns in the Field: Results from a Statewide Turnout Experiment in Michigan," *Political Research Quarterly* 59 (March 2006): 85–97; David Niven, "The Mobilization Solution? Face-to-Face Contact and Voter Turnout in a Municipal Election," *Journal of Politics* 66 (August 2004): 868–84.

70 Alan S. Gerber, Donald P. Green, and Ron Shachar, "Voting May Be Habit-Forming: Evidence from a Randomized Field Experiment," *American Journal of Political Science* 47 (July 2003): 540–50.

71 David W. Nickerson, "Quality is Job One: Professional and Volunteer Voter Mobilization Calls," *American Journal of Political Science* 51 (April 2007): 269–82; also see David W. Nickerson, "Volunteer Phone Calls Can Increase Turnout: Evidence from Eight Field Experiments," *American Politics Research* 34 (May 2006): 271–92.

72 Peter W. Wielhouwer and Brad Lockerbie, "Party Contacting and Political Participation, 1952–90," *American Journal of Political Science* 38 (February 1994): 211–29.

73 Joseph Gershtenson, "Mobilization Strategies of the Democrats and Republicans, 1956–2000," *Political Research Quarterly* 56 (September 2003): 293–308; also see Weilhouwer, "Grassroots Mobilization."

74 Nickerson, Friedrichs, and King, "Partisan Mobilization Campaigns in the Field."

75 David Niven, "The Limits of Mobilization: Turnout Evidence from State House Primaries," *Political Behavior* 23 (December 2001): 335–50; David Niven, "The Mobilization Calendar: The Time-Dependent Effects of Personal Contact on Turnout," *American Politics Research* 30 (May 2002): 307–22. In contrast, Hillygus found that being contacted by a party did nothing to alter the intention of those who planned to sit out the 2000 presidential election; see D. Sunshine Hillygus, "Campaign Effects and the Dynamics of Turnout Intention in Election 2000," *Journal of Politics* 67 (February 2005): 50–68. The reader should note that both studies by Niven are based on data from primary rather than general election campaigns.

76 Irwin W. Gertzog, "The Electoral Consequences of a Local Party Organization's Registration Campaign," *Polity* 3 (Winter 1970): 247–64.

77 Samuel L. Popkin, *The Reasoning Voter: Communication and Persuasion in Presidential Campaigns* (Chicago, IL: University of Chicago Press, 1991), 8.

78 Gelman and King, "Why Are American Presidential Election Campaign Polls So Variable When Votes Are So Predictable?"; also see Kevin Arceneaux, "Do Campaigns Help Voters Learn?"

79 To the surprise of many critics, campaign ads appear to be a good source (and in some cases a better source than newspapers or TV news) of information about candidates' issue positions. See Thomas E. Patterson and Robert D. McClure, *The Unseeing Eye: The Myth of Television Power in National Politics* (New York: G.P. Putnam's Sons, 1976); Marion Just, Ann Cigler, and Lori Wallach, "Thirty Seconds or Thirty Minutes: What Viewers Learn from Spot Advertisements and Candidate Debates," *Journal of Communication* 40 (Summer 1990): 120–33; Craig Leonard Brians and Martin P. Wattenberg, "Campaign Issue Knowledge and Salience: Comparing Reception from TV Commercials, TV News, and Newspapers," *American Journal of Political Science* 40 (February 1996): 172–93; Freedman, Franz, and Goldstein, "Campaign Advertising and Democratic Citizenship," 723–41; Ansolabehere and Iyengar, *Going Negative.*

80 A recent look at learning that takes place over the course of a nonpresidential campaign is Stephen C. Craig, James G. Kane, and Jason Gainous, "Issue-Related Learning in a Gubernatorial Campaign: A Panel Study," *Political Communication* 22 (October–December 2005): 483–503.

81 Some studies indicate that people who are more active or knowledgeable to begin with are the ones most likely to acquire information during the campaign; see Craig, Kane, and Gainous, "Issue-Related Learning in a Gubernatorial Campaign"; Daniel Stevens, "Separate and Unequal Effects: Information, Political Sophistication and Negative Advertising," *Political Research Quarterly* 58 (September 2005): 413–25. Others report that exposure to campaigns helps to narrow the so-called "knowledge gap"; see R. Michael Alvarez, *Information and Elections* (Ann Arbor, MI: University of Michigan Press, 1997); Freedman, Franz, and Goldstein, "Campaign Advertising and Democratic Citizenship"; Arceneaux, "Do Campaigns Help Voters Learn?" Mixed results are reported by Thomas M. Holbrook, "Presidential Campaigns and the Knowledge Gap," *Political Communication* 19 (October–December 2002): 437–54.

82 William G. Mayer, "In Defense of Negative Campaigning," *Political Science Quarterly* 111 (Fall 1996): 450. Also see John G. Geer, *In Defense of Negativity: Attack Ads in Presidential Campaigns* (Chicago, IL: University of Chicago Press, 2006).

83 Ansolabehere and Iyengar, *Going Negative.*

84 Craig L. Brians and Martin P. Wattenberg, "Campaign Issue Knowledge and Salience: Comparing Reception from TV Commercials, TV News, and Newspapers," *American Journal of Political Science* 40 (1996): 172–93; Kahn and Kenney, *No Holds Barred.*

85 John G. Geer, "Assessing Attack Advertising: A Silver Lining," in *Campaign Reform: Insights and Evidence,* ed. Larry M. Bartels and Lynn Vavreck (Ann Arbor, MI: University of Michigan Press, 2000); Darrell M. West, *Air Wars: Television Advertising in Election Campaigns, 1952–2004,* 4th ed. (Washington, D.C.: CQ Press, 2005); Geer, *In Defense of Negativity.*

86 George E. Marcus and Michael B. MacKuen, "Anxiety, Enthusiasm, and the Vote: The Emotional Underpinnings of Learning and Involvement during Presidential Campaigns," *American Political Science Review* 87 (September 1993): 672–85.

87 Brians and Wattenberg, "Campaign Issue Knowledge and Salience." On the other hand, the results of an experimental study involving college students revealed little difference in the recall of positive and negative radio ads; moreover, the specific things that subjects recalled about the negative ads were more likely to be in error. See John G. Geer and James H. Geer, "Remembering Attack Ads: An Experimental Investigation of Radio," *Political Behavior* 25 (March 2003): 69–95.

88 Richard R. Lau, "Two Explanations for Negativity Effects in Political Behavior," *American Journal of Political Science* 29 (February 1985): 119–38. Allyson L. Holbrook, Jon A. Krosnick, Penny S. Visser,

Wendi L. Gardner, and John T. Cacioppo, "Attitudes toward Presidential Candidates and Political Parties: Initial Optimism, Inertial First Impressions, and a Focus on Flaws," *American Journal of Political Science* 45 (October 2001): 930–50.

89 Larry M. Bartels, "Uninformed Votes: Information Effects in Presidential Elections," *American Journal of Political Science* 40 (February 1996): 194–230.

90 Scott L. Althaus, "Information Effects in Collective Preferences," *American Political Science Review* 92 (September 1998): 545–58. Also see Richard R. Lau and David P. Redlawsk, "Voting Correctly," *American Political Science Review* 91 (September 1997): 585–98.

91 This is often measured with a survey question asking people whether things (in the country/state/district) are "heading in the right direction" or "off on the wrong track"; see "Direction of the Country," available from the PollingReport.com website, www.pollingreport.com/right.htm.

92 For overviews on the topic of campaign spending, see John C. Green, "Money and Elections," in *The Electoral Challenge: Theory Meets Practice*, ed. Stephen C. Craig (Washington, D.C.: CQ Press, 2006), 58–78; Michael J. Malbin, ed., *The Election after Reform: Money, Politics, and the Bipartisan Campaign Reform Act* (Lanham, MD: Rowman & Littlefield, 2006).

93 Bruce Bimber and Richard Davis, *Campaigning Online: The Internet in U.S. Elections* (New York: Oxford University Press, 2003); Dennis W. Johnson, "Campaigning on the Internet," in *The Electoral Challenge: Theory Meets Practice*, ed. Stephen C. Craig (Washington, D.C.: CQ Press, 2006), 121–42.

94 David A. Dulio and Erin O'Brien, "Campaigning with the Internet: The View from Below," in *Campaigns and Elections American Style*, 2nd ed., ed. James A. Thurber and Candice J. Nelson (Boulder, CO: Westview, 2004), 173–94.

5

Political Management and Political Communications

Lynda Lee Kaid

Political management has long-standing ties to applied political communications and to political communication as an academic discipline. From both the applied and theoretical perspectives, political communication traces its roots to the classic writing of Aristotle, Plato, Quintillian, and Cicero.[1] In more modern contexts, the study of political communication as a theoretical and scholarly discipline is derived from a melding of multidisciplinary work in communication, political sciences, psychology, sociology, and marketing.[2] Among the many definitions of *political communication*, Steve Chaffee's simple and straightforward one is perhaps the best: the "role of communication in the political process."[3]

As an academic area of study, political communication developed into its own cross-disciplinary field in the 1950s, according to Dan Nimmo and Keith R. Sanders in their seminal *Handbook of Political Communication*.[4] Nimmo in his early work, *The Political Persuaders*, helped to introduce the intertwining of communication and political consultants in the political process.[5] Bibliographic resources, journals, and classes devoted to the topic of political communication also emerged, and particularly important was the establishment in 1973 of the political communication division in the International Communication Association, which for nearly two decades functioned as the major scholarly venue devoted to political communication. Later, the American Political Science Association and the Speech Communication Association (now the National Communication Association) followed suit by establishing similar divisions devoted to political communication.

Joseph Napolitan, a founder of the American Association of Political Consultants, proclaimed more than three decades ago that a "political consultant is a specialist in political communication."[6] As such, Napolitan argued, the job of a political consultant is to define the message that needs to be communicated, select the vehicles of communication, and implement the communication process. This chapter concerns particularly the contributions of the discipline of political communication to political management, to the communication of a candidate's message through appropriate channels to citizens, or voters. The chapter considers these contributions in five main topic areas: political speaking, political debates, political advertising, new technologies, and political news.

Political Communication as Public Speech and Rhetoric

Early studies of communication in political contexts were devoted to analyzing political speaking and debating. The famous Lincoln–Douglas debates, of course, received attention, but scholars also considered the effects of public speaking in non-campaign contexts, such as Lincoln's famous 1863 Gettysburg Address,[7] Martin Luther King's "I Have a Dream" speech in 1963, the speeches of "great communicator" Ronald Reagan, and presidential inaugural and state of the union speeches.[8] Whether aware of it or not, when a political consultant coaches a candidate or public figure on giving an effective speech, the principles involved are derived from classical rhetorical theory that stressed the five canons of rhetoric: invention (ideas), arrangement (organization), elocution (style), memory, and delivery.[9]

The study of political communication as political speeches and rhetoric is primarily concerned with analysis of political messages. Currently, such study often focuses attention on political speaking as manifested in *genres* of speech making. For instance, scholars study inaugural addresses and state of the union addresses of presidents and state governors.[10] Analyses have also been focused on the specialized genre of apologia as exemplified by Richard M. Nixon's famous "Checkers" speech in the 1952 presidential campaign, Edward Kennedy's speech apologizing for the 1969 Chappaquiddick incident, and Bill Clinton's acknowledgment of his affair with White House intern Monica Lewinsky in 1998.[11] Scholars have, for instance, identified four major strategies that are useful in successfully restoring an image: denial, bolstering, differentiation, and transcendence.[12]

Political consultants and managers can also benefit from discussions of the principles of speechwriting[13] and from application of dramatistic analysis to political campaigns. The latter work also incorporates the study of group interactions and contributes to understanding how the meaning of political messages may "chain out" and acquire multiple interpretations in political audiences.[14]

Political Communication as Political Debates

Although the previously mentioned Lincoln–Douglas debates are among the most famous examples of the debate mode of political communication, the inclusion of television in the debate equation made debates the quintessential modern democratic forum. From the first television encounter between Kennedy and Nixon in 1960, televised debates have captured the attention of political candidates, political consultants, the news media, and the public. The 1960 "Great Debates" were subjected to voluminous study by political communication specialists from multiple disciplinary perspectives, and these analyses spawned many interpretations of Kennedy's success in the encounters.[15]

For a variety of reasons, there was no recurrence of televised presidential debates until 1976. The Federal Communication Commission's reinterpretation of the Equal Time Provision in 1975 opened the floodgates for televised political debates, and every presidential election since 1976 has featured some type of debate encounter between presidential contenders. In the 1980s presidential debates became a staple of presidential primaries, and the practice of live and mediated (on both radio and television) candidate encounters spread to races below the presidential level. In presidential campaigns, debates draw the largest television audience of any single campaign event.[16] Debates are also now a common feature of campaigns, both in primary and general election campaigns, for state governor, for US Senate, for US Congress, and for many other contested electoral positions.

Because of the long hiatus of campaign debating between 1960 and 1976, many classic books about political campaigning had little or nothing to say about the strategic importance of political debates and offered candidates and their managers little or no advice about the role debates could play in campaign communication.[17] However, in recent years, political communication scholarship has had much to offer political managers about successful strategies for political debating.

Initially, of course, a candidate must decide whether or not to participate in a debate. Steve Chaffee outlined the conditions under which voters find debates useful: (1) when at least one of the candidates is relatively unknown; (2) when many voters are undecided; (3) when the race appears close; and (4) when party allegiances are weak.[18] Judith Trent and Robert Friedenberg have outlined the conditions under which political candidates benefit and/or lose from participating in debates. Deciding whether to debate, they suggest, depends on evaluating the closeness of the election, the advantages of debating, how capable the candidate is as a debater, the number of candidates who will participate in the debate, and the extent to which the candidate can control the debate elements (timing, location, format, topics, and so forth).[19] Trent and Friedenberg also provide good analyses of how debates may influence voter learning about campaign issues and their potential persuasive effects on perceptions of candidate images.[20] Specific debate advice has also been offered by Myles Martel about the physical context of a debate encounter (sitting vs. standing, eye contact strategies, candidate dress and movement tactics), strategies for confronting arguments, denials, handling apologies, use of humor, opening and closing speeches, and strategies for choosing formats and panelists.[21]

There is strong evidence that debates contribute to voter learning about political issues and to candidate image formulations. In the end, however, it is also important for political managers to know that research shows that overall debates are unlikely to result in very substantial changes in voting intentions.[22] More commonly, debates reinforce pre-existing attitudes of voters; but debates may sometimes affect the votes of a small percentage of viewers. Some elections are decided by small percentage margins, thus making debate effects potentially pivotal to electoral outcomes. Debate exposure may also have some latent effects on the political system, increasing a voter's sense of political efficacy and lessening cynicism.[23]

Finally, most political communication investigations on political debates focus on the presidential level. We know very little about the practices and effects in debates below the presidential level. However, managers may find the report of a national survey of voters produced by the Debate Advisory Standards Project to be useful in understanding "best practices" for state and local debates.[24]

Political Communication as Political Advertising

Political advertising represents one of the areas where the ties between political communication research and political management have been the strongest. Because political advertising is the major form of communication between candidates/parties and voters in modern campaigns, political communication research has offered findings that can be directly applied to political campaign situations. From the earliest empirical research focused on political advertising, researchers found that televised political advertising defied the general conclusions of the limited effects model of communication.[25] For instance, political communication scholars discovered that televised political advertising, because it appeared in commercial breaks as interstitial programming, could overcome partisan selectivity and ensure exposure of the candidate's message to a broad range of voters.[26]

Political communication researchers have extensively analyzed political advertising, breaking down the "videostyle" of ads into the verbal, nonverbal, and video production techniques that represent an ad's content and structure.[27] Researchers also quickly found other reasons to reinforce the confidence of political consultants in the power of political advertising messages, verifying that political advertising could have direct effects on voter issue knowledge, image perceptions of political candidates, and sometimes on voting decisions.[28] Such effects appear to be the greatest on voters who are undecided and who have low levels of involvement or awareness of the political campaigns or political issues at stake.[29]

Political advertising research has also provided evidence that ads that focus on candidate issue positions are more successful than ads that contain primarily candidate image or personality information.[30] The superiority of issue advertising appears to be particularly clear when the issues involved are those over which the candidate's political party claims "ownership." Historically, this has meant that Democrats receive more credit for being successful in achieving results related to economic and social issues, whereas Republicans have appeared to "own" foreign policy.[31]

The extent to which political advertising generates emotional responses in viewers is also related to its effects on viewers. For instance, emotional content can affect recall of information in an ad.[32] Emotional responses generated by ad exposure may influence how viewers respond to and evaluate a candidate.[33] This is especially true for emotional responses that rely on fear appeals.[34]

Negative Advertising Effects

The effects of negative advertising present a special case in the study of political communication, and the growing use of such advertising in political campaigns at all levels has spurred considerable popular, professional, and scholarly interest in the subject. The use of negative advertising by political action committees (PACs) and independent groups has grown especially heavy in the aftermath of Congressional passage in 2002 of the Bipartisan Campaign Reform Act (BCRA). Record levels of negative political advertising were hallmarks of the 2004 presidential campaign and the 2006 mid-term elections in the United States.[35] (See also Chapter 11, by Steve Billet, on "monster" PACs, and Chapter 14, by Nicholas J. O'Shaughnessy and Stephan Henneberg, on the selling of the presidency.)

The use of negative advertising by independent groups has long been considered an effective strategy in political campaigns. Early research on negative advertising demonstrated that independent groups were more successful in attracting voter confidence for their negative attacks against a political candidate.[36] The use of independent groups as sources of negative advertising has been a staple of advertising strategy for several decades, although some recent research suggests that the increased frequency of such advertising may be decreasing the reliability of this finding.[37]

Of course, "going negative" always carries some risk of backlash,[38] although using comparative ads,[39] humor,[40] or focusing criticism of opponents on their issue positions, rather than on image or character traits, may help to overcome the risk of backlash and heighten the effectiveness of negative ads.[41]

Nonetheless, there is a substantial body of research that validates the effectiveness of negative advertising. Even though such advertising may sometimes lessen the evaluation of the sponsoring candidate, the negative effect on the opponent's evaluation is often even more severe, making the outcome a good one for the attacking candidate, especially since exposure to negative advertising is very effective in embedding negative information about the opponent in the voter's mind.[42] Research also suggests that a candidate who is attacked must not delay in his/her response to the attacks, making the process of rebuttal a crucial campaign dynamic.[43] In addition to direct rebuttals, a candidate who expects to be attacked by an opponent can also help to blunt the effect of an attack by engaging in inoculation early in the campaign.[44] Candidates who can successfully use political advertising to get their own message out first, staking out a positive position on the issues of potential vulnerability, can be more successful in surviving attacks when they do come. Meta-analysis shows some of these effects to be small, but studies that pit negative ads directly against other ads, as measured in such studies, do not provide a thorough investigation of negative advertising effects.[45]

Finally, while journalists, and even some researchers, have charged that political advertising on television is a blight on democracy and serves to dampen voter participation in politics, the evidence for such charges is limited. A few studies have demonstrated small decreases in voter turnout in races where voters were exposed to negative advertising.[46] Other studies have found no such effects, or even positive effects on voter interest and participation as a result of exposure to negative advertising.[47]

Political Communication and New Technologies

New technological developments are rapidly reshaping the political communication landscape. Candidates, parties, interest groups, and voters increasingly rely on the Internet to communicate political information and to attempt to persuade others to their viewpoints. (See also Chapter 13, by Emilienne Ireland, on online campaigning.) In addition to the use of e-mail for contact and organizational purposes, political campaigns and government organizations quickly began to use the Web as an information distribution mechanism. The virtually unlimited space at an almost free cost was, and remains, an irresistible combination. Bill Clinton's 1992 campaign was the first presidential campaign to take advantage of the Web to distribute materials. Following the 1996 election year researchers at Rutgers University outlined the structural capabilities of the Web to enhancing democratic activity:

> (a) inherent interactivity; (b) potential for lateral and horizontal communication; (c) point-to-point and non-hierarchical modes of communication; (d) low costs to users (once a user is set up); (e) rapidity as a communication medium; (f) lack of national or other boundaries; and (g) freedom from the intrusion and monitoring of government.[48]

It is now virtually unthinkable for any political candidate, political leader, political or government organization to forgo a Web presence. Campaign websites are the hub of modern campaigning, providing unlimited opportunities for communication with news media and the public and incorporating opportunities for fundraising, interactivity, and citizen feedback as well. While the Internet has not yet provided the kind of democratic "public sphere" that some researchers have idealized,[49] it has nonetheless opened up new potential for candidate, citizen, and news media interaction in the form of blogs, Vlogs such as YouTube, and social networking sites like Facebook and MySpace. Other forms of new technology are also developing into important political management tools, including cell phones, podcasting, RSS (Really Simple Syndication) feeds, and even campaigning in virtual sites such as Second Life. Research on these new political communication channels and formats is still in its infancy, but there are many avenues for future development, and political communication researchers will undoubtedly continue to advance our understanding of the political contributions of these new technologies.

Political Communication and News Media

Political speeches/rhetoric, debates, advertising, and most aspects of new technologies are all primarily *controlled* communication; they are generated by a source (usually a candidate, a political leader, a political group, a government organization, or even a citizen). Political communication also encompasses the study of *uncontrolled* communication. Of course, the most common form of uncontrolled communication in the political system is represented by the news media.

Political consultants and managers often make concentrated and Herculean efforts to influence political news, most overtly through production of print and video news releases and the staging of campaign events (sometimes referred to as pseudo-events). Political communication researchers have learned a great deal about the interaction of political actors with the news media by studying the content of news media coverage of political campaigns and other political issues and events. Such research has verified the frequently observed news media practice of limiting quotations and coverage of actual messages of political figures to "sound bites." In modern presidential campaigns, the average sound bite a candidate can expect to receive when speaking about a campaign issue or event is 7–8 seconds.[50]

In addition to shortening the time for candidates to speak, the news media also focus little of their coverage on real or substantive public issues, preferring instead to fill news time with discussions of campaign strategy, analyzing the campaign as a "horserace."[51] Breaking through the wall of journalistic narcissism that focuses more on what journalists think than on what candidates say and casting campaign news in a continuously negative light presents modern campaigns with difficult challenges.[52]

Political communication scholars have also built a strong case for two other aspects of news media coverage of political campaigns. The first area is represented by the agenda-setting research tradition. Max McCombs and his colleagues have developed over many years convincing evidence that the mass media set the public's agenda of issues.[53] In other words, the issues that the media choose to cover and their relative importance (agenda lists in order of importance) become the issues that the public judges to be important. The first empirical testing of this agenda-setting relationship was conducted during the 1968 presidential campaign in North Carolina with undecided voters. Since that initial study, a voluminous research tradition has evolved, providing research to indicate that agenda-setting effects are strongest for voters who are heavy media users and who have a high need for orientation.[54]

The second convincing area of research on news media effects is framing research. Framing is the study of how the news media present issues or candidates to the public. Some agenda-setting researchers see framing as conceptually linked to agenda-setting and argue that framing is presentation of specific attributes related to an issue.[55] Others, such as Robert Entman, argue convincingly that framing constitutes its own conceptual base and derives from the media's concentration on some aspects of an issue over others: "to frame is to select some aspects of a perceived reality and make them more salient in a communicating text."[56] William A. Gamson and Andre Modigliani define framing as "the central organizing idea or story line that provides meaning to an unfolding strip of events."[57] Still other researchers stress the need to view framing as a separate concept and to consider the importance of audience frames as well as media frames.[58] All of these approaches provide a way of analyzing media coverage of political events and help scholars and practitioners to understand the approaches and routines that guide journalistic decisions about how to cover political candidates, issues, and events.

Conclusion

Whether focusing on controlled media such as speeches, debates, ads, or new technologies or uncontrolled media such as news in print or on television, political communication is at the nexus of political campaigning and of the relationship between citizens and their leaders in the governing process. As technology continues to evolve and develop new ways for citizens to interact with their governments and their leaders and to monitor and hold them accountable for the success and failure of public policies, those governments and leaders must also embrace new technologies to develop effective ways to listen to citizens and to serve their needs. Political consultants and managers will play important roles in making these future interactions successful. The maintenance of democratic life at every level and in every part of the world will depend upon that success.

Notes

1 Aristotle, *Aristotle's Rhetoric: Or, The True Grounds and Principles of Oratory; Showing the Right Art of Pleading and Speaking in Full Assemblies and Courts of Judicature* (London: Robert Midgley, 1685); Quintilian, *Instituto Oratoria*; and Paul Newall, *An Introduction to Rhetoric and Rhetorical Figures*, Galilean Library website, 2005, http://galilean-library.org/int21.html.
2 See Dan Nimmo, *The Political Persuaders* (Englewood Cliffs, N.J.: Prentice-Hall, 1970); Bruce I. Newman, ed., *The Handbook of Political Marketing* (Thousand Oaks, CA: Sage Publications, 1999); and Dan Nimmo and Keith R. Sanders, eds, *Handbook of Political Communication* (Beverly Hills, CA: Sage Publications, 1981).
3 Steven Chaffee, ed., *Political Communication* (Beverly Hills, CA: Sage Publications, 1975), 15.
4 Nimmo and Sanders, *Handbook of Political Communication*.
5 Nimmo, *The Political Persuaders*.
6 Joseph Napolitan, *The Election Game and How to Win It* (Garden City, N.Y.: Doubleday, 1972), 2.
7 Douglas L. Wilson, *Lincoln's Sword: The Presidency and the Power of Words* (New York: Knopf, 2006).
8 See examples of many well-known American speeches at the American Rhetoric website, http://www.americanrhetoric.com/; and George A. Kennedy, *A New History of Classical Rhetoric* (Princeton, N.J.: Princeton University Press, 1994).
9 Newall, *An Introduction to Rhetoric and Rhetorical Figures*.
10 Karlyn Kohrs Campbell and Kathleen Hall Jamieson, *Deeds Done in Words: Presidential Rhetoric and the Genre of Governance* (Chicago, IL: University of Chicago Press, 1990); and Donna R. Hoffman and Alison D. Howard, *Addressing the State of the Union: The Evolution and Impact of the President's Big Speech* (Boulder, CO: Lynne Rienner Publishers, 2006).
11 Kurt Ritter and Martin J. Medhurst, eds, *Presidential Speechwriting: From the New Deal to the Reagan Revolution and Beyond* (College Station, TX: Texas A&M University Press, 2003); William L. Benoit, *Accounts, Excuses, and Apologies: A Theory of Image Restoration Strategies* (Albany, N.Y.: State University of New York Press, 1995); and Sharon D. Downey, "The Evolution of the Rhetorical Genre of Apologia," *Western Journal of Communication* 57 (1993): 42–64.
12 B.L. Ware and Wil A. Linkugel, "They Spoke in Defense of Themselves: On the Generic Criticism of Apologia," *Quarterly Journal of Speech* 59 (1973): 273–83.
13 Ritter and Medhurst, *Presidential Speechwriting*.
14 Ernest G. Bormann, "Fantasy and Rhetorical Vision: The Rhetorical Criticism of Social Reality," *Quarterly Journal of Speech* 58 (1972): 396–407; Ernest G. Bormann, "The Eagleton Affair: A Fantasy Theme Analysis," *Quarterly Journal of Speech* 59 (1973): 143–59; and Dan Nimmo and James E. Combs, *Mediated Political Realities*, 2nd ed. (New York: Longman, 1990).
15 Sidney Kraus, ed., *The Great Debates: Background, Perspective, Effects* (Bloomington, IN: Indiana University Press, 1962).
16 Mitchell S. McKinney and Diana B. Carlin, "Political Campaign Debates," in *Handbook of Political Communication Research*, ed. Lynda Lee Kaid (Mahwah, N.J.: Lawrence Erlbaum, 2004), 203–34.
17 For instance, debates are not even mentioned in early campaign management texts such as Robert Agranoff, *The Management of Election Campaigns* (Boston, MA: Holbrook, 1976) and Edward Schwartzman, *Campaign Craftsmanship* (New York: Universe Books, 1972).
18 Steven H. Chaffee, "Presidential Debates: Are They Helpful to Voters?" *Communication Monographs* 45 (1978): 330–46.
19 Judith Trent and Robert Friedenberg, *Political Campaign Communication: Principles and Practices*, 6th ed. (Lanham, MD: Rowman & Littlefield, 2007).
20 Ibid.
21 Myles Martel, *Political Campaign Debates: Images, Strategies, Tactics* (New York: Longman, 1983).
22 McKinney and Carlin, "Political Campaign Debates."
23 Lynda Lee Kaid, Mitchell S. McKinney, and John C. Tedesco, *Civic Dialogue in the 1996 Presidential Campaign: Candidate, Media, and Public Voices* (Cresskill, N.J.: Hampton Press, 2000).
24 Ronald A. Faucheux, "What Voters Think About Political Debates: Key Findings from a Nationwide Voter Poll," *Campaign and Elections* 23 (2002): 22–4ff.
25 Joseph Klapper, *The Effects of Mass Communication* (New York: Free Press, 1960).
26 Charles K. Atkin, Lawrence Bowen, Oguz B. Nayman, and Kenneth G. Sheinkopf, "Quality Versus

Quantity in Televised Political Ads," *Public Opinion Quarterly* 37 (1973): 209–24; Stuart H. Surlin and Thomas F. Gordon, "Selective Exposure and Retention of Political Advertising," *Journal of Advertising* 5 (1976): 32–44.

27 For a more detailed description of the elements of videostyle, see Lynda Lee Kaid and Anne Johnston, *Videostyle in Presidential Campaigns: Style and Content of Televised Political Advertising* (Westport, CT: Praeger, 2001).

28 Lynda Lee Kaid, "Political Advertising," in *The Electoral Challenge: Theory Meets Practice*, ed. Stephen C. Craig (Washington, D.C.: Congressional Quarterly Press, 2006), 79–96; Lynda Lee Kaid, "Political Advertising," in *The Handbook of Political Communication Research*, ed. Lynda Lee Kaid (Mahwah, N.J.: Lawrence Erlbaum, 2004), 155–202; and Michael M. Franz, Paul F. Freedman, Kenneth M. Goldstein, and Travis M. Ridout, *Campaign Advertising and American Democracy* (Philadelphia, PA: Temple University Press, 2008).

29 Donald T. Cundy, "Political Commercials and Candidate Image: The Effects Can Be Substantial," in *New Perspectives on Political Advertising*, ed. Lynda Lee Kaid, Dan D. Nimmo, and Keith R. Sanders (Carbondale, IL: Southern Illinois University Press, 1986), 210–34; Michael T. Rothschild and Michael L. Ray, "Involvement and Political Advertising Effect: An Exploratory Experiment," *Communication Research* 1 (1974): 264–85; and Nicholas A. Valentino, Vincent L. Hutchings, and Dmitri Williams, "The Impact of Political Advertising on Knowledge, Internet Information Seeking, and Candidate Preference," *Journal of Communication* 54 (2004): 337–54.

30 Lynda Lee Kaid, Mike Chanslor, and Mark Hovind, "The Influence of Program and Commercial Type on Political Advertising Effectiveness," *Journal of Broadcasting & Electronic Media* 36 (1992): 303–20; Lynda Lee Kaid and Keith R. Sanders, "Political Television Commercials: An Experimental Study of the Type and Length," *Communication Research* 5 (1978): 57–70; Esther Thorson, William G. Christ, and Clarke Caywood, "Effects of Issue-image Strategies, Attack and Support Appeals, Music, and Visual Content in Political Commercials," *Journal of Broadcasting & Electronic Media* 35 (1991): 465–86; Esther Thorson, William G. Christ, and Clarke Caywood, "Selling Candidates Like Tubes of Toothpaste: Is the Comparison Apt?" in *Television and Political Advertising, Volume 1*, ed. Frank Biocca (Hillsdale, N.J.: Lawrence Erlbaum Associates, 1991), 145–72.

31 Stephen Ansolabehere and Shanto Iyengar, "Riding the Wave and Claiming Ownership Over Issues: The Joint Effects of Advertising and News Coverage in Campaigns," *Public Opinion Quarterly* 58 (Fall 1994): 335–57; William Benoit, "Political Party Affiliation and Presidential Campaign Discourse," *Communication Quarterly* 52 (2004): 81–97; and William L. Benoit and Glenn J. Hansen, "Issue Adaptation of Presidential Television Spots and Debates to Primary and General Audiences," *Communication Research Reports* 19 (2002): 138–45.

32 Annie Lang, "Emotion, Formal Features, and Memory for Televised Political Advertisements," in *Television and Political Advertising*, ed. Frank Biocca (Hillsdale, N.J.: Lawrence Erlbaum Associates, 1991), 221–43.

33 Lynda Lee Kaid, "The Effects of Television Broadcasts on Perceptions of Political Candidates in the United States and France," in *Mediated Politics in Two Cultures: Presidential Campaigning in the United States and France*, ed. Lynda Lee Kaid, Jacques Gerstlé, and Keith R. Sanders (New York: Praeger, 1991), 247–60; Lynda Lee Kaid and Mike Chanslor, "The Effects of Political Advertising on Candidate Images," in *Presidential Candidate Images* ed. Kenneth L. Hacker (Westport, CT: Praeger, 2004), 133–50; Lynda Lee Kaid and John C. Tedesco, "Tracking Voter Reactions to Television Advertising," in *The Electronic Election: Perspectives on the 1996 Campaign Communication*, ed. Lynda Lee Kaid and Dianne G. Bystrom (Mahwah, N.J.: Lawrence Erlbaum, 1999), 233–46; John C. Tedesco, "Televised Political Advertising Effects: Evaluating Responses During the 2000 Robb–Allen Senatorial Election," *Journal of Advertising* 31 (1992): 37–48; and John C. Tedesco and Lynda Lee Kaid, "Style and Effects of the Bush and Gore Spots," in *The Millennium Election: Communication in the 2000 Campaigns*, ed. Lynda Lee Kaid, John C. Tedesco, Dianne Bystrom, and Mitchell S. McKinney (Lanham, MD: Rowman & Littlefield, 2003), 5–16.

34 Ted Brader, "Striking a Responsive Chord: How Political Ads Motivate and Persuade Voters by Appealing to Emotions," *American Journal of Political Science* 49 (2005): 388–405.

35 Lynda Lee Kaid and Daniela V. Dimitrova, "The Television Advertising Battleground in the 2004 Presidential Election," *Journalism Studies* 6 (2005): 165–75; L. Patrick Devlin, "Contrasts in Presidential Campaign Commercials of 2004," *American Behavioral Scientist* 49 (2005): 279–313; and "U.S. Advertising Spending Rose 4.6% in 2006," *Nielsen Monitor-Plus Reports*, 2007.

36 Gina M. Garramone, "Voter Responses to Negative Political Ads," *Journalism Quarterly* 61 (1984): 250–9; Gina M. Garramone, "Effects of Negative Political Advertising: The Roles of Sponsor and Rebuttal," *Journal of Broadcasting & Electronic Media* 29 (1985): 147–59; Gina M. Garramone and Sandra J. Smith, "Reactions to Advertising: Clarifying Sponsor Effects," *Journalism Quarterly* 61 (1984): 771–5;

Fuyuan Shen and H. Denis Wu, "Effects of Soft-money Issue Advertisements on Candidate Evaluations and Voting Preference: An Exploration," *Mass Communication & Society* 5 (2002): 295–410; and Michael Pfau, Lance Holbert, Erin Alison Szabo, and Kelly Kaminski, "Issue-advocacy Versus Candidate Advertising: Effects on Candidate Preferences and Democratic Process," *Journal of Communication* 52 (2002): 301–15.

37 Lynda Lee Kaid, Juliana Fernandes, Feng Shen, Hyun Yun, Yeonsoo Kim, and Abby Gail LeGrange, "Effects of Message Content and Sponsorship on Political Advertising," Paper scheduled for presentation at the International Communication Association Conference, Montreal, May 2008.

38 James B. Lemert, Wayne Wanta, and Tien-Tsung Lee, "Party Identification and Negative Advertising in a U.S. Senate Election," *Journal of Communication* 49 (1999): 123–34; S. Merritt, "Negative Political Advertising," *Journal of Advertising* 13 (1984): 27–38; and Brenda S. Sonner, "The Effectiveness of Negative Political Advertising: A Case Study," *Journal of Advertising Research* 38 (1998): 37–42.

39 Patrick Meirick, "Cognitive Responses to Negative and Comparative Political Advertising," *Journal of Advertising* XXXI (2002): 49–62; Bruce E. Pinkleton, "The Effects of Negative Comparative Political Advertising on Candidate Evaluations and Advertising Evaluations: An Exploration," *Journal of Advertising* XXVI (1997): 19–29; and Bruce E. Pinkleton, "Effects of Print Political Comparative Advertising on Political Decision-making and Participation," *Journal of Communication* 48 (1998): 24–36.

40 Michael Pfau, Roxanne Parrott, and Bridget Lindquist, "An Expectancy Theory Explanation of the Effectiveness of Political Attack Television Spots: A Case Study," *Journal of Applied Communication Research* 20 (1992): 235–53.

41 Kaid and Tedesco, "Tracking Reactions"; William J. Schenck-Hamlin, David E. Procter, and Deborah J. Rumsey, "The Influence of Negative Advertising Frames on Political and Politician Accountability," *Human Communication Research*, 26 (2000): 53–74; Michael Pfau and Michael Burgoon, "The Efficacy of Issue and Character Attack Message Strategies in Political Campaign Communication." *Communication Research Reports* 2 (1989): 52–61; Brian L. Roddy and Gina M. Garramone, "Appeals and Strategies of Negative Political Advertising," *Journal of Broadcasting & Electronic Media* 32 (1988): 415–27; and Kim Fridkin Kahn and John G. Geer, "Creating Impressions: An Experimental Investigation of Political Advertising on Television," *Political Behavior* 16 (1994): 93–116.

42 Stephen Ansolabehere and Shanto Iyengar, *Going Negative: How Political Advertisements Shrink and Polarize the Electorate* (New York: The Free Press, 1995); Michael Basil, Caroline Schooler, and Byron Reeves, "Positive and Negative Political Advertising: Effectiveness of Ads and Perceptions of Candidates," in *Television and Political Advertising*, ed. Frank Biocca (Hillsdale, N.J.: Lawrence Erlbaum Associates, 1991), 245–62; Craig L. Brians and Martin P. Wattenberg, "Campaign Issue Knowledge and Salience: Comparing Reception From TV Commercials, TV News, and Newspapers," *American Journal of Political Science* 40 (1996): 172–93; Chingching Chang and Jacqueline C. Bush Hitchon, "When Does Gender Count? Further Insights into Gender Schematic Processing for Female Candidates' Political Advertisements," *Sex Roles* 51 (2004): 197–208; Karen Johnson-Cartee and Gary Copeland, "Southern Voters' Reaction to Negative Political Ads in 1986 Election," *Journalism Quarterly* 66 (1989): 888–93, 986; Lang, "Emotion, Formal Features,"; John E. Newhagen and Byron Reeves, "Emotion and Memory Responses for Negative Political Advertising: A Study of Television Commercials Used in the 1988 Presidential Election," in *Television and Political Advertising*, ed. Frank Biocca (Hillsdale, N.J.: Lawrence Erlbaum Associates, 1991), 197–220; Kim Fridkin Kahn and Patrick J. Kenney, "Do Negative Campaigns Mobilize or Suppress Turnout? Clarifying the Relationship between Negativity and Participation," *American Political Science Review* 93 (1999): 877–89; Kahn and Geer, "Creating Impressions,"; Shen and Wu, "Effects of Soft-money"; Spencer F. Tinkham and Ruth Ann Weaver Lariscy, "A Diagnostic Approach to Assessing the Impact of Negative Political Television Commercials," *Journal of Broadcasting & Electronic Media* 37 (1993): 377–400; Lynda Lee Kaid and John Boydston, "An Experimental Study of the Effectiveness of Negative Political Advertisements," *Communication Quarterly* 35 (1987): 193–201; and Amy E. Jasperson and David P. Fan, "An Aggregate Examination of the Backlash Effect in Political Advertising: The Case of the 1996 U.S. Senate Race in Minnesota," *Journal of Advertising* 31 (2002): 1–12.

43 Roddy and Garramone, "Appeals and Strategies."

44 Michael Pfau and Michael Burgoon, "Inoculation in Political Campaign Communication," *Human Communication Research* 15 (1988): 91–111; and Michael Pfau and Henry C. Kenski, *Attack Politics: Strategy and Defense* (New York: Praeger Publishers, 1990).

45 Richard R. Lau, Lee Sigelman, Caroline Heldman, and Paul Babbitt, "The Effects of Negative Political Advertisements: A Meta-analytic Assessment," *American Political Science Review* 93 (1999): 851–75.

46 Ansolabehere and Iyengar, *Going Negative*; and Lemert, Wanta, and Lee, "Party Identification."

47 Franz, Freedman, Goldstein, and Ridout, *Campaign Advertising and American Democracy*; Steven E. Finkel and George G. Geer, "A Spot Check: Casting Doubt on the Demobilizing Effect of Attack Advertising," *American Journal of Political Science* 42 (1998): 573–95; Paul Freedman and Kenneth Goldstein,

"Measuring Media Exposure and the Effects of Negative Campaign Ads," *American Journal of Political Science* 43 (1999): 1189–208; and Lynn Vavreck, "How Does it All 'Turnout'? Exposure to Attack Advertising, Campaign Interest, and Participation in American Presidential Elections," in *Campaign Reform: Insights and Evidence*, ed. Larry M. Bartels and Lynn Vavreck (Ann Arbor, MI: University of Michigan Press, 2000), 79–105; and Martin P. Wattenberg and Craig L. Brians, "Negative Campaign Advertising: Demobilizer or Mobilizer?" *American Political Science Review* 93 (1999): 891–9.

48 B.R. Barber, K. Mattson, and J. Peterson, *The State of "Electronically Enhanced Democracy": A Survey of the Internet* (New Brunswick, N.J.: The Walt Whitman Center or the Culture and Politics of Democracy, 1997), 8.

49 John C. Tedesco, "Changing the Channel: Use of the Internet for Communicating about Politics," in *The Handbook of Political Communication Research*, ed. Lynda Lee Kaid (Mahwah, N.J.: Lawrence Erlbaum, 2004), 507–32; W. Lance Bennett and Robert M. Entman, "Mediated Politics: An Introduction," in *Mediated Politics: Communication in the Future of Democracy*, ed. W. Lance Bennett and Robert M. Entman (Cambridge: Cambridge University Press, 2001), 1–32; and D. Resnick, "Politics on the Internet: The Normalization of Cyberspace," in *The Politics of Cyberspace*, ed. C. Toulouse and T. Luke (New York: Routledge, 1998), 48–68.

50 Daniel Hallin, "Sound Bite News: Television Coverage of Elections, 1968–1988," *Journal of Communication* 42 (1992): 5–24; and Stephen J. Farnsworth and S. Robert Lichter, *The Nightly News Nightmare: Television's Coverage of U.S. Presidential Elections, 1988–2004*, 2nd ed. (Lanham, Md.: Rowman & Littlefield, 2006).

51 Doris Graber, "Press and Television as Opinion Resources in Presidential Campaigns," *Public Opinion Quarterly* 40 (1976): 285–303; Thomas E. Patterson, *Out of Order* (New York: Knopf, 1993); and S. Robert Lichter and Richard E. Noyes, *Good Intentions Make Bad News* (Lanham, MD: Rowman & Littlefield., 1995).

52 S. Robert Lichter, Richard E. Noyes, and Lynda Lee Kaid, "No News or Negative News: How the Networks Nixed the '96 Campaign," in *The Electronic Election*, ed. Lynda Lee Kaid and Dianne G. Bystrom (Mahwah, N.J.: Lawrence Erlbaum, 1999), 3–13; and Farnsworth and Lichter, *The Nightly News Nightmare*.

53 Maxwell McCombs and Donald Shaw, "The Agenda-Setting Function of the Mass Media," *Public Opinion Quarterly* 36 (1972): 176–87.

54 David Weaver, Maxwell McCombs, and Donald L. Shaw, "Agenda-Setting Research: Issues, Attributes, and Influences," in *The Handbook of Political Communication Research*, ed. Lynda Lee Kaid (Mahwah, N.J.: Lawrence Erlbaum, 2004), 257–82.

55 Weaver, McCombs, and Shaw, "Agenda-Setting Research."

56 Robert Entman, "Framing: Towards Clarification of a Fractured Paradigm," *Journal of Communication* 43 (1993): 52.

57 William A. Gamson and Andre Modigliani, "The Changing Culture of Affirmative Action," *Research in Political Sociology* 3 (1987): 137–77.

58 Dietram A. Scheufele, "Framing as a Theory of Media Effects," *Journal of Communication* 49 (1999): 103–22.

6

Political Management and Marketing

Wojciech Cwalina, Andrzej Falkowski, and Bruce I. Newman

Politicians are in the business of selling hope to people. This hope is related to convincing people that it is this particular politician or political party that guarantees, as Jenny Lloyd[1] puts it, successful management of national security, social stability and economic growth on behalf of the electorate. From this perspective, the major challenge to the political market is to connect a politician's words, actions and vision into a realistic transformation of the electorate's dreams and aspirations.[2]

Mainstream and Political Marketing

The first conceptualizing efforts related to political marketing referred to or represented the attempts of transferring the classical product marketing onto the plane of politics,[3] defined by Stephan Henneberg[4] as "instrumental" or "managerial" interpretation of political marketing activities. The starting point for this approach was the assumption that it would be a gross mistake to think that election campaigns have taken on marketing character only in recent years. Campaigning for office has always had a marketing character, and what has only increased in the course of time is the sophistication and acceleration of use of marketing methods in politics.[5] From this perspective, political marketing was defined as "the process by which political candidates and ideas are directed at the voters in order to satisfy their political needs and thus gain their support for the candidate and ideas in question."[6] Applying mainstream marketing to politics was justified by a number of similarities, meaning similarities of concepts (e.g. consumers, market segmentation, marketing mix, image, brand loyalty, product concept and positioning) and similarities of tools (e.g. market research, communication, advertising). On the other hand, attempts were made to prove that the differences between them were only ostensible and that they disappeared under a more thorough analysis.[7]

One of the consequences of identifying political marketing as product marketing was that candidates or political parties were often compared to particular consumer products, such as toothpaste or bars of soap. The media played an important part in popularizing that myth. However, as Alex Marland[8] demonstrates, such comparisons are outdated and hardly appropriate in modern marketing. He stresses that politicians are not consumer products that one can own. As Nicholas O'Shaughnessy[9] puts it, "politics deals with a person, not a product." Rather, they should be treated as vendors hired for a particular period of time—like doctors or lawyers.

According to Bruce Newman[10] in reality the candidate is rather like a service provider, whereas parties can be compared with service-providing companies.[11] From this perspective, a candidate offers a service to voters, much in the same way that an insurance agent offers a service to consumers. In this case, the insurance policy becomes the product sold by the agent. Therefore, to convey impression that the marketing of candidates is similar to traditional fast moving consumer goods marketing (FMCG) is to oversimplify and minimize the uniqueness of the marketing application to politics.

First of all, as Newman[12] proves, consumers of soap do not spend nearly as much time and effort in the decision to buy one brand over another as a voter does when deciding to cast a ballot for a candidate. As a result, a buyer of soap will be less involved in the acquisition of information than a voter is. Second, by taking note that a candidate is really a service provider, the distinction between campaigning and governing becomes clearer. The actual delivery of a service that a candidate offers to the voter does not occur until he or she begins to govern. Finally, candidates operate in a dynamic environment, fast, changing and full of obstacles that present marketing challenges that require flexibility. According to Newman,[13] like corporations around the world that alter their services to respond to a more demanding consumer in the commercial market-place, candidates have to respond to the fast-paced changes that take place in the political marketplace.

These clearly defined differences between political and product marketing presented above, notwithstanding some differences, suggest that political marketing may have much more in common with service and nonprofit organization marketing than with product marketing.[14] This approach is defined by Henneberg[15] as "functional" marketing analysis of political man-agement. Service marketing incorporates a whole host of strategic issues that are not applicable in the marketing of products because services have unique characteristics that products don't have. Services are intangible (no physical product is exchanged and repeat purchases may be based on reputation and recollection of previous services), heterogeneous (the provision of services is variable—depending on the service provider, the quality of the service can vary), perishable (they are instantaneous and cannot be stored for any length of time), inseparable (service requires presence of producer and the production of it often takes place at the same time as consump-tion—either partial or full), non-standardized (there is difficulty in consistency of service deliv-ery) and they haven't any owner (customer has access to but not ownership of service activity or facility).[16] These characteristics can be referred, to a large extent, to the area of politics.[17] Besides, what Hans Bauer and his colleagues[18] stress is that,

> when referring to political party as an association of citizens, it is important to remember that according to the parties' view of themselves, their services have no "consumers". Instead, the parties' efforts are aimed at inducing citizens to put their political ideologies into practice in every aspect of their daily lives.

These authors stress that one of the major strategies used by political parties to win support should be reducing voters' risk and uncertainty by gaining their trust and developing one's reputation.

This approach seems analogous to the concept of perceived service quality and relationship marketing introduced and developed by Christian Grönroos.[19] He also introduced the concept of interactive function to cover the marketing impact on the customer during the consumption of usage process, where the consumer of a service typically interacts with systems, physical resources and employees of the service provider. From this perspective, the goal of a company (and political party or candidate too) is to establish, maintain and enhance relationships with customers and other partners, at a profit (voters and other political power brokers), so that the objectives of the parties involved are met. And, this is achieved by a mutual exchange. An integral element of the relationship marketing (but also political marketing) approach is the "promise concept." A firm that is preoccupied with giving promises may attract new customers and initially build relationships. However, if promises are not kept, the evolving relationship cannot be maintained and enhanced.

However, these clear similarities between service and political marketing do not mean that they are identical. As elements distinguishing political marketing Lloyd[20] suggests the following: (1) political outcomes are standardized at the point of "production," whereas variations arise from the way they are perceived, based upon electors' experiences and expectations; (2) political outcomes may refer to individuals or groups and they either function independently or sum up; and (3) voters are stakeholders in the resources that create political outcomes.

To sum up, despite many similarities between political marketing and a mainstream (product, service, not-for-profit and relationship) marketing, identifying them cannot be justified. In order to understand the specificity of marketing actions in politics, one should take a closer look at the differences between mainstream and political marketing. A detailed analysis was conducted by Andrew Lock and Phil Harris[21] who point out seven major differences between the two spheres:

1 Those eligible to vote always choose their candidate or political party on the same day when the voting takes place. Consumers, on the other hand, can purchase their products at different times, depending on their needs and purchasing power. Moreover, although there are similarities between opinion polls and brand shares' tracking methods, the latter are based on actual purchasing decisions while the former are based on hypothetical questions.

2 While the consumer purchasing a product always knows its price, the value expressed in financial terms, for the voter there is no price attached to the ability to make a voting decision. Taking a voting decision may be the result of analyzing and predicting the consequences of this decision (psychological cost), which can be considered as possible losses and gains in the long-term perspective between elections.

3 Voters realize that the choice is collective and that they must accept the final voting result even if it goes against their voting preferences.

4 Winner takes all in political elections. This is the case especially in countries such as the UK where the electoral system is "first past the post" or in presidential elections in Poland.

5 The political party or candidate is a complex intangible product that the voter cannot "unbundle" to see what is inside. Although in commercial marketing there are also products and services that the consumer cannot unpack and check while buying them, the proportion of such packets that cannot be unpacked on the political market is much greater. Besides, consumers may change their minds and exchange products or services almost immediately for others, if they do not like ones that they have purchased; such exchanges may be quite expensive, though. If the voter decides to change their mind, they have to wait till the next election, at least a few years.

6 Introducing a new brand in the form of a political party is quite difficult and always remote in time.

7 In mainstream marketing brand leaders tend to stay in front. In political marketing, one can often witness a situation when, after winning elections, a political party begins to lose support in public opinion polls.

In addition to this, Newman[22] points to further differences between mainstream and political marketing, stressing that in business the ultimate goal is financial success, whereas in politics it is strengthening democracy through voting processes. Using various marketing strategies in economic practice is the result of conducting market research that promises satisfactory financial profits. In politics, on the other hand, a candidate's own philosophy often influences the scope of marketing strategies. This means that although marketing research may suggest that a politician's chances will increase if he or she concentrates on particular political or economic issues, they do not have to follow these suggestions if their own conception of political reality is incongruent with these issues. The distinguishing feature of political marketing is continuous and increasing use of negative advertising, attacking directly rival political candidates.[23]

The differences between mainstream and political marketing are big enough to make one think about developing an independent concept for studying voting behaviors. Despite the fact that as Lock and Harris[24] conclude, political marketing is at a "craft" stage, the assumption that there is direct transferability of mainstream marketing theory to political marketing is questionable. They claim that political marketing has to develop its own frameworks by adapting the core marketing literature and develop its own predictive and prescriptive models.

Newman[25] believes that the key concept for political marketing is the concept of "exchange." When applying marketing to politics, the exchange process centers on a candidate who offers political leadership in exchange for a vote from the citizen. In other words, when voters cast their votes, a transaction takes place. They are engaged in an exchange of time and support (their vote) for the services and better government the party or candidates will offer after the election. Aron O'Cass[26] believes then that "marketing is applicable to political processes as a transaction occurs and is specifically concerned with how transactions are created, stimulated and valued." In this way, marketing offers political parties and candidates the ability to address diverse voter concerns and needs through marketing analyses, planning, implementation and control of political and electoral campaigns. According to Dominic Wring,[27] political marketing is "the party or candidate's use of opinion research and environmental analysis to produce and promote a competitive offering which will help realize organizational aims and satisfy groups of electors in exchange for their votes."

The emphasis on the processes of election exchanges cannot obscure the fact that political marketing is not limited only to the period of the election campaign. In the era of permanent campaign, in reality there is no clear difference between the period directly before the election and the rest of political calendar.[28] Tough endless campaigning secures politicians' legitimacy by stratagems that enhance the governor's credibility.[29] Taking this into consideration, Lock and Harris[30] define political marketing as

> a discipline, the study of the processes of exchanges between political entities and their environment and among themselves, with particular reference to the positioning of those entities and their communications. Government and the legislature exist both as exogenous regulators of these processes and as entities within them.

Political marketing should then have strong emphasis on long-term interactive relationship, and not only on simple exchange. It should also focus on party allegiance, electoral volatility, civic duty, government quality, responsible legislature or new public management.[31]

Political marketing refers then to the processes of exchanges and establishing, maintaining and enhancing relationships between objects in the political market (politicians, political parties, voters, interests groups, institutions), whose goal is to identify and satisfy their needs and develop political leadership.

Political Marketing Orientation

Together with the development of political marketing and the changes in the voter market, there also took place, the evolution of the marketing approach to political campaigns. Newman[32] discussed in four stages how American presidential campaigns have gone from organizations run by party bosses (the party concept), through organizations that have only one goal: to find the best possible candidate to represent the party (the product concept). Next, the organization shifts from an internally to an externally driven operation (i.e. focus on the voter's reaction to the candidate—the selling concept) to an organization run by marketing experts. This type of organization identifies voter's needs and then develops political platforms to meet those needs (the marketing concept).

A similar approach to the evolution of marketing in politics was proposed by Jennifer Lees-Marshment[33] for British political parties. She points to three stages, from product-oriented party to sales-oriented party to market-oriented party.

What is crucial for the specificity of political marketing is defining what "political product" actually is. Patrick Butler and Neil Collins[34] believe that it can be described as a conglomerate consisting of three parts: the multicomponent (person/party/ideology) nature of offer; the significant degree of loyalty involved; and the fact that it is mutable, i.e. it can be changed or transformed in the post-election setting. According to Lees-Marshment,[35] a party's "product" is its behavior that "is ongoing and offered at all times (not just elections), at all levels of party. The product includes the leadership, MPs (and candidates), membership, staff, symbols, constitution, activities such as party conferences and policies."

Then, according to Newman,[36] the real "political product" is the campaign platform. It consists of a number of elements, including: (1) the general election program of the candidate based on the political and economic guidelines of the party he or she belongs to or the organization set up for the time of the elections; (2) his or her positions on the most important problems appearing during the campaign; (3) the image of the candidate; (4) reference to his or her political background and the groups of voters supporting the candidate (e.g. labor unions, associations, non-governmental organizations etc.) or the authorities. Such a platform is flexible and evolves together with the development of the voting campaign and changes in the voting situation.

Philip Kotler and Neil Kotler[37] state that to be successful, candidates have to understand their markets, that is, the voters and their basic needs and aspirations and the constituencies they represent or seek to represent. Marketing orientation means that candidates recognize the nature of the exchange process when they strive for votes. If a candidate is able to make promises that match the voters' needs and is able to fulfill these promises once in office, then the candidate will increase voter, as well as public, satisfaction. It is obvious then that it is the voter who should be the center of attention during political campaigns.

Philip Kotler and Alan Andreasen[38] propose that the difficulty in transposing marketing into public and nonprofit organizations is a function of how organization-centered (internally oriented) such organizations are as opposed to customer-centered (externally oriented). An organization-centered orientation counters the organization's ability to integrate marketing. From this perspective, marketing is viewed as a marketing mindset of customer-centeredness, and is seen in organizations that exhibit customer-centeredness, heavy reliance on research, are biased toward segmentation, define competition broadly, and have strategies using all elements of the marketing mix.

One should stress that "marketing orientation" is not the same as "market orientation."[39] "Market orientation" refers to acceptance of the importance of relationships with all stakeholders, and aims toward being responsive to internal and external markets in which organization operates. The emphasis here is on building and maintaining stakeholder relationships by the entire organization. With politics, political market orientation refers to "all party members' responsibility for taking part in both development of policies and their implementation and communication."[40] There are three key elements in this approach: organization-wide generation of market intelligence, dissemination of the information throughout the organization and an organization-wide responsiveness to it (member participation and consistent external communication). According to O'Cass,[41] market orientation is the key mechanism for implementing the marketing concept, while marketing orientation is the underlying mindset/culture of approaching the operations and processes of the organization through marketing eyes. As such, a marketing orientation is a necessary prerequisite for both being market oriented and adopting the marketing concept. The essence of marketing is a marketing mindset of customer-centeredness, which is fundamentally a marketing orientation.

Another important distinction for marketing orientation in politics is juxtaposing market-driven versus market-driving business strategies.[42] The aim of a market-driven organization is to possess a culture that focuses outward on the customer in an attempt to build and sustain superior customer value. Hence, a market-driven organization is one that aims to satisfy consumers through responding to their needs which are derived through market research and market scanning. This suggests that as a longer-term strategic option, the focus on being market-driven leads to managerial complacency in that the focus remains on the existing customer base without being aware of the changing nature of the consumer base in the future. Market-driving organizations anticipate the changing nature of the market in the future and developing strategies to adapt the organization to ensure long-term success. As Peter Reeves, Leslie de Chernatony and Marylyn Carrigan[43] suggest, in the political marketplace, there is currently a move toward a market-driven standpoint in that the political parties attempt to design their brand on the basis of the needs of the electorate through market research and polling evidence. Political parties also need to be market-drivers in predicting and taking action on longer-term programs, which are not immediately important, but will have longer-term consequences. In other words, successful political marketing requires a balanced approach. Driving the market or being driven by it, are antagonistic concepts on a continuum, but this is not the case in political marketing orientation. These two dimensions, as Henneberg[44] demonstrates, constitute the specific strategic posture a political party or candidate holds and their behavior on the political marketplace: the relationship builder (high in market-driving and high in market-driven), the convinced ideologist (high/low), the tactical populist (low/high) and the political lightweight (low/low).

The political arena is very diverse. It consists of groups of various interests, likings, preferences and lifestyles. More efficient and successful political campaigns need to accommodate this diversity by creating strategies for various market segments. There are issue-oriented voters but there are also voters influenced by the candidate's personal charm. The politicians often face a difficult task then; they have to build a voting coalition based on and reflecting a certain compromise among various social groups. This requires a lot of skill on the part of the candidate in creating a cognitive map of different opinions, emotions or interests. Then the candidate has to assign them to particular groups and refer to such a map while constructing his or her information messages in order to establish the foundations of the agreement between various voter groups and the candidate.

Lock and Harris[45] point out that political marketing is concerned with communicating with party members, media and prospective sources of funding as well as the electorate. Then, Kotler and Kotler[46] distinguish five factors playing key roles in organizing political campaigns and establishing a political market that they call voting market segments: (1) active voters who are in the habit of casting ballots in elections; (2) interest groups, social activists and organized voter groups who collect funds for election campaigns (for example labor unions, business organizations, human rights groups, civil rights or ecological movements); (3) the media that make the candidate visible; (4) party organizations that nominate a candidate and express opinions on him or her and provide the resource base for the campaign; and (5) sponsors, private persons making donations for the candidate and campaign. Among these five elements it is the media that is most important for the success of a political campaign. The media influence the ultimate image of the candidate in the direct process of communication with voters. The media's influence on voting preferences can be either open or hidden.[47]

It should be emphasized that political marketing should not be identified with political management. Above all, political management includes not only the activities undertaken for conducting campaigns, but also lobbying and government relations, grassroots politics, fundraising, issues management and advocacy, corporate and trade association public affairs and crisis management. It also includes handling the media, developing communications strategy and using the new media as political and communication tools. Political management also deals with issues related to political leadership and understanding and appreciating the ethical dimensions of public life. Furthermore, political marketing strategies go into a level of detail that political management doesn't because of its focus on consulting.[48]

Political marketing campaigns are integrated into the environment and, therefore, they are related to the distribution of forces in a particular environment.[49] It can then be stated that the environment in which marketing and political campaigns take place consists of three fundamental component groups: (1) technological elements (direct mail, television, the Internet and other means of voting communication, e.g. spots); (2) structural elements connected mainly with the election law, but also with the procedure of nominating candidates, financial regulations for the campaign, and conducting political debates; and (3) the forces influencing the development of the campaign (candidate, consultants, media, political parties, interest groups setting up political and election committees, polling specialists and voters).

Each of these elements represents an area where dynamic changes have taken place in the past few decades. These changes facilitate the development of marketing research and are becoming more and more important for the election process. Technological changes, for instance, have revolutionized a candidate's contacts with voters (for example, through e-mail, cable televisions or cell phones). Structural changes in the development of political campaigns made candidates pay more attention to marketing strategies and rely more on the opinions of the experts developing them.

Political Marketing Concept

In order to understand political marketing, one should also understand specific political marketing concepts. Above all, marketing as a process involves creating exchange, where the two sides involved are the candidate or party and the voters or/and other market segments. The majority of political marketing strategies are analyzed with reference to the classic 4Ps marketing model.[50] More extended approaches go beyond the marketing mix, trying to relate it to service and relationship marketing, nonprofit organization marketing, as well as knowledge of political science, communication analyses and psychology.[51]

In his model Newman[52] introduces a clear distinction between the processes of a marketing campaign and those of a political campaign, although both campaigns are closely connected. The marketing campaign is the heart of the model because it contains the marketing tools that are used to get the candidate successfully through the four stages of the political campaign (preprimary, primary, convention and general election). There are three parts to the marketing campaign: market (voter) segmentation, candidate positioning and strategy formulation and implementation.

Voter Segmentation

The major challenge for a marketing campaign is the candidates' realization that they are not in a position to appeal to all voters of every persuasion. This means that the candidate must break down the electorate into segments or groupings and then create a campaign platform that appeals to these targets. The process of dividing the whole electorate into many different groups is called voter segmentation.[53] The goal of segmentation is to recognize and assess voter needs or characteristics, which become the foundation for defining the profile of the voters in order to plan efficient communication with them. In other words, marketing planning aims at identification and creation of competitive advantage, and, in the case of politics, its goal is to determine how to generate and retain public support for party/candidate policies and programs.[54]

The basic division in the case of segmentation is the division into a priori and post hoc segmentation.[55] A priori segmentation involves the researcher choosing some cluster defining descriptor (e.g. demographic or psychological characteristics) in advance of the research itself. In post hoc segmentation there is no pre-judgment by choosing the bases at the outset. Respondents are placed into groups, by using statistical techniques, according to their similarity with those in the same group, and dissimilarity with those in other groups.[56]

With political marketing, one may distinguish two levels of voter segmentation. The primary segmentation focuses on dividing voters based on the two primary criteria: (1) the power of voter partisanship (continuum from heavy partisans to floating voters); and (2) time of voting decision (pre-campaign deciders, campaign deciders, last-minute deciders). Voter partisanship is the criterion of dividing the market into electorates and the candidates develop such a platform of their campaign that promotes problems that are relevant for their voters and one that can attract voters from rival electorates, which are not very remote ideologically. The time of voter decision taking allows one to distinguish such a group of voters that are uncertain about whom to support.[57] Primary segmentation, is just a type of a priori segmentation allowing one to initially select those voter groups with which communication may be successful, which influences the planning of marketing strategies and helps one allocate well the resources for marketing campaigns.

From the perspective of the whole marketing campaign, the goal of the marketing campaign should be to reinforce the decisions of the supporters and win support of those who are uncertain and whose preferences are not crystallized as well as those who still hesitate or have poor identification, for a candidate or party that is close ideologically.[58] It is these groups of voters that require more study—the secondary segmentation. It can be both a priori and post hoc segmentation. Besides, it may only focus on analyzing the voters' individual characteristics or whole sets of them. In political marketing, the segmentation methods that are most frequently used refer to four groups of variables:[59] geographic,[60] demographic,[61] behavioristic and psychographic.[62] Some approaches to political market segmentation go beyond these groups of variables and are based on more complex models,[63] and also refer to benefit segmentation applied in mainstream marketing.[64]

Positioning and Candidate Image

After identifying voting segments, one needs to define the candidate's position in each of them in the multi-stage process of positioning. It consists in assessing the candidate's and the opponents' strengths and weaknesses. The key elements here include: (1) creating an image of the candidate emphasizing his or her particular personality features; and (2) developing and presenting a clear position on the country's economic and social issues. These elements may be used combinely for positioning politicians or, as Gareth Smith[65] puts it: *positioning via policies on issues* or *image and emotional positioning*.

Similar to brand images, political images do not exist apart from the political objects (or the surrounding symbolism) that impact on a person's feelings and attitudes about the politician. Based on the analogy between a political party and brand,[66] one may use the same marketing tools to develop their integrated images. The brand equity pyramid is a standard tool for understanding a brand's associations and customers' (voters') response. Kevin Lane Keller's brand pyramid[67] establishes four steps (establishing identity; establishing the meaning of the brand; developing positive responses to brand identity and meaning; and developing loyalty) in building a strong brand, where each step is conditional on successfully achieving the previous step.[68] Political parties can build their brands more effectively in a way that strikes the appropriate balance between the ideological or voter-driven strategies.[69]

In sum, a politician's image consists of how people perceive him or her based on characteristics, leadership potential and surrounding messages that are conveyed through the mass media and by word-of-mouth in everyday communication with friends and family. The term "candidate image" means creating a particular type of representation for a particular purpose (e.g. voting), which, by evoking associations, provides the object with additional values (e.g. socio-psychological, ethical or personality) and thus contributes to the emotional reception of the object.[70] The values by which the constructed object is enriched may never be reflected in his or her "real" features—it is enough if they have a certain meaning for the receiver. However, in order for such an image to be reliable and for the candidate to be efficient in his or her actions he or she needs a balanced personality and oratorical skills.

The most important issue about any image is selecting those features that will lay foundations for further actions. Such characteristics include personality features that can refer to people's beliefs connected with human nature (especially integrity and competence) or be a consequence of social demand in a given moment of time and particular socio-political situation when the campaign is conducted.[71] They are the core around which peripheral features are placed; they are less relevant for the voters but important for the candidate's realistic image.

Another stage in creating the image is "translating" the characteristics into behaviors that illustrate them or are perceived as if they did. In politics, an image is created through the use of visual impressions that are communicated by the candidate's physical presence, media appearances, and experiences and record as a political leader as that information is integrated in the minds of citizens. A candidate's image is also affected by endorsements of highly visible people in the country who support him.

Strategy Formulation and Implementation

According to Newman,[72] in order to position the candidate in voters' minds, one should apply the political marketing mix used for the implementation of a marketing strategy. For a company marketing a product, the 4Ps include the following components: product, promotion, price and place. Despite the fact that in Newman's proposal political 4Ps are to a large extent compatibles with those mentioned above, it seems necessary to redefine them following political marketing's theoretical development and the specificity of political campaign strategies. The political marketing mix consists of the following: product, push marketing, pull marketing and polling.

Product, as it was presented above, is defined in terms of candidate leadership and campaign platform, particularly issues and policies advocated. Push marketing primarily refers to the grassroots effort necessary to build up a volunteer network to handle the day-to-day activities in running the campaign. The grassroots effort that is established becomes one information channel that transmits the candidate's message from the party organization to the voter, and feedback from the voters to the candidate. The goal here is then not only the distribution of the candidate's message, but also an attempt to establish and/or enhance relationships with voters and other political power brokers.

Pull marketing becomes a second information channel for the candidate. Instead of the person-to-person channel used with a push marketing approach, this channel makes use of media outlets such as television, radio, newspapers, magazines, direct mail, the Internet and any other form of promotion that is available.

Polling represents the data analysis and research that are used to develop and test new ideas and determine how successful the ideas will be. Polls are conducted in various forms (benchmark polls, follow-up polls, tracking polls) throughout the whole voting campaign and implemented by various political entities between the campaigns. One should also note the growing importance of polling specialists. The results of their analyses given to the general electorate not only reflect the electorate's general mood, but they also influence the forming of public opinion.[73]

The foundations of marketing strategy implementation are organizational tasks connected with assembling staff for the campaign team, defining their tasks, monitoring their activities where soliciting funds for the campaign plays an important role. The structural shifts refer to primary and convention rules, financial regulations and debates.

Ethical Implications for Democracy

The foundation of democratic societies is their citizens' freedom, which helps to create more and more sophisticated marketing strategies whose goal is to make the voter vote for a certain political option. We face then a paradoxical situation because a side product of these strategies is the limitation of the voter's choice in voting decisions.[74]

The character of limiting freedom in democratic states is different from totalitarian states. In the latter, this limitation is imposed from outside. The whole legal structure, including state laws and rulings, had efficiently inhibited the freedom of citizens in East-Central Europe. The citizens were aware of the limitations imposed by the state. In democratic countries, however, these limitations come from inside, through creating in one's mind a certain picture of a part of reality, stimulating certain behaviors. The character of such internal limitation is much more dangerous than external limitation, because one does not often realize that he or she is being limited in his or her freedom, and there are no formal ways to oppose these limits. As in totalitarian states, political organizations in democratic countries can achieve their goals through dishonest competition or falsifying the results of political elections. This falsifying, however, does not take place outside the voters but inside them, when false images and false memories of a candidate are created in their minds.

Political marketing has also been criticized from the ethical standpoint as undermining democracy because of its ability to promote populism, and people with right appearances, and to manipulate and mislead the voter. O'Shaughnessy[75] argues that the rise of political marketing contributes to the misperception of political processes and the ease with which solutions can be traded and implemented. As campaigns are conducted primarily through mass media and citizens participate in them as a media audience, Harris[76] states that we witness a shift from citizenship to spectatorship. Groups competing for power do not concentrate on solving real problems, but on respecting the symbolic commitments and showing competing desires and ambitions of parties interested in the programs. In this way, as Newman[77] observes in the title of his book, democracy is on the verge of "*an age of manufactured images*" or, in other words, tabloidization.

However, as O'Shaughnessy[78] claims, the application of ethical frameworks does not generate any final answers, as no ethical debate is ever final. Political marketing has also a positive influence on the stability and development of democracy. O'Shaughnessy[79] points out that—at least to some extent—it can support the growth of an issue-oriented "political nation": distinguished from the older base of political support by greater commitment to narrower issues, and the possession, via direct mailings, of detailed and intimate information. Besides, it contributes to filtering down of knowledge of marketing's various tools and techniques and transfusion of power from elected to non-elected, to staffers and civil service.[80]

As it was mentioned before, political marketing is not only limited to the activities taken up by politicians and political parties during elections. It can and should be used to establish, maintain and enhance relationships between the ruling and various social groups: "ordinary" citizens, non-governmental organizations, lobbyists and other politicians and political parties. And this can be achieved by a mutual exchange and fulfillment of promises.

It seems that the near future will bring efficient and beneficial application of political marketing's theory and practice to democratic institutions and mutual relations between states and organizations (e.g. the UN or European Union parliament) on the international scene.

Notes

1 Jenny Lloyd, "Square Peg, Round Hole? Can Marketing-Based Concepts Such as 'Product' and the 'Marketing Mix' Have a Useful Role in the Political Arena," in *Current Issues in Political Marketing*, ed. Walter W. Wymer Jr. and Jennifer Lees-Marshment (Binghamton, N.Y.: Haworth Press, 2005), 35.

2 Bruce I. Newman, *The Mass Marketing of Politics: Democracy in an Age of Manufactured Images* (Thousand Oaks, CA: Sage Publications, 1999).

3 See e.g. David M. Farrell and Martin Wortmann, "Parties Strategies in the Electoral Market: Political Marketing in West Germany, Britain and Ireland," *European Journal of Political Research* 15 (1987): 297–318. Phillip B. Niffenegger, "Strategies for Success from The Political Marketers," *Journal of Services Marketing* 2 (3) (1988): 15–21. Philip Kotler, "Overview of Political Candidate Marketing," *Advances in Consumer Research* 2 (1975): 761–9. Avraham Shama, "Applications of Marketing Concepts to Candidate Marketing," *Advances in Consumer Research* 2 (1) (1975): 793–801.

4 Stephan C.M. Henneberg, *Generic Functions of Political Marketing*, (Bath: University of Bath School of Management Working Paper Series 19, 2003), 5.

5 Philip Kotler, "Overview of Political Candidate Marketing," 761. Philip Kotler and Neil Kotler, "Political Marketing: Generating Effective Candidates, Campaigns, and Causes," in *Handbook of Political Marketing*, ed. Bruce I. Newman (Thousand Oaks, CA: Sage Publications, 1999), 3.

6 Shama, "Applications of Marketing Concepts to Candidate Marketing," 793.

7 See Kotler, "Overview of Political Candidate Marketing," 766–8. John Egan, "Political Marketing: Lessons from the Mainstream," *Journal of Marketing Management* 15 (6) (1999): 498–502.

8 Alex Marland, "Marketing Political Soap: A Political Marketing View of Selling Candidates Like Soap, of Electioneering as a Ritual, and of Electoral Military Analogies," *Journal of Public Affairs* 3 (2) (2003): 106–7.

9 Nicholas J. O'Shaughnessy, "America's Political Market," *European Journal of Marketing* 21 (4) (1987): 63.

10 Bruce I. Newman, *The Marketing of the President: Political Marketing as Campaign Strategy* (Thousand Oaks, CA: Sage Publications, 1994), 9.

11 See Hans H. Bauer, Frank Huber and Andreas Herrmann, "Political Marketing: An Information-Economic Analysis," *European Journal of Marketing* 30 (10/11) (1996): 156.

12 Newman, *The Marketing of the President*, 9.

13 Ibid., 9–10.

14 See Jenny Lloyd, "Square Peg, Round Hole?" 31–32; Philip Kotler and Alan Andreasen, *Strategic Marketing for Nonprofit Organizations* (Englewood Cliffs, N.J.: Prentice-Hall, 1991); Margaret Scammell, "Political Marketing: Lessons for Political Science," *Political Studies* 47 (4) (1999): 718–39.

15 Henneberg, "Generic Functions of Political Marketing," 5.

16 See Leonard L. Berry, "Services—Marketing Is Different," *Business* 30 (3) (1980): 24–9; Anthony Kearsey and Richard J. Varey, "Managerialist Thinking on Marketing for Public Services," *Public Money & Management* 18 (2): 52.

17 Patrick Butler and Neil Collins, "Political Marketing: Structure and Process," *European Journal of Marketing* 28 (1) (1994): 20–21.

18 Bauer et al., "Political Marketing: An Information-Economic Analysis," 156.

19 Christian Grönroos, "From Marketing Mix to Relationship Marketing: Towards a Paradigm Shift in Marketing," *Management Decision* 32 (2) (1994): 4–20; Christian Grönroos, "Marketing Services: The Case of a Missing Product," *Journal of Business & Industrial Marketing* 13 (4/5) (1998): 322–38.

20 Lloyd, "Square Peg, Round Hole?," 37–9.

21 Andrew Lock and Phil Harris, "Political Marketing—*Vive la Différence!*," *European Journal of Marketing* 30 (10/11) (1996): 14–16.

22 Newman, *The Marketing of the President*, 10–11.

23 O'Shaughnessy, "America's Political Market," 63.

24 Lock and Harris, "Political Marketing," 16.

25 Newman, *The Marketing of the President*.

26 Aron O'Cass, "Political Marketing and the Marketing Concept," *European Journal of Marketing* 30 (10/11) (1996): 38.

27 Dominic Wring, "Reconciling Marketing with Political Science: Theories of Political Marketing," *Journal of Marketing Management* 13 (7) (1997): 653.

28 See Phil Harris, "To Spin or not to Spin that is the Question: The Emergence of Modern Political Marketing," *Marketing Review* 2 (1) (2001): 38–9; Newman, *The Mass Marketing of Politics*.

29 Dan Nimmo, "The Permanent Campaign: Marketing as a Governing Tool," in *The Handbook of Political Marketing*, ed. Bruce I. Newman (Thousand Oaks, CA: Sage, 1999), 75.

30 Lock and Harris, "Political Marketing," 21.

31 See Bauer et al., "Political Marketing," 156–9. Patrick Butler and Neil Collins, "A Conceptual Framework for Political Marketing," in *Handbook of Political Marketing*, ed. Bruce I. Newman (Thousand Oaks, CA: Sage, 1999), 55–56; Neil Collins and Patrick Butler, "When Marketing Models Clash with Democracy," *Journal of Public Affairs* 3 (1) (2003): 52–62; Wojciech Cwalina and Andrzej Falkowski, *Marketing Polityczny: Persepektywa Psychologiczna [Political Marketing: A Psychological Perspective]* (Gdansk, Poland: GWP, 2005), 551–88. Jennifer Lees-Marshment, "Political Marketing: How to Reach That Pot of Gold," *Journal of Political Marketing* 2 (1) (2003): 22–4.

32 Newman, *The Marketing of the President*, 31–4.

33 Lees-Marshment, "Political Marketing: How to Reach," 14–21; Jennifer Lees-Marshment, "The Product, Sales and Market-Oriented Party: How Labour Learnt to Market the Product, Not Just the Presentation," *European Journal of Marketing* 35 (9/10) (2001): 1074–84.

34 Butler and Collins, "Political Marketing," 21–23; Butler and Collins, "A Conceptual Framework for Political Marketing," 58–9.

35 Lees-Marshment, "Political Marketing: How to Reach," 14–15.

36 Newman, *The Marketing of the President*, 9–13.

37 Kotler and Kotler, "Political Marketing," 3–4.

38 Kotler and Andreasen, *Strategic Marketing for Nonprofit Organizations*.

39 See Ajay K. Kohli and Bernard J. Jaworski, "Market Orientation: The Construct, Research Propositions, and Managerial Implications," *Journal of Marketing* 54 (2): 1–18. John C. Narver and Stanley F. Slater, "The Effect of a Market Orientation on Business Profitability," *Journal of Marketing* 54 (4): 20–35.

40 Robert P. Ormrod, "A Critique of the Lees-Marshment Market-Oriented Party Model," *Politics* 26 (2) (2006): 113. See also Robert P. Ormrod, "A Conceptual Model of Political Market Orientation," in *Current Issues in Political Marketing*, ed. Jennifer Lees-Marshment and Walter Wymer (Binghampton, N.Y.: Haworth Press, 2005) 47–64.

41 Aron O'Cass, "The Internal-External Orientation of a Political Party: Social Implications of Political Party Marketing Orientation," *Journal of Public Affairs* 1 (2) (2001): 137–8.

42 See Stecey Barlow Hills and Shikhar Sarin, "From Market Driving to Market Driven: An Alternative Paradigm for Marketing in High Technology Industries," *Journal of Marketing Theory and Practice* 11 (3) (2003): 13–24; George S. Day, "What Does It Mean to Be Market-Driven?" *Business Strategy Review* 9 (1) (1998): 1–14.

43 Peter Reeves, Leslie de Chernatony and Marylyn Carrigan, "Building a Political Brand: Ideology or Voter-Driven Strategy," *Brand Management* 13 (6) (2006): 424–5.

44 Stephan C.M. Henneberg, "Leading or Following? A Theoretical Analysis of Political Marketing Postures," *Journal of Political Marketing* 5 (3) (2006): 29–46.

45 Lock and Harris, "Political Marketing," 20.

46 Kotler and Kotler, "Political Marketing", 4–5.

47 See Cwalina and Falkowski, *Marketing Polityczny*, 264–90; Lynda Lee Kaid and Christina Holtz-Bacha, eds, *The Sage Handbook of Political Advertising* (Thousand Oaks, CA: Sage Publications, 2006); Newman, *The Marketing of the President*, 56–8.

48 See Chapter 1, Dennis W. Johnson, "American Political Consulting: From its Inception to Today."

49 See Wojciech Cwalina, Andrzej Falkowski and Bruce I. Newman, *A Cross-cultural Theory of Voter Behavior* (Binghamton, N.Y.: Haworth Press, 2007); Newman, *The Marketing of the President*, 42–60; Scammell, "Political Marketing," 728–31.

50 See Harris, "To Spin or not to Spin that is the Question," 36–8; Kotler and Kotler, "Political Marketing", 13–17; Niffenegger, "Strategies for Success from the Political Marketers," 16–20; Wring, "Reconciling Marketing with Political Science," 654–60.

51 E.g. Henneberg, "Generic Functions of Political Marketing," 11–22; Lees-Marshment, "Political Marketing: How to Reach," 1–32; Lees-Marshment, "The Product, Sales and Market-Oriented Party," 1074–84; Newman, *The Marketing of the President*.

52 Newman, *The Marketing of the President*.

53 Paul R. Baines, "Voter Segmentation and Candidate Positioning," in *The Handbook of Political Marketing*, ed. Bruce I. Newman (Thousand Oaks, CA: Sage, 1999), 405–8.

54 Paul R. Baines, Phil Harris and Barbara R. Lewis, "The Political Marketing Planning Process: Improving Image and Message in Strategic Target Areas," *Marketing Intelligence & Planning* 20 (1) (2002): 6–8.

55 Yoram Wind, "Issues and Advances in Segmentation Research," *Journal of Marketing Research* 15 (3) (1978): 317–37.

56 Gareth Smith and John Saunders, "The Application of Marketing to British Politics," *Journal of Marketing Management* 5 (3) (1990): 301.

57 See Stephen Chaffee and Rajiv N. Rimal, "Time of Vote Decision and Openness to Persuasion," in *Political Persuasion and Attitude Change*, ed. Diana C. Mutz, Paul M. Sniderman and Richard A. Brody (Ann Arbor, MI: University of Michigan Press, 1996). Bernadette C. Hayes and Ian McAllister, "Marketing Politics to Voters: Late Deciders in the 1992 British Election," *European Journal of Marketing* 30 (10/11) (1996): 127–39.

58 For more detailed discussion see Bruce I. Newman and Jagdish N. Sheth, *A Theory of Political Choice Behavior* (New York: Praeger, 1987).

59 Smith and Saunders, "The Application of Marketing to British Politics," 300–1.

60 E.g. Ronald J. Johnston, Charles J. Pattie and J. Graham Allsopp, *A Nation Dividing? The Electoral Map of Great Britain 1979–1987* (London: Longman, 1988).

61 E.g. D.A. Yorke and Sean A. Meehan, "ACORN in the Political Marketplace," *European Journal of Marketing* 20 (8) (1986): 63–76.

62 E.g. Cwalina and Falkowski, *Marketing Polityczny*, 62–9.

63 See e.g. Cwalina et al., *A Cross-Cultural Theory of Voter Behavior*. Wojciech Cwalina, Andrzej Falkowski, Bruce I. Newman and Dejan Verčič, "Models of Voter Behavior in Traditional and Evolving Democracies: Comparative Analysis of Poland, Slovenia, and U.S.," *Journal of Political Marketing*, 3 (2) (2004): 7–30; Bruce I. Newman, "A Predictive Model of Voter Behavior: The Repositioning of Bill Clinton," in *The Handbook of Political Marketing*, ed. Bruce I. Newman (Thousand Oaks, CA: Sage, 1999), 259–82; Bruce I. Newman and Jagdish N. Sheth, "A Model of Primary Voter Behavior," *Journal of Consumer Research* 12 (2) (1985): 178–87.

64 E.g. Paul R. Baines, Robert M. Worcester, David Jarrett and Roger Mortimore, "Market Segmentation and Product Differentiation in Political Campaigns: A Technical Feature Perspective," *Journal of Marketing Management* 19 (1–2) (2003): 225–49; Paul R. Baines, Robert M. Worcester, David Jarrett and Roger Mortimore, "Product Attribute-Based Voter Segmentation and Resource Advantage Theory," *Journal of Marketing Management* 21 (9) (2005): 1079–115.

65 Gareth Smith, "Positioning Political Parties: The 2005 UK General Election," *Journal of Marketing Management* 21 (9) (2005): 1139–44. See also Richard M. Johnson, "Market Segmentation: A Strategic Management Tool," *Journal of Marketing Research* 8 (1) (1971): 13–19.

66 Leslie de Chernatony and Jon White, "New Labour: A Study of the Creation, Development and Demise of Political Brand," *Journal of Political Marketing* 1 (2/3) (2002): 45–52.

67 Kevin Lane Keller, "Building Customer-Based Brand Equity: A Blueprint for Creating Strong Brands," *Marketing Management* 28 (1) (2001): 35–41.

68 See Wojciech Cwalina and Andrzej Falkowski, "Cultural Context of the Perceptual Fit of Political Parties' Campaign Slogans: A Polish Case," in *Political Marketing: Cultural Issues and Current Trends*, ed. Kostas Gouliamos, Antonis Theocharous, Bruce I. Newman and Stephan C.M. Henneberg (Binghamton, N.Y.: Haworth Press, 2008).

69 Reeves et al., "Building a Political Brand," 426.

70 See Wojciech Cwalina, Andrzej Falkowski and Lynda Lee Kaid, "Role of Advertising in Forming the Image of Politicians: Comparative Analysis of Poland, France, and Germany," *Media Psychology* 2 (2) (2000): 121. Andrzej Falkowski and Wojciech Cwalina, "Methodology of Constructing Effective Political Advertising: An Empirical Study of the Polish Presidential Election in 1995," in *The Handbook of Political Marketing*, ed. Bruce I. Newman (Thousand Oaks, CA: Sage, 1999), 286.

71 Wojciech Cwalina and Andrzej Falkowski, "Morality and Competence in Shaping the Images of Political Leaders," Paper presented at the 4th International Political Marketing Conference: "Political Marketing Concepts for Effective Leadership Behavior," Sinaia, Romania, April 19–21, 2006.

72 Newman, *The Marketing of the President*, 86–130.

73 See e.g. M. Margaret Conway, "The Use of Polls in Congressional, State, and Local Elections," *Annals of the American Academy of Political and Social Science* 472 (1984): 97–105; Dennis Kavanagh, "Speaking Truth to Power? Pollsters as Campaign Advisors," *European Journal of Marketing* 30 (10/11) (1996): 104–13; Eric W. Rademacher and Alfred J. Tuchfarber, "Preelection Polling and Political Campaigns,"

    in *The Handbook of Political Marketing*, ed. Bruce I. Newman (Thousand Oaks, CA: Sage, 1999), 197–221.

74 Cwalina et al., *A Cross-cultural Theory of Voter Behavior*.

75 Nicholas J. O'Shaughnessy, "High Priesthood, Low Priestcraft: The Role of Political Consultants," *European Journal of Marketing* 24 (2) (1990): 7–23.

76 Harris, "To Spin or not to Spin that is the Question," 46–7.

77 Newman, *The Mass Marketing of Politics*.

78 Nicholas O'Shaughnessy, "Towards an Ethical Framework for Political Marketing," *Psychology & Marketing* 19 (12) (2002): 1092–3.

79 O'Shaughnessy, "America's Political Market," 64–5.

80 See also Collins and Butler, "When Marketing Models Clash with Democracy," 52–62.

Part 2

American Campaigns and Elections

7

The Permanent Campaign

David A. Dulio and Terri L. Towner

A pair of prominent Republicans whose names frequently surface in speculation about possible 2008 presidential candidates joined Granite Staters at a breakfast yesterday.[1]

The above report from the influential *Union Leader* in Manchester, New Hampshire, would not seem unusual given the Granite State's important place at the beginning of the presidential selection process; any potential candidate looking to win his or her party's nomination for the presidency must court New Hampshire voters. The important aspect of this report is not the activity, but the date—this appeared in the *Union Leader* on September 1, 2004, a full four years and two months before the 2008 election, and two months before the election being contested at the time between George W. Bush and John Kerry.

This anecdote epitomizes the permanent campaign. However, it is not unusual. Consider just a few examples: on Sunday, August 29, 2004, Hillary Clinton was asked by Wolf Blitzer on CNN what her plans were for 2008; and on September 3, 2004, the *Houston Chronicle* ran a story describing the "wide-open field" for Republicans for the 2008 race;[2] and the *New York Times* ran the following headline on September 1, 2004—"Possible Contenders for 2008 Begin the Wooing in 2004."[3] What is more, this type of scene has played out for years. Media outlets have also been guilty of asking voters their thoughts on candidates for the next election before the current cycle was finished. In 1995, a Gallup/CNN/*USA Today* survey asked respondents if they thought Colin Powell should run for president in 2000 if he did not get into the 1996 contest. In September 1996, an ABC News/*Washington Post* poll asked potential voters if they would be satisfied with Al Gore and Jack Kemp as a slate of candidates in 2000; importantly, roughly seven in ten said it was "too early" to judge the candidates.[4]

In this chapter, we explore the nature and influence of the permanent campaign in the United States.

What Is the Permanent Campaign?

Since the 1970s, the "permanent campaign" has been an important, yet understudied feature of American politics. In 1976, President-elect Jimmy Carter's pollster, Patrick Caddell, advised him of a new tactic for presidents in their first term—governing by garnering public support—and that it required a continuing political campaign, thus articulating the meaning of a never-ending or permanent campaign. Sidney Blumenthal, a journalist turned Clinton administration official, however, is often credited with coining the term "the permanent campaign" with a book of the same title in 1982. According to Blumenthal, the permanent campaign refers to a policymaking environment where government was remade "into an instrument designed to sustain an elected official's popularity," hence lessening the distinction between campaign and governing.[5] Simply put, elected officials propose policy that is consistent with public sentiment to maintain public approval in order to prevail in the next presidential or congressional election.[6] Drawing on Blumenthal's permanent campaign hypothesis, political consultants began to use the term to solicit business from potential candidates. In 1983, for example, Democratic campaign consultant Walter (Wally) Clinton pitched the following:

> Whether we like it or not, the day of the "Endless Campaign" is here. No longer can an incumbent simply go about his or her business after winning an election, waiting until a few months before the new election to think about campaigning. In fact, any official who intends to stay in office would be wise to view his or her victory speech on election night as a kick off speech for the next election.[7]

Therefore, in the quest for votes, the time between the previous election and the next election begins to narrow as incumbents and challengers hire political consultants, conduct fundraisers, poll the public for policy sentiment, and stump for votes long before the upcoming election. Today, the permanent campaign is considered to describe the current state of American electoral politics. Specifically, campaigns lack convenient starts and stops; campaigning is now a non-stop process in more than one respect. As the Wally Clinton memo makes clear, the modern permanent campaign often begins as soon as the last election ends (or as the media examples that began this chapter demonstrate, even before the current cycle ends); but as Patrick Caddell and Sidney Blumenthal also illustrate, it also extends into how elected officials make policy.

Immediately following Blumenthal's important work, scholars did not devote much attention to the phenomenon. More recently, however, academics, pundits, and journalists alike have begun to pay more attention.[8] Much of this attention has coincided with the presidency of Bill Clinton, whose administration was described as taking the permanent campaign to new heights, and who was dubbed as the first true "permanent campaign" president.[9] Since Clinton, the permanence of the permanent campaign has been revisited given the approach of the administration of and advisors to his successor, George W. Bush.

Structural Components of the Permanent Campaign

The permanent campaign did not emerge simply because of elected officials' need for public approval. In fact, the permanent campaign is well established in the US for other reasons as well. Several structural factors and changing processes have contributed to the rise of the permanent campaign, such as the decline of the party organizations, the ever-widening presidential primary period, and the growth of technology and new media.[10] First and foremost, however, is the structure of the American political system. The Framers themselves sowed many of the seeds of the permanent campaign, granting only two-year terms to legislators in the House of Representatives and four-year terms to the president. In their desire to ensure a government by the people and a quick replacement of legislators who did not meet their constituent's expectations, the Framers of the Constitution ultimately guaranteed elected officials would be subject to "frequent" elections.

As a result, American voters are expected to go to the ballot box more than anyone else in the world. Beyond the nationwide elections in even-numbered years to select representatives at the federal level, some states, particularly New Jersey, Virginia, Louisiana, and Mississippi, occasionally hold statewide elections in odd-numbered years. For example, in 2007, three states held gubernatorial elections, and voters in four states elected state legislators. Moreover, several major cities hold their mayoral elections in odd-numbered years. Then, there are primary and local elections that take place below the public's radar at odd times of every year. For instance, one county in Michigan—Calhoun County—had four separate elections in 2007 ranging from school board to several ballot propositions. Along with regularly scheduled "on-year," "off-year," and in some places "odd-year" elections, voters are more commonly voting in "special elections," which are held when seats in the US House and state legislatures are vacant due to death, resignation, or removal from office. Put simply, as Anthony King so aptly states, "Indeed there is no year in the United States—ever—when a major statewide election is not being held somewhere."[11] Furthermore, not only do Americans vote often, but they also vote individually for dozens of elected posts, ranging from governors and mayors to officials serving as county tax auditors, city board members, police commissioners, and district board advisors. Thus, an important piece of the permanent campaign is that Americans are called to vote more often than any other citizenry in the world.

The permanent campaign has also emerged due to reforms to political processes during the past thirty years. Specifically, as Norman J. Ornstein and Thomas E. Mann suggest, the function of political parties has changed.[12] Political parties rarely recruit candidates for public office, and they control the nomination of candidates less often than they did in their heyday. Rather, the mechanism for selecting candidates to run in a general election is mainly the primary election. This holds true for most elective offices, but is most pronounced and noticeable at the presidential level. As a result, in their efforts to build support for their candidacies, presidential candidates begin campaigning early to gain the attention of voters and other political leaders, create momentum, raise funds, and even mobilize voters. Not surprisingly, the increased importance of the political primary has led to significant changes in the primary calendar. Traditionally, in presidential elections, the primaries and caucuses have occurred between February and June of the election year, with Iowa and New Hampshire leading the pack of nominating contests. Recently, however, since presidential primaries garner much attention, states have begun to frontload their primaries in the attempt to increase their importance in the primary process. In the 2004 presidential elections, for example, nine states voted before February 5. For 2008, twenty states moved their nomination contests to February 5, creating the largest "Super Tuesday" to date, which some have dubbed "Giga Tuesday" or "Super Duper Tuesday." As such, New Hampshire and Iowa's primaries were forced to move to early January. This has created what amounts to a national primary, resulting in nominations being decided earlier and earlier in every successive presidential cycle. The frontloading trend can be clearly seen in Figure 7.1, which illustrates the pace at which primary delegates—the currency of presidential primaries—have been chosen and the start date of nominating battles in 1976—before the push toward frontloading—and 1996 to 2008. The key to seeing the changes in the figure are (1) where the lines begin in the lower left corner—this is the date of the first primary or caucus; and (2) the slope of the line. Notice how in 1976 the line does not begin until late February and it is a gentle slope upward. This means that primaries and caucuses began later and took longer to pick a nominee—it was early May before a majority of delegates had been assigned. In 2008, the line begins earlier than ever before, and is very steep—a majority of delegates were chosen by the beginning of February—a point at which less than 10% of delegates had been chosen in the last three cycles, and before any delegates had been selected in 1976.

Another, often overlooked, component of the permanent campaign is the role of mass media in modern politics. The media devote substantial amounts of time to covering the candidates and

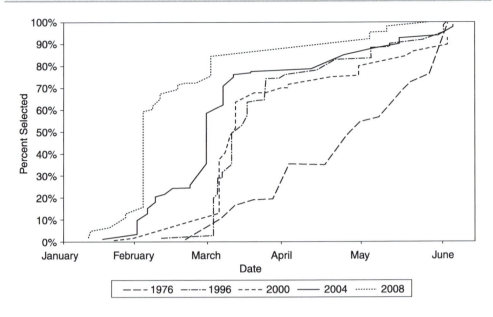

Figure 7.1. Frontloading in Republican Presidential Primaries

Source: 1976 data are estimates taken from William G. Mayer and Andrew E. Busch, *The Frontloading Problem in Presidential Nominations* (Washington, D.C.: Brookings Institution Press, 2004); data on nominating contest dates (1996–2008) taken from Nelson W. Polsby and Aaron Wildavsky, *Presidential Elections: Strategies and Structures of American Politics*, 12th ed. (Lanham, Md.: Rowman & Littlefield, 2008); data on number of delegates per contest (1996–2008) are taken from *National Party Conventions 1831–2004* (Washington, D.C.: CQ Press, 2005).

their campaigns, as well as presidential debates and party conventions, primarily focusing on "horse-race" aspects (for example, who's winning, who's losing, who's catching up), opinion polls, campaign strategies, and candidates' images. Traditionally, media coverage of the presidential campaign occurs between the formal primary period, usually February of the election year, and when the polls open in November.[13] This is no longer the norm, however. Campaign coverage has become an endless horse-race as candidates campaign early and the formal campaign periods widen, with campaign news occurring long before the traditional campaign period (for example, February to the November general election) as well as the pre-campaign period (for example, time between the mid-term elections and the traditional campaign period). As Figure 7.2 illustrates, a majority of network television (that is, ABC, CBS, CNN, NBC, and Fox News) coverage begins at least two years prior to the presidential election. Some campaign news, however, is reported immediately following the last general election and in some cases, *before* the current general election is even contested. On April 15, 2004, for example, Fox News reported that former Minnesota governor Jesse Ventura would seek to run an independent race for the White House in 2008, four years and seven months *before* the 2008 election, and seven months *before* the current 2004 presidential election. As such, journalists simultaneously wrap up the current election *and* report on the next election, with little gap, if any, in presidential campaign news between elections (see Figure 7.2).

Campaigning has become a 24/7 obsession, particularly with the dawn of the competitive twenty-four-hour cable news industry, that continues to fuel the permanent campaign. Unlike a nightly network or local news program, the twenty-four-hour format allows for more news time, broadcasting round-the-clock discussion of who's ahead and who's behind or simply repeating versions of the same wire copy. The emergence of political news "all day, every day" is in line with Stephen Hess's early·remarks regarding changing technology, components, and

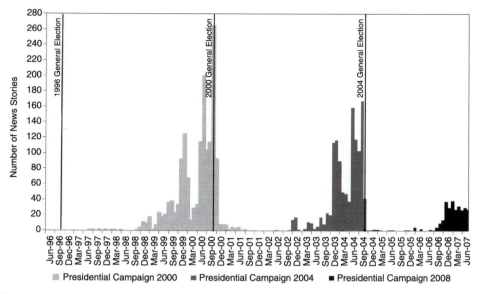

Figure 7.2. Number of Television News Stories on the 2000, 2004, and 2008 Presidential Campaigns

Source: Vanderbilt Television News Archives.

Note: These news stories represent ABC, CBS, CNN, and NBC evening news and special programs, and Fox News reports.

economics of the media: "[These changes] affect why and how politics and government came to be reported as part of a permanent campaign."[14] From CNN's meager beginnings as the "Chicken Noodle News," the twenty-four-hour cable news industry, presently consisting of CNN, MSNBC and Fox News, has become extremely popular among the viewing public. Politics has also become a branch of entertainment. Today, viewers can choose from a broad range of shout shows and talking heads: Fox News' *The O'Reilly Factor, Hannity & Colmes,* and *The Beltway Boys;* MSNBC's *Countdown with Keith Olbermann, Hardball with Chris Matthews,* and *Meet the Press;* and CNN's *The Situation Room* and *Anderson Cooper 360°.* If 24-hour cable news is too much volume and hype, viewers can switch over to ABC's *20/20, Nightline, Primetime,* and *Good Morning America;* CBS's *The Early Show, 60 Minutes,* and *Face the Nation;* and NBC's *Today* and *Dateline* as well as their local news. For softer news, viewers can now be entertained by humorous political television shows on television—*The Daily Show, The Colbert Report,* and *Real Time with Bill Maher*—and catch candidates visiting Oprah Winfrey during the day and Jay Leno and David Letterman during late-night. It is clear that the media embrace the permanent campaign because it provides journalists with the constant drama and conflict they seek to deliver to their audiences. As a result, twenty-four-hour politicized news has an insatiable appetite for campaign news, creating a permanent punditry craving new political conflict, drama, and controversy.

Meanwhile, with new technology, the massive growth of the Internet has created a "permanent online campaign." Websites, chat rooms, forums, blogs, social networks (for example, MySpace and Facebook), streaming video sites (for example, YouTube or Brightcove) and online newspapers provide potential voters with the latest campaign news twenty-four-hours a day as well as function as a permanent archive of the candidates themselves and their campaign activities. All of the US House members and senators have official websites and nearly all have campaign websites, allowing them to reach their constituents year-round rather than relying on mailing newsletters near election time. All 2008 presidential candidates had regularly updated websites, some of which were up and running before officially announcing their candidacy. For example, former Senator Fred Thompson (Republican-Tennessee) used his campaign website in the summer of

2007 to explore (that is, "test the waters") a possible presidential bid, and later announced his candidacy in September 2007. Candidates also use their websites to solicit money, respond quickly to media events, provide information about their platforms, and post timely videos and blogs. For instance, in January 2007, Sen. Hillary Clinton (Democrat–New York) announced her Democratic presidential bid with a webcast posted on her website, and Sen. Barack Obama (Democrat–Illinois) garnered support for his presidential bid via web bloggers.

Not to be outdone, radio also continues to play an important role in the permanent campaign, particularly with the rise in Internet radio, podcasting, and satellite broadcasts. According to Media Monitors, which tracks radio advertising, 2008 presidential candidates, former Massachusetts governor Mitt Romney (Republican) and former New York City mayor Rudy Giuliani (Republican), had run close to 1,000 radio spots nationwide before June 2007. In September 2007, XM Satellite Radio debuted its twenty-four-hour, commercial-free radio channel called "P.O.T.U.S. '08" (which stands for "President of the United States") dedicated to the 2008 presidential election for people with XM radios. Gone are the days of quiet politicking, with its occasional Sunday morning political shows and newspaper coverage three months before the election; now the public can switch on their television, computer, and radio for all-day, year-round access to the latest political news.

As the media have expanded, the number of media polls has also exploded over the past few decades, becoming a prominent feature of election news coverage.[15] Traditionally, throughout the campaign period, the media use public opinion polls to explain voter's opinion, fuel horse-race coverage and frame images consistent with the candidates' positions. As the permanent campaign has become more prevalent, however, polling has become more consistent, actively polling throughout the campaign period and beyond. As Karlyn Bowman notes, for example, the presidential job approval question (for example, "Do you approve or disapprove of the way George W. Bush is handling his job as president?") has been asked more and more frequently by polling outlets, providing further evidence of a permanent campaign.[16] Between 1950 and 1980, no more than four pollsters asked less than fourteen job approval questions during the president's first 100 days in office.[17] As Table 7.1 illustrates, this is no longer the case. In President George W. Bush's second term, twenty-one pollsters asked fifty-one job approval questions once every 3.8 days in the president's first 100 days in office. This is a tremendous increase since the days of Presidents Johnson, Nixon, and Ford, ultimately strengthening the permanent campaign hypothesis.

A deep-seated democratic tradition of frequent elections, the increasing role and frontloading of political primaries, and the growth of twenty-four-hour media are just a few of the major factors that perpetuate the permanent campaign. The permanent campaign, however, has taken on a broader meaning that encompasses behaviors and activities, such as the techniques and strategies of campaigning, that politicians use throughout their terms in office. As discussed below, these behavioral components range from politicians' continued use of advanced techniques of pollsters and campaign consultants to their endless demand for campaign money.

Behavioral Components of the Permanent Campaign

A critical aspect of the permanent campaign in the United States is the behavior of candidates and elected public officials. Clearly illustrated by the example that began this chapter—potential Republican presidential candidates for 2008 laying the groundwork for a run for office in 2004—is the fact that candidates are perpetually in campaign mode. Much of this follows from the structural components of the permanent campaign noted above. However, much of this is also an attitude taken on by candidates and elected officials. As Anthony King notes, candidates and elected officials in the United States "run scared."[18] While the structural factors set the stage

Table 7.1. Number and Frequency of Presidential Job Approval Questions during the First 100 Days in Office by News Organization

	1997	2001	2005
President	Clinton	G. W. Bush	G. W. Bush
Number of days	27	44	51
Frequency	4.7	4.5	3.8
	ABC News	ABC News/*WP*	ABC News/*WP*
	ABC News/*WP*	CBS News	American Research Group
	American Viewpoint	CBS News/*NYT*	*Associated Press*/Ipsos
	CBS News	Fox News	CBS News
	CBS News/*NYT*	Gallup	CBS News/*NYT*
	Gallup	Gallup/CNN/*USA Today*	Fox News
	Gallup/CNN/*USA Today*	Harris	Gallup
	Harris	*LAT*	Gallup/CNN/*USA Today*
	LAT	NBC News/*WSJ*	Greenberg Quinlan Rosner
	NBC News/*WSJ*	Pew	Harris
	Pew	PSRA/*Newsweek*	Marist College Institute
	PSRA/*Newsweek*	Public Opinion Strategies/BAPAC	NBC News/*WSJ*
	Time/CNN/Yankelovich	Reuters/Zogby Poll	*NYT*
		The Tarrance Group	Pew
		Time/CNN/Harris Interactive	PSRA/*Newsweek*
		Time/CNN/Yankelovich	Quinnipiac Univ. Polling
		TIPP/Investor's Business Daily/	Tarrance Group and Lake, Snell,
		Christian Science Monitor	Perry, Mermin Assoc./George
		WP/Kaiser/Harvard University	Washington University
		Zogby	Time/SRBI
			Winston Group
			WP/ Henry J. Kaiser Family
			Foundation/Harvard University
			Zogby

Source: The authors gathered the data in this table from The Ipoll Databank at the Roper Center for Public Opinion Research. This table was adapted from Karlyn Bowman, "Polling to Campaign and to Govern," in *The Permanent Campaign and Its Future*, ed. Norman J. Ornstein and Thomas E. Mann (Washington, D.C.: American Enterprise Institute and The Brookings Institution, 2000), 65.

Note: Question wordings are not identical.

for the permanent campaign, the attitude and behavior of running scared reinforces the idea, leading to important consequences that perpetuate it, including campaign organizations that fail to shut down between election cycles, and the constant chase for campaign cash by candidates for office.

A central component to this aspect of the permanent campaign is a perception of vulnerability on the part of elected officials who intend to seek reelection. King's argument that candidates run scared is based on their feeling of uncertainty about their electoral prospects. In part, this is because of structural factors we noted previously—short terms of office and the direct primary. Candidates often feel vulnerable simply because they have to face reelection and go before the voters so soon after being elected. Moreover, because of the primary system that exists, many elected officials often assume that there is a challenger lurking in the weeds, and that they need to take steps to ward off this possibility. In the case of members of the House of Representatives, these factors come together to put enormous pressure on a candidate seeking reelection. A two-year term and a possible primary means that an incumbent member of the House may have to face the voters as early as fifteen months after taking office. For instance, a candidate elected to the US House of Representatives from Texas in 2008 would begin his or her term in January

2009, but could face a primary challenge as early as March 2010, the traditional date of the Texas primaries (these dates, of course, are different in each state).

As students of congressional elections know well, the number of elected officials who actually *lose* a primary challenge is very small—since 1990 only forty-two members of the House and four members of the Senate have lost in a primary. The two years during this time with the highest numbers of House incumbents losing in primaries were the heavy anti-incumbent cycles of 1992 and 2002, which saw nineteen and eight incumbents defeated, respectively. Amid the anti-Republican and anti-war sentiment of 2006, however, only two incumbents fell victim to a primary challenge, and one of these was a Democrat; in the Senate, the one incumbent who lost a primary in 2006 was Joe Lieberman (Democrat-Connecticut) who went on to win the general election as an Independent.

However, "what matters is not political scientists' statistics concerning incumbents' electoral success rates, but congressmen's and senators' subjective awareness of how uncertain the world of politics is and how much they personally stand to lose."[19] This is not a new phenomenon, however. Richard F. Fenno, Jr, during his work in the 1970s, discovered that words such as "worry" and "fear" often appeared in his interviews with many members of the House who were seeking reelection.[20] Even in the Senate, where members serve six-year terms, this fear can be pervasive; as King notes "even if individual senators do not feel themselves to be under continuing electoral pressure, the Senate as a whole does. *It*, the Senate, may not be up for reelection every two years; but one in three of *them* are."[21]

These feelings of vulnerability to a challenge—either in a primary or general election—lead candidates to engage in activities to protect themselves and also reinforce the permanent campaign. These include, but are not limited to, campaign organizations that never shut down and a constant chase for campaign cash. Students of campaigns and elections know that most campaigns today employ professionals to provide services that candidates demand, including survey research, media advertising (that is, television, radio, and mail), campaign management, fundraising, opposition research, and others. In this aspect of the phenomenon, it is *after* election day when the permanent campaign takes over.

Often, elected officials keep part, if not all, of their campaign organization up and running. Sometimes the campaign organizations are small and may only consist of a part-time staffer,[22] who works to keep tabs on the issues that are important to the officeholder's constituency and any potential challengers. Other campaign organizations that are in place between election cycles are larger in scope and carry out more political operations. These larger organizations may continue to conduct survey research to precisely measure the mood of the electorate, test potential election match-ups, or simply provide the officeholder with information about his or her constituents. Other more substantial permanent organizations may also continue to hold events, include more staff—including consultants and other aides such as accountants and lawyers—and even keep a campaign car.[23] Paul S. Herrnson estimates that the typical incumbent from the House of Representatives spends more than $200,000 on "organizational maintenance" between elections; some even go further, as illustrated by the $1.1 million former House minority leader Richard Gephardt (Democrat-Missouri) spent on staff, rent, office equipment and supplies, and other resources during 2002 alone.[24] Moreover, many elected officials "keep at least an embryonic campaign organization permanently in place, often as personal staff" in their official office.[25] Elected officials in Congress for instance, engage in what amounts to campaign activity through their official duties by using the franking privilege to send out mailings to their constituents describing their efforts to represent the interests of their district or state.

It is less likely that challenger candidates have campaign organizations up and running between election cycles since they may not decide until late in the game that they are even going to run. Candidates who lose in one election cycle, however, may also try to maintain some semblance of a campaign organization so they can prepare for another run. Take for instance

Mary Jo Kilroy who ran in Ohio's fifteenth congressional district in 2006; she narrowly lost to Representative Deborah Pryce (Republican), but was conducting polling in her district as early as the middle of 2007 in preparation for her 2008 run.

If a candidate is going to engage in this aspect of the permanent campaign and either keep a campaign organization up and running or simply start campaigning early, the one thing they need more than anything is money. In fact, one "must-have" staffer in a campaign organization that is going to be maintained through the off-year of the election cycle is a fundraiser. Others in this volume will discuss money in modern campaigns, but suffice it to say that candidates today need large sums to even mount a serious challenge. Because of the dollars needed to compete and purchase the expensive services that are part of campaigns today (polling, television ads, direct mail pieces, and so forth), and the worry most incumbent candidates have about their reelection, the dash for campaign cash is never-ending.

Many incumbent members—both in the US House and Senate—raise money throughout their terms not only because they want to be able to keep up a campaign organization through the election cycle, but also so they can build a large campaign "war chest" that scares off potential challengers. As of the middle of 2007, for example, Representative Marty Meehan (Democrat-Massachusetts) had a war chest of over $5 million at his disposal. This figure is rare, but the practice is not—elected officials grab as much cash as they can, often starting to raise money immediately after the prior campaign.

As with other aspects of this piece of the permanent campaign, incumbent candidates are more likely to be active here, and today they are raising more money earlier than at any point in history. A study by Anthony Corrado illustrates this aspect of the larger phenomenon nicely. In the first six months of the 1980 election cycle (that is, January to June of 1979), incumbents seeking reelection to the US House of Representatives raised $6.4 million in total, which turned out to be less than one-quarter of all the money raised by incumbents during that election cycle.[26] This is compared to the funds raised in the first six months of the 1998 election cycle: during this period, all incumbents had raised nearly $55 million, which translated into nearly 40% of all money raised by incumbents in that cycle.[27] Moreover, incumbents *spend* a good deal of the money they raise in the off-year before they were to face the voters. In 1979—the year before the election—all incumbent candidates raised a total of $16.9 million for their reelection bids; of this total they spent $12.6 million. This is in comparison to their opponents in the general election who raised $37.8 million and spent $36.3 million in *total* over the two-year period. In other words, "Legislators' off-year activity was the equivalent of about 45% of their general election opponents' final receipts and about a third of their final expenditures."[28] In 1997, incumbents raised a total of nearly $116 million and spent almost $71 million in that first year of the 1998 cycle. This is compared to the nearly $80 million and $78 million all challengers raised and spent, respectively, throughout the 1998 cycle.

This type of activity has only continued to explode in more recent election cycles. In 2000, the average incumbent in the House of Representatives raised $179,067 during the first six months of the election cycle; this ballooned to $318,139 in the first six month period of the 2008 campaign.[29] Challengers, on average, have also shown tremendous increases in early fundraising over the last four elections increasing their receipts during the first six months of the 2000 cycle from $60,951 to $107,567 in the first six months of the 2008 cycle.[30] Not only are incumbents raising enough money to pay for the campaigns they will wage in the next year and a half, and to keep their campaign organizations running in the off-year, but they continue to dwarf their challengers in fundraising. It is this year-round dash for cash that enables candidates to engage in activities that keep the permanent campaign going.

The Permanent Campaign in the White House

Nowhere is the permanent campaign more evident than in the White House. As we noted above, the frontloaded nature of the presidential primary season may be the clearest example of just how permanent campaigning is in the United States, with speculation about who might run for office beginning more than four years ahead of an election, and candidates announcing they are going to run for president more than two years in advance of election day (for example, Senator Joe Biden (Democrat-Delaware) announced that he would seek his party's nomination for president in 2008 in May 2005). Moreover, sitting presidents have always taken actions during their time in the White House to try and ensure their reelection after they first get into office; they run scared too.

At the time, it was argued that Bill Clinton helped the permanent campaign reach its peak with his activities in office—continuous polling of the attitudes of the American public—and with those with whom he surrounded himself—a bevy of professional campaign consultants including Stanley Greenberg, James Carville, Paul Begala, Mandy Grunwald, Mark Penn, Robert Squier, Hank Sheinkopf, Marius Penczer, and Dick Morris.[31] One analysis shortly after his presidency ended concluded that "President Clinton set a new record with the sheer number of external consultants he employed."[32] Not only did Bill Clinton utilize consultants for advice, those consultants seem to have "participate[d] in devising policy strategy to a greater extent than normal."[33]

This was before the presidency of George W. Bush, however. Conventional wisdom has likely shifted to place President Bush at the top of the list of presidents who excelled at the permanent campaign. Bush has continued some of the efforts of his predecessor, including having individuals from his campaigns around—most notably Karl Rove. But there is a main difference between how Bill Clinton and George W. Bush used their political consultants during their time in office—the consultants working for Clinton were paid by the Democratic National Committee (or even by the Clinton–Gore reelection campaign),[34] while Rove was formally on the President's White House Staff, first as Senior Advisor to the President in charge of political operations in the White House and Bush's top political advisor, and then as Deputy Chief of Staff later in the Bush presidency.

Both Bill Clinton and George W. Bush, however, took actions during their first term of office illustrative of the permanent campaign and running scared. For instance, the Democratic National Committee, with the help of the consultants Clinton kept close to his side, began running issue advertisements during 1995 for the president's reelection effort. Not long after Bush was inaugurated in 2001, Rove set out to create a plan for Bush's reelection in 2004. These steps included an effort to increase the election day turnout of evangelical Christians by roughly 4 million from their 2000 levels, as well as using the newly created Office of Strategic Initiatives to help increase the president's political standing among the electorate.

These examples make it seem as though political consultants in the White House are a modern phenomena. Nothing could be further from the truth. In fact, every president since Nixon has utilized the services of pollsters and political consultants during their terms of office.[35] How they have used these individuals and the extent of their work and advice has certainly varied, however.[36] In addition, the George W. Bush White House was not the first to use the executive branch to work toward reelection of the president. The Office of White House Communication has also served as a place for White House staff to engage in political activity advancing the president's reelection efforts. As John Maltese notes in his study of that office, the Office of Communications

> is charged with long-term public relations planning, the dissemination of the "line-of-the-day" to officials throughout the executive branch, and the circumvention of the White House press corps

through the orchestration of direct appeals to the people. . . . The goal is to set the public agenda, to make sure all parts of the presidential team . . . are adhering to that public agenda, and to aggressively promote that agenda through a form of mass marketing.[37]

This brings us to a final aspect of the permanent campaign that takes us back to Blumenthal's original definition of the concept—that a continuous campaign "remakes government into an instrument designed to sustain an elected official's popularity"[38]—and Caddell's advice to President Carter in 1976. In addition to his recommendation that Carter convene a working group to begin planning the 1980 reelection effort, Caddell advised that it was "important to recognize that we cannot successfully separate politics and government. . . . Essentially it is my thesis that governing with public approval requires a continuing political campaign."[39] In short, in order to govern effectively, elected officials must act as if they are in a political campaign while they are in office. This next aspect of the permanent campaign is likely the most controversial. Not only are presidents (as well as other elected officials) working toward reelection while in office, but they are blurring, if not obliterating the line between campaigning and governing, two centerpieces of democratic governance. As Hugh Heclo notes, the permanent campaign is "a nonstop process seeking to manipulate sources of public approval to engage in the act of governing itself."[40]

Campaigning Extends to Governing

Heclo's use of the word "manipulate" illustrates the widely held notion that Caddell's and Blumenthal's conception of the permanent campaign is less than desirable. The complaints that each of the last two presidents have been "poll driven"—they simply take a poll to find out what position to take[41]—only advances that belief. Some of those involved in the activities, however, would argue that campaigning to govern is a necessity in modern politics. Bill Clinton advisor Dick Morris argues that presidents must be part of the permanent campaign so they can continue to build public support, which allows them to make strides in implementing their agenda:

> Power . . . comes from a majority of the voters . . . Unless you are tapped into a power source of the majority of voters supporting your position, you can't effectively sustain it in our system—you can't get it passed; and if it's passed, you can't implement it; if you implement it, it can't work. The process at every level requires popular support.[42]

In other words, "Each day is election day in modern America."[43]

In order to take the advice of Caddell, Morris, and the other campaign consultants that frequent the West Wing of the White House more and more in modern administrations, tactics and techniques that have traditionally been associated with election campaigns are used for governing purposes. Included in this list is certainly survey research data. It is clear from several investigations that public opinion plays a vital role in the modern White House.[44] As Bowman points out, the use of polling among politicians has grown due to its ability to scientifically measure and predict public opinion.[45] As evidence of the permanent campaign in the executive branch, some scholars have shown that more and more polling is conducted under White House direction.[46] How presidents use the information they gather from public opinion polls, however, can be debated. Is polling data used to help presidents find politically expedient positions on issues (in other words, to pander for support)? Or is polling data used for less upsetting purposes such as agenda setting, defining the president's message, and framing issues? The answers to these questions are beyond the scope of this chapter, but have been addressed elsewhere.[47]

The use of campaign techniques to govern goes beyond polling. In both the White House and offices of other elected officials such as members of Congress, many examples of activities that were once thought to be in the realm of campaigns can be found trying to advance the progress of specific pieces of legislation or a governing agenda in general. These include campaign-like events, long-term strategic initiatives such as those from the Office of Communications in the White House, "war rooms," television advertising, rapid response to opponents' arguments, and others. Two examples provide an illustrative picture.

The Clinton administration, at the time, set (and in some ways still is) the standard for the permanent campaign. For instance, it was Bill Clinton who used television advertisements to tell the public about his policy ideas and why they should support his programs. Specifically, as the battle over the federal budget between Clinton and the Republican Congress heated up in late 1995, the administration ran ads focused on that topic. According to Morris: "during that period, . . . our intent in running those ads was to win the legislative fight."[48] Of course, these ads were also beneficial to Clinton's reelection campaign that would follow in 1996.

Additionally, in both the White House and on Capitol Hill, "war rooms" have been used to establish and plot strategy for major legislative battles. The Clinton administration again led the way here with its efforts on health care and the Clinton economic plan.[49] Certainly the term is more familiar because of the Academy Award-nominated documentary—*The War Room*—about war rooms in the 1992 Clinton campaign. Interestingly, because of the association with an electoral campaign tactic, the use of the term "war room" was forbidden inside the Clinton White House; but the practice was used many times.[50]

Both parties on Capitol Hill have also used "war rooms" during difficult legislative fights. During the debate over a "patients' bill of rights" in 2001, for example, Senate Democrats created an "Intensive Communication Unit" (ICU) responsible for coordinating media efforts.[51] Not to be outdone, Senate Republicans also set up their own communications center, dubbing it the " 'Patients First Delivery Room,' a reference to their party's slogan for [the] debate, 'Patients First.' "[52] Interestingly, 2001 was not the first time Democrats used an "ICU" during a health care debate. Two years prior when a previous version of the legislation was being considered, they had created an "ICU" that served as "a war room for political and media strategy."[53] One journalist's description of the tactics illustrated how, in the modern Congress, campaign techniques fit nicely with governing on Capitol Hill: "Dueling pep rallies, ad campaigns and procedural maneuvering marked the first day of Senate debate over HMOs [health maintenance organization] . . ."[54] More recently Republicans in the House during the 108th Congress created a "War War Room" during debate about the Iraq war.

Conclusion

The permanent campaign in the United States is here to stay. In fact, it will likely only become more pronounced. As we have noted, the permanent campaign is entrenched in US politics because of structural and political factors. Some factors will not change—short terms of office for our representatives, for example. Others are unlikely to change; consider one of the main culprits of the permanent campaign—frontloading of presidential primaries. Unless some variation of a national or regional primary is instituted (an unlikely scenario in our federal system) states will continue to shift their dates up in the calendar to gain relevancy and importance in the presidential selection process. In addition, the pressure to win elections—from candidates themselves, but also from political parties and outside interest groups—is great. To this end, elected officials will continue to engage in behaviors that benefit their own self-interest and make it more likely that they will be victorious on election day—continually campaigning between election cycles and engaging in the kind of governing practices envisioned by Patrick Caddell fit this mold nicely.

Beyond a near certainty of this phenomenon growing in strength in US politics are important consequences of the permanent campaign. While certainly not an exhaustive list, we see consequences of the permanent campaign in two important areas—those that affect the public and those that affect governing. First, the impact on the public is far reaching and stems from several elements of the permanent campaign. The fact that Americans vote more than citizens in any other nation certainly has an impact on voter turnout in the US; with so many elections there is a certain amount of fatigue in the electorate. Voter fatigue is only heightened with the perpetual attention the media pay to elections, and is heightened even more when the public sees elected officials campaigning in the middle of the period when they are supposed to be engaged in governing. In short, these factors associated with the permanent campaign may lead to a sense of "enough is enough" among the electorate, where we continue to see low voter turnout and low levels of interest in politics among the American people.

Potentially more important are the effects the permanent campaign may have on governing. Continual campaigning, the adoption of the Caddell-style governing campaign, and use of campaign techniques to govern may have detrimental effects on policymaking. Clearly, the line between the campaign season and a governing period is disappearing, if it is still there at all. In addition, the short terms of office and primaries noted earlier systematically create shorter periods where elected officials can engage in governing. Included here are the effects of elected officials not focusing on the job at hand. After election day has produced a winner and that candidate is turned into an elected official, upon swearing in they are supposed to turn to the job of representing their constituents. However, with the pressure to win that is felt from several points, officeholders may neglect the people's business to focus on their campaign. Consider several of the contenders for the presidency in 2008: Senators Joe Biden, Sam Brownback (Republican-Kansas), Hillary Clinton, Christopher Dodd (Democrat-Connecticut), Barack Obama, John McCain (Republican-Arizona), as well as Representatives Duncan Hunter (Republican-California), Dennis Kucinich (Democrat-Ohio), and Ron Paul (Republican-Texas) and New Mexico Governor Bill Richardson (Democrat). Each of these individuals held office at the start of the nomination process, which dated back to early 2007 or late 2006. The time that these candidates spent on the campaign trail was time that they could not spend in their Senate, House, or governor's offices. Those candidates who are legislators also missed out one of the most important responsibilities they have—casting votes—as senators in the race missed between roughly 10 and 50% of all votes taken in their chamber and House members were absent for between roughly 10 and 30% of the votes during the first nine months of the 110th Congress.[55]

Moreover, as Norman Ornstein and Thomas Mann argue, "Campaigning intrinsically is a zero-sum game with a winner and a loser. Governing, ideally, is an additive game that tries to avoid pointing fingers or creating winners and losers in the policy battles."[56] When elected officials are continually looking at a policy decision through the lens of the electoral context that is right around the corner because they may face a primary challenge and are running scared, the results of the policymaking may have to be questioned.

Notes

1 "GOP Leaders Court NH Delegation," *The Union Leader* (Manchester, N.H.), September 4, 2004, A14.
2 "2004 Republican Convention New York: 2008 Hopefuls Subtly Testing the Waters during Convention," *The Houston Chronicle*, September 3, 2004, A20.
3 "Possible Contenders for 2008 Begin the Wooing in 2004," *New York Times*, September 1, 2004, 1.
4 Karlyn Bowman, "Polling to Campaign and to Govern," in *The Permanent Campaign and its Future*, ed. Norman J. Ornstein and Thomas E. Mann (Washington, D.C.: American Enterprise Institute and The Brookings Institution, 2000), 54–74.

5 Sidney Blumenthal, *The Permanent Campaign* (New York: Simon and Schuster, 1982), 7.

6 David Mayhew, *Congress: The Electoral Connection* (New Haven, CT: Yale University Press, 1974).

7 Wally Clinton, "Endless Campaign," pamphlet, The Clinton Group, Washington, D.C., November 1983.

8 See for instance, Norman J. Ornstein and Thomas E. Mann, eds. *The Permanent Campaign and its Future* (Washington, D.C.: American Enterprise Institute and The Brookings Institution, 2000); Corey Cook, "The Permanence of the 'Permanent Campaign': George W. Bush's Public Presidency," *Presidential Studies Quarterly* 32 (4) (December 2002): 753–64; Kathryn D. Tenpas and James McCann, "Testing the Permanence of the Permanent Campaign: An Analysis of Presidential Polling Expenditures, 1977–2002," *Public Opinion Quarterly* 71 (3) (2007): 349–66.

9 Charles O. Jones, "Preparing to Govern in 2001: Lessons from the Clinton Presidency," in *The Permanent Campaign and it Future*, ed. Norman J. Ornstein and Thomas E. Mann (Washington, D.C.: American Enterprise Institute and the Brookings Institution, 2000), 185–218.

10 Ornstein and Mann, eds. *The Permanent Campaign and its Future.*

11 Anthony King, *Running Scared: Why America's Politicians Campaign Too Much and Govern Too Little* (New York: Free Press, 1997), 2.

12 Ornstein and Mann, eds. *The Permanent Campaign and its Future.*

13 Marion Just, Anne Crigler, Dean Alger, Timothy Cook, Montague Kern, and Darrell West, *Crosstalk: Citizens, Candidates, and the Media in a Presidential Campaign* (Chicago, IL: University of Chicago Press, 1996); Matthew Kerbel, *Edited for Television: CNN, ABC, and American Presidential Elections*, 2nd ed. (Boulder, CO: Westview, 1998); Thomas Patterson, *The Mass Media Election: How Americans Choose their President* (New York: Praeger, 1980).

14 Stephen Hess, "The Press and the Permanent Campaign," in *The Permanent Campaign and Its Future*, ed. Norman J. Ornstein and Thomas E. Mann (Washington, D.C.: American Enterprise Institute and the Brookings Institution, 2000), 44.

15 Bowman, "Polling to Campaign and to Govern," 54–74.

16 Ibid., 64.

17 Ibid., 65 (see Table 3.1).

18 Ibid.

19 Ibid., 51.

20 Richard F. Fenno, Jr., *Home Style: House Members in Their Districts* (Boston, MA: Little, Brown, 1978).

21 King, *Running Scared*, 32.

22 Paul S. Herrnson, *Congressional Elections: Campaigning at Home and in Washington*, 4th ed. (Washington, D.C.: CQ Press, 2004).

23 Ibid.

24 Ibid.

25 Gary C. Jacobson, *The Politics of Congressional Elections*, 6th ed. (New York: Longman, 2004), 85.

26 Anthony Corrado, "Running Backward: The Congressional Money Chase," in *The Permanent Campaign and Its Future*, ed. Norman J. Ornstein and Thomas E. Mann (Washington, D.C.: American Enterprise Institute and the Brookings Institution, 2000), 75–107.

27 Ibid., 81 (see Table 4.2).

28 Ibid., 83.

29 Campaign Finance Institute, "Democratic Incumbents Up, Republicans Down," http://www.cfinst.org/congress/pdf/2007_Q2_Table1.pdf. Accessed September 14, 2007.

30 Ibid.

31 Kathryn Dunn Tenpas, "The American Presidency: Surviving and Thriving amidst the Permanent Campaign," in *The Permanent Campaign and its Future*, ed. Norman J. Ornstein and Thomas E. Mann (Washington, D.C.: American Enterprise Institute and the Brookings Institution, 2000), 108–33.

32 Ibid., 113.

33 Charles O. Jones, "Campaigning to Govern: The Clinton Style," in *The Clinton Presidency: First Appraisals*, ed. Colin Campbell and Bert A. Rockman (Chatham, NJ: Chatham House Publishers, 1996), 45.

34 Tenpas, "The American Presidency," 108–33.

35 Ibid.

36 Ibid.; Stephen K. Medvic and David A. Dulio, "The Permanent Campaign in the White House: Evidence from the Clinton Administration," *White House Studies* 4 (3) (2004): 301–17.

37 John Anthony Maltese, *Spin Control: The White House Office of Communications and the Management of Presidential News* (Chapel Hill, NC: University of North Carolina Press, 1992), 2.

38 Blumenthal, *The Permanent Campaign*, 7.

39 Ibid., 56.

40 Hugh Heclo, "Campaigning and Governing: A Conspectus," in *The Permanent Campaign and its Future*, ed. Norman J. Ornstein and Thomas E. Mann (Washington, D.C.: American Enterprise Institute and the Brookings Institution, 2000), 17.

41 For evidence to the contrary, see Medvic and Dulio, "The Permanent Campaign in the White House," 301–17.

42 Ibid.

43 Dick Morris, *The New Prince: Machiavelli Updated for the Twenty-first Century* (Los Angeles, CA: Renaissance Books, 1999), 75.

44 Tenpas, "The American Presidency," 108–33; Bowman, "Polling to Campaign and to Govern," 54–74; Lawrence R. Jacobs and Robert Y. Shapiro, *Politicians Don't Pander: Political Manipulation and the Loss of Democratic Responsiveness* (Chicago, IL: University of Chicago Press, 2000).

45 Bowman, "Polling to Campaign and to Govern," 54–74.

46 Tenpas and McCann, "Testing the Permanence of the Permanent Campaign," 349–66; But see Shoon Kathleen Murray and Peter Howard, "Variation in White House Polling Operations: Carter to Clinton," *Public Opinion Quarterly* 66 (4) (2002): 527–58.

47 For example, see Jacobs and Shapiro, *Politicians Don't Pander*; Medvic and Dulio, "The Permanent Campaign in the White House," 301–17; Shoon Kathleen Murray, "Private Polls and Presidential Policymaking: Reagan as a Facilitator of Change," *Public Opinion Quarterly* 70 (4) (2006): 477–98.

48 Medvic and Dulio, "The Permanent Campaign in the White House," 301–17.

49 Tenpas, "The American Presidency," 123–24.

50 Bob Woodward, *The Agenda: Inside the Clinton White House* (New York: Simon & Schuster, 1994), 259.

51 "Daschle's 'Intensive Care Unit' to Attend to Patients' Rights," *Washington Post*, June 18, 2001, A15.

52 "Patients' Rights Vote in View; Details Argued as PR War Rages," *The Atlanta Journal and Constitution*, June 21, 2001, 3A.

53 "Debate Begins on Patients' 'Bill of Rights'," *Star Tribune* (Minneapolis), July 13, 1999, 1A.

54 "Senate Starts Debating Patients' Bill of Rights," *St. Louis Post-Dispatch*, July 13, 1999, A4.

55 "The U.S. Congress Votes Database," available from *The Washington Post* website, www.washingtonpost.com. Accessed October 3, 2007.

56 Ornstein and Mann, *The Permanent Campaign and its Future*, 225.

8

Political Management and the Technological Revolution

Stephen K. Medvic

Those seeking to obtain and maintain power have always harnessed technology to support their efforts. The present era is not different in this respect. What is unique, however, is the relatively recent development of a class of professional managers who are skilled, if not formally trained, in the use of technology to achieve political goals. They do not seek power for themselves, but for those who pay for their assistance. Some of these managers are primarily technicians; others provide strategic guidance. Nevertheless, the interplay of technology and politics can best be studied by observing these professional political managers, for it is they who adopt technological means for political ends.

Though the political use of technology has a long history, this chapter begins in the mid-nineteenth century and traces developments in political management and technology through to the present. This period of time constitutes what James Beniger calls the "Control Revolution."[1] That revolution is "a complex of rapid changes in the technological and economic arrangements by which information is collected, stored, processed, and communicated, and through which formal or programmed decisions might effect societal control."[2] It is within this period that political consultants begin to emerge as central figures in campaigns.

This chapter will focus on campaign management, but the techniques used by political consultants are now routinely used by those in public office and by interest groups to wage a "permanent campaign" to secure public support for their agendas. Given that political actors now engage in constant campaigning, not just for office, but in governing as well, consultants and technology have become essential elements in the political process. However, a word of caution is due before we explore their effects. Consultants have been shown to give an advantage to at least certain kinds of candidates who employ them, but the influence is relatively marginal.[3] Furthermore, technology's impact in politics is undeniable, but it is not an autonomous agent that *imposes* change on political actors or a political system.[4] As a result, we should be careful not to engage in mythologizing professional political operatives or fall victim to technological determinism. Indeed, it is a central goal of this chapter to provide a measured account of how consultants and technology function in politics.

A Brief History of Technology in Campaigns

The use of technology for political management emerges from the "crisis of control" created by the Industrial Revolution. According to Beniger, the mass production and distribution of goods made it difficult, if not impossible, for producer and consumer to communicate; this, in turn, made supply-and-demand equilibrium elusive. The increasing speed with which goods could be sent further complicated matters. Thus, the need arose for communication and information-processing technology that could resolve the control, or coordination, crisis.[5]

One response to this crisis was bureaucratization and its companion, rationalization. The latter is the process of controlling information by reducing the amount of it that needs to be processed. Standardized forms are an example of a rational means of processing information.[6] Bureaucracies have for centuries formed to manage complex systems, but modern bureaucratic organization emerged during industrialization.[7] And it should be said that bureaucracy is a technological response to the control crisis inasmuch as it fits the definition of technology Beniger employs—namely, "any intentional extension of a natural process," including matter, energy and information processing.[8]

In addition to bureaucratization and rationalization, the development of communication and information-processing technologies helped address the control crisis and launched what Beniger calls the "Control Revolution." The most significant technological innovations of this sort include "photography and telegraphy (1830s), rotary power printing (1840s), the typewriter (1860s), transatlantic cable (1866), telephone (1876), motion pictures (1894), wireless telegraphy (1895), magnetic tape recording (1899), radio (1906), and television (1923)."[9] Each of these would come to influence politics, but not until political operatives applied them to the campaign process.

Elsewhere, I have argued that the political parties developed a "nation-centered group management" model for handling presidential campaigns in the mid-nineteenth century.[10] Though political entrepreneurs such as Martin Van Buren, John Easton and Thomas Hart Benton were influential within their party organizations, the task of managing a nationwide presidential campaign was too complicated for one person to handle. Thus, groups of party leaders managed the campaigns of their nominees. This was, in essence, a bureaucratic response to the complexity of the electoral environment (as was the creation of party national committees, first undertaken by the Democrats in 1848).

By the 1880s, individual managers began assuming responsibility for running presidential campaigns, a task made possible by the availability of communication and information-processing technology. The presidential campaign managers of this era, such as Mark Hanna of Ohio, served as the chairpersons of their respective national parties. This gave them a bureaucracy to rely upon for campaign logistics and organization. Indeed, for the 1896 campaign of William McKinley, Hanna developed a sophisticated organization with various departments that "appealed to different constituencies—Germans, blacks, wheelmen, even women."[11] But campaigns were no longer solely about mass mobilization as they had been in the mid-nineteenth century. Organization mattered, as it still does, but as President Grover Cleveland recognized in 1882, the campaign had become "one of information and organization."[12] To those, he might have added communication, as voters increasingly wanted candidates to speak to them directly. Nevertheless, the period from 1880 to 1896 was something of a campaign purgatory, with pressure to maintain the republican taboo on candidates campaigning for themselves and yet to satisfy the democratic demand that candidates actively run for office in full view of the public.

The telegraph had begun influencing campaigns by at least the 1850s, but it was particularly prominent by the end of the century. To take but one example, Gil Troy notes that Benjamin Harrison refused to take to the stump in 1888 but would leave his house a few times a day to meet well-wishers at a park near his home where he would "listen to the greetings, and respond.

Afterward, Harrison edited these speeches and sent them out on the Associated Press wires for publication the next day."[13] Though he was committed to the republican practice of standing, rather than running, for office, the times also required direct communication on the part of candidates. The telegraph made it possible to communicate to a wide audience from the comfort of one's front porch.

After 1900, however, most candidates actively courted voters, though incumbents were far more reluctant to do so than challengers. Nevertheless, the result was an increase in the use of transportation in presidential campaigns. William Jennings Bryan, the Democratic nominee in 1896 (as well as 1900 and 1908), had broken new ground by speaking at campaign stops from the back platform of a train during a tour that covered "twenty-seven states, over 18,009 miles, in 600 speeches, averaging 80,000 words each day."[14] Whistle-stop campaigning would be, more or less, a central part of presidential campaigns until air travel became widespread in the 1960s.

A much more efficient mechanism for reaching large audiences than traveling around the country by train emerged in the first two decades of the twentieth century. Radio first made its mark in the world of politics when KDKA in Pittsburgh broadcast the results of the 1920 presidential election between Warren Harding and James Cox. In 1921, New York Mayor John Hylan became the first candidate to use radio in a campaign; the following year, Senator Harry New of Indiana used a radio address from Washington to solidify support back home in the lead up to a tough primary (which he lost anyway).[15] In his study of the political use of radio, Douglas Craig notes that the new broadcast technology was used in the 1924 presidential campaign, but that 1928 would be the "first true radio election."[16] Not only did the parties spend considerable amounts of money on radio in that year (the Democrats budgeted $600,000 for radio—or more than $7 million in 2007 dollars—while the Republicans allocated $350,000), but they targeted some of that spending to reach at least one particular group.[17] According to Craig, "Both the RNC [Republican National Committee] and the DNC [Democratic National Committee] booked large amounts of time during the morning to reach women at home."[18] Ultimately, as Gil Troy argues, the 1928 Democratic nominee Al Smith was "defeated by a medium [that is, radio] that had previously been kind to him . . . Smith's radio speeches were less effective than his personal appearances . . . His voice, when amplified, became 'tinny . . .' For better *and* for worse, Smith's voice became his calling card."[19]

Radio brought the candidates into every living room in the country and voters were able to judge them in ways that had previously been available only to those who could hear the candidates in person. As the example of Al Smith suggests, the basis for the voters' judgments would likely be matters of style, such as a candidate's accent, rather than substance. Furthermore, every public utterance had the potential of being broadcast to millions of individuals. Thus, candidates became far more conscious of their choice of words and tone of voice than they had ever been.

It may be no coincidence, then, that the first professional campaign managers appeared in the 1930s. The tactics they employed were drawn from the relatively young field of public relations.[20] During World War I, the United States had established the Committee on Public Information in an attempt to influence public opinion about the war effort. A number of the Committee's members, including Edward Bernays, would help establish public relations as a profession. At roughly the same time, business interests were recognizing the need "to 'sell' the social system which sustains the large corporation, to build a public opinion favorable to legislation fostered by segments of business enterprise, and occasionally to intervene directly in political campaigns."[21]

Professionally managed campaigns first emerged in California. This, too, is perhaps no surprise. Given the size of the state, as Robert Pitchell noted, statewide campaigns were forced to organize according to rational principles. Furthermore, the early success in California of the Progressive movement's campaign for direct legislation and particularly active interest groups in California also contributed to the demand for professional management of politics.[22] Of course, the weak party system in California (made weaker still by Progressive reforms) "created a partial vacuum in campaign techniques for shaping and mobilizing public sentiment."[23] Professional managers simply filled that vacuum.

Alan Ware has maintained that professional campaign handlers might have emerged even in the presence of strong parties. To illustrate the point, he offers an analogy that, for the purpose of this chapter, is all the more interesting because of its reference to technology. Arguing that professional campaign managers could only have surfaced in the absence of political parties, says Ware, is like arguing that the railway system could only have developed in nineteenth-century Britain if the canal system was weak. But the canal system was operating effectively when the more efficient rail system supplanted it.[24] Similarly, professional campaign operatives offered a more efficient way to reach a large number of voters than did parties, so candidates were likely to utilize their services regardless of the health of the party system.

The appeal of professional campaign managers for candidates was twofold. They were obviously creative and clever and their campaign plans were rational. The strategies they prepared for candidates seemed to offer a direct path to victory. But professional operatives provided more than sound campaign strategy. As Stanley Kelley, Jr has written:

> It is primarily as the member of a skill group that the public relations man [sic] comes to campaigns and public discussion . . . the value put on his services by those who employ him derives from his specialized knowledge of, and experience with, the methods and instruments of mass communication.[25]

Campaigns and the technologies necessary to run successful bids for office, simply became too complex for amateurs to run.[26]

The first, and most successful, firm to offer candidates the skills required to manage a modern, communication-based campaign was Campaigns, Inc., run by Clem Whitaker and Leone Baxter. Whitaker and Baxter controlled every aspect of a campaign, including strategy, finances, organization and communication. To disseminate a candidate's message, they relied on every medium available. Radio, of course, was vital to any serious operation, but Whitaker and Baxter also used pamphlets, letters, postcards, billboards and newspaper advertisements.[27]

We often forget that by the 1930s, images were also part of the campaign arsenal. In 1924, according to Troy, President Coolidge "spoke to the nation in the modern language of photography. In their newspapers and movie theatres, Americans enjoyed seeing their President chopping trees, pitching hay, or greeting such visitors as Henry Ford and Thomas Edison at the White House."[28] "Of course," Troy continues, "these apparently unguarded moments were carefully staged."[29]

Before widespread access to television, people had become accustomed to motion pictures at their movie theaters. In the 1934 California gubernatorial campaign, an organized effort to defeat socialist candidate Upton Sinclair used movie shorts—five-minute films played prior to the feature presentation—to raise doubts about him. In these shorts, called *California Election News* and produced by (but not credited to) MGM, an "inquiring cameraman" roamed California asking voters whom they supported. Those backing Republican Governor Frank Merriam were inevitably clean cut and well spoken while Sinclair voters were outcasts, "the gap-toothed bum and the sneaky-eyed foreigner."[30] To many, the arguments for Merriam were not particularly persuasive. But, as Greg Mitchell writes in his magnificent history of the campaign, "this was a new political medium—a visual medium. The spoken word might rule the radio, but in the darkened theater moviegoers identified with images projected on the big screen."[31]

Technological change was rapid in the first half of the twentieth century. Indeed, Bruce Bimber argues that, unlike earlier information revolutions that were based on institutional developments (that is, the creation of the national postal system in the early nineteenth century) or socio-economic changes (that is, the dramatic increase in the amount of communication in the late nineteenth century), the information revolution of the early twentieth century was entirely the result of technological advances.[32] The most significant of these was the advent of television.

Though television sets were commercially available before World War II, their high cost discouraged many people from buying them. In the decade following the war, however, television ownership skyrocketed. In 1950, just 7% of American households owned a television set, a number that would jump to 82% by 1957.[33]

Though Kathleen Hall Jamieson notes that presidential candidates were conscious of television during the 1948 campaign, and even purchased time to deliver speeches on the air, the presidential campaign of 1952 is usually said to be the first in which television played a significant role.[34] Jamieson reports that Republicans spent at least $800,000 on television ads, compared to the Democrats' paltry $77,000, but that Democrats far outspent Republicans on time to air speeches.[35] Thus, while television had arrived as a vital campaign tool, it was still often used in a simplistic manner. Much of the time, candidates and their surrogates spoke directly into the camera and even many of Dwight Eisenhower's ads featured the General answering questions as a talking head.

Nevertheless, the campaigns realized that television was a powerful medium. Thus, when questions arose about an alleged secret slush fund established for Vice-Presidential candidate Richard Nixon's personal use, the campaign purchased time following the popular Milton Berle Show for Nixon to defend himself. The result was the famous "Checkers Speech" in which Nixon denied receiving improper gifts, but did admit to having been given a dog, named Checkers, that his children loved and that they would not return.[36] The speech helped Nixon weather the slush fund controversy and saved his political career.

Television was also essential to John F. Kennedy's presidential bid in 1960. Young and energetic, Kennedy was also considered inexperienced. Furthermore, some voters were uncomfortable with his Catholicism. Television gave Kennedy an opportunity to convey his competence and to allay concerns about his faith. He did so by appearing before groups that might be thought less than friendly, including primary voters in Wisconsin and West Virginia and Protestant ministers in Houston. Many of these appearances were televised, particularly in targeted primary or general election swing states. The Houston appearance was broadcast live throughout Texas and the national media later used clips of it in their reports. The Kennedy campaign also taped the event for use in ads and at future events.[37] Of course, Kennedy's performance in the nationally televised debates with Nixon also helped tremendously. Though the influence of television in the 1960 election is hard to measure, and may have been overstated in analyses of the race, it certainly had a positive impact on Kennedy's campaign. As Theodore Sorensen wrote:

> Kennedy's style was ideally suited to this medium. His unadorned manner of delivery, his lack of gestures and dramatic inflections, his slightly shy but earnest charm, may all have been handicaps on the hustings, but they were exactly right for the living room.[38]

The 1960 campaign made it difficult to avoid two conclusions. First, a candidate's style was now as important as (if not more than) his or her issue positions and policy proposals. Second, the effective use of television required the assistance of campaign operatives with specialized skill. Both conclusions led to the emergence of a new breed of campaign professional, the political consultant. Unlike campaign managers, consultants worked on numerous campaigns simultaneously and did not handle the day-to-day functions of a campaign (unless they were running a presidential campaign). Initially, consultants were generalists who gave advice about every aspect of a campaign, including the basic campaign strategy that would be implemented. Eventually, however, consultants began to specialize in particular aspects of campaigns, such as advertising, fundraising or polling.[39]

The complaint—heard from the earliest years of political television—that candidates are packaged and "sold" like products such as soap and cereal, might have arisen because the people selling the candidates were also those who sold soap and cereal. Candidates' media operations were initially handled by advertising agencies whose primary clientele were corporations. By the mid-1960s, however, these agencies were creating campaign spots that were uniquely political. As the famous "Daisy Girl" ad of 1964 illustrates, advertising experts recognized the importance of emotional, as opposed to purely rational, appeals to voters.[40] As editing techniques and equipment became more sophisticated, these appeals became more effective.

Advertising also benefited, as did campaign strategy generally, from the development of scientific polling. Presidents had relied on polls, to a greater or lesser extent, to understand the sentiments of the citizenry at least since Franklin Roosevelt's administration. Indeed, George Gallup had made a name for himself by producing a poll that accurately predicted the outcome of the 1936 election. But candidates did not use polls to steer their campaigns until Jacob Javits hired Elmo Roper to help with his congressional campaign in 1946.[41] The first presidential campaign to rely heavily on polling for strategic insight was the 1960 Kennedy effort.[42] By 1962, two-thirds of Senate candidates, but only 10% of House candidates, used professional pollsters.[43] Within a relatively short period of time, all serious candidates for offices at nearly any level of prestige would hire a professional pollster.

Polling required even more specialized skill than did advertising. Knowledge of statistics was a prerequisite for conducing polls, as was an understanding of valid survey research methods. By 1970, pollsters were also making use of a complicated technology called the computer. To that point, computers were mostly a novelty item in campaigns, primarily due to the prohibitive cost of using them in any significant way. James Perry noted that Arkansas Governor Winthrop Rockefeller leased a computer from IBM for his 1968 reelection campaign for an estimated $10,000 a month (or $59,000 in 2007 dollars).[44] Even if campaign operatives had access to computers, some doubted the value of the technology. As late as 1970, Dan Nimmo wrote that pollsters were "assisted by the helpful but rarely necessary mystique of computers."[45] At roughly the same time, however, the development of the microprocessor made computers more versatile, more powerful and, eventually, smaller. By the early 1980s, personal computers were becoming widely available and were far more useful for business activity, including campaign consulting.[46]

Computers enabled political consultants to operate more efficiently and far more rapidly. For pollsters, Computer Assisted Telephone Interviewing (or CATI) systems helped manage the thousands of phone calls interviewers must make to conduct a poll. Gary Selnow argues:

> As an interviewing aid and coordinator, CATI is a wizard:
>
> - Its dialing and number management keeps the calls moving along.
> - Question sequencing focuses questionnaires and reduces mistakes and disruptions in the flow.
> - It checks for ineligible responses and thus helps reduce errors.
> - It notes times and dates for each interview and clocks completion times. This helps management identify and work with particularly slow or fast interviewers.[47]

As Selnow notes, CATI's most important feature is its data management capability. As interviews are completed, CATI collects the responses and builds a database for immediate analysis upon completion of the poll.[48] In the fast-paced world of political campaigns, the rapid production of poll results is essential. Indeed, tracking polls—or polls conducted over a series of days in which each new day's results replace the results of the first day in series, producing a rolling average—would be nearly impossible without CATI software. When used to determine the effectiveness of campaign tactics, particularly with respect to campaign ads, tracking poll results can mean the difference between winning and losing a close contest. Thus, computers have provided political consultants with the ability to guide campaigns with far more precision than was possible just thirty years ago.

As CATI's data management feature suggests, computers became valuable not only for polling but also for voter contact. Databases containing information about tens of thousands of voters could be built and utilized for voter persuasion and mobilization. Parties and campaigns could collect demographic, political and (eventually) consumer data on voters throughout a district, state or the entire nation. The sources of data are many. Campaigns and the parties build some datasets "in-house." A primary source of such data is door-to-door canvassing, where voters will be identified by, among other things, whether they support the candidate, are undecided or oppose the candidate. Other datasets are purchased from list vendors or imported from voter registration rolls or the Census Bureau.[49] Again, this data will be analyzed and used for targeted messages to various types of voters during the campaign and for mobilizing supporters on election day.

Parties, candidates and fundraising consultants also began to use databases to maintain lists of contributors and potential contributors. Because a vast amount of information can be stored in databases, fundraisers possess a great deal of knowledge about potential donors. This includes occupations, past contributions, interests and even personal facts such as birthdays. Armed with such information, fundraisers are better able to cultivate the kinds of relationships that produce big contributions.

By the 1980s, then, computers were widely used in campaigns. At the same time, other technologies that would change the nature of campaigning were also emerging. For example, the videocassette recorder, or VCR, came into market circulation in the late 1970s and was first used in a campaign in the 1982 Senate race in Missouri. According to media consultant Paul Curcio, Democratic challenger Harriet Woods used a VCR that year to tape an ad by Republican senator John Danforth and used a clip from that ad in her own spot. In the following election cycle, campaigns across the country used VCRs in this manner. The VCR, therefore, made possible "the back-and-forth arguments between campaigns' advertisements" that have come to be standard fare in campaigns.[50]

Though cable television had been available for some time prior to 1980, that year marked its political coming of age. It was in 1980 that a twenty-four-hour news channel called the Cable News Network, or CNN, debuted. The new media outlet would become a major actor in the world of journalism eleven years later, during the first Gulf War. But the very creation of such a network altered the way campaigns, at least those commanding national attention, thought about "free" (or "earned") media coverage. Campaigns would now not only have to respond to news that could break at any moment during the day or night, but they could also make news around the clock.

Cable television, in general, would also have some impact on how campaigns allocated "paid" media (that is, advertising). As channel offerings proliferated on cable, campaigns found it more and more useful to target voters with ads on particular channels. This process came to be known as "narrowcasting," a tactic that on radio pre-dates cable by a number of years. Candidates seeking to reach women voters might advertise on Lifetime; those with a message for African-Americans could turn to Black Entertainment Television; and those wanting access to business-oriented voters could buy time on CNBC.

There would be an explosion of new technology in the 1990s and political operatives would fairly quickly find campaign uses for most of it. These technologies have been valuable in terms of both campaign organization and communication. For instance, mobile telephones, which had first become available as "car phones" in the 1980s, were ubiquitous by the end of the century. "Cell phones," as they have come to be known, allowed campaign staffers to communicate instantly with one another from any location. Field operations and advance work were made more efficient through the use of cell phones, but press relations were also significantly affected. Journalists could reach campaign spokespersons at any time and press secretaries could alert reporters to developments as they were unfolding. Eventually, cell phones would allow campaigns to communicate directly with voters.

Various other technologies also appeared in campaigns in the 1990s. For instance, candidates began using multimedia formats to communicate with voters. The digital video disc (or DVD) provided an interesting new mechanism for disseminating messages and within a few years of their availability in the mid-1990s, the cost of DVDs had fallen sufficiently to make their use in campaigns commonplace. In the late 1990s, the personal digital assistant (or PDA) made campaign scheduling more efficient but was also a valuable tool for mobile e-mailing. Even more important, however, was the use of PDAs for data entry during canvassing and get-out-the-vote (GOTV) operations.

The 1990s ushered in what Bimber argues is the fourth information revolution. The Internet, of course, has taken a lead role in this latest transformation. The key characteristics of our new era, according to Bimber, are the proliferation of information and the attendant "postbureaucratic forms of politics."[51] That is, "the structure of group politics is organized around not interests or issues, but rather events and the intensive flow of information surrounding them."[52] In addition to groups, individuals have also become influential political actors as "bloggers"— those who write web-logs, or "blogs"—and as amateur video producers who are able to distribute their work via websites such as YouTube. The result is a fragmented political environment in which traditional campaign organizations have lost a great deal of control over the flow of communication.

Campaign Technology Today

Discussions of technology and political management today inevitably revolve around the Internet. Though other technologies, including older ones such as television and telephones, continue to play an important role in campaigns, the Internet has begun to dominate the attention, if not yet the resources, of political operatives and observers. This is, perhaps, because the Internet is the first fully interactive technology. The possibilities for communication with voters have only just begun to be explored.

Kirsten Foot and Steven Schneider have identified four practices that web campaigning accommodates—informing, involving, connecting and mobilizing.[53] Each of these practices, of course, is as old as campaigning itself. But the Internet has enhanced a campaign's ability to employ them by using a number of production techniques, namely co-production, convergence and linking. Co-production occurs when multiple actors collaborate to create a web object; convergence is the merging of online and offline forms of communication; and linking provides a connection between two web objects.[54]

Campaigns seek to provide the electorate and the media with a justification for electing one candidate and/or defeating another. This requires the dissemination of abundant, if selective, information. Campaign websites have become the primary source of information about a candidate, including familiar campaign literature such as position statements, press releases and biographies. In 2004, 71% of all US Senate candidates and 68% of all US House and gubernatorial candidates had websites.[55] Though the information on those sites may be traditional, the Internet's presentation of that information is novel. Through linking, for example, the web allows campaigns to provide evidence for their claims from independent sources. It also allows those interested in probing beyond bullet points and vague policy statements to download longer and more detailed policy papers.[56]

Visitors to candidate websites are also given ample opportunities to get involved in the campaigns. One way in which they are often invited to become involved is by contributing money to a campaign. The Internet has made that process more efficient and campaign websites have been designed to make the process of contributing as easy as possible. Clicking on the large "CONTRIBUTE" or "DONATE" button that all candidate homepages prominently display allows an individual to make a donation using a credit card in a matter of minutes. If the potential supporter would rather volunteer his or her time, attend (or even plan) an event, comment on the campaign, or simply add his or her name to a list of supporters, a website will facilitate these forms of involvement as well (see Figure 8.1).

It should be noted that campaigns are not passive with respect to Internet fundraising. That is, they do not simply wait for self-motivated supporters to visit the candidate's website to contribute. Instead, potential contributors are driven to websites by e-mails that sound similar to

Source: www.joinrudy2008.com, September 30, 2007.

Source: www.hillaryclinton.com, September 30, 2007.

Figure 8.1. Presidential Campaign (2008) Websites "Involving" Supporters

emotional direct mail solicitations. When an opponent says something controversial or positive new polling numbers are released, the campaign will attempt to capitalize by sending mass e-mails asking for donations. There is often a sense of urgency, particularly near the end of fundraising reporting periods, as the following example from the 2008 Mitt Romney for President campaign illustrates.

Stephen:

The clock is ticking. We are nearly 24 hours away from the end of the third fundraising quarter. We must finish this quarter strong and approach the end of the year fully energized.

We defied expectations the first quarter of this year, and it was a great turning point in the campaign. It helped provide the resources to win the debates and propel us into the lead in the early states. Yet now the race is in sprint mode, and it's neck and neck.

We need a strong finish to this quarter to ensure we have the resources necessary to continue our momentum and to win. Please contribute any amount you can today at www.MittRomney.com/Act.

Please don't wait: www.MittRomney.com/Act.

Your early and continued support has proven we're the strongest campaign and that we're prepared to win. Now, let's show the world.

Our strong position in the early primary and caucus states illustrates that my message of conservative change in Washington is resonating. I am thankful for supporters like you, without whom we would not be where we are today. If you could make one donation of any amount at our website www.MittRomney.com/Act or by phone at 857-288-6418, it would mean the world to me. Your contribution will go directly toward spreading my vision for change.

With your continued support, we're headed to the White House.

Governor Mitt Romney

P.S. I have told one of my aides that you might be calling. He can be reached at 857-288-6418.[57]

While there are similarities between e-mail and direct mail fundraising solicitations, there are also significant differences. As Larry Biddle, the deputy finance director for Howard Dean's 2004 presidential bid, explains:

E-mails . . . must be short, and direct mail long . . . Online requires a direct line of attack, a quick read and reiteration of the need two or three times—usually in less than 100 words. The average bloke looks at an e-mail for 20 to 30 seconds and then decides what to do. Direct mail donors love long, interesting stories.[58]

The Dean campaign, of course, became renowned for its use of the Internet.[59] Roughly 40% of its fundraising total of almost $53 million was raised online.[60] Just as importantly, the Dean campaign appears to have mastered the practice of connecting. "Campaign organizations engage in connecting when they provide bridges on or to the Web between two (or more) political actors," write Foot and Schneider. "Whereas the aim of involving is cultivating site visitors' relationships with the campaign, the aim of connecting is to facilitate site visitors' interaction with other political actors."[61] An example of connecting is when campaigns provide links between the campaign and other political actors such as interest groups or parties. The Dean campaign famously used the website Meetup.com to connect its supporters to one another in locations around the country. Of course, the campaign also had to maintain contact with the local Dean Meetup groups. It did so, according to the director of Dean's National Meetup operation, by making "a concerted effort to maintain constant dialogue with our grassroots leaders using every available technology (that is, phone, conference call, mail, instant-message, and digital video)."[62]

Finally, campaigns must mobilize supporters, both to advocate on behalf of the candidate and, ultimately, to vote. A campaign might, for instance, offer features that enable supporters to send their friends e-postcards that promote the candidate and direct the friends to the candidate's website. They can also make "e-paraphernalia," such as screensavers, graphics and desktop wall-paper, available to supporters; they can facilitate communication between supporters and the public through letters to the editor, talk radio or blogs. And they can provide materials online that help supporters organize and hold campaign events like fundraisers or house parties that promote the candidate.[63] Clearly many of the practices of web campaigning overlap so that, for example, involving supporters in the campaign can take the form of mobilization or supporters may be mobilized to offer opportunities for others to connect with each other and the campaign.

At this time, the Internet is underutilized for GOTV. "The online tools that would let activists do effective campaign work on their own," says the former organizing director for MoveOn.org, Zach Exley, "are only beginning to be developed . . . A hastily constructed contribution page will still take contributions. But it's much more difficult to build a web tool to accept a contribution of [volunteer] time effectively."[64] Ultimately, Exley argues that operatives with *offline* experience in field organizing will have to help create those tools.

Indeed, each of the Internet campaign practices described above—informing, involving, connecting and mobilizing—takes place offline as well. When campaigns undertake those practices offline, they nonetheless rely on a range of available technologies. Perhaps the most important of these is the personal computer. Databases, in particular, have become extremely valuable not only for fundraising purposes but also for voter contact and mobilization. Both the RNC and the DNC have built enormous files with personal information about tens of thousands of voters. As of 2004, each party's file—named Voter Vault and Demzilla for the Republicans and Democrats, respectively—contained 165 million names with as much as 400 pieces of information per name.[65] (The Democrats have since created a new list, called VoteBuilder.) These lists help the parties in a process called microtargeting, where voters are targeted based on the connection between their consumer preferences and lifestyle profiles, on the one hand, and their political predispositions on the other. The jury is still out on whether or not this tactic is successful, but for our purposes the point is that it could not be implemented without the assistance of computers.

As noted above, computers also make efficient polling possible. Without CATI systems, polling results would take days, if not weeks, to obtain and analyze. Tracking polls are inconceivable without CATI software. Beyond polling, computers also enable campaigns to place "robocalls," or automated telephone calls carrying pre-recorded messages, typically from a well-known figure who is likely to be popular in the home to which the call is made. Robocalls are usually used near election day to help motivate voters to cast a ballot. Like microtargeting, there is little evidence to suggest that robocalls work to either persuade voters or mobilize them (and some evidence that they have no effect at all).[66] But they have become a standard part of campaign communications.

Another increasingly common form of communication with voters is text messaging via cell phones. Many of the major presidential candidates in 2008 had options on their websites for visitors to sign-up to receive texts from the campaign. Newer technology is even making it possible for candidates to leave voicemails on supporters' cell phones. Where possible, candidates are also using video as opposed to mere text (that is, "vlogging," or video-blogging). And candidate speeches and other messages are now routinely available for downloading as podcasts.

Technology has also improved voter mobilization efforts. Well-funded campaigns now use PDAs to record information gathered during voter canvasses. That data, often in conjunction with maps provided by geographic information systems (GIS), can then be used for follow-up voter contact and, ultimately, GOTV. On election day, PDAs are used to communicate with precinct-level volunteers about who has—and more importantly, who has not—voted, improving the parties' success in getting every possible supporter to the polls.

As of this writing, no campaign has used recent advances in technology as effectively as the 2008 presidential campaign of Barack Obama. By the end of May 2008, Obama had raised nearly $300 million, from more than 1.5 million donors, and the great majority of that money was raised online. In addition, the campaign energized many first-time voters and amassed an enormous database of supporters. It engaged those supporters by using social networking sites such as Facebook and MySpace and communicated to them through YouTube, podcasts, and text-messaging, as well as blogs and micro-blogs (such as Twitter). Obama has also spent more money than any of his opponents on Internet advertising. Those he has followed the lead of Howard Dean in promoting grassroots activism, he has gone far beyond what Dean was able to accomplish. There is no doubt that the success of Obama enjoyed in 2008 was due, in large measure, to his masterful use of new technologies.

Just as technology allows campaigns to reach voters more efficiently, it must be said that it also enables voters to avoid campaigns. It has become difficult to conduct polls, for example, because of "caller identification" devices that enable those receiving telephone calls to avoiding answering those from phone numbers they do not recognize. In addition, it is not currently possible to randomly contact respondents via cell phone, a problem for pollsters that will only increase as more people replace their landline telephones with cell phone services. Even campaign ads on television are more easily avoided as digital video recorders allow voters to skip commercials when watching programs they have recorded. Technology, then, can be as much an obstacle as an asset for the campaign professional.

Concluding Thoughts

Before reflecting on the impact of technology in campaigns, it should be noted that interest groups and lobbyists use many of the same techniques to advance their legislative agendas that candidates use to get elected. For example, interest group websites prominently display "Take Action" buttons that allow visitors to the site to, among other activities, quickly produce a personalized e-mail expressing an opinion about an issue of importance to the organization. The message is then sent automatically to the person's representative in Congress or in a state legislature.[67]

Once in office, elected officials, particularly presidents and governors, employ campaign tools and techniques to govern. Polling, for example, is now ubiquitous and helps frame policy proposals, while political parties often air television ads during legislative disputes. The result is a "permanent campaign" in American politics (see Chapter 7, by David Dulio and Terri L. Towner).

Of course, the number of actors influencing politics has proliferated as the amount of information has increased and the technology for producing (and receiving) that information has become widely accessible. Today, an individual with a digital video camera can produce a YouTube video that can significantly alter the dynamics of a US Senate race and damage the career of sitting Senator (for example, the 2006 George Allen "macaca" video).[68] Furthermore, unknown individuals frequently have an effect on major political stories, as when a conservative blogger revealed as fraudulent the document at the heart of a 2004 CBS News story on George W. Bush's alleged failure to report for National Guard duty.[69] And entirely new organizations can form seemingly overnight, as MoveOn.org did when a husband and wife sent 100 e-mail petitions during the Clinton impeachment asking Congress to censure the President and then "move on." Within a month of sending the original e-mail, MoveOn had 300,000 signatures and a new force in American politics had been born.[70] Though Richard Davis predicted that the actors who dominate politics offline will continue to dominate politics online, nontraditional actors are increasingly exercising influence in campaigns.[71]

The current postbureaucratic political environment, to use Bimber's terminology, has led to a new crisis of control. This crisis does not affect society in general, as the control crisis of the nineteenth century did, but rather relatively large (and bureaucratic) organizations, including political campaigns. Messages now come from a variety of sources and voters get fragmented information about candidates from the campaigns, the parties, interest groups in all their forms (including 527 organizations) and the range of media outlets now producing politically relevant material. Perhaps in response to this situation, decentralized networks of politically aligned organizations, operatives and activists have begun to form. These are often referred to as "party networks."[72]

Regardless of how American politics is practiced in the future, it will undoubtedly rely upon technology. And given the rapid advances of technology, candidates will continue to require the skills and experience of professional political operatives. At the same time, non-professionals will find it even easier to make their mark on campaigns.[73] As a result, campaigns are likely to be dynamic and, indeed, thrilling affairs for decades to come.

Notes

1 James R. Beniger, *The Control Revolution: Technological and Economic Origins of the Information Society* (Cambridge, MA: Harvard University Press, 1986).

2 Ibid., vi.

3 Stephen K. Medvic, *Political Consultants in U.S. Congressional Elections* (Columbus, OH: Ohio State University Press, 2001); David A. Dulio, *For Better or Worse: How Political Consultants are Changing Elections in the United States* (Albany, N.Y.: State University of New York Press, 2004).

4 John Street, *Politics and Technology* (New York: The Guilford Press, 1992), 5, 23–45.

5 Beniger, *The Control Revolution*, 10–13. The political predicament of the time was a "crisis of integration"; see Paul Goodman, "The First American Party System," in *The American Party Systems: Stages of Political Development*, ed. William Nisbet Chambers and Walter Dean Burnham (New York: Oxford University Press, 1967).

6 Beniger, *The Control Revolution*, 15–16.

7 Ibid., 14.

8 Ibid., 9.

9 Ibid., 7.

10 Stephen K. Medvic, "Campaign Organizations and Political Consultants," in *Guide to Political Campaigns in America*, ed. Paul S. Herrnson (Washington, D.C.: CQ Press 2005), 162; and Stephen K. Medvic, "Is There a Spin Doctor in the House? The Impact of Political Consultants in Congressional Campaigns," PhD dissertation, Purdue University, 1997, 28.

11 Gil Troy, *See How They Ran: The Changing Role of the Presidential Candidate* (New York: The Free Press, 1991), 105.

12 As quoted in Troy, *See How They Ran*, 94.

13 Ibid., 95.

14 Ibid., 104.

15 Douglas B. Craig, *Fireside Politics: Radio and Political Culture in the United States, 1920–1940* (Baltimore, MD: The Johns Hopkins University Press, 2000), 140–41.

16 Craig, *Fireside Politics*, 150.

17 Ibid., 147.

18 Ibid., 148.

19 Troy, *See How They Ran*, 155.

20 For a comprehensive history of public relations, see Stuart Ewen, *PR! A Social History of Spin* (New York: Basic Books, 1996).

21 Stanley Kelley, Jr., *Professional Public Relations and Political Power* (Baltimore, MD: The Johns Hopkins Press, 1956), 13.

22 Robert J. Pitchell, "The Influence of Professional Campaign Management Firms in Partisan Elections in California," *Western Political Quarterly* 11 (1958): 278–9.

23 Ibid., 279.

24 Alan Ware, *The Breakdown of Democratic Party Organization, 1940–1980* (Oxford: Clarendon Press, 1988), 10.

25 Kelley, *Professional Public Relations and Political Power*, 4.

26 See Frank I. Luntz, *Candidates, Consultants, and Campaigns: The Style and Substance of American Electioneering* (New York: Basil Blackwell, 1988), 42–3.

27 Kelley, *Professional Public Relations and Political Power*, 54.

28 Troy, *See How They Ran*, 149.

29 Ibid.

30 Greg Mitchell, *The Campaign of the Century: Upton Sinclair's Race for Governor of California and the Birth of Media Politics* (New York: Random House, 1992), 371.

31 Ibid.

32 Bruce Bimber, *Information and American Democracy: Technology in the Evolution of Political Power* (New York: Cambridge University Press, 2003), 75.

33 Harold Mendelsohn and Irving Crespi, *Polls, Television, and the New Politics* (Scranton, PA: Chandler Publishing Company, 1970), 264.

34 Kathleen Hall Jamieson, *Packaging the Presidency: A History and Criticism of Presidential Campaign Advertising* (New York: Oxford University Press, 1984), 34.

35 Ibid., 43.

36 Ibid., 69–79.

37 Ibid., 133–6.

38 Theodore C. Sorensen, *Kennedy* (New York: Harper & Row, 1965), 195.

39 For a general introduction to political consulting, see Dan Nimmo, *The Political Persuaders: The Techniques of Modern Election Campaigns* (Englewood Cliffs, N.J.: Prentice-Hall, 1970); Larry J. Sabato, *The Rise of Political Consultants: New Ways of Winning Elections* (New York: Basic Books, 1981); Luntz, *Candidates, Consultants & Campaigns*; and Dennis W. Johnson, *No Place For Amateurs: How Political Consultants Are Reshaping American Democracy*, 2nd ed. (New York: Routledge, 2007).

40 See, for example, Tony Schwartz, *The Responsive Chord* (New York: Anchor Press Doubleday, 1973).

41 Jacob K. Javits, "How I Used a Poll in Campaigning for Congress," *Public Opinion Quarterly* 11 (1947): 222–6.

42 Lawrence R. Jacobs and Robert Y. Shapiro, "Issues, Candidate Image, and Priming: The Use of Private Polls in Kennedy's 1960 Presidential Campaign," *American Political Science Review* 88 (September 1994): 527–40.

43 Louis Harris, "Polls and Politics in the United States," *Public Opinion Quarterly* 27 (1963): 3.

44 James M. Perry, *The New Politics: The Expanding Technology of Political Manipulation* (New York: Clarkson N. Potter, Inc., 1968), 140.

45 Nimmo, *The Political Persuaders*, 76.

46 Luntz, *Candidates, Consultants & Campaigns*, 200–3.

47 Gary W. Selnow, *High-Tech Campaigns: Computer Technology in Political Communication* (Westport, CT: Praeger, 1994), 59.

48 Ibid., 60.

49 Ibid., ch. 5.

50 Paul Curcio, "Use of VCRs in Campaign Advertising," unpublished manuscript received by personal e-mail, September 28, 2007.

51 Bimber, *Information and American Democracy*, 21.

52 Ibid., 22.

53 Kirsten A. Foot and Steven M. Schneider, *Web Campaigning* (Cambridge, MA: The MIT Press, 2006), 22–3.

54 Ibid., 35.

55 Philip N. Howard, *New Media Campaigns and the Managed Citizen* (New York: Cambridge University Press, 2006), 26–8.

56 Foot and Schneider, *Web Campaigning*, 57–9.

57 E-mail message, "Thanks Stephen," from "Mitt Romney" (info@mittromney.com), September 29, 2007.

58 Larry Biddle, "Fund-Raising: Hitting Home Runs On and Off the Internet," in *Mousepads, Shoe Leather, and Hope: Lessons from the Howard Dean Campaign for the Future of Internet Politics*, ed. Zephyr Teachout and Thomas Streeter (Boulder, CO: Paradigm Publishers, 2007), 172.

59 See Zephyr Teachout and Thomas Streeter, eds, *Mousepads, Shoe Leather, and Hope: Lessons from the Howard Dean Campaign for the Future of Internet Politics* (Boulder, CO: Paradigm Publishers, 2007).

60 Monica Postelnicu, Justin D. Martin and Kristen D. Landreville, "The Role of Campaign Web Sites in Promoting Candidates and Attracting Campaign Resources," in *The Internet Election: Perspectives on the Web in Campaign 2004*, ed. Andrew Paul Willliams and John C. Tedesco (Lanham, MD: Rowman & Littlefield, 2006), 105.

61 Foot and Schneider, *Web Campaigning*, 103.

62 Michael Silberman, "The Meetup Story," in *Mousepads, Shoe Leather, and Hope: Lessons from the Howard Dean Campaign for the Future of Internet Politics*, ed. Zephyr Teachout and Thomas Streeter (Boulder, CO: Paradigm Publishers, 2007), 116.

63 Foot and Schneider, *Web Campaigning*, 135.

64 Zack Exley, "An Organizer's View of the Internet Campaign," in *Mousepads, Shoe Leather, and Hope: Lessons from the Howard Dean Campaign for the Future of Internet Politics*, ed. Zephyr Teachout and Thomas Streeter (Boulder, CO: Paradigm Publishers, 2007), 219.

65 Lev Grossman, "What Your Party Knows About You," *Time*, October 18, 2004, http://www.time.com/time/printout/0,8816,995394,00.html. Accessed July 5, 2007.

66 Donald P. Green and Alan S. Gerber, *Get Out the Vote! How to Increase Voter Turnout* (Washington, D.C.: Brookings Institution Press, 2004), 77.

67 See Richard Davis, *The Web of Politics: The Internet's Impact on the American Political System* (New York: Oxford University Press, 1999), ch. 3.

68 Tim Craig and Michael D. Shear, "Allen Quip Provokes Outrage, Apology," *The Washington Post*, August 15, 2006.

69 Journalism.org, "Memogate: CBS News and the Texas National Guard Story," January 15, 2006, http://www.journalism.org/node/105. Accessed October 5, 2007.

70 Gary Wolf, "Weapons of Mass Mobilizaiton," *Wired*, September 2004, http://www.wired.com/wired/archive/12.09/moveon.html. Accessed October 5, 2007.

71 See Davis, *The Web of Politics*, 5.

72 John Bibby, "Party Networks: National–State Integration, Allied Groups, and Issue Activists," in *The State of the Parties: The Changing Role of Contemporary American Parties*, 3rd ed., ed. John C. Green and Daniel M. Shea (Lanham, MD: Rowman & Littlefield, 1999).

73 For a polemical treatment of this possibility, see Jerome Armstrong and Markos Moulitsas Zúniga, *Crashing the Gate: Netroots, Grassroots, and the Rise of People-Powered Politics* (White River Junction, VT: Chelsea Green Publishing, 2006).

9

Message Testing in the Twenty-First Century

Brian C. Tringali

American voters are barraged with messages day in and day out—not just by campaigns, but by those selling more conventional products as well. In 2002 alone, the top five network television advertisers (General Motors Corp., Procter & Gamble, Johnson & Johnson, Ford and Pfizer) spent $2.8 billion on network air time. So how can political campaigns compete with all those big advertising dollars? They can compete for the attention of the voter only by adopting some of the same techniques used on Madison Avenue in their own campaigns.

This chapter illuminates some of these more sophisticated techniques for discerning what works and what does not work when speaking to the voters. A message that scores well in a poll may or may not be a message that moves voters; a multiple regression equation can provide the critical insight. Further, this chapter focuses on ways to evaluate advertising based upon its influence on both *affect* and *cognition*, as well as a little bit about *deliverability*.

The methodology for message testing employs both focus group and survey research in an effort to chart a course for convincing the part of the electorate that remains malleable. Combining qualitative research (focus group) and quantitative research (survey) is uniquely powerful.

None of this, however, is meant to take the *art* out of the advertising business. Today's media gurus are truly artists. Dissecting every word and gesture in an ad will do nothing but ruin the artists' product.

In the years of doing this kind of message testing, we have learned that *what moves the electorate is either new information or old information made to sound like new.* Voters evaluate candidates in much the same way as consumers make a purchasing decision. It is only in the comparison of the products that a final decision to buy or support is reached.

What Are We Measuring?

Years ago, someone told me that the only thing anyone who works on a campaign should worry about is winning on election day. Anyone who has ever worked on a campaign knows that almost everyone who walks through the door of the headquarters has another agenda besides winning. To that end, the only thing we should really care about measuring in political research is what messages give the voters themselves a reason to vote on election day. Sometimes these messages have to do with voting for the candidate of choice and sometimes they have to do with turning out on election day.

Campaigning, therefore, is about communicating a "reason to vote" that is tailored to each particular target audience at the time they are most attentive and through the medium that they are most likely to be attuned. My "reason to vote" could be very different from yours. It is finding this "reason to vote" that should be at the heart of every research endeavor in the campaign.

In campaign research we *care about motivating the electorate to vote for our candidate and show up to do so on election day*. From a research perspective, nothing else is of importance in a campaign.

As a result, when we are conducting research, we want to utilize messages that move a portion of the electorate toward voting for one particular candidate and/or away from voting for other candidate(s). The nuance here is that we are interested in messages that either by themselves or in combination motivate a voter to "switch" to another candidate, but we also are interested in messages which help to "solidify" vote decisions.

Whether testing through qualitative or quantitative means, the focus on messages that cause a voter to "switch" or "solidify" is the same. In qualitative research, we are exploring the words and phrases that are influential to the electorate (or some portion of it), as well as the way voters think about the messages and relate them to their vote decision. In quantitative research we are exploring the power of these messages to move voters either toward or away from our candidate. While both types of research are useful, only quantitative research allows the researcher to generalize the findings to the electorate.

No matter how many voters are in the room and no matter how many times we hold a focus group, our findings can never claim to represent the electorate or any portion of that electorate. Those who show up for focus groups are never a representative sample of the population under study. We liken focus group participants to those who sat in the front row of your fifth grade class and raised their hands to tell the teacher she forgot to give homework that day. Clearly, their views are not representative of the entire class.

What Messages Should Be Tested?

Just because an issue may be important in Washington, D.C. or among policy makers does not make it an important issue in a campaign. The only issues we care about in campaigns are the ones that draw a distinction between the candidates. That means that if both candidates hold the same position on an issue, our respective positions are not going to help voters make a decision.

Prior to conducting research, the campaign plan should already be put together. Certainly, by the time we get to the message testing portion of the campaign, you should have a good idea about what your opponent is going to say and what you are going to say during the last few months. A message grid (see Figure 9.1), which points out the major messages that are likely to be communicated, is a good starting point for this inventory.

Candidate A on Candidate A	Candidate A on Candidate B
Candidate B on Candidate A	Candidate B on Candidate B

Figure 9.1. Strategic Message Grid

The goal here is to have a list of messages that will form the central decision points for the malleable portion of the electorate. These messages should correspond to the message grid in that we are testing: (1) what our candidate says about himself; (2) what our candidate says about his opponent; (3) what our opponent says about himself; and (4) what our opponent says about our candidate.

If we have been honest with ourselves during the planning process, this should be the comparison that the voters are likely to see in the final months of the campaign. The best thing about starting with the grid is that it forces us to include both positive and negative messages about each of the candidates. Even better, the grid forces us to simplify our messages by forcing them to fit in the boxes.

The Focus Group Methodology

Bruce L. Berg describes focus groups as an interview framework in a group setting.[1] But focus groups are so much more than that. If the numbers of erasers in a classroom of first graders is quantitative information, then the smell of that same classroom after recess with chalk dust in the air is qualitative information. In a Proustian sense, this odor carries with it a universal definition for almost all of us.

Focus groups attempt to give the researcher a glimpse of these underlying meanings that we all attach to messages and images. The focus group methodology begins by making a decision about who to invite to participate in focus groups. Those attending are often limited to the malleable portion of the electorate. Bill Clinton's campaigns did a good job of recognizing that in many cases these malleable voters tend to be suburban women with families who are habitual ticket-splitters. The "screener" used to recruit participants for these types of focus groups needs to help us find only those who have not completely made up their minds about the contest.

Because of the unique objectives of the now famous Clinton "triangulation" strategy, those conducting focus groups for Clinton's presidential campaigns decided to use a mall intercept strategy. By taking every "Nth" person who walked through a shopping mall on a Saturday morning and asking them to watch a few commercials, the Clinton campaign was able to find those busy suburban women. The messages shown to those recruited were concerned only with either solidifying favorable opinions toward candidate Clinton or getting those who were "undecided" or leaning to voting for his opponent to "switch" to Clinton.

Much of this early effort toward message development has to do with understanding the words or images that are most effective in moving voters. A voter is impacted by a message at two levels: *affect*, which is their emotional reaction to the message and *cognition*, which is their thought process with regard to the message. But *deliverability* is important too in that some messages are simply harder to communicate; either because of their complex nature or because voters are less familiar with them.

Affect

A respondent's emotional reaction is likely to come first. An example of this is when we hear a song on the radio for the first time. Research supports the idea that the first three or four times we hear a song on the radio, we decide whether we like the tune or not. It is only after making this "like" or "not like" decision that we begin to listen to the words. This *affect* reaction is primarily an emotional one, in which we will listen to the tune of a song we like, but we are unlikely to make the commitment to really listen further if the song does not pass this test for us.

By the time we have heard a particular song eight or ten times, we usually have internalized the message of the song. This research is the basis for the belief that we all need to hear a particular television ad between ten and twelve times.

Affect, therefore, acts as a hurdle for listening to the *cognitive* portion of a message. When the National Conservative Political Action Committee (NCPAC) ran stark and sinister-looking negative advertising during the early 1980s against many then members of Congress, their television spots were not well received. Therefore, much of the cognitive message was lost. The reason for this had everything to do with the style of their message delivery.

NCPAC's television advertising tended to be very stark. Typically, it featured a black background with white lettering scrolling across the screen. The information being conveyed was negative in nature, and the background music was always very sinister too. It typically gave the viewer the feeling that an attack was pending—like something out of the 1970s movie classic *Jaws*.

To be effective, messages to the voters must pay attention to the social mores of the local population. In the South, politics is a blood sport where a candidate is expected to run a fairly negative campaign as proof to the voters that he/she really wants the office. But in a state such as Minnesota, even the use of a grainy photograph of your opponent in one of your ads will cause a serious uproar. The late Speaker of the House Thomas P. "Tip" O'Neill, Jr, was right in that "politics is local." This is true not only in issues but also in tone.

Cognition

If *affect* is the heart's reaction to messages and images, then *cognition* can be described as the head's reaction. Cognition is, simply put, the brain's sorting out of the informational content of messages and coming to a decision based on it. For campaigns, the decision we care about is who you will vote for in the election under study. The only objective of research is to discern this "reason to vote."

Focus groups are helpful in identifying not so much which messages are likely to move the individual voters, but why they are likely to be moved by those messages. So with this methodology, we get a feeling for why messages might work, as well as the reasons behind them. It has been our experience over the years that the messages most likely to move the voters do something to reinforce or alter the respondents' framework of trust.

Former Republican media consultant Roger Ailes, in his book *You Are The Message*, argued that the individual will vote for the candidate who he or she likes the most.[2] Getting voters to change their mind as we approach election day usually requires changing which of the candidates they trust the most. It follows, then, that messages that focus on trust, or have trust as an underlying theme, are the most likely to move the electorate during the course of the campaign.

While during the beginning of the campaign season many of the commercials seem to be about which candidate you (as the voter) *like* the most, the end of the campaign season is often about which of the candidates you *trust* the most. Campaigns are run based on the recognition that voters receive messages first based upon *affect* and then based upon *cognition*.

Testing Advertising

The pioneer for using dial testing in the political realm was David Hughes, then a business professor at the University of North Carolina-Chapel Hill. Hughes used his *Perception Analyzers©* with scores of students and corporate clients to develop a technique of analysis, not just the tool to do it with. This technique allowed Hughes to analyze *affect* as a separate impulse from *cognition*. More importantly, Hughes was able to support the idea that this methodology was sound in terms of validity and reliability.[3]

Dial testing devices are now used routinely in political campaigns. With campaigns spending millions of dollars on television advertising, it is usually a good investment for these campaigns to test their ads before they are seen on your television or even on a web site.

Sometimes this testing can reveal simple problems that are almost common sense. In a focus group in the Detroit media market years ago, the candidate was pictured shoveling manure into the back of a pickup truck. Unfortunately, the pickup truck the media firm used that day of filming was manufactured in Japan. It took the focus group participants about two seconds to identify the problem. (Of course, today that pickup truck of the same manufacturer was probably assembled in a suburb elsewhere in the country.)

Most of the time, dial testing of advertising is a little less cut and dry. EKG-like scales are produced by each participant of the large audience (a whole theater full at times) dialing first for whether they find the message(s) "believable" (*affect*) and then whether the message(s) would make them more likely or less likely to vote for the candidate (*cognition*). Usually, a string of ads are tested together, so respondents give their impressions on *affect* for every ad prior to reviewing the ads for *cognition*.

This methodology, of course, does not reflect the way that the average viewer looks at any type of advertising. We get away with this methodological short cut because we are asking the respondents to focus on the advertising in a very unnatural way. We are asking them to stay focused on the television screen and respond to both what they hear and what they see. The theory is that this approach is a good approximation for what happens after you have seen the ad multiple times.

The compilation of both *affect* curve and *cognition* curve usually reveals key trigger points during the course of the ad or series of ads. These trigger points might include a buzzword or turn of phrase, or a key statistic used, or maybe just the look the candidate gives the camera at the end. Most ads can be improved to a degree by the use of this technique, but we have learned to be careful in not overly directing ads. *Media, even of the campaign variety, is still an art form and should be respected as such.*

With more and more focus group respondents tending to be regulars at the focus group facility, we must be careful of the respondents who turn from criticism to critique. Some respondents feel they are well informed enough to stop responding to an ad and begin to correct camera angle, lighting and other production values. Roger Ailes once commented that real power would be "coming back (to life) as a full-time focus group participant."

Through the years of using this methodology, we have learned to be careful about making sure we get a positive *affect* response, so that we do not block the individuals' ability to have a *cognitive* response. With respect to the curves, we need to have a largely positive response—meaning that we are largely above the neutral position throughout the test—on both *affect* and *cognition*. Tests in which individuals have a negative *affect* response are not helped by a positive *cognitive* response because the voters have literally tuned out the campaign (see Figure 9.2).

Think of the positive *affect* response as a prerequisite for any *cognitive* response at all. Today, you see candidates delivering negative messages about their opponents in commercials with smiles

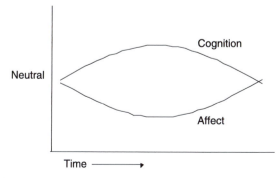

Figure 9.2. Dial Test: Response to a Typical "Negative" Ad

on their faces for this very reason. One of the most underused methods for getting over the same hurdle is humor—something used all too sparingly in campaigns.

Deliverability

It is important to also discuss the deliverability of messages. Not all messages are created equal in terms of the ability to be communicated. Campaign advertising depends a great deal on the short sound bite. While many complain about how this reality has "dumbed down," our political discourse in the United States also requires that a candidate or campaign hone their message prior to speaking to the voters. We all lead busy lives and none of us has time to hear someone ramble on and on about themselves or their ideas.

As part of the debriefing process when testing ads, some attention is paid to the ability of respondents to recall content of the ads and the ability of the ads to convey broader messages. If an ad is designed to speak to trust, we need to evaluate the ad or ads for the ability to communicate this message.

Sometimes this is done by survey methodology. Prior to looking at a series of ads, respondents are asked a series of attitudinal and demographic questions. After respondents review the ads, a post-test series of questions are reviewed so that the research team can evaluate who moved on the key questions under study, but also as a way to get a start on understanding why respondents moved during the course of the ads being reviewed.

This pre- and post-test evaluation takes place before any general discussion occurs. In that way, we do not allow any outside influence on respondent reaction, which helps us avoid one of the biggest problems with traditional focus groups—the dominant participant. Sometimes only those who move during the course of testing are retained for the debriefing portion of the electronic focus group test.

But some issues, particularly complicated ones, require more time to be understood. A commercial that attempts to address problems with our Social Security system or the difficulties with immigration reform is likely to be more difficult to boil down to 60 seconds, let alone 30 seconds. As a result, campaigns today tend to use the Internet for these more detailed discussions. This tends to reinforce the reality that those who understand the issues will continue to be those who understand the issues, and those who do not will continue to be less informed. It also suggests an additional reason why the more complicated issues are only going to take longer to reach a consensus in the future.

The concept of *deliverability* adds a third dimension to the testing of messages (see Figure 9.3). The result is that we can look beyond a linear plane to display our testing results in three dimensions as well. The goal here is to maximize our results so that we end up only communicating with voters with advertising that is the best it can be in terms of (1) *affect*, (2) *cognition* and (3) *deliverability*. With this type of rigorous approach to testing, only the best possible ads will be viewed by the voters.

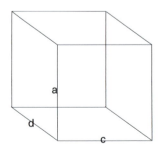

Figure 9.3. Dimensions of Message Testing

No matter how many focus groups we conduct, we still cannot generalize our findings to the total electorate. Those who show up for focus groups will never give us a representative sample of any subgroup of American society. How normal can the people be who take several hours out of their busy lives to show up at a remote office site in a shopping mall to talk about politics?

The Survey Methodology

The only way to be able to project our findings to the total electorate is to take a survey of registered voters in a given congressional district, state or nationwide. No matter what we think we know from the focus group findings, we test the refined messages that come out of the focus groups in a quantitative survey. We need a random sample of all those who might vote in a particular election. At The Tarrance Group, we use a stratified cluster design for our sampling methodology and draw the regional quotas based upon the history of turnout in similar elections.

Why not just sample those who have not made up their minds about a particular election? First, we want to understand the ability of the messages tested to move all the key target groups within the electorate. Messages must be measured for their ability to *solidify* voters who are already voting for our candidate, not just the *switchers*. That also means we can keep an eye on messages that might energize our opponent's base of support.

Second, no matter what the main objective of the survey (message testing in this case), we want to use the survey as a predictive model. In fact, we use turnout model equations to project the outcome of elections at various turnout levels. We monitor this information throughout the course of the campaign. Targeting information allows us to develop projected vote goals by region and target group so that we can continue to monitor our progress throughout the campaign.

Questionnaire Design

While the campaign plan has identified the messages likely to contrast the two candidates and focus groups have confirmed the proper language likely to appeal to the voters, the next step is to design the survey to confirm that these messages can move the voters.

Questionnaire design is fairly straightforward for message testing. We want an initial ballot to appear early in the questionnaire design. This ballot needs to include all of the candidates who have qualified. In addition, it should appear in the proper sequence—so if we are conducting the research for a congressional campaign, the presidential and senatorial ballots will precede it.

After an initial ballot, we test a series of messages, just as they are likely to appear in our advertising or other communication with voters. The closer we get to actual language, the more confidence we can have in the results. A positive message might be something along the following lines:

> Would you be more likely or less likely to vote for Congressman X if you knew that while a state senator, he was the author of the Human Life Amendment, protecting the sanctity of the unborn?

A negative statement might be phrased something like the following:

> State Senator X was convicted of drunk driving charges four years ago and attempted to use his office to avoid appearing in court. Do you believe or not believe that statement?

119

One of the most important steps a researcher should take in order to protect his integrity and that of his client, is to require proof of all charges before designing the research project. No question should be asked without documented proof that has appeared in the public domain.

No legitimate pollster conducts so-called "push polls." These are thinly veiled attempts at telemarketing, which ask several thousand respondents a night a series of damaging questions and almost never include demographics questions. No one cares what the respondent on the other end of the line says in this case. This kind of telemarketing ploy is designed to damage the reputation of the opponent only. It seriously impedes the work of legitimate polling organizations and is, by definition, unethical.

However, questions that *push* respondents with legitimate information are useful to political pollsters. They are legitimate to the degree that they are likely to appear in the communication of the campaign—either positive or negative in nature—and that they represent the facts. Exaggerated attacks are of no use to a legitimate pollster and/or his clients.

Our preference is for message language to approximate a more *affect*-oriented question to the respondents. Therefore, we might be more inclined to ask respondents if they believe the information they have been read. With that in mind, we can use the second ballot to determine the *cognitive* impact on their vote decision. In fact, movement on the ballot is the best way to unearth the impact of *cognitive* decision-making.

Our goal is to randomize a series of messages before we introduce a second ballot. We then quantify a switch variable based upon the movement of respondents between the first and second ballot tests in the survey. The goal of the campaign is not to move the entire electorate. *The goal of the campaign is to move the malleable portions of the electorate toward their own candidate, while reinforcing the voters who are already with them and not raising the ire of the other candidate's base of support.* We do this by communicating a series of messages that correspond with the series of messages being stated in the survey instrument (see Figure 9.4).

While the results of the message statements alone would reveal how voters think they would react to a piece of information, too often voters hear a message and do not actually have it impact their vote. Perhaps when weighed against other pieces of information this one message has relatively little impact. The only way to understand the ability of a message to move a respondent on the ballot is to ask the ballot again.

A specific example might help one to see the importance of this principle.

US Senator David Vitter (Republican-Louisiana), when he was a promising young member of Congress, periodically was faced with the prospect of a primary election fight against David Duke. Almost every political junkie knows that Duke is a former leader of the Ku Klux Klan. If we were to ask the question, "Would you be more likely or less likely to vote for David Duke if you knew he was once active in a white supremacy group" about 90% of the voters in this congressional district would tell us they would be less likely to vote for him. The problem is that the voters already know that information and, therefore, it is not a message the campaign

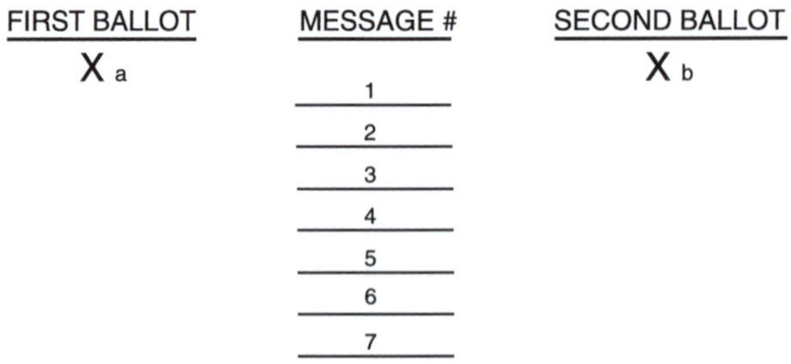

FIRST BALLOT	MESSAGE #	SECOND BALLOT
X_a		X_b
	1	
	2	
	3	
	4	
	5	
	6	
	7	

Figure 9.4. Questionnaire Design for Message Testing

should spend money communicating. Traditional survey work just does not reveal the problem, although common sense does.

Multivariate Analysis

How do we determine which messages are likely to move those who are malleable in the particular election under study? Multivariate analysis offers a solution through multiple regression. Earl R. Babbie in his *The Practice of Social Research* gives a clear definition:

> Regression analysis represents the relationships between variables in the form of equations, which can be used to predict the values of a dependent variable on the basis of values of one or more variables . . . A multiple regression analysis results in a regression equation, which estimates the values of a dependent variable from the values of several independent variables.[4]

Multiple regression offers a way of revealing what messages (questions) move people from point A to point B on the (survey) ballot. If our goal is to move voters, we are far less concerned with messages that voters *say* will move them and more interested in what actually moves them.

In order to reveal which messages move the respondents and then generalize those findings to the total population, we must first construct a new variable to reveal those who are switching on the ballot. This *switch* variable is the centerpiece of the regression equation. Those who switch toward our candidate are placed on the top of the variable and those who switch away from our candidate are placed on the bottom of the variable (see Figure 9.5).

Switched to Candidate A.........….....…....1

Stayed with Candidate A......................2

Other/Candidate A 3

Stayed Undecided.............................4

Other/Candidate B.............................5

Stayed with Candidate B.....................6

Switched to Candidate B.....................7

Figure 9.5. Switch Variable Construct

By creating the switch variable this way, we allow movement toward our candidate to be expressed in positive Beta scores. Movement away from our candidate is expressed in negative Beta scores. This makes it easier to interpret the results. Beta scores are used to express the strength of the relationship between the variable in question and, in this case, movement on the ballot. Betas are a form of interval level data that reveal the strength of the relationship between variables.

A regression equation is built by setting up the movement on the ballots as a function of the messages contained in the questionnaire between those two ballot questions. Since there is no other information given to the respondent between the two ballots, this is a safe argument to make. Still, academics tend to use a "tea pot" approach, which includes the demographics and other key attitudinal questions from the survey. We usually run the regression with only the messages and then look to the cross tabulations to determine which demographic groups have been moved or not moved as the case may be (see Figure 9.6).

$$\text{Switch A} = f\,(m1,\ m2,\ m3\ \ldots\ m7)$$

Figure 9.6. Multiple Regression Equation

What is interesting here is that often what moves the electorate is not one message, but a series of messages—often built around one theme. *The most important thing we have learned about moving voters is that new information—or at least old information packaged in a new way—is more likely to move the electorate than anything else.* In other words, if voters have already factored a certain piece of information into their vote decision, then why would the campaign spend the money to communicate that message to them again?

It might help to demonstrate an example of just how multiple regression can be used as a guiding light to sort through a quagmire of messages.

Distilling a Message: An Example

In early 2003, Citizens for a Sound Economy (CSE) (they have since combined with Empower America and now call themselves Freedom Works) contracted The Tarrance Group to conduct a series of telephone surveys. The objective of the research was to discover the impact of various messages surrounding President Bush's pending tax reform package.

Indeed, several messages were deemed to be key as revealed in the research. The most important of these messages were the annual tax savings likely to go to married couples, families with children, and seniors. These messages were used as central points in communication surrounding the issue not just by CSE, but by all those who favored passage. That package was eventually signed into law during the spring of 2003, but not before the president had visited several states to lobby for his package.

The survey provided some important insights. In the initial ballot of support for the president's pending tax reform package a simple majority (50%) of the voters were found to be in favor, based upon a national survey conducted in early March among 1,007 registered voters. Thirty-four percent of the voters were opposed to the president's plan based upon their current level of information.

In this specific example, only positive messages were communicated to the respondents. After hearing fifteen separate messages, respondents were asked a second ballot. On this second ballot, 63% of the voters were now supportive, but 31% remained opposed. All regressions assume a perfect ability to communicate and that the only messages being communicated are those that appear in the questionnaire. While this was not going to be the case with the president's package, the results were helpful in determining which messages to communicate from a positive standpoint.

In this case, only three messages were revealed as instrumental in moving the electorate. A normal survey would have found that each of the messages was about equally appealing if we were to rely only on what respondents told us they saw as most positive. But the multiple regression equation revealed that the tax benefit to married couples was almost three times as important in moving voters on the president's package as the tax benefit to families with kids. And while the benefit to seniors has influence in moving the electorate, it was not nearly as important as the other two (see Figure 9.7).

Perhaps more important are the messages that were thrown out by the regression equation. In almost each case, these were far more complex arguments in support of the president's package. Although the analysis itself may be a bit complicated, its use often points the researcher toward the simpler arguments to be made with the voters.

Minorities and those with lower income levels were among those most likely to be persuaded by these messages. Democratic leaders who stood against this package in both the House and the Senate claimed to be standing up for the groups most likely to be persuaded by these positive messages.

#	Message	+%/ −%	Beta Score
Q22	46 million married couples will get about $1,716	60/37	0.422
Q23	More than 34 million families with kids get about $1,473	62/36	0.152
Q25	13 million seniors will get about $1,384	63/34	0.057

Figure 9.7. Multiple Regression Analysis

Source: National survey by CSE on March 4–6, 2003.

Using the Methodology on the Internet

Both the qualitative and quantitative approaches to message testing are easily adapted to the Internet. Long-term, online approaches to research are someday going to be the preferred methodology. For now, the problem with this method of inquiry is one of sample—as not all voters have access to the Internet, as opposed to phones. But the Internet may be the best way to get around another rising problem with phones in that young people no longer tend to have access to a landline phone but they are a lot more likely to have daily access to the Internet.

While access to the Internet is improving among various demographic segments, voters as a group are actually lagging behind the total population. There are some exceptions to this rule. In Minnesota, for instance, a significant percentage of voters have access to the Internet and check it at least once a week.

Now that television and radio advertising is being edited digitally and bandwidth into homes is increasing, it is no problem to send commercials online. In fact, respondents do not even have to have the same software to view the ads. The same can be said for articles and mail samples, as they are easily viewed by virtually everyone with online access. Therefore, providing campaign messages in the form they are likely to be seen by the voters is no problem over the Internet.

The same format is used to show respondents messages. A ballot appears on the screen early. Messages are tested first for *affect* and then for *cognition* in the format chosen by the researcher. Afterward, a second ballot test is presented before any real discussion about the advertising spots or campaign messages is introduced. Even specific questions about *deliverability* can be measured online. This "clean" examination of the respondent's reactions to stimuli must be maintained.

Online research has some distinct advantages. One of the most important for the researcher is control of the medium. Computer users are a lot less likely to be doing other things while they are online. But, when a respondent is pulled away by other tasks, it tends to be less disturbing to data gathering than other methods. Respondents can simply go back to where they left off in the process before they were pulled away. There is no inherent cost because of the interruption.

The cost per respondent is relatively cheap for online research. Once the study is programmed, the additional cost of adding respondents is low. Overall costs tend to be comparable to a smaller benchmark survey. Most close observers of this kind of research expect the costs to continue to drop rapidly in the coming years, making it an even cheaper option in the near future.

The ability to gather research quickly is an important feature of online research. A research project can be conducted during the course of an afternoon. Or, as is more common, the research can be left online to allow a larger sample of respondents. When larger samples are taken, the methodology can allow respondents to get online at their leisure—even if it is three in the morning.

The ability to tailor the research instrument as the project gathers information is even easier. Advertising can be refined and edited as the project goes along each day. Respondents can be asked to comment about other respondents' comments or be encouraged to hold a dialog with those other respondents.

Clients can actually monitor the data gathering process. While this is possible with telephone surveys, monitoring research online can be done at the clients' leisure. With telephones, the client has to typically call in during evening hours from home. In addition, split screen technology allows the client to not only view the research as an ongoing process, but also participate to the extent that he/she wishes. Clients can directly interact with the moderator with their thoughts and ask that certain avenues of questioning be probed.

Perhaps most importantly, online data collection allows the researcher to combine both focus group and survey techniques. In other words, the keyboard allows respondents to give a tremendous amount of qualitative information at the same time that quantitative responses are being gathered. This is the real power of the Internet, particularly when we take into account the speed with which this information can be gathered.

Campaign Simulation

Message testing is really about simulating the messages voters might expect to hear and see during the campaign season about a particular race. Once the researcher decides which methodology to use—be it focus group, survey or online—the goal is to present to the respondent that series of messages in a way that is as close to how the voters are going to see and hear the messages as possible. This tends to be done in small chunks, so that early in the process a sample of voters will hear about our candidate's background and later in the year another sample of voters will hear about the vulnerabilities of our opponent.

It should come as no surprise that winning campaigns tend to run better research components. Many of our stronger campaigns have tended to put together a series of evenings where a small audience is allowed to view an entire campaign of advertising and mail. In these situations, the campaigns often go to the trouble of hiring an outside media firm to produce mail and advertising on behalf of our opponent. These firms are given access to research and paid a fee for the project alone.

The combined test reel of campaign ads that results puts our advertising campaign against a potential series of ads from the opponent. It is amazing how close to final product these reels tend to be in the end. Respondents, therefore, are treated to the campaigns' messages as they are likely to appear from both sides. The advertising spots are presented in an alternating format, just as they are likely to occur during the course of the campaign.

These campaign simulations are extremely helpful. Most obviously, it is nice to see if our side wins at the end of the evening. What is most useful from a research perspective is to be able to adjust messages after we have gathered our research. This allows us to identify our weaker points and make adjustments, as well as identify our strong points so that we can better take advantage of the upper hand when we have it. Throughout the course of all of these messages, there are always key *trigger points* that are identified.

It has been our experience that when we win these campaign simulations, we win in November. But, when we lose the exchange, we have an opportunity to go back and re-tool our efforts. Win or lose during the experiment, we always end up making important adjustments to our messages—sometimes in the form of substance and sometimes just in terms of style.

One of the real secrets of campaigns today is just how research driven they have become. When a candidate says, "I never pay attention to polls," you can bet he/she is obsessed by them. But those who downgrade what we do for a living are correct in that too much emphasis is placed on the predictive aspect of campaign research. Most of what campaign research offers is strategic in nature.

Message testing is one of these strategic benefits that a good pollster can offer a campaign. But message testing and strategic polling are not something to be used to tell candidates what their positions should be. Rather, the goal of message testing is to give candidates and campaigns insights into how best they can sell their positions (as opposed to their opponent's positions) to the electorate.

Campaigns create messages to give voters a choice, not just between candidates, but between ideas about how we govern ourselves. The best campaigns offer choices about the candidates' visions of the future. And as V.O. Key, Jr, once wrote about America, the voters are much smarter than we give them credit for being.[5]

Notes

1 Bruce L. Berg, *Quantitative Research Methods for the Social Sciences*, 2nd ed. (Needham Heights, MA: Allyn & Bacon, 1995).
2 Roger Ailes and Jon Kraushar, *You Are the Message* (New York: Bantam Doubleday, 1995).
3 David G. Hughes, "Validating Realtime Measures of Television Stimuli," Kenan–Flagler Business School, University of North Carolina, June 19, 1995.
4 Earl R. Babbie, *The Practice of Social Research*, 2nd ed. (Belmont, CA: Wadsworth Publishing Company, 1979).
5 V.O. Key Jr, *Politics, Parties, and Pressure Groups*, 5th ed. (New York: Ty Crowell Co., 1964).

10

The New Media in Political Campaigns

What the Future Holds

Peter Fenn

It is truly extraordinary how far political media has come in the past twenty-five years. From the "stone age" of taking weeks to shoot and produce spots to the modern "tech age" of high-quality digital video; from time-consuming editing to instant changes with computer wizardry; from mere guesswork to a growing body of research about our audiences, focus groups, testing, and audience targeting. All in just one generation!

Nothing could illustrate this change more than a serendipitous encounter with one of our country's truly honorable senators. I was on a flight in the late 1980s with former senator Thomas F. Eagleton of Missouri, a thoughtful and wonderfully humane man. We talked about politics and campaigns and the incredible impact of television ads. Tom spoke wistfully of shooting his commercials during the summer break and airing them a few months later. Back then, campaigns never started before Labor Day. How about a quick response ad to an attack? Always with the candidate to camera, cut and produced at the local television studio, a challenge to get it done and ready to air while it was still relevant—a time crunch.

Not anymore. We are in the era of the "instant commercial." Now, Avid and Final Cut editing and immediate satellite or digital transmission to television stations have made the creation and distribution of television spots something that takes hours, not days or weeks. And if you've got no television spots produced by Labor Day? Well, we're in a different age now.

Political media has changed so much, so fast, and new technologies and advertising platforms such as the Internet and digital video recorders like TiVo are promising to create even more change in the years to come. Everyone is a producer, director, editor, and creative force with YouTube, Facebook, MySpace, and video blogs galore. The fragmentation of the television audience, the high cost of television/radio/print advertising, and modern society's saturation of sound and images are what I believe to be the three key trends driving changes in political media in the early part of the twenty-first century. In response to these changes, more than ever before, campaigns must focus on how to reach the people they want, and somehow grab their attention—at the lowest cost possible. To do this, there are a host of new media techniques and strategies already in place and on the horizon that will vastly change the way political media campaigns are run.

This chapter explores these changes in the political media landscape, discusses how media professionals can get ahead of the curve, and what the future holds for getting out the right messages to the right people at the right price. It has been an exciting forty plus years since Lyndon Johnson's 1964 "Daisy" ad revolutionized political media—but we ain't seen nothing yet.

How the Landscape is Changing Advertising

Not that long ago, there were just three television networks, and a healthy media buy could pretty much guarantee a campaign would hit most of the television-watching country enough times to make an impact. Reaching viewers was relatively cheap, because there were only a few places they could be found. Before the age of remote controls, TiVo, and literally hundreds of cable networks, campaigns could be pretty sure that advertisements were being seen and that people weren't just changing the channel every time a commercial came on. Not anymore. The world is different now. Fragmentation of the audience, increased cost, and an ad-saturated society have changed all of this. Joseph Jaffe, in his 2005 book *Life After the 30-Second Spot*, points out that the average American is exposed to 3,225 messages every day.[1] Now that's clutter! People can and do watch television shows, movies, and other content on their computers, on their iPods, and on their cell phones. Furthermore, the advent of "Internet TV," with its consumer-created content, has revolutionized modern media.

Audience Fragmentation

Cable television stations pitch themselves as the perfect place to capture specific audiences. Want to reach a "higher concentration of affluent/managerial adults than local newspapers, radio, and broadcast news?" Then advertise on the Arts & Entertainment Network, A&E; The Cartoon Network is "a great place for reaching kids, [and] it's also perfect for targeting the parents of small children"; "CNN is especially powerful in reaching homeowners"; "Comedy Central appeals primarily to men 18–34"; The Food Network "offers a fresh opportunity to bring products to the attention of the highly coveted female audience aged 25–54 who purchase for the home and family"; CNN Headline News viewers "are 40% more likely to be in households earning over $60,000 than the average television viewer"; and Nickelodeon "delivers more kids than all the broadcast networks combined."

The options and combinations are endless. From 1990 to 2006, primetime broadcast viewing declined from 74.8% of people watching television to 43.7%. Total network viewing dropped from 71.5% to 38.9%. Meanwhile, ad-supported cable increased its share of primetime viewers from 16.4% to 45.8% and its total share from 19.5% to 49.5%. In 1971, the World Series captured a 59 share (59% of people watching television at the time were watching the World Series). By 2007, the share had fallen to 24.5. The top programs have fewer viewers: the comedy show *I Love Lucy* won the 1952–1953 season with a 67.8 rating; the 2002–2003 season was won by a crime solving show called *CSI*, with just a 14.6 rating. Viewers are leaving the "Big Three" networks— CBS, NBC, and ABC—and going to the wide world of cable, with hundreds of channels and niche programs to choose from. With this kind of proliferation of viewership, getting a television spot to reach a critical mass is nearly impossible, especially if you have to work within any sort of budget.[2]

It isn't just television. Newspaper readership has declined precipitously over the past thirty years, especially among the younger generations. In 1972, 47% of survey respondents ages eighteen to twenty-nine said they read a newspaper every day, according to the National Opinion Research Center. By 2000, that number had dropped to just 18%. Readership is declining for other age groups as well, except for the very oldest age group studied, seventy-three to seventy-seven. I teach a graduate class in campaign advertising at the Graduate School of Political Management at the George Washington University. Each year, my class consists of twenty-five students, most of whom split their time between school and jobs on Capitol Hill, at K Street lobbying firms, in trade associations, and with various campaigns. Two years ago, I asked the group how many read a hard copy of the newspaper almost every day. Five raised their hand. Then I asked how many read it online. All twenty-five, including the five who read the hard copy, raised their hands. Last year when I asked the same question, the number reading the hard copy was down to two. People are still getting their news; now they're just getting it in very different ways.

The world of radio has changed dramatically, as well. In 1968, there were about 6,500 stations across the United States. The number of radio stations has more than doubled to 13,500, with a tremendous increase in FM and educational stations. Most cars are now equipped with CD players, reducing the likelihood that many potential listeners are even tuning in to radio. Many are also compatible with MP3 players. XM and Sirius satellite radio let listeners tune in to an incredible variety of stations featuring any type of music imaginable as well as sports and news/talk without commercials. The newest technology to the scene, HD radio, is increasing the variety of stations among which consumers can choose. These various devices may become standard in cars (and also at home) for a marginal cost. What all this means, of course, is that it is becoming increasingly difficult for advertisers to reach their audiences.

The sheer number of media choices has grown tremendously with the rise of the Internet, cable/digital television, and the proliferation of radio stations. Our target audiences are hard to find and can't all be found in one place anymore. This audience fragmentation has made it vastly more difficult to get our messages out to the people we want in sufficient enough numbers to really make an impact. But this is not all doom and gloom for advertisers. As in the earlier cable example, audience fragmentation has made it easier to reach a more specific audience and has decreased dollars wasted on audiences that don't need to be reached.

Cost

Even as the audience has grown smaller and smaller, the cost of primetime television commercials has increased dramatically. During the 2006 election cycle in the Minneapolis market, the popular doctor/hospital show *Grey's Anatomy* reached 26.5% of adults aged thirty-five and over with their televisions on. The cost for a 30-second candidate ad: $20,000. While daytime and late-night spots are substantially more affordable—costs ranged from $300 for the least expensive daytime to $800 for the most popular late night and midday shows—it's hard to saturate a market this way and really impact the target audience. Because reaching "everyone" has become so difficult and cost-prohibitive, campaigns are left to settle for reaching "someone."

Part of what has driven up the cost of television advertising has been the price gouging of candidates by local television stations as campaigns heat up. A thirty-year-old federal law is designed to protect candidate ad rates by requiring stations to charge them the Lowest Unit Rate (LUR) as printed on their rate cards—a rate no higher than the cost of what any other advertiser pays, even the year-round bulk-buying product advertisers. However, stations are allowed to set rules and policies regarding this rate that can make it unattractive to candidates, such as by including a provision that if a higher-paying advertiser comes along, anyone paying the LUR rate can be bumped to another time slot. While product advertisers care mostly about the number of viewers, and moving an ad a week earlier or later is not a big issue, for political campaigns, the time slot is crucial. During the fast-paced campaign season, stations took advantage of this and steered advertisers towards paying a higher non-preemptible rate. The result? Candidates paid at rates an average of 65% higher than the LUR rate on the stations' rate cards.

On another front, soft money, until it was banned at the federal level in 2002, had contributed to an explosion of issue ads: in 2000, these ads accounted for approximately half of all political spending. After 2002, issue ads by 527 organizations filled the soft money void and filled the air waves. These ads, incidentally, are not subject to the federal LUR protection and "issue" rates are often 20–30% higher than the normal, retail rates charged. For organizations producing these ads in support of a candidate, the cost to place them could grow astronomically. Now candidates have to fight on many fronts—they have to respond to their opponent's advertisements, but they also must respond to a wide variety of issue ads, each focused on a different topic, each needing another expensive ad produced and a costly media buy.

One thing is certain: more and more money will continue to be spent on elections, most of it on media and more groups will surface to channel that money. Recent campaign finance laws have become the Mercedes Protection Act for owners of media outlets.

All of these factors have made television advertising extraordinarily expensive for reaching enough viewers with the candidate's message. But cost and audience fragmentation aren't the only issues to worry about.

Media Saturation

In their 1999 book, *Net Worth*, John Hagel III and Marc Singer[3] wrote that the average US consumer "receives roughly 1 million marketing messages a year across all media." Seth Godin's *Permission Marketing* (1999) adds:

> An hour of television might deliver forty or more, while an issue of the newspaper might have as many as one hundred. Add to that all the logos, wallboards, junk mail, catalogs, and unsolicited phone calls you have to process every day, and it's pretty easy to hit that number.[4]

US News and World Report in 2001 noted that

> since 1965, the average news sound bite has shrunk from forty-two seconds to just eight. The average network television ad has shrunk from fifty-three seconds to twenty-five. Fifteen-second ads are now commonplace, and five-second ads are on the rise.

A survey by the Newspaper Advertising Bureau found that in 1965, 34% of adult evening television viewers were able to name a brand or product advertised in a program they had just seen the night before. By 1990, that number had dropped to just 8%. According to the American Academy of Advertising, 19% of television viewers change the channel during a commercial, 14% mute the television, 53% alternate their attention with another activity, and 6% ignore the commercial altogether. That leaves precious few viewers really paying attention!

Clearly, we are bombarded with sounds and images in today's society: billboards, ads on the sides of buses and the tops of taxi cabs, radio advertising, newspapers, television, video games, product placement in movies and television, the Internet, blast e-mails, inserts in our utility bills, catalogs, and telemarketers' phone calls. The list is practically endless. For one name, one candidate, one idea to stick out from all of the rest, it is harder than it used to be. According to Godin, it's a catch-22. The more we advertise, the more we add to the clutter, and the more difficult we make it for any one message to stand out and make an impression. But refusing to advertise certainly isn't the answer. Godin writes: "The more [you] spend, the less it works. The less it works, the more [you] spend."

The answer? Finding new tactics to cut through the clutter, new ways to capture an audience— before the opponent finds them. That doesn't just mean spending *more*, it means spending *smarter*. More than ever before, *bad* advertisements aren't enough. They'll simply be lumped in with the other 3,224 messages consumers are exposed to in a particular day, and the audience won't remember them. The more messages there are, the more compelling a message needs to be to stand out. Making high-quality, memorable, interesting advertisements becomes crucial. High production quality is a given. And the real goal is finding new vehicles for imparting the message, beyond expensive traditional television advertising, and beyond the traditional 30-second static spots.

One of the other major problems political ads have is that they don't have the luxury of months of repetition as product advertisers often do—they need to change weekly, with the fast

129

pace of the campaign, and the last four to six weeks before the election is the window for making that critical impression, not months or years. This time crunch demands ads that are memorable, contain a strong and easily understood message, and penetrate to the target audience. Political campaigns also don't have the luxury of big budgets that product advertisers do. And in politics, you don't have multiple chances to get your message right. The backlash to a bad ad is much more severe for candidates. If Coke, for instance, ran an ad that people didn't like, how many of them would really switch to Pepsi? But people are much less loyal to candidates than to consumer products, especially in primaries, and the result could be losing the election. Thus, political consultants need to be more creative than regular ad agencies, more able to stretch their production dollars, and smarter about their media buying strategies.

How can candidates and their political media firms overcome these three challenges of audience fragmentation, rising advertising costs, and media saturation? And given these challenges, what might the future of political advertising look like in the years to come?

Responding to the Challenges

Each of the three challenges presents a question that political advertisers need to answer. Audience fragmentation: "How do we get our message to the people we want?" Media saturation: "Once we know how to reach our target audience, how do we grab their attention?" Cost: "Once we know how to reach our audience and make an impact, how do we do so without breaking the bank?" Coming up with the answers to these three questions is the challenge for political advertisers today and in the near future, as technology presents us with more and more options and more and more possibilities.

How do we reach the people we want? Traditional political campaigning relies on television and radio commercials, direct mailings, and grassroots movements to rally support. And all of these are still important today, even with the changing landscape. The keys are to use these "old methods" better while exploring and developing new methods for reaching voters as well.

Television

It used to be that campaigns could reach network news watchers, usually the most informed portion of the electorate and the most likely to vote, not only through advertising but through the creation of photo opportunities and rallies designed to gain media coverage, speeches and sound bites that would lead to news stories. This was free advertising, as we used to think of it. But even this has begun to dry up. A 2003 survey by the University of Southern California and the University of Wisconsin at Madison, as reported in the *Washington Post*, examined over 10,000 non-network newscasts from the final seven weeks of the 2002 campaign season. It found that fewer than half contained any stories at all on the upcoming political contests, and that only 7% of the news programs contained three or more stories about the campaign. Even those stories were less informative—the average quotation from a political candidate in the news, according to a 1999 study by S. Robert Lichter, Richard E. Noyes, and Lynda Lee Kaid, shrunk from 43 seconds in 1968 to only 8.2 seconds in 1996, similar to sound bites overall.[5] So, if a candidate wanted to be on television, odds were he or she would have to pay for the privilege. By and large, they did. The USC/Wisconsin study found that over 80% of the programs examined contained at least one political ad and 49% contained more than three.

This advertising isn't reaching the right people or many people at all. Political consultant Dick Morris writes that television advertising is quickly becoming like radio advertising is today—"a good way to reach 40 or 50% of the voters, but [a medium] that never reaches the half that don't listen to the radio."

Like radio advertising, television advertising needs to move from a broad-based "hit everyone" model to a more targeted approach. The proliferation of cable channels does, as the earlier marketing pitches illustrate, allow for targeting of specific audience groups. Hit Lifetime with an ad aimed at women, ESPN with an ad aimed at sports fans, or CNN with an ad aimed at news-watchers.

The upside of using cable is that it is cheaper and ads can be tailored specifically for the audience. Nevertheless, cable is also able to localize advertising in many markets to target voters in specific counties, cities, and ZIP codes, reducing the cost and allowing advertisers to tailor their messages by geographic region. Television is no longer a place where everyone can be found. The key now is to use it for specific audiences, and to create specific messages to reach those audiences. The other factors, of course, are the number of people actually watching and the cost per persuadable voter of the communication.

Newspapers

Similarly, since newspaper readership is down, the key here is to think less about general audiences and more about specific targeting. Spanish-language and other foreign-language newspapers aimed at non-English speaking voters can be a start; college newspapers to help get out the youth vote and present messages appealing to young people; sports newspapers; and others.

In addition, more and more newspapers are finding their readership on the Web and most have their own strategies to make their sites revenue-producers. While many political consultants in the past have rejected newspaper ads for candidates, they are now finding that newspaper websites may be better for targeting their message—placing ads on the events of the day, creating short television-type spots that can be viewed online, and linking potential voters, volunteers, and contributors to their website. Most sites also allow for target by content placement (for example, in the politics section), by geography (in a specific Designated Market Area), by demographic (age, gender, income, and others) or by ISP or e-mail address.

With both television and newspapers, these new strategies create more work for campaign professionals. Before, one set of ads could be developed for network television; with a targeted approach, many sets may be needed, focusing on a variety of issues, with a variety of approaches. While this is hard work, it should pay off in the end—as campaigns will have a better chance of reaching the *right* people with the *right* messages, instead of just shooting in the dark and hoping to hit the target. Nevertheless, we have to be careful not to target messages that are diffuse and "too specific" and don't move voters. In other words, ads that are "off" message and confuse voters.

Direct Mail and List Maintenance

Direct mail has seemingly been around forever. But the new information technologies have the potential to really revolutionize mailing lists and other direct appeals. Certainly computers have led to the first wave of transformation—mailing lists move from index cards to Excel spreadsheets, volunteers go from hand-addressing envelopes to printing out a mail merge, new names get *imported*, not scribbled down onto a napkin and transferred to a cabinet somewhere. The time saved has been extraordinary, and has freed up hands and minds for less tedious tasks. This, however, is only the tip of the iceberg.

Spreadsheets have the power to sort and cluster voters by as many categories of information as can be collected. Mailings targeted to one gender, a specific age group, voters in a specific neighborhood, perhaps income and employment, can all be executed at the click of a button. The increasing ability to collect more information on the voting habits of members of specific households even takes the targeting beyond groups and into the homes. The building of computer files on who votes, how often, what their interests are, what organizations they belong to and contribute to, and seemingly endless other bits of information is revolutionizing our politics. Keeping and manipulating files with tens of millions of data elements, impossible a decade ago, can be done cheaply and easily once files have been built. This has created a whole new industry called microtargeting, which will prove increasingly effective.

Thus, the Internet has made list sharing instantaneous and highly efficient for gaining information . . . Googled anyone lately?

Movies

Lately, going to the movies has become more of a "commercial" experience than ever before. Not only are there a half-dozen movie trailers for upcoming films, but now there are actual product commercials before the movie. How long viewers will tolerate ads before movies is an open question but clearly there is a great deal of testing going on and there is no doubt that there is a captive audience. And once the movie starts, there are often dozens more "mini-commercials" through product placement. Computers, cars, soft drinks, and hundreds more products are paying money to appear in movies, catch an audience's eye, and be associated with the movie and its characters. This is nothing new—think Aston Martin/James Bond—but now it's being done to a much greater extent. Entire shows, like *Extreme Home Makeover*, are built around product placements.

While it seems like a stretch to extend this practice toward politics and politicians, it is not impossible to imagine cutting together a 40–50-second bio spot to play on the big screen before a movie. As audiences become harder and harder to reach, tactics like these may become the best ways to guarantee reaching a critical mass of people in some markets—and can be targeted toward the specific audience of a particular movie. Action movies and romantic comedies appeal to different demographics and the ads could be customized to do the same. A bit far-fetched, maybe, but look at today's reality television and movies in which politicians appear as themselves, make statements, and make appeals through pop culture.

Branding Content

Advertising Age writes that Sony is trying "to turn the children's Play Doh character into a sponsored television character in a half-hour sitcom with Sony products in it." Like Federal Express in the movie *Cast Away*, or Coca-Cola in the television series *American Idol*, the step beyond product placement is the complete integration of advertising and entertainment into branded content. As a producer quoted in *Playback* magazine says: "If you can create a piece of entertainment that has some inherent product identification it can be a win–win for everybody." Creating entertainment based around a product or service, or featuring that product or service, is a way to not only avoid losing the audience members who tune out commercials (or skip them completely using their DVR systems), but also to create positive identifications because of the associated content.

Like product placement, while it may not seem an obvious direction to go in for politicians, it's not impossible to imagine placing candidates on talk shows or guest spots on television during their campaigns. Beyond *Nightline* and *Meet the Press*, and late-night comedians such as Jay Leno and David Letterman, walk-ons in sitcoms or dramas—as long as they stay consistent with the candidate's image and views—could be a way to reach new audiences and create positive associations (and, of course, gain some press for the "stunt"). Linking candidates to an increasingly popular culture goes a long way to adding to their likeability factor. The 2003 HBO series *K Street* made widespread use of candidates and officeholders in its episodes.

The Internet

No discussion of the future of political advertising could possibly ignore the Internet and the tremendous impact it has had and will continue to have in reaching voters. (For more on the Internet and campaigning, see Chapter 13, by Emilienne Ireland.) To begin with, use of the Internet is exploding. A recent UCLA study showed that 71% of Americans use the Internet. Obviously, not all of them use it often enough that it can be a useful political tool, but many of them do, and a critical mass of people are relying on the Internet for political information. According to the Pew Internet and American Life Project, 46% of Internet users get political news and information online (survey conducted November 2006).[6] From November 2002 to November 2006, the number of adults with high-speed Internet at home grew by 265%, from 17% to 45%, extraordinary gains that illustrate how quickly the Internet has taken hold in American society. Furthermore, the number of Americans getting *most* of their political news online has doubled since 2002 and grown fivefold in the last decade. Further, 23% of these "online citizens" became online political activists, posting content on blogs, creating original content, and forwarding other consumer-created content. The use of the Internet is exploding and has nowhere to go but up. All of the 2008 presidential campaigns have relied on an extensive Internet fundraising and communications strategy. Hillary Clinton even announced her candidacy on her website.

Gary Selnow of San Francisco State University declared that the Internet is the "master medium." Like newspapers, it can deliver text and photos. Like radio, it can deliver audio. Like television, it can deliver audio, text, and video. And like direct mail, it can deliver text messages via e-mail. And it is interactive and instantaneous. Unlike radio or television, the Internet is an active and engaging media.

Campaign initiatives on the Internet can be divided into three broad and somewhat-overlapping categories: Internet advertising, e-mail, and candidate websites. We can look at each of these separately.

Internet Advertising

In a 2001 paper on the effectiveness of political advertising on the Internet, Michael Bassik writes that online advertising is likely to increase dramatically in the future. This is partly due to cost, because "campaigns can purchase 1,000 targeted ad impressions at an average cost of $35, which is considerably less than buying time slots on network television." It is also partly due to the technological ability to target online ads toward specific groups of voters in a way that television really cannot. Bassik observes that through using demographic targeting (demotargeting) and geographic targeting (geotargeting), precisely defined audiences can be reached: "Demotargeting technology can literally help a campaign to serve its ads exclusively to Republican females who make over $50,000 a year while geotargeting can ensure that such ads are only served in swing states."

Ads on websites are relatively inexpensive to make and place and can be targeted to a specific population, making them an important weapon in the advertising arsenal. The future may very well see the advent of the "Compu-television" which provides everything through one box and allows digital, high-resolution Internet as well as television and games and movies. In addition, there may be a greater interactive capability with the new technology that may allow viewers to watch and be a part of candidate forums and town meetings. This would give new meaning to the "call-in" shows, allowing for more audience participation and involvement, with people on screen. The CNN/YouTube US presidential nomination primary in 2007–2008 were a clear step in this direction.

133

E-mail

Shortly after the 2000 election Larry Purpuro, deputy chief of staff of the Republican National Committee, said: "As a campaigning tool, e-mail is going to be what I would consider a tactical nuclear weapon in the future." The political parties in 2000 collected hundreds of thousands of e-mail addresses, in databases that will grow with each campaign and develop into a truly valuable tool for hitting potential voters in a brand new way.

Dick Morris observed that "e-mail campaigning will leave television in the dust" once the collection of addresses has been completed: "Only the absence of a telephone book for the Internet is stopping it from happening already."

Morris explains how advertising will have to change once these e-mail campaigns take hold in order to really compel potential voters to read the e-mails and actually hear the messages:

> Will voters reject unwanted e-mail from politicians as spam? Not if the e-mails are sufficiently customized to address the needs, concerns and opinions of each individual voter. Will the e-mails be redundant and boring? Political consultants will soon realize that repetition on the Internet is deadly and condensation—a key for the 30-second television ad—is counterproductive online. Repeat the same short message over and over and over and you will lose your audience to another e-mail or website that offers new, humorous, attractive, interesting material each day.

Sending e-mails is virtually costless. If nothing else, it is a great fundraising and organizing tool for campaigns. We'll see how the spam problem works itself out.

Candidate Websites

It's pretty much a given these days that candidates will have websites. But the quality of such websites varies widely. A lot of campaigns waste the opportunity to create a portal that does something unique and different from a television ad or a radio spot. Obviously, anyone who clicks onto a web page is already someone with an interest in politics and in the candidate. The key, therefore, is providing information specifically targeted to people with an interest in the race—access to position papers, candidate videos, speeches, and so forth. When individuals visit the web page, there is a good chance they are the persons a campaign would want to reach. The key then is rising above the clutter and grabbing their attention and keeping it. New, exciting, constantly updated content is crucial.

How do we grab our audience's attention? Technology has been both a boon and a bane to political advertising. A boon because commercials are easier to cut together, it's easier to target exactly who the ads will reach, and special effects have made just about anything possible. But a bane, because advertisements are now everywhere, and getting people to pay attention has replaced simply getting on the air as the biggest challenge today. Candidate websites provide the best illustration of this double-edged sword—technology has made creating a web page easy. But the sheer amount of information available on the Internet means that to get visitors to come, and to stay, we need to rise above the rest of what is out there and, more than before, give people a *reason* to listen to what we have to say.

There are two key trends that advertisers must take advantage of in order to grab an audience and keep it coming back—*interactivity* and *customized information*. By interactivity, I refer to two-way communication. Television commercials—and most current incarnations of candidate websites—are one-way in nature. We provide information, and hope someone out there receives it, although we can never quite be sure. Technology has made two-way communication possible now, and this interactivity holds the key to really providing content that potential voters will listen to and be affected by. By customized information, I refer to taking advantage of the targeting capabilities of technology to provide information that is tailored toward each individual voter or group of voters—information that we can be more certain is actually relevant to their lives and can actually make an impact.

Interactivity

Interactivity—giving the public an opportunity to provide feedback, contact the candidate directly, pose questions and comments, participate in polls and surveys—provides a way to get potential voters more involved in a campaign, to allow them to feel like they have a stake in the process, and to canvass public reaction to issue positions and messages, potentially giving campaign professionals valuable information that can be used to alter or re-focus campaign themes and platforms.

In addition, providing ways for the public to interact with the campaign makes potential voters see the candidate more favorably. In 2002, Lynda Lee Kaid observed:

> Research has shown that the level of interactivity on a candidate's website affects the perception of the candidate. [The 1998 study] find[s] that candidates with high levels of interaction on their sites were perceived as more sensitive. Apathetic users, in particular, were more likely to see increased interactivity as a sign of greater candidate responsiveness and trustworthiness.[7]

Thus, by simply having an interactive website, a candidate appears more appealing. On the Internet, the types of interactivity are almost limitless. In looking at the 2000 presidential election William Benoit and Pamela Benoit of the University Missouri write:

> Candidates can (and do) include informal polls on their websites to assess the opinions of voters who visit their sites. Candidates can solicit feedback about their messages or policy positions through a website. Candidates can, themselves or through a staff person, interact directly with voters. Candidates can include a chat room so that interested voters can interact in "virtual space"—and the campaign can monitor and learn from those discussions. The Internet is more interactive than any other medium besides face-to-face interaction (and perhaps the telephone). And the World Wide Web is clearly more efficient than dyadic interaction, which, by definition, is one-on-one contact. Depending only on the increasingly sophisticated hardware and software, thousands (or more) of voters can interact with a candidate's website simultaneously.[8]

Even outside of the Internet, there are ways for campaigns to incorporate interactivity into their arsenal of tactics—call-in radio or television programs (or purchasing television time for a call-in question-and-answer session), live town meetings (which could even be simulcast on the Internet), personal appearances, meet-ups, and others. But clearly the Internet is where the future of interactive campaigning lies. Through webcasts, chat rooms, question-and-answer interfaces, online polls and surveys, and live feeds of candidates "in action," there is a vast and largely untapped potential to really get voters involved in campaigns to a much greater extent than they have been before.

Customization

Customization is where the true value of the Internet can be unleashed. The Internet provides the perfect technological interface for providing information tailored to each user's specific needs, and designed to address the issues most salient to his or her decision as to which candidate to vote for. Benoit and Benoit elaborate:

> The ability to personalize messages through e-mail, to obtain direct (virtual) access to voters, and to permit voters to seek out information that interests them personally is very important.
> Candidate web pages can include position statements and discussions of accomplishments in each issue area, and visitors who care about issues have the power to choose which topics to

explore, and how much time to spend on each. Thus, if a web page is well-designed, individual voters have the power to learn about the topics that matter most to them—and to ignore or skim the topics of little or no interest. No other medium has this incredible potential to permit a multitude of diverse auditors to *each* tailor a rhetor's message to suit their own individual interests and concerns.[9]

The Internet also allows for greater depth than other media: a voter can be given the ability to delve as deep as he or she might like regarding any particular issue, through videos, position papers, and policy proposals—beyond the thirty-second sound bite.

Technology allows us to let Internet users "customize" their candidate "home pages" with the information they are most interested in, and opt to be notified when information in their areas of interest is added or changed. It also allows for real-time feedback—"You just watched Barack Obama's video on taxes. What did you think?"—that can help campaign professionals determine which messages are working most effectively.

Cutting through the Clutter

So a campaign has found its target audience; so has everyone else. And you're using the latest technologies to create interactive and customized experiences for potential voters. But so is everyone else. In the future, this will all be the baseline, like television advertising is today. Everyone has commercials. The key is to cut through the morass of images and information available, and make yours stand out. This means that, more than ever, quality is key. A campaign's videos need to be well-done, messages need to be compelling, and the candidate needs to stand out. Yours has to be the one who people want to pay attention to and become involved with.

In the 2004 presidential campaign, former Vermont governor Howard Dean experimented with a website called MeetUp.com to form an online community of supporters who gather in person in support of their candidate. Creating a community around a candidate and a campaign is something that had not really been done before, and it is now accepted strategy. The Internet is terrific for bringing supporters together and forming a community, or passing along information about volunteer opportunities, ways to help the campaign, spreading the word, and especially fundraising. The last of these is key. If nothing else, the Internet makes it easier to collect money via credit cards from a wide range of people who may not otherwise be inclined to donate. Obviously, it is important to use websites to drive these donations. The past few election cycles have shown that the Internet is a fundraiser's dream. And this is not likely to slow.

Bandwidth and connection speeds are growing such that e-mailing videos and commercials directly to supporters is a growth industry and can help spread the word quickly and without excessive cost. The new word is "viral" video.

Longer-form stories—beyond thirty-second commercials—can have a place on the Internet, as can candidate journals, and other frequently updated material that can make the website not only deep but also timely and ever-changing. Having a site where there is a consistent addition of fresh material can lure visitors back multiple times, and keep them involved in the campaign.

Managing the Cost

The more campaigns can rely on the Internet, the bigger the savings. Producing Internet banner ads is cheaper than television commercials, bandwidth on the Internet is cheaper than buying time on network or cable television, live feeds of the candidate are cheaper than having him or her travel to three different cities a day. Of course, it is unreasonable to expect that television advertising will go away, or that candidates will stop campaigning in person. Costs will not fall dramatically in the "old ways" we continue to pursue—although targeting audiences on cable can often be cost-effective. But the new ways simply will not be that expensive, especially compared to the potential benefits.

But more important than the cost savings of the Internet directly are the potential cost savings that information technologies can provide with regard to tactics and research. Technology has already made collecting and maintaining computer lists easier and cheaper, has allowed for the customization and targeting of direct mailings, has let campaign professionals make changes to commercials quickly and get response ads on the air almost instantly, and has freed up workers to be proactive in gathering support rather than hand-addressing envelopes from names scrawled on index cards in a file cabinet.

The next cost-saving tool that has yet to be exploited is "instant feedback." The Internet allows for the gathering of statistics on what advertisement drives the most click-throughs to the web page, what content yields the greatest amount of fundraising, what pages on the site are most popular and, through online polling, what people prefer. All this comes instantly, without having to engage costly focus groups and external polling resources. Instant feedback can help make ads and other content more effective, isolate what works from what doesn't and create a feedback loop where the materials get stronger and stronger as the visitors increase and provide more and more input. This is the next wave of how information technology can revolutionize political campaigns, and whoever takes full advantage of it first will have a true competitive edge.

Conclusion

Network television is no longer the answer. Or at least it's not the only answer. Audiences are shrinking, cable and the Internet are taking over, and no one watches commercials the way they used to a quarter century ago. The public expects to see campaign ads on television, and for now they will. As my creative colleague, Republican Mike Murphy puts it: "Right now we consultants buy and buy television—we drop the piano on the mouse." But the future holds more in store. We now have the ability to hone in on target audiences more than ever before, to transmit content and messages faster and more inexpensively than ever before, and to use the new information technologies to dramatically change the way we do business and make political advertising more effective than it's ever been. The fragmentation of the audience, the increased cost of television advertising, and the saturation of the public with images and logos can be seen as negatives—or they can be seen as the impetus for change. We can overcome these challenges by making the old ways better, and by turning to new ways: in-theater advertising, product placement, better ads, branded content, e-mail lists, and, of course, the Internet. On Madison Avenue, the keys to the future are interactivity and customization. On Pennsylvania Avenue, it shouldn't be any different. The opportunities are tremendous; the new technologies we have at our fingertips today were unimaginable just a generation ago.

But we can't get carried away and forget that beneath it all is still the message, and the candidate. The wrong message or the wrong candidate, and no amount of technology can save the campaign. But the right message—a compelling story that grabs the voters in just the right way—can now be sent to more people, more quickly and more effectively than ever before.

What will it all look like twenty years from now? Probably nothing like the vision I've presented in this chapter. New technologies we can't even fathom today will have taken hold; new ways to communicate will be revolutionizing the world like the Internet is today. The constantly changing landscape is what makes this field so fascinating to be a part of—and seeing these visions of the future turn into reality is what keeps me excited to go to work each morning.

What the future holds? I can't wait to see.

Notes

Special thanks to Jeremy Blachman and Erica Kraus for their assistance in preparing this chapter.

1 Joseph Jaffe, *Life After the Thirty-Second Spot: Energize Your Brand with a Bold Mix of Alternatives to Traditional Advertising* (Hoboken, N.J.: John Wiley, 2005).
2 Cabletelevision Advertising Bureau, "The Big Erosion Picture," http://onetvworld.org.
3 John Hagel III and Marc Singer, *Net Worth* (Cambridge, MA: Harvard Business School, 1999).
4 Seth Godin, *Permission Marketing: Turning Strangers into Friends and Friends into Customers* (New York: Simon and Schuster, 1999).
5 S. Robert Lichter, Richard E. Noyes, and Lynda Lee Kaid, "No News or Negative News: How the Networks Nixed the '96 Campaign," in *The Electronic Election: Perspectives on the 1996 Campaign Communication*, ed. Lynda Lee Kaid and Diane G. Bystrom (Mahwah, N.J.: Lawrence Erlbaum, 1999), 3–13.
6 See also, Lee Rainie and John Horrigan, "Election 2006 Online," Pew Internet and American Life Project, January 17, 2007, http://www.pewinternet.org/pdfs/PIP_Politics_2006.pdf.
7 Lynda Lee Kaid, "Political Advertising and Information Seeking: Comparing Exposure via Conventional and Internet Channels," *Advertising Age* 31 (1) (2002): 27–36.
8 William Benoit and Pamela Benoit, "The Virtual Campaign: Presidential Primary Websites in Campaign 2000," *American Communications Journal* 3 (3) (2000).
9 Ibid.

11

The Rise and Impact of Monster PACs

Steven E. Billet

Political action committees (PACs) are one of the constants of American campaign finance. From the time of their rise to prominence in the mid-1980s, PACs increased in number and activity, leveling off by the end of the 1980s at around 4,000 federally registered PACs.[1] PACs accounted for around 34% of the hard dollars reported by congressional races in the 2006 election cycle, around $320 million. PAC contributions have remained very stable in the mix among all types of contributions to candidates for Congress. Since 2000, they have stood between 33 and 34% of total contributions to congressional candidates.[2]

It would be a mistake, however, to assume that the PAC arena is static. The passage and implementation of the Bipartisan Campaign Reform Act (BCRA) in 2002, its interpretation in the courts, its implementation by the Federal Election Commission (FEC), and the ever-competitive US electoral world, have all driven PACs into new spheres of activity unimaginable a decade ago. This chapter is an examination of one of the more important and dramatic changes in the PAC world in the last few election cycles: the rise of Monster PACs.

PACs are organizations created by groups to collect and distribute contributions to political candidates. Customarily, PACs are formed by labor unions, corporations, and trade and membership associations. These PACs are referred to as "affiliated" PACs, since they are sponsored and supported by an interest group. A second group of PACs are classified as "unaffiliated" and operate as free-standing entities without the support of a sponsoring organization. Many unaffiliated PACs are ideological groups. PACs are created primarily to provide financial support to political candidates—commonly in the form of direct contributions. Increasingly, groups have been supporting candidates in other ways. Support in the "other" category often includes activities undertaken independent of the target campaigns.

A Monster PAC is any group registered as a multi-candidate committee with the FEC that raises and spends more than $2,000,000 in any election cycle.[3] Admittedly, this is a somewhat arbitrary standard but is based on the notion that a $2 million PAC is able to "max-out" (that is, spend as much as legally possible) on the campaigns of half the incumbent members of at least two full committees in the House and Senate while making additional contributions to congressional leaders, ten of their Leadership PACs, and the party organizations.[4] Even for the smallest of the Monsters, this would leave over $500,000 for independent expenditures and other campaign activity.

There were seventy-two PACs that raised and spent over $2 million for the 2005–2006 election. In the 1995–1996 cycle, there were only twenty-seven. In the 1985–1986 cycle there were just three. These figures do not include organizations established under section 527 of the Internal Revenue Service or Leadership PACs, nor do they include committees directly affiliated with former or present public officials.[5] In terms of money raised, the Monster PACs in 2006 range from the largest, EMILY's List at $34 million, to the smallest, the American Society of Anesthesiologists at just over $2 million per cycle. The categories of PACs include seventeen corporate, thirty labor, eighteen trade or membership organizations and seven in a category referred to as "NeoPACs." NeoPACs include a diverse group including EMILY's List, ActBlue, the National Right to Life Committee, Americans Coming Together, and Moveon. The NeoPACs include several organizations that have been leaders in the creation of Monster PACs. These are discussed later in this chapter.

Monster PACs have fundamentally changed the calculus of campaign giving over the last decade. They have embraced the idea that interest groups can extend and deepen their impact in the electoral arena by funding activities well beyond writing checks for individual races. Indeed, for most non-Monsters, check writing remains the most prominent feature of their operations. It is commonplace for Monster PACs, on the other hand, to recruit candidates, to mobilize support for favored candidates, to run parallel campaigns in support of those candidates, and to train operatives for campaigns. The most effective groups align these activities to support and advance their public policy goals. In many ways the groups have taken on the trappings of political parties.

Why Are They So Different?

The most obvious difference between Monster PACs and the rest is their size. They are large PACs and they are growing at a remarkable pace. A comparison between the seventy-two Monsters and other categories of PACs from the 2005–2006 cycle is instructive. The Appendix to this chapter (p. 147) provides a list of all seventy-two PACs that raised more than $2 million during 2005–2006. The average disbursal for Monsters was over $5.1 million in 2005–2006. The seventy-two PACs accounted for over $370 million in disbursements during the 2005–2006 cycle. Of this amount, $147 million was contributed directly to congressional candidates. These contrast markedly from the averages for federal PACs in the three major categories of PACs. Those figures are shown in Table 11.1. On average, Monster PACs gave just 37.5% of their contributions directly to candidates. Of the top fifteen, only ActBlue, a conduit that passes along all its contributions, and the American Federation of Teachers gave more than 50% of their contributions directly to candidates for Congress. If one calculates the percentage of direct contributions for the top fifteen Monsters and removes ActBlue from the list, the average direct contribution is well under 10%. Even so, and in spite of their emphasis on indirect contributions, the Monster PACs account for an impressive 46% of all PAC dollars contributed to congressional races.[6]

The tendency to spend PAC money on campaign activity other than direct contributions is not uniform across the different categories of PACs. Table 11.1 shows that in 2005–2006, labor union PACs had a much greater likelihood to do other things with their money. Corporations and trade and membership associations continue to give 67 and 63% respectively for all PACs listed in the reports of the FEC.[7] This is certainly consistent with the tendencies of both categories of actors to take a more conservative approach to PAC activity (compared to labor) and reflects labor's prominence among the Monster PACs.

One interesting question concerning the rise of Monster PACs relates to exactly when they began to emerge. There has been a noteworthy increase in the number of $2 million plus PACs over the last two decades. But it is not so clear when they shifted their contribution pattern to an emphasis on activity other than direct contributions. Table 11.2 was constructed to make that determination, examining the difference in contribution patterns between the 1997–1998 cycle

Table 11.1. PAC Disbursements and Contributions (2005–2006)

	Corporations (1871)	Labor (306)	Trade/Member Association (1003)	Monster (72)
Disbursements	$276,251,625	$198,289,209	$210,810,463	$370,251,027
Average	$147,649	$1,291,786	$209,971	$5,142,514
Contributions to all Candidates	$204,604,068	$72,660,217	$132,223,211	$147,047,537
Average	$109,355	$473,356	$131,828	$2,042,327
	(67%)	(37%)	(63%)	(39%)

Source: CQ Money Line 2007.

Table 11.2. Percentage of PAC Contributions Given to Congressional Candidates (1997–1998 and 2005–2006)

Percentile	Years	Business Percentage	Labor Percentage	Trade/Membership Association Percentage	Average Percentage for All
Top Ten					
	2005–2006	68	26	52	39
	1997–1998	58	57	49	60
75th Percentile					
	2005–2006	83	31	67	57
	1997–1998	63	31	67	53
50th Percentile					
	2005–2006	100	25	67	60
	1997–1998	33	33	60	45

Source: CQ Money Line 2007.

and the 2005–2006 cycle. While the results are not conclusive, there are a number of noteworthy findings contained in the information.

Table 11.2 was constructed by examining the average contributions of the top ten PACs in three categories, corporate, labor, and trade and membership associations. In addition, the table shows the average of contributions made by ten PACs at the 75th and the 50th percentile for each group. The table shows that there was a clear movement of PACs away from direct contributions for the totals shown between 1997–1998 and 2005–2006. No doubt, that the labor sector shows the greatest movement among the top ten PACs, indicative of its greater emphasis on other contributions when comparing the totals for the two cycles examined. Trade and membership associations also show some noteworthy differences between the 75th percentile and their top ten group. There is little of note related to changes in the corporate arena, indicative of their risk averse approach to campaign finance activity.

The Emergence of Monster PACs

In the last few election cycles we have seen the emergence of a growing number of PACs that spend unprecedented amounts of money on election campaigns. Certainly, these include groups such as MoveOn, Americans Coming Together, and ActBlue. But the community of Monsters includes older, more established PACs such as the National Association of Realtors, the Service Employees International Union, and the National Rifle Association. These groups have been

141

prominent in the PAC community for many years and have steadily grown their PACs. All raised more that $9 million in the last election cycle. This section will examine a sampling of the Monster PACs including a few of the NeoPACs.

For Monster PACs, political contributions are about more than writing checks to candidates. In addition to their expanded arena of contribution activity, Monster PACs often establish other contribution organizations under various parts of the Internal Revenue Code. The attraction of this approach relates to the lack of restrictions on the money they can spend in support of a candidate or a cause. The BCRA, while eliminating soft money activity by federal candidates and parties, failed to ban unlimited soft money contributions that were not funneled through the national party organizations or through federal candidates.[8] (For more on BCRA, see Chapter 12, by Anthony Gierzynski.)

MoveOn.Org

MoveOn.org has set a new standard for groups advocating on behalf of partisan candidates since its organization in 1998. MoveOn was first established during the controversy surrounding the impeachment of President Bill Clinton. The name derives from their online petition entitled, "Censure President Clinton and Move On to Pressing Issues Facing the Nation."

The campaign caught on and MoveOn continued after an early surge by creating a political action committee intended to collect and distribute campaign funds to Democratic candidates. All of MoveOn's contributions go to support Democratic candidates for public office. The fundraising prowess of MoveOn is illustrated in Table 11.3.

MoveOn is presently number two among PACs based on information from the 2005–2006 cycle.

Like many other NeoPACs, MoveOn is much more than a PAC. Its suite of organizations include MoveOn.org Civic Action, a 501(c)(4) non-profit organization "engaged in a campaign to reform the media and other work aimed at bringing real people back into the democratic process by making sure legislators hear their voices."[9] During the 2006 election, MoveOn spent $12.6 million on negative campaign ads through its 527 organization, mostly opposing the candidacy of President Bush and Republican Party policies. The MoveOn 527 received a large percentage of its funding from financier George Soros and Peter Lewis, the chairman of the Progressive Corporation.

MoveOn has not been shy about the positions it takes on the issues of the day, even when those positions create discomfort for mainstream Democrats. Particularly interesting was an issue advertisement MoveOn ran in September, 2007, entitled "General Petraeus or General Betray Us." Democrats in the Congress were decidedly uncomfortable with the ad and critical of the piece. The ad ran just prior to testimony given by General David H. Petraeus updating the Congress on the state of the US military effort in Iraq. The episode illustrates the tendency among some Monster PACs to act independently and look more like political parties than PACs.

Table 11.3. MoveOn Political Action Financial Reports

	Receipts	Total Spent to Candidates	Contributions
1997–1998	$12,000	0	0
1999–2000	$2,290,268	$2,281,661	$109,983
2001–2002	$1,250,767	$1,014,448	$126,991
2003–2004	$31,870,607	$30,043,750	$204,442
2005–2006	$27,696,912	$28,135,112	$784,186

Source: Opensecrets 2007.

Emily's List

Emily's List is currently America's largest PAC. Unlike the vast majority of the Monster PACs, EMILY's List is not a lobbying organization, but focuses all of its energies on creating a "pro-choice" America among the country's elected officials. The Emily's List website proclaims:

> We are dedicated to building a progressive America by electing pro-choice Democratic women to federal, state, and local office. We are a network of more than 100,000 Americans—from all across the country—committed to recruiting and funding viable women candidates; helping them build and run effective campaign organizations; training the next generation of activists; and mobilizing women voters to help elect progressive candidates across the nation.[10]

Started in 1985, EMILY's List takes credit for helping elect pro-choice Democrats to sixty-nine seats in the House of Representative, thirteen senators and eight governors.[11] Its method of operation is an illustration of how Monster PACs have moved beyond the direct contribution world to embrace activities more closely identified with political parties. Through a variety of programs, EMILY's List runs a get-out-the-vote program, trains campaign workers and candidates, and recruits promising candidates to run for office—far beyond the arena most often identified with traditional, check-writing PACs.

The contribution pattern of EMILY's List provides a lucid illustration of the tendency of Monster PACs to spend their money on things other than direct contributions. Table 11.4 shows that EMILY's List has never spent more than 2% of its total PAC income on direct contributions, choosing instead to devote most of its considerable bank account to supporting grassroots operations and the training of candidates and campaign operatives. Like so many other large PACs, EMILYs's List supplements its PAC contributions with one of America's larger 527 organizations, funded with $11.8 million in the 2006 cycle.

Service Employees International Union (SEIU) Committee on Political Education (COPE)

If there was a poster child for Monster PACs, the SEIU would be it (see Table 11.5). The SEIU has grown to nearly ten times its size since 1998 raising $23.4 million in 2005–2006. During the same period of time, it established one of the country's leading 527 organizations, the SEIU Political Education and Action Fund. It raised over $22.8 million in the last cycle.[12]

The SEIU is proof that bigger is better. With 1.9 million members, the union is able to take advantage of a dues deduction system for all its members. How do you raise $23.4 million for a PAC and $22.8 million for a 527? You deduct a little more than a dollar a week from the union members' paychecks.

Table 11.4. EMILY's List PAC

	Receipts	Total Spent to Candidates	Contributions
1997–1998	$14,237,394	$13,867,394	$236,221
1999–2000	$21,201,339	$21,466,049	$233,746
2001–2002	$22,682,406	$22,767,521	$202,940
2003–2004	$34,128,818	$34,175,207	$125,535
2005–2006	$34,118,930	$34,260,714	$268,436

Source: Opensecrets 2007.

Table 11.5. SEIU Committee on Political Education

	Receipts	*Total Spent*	*Contributions to Candidates*
1997–1998	$2,430.129	$2,450,449	$1,300,099
1999–2000	$5,102,664	$4,193,052	$1,861,649
2001–2002	$8,371,266	$7,101,432	$1,883,162
2003–2004	$14,716,632	$12,461,614	$1,985,000
2005–2006	$23,371,467	$9,759,151	$1,447,833

Source: Opensecrets 2007.

Table 11.6. National Realtors Association Political Action Committee (RPAC)

	Receipts	*Total Spent*	*Contributions to Candidates*
1997–1998	$2,928,559	$2,847,464	$2,475,983
1999–2000	$4,258,917	$4,031,656	$3,423,441
2001–2002	$5,193,903	$5,441,276	$3,648,526
2003–2004	$7,738,250	$7,349,116	$3,787,083
2005–2006	$9,644,561	$8,800,261	$3,752,005

Source: Opensecrets 2007.

The National Association of Realtors (NAR)

Whenever a survey of the most effective PACs in Washington is discussed, the Realtors invariably make the list. The NAR has grown in both scale and scope; tripling its size since 1998 and adopting a targeted independent expenditure program to support specific candidates. When questioned about the notion that it started to look more like a political party than an interest group, its PAC director admitted that there is unchallenged discussion within the organization about the creation of "The Realtors Political Party."[13]

While the Realtors are not likely to start their own party, they use the term to describe their goal of creating a pro-realtor majority in the Congress. The National Association of Realtors was actually one of the first organizations to create a PAC, long before the passage of the Federal Election Campaign Act in 1971. Their growth has been steady and a credit to decades of work. In addition, NAR has a large political staff.

The NAR is a prime example of an organization that gradually grew to Monster PAC status, shifting its emphasis away from direct contributions and toward indirect support for candidates. This is illustrated in Table 11.6. In the 1997–1998 election cycle, its PAC distributed just under 87% of its total receipts directly to congressional candidates. This figure grew through the period examined, but at a much slower rate than the group's total receipts. By the 2005–2006 election, the NAR gave just under 40% directly to candidate campaigns.

Where did the rest of the money go? One interesting place was a series of congressional races where the Realtors felt they could have an impact on the race and where they thought they had much at stake. In 2005–2006 the Realtors pushed just over $4 million into independent expenditures to help on six races.[14] In addition to its PAC, the Realtors maintained a somewhat smaller 527 organization that contributed just under $2.5 million in the 2005–2006 election cycle.

ActBlue

ActBlue is far different from most PACs and unlike any other of the Monster PACs or the NeoPACs. ActBlue is best described as a "fundraising facilitator" for people who want to make contributions to individual Democratic candidates. It provides a cogent example of just how powerful the Internet is becoming as a fundraising vehicle for parties, interest groups, and candidates. ActBlue maintains a website that provides a comprehensive list of Democratic candidates running for office on its contribution page. Potential contributors simply scroll through the list of Democratic candidates and make a contribution via credit card. The organization lacks the traditional trappings of a PAC. It has no agenda beyond that of funding Democratic candidates and serve as a conduit for people who want to make contributions. Nearly all the money channeled to candidates by ActBlue comes in amounts of less than $200.

Beyond maintaining the website, ActBlue does not have to worry about all the normal PAC functions such as communications programs, regular solicitations, or where the money is spent. The group does not have a lobbyist, nor is it connected to an advocacy organization. It is just a free-standing fundraising organization without a formal attachment to the Democratic Party. ActBlue raised over $26 million in the 2005–2006 election cycle. Consider this description from its website:

> ActBlue is a political committee that enables anyone—individuals, local groups and national organizations—to fundraise online for the Democratic candidates of their choice. . . . You need only choose your candidates and make your ask. By providing all the technical, financial and compliance systems, ActBlue enables every progressive campaign organization and individual to make the most of their networks—rapidly raising otherwise untapped millions for Democrats in the closest races.[15]

The long-term vision for this organization for the 2007–2008 cycle is considerable. ActBlue's goal for the cycle is to reach the $100 million level, extending its support to state-level races in all fifty states. This ambitious agenda is directed at the need for Democrats to secure or expand majorities in state legislatures in anticipation of redistricting that will occur after the 2010 census.[16]

How Did We Get Here and Where Are We Going?

As an occasional advisor to PACs, it is sometimes amusing for me to see how often the managers and board members of smaller PACs express their desire "to build a million dollar PAC," a magical goal for many PACs. The managers would then describe how they needed a great new solicitation plan, fundraising firm, or inducement scheme. Most PACs, of course, never approach the million dollar level. A closer look at the Monsters' operations shows us much about how effective PACs operate.

One of the distinctive characteristics of all the Monsters is their communication operations. They communicate frequently through their websites and their newsletters. It is about much more than just asking for contributions. It is often about creating and eventually leveraging a political culture. Certainly, many of the groups have large memberships and these create an advantage for them. But many of them maximize participation by spending enormous effort talking to their target audiences.

The Hong Kong and Shanghai Banking Corporation (HSBC) is a great example. HSBC has a relatively small restricted class: those people it is permitted to solicit legally. Yet the organization has built one of America's largest corporate PACs by paying particular attention to its ongoing communications program. Its PAC director has repeatedly told me how it spends eleven months of every year communicating with its management corps about the political circumstances of the company and then one month asking for contributions to its PAC. Since the 1997–1998 cycle the PAC has quadrupled its size to over $2.3 million.[17]

Convincing people to turn over their hard-earned cash is easier for some groups than it is for others. Many of the single-issue groups such as the National Rifle Association or EMILY's List address issues that have substantial and emotional bases of support. Certainly, some of the NeoPACs benefit by tapping into highly motivated partisan and ideological sectors of the population. In both of the above cases, there exists a substantial portion of the public that is "ready for the picking." The PACs target people that already have a strong inclination to get involved and to give. For others, but particularly corporations and many of the trade and membership associations, the situation is more challenging. The distance between their primary *raison d'être* and the need for effective political engagement is not so immediate or apparent. Corporations are in the business of making money, trade and membership organizations generally more concerned with the defense or advancement of their professions. Creating a sufficient political commitment and an attendant political culture to create and maintain a large PAC for these groups is often far more challenging than it is for the single issue or partisan organizations. This suggests an even greater need to establish and nurture an effective communications program.

Another characteristic of many of the Monster PACs relates to their level of executive involvement in the overall PAC effort. It is important that potential donors to the PAC understand that senior management is fully committed to the goals of the PAC, that they contribute generously to it, and that they let everyone in the organization know how important the PAC is to the success of the organization and its political goals. Given the high level of transparency of the current system, where anyone can access the public reports of the FEC, it is easy for the rank and file of any organization to find out if senior management is "walking the walk." Successful PACs understand this.

Monster PACs certainly have a more sophisticated understanding of the political world than most PACs, interest groups, or advocacy organizations. The groups I have examined all have coherent strategies that reflect the organization's overall goals and objectives. All of them have well-developed budgets or forecasts that allocate projected income to specific races early in the election cycle. All have and communicate explicit contribution criteria to their organization. Most have reasonably transparent internal procedures and decision-making that involves significant parts of their PACs membership. All have a solid understanding of the electoral arena and know details about a large number of the races at any given moment. In short, they set a standard for effective PAC operation and establish a model for any other PACs or campaign funding organization, Monster or not.

It is perhaps a bit ironic that the dramatic increase in the number of Monster PACs may have been the result of a miscalculation on the part of PAC managers around the time the BCRA passed. Many PAC managers and observers believed at that time that the elimination of "soft money" contributions to political parties would increase demand for funding from PACs, to fill a presumed shortfall in campaign cash after BCRA's passage. There was much discussion during the final stages of BCRA's consideration about how PACs might fill the void. Many prepared for the projected onslaught of increased requests and redoubled their efforts to increase substantially their receipts. In the end, the party organizations essentially made up for the lost soft dollar contributions with hard dollar contributions, leaving a few of the well-prepared PACs with large surpluses that eventually found their way back into the system through independent expenditures and other non-direct contributions.

Having a large and well-organized PAC has apparent advantages for groups trying to influence elections and the policy world. There is no doubt that there is a strong correlation between the very largest of the Monster PACs and groups considered to be some of Washington's most powerful. I would not be surprised to see the question above about creating a million dollar PAC change in the coming years. Instead, interests will start asking how to create their own Monster PACs.

Appendix 11.1. Monster PACs (2005–2006)

PAC Name	Type	Total Receipts	Total Disbursements	Congressional Race Contributions	Percentage to Candidates
EMILY'S List	NeoPAC	$34,118,930	$34,260,714	$1,781,210	5
Moveon. org Political Action	NeoPAC	$27,696,912	$28,135,112	$6,873,909	24
Service Employees International Union Committee on Political Education (SEIU COPE)	Labor	$23,371,467	$9,759,151	$1,960,333	20
ActBlue	NeoPAC	$15,974,073	$15,793,232	$15,382,591	97
American Federation of State County & Municipal Employees—PEOPLE, QUALIFIED	Labor	$14,527,366	$14,421,920	$2,932,686	20
DRIVE—Democrat Republican Independent Voter Education—PAC for International Brotherhood of Teamsters	Labor	$12,008,757	$11,782,624	$2,845,609	24
UAW V-CAP (UAW Voluntary Community Action Program)	Labor	$11,370,844	$13,444,980	$2,535,800	19
National Rifle Association of America Political Victory Fund	Trade	$11,245,144	$11,188,283	$1,184,128	9
America Coming Together	NeoPAC	$11,062,378	$15,225,829	0	0
National Association of Realtors Political Action Committee	Trade	$9,644,561	$8,800,261	$4,344,005	41
1199 Service Employees International Union Federal Political Action Fund	Labor	$8,942,585	$9,151,568	0	0
American Federation of Teachers AFL–CIO Committee on Political Education	Labor	$8,303,534	$7,189,667	$3,578,950	51
Voice of Teachers for Education/ Committee on Political Education NY State United Teachers (VOTE/COPE) of NYSUT	Labor	$7,992,827	$8,728,212	0	0
International Brotherhood of Electrical Workers Committee on Political Education	Labor	$7,916,459	$8,173,779	$4,012,125	49
CWA-COPE Political Contributions Committee	Labor	$6,807,046	$6,957,073	$1,891,805	27
American Association for Justice Political Action Committee (AAJ PAC)	Trade	$6,444,752	$6,318,892	$3,417,000	54
United Food & Commercial Workers International Union Active Ballot Club	Labor	$5,851,054	$4,986,059	$1,939,878	38
Dealers Election Action Committee of the National Automotive Dealers Association	Trade	$5,777,268	$6,007,122	$3,311,100	55
NEA Fund for Children and Public Education	Labor	$5,344,647	$5,350,748	$2,585,222	48
United Parcel Service Inc. Political Action Committee	Corporate	$4,778,387	$5,115,056	$3,187,287	63
International Union of Painters and Allied Trades Political Action Together Political Committee	Labor	$4,494,600	$4,222,491	$1,683,940	40
International Brotherhood of Electrical Workers Local 98 Committee on Political Education	Labor	$4,324,515	$2,906,226	$12,300	1

(Continued Overleaf)

Appendix 11.1. Continued

PAC Name	Type	Total Receipts	Total Disbursements	Congressional Race Contributions	Percentage to Candidates
Build Political Action Committee of the National Association of Home Builders	Trade	$4,172,134	$3,980,809	$3,526,500	88
Machinists Non-Partisan Political League of the International Association of Machinists & Aerospace Workers	Labor	$3,996,631	$3,777,768	$2,482,509	66
American Medical Association Political Action Committee	Trade	$3,814,158	$3,813,509	$2,139,850	55
Credit Union Legislative Action Council of CUNA	Trade	$3,754,562	$3,880,725	$2,864,220	74
Pfizer Inc. PAC	Corporate	$3,666,564	$3,678,493	$2,161,450	59
National Air Traffic Controllers Association PAC	Labor	$3,610,952	$3,290,261	$3,246,570	98
NJ State Laborers PAC/Laborers Political League	Labor	$3,572,259	$3,401,212	$19,000	1
American Resort Development Association Resort Owners Coalition PAC (ARDA-ROC PAC)	Trade	$3,468,168	$2,469,083	$958,828	4
International Association of Firefighters Interested in Registration and Education PAC	Labor	$3,430,425	$3,070,211	$2,339,650	77
Laborer's Political League-Laborer's International Union of N.A.	Labor	$3,389,570	$3,477,592	$2,874,900	83
Engineers Political Education Committee (EPEC)/International Union of Operating Engineers	Trade	$3,354,286	$2,340,085	$2,300,480	97
American Bankers Association PAC (BANKPAC)	Trade	$3,341,770	$3,331,165	$3,273,000	98
Gay and Lesbian Victory Fund	NeoPAC	$3,333,643	$3,350,706	$9,000	<1
Federal Express Political Action Committee	Corporate	$3,248,346	$3,278,561	$2,232,400	67
National Right to Life Political Action Committee	NeoPAC	$3,207,226	$3,058,014	$18,357	<1
American Hospital Association PAC	Trade	$3,151,798	$2,643,593	$2,304,665	89
National Beer Wholesalers Association Political Action Committee	Trade	$3,125,013	$3,162,189	$3,149,500	99
Sheet Metal Workers' International Association Political Action League	Labor	$3,123,303	$2,991,767	$2,187,015	73
Carpenters Legislative Improvement Committee United Brotherhood of Carpenters and Joiners	Labor	$3,019,230	$3,362,834	$2,882,500	85
National Federation of Independent Business/Save America's Free Enterprise Trust	Trade	$3,005,961	$3,286,976	$908,435	27
WAL-MART Stores Inc. PAC for Responsible Government	Corporate	$3,002,453	$2,787,072	$1,735,050	63
Committee on Letter Carriers Political Education (Letter Carriers Political Action Fund)	Labor	$2,979,395	$2,798,985	$1,812,900	64

United Association Political Education Committee	Labor	$2,913,414	$2,370,718	$1,570,250	67
United Transportation Union Political Action Committee (UTU PAC)	Labor	$2,886,219	$2,897,059	$1,430,000	48
Club for Growth Inc. PAC	Trade	$2,854,120	$2,746,429	$16,553	<1
California Real Estate Political Action Committee/Federal (CREPAC/FEDERAL) AKA "99 CLUB"	Trade	$2,781,837	$1,673,941	0	0
Action Committee for Rural Electrification (ACRE) National Rural Electric Coop. Association	Trade	$2,696,152	$2,297,114	$1,444,673	61
AT&T Inc. Federal Political Action Committee (AT&T Federal PAC)	Corporate	$2,663,714	$2,651,595	$2,640,682	99
Deloitte & Touche Federal Political Action Committee	Corporate	$2,628,852	$2,426,664	$2,224,117	92
New York State Laborers' Political Action Committee	Labor	$2,563,700	$2,468,695	$5,500	<1
Valero Energy Corporation Political Action Committee	Corporate	$2,500,113	$2,335,345	$1,034,650	43
United Steelworkers Political Action Fund	Labor	$2,452,958	$1,549,474	$1,293,250	87
Air Line Pilots Association PAC	Labor	$2,445,237	$1,937,028	$1,795,000	95
Laborers' District Council of the Metro Area of Philadelphia and Vicinity PAC	Labor	$2,388,846	$2,003,275	$12,150	<1
Koch Industries Inc. Political Action Committee (KOCHPAC)	Corporate	$2,387,844	$2,040,735	$1,716,500	85
American Postal Workers Union Committee on Political Action	Labor	$2,372,553	$1,929,697	$1,747,950	89
HSBC North America Political Action Committee (H-PAC)	Corporate	$2,321,219	$2,371,699	$1,110,051	46
Anheuser-Busch Companies Inc. Political Action Committee	Corporate	$2,292,104	$1,488,240	$1,376,660	93
Union Pacific Corp. Fund for Effective Government	Corporate	$2,266,940	$2,318,397	$1,755,233	78
National Association of Insurance and Financial Advisors Political Action Committee	Trade	$2,256,014	$2,443,243	$1,866,050	76
Bank of America Corporation State and Federal Political Action Committee	Corporate	$2,197,765	$2,151,986	$764,830	39
International Association of Bridge Structural Ornamental & Reinforcing Iron Workers (IPAL)	Labor	$2,141,529	$2,020,753	$1,678,650	85
Burlington Northern Santa Fe Corporation RailPAC (BNSF RAILPAC)	Corporate	$2,133,562	$2,087,726	$1,659,000	81
Mason Tenders District Council of Greater New York and LI PAC	Labor	$2,130,387	$2,112,425	$37,000	2
Smithkline Beecham Corporation Political Action Committee (GLAXOSMITHKLINE PAC)	Corporate	$2,127,982	$2,209,574	$1,584,913	73
General Electric Company Political Action Committee	Corporate	$2,110,636	$2,396,709	$2,005,450	83

(Continued Overleaf)

Appendix 11.1. Continued

PAC Name	Type	Total Receipts	Total Disbursements	Congressional Race Contributions	Percentage to Candidates
National Committee for an Effective Congress	NeoPAC	$2,070,929	$1,990,234	$802,333	40
Lockheed Martin Employees' Political Action Committee	Corporate	$2,050,561	$2,254,567	$2,221,173	96
JP Morgan Chase & CO. PAC	Corporate	$2,036,631	$2,060,896	$1,050,912	52
American Society of Anesthesiologists Political Action Committee	Trade	$2,034,981	$1,876,200	$1,317,350	68
Totals and Average		**$389,472,752**	**$370,261,027**	**$147,047,537**	**37.5**

Source: CQ Money Line 2007.

Notes

1 The number of PACs reported by the FEC generally runs at about 4,100. These 4,100 are only those PACs that were *active* during the reporting period. The *total* number of PACs registered with the FEC at any given time is usually a good deal larger; normally around 4,800. A substantial number of PACs are inactive and are not included in the FEC official count.
2 Michael J. Malbin and Sean A. Cain, "The Ups and Downs of Small and Large Donors," The Campaign Finance Institute, http://www.cfinst.org/books_reports/SmallDonors/Small-Large-Donors_June2007.pdf.
3 A multi-candidate committee is defined by the FEC as a separate segregated fund that has "been registered at least 6 months, has more than 50 contributors and, with the exception of state party committees, has made contributions to at least 5 candidates for federal office." Federal Election Commission, *Guide for Corporations and Labor Organizations* (Washington, D.C.: Government Printing Office, 2007).
4 The term "max-out" refers to the practice contributing the allowable limit to a political campaign. In this instance, maxing out means that a contributing PAC gives $5,000 in both the primary and general election campaigns to the candidate.
5 "PACs and 527s," available from CQ Money Line website, http://moneyline.cq.com/pml/home.do.
6 These figures were drawn from FEC reports, Annex 1, and information on the Campaign Finance Institute webpage.
7 "PACs and 527s," available from CQ Money Line website, http://moneyline.cq.com/pml/home.do.
8 "Bipartisan Campaign Reform Act of 2002," available from FEC website, http://www.fec.gov/pages/bcra/bcra_update.html.
9 "About the MoveOn Family of Organizations," available from MoveOn website, http://www.moveon.org/about.html.
10 "Who We Are," available from EMILY's List website, http://www.emilyslist.org/about/.
11 Ibid.
12 "PACs and 527s," available from CQ Money Line website, http://moneyline.cq.com/pml/home.do. Also see SEIU website, http://www.seiu.org.
13 Scott Reiter, PAC Director, National Association of Realtors, interview in Washington, D.C., April, 2007.
14 The six winning races where PAC dollars were spent on behalf of candidates were Rep. Heather Wilson (Republican-New Mexico, 1st District), $797,919; Rep. Melissa Bean (Democrat-Illinois, 8th District), $501,753; and Sen. Ben Nelson (Democrat-Nebraska), $208,881. The three losing races were for Rep. Anne Northup (Republican-Kentucky, 3rd District), $1,040,460; Sen. Jim Talent (Republican-Missouri), $985,485 and the losing senate primary of Ed Case (Democrat-Hawaii), $638,202.
15 "ActBlue Home," available from ActBlue website, http://www.actblue.com/support.
16 Ibid.
17 Micela Isler, vice president of government relations, HSBC, interview held Washington, D.C., April, 2007. The HSBC PAC came to its lofty position as one of the Monsters through the acquisition of Household Finance. Household Finance started the program long before the HSBC acquisition.

12

The Promise and Futility of American Campaign Financing

Anthony Gierzynski

The landscape of campaign financing in the United States is an ever-changing one. Reformers continue to devise new ways to regulate the behavior of contributors and spenders at the national, state, or local level in order to fight corruption (real or perceived) and/or to redress the inequities inherent in the private financing of campaigns. More often than not their efforts at reform are overturned by the courts in the name of freedom of speech or side-stepped by the seemingly endless ability of givers and spenders of campaign money to adapt to any new obstacle in campaign finance law. All the while political money, driven by its purpose to either attain access to the government or attempt to reshape the government, continues to flow via one path or another to where the power resides in the system, feeding the advantages of incumbency and carving out an electoral landscape that is dominated by lop-sided contests and a small number of hyper-contested races that are immersed in a sea of money. This chapter maps out this ever-changing terrain of campaign finance in the United States, first discussing the context of campaign finance—namely campaign finance law—and then focusing on the issues that arise from the American system of privately financed election campaigns.

Context: Campaign Finance Law

Those who make the rules that govern the financing of political campaigns are faced with a dilemma. They can either choose to allow those with money the freedom to dispense it as they see fit, or they can choose to create a system in which no side in a campaign or any interest in the political process has a decisive advantage. Choosing one of these options makes it near-impossible to attain the other. Unless wealth is evenly distributed in a society, free campaign finance systems *will* result in political inequality. On the other hand, if political equality is desired, freedom to give or spend *will* have to be restricted. A system can aim for some middle ground between these two extremes, though doing so will require it to balance how much to trade off of one of these values for the other. The United States has chosen a system that favors the freedom side of this fundamental choice about elections. It is a choice that has been made largely by the US Supreme Court through its interpretation of the First Amendment.

The Court Sets the Boundaries

The Supreme Court in its 1976 decision, *Buckley v. Valeo*,[1] set the boundaries that have constrained campaign finance law in the United States ever since. In the *Buckley* decision the court famously (or infamously, depending on your views) equated campaign spending with speech. While governments were allowed to limit contributions, the Court ruled that they could not limit candidate spending, independent spending by groups or individuals, or contributions candidates made to their own campaigns. The Court also limited government regulation to the area of express advocacy, defined as campaign communications that directly and explicitly advocate the election or defeat of a candidate. Everything else was considered "issue advocacy" and protected by the First Amendment. The ruling—and subsequent rulings reinforcing the *Buckley* precedent—has made it extremely difficult for Congress, state or local governments to pursue political equality over the freedom to spend. In its two most recent rulings on campaign finance the Court demonstrated that, with the arrival of the two new Bush appointees, this bias in favor of freedom to spend will continue, perhaps even more strongly so than before.

In *Randall v. Sorrell*[2] the Supreme Court struck down a Vermont law that had limited candidate spending as well as contributions, reversing a decision by the Second Circuit Court of Appeals that had upheld both types of limits in the law. While the decision was fractured—the Court issued six separate opinions—it was clear that there is a majority on the Court that will not only continue to insist on the notion that spending limits are a violation of the First Amendment, but that it will also strike down *contribution* limits that, in their opinion, are too low, facts to the contrary notwithstanding.[3]

In *Federal Election Commission v. Wisconsin Right to Life*[4] the Court issued a ruling that has hamstrung the Bipartisan Campaign Reform Act (BCRA). In the decision the Court reversed itself on the constitutionality of restrictions on issue advertising,[5] reopening a major pathway for soft money (unregulated corporate, union, and other wealthy individuals or group contributions) to influence elections. The BCRA had attempted to rein in the abuse of "issue advocacy" by defining any ad that included the name or likeness of a candidate which aired in the thirty days before a primary election and the sixty days before a general election as express advocacy. The Court replaced the BCRA definition with the position of Chief Justice John G. Roberts, Jr that express advocacy ads are those that are "susceptible of no reasonable interpretation other than as an appeal to vote for or against a specific candidate." All others are considered issue ads and thus beyond the reach of regulators. As a result, the 2008 election is already witnessing the return of campaigns waged by organizations funded out of unregulated and undisclosed sources.

Federal Law

Federal campaign finance law regulates contests for the presidency and Congress. State and local laws govern the rest of the elections held in the United States.

Presidential Fundraising

While the Court made it clear that spending limits were unconstitutional, it has raised no objection to limits that accompanied a voluntary public funding system. From 1976 to 2000 the dual public funding system for presidential nomination and general election campaigns worked quite well to establish a relatively equal playing field. During the nomination qualified candidates received matching funds for the first $250 of any individual contribution. In return the candidates for the Democratic and Republican Party nominations who accepted the public funds agreed to follow spending limits set for each state as well as an overall spending limit. During the general election the parties' nominees decide whether to accept total public funding for their campaigns. Starting in the 1990s the effectiveness of this public funding system has eroded dramatically.

First, the political parties and interest groups discovered that they could use the soft money and issue advocacy loopholes to spend practically unlimited amounts of money on behalf of their party's nominee during the general election period. The BCRA attempted to address this end run around the rules by banning soft money and reigning in "issue advocacy," but soft money contributors found an alternative route for their money—527 committees. As seen, the Court has invalidated the BCRA attempt to regulate issue advocacy. So, while the nominees of both parties have accepted public funding for general elections through 2004, the effectiveness of the public funding mechanism has been severely weakened. In the 2008 cycle a number of candidates on both sides have taken to collecting contributions for both the general election and the nomination contest, a clear indication that this may be the first presidential campaign since Watergate in which any major presidential candidate forgoes public funding.

Second, because of the spending limits, the front-loading of the primary nomination contests, and the ease of which candidates were raising large sums of money, the public funding system for the presidential nomination of the parties has lost much of its power to induce candidates to participate in the system. In 2000, George W. Bush was the first major candidate to opt out of the public funding system for the nomination contest. In 2004 two major Democrats opted out, Howard Dean and John Kerry. In 2008, Obama, McCain, Clinton, Romney, Fred D. Thompson, and Giuliani opted out of public financing in the primaries, and Obama also opted out in the general election.

Because the public funding system for the nomination has failed to keep pace with the demands of the nomination contest there has been a move to fix it. One proposal by the Campaign Finance Institute's Task Force on Financing Presidential Nominations suggests a number of changes including increases in the spending limits, a 3 to 1 match for the first $100 of a contribution, and an escape hatch, among other things.[6]

Congressional Elections

Congressional candidates fund their campaigns with contributions from individuals, political action committees (PACs), and political parties. Individual contribution limits were increased by the BCRA and indexed to inflation (in 2008 the limit is $2,300 per election). For candidates facing wealthy self-financed candidates, individual contributions limits are higher (due to the so-called "millionaire amendment" to the BCRA). In Senate races that involve self-financed candidates who exceed two to four times the threshold of $150,000 plus four cents times the number of eligible voters in a state, the individual contribution limit for the opponent of the self-finance candidate is tripled. It is set at six times the limit if the self-financed candidate exceeds four to ten times the threshold, and the limits are removed in cases where the self-financed candidate exceeds ten times the threshold. The individual contribution limit for House candidates facing a self-financed candidate who contributes $350,000 or more to the campaign is tripled.

PACs are limited to $5,000 per election. Party direct contributions to Senate candidates are limited to $17,500, and $5,000 to House candidates. Parties are also allowed to make a limited amount of coordinated expenditures on behalf of congressional candidates or they can spend an unlimited amount of money independently of the candidate (the BCRA mandated that the parties must choose one or the other in each district). Coordinated expenditure limits are adjusted by inflation and for Senate contests by the population of the state. The limits for House contests are $81,800 in states with more than one House seat and $163,600 in states with only one House seat. The limits for Senate contests vary from $163,600 to $4.4 million.[7] A 1996 decision by the US Supreme Court in *Colorado Republican Federal Campaign Committee v. Federal Election Committee*[8] allowed the parties to spend unlimited amounts of hard money independently on behalf of congressional candidates. Expenditures are considered independent if they are spent without the candidate's knowledge or consent.

There is no public funding for congressional campaigns, though many reform groups—including, the New York University Law School's Brennan Center for Justice, Common Cause, Democracy Matters, Public Campaign, Public Citizen, and US PIRG—continue to push for it and legislation to that effect has been introduced in the Senate by assistant majority leader Richard J. Durbin (Democrat-Illinois) and Senator Arlen Specter (Republican-Pennsylvnia).

State and Local Laws

The financing of state and local elections is governed by state and/or local statutes operating within the limits set by the Supreme Court. State laws regulating campaign finance vary widely from statutes that require little more than public disclosure to statutes that set up public financing systems with strict limits on contributions. While change in federal campaign finance law has been rare, it is commonplace at the state level. Between 1992 and 2002, twenty-two states made changes in their campaign finance laws, either adopting limits on individual contributions or reducing the limits already in place, increasing disclosure requirements, or adopting public financing.[9] Four states—Maine, Vermont, Arizona and Massachusetts—adopted the so-called "clean elections" public financing programs that attempt to eliminate most private money from elections (although Vermont's law is now defunct and Massachusetts has struggled with the funding of its law). Under these "clean election" laws, candidates qualify for public funding if they are able to raise a specified number of small contributions ($5 in Maine and Arizona). As part of accepting the public funds, candidates agree to spending limits and raising no additional private money. To encourage participation in the public financing system these states also lower contribution limits for those who choose not to participate.

Fourteen states have some form of public funding for gubernatorial elections. Minnesota and Wisconsin have had since the 1970s partial public financing with corresponding expenditure limits for state legislative candidates who agree to campaign spending limits and meet eligibility requirements. These candidates can receive public funds to cover campaign expenses.

States have also attempted to deal with a number of other campaign finance issues. Oregon, for example, enacted a law that restricted the percentage of money candidates could raise outside of their district. Minnesota tried to mitigate the impact of independent expenditures by adjusting public funds and spending limits for candidates, and Missouri prohibited incumbents from carrying over excess campaign funds from the previous election. Arkansas, Virginia, Minnesota, Ohio, and Oregon give tax credits to citizens who make small contributions of $25 to $50 to candidates who abide by expenditure limits.[10]

Local governments have also been active, testing different approaches to regulating campaign finance. The two largest cities in the United States, New York and Los Angeles, have adopted systems of public funding with corresponding spending limits for city candidates. Qualified city council candidates in both cities who are willing to abide by spending limits receive public funds to match contributions of a certain size. Seattle had a partial public funding system with expenditure limits in place until Washington voters passed an initiative that prohibited public funding of campaigns in the state.[11] One city, Albuquerque, New Mexico, had mandatory spending limits in place between 1974 and the late 1990s in defiance of *Buckley* because the statute had never been successfully challenged until then.[12]

Many state and local innovations in campaign finance law have been invalidated by court rulings before or shortly after they took effect. Vermont's "clean elections" law, Oregon's out of state provision, Minnesota's attempt to regulate independent expenditures, and Missouri's ban on carry over funds were ruled unconstitutional. Nonetheless, states continue to try new ways of regulating campaign finance and elections have taken place under the law of some of these innovations—Maine and Arizona's "clean election" laws still stand, and before striking down the Vermont contribution limits as too small, the US Supreme Court had upheld Missouri's strict contribution limits.[13]

Issues

The common thread among most of the legislated changes in campaign finance law is an attempt to bolster political equality in the broadest sense of the word. Either they were designed to fight corruption or the appearance of corruption (corruption meaning that those who give money exercise undue influence) or to make election contests fairer (or both). The philosophy behind governmental regulation of campaign finance practices is that a private system of financing campaigns will, if left to itself, create political inequality in' elections and in governance that undercut the democratic nature of the political system. The record in the United States has borne out that claim empirically, as issues of inequality regularly dominate the concerns about how elections are financed in the US.

Corruption and/or the Perception of Corruption: Who Gives and What Do They Get?

The problem with inequality arises in who gives money to candidates and parties. While giving money to candidates or parties is not, as some claim, the equivalent of buying them, those who give to election causes do have greater access to law makers (and access is critical in a pluralist system). Their contributions have been found to affect the effort that law makers put into supporting or opposing legislation, and contributions have been found to influence votes on legislation that is less visible to the public or more important to the interests of the contributors.[14]

That being said, analyses of contributions consistently find that most of the money given to candidates and political parties comes from the business sector and/or wealthy Americans.[15] Figure 12.1 shows the sources of contributions to federal candidates and parties from 1990 to 2004 by the business/corporate sector, professionals, labor unions, ideological and single interest groups, and others. The domination of the business/corporate sector is quite obvious—roughly six of every ten dollars contributed comes from the business/corporate sector. This is true at the state level as well, as the contributions to state party organizations in 2004 illustrates in Figure 12.2. While 2004 saw a jump in small contributions to campaigns, the bulk of money used by parties, candidates, and groups came in the form of large contributions and was provided by those higher up on the income scale.

Figure 12.3 shows the make up of the money from 527 committees by the size of the contributions. Over one-half (56%) of the money raised by 527 committees came in contributions in the size of $2 million or more. Surveys consistently find that most contributors to political campaigns are people who come from households with the highest income levels. Figure 12.4 shows who makes individual contributions to candidates, parties, or groups by household income level. Those who made contributions were more likely to have higher household income; 44.3% of those who contributed had household incomes of $80,000 or more.

Some political observers hold out hope that the Internet will reduce the dependence on large contributors; the record to this point has yet to support that optimism. An analysis of contributions to candidates for presidential nomination through the third quarter of 2007 by the Campaign Finance Institute found that despite the increase in use of the Internet to raise

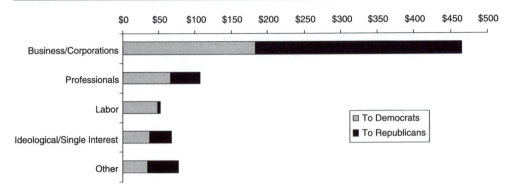

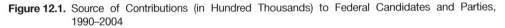

Figure 12.1. Source of Contributions (in Hundred Thousands) to Federal Candidates and Parties, 1990–2004

Source: Calculated by author from data available by the Center for Responsive Politics, http://www.crp.org/bigpicture/sectors.asp?Cycle=All&Bkdn=DemRep&Sortby=Sector.

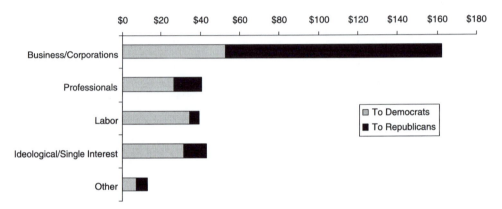

Figure 12.2. Sector Contributions (in Millions) to State Party Organizations, 2004

Source: Calculated by author from data provided by The Center for Public Integrity, http://www.publicintegrity.org/partylines/.

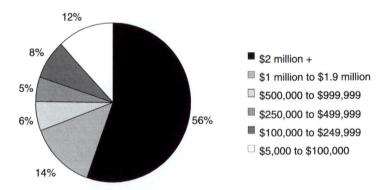

Figure 12.3. Distribution of Contributions to 527 Committees by Size of Contribution, 2004

Source: Steve Weissman and Ruth Hassan, "527 Groups and BCRA," in *The Election after Reform: Money, Politics, and the Bipartisan Campaign Reform Act,* ed. Michael Malbin (Lanham, Md.: Rowman & Littlefield Publishers, 2005).

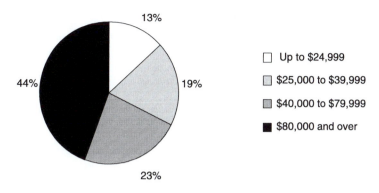

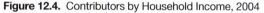

Figure 12.4. Contributors by Household Income, 2004

Source: American National Election Studies, 2004.

money, only 21% of the total amount raised from individual contributions came in contributions of $200 or less.[16]

The BCRA ban on soft money, however, does seem to have led to a rise in dependence of the national party committees on small contributions (and a concomitant decline in the dependence on large contributors). Contributions of $200 or less constituted 33 and 35% of the total receipts of the Democratic and Republican national committees in 2006, respectively. The comparable figures for 2002 (the last election before the BCRA took effect) were 14% for the Democratic committees and 27% for the Republican committees.[17]

Uneven Races, Unequal Choice

The odds of winning an election must be roughly equal in order for electoral races to be said to be fair contests between opposing political viewpoints—if the odds are stacked in favor of one side the election winners will owe their victory not to the fact that their issue positions are the ones most preferred by the electorate, but to their advantages in other areas unrelated to governing. Ultimately, when the answer to the question "Why did the candidate win?" is "Because they had more money," the legitimacy of elections and the governments they choose is questionable. Additionally, from the point of view of the voters, unequal or lopsided contests deprive voters of a meaningful say in governance, contributing to cynicism about elections and the responsiveness of public officials.

As one eminent political scientist put it years ago, "[a]bove everything, the people are powerless if the political enterprise is not competitive. It is the competition of political organizations that provides the people with the opportunity to make a choice. Without this opportunity, popular sovereignty amounts to nothing."[18] The relatively unregulated private system of financing elections in the United States has contributed to a situation were the odds are stacked in favor of certain types of candidates—namely, incumbents—and has given a consistent financial edge to the Republican party.

Incumbents versus Challengers

Most incumbent candidates running for reelection to legislative bodies have tremendous advantages in the amount of money they can spend. The typical candidate who challenged a sitting senator in 2004 was only able to raise enough funds to spend a little over one-third (36.4%) of what the typical incumbent senate candidate spent. The typical candidate challenging a US House incumbent was only able to spend a little over one-fourth (26.7%) of their incumbent opponent. Even in competitive races, incumbents had an overwhelming advantage: senate challengers in close races were able to raise just 55% of what incumbent senators in those races collected, and House challengers just 47% of incumbent representatives' total revenues.[19]

As Figure 12.5 shows, this disadvantage for candidates running against House incumbents has gotten worse since 1976; the last time challengers spent at least one-half of what incumbents spent (marked by the 50% line in the graph) was 1980. The jump in spending for candidates challenging sitting senators in 1994 and subsequent elections can be attributed to the fact that a number of senate challengers spent large amounts of their own personal money in these years.[20] The downward trend, however, returned in 2004 despite continued self-financing,[21] with the average challenger only spending 36% of what incumbents spent—the greatest disadvantage for senate challengers vis-à-vis incumbents for the entire time frame. According to reports filed through mid-October, senate and House challengers faired a bit better in the intensely fought-out 2006 election.

This incumbent–challenger financing imbalance also holds true for state legislative seats. Figure 12.6 shows challenger spending as a percent of incumbent spending for state House and senate candidates for 2004. In most of these cases, challengers had difficulty raising as much as one-half of what incumbents raised and in many cases failed to raise even one-third of what the typical incumbent raised. Challengers do better in states where the amount of money involved in legislative contests is relative small, such as Arkansas, Montana, and South Dakota, and in Arizona where legislative campaigns are publicly funded. This pattern of a lopsided incumbent advantage in campaign money can be found in any year for almost any state and there is plenty of evidence to show that this imbalance is worsening.[22]

While not as visibly lopsided as legislative contests, incumbent governors are able to raise and spend more money than the typical challenger. Figure 12.7 shows the average spending by incumbent governors and their challengers for elections between 1997 and 2004. On average, challengers have been able to spend about 74% of what incumbents have spent. In an earlier analysis of gubernatorial elections between 1997 and 2000, I found that, after controlling for a

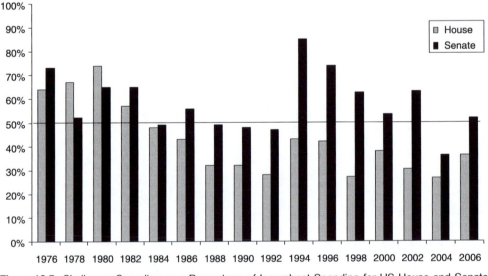

Figure 12.5. Challenger Spending as a Percentage of Incumbent Spending for US House and Senate Races from 1976 to 2006 (General Election Candidates Only)

Source: Produced by author from data presented in Norman J. Ornstein, Thomas E. Mann, and Michael J. Malbin, *Vital Statistics on Congress, 1997–1998* (Washington, D.C.: Congressional Quarterly Press, 1998) and the Federal Election Commission, http://www.fec.gov/.

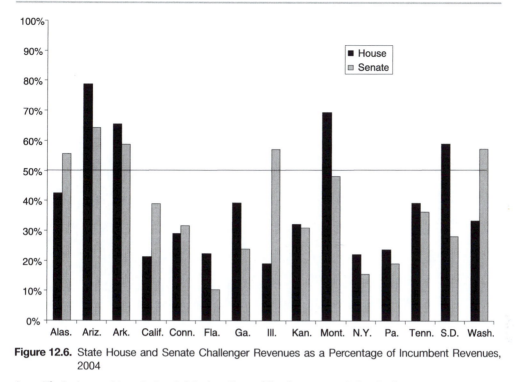

Figure 12.6. State House and Senate Challenger Revenues as a Percentage of Incumbent Revenues, 2004

Source: The Institute on Money in State Politics, http://www.followthemoney.org/index.phtml.

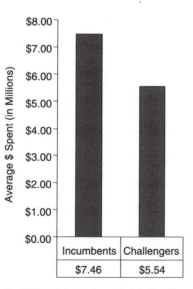

Incumbents	Challengers
$7.46	$5.54

Figure 12.7. Average Spending (in Millions) in Gubernatorial Elections by Incumbent Governors and Challengers, 1997–2004

Sources: Gubernatorial Campaign Expenditures Database, compiled by Thad Beyle and Jennifer Jensen, secretaries of state and state ethics committees, and The National Institute on Money in State Politics.

number of other factors that are related to fundraising levels—gross state product, candidate quality, competitiveness of the race, strictness of campaign finance laws, party, and so forth—incumbents raised, on average, $1.6 million more than challengers.[23]

159

Democrats versus Republicans

Republicans typically hold a large financial advantage over Democrats in fundraising for elections. This is especially true of the national political party organizations and of presidential and gubernatorial candidates.[24] The 2004 election, however, was unique in a number of ways that require closer examination. George W. Bush's $35 million campaign finance advantage during the nomination phase of the election gave the president an upper hand in getting his message out and organizing his campaign early.[25] While John Kerry had to spend nomination-phase money in the competition to win his party's nomination, the Bush campaign was allowed to spend its superior resources freely at that time on communicating with voters (including a $40 million, six-week television assault on Kerry immediately following Super Tuesday in March) and on organizing the Republican voter mobilization effort that garnered the party an additional 10.5 million votes over their total for 2000 (Democrats increased their vote by 6.8 million over 2000).[26] This advantage in campaign funds was exacerbated by the extra five weeks the Bush campaign had to spend his nomination-phase money because of the later date of the Republican National Convention (public funding and the corresponding spending limits take effect shortly after candidates accept their party's nomination at their party's conventions).[27] It was during this five-week period that Kerry—who was conserving his public funds to avoid an end of the election campaign shortfall like the one that plagued the Gore campaign in 2000—fell victim to the negative (and false) attacks from the "Swift Boat Veterans for the Truth" 527 committee.

To get the full picture on the 2004 presidential contest it is important to look beyond just what the candidates raised to what their party organizations and 527 committees raised. With bitterness left over from the 2000 presidential election, a high level of ideological polarization, discontent about the war in Iraq, and the further development of the Internet as a fundraising tool, more money than usual flowed into Democratic party and Democratic candidate accounts in 2004 reducing the traditional gap between the parties. In the 2003–2004 reporting cycle, the Democrat National Committee (DNC) actually raised $2 million more than the Republican National Committee (RNC). Between 2001 and 2002, however, the RNC raised $170.1 million while the DNC only raised $67.5 million. That is a $102.6 million advantage for the RNC which used the money in an early start up for the Bush reelection campaign, spending millions of dollars beginning in 2001 devising and testing new ways to reach voters for the 2004 election.[28] Republicans were also able to raise $29 million more (51% more) than Democrats did for their party's 2004 nominating convention.[29]

In response to the BCRA of 2002, which banned soft money (unregulated money used by the parties to run issue ads and voter mobilization programs), a number of Democratic leaders channeled their efforts into 527 committees (named after the IRS tax-code section used to regulate them). Contributions to and expenditures by 527 committees in 2004 were not limited by the Federal Election Commission (FEC) as long as the groups did not formally endorse a candidate or coordinate their efforts with the parties or candidates. These committees could thus raise unlimited sums of money from wealthy individuals, corporations, and labor unions. Democrats had an advantage among major 527 committees trying to influence the presidential race in 2004, out-raising major Republican 527s' $181.8 million to $64.5 million, a $117.3 million advantage.[30]

It is questionable whether this money helped to eliminate the disadvantage the Democrats' presidential bid faced in candidate and party money. In order for it to do so, this 527 money would have to be considered as de facto party or candidate money, which it is not. The parties and presidential candidates did not have control over the spending of this money; candidates and parties, by law, cannot coordinate with 527 committees. So, any advantage provided by having independent groups spend money to support or oppose candidates is minimized by the lack of control and coordination, which results in an unclear message and inefficient and overlapping administration of the effort. This was best illustrated by the fact that no 527 came to the aid of John Kerry when the "Swift Boat Veterans" attacked his war record immediately following the Democratic National Convention, an attack that had serious consequences for the Kerry campaign.[31] It is also driven home by comments of those involved such as the one made by Harold Ickes to *Washington Post* reporters. Ickes, "who ran the Media Fund, a 527 organization that raised about $59 million in support of Kerry, said the federal election law prohibiting communication with the Kerry campaign created insurmountable obstacles in crafting effective, accurate responses to anti-Kerry ads."[32]

The complete picture of money involved in the 2004 presidential election is summarized in Figure 12.8. The Republican's candidate, Bush, had an advantage in fundraising in the nomination phase of the election, an advantage that was exacerbated by the fact that Bush had no real opposition during the nomination phase and by the extra five weeks that his campaign had to spend this money because of the timing of the two parties' national conventions. The Republicans had a money edge for their national convention—which showcases the party's nominee and is an important fundraising opportunity. The RNC had a $100 million advantage over the DNC between 2001 and the 2004 election. While the Democrat's presidential bid had an advantage in 527 committee money, its use could not be coordinated with the party or the Kerry campaign.

In all, the Republican's bid to hold on to the presidency had a $47.2 million edge on the Democrats if money raised by major 527 committees is counted, and a $117.3 million edge if 527 money is excluded. Either way, in such a close race as the 2004 presidential election, the inequality in campaign money between the Republicans and Democrats, characteristic of most US elections, was an important factor in the outcome of that election.

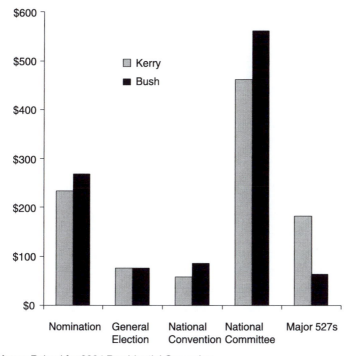

Figure 12.8. Money Raised for 2004 Presidential Campaign

Sources: Federal Election Commission and The Center for Public Integrity "527s in 2004 Shatter Previous Records for Political Fundraising," http://www.publicintegrity.org/527/report.aspx?aid=435&sid=300. Accessed September 27, 2005.

The fundraising advantage for Republicans is not limited to the 2004 presidential contest. At the national level Republican committees have long had a significant financial advantage over their Democratic counterparts. Between 2003 and 2004 the Republican's party committees raised $782.4 million federal dollars,[33] $103.6 million more than the Democratic Party committees' total of $678.8 million; the DNC and the Democratic Senatorial Campaign Committee (DSCC) raised slightly more than their Republican counterparts, but the National Republican Campaign Committee (NRCC) and Republican state and local party committees raised substantially more federal money than their counterparts.

The Republican Governors' Association—which had previously been counted as part of the party's nonfederal (soft money) operation and organized as a 527 committee for 2003 to 2004—out-raised the Democratic Governors' Association (another 527 committee) by about $10 million ($34 million to $24 million).[34]

The 2004 election was historically unique in that both the DNC and the DSCC out raised their Republican counterparts (the RNC and NRSC (National Republican Senatorial Committee)). The question is whether this is indicative of the future or whether RNC and NRSC will reassert their advantage in 2008. The 2006 midterm election saw the RNC out raise the DNC $243 million to $131 million, though the NRSC lagged behind the DSCC once again. Overall, Republicans will likely continue to hold the advantage because they draw from more reliable sources of campaign money, namely, corporate interests and upper income Americans. The Democrats' majority status in Congress, for as long as it continues, will moderate the advantage to some degree (those who contribute want access to those in power and will therefore contribute to the party in power even if it goes against their ideology). Figure 12.9 shows the historical perspective on party fundraising, reporting the federal receipts for the two major parties' committees since 1978. The average election cycle cash advantage of the Republican party committees during this time frame was $145 million.

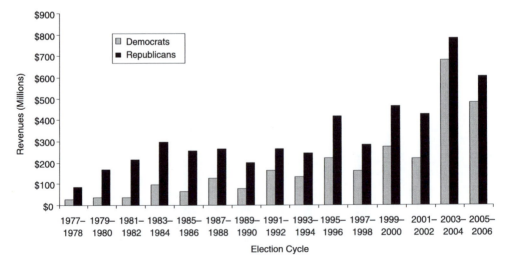

Figure 12.9. Money Raised for Federal Campaigns by Democratic and Republican Party Committees, 1977–2006

Source: Federal Election Commission, "Party Financial Activity Summarized for the 2006 Election Cycle," http://www.fec.gov/press/press2007/partyfinal2006/20070307party.shtml and Norman J. Ornstein, Thomas E. Mann, and Michael J. Malbin, *Vital Statistics on Congress, 1997–1998* (Washington, D.C.: Congressional Quarterly Press, 1998).

Ballot Measures, Judicial Candidates

Attention to campaign finance practices has begun to extend beyond executive and legislative contests, to the financing of ballot measures and state judicial campaigns. Twenty-four states permit citizens to put policy questions on the ballot via the initiative process and twenty-four states (many of which are those that allow for initiatives) allow for popular referendums, which allow voters to repeal acts of the legislature; most states are required by their constitutions to put changes to their constitution on the ballot.[35] The number of initiatives placed on the ballot in the states exploded in the 1990s—there were 458 initiatives on the ballot between 1990 and 2000, more than three times as many as in the 1940s, 1950s, and 1960s—with the increase in the use of the initiative concentrated in six states.[36]

The process of getting a question on the ballot is expensive, requiring significant amounts of money to obtain the number of signatures required to put questions on the ballot and to educate the public about the effect of voting for or against the proposition (and this is especially true in the states where the process is most used). As a consequence successful ballot measures need to be supported by organizations and well-financed groups or individuals. In other words, it is a process that seems designed for interest groups, especially those with money.[37] As Richard Ellis showed, initiative and referendum is the realm of interest groups, politicians, initiative activists, and the very rich. While average citizens do endeavor to put questions on the ballot, "the best place to find amateur citizen initiatives is not on the ballot, but in the large number of initiatives that get filed but never make it to the ballot."[38] Major imbalances in the funding of these campaigns do occur, especially when the issue affects the interests of corporations. In 1978, the Supreme Court ruled in *First National Bank of Boston et al. v. Bellotti* that states could not limit business spending on the debate over ballot questions.[39]

Thirty-nine states hold elections for their state judges and the role of money in such elections is attracting increased attention from scholars and political observers. Of particular concern or interest are the small subsets of judicial contests that are heavily contested and as a consequence require increasingly high levels of campaign contributions. The money for these contests comes mainly from parties that have cases before the court and from lawyers and big businesses whose interests are affected by the judges' decisions, a fact that raises concerns of political corruption.[40] Adding to that concern is the fact that the outcome of judicial contests *is* influenced by that campaign spending.[41]

Conclusion

In the past several decades the United States has witnessed constant changes in the landscape of campaign finance created by changes in the law, the behavior of contributors and spenders, and political and technological changes. How the landscape of campaign finance in the United States will change next is anybody's guess and certainly a source of fascination for those of us who study it. What impact will the current conservative Supreme Court have on campaign finance laws at the national, state, and local level? How will reformers respond? How will contributors, candidates, and parties adapt to such changes? Has the Internet reached its full potential in terms of its impact on fundraising? If the current party polarization continues, what impact will that have on the fundraising advantage of the Republicans? Whatever happens, the role of money in electoral politics will undoubtedly continue to generate concerns about the quality of democracy in the United States.

Notes

1 424 U.S. 1 (1976).

2 548 US ____ (2006).

3 The justices ignored the record established by the state of Vermont (see the dissenting opinion of Justice John Paul Stevens).

4 551 US ____ (2007).

5 See *McConnell v. Federal Election Commission*, 540 U.S. 93 (2003).

6 Campaign Finance Institute Task Force on Financing Presidential Nominations, "So the Voters May Choose . . . Reviving the Presidential Matching Fund System," http://www.cfinst.org/president/pdf/ VotersChoose.pdf. Accessed December 9, 2007.

7 R. Sam Garrett and L. Paige Witaker, "Coordinated Party Expenditures in Federal Elections: An Overview," A Congressional Research Service Report for Congress, April 13, 2007, http://fpc.state-.gov/documents/organization/84325.pdf. Accessed December 10, 2007.

8 518 U.S. 604 (1996).

9 Christopher Witko, "Explaining Increases in the Stringency of State Campaign Finance Regulation, 1993–2002," *State Politics and Policy Quarterly* 7 (4) (Winter 2007): 369–93.

10 See Council of State Governments, *The Book of the States, 2000–2001*, vol. 31 (Lexington, KY: Council of State Governments, 2000).

11 Carolyn M. Van Noy, "The City of Seattle and Campaign Finance Reform: A Case Study." *Public Integrity* II (IV) (Fall 2000): 303–16.

12 See *Homans v. City of Albuquerque* 264 F.3d 1240, 1243–44 (10th Cir. 2001). For an analysis of the effect of these limits see Anthony Gierzynski and Donald Gross, "Spending Limits in Practice: The Case of Albuquerque," Paper presented at the 2007 Annual Meeting of the Midwest Political Science Association, April 12–15.

13 *Nixon v. Shrink Missouri Government PAC*, 528 U.S. 377 (2000).

14 Richard L. Hall and Frank W. Wayman, "Buying Time: Moneyed Interests and the Mobilization Bias in Congressional Elections," *American Political Science Review* 84 (1990): 797–820; Laura I. Langbein and Mark A. Lotwis, "The Political Efficacy of Lobbying and Money: Gun Control in the U.S. House, 1986," *Legislative Studies Quarterly* 15 (August 1990): 413–40; Stacy B. Gordon, *Campaign Contributions and Legislative Voting: A New Approach* (New York: Routledge, 2005).

15 Jacob S. Hacker and Paul Pierson, *Off Center: The Republican Revolution and the Erosion of American Democracy* (New Haven: Yale University Press, 2005); Anthony Gierzynski, *Money Rules: Financing Elections in America* (Boulder, CO: Westview Press, 2000); Sidney Verba, Kay Lehman Schlozman, and Henry E. Brady, *Voice and Equality: Civic Voluntarism in American Politics* (Cambridge, MA: Harvard University Press, 1995); The Center For Responsive Politics, "The Big Picture: The Money Behind the Elections," http://www.crp.org/bigpicture/index.asp. Accessed September 26, 2005; Peter L. Francia, Paul S. Herrnson, John C. Green, Lynda W. Powell, and Clyde Wilcox, *The Financiers of Congressional Elections, Investors, Ideologues, and Intimates* (New York: Columbia University Press, 2003).

16 Campaign Finance Institute, "Large Donors Dominate Record-Setting Presidential Fundraising," October 17, 2007, http://www.cfinst.org/pr/prRelease.aspx?ReleaseID=164. Accessed December 10, 2007.

17 Anthony Corrado and Katie Varney, "Party Money in the 2006 Elections: The Role of National Party Committees in Financing Congressional Campaigns," A Campaign Finance Institute Report, 2007, www.CFInst.org. Accessed December 8, 2007.

18 E.E. Schattschneider, *The Semi-Sovereign People: A Realist's View of Democracy in America* (New York: Holt, Rinehart, and Winston, 1960), 140.

19 Campaign Finance Institute, "House Winners Average $1 Million for The First Time; Senate Winners Up 47%," press release, November 5, 2004, http://www.cfinst.org/pr/110504a.html.

20 Gierzynski, *Money Rules*.

21 Gary C. Jacobson, "The First Congressional Elections after BCRA," in *The Election after Reform: Money, Politics, and the Bipartisan Campaign Reform Act*, ed. Michael Malbin (Lanham, MD: Rowman & Littlefield Publishers, 2005).

22 Gierzynski, *Money Rules*; Gary Moncrief, "Candidate Spending in State Legislative Races," in *Campaign Finance in State Legislative Elections*, ed. Joel A. Thompson and Gary F. Moncrief (Washington, D.C.: CQ Press, 1998), 37–58; Robert E. Hogan and Keith E. Hamm, "Variations in District-Level Campaign Spending in State Legislatures," in *Campaign Finance in State Legislative Elections*, ed. Joel A. Thompson and Gary F. Moncrief (Washington, D.C.: CQ Press, 1998), 59–79.

23 Anthony Gierzynski, "Gubernatorial and State Legislative Elections," in *Financing the 2000 Election*, ed. David Magleby (Washington, D.C.: Brookings Institute Press, 2002), 188–212.

24 See discussion below regarding political party finances. In the past five presidential contests the Republican nominee for president out-raised the Democratic nominee during the nomination phase. And, once incumbency, competitiveness, gross state product, and other important factors are controlled for, Democratic gubernatorial candidates raise, on average, about $1.1 million less than Republican gubernatorial candidates (see Gierzynski, "Gubernatorial and State Legislative Elections," 188–212).

25 Federal Election Commission, "2004 Presidential Campaign Financial Activity Summarized," February 3, 2005, http://www.fec.gov/press/press2005/20050203pressum/20050203pressum.html. Accessed September 22, 2005.

26 Thomas B. Edsall and James V. Grimaldi, "On Nov. 2, GOP Got More Bang For Its Billion, Analysis Shows," *The Washington Post*, December 30, 2004, A01.

27 The 2004 Democratic National Convention took place between July 26 and the 29, the Republican National Convention between August 30 and September 2.

28 Edsall and Grimaldi, "On Nov. 2, GOP Got More Bang For Its Billion, Analysis Shows."

29 Federal Election Commission, "2004 Presidential Campaign Financial Activity Summarized."

30 The Center for Public Integrity "527s in 2004 Shatter Previous Records for Political Fundraising," http://www.publicintegrity.org/527/report.aspx?aid=435&sid=300. Accessed September 27, 2005. Edsall and Grimaldi, "On Nov. 2, GOP Got More Bang For Its Billion, Analysis Shows."

31 Gerald M. Pomper, "The Presidential Election: The Ills of American Politics After 9/11," in *The Election of 2004*, ed. Michael Nelson (Washington, D.C.: CQ Press, 2005), 42–68.

32 Edsall and Grimaldi, "On Nov. 2, GOP Got More Bang For Its Billion, Analysis Shows."

33 Federal money is money that can legally be spent on campaigns for federal offices, for example, the presidency, U. S. Senate and U. S. House.

34 Anthony Corrado, "Party Finance in the Wake of BCRA: An Overview," in *The Election after Reform: Money, Politics, and the Bipartisan Campaign Reform Act*, ed. Michael Malbin (Lanham, MD: Rowman & Littlefield Publishers, 2005).

35 The National Conference of State Legislatures, "Initiative, Referendum and Recall," http://www.ncsl.org/programs/legismgt/elect/initiat.htm. Accessed July 5, 2007.

36 Richard J. Ellis, *Democratic Delusions: The Initiative Process in America* (Lawrence, KS: University Press of Kansas, 2002); The National Conference of State Legislatures, "Initiative and Referendum in the 21st Century: Final Report and Recommendations of the NCSL I&R Task Force," July 2002, http://www.ncsl.org/programs/legismgt/irtaskfc/IandR_report.pdf. Accessed July 5, 2007.

37 Betty H. Zisk, *Money, Media and the Grass Roots: State Ballot Issues and the Electoral Process* (Newbury Park, CA: Sage Publications, 1987).

38 Ellis, *Democratic Delusions*, 119.

39 435 U.S. 765 (1978). Gierzynski, *Money Rules*.

40 Henry R. Glick, *Courts, Politics and Justice* (New York: McGraw Hill, 1993); Adam Liptak and Janet Roberts, "Campaign Cash Mirrors a High Court's Rulings," *The New York Times*, October 1, 2006, 1.

41 Melinda Gann Hall and Chris W. Bonneau, "Does Quality Matter? Challengers in State Supreme Court Elections," *American Journal of Political Science* 50 (1) (January 2006): 20–33.

13

Campaigning Online

Emilienne Ireland

Online campaigning has fundamentally changed in the past two presidential campaign cycles. In 2000, campaign websites were considered new, and there were still candidates for United States Senate who did not have campaign-funded websites. A practical primer that I co-authored in 2001 opened not by describing campaign websites, but by making the case that a campaign website was a necessary component of an effective campaign.[1]

Since then, campaign websites have become ubiquitous, and are considered an essential campaign tool. What today's campaign managers may not yet realize, however, is that the definition of an effective Internet campaign in 2000 was fundamentally different from what it is today. The difference is that the Internet itself, and the behavior of those who use it, has changed fundamentally.

That change is seen in the rise of political networking and content production by ordinary voters, independent of the campaigns and candidates they support. Campaigns must still create campaign themes, strategies, and tactics, but they also must be flexible enough to address the many new sources of information that have emerged in the last eight years.

After a brief review of the state of online campaigns in 2000, this chapter will explore the current state of online campaigning as Campaign 2008 steps into high gear.

Campaign 2000: The Way We Were

It is sometimes hard to remember how much the Internet has reshaped the public space that formerly had been defined by television, newspapers, and radio. As the public space has become transformed, so have relations among the various political actors in that space.

In the 2000 campaign cycle, Democrats were lagging behind Republicans in online campaigning effectiveness. By 2008, they had not only leveled the playing field but apparently surpassed the Republican Party online. For example, in October 1999, I co-authored a report analyzing campaign websites for United States Senate candidates in terms of the most basic criteria for website effectiveness, including the ability to accept online donations, sign up volunteers, and collect e-mail addresses.

The report found that Republican sites were roughly twice as effective and Internet-savvy as those of Democrats or Independents.[2] It is worth noting, however, that in those early days, about 70% of the declared United States Senate candidates had no campaign website whatever.[3]

Among the intrepid few campaigns that did have websites, 62% of the Republican candidates were able to accept online donations, compared to only 17% of the Democrats. When judged by ability to collect e-mail addresses and recruit volunteers online, the Republicans also were ahead.

This gap in Internet skills between the two major parties did not cause much concern in the early days of the Internet. The attitude of most campaign consultants at that time was expressed in a remark by pollster Mark Mellman: "The truth is, as a tool of political communication, the Internet today is of marginal value, but increasing value."[4]

Early Online Pioneers: Bradley, McCain, and Dean

Back in 2000, campaigns at all levels had to be reminded about the fundamentals: start with a strong website, constantly publicize the site, integrate online and offline efforts, don't hide the "Donate" button, make sure donating is simple and easy, provide a choice of payment options, adopt a privacy policy, send regular e-mails to supporters, and keep the website updated.[5]

Two campaigns in that cycle stood out for their awareness of greater possibilities. While neither senators Bill Bradley (Democrat-New Jersey) nor John McCain (Republican-Arizona) won their party's presidential nomination, they showed campaigns from the top to the bottom of the ballot that the Internet was here to stay.

Several presidential campaigns in 2000 featured volunteers on their websites, including photos and personal statements about why they supported the candidate. Team Bradley was especially effective at doing this, and Bradley's site allowed visitors to browse through volunteer pages by state and city. This made it easy to find snapshots of neighbors in your own or nearby communities, alongside their personal comments about Bill Bradley and why they supported him on a particular issue. In retrospect, this was the precursor of "social networking" that has become so ubiquitous today.

Likewise, former representative Tom Campbell (Republican-California), running against incumbent Dianne Feinstein (Democrat-California) for her US Senate seat in 2000, included a "Town Hall" feature that showed he was confident, open to dialog, and responsive to constituents. Every day, he personally answered five e-mails from constituents on his website, and even archived each dialog by topic so voters could read his responses to previous questions.

At the time, a colleague and I noted admiringly that

> Campbell's Town Hall was not an unmoderated free-for-all "chat room" that allowed visitors to post irrelevant and potentially damaging messages on his site. Far from it. Campbell stayed in control and on message by posting questions and answers he specifically chose as relevant to his campaign.[6]

Little did we realize that blogs, the ultimate in visitor messaging and the opposite of the traditional tightly controlled campaign message, would become so ubiquitous and so powerful so quickly.

John McCain's contribution to the 2000 presidential campaign was in the field of fundraising. Indeed, the "McCain Effect" was a term used to describe his explosion of fundraising over the Internet after his surprise upset of George W. Bush in the New Hampshire primary. His "Straight Talk Express" raised the unheard-of amount of $6.4 million online that cycle[7] because Team McCain was not afraid to take the best of offline direct mail and telemarketing strategies and adapt them to the new online technology.

Much has been written about how, in the 2004 campaign cycle, former Vermont governor Howard Dean and his team used the Internet to raise record sums of money, interface with constituents all across the country, and bring a dark horse candidate in 2003 almost to the brink of success as the 2004 presidential primary season began. While Dean did not survive the early 2004 primaries, the eventual Democratic candidate, senator John F. Kerry (Massachusetts), went on to use many of the techniques pioneered by Team Dean.

Campaign 2008: Online Campaigning Comes of Age

By 2007, political pundits such as David Brooks of the *New York Times* are still grousing about the "netroots self-righteousness and bullying," and insist that "both liberals and Republicans have an interest in exaggerating the netroots' influence, but in reality that influence is surprisingly marginal."[8] Despite the protests of pundits, however, the role of the Internet in public life has changed dramatically, and political leaders all know it.

In August 2007, bloggers touted their political relevance when nearly all of the Democratic presidential candidates attended the YearlyKos convention of liberal bloggers, while not even one candidate visited the Democratic Leadership Council's National Conversation that met a few days later.[9] According to *The Politico*, the 2008 National Republican Senatorial Committee Internet Guide included this warning from the NRSC Chair, senator John E. Ensign (Republican-Nevada): "It is critical that Republicans not let Democrats continue the edge" in Internet tactics and strategies. "They have had an edge on us."[10]

If Ensign's assessment is accurate, how is it that Republicans entered the Internet age in a dominant position and have since fallen behind? The answer may be that the Internet itself has profoundly changed in the years since the 2000 campaign, and the corporate-style top-down management savvy that served the Republican Party well in those early Internet days is out-of-date and ineffective in today's open-source, many-to-many, user-driven and user-controlled Internet.

In the past eight years, the gap has widened between old and new media and old and new strategies for campaigning online. This chasm between the Internet on one hand, and newspapers, television, and radio on the other is not one of technology, but of culture. The Internet has provided powerful organizing and mass-publishing tools to loosely coordinated, informal, and fluid groups of political activists at the same time that traditional media (such as television, newspaper, and radio) have become ever more centralized, uniform, and tightly controlled by large corporate interests.

On the Internet, acephalous, collaborative, many-to-many forms of communication, participation, and sharing are replacing the command-and-control, extractive, one-way broadcast, top-down institutions of twentieth-century business and political life. Blogs, YouTube, Ebay, MySpace, Facebook, Wikipedia, Flickr, and Craig's List are collectively part of a phenomenon called "Web 2.0," which political strategists in Campaign 2008 and beyond will have to understand if they are to be effective.

How Web 2.0 Is Reshaping Politics

In the early days of the web, even the best campaign websites were essentially isolated "information silos" that could collect and display information online but were incapable of reciprocally exchanging information with other systems. Such information silos tend to be inward-focused and unable to take advantage of the power of the Internet to interconnect individuals, groups, and business processes.

Recent years have seen the rise of mass collaboration and information sharing tools, loosely termed "Web 2.0." Technologies such as blogs, social bookmarking, wikis, podcasts, RSS feeds (and other forms of many-to-many publishing), social software, web application programming interfaces (APIs), and online web services such as eBay and Gmail provide advantages over read-only websites.

While the early web mainly allowed only vertical communication—narrowly circumscribed, top-down and bottom-up—today's Web 2.0 Internet provides a platform for efficient, inexpensive, open and collaborative peer-to-peer content production and distribution on a mass scale.

Commenting on the increasingly participatory, collaborative nature of today's Internet, open-source advocate Tim O'Reilly cites the philosophy and strategy of Google CEO Eric Schmidt: "Don't fight the Internet," which in practical terms means "to embrace the network, to understand what creates network effects, and then to harness them in everything you do." O'Reilly adds: "Web 2.0 is ultimately based on trust. [Architectures of participation] do ultimately rely on trust. What we're really talking about is understanding the dynamics of the network economy."[11]

The many-to-many paradigm was responsible for the biggest political realignment seen in the past few years, when the Democrats defied all expectations to take back control of the US Senate in 2006. At a campaign event, incumbent senator George Allen (Republican-Virginia) made the same kind of racist remark that other politicians may have made with impunity in the past when they could safely assume that only their supporters could hear them. Allen was being shadowed by a college student, who was a staffer from his rival's campaign. The student, an American citizen of Indian heritage, using a digital recorder captured Allen giving a speech before a friendly crowd of rural supporters. Allen turned toward the student, saying: "This fellow here, over here with the yellow shirt, macaca, or whatever his name is. He's with my opponent. He's following us around everywhere . . . Let's give a welcome to macaca, here. Welcome to America and the real world of Virginia." The resulting video was broadcast to the world via YouTube, and Allen's "macaca" moment became his "macacalypse."

After Senator Allen made his infamous "macaca" remark, his opponents at the Jim Webb for Senate campaign did not immediately release the damaging video online. Instead, they held it over the weekend, while online buzz grew over the impending release of a political bombshell. When the Webb campaign tipped off the *Washington Post*, the "Post reporter was sort of like, 'I don't know if this is news. I don't know if we are going to write about it,' " said Webb campaign manager Jessica Vanden Berg.[12]

The campaign did not put the video on YouTube, the file-sharing service, until the *Post* published a short story online. However, bloggers kept the story alive and helped it spread. The macaca frenzy was born, and Allen lost what was initially viewed as an easy re-election. His loss was just enough to tip the balance of power in the Senate to the Democrats.

Web 2.0: Potential Pitfalls for Candidates

The new participatory, many-to-many Internet provides increased risks for political campaigns in three areas: greater accountability for past statements, greater danger of going off-message, and greater danger that the private becomes public.

Brooks Jackson and Kathleen Hall Jamieson[13] note that the Internet provides voters with more information that is more easily retrievable than ever before. This makes it easier to hold candidates accountable for discrepancies between past and present statements. At the same time, the Internet blurs the boundaries between campaigns and supporters, allowing supporters potentially to either broadcast a campaign's message or hijack it. Such blurred boundaries may seem advantageous to the campaign by providing deniability when supporters say things the campaign wants said but cannot say itself. As a leaked excerpt from the National Republican Senatorial Committee (NRSC) *Internet Guide* noted: "Blogs are sometimes more likely to discuss controversial issues that mainstream media shies away from and getting a blog to post on an issue might be the final justification a reporter needs to write a potentially damaging story on your opponent."[14] The "macaca meltdown" suggests that Democrats are likewise aware of these tactics.

Mass-scale political communication and action undertaken by loosely organized groups of individuals accountable to and controlled by no one in particular can, however, produce headaches for campaigns.

For example, the wildly successful Guy Fawkes Day fundraising on November 5, 2007 organized by supporters of Republican presidential candidate Ronald E. Paul is a more egregious example of "going off-message" than most campaign managers could imagine in their worst nightmares. Suffice it to note that Guy Fawkes was executed in England in 1606 after a failed attempt to blow up the British Parliament and assassinate King James I, along with most of the Protestant aristocracy.

While the memory of Fawkes is not universally reviled (Fawkes was ranked 30th in the 2002 list of "100 Greatest Britons", sponsored by the BBC and voted for by the public,[15] and has been said to be "the only man to ever enter Parliament with honourable intentions"), he was undeniably a traitor, would-be assassin, and terrorist. This most definitely is *not* a suitable fundraising theme for a post 9–11 American presidential candidate.

A group of Ron Paul supporters, however, thought otherwise. They put up a simple website[16] and on November 5, 2007, broke records by raising over $4 million online in one day for their candidate. While the campaign was delighted at the success of the fundraising effort, campaign spokesman Jesse Benton felt compelled to clarify that Mr. Paul did not support blowing up government buildings. "He wants to demolish things like the Department of Education," Mr. Benton said, "but we can do that very peacefully, in a constructive manner."[17] The following day the *New York Times* duly issued a correction to its initial report of the event: "the organizers . . . were supporters of Mr. Paul, who has mentioned the British rebel Guy Fawkes in speeches; Mr. Paul's campaign was not involved."[18]

Although the bizarre message of the Guy Fawkes Day campaign apparently has not damaged the Ron Paul campaign (possibly because the candidate is hardly positioning himself as a mainstream candidate), this story easily could have had a different ending.

Howard Rheingold introduced the notion of "smart mobs"[19] as a form of of intelligent self-structuring social organization "consisting of people who are able to act in concert even if they don't know each other . . . because they carry devices that possess both communication and computing capabilities." In Rheingold's view, a smart mob behaves in an intelligent or efficient manner because of the power and ease of technologically mediated networking. Despite this benign view of the phenomenon, campaign managers are well advised to remember that however smart they may be, Internet swarms can also behave as mobs in the familiar sense.

Yet another way that the web blurs boundaries is between public and private discourse, so that conversations that were once considered inappropriate for public airing now appear on the public Internet. According to research at Kansas State University, some 20% of a study sample of YouTube videos were "private conversations" directed through the public medium.[20] In some respects, the Internet as currently constituted functions as a neutral amplification device that can project onto a large screen what in former times might have been private comments and conversations.

Web 2.0: Potential Benefits for Candidates and Voters

Given these potential dangers for political campaigns in the era of Web 2.0, what are the potential benefits? For campaigns, these include new ways to reach and engage voters, increased participation by younger voters, and greater access to earned media attention, both online and offline. For the public at large, benefits include access to more substantive information about candidate's positions, as opposed to stories focusing mainly on the horse race aspects of the campaign. Equally important, private citizens are increasingly using the new Internet tools to creatively shape the political debate. After nearly a century of interacting with mass media mainly as passive consumers, ordinary individuals are finding the power of their own voices on the Internet.[21]

A 2007 study noted that presidential candidate websites "have fully embraced politics as a two-way conversation with voters."[22] Reading between the lines, it was clear that most of these campaigns were encouraging not only two-way, but many-to-many (voter-to-voter) discourse: "All candidates offer at least one way for users to 'converse' with the candidate or the campaign. The majority even let voters talk to each other."[23]

Those of us who analyze the political arena still tend to measure supporters' political participation by their level of volunteering and making contributions to the campaign. In the era of Web 2.0, however, such traditional forms of campaign involvement are hardly the only way people can participate. In fact, rising generations of voters appear to be moving away from such hierarchical, non-creative, and non-expressive ways of contributing support, preferring instead to produce and mass-broadcast their own message about the campaign, whether through blogs, videos, or other media. Internet scholar Henry Jenkins notes that even as early as 2005, "more than one-half of all American teens—and 57% of teens who use the Internet—could be considered media creators."[24]

Even among political web pundits, we see the same tendency to discount or overlook many-to-many political action on the web. For instance, when Jerome Armstrong, founder of MyDD.com, often cited as the "Blogfather of the progressive netroots," posted his list of stand-out moments showing how the Internet impacts the modern campaign,[25] commenters complained that the list neglected to mention some of the most effective examples—such as the "I'm So Pretty" video lampooning John Edwards, who appeared to be primping in front of a mirror for two entire minutes—simply because they were not produced by a campaign. Significantly, other commenters then noted that it was impossible to be sure the video had not in fact been produced by an opposing campaign, which then allowed "independent supporters" to take credit (and blame) for it.

Another example of the boundary-blurring, ambiguous, yet important role of "unaffiliated supporters" in modern campaigns is seen in the Fred Thompson exploratory campaign. Thompson, a former Republican senator from Tennessee, was the subject of a formal Federal Election Commission (FEC) complaint for allegedly running what was, in effect, an online presidential website at a time when he still had not filed as a candidate with the FEC. As reported by the Pew Research Center's Project for Excellence in Journalism:

> Thompson accomplished his voter involvement activities online without ever explicitly stating that he is running for president or asking for votes. He didn't have to. Instead, the site let his online supporters do the campaigning for him by networking with each other.[26]

Despite the myriad new ways the Internet enables candidates to evade accountability for their actions, they are by no means getting a free ride. The Internet allows voters to compare candidates head-to-head on the issues, in depth, as never before. For instance, the popular "YouChoose08" section of YouTube[27] allow voters to play a video clip showing exactly what a candidate has said about a specific issue, and then compare it to video clips of other candidates. Visitors also can view replays of the presidential debates online at their convenience. While it is true that candidates are feeling increased pressure from this new level of scrutiny, the trade-off is a better informed, more engaged citizenry, and presumably, greater transparency in the campaign process.

Social Networking: Reaching Out to the Rising Generation

It is precisely in the new arena of collaborative, participatory, many-to-many politicking that NRSC chair John Ensign's rueful remark about the "Democratic edge" appears to be justified. A

December 2007 snapshot of YouTube cumulative daily viewership by campaign showed that top-tier Democratic candidates were making good use of this medium, with Obama, Edwards, and Clinton garnering 5.0, 3.6, and 3.0 million daily video views, respectively. By contrast, on the Republican side, the top-tier candidates were lagging behind. Long-shot candidate Ron Paul far outdid his rivals, with 7.4 million daily views, compared to Mitt Romney's 2.9 and Rudy Giuliani's 1.1 million.[28]

A December 2007 snapshot of Facebook supporters for the candidates showed a similar disparity between Democrats and Republicans, with the top-tier Republican Party candidates generating far less interest than their Democratic counterparts. Obama, with over 170,000 supporters, led the Democrats, followed by Clinton (55,567) and Edwards (25,385). On the Republican side, Ron Paul again led the field, with 43,811 supporters, while none of the remaining candidates matched the Facebook support of any of the three leading Democratic candidates. After Paul, the Republican Party candidates with the most Facebook support were Romney (22,259), Thompson (19,099), and Mike Huckabee (15,125).[29]

Despite the demonstrated success of Democratic campaigns in using social networking tools and virtual communities for outreach, it is occasionally apparent that their Internet strategists have not read the whole playbook. For instance, Clinton campaign advisors Mandy Grunwald and Mark Penn fumbled when they tried to disparage Obama's success at recruiting young supporters by comparing them to members of Facebook, a leading online social networking community. "Our people look like caucus-goers," Grunwald said, "and his people look like they are eighteen. Penn said they look like Facebook."[30]

This stinging insult to both Obama supporters and Facebook members provoked a storm of indignation among certain bloggers. Well, at least from one blogger, Peter Erickson, who wrote:

> On Monday, I posted on One Million Strong about top advisers to the Clinton campaign disparaging Facebook and arguing that Obama's young supporters are not caucus-goers . . . After cross-posting on MyDD and DailyKos, I was eventually invited to post on TechPresident, a group blog that covers the intersection of technology and politics. From there, the story was picked up by ABC News' The Note, which quoted my post, followed by another ABC blog Political Punch, Wonkette, and finally was broadcast on CNN (video here). There is also now a petition on Facebook protesting the comments. Rick Klein's post on The Note on ABC News has drawn over 2,000 comments.[31]

Not content merely to savor the moral victory of prompting an "Official Petition Against Hillary Clinton" on Facebook.com, Erickson, an Obama supporter, unflinchingly delivered the *coup de grâce*. Slyly alluding to the "older" profile of both Clinton and her voter base, he cited a *BusinessWeek* article titled "Fogeys Flock to Facebook," which revealed that more than 41% of all Facebook visitors are age thirty-five and older."[32]

Web 2.0, therefore, is not merely a change in technology; it is a clash of generations and of cultures. The dismissive attitude sometimes displayed by campaign strategists toward the unwashed masses of Facebookers, bloggers, citizen journalists, bloviators, and blowhards is shared by some pundits and experts who earned their credentials and status the old-fashioned way. A *Newsweek* article on Andrew Keen's book, *The Cult of the Amateur*, describes his disgust with the whole collaborative, participatory, many-to-many Web 2.0 phenomenon:

> In his view, the entire Internet movement involving "collective intelligence," "citizen journalism" and "the wisdom of crowds" is a cultural meltdown, an instance of barbarians at civilization's gates. He considers Wikipedia, the popular Internet-based encyclopedia written and vetted by anyone who cares to contribute, as no more reliable than the output of a million monkeys banging away at their typewriters . . . In Keen's view, sites like Wikipedia, along with blogs, YouTube and iTunes, are rapidly eroding our legacy of expert guidance in favor of a "dictatorship of idiots." Reliable sources

of information . . . are under siege from an explosion of self-appointed writers, broadcasters and filmmakers whose collective output, charges Keen, is garbage. What's more, he notes, in the war for eyeballs and ad revenues, the amateurs are winning.[33]

Apparently, the growing menace of this dictatorship of Internet idiots was somehow overlooked by the team of scientists and business leaders who authored a December 2007 article in *Scientific American:* "The Semantic Web in Action: How the Internet is Getting Smarter."[34] They describe advances in medicine, commerce—and social networking systems—that will be enabled by the next wave of intelligent web software, ontologies, and data formats.

For the modern campaign strategist, it really doesn't matter whether the new forms of online information production and sharing are moronic or magnificent. They are here to stay. Campaign strategists and other pundits must learn to use them effectively. After all, even Andrew Keen, committed foe of Internet idiocy, has his own blog and podcast.

Welcoming Bloggers into the Campaign

In the early days of online campaigning, a candidate could get bad publicity in a local newspaper simply because someone was able to follow a trail of links from the campaign site to another site, then another site, and finally end up on a porn site. People are more savvy about the Internet now, and understand the candidate cannot control the content of every site on the Internet.

Likewise, before Howard Dean popularized the campaign blog in his 2004 campaign, blogs were often considered too risky for mainstream campaigns. Now all the top-tier presidential campaigns have them. In addition, website visitors now expect to be allowed to participate in the blog discussion. As reported in a Pew study, thirteen of the fifteen official presidential candidate blogs allowed comments, and seven of the nineteen candidates hosted citizen-initiated blogs.[35]

Observing the rising importance of blogs and other online information sources in presidential campaigns, a Pew study of campaign websites warned against "the role of the Web in particular as a way of sidestepping the scrutiny of traditional journalism."[36]

However, bloggers across the political spectrum tend to see traditional journalism, in an age of increasing media consolidation, as often providing less scrutiny than blogs, not more. There is some support for this view in the Harvard University's Shorenstein Center's report that most political news stories in the traditional media focus on the horse race aspects of the campaign (63% of stories) or the candidate's personal life (17%), and not positions on the issues (15%) or voting records (1%).[37]

Although the same study found that 77% of Americans say they want more coverage of the candidates' positions on issues, some newspaper journalists say that what these readers are saying does not square with what they actually do. In a 2007 Politics Online panel featuring both bloggers and traditional journalists, David Plotz, deputy editor of online magazine *Slate* (owned by the *Washington Post*) insisted that "Web traffic shows that horse race is what readers want," and that they don't want "to eat their vegetables."[38]

Campaigns today must actively reach out to the netroots. They have to think about providing ready-to-use content for bloggers, and to make their communications staff readily available to bloggers and other online content creators. This new campaign messaging strategy was spelled out with stunning clarity in a leaked excerpt from the NRSC *Internet Guide*:[39]

Old method of communicating campaign message to public:

1 Campaign decides on press release and talking points on certain issue,
2 Press secretary sends mass e-mail/fax of press release to mainstream media (MSM),

3   Possible news story on issue/race/candidate/opponent,

4   RESULT: Voters hear about issue/race/candidate/opponent through local newspaper or local news station.

New method of getting campaign's message to public:

1   Campaign decides on message points and strategy for certain issue,

2   ePress Secretary sends talking points and information to the blog editors that they have established relationships with,

3   Campaign e-mails specific message to supporters—utilizing "forward to a friend" website features to take advantage of viral nature of e-mail,

4   Candidate posts video on message,

5   Blog community posts opinions on issues related to the race and the candidate,

6   More blogs link to the first blog and give their own opinions on the issue/ candidate/opponent,

7   Buzz builds around issue/candidate/opponent in online community,

8   MSM (mainstream media) hear about buzz and write story about issue/candidate/opponent,

9   RESULT: Voters hear about issue/candidate/opponent through blog community, local newspaper, local news station, national media, e-mail, website, etc.

For Democratic candidates, the relationship between the campaign and bloggers is more independent, according to Markos Moulitsas Zúniga, founder of popular liberal blog DailyKos. com. In an interview he explains why, among supporters of Democratic campaigns, the old system of top-down control of content production has given way to the new collaborative, many-to-many, participatory model:

> I often say that the blogosphere is really the first medium that plays to our strengths as liberals. If you look at the progressive blogosphere and the conservative one, they operate in dramatically different styles. The conservative blogosphere is a top/bottom machine. Most of the major blogs do not have comments. It's a messaging machine. . . . So, it's very effective when they focus on any one story line, because—it's an echo chamber, sure, but it creates a sort of megaphone effect where they can really blast out a singular message across television, radio, the Internet, print, and newspapers. And that is very, very powerful. So, I'm not saying this as a value judgment, saying ours is better and theirs sucks, because they're very effective at doing what they're doing.
>
> Now, on our side, we've been at a disadvantage in the media world, because everybody jokes that liberals do not work from the same playbook. Will Rogers saying, "I'm not a member of an organized party, I'm a Democrat." This notion that we're not going to follow: "Don't tell me what to think, I'll think for myself." Obviously, that's been a problem in a world that has been increasingly dominated by the talking points and by being able to properly message. . . . So, we have a medium that doesn't necessarily require that sort of singularity of message, that actually encourages what we love to do the most, which is just to sit there and argue, fight, and debate. And sure, when the elections come—when the time comes, we can actually get together and work for campaigns and work for elections.[40]

Conclusion: Don't Fight the Internet, Embrace It

The online strategies of the political sector typically lag behind those of the commercial sector, which already has moved beyond two-way dialogue to many-to-many communication. The political sector as a whole in the 2008 campaign cycle appears to be reluctantly adopting two-way conversation between supporters and campaigns, a first step toward the many-to-many conversation that is at the heart of Web 2.0. Meanwhile, a recent Pew study says that the majority of presidential campaigns are going even further toward Web 2.0 by allowing supporters to talk to each other.[41] The 2008 election will be the first in which voter-generated content affects the course of most campaigns.

In the early days of the Internet, campaigns typically had little or no Internet strategy, and viewed the Internet as a fulfillment device or an e-commerce tool, incapable of persuasion. Early online campaigns, therefore, were implemented by young programmers with minimal strategic input from the campaign.

As veteran strategists schooled in the offline aspects of campaigning saw the monies raised and the communication possibilities opened, they rushed into the online campaigning sector, but had as little success as early movie producers who tried to use the same staging and blocking techniques they had learned in the world of staged dramas.

As Campaign 2008 unfolds, the full range of many-to-many communication, fundraising, and volunteering opportunities are coming to fruition. Younger web-savvy strategists are coming of age, and the boomer generation of politicos is hiring them and starting to give them a place at the strategy table. Given how fast technology is changing, it is hard to predict where this is all leading. But for now, the innovations of Web 2.0 have made politicians more accountable, campaigns more interactive, and the public more engaged.

Notes

1 Emilienne Ireland and Phil Tajitsu Nash, *Winning Campaigns Online*, 2nd ed. (Bethesda, MD: Science Writers Press, 2001).
2 Emilienne Ireland and Phil Tajitsu Nash, "Campaign 2000: Parties Vie for Internet Dominance," *Campaigns and Elections* 20 (9) (1999): 62–5.
3 In a field of 102 candidates, only thirty-one had campaign websites. I did not include the thirty-seven public officeholder sites provided at taxpayer expense, because candidates cannot legally accept donations, recruit volunteers, or collect any campaign data from such sites.
4 Mellman quoted in Dennis W. Johnson, *No Place for Amateurs: How Political Consultants Are Reshaping Democracy* (New York: Routledge, 2001), 28.
5 Emilienne Ireland, "Secrets of Successful Online Fundraising: Tips for Increasing Donations," *Campaigns & Elections* 22 (6) (August 2001): 47.
6 Ibid.
7 Ibid.
8 David Brooks, "The Center Holds," *New York Times*, September 25, 2007.
9 Ibid.
10 Carrie Budoff, "GOP Issues Rules to Avoid Macaca Moments," *Politico.com*, June 13, 2007, http://www.politico.com/news/stories/0607/4483.html.
11 Tom O'Reilly is founder of O'Reilly Media and a supporter of the free software and open source movements. Comment is available at http://radar.oreilly.com/archives/2006/07/levels_of_the_game.html.
12 Michael Scherer, "Salon Person of the Year: S.R. Sidarth," Salon.com, December 12, 2006, http://www.salon.com/opinion/feature/2006/12/16/sidarth/.
13 Brooks Jackson and Kathleen Hall Jamieson, *unSpun: Finding Facts in a World of Disinformation* (New York: Random House, 2007).
14 Excerpts from National Republican Senatorial Committee (NRSC) Campaign Internet Guide, http://www.politico.com/pdf/PPM44_nrscexcerpts.pdf.
15 BBC News, "100 Great British Heroes," BBC News website, August 21, 2002, http://news.bbc.co.uk/2/hi/entertainment/2208671.stm.
16 "Remember the 5th of November," http://www.thisnovember5th.com/.
17 David D. Kirkpatrick, "Guy Fawkes Day Helps Raise Millions for Paul," *New York Times*, November 5, 2007.
18 David D. Kirkpatrick, "Candidate's Pleased to Remember This Fifth of November," *New York Times*, November 6, 2007.
19 Howard Rheingold, *Smart Mobs: The Next Social Revolution* (Cambridge, MA: Perseus Publishing, 2002), xii.
20 Michael L. Wesch, "Why WeTubed on YouTube: Vlogging and Participant Observation in a Digitally Mediated Community," Paper presented at the 106th Annual Meeting of the American Anthropological Association, December 1, 2007.

21 Doc Searls and David Weinberger presciently wrote about this nearly a decade ago. See "Markets Are Conversations," in *The Clue Train Manifesto: The End of Business as Usual*, ed. C. Locke, R. Levine, D. Searls, and D. Weinberger (Cambridge, MA: Perseus Publishing, 2000).

22 Pew Research Center's Project for Excellence in Journalism, "Candidate Web Sites, Propaganda or News?—A PEJ Study," July 12, 2007, 2, http://www.journalism.org/node/6370.

23 Ibid., 3.

24 Henry Jenkins et al., "Confronting the Challenges of Participatory Culture: Media Education for the 21st Century," *MacArthur White Paper*, 6, http://www.digitallearning.macfound.org/atf/cf/%7B7E45C7E0-A3E0-4B89-AC9C-E807E1B0AE4E%7D/JENKINS_WHITE_PAPER.PDF. Jenkins cited a 2005 study, A. Lenhardt and M. Madden, *Teen Content Creators and Consumers*, Pew Internet and American Life Project, 2005, www.PewInternet.org/PPF/r/166/report_display.asp.

25 Jerome Armstrong, "The 2008 Internet-Based Standouts," MyDD.com, August 4, 2007, http://www.mydd.com/story/2007/8/4/11426/98308.

26 Niki Woodard, "Fred Thompson's Campaign Web Site Was Already in Full Swing," Pew Research Center's Project for Excellence in Journalism, September 7, 2007, http://www.journalism.org/node/7367.

27 Available at http://www.youtube.com/youchoose.

28 "YouTube Stats," http://www.techpresident.com/youtube. Accessed December 9, 2007.

29 "Facebook Supporters," http://techpresident.personaldemocracy.com/scrape_plot/facebook. Accessed December 9, 2007.

30 Roger Simon, "Jefferson Jackson a Warm-up for Iowa," Politico.com, November 11, 2007, http://www.politico.com/news/stories/1107/6815.html.

31 Peter Erikson, "One Million Strong Starts Facebook Fire," OneMillionStrong.us, November 14, 2007, http://www.onemillionstrong.us/showDiary.do?diaryId=198.

32 Aaron Ricadela, "Fogeys Flock to Facebook," *Business Week*, August 6, 2007.

33 Steven Levy, "Invasion of the Web Amateurs," Newsweek.com, August 21, 2007, http://www.newsweek.com/id/36171/.

34 Lee Feigenbaum, et al., "The Semantic Web: How the Internet is Getting Smarter," *Scientific American* 297 (6) (December 2007): 90–7.

35 "Candidate Web Sites, Propaganda or News?—A PEJ Study," 1.

36 Ibid.

37 Joan Shorenstein Center Project for Excellence in Journalism, "The Invisible Primary—Invisible No Longer: A First Look at Coverage of the 2008 Presidential Campaign," October 29, 2007, 6, http://www.journalism.org/node/8187.

38 Drew Clark, "Web 2.0 Gives Birth to Politics 2.0," Gigaom.com, March 19, 2007, http://gigaom.com/2007/03/19/web-20-gives-birth-to-politics-20/.

39 Excerpts from NRSC *Campaign Internet Guide*, http://www.politico.com/pdf/PPM44_nrscexcerpts.pdf.

40 Dylan Tweney, "Controlled Chaos: An Interview with Kos," Wired.com, May 8, 2007, http://blog.wired.com/business/2007/05/controlled_chao.html.

41 "Candidate Web Sites, Propaganda or News?" 1.

The Selling of the President 2004

A Marketing Perspective

Nicholas J. O'Shaughnessy and Stephan C. Henneberg

Contextual Background: The Market Conditions

In order to provide a framework, the 2004 US presidential election will be introduced initially by identifying the contextual background that characterizes the "market conditions" in which the relevant marketing exchanges are played out. All products and offerings operate in a marketplace and each market is different with its own private ecology and exchange structures. There are facts of market context, some of recent historical evolution, some traditional. They can be codified in legislation (party and campaign funding rules), based on social contracts of mutual agreements between actors, or are engrained in the attitudes and interpretations of relevant parties (the "brand" perception of what certain parties or candidates represent).[1] The analogy is with socio-cultural and legal trading conditions in a commercial context, the non-negotiable givens of a situation. However, elections take place in a dense *public* context, historical memory combined with new developments; in the 2004 US presidential election it can be shown that changes in media and society determined the character of the campaign. We will specifically focus on the following: speed of riposte, decline of hard news, climate of antipathy, and the new media reality.

Speed of Riposte

Politics differ from consumer marketing campaigns in the intensity of the interaction process. There is less predictability, more fluidity in the cognitive environment with a speed of response and anticipation unthinkable in consumer marketing: as will be shown, the Internet, blogosphere (for example, "Little Green Footballs," a very right-wing website), cable television, video tele-phone and satellite technology all create a mobile environment where instant imagery replaces deliberation. New developments are commented on by opponents nearly instantaneously. Otherwise, a perception by the media and voters exists that if a certain news item or accusation is not dealt with by the opposition candidate, it must either be "true" or at least must have wrong-footed the campaign, something that also negatively affects their interpretation of this specific candidate. A quick-rebuttal capability is now seen as one of the core elements of any election campaign.[2]

Decline of Hard News

The phenomenon of the decline of "hard news" as a proportion of US media[3] manifests itself quantitatively: even in the 2000 election there were four times as many local campaign ads as television political stories. The media in 2004 were also more likely to reproduce without comment press releases and imagery, particularly video footage, created by the government itself (and seldom disclosed as such, that is, resembling deception). Thus, up to a third of news directors admitted to taking news feeds as part of the news-management activities of parties, and feed material had increased from 14 to 23% in the years 1998–2002, while the number of investigative reporters had been halved and media corporations were looking for profit margins of 40% with the expected results regarding source quality and content choice.[4] They achieved these margins by substituting celebrity gossip and government-inspired narratives at the expense of traditional news, for example, foreign coverage on mainstream news and media was halved from 1989 to 2003.[5] The political ramifications of this were considerable. Mass media were less likely to solicit controversy and thus imperil advertising revenues, and in practice this meant a failure to license criticism of the Bush regime. Prestige liberal figures associated with the old dispensation (anchors Dan Rather, Tom Brokaw, and Ted Koppel) were soon discarded. Thus, mass media were now easier to manipulate by a media savvy regime and sophisticated "news–management" by campaigning candidates.[6]

Climate of Antipathy

A fact of the political marketplace was the ingrained, negative perception of the Democrat offering ("brand") by the media and large sections of the citizens, which had to be overcome if they were to win. Deep wells of antipathy existed in the 2004 election for political marketers to exploit. This relates to political correctness, secularism, welfarism, affirmative action, redistribution, racial and minority privileges. The Democrats had "brand baggage": the incubus of big government, the high-tax/high-spend accusation, their associations with bohemian big city morality. Thus, Bush advertising could portray Kerry as pro-big government, a man who would increase gasoline tax by 50%.[7] The enigma of blue-collar Republicanism may be viewed by some as an example of Marxist "false consciousness." But much Republican rhetoric successfully tapped into the Zeitgeist of the era and the specific antipathies pathologically engrained in it, its anti-intellectualism and distrust of liberalism, particularly by activating the latent fear that "that which tolerates all teaches nothing." There was also the broader historical context, another aspect of the market condition, of the re-emergence of a vociferous American right in the aftermath of Richard Nixon's 1968 "Southern" strategy. This came to have two distinct strata, a populist one founded in traditional "bible belt" evangelical Christianity (represented by Jerry Falwell or Ralph Reed), and an intellectual one, the so-called "neo-cons" (neo-conservatives), former liberals (such as Irving Kristol or Paul Wolfowitz) who had migrated to the free-market economic right in the late twentieth century and embraced the assertion of American "hard" power across the globe.

A New Media Reality

A critical part of the market conditions in 2004 was the coming of age of new media (Internet bloggers), the reinvention of old ones (talk radio) and the rise of partisan television news. For political marketers to succeed they had to understand these changes in communication channels and learn how to operate them. Again market conditions favored Republicans; the new media were unabashedly right wing. What these new media possessed in common was a culture of right-wing polemic,[8] something they did not of course originate but which they brought to new levels of vigorous outrage. Then there was the rise of what can be labelled "tabloid television." Underlying this phenomenon is really the media of hyperbole in which any idea of presenting "objective truth" has been suborned by the dictates of ideology which is fed by the denizens of 500 rightist think tanks[9] and a broad conservative infrastructure, thereby privileging the representatives of partisan information structures. The tone of public political discourse had coarsened in consequence. For example, one anti-war professor was berated by a Fox television anchor as an "obnoxious, pontificating jerk. . . . A self-absorbed, condescending imbecile. . . . An Ivy League intellectual lilliputan."[10] Fox TV and related mass media were thus the arbiters of this new context: its heroes (and antecedents) were in particular Bill O'Reilly and Rush Limbaugh, as well as Anne Coulter, Sean Hannity, Michael Savage, Oliver North, G. Gordon Liddy, and Ronald Reagan.

This new milieu obviously favored Republicans since it did the job of stigmatizing Democrats. A social climate is created, characterized in the view of some by chauvinism and a meanness of civic tone: the "formal" political marketing communication campaign did not have the labor of changing this climate or questioning the new values, merely reflected them. It was a saturated realm, a public space ostensibly colonized by Republican sympathisers with (in effect) free media publicity for the Republicans' product.[11] If the earlier concentration of media historically had produced a liberal outlook, its later fragmentation at the end of the millennium led to a conservative one. This really constituted retail negative advertising for the Republicans on a grand scale without the Republicans being (at least formally) involved. There is perhaps no obvious parallel in consumer life.

Such distortions were magnified by the political coming-of-age of talk radio, from which 22% of Americans derived their daily news, fifteen million alone listening to Limbaugh.[12] This medium—a renaissance rather than an invention, since the demagogue Father Charles Coughlin had dominated it for similar purposes in the 1930s—is unabashedly partisan: the top forty-five AM radio stations broadcast 310 "conservative" hours of political talk to five hours of "liberal."[13] Their impact on the outcome of the 2004 election is suggested by this account of the progress of a libel:

> One of the conservative talking points in the last election was that terrorists supported the candidacy of John Kerry. According to *Media Matters*, this pearl originated on Limbaugh's radio show in March 2004 and repeatedly surfaced in mainstream news. In May 2004, CNN's Kelli Arena reported "speculation that al-Qaeda believes it has a better chance of winning in Iraq if John Kerry is in the White House;" in June it migrated to Dick Morris's *New York Post* column. Chris Matthews mentioned it in a July edition of "Hardball." In September, Bill Schneider, CNN's senior political analyst, declared that al-Qaeda "would very much like to defeat President Bush," signaling that Limbaugh's contrivance was now embedded firmly in the national consciousness.[14]

Hence, what we saw embedding the 2004 US presidential election and its political marketing management was the creation and sustenance of a distinct social and political "climate," and its weather was Republican.

After the general socio-political environment has been introduced in which the US presidential elections were enacted, the chapter will now look at selected and salient aspects of the political marketing mix. Initially the "product" offering will be covered by focusing on the aspects of the "persona" and "values." Different characteristics of the "promotions," that is, the communication aspect visible in the election campaign, as well as "price" and "packaging" of the offering will be discussed.

Political Marketing Mix: Product (1)—Persona

Identity Manufacturing

Any offering must be clear about its function, about the problem it is solving, that is, the service it is rendering. Its image must be differentiated even if it is not unique. The product "Kerry" was neither of these things. Kerry was in many ways an unknown with no public visibility or record beyond the "political nation." His offering (in terms of personal characteristics but also policy stances) was ill-defined for most voters at the beginning of the campaign. The Republican achievement in this campaign was to foist an identity upon him by stereotyping him as the ultimate weak liberal and airbrushing out all nuances: he would go "whichever way the wind blows" according to a Republican advertisement that made cruel metaphoric use of the imagery of him windsurfing.[15] This was not without precedent: the aspiration to create an anti-type, in this case the paternalistic, sanctimonious liberal, or soulless political technocrat, had been achieved by Republicans before, for example, in their 1988 campaign against Dukakis.[16] In 2004, they would repeat it.

Incumbent Effect Revisited

In general the US presidency embodies a role that is in part symbolic—it represents, speaks for and even personifies the nation and is a fountainhead of normative wisdom, a "bully pulpit" in the famous words of Teddy Roosevelt. Successful incumbency offers the pleasure of the familiar: it is the brand we know. Constant brand visibility is the consequence of what amounts to a perpetual marketing campaign,[17] aided by the best speechwriters and advertising executives and the best funding: the power of the American presidency is the power of attention getting.

Nor should we discount the power of the "9/11 President" in this election; this was naturally part of the overall context of the electoral campaign. Countries whose cherished myths (in this case this was the invulnerability of the homeland) are destroyed exhibit certain traits; resulting hyper-patriotism is followed (potentially) by paranoia. Bush exploited this, with a "reminder strategy," mentioning 9/11 eight times in one electoral press conference and with his advertising also shamelessly exploiting the event with "footage of the charred hulk of the World Trade Center and flag draped remains."[18] Republicans successfully used the presidency as a "patriotism signifier" (a "brand cue") and insinuated, even actively promulgated the idea that to be against Bush was to be unpatriotic. There are clear market advantages to the "patriotism brand" in time of war (that is, a high involvement environment that mobilises citizens), hence a Republican advertisement featuring the Bushes with the message that the solemn duty of the President was to "protect the nation." Republicans had apparently mutated—ceasing to be a party and becoming the embodiment of the nation.

Personality

Certain perceived character traits are a necessary condition for success in presidential elections. They provide the cognitive "cues," the short-cuts and heuristics that voters (and the media) use to assess complex offerings like "policies."[19] What American voters apparently want is both a hero and a warm everyman.[20]

A well-known politician is also and maybe foremost a brand; and a president completing a first term is a very well-known brand indeed. The problem this presents for the challenger is that its brand often has to be created virtually from scratch except in rare cases. Even here, political marketing management cannot merely re-engineer the publicly understood persona because it comes to us with a visible, recorded and remembered history. If there is such a thing as a political "product" at the US presidential level, then personality is its core feature. But the process, the intense pressure and scrutiny of the campaign itself does also expose certain key truths about a candidate and candidacy that were hitherto invisible.

Offerings Compared: Kerry and Bush

The 2004 US presidential election was a contest between two members of America's political elite, one of whom was successfully self-cast as "down home," the candidate "would you split a beer with" test. On the other hand, there was a failure to ignite imagery of a softer, gentler Kerry. He emerged as a driven man but the resulting attacks should have been anticipated. The relaxedness of Bush contrasted with the unrelaxedness of Kerry. A public Kerry emerged who appeared to many—by no means was this a universal judgment—a tedious, agonized, cerebral patrician. People spoke of a "charisma deficit." Consequently, Kerry represented (that is, was perceived as) an "offering" that was not sure about its value to the electorate. A vote is a vote "for," but it is also of course a vote "against." The balance between the two is dependent on the electoral context and on the offerings. Voters were not sure what Kerry really believed in, what he was about. The ambiguities of Kerry's career—war hero, but also anti-war protester—made them ask who or what was the "real" Kerry? Here was a character too complex for political purposes; the "rambling," "nuanced" old Kerry[21] and an offering without clear value proposition. It can be argued that this was partly a result of his wishing to appear all things to all people, that is, resembling a fully differentiated targeting strategy with contradicting segment offerings. Kerry appeared to offer no self-explanation, no "narrative" holding his offering as a persona together. He appeared to "think what he was saying, not saying what he felt."

Bush on the other hand epitomised the "permanent campaign." Bush's unreflective self-confidence, his "golf persona," cohere with US values. His lack of nuance was interpreted as evidence of authenticity. Bush appeared also "tough"[22] and a conviction politician, a leader. In political market exchanges we are in fact "buying" a relationship.[23] It is therefore not only credibility but attractiveness that is important, and the basis of attractiveness is similarity. The candidate enters into an imagined social relationship with the citizens, a personalized conversation with the voter. This election was hence the story of two contrasting brands, known and unknown: the one cheerful/common/unintellectual, the other dour/elite/cerebral (objectively of course such extraneous dimensions of personality should be irrelevant to the job description, but whoever said democracy was, or ought to be, rational).

Coherent Narrative

The election affirmed the importance of consistency and coherence in a candidate's record and public case. Clarity is a political asset in a campaign (ambiguity a cost), and Bush presented a coherent narrative to American voters.[24] Pennington and Hastie have demonstrated how important this is in persuasion, that is, how we make sense of things and interpret them.[25] For example, they show how jurors make sense of confusing realities by weaving them into a narrative. The same has been demonstrated in organizational settings. Bush was "strong"—an important quality in presidential candidates—in the limited sense that he was consistent and also coherent. Kerry by contrast offered a fragmented, incoherent, even contradictory story. This is a case of offering and consequently message coherence and clear differentiating dimensions: Kerry's was an indeterminate brand offering, a vague definition product with unclear services rendered.[26] The "flip-flop" charge proved to be Kerry's Achilles heel (epitomized by Kerry's "windsurfing" as used metaphorically by the Republicans in their ads): he voted for the Iraq war and therefore could not credibly convert this war (or the general "war against terror") into political capital. In particular his tortured, tortuous explanation—"I voted for the bill before I voted against it"—was turned by Republicans into an attack advertisement and his alibi for his

Iraq war votes featured in a Republican National Committee website documentary.[27] The analogy is with a product whose core functions and value-in-use are obscure.

Political Marketing Mix: Product (2)—The Salience of Value(s)

Any consumer product or service, any offering is not just utilitarian, the sum of its functions. It is something more: a social expression and therefore a value articulation. Does it cohere with current social norms, or capture some ephemeral public mood? Is the offering upgraded to track these values as they change or erode? If this is true of the classical consumer offering, how much more can the same be said of the political offering? People are not just looking for technical competence, or technical solutions to political issues. This explains much seemingly extracurricular matter in American political conflict such as the battles over the abortion laws. Thus, one Bush advertisement asked "whether Kerry's priority on abortion issues are yours?" adding that Kerry "voted against parental notification."[28] Values are part of the political offering—voters seek affirmation and many political issues are issues simply because of their value symbolism. A politician therefore "sells" value affirmation.

Marketing is concerned with exchanges that are facilitated by value transactions. Consumer products in comparison do not "do" values except in the most general and attenuated sense as with for example "Fair Trade" campaigns. However, the specific value embedded in a political offering is often linked to a more general system of "values," that is, general normative belief patterns. Critical to the US presidential election in 2004 was the question of such values, their symbolization aspects and the role of the non-negotiable absolutes. For Amitai Etzioni values are the great mobilizing force of modern politics[29] after cleavage structures have lost their hold on the electorate, and liberal intellectuals (and political marketers) ignore their salience in voter decision processes at their peril.

Notions of a rational voter lead merely to a rented allegiance and not the creation of converts: "it's the economy stupid" was a winning formula for Clinton but the election under question exposed the limitations of this nostrum.[30] A US presidential election is always, *inter alia*, a referendum on values. Thus, value stances are a core part of the presidential job specification since a key role of the president is, and to an extent has always been, to articulate normative values— what we believe as a people—as a force for cohesion in a highly individualistic and pluralist society. Much success in political marketing arises not just from the creation of image or perceived competence, but from the ability to express majoritarian ideals lucidly (Reagan's ability to achieve just that springs to mind). More specifically, the mobilization against Kerry represented a replay of some aspects of the "culture wars" of the 1960s but if anything partisanship this time was magnified by the legacy of the more recent "value civil wars" and related ideological fissures over issues such as abortion.

To exemplify the point, choosing just one topic: all this is pre-eminently true of gay marriage. Part of the value package conservative American politicians expect to "market" is that marriage is for men and women ("God created Adam and Eve not Adam and Steve"). The issue was of particular salience to the minority Christian Right: would it also be salient to a majority of voters? In 2004 it indeed became a very public issue: the Massachusetts Supreme Court had legalized same sex marriage in November 2003, and on July 14, 2004, the Senate rejected the Federal Marriage Amendment.[31] The election became a referendum on moral values though there was (ostensibly) no pre-existing Republican master plan to do this. No pundit foresaw the impact the gay marriage issue would make. The unpredictable can gatecrash the election agenda and force-feed its themes into the campaign. Gay marriage shot to the top of the political agenda with an onrush of images of exuberant gay weddings. Yet some issue stands are (or can be turned into) value markers, and gay marriage was one such issue. They serve not only as a powerful cue but also as a *pars pro toto*: general ideological or value distinctions are represented in one (dominant) particular issue (or offering component). The mobilization of the Christian Right generated an extra four million (critical) extra voters who had stayed home in 2000.[32] Perhaps self-mobilization would be a more accurate term. They had been persuaded that Bush spoke for them.

As a group they had a strong collective identity and they voted only on value issues. Such politicized Christianity is not unique to the US but the pervasiveness of its influence probably is. Thus, the Bush decision to support a constitutional amendment banning gay marriage (on February 24, 2004, two weeks after a series of legalized gay weddings in San Francisco had received national publicity) proved critical. The issue of same sex marriage was then cunningly placed on the poll ballot in thirteen states.[33] For the political consultant and theorist Tony Schwartz[34] "resonance" is the main, indeed the only, quality that a political commercial should strive for. Gay marriage resonated, striking many as an attack on core American values, its way of life, in ways that comfort issues such as a national health service or the continuity of income tax simply did not.

The experience of the 2004 US presidential campaign thus also emphasized the importance in politics of non-economically based voter decision making, challenging the force of much that has been written on the rational choice model in this area.[35] The catastrophe of the Iraq war with its stream of morbid news, or the fact that Bush had presided over the highest rate of increase in joblessness in seventy years, were not the most persuasive arguments for American voters in 2004. This election at least exposed the limitations of the economic appeal and the anachronism of such earlier American campaign nostrums as "are you better off now than you were four years ago?" Irrelevant also were new ideas, new policies. Voters wanted reassurance and the triumph of old certitudes.

Political Marketing Mix: Promotion

527 Communication

Another phenomenon we would like to highlight in our discussion of the political marketing mix as part of the chapter of the 2004 US presidential election is the colonization of this campaign and especially the communication arena by political "immigrants," that is, non-traditional political actors and organizations. The "external" so-called 527 groups were the *sotto voce* of the election, deflecting opprobrium for negative campaigning away from the candidates. Such groups are ostensibly unconnected to the campaign and therefore not bound by campaign finance rules.

Much of the work of political marketing practitioners is less than dignified. Fundamentally, it may involve deprecating the rival brand but the danger here is that one self-incriminates. The merit of 527s is that they do this work without monetary or ethical and reputational cost for the campaign (or it is at least believed that this would be the case). There is no analogy to this in consumer or business marketing campaigns, which are ordinarily a unitary effort by a single company. Consumer marketing campaigns for example may lie, but they do not libel. Thus, "The Swift Boat ads—a first round charging that Kerry had lied to win his medals, then a second batch accusing him of betraying his mates by calling them war criminals—were misleading, but they were very effective."[36] Similarly, but this time assisting Kerry, the "Texans for Truth" showed an ex-National Guard officer questioning Bush's military service record in Alabama.[37]

Advertising Content: Negativity

Comparative (negative) advertising exists on the margin of consumer marketing and as a strategy it is perceived as high risk/high reward. The fear on the part of many businesses is that if they deploy this (if it is legal in their specific markets), they will degrade the collective image of their entire industry and eventually suffer, whatever short-term gains the individual comparative campaign might have gained for them. By contrast, in politics comparative (and especially what has come to be known as negative or attack) advertising has come to be the paradigm of choice among political campaigners. Negativity may even on occasion become an index of political virility, and the quality of the campaign is implicitly viewed, probably erroneously, as a surrogate indicator of leadership competence. The 2004 US election confirmed the remorseless advance of negative polemic in American campaigning. In the two main waves of new advertisement launches (April/May and October), ads focusing on the opponent outnumbered ads focusing on the position of the actual candidate by 3 to 1.[38] The course of the campaign affirmed the relevance of the social anthropologist Mary Douglas's insight into the nature of persuasion, that is, that we define ourselves via what we stand against rather than what we stand for.[39] In 2004, 75% of George Bush advertisements were negative and the inference was that this had been "the most negative and most expensive air wars in political history."[40]

Politicians, campaign managers and citizens claim to resent negative campaigns but these are perceived to be usually effective. Stephen Ansolabehere and Shanto Iyengar[41] point out that negative advertising works powerfully for Republicans (it confirms their essentially misanthropic world view), and it shrinks and polarizes the electorate and reinforces political partisanship. As such, it freezes out the political center and yet paradoxically does actually educate voters in campaign issues.

In 2004 there were two presidential campaigns: the official one, which was still subject to constraints and unwritten conventions (for example, the Republican "wolf" advertisement on the terrorist menace that was a rehash of the "bear" advertisement of the Reaganite cold war or the use by Republicans of apocalyptic World Trade Center imagery).[42] Second, the unofficial campaign, in which rules and ethical considerations were marginal. Here the abovementioned 527 groups' advertisements were remorseless in their intensity. Their polemical advertising themes focused on for example:

> *Shock*: a U.S. infantryman with a stump in place of an arm, from "Operation Truth";
> *Tragedy*: MoveOn.org featured a grieving mother who had lost her son in Iraq;
> *Anger*: Progress for America featured images of Bin Laden and terrorists; the 9/11 attacks were remembered via the phrase "Would you trust Kerry?" In "Quagmire" MoveOn.org shows an actor as a soldier sinking into sand.
> *Fear*: "Win Back Respect" created commercials warning of a return to the draft.[43]

The main political media in the United States has now become, at least in presidential campaigns, 15–30-second attack advertising spots. The context in which they appear is thus straight consumer advertising: a typical ad sequence for viewers might be: diapers, washing up liquid, presidential candidate, home insurance. Like all other forms of advertising these political ads face two problems: (1) to be noticed; and (2) to be remembered. They must strive to distinguish themselves from the contextual clutter. Advertising is (often if not usually) a delicate balancing act, for it can neither consistently violate nor uncritically replicate social norms.

In politics negativity is often prevalent. These negative or attack ads by 527 organizations work because they break through the "noise" of other forms of commercial solicitation.[44] The significance of these "commercials" sometimes lies not so much in the immediate, and often local, audience exposure to them but in their mass media replication, that is, the alacrity with which television news recreates them as a political "story," thus ensuring high visibility and making them into "election news" that is transmitted to the voters. Besides any "direct" effect of political advertising, the 2004 US presidential election highlighted the ever more prominent (or dominant) impact of "mediated" advertising: that is, advertising that is not meant to work directly but that is meant to create a news story. This news-management multiplies its reach, gives it credibility by piggy-bagging on a credible source medium, and provides it with a rich network of associations within the election campaign: thus the *Newsweek* team describe the progress through the American media of the "Swift Boat Veterans" advertising campaign:

> The old-fashioned mainstream press was ignoring the claims of the Swifties, but on Fox News, the "fair and balanced" cable network whose viewership was roughly 80% pro-Bush, the Swifties were getting plenty of air time. And not just on Fox . . . the Swifties had brought only a few hundred thousand dollars' worth of ads, but each played over and over—free—on the cable channels, CNN and MSNBC as well as Fox. The Swift Boat charges were the source of constant debate in the blogosphere.[45]

Impact of Political Advertising

In general political advertising constitutes a signaling or telegraphy device: what is the core of the candidate's case, the essence of his/her image, the key issue positions? The aim is to be invasive, to colonize the attention of the "turned off," that is, low involvement citizen.[46] They achieve this by eschewing any rational advocacy and appealing to emotion in its most visceral and elemental form, a strategy employed in the commercial as well as the political sphere.[47] Thus,

> The sound of laughter at a media dinner as a tuxedo-clad President Bush makes light of the search for Iraqi weapons gives way to the plaintive voice of Brooke Campbell describing what happened thirty-six days later. "My brother died in Baghdad on April 29," she says. "I watched President Bush make a joke, looking around for weapons of mass destruction. My brother died looking for weapons of mass destruction." The intensity of the Georgia woman's lament, in a television ad being financed by "MoveOn" political action committee (PAC) is matched by that of Ashley Faulkner, whose mother was killed in the 2001 World Trade Center attack. "He's the most powerful man in the world, and all he wants to do is make sure I'm safe," the Ohio teenager says in an ad from the Progress for America Voter Fund. The spot shows a still photo of a choked-up president hugging her.[48]

Political Marketing Mix: Packaging

Judicious attention to symbolism was another aspect of Bush and his permanent campaign before and during the actual election. These symbols were only part of the carnival; critical too was the generation of the "tableaux"—vividly arranged, emotionally charged public imagery such as the "mission accomplished" arrival on the flight deck of the USS *Abraham Lincoln*[49] or Bush's unheralded appearance at an army Baghdad Christmas dinner. Symbolism took center stage after 9/11, e.g. in the "dead or alive" poster the dollar bills for Afghan children stuffed into envelopes by American kids, or the firemen raising the flag in imitation of Iwo Jima.[50] The newly emergent symbol system stressed pugnacity, such as the rows of square-jawed warriors as backdrops to Bush perorations, or the massive American eagle decorating the command center in Qatar. This stage set had actually been designed by Hollywood art director George Allison at a cost of $200,000.[51] Monetary cost was not a consideration. The landing on USS *Abraham Lincoln*, with "commander in chief" inscribed beneath the cockpit and the huge "mission accomplished" banner, cost even more: $1 million.[52] The emerging methodology of image management was not of course perfect and there were occasional lapses of image control, as with the leaked image of flag-draped coffins in serried ranks aboard a giant cargo plane.

The Bush-era's self-presentation condensed into a set of rhetorical formulae. Republican linguistic strategies that could be summarized in Victor Klemperer's phrase as "*language which thinks for you.*[53] There was now a distinct new rhetorical currency employing words such as "freedom." Thus, symbolic packaging and imagery were critical to the Republican strategy. Symbols of inclusion were central to this approach. To proclaim their "broad tent" credentials at the stage-managed convention, their "liberals" (George Pataki, Rudolph Giuliani, Arnold Schwarzenegger) were all on show. Similarly "in 2004 the Bush/Cheney campaign website had a page titled 'Compassion' devoted mainly to photos of the president with black people, Colin Powell included."[54]

In fact, writing in *Time* magazine, the journalist Joe Klein appeared to suggest that packaging was the essence of the Bush political ethos—not one instrument of governing but the core art, and certainly not followed up with actual offering (policy) implementation.[55] For example "there are grand pronouncements and, yes, crusades, punctuated with marching words like evil and moral and freedom."[56] Thus, "Bush opposed a department of home security, then supported it as a campaign ploy—and then allowed it to be slapped together carelessly . . ." while "the White House proposed a massive Medicare prescription-drug plan and then flat out mis-represented the true cost."[57] Similar criticisms applied to the war in Iraq, its inception, conduct and attempted termination.

Political Marketing Strategy

After having elaborated on some of the political marketing mix variables that specifically characterize the 2004 US presidential election campaign, the focus of this chapter's analysis is now on the strategic aspects of the campaign. In the following, strategic electioneering aspects such as rebuttal capabilities, segmentation and targeting, but also the strategic employment of guerrilla marketing will be highlighted. In consumer marketing the strategy gives structure, coherence and focus to the marketing activities but in the absence of an imagined strategy there is a default strategy, which implies becoming the victim of circumstances. It would be simplistic to say that in this election the Bush people had a working strategy and the Kerry people did not. But the Bush people had a much clearer strategic marketing orientation, and they had a covert as well as an overt strategy.

Failure to Anticipate

One lesson in presidential marketing strategy that this 2004 election illuminates is in particular the need for candidates to fully think out strategically their areas of vulnerability well before the beginning of the campaign. Kerry naturally began the campaign by vaunting his war record, making the contrast between him and Bush implicit, saluting the Democrat Convention as he told them that he was "reporting for duty." The imagery was contrived to suggest the Swift Boat (and JFK?) connection, with Kerry arriving in Washington by boat, and a vaguely nautical convention set with a phalanx of old comrades in arms. Later in the convention even admirals were to join them.[58] But he was vulnerable through the inherent contradiction in his Vietnam–era role, and his post-service militant peace activism that effectively negated the value of that service in the eyes of many.

Political campaigns—including this one—often fail to gauge the innate plasticity (or ambiguity) of symbolism. Meaning is always negotiated, and we can never foreordain the interpretation of symbols. Hence the fiasco of Michael Dukakis's "Snoopy helmet" tank journey[59] and of Kerry's athletic windsurfing. Thus, the "Swift Boat Veterans" set their trap[60] and Kerry had no strategic rebuttal. These fraudulent claims were celebrated by the "new" media. Their later exposure by the "old" media was judicious but frankly irrelevant. Thus, the Bush campaign and its acolytes systematically sabotaged Kerry's veteran posture and strategy, taking attention not only away from Bush's non-participation in the war but also from that mysterious "missing year" as well as the Killian report (which claimed Bush to have been derelict of duty during his Air National Guard time, a claim that later was shown to be inauthentic).[61] The Republican achievement was to make Kerry's heroism an issue while neutralizing the record of their own candidate.

The enigma of the campaign is the question why Kerry, like Dukakis against another George Bush, failed to hit back. Such an attack should have been anticipated, there should have been capabilities existent in his campaign organizations that would allow him to instantaneously deal with the threat (and maybe even turn it to his advantage). That such strategic capability (for example, something like the UK Labour Party's "Excalibur" database for rebuttal purposes)[62] did not exist was a strategic blunder. It was a failure of Kerry's campaign managers,[63] a failure in his strategic political marketing management. His advisors' and experts' passivity harmed their candidate. According to Evan Thomas and his colleagues staffers Robert Shrum and Mary Beth Cahill advised a "dignified" silence whereas Kerry's pollster Mark Mellman was more nervous and indeed polls began to dip. Dukakis had assumed a similar mute dignity in the face of defamatory Republican advertising in 1988.[64] This suggests at some level a failure of Democrat campaign managers to understand a core element of their native political and social culture, its civic aggression.

Renaissance of Targeting

Another strategic marketing issue is related to targeting: this campaign saw a re-affirmation of this old campaign discipline.[65] The targeting of political advertising was parsimonious and precise, and in the right places—the key state of Ohio for example was a prime target for campaign activities (targets were mainly the "swing states," defined by a winning margin of less than three percentage points in the 2000 presidential election). There were half a million airings in three to six states (with the consequence that 60% of all voters nationwide were virtually excluded from any exposure to political television commercials). An example of the intensity of this targeting was Santa Fe, New Mexico: voters there received 5,000 airings of the commercials from September 24 to October 2, 2004.[66] The role of doorstep campaigning (that is, micro-targeting) was also re-affirmed. Furthermore, the uses of the Internet as a targeting device in this campaign were also intriguing even if they were not critical to victory or defeat. The Howard Dean candidacy in particular was largely governed by the Internet but Dean also exposed its limitations since it emerged as a vehicle for minority partisanship, not the solicitation of a national following.[67]

Strategic Guerrilla Marketing

Much of the perceptual engineering that enters a presidential campaign and its run-up would be enlisted in consumer marketing under the once vogue heading of "guerrilla marketing"[68]: everything from the "pre-campaign campaign" to the staging of "faction" events reported by the media under the ostensible appearance of authenticity, but in fact planned and packaged. But some of what is done would be merely inflammatory—or illegal—in the non-political circumstances of consumer marketing. For example, the *New York Times* exposed the supposedly US-made boxes of goods that were the backdrop to a Bush speech had their "Made in China" stickers pasted over.[69]

Guerrilla marketing is a relatively recent genre and represents the attempt to get attention by bypassing orthodox marketing channels and methodologies. The consumer is surprised, even ambushed, into giving product claims a hearing. However, political campaigns go beyond this, and the 2004 case example of the US presidential election showed how this was used in a strategic way. The principal campaigns accommodated their own pseudo-terrorist wing as part of their campaign organization, who were doing everything from pasting the image of Kerry into a photograph of "Hanoi" Jane Fonda at an anti-Vietnam war rally, to spreading rumors in Bush's initial run for the Republican nomination in 1999 that Senator McCain had fathered a black child via a prostitute.[70]

The Bush campaign also brought in its wake an army of partisan and Internet-literate camp followers ready to assault any of Bush's media-domiciled critics. When CBS apparently surfaced a contemporary document exposing Bush's unofficial absence from his Air Guard squadron, the CBS producer Mary Mapes found that "within a few minutes, I was visiting web sites I had never heard of: Free Republic, Little Green Footballs, Power Line. They were hard-core, politically angry, hyper-conservative sites, loaded with vitriol about Dan Rather and CBS."[71] In the same vein, "the White House had sent out talking points about how to attack Brent Scowcroft after Bush the Elder's National Security Adviser went public with his opposition to the war in *New York* magazine."[72] Ultimately, it becomes more difficult to see the marketing parallel as such communications, based on the strategic use of guerrilla marketing, morph into propaganda by this stage.

The attempts at guerrilla marketing were a disposable tool to be used and then discarded within a strategic framework, representing the attempt to create a "for the moment" fleeting public impression whose later exposure would be ignored by most of the relevant publics. In fact, many of these assertions were exposed. Thus, *New York Times* columnist Frank Rich:

> When an army commander had troops sign 500 identical good-news form letters to local news-papers throughout America in 2003, the fraud was so transparent it was almost instantly debunked. The fictional scenarios concocted for Jessica Lynch and Pat Tillman also unravelled quickly, as did last weekend's Pentagon account of ten marines killed outside Fallujah on a "routine foot patrol."[73]

But such exposés did little political damage until the post-Hurricane Katrina context brought forward a new, more publicly sullied image of Bush, where both the competence and the integrity of this presidency became more publicly contested.

Part of this process of guerrilla marketing was of course the creation of a climate of fear and in the eyes of some critics a concomitant fabrication of crisis: according to Frank Rich:

> Keith Olbermann of MSNBC recently compiled thirteen "coincidences" in which a "political downturn for the administration" from revelations of ignored pre-9/11 terror warnings to fresh news of detainee abuse, is followed by a "terror event"—a change in alert status, an arrest, a warning.[74]

In the words of one commentator: "What sets Bush apart is not the crises he managed but the crises he fabricated."[75]

Explaining 2004: Political Marketing and the Psychology of Persuasion

The previous sections provided a selective description of the 2004 US presidential election by looking at characteristic phenomena of the framing market context, the use of political marketing instruments, as well as some strategic peculiarities. Throughout, concepts of political marketing were explicitly or implicitly used to structure this description. However, it is neces-sary to further integrate the descriptive findings within an analytical section that crystalizes and condenses points of departure for further insights that also point to resulting research issues in political marketing as well as comparisons with "traditional" political science studies of the same campaign. We will focus in the following on two aspects that we believe need further elucidation because they may become more prevalent in future election campaigns, also outside the United States.

Fantasies and Myths

Political persuasion, it can be argued, may rest on an invitation to share a fantasy, where voters and citizens become co-conspirators in their own self-deceit.[76] The notion of people willingly misled strikes at the root of notions of humans as (ir)rational decision makers, yet that is what arguably happened in this specific election campaign. For example, the existence of weapons of mass destruction or a Hussein–Bin Laden link were conclusively disproved. However, voters were reluctant to unlearn what they had become pre-committed to: they had accepted an invitation that they could easily have rejected. This may point toward an important analogy: consumer marketing—and particularly advertising—sometimes rests less on overt didacticism than on the similar co-production of fantasy: the consumer is not harangued into acceptance, but seduced into a reverie of possession and possibility. Many critics of marketing too easily assume therefore a naive consumer.[77] However, more sophisticated perspectives give us notions of the consumer as knowing and consciously led. For example, an earlier study by O'Shaughnessy of "green" labeling of detergents suggested that many consumers accepted that such labels were often essentially bogus but still bought the product because they valued the fact that the issue was being addressed even at the symbolic level.[78] People had invested emotional capital in a proposition that had been knowingly falsified.

By analogy, when they wished to believe in Bush, they merely filtered out all the negative propaganda. Political spaces are an edited realm in voters' consciousness, for they see what they want to see. Political "realities" are co-produced (a characteristic of essentially every service offering). In effect what we witnessed in the American political marketplace of 2004 can be subsumed under what in the physical sciences is known as the "polarization effect": the anger of his Democrat critics would simply solidify and not undermine the Bush powerbase. Examples of the success of the myth-making apparatus of the Bush presidency in selling fictions as established facts to the American public include for example reports that

1. 72% of Bush supporters believed Iraq had weapons of mass destruction; 75% of Bush supporters believed that Iraq was providing support to al Qaeda.[79]
2. Bush had convinced Americans that the US was pursuing war against the right enemy in the right place; indeed, 42% of Americans thought Saddam was personally responsible for 9/11.[80]

Meta Strategy: The Permanent Campaign Revisited

For journalist Joe Klein, all of the faults and problems of the 2004 US presidential campaign can be attributed to one conceptual foundation—the idea of the permanent campaign, first espoused by Carter's pollster Pat Caddell in 1976, and probed by Sidney Blumenthal in his analysis of the presidency of Ronald Reagan and by degrees elevated to the commanding orthodoxy of US government.[81] (See Chapter 7, by David Dulio and Terri L. Towner on the permanent campaign.) Klein criticized the "tendency of [Karl] Rove's message apparatus to see war as part of the permanent campaign."[82] Thus, congressional endorsement of the attack on Iraq, and earlier reference to the UN, were sought in light of polling data (that is, political market research). The war was first a rhetorical opportunity to be seized and then an embarrassing fact to be massaged.

The institutionalization of the permanent campaign is of particular relevance to the Bush triumph in 2004. The idea is that the tools used to conduct office are identical to those used to gain it:[83] political marketing essentially as campaigning, a radical departure from traditional practice (and a radical departure from marketing theory that perceives service delivery, that is, the implementation of promises, to be the most pivotal marketing aspect of services offerings). While many consumer marketing campaigns are also "permanent," the parallel is however an inexact one. The marketing of a government is the marketing of a highly complex offering whose communication channels one can influence but—unlike the case of consumer product marketing—not control. The demarcation between government and electioneering does not disappear within a permanent campaign but it is much reduced. In consequence government is seen in an entirely different way, as a means to the end of winning the next election and everything therefore is subordinate to the needs of communication and political marketing activity. Policies, political actions and politicians may be chosen not for their relevance but for their rhetorical resonance as part of a reductionist political marketing perspective.

Much of what is exemplified by the 2004 US presidential campaign does however transcend the domain of political marketing, and political marketing theory at some stage must become conceptually inadequate as a descriptor. For example, post-election exposures of the methodology of Bush's permanent campaign included that of the "journalist" and male prostitute James Guckert (aka Jeff Gannon) planted at White House briefings to ask favorable questions. Then there was the effective bribing of conservative television journalist Armstrong Williams.[84] According to the New York Times: "The agencies spent a whopping $88 million spinning reality in 2004, splurging on PR contracts."[85] There was also the creation of pre-packaged "news" videos:

> The auditors denounced a pre-packaged television story disseminated by the education department. The segment, a "video news release" narrated by a woman named Karen Ryan, said that President Bush's program for providing remedial instruction and tutoring to children "gets an A-plus." Ms Ryan also narrated two videos praising the new Medicare drug benefit last year.[86]

Thus, the story of this election does not begin with the campaign proper but with the entire history of the George Bush permanent campaign from 2000 and indeed before. The focus of much research in political marketing and political science on the phenomenon of campaign therefore needs to be revisited. Furthermore, campaigns have to be seen as consisting not of objective activities and tools but of subjective interpretations and perspectives. A part of the permanent campaign process was about the right to interpret, and with this came prohibition: "This highly secretive White House has also tried to circumvent the mainstream press by limiting reporters' access, keeping President Bush's press conferences to a minimum and going over the head of the national media to local outlets."[87] The administration seemed to some observers to be creating its own parallel universe of positive imagery and rhetorical uplift, something that also characterizes commercial marketing campaigns, but an idiom that is dangerous when applied so radically to politics. Thus, one of Bush's advisors "dismissed a reporter he was talking to as a member of the 'reality-based community,'" a supposedly obsolete life-form given the aide's assertion that "we're an empire now, and when we act, we create our own reality."[88]

New York Times columnist Frank Rich spoke of "an alternative reality built on spin and outright lies."[89] With this comes the phenomenon of the institutionalization of "spin" (arguably an ill-defined concept) which is an important characteristic of the permanent campaign. For the veteran commentator Walter Lippmann, whose Washington experience was to span most of the twentieth century, what really mattered in public life was not the fact but the received public idea of the fact,[90] and this understanding is in our conceptualization the essence of the concept of spin. Events have loose texture: they can always be opened up to fresh interpretation, so persuasion is the political skill. For example, the successful attribution of blame to others is clearly critical in politics and an example of this art of "spin." Events of the Bush era could have received a very different interpretation. 9/11 itself, the reason Bush was re-elected, could have been a disaster, an indictment of gross incompetence—of warnings missed, of ignorance, of miniature attention spans. It would be plausible to argue that two ostensibly very different events, 9/11 and the post-election Hurricane Katrina disaster, illuminate exactly the same set of weaknesses in his regime. Yet 9/11 was in popularity terms a triumph, and even now nobody really associates the two events together as a unitary symbol of ineptitude. 9/11 was successfully blamed, in so far it was blamed, on the previous (Clinton) regime.

Conclusion

In general, in 2004 contextual factors relevant for the political marketing campaign were heavily weighted toward Bush; his managers also exhibited a deft conceptual understanding and pragmatic applied management of the concept of the perpetual political marketing campaign. The success of the real campaign has therefore to be explained in terms of the effectiveness of the pre-campaign; but it was also bolstered by key strategic marketing errors on Kerry's part, particularly the military-heroic posture which, since he had been also war anti-hero as well as hero, lacked authenticity and was perceived as such. Subsequently, the use of political marketing deteriorated on occasions into ruthless pursuit of enemies. Via smart use of these marketing instruments and the "art of the advocate" George Bush overcame critical flaws in his record. There were of course serious defects in Kerry's public case (that is, his "offering" to the voters and donors). The Bush people and his retinue were, we maintain, more effective advocates and, specifically, more effective political marketers.

This 2004 US presidential election illustrated how a politician can still win office in spite of the disasters he is persuasively accused of, at least by some, presiding over: Bush survived a vitriolic and global propaganda campaign against him that was external to the election. Media phenomena such as Jib-Jab.com or the "documentary" *Farenheit 9/11* are just some examples of the adverse environment Bush faced in his re-election endeavor. The irony of the presidential campaign in 2004, as we have discussed, was that the war hero was made the villain, the war dodger was enabled to proceed through the campaign exuding moral superiority. Later events that seriously exposed the social character of his government (the Iraq occupation, Hurricane Katrina, Scooter Libby) lay in the future and are therefore not a template by which we should judge this campaign.

Notes

1 G. Smith, "The 2001 General Election: Factors Influencing the Brand Image of Political Parties and their Leaders," *Journal of Marketing Management* 17 (2001): 989–1006.

2 Bob Franklin, *Packaging Politics* (London: Edward Arnold, 1994); Bruce I. Newman, *The Mass Marketing of Politics: Democracy in an Age of Manufactured Images* (Thousand Oaks, CA: Sage Publications, 1999).

3 Sheldon Rampton and John Stauber, *Weapons of Mass Deception: the Uses of Propaganda in Bush's War on Iraq* (New York: Tarcher/Penguin, 2003).

4 *New York Times*, March 26, 2005.

5 Rampton and Stauber, *Weapons of Mass Deception*.

6 Kathleen Hall Jamieson, *Packaging the Presidency: A History and Criticism of Presidential Campaign Advertising*, 2nd ed. (New York: Oxford University Press, 1992); Franklin, *Packaging Politics*.

7 Evan Thomas and *Newsweek* staff, *Election 2004* (New York: Public Affairs, 2004).

8 Craig Crawford, *Attack the Messenger* (New York: Rowman & Littlefield, 2005).

9 Rampton and Stauber, *Weapons of Mass Deception*.

10 Ibid., 176.

11 David Brock, *The Republican Noise Machine* (New York: Crown Publishing, 2004).

12 Robert R. Kennedy, *Crimes Against Nature* (New York: Harper Perennial, 2005).

13 Donald Warren, *Radio Priest: Charles Coughlin, the Father of Hate Radio* (New York: The Free Press, 1996).

14 Kennedy, *Crimes Against Nature*.

15 *USA Today*, September 27, 2004.

16 Nicholas J. O'Shaughnessy, *The Phenomenon of Political Marketing* (New York: St. Martin's Press, 1990); Kathleen Hall Jamieson, *Dirty Politics* (New York: Oxford University Press, 1992); *New York Times*, September 12, 2004.

17 Sidney Blumenthal, *The Permanent Campaign* (New York: Simon and Schuster, 1982).

18 Maureen Dowd, *New York Times*, March 9, 2003; *Guardian*, March 5, 2004; *USA Today*, September 27, 2004; Thomas et al., *Election 2004*.

19 Ronald Rapoport, Kelly L. Metcalf and Johns Hartman, "Candidate Traits and Voter Inferences: An Experiential Study," *Journal of Politics* 51 (4) (November 1989): 917–32.

20 Thomas et al., *Election 2004*.

21 Ibid.

22 *Daily Telegraph*, October 11, 2004.

23 D.P. Bannon, "Relationship Marketing and the Political Process," *Journal of Political Marketing* 4 (2) (2005): 85–102.

24 Linda Colley, *Guardian*, September 27, 2004; Errol Morris, *New York Times*, January 18, 2005.

25 N. Pennington and R. Hastie, "A Theory of Explanation-based Decision Making," in *Decision Making in Action: Models and Methods*, ed. C. Klein, J. Orasanu, R. Calderwood and C.E. Zsambok (Norwood, N.J.: Ablex, 1993).

26 S.L. Vargo and R.F. Lusch, "Evolving to a New Dominant Logic for Marketing," *Journal of Marketing* 68 (1) (2004): 1–17.

27 Thomas et al., *Election 2004*.

28 *USA Today*, September 27, 2004.

29 Noted in O'Shaugnessy, *The Phenomenon of Political Marketing*.

30 Bruce I. Newman, "Image-manufacturing in the USA: Recent U.S. Presidential Elections and Beyond," *European Journal of Marketing* 35 (9) (2001): 966–70.

31 *Washington Post*, November 8, 2004.

32 Ibid.

33 Ibid.

34 Tony Schwartz, *The Responsive Chord* (New York: Basic Books, 1973).

35 J. Bartle and D. Griffiths, "Social-psychological, Economic and Marketing Models of Voting Behaviour Compared," in *The Idea of Political Marketing*, ed. N. J. O'Shaughnessy and S. C. Henneberg (Westport, CT: Praeger, 2002), 19–37.

36 Thomas et al., *Election 2004*, 176. However, it transpired in this specific case that the 527 group involved was not fully independent of the Republican campaign: Bush's leading lawyer Benjamin Ginsberg had contacts with the Swift Boat Veterans and had to resign when these contact became known.

37 *USA Today*, September 27, 2004.

38 Stanford University Political Communication Lab, http://pcl.stanford.edu/campaigns/campaign2004/archive.html. Accessed June 2, 2006.

39 Mary Douglas, *Natural Symbols* (New York: Pantheon Books, 1982).

40 Thomas et al., *Election 2004*.

41 Stephen Ansolabehere and Shanto Iyengar, *Going Negative: How Political Advertisements Shrink and Polarize the Electorate* (New York: Free Press, 1995).

42 Thomas et al., *Election 2004; USA Today*, September 27, 2004.

43 *USA Today*, September 27, 2004.

44 *New York Times*, October 17, 2004.

45 Thomas et al., *Election 2007*, 114–15.

46 Bernard B. Berelson, Paul F. Lazarsfeld and William N. McPhee, *Voting: A Study of Opinion Formation in a Presidential Campaign* (Chicago, IL: University of Chicago Press, 1954); Michael X. Delli Carpini, "In Search of the Informed Citizen: What Americans Know About Politics and Why it Matters," The Pew Charitable Trust, Paper presented at the *Transformation of Civic Life* Conference, (Nashville, Tenn., 1999).

47 Ansolabehere and Iyengar, *Going Negative*; B. Shiv and A. Fredorikhin, "Heart and Mind in Conflict: The Interplay of Affect and Cognition in Consumer Decision Making," *Journal of Consumer Research* 26 (1999): 278–92.

48 Howard Kurtz, *Washington Post*, October 26, 2004.

49 Rampton and Stauber, *Weapons of Mass Deception*.

50 *New York Times*, October 11 and 14, 2001; *Daily Telegraph*, January 16, 2002.

51 *Guardian*, March 26, 2003.
52 Rampton and Stauber, *Weapons of Mass Deception*.
53 Victor Klemperer, *The Language of the Third Reich* (London: Athlone Press, 2000).
54 Frank Rich, *New York Times*, September 18, 2005.
55 *Time*, November 7, 2004.
56 Frank Rich, *New York Times*, October 30, 2005.
57 Klein, *Time*, November 7, 2004.
58 Thomas et al., *Election 2004*.
59 O'Shaughnessy, *The Phenomenon of Political Marketing*; Jamieson, *Packaging the Presidency*.
60 *New York Times*, September 12, 2004.
61 Terry McAuliffe (head of the Democratic National Committee) actually claimed that these documents may have been created by the White House campaign itself as a smokescreen to discredit any information on Bush's military service (*New York Observer*, September 20, 2004).
62 Andy McCue, "Election '05: High-tech Campaigning Replaced by Fancy Databases," *Silicon.com*, April 27, 2005.
63 Thomas et al., *Election 2004*.
64 Jamieson, *Dirty Politics*.
65 McCue, "Election '05."
66 *New York Times*, October 4, 2004.
67 Nicholas J. O'Shaughnessy, *Politics and Propaganda: Weapons of Mass Seduction* (Manchester: University of Manchester Press, 2004).
68 Jay Conrad Levinson, *Guerrilla Marketing Weapons* (New York: Penguin Books, 1990).
69 *New York Times*, January 23, 2003.
70 Thomas et al., *Election 2004*.
71 Mary Mapes, "60 Minutes is Going Down." *Vanity Fair*, January 2006; extracted from Mary Mapes, *Truth and Duty* (New York: St Martin's Press, 2005), 307.
72 Joe Klein, *Time*, November 7, 2004.
73 *New York Times*, December 11, 2005.
74 Ibid.
75 Harold Meyerson, *Washington Post*, January 13, 2005.
76 O'Shaughnessy, *Politics and Propaganda*.
77 John Kenneth Galbraith, *The Affluent Society* (New York: Houghton Mifflin, 1958).
78 O'Shaughnessy, *Politics and Propaganda*.
79 *New York Times*, October 31, 2005.
80 *New York Times*–CBS survey, *New York Times*, March 9, 2003.
81 *Time*, November 7, 2004; Blumenthal, *The Permanent Campaign*.
82 *Time*, November 7, 2004.
83 Blumenthal, *The Permanent Campaign*.
84 Maureen Dowd, *New York Times*, February 17, 2005; *New York Times*, October 1, November 11, and December 23, 2005.
85 *New York Times*, March 13, 2005.
86 *New York Times*, October 1, 2005.
87 *New York Times*, November 11, 2005.
88 *New York Times*, October 30, 2005.
89 Ibid.
90 W. Lance Bennett, *News: The Politics of Illusion*, 3rd ed. (London: Longman, 1996).

15

What Drives the Cost of Political Advertising?

Robin Kolodny and Michael G. Hagen

A critical component of most political campaigns in America is television advertising. There is no doubt that television advertising costs a lot of money. But what exactly determines the cost of advertising, and does the high price affect all electoral actors similarly? This chapter addresses this question head on, using comprehensive data about television advertising in five major contests in the Philadelphia area in 2006. We open up the "black box" of political advertising pricing to explain what political actors are up against in the communications marketplace. While political campaigns are being waged, commercial interests do not recede. Therefore, decisions about purchasing political advertising require a complicated investigation of a variety of factors: what the target audience is watching; competition for the target audience; incentives from the stations to buy early or in bulk; requirements from the federal government that broadcasters make available some time for political candidates; and the competitive political environment for the individual campaigns. Our study shows that candidates indeed get a break on the price of political advertising and that political parties and interest groups need to be much more creative to have the same advertising coverage for their money.

Who Purchases Political Advertising?

Obviously candidates for office try to purchase political advertising to enhance their prospects of electoral victory. In addition, political parties and interest groups often engage in television advertising to promote the election or defeat of a particular candidate. In the case of political parties, the impetus for political advertising is to either hold on to the institution related to the contest (for example, US Congress and US Senate) or to recapture the majority from a status of being the minority. Thus, political parties are likely to advertise in the most closely contested races emphasizing any one of a variety of issues believed to be important to that set of constituents. In the case of interest groups, television advertising serves the dual purpose of enhancing the likelihood that the group's desired candidate wins while promoting the group's issue to the electorate. While these three actors are trying to influence the same race in the same media market, the prices they will pay for essentially the same product (thirty seconds of advertising time) will vary due to distinctions made between them in current law, their negotiating power with the stations, and the market in general.

194

Collecting Station Records: Philadelphia 2006

Our study takes as its point of departure previous work conducted by the Center for the Study of Elections and Democracy (CSED). For the 2006 elections, Kolodny was asked by CSED to gather information on electioneering activity in Philadelphia for two high profile races: the US Senate race in Pennsylvania and the US House race in Pennsylvania's 6th congressional district. Kolodny previously collected data for CSED studies for Pennsylvania's 13th congressional district in 1998, 2000, and 2004 races.[1] Hagen has used advertising data extensively in his work on the effects of campaigns in presidential elections.[2] We decided to pool our experience and collect station records from all the high-level competitive races in the Philadelphia media market in 2006 in an effort to develop a detailed understanding of both the exposure and cost of campaign advertising for prospective voters.

Our researchers obtained the records on political advertising from the Philadelphia affiliates of the major national broadcast networks—WPVI/ABC, WCAU/NBC, KYW/CBS, and WTXF/Fox—from two independent broadcast stations—WPHL and WPSG—and from Comcast, the major cable provider in the Philadelphia region.[3] Here, we present information from the first four major stations. We collected information about advertising sponsored by the candidates in the following five races: (1) US Senate: Rick Santorum (Republican) and Bob Casey (Democrat); (2) Pennsylvania Governor: Ed Rendell (Democrat) and Lynn Swann (Republican); (3) US House, 6th congressional district of Pennsylvania: Jim Gerlach (Republican) and Lois Murphy (Democrat); (4) US House, 7th congressional district of Pennsylvania: Curt Weldon (Republican) and Joe Sestak (Democrat); (5) US House, 8th congressional district of Pennsylvania: Mike Fitzpatrick (Republican) and Patrick Murphy (Democrat).

We also gathered information about airtime purchased by the parties and by interest groups in these races: (1) US Senate: National Republican Senatorial Committee (NRSC) (sponsored jointly with Santorum), Pennsylvania Democratic Party (sponsored jointly with Casey), American Taxpayers Alliance, Softer Voices, US Chamber of Commerce; (2) US House: National Republican Congressional Committee (NRCC), Democratic Congressional Campaign Committee (DCCC), Republican National Committee (sponsored jointly with Weldon), US Chamber of Commerce. The station records also included information about the handful of ads aired during the campaign, sponsored by the United Food and Commercial Workers, which did not target a specific race.[4]

The records that were collected differ in format from station to station, but they all contain the same basic elements. The records are of two types: confirmation contracts and invoices. Confirmation contracts, negotiated with stations by advertising agencies on behalf of sponsors, list spots scheduled to air in the future. When changes are made to a confirmation contract before the scheduled spots begin to air, as frequently occurs, a new version of the contract is created.[5] We found at least several versions of most contracts. For the analysis we report here we rely on the information available in the last available version of each confirmation contract. We obtained confirmation contracts from the 2006 political files of WPVI/ABC and WCAU/NBC.

Each confirmation contract specifies the spots purchased for a specified range of dates. The list of spots is generally organized by program, time slot, and calendar week. For each program each week, the contract lists the total number of spots to be aired, the range of dates on which they will air, the days of the week on which they will air, the class of the airtime purchased, the price per spot, and the length of the spots. Each revised contract also indicates the date on which the original contract was settled.

An invoice is printed after the last day of a contract's schedule, detailing the spots specified in that contract that were actually aired. The invoice identifies each individual spot separately, listing the date, exact airtime, scheduled time slot, length, unit price, class of airtime (for WTXF/Fox), and a brief description of the ad aired. Invoices were collected for KYW/CBS,

195

WPVI/ABC, and WTXF/Fox. Our coders entered into spreadsheets all the information available for each spot specified in each contract (for WCAU/NBC) or invoice (for the other three stations).

Paying for the Audience

Broadcast stations generate virtually all their revenue from sales to advertisers, on what is known as the "spot" television market. The prices stations charge can vary enormously, from $50 or less to $200,000 or more. Stations publish their prices on "rate cards." Rate cards change frequently (as often as weekly during election season), however, and many buyers and sellers—particularly when campaign advertising is involved—regard them only as starting points for negotiations. In practice, prices often are set in negotiations between stations and advertisers, or their representatives.[6] To the extent that the spot television market is open and competitive, prices are heavily influenced by supply and demand.

What television stations supply and advertisers demand are eyes and ears, and the opportunity to place a video and audio message in front of their target audience. By itself, without an audience, television airtime is of no value to an advertiser. Television stations should be understood to be in the business of creating audiences and selling them to advertisers. For a commercial advertiser, the audience consists of potential purchasers of goods and services; for a political campaign, of course, the audience is comprised of potential voters. Both types of advertisers want to convey their message to as many people to whom their message might appeal as possible. The price a station can charge for a spot depends on the size and character of the audience likely to be tuned in at the moment the spot airs.

Some of the elements that determine the size of the television audience in general, and therefore the price of advertising in general, have less to do with television than with the rhythms of people's everyday lives. At 5:00 a.m. on a weekday, for instance, just 15% of American households have a television on (Figure 15.1).[7] By 7:00 a.m., more than a quarter have tuned in, and the percentage hovers between 25 and 30 until 3:00 p.m. After 3:00 p.m., as children come home from school and adults come home from work, many turn on their televisions. The audience peaks at 9:00 p.m., when nearly two-thirds of American households are watching television.

The trajectory of prices typically paid over the course of the day by the 2006 campaigns in Philadelphia tracks hour-to-hour changes in the size of the television audience very closely. The median price of a thirty-second spot was lowest early in the morning, then rose to between $700 and $1,200 between 6:00 a.m. and 9:00 a.m. Prices dipped a bit during the later hours of the morning, as the workday began and the audience declined slightly. The daily jump in prices began, just as the surge in the audience began, at 3:00 p.m., though the price increase was not as sharp until 8:00 p.m., the start of prime time. The median price of a spot at 7:30 p.m. was $3,000; the median price peaked at 9:00 p.m. at $9,000. Like the audience, prices declined swiftly between 9 p.m. and 11 p.m., although it is worth noting that the median price for an ad during the late local news was $3,750, substantially higher than for the early evening newscasts at 5:00 p.m. and 6:00 p.m.

The price of prime-time advertising also varies systematically over the week, in parallel with the ebb and flow of the prime-time audience. Again, the flow of the audience reflects the competition between television and other aspects of life: the prime-time television audience is smallest on Friday and Saturday evenings, when alternative opportunities for entertainment are most readily available (Figure 15.2). Accordingly, the political campaigns in Philadelphia paid less for advertising on Friday and Saturday evenings than for any other. Ad prices on other days do not strictly parallel the size of the audience, however. The television audience is typically a bit

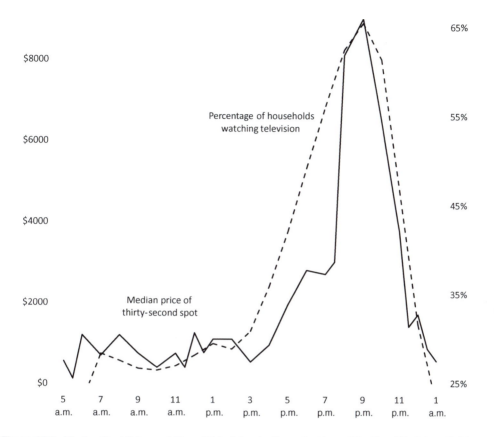

Figure 15.1. Median Spot Price and Size of Television Audience by Hour of the Day (Weekdays Only)

smaller on Thursday than earlier in the week, but ad prices were higher. The size of the overall audience obviously is not the only consideration influencing the prices campaign advertisers paid.

Day and time are necessary but not sufficient explanations for variation in the price of advertising. As everyone knows, some television programs are more popular than others. Advertisers obviously will have to pay more for a spot on a hit show than for one on other stations at the same time. Figure 15.3 displays, for instance, three pairs of spots purchased by the NRCC to air near the end of the 2006 campaign. Each pair aired almost simultaneously, on different stations. For *ER*, among the twenty most highly-rated shows on television in 2006, the NRCC paid many times the price it paid for the late evening local news on the Fox network affiliate. For *Lost*, even more highly rated than *ER*, the NRCC paid more than twice what it paid for another respectably rated entertainment show, *Jericho*.

The widest gap by far, however, was between a spot during a Philadelphia Eagles game and a NASCAR race on October 29. The price for a spot during an Eagles game is enormous in part, of course, because these games draw huge audiences in Philadelphia. What is more, they draw huge audiences of men. Because men are more likely than women to be watching television for weekend sports than at almost any other time during a week, advertisers who want to reach men pay a premium. As it happens, football fans were particularly pursued, despite their high price tag, by Pennsylvania's gubernatorial candidates in 2006—one a member of the NFL Hall of Fame (Lynn Swann) and the other employed as an analyst on Eagles post-game shows (Ed Rendell).

197

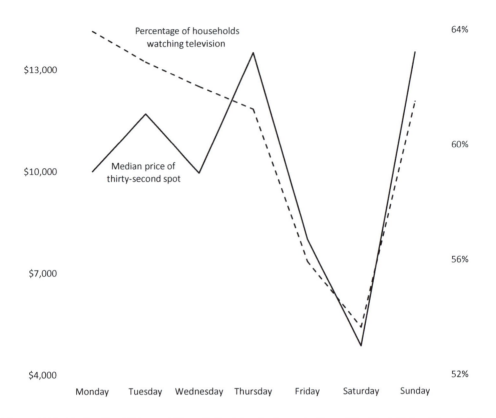

Figure 15.2. Median Spot Price and Size of Television Audience by Day of the Week (Prime Time Only)

We can show that the character as well as the size of the television audience matters by recognizing how the character of the audience changes over the course of a typical weekday. As Figure 15.4 shows, the campaigns in Philadelphia spent a great deal more on advertising during the late afternoon and evening hours than earlier in the day. This is no doubt due, in part, to the increase in the size of the overall television audience obvious in Figure 15.1. Two additional features of the late afternoon are noteworthy, however. The first is that the campaigns actually spent more on advertising between 5:00 p.m. and 8:00 p.m. than between 8:00 p.m. and 11:00 p.m. Those late afternoon spots aired during the major stations' local newscasts and also during syndicated shows aired between 7:00 p.m. and 8:00 p.m.: *Wheel of Fortune, Jeopardy, Entertainment Tonight*, and so on. The second feature of that "daypart" is that while percentage of adults under the age of fifty-five grows substantially during the late afternoon—from 14 to 22%—the percentage of adults fifty-five and older watching television grew much more—from 22 to 39%. What is distinctive about older people, as anyone who has worked in electoral politics will attest, is that they vote. That makes the eyes and ears of older people especially valuable to political campaigns.

Clearly, the first two factors that drive the cost of advertising are which program and station voters watch and what time of day voters are watching. Political advertisers must guess when they will find their target audience. The audience sought by political advertisers is also sought by other types of advertisers. Therefore, political advertisers face a number of market variables that can drive the price of an ad up or down while having finite resources to pay for ad time when the orders are placed. The next sections explore particular market factors unique to political advertisers.

Figure 15.3. Prices for Selected Concurrent Programs

Note: All spots purchased by the NRCC.

Classes of Airtime

Contracts between stations and advertisers frequently do not guarantee that an advertiser's message will be aired on the date and at the time specified. Many contracts reserve for the station the right to preempt a spot at the station's discretion. Such contracts permit stations to entertain a higher bid for a particular spot even after it has ostensibly been sold. If a spot is preempted, the station will either reschedule the advertiser's ad to a later time and day when an audience of comparable size and composition is likely to be watching (the rescheduled spot is known as a "make-good") or will rebate to the advertiser the price paid for the spot.

Advertisers often can pay a premium, however, to exert more control over the specific day and time a message will air. The size of the premium depends on the degree of control. For relatively small increases in price, a station may agree to notify the advertiser a week or two in advance that a spot will be preempted. At a much higher price a station will guarantee that an advertiser's message will be aired on a specific date and at a specific time. The categories into which these different contract terms fall are known as "classes." The number of classes varies from station to station, but the most important distinction is between "preemptible" and "nonpreemptible" airtime.

The issue of preemption is particularly critical for campaign advertisers. Any advertiser who wishes to air a time-sensitive ad—a retailer announcing a weekend sale, for instance—might opt to pay for nonpreemptible airtime in order to ensure that the ad airs at an optimal time. Political campaigns face especially tight constraints. During the closing weeks of the campaign, when most campaign advertising is aired, every ad is time-sensitive. A make-good that airs after election

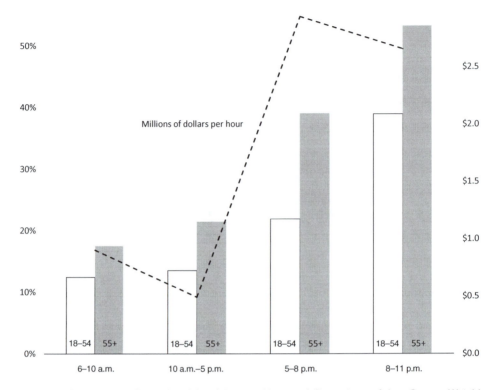

Figure 15.4. Spending on Campaign Advertising per Hour and Percentage of Age Groups Watching Television by Daypart (Weekdays Only)

day is obviously of no value whatsoever to a campaign and neither is a rebate. Campaign advertisers frequently feel compelled, therefore, to purchase nonpreemptible airtime.

The price can be steep. Figure 15.5 shows the prices charged by WCAU/NBC for preemptible and nonpreemptible spots aired during three programs during the last two weeks of the campaign. On the Friday night before the election, a nonpreemptible spot during *Law & Order* cost $8,000, a full 23% more than a preemptible spot during the same program. The premium for a nonpreemptible spot during *The Biggest Loser* on October 25 was 63%. And for a nonpreemptible spot during the *Football Night in America* pregame show on October 29 a campaign paid $7,000, well over double the price of a preemptible spot. For the assurance that their ads will air as scheduled, campaign advertisers pay a great deal of money.

Legal Status of the Advertiser

Federal law and regulations impose special constraints on television stations when they set prices for campaign advertising. The Federal Election Campaign Act of 1971 requires that television broadcast stations, cable systems, and direct satellite systems offer airtime during a campaign to all candidates at their "lowest unit charge" (LUC). This entitles a candidate, during the sixty days preceding a general election, to pay the lowest rate a station charges any of its advertisers for airtime comparable to that sought by the candidate. Candidates for any office at any level of government qualify for the lowest charge, but political parties, interest groups, and political action committees do not. Parties and groups therefore pay more for airtime than candidates, other things equal.

Figure 15.5. Prices by Class for Selected Programs

Note: All spots aired on WCAU/NBC.

The prices paid in Philadelphia in 2006 amply illustrate the impact of the difference in legal status. One appropriate point of comparison is between the prices paid by the Santorum re-election campaign and by Softer Voices, an issue advocacy group that aired ads in late September and early October praising Senator Rick Santorum and criticizing his Democratic opponent, Bob Casey. Figure 15.6 shows typical prices paid for comparable spots by the two organizations. In each case the candidate's campaign paid considerably less than the interest group—from 10% to nearly 50% less.

Similar differences are evident between the prices paid by the parties' House campaign committees and their House candidates (Figure 15.7). In each of these three examples, all from late October, the House candidate paid between 9 and 31% less than his party for a comparable spot. Differences of this magnitude are typical of spots aired by candidates and parties during the same program late in the campaign. The legal requirement that candidates be offered the LUC works to reduce the price of advertising to candidates but constrains the ability of parties and groups to promote their favored candidates.

Price Increases

The price of campaign advertising may rise as election day approaches. In a market in which many campaigns wish to purchase airtime, the demand for spots may naturally drive prices up. Some observers contend that price increases reflect not so much the forces of an open market but the leverage enjoyed by an oligopoly. Stations, knowing that campaigns depend upon television to reach certain segments of the electorate, may take advantage of the small number of television

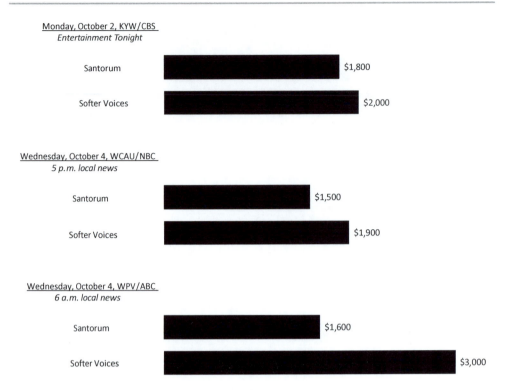

Figure 15.6. Prices by Senate Sponsor for Selected Programs

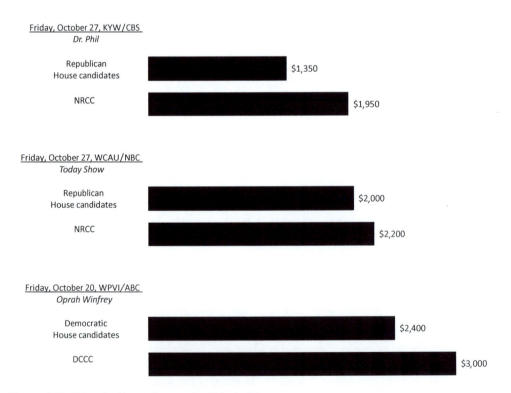

Figure 15.7. Prices by House Sponsor for Selected Programs

outlets in a market by charging political campaigns more than their regular advertisers, especially near the end of the campaign.[8] One of the few previous studies of campaign advertising costs, based on analyses of political advertising sales logs at ten local television stations (Philadelphia's KYW/CBS among them) and interviews with campaign consultants and television station executives, reported:

> Local television stations across the country systematically gouged candidates in the closing months of the 2000 campaign, jacking up the prices of their ads to levels that were far above the lowest candidate rates listed on the stations' own rate cards.[9]

Whatever the explanation, prices in Philadelphia did rise as the 2006 campaign wore on. Figure 15.8 traces changes from mid–September through election day in the rates the four stations charged candidates for spots airing between 6:00 p.m. and 6:30 pm. Three of the stations air a newscast during the time slot. The large differences among the rates charged by the four stations on a given date mainly reflect differences in their ratings: WPVI/ABC consistently wins the ratings competition among local newscasts, and the syndicated *Simpsons* aired by WTXF/Fox during the time slot trails the newscasts in the ratings. The price of a spot on the *Simpsons* was about 40% higher during the last two weeks of the campaign. Prices for all three newscasts rose markedly around October 1. The increases were between 20 and 30% on WPVI/ABC and WCAU/NBC, 75% on KYW/CBS. The CBS affiliate charged another 80% more for spots during their 6:00 p.m. newscast on the eve of the election. A campaign developing plans for television advertising would be well advised to anticipate substantial increases in the cost of airtime as election day approaches.

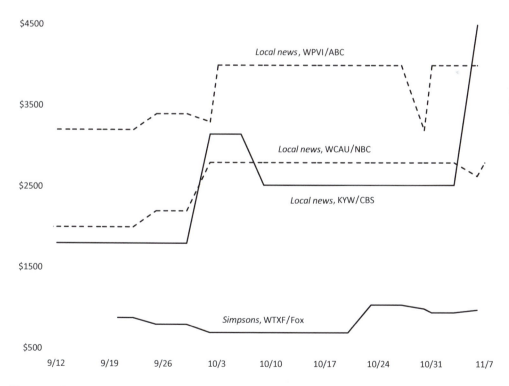

Figure 15.8. Average Price for 6 p.m. Weekday Programs by Air Date (Spots Purchased by Candidates Only)

The Timing of the Buy

We noted when comparing costs across sponsors above the importance of taking into account differences among sponsors in the distribution of their spots over the hours of the day, the days of the week, and the programs on the air. Periods of the campaign may differ in the same way. Just 5% of Philadelphia's political advertising in early October appeared during prime time, but a month later 10% aired in prime time. Because prime-time ads are more expensive, the average cost of a spot overall would have increased even if the cost of a spot purchased for a particular program had remained constant. Assessing temporal changes in the cost of advertising also requires the distinction among types of sponsors to be maintained. As we have seen, different sponsors pay different rates for airtime. Different sponsors also advertise at different times during the campaign. On the most expensive station in Philadelphia, for example, the first sponsors to advertise were the gubernatorial candidates, who paid the lowest prices, beginning in early September. The sponsors paying the highest prices, the House campaign committees (the DCCC and the NRCC), did not begin advertising until October. The Rendell and Swann campaigns did pay more for WPVI/ABC spots in mid-October—about $1,750 per thirty-second spot—than in mid-September, when they paid closer to $1,300 per spot. When the DCCC and NRCC advertising campaign began in mid-October, however, their average spot was priced at over $2,600, and the committees' ad campaigns entailed a substantially higher volume of ads. An average calculated without regard to the difference in price paid by the two types of sponsors would greatly exaggerate the increase in price from September to October.

The time advertisers buy is another crucial variable in determining the ultimate cost to them. We consider the parties first. Both parties purchased most of the airtime they used to support their House candidates in July and August, although neither party's ads were aired until October. The DCCC made its major purchases on KYW/CBS and WCAU/NBC in mid-July and on WPVI/ABC in mid-August, all for spots to air October 10 through election day. The NRCC made its major purchases on all three stations in early August, for airtime beginning October 2. The DCCC made one small, additional purchase on each station in mid-September. The NRCC, too, made small purchases later, one in late September from WCAU/NBC for spots airing throughout October, followed by weekly purchases for flights of spots to air over the week that followed.

The prices the parties paid for the spots they purchased in July and August varied little with the dates in October when their ads aired. The prices the NRCC paid did vary, however, with the date on which the spots were purchased. Figure 15.9 displays some typical examples, all aired on WCAU/NBC. Each pair of ads aired during the same program on the same day but were purchased on different dates. The spots purchased in October were substantially more expensive than those purchased in August—between 50 and 100% more expensive.

The candidates, in contrast to the parties, mainly lived hand to mouth: most of the spots the candidates purchased were bought just a week or two prior to the date the spots aired. The relationship between a spot's cost and its purchase date is very much the same as the relationship between its cost and its air date. The LUC regulations did not prevent prices from rising. We limit our analysis here to the two stations for which we can distinguish preemptible from nonpreemptible airtime. In a span of two weeks in late September and early October, the average price candidates paid for thirty non-preemptible seconds on WPVI/ABC increased 22%—about $400. The price increase on WCAU/NBC began earlier, ended later, and amounted to more— $440, which on the less expensive NBC affiliate represents an increase of 36%. Unlike parties and interest groups, candidates are not in a position to realize significant cost savings by purchasing airtime far in advance. They simply don't have the cash-on-hand to make such a commitment of resources.

Figure 15.9. Prices by Purchase Date for Selected Programs

Note: All spots sponsored by the NRCC and aired on WCAU/NBC.

Conclusion

It is neither mere modesty nor habit that prompts us to point out that our study has limitations. Philadelphia is just one media market—the fourth largest in the nation, and one in which hundreds of millions of dollars have been spent over the past few election cycles by candidates for offices at all levels of government, but just one. The 2006 election cycle is just one cycle—one that swept the Republicans out of and the Democrats into control of the US House and the US Senate (and the Pennsylvania House), altering the course of government policy, but just one. In combination, Philadelphia in 2006 was an extraordinary focal point for campaign activity, in connection with one of the most-watched Senate campaigns in the country, three of the most competitive House races, and a gubernatorial race that was well funded, if not very competitive. The $36 million spent at four television stations by those campaigns in one city is probably not typical for an off-year election.

On the other hand, there could have been more. Lynn Swann might have mounted a better-financed challenge to governor Ed Rendell, to which Rendell would have responded, no doubt, by raising and spending even more money. Senator Rick Santorum might have stayed close enough to Bob Casey in the polls to keep the money coming in from individual contributors and to ensure more support from the NRSC. Representative Curt Weldon, Republican of Pennsylvania's 7th district, might have spent more on television advertising if the newspapers had not featured photos of the FBI carrying boxes from his daughter's house, looking for evidence that he had used his office inappropriately. If the amount of money advertisers can spend influences the price of television airtime, the relatively modest price increase we observe—at three of the four stations, at least—may reflect a weaker market for sellers than might have emerged. This is just one illustration of how our results might be bound by space and time and circumstances.

Our focus on alternative sources of information about costs should not be allowed to obscure the substantive findings based on station records themselves. The substantive results we report here mainly confirm the received view of campaign advertising on television, broadly speaking. We believe we are able to measure differences in cost more precisely and more systematically than has been possible before, however, and the magnitudes of the differences we find are worth highlighting. The parties did pay more than candidates for comparable airtime in Philadelphia in 2006, but the difference was not enormous. The candidates did rely overwhelmingly on non-preemptible spots during the sixty days prior to the election, when they were legally entitled to each station's LUC, although they did purchase some preemptible spots for the most expensive programs. It appears that the price paid for airtime by the parties did rise very substantially, but it also appears that the parties largely mitigated the increase by purchasing most of their spots before the prices went up. Despite the federal regulations, the stations also raised the prices for candidates inside the sixty-day period, though less than the prices for parties. A deeper understanding of how the federal regulations shape—and do not shape—the spot market in television advertising will be a central goal of our continuing work in this area.

Finally, our analysis entirely excludes advertising on cable television, the next big frontier in political advertising. While we do not have detailed analysis to present here, we can say that candidates, political parties, and interest groups spent a combined $3.6 million in cable advertising in the five races we studied. There are clear reasons for this significant investment in cable, especially for congressional candidates in a major metropolitan area. Cable allows an advertiser to target advertising to a very narrow geographic region. This eliminates the "waste" of advertising dollars spent to broadcast an ad to many viewers who are unable to cast a vote in the race at hand. Cable is also very, very cheap compared to broadcast advertising. This allows political advertisers to repeat an ad many times for the same price as one airing on a major broadcast show. However, part of the reason for the discounted rates is the smaller viewership that accompanies the shows found on cable. What remains unknown is the propensity of voters to watch cable television or broadcast television. We expect that cable advertising will receive more attention in future election cycles, especially if evidence is found that voters consume this medium more.

Notes

1 Robin Kolodny, Sandra Suárez, and Kyle Kreider, "The 2000 Pennsylvania Thirteenth Congressional District Race," in *Election Advocacy: Soft Money and Issue Advocacy in the 2000 Congressional Elections*, ed. David B. Magleby (Provo, UT: Center for the Study of Elections and Democracy, Brigham Young University, 2001); Robin Kolodny, Sandra Suárez, and Michael Rodríguez, "Pennsylvania Thirteenth District," in *Outside Money: Soft Money and Issue Ads in Competitive 1998 Congressional Elections*, ed. David B. Magleby and M. Holt. (Provo, UT: Center for the Study of Elections and Democracy, Brigham Young University, 2001); Robin Kolodny and Diana Dwyre, "A New Rule Book: Party Money after BCRA," in *Financing the 2004 Election*, ed. David B. Magleby, Anthony Corrado, and Kelly D. Patterson (Washington, D.C.: Brookings Institution Press, 2006); Robin Kolodny, Sandra Suárez, and Justin Gollob, "Why Context Matters: The Pennsylvania Thirteenth Congressional District Race," in *Electing Congress: New Rules for an Old Game*, ed. David B. Magleby, J. Quin Monson, and Kelly D. Patterson (Upper Saddle River, N.J.: Prentice-Hall, 2007).
2 Richard Johnston, Michael G. Hagen, and Kathleen Hall Jamieson, *The 2000 Presidential Election and the Foundations of Party Politics* (New York: Cambridge University Press, 2004); Michael G. Hagen and Richard Johnston, "Conventions and Campaign Dynamics," in *Rewiring Politics: Presidential Nominating Conventions in the Media Age*, ed. Costas Panagopoulos (Baton Rouge, LA: Louisiana University Press, 2007).
3 For the analysis reported here we have focused mainly on the four major broadcast stations.

4 We did not gather information about the small purchases made in connection with the races for Pennsylvania's 13th district seat in the US House and New Jersey's US Senate seat.

5 Although we have not yet investigated these changes in depth, most appear to have been minor, and most were initiated by the stations, as their schedules changed, rather than by sponsors, as strategic imperatives changed.

6 In practice, employees of a station and an advertiser might never communicate directly; in many cases, at least, their business is transacted by brokers and buyers working on their behalf.

7 These figures are based on national ratings data collected between September 27 and November 28, 2004. See Jana Steadman, *TV Audience Special Study: African-American Audience*, Nielsen Media Research, summer 2005.

8 Craig Holman and Luke P. McLoughlin, *Buying Time 2000: Television Advertising in the 2000 Federal Elections* (New York: Brennan Center for Justice at New York University School of Law, 2001); Jonathan Krasno and Kenneth Goldstein, "The Facts About Television Advertising and the McCain–Feingold Bill," *PS: Political Science and Politics* 35 (2) (2002): 207–12; David B. Magleby, ed., *The Other Campaign: Soft Money and Issue Advocacy in the 2000 Congressional Elections* (Lanham, MD: Rowman & Littlefield, 2002); J. Quin Monson and Stephanie Perry Curtis, "Appendix B—Methodology" in *eSymposium: The Noncandidate Campaign: Soft Money and Issue Advocacy in the 2002 Congressional Elections* (Washington, D.C.: American Political Science Association, 2003).

9 Paul Taylor, *Gouging Democracy: How the Television Industry Profiteered on Campaign 2000* (Washington, D.C.: Alliance for Better Campaigns, 2001).

16

Running for Office

The Candidate's Job Gets Tougher, More Complex

Ronald A. Faucheux

There's nothing quite like running for office. It is an increasingly difficult and complex undertaking, requiring enormous personal dedication, discipline, time, energy and preparation. There is nothing quite like it.

Deciding to run is an easy equation for some, a logical next step. Occasionally, circumstances create candidacies. But for most newcomers and challengers, the decision can be knotty.

Even though it's easy to become consumed in the ego trip of being the center of attention, the intense personal commitment required of candidates is a matter that demands reflection and sober assessment. Candidacy brings high ups and low downs—every day. At two o'clock, a candidate may feel like the Master of the Universe. By four o'clock, he's looking for Dr Kevorkian's phone number.

The instability and uncertainty of political campaigns, even carefully planned ones, and the extraordinary mix of emotions tangled within the process, strain even the strongest candidates. The long hours of hard work and being away from home add increased pressure on candidates. Losing the election, after taking all of that abuse and spending all of that time, can wrack otherwise sane people with bitterness and leave emotional scars. In politics, there's pain with every gain.

Once someone makes the decision to run, it can be a relief. It may even be the most euphoric moment of the campaign, matched only by the elation of a victorious election night. Those first few days when candidates tell themselves, "Yes, I can do it! Yes, I'm gonna do it!" are remarkably fanciful. But once the novelty wears off and the slugfest begins, feelings shift. It begins to feel as if a sword hangs over one's head, dangling on a thin thread, just waiting for any loon with a printing press or a website or a thousand rating points of television time to clip it, and your career, in one fell snip. Just ask Bill Clinton how he felt when he heard that Gennifer Flowers was calling a press conference. Or how George W. Bush felt a few days before the tight 2000 election when the story of an old drunken driving offense was about to break.

The pendulum swings wider for political candidates than it does for most other mortals. Campaigns provide a unique view of society, revealing a cross section one cannot see anywhere else. They bring out the best and worst in many people. When it's the best, it's touching and inspiring; when it's the worst, it's excruciating. Candidates report that there is nothing more touching than when young children hand them their weekly allowance of quarters, nickels and pennies to help the campaign. On the other hand, they report that there is nothing more infuriating than when they find out that one of their own cousins has been caught passing out leaflets for the opposition.

New World

A scene in "The Wizard of Oz" has a young Dorothy confiding suspicions to her little dog about being magically taken from a simple place called home to an inscrutable, more vivid, new world. "Toto," she says, understating her fears, "I have a feeling we're not in Kansas anymore."

The same can be said about how political campaigning across the globe has changed into a new world of politics that is filled, like Oz, with inscrutable opportunity—and danger.

Technology and regulation have driven the biggest changes. Websites, blogs, e-mail, satellites, desktop publishing, digital video editing, micro-targeting, text messaging, Blackberries, twenty-four-hour cable news channels and phone bank predictive dialers have sped up the pace of campaigns and increased the costs. Enactment of campaign finance regulations—disclosure, contribution limits, public financing—plus liberalized absentee voting and vote-by-mail, have combined with the effects of technology and produced more expensive, professional, technology-driven campaigns.[1]

These transformations have ushered in a new era of communications, both mass and peer-to-peer, reflecting the pressures of media messaging and the implications of commonly shared theories of voting and campaign strategy-making.[2]

Throughout the 1980s, information emerged as the power tool of campaigning, be it about policy or candidate records and backgrounds. And with it, going into the 1990s, the new concept of disciplined, poll-tested, research-based, message-driven politics was born. It has been honed ever since.

Political consultants now accept the notion that every campaign positions itself by conveying a message—which is, in effect, the rationale they provide to voters to persuade them to cast their ballots one way versus another.

This concept emerged from the simple idea that the voting decision is a *choice*. Voters don't elect the best man or woman for the job but, instead, simply pick between the available alternatives on the ballot, available on that day, for any specific office. To make such a choice, it follows that voters focus on the differences—rather than the similarities—between candidates.

Contrast, therefore, became the centerpiece of message-making, and contrast necessarily meant some measure of attack. This, together with the ready retrieval of opposition research—computerized and neatly documented—and an increasingly fractured media marketplace, gave rise to an explosion of negative advertising.

Surveys show that many good people are declining to run for office because they are repelled by the negativity, scrutiny and expense of the process. One poll of political candidates, winners and losers in state legislative elections, taken for the University of Maryland through a grant from The Pew Charitable Trusts, found that a solid 81% of the candidates surveyed thought that press scrutiny discouraged people from running for office while 79% thought campaign costs did as well.[3]

Political campaigns offer participants a cross-section glimpse of society that is both penetrating and unique. They demand much, and the quest to win is often destructive. By nature of the electoral process, campaigns yield more losers than winners. They are messy, confusing and ephemeral, and occasionally silly, mindless and ferocious, but they provide the pivot upon which our democracy turns. Without them, free government—for, by and of the people—could not exist.

Political competition, like war, is not for the squeamish or thin-skinned. Career advancement demands focus and determination. The best political candidates are tough operators, able to throw as many punches as they take. But when they walk into the spotlight, whether it's in a race for school board or president of the United States, they should always remember, as Edmund Burke once observed, that they "sit on a conspicuous stage" and the whole world marks their demeanor.

In modern politics, running for office demands three very important things: preparation, focus and discipline.

Career Choice

Running for office is a career choice that dramatically changes the lives of many of the people who make it. It is not a decision to be taken lightly. Sudden flashes of egomania and shallow ambition may spawn some candidacies, but the decision to run requires careful thought and deep reflection. It requires a realistic understanding and a sustaining purpose. That's true whether it is a first time run or an experienced officeholder trying to step up the career ladder.

Some candidates run just to run, simply to get into public life, without much regard for the job itself. When this is the motivation, it often shows. Once the press and voters begin to sense a candidate's lack of interest in anything but himself or herself, it becomes increasingly difficult for that candidate to be taken seriously.

Public office is not for everyone and some people only fit certain positions. A middle-aged business executive who enjoys managing large organizations may love being mayor of a big city, but may be bored serving in a state legislature. A young idealist who's motivated by strong issue commitment may find serving in Congress a dream come true, but may abhor being a sheriff or clerk of court.

At the end of the movie *The Candidate*, young Bill McKay (played by Robert Redford), having just been elected to the US Senate after a storybook come-from-behind finish, looks up in puzzlement and asks his campaign manager, "What do we do now?"

Unfortunately, many candidates run without a clue as to what they want to do with the job. An oft-repeated example was Senator Edward M. Kennedy's unsuccessful bid to capture the 1980 Democratic presidential nomination. Sure, Kennedy wanted it. But because he couldn't readily articulate why he wanted it, his early days on the hustings were nonstarters. His performance in the celebrated CBS interview conducted by family friend Roger Mudd, when Kennedy couldn't give a coherent argument as to why he wanted to be president, sharpened the point.

While some candidates may want the jobs they seek, many of them don't know what they want to do with them should they win their elections. Not only is that void a violation of the civic spirit that public service should be based upon, it is also a political weakness.

Running for office is a tough experience and requires clear dedication. The naive believe they can simultaneously run for office and keep demanding jobs or businesses going at full speed. They don't understand that few things in life are as consuming as a candidacy, especially for a national, statewide or major district office.

Unless it is a lopsided contest or one for a low-level office in a tiny district, campaigning takes an enormous amount of time. There is always something a candidate could be doing to advance the cause: one more hand to shake, phone call to make, dollar to raise, briefing paper to read, speech to make, thank you letter to write or strategy meeting to attend. If a politician thinks he or she can run in a major, competitive election and be a part-time candidate, he or she needs to think again. Candidates need to be prepared to live, eat and breathe campaigning. Or they need to be prepared to lose.

No candidate is perfect. Everyone has flaws and weaknesses. In politics, any hint of imperfection may be magnified into a gaping canyon. Thanks to television, those cracks can be exploited by the opposition day in, day out—100 times a day—in living color, in the living rooms and on the computer screens of your family, friends and neighbors. Add to that an increasingly aggressive news media and Internet blogs, and being a candidate starts looking less and less appealing to many people who want to live normal lives without constant public scrutiny.

Modern candidates must ask themselves whether they can afford to lose the elections they are contemplating. Some people, because they've already lost elections, or because of the circumstances of the race, may not be able to survive a loss with their political careers intact. This is particularly important when it comes to finances. If you figure the only way you can fund a campaign is largely with your own money or on your own borrowing power, candidates need to make sure that if they lose they still can afford to feed their families. Some candidates who throw caution to the wind are elected; others have their houses repossessed.

Electoral victory usually stirs ambition to move up the career ladder. What begins as a part-time commitment to serve on a local school board may grow into a desire to run for county supervisor, then Congress, governor and even president.

Financing is an obstacle that keeps many people—particularly those who lack personal wealth and connections—out of public office. For some, raising money can be an experience that falls somewhere between having a root canal and cleaning a bathroom floor. Most candidates hate it. They wake up each morning dreading that they have to ask strangers and, worse, friends and relatives, for cash.

If a candidate is not a multimillionaire, or a powerful incumbent with lobbyists begging for the chance to hand them a PAC check, fundraising is a hard business. Candidates without ready money sources, and who detest asking for money, will often find themselves running under-financed campaigns.

Politics is hard on the families of candidates, who are often asked to make major personal sacrifices. Children, spouses, parents, even siblings are drawn into not just the excitement but also the agony of nonstop campaigning.

Remember 1992 presidential candidate Ross Perot ranting about Republican dirty tricksters disrupting his daughter's wedding? Candidates and their families are subject to cruel jokes, gossip and innuendo. It's open season on the way they look, act, think, dress and talk. Everything they do is going to be ridiculed by someone, somewhere.

Campaigns routinely spend time and staff hours doing research on their opposition (as well as research on themselves, to anticipate the coming attacks). At its best, such research is precisely accurate and helps inform candidates, the news media and the public on the facts related to issues and a rival's public record. At its worst, it is unnecessarily personal, sloppy and "used ruthlessly for character assassination, and becomes the indispensable weapon of 'gotcha' campaigning."[4]

Political research may include inquiry into legislative voting records, absenteeism (missed roll call votes by legislators), bill sponsorships, committee and leadership assignments, patronage and "pork-barrel" government spending, questionable campaign contributions, official mailings funded by tax dollars, government-paid travel, media coverage and quotes, public records, verbal gaffes and contradictions, public statements and positions.[5] In recent elections, lawsuits filed against candidates and private business practices have also come into play. Researchers will tell you their jobs are about finding "votes, quotes and anecdotes" that have political currency.

Complex Task

Running for office is a complex task. Before candidates can start public campaigning, they need to get their personal and business affairs in order. Campaigning consumes mental capacity and physical energy, making it difficult to do other things. It takes undivided attention.

Candidates must be careful that they check all applicable election laws and set up a legal compliance system before they accept or spend any funds or engage in campaigning. There are many regulations candidates and committees must obey. In most jurisdictions, candidates have to file timely campaign finance reports. In some, personal income disclosure statements are required. Every candidate must, at some point, officially file his or her candidacy with a party committee, a board of elections, the secretary of state or a combination of some or all of these entities.

Missing a deadline can be embarrassing, and politically costly in that it can even extinguish promising candidacies before they begin. If tardiness involves candidate qualification papers, it may knock a candidate out of the race. In 1994, a frontrunning congressional candidate in Indiana failed to file her candidacy papers on time—despite warnings—and was disqualified from a race she may have won.

To assist their efforts, candidates need three things: (1) good legal advice; (2) experienced staff assistance to handle all financial reporting and compliance accounting; and (3) a reliable vetting process to ensure that all campaign materials are factually accurate and politically acceptable as well as to review campaign contributions to make sure they are legally proper and politically defensible.

Every modern candidate, no matter how smart or seasoned, needs outside advice that is based on objective understanding of the political landscape and broad experience in the technical aspects of modern campaigning.[6] There are three functions in campaigns that should be handled by professionals: (1) research; (2) communications; and (3) strategy. They each require technical expertise that most candidates do not possess.

Research includes public opinion surveys—which should be conducted by professional polling firms—and opposition research, which can be handled by in-house staff or a consulting firm. In larger races, candidates will also need policy research personnel. Solid, reliable, accurate research is the key to message-making and message-making determines how a campaign frames the choice it presents to the voters.

A campaign's media consultant serves as its advertising and public relations agency. Though capabilities vary, most good consultants provide strategy advice as well as produce and place (buy time and space for) ads. Some are highly experienced in politics and will assume the role of chief communications strategist. It's important for candidates to hire media consultants with strong political backgrounds to blend technical expertise, creativity and strategic capacity.

Campaign communications include "paid" media (television, radio, billboard, newspaper and Internet advertising) and "earned" media (press relations, events, editorial boards and blogs). In smaller races, media consultants may also serve as de facto press secretaries. In larger campaigns, a full-time press secretary is usually employed. In the largest statewide and national campaigns, both a communications director and a press secretary will be needed, together with supporting staff.

General consultants are often hired to serve as strategists, advisers and planners. They may be experienced professionals who have advised campaigns across the nation or they may be local operatives with knowledge of the local terrain. Availability and budget will determine who to hire and what role they should play.[7]

In many races, the pollster, media consultant or even campaign manager will assume the strategy function, eliminating the need for a separate general consultant.

In addition to general consultants, pollsters and media consultants, specialized consultants may also be needed for:

- Fundraising (writing a plan, soliciting political action committees, organizing events and so forth).
- Direct mail (writing copy, designing the pieces, overseeing the print production process, quality control, coordinating postal regulations, handling the mail drop).
- Telephone contact (hiring professional phone centers to make persuasive calls, recruitment calls, voter ID calls and get-out-the-vote calls).
- Online activities (design and maintenance of your Internet presence).

- Database management (setting up the hardware and software needed to keep track of voters, volunteers, contributors and correspondence).

Hiring Consultants

Hiring campaign consultants is a particularly difficult decision for most candidates. The increased number of firms that call them "political consultants" has intensified business competition and made the hiring process more complex.

In evaluating possible consultants, many factors come into play. "Chemistry is critical," said Arthur J. Hackney, a media consultant based in Washington, D.C.:

> If you and a consultant don't spark personally, it won't be a good fit. . . . A candidate needs a consultant who can lay it on the line, read your heart and translate your fire into media that burns just as brightly. Your consultant must be the one voice you hear forsaking all others, until-death-do-you-part.[8]

"Candidates should feel comfortable with the consultant they hire," said Tony Payton, a consultant based in Arlington, Virginia. "They ought to feel like they're on the same wavelength." To explain his point, Payton recalled the story of an Arkansas candidate whom "once told me it was important for the candidate and consultant to match noses. I never knew what he meant, but I think it was that things should smell the same to both of them."[9]

Florida-based pollster Dave Beattie has in focus groups sponsored by The Pew Charitable Trusts asked numerous candidates about picking consultants. He's found that

> most candidates rehired a consultant because they liked their personality. Consultants can maximize their chance of being hired—getting referrals and retaining the candidate's trust—by realizing that personality does matter and there are some candidates that would be better served by someone with a different personality.[10]

Another criterion to consider is the ability of a consultant to be strictly objective, unaffected by the emotions of the moment. This is especially important when it comes to hiring pollsters and analysts. They will be called upon, over and over, to look beyond personal friendships and partisan affiliations for the hard reality presented in their data. That's not always easy to do when the candidate has a need for affirmation or, even worse, hero-worship.

The hiring process can take time, and is often frustrating for candidates who don't know what to look for in the stream of ad firms, pollsters, general consultants, direct mail producers, fundraisers and telephone vendors who come calling, seeking business. Nonetheless, it is crucial to winning the election. "Your campaign is a matter of political life or death: Hire someone like you would a brain surgeon, not based just on price," ominously advises media consultant Karl Struble.[11]

In addition to chemistry, confidence and objectivity, creativity and competence are also considerations, especially when reviewing possible media consultants, who will in effect serve as the campaign's advertising agency and communications ramrod.

Selecting a media consultant is "a big decision for candidates. Treat it that way," recommends consultant Jim Duffy.[12] It can also be a time-consuming decision. Most media firms send potential clients reels of ads they've produced as a way to promote their abilities. "Don't just look at the promotional reels," cautions Duffy. "Talk to the firm's winners and losers, find out how much time they spent on each race. Don't just talk to the candidates, talk to the campaign managers as well. You want to know how involved they were in the races."

"Pay special attention not just to the quality of the ads," emphasizes Struble, but also "look to see if there is a consistent strategic thread to the reel and if the quality diminishes as the campaign progresses." Media strategist Ray Strother, a former president of the American Association of Political Consultants, reinforces the notion that candidates should not evaluate spots in a vacuum, but should look at the larger political context in which they were produced. "Don't fall in love with one cute commercial. Ask questions," he advises.[13]

In judging a consultant's past work, a candidate should remember, says Dan Payne, a Boston-based media consultant, that "it's the work you're paying for, not the presentation, size of the firm or size of the name." Payne advises candidates to ask themselves, "What role do you, the candidate, want to play in creating and delivering messages? How flamboyant or conservative is your style; how daring or safe do you need to be to win?"[14]

"With their own success depending so heavily on hype, it's not surprising that candidates often go with the consultant they see on TV, not stopping to think about who's going to be the star of their show," says media consultant John Franzen. "Better to seek out someone who stays studiously behind the scenes, putting the focus on you and refusing to feed the journalists' obsession with campaign process. Also, when crunch time comes, it doesn't help to have the superstar consultant if you can't get him or her on the phone." To avoid bringing on "the overrated and the overextended," suggests Franzen, "there's really no substitute for talking to as many of the consultant's former clients as possible, the winners and the losers."[15]

When hiring media firms, candidates must always keep in mind that the consultant's role in a campaign consists of three distinct components: devising messages and communication strategies; creating and producing ads; and buying the time for those ads and handling the paperwork of media placement.

"Find out if the media placement is done in-house or contracted out," says media consultant Gary Nordlinger. "One is not necessarily better than another, but find out about the buyer and his or her experience. Chances are this person will be handling your largest single expenditure."[16]

Another issue, says Nordlinger, is how fast can the firm turn around spots? In an increasingly competitive world of political media politics, with attacks and counterattacks hurling back and forth, this can be a serious matter. A firm that isn't overextended with too much work, or perhaps one with in-house facilities to do quick post-production chores, may be in a better position to give your campaign the rapid response capability it will need.

Production costs, in addition to the time buys, can be a major budget item that candidates often find difficult to understand. "Be sure to get a handle on production costs. A TV spot can cost from $1,000 to $100,000," says Nordlinger.

One of the most perplexing decisions candidates for statewide and local offices face is whether they should hire campaign consultants from out of state. Out-of-state consultants often offer one big advantage: they have a broad, national perspective on what works and what doesn't in campaigning. They tend to understand the cutting edge of technique and have access to the best available technical talent. They also bring disadvantages: first, distance—they may not be there, in person, when you want them; second, busy schedules—if they're really hot, they may take on too many clients to give all of them adequate attention; third, local knowledge—they may not understand the nuances and customs of the political culture and, worse, may not want to spend the time or effort to learn them.

Local consultants, too, bring both benefits and baggage. Their benefits: first, proximity—they're usually only a short drive away; second, cost—in many cases, they're less expensive than top national practitioners; and third, local knowledge—they grasp the personalities, subtleties and traditions from day one. Their baggage: they may lack national perspective and an appreciation of advanced techniques used across the nation; their access to technical talent and technologies may be limited; they may be too immersed in the local scene and, as such, may have too many personal conflicts and lack objectivity.

There is no easy answer to the question as to whether you should stay home or go out of town to hire campaign consultants. But these factors must be considered by candidates as they ponder their options.

In political campaigning, one size does not fit all. There's no magic wand, no infallible formula. Each race has its own heart and soul, and must be viewed with particularity and sensitivity. Consultants who understand this reality should never be ruled out just because they're from out of state; but those who don't should be given the boot from the beginning.

In some cases, a team approach will give you the best of both worlds: a combination of the best local and national talent. A candidate may decide, for example, to hire an out-of-state pollster—for national expertise—along with local media consultants—for local expertise. There are certain venues in the United States and in a number of countries around the world that lack adequate local talent. In that instance, candidates may be forced to look out of town. Even in that case, candidates may want to mix national consultant advice with that of a local campaign manager or frequent consultations with smart, loyal, hometown politicians.

Candidates also need to be mindful of the issues involved in compensating consultants. Most media consultants are compensated, in whole or in part, through commissions on advertising buys. As an advertising industry standard, television and radio stations and networks, as well as many newspapers and billboard companies, usually build into the cost of each ad a 15% commission. Typically, that commission is given to the agency that places the buy.

Of course, the commission can be negotiated between the campaign and the consultant. In some large campaigns where there are plenty of consultants competing for the business, campaigns attempt to reduce the commission percentages. However, some media consultants—particularly the most experienced ones who are the highest regarded—will refuse to reduce their commissions in many races, especially the more competitive, time-consuming ones.

In addition to media commissions, media consultants may also receive an upfront or monthly retainer fee to cover strategic advice over and above the advertising services they provide. Out-of-pocket expenses (travel, for example) are usually billed extra.

Most general consultants charge by the hour or by a monthly retainer. Since their primary function is to provide strategic advice and political coordination—not specific deliverables, such as an ad, a poll or a mail piece—this makes sense. In some cases, general consultants will take a portion of the media commissions either in lieu of retainers or in addition to them.

Pollsters provide specific products, namely polls that quantify voter attitudes based on a scientific sample. They can also provide micro-targeting analysis, focus groups and qualitative interview studies. Usually, they charge set prices for these deliverables.

The cost of a typical telephone poll is based on two things: the length of the survey questionnaire and the size of the sample. Open-ended questions that probe survey responses add cost. The cost of focus groups may be affected by how many are conducted, where they are and how difficult the participants are to select. Pollsters who also serve as day-to-day strategy advisers are often paid monthly retainer fees in addition to charging for specific research studies.

Message Presentations

Every campaign needs a public rationale, a compelling reason voters should vote their way. That's the campaign's message—and it is largely based on personal and issue distinctions between each candidate and their opposition. A well-crafted, research-driven message will frame the central choice presented to voters; it will position a candidacy relative to the opposition and the political environment. Candidates must internalize their campaign messages, feel comfortable with them and understand how to communicate them to voters and the news media.

Public presentations—speeches, media interviews, debates—are important elements in modern campaigns. As such, candidates need to be well prepared for these events. They need to understand the mechanics and the substantive messages for each method of communicating messages.

Though speeches can be written or outlined by consultants, communications personnel or professional speechwriters, they must closely reflect the candidate—his or her speaking ability and unique language formulations as well as personal values and philosophies. Speech-making is a staple in every campaign. It requires plenty of preparation. Woodrow Wilson was once asked how long it took him to prepare a fifteen-minute speech. He responded, "Two weeks." How long for a thirty-minute speech? "One week." How about a two-hour speech? "I'm ready now," smiled the scholarly president.

It takes time for candidates to assemble their thoughts in a coherent way. It takes time to figure out what goes in and what stays out of a speech. It takes time to get the timing right so that each speech is, as Winston Churchill advised, long enough to cover the subject but not so long that people lose interest.

Speeches must be unique to each candidate's strengths and weaknesses and should also reflect the campaign's central message. They should help create an emotional connection to the audience and should be delivered with passion and enthusiasm.

Media interviews, especially in elections for major statewide and national offices where there is the most intense press coverage, are crucial to a candidate's success. Candidates must understand how to get their messages across in short sound bites on television, radio and in print media formats.[17] That requires preparation.

To assist candidates plan and practice speeches, media interviews and debates, candidates often hire professional media trainers.[18] Close elections are won, in some instances, by candidates who win the nightly news sound bite exchanges. Understanding the rules of the road, and the technical constraints of both electronic and print media, is critical. It's something every candidate must learn. Regardless of a candidate's personal facility for communicating to the mass public, it usually requires specialized training to ensure that a candidate can handle the demands of media inquiry.

Candidates need not only a firm grasp of their own messages—arguments, proposals, explanations, issue specifics—but they must also understand how their rivals will rebut their claims and statements. In addition, candidates also need to be ready to rebut their opponents as well.

In effect, candidates must always be prepared to debate—even when there is no formal debate looming on their schedules. Every speech, public meeting, media interview presents an opportunity to deal with the numerous arguments and counterarguments involved in a candidacy. Knowing how to debate and what to say, even when a candidate doesn't actually have to debate, is a wise start for any candidacy.

There was a time when candidates spent countless hours agonizing over whether to debate. The old rule of thumb was that frontrunners had everything to lose by debating, and underdogs had everything to gain. Since most elections have frontrunners, debates were often shunned.

But in recent times, debates have become a fixture of campaigning. Ever since 1984 when incumbent President Ronald Reagan, who enjoyed a big lead in the polls, consented to debate his underdog opponent, Walter Mondale, the incumbent/frontrunner no-show excuse was obliterated.

Now, voters and the news media expect all candidates to debate, whether they're running for town alderman or president. When candidates won't debate, they become suspect and subject to attack. Candidates who have good reason not to debate have to weigh the damage done by refusing alongside the risk of doing it.

A 2002 nationwide voter survey conducted for The Pew Charitable Trusts and the Center for American Politics and Citizenship at the University of Maryland found that 57% of the respondents would be less likely to vote for a candidate for a major statewide office, and 55% of the respondents would be less likely to vote for a candidate for a district or local office, who had refused to debate his or her opponent. By any measure, in any situation, that's a large segment of the electorate to risk offending.[19]

This poll also found that 83% of voters believe there should be multiple debates in major statewide elections, such as those for US senator and governor, and that 62% believe the same for district and local races, such as those for the US House, state legislature, mayor and county council.[20]

According to the survey, voters like debates because they provide them an opportunity to find out where candidates stand on the issues and how the rivals differ. Voters also say they are more interested in debate substance—the candidates' knowledge and positions on the issues—than style—the candidates' physical appearance and speaking ability. While most voters say they don't care about each combatant's capacity to land attacks on his or her rival, voters do expect the candidates to keep cool and calm throughout the encounter.

Experienced campaigners, as well as newcomers, often get the jitters before they walk on stage to debate. Fear of being surprised with an unexpected attack, or being hit with a question for which one doesn't know the answer, sets off butterflies in the stomachs of even the toughest combatants. In preparation sessions, campaign staff and media consultants should be sensitive to the trepidation with which most candidates approach debates and encourage their clients to relax and "be themselves" as they attempt to connect with the audience and deliver clear, compelling messages.

It is essential for candidates to understand the unique dynamics of a debate. Unlike a regular campaign speech, where one can say whatever he or she wants without fear of immediate rebuttal from an opponent, in a debate one has to be constantly prepared for the comeback. As such, candidates must think through arguments in terms of an interrelated three-part process: (1) making a point; (2) anticipating a rebuttal from an opponent; and (3) preparing a response to an opponent's rebuttal.[21]

Because of the strict time limits that are part of most debates. Candidates need to be able to make their points quickly, without hesitation, wasted words or unnecessary pauses. Before candidates walk into a debate, they need to know what they want to say, they need to have a good idea of what their opponent will say and they need to devise answers to all possible opposition claims, both positive and negative.

Candidates need to have a strategic endgame before they begin debate preparations. The goal of a political debate is not to win the debate. It is to win the election. Often, candidates debate to accomplish one or all of these strategic goals: (1) sharpen their campaign's overall message; (2) draw clear distinctions between their positions and those of their opponent on select issues; (3) address voter skepticism or confusion by demonstrating a personal quality or strength, or inoculating against a perceived personal weakness.

Debates are opportunities to frame the ultimate choice for voters by explaining and illustrating themes and messages. For example, when former California governor Ronald Reagan debated president Jimmy Carter in 1980, his first task was to demonstrate his own capacity to be a strong national leader and, in so doing, to define a contrast that would be unfavorable to Carter, who was perceived by many voters as being weak and timid. Pre-debate polls showed that a large percentage of the electorate was still skeptical of the sixty-nine-year-old ex-actor's ability to protect the peace and to handle the complex duties of the presidency. Reagan accomplished this first task by the way he handled himself, by the way he looked and by the strength and reasonableness he conveyed.

His second task was to draw out public dissatisfaction with the weakened economy and to turn it full-force against Carter's re-election. He did this repeatedly with specific attacks on a variety of issues. He capped his case with the now-famous line, a killer close that has been copied by hundreds of candidates since then: "Are you better off now than you were four years ago?"

Debates, by themselves, rarely win elections. But they can nonetheless play a role in a campaign's outcome. Most importantly, they can underscore and reinforce a candidate's strengths or weaknesses. How that relates to what has happened before the debate, and what is to happen after the debate during the rest of the campaign, is what is important.

Things to Do

In the modern world of campaigning, candidate preparation is the key to smart, effective campaigns. In their effort to prepare for candidacy, people running for office have a long list of tasks they must perform. These tasks include the following:

1 *Develop a fundraising plan.* Put the fundraising team in place, schedule call-time to reach potential donors and starting to ask for money. Unfortunately, most candidates can't get very far without the resources to convey messages to the public. The finance plan and fundraising strategy need to be given as much attention as the political plan and strategy.

   Regardless of the size of a campaign's fundraising apparatus, in most campaigns—except, perhaps, in large races that are targeted by major national parties for their political significance—the candidate still has to ask for much of money personally. There's no getting around it. It takes plenty of direct candidate pleas, on the phone and in person, to get the dollars needed to fund increasingly expensive campaigns.

   Campaign finance reforms that lower allowable contributions have complicated the burden of raising money. The lower the applicable legal contribution caps, the more time it takes. That's why candidates running for federal offices, as well as state and lower offices that have low donor caps, are required to spend so much "call time" dialing for dollars.

2 *Learn the issues.* Everybody has opinions on issues. Not many people have deep knowledge of issues. Most newcomers and challengers, especially those who do not yet hold public office, have serious information gaps compared with those who do. Before someone goes public with a candidacy, they need to research the important policy issues and have a working knowledge of them.

3 *Find a campaign manager.* This can be a difficult position to fill. It's a tough job that requires endless hours and total commitment. The candidate has to believe in the manager, and the manager has to believe in the candidate.

4 *Hire personal staff.* In addition to hiring professional consultants and staff to run organizational operations, most campaigns are large enough to require the hiring of a personal assistant to the candidate as well as a scheduler. These are two very important jobs. The personal assistant's job is to keep the candidate on track and on time. A key function of the job is to serve as the candidate's driver to save the candidate time and stress. The scheduler is in charge of the campaign's most precious resource: the candidate's time. A good scheduler must juggle conflicting requests as a matter of course and take all the flak for saying no. Every meeting the candidate attends, whether it's a private one-on-one or a public speech before a large audience, needs to be entered on the schedule with full information.

5 *Set up an office.* Campaigns have all the trappings of most businesses. They need offices, telephones, fax machines, computers, software, medical insurance, parking and personnel staffing. They also need strict financial management, accounting and legal compliance.

6 *Establish a strategy inner circle.* This is usually a tight-knit group with a minimum of three or four people and a maximum of seven or eight people. This group would normally include the candidate plus the pollster, media consultant, general consultant (if there is

one), campaign manager and a few other trusted advisers. It should encompass a variety of viewpoints. Campaign strategy, tactics and management issues must be discussed and deliberated at these sessions. They are crucial to a campaign's decision-making process.

Candidates need to be—and feel—in control. They need to maintain cool in every crisis. Knowing that help and advice is always a quick call away can be calming and reassuring in situations that could otherwise spin out of control.

7 *Develop an organizational chart.* A campaign's operational apparatus must cover the functional aspects from field organization to office management, material distribution to coalition outreach, fundraising to mass communications, legal compliance to research, candidate scheduling to press relations.

8 *Establish a graphic "look" for a campaign.* Early on, it is important for candidates to select a consistent graphic theme with colors, type fonts, photos, layout and design. Getting good photographs of the candidate is critical to image presentation.

Strategic Context

A political campaign should not be merely a series of events and activities haphazardly sequenced and arbitrarily timed. It should be rolled out with clear purpose as part of a logical plan.

Most candidates know they must have a coherent message, take polls, use modern database software, distribute literature, produce advertising, send out mail, make phone calls, identify and persuade swing voters, turn out supporters on election day—but figuring out when to do what, and to what degree and in what order, is something that often mystifies. Solving the strategy puzzle requires the ability to think strategically. And that's the key to victory.

This process is not unlike planning for war. "The political world speaks in military tongues because war provides a useful model for political activity," elaborates political scientist John J. Pitney Jr, who cites one of history's greatest military strategic wizards Carl von Clausewitz ("War is a clash between major interests, which is resolved by bloodshed—that is the only way in which it differs from other conflicts") as evidence for his thesis.[22]

The strategy-making process in politics can be made less mystifying and more rational if candidates understand the elements of what a strategic battle plan should be.

Every campaign needs four basic strategies: a positioning strategy (which is, in effect, the campaign message); a message sequence strategy (the order in which a campaign presents the positive, comparative and negative components of its message); timing and intensity strategy (what a campaign does when); and a mobilization/persuasion strategy (targeting voters to reach "persuadables" and "undecideds" vs. organizing and turning out "favorables"). In addition, there are opportunity strategies that are used to exploit situational advantages or to overcome existing or anticipated obstacles through a special maneuver.

The essence of political strategy is to concentrate one's greatest strength against the point of the opposition's greatest weakness. This is done through developing and delivering of messages that present voters with a choice based on candidate differences that are clear, believable and connected to reality.

Campaign messages may be based on: (1) personal virtues and flaws of the candidates, such as experience, competence, independence, integrity, compassion, stability, preparation; (2) ideological and partisan differences that may be based on notions of one candidate being liberal, conservative, moderate, radical, extreme, wishy-washy, inconsistent or pragmatic; (3) situations that may include big ideas such as change vs. the status quo, the right track vs. wrong track, progress vs. stagnation; or (4) a combination of any of the above.

For example, Bill Clinton's strategy in his 1996 re-election campaign was to enhance differences between himself and his Republican opposition on issues that benefited Democrats

(Medicare, Medicaid, education, environment) and to blur differences on issues that benefited Republicans (crime, taxes, balanced budget, welfare reform, family values). By enhancing differences on favorable issues, he was playing to his natural strengths. He was, in effect, mobilizing his base. By blurring differences on less favorable issues, and by co-opting elements of Republican rhetoric, he was able to take many of these issues off the table, which made it easier for him to persuade swing voters to jump on his bandwagon.

The tactics Clinton used to implement this strategy included early "positioning" television spots in targeted markets ("Gingrich and Dole on Medicare") and a series of speeches ("the era of big government is over"), legislative proposals (school uniforms, opposition to teenage smoking) and bill signings (welfare reform).

In the 2000 presidential election, polls showed that George W. Bush's strengths were related to his personality, leadership skills and family's values. Al Gore's strengths were related to policy issues and the incumbent administration's economic track record. It made sense for Bush to stress his strong points and to frame the election's choice around them. Gore's campaign, as a counterpoint, stressed his strong points, especially policy issues, as a way to frame the choice presented to the voters.

A criticism of Gore's campaign was that he didn't focus enough attention on the "track record" aspect of his message. Many strategists during, and especially *after*, the election speculated that Gore would have run a better race had he figured out a way to tie himself tighter to the improved national conditions that occurred during the Clinton–Gore administration ("You're better off than you were eight years ago") while keeping his distance from Clinton's personal behavior.

Inoculation is an important element of a positioning strategy; it is a way to blunt existing or potential weakness before it is allowed to kill a candidacy. When Franklin D. Roosevelt (FDR) was planning a political comeback after his polio affliction, he realized two things: (1) being a severely crippled paraplegic could be a major campaign liability; and (2) an aristocratic candidate born into wealth and privilege could have trouble winning the trust of the masses. So during the years before his re-entry into elective politics, Roosevelt developed a persona as a man of action, a strong, bold leader for change and a friend of poor, forgotten people. When opponents attacked him for "moving the country too fast," and when the rich criticized him for "betraying their class," it played right into his hands. His strengths were positioned in such a way that they also overcame his potential weaknesses.

How Many Actors on Stage?

Once upon a time, campaigns were about people who wanted to get elected to public office. It was a fairly simple concept. But now, there are new contestants in the campaign ring. Interest groups and political party committees are running their own campaigns—separate and apart from those of the candidates. This is especially true in major congressional and statewide elections that have national implications and in key state legislative races that may determine party control.

Independent campaigns usually center on issues that the sponsoring organization wishes to promote and, by so doing, seek to help candidates who agree and harm those who don't. They are the "x-factor" of modern political strategy that, according to Republican strategist Whit Ayres, gives "almost everybody involved in campaigns heartburn at one time or another."[23]

Traditional notions of issue advocacy—public campaigns aimed at influencing legislative and governmental decision-makers—differ from this new brand of electoral advocacy, which is aimed at influencing voters during an election. Of course, political party entities, as well as many of the groups that pioneered issue advocacy and grassroots lobbying—regulated industries, organized labor, trial lawyers, environmentalists, term limit advocates, pro-life and pro-choice activists, to name the major players—are now mounting expensive, sophisticated, high-profile "independent expenditure" campaigns that are designed to elect and defeat candidates on election day.

After watching what has happened in recent elections, candidates and political consultants have mixed feelings about this trend. Of course, some independent expenditures prove to be politically effective. But some backfire and get campaigns off track. "It's a very disconcerting trend," says Republican pollster Ed Goeas, president of The Tarrance Group. "I think we'll reach a point in the future where you may see the bulk of the campaign being run from outside of [candidate] campaigns in terms of developing the messages, delivering the messages and determining what the messages are."[24]

"Candidates are losing control of their own campaigns," observes Democratic analyst Mark Mellman. "We have independent groups that decide what the message is going to be, decide what the timing is going to be. . . . It is a very uncomfortable position to be in." Consultant Jim Duffy echoes Mellman's thoughts: "As candidates lose control and as advocacy groups take over, candidates become props in campaigns."[25]

"We're going to have to be quicker on our feet as operatives, as planners," says Alan Secrest, president of the Cooper & Secrest polling firm. "Your antennae are going to have to be that much better. You're going to have to be that much farther ahead of the curve whether through research, or through word of mouth or through your own experience." Consultants and managers, counsels Secrest, need to learn to be more disciplined "in terms of the job you do on behalf of your candidates . . . in introducing yourself and sometimes in introducing your opponent as well."[26]

Message discipline isn't always easy to maintain, warns Secrest, because "oftentimes we don't know where that third party money is going to come from and where it's going to land." In addition, he advises candidates to consider starting earlier with larger media buys and greater spot repetition so they can get their "message through before some of these distractions come into place."

Former Republican media consultant Ann Husted reinforces Secrest's point: "The best way for candidates to protect themselves is to set the agenda and tone of what you want your campaign to be about before outside groups come in."[27]

Laments Duffy: "Regardless of which side you're on, whether you're helped or hurt, you can't see what's happening as a good thing. Treating candidates as a mere pass-through diminishes the process." Diminishing candidates in the electoral process, it could also be argued, subsequently diminishes their capacity for leadership in the governmental process.

"Campaigns are supposed to be a reflection of candidates," says Mellman. But "if the campaigns are controlled by outside groups who ostensibly have never met, have no idea about and no coordination with those candidates, then those campaigns are not proper reflections of those candidates."

The implications of crowding the political field with outside players are far-reaching and go to the heart of voter participation. In the end, concludes Mellman, this trend makes "it harder—not easier—for people to make judgments about the choices they want in elections."

And all that—together with the personal, financial and professional pressures—makes being a candidate a harder job in today's politics than it has ever been.

But no matter how tough of a job running for office is in today's political environment, somebody's got to do it. And thankfully, many strong, capable, honest people do.

Notes

1 Daniel M. Shea and Michael John Burton, *Campaign Craft: The Strategies, Tactics and Art of Political Campaign Management* (Westport, CT: Praeger, 2001), 1–4.

2 Ronald A. Faucheux, ed., *Winning Elections: Political Campaign Management, Strategy and Tactics* (New York: M. Evans and Co., 2003); Michael McCurry, "Mass Media Politics: Historic Perspective," in *Winning Elections*, ed. R. Faucheux (New York: M. Evans and Co., 2003), 470–4.

3 Ronald A. Faucheux and Paul S. Herrnson, *The Good Fight: How Political Candidates Struggle to Win Elections Without Losing Their Souls* (Washington, D.C.: Campaigns & Elections, 2000), 137.

4 Dennis W. Johnson, *No Place for Amateurs: How Political Consultants Are Reshaping American Democracy* (New York, London: Routledge, 2001), 60.

5 Shea and Burton, *Campaign Craft*, 59–71.

6 James A. Thurber and Candice J. Nelson, eds, *Campaign Warriors: Political Consultants in Elections* (Washington, D.C.: Brookings Institution Press, 2000), 10–12; Candice J. Nelson, James A. Thurber and David A. Dulio, "Portrait of Campaign Consultants," in *Campaign Warriors: Political Consultants in Elections*, ed. J.A. Thurber and C.J. Nelson (Washington, D.C.: Brookings Institution Press, 2000), 10–36.

7 Dennis W. Johnson, "The Business of Political Consulting," in *Campaign Warriors: Political Consultants in Elections*, ed. J.A. Thurber and C.J. Nelson (Washington, D.C.: Brookings Institution Press, 2000), 37–48.

8 Ronald A. Faucheux, *Running for Office: The Strategies, Techniques and Messages Modern Political Candidates Need to Win Elections* (New York: M. Evans and Co., 2002), 122.

9 Ibid.

10 Ibid.

11 Ibid., 125.

12 Ibid., 124.

13 Ibid., 125.

14 Ibid.

15 Ibid., 127.

16 Ibid., 128.

17 Shea and Burton, *Campaign Craft*, 172–81.

18 Jeff Ansell, "Picking a Media Trainer," in *Winning Elections: Political Campaign Management, Strategy and Tactics*, ed. R. Faucheux (New York: M. Evans and Co., 2003), 462–3.

19 Ronald A. Faucheux, ed., *The Debate Book* (Washington, D.C.: Campaigns & Elections Publishing Co., 2002), 86.

20 Ibid., 84.

21 Faucheux, *Running for Office*, 156–7.

22 John J. Pitney, Jr, *The Art of Political Warfare* (Norman, OK: University of Oklahoma Press, 2000).

23 Faucheux, *Running for Office*, 187.

24 Ibid., 188.

25 Ibid., 196–7.

26 Ibid., 192

27 Ibid., 194.

17

The War of Ideas, Wedge Issues, Youth Recruitment, and Money

Kathleen Barr

American politics is in a perplexing place. Recent presidential elections have been decided by razor-thin margins, political rhetoric is divisive and sectarian, and public opinion is sharply divided between the two major parties. Yet as recently as 2006 the Republican Party controlled every branch of federal government, held a majority of state legislatures and statehouses, and had pushed political debate further to the right continuously for thirty years.[1] This seeming paradox existed because over the past thirty years Republicans and conservatives have built an infrastructure for winning political power superior to that of the Democrats and progressives, enabling conservative electoral and political success out of proportion to its strength and at variance with public opinion on the issues.

This is indeed a new phenomenon. In the first half of the twentieth century, there was no cohesive American conservative movement or ideology.[2] Conservatism's growth in America began when thinkers and leaders such as William F. Buckley, Jr, Russell Kirk, and Barry Goldwater brought together anti-communists, libertarians, and moral traditionalists, providing an ideological base for the conservative movement. From this base, American conservatives built a powerful infrastructure of think tanks, media outlets, and grassroots leadership that has impacted US public opinion and turned the Republican Party into a modern conservative powerhouse. Conversely, "liberal" is today a moniker that receives as little respect as "conservative" had before the 1970s, despite strong public support on progressive core issues such as health care, education, and the environment. Democrats grapple for a plan and progressive activists are badly splintered, despite the party's success taking back power in the US Senate in 2006. If conservatives and the Republican Party maintain their organizational superiority, US politics and policy will continue in a rightward movement. However, progressives and Democrats can win back political power by implementing a plan using lessons learned from the modern conservative resurgence.

The Conservative Movement

A handful of intellectuals in the 1940s and 1950s laid the foundation for the modern conservative coalition. In the first half of the twentieth century, ideological factions that today make up the conservative coalition—libertarians, traditionalists, and defense hawks—existed in disharmony and the Republican Party was by no means a conservative stronghold. A series of writings helped change that. In 1940, Friedrich von Hayek published *The Road to Serfdom*, a treatise against big government; in 1950 William F. Buckley, Jr, wrote *God and Man at Yale*, attacking the Republican Party and America's dominant liberal politics, and in 1953, Russell Kirk published *The Conservative Mind*, arguing that conservatism was the true American tradition. In 1962, Frank Meyer built upon these writings with *In Defense of Freedom*. Arguing that virtue and freedom are intertwined, Meyer paved the way for an ideological cohesion between the traditionalists, libertarians, and anti-communist internationalists, and helped fuse together a conservative ideology in America.[3]

The ideas of conservative intellectuals caught fire in the 1960s and 1970s with Americans increasingly unsettled by permissive social mores, the looming threat of communism, and unsettled economic times. In the 1960s, traditionalists began to flock to the Republican Party, disturbed by Democrats' affiliation with the women's movement, civil rights, and increasingly permissive social attitudes. The threat of communism motivated many isolationist conservatives to embrace an interventionist foreign policy and compromise small government in favor of increased defense spending. And when in the 1970s massive inflation and unemployment seemed to indicate a failure of traditional liberal Keynesian economics, libertarians and others were drawn to "supply-side" economics, which became an integral part of the conservative platform. Previously divided among both parties, libertarians, anti-communists, and traditionalists abandoned the Democrats in droves in the 1970s.[4] Today, the base of American conservatism is shaped by the ideas of Meyer, Buckley, and Hayek, and the politics of Goldwater and Reagan.

Follow the Money

Strategic, ongoing, and significant funding from philanthropists and self-interested corporations is a primary factor behind the conservative revolution. Beginning in the 1960s, conservative foundations began to invest millions of dollars in ideological think tanks and organizations. Conservative giving is led by "The Big Five": the Richard M. Scaife family of foundations, The Lynde and Harry Bradley Foundation, The John M. Olin Foundation, The Charles G. Koch Foundation, and the Coors family foundations. Nearly all well-known—and hundreds of less well known—conservative think tanks, publications, leadership training programs, legal foundations, and advocacy organizations are in part funded by money from The Big Five. In addition, dozens of other foundations fund conservative groups. From 1985 to 2005, the top thirty-six conservative foundations granted out a total of $2.8 billion just under half of which went to groups with public policy or political agendas.[5] In addition, beginning in the 1970s, wealthy corporations began to donate large sums of money to conservative political organizations. Frightened by the success of Ralph Nader's consumer movement and the growing strength of environmentalists, companies such as Citibank, General Electric, and General Motors began to donate increasingly large sums of money to the Republican Party, the Heritage Foundation, American Enterprise Institute, and other conservative institutions.[6]

Foundation and corporate funding have built a successful conservative movement for four reasons. First, foundations fund right-wing work at every stage in the process, from national and state think tanks to grassroots activist groups.[7] Second, conservative funding is deep and dependable. These foundations often give donations in increments of one million dollars or more (an amount almost unheard of from progressive funders), give funding toward "general support" rather than specific projects, and give for many consecutive years. Third, conservative foundations have no qualms giving to blatantly political organizations or media organizations,[8] such as the Heritage Foundation and Young America's Foundation. Both funders and organizations expertly exploit IRS loopholes that regulate their "charitable," tax-exempt statuses.

Funding from individual donors is also crucial to the conservative movement's strength. In 1957, conservative activist Richard Viguerie pioneered fundraising through direct mail,[9] today one of the most important tactics in political campaigns. The Right strategically diversifies its funding today: for example, two-thirds of the Heritage Foundation's budget comes from individual donors[10] and in the 2004 presidential primaries, 51% of George W. Bush's contributions came in amounts of under $200 in the post–Super Tuesday portion of the race.[11] Rather than rely solely on big donors, the Right recognizes the potential of the grassroots' pocketbooks.

The War of Ideas

Since the 1970s, conservative policy has infiltrated and increasingly shaped mainstream public opinion and policy due to a powerful network of conservative think tanks and media outlets. This network, today led by the Heritage Foundation and Fox News Channel, researches, develops, packages and publicizes policy ideas to create an "echo chamber" that, more often than not, makes its way into the mainstream media and public opinion. In *The Republican Noise Machine*, former conservative David Brock contends that the right wing spends about $300 million per year on this "war of ideas."[12] Each of The Big Five, and innumerable other foundations, have contributed millions to the war of ideas, including $57.9 million to the Heritage Foundation and $40 million to the American Enterprise Institute in the past twenty years.[13]

Think Tanks

Conservative think tanks are well-funded, particularly compared to progressive think tanks. The annual budgets of the top five conservative think tanks—Heritage Foundation, Center for Strategic and International Studies, American Enterprise Institute, Cato Institute, and American Legislative Exchange Council—are approximately $103.1 million. By contrast, the annual operating budgets of the top five progressive think tanks—Center on Budget and Policy Priorities, Center for American Progress, Center for Policy Analysis, Economic Policy Institute, and the Institute for Policy Studies—are approximately $21.8 million.[14]

Well-funded conservative think tanks have had a significant impact on public opinion and policy-making. One measure of impact is media exposure. According to a 2005 study by Fairness and Accuracy in Reporting (FAIR), conservative think tanks far outnumber centrist and progressive counterparts in total number of media attributions or appearances.[15] The study, based on a Lexis Nexis search of major papers and television and radio transcripts, found that 50% of media attributions are from conservative or center-right think tanks, compared to 16% from progressive or center-left think tanks. Of the top five most-cited think tanks in the media, four are conservative (Heritage Foundation, American Enterprise Institute, Center for Strategic and International Studies, and Cato Institute rank second, third, fourth and fifth). The most frequently cited think tank is the centrist Brookings Institution. Of the top ten, only one is progressive—the Economic Policy Institute, which ranks ninth, and two (Brookings and the Carnegie Endowment) are centrist. The remaining seven are conservative or center-right think tanks.

Conservative think tanks also exert their influence directly on Capitol Hill and the White House. From 1999 to 2001 conservative foundations gave a total of $254 million to public policy work, 46% of which went to think tanks.[16] The Heritage Foundation is particularly well-known for its overt mission to influence public policy. Since 1980, when the twenty-volume Heritage series "Mandate for Leadership" became the blueprint for the Reagan White House to its input into Newt Gingrich's "Contract with America," the Heritage Foundation has had its hand in substantial policy emanating from the White House and Congress.

Media

In addition to prominence in the mainstream media, conservatives have amplified their voice through conservative newspapers, magazines, websites, television networks, and radio shows. Conservative Matt Labash, in an interview with JournalismJobs.com, stated:

> We've created this cottage industry in which it pays to be un-objective . . . it's a great way to have your cake and eat it too. Criticize other people for not being objective. Be as subjective as you want. It's a great little racket.[17]

Top publications include the *National Review*, the *Weekly Standard*, and the *Washington Times*, as well as Fox News Channel and Radio America. Conservatives also blanket college campuses with conservative newspapers, supported by the Intercollegiate Studies Institute's Collegiate Network. Conservative "media watchdog" Accuracy in Media documents "liberal media bias" on a daily basis. Media has proven a powerful way for the conservatives to influence mainstream politics, the political parties, traditional media outlets, and American public policy.

Conservative publications began to appear in the 1940s; by the late 1960s, the publications, their ideas, and the concept of a "liberal media bias" were flourishing among conservatives and beginning to enter the mainstream. The most influential publication, *The National Review*, was founded by William F. Buckley, Jr in 1955, followed by *The Public Interest* founded in 1965 by Irving Kristol and Daniel Bell, and the favorite conservative opinion magazine, *The American Spectator*, founded under its current name in 1977 by R. Emmett Tyrell. In 1995, William Kristol, Fred Barnes, and John Podhoretz founded the *Weekly Standard* with funding from media mogul Rupert Murdoch. Today, *The Weekly Standard* is the most influential publication for conservatives, hand-delivered to the White House, policymakers, and politicians weekly. Today, print outlets are still crucial to the conservative echo-chamber, but radio, television, and Internet media such as Fox News Channel, Radio America, and The Drudge Report have amplified the reach of conservative propaganda.

Conservative foundations, corporations, and billionaires deserve much of the credit for the proliferation of right-wing media. *The American Spectator*, infamous for publishing the article by David Brock that characterized Anita Hill "a little bit nutty and a little bit slutty" during the Clarence Thomas Supreme Court hearings, received $6.1 million from the Scaife, Bradley, Olin, and Carthage Foundations from 1985 to 2000. National Affairs, which publishes *The National Review* and *The Public Interest*, and the Intercollegiate Studies Institute have received $8.1 million and $18 million, respectively, from foundations since 1985.[18] The Reverend Sun Myung Moon's Unification Church has spent $1 billion subsidizing *The Washington Times; The National Review* received start-up funds from William F. Buckley's oil company executive father,[19] and *The Weekly Standard* and *The New York Post* are bankrolled by Rupert Murdoch.[20] The "liberal bias watchdog" organization, Accuracy in Media, has been funded by Union Carbide and Mobil Oil, while Murdoch spent $400 million to keep Fox News afloat until it turned a profit in 2001.[21]

The Ground Troops

Despite the popular image of the 1960s as monopolized by the radical left, the seeds of the conservative grassroots began to sprout at this same time. On college campuses, young conservatives organized Young Americans for Freedom (YAF), in suburban America housewives and small business owners became politically active, anti-communists and xenophobes organized the John Birch Society and the Minutemen, and previously apolitical American churches began to awaken to the power of politics and faith.[22] Enduring today, and most crucial to today's conservative movement, are the Religious Right and youth activist groups.

Youth Recruitment and Leadership Development

Beginning in the 1950s numerous conservative student groups were active on college campuses. William F. Buckley's YAF, the Intercollegiate Society for Individualism, and numerous local Republican clubs sprung up on campuses; in the 1960s, Barry Goldwater's run for president mobilized thousands of young conservative activists.[23] Religion strongly influenced the conservative student movement, as did the growing conservative intellectual network of anti-communist, pro-capitalism thinkers.[24] The conservative's successful youth recruitment and leadership development is one of the most important factors contributing to today's conservative hegemony. Alumni of Barry Goldwater for President, College Republicans, YAF, the Intercollegiate Studies Institute, and the Leadership Institute reads like a who's who of conservative leaders: Karl Rove, Ralph Reed, Ann Coulter, Grover Norquist, G. Gordon Liddy, and Senator Mitch McConnell (Republican-Kentucky) are just a few.

The recruitment and leadership training arm of the Right is very well-funded. In the early years, the Leadership Institute, YAF, and others relied heavily on The Big Five foundations. Today, Bradley and Scaife still lead the way, but at least seventy foundations contribute to these groups.[25] Top givers include the Kirby Foundation, Lilly Endowment, Jaquelin Hume Foundation, and Murdock Charitable Trust. Their support is deep and broad. Of the seventy foundations, one-third give $100,000 or more annually, 37% donate over multiple years, and 40% donate to two or more leadership development groups. Each organization—and several newer groups including Young America's Foundation and the Center for the Study of Popular Culture—is also funded by thousands of small donors. In 2003, Young America's Foundation's budget was $12 million, the Intercollegiate Studies Institute's was $11.6 million, and the Leadership Institute's was $9.1 million.[26] In addition, the College Republican National Committee spent $30 million from 2001 to 2005 on partisan political activities,[27] including recruitment and training of activists.

Thanks to significant funding, the conservative training arm has reached tens of thousands of activists and produced many of today's leading conservatives. Dozens of members of Congress, more than 220 state legislators, and hundreds of prominent activists are graduates of these conservative training programs.[28] Since 1979, the Leadership Institute alone has trained 40,000 people and alumni, including "152 current state legislators [and] 82 graduates in TV news,"[29] the College Republicans have chapters on more than 1,000 campuses nationwide, and alumni of Goldwater's presidential run and YAF serve in Congress, on the courts, as editors of newspapers and television networks, and direct the top conservative think tanks.[30] Training is coordinated to reach the most potential leaders in an efficient way. Staff, advisors, and trustees overlap between all of these groups as well as other prominent conservative groups. In addition, the now infamous "Wednesday Meeting" chaired by Grover Norquist brings together everyone from top conservative operatives to "student activists fresh off the Greyhound bus" in order to coordinate strategy.[31]

The conservative leadership training programs successfully produce skilled conservative activists. The Leadership Institute offers courses on effective television techniques, grassroots communications, public speaking, get-out-the-vote, and more, run by experienced political operatives, such as Genevieve Wood, former Republican National Committee staff (a trainer for "Effective Television Techniques"), or Ron Nehring, vice chair of the California Republican Party (a trainer for "Grassroots Communications"). The Young America's Foundation "Club 100" rewards students with points toward a visit to the Reagan Ranch for each action they take. At the Ranch, students are treated to workshops with top conservative activists.

Conservative training programs also foster a sense of community and feeling that being conservative is "cool" by bringing together young people for both work and fun, and allowing them to rub shoulders with the top conservative operatives. Today, more than any time in the past, being a young Republican can be hip. Gone are the days of the 1980s' television sitcom *Family Ties* character Alex P. Keaton, the stereotyped, uptight, and buttoned-down young Republican. In *The Right Nation*, John Micklethwait and Adrian Wooldridge describe two conservative activists, Dustin and Maura, as "look[ing] like a couple of twenty-somethings in a creative writing course: a sprawl of slightly scruffy sweatshirts, jeans and sneakers . . ." and later record overhearing as "[o]ne young CPAC [Conservative Political Action Conference] activist boasted to a group of friends that he had Rove's cell phone number in the same excited tones that other students might use to boast of having Britney Spears'." In 2006, nearly half of CPAC attendees were young people, rubbing shoulders with Senator Rick Santorum (Republican-Pennsylvania) and Grover Norquist. A group of four students, just outside the CPAC exhibit hall, excitedly took out cell phones to call their parents after taking pictures with G. Gordon Liddy and nearly knocked over Senator John Cornyn (Republican-Texas), cameras out and ready, as he walked by. "This is the best day of my life," said one of the young ladies as Cornyn walked off. As the oratory wound down, talk turned to what D.C. bars to check out that night.[32] Youth recruitment and training is one of the primary factors behind the strength of today's conservative movement. With the help of foundations, conservative leaders have built a network of interconnected leadership training programs to recruit and train tens of thousands of new conservative leaders.

The Politicized Religious Right

The Religious Right is now a potent grassroots force in the conservative coalition, but as recently as the 1970s that was not the case. While a handful of Christian conservative leaders as early as the 1940s were urging evangelicals to become politically active,[33] E.J. Dionne, Jr notes that "[u]ntil the 1970s, a polite disrespect for politics characterized much of the fundamentalist and evangelical movement."[34] However, in the 1950s and 1960s, church membership grew, particularly in evangelical and fundamentalist churches. In the 1960s and 1970s, religious leaders and followers, alarmed by permissive social mores, the 1973 Supreme Court decision of *Roe v. Wade* permitting abortions, the women's movement, and the looming communist threat, began to join the political Right.[35] Further, influential conservatives such as Paul Weyrich and William F. Buckley, both deeply religious, built ties with the reverends Jerry Falwell and Pat Robertson, bringing them and their followers into the new conservative Republican fold.[36]

Today, the Religious Right is the base of the conservative political movement. The most religious Americans are reliable Republican voters. In 2004, 78% of Evangelical/Born-Again voters cast ballots for George W. Bush, as did 58% of weekly church-goers.[37] In addition, evangelicals are an important grassroots force, both in building public support for conservative policy and in turning out other voters. The Christian Coalition, founded by Pat Robertson, claims a membership of two million and, while perhaps its most influential years have passed it by, was very active in the 2004 elections, distributing more than seventy million voter guides in all fifty states.[38] Focus on the Family, founded by James Dobson, is a newer and arguably more influential Christian Right force in politics, thanks in part to nearly $3 million in grants from Olin, DeVos, Bradley, and other conservative foundations in its first five years.[39] Focus on the Family claims to reach more than 200 million people worldwide every day with its radio show and produces ten monthly magazines with a total of 2.3 million subscribers.[40] (See also Chapter 18, by Mark J. Rozell, on the Christian Right in America.)

Conclusion

By the beginning of the twenty-first century, the conservative coalition was diverse and powerful—but not infallible. By 2006, we began to see the disintegration of the right-wing coalition, a movement strong thanks to fifty years of smart organizing, not intrinsic power or a monopoly on public opinion. Despite Meyer and Buckley's justifications for fusing economic, social, and religious conservatives, libertarians and neoconservatives, Wall Street and Main Street, the conservative coalition is a tenuous network of diverging interests, the disagreements between which we are witnessing in the 2008 Republican presidential primary. Despite the recent cracks, however, conservative leaders and institutions built a well-organized, results-oriented coalition from which progressives must learn lessons. The agenda of the far-right is out of touch with public opinion. By creating and implementing a plan to out-organize conservatives, progressives can implement a strategy to take back power in America with a populist,[41] progressive agenda.

A Progressive Action Plan

Over the past ten years, the call for a progressive action plan to take back power in American politics has grown from a whisper to a loud yelp. However, we need a lion's roar. It is trendy to embrace George Lakoff's "framing" or talk approvingly about the new Democracy Alliance's call for rich progressives to pony up, but the actual work of implementing a comprehensive action plan is being led by the few. Perhaps this is yet another symptom of the Left's tunnel vision issue-based politics, perhaps it is simply that progressives are fed up with Democrats, or perhaps it is a lack of direction. Regardless, progressives can and must take back power.

There is hope for a progressive reemergence in American politics—public opinion is on our side. One need only look at the results of the 2006 congressional elections, 2004 initiatives, legislative victories in states, and the many failures of Republicans at the federal level. In 2004, Colorado, Nevada, and Florida voted for George W. Bush in the presidential election, but their residents overwhelmingly voted in favor of a renewable energy initiative in Colorado and minimum wage hikes in Nevada and Florida. In the states, progressives are winning campaigns for public financing of elections (Arizona, Connecticut, Oregon, New Mexico, North Carolina), renewable energy (California, Maryland), affordable housing (Illinois, Washington, North Carolina, Virginia), minimum wage increases (New Jersey, Illinois), reduced air pollution and greenhouse gas emissions (New Jersey, New York, Maine, New Hampshire, Connecticut), and more. Further, the Bush administration has tried and repeatedly failed to defund popular programs such as Head Start, Medicaid, and Medicare, open up wilderness areas to oil drilling, or to privatize Social Security, and relax pollution laws.

The above examples should give progressives confidence that they can and must take back power in American politics. Right-wing Republicans are out of step with America, too beholden to big corporations and radical religious groups to represent the people. However, they had organized in a manner superior to progressives for fifty years, and created an infrastructure for success. But despite their money, think tanks, media, and organization, they are fallible and are beginning to fall. If progressives learn from conservatives' tactical successes and create a superior infrastructure, we can take back our government. Following is a plan to do so.

Funding and the War of Ideas

Today, there are many left-liberal and progressive think tanks, but they do not have the resources, direction, or visibility to have a significant impact on American politics or public opinion. Excellent organizations such as the Center on Budget and Policy Priorities, the Urban Institute, and the Center for Policy Alternatives have been around for years. However, they have nowhere near the dominance in media, on public opinion, or with government that conservative groups have, for three primary reasons: funding, focus, and visibility.

Focused funding from charitable foundations gives conservative think tanks a significant political advantage over progressive institutes. Recent analyses suggest that the amount of foundation funding directed toward progressive policy institutes is not the reason they are less effective, but the type and scope of funding. While conservative foundations heap unrestricted grants upon conservative think tanks, center and left foundations shun grant requests for "general support" and fund only proposals for specific, time-limited projects.[42] For example, in 2000 the generally progressive Mott Foundation, gave slightly more to policy institutes ($7.45 million) than the conservative Bradley Foundation ($6.53 million), but most of its funding was devoted primarily to specific projects. By contrast, the majority of Bradley's funding went to general support. When viewed in this light, Bradley outspent Mott by about eight to one: $3.8 million to $460,000.[43]

Second, left think tanks do not create or disseminate their work in a deliberately political way, which conservative think tanks do so aggressively. In the 1970s and 1980s, as conservative funders such as Scaife, Coors, Olin, DeVos, and Koch invested heavily in overtly political organizations, liberal and moderate foundations began to scale back from political groups.[44] Today, the aim of the largest conservative think tanks is overtly political and public. Conservative researchers appear on television to debate policy, meet with elected officials, and print policy recommendations in publications that reach millions. For example, in 2004 the Brookings Institution spent 3% of its $39 million budget on communications, while the Heritage Foundation spent 20% of its $33 million 2002 budget on public and government affairs.[45] If progressives hope to have heft in the war of ideas, foundations must rethink their role and giving habits.

Aside from foundation funding, however, the Right's war of ideas does enjoy superior financial resources, thanks to wealthy corporations and successful fundraising from individuals. As stated above, the combined budget of the five largest conservative think tanks is nearly five times that of the five largest progressive think tanks ($103.1 million compared to $21.8 million).[46] While the newer Center for American Progress is much touted as a solution to this problem, its budget today is approximately $10 million—far larger than most progressive think tanks, but only about one-quarter of the Heritage Foundation's budget.

If progressives rely primarily on foundation support and rich philanthropists, we will forever be lagging far behind the financial heft of the Right. The Heritage Foundation's budget does not dwarf that of the Center for American Progress because of a dearth of foundation funding, but because oil companies, the pharmaceutical industry, and other big business will always have more money than any left-friendly foundation or individual and because of the success of individual donor programs. Progressives should think creatively about fundraising for our agenda. First, founding or forming alliances with socially responsible corporations—a strategy that exists in its infancy—should be greatly expanded. For companies such as Earthtones, the environmental phone company, and Working Assets, the wireless, credit card, and long distance service, funding progressive causes is integral to their missions. As discussed in William Greider's *The Soul of Capitalism*, progressives need not be at odds with business, but should harness the potential for joint progress.

In addition, progressives and Democrats must greatly ramp up their fundraising from individual donors. The 2004 election saw a glimmer of hope here for the Democrats, when Howard Dean ran a campaign financed primarily by small, Internet donations and a new firm, Grassroots Campaigns, raised tens of millions of dollars for Democrats from 750,000 individual donors through door-to-door and street canvassing. The primary race for the 2008 presidential election is also witnessing massive amounts of giving from individual donors. Many progressive groups have for years heavily invested in fundraising from individuals donors, but far too many rely on foundation support, which both restricts their ability to engage in political activities and also often forces them to compromise their missions at the whim of the foundation community. Grassroots fundraising is often difficult and the up-front costs seemingly prohibitive, but if progressives work together to implement outreach campaigns, the rewards will be a stronger, better-funded movement. For example, the New Progressive Coalitions' political "mutual funds," where small to medium-sized donors buy shares in pre-vetted organizations, thereby pooling their support, is a step in the right direction.

Progressives have slowly begun to remedy their disadvantage in the war of ideas, but have far to go. A set of political think tanks have recently opened. In 2003, former Clinton White House chief of staff John Podesta founded the Center for American Progress, now the second largest progressive think tank and home to a number of high-quality thinkers, while David Sirota founded the Progressive Legislative Action Network. In 2005, Simon Rosenberg, president of the New Democrat Network, and strategist Rob Stein formed the Democracy Alliance, a progressive clearinghouse with the goal of raising $200 million from wealthy donors to fund think tanks and advocacy groups.[47] These are all positive moves; however, the size and reach of the new think tanks is still miniscule compared to that of the conservative groups. The Center for American Progress at $10 million, is by far the largest, but has a budget just one-quarter of the Heritage Foundation. Until progressives expand their fundraising plan beyond rich progressives and foundations, they will be disadvantaged in the war of ideas.

The best ideas do no good unless they are disseminated widely. The "Republican Noise Machine," as coined by David Brock, is very successful. The basic infrastructure for progressives exists to do the same, but it must be used. Progressive publications such as *The Nation*, *Mother Jones*, and *The Progressive*, high-traffic blogs such as Daily Kos, and media watchdogs such as Media Matters and Fairness and Accuracy in Reporting exist, but are inadequately funded and shunned by mainstream Democrats. When funders, think tanks, and leaders work together to both improve progressive publications and strengthen their circulation, they will play a significant role in the progressive action plan.

A Progressive Issues Platform and Message

Progressive issues should be populist and vice versa. With the exception of a set of "wedge" issues discussed below, progressives' issues are popular with the public, but leaders and activists fail to communicate in a way that resonates with the public while also getting side-tracked both by hot-button wedge issues. Progressives should package a platform of issues that unites rather than divides a majority of Americans. All too often, politicians based their issues platforms on polls that ask voters about programs—Social Security, vouchers, welfare reform, the war in Iraq. While these polls are instructive, they can be misleading. For example, polls show the vast majority of Americans support strong gun control laws—but a values-based poll shows that that same majority reacts negatively on a cultural level to politicians who support additional federal gun laws. Americans value freedom, opportunity, hard work, security, community, and individuality; instead of talking about education, Social Security, or wages in terms of statistics and policy proposals, Democrats must learn to talk about issues using words that resonate with Americans' values.

Wedge Issues

In addition to packaging their core issues, Democrats must take away from conservatives their ability to use the wedge issues of abortion, gay marriage, and guns to rally cultural support. As noted by *The Economist*, "History is full of great generals who won their wars by staging strategic retreats."[48] Taking positions on these issues that are out of step with popular opinion and dependent on the judiciary has been a recipe for Democratic disaster; the effect has been falling support for Democrats among working-class people, suburban parents and church-goers. To some extent, portraying Democrats as out of touch with regular Americans is justified. E.J. Dionne, Jr wrote in 1991:

> The Sixties Left and the Eighties Right ... both profoundly mistrusted the decisions that a democratic electorate might arrive at. The Left increasingly stopped trying to make its case to the voters and instead relied on the courts to win benefits for needy and outcast groups.

231

A reliance on the judiciary to enforce contentious social issues—notably abortion—helps portray Democrats as elitist and out of touch with Americans by violating central democratic, populist American principles, and provides conservatives' powerful ammunition to win votes.

Reproductive Rights

Abortion is the wedge issue that has been most destructive for Democrats and a golden ticket for conservatives. In "A Heretical Proposal," the *Economist* notes that "in political terms, *Roe* [*vs. Wade*] has been particularly disastrous for the Democrats . . . a lightning-rod for conservatives . . . but imagine if *Roe* were overturned . . . The conservative coalition would be split asunder."[49]

Americans generally support a woman's right to choose and oppose attempts to illegalize abortion, but are at the same time turned off by Democrats' rhetoric on this issue. In contrast to the immovable positions take by pro-life and pro-choice groups, polling shows that most Americans hold more middle-of-the-road views on reproductive rights, torn between a respect both for life and for women's right to privacy and autonomy.[50] Just 21% of American adults favor making abortion illegal,[51] and polls consistently find that more than 80% say that abortion should be sometimes or always legal.[52] However, support for unrestricted abortion is not strong and the fact that only a slim majority (53%) of Americans identify as pro-choice[53] should give Democrats pause. The pro-choice movement's rhetoric does not play well with most Americans, while the conservative's choice of "partial-birth" abortion as a focal issue has been an excellent tool for public sympathy: up to 70% of Americans favor making this procedure illegal, with exceptions if the mother's life is in danger.[54] Conservative strategists did not choose "partial-birth" abortion (or name it as such) because it is a significant issue—only 0.015% to 0.076% of abortions in the US qualify as "partial-birth"[55]—but because it is a great way to rally the base and make Democrats look amoral.

Democrats and progressives should revise their stance on the issue to be more in line with public opinion, stop relying on *Roe v. Wade*, and accept taking this issue back to the people. Americans strongly support legal abortion. In the long run, allowing voters and their representatives to make laws regarding abortion will both protect a woman's right to choose and strengthen the Democrats' support with more voters. The *Economist* article points out that the US is the only comparable country that has not settled the abortion issue by consulting the electorate through their legislative representatives or referendum, which in nearly all other rich countries has led "broadly, [to] the triumph of abortion rights. Because abortion was legalized democratically . . . abortion became a settled right." If Democrats ever expect to gain back the vote and trust of a majority of Americans, they must stop being scared of populist sentiment and shackled by the tunnel-vision abortion rights organizations. Allowing the people to make decisions on abortion rights will lead to broad-based protections and help dissipate this cultural issue that works to the benefit of Republicans.

Pro-choice activists may argue—incorrectly—that this action will lead to illegalized abortion in many states. The fact is abortion options are already rare or non-existent in socially conservative states. For example, although there are 1,819 abortion clinics in the US, there are only two in North Dakota and South Dakota and three in Kentucky and Wyoming—but fifty-one in Hawaii and 400 in California.[56] There are both more clinics in progressive states and more per capita: one per 89,734 people in California and one per 24,761 people in Hawaii, but just one per 317,183 people in North Dakota.[57] Pro-choice advocates will also point out that twenty-four states have on the books "trigger" laws to outlaw abortion if *Roe v. Wade* is overturned. Setting aside whether or not trigger laws can be enforced,[58] it is likely that, without the cover of voting for an unenforceable law, many of these laws would be overturned or elected officials in favor of banning abortion would be thrown out of office. The same argument holds: disowning *Roe* and allowing the people to decide the law is both strategic and ultimately the best move to preserve freedom of choice.

Gay Marriage

Conservatives have successfully exploited the issue of gay marriage to rally their base and win votes from cultural conservatives over the past several years. In 2004, George W. Bush and John Kerry faced questions over support for gay marriage and civil unions; while Bush's blanket opposition to any formal union excited his base, Kerry's answer—in support of civil unions but against gay marriage—both irritated those on the left and fed into the right's portrayal of him as a "flip-flopper." Polling informs us why. About 45% of Americans support civil unions and 39% support gay marriages, while opposition is 51% and 56%, respectively.[59] It appears most Americans, whether for or against, do not see much difference between civil unions and gay marriage.

America is clearly not ready for gay marriage and Democrats and progressives must recognize this and refuse to play into debating this issue with conservatives. Far from a sell-out position, setting gay marriage aside for now is the smart thing to do. First, it will eliminate a conservative wedge issue. According to the 2004 National Election Pool, 34% of voters believed that there should be no legal recognition of gay and lesbian relationships, and 70% of those voters voted for Bush. A majority of voters in favor of civil unions but against gay marriage also voted for Bush.[60] Further, 22% of 2004 voters indicated "moral issues" as the issue most important in their choice for president—more than any other issue—and 80% of those that said this voted for Bush. While opposition to gay marriage is obviously not the only issue that caused these voters to choose Bush over Kerry, Democrats should take serious note of these figures.

Second, public opinion is on the path toward acceptance of gay marriage already. In 2004, 39% of Americans supported gay marriage, but in 1996 only 27% did. Today, 56% oppose gay marriage, but ten years ago 68% did.[61] Public opinion is trending this way due to simple demography. Today's young adults are part of the most diverse generation in American history and have grown up with popular gay-friendly television shows *Will and Grace* and *Ellen*, and a society where gay-bashing is seen increasingly akin to racial bigotry. According to the Pew Center for People and the Press, 42% of people between eighteen and twenty-nine years of age are in favor of gay marriage, compared with 25% of those between fifty and sixty-four years and 35% of thirty to forty-nine year olds. A Fox News poll found that 58% of eighteen to twenty-nine year olds think gay marriage should be legal, compared to 41% overall. Conservatives cannot compete with demography. All indications are that in ten years, a majority of Americans will support gay marriage and in the next twenty-five years gay marriage will be legal and socially accepted.

Democrats and progressives should focus on gay rights issues, such as employment discrimination and hate crimes, which impact more gay Americans and also have strong public support. It is legal in thirty-three states to fire a person because of his or her sexual orientation, and according to the Federal Bureau of Investigation (FBI), law enforcement reported 1,407 hate crimes against gay, lesbian, or bisexual Americans in 2004.[62] Democrats should fight to end these egregious civil rights violations—these goals are also supported by the vast majority of Americans.[63] But right now the public is too divided on the issue of gay marriage for Democrats to take up the bullhorn. More importantly, the Right is too skilled at using this issue as a political tool. Progressives should position themselves as the populist party that listens to and accepts public opinion.

Guns

Gun control is an issue of local policy and individual rights that runs into opposition from Democrats' so-called "mommy complex." The cultural and political landscape is entirely different in Montana and Alabama than in New York City, Philadelphia, or Los Angeles, and on this issue the same rules cannot apply. US Senate candidate Bob Casey, Jr (Democrat-Pennsylvania) running in a state often characterized as "Philadelphia and Pittsburgh with Alabama in between," knows this. While he strongly supports enforcing existing laws, he opposes increased regulation on firearm ownership.[64] Statewide, about 40% of Pennsylvania voters strongly favor additional gun control laws, while one-quarter opposes new laws. But opinion varies wildly between voters in and around the two major cities and everyone else. Among registered Democrats, support for additional gun control polls at 62% in Philadelphia and 68% in the closest four southeastern counties. Conversely, only 27% of registered Democrats in rural Southwest Pennsylvania strongly support additional gun laws.[65]

Finally, and most importantly for Democrats to realize, federal gun control is a battle they can only lose. First, bearing arms is an American right. The Second Amendment[66] is clearly viewed by Americans as protecting the right to own a gun: nearly three-quarters (72%) of Americans say the Second Amendment guarantees the inalienable right to own a gun.[67] No progressive can justify abortion, free speech, or the right to food or health care using the Constitution while railing against guns. Second, public opinion is increasingly on the side of the National Rifle Association. In 1990, 78% of Americans thought that gun laws should be stricter; today, only 54% do. Second, voters see guns as a cultural issue and therefore gun control positions as a cultural attack. As James Carville and Paul Begala note in their book *Take It Back*, "gun control is more about culture than about crime, especially in noncoastal America."[68] They base this on a poll showing that, while Americans overwhelmingly support banning assault weapons, those same people agreed with the statement "When I hear a politician talk about gun control, it makes me think he doesn't share my values."[69] Carville and Begala continue, "when a Democrat takes a position on gun control—even a position that most folks agree with—millions of Americans resent them and worry about whether the position is really an attack on their culture." This situation only plays into conservatives' portrayal of Democrats as elitist snobs from big east coast cities. Democrats should not fall into the trap of justifying those stereotypes.

"If middle-class folks aren't getting jacked up about abortion, they might pay attention to how the GOP is robbing them blind on economic issues," argue Begala and Carville.[70] The same could be said for deeply religious Americans or the issues of gay marriage and guns. Democrats and progressives perennially wonder why they have lost the "Joe Sixpack" and religious votes to Republicans, but when looking at the fight over cultural issues, the answer to that question is clear. As pollster Stanley Greenberg wrote of the 2004 election, "Bush's determined culture war . . . [forced] people to choose sides . . . turned the heads of many swing blue-collar voters . . . and eroded Kerry's Catholic support."[71] Democrats must develop more strategic positions on abortion, gun control, and gay rights. By relying on the judiciary on abortion and gay marriage, Democrats' positions alienate the public. This is a disastrous path. To win back the public, Democrats must start to trust the voters. While progressives should never stray from core values of freedom and justice, they must think about how to win strategically while being the truly democratic party.

Youth Recruitment and Leadership Development

Youth recruitment and leadership development is a strategy that the Right borrowed from the Left. It is time the Left take it back. College campuses are a bevy of progressive activism. Students concerned with poverty volunteer with Oxfam USA and the One Campaign, environmentalists join the Sierra Student Coalition, the student Public Interest Research Groups (PIRGs), or Rainforest Action Network, living wage campaigns abound on campus, women's rights groups organize Take Back the Nights and NARAL chapters, and student branches of the American Civil Liberties Union (ACLU), the National Association for the Advancement of Colored

People (NAACP), and Amnesty International exist on hundreds of campuses. Beyond that, college students organize hundreds of local political efforts, as well as service-oriented volunteer programs.

In addition, recent years have seen an increase in non-campus youth political activities. In addition to organic efforts, organizations such as the Oregon Bus Project, Forward Montana, the League of Young Voters, the Hip Hop Political Caucus, and many others have reached out to young adults to organize around issues of economic insecurity, community violence, health care, immigration, elections, and more.

However, progressive youth activism is too frequently disjoined from overall progressive political power-building, and too little is electoral or focused on building political power. For instance, the College Republicans have chapters on 1,000 campuses and spent out more than $30 million from 2001 to 2004, while the College Democrats spent out just $210,038 from 2000 to 2004.[72] Beyond partisan politics, the size difference between conservative political groups such as Young America's Foundation and the Leadership Institute and progressive groups such as Campus Program (Center for American Progress) and Young People For (People for the American Way) is astounding: in 2003, Young America's Foundation's budget was $12 million and the Leadership Institute's $9.1 million. Compare that to the current $1.5 million budget of Campus Progress or the $1 million budget of Young People For. PIRG and other national networks that prioritize youth organizing are a start toward building a skilled set of young progressive leaders, but more needs to be done. Following the success of the Right, progressives should invest serious sums of money in youth recruitment, develop a network for internships and jobs, and train young people to be skilled and politicized progressive leaders.

A Strategic Coalition

Much has been made of the red (Republican) and blue (Democratic) divide. Since 2000, televisions have shown the US map, with wide swaths of red states with small enclaves of blue states broadcast hugging the Atlantic and Pacific coasts. The tale of "Two Americas" is exaggerated, but Democrats do need to be alarmed that so much of middle America, working-class people, and the booming exurbs are voting Republican. Today, the Democrats' base consists of African-Americans, the secular, the highly-educated, urban Americans, and working-class union members. In addition, young people and Latinos lean Democratic. To win back America, however, Democrats must think about how to solidify or increase support from these voters.

The culture war is a significant reason why Democrats have lost support from working-class whites, Catholics, and Protestants. White working-class men were the backbone of the Democrat's New Deal coalition, but by the 1980s, 61% voted for Ronald Reagan[73] and in 2004 George W. Bush won the white working-class vote by twenty-three points over John Kerry.[74] Catholics, once a Democratic mainstay, now lean Republican: in 2004, 52% of Catholics voted for Bush and 47% for Kerry. White Protestants began to defect from the Democratic Party in the late 1970s: Jimmy Carter, himself a "born-again Christian," won 52% of the white evangelical Protestant vote in 1976, but by 1984, 80% of their vote went to Reagan.[75] Further, Hispanics, the fastest growing ethnic group in America, are largely Catholic. In 2004, 44% voted for Bush— nine points more than voted for him in 2000 and twenty-three points more than voted for Dole in 1996.[76] While the culture war is not the only reason Democrats have lost support from working-class and religious whites, and are quickly losing the Hispanic vote, it is a major factor.

In addition to a comprehensive youth leadership plan, Democrats must devote significant resources to securing and turning out the youth vote. In a significant shift from the 1990s and early 2000s, today's eighteen to twenty-nine year olds are a strongly Democratic voting bloc. In 2000, young voters went for Gore over Bush by only two percentage points, but in 2004, 54% of young voters cast ballots for John Kerry, nine points more than voted for Bush. In Wisconsin and

New Hampshire, the youth vote gave Kerry his margin of victory, and nearly did so in Iowa and Nevada.[77] In 2006, the youth vote's Democratic leanings grew: that year, 60% of eighteen to twenty-nine year olds voted for Democrats while just 38% voted for Republicans, the largest margin of any age group. In the states of Montana and Virgina, the second congressional district of Connecticut, and the ninth congressional district of Indiana, and several other races, eighteen to twenty-nine year olds' vote choice and increased turnout over previous years made the different for the Democratic candidates, now Senators Jon Tester (Montana) and Jim Webb (Virginia), and Representatives Joe Courtney (Connecticut) and Baron Hill (Indiana).[78]

Did young people suddenly have a progressive epiphany between 2000 and 2006? Between 2000 and 2004, there was no major ideological change—eighteen to twenty-nine year olds' party identification remained about evenly split between Democrats, Republicans, and Independents.[79] It seems the reason for stronger Democratic support at the polls in 2004 was due to higher young voter turnout—that year 4.3 million more eighteen to twenty-nine year olds voted than did in 2000.[80] In fact, the size of the youth vote (20.1 million) rivaled the size of the over-sixty-five vote (22.3 million) in the 2004 elections.[81] In swing states where youth turnout was highest, support for Kerry was also highest. Further, young single women and African-Americans, the most reliably Democratic young voters, led the increase in youth turnout.[82]

The story changed in 2006, however. Not only did eighteen to twenty-nine year olds vote overwhelmingly for Democrats in the midterm elections (by 22 points) but we also began to see a shift in party identification. No longer split evenly between the two parties and independents, by the 2006 elections 43% of eighteen to twenty-nine year olds identified as Democrats, compared to 31% as Republicans and 19% as Independents.[83] Again, as in 2004, young voter turnout played a significant part in Democratic vote totals.[84]

Young adults are a crucial bloc for Democrats to engage and mobilize. They constitute a huge group,[85] are voting in growing numbers, and are increasingly Democratic. Despite the accepted adage that young people do not vote, the turnout jumps in 2004 and 2006 and their impact on Democratic victories should spur Democrats to invest heavily in young voter turnout in 2008 and beyond.

Conclusion

To take back political power in America, progressives must organize an infrastructure superior to that of conservatives. Today the progressive coalition is a splintered set of provincial interests, including women's groups, advocates for the poor, racial minority lobbies, environmental groups, youth advocates, and more. By investing in a stronger infrastructure of think tanks and media outlets, grassroots leadership and activism, a thoughtful issues platform, and a strategic coalition, progressives can work together to win political power.

There is reason for optimism—today, progressives have identified their weaknesses and are beginning to devote resources toward building a strategic coalition and infrastructure. Optimism comes from new groups like the Center for American Progress, Young People For, Forward Montana, the Oregon Bus Project, Rockridge Institute and Longview Institute, Institute for America's Future, Center for Progressive Leadership, the Take Back America conference, and more. Wealthy progressives such as Andy Rappaport, Peter and Jonathan Lewis, Jonathan and George Soros, and the members of the Democracy Alliance are committing millions to progressive infrastructure-building, and intellectuals such as George Lakoff and the Center for Policy Alternatives are beginning to break through to activists on the need to frame a message that encompasses the basic beliefs running beneath the disparate progressive coalition. The successes of 2004 and 2006 bode well for resource-building, and activists on the ground have made attempts at building more strategic coalitions—groups active in the 2004 elections such as Voices for Working Families and America Votes began to bridge the identity gap. The desire, knowledge, and initial action are there, as are initial victories in the 2006 elections. It remains to be seen whether progressives can organize a true movement to take back power in America.

Notes

1 John Micklethwait and Adrian Wooldridge, *The Right Nation* (New York: Penguin Books, 2004), 414–17.
2 Lee Edwards, *The Conservative Revolution* (New York: The Free Press, 1999), 75; Alan Crawford, *Thunder on the Right* (New York: Pantheon Books, 1980).
3 Paul Gottfried and Thomas Fleming, *The Conservative Movement* (Boston, MA: Twayne Publishers, 1988), 1. Friedrich von Hayek, *Road to Serfdom* (New York: Routledge, 2006, 1944); William F. Buckley, Jr., *God and Man at Yale: The Superstitions of "Academic Freedom"* (New York: Gateway Editions, 1978, 1951); Russell Kirk, *The Conservative Mind: From Burke to Eliot*, 4th ed. (New York: Equinox Books, 1973, 1953); Frank S. Meyer, *In Defense of Freedom: A Conservative Credo* (Chicago, IL: H. Regnery Co., 1962)
4 Edwards, *The Conservative Revolution*, 3.
5 Media Transparency, "The Strategic Philanthropy of Conservative Foundations," http://www.mediatransparency.org/conservativephilanthropy. Accessed February 1, 2006.
6 John B. Judis, *The Paradox of American Democracy* (New York: Routledge, 2000), 124.
7 People for the American Way Foundation, "Buying a Movement: Right-Wing Foundations," http://www.pfaw.org/pfaw/general/default.aspx?oid=2052.
8 Andrew Rich, *War of Ideas*, (Stanford, CA: Stanford Social Innovation Review, 2005), 18.
9 Edwards, *The Conservative Revolution*, 152–3.
10 Heritage Foundation Annual Report 2004, www.heritage.org.
11 The Campaign Finance Institute, "Wrap-Up Analysis of Primary Funding," http://www.cfinst.org/pr/100404.html.
12 David Brock, *The Republican Noise Machine* (New York: Crown Publishing, 2004), 380.
13 Media Transparency, "Recipients," www.mediatransparency.org. Accessed February 1, 2006.
14 Figures from 2003 or 2004 IRS 990 forms, except the Heritage Foundation (from 2004 Annual Report).
15 Michael Dolny, "Right, Center Think Tanks Still Most Quoted," *Fairness and Accuracy in Reporting Extra!* (May/June 2005): 1.
16 Jeff Krehely, Meaghan House, and Emily Kernan, "Axis of Ideology," *National Committee for Responsive Philanthropy* (March 2004): 2.
17 Brock, *The Republican Noise Machine*, 10.
18 Media Transparency, "Recipients."
19 Micklethwait and Wooldridge, *The Right Nation*, 50.
20 Sheldon Rampton and John Stauber, *Banana Republicans* (New York: Penguin Group, 2004), 68.
21 Brock, *The Republican Noise Machine*, 381.
22 David Farber and Jeff Roche, *The Conservative Sixties* (New York: Peter Lang Publishing, Inc., 2003), 7.
23 Edwards, *The Conservative Revolution*, 104.
24 Gottfried and Fleming, *The Conservative Movement*, 22.
25 Iara Peng, "Conservative Leadership Development," *Young People For* (January 2006): 1.
26 Ibid.
27 The Center for Public Integrity, www.publicintegrity.org. Accessed February 10, 2006.
28 Peter Murray, "Winning from Within," *Center for Progressive Leadership* (February 2006): 2.
29 The Leadership Institute, Youth Leadership School promotional materials.
30 Edward, *The Conservative Revolution*, 138–9.
31 Micklethwait and Wooldridge, *The Right Nation*, 16.
32 Based on personal observation during attendance at CPAC 2006 on Thursday February 9, 2006.
33 Scott Flipse, "Below the Belt Politics," in *The Conservative Sixties*, ed. David Farber and Jeff Roche (New York: Peter Lang Publishing, Inc., 2003), 132.
34 E.J. Dionne, Jr., *Why Americans Hate Politics* (New York: Simon & Schuster, 1991), 209.
35 James T. Patterson, *Grand Expectations* (New York: Oxford University Press, 1996), 328–30.
36 Flipse, "Below the Belt Politics," 127.
37 National Election Pool, National Exit Poll, 2004.
38 Christian Coalition, www.cc.org. Accessed February 12, 2006.

39 Media Transparency, "Recipients."

40 Focus on the Family, www.family.org. Accessed March 17, 2006.

41 *Populist* is used to describe a political agenda based on the rights, wisdom, or virtues of common people.

42 Rich, "War of Ideas," 20.

43 Ibid., 22.

44 Ibid., 21.

45 Ibid., 25.

46 Figures from 2003 or 2004 IRS 990 forms, except the Heritage Foundation (from 2004 Annual Report).

47 Thomas Edsall, "Rich Liberals Vow to Fund Think Tanks," *The Washington Post*, August 7, 2005, A01.

48 Lexington, "A Heretical Proposal," *The Economist*, December 10, 2005, 40.

49 Ibid.

50 William Saletan, *Bearing Right*, (Berkeley, CA: University of California Press, 2003), 1–7.

51 CBS News/New York Times Poll. January 20–25, 2006

52 CNN/USA Today/Gallup Poll. November 11–13, 2005.

53 CNN/USA Today/Gallup Poll. January 6–8, 2006.

54 CNN/USA Today/Gallup Poll. January 10–12, 2003.

55 Figures are based upon total abortions per year in the U.S. (1.31 million, according to both the Alan Guttmacher Institute and the National Right to Life Committee) and estimated numbers of "partial-birth" abortions, ranging from the pro-choice Guttmacher Institute's estimate of 2,000 and an estimate of 5,000 to 10,000 from Dr Curtis Cook, a pro-life doctor at Michigan State University College of Human Medicine.

56 Lawrence Finer and Stanley Henshaw, "Abortion Incidence and Services in the United States in 2000," *Perspectives on Sexual and Reproductive Health* 35 (1) (2003): 10.

57 State population statistics from the 2004 U.S. Census Bureau.

58 Some legal articles suggest "trigger" laws are valid once the prohibitive law has been overturned: see most recently: Richard H. Fallon, Jr., "Making Sense of Overbreadth," *Yale Law Journal* 100 (1991): 853, 876. However, others suggest that the question is unsettled: see Charles Nesson and David Marglin, "The Day the Internet Met the First Amendment," *Harvard Journal of Law and Technology* 10 (1996): 113–35.

59 Quinnipiac University poll, Dec. 7–12, 2004 and CNN/USA Today/Gallup, April 29–May 1, 2005.

60 National Election Pool, 2004 Exit Poll Survey.

61 CNN/USA Today/Gallup Poll. April 29–May 1, 2005.

62 Human Rights Campaign, "Statewide Anti-Discrimination Laws and Policies," www.hrc.org. F.B.I., "Hate Crime Statistics," www.fbi.gov. Accessed March 12, 2006.

63 Seventy-five percent of Americans support hate crime legislation to protect gays and lesbians (The Gallup Organization, April 7, 1999); nearly 90% favor equal opportunity employment (The Gallup Organization, May 15, 2003).

64 Lancaster County Action 2004 Voter Guide Questionnaire, November 2, 2004.

65 Center for Politics and Public Affairs, Franklin and Marshall College, "Wedge Issues in the Democratic Primary, March 5, 2002," www.fandm.edu/x2348.xml.

66 The Second Amendment reads "A well regulated militia, being necessary to the security of a free state, the right of the people to keep and bear arms, shall not be infringed."

67 Gary Langer, "The Silly Season," ABC News, May 1, 2003.

68 Paul Begala and James Carville, *Take It Back: A Battle Plan for Democratic Victory* (New York: Simon & Schuster, 2006), 48.

69 Ibid.

70 Ibid., 45.

71 Stanley Greenberg, *The Two Americas: America's Current Political Deadlock and How to Break it* (New York: St Martin's Press, 2004), 313.

72 Center for Responsive Politics, www.opensecrets.org. Accessed February 10, 2006.

73 John B. Judis and Ruy Teixeira, *The Emerging Democratic Majority* (New York: Scribner, 2002), 22.

74 National Election Pool, 2004 Exit Poll Survey.

75 Judis and Teixeira, *The Emerging Democratic Majority*, 24.

76 Hispanics voted 53% Kerry, 44% Bush (National Election Pool, 2004 Exit Poll); 62% Gore, 35% Bush in 2000, and 72% Clinton, 21% Dole in 2000 (Voter News Service).

77 Center for Information and Research on Civic Learning and Engagement, "2004 Youth Voting Map," http://www.civicyouth.org/Map.htm.

78 Young Voter Strategies, *Young Voter Mobilization Tactics*, 2007.

79 In 2000, 36.1% of eighteen to twenty-nine year olds identified as Democrat, 34.7% as Republican, and 29.2% as Independent; in 2002, 36.7% identified as Democrat, 39.2% as Republican, and 24.1% as

Independent. In 2004, 36.9% identified as Democrat, 34.5% as Republican, and 28.6% as Independent (National Election Pool Exit Poll, 2000–2004).

80 U.S. Census Bureau, 2004 Current Population Survey, November Voting and Registration Supplement.

81 Ibid.

82 African-American eighteen to twenty-nine year olds' turnout jumped by 11 percentage points from 2000 to 2004, more than any other racial or ethnic group, and eighteen to twenty-nine year old women increased their turnout by ten percentage points. Fifty-two percent voted, higher than their male peers and than young adults overall.

83 National Election Pool Exit Poll, 2006.

84 In 2006, 1.9 million more eighteen to twenty-nine year olds voted than in 2002, according to the U.S. Census Bureau, making it the second election in a row with increased young voter turnout—the first time we had seen two consecutive increases in eighteen to twenty-nine year olds' turnout in twenty-four years.

85 According to Rock the Vote tabulations of U.S. Census Bureau 2000–2050 projections for the year 2008, there will be approximately forty-four million eighteen to twenty-nine-year-old citizens in 2008.

18

The Religious Right in American Politics

Mark J. Rozell

Perhaps no movement in contemporary US politics is more misunderstood than the Christian Right. Interpretations of this movement vary dramatically. Defenders of the movement see it as an important voice in US politics trying to restore moral order to an increasingly secular society that tolerates behavior that would have been unthinkable a generation ago. Opponents see the Christian Right as an intolerant group that wants to make everyone else live by its own narrow moral code. Defenders see the movement as a counterpoint to the dominant liberal creed promoted by the mainstream media, higher education, public schools, and Hollywood. Opponents perceive the Christian Right as firmly in control of the Republican Party and at the center of policy decisions when the party has controlled either Congress or the White House.[1]

There is a great deal of exaggeration on both sides when it comes to the Christian Right. It is important therefore to demystify this movement because many observers make a bit too much of it. This chapter thus steps back from all the controversy and tries to explain in a less heated fashion what this movement is, its role in US politics, and its influence on policy.

The Christian Right is comprised largely of evangelical and born-again Christians who are socially conservative and politically active. The movement includes other religious conservative groups as well, especially traditional Catholics who are active in pro-life politics. Most scholars trace the origins of the modern Christian Right to the 1970s when certain secular conservative leaders saw the potential for forming a powerful political alliance on the Right that would include pro-business groups, anti-tax, anti-Communist, and social conservative activists.[2] Although many correctly refer to the Christian Right primarily as a social movement, today it is also a leading interest group and a strong faction within the Republican Party.

As an interest group the Christian Right is formidable in size and potential influence. Scholars generally places the size of the core constituency of the Christian Right between 14–18% of the US voting population, and thus on a par with the African-American vote, with the Latino vote, and larger than the labor union household vote.[3] In its role as a party faction, the Christian Right exerts significant influence on Republican platforms and nominations. Despite these three roles for the Christian Right, the policy influence of the movement has been limited since its formation.

By 1972, neither national party had ever mentioned the word "abortion" in its party platform. But the 1973 *Roe v. Wade* Supreme Court decision that legalized abortion as a privacy right changed this landscape and gave a powerful impetus for social conservatives to become involved in politics. Also in the 1970s, social conservatives in a number of communities had organized in local politics on a variety of issues. Most of this political activity was centered on public school teaching materials and efforts by some communities to adopt anti-discrimination laws to protect gays and lesbians.

In 1978 the Rev. Jerry Falwell, pastor of Thomas Road Baptist Church in Lynchburg, Virginia, organized a statewide pastor-led campaign to oppose a horse-track betting referendum in the state. He succeeded in helping to narrowly defeat the referendum and said immediately after that his organizational effort to mobilize religious leaders in politics was a portent of "future endeavors together."[4] This was an important acknowledgment because Falwell had earlier taken the more traditionally separationist view that religion and politics should not mix. He, like most conservative Protestant leaders of that time, had warned parishioners against getting involved in "matters of this world" and to let God work His will on society.[5]

Falwell and others changed their minds after *Roe v. Wade* and in response to what they perceived as an increasingly secular culture that disrespected the views of religious people. In interviews with a number of religious conservative leaders, time and again they said that they had come to realize that they were God's stewards in this world and that it was their moral duty to take up political activity to try to stem the moral decline of the United States. Many interviewees said that their largest challenge was convincing parishioners to get out of the pews and into politics after having communicated a different message for so long. Thus, it wasn't easy at first to mobilize the Christian Right, but a combination of factors converged to make this happen.[6]

Ironically, it was Jimmy Carter in 1976 who helped energize this potential constituency when he campaigned openly as a born-again Christian who was guided in his public life by his faith. Many Southern evangelicals who had been previously apolitical rallied to his candidacy, only to eventually reject Carter because of disappointment with his social policies.

Because of Carter's electoral success at mobilizing many previously apolitical evangelicals, a group of secular conservative leaders saw an opportunity. They believed that they could build a powerful coalition of secular and religious conservative groups that would make the Republicans the dominant party for years. They reached out to Falwell, who formed a national organization called the Moral Majority. They convinced Republican candidate Ronald Reagan to make direct appeals to conservative evangelicals on the belief that, if successfully mobilized, this group could deliver millions of new votes to the Republican Party. Reagan did exactly that and thus the Christian Right became firmly entrenched in the Republican Party.[7] The 1980 Republican Party landslide surprised most observers, and few ultimately disputed Falwell's claim that his Moral Majority had helped to mobilize for the Republican Party nearly four million previously apolitical evangelical voters. Falwell was an instant major player in US politics and the Christian Right was the big story of the newly resurgent Republican Party. Although Reagan did not forcefully push the social issues agenda in his two terms as president, the Christian Right had nonetheless achieved legitimacy by having a voice in the administration.

Before returning to the story of the evolution of the movement, I want to address the size and potential electoral impact of the Christian Right in US politics.

Size of the Christian Right

Although scholars put the Christian Right vote nationally at about 14–18% in general elections, the percentage goes way up in some states, particularly in the South, and way down in others, especially in the Northeast. Over the past three decades popular accounts have tended to characterize the Christian Right at various times either as "taking over" American politics or on the verge of extinction. The real story of the movement is one of continuity, although like with all movements, interest groups, and party factions, its fortunes rise or fall depending on a variety of circumstances at any period in time. The core constituency of the Christian Right has remained fairly stable over the past three decades, even though the movement has turned out to vote more heavily in some elections (such as 2004 and 1996) than in others (most notably in 2000 when its participation was way down).

The key power of the Christian Right is within the Republican Party, where the movement has succeeded in helping to nominate social conservative candidates for various offices, and led platform and rules committees. In the early period of Christian Right mobilization there was a fierce battle for party control between social conservatives and party moderates.[8] It is widely acknowledged that over time, the social conservatives won. But the story is a little more complicated than one group ousting another. What actually has happened is that the Christian Right had learned over time how to play the political game much smarter, and thus became a stronger force in the Republican Party and US politics. Nonetheless, the battle between party moderates and the social conservatives continues.

The first wave of the Christian Right, generally from the 1970s to the end of the 1980s is widely seen as a failure. By the end of the 1980s two terms of the Reagan presidency had delivered very little on social policy, the Moral Majority was bankrupt and disbanded, and most coverage of the evangelical movement focused on several high-profile televangelist scandals. The Rev. Marion G. (Pat) Robertson of the 700 Club had run for president in 1988 only to be soundly defeated after running the most expensive primary campaign up to that point. The socially moderate George H.W. Bush succeeded Reagan, leaving the Christian Right little to hope for. Many scholars and journalists had started writing the obituary of the Christian Right. Whether or not they thought the Christian Right was defunct, scholars agreed that the movement had failed to that point due to a lack of political sophistication among the leaders who tended to use extreme rhetoric and eschew the necessity of compromise.[9]

Yet the movement endured. In 1989, Robertson formed a new organization, the Christian Coalition. He chose as its political director Ralph Reed, a young political operative who could give a fresh look to the Christian Right. Unlike Falwell and some of the other early leaders of the movement, Reed could speak the secular language of politics as well as communicate with fellow evangelicals.

Thus, the second wave of the Christian Right began and it took on a much different look than the Moral Majority-led first wave. After his defeat in the 1988 Republican Party presidential contest, Robertson decided to convert his large campaign contributors list into a national grassroots organization. The Christian Coalition made a major effort to build state, county, and local organizations around the country. Reed recruited state and local leaders whose backgrounds were in business, interest group politics, or civic activity—a major shift from the Moral Majority strategy of recruiting local pastors.

This shift in strategy enabled the Christian Coalition to build a broadly ecumenical organization. The national lobbying office included people from a variety of religious backgrounds and at one point its legislative director was Jewish. Research suggests that state and local chapters in many parts of the country were similarly diverse.[10] Leaders and supporters of the Christian Coalition may not have agreed on religious doctrine, but they did agree to work together to support pro-life Republican candidates for public office.

The "second coming" of the Christian Right in the 1990s evidenced a politically maturing movement that had learned from the mistakes of the first wave. Reed, who himself had once compared his political tactics to guerrilla warfare and boasted that he ambushed opponents and left them in body bags, recanted the use of such language and wrote to supporters that "phrases like 'religious war' and 'take over' play to a stereotype of evangelicals as intolerant." He urged followers to avoid using threatening-sounding language: "We must adopt strategies of persuasion, not domination."[11] Reed was not alone in this sentiment. Studies of the Christian Right in the 1990s found the rhetorical appeals of leaders to sound more moderate, the issue-appeals more broad-based, and the organizations of the movement had built more broadly ecumenical bases and strong grassroots networks than the first wave of the movement.[12]

A telling case was that of Anne Kincaid, who had been the leading pro-life organizer in Virginia for years. She became active in the 1980s and in her various efforts as a movement leader for the Family Foundation, state director for Pat Robertson's presidential campaign, among other posts, she was known for using extreme-sounding issue appeals, carrying pictures of aborted fetuses to editorial offices and to political rallies. She had a special appeal to group activists, in large part due to her own charisma and a compelling personal story of having fallen as a young adult and then changed her life after discovering her faith. But in terms of political impact outside the movement, she was considered a fringe figure and not influential. By the early 1990s she changed her language and tactics and her political stature grew enormously. In 1993 many credited her with delivering critical support among religious conservatives for George Allen's successful Republican gubernatorial nomination campaign, even though Allen professed that he was a moderate on abortion. After winning the general election Allen appointed Kincaid his director of constituent services and she later went on to run a number of Republican Party candidate campaigns in the state. It was no exaggeration when opponents and political observers referred to her as the most formidable political strategist in the state. In an interview she reflected on her transformation from fringe activist to influential Republican Party leader:

> I can remember using rhetoric that I don't use anymore, that sounded inflammatory. "Onward Christian Soldiers" scared people. So you don't talk that way. Some still talk about witchcraft and the feminist movement. Yes, the Bible says that "rebellion against men is of witchcraft." It's all Biblical tenets, but the layman doesn't understand that. So it makes you sound like you've lost your marbles.
>
> The point is that you have to know your audience. That's not deception. . . . Unless you're talking to a Christian audience, you don't put all the rhetoric out there that others won't respond to. I learned this lesson the hard way.[13]

In the 1980s it was nearly unthinkable that major Christian Right figures would have backed a Republican Party candidate who, like Allen, professed his view on abortion was one of "reasonable moderation" and said that he favored abortion rights in the first trimester and in cases of rape, incest, and threat to the life of the woman. Yet that was Allen's public stand, and Kincaid and a number of other pro-life leaders in Virginia supported him because they believed that he could win and perhaps achieve some secondary limitations on abortion such as parental consent and notification. In the 1980s the same movement leaders in Virginia had given their support in statewide campaigns to purist-type social conservative candidates, all of whom lost and were thus in no position to deliver any goods at all to the Christian Right.[14]

The example of the evolution of the Christian Right in Virginia is not unusual. Indeed, a series of studies of the electoral impact of the movement in federal elections showcases the many states in which similar developments occurred.[15]

To sound more mainstream, many leaders of the Christian Right adopted the rights-based language of liberalism to describe their aspirations. Thus, rather than denouncing "infanticide," "murder of the unborn," or making comparisons of abortion-rights to the Holocaust, leaders framed the issue as defending the rights or equality for the unborn. Rather than espouse the desire to "take-over" Republican Party party committees or policy making institutions, leaders said they merely wanted not to be discriminated against in politics because of their status as Christians, or that they were angling only for a "place at the table" in American politics. Movement leaders have asserted that the goals of the Christian Right were really no different from those of the 1960s civil rights movement: that Christian pro-lifers should be treated fairly, with dignity, not discriminated against.[16]

Such language certainly has been couched for broader public consumption and clearly Christian Right leaders are not so mainstream-sounding when speaking among themselves or directly to their own supporters. And of course, by making so many public pronouncements over the years, such leaders as Falwell and Robertson have been prone to let loose some terribly impolitic statements, the kind that, to paraphrase Kincaid, make them sound like they've lost their marbles.

One interesting tack in the 1990s was to promote overturning *Roe v. Wade* on the grounds that legalizing abortion was bad constitutional law, rather than insisting that abortion is immoral. Reed himself argued that he merely wanted the issue of abortion remanded to the states, in keeping with the constitutional framers' notion of federalism, rather than to have the Supreme Court mandate a one-size-fits-all approach.[17] Other major movement figures such as Robertson and Phyllis Schlafly made similar appeals.

Of course, presumably such a change would lead to abortion restrictions by many of the states and there is no doubt that this outcome is the purpose, not to restore the constitutional framers' view of federalism. For example, in 2006, the South Dakota state legislature passed a law outlawing all abortions, except in cases of threat to the life of the woman. Although clearly unconstitutional, this action showcased the potential payoff for the Christian Right of the federalism strategy—and it is possible that a newly constituted Supreme Court will one day overturn *Roe v. Wade*. But the key point is that leaders in the movement eventually understood that to be effective meant sometimes avoiding moralistic appeals and finding other more clever strategies to effect moralistic goals.

Another good example was the recognition by many leaders in the movement that abortion rights can be more effectively reduced in the current political climate by focusing on secondary restrictions: parental notification, parental consent, no taxpayer funding, no late-term abortions, mandatory waiting periods and counseling for those seeking abortion, and restrictions on what health care professionals and educators can tell young women about abortion options. Many of these issue positions are popular with voters outside of the Christian Right. Thus, in areas where the Christian Right position on an issue has dovetailed with broader public sentiment, the movement has had some successes at the state level.

Robertson himself signaled to the movement that it was necessary to focus energy on the politically feasible when it came to abortion restrictions. In a November 4, 1993, appearance on ABC television's *Nightline*, Robertson explained:

> I would urge people, as a matter of private choice, not to choose abortion, because I think it is wrong. It's something else, though, in the political arena to go out on a quixotic crusade when you know you'll be beaten continuously. So I say let's do what is possible. What is possible is parental consent.[18]

Pro-choice leaders have referred to this strategy as "death by a thousand little cuts"; that all of the many secondary abortion restrictions around the country are slowly adding up to a serious withering away of abortion rights.

Of course, all of these signals from movement leaders would be ineffective unless the grassroots activists in the Christian Right agreed with the sentiments that it is important to focus on the politically feasible and not the ideal. For many activists in the Christian Right, to compromise on abortion is to consent to the ultimate sin. But there is evidence that the signals from the leadership indeed have had a real impact on many grassroots activists.

Religion writer Ed Briggs has suggested that it is also possible that the changing face of fundamentalism in the US has made the grassroots activists more open to the message of focusing on the politically possible. That is, fundamentalism has developed something of a "soft-side, becoming mainstream." Thus, as fundamentalists increasingly accept the proposition that it is fine to partake in "matters of this world," many become much more receptive than ever to appeals to be realistic about the political world.[19] Kincaid agreed with this sentiment when she said that the biggest challenge for her and other movement leaders initially was "getting people out of the pews" once in a while to participate in politics.[20]

Over time, Christian Right organizations largely succeeded at reaching their core constituency and convincing as many as possible of the need to get involved in politics. As these new activists entered the political world and many participated in training sessions and local political organizations, they became more knowledgeable about how to mobilize and to be effective. As scholar Jon A. Shields accurately shows in his study of what he calls the "democratic virtues of the Christian Right," the early wave of evangelical mobilization radicalized the anti-abortion movement, but by the mid-1990s these activists either became moderated or they abandoned political activity altogether.[21]

Political organizing has further led social conservative activists to come into contact more frequently with other, primarily Republican Party-based, constituencies. Studies of Christian Right activists in the Republican Party in the 1990s showed that the Christian Coalition had achieved its goals of bringing social conservatives into the mainstream of the party and forging a broad-based coalition of social and secular conservatives. Pro-gun rights and anti-tax activists did not share the same commitment to social issues as the religious conservatives in the party, but these groups were willing to come together to support each other's favored candidates. In many cases, religious conservative leaders and activists worked for the elections of moderate Republican Party nominees, with the understanding that such loyalty to the party despite policy differences would be rewarded with support from the moderates for future social conservative candidates and issues.[22]

Thus, the story of the "second coming" of the Christian Right has been that of a largely transformed movement. The first wave of the movement was characterized by religiously exclusionary outreach, extreme-sounding rhetoric, the taking of absolutist positions on moral issues, the refusal to compromise on principles, and a lack of effective coalition building. The new wave Christian Right activism emerged with a much more sophisticated and effective approach to politics. Group leaders, and even many activists, recognize the need to build a broadly ecumenical movement, to adopt mainstream-sounding rhetoric, to focus on incremental goals on some issues, to accept the necessity of compromise, and to build coalitions with various groups.

The Christian Right transformation was remarkable and surprised observers who had declared the demise of the movement back in the late 1980s. Perhaps the act of unifying the various religious groups that make up the Christian Right was made much easier by the existence of Bill and Hillary Clinton in the White House in the 1990s. Common enemies can sometimes do more to unite feuding allies than any well-thought-out strategies.

But in 2000, with the Clintons soon to leave the White House, and many prominent Republicans competing to be the next occupant of that residence, the potential existed for the movement to splinter. That did not happen. Even with some prominent Christian Right figures seeking the Republican Party nomination (for example, Gary Bauer, Alan Keyes, Pat Buchanan), and one eventually running on the general election ballot as an Independent (Buchanan), movement leaders and activists mostly united behind the candidacy of Texas Governor George W. Bush, who was then running as a moderate on abortion. The act of backing Bush was one of political pragmatism; of supporting a candidate who was not ideal on all of the social issues but could win office and deliver some of what the Christian Right wanted.

The New Millennium: What Does the Christian Right Want?

From its inception, the Christian Right has been motivated by a desire to restore what it considers "traditional morality" to public policy. In this regard, much of the movement's activities have been reactive to policy changes. For example, Christian Right activists have sought to reinstate legal restrictions on abortion, protect religious expression in public institutions, and limit the expansion of gay rights. Although some of its goals have been proactive, such as support for school vouchers and faith-based social service providers, the level and intensity of Christian Right activity are explained in large measure by policy shifts away from traditional morality. Such a shift occurred in 2004: the legalization of same-sex marriage in Massachusetts and the fear that other states would follow suit. This change provided a powerful motivation for movement activity. Observers characterized the 2004 contest as the "values campaign" in large part because of the surge in voting by conservative evangelicals and Catholics, the increased Republicanism of these groups, and Bush's narrow victory that would not have been possible without the Christian Right mobilization.[23]

Significantly, the Christian Coalition had largely faded in importance by the new millennium and in the 2004 election few were talking of its activities other than to suggest that the once-powerful player had become nearly defunct. The Christian Right movement nonetheless survived and succeeded in 2004 without the leadership of the Christian Coalition. New groups were formed at the state and local levels to pick up the role formerly played by the Christian Coalition. Some of the new groups were specific to the 2004 campaign and centered around the anti-gay marriage referenda. Other new groups might have a longer life in electoral politics. The "values campaign" of 2004 seemed to have expanded the movement's organizational infrastructure.

It was the marriage issue that gave focus to the movement's activities in 2004. While these state-level efforts were important in their own right, they had implications for the rest of the ballot, especially President George W. Bush's reelection bid and a number of close congressional contests.

Although observers acknowledged the strength of the Christian Right in 2004, the movement learned in 2006 that what one election cycle delivers, the next can take away. Given widespread dissatisfaction in the country with the Bush presidency, the Republican Party suffered major losses in the midterm elections and saw party control in both houses of Congress switch to the Democrats. Yet again the Christian Right lost influence, as the Bush presidency could no longer muster majorities for its agenda and, even before the Democrats took back Congress, the administration had not worked very hard at delivering on the social issues. The one major advance of the Christian Right perhaps was the appointments of two conservative judges to the US Supreme Court as well as a number of conservatives placed on lower federal courts.

As with all movements, there is internal competition over leadership and presently there is no single Christian Right group that commands the power once held by the Christian Coalition. The passing of Jerry Falwell and the declining influence of Pat Robertson and Ralph Reed have left a void not yet filled by any single personality, although some figures such as Dr James Dobson (Focus on the Family) and Richard Land (Southern Baptist Convention) have become more overtly political in recent years and now command increased influence in the movement.

What Does the Christian Right Get?

There is considerable debate over the extent of the Christian Right influence on policy in the United States. A few years ago the editor of *National Review* wrote that "the Christian Right has infiltrated and taken over the White House in the person of George W. Bush" and that the movement could not have done better had Jerry Falwell or Pat Robertson hand-picked the occupant of the Oval Office.[24] This statement comes as a complete surprise to the many Christian Right leaders and activists who are thoroughly disgruntled with the lack of social issue energy out of the Bush White House, just as they had been disgruntled with the same lack of commitment to social issues from the Reagan and former Bush White Houses as well.

Generally the movement has had modest policy success at best at the federal level. After three decades of political activity by the Christian Right, US public opinion has actually become more liberal on a variety of social issues, especially gay rights. And the younger cohorts are especially libertarian in their social issues views, suggesting that the future of the Christian Right may be diminished by generational replacement.[25]

The Christian Right has had its major influence in areas where it has been able to forge a consensus for its issues positions with the broader public. Thus, for example, many states have enacted such restrictions on abortion as parental notification, parental consent, no taxpayer funding for abortion services, and no late-term abortions. Although the public still strongly favors abortion as a constitutional right, various secondary restrictions are overwhelmingly favored by the public and thus the Christian Right has succeeded over time in enacting many such restrictions. When the movement strives to achieve its ultimate goal such as eliminating abortion, the public and political leaders hold the Christian Right back.

The Christian Right has gone through two distinct phases: the first in the 1970s and 1980s was characterized by extreme rhetoric, refusal to compromise on moral issues, the inability to form coalitions, a lack of ecumenism, and a lack of organizational power at the grassroots. The "second coming" of the Christian Right began in the late 1980s with the founding of the Christian Coalition and the recognition by movement leaders of the need to build a broadly ecumenical movement with grassroots networks, and to develop political coalitions and to accept the necessity of incremental gains in policy. The movement became more successful as a result of becoming more politically sophisticated.

But becoming sophisticated meant accepting incrementalism and compromise and these have been hard for many core activists to accept. Earlier movements such as labor, feminism, and civil rights have all profoundly changed the laws and society in the US. The Christian Right has had nowhere near the kind of impact of these movements. And its future prospects are not likely to be different either. Let me close by illustrating the limits of the movement when it comes to its most important issue: abortion.

Abortion and the Future of the Christian Right

If *Roe* is overturned, even many in the core constituency of the Christian Right will be uncomfortable with that outcome. Public opinion data show that most evangelicals and traditional Catholics do not support eliminating all abortion rights. Indeed, a surprising number of people in these groups favor legal abortion rights under certain circumstances or even in all circumstances. According to the combined General Social Survey (GSS) data from 2000–2004, only 9% of Catholics and 12% of evangelicals favor eliminating abortion rights in all cases, and only 8% of Catholics and 11% of evangelicals favor eliminating abortion in all cases except to protect the health of the woman. Yet 28% of Catholics and 21% of evangelicals would allow abortion under any circumstance.

To break it down even further, among evangelicals who believe that the Bible is literally true word-for-word, only 17% oppose all abortion, and another 15% would only allow the one exception for the health of the woman. Yet 15% of this group would allow abortion in any circumstance. Among regular church-going Catholics (nearly every week or more), merely 17% oppose all abortions and another 10% would allow it only to protect the health of the woman. Yet 17% of this group would allow abortion under any circumstance.

These data suggest that overturning *Roe* could actually splinter the core constituencies of the Christian Right. Clyde Wilcox and Carin Larson report that in interviews with Christian Right activists, some told stories of why they personally opposed eliminating abortion rights in all cases. In their discomfort they asked interviewers to turn off the recording device and requested that this information not be communicated to others in the movement. In one case a woman said that she favored the exception for rape, another said to protect the health of the woman; both had personal experiences to explain why they favored these conditions.[26] Although anecdotal of course, these personal stories dovetail with the picture in the GSS data: even among the core constituencies of the Christian Right, many become very uncomfortable when presented with the reality of all abortion rights being eliminated.

Thus, what would a post-*Roe v. Wade* environment look like in the United States? In the short-term, such a development will be celebrated by the Christian Right as a major victory. But as the states take up the issue of abortion, the reality becomes much more complicated. Certainly several states will outright ban abortion, but many more will quickly act to establish abortion as a basic right.

In 1989, the pro-choice community experienced a significant resurgence in the wake of a Supreme Court decision (*Webster v. Reproductive Health Services*) that many perceived as a threat to the future of abortion rights. If the reaction to that court decision is at all a guide, then the pro-choice movement will likely experience a major resurgence in support should *Roe v. Wade* be overturned. That decision temporarily energized pro-choice activists around the country and caused many state-level Republican Party candidates to rethink their opposition to abortion rights. The Christian Right reemerged with its newer and more effective strategies in the 1990s, but it is hard to imagine that the movement would be able to do the same in an environment in which abortion is remanded to the states and the stakes of the issue are not merely over secondary restrictions such as prohibiting late-term abortions or requiring parental consent.

The Christian Right has achieved successes at the state level on abortion policy exactly when the movement's position has dovetailed with that of broader public opinion. Thus, as Robertson had signaled in the early 1990s, secondary restrictions are politically possible, and his view is validated by the largely popular abortion restrictions since enacted by many states. The political calculation though changes dramatically when the debate focuses on whether to eliminate the right to abortion altogether or under a variety of circumstances.

Strong overall national public opinion support for abortion rights suggests that overturning *Roe v. Wade* will indeed be hugely unpopular. The 2000–2004 GSS data show that only 8% of the public favors eliminating all abortion rights. Further, 89% of the public favors abortion rights in cases of threat to the health of the woman, 79% in cases of rape, and 77% in cases of known defect of the fetus. And the GSS data foretell the likelihood that the core constituencies of the Christian Right will seriously fragment over the issue in a post-*Roe* environment.

Quite possibly too, the Republican Party in many parts of the country will bear the political costs for the likely public outcry. If these events were to happen, it is plausible that many in the

Table 18.1. Public Attitudes on Abortion Exceptions, 2000–2004

	Attitudes on Abortion Rights	
	Oppose	*Support*
Woman's health is in danger	11.3	88.7
Fetus is severely defected	22.7	77.3
Pregnancy is the result of rape	20.7	79.3
Family is too poor to support additional children	57.5	42.5
Single woman does not wish to marry	59.7	40.3
Married couple wants no more children	58.0	42.0

Source: Combined GSS Data 2000, 20002, 2004.

Republican Party will rethink the party's relationship with the Christian Right. In the long run overturning *Roe v. Wade* might be the worst outcome possible for the Christian Right.

As this possible scenario makes it clear, the role of the Christian Right in US politics is always evolving and changing. It is difficult to predict its future impact because so many factors affect the standing of the movement. One thing does seem certain though, and that is that much of the core constituency of the Christian Right is now firmly committed to political activism over the long term. Whether in the future the movement is successful or not, the Christian Right is here to stay.

Notes

1 Clyde Wilcox, Mark J. Rozell, and John C. Green, "The Meaning of the March: A Direction for Future Research," in *The Christian Right in American Politics: Marching to the Millennium*, ed. John C. Green, Mark J. Rozell, and Clyde Wilcox (Washington, D.C.: Georgetown University Press, 2003), 277–80.

2 See Clyde Wilcox, *God's Warriors: The Christian Right in 20th Century America*. (Baltimore, MD: The Johns Hopkins University Press, 1992).

3 See Clyde Wilcox, Rachel Goldberg, and Ted G. Jelen, "Full Pews, Musical Pulpits: The Christian Right at the Turn of the Millennium," *The Public Perspective* (May/June 2000): 36–9. Numerous surveys and exit polls have estimated the size of the Christian Right as a percentage of the adult voting population.

4 Jospeh Gatins and Ed Briggs, "Churchmen See Future Alliances," *Richmond Times-Dispatch*, November 9, 1978, B2.

5 Mark J. Rozell and Clyde Wilcox, *Second Coming: The New Christian Right in Virginia Politics* (Baltimore, MD: The Johns Hopkins University Press, 1996), ch. 2.

6 Ibid.

7 See Kenneth Wald, *Religion and Politics in the United States*, 4th ed. (Lanham, MD: Rowman & Littlefield, 2003), ch. 7.

8 Duane M. Oldfield, *The Right and the Righteous: The Christian Right Confronts the Republican Party* (Lanham, MD: Rowman & Littlefield, 1996).

9 See Matthew Moen, "The Changing Nature of Christian Right Activism," in *Sojourners in the Wilderness: The Christian Right in Comparative Perspective*, ed. Corwin Smidt and James Penning (Lanham, MD: Rowman & Littlefield, 1997), 21–40.

10 Clyde Wilcox, Mark J. Rozell, and Roland Gunn, "Religious Coalitions in the New Christian Right," *Social Science Quarterly* 77 (September 1996): 543–58.

11 Joe Taylor, "Christian Coalition Revamping Image," *Richmond Times-Dispatch*, December 7, 1992, B4.

12 Moen, "The Changing Nature of Christian Right Activism," 21–40; Mark J. Rozell, "Growing Up Politically: The New Politics of the New Christian Right," in *Sojourners in the Wilderness*, ed. Corwin Smidt and James Penning (Lanham, MD: Rowman & Littlefield, 1996) 235–48; Rozell and Wilcox, *Second Coming*; Clyde Wilcox and Carin Larson, *Onward Christian Soldiers: The Religious Right in American Politics*, 3rd ed. (Boulder, CO: Westview Press, 2006).

13 Author interview with Anne Kincaid interview, November 17, 1993, Richmond, Virginia.

14 Rozell and Wilcox, *Second Coming*.

15 See Mark J. Rozell and Clyde Wilcox, eds, *God at the Grass Roots: The Christian Right in the 1994 Elections* (Lanham, MD: Rowman & Littlefield, 1995); Mark J. Rozell and Clyde Wilcox, eds, *God at the Grass Roots 1996: The Christian Right in American Elections* (Lanham, MD: Rowman & Littlefield, 1997); John C. Green, Mark J. Rozell, and Clyde Wilcox, *Prayers in the Precincts: The Christian Right in the 1998 Elections* (Washington, D.C.: Georgetown University Press, 2000); John C. Green, Mark J. Rozell and, Clyde Wilcox, eds, *The Christian Right in American Politics*: Marching to the Millennium (Washington, D.C.: Georgetown University Press, 2003); John C. Green, Mark J. Rozell and Clyde Wilcox, eds, *The Values Campaign?: The Christian Right and the 2004 Elections* (Washington, D.C.: Georgetown University Press, 2005).

16 Rozell, "Growing Up Politically," 235–48.

17 Ralph Reed, "What Do Christian Conservatives Really Want?" Paper presented at the Colloquium on the Religious New Right and the 1992 Campaign, Ethics and Public Policy Center, Washington, D.C, 1993.

18 ABC *Nightline* transcript.

19 Author interview with Ed Briggs, December 9, 1993, Richmond, Virginia.
20 Kincaid interview.
21 Jon A. Shields, "The Democratic Virtues of the Christian Right." Doctoral dissertation prepared for the Department of Politics, University of Virginia, Charlottesville, Virginia, 2006.
22 Mark J. Rozell, Clyde Wilcox, and John C. Green, "Religious Constituencies and Support for the Christian Right in the 1990s," *Social Science Quarterly* (December 1998): 815–20.
23 See Green, Rozell, and Wilcox, *The Values Campaign?*
24 Richard Lowry quoted in the *Washington Post*, August 10, 2003.
25 Mark J. Rozell and Debasree Das Gupta, "The Christian Right and the Politics of Abortion." Paper delivered at the conference, "Fundamentalism and the Law," Cardozo Law School, New York, March 14–15, 2006. Data compiled by the authors.
26 Wilcox and Larson, *Onward Christian Soldiers*, 143.

Part 3

Campaigns Worldwide

19

Television Campaigning Worldwide

Fritz Plasser and Günther Lengauer

Television has been regarded as the driving force for changing campaign practices worldwide. Despite the rise of the Internet, web-based videos and televised debates shown on the web as well as declining audiences of nightly television news programs and the ongoing fragmentation of media markets and styles of news consumption, it would be premature to announce the post-television-campaign era. Television is here to stay and will remain the dominant medium and arena for campaign information and persuasion for the near future. It is estimated that in 2006 around 1.2 billion television households existed worldwide and 700 million people used the Internet worldwide. Although a digital convergence can be foreseen between television and Internet, this does not mean that the presence of television news, interviews in television studios, live television debates and political television advertisements will lose their importance.

Television campaigning takes place on *two* different levels: free and paid media. Free or earned media (publicity and public relations) means exposure in daily news programs or partly mediated talkshow formats and televised debates. This kind of television presence is based on professional news management, spin control, camera-ready scripted event marketing, strict message discipline and impression management. Paid media (advertising) on the other hand means to deliver unmediated campaign messages to potential swing and target voters without interference of critical journalists, political opponents or editorial policies.[1] Paid media is synonymous with television advertising in the United States while in other countries we have to distinguish between free air time allocated under provision of law and television advertising paid for by candidates or political parties.

Looking at the percentage of television households in the respective countries, there is striking evidence for a global penetration of societies by television with the exception of some African countries where access to television is confined to economically more developed urban regions. Television penetration is almost universal. Television is also the medium that is most often tuned in to get news about political events and affairs. Comparing the primary source of news in thirty-five countries we found striking evidence for the dominant position of televised news programs as central source of political information. Televised news programs seem to be the dominant way of connecting people with current political affairs and framing political reality in the respective countries. While reported news in newspapers plays an important role for placing breaking television news in context and providing background information to interested readers, the most important source of political news is television. In virtually all countries from which data are available, television is considered the most important provider of political information (see Table 19.1).

Table 19.1. Political Information Habits Worldwide

Medium most often turned to for news (in percentages)	Television	Newspapers	Radio
Anglo America			
Canada	52	26	12
United States	67	17	7
Latin America			
Argentina	68	10	19
Bolivia	69	9	20
Brazil	78	11	7
Chile	71	18	9
Colombia	65	10	20
Guatemala	63	19	15
Honduras	73	10	17
Mexico	72	10	14
Peru	72	7	18
Venezuela	75	19	5
Western Europe			
Austria	56	25	12
France	61	18	17
Germany	56	28	11
Italy	74	20	2
United Kingdom	60	24	11
Eastern Europe			
Bulgaria	81	7	7
Czech Republic	62	22	10
Hungary	74	24	2
Poland	83	7	7
Russia	84	6	8
Ukraine	75	10	12
Asia-Pacific			
Australia	69	18	7
India	61	14	16
Indonesia	92	5	3
Japan	71	24	2
Philippines	77	6	16
South Korea	70	17	1
Africa			
Egypt	80	9	9
Ghana	22	6	69
Kenya	17	7	73
Mali	37	4	55
Senegal	32	5	62
South Africa	54	11	28
Uganda	2	4	88

Sources: The Pew Research Center for the People and the Press, "Pew Global Attitudes Project," Washington, D.C., 2002, http://pewglobal.org; Fritz Plasser with Gunda Plasser, *Global Political Campaigning: A Worldwide Analysis of Campaign Professionals and Their Practices* (Westport, Conn.: Praeger, 2002), 196–203

Note: Other minor sources of news information not added in.

The ubiquitous status of the medium television, although it gets increasing competition through the Internet in some technologically advanced countries such as the United States, Australia or South Korea, is reflected worldwide in the overwhelming importance placed upon television by candidates and political parties in their communication and campaign strategies. As television news broadcasts are watched by almost 70% of Australian voters on an average weeknight during a federal election campaign, the parties' strategies concentrate on TV-*grabs*, the Australian codeword for constructing camera-ready events. Since television has become the driving force of Australian campaigns, itineraries of the parties' top candidates crossing the continent by plane are first oriented to get free coverage in the national media and second to provide targeted messages to regional constituents. Also throughout Latin America the focus of campaign activities has shifted from mass rallies, parades and intensive discussions in public places to scripted events (*escenarios mediatiocos*), television interviews and televised leaders' debates. In Latin America this is referred to as an impoverishment of the public space and a relocation of election campaigns to the television studio.

The television-centeredness of Russian candidates and their struggle to control the flow of news of the dominant, state- and Kremlin-affiliated television stations, are characteristic of campaign practices in today's Russia, where elections are fought almost exclusively on television with strong interference by the government. Even Asian campaigns are two-tier campaigns combining culturally bound, clientelistic styles of voter mobilization with media-driven, high-tech campaigning, as can be seen by the intrusion of television campaigning into traditional Indian electoral politics.[2] Also Western and Eastern European parties and candidates spend considerable time and effort on free or earned television campaigning: organizing press conferences, orchestrating the message of the day, trying to put spin on media reports, creating camera-ready events and participating in political talkshow and debate formats. Getting free or earned television coverage and spinning the news are also driving motives of American candidates, supplemented by relentless airing of thirty-second television spots in select media markets to deliver the central campaign messages to target voters.

Campaigns and Television News

The Pew Global Attitudes Project[3] shows that in Eastern Europe television is the dominating source of news for about eight out of ten people. In Latin America and Asia this holds true for approximately seven out of ten people whereas in Western Europe and North America about six out of ten people primarily turn to television to get political and electoral information. With about 40%, only in Africa is this ratio significantly lower. Particularly countries in West and East Africa remain radio-centric information systems, whereas countries in southern and northern Africa have already turned into television-centric societies. Consequently, a vast majority of contemporary societies on all continents present themselves as advanced "sound-bite societies" where televised news is the primary source of electoral and campaign information. Although the levels of modernization of media- and television-centered democracies differ worldwide, television prime time news can be considered a global phenomenon and the central political arena for election campaigns in the twenty-first century.

What Jay G. Blumler and Dennis Kavanagh[4] introduced as the evolutionary phasing model of political communication after World War II can also be applied to the dynamics of broadcasting systems in general and television news in particular.[5] In the 1980s and early 1990s the rapid expansion of cable and satellite technology accompanied by political deregulation increased the dominant status of television and created a "multi-channel public,"[6] characterized by increasing commercialization and highly competitive television markets. Accelerating news cycles and an increasing breaking news character fostered by heightened market competition are strengthening the dynamic character of news as well as the rivalry among politicians to vie for the attention of editors, reporters and audience.[7]

Since 2000 all European public service monopolies of television have been eroded and transformed in dual or even completely deregulated commercial systems and state-control over television systems has been eroded by far-reaching political deregulation. After the fall of the Soviet Empire and the rise of new democracies in Eastern Europe in the early 1990s national broadcasting systems were also remodeled on the principles of a dual market idea. However, an oligarchic ideology that characterizes evolving business structures in Eastern Europe is also partially transferred to the television systems. A similar structure of highly intertwined networks between state authorities and media corporations is also inherent to television systems in Latin America. After decades of dictatorship and censorship the editorial boards gained autonomy. However, capital-strong multimedia entrepreneurs entered into arrangements with their governments[8] and state control still remains a significant force in these television markets.

Particularly North Atlantic and Western European societies can be classified as postmodern media-centered democracies that have already entered the third era of political communication[9] and are characterized by a significant level of accordance referring to the operational logic of political campaigning and journalism. However, these societies and systems are still characterized by contextual differentiations that form distinct models of media and politics—Liberal, Polarized Pluralist and Democractic Corporatist Models.[10] "The adjustment by the news media and journalism to the new scenarios is progressing at different speeds in different national and continental contexts."[11]

Competing, however not mutually exclusive concepts of modernization (from neo-Marxist economic determinism to Weberian cultural determinism), globalization (capitalist global markets, cross-continental communication networks), and postmodernization (postmaterialist value change) form the theoretical foundation for transformational and potentially transnational converging processes affecting national political communication systems and cultures in general and television news in particular. These trends and underlying forces are commonly condensed and superficially labeled as "Americanization."[12]

Currently ascertainable and prevailing trends in election coverage of increasing personalization, game-centeredness or an increasing antipolitics bias are mainly discussed and empirically documented for the United States as the international role model of a deregulated and highly professionalized political communication system and culture. Nevertheless, it is unclear to what extent television news globally correspond to these patterns and trends, taking into consideration that diverse contextual systemic, political, socio-cultural and economic-technological settings may limit the power of transnational homogenization. It is still not clarified whether we have to speak of tendencies in election coverage toward global universalism, national and cultural particularism or forms of transnational hybridism.

From a transnational perspective, comparable data on election coverage are extremely rare.[13] Recent studies speculatively conclude that relatively stable differences in political, electoral and media systems prevent the political communication systems and cultures from adopting transatlantic features and patterns.[14] Only a few studies identify at least partially cross-national trends and correspondence referring to TV coverage in general or campaign coverage in particular.[15]

On the primary level of analysis this investigation will give some answers to the question whether the structure of the continental Western European style of election reporting compared to the US television coverage of election campaigns is primarily shaped by country specific systemic and cultural settings or whether it is more driven by transnational patterns of an emerging journalistic logic in media-centered democracies referring to the third age of political communication. On the secondary level of analysis this additional global compilation of empirical evidence will investigate to what extent the recent styles of television election coverage differ or correspond in various parts of the world.

256

The primary investigative focus of this chapter is based on a comparative content analysis[16] conducted by the authors analyzing and directly comparing the television election coverage of recent parliamentary election campaigns in Germany (2005), Italy (2006), Austria (2006) and the presidential election campaign in the US (2004).[17] The secondary investigative focus builds a compilation of content analyses data from sixteen countries representing recent styles of national television election coverage from all continents.[18] The data sets of these international studies have been re-calculated and re-categorized by the authors in order to ensure the greatest possible conceptual and methodological levels of correspondence with the data of the primary analysis. All analyses focus on television election coverage in the final phase of national campaigns and cover a representative sample of the most eminent evening newscasts on private and public or state-owned channels. The compiled studies were all conducted by scientific teams and supervised by experts in content analysis following international standards of empirical social research. The selected studies were conducted by university or human rights institutes, national electoral commissions, the Organization for Security and Co-operation in Europe (OSCE) or the European Union Commission and globally operating media research institutes.[19] Despite its limitations caused by varying periods of observations, numbers of observed television newscasts or slightly different codebook definitions, this integrative analysis allows at least rough insights and provides an overview of potential transnational phenomena in television election coverage.

Personalization in Television News

The phenomenon of *personalization* refers to an increasing focus on candidates at the expense of their parties or even policy issues in the television coverage,[20] even in election campaigns that are based on party-centered political and election systems. Despite highly different election campaigns (presidential, senatorial and parliamentary races) taking place within diverging electoral systems (from first-past-the-post to proportional representation) that may account for significant variations in the actual levels of personalization in television news, we find strikingly corresponding patterns over the globe. Not only in countries with highly candidate-centered campaigns and electoral systems do politicians outnumber their parties as the main protagonists in election and campaign reports, these patterns are also evident in countries with party-centered systems (see Table 19.2).

Corresponding with the level of personalization of the electoral and political systems, in this transnational comparison candidate-centered presidential and senate races in the US, Venezuela and the Philippines are the most personalized ones on television news. On US television the 2004 presidential candidates George W. Bush and John F. Kerry were ten times more salient than their parties in the final stages of the election campaign. The Australian level of individualization on television may also be directly explained by the highly personalized voting system. However, even in Italy, where the party list election system was reintroduced in 2005, the individual representation of the political elite, personified by Silvio Berlusconi and Romano Prodi, dominates over the significance of their party blocs "Casa delle Libertá" and "L'Unione." The least personalized portrayal of election campaigns is offered by Austrian and German television news. However, even in these clearly party-driven political and election systems, candidates are more salient than their parties in the television coverage.

Table 19.2 illustrates that the level of candidate-centered reporting in proportional representation systems does not differ fundamentally from the coverage in highly personalized election systems. Despite their party-centered proportional voting systems, Austrian, German or Italian news coverage displays a significant and dominating level of personalization and individualization. This institutional and systemic party-centrism is not correspondingly reflected by its election coverage on prime time news. At this state of analysis we can recapitulate that the systemic

Table 19.2. Main Protagonists in Election Reports—Candidates versus Parties

	Candidates as main protagonist (%)	Parties as main protagonist (%)
USA 2004[a]	91	9
Philippines 2007[b]	78	22
Venezuela 2006[b]	76	23
Italy 2006[a]	70	30
Australia 2001[b]	69	31
Canada 2000[b]	67	33
Germany 2005[a]	64	36
Austria 2006[a]	58	42

Sources: EU EOM—European Union Election Observation Mission, "Final Report. Presidential Elections Venezuela 2006," Caracas, 2006, http://www.eueomvenezuela.org; CMFR—Center for Media Freedom & Responsibility, "CMFR Monitor of News Media Coverage of the 2007 National Elections," Makati City, 2007, http://www.cmfr.com.ph/_documents/CMFR_Monitor_of_2007_Elections_Media_Coverage__Fourth_Period_final.doc; David Denemark, Ian Ward and Clive Bean, "Election Campaigns and Television News Coverage: The Case of the 2001 Australian Election," *Australian Journal of Political Science* 42 (1) (2007): 89–109.

Notes:
a Data retrieved from the primary analysis.
b Data retrieved from the secondary analysis.

context may moderately limit the level of transnational concordance referring to candidate-centrism. However, it obviously does not hinder the emergence of a general personalized and individualized style of electoral reporting on a cross-national scale.

Antipolitics Bias on Television News

Pundits frequently conclude that election news is dominated by an intensifying negative tone and disdain based on "an automatic skepticism—some call it cynicism."[21] Thomas Patterson speaks of an increasing "antipolitics bias" of the US media and W. Lance Bennett additionally concludes that the news focus has increasingly shifted away from trusted authorities to portrayals of mistrusted and failing politicians.[22] Gianpietro Mazzoleni and Winfried Schulz argue that this rise of adversarial spirit is due to the growing competition among media organizations and political actors "for public consent and legitimation in the same political arena."[23]

The global examples presented here and the compiled empirical evidence demonstrate that an antipolitics bias is far from being an exclusive US phenomenon.[24] As far as the situation in Western Europe is concerned, we find that in all countries examined here (Austria, Germany, Italy) the balance of positive and negative evaluations of the chancellor candidates as well as their parties in the electoral coverage is clearly negative on a cumulative level. The adversarial tone toward the front-runners and their parties in the Italian television coverage is even more accentuated than in the United States with its strong negative campaigning and mutual attack tradition. The prototypical examples of the North Atlantic logic of election coverage (Canada, Great Britain) also reflect a negative spin toward political actors during the parliamentary election campaigns of 2000 and 2005.[25]

In contrast, the picture on Eastern European television is much more diverse: In these countries, the ownership-structure of television channels seems to have some impact on the tone of the coverage. In the 2004 Russian presidential election campaign and in the 2004 Belarus parliamentary election campaign the ruling government and the incumbent president were presented highly positively by the state-controlled television news, whereas the opposition was mainly portrayed in a clearly negative light.[26] Private channels portrayed the election campaigns and their protagonists with more ambivalence in their tonality. Thus, the private Russian channel

Ren TV portrayed President Vladimir Putin predominantly negatively, whereas opponent candidates were positively covered. During the 2006 Ukraine election campaign the state-owned channel *UT 1* reported mainly positively about the administration and the incumbent president and ambiguously toward the opposition, whereas the strong private television sector reported more ambivalently about the government as well as the opposition.[27]

As far as the tone of the coverage is concerned, we can see two patterns forming the Latin American as well as the African style of election reporting on television: whereas the portrayal of the presidential candidates in Chile 2006[28] was clearly negative in tone, the presidential candidates in Mexico 2006 (except for the leftist candidate Obrador who was covered slightly negatively) and Venezuela 2006 were mostly covered in a positive tone.[29] A similar ambiguous portrayal referring to political parties is drawn in the African election coverage on television: whereas in South Africa[30] the prime time television news reports mainly critical about the contesting parties, the coverage of candidates and parties in Tunisia 2004 and Egypt 2005 were mainly positive.[31] Similar to the situation in Belarus or Russia, television news in Tunisia and Egypt is almost solely state-controlled. In these countries, political instrumentalization by the government is accompanied with a significant level of political parallelism in state-owned and -controlled television news. For example, television news in African and Latin American countries with higher levels of press freedom and less state-control—such as South Africa or Chile—seem to report more consistently critical on political elites and election campaigns.[32]

On a global scale there emerges no standardized and universal model of political skepticism and antipolitics bias in prime time television news. However, the patterns don't differ so much along regional, cultural or electoral settings, but rather according to the level of press freedom and the level of state-control. The "modernization" of political communication seems to go hand in hand with an increasing antipolitics bias, as detected for Western European and North Atlantic countries as well as for emerging media-democracies in Africa or Latin America.

Policy versus Non-policy Focus in Television News

One of the most prominently discussed indicators of recent electoral television coverage that can be extracted from previous research is the so-called *game schema, non-policy* or *strategy focus*.[33] It describes a portrayal of politics in a depoliticized way, lacking policy-relevance and rather depicting winners and losers, horse race scenarios or speculations about the election outcome. Politics is portrayed as a competitive game or a journalistic search for the story behind the story and campaign hoopla to heat the race character and to deconstruct political public relations strategies. Contrastingly, the *policy focus* describes a policy and issue-centered reflection of campaigns "within the context of policy and leadership problems and issues"[34] and their potential solutions. Findings of longitudinal content analyses of television news in the United States and Germany[35] substantiate high levels of transnational accordance and confirm an underlying long-term trend in television coverage towards "game- and non-policy-centered" reporting.

Table 19.3 offers an overview of non-policy structures of televised election coverage in thirteen countries. This compilation shows that in all societies investigated, election reports on TV are penetrated by a high level of non-policy topics. In the US, Italy, Germany and Great Britain at least every second report is built around a non-policy focus. The level of non-policy relevant campaign information is even higher in the surveyed Latin American and African countries, the Philippines and Russia, but also in Austria and Canada. As far as game-centrism is concerned there emerge no clear underlying cultural or regional patterns. Nonetheless, the dominance of the non-policy focus on television news is far from being a phenomenon unique to the US. There seems to emerge a more or less global pattern of non-policy centrism in television election coverage. Obviously this phenomenon is less explicable by the systemic and contextual framework of election campaigns, but rather by a globally established journalistic logic that

Table 19.3. Non-policy Topics as Main Objects of Election Reporting

	Non-Policy Reports (%)
Namibia 2004[b][c]	94
Canada 2000[b]	72
Brazil 2006[b]	70
Russia 1995[b]	70
South Africa 2004[b][c]	63
Austria 2006[a]	62
Venezuela 2006[b]	60
Chile 2006[b]	59
Philippines 2007[b]	56
USA 2004[a]	52
Italy 2006[a]	51
Germany 2005[a]	50
Great Britain 2005[b]	50

Sources: Canadian Election Study, "2000 Data Set," University of Montreal, 2000, http://www.ces-eec.umontreal.ca/surveys.html#2000; Center for Media Freedom and Responsibility, "CMFR Monitor of News Media Coverage of the 2007 National Elections," Makati City, 2007, http://www.cmfr.com.ph/_documents/CMFR_Monitor_of_2007_Elections_Media_Coverage_Fourth_Period_final.doc; Asociación Latinoamericana para la Comunicación Social, "Monitoreo de los principales Medios de Comunicación Social de Alcance National: Chile. Elección Presidencial 2006," Santiago de Chile, 2006, http:observatoriodemedios.org.ve/docs/elecciones_2006.doc; Deacon et al., *Reporting the 2005 UK General Election* Cloughborough University: Communication Research Centre, August 2005; Denmark et al., "Election Campaigns and Television News: The Case of the 2001 Australian Election," Australian Journal of Political Science 42 (1) (2007): 89–109; European Union Election Observation Mission, "Final Report: Presidential Elections Venezuela 2006," Carcas, 2006, http://www.eueomvenezuela.org; Media Tenor, "Media's Perception of Political Parties in South Africa in the Run-up of the National Elections in April 2004" and "Media's Perception of Political Parties in Namibia in the Run-up of the Elections in November 2004," both Pretoria, 2004, http://www.mediatenor.co.za; Sarah Oates and Laura Roselle, "State-Controlled and Commercial Television Channels. Russian Elections and TV News: Comparison of Campaign News," *The Harvard International Journal of Press/Politics* 5 (2) (2000): 30–51; Mauro P. Porto, "Trends in Brazilian Election News Coverage." Paper presented at the Annual Conference of the International Communication Association (ICA), San Francisco, May 2007.

Notes:
a Data retrieved from the primary analysis.
b Data retrieved from the secondary analysis.
c Coding units were statements instead of reports.

increasingly brings the game character of politics to prominence. Still discernible country specific variations are more likely to be due to campaign specific dynamics and climaxes and less likely to be put down to diverging cultural or legal frameworks. To summarize, it can be stated that electoral reports in the final stages of campaigns predominantly focus on politics as a competitive game and thrust public policy relevant information into the background on a fairly global scale. Despite differing campaign climaxes, election discourse cultures and policy debates on hand, non-policy information is prominently presented to the audience by television news worldwide.

Although this chapter only provides a snapshot of a few selected indicators, it offers valuable insights about the current state of worldwide electoral and campaign discourse on television news in diverging legal, political, economic and socio-cultural settings. First, it can be concluded that election coverage is characterized by significant levels of personalization and game-centrism on a global perspective. Common patterns arise that are partially leveled, however not abolished, by variations due to differing levels of candidate-centered electoral and political systems, situational factors or the suspense-level of electoral races. Second, as far as the tonality of electoral coverage is concerned, it can be stated that there emerges a general antipolitics bias in Western European and North Atlantic media-democracies. However, on a global scale substantial differentiations arise that seem to be best put down to the level of state-control and power relations within the television systems. Third, the phenomena of game- and candidate-centrism and of an antipolitics bias are transnationally discernible features of election coverage that are not limited to the US and thus cannot be interpreted as features of some kind of "American Exceptionalism" in political communication.[36]

Apart from some variations in election reporting and the leveling forces of differing contextual frameworks, there seems to arise a common ground for a transnational operational logic of political television journalism that is primarily driven by a pragmatic, news value oriented, approach. Daniel C. Hallin and Paolo Mancini[37] conclude that the "media system increasingly operates according to a distinctive logic of its own" and name it a "professional or commercial logic." Based on the empirical evidence presented here—it can be concluded that transnational forces of convergence concerning technological innovation, professionalization and commercialization may not only change the formal structure of media systems, but also affect their operational logic.

The depicted phenomena neither should be interpreted as tendencies toward a universal standardization, nor as evidence for idiosyncratic particularism on a national level. What best characterizes the ongoing transformation of covering election campaigns is a form of hybridization[38] that reflects transnational trends of journalistic pragmatism and professional news value orientations as well as national or cultural norms and specifics.

Access to Political Television Advertising

Contrary to the mediated portrayal of campaigns in the nightly evening news guided by professional journalistic norms and values, political television advertising is an opportunity for campaigners to deliver their messages, pictures and emotions unmediated. In eighty countries worldwide legal frameworks provide at least some free air time for political parties or candidates, either paid by the state or by the networks themselves. Countries without free television air time provisions are Austria, Belarus, Costa Rica, Ecuador, Honduras, Indonesia, Malaysia, Nicaragua, Singapore, South Africa, Switzerland, the United States and Venezuela. Generally, free television time segments are allocated either proportionately to the parliamentary strength of the respective parties, equally to all registered political parties campaigning for parliamentary seats or according to special rules of graded allocation defined by prevailing electoral laws. Free air time may be given exclusively to political parties or exclusively to candidates. In some countries free air time is only provided by public broadcasting stations or state-owned television channels, whereas in other countries free air time segments are also allocated on private commercial networks. Almost half of the countries where free air time provisions exist allocate the available time proportionally. Equal time provisions can be found especially in Northern European countries and in the majority of Eastern European countries.

In 2007 there are at least sixty-five democratic countries worldwide that allow political parties or candidates to buy television air time. Thirty years ago, only four countries (the United States, Australia, New Zealand and Japan) permitted the purchase of air time for political television advertisement. Similar to the regulations regarding access to free political advertising time on television, there are various rules and limits on the total amount of air time, frequency, format and content of television spots purchased by political parties and candidates. While access to paid political advertising seems to be a standard campaign feature in North America, Australia, Latin America and Eastern Europe, it is a rare exception in Western Europe, Asia and Africa, where the majority of countries strictly ban any form of paid political television advertising (see Table 19.4).[39]

Starting with East Asia we will illustrate select country and area specific practices of political television advertising. The *Japanese* framework is remarkable because it distinguishes between the strictly regulated access of individual candidates to political television, and the comparably

Table 19.4. Access to Paid Political Television Advertising Worldwide

Anglo America	Latin America	Western Europe	Eastern Europe/CIS	Asia-Pacific/Caribbean	Africa
Canada	Argentina	Austria[a]	Albania	Aruba	Botswana
United States	Colombia	Denmark[a]	Armenia	Australia[a]	Gambia
	Costa Rica[b]	Finland[a]	Azerbaijan	Bahamas	Ghana
	Dominican	Germany[a]	Bulgaria	Barbados	Lesotho
	Republic	Greece[a]	Estonia[a]	Indonesia[b]	Malawi
	Ecuador	Italy[b]	Georgia	Japan[c]	Mozambique
	El Salvador	Malta	Hungary	Mauritius	Namibia
	Guatemala	Netherlands[a]	Latvia	New Zealand	Uganda
	Honduras		Lithuania	Philippines	
	Mexico[a]		Macedonia	Samoa	
	Nicaragua		Mongolia	South Korea	
	Panama		Montenegro	Taiwan	
	Paraguay		Poland	Vanuatu	
	Peru		Romania		
	Uruguay		Russia		
	Venezuela		Serbia		
			Ukraine		

Sources: Lynda Lee Kaid and Christina Holtz-Bacha. "Political Advertising in International Comparison," in *The Sage Handbook of Political Advertising*, ed. Lynda Lee Kaid and Christina Holtz-Bacha (Thousand Oaks, Calif.: Sage, 2006), 3–14; Michael Pinto-Duschinsky, "Financing Politics: A Global View," *Journal of Democracy* 13 (4) (2003): 69–86; Fritz Plasser with Gunda Plasser, *Global Political Campaigning: A Worldwide Analysis of Campaign Professionals and Their Practices* (Westport, Conn.: Praeger, 2002), 206–08.

Notes:
a In private TV-stations only.
b Out of the official election campaign period only.
c For political parties only.

permissive access of political parties to buy and air political advertisements. Prevailing law allows candidates only a limited number of television appearances according to the number of candidates per constituency. To get the attention of potential voters of their home district, Japanese candidates announce their scheduled television appearances at campaign meetings, via posters or by telephone calls to core voter groups. Formats and styles of televised candidate presentations are strictly regulated by restrictive rules.

While Japanese candidates have only rare and strictly regulated access to political television, political parties are allowed to buy and air political television spots to an unlimited extent. These party-produced television spots have an average length of fifteen to thirty seconds but must not mention the name or record of individual party candidates, and should emphasize only policy or programmatic positions. Television spots prefer a formal style of addressing the audience. According to political cultural traditions, there are no negative spots and, therefore, televised spots lack the hard-hitting approach of political television spots common in the United States, Israel and Australia or the vividness of Latin American television advertisement.[40] Contrary, *Taiwan* is an example of a country with only minor regulations on political television advertising. While the state provides limited free air time for political parties and presidential candidates on land-based television stations, there is unlimited access to paid political television advertising on cable television stations.[41] As a result, candidates spend enormous sums for television advertisements on cable stations. This practice consequently fostered rising campaign expenditures and extensive spending by well-funded candidates.[42]

A combination of limited access to free television advertising on public broadcasting channels and unlimited opportunities to buy political air time on commercial stations characterizes the situation in *Australia*. There are no limits on the total amount, frequency, length and content of paid political television advertising in private, commercial networks. The average length of Australian political television spots is fifteen to thirty seconds. Although the law prohibits printing, publishing or distributing any electoral advertisement containing a statement that is untrue or deceptive, the bulk of aired television spots can be regarded as hard-hitting, negative advertisement criticizing or attacking opponent parties and candidates.[43] Targeted ad campaigns foster rising campaign expenditures. Approximately $30 million have been spent on broadcast advertising during the parliamentary campaign 2004.

A different way of regulating political television advertisements has been taken by *Canada*. Every broadcaster in Canada is required to make available a fixed contingent of air time for purchase by registered political parties during federal elections. The allocation of this time is to be based on the decision of the Broadcasting Arbitrator. In addition, television stations are required to allocate free time segments for the transmission of advertising programs produced and directed by political parties. Starting in the mid-1990s, Canadian political advertising has adopted select styles and arguments found in American campaign ads without becoming entirely "Americanized."[44] In the recent parliamentary election Canadian parties spent about $30 million on political television advertising.

Practices of Political Television Advertising

With only two exceptions (Brazil and Chile), where paid political television advertising is prohibited by law, Latin American political parties and candidates face only minor restrictions when launching massive and highly expensive television advertising campaigns. *Brazilian* parties and candidates are provided a daily *horario gratuito eleitoral* on all television channels funded by the state.[45] In addition to the 1.4 daily hours devoted to the broadcasting of presidential candidates' programs, which are aired in two time sets (one at 1:00 p.m., the other at 8:30 p.m.), the law added twenty-five minutes for the broadcasting of fifteen-, thirty-, or sixty-second spots aired during regular commercial breaks.[46] On the average 40% of Brazilian voters (almost forty million viewers) watch these advertising segments regularly. Rising production costs, expensive production techniques and the colorful and rhythm-driven *samba* atmosphere of Brazilian political advertising have increased advertising expenditures. As Brazilian media consultants have to produce comparatively long advertising programs, they rely on sequences of short video clips (*insercoes*), designed to entertain the audience and to avoid saturation. The serial production of professional video clips consequently increases the production costs, despite the fact that air time for a *horario gratuito* is provided free of charge.[47]

As Latin American campaigns are concentrated on television advertising either using free air time or buying fifteen- to sixty-second spots from commercial television stations, overall campaign expenditures are spiraling up. Total campaign expenditures at the Brazilian presidential election 2006 reached almost $500 million. Brazilian candidates on the average spend almost 60% of the available campaign budget on producing vivid television sequences to be aired during the *horario gratuito* and commercial breaks. In *Ecuador* and *Costa Rica* between 80 and 90% of overall campaign expenditures have been spent on television advertising in recent elections. Since 1983 overall expenditures in *Argentine* presidential elections have doubled each election cycle. Excessive spending on political advertising is also a signature of campaigning in *Venezuela*, once estimated to have the highest per capita spending on political advertising in the world.[48]

In contrast to the regulatory practice in most Latin American democracies, *Mexico* has introduced comparatively strict regulations of access to political television.[49] According to the current legislation, political parties have access to both television and radio. Time on television and radio can be used either in form of government provided free time or by buying contingents of air time from the corresponding office at the Instituto Federal Electoral (IFE). Although the regulation declared that in any case the expenses for paid television advertising may not exceed 20% of the public funding in electoral years, Mexican parties and presidential candidates spend 60% of their available campaign funds (between $150–170 million) on political television advertising.[50] According to IFE about 750,000 paid radio and television spots have been aired during the last six months of the presidential campaign 2006.

The *United States* is one of few countries worldwide where there are no free air time provisions for congressional and presidential candidates.[51] Signature of American election campaigns is the excessive use of paid television advertisements, where candidates invest 60% of their budgetary resources on the average.[52] In the election year 2004 presidential and congressional candidates, political parties and affiliated interest groups spent the record sum of $1.6 billion for television advertising. This is more than twice as much spent in the election year 2000 for political television advertising. In the congressional election year 2006 according to data from Nielsen Media Research a total of $2.3 billion has been spent for political television advertising. Experts estimate that during the eighteen months prior to the presidential election in 2008 about $3 billion would have been invested in paid political television advertising by candidates, parties and interest groups (see Table 19.5).

One striking feature of American political advertising practices is the huge amount of thirty-second spots aired in competitive battleground states and closely contested districts.[53] Within ten years the number of aired political commercials increased ten times. Consequence is an *advertising clutter* experienced by voters watching daily more than 100 political spots during primetime, as is the case in select media markets of battleground states with synchronous air wars between the presidential contenders, senatorial candidates and well-funded congressional candidates fighting for open seats.

Quite different is the overall situation in Western Europe, where access to paid political television is the rare exception. In *Germany*, the two public broadcasting channels ARD and ZDF provide political parties with free air time. At the parliamentary election 2005 the two major political parties were allowed to air a total of thirty-two ninety-second spots on the two public broadcasting stations.[54] In addition to limited free time segments in the public broadcast channels, German political parties are allowed to buy air time in private channels. Yet, for budgetary reasons German campaigners only make reluctant use of this possibility. During the election campaign 2002 only about 600 thirty-second spots were aired in private television channels. In 2005 the German parties invested even less in paid television advertising. A similar restraint was also noticeable among *Austrian* political parties at the recent parliamentary election campaign 2006, where only 3% of the advertising budget was invested in the purchase of air time at private channels.

Table 19.5. Intensity and Expenditures of Political TV Advertising in the US

	Number of TV spots on air	Expenditures (in millions of US$)
1996[a]	235,000	315
1998	302,000	500
2000[a]	970,000	771
2002	1,500,000	996
2004[a]	1,950,000	1,600
2006	2,630,000	2,300

Source: TNS Media Intelligence, "Political Television Ad Spending Sets Record for 'Off-Year' Elections," news release, November 10, 2005, http://www.tns-mi.com/news/11102005.htm.

Note:
a Presidential election year.

In 2000, the *Italian* parliament enacted a law banning paid political television advertising during election campaigns. According to the new law, political advertising may only be aired free of charge, providing equal opportunities (*par condicio*) to all candidates and political parties. The public broadcasting channel RAI is obliged to air political advertisements while the private stations can refuse them. However, this prohibition to air paid political advertisements did not keep Berlusconi and his Forza Italia from waging large-scale television advertising campaigns on his television channels during the months prior to the official campaign periods in 2001 and 2006.[55]

The majority of Western European democracies have placed a ban on paid political advertising on public, as well as private, commercial networks. An example of strict regulations on political television advertising practices is *France*, where state authorities defined numerous rules regarding access to political television, as well as style and content of political television advertising. French political parties and presidential candidates have limited access to free air time for their political broadcasts (*clip politique*) on the public channels (France 2, France 3 and France 5), whereas detailed regulations on time, production, format, placement, special effects and settings are quite restrictive.

Paid political television advertising is also prohibited in *Israel*. Political parties are provided with free air time on both of the two national television networks. Free air time is limited to ten minutes for each party or list of candidates, plus three minutes per seat won in the previous elections. Since 1996 hard-hitting advertising campaigns—professionally crafted by American overseas consultants—transformed the traditional style of Israeli video politics into aggressively fought air wars, comparable to television advertising practices in the United States.[56]

Contrary to the fairly restricted situation in Western Europe, virtually all East Central European countries allow political parties to buy air time on both public and private television channels. However, there are striking differences regarding paid political advertising practices within the respective countries. In the *Czech Republic* all political parties are allowed a total of twenty-one hours of broadcast and television time, which is divided among them equally. The actual time of presentation for each party is determined by lot. Paid political television advertising is banned by law as is the case in *Slovakia*. Political television advertising seems to play a far more important role in *Romanian* presidential elections, using fast-paced television spots for image-building of candidates as well as for hard-hitting attacks on opponents. Intensive use of limited, state-provided, free air time on public television stations and paid advertising on private channels is common in *Poland*. Especially during presidential election campaigns candidates rely on massive television advertising campaigns, using professional production techniques and strategies of negative political advertising, observable during the recent Polish parliamentary campaign.

In *Russia*, political parties and presidential candidates are provided with a limited amount of free air-time segments (*predvybornyje roliki*), allocated equally among registered parties on both channels of the state-owned television network. Additionally, political parties and candidates are allowed to buy air time as well up to thirty minutes on the state-controlled networks.[57] In contrast to excessive spending practices during the presidential campaign of 1996, expenditures on political television have been regarded as moderate during the parliamentary and presidential campaign cycle 1999–2000 and 2003–2004. Acting president Vladimir Putin refrained from using free time segments or buying time slots for political advertisements. According to Sarah Oates[58] "this would have been completely unnecessary, given the primary news programs in the country devoted a huge amount of time promoting his candidacy" (see Table 19.6).

Styles of Political Television Advertising

Apparently, there are striking differences between American *issue-advocacy ads*, French *clips politiques*, Greek *poli-spots* and German *Wahlwerbesendungen* regarding format, content and visual

Table 19.6. Access to Political Television in Thirty-Seven Countries

	Purchase of Time on Commercial TV	Purchase of Time on Public TV	Free Time on TV	Leaders' TV debates
Argentina	Yes	Yes	Yes	Yes
Australia	Yes	No	Yes	Yes
Austria	Yes[a]	No	No	Yes
Bolivia	Yes	Yes	Yes	Yes
Brazil	No	No	Yes	Yes
Bulgaria	Yes	Yes	No	Yes
Canada	Yes	Yes	Yes	Yes
Chile	No	No	Yes	Yes
Columbia	Yes	Yes	Yes	Yes
Czech Republic	No	No	Yes	Yes
Finland	Yes	No	Yes	Yes
France	No	No	Yes	Yes
Germany	Yes	No	Yes	Yes
Greece	Yes	No	Yes	Yes
India	No	No	Yes	No
Indonesia	No[b]	No	Yes	No
Israel	No	No	Yes	Yes
Italy	Yes[b]	No	Yes	Yes
Japan	Yes[c]	No	Yes	No
Mexico	Yes	No	Yes	Yes
Netherlands	Yes	No	Yes	Yes
Norway	No	No	Yes	Yes
Poland	Yes	Yes	Yes	Yes
Portugal	No	No	Yes	Yes
Romania	Yes	Yes	Yes	Yes
Russia	Yes	Yes	Yes	No
South Africa	No	No	No	No
South Korea	Yes	Yes	Yes	Yes
Spain	No	No	Yes	Yes
Sweden	No	No	Yes	Yes
Switzerland	No	No	No	No
Taiwan	Yes	Yes	No	Yes
Ukraine	Yes	Yes	Yes	Yes
United Kingdom	No	No	Yes	No
United States	Yes	No	No	Yes
Uruguay	Yes	Yes	Yes	Yes
Venezuela	Yes	Yes	No	No

Sources: Fritz Plasser with Gunda Plasser, *Global Political Campaigning: A Worldwide Analysis of Campaign Professionals and Their Practices* (Westport, Conn.: Praeger, 2002), 205; Lynda Lee Kaid and Christina Holtz-Bacha, "Political Advertising in International Comoparison," in The Sage Handbook of Political Advertising, ed. Lynda Lee Kaid and Christina Holtz-Bacha (Thousand Oaks, Calif.: Sage, 2006), 8–12; Stephen Coleman, *Televised Election Debates: International Perspectives* (Houndmills: Palgrave Mcmillan, 2000).

Notes:
a Only on private channels, mainly German private TV-stations with special "Austrian windows" during their commercial breaks.
b Only on private channels outside the official campaign period.
c Only accessible for political parties.

elements. The contrast between video styles may be even more pronounced when watching rhythm-driven Brazilian *insercoes* or ten minutes of a highly formalized television self-presentation of Japanese district candidates. After intensive comparative studies of political television spots in established Western and evolving European democracies, Lynda Lee Kaid, the principal investigator of this long-term research program summarizes the central findings as follow:[59]

1 Most countries concentrate the content of their ads on issues. Korea and Turkey are exceptions.

2 The political broadcasts across countries are overwhelmingly positive, not negative in their focus. The United States, Australia and Israel are the notable exceptions.

3 Despite the emphasis on issues and positivism, most leaders and parties rely on emotional, rather than logical of source credibility proof, to make their points. Exceptions are France, Britain and the United States, where logical appeals dominate.

4 Candidates and leaders across all countries are rarely the main speakers in their party broadcasts, relying instead on anonymous announcers to make their pitch.

5 Most parties and leaders have deemphasized the political party in their ads. France, Britain and Greece are exceptions.

6 While earlier research found substantial differences in production styles, there is an increasing similarity in these across countries as well.

A closer look at country specific differences disproves the assumption of a unique American video style regarding the emphasis of negative appeals. In all other countries studied, political TV spots overwhelmingly accentuated the positive approach refraining from direct attacks on opponents. According to William L. Benoit[60] "acclaims are more common than attacks." But these patterns seem to be in flux, concentrating on changes in video styles over time. Israel is a striking example for profound changes of video styles related to the involvement of leading American media consultants in the parliamentary election campaigns 1996 and 1999. Before 1996, Israel aired its political television spots each evening during prime time during the last three weeks of a campaign. They have been characterized as a nightly rolling debate between parties and candidates, responding to issue positions in an interactive way. This style of instant rebuttal, without using the modus of attack and counterattack, has changed dramatically during the 1996 campaign, when American consultants took command of the advertising strategies and transformed rolling debates into relentless attacks of opponents, introducing the American format of hard-hitting thirty-second spots, which culminated during the 1999 air war in an unprecedented way.[61]

Similar tendencies can be found in Australia, where the video style of political advertisements in recent parliamentary election campaigns concentrated on negative imputations and direct attacks, clearly inspired by attack lines from previous American presidential campaigns. Negativity seems to play an increasing role in Russian political television advertising. Russian political television advertising has undergone massive changes in the direction of a distinct video style, characterized by exploiting the traumatic past in a highly selective manner, using emotions and collective memories for defamation of specific policies and attacking the integrity of opponents via *dirty technologies* (*chernaya tekhnologiya*), the Russian term for negative campaigning. Even in Latin America traditional video styles, based on music, folklore and emotional appeals of leaders delivering speeches to cheering crowds have been transformed in the meantime and were replaced by emphasizing the contrast, addressing opponents' weaknesses and stirring up negative emotions, such as anger and resentment.[62]

While some countries imposed restrictions on production style and content of political television advertisements by forbidding negative campaign messages, personal attacks or hate speeches, other countries refrained from interfering with the content of political commercials. France, Italy, Finland and Turkey set specified rules for the production of television advertisements. In Latin America, Brazilian and Mexican electoral laws contain explicit guidelines for production. Also in Japan and South Korea we find detailed regulations regarding production style, format and content of televised political advertisement. The variety of political television advertising becomes clear, when comparing the most common formats of political television advertising. While the American standard format of thirty-second spots may be common practice in Canada,

Australia and some Latin American countries, most common formats vary between ninety seconds to ten minutes. This results in a multiplicity of production styles despite some general commonalities regarding formal aspects and the growing sophistication of professional video politics.[63]

Summarizing our worldwide exploration of practices of political television advertising we reach the following tentative conclusions: first, the degree of access to political television advertising seems to have a major impact on prevailing campaign practices. If political parties get the chance to reach sufficient voters by frequently televised advertisements, they may concentrate their resources and communication strategies on television advertising instead of relying on more traditional forms of campaign communication. This pattern can be observed in countries with unlimited access to paid political television advertising as the United States, as well as in countries where parties are not permitted to buy air time but are provided with considerable free air time as in Brazil. Apparently, it is the sheer amount of available air time either provided by the *market model* (paid political television advertising) or the *public interest model* (free air time provided by the state), which stimulates an intensive use of television advertising.[64] Second, the multiplicity of different regulatory frameworks, formats, production styles and the total amount of political television advertising is contrary to assumptions about a worldwide standardization or Americanization of campaign communication.[65] With the exception of the United States and Brazil, where television advertising has become the signature of election campaigns, television advertising is an important, but not the sole feature of campaign practices worldwide.

Notes

1 Marjorie Hershey, "Campaigns, Elections and the Media," in *Encyclopedia of Media and Politics*, ed. Todd M. Shaefer and Thomas A. Birkland (Washington, D.C.: CQ Press, 2007), 34–7.
2 Fritz Plasser with Gunda Plasser, *Global Political Campaigning. A Worldwide Analysis of Campaign Professionals and Their Practices* (Westport, CT: Praeger, 2002), 267–80.
3 The Pew Research Center for the People and the Press, "Pew Global Attitudes Project," Washington, D.C., 2002, http://pewglobal.org. Eastern Europe countries surveyed: Bulgaria, Czech Republic, Poland, Russia, Slovak Republic, Turkey, Uzbekistan, Ukraine. Latin American countries surveyed: Argentina, Bolivia, Brazil, Guatemala, Honduras, Mexico, Peru, Venezuela. Asian countries surveyed: Bangladesh, China, India, Indonesia, Japan, Jordan, Lebanon, South Korea, Pakistan, Philippines, Vietnam. Western European countries surveyed: France, Germany, Italy, Great Britain. North American countries surveyed: Canada, USA. African countries surveyed: Angola, Egypt, Ghana, Ivory Coast, Kenya, Mali, Nigeria, Senegal, South Africa, Tanzania, Uganda.
4 Jay G. Blumler and Dennis Kavanagh, "The Third Age of Political Communication: Influences and Features," *Political Communication* 16 (3) (1999): 209–30.
5 Pippa Norris, *A Virtuous Circle: Political Communications in Postindustrial Societies* (New York: Cambridge University Press, 2000), Plasser, *Global Political Campaigns*.
6 Winfried Schulz, "Wahlkampf unter Vielkanalbedingungen," *Media Perspektiven* 8 (1998): 378–91.
7 W. Lance Bennett, *News: The Politics of Illusion*, 7th ed. (London: Pearson Longman, 2006).
8 Plasser, *Global Political Campaigns*.
9 Blumler and Kavanagh, "The Third Age of Political Communication."
10 Daniel C. Hallin and Paolo Mancini, *Comparing Media Systems. Three Models of Media and Politics* (Cambridge: Cambridge University Press, 2004).
11 Gianpietro Mazzoleni and Winfried Schulz, " 'Mediatization' of Politics: A Challenge for Democracy?" *Political Communication* 16 (1999): 257.
12 Jay G. Blumler and Michael Gurevitch, " 'Americanization' Reconsidered: UK–U.S. Campaign Communication Comparisons Across Time," in *Mediated Politics: Communication in the Future of Democracy*, ed. W. Lance Bennett and Robert M. Entman (Cambridge: Cambridge University Press, 2001), 380–403.
13 Frank Esser, Carsten Reinemann and David Fan, "Spin Doctors in the United States, Great Britain, and Germany: Metacommunication about Media Manipulation," *The International Harvard Journal of Press/Politics* 6 (1) (2001): 16–45; Frank Esser and Paul D'Angelo, "Framing the Press and Publicity Process in U.S., British, and German General Election Campaigns: A Comparative Study of Metacoverage," *The*

Harvard International Journal of Press/Politics 11 (3) (2006): 44–66; Holli A. Semetko, "Political Balance on Television: Campaigns in the United States, Britain and Germany," *The Harvard International Journal of Press/Politics* 1 (1) (1996): 51–71; Holli A. Semetko, Jay G. Blumler, Michael Gurevitch and David H. Weaver, *The Formation of Campaign Agendas: A Comparative Analysis of Party and Media Roles in Recent American and British Elections* (Hillsdale, N.J.: Erlbaum, 1991); David L. Swanson and Paolo Mancini, ed., *Politics, Media, and Modern Democracy: An International Study of Innovations in Electoral Campaigning and their Consequences* (Westport, CT: Praeger, 1996).

14 Barbara Pfetsch, "Political Communication Culture in the United States and Germany," *The Harvard International Journal of Press/Politics* 6 (1) (2001): 46–67; Juergen Wilke and Carsten Reinemann, "Do the Candidates Matter? Long-term Trends of Campaign Coverage—A Study of the German Press since 1949," *European Journal of Communication* 16 (3) (2001): 291–314.

15 Anne Cooper-Chen, "Televised International News in Five Countries: Thoroughness, Insularity and Agenda Capacity," *International Communication Bulletin* 24 (1–2) (1989): 4–8; Andreas Genz, Klaus Schoenbach and Holli A. Semetko. " 'Amerikanisierung?' Politik in den Fernsehnachrichten Während der Bundestagswahlkämpfe 1990–1998," in *Wahlen und Wähler: Analysen aus Anlass der Bundestagswahl 1998*, ed. Hans-Dieter Klingemann and Max Kaase (Wiesbaden: Westdeutscher Verlag, 2001), 401–13; Günther Lengauer, *Postmoderne Nachrichtenlogik. Redaktionelle Politikvermittlung in Medienzentrierten Demokratien* (Wiesbaden: VS Verlag, 2007); Joseph Straubhaar, Carrie Heeter, Bradley Greenberg, Leonardo Ferreira, Robert Wicks and Tuen-Yu Lau, "What Makes News: Western, Socialist, and Third-World Television Newscasts Compared in Eight Countries," in *Mass Media Effects Across Cultures*, ed. Felipe Korzenny and Stella Ting-Toomey, (Newbury Park, CA: Sage, 1992), 89–109.

16 For the content analysis tests of reliability and validity were conducted. The average intercoder-reliability resulted in a coefficient of 0.852 on an average. Additionally, a validity test was computed that shows the correspondence of the conception of the researchers and its operationalization by the coders. The validity-coefficient reaches 0.882 and thus reflects a sufficiently high level of accordance.

17 A total population of 775 election and campaign reports (published in the final six weeks of each election campaign) was analyzed. The selection of countries on this primary level of analysis was based on Hallin and Mancini's three models of media and politics (U.S.—North Atlantic Model; Italy—Mediterranean Model; Germany and Austria—Northern European Model) in order to ensure the greatest possible diversity in contextual political communication settings among postmodern media democracies.

18 North America: Canada—parliamentary elections 2000. Latin America: Venezuela—presidential elections 2006; Mexico—presidential elections 2006; Chile—presidential elections 2006; Brazil—presidential elections 2006. Eastern Europe: Belarus—parliamentary elections 2004; Russia—presidential elections 1995/2004; Ukraine—parliamentary elections 2006. Africa: South Africa—parliamentary elections 2004; Namibia—parliamentary elections 2004; Tunisia—parliamentary elections 2004; Egypt—parliamentary elections 2005. Asia-Pacific: Philippines—senatorial elections 2007; Australia—parliamentary elections 2001. Western Europe: Great Britain—parliamentary elections 2005.

19 University or human right institutes studies: Australia 2001; Philippines 2007; Brazil 2006; Russia 1995; Egypt 2005; Tunisia 2004; Chile 2006; Mexico 2006. OSCE/ODIHR studies: Belarus 2004; Russia 2004; Ukraine 2006. EU-EOM studies: Venezuela 2006. Electoral Commission studies: Great Britain 2005; Canada 2000. Media Tenor studies: Namibia 2004; South Africa 2004.

20 Bennett, *News*; Gideon Rahat and Tamir Sheafer, "The Personalization(s) of Politics: Israel, 1949–2003," in *Political Communication* 24 (1) (2007): 65–80.

21 Bennett, *News*, 6.

22 Thomas E. Patterson, *Out of Order* (New York: Knopf, 1993), 19; Bennett, *News*.

23 Mazzoleni and Schulz, " 'Mediatization' of Politics," 257.

24 See also Wolfgang Donsbach, "Drehbücher und Inszenierungen: Die Union in der Defensive," in *Kampa. Meinungsklima und Medienwirkung im Bundestagswahlkampf 1998*, ed. Elisabeth Noelle-Neumann, Hans-Matthias Kepplinger and Wolfgang Donsbach (Freiburg: Alber, 1999), 141–80; Genz, Schoenbach and Semetko, " 'Amerikanisierung?'

25 Canadian Election Study, "2000 Data Set," University of Montreal, 2000, http://www.ces-eec.umontreal.ca/surveys.html#2000; David Deacon *et al.*, *Reporting the 2005 UK General Election* (Loughborough University: Communication Research Centre, August 2005).

26 OSCE/ODIHR—Office for Democratic Institutions and Human Rights, "Russian Federation Presidential Election 14 March 2004," Warsaw, 2004, http://www1.osce.org/documents/odihr/2004/06/3033_en.pdf; "Republic of Belarus Parliamentary Elections 17 October 2004," http://www.osce.org/documents/odihr/2004/12/3961_en.pdf.

27 OSCE/ODIHR—Office for Democratic Institutions and Human Rights, "Ukraine Parliamentary

Elections 26 March 2006," Warsaw, 2006, http://www1.osce.org/documents/odihr/2006/06/19631_en.pdf.

28 Asociación Latinoamericana para la Comunicación Social, "Monitoreo de los principales Medios de Comunicación Social de Alcance Nacional: Chile. Elección Presidencial 2006," Santiago de Chile, 2006, http://observatoriodemedios.org.ve/docs/elecciones_2006.doc.

29 Sebastián Valenzuela and Maxwell McCombs, "Agenda-setting Effects on Vote Choice: Evidence from the 2006 Mexican Election." Paper presented at the Conference of the International Communication Association, San Francisco, May 2007; European Union Election Observation Mission, "Final Report. Presidential Elections Venezuela 2006," Caracas, 2006, http://www.eueomvenezuela.org.

30 Media Tenor, "Media's Perception of Political Parties in South Africa in the Run-up of the National Elections in April 2004," Pretoria, 2004, http://www.mediatenor.co.za.

31 The Tunisian League for the Defense of Human Rights, "Monitoring the Coverage of the October 2004 Legislative and Presidential Elections in Tunisia," Tunis 2004, http://www.cmpd.eu.com/reports/tunisia_2004.pdf; Cairo Institute for Human Rights Studies, "Media and Parliamentary Elections. Monitoring the Media Coverage of Egypt's Parliamentary Elections (October 27–December 3, 2005)," Cairo, 2006, http://www.cihrs.org/Release/PDF/36_68200634546.pdf.

32 Freedom House, "Freedom of the Press 2007," Washington D.C., 2007, http://www.freedomhouse.org/template.cfm?page=16.

33 Joseph N. Capella and Kathleen Hall Jamieson, *Spiral of Cynicism: The Press and the Public Good* (New York: Oxford University Press, 1997); Thomas E. Patterson, *Doing Well and Doing Good: How Soft News and Critical Journalism are Shrinking the News Audience and Weakening Democracy—and What News Outlets Can Do About It* (Cambridge, MA: Joan Shorenstein Center on the Press, Politics and Public Policy, Harvard University, 2000); Patterson, *Out of Order*.

34 Patterson, *Doing Well and Doing Good*, 74.

35 Genz, Schoenbach and Semetko, " 'Amerikanisierung?' " Patterson, *Doing Well and Doing Good*; Winfried Schulz and Reinmar Zeh, "Changing Campaign Coverage of German Television. A Comparison of Five Elections 1990–2005." Paper presented at the Annual Conference of the International Communication Association (ICA), San Francisco, May 2007.

36 Michael Schudson, "Social Origins of Press Cynicism in Portraying Politics," *American Behavioral Scientist* 42 (6) (1999): 998–1008.

37 Daniel C. Hallin and Paolo Mancini, *Comparing Media Systems: Three Models of Media and Politics* (Cambridge: Cambridge University Press, 2004), 253.

38 See also, Plasser, *Global Political Campaigning*.

39 Ibid., 206.

40 Ibid., 208.

41 Jinyoung Tak, "Political Advertising in Japan, South Korea, and Taiwan," in *The Sage Handbook of Political Advertising*, ed. Lynda Lee Kaid and Christina Holtz-Bacha, (Thousand Oaks, CA: Sage, 2006), 293–5.

42 Christian Schafferer, "Electoral Campaigning in Taiwan," in *Election Campaigning in East and Southeast Asia: Globalization of Political Marketing*, ed. Christian Schafferer, (Aldershot: Ashgate, 2006), 29–54.

43 Julianne Stewart, "Political Advertising in Australia and New Zealand," in *The Sage Handbook of Political Advertising*, ed. Lynda Lee Kaid and Christina Holtz-Bacha (Thousand Oaks, CA: Sage, 2006), 275–8.

44 Paul Nesbitt-Larking and Jonathan Rose, "Political Advertising in Canada," in *Lights, Camera, Campaign!*, ed. David A. Schultz (New York: B&T, 2004), 284–7.

45 Mauro P. Porto, "Framing Controversies: Television and the 2002 Presidential Election in Brazil," *Political Communication* 24 (1) (2007): 20–1.

46 Mauro P. Porto, "Political Advertising and Democracy in Brazil," in *The Sage Handbook of Political Advertising*, ed. Lynda Lee Kaid and Christina Holtz-Bacha (Thousand Oaks, CA: Sage, 2006), 133–4.

47 Plasser, *Global Political Campaigning*, 213.

48 Ibid., 214.

49 Jose-Carlos Lozano, "Political Advertising in Mexico," in *The Sage Handbook of Political Advertising*, ed. Lynda Lee Kaid and Christina Holtz-Bacha (Thousand Oaks, CA: Sage, 2006), 259–68.

50 Ulises Beltran, "The Combined Effect of Advertising and News Coverage in the Mexican Presidential Campaign of 2000," *Political Communication* 24 (1) (2007): 41–2.

51 Lynda Lee Kaid, "Political Advertising in the United States," in *The Sage Handbook of Political Advertising*," ed. Lynda Lee Kaid and Christina Holtz-Bacha (Thousand Oaks, CA: Sage, 2006), 37–64.

52 Kenneth Goldstein and Patricia Strach, eds, *The Medium and the Message: Television Advertising and American Elections* (Upper Saddle River, N.J: Prentice Hall, 2004).

53 Darrell M. West, *Air Wars. Television Advertising in Election Campaigns, 1952–2004*, 4th ed. (Washington D.C.: CQ Press, 2005).

54 Christina Holtz-Bacha and Eva Maria Lessinger, "Wie die Lustlosigkeit Konterkariert Wurde: Fernsehwahlwerbung 2005," in *Die Massenmedien im Wahlkampf: Die Bundestagswahl 2005*, ed. Christina Holtz-Bacha (Wiesbaden: VS Verlag, 2006), 170.

55 Gianpetro Mazzoleni, "TV Political Advertising in Italy: When Politicians are Afraid," in *The Sage Handbook of Political Advertising*, ed. Lynda Lee Kaid and Christina Holtz-Bacha (Thousand Oaks, CA: Sage, 2006), 254–5.

56 Dan Caspi and Baruch Leshem, "From Electoral Propaganda to Political Advertising in Israel," in *The Sage Handbook of Political Advertising*, ed. Lynda Lee Kaid and Christina Holtz-Bacha (Thousand Oaks, CA: Sage, 2006), 109–28.

57 Daphne Skillen, "Russia," in *The Media and Elections*, ed. Bernd-Peter Lange and David Ward (Mahwah, N.J.: Erlbaum, 2004), 123–43.

58 Sarah Oates, "A Spiral of Post-Soviet Cynicism: The First Decade of Political Advertising in Russia" in *The Sage Handbook of Political Advertising*, ed. Lynda Lee Kaid and Christina Holtz-Bacha (Thousand Oaks, CA: Sage, 2006), 309–24.

59 On Western Europe: Lynda Lee Kaid and Christina Holtz-Bacha, eds, *Political Advertising in Western Democracies: Parties and Candidates on Television* (Thousand Oaks, CA: Sage, 1995); Lynda Lee Kaid and Anne Johnston, *Videostyle in Presidential Campaigns: Style and Content of Televised Political Advertising* (Westport, CT: Greenwood Press, 2001). On evolving European democracies: Lynda Lee Kaid, ed., *Television and Politics in Evolving European Democracies* (Commack, N.Y.: Nova Biomedical, 1999). Long-term research: Lynda Lee Kaid and Christina Holtz-Bacha, "Television Advertising and Democratic Systems Around the World: A Comparison of Videostyle Content and Effects," in *The Sage Handbook of Political Advertising*, ed. Lynda Lee Kaid and Christina Holz-Bacha (Thousand Oaks, CA: Sage, 2006), 445–57.

60 William L. Benoit, *Communication in Political Campaigns* (New York: Peter Lang, 2007), 163.

61 Caspi and Leshem, "From Electoral Propaganda to Political Advertising in Israel," 109–28.

62 Plasser, *Global Political Campaigning*, 95.

63 Kaid and Holtz-Bacha, "Television Advertising and Democratic Systems Around the World," 445–57.

64 Plasser, *Global Political Campaigning*, 236–7.

65 Fritz Plasser, "Par et Impar: Wahlkommunikation in den USA und Europa im Vergleich," in *Medien und Kommunikationsforschung im Vergleich*, ed. Juergen Wilke et al. (Wiesbaden: VS Verlag, 2008, 155–77).

20

Mobile Technology and Political Participation

What the Rest of the World Can Teach America

Julie Barko Germany and Justin Oberman

In the realm of American politics, the first decade of the twenty-first century has become synonymous with the "web campaign." Political candidates, organizations, and parties have turned to the Internet to raise money, register voters, mobilize volunteers, persuade, and earn media. From where we sit, writing this chapter during the summer before the 2008 primaries, running an American political campaign is no longer a question of having a website or sending e-mail.

Instead, the campaign web presence is evolving into a cohesive online and off-line effort that combines political management with technology-powered tools, applications, and media. Books such as *The Revolution Will Not Be Televised* by Joe Trippi, *Crashing the Gate: Netroots, Grassroots, and the Rise of People-powered Politics* by Jerome Armstrong and Markos Moulitsas Zuniga, *Burning at the Grassroots: Inside the Dean Machine* by Dana Dunnan, and *The Political Promise of Blogging*, edited by Daniel Drezner and Henry Farrell[1] look at the ways voters engage in politics through blogs and social networking sites. Recent studies by the George Washington University Institute for Politics, Democracy & the Internet (IPDI) have provided a body of research about people engaging in online politics, and have helped turn donors of small, online fundraising contributions into a new invisible primary. As the presidential campaigns geared up for the 2008 primaries, every new utility and online tactic made the news, and blogs such as TechPresident.com and TechRepublican.com covered online campaign news and strategy. To date, the Internet has become one of the most hyped—and most promising—tools in the political sphere. (See Chapter 13, by Emilienne Ireland on the use of the Internet in campaigns.)

While American politicos have worked to turn online campaigning into a craft and a science, many American candidates, issue groups, and political non profits have until recently ignored a tool that the rest of the world has embraced: the mobile phone—a technology that weighs (and costs) considerably less than a computer and that has the ability to mobilize hundreds of thousands of people within seconds. In fact, over the course of the last decade, mobile phones have fueled revolutions and mass protests across the globe, becoming less a tool of the political establishment and more a grassroots medium for a polarized and often unhappy electorate. The timeline for many of these major events peaks around critical elections, and the events themselves are as geographically different as they are politically diverse. In January, 2001 Filipino citizens rallied through text messages, radio, and television. Their mass protests in Manila led to the resignation of President Joseph Estrada, and People Power II, as it came to be called, has become the poster child for mobile-powered political movements. A year later, in April 2002, Hungarian political parties used text messaging to launch dueling negative campaigns. On election day, voter turnout exceeded 71% at the polls. Text messages turned out mass protests in Spain the week of elections in March 2004. The protesters mobilized the day before voters went to the polls, a day in which all organized political activities are banned. The message was powerful and immediate: the government was lying about the Madrid train bombings. The protests led to the upset of the incumbent Popular Party by the Spanish Socialist Labour Party. Similar protests occurred during the Orange Revolution in Ukraine in 2004.

Since then, mobile penetration has increased, mobility has become more affordable, and mobile-powered political events, elections, and protests have occurred with regularity around the world and, slowly at first but with more regularity, in the United States. This chapter looks at some of the lessons we have learned from observing many of these events and talking with participants. Most of our examples look at the role text messaging has played in political events and elections. However, as mobile technology evolves, we anticipate that other features, including photos, ring tones, instant messaging, and file sharing may also be used in politics.

As many of these "peak" events illustrate, when the right conditions exist, mobile technology has played a role in many of the largest people-powered political movements of the last ten years. In 2004, technology author and thinker Howard Rheingold wrote,

> The alphabet made empires and armies possible, the printing press made democracy and science possible; railroads and telephones, corporations and bureaucracies co-evolved. Now the fusion of the mobile telephone, the PC, and the Internet is beginning to make new forms of collective action possible on new scales, at new tempos, in new places, with groups that had not been able to organize before.[2]

On a global scale, mobile technology may be the most effective grassroots organizing tool of the early twenty-first century. Determining what those "right" elements comprise varies, according to the time, political climate, and emphatically the individual users or mobile political participants.

At the same time, mobile phones possess some very specific characteristics that make them an ideal grassroots tool. First, mobile phones are individual and customizable. We store intimate photos of our friends and family on them, load ringtones that reflect our favorite music, and use them to communicate in very personal ways. Second, the mobile phone is an incredibly personal tool and it enables conversations—voice and text message—that are as individual as the people engaged in the conversation. Historically, many of these successful, mobile-driven political events have evolved from word-of-mouth messages passed from one individual to the next, instead of being blasted or broadcast from one source, such as a political campaign or advocacy group. Even in other countries, the data features of mobile communication are mostly used to quickly spread information or chat with someone personal, such as a coworker, close friend, boyfriend or girl-friend. Third, mobile phones are ubiquitous. People across different demographics and skill levels find them easy to use and carry their mobile phones with them everywhere they go—bathrooms, dinner tables, meetings, and bedrooms. Finally, the mobile phone is a tool of immediacy. We use phones to call and text people when we anticipate an immediate response.

Many of these characteristics feel inherently democratic: personal interaction, individual choice, engagement. In fact, when political scholars and activists talk about mobile technology in the political space, they often emphasize its democratizing ability. During an era of decline in political participation, mobile technology appears to have assisted in voter turn out, protests and demon-strations, and even in spreading political humor. Computers and Internet connections are not financially feasible for many populations around the world: mobile phones are pocket sized com-munication and information gathering tools that cost considerably less and are much less difficult to operate. However, we believe that possessing an unfaltering faith in mobile technology's ability to democratize the planet often naively undervalues the role that government and political party control currently play in the process.

Elements of the Mobile Revolution

In January 2001, hundreds of thousands of Filipino citizens poured onto the Epifanio de los Santos Avenue, a major highway that circles Manila. They were protesting a vote in the impeachment trial of then President Joseph Estrada to block evidence of political corruption. On January 17, a text message began circulating, telling people to "GO 2EDSA. WEAR BLACK," compelling 100,000 protesters to comply over the course of the day. Within the next twenty-four hours, the numbers tripled, fueled by a combination of over seventy million text messages and the radio and television coverage that the early push of protesters garnered. Despite protests from President Estrada claiming that he would not resign office, by noon on January 20, Gloria Arroyo took the oath of office and became the new president of the Philippines. Her story did not endure as victoriously as it began, due in large part to the role that mobile technology played in uncovering corruption in her own administration. (On elections in the Philippines, see Chapter 26, by Louis Perron.)

People Power II or EDSA II, as the peaceful revolution has been called, is one of the earliest, often cited examples of how people used mobile technology for mass political action. Glossing over the surface of this story, as many American mobilists and politicos do, it is tempting to become drunk on the power that mobile technology has in the political space, particularly when it comes to mobilizing immediate action. Our experiences have reflected that more than a few political minds are drawn to mobile technology because is resembles an ultra-effective e-mail delivery service that political groups and campaigns can use to pound voters with a carefully sculpted barrage of text message after text message to "donate now" or "protest now." The context in which political events such as People Power II occur is imperative. That context includes such factors as mobile phone adoption, cultures of technology usage, and political dynamics.

Mobile Phone Adoption

Technology adoption was an important part of the People Power II context, and it provides a backdrop for the other examples used in this chapter. Mobile phone penetration and text message usage was becoming ubiquitous in the Philippines during the protests. Similar mobile-enabled revolutions and mass protests would not have occurred without a citizenry that relied on mobile technology the way many Americans rely on landline telephones, e-mail, and instant messaging.

In 2005, when we worked together on a publication entitled *The Politics-to-Go Handbook: A Guide to Using Mobile Technology in Politics*,[3] the United States was one of the three largest mobile phone markets in the world, representing 20% of the global market in revenue and 12% of the global market in number of mobile phone subscribers. At the time, however, the mobile climate in the United States did not feel as innovative or as advanced as markets in Europe and Asia. Users outside the United States were migrating to the more advanced Third Generation (3G) and Fourth Generation (4G) mobile networks, and they had fancier, more colorful handsets. Their mobile networks seemed more open, and users seemed more active. In this context, it is not unsurprising that countries with actively mobile populations were amongst the first to develop mobile-powered political activities.

Many aspects of mobile penetration—from network decisions about which services to offer to consumer choices about which handsets to purchase and which features to use—have been difficult to predict in the United States. How does an organization reach people via mobile devices? In *Politics-to-Go*, Oliver Starr, a mobile entrepreneur and blogger, wrote:

> While certain rules clearly apply to large groups and various predictions can be made to within a few percentage points of accuracy given the appropriate analysis, the public isn't swayed one group at a time or one community at a time, but one individual at a time. . . . You might have a nice unit with a bigger screen and you may have public funds to subsidize calls, but when your fingers start depressing the keys on the keypad you've entered one of the most democratic mediums on the planet.[4]

At the time, Starr was attempting to explain a blossoming that was occurring in the mobile industry and among the citizen-users it equipped. He also wanted to explain some of the difficulties marketers face when trying to tackle the mobile market. Mobile marketing has been much hyped over the past few years. Adoption of mobile marketing tactics has occurred slowly, as users have warmed to mobile devices and the myriad ways companies and political groups can use mobile devices to market to them. That was 2005.

By mid-2007, 243.4 million Americans are mobile phone subscribers, and mobile phone penetration is 81%. Over 12% of American households no longer purchase landlines, relying solely on mobile devices for telephonic communication. Mobile users send 240.8 billion text messages a year. This number has quadrupled since the publication of *Politics-to-Go* in 2005. Revenues from data plans have doubled during that time, from $8.5 billion in 2005 to $19.2 billion in 2007. Americans talk on their cell phones almost two trillion minutes a year.[5] In today's climate of rapid adoption, mobile marketing and mobile-powered politics are beginning to be staples.

Cultures of Technology Usage

Mobile culture has slowly trickled into the American consciousness. It has only been within the past year, for example, that US mobile providers have addressed unlimited text messaging as a desired service, and it has only been within the last few years that television and the mainstream media have incorporated mobile technology into their reality programs, game shows, and news delivery service. Most of these ads and mobile programs, it is important to note, focus on mobile technology as a tool for youth, young parents, and busy urban professionals.

There are no doubt substantial differences in the ways that the United States and the rest of the world use and perceive the mobile medium. These differences are rooted in the different ways technology is perceived, amongst other things. This is especially the case when it comes to personal computers, mobile devices, and the Internet.

Mobile culture in Japan illustrates this point, since mobile phone use in Japan is more pervasive than it is anywhere else in the world. A lot of the new technology and social software built for the mobile phone, or as it's called in Japan, *keitai*, was and is developed in Japan. Consequently, these new tools and software are adopted in Japan before the shops in any other country begin to sell them. Japanese consumers can do a wide variety of things with their *keitai*, and in highly social spaces. For example, Japanese citizens can buy train fares using their *keitai*, as well as take pictures of barcodes to compare shop prices right from the store. Anywhere you go in Japan you will see Japanese citizens using their cell phones for something. Academics studying the cultural implications of the new technology have coined the term "*keitai* culture" to help explain the phenomenon. Pop-culture news and media have even picked up the term in an act of postmodern legitimacy. In Japan, more connections are made to the Internet through *keitai* than through any other broadband option.[6]

Some experts attribute the rapid development of the mobile medium in Japan to a direct reaction to the digital divide. The cost of broadband was substantially more expensive than the mobile i-mode network. Consequently, many Japanese interact with the Internet via their *keitai*. When Japanese mobile users want to send a message to other mobile users, for example, they are more likely to send messages by means of e-mail than text message. *Keitai* is seamless with everyday life, while the computer requires abrupt attention to a specific location. In the word of *keitai* culture expert Mizuko Ito, *keitai* "functions more as a medium of lightweight 'refreshment' analogous to sipping a cup of coffee or taking a cigarette break." It is a small moment of our lives with tremendous importance.[7]

By contrast, most American mobile users and businesses perceive mobile technology as "second-rate" Internet access, something good to have when you don't have your personal computer or laptop. The Japanese model teaches us that the American way of thinking about and perceiving the Internet is not the only way and that "portable, lightweight engagement" to quote Ito again, "form[s] an alternative constellation of 'advanced' Internet access characteristics that stand in marked contrast to complex functionality and stationary immersive engagement."[8] The differences here are between networked infrastructures that base themselves on a cross-cultural universal model (the PC Internet) and a network built on a true network of shifting localities and cultures (the mobile medium). Neither one is better than the other. That is not the point here. The point is to show that they are different and that problems only occur when one discourse dominates the way we perceive the other.

Political Dynamics

Another part of that context, a highly charged political climate, simply cannot be forged. During People Power II, the political-economic environment, including political and social opposition groups powered by the middle class was imperative. Mobile revolutions tend to begin in a highly charged, polarized political environment in which a large percent of the population feel oppressed by or lied to by the government. Text messages help to galvanize and activate these populations, and their efforts, from protesting to voting to spreading rumors, increase in strength as they garner more media coverage.

The Spanish general election in March 2004 illustrates this point. For many Spaniards, the Madrid train bombings that occurred on March 11, 2004, days before the general election, are as painful as many Americans' memories about the attack on the World Trade Center buildings on September 11, 2001. The government did not share information about the bombings, fueling rumors and resentment around the country. Much of this energy centered in Madrid, where text messages rose 20% above normal on March 13, the day before the election and a day when political organizations are required by law to refrain from political activities. By the end of the day, called 13M in text messaging shorthand, more than 5,000 people gathered in spontaneous protests. The biggest upset, however, occurred the next day, when text messages rose 40%: many of those messages urged Spaniards—particularly young people—to vote. Voter turnout exceeded 77%. The increase in voters, possibly propelled by a rise in voting-themed text messages, led to the election of the opposition Spanish Socialist Labour Party.

Political climate also includes the ways in which mobile technology is used for political purposes. Most of the examples used in this chapter have several elements in common. Like 13M in Spain or People Power II in the Philippines, mobile revolutions tend to occur when they play on individual political sentiment and emotions, and they reflect immediate events, such as corruption charges or catastrophes. Almost all of these mobile revolutions appear to be people-powered: calls to action, rumors, and political messages spread from cell phone to cell phone, from individual to individual. Through our observations, some of the most effective mobile-powered events are not controlled and disseminated like American political e-mail—single messages carefully controlled, crafted, and broadcast by one political group to a mass audience. They are personal, sent from one friend, family member or work associate to another, and sometimes personalized. Finally, most of the text message waves, along with the events or actions they encourage, appear to be spontaneous. Instead of being planned out months or weeks in advance the way American political groups typically run protests, political fundraisers, or get-out-the-vote activities, these events occur in the immediate, polarized, emotional moment.

This is not always the case, however. During the early stages of the 2002 parliamentary elections in Hungary, for example, text messages were used to organize a few protests and spread a few political messages. It was not until after the first round of elections, when the Hungarian Socialist Party and the opposition party, Fidesz, received almost the same amount of votes, that the political parties focused their attentions on text messaging as a platform for their messages. The content of those messages appears to have been rumor-fueled, negative repartee, which sociologist and researcher Endre Danyi calls "black propaganda" and "viral political marketing."[9] The political parties designed the text message campaigns, but the message recipients altered messages, using their own creativity and wit to create new messages, which they in turn forwarded to their friends. Traffic rose as Hungarian voters sent each other more than one million text messages a day leading up to the election. To some degree, these were effective. Voter turnout exceeded 71%. The results for the two major parties, however, remained almost identical.

Mobilization vs. Persuasion

Several notable technology authors, including Howard Rheingold, author of *SmartMobs*, and McKenzie Wark, author of *A Hacker Manifesto*,[10] believe that mobile phones have the greatest political potential when they do what they were designed to do in the first place, namely, to create and send communications from one person to another. When tied to an immediate message or event, many of these messages have the potential to spread virally, inciting friend after friend to take an action and forward the message. That is precisely what occurred during the People Power II movement in the Philippines, during Hungarian elections in 2002, and preceding Spanish elections in 2004.

Examples such as these suggest that mobile adoption has greatly influenced politics itself. However, mobile technology is not always a political tool. For example, *keitai* culture in Japan is decidedly apolitical. The country with the most pervasive use of the most advanced phones and social software does not use the technology politically in any substantial way. Yet, when a country such as the Philippines or various regions in Africa adopt the mobile phone, it becomes political almost immediately.

Why is this the case? Perhaps because *when it comes to integrating the mobile medium into politics just focusing on the technology is not the right way to go.* As seen, mobile communications are located in the very social, cultural, and historical contexts in which they are physically used. No one in the Philippines, for example, signed up to receive any text message alerts should a need for social or political protesting arise. Yet the text message flurry that led to the People Power II demonstration was spread by no other means than the insanely viral communication of peer-to-peer/friend-to-friend networks. Mobile technology was used exactly how it was meant to be used: the political momentum against President Estrada was already in place, and text messaging was merely the tool used to organize around a cause.

Caught in highly charged political moments, mobile-powered politics does not persuade the undecided. Rather, it motivates the already persuaded. As political organizations across the globe continue to find ways to incorporate mobile technology into their grassroots programs, it is important to focus on mobilization through cell phones, not marketing to undecided voters. In June 2006, for example, Catalans voted on a referendum that would give their region in Spain greater autonomy. The Catalan Socialist Party (PSC), the Catalan arm of the ruling Spanish Socialist Labour Party (PSOE), designed a mobile strategy to encourage people to vote "*Sí*" on the referendum. The PSC set up Bluetooth booths at four political events preceding the referendum that gave political activists the opportunity to download videos, ringtones, and images displaying the word "*Si*" that they could then forward to their friends. and family to thus help spread the "*Si*" message on the street. Supporters could send their own, personalized text messages, which were then projected on a screen at the events. Participants also received a message from someone else. The final rally was streamed live to 3G mobile phones in Spain.[11] On the day of the referendum, almost three out of four voters cast a "*Si*" ballot.[12]

Another example occurred in the spring of 2007, when text messages fueled protests in Xiamen, China. Earlier that year, in November, a chemical plant announced that it was building a factory to process two toxic substances found in polyester a few kilometers away. In March, a Xiamen University professor, Zhao Yufen, gave a speech suggesting that the plant was too close to the city and ought to be moved further away. Later that month, on March 25, citizens began circulating text messages about the issues, telling recipients, "For our children and grandchildren, act! Participate among 10,000 people, June 1 at 8 a.m., opposite the municipal government building! Hand tie yellow ribbons! SMS all your Xiamen friends!"

The news spread through the online and news media, and on May 30, the government announced it was postponing the project. The next day, a *Xiamen Daily* editorial claimed that the text messages were misleading the public and trying to create an environment of hostility between citizens and the government. At 8 a.m. on June 1, protesters began gathering.[13] Some reports suggested that thousands of protesters came together; other sites claim as many as one million people sent and received text messages.[14] Another blog, Global Voices, reported that the Chinese government shut down the mobile networks in an attempt to control the protests.[15]

Both of these examples reflect many of the elements of effective mobile politics. The mobile movements surrounding both the Catalonia referendum and the Chinese chemical plant protest played on very personal concerns, such as regional pride and safety, and immediate events. They both mobilized citizens for collective action—voting and protesting. Yet both relied on the power of word-of-mouth networks to carry the mobile messages, instead of faceless organizations blasting text messages to a public that may not want to receive them. Finally, both events asked recipients to take actions—actions that were at once very personal and contagiously collective.

The American Mobile Context

All of the examples we have used to illustrate mobile technology as an advocacy tool have occurred outside the United States. To date, the United States has trailed other countries in mobile adoption—particularly text messaging. In an October 2006 article titled "Why We Don't Get the (Text) Message," for CNN Money, Paul Kedorsky writes: "Consider this anomaly: Ecuador, with a per capita GDP of $4,300, has the United States beat when it comes to a critical wireless technology. Americans may be ten times as wealthy, but Ecuadorians send four times as many text messages."[16] One of the primary reasons Americans have adopted text messages and mobile telephony slower than the citizens of other nations stems from context.

In the United States, through the last decade, households possessed multiple telephone lines and computers. Many teenagers had their telephones in their rooms—if not their own telephone lines. Within the last seven years, this has changed, and instead of receiving their own telephone lines, teenagers and elementary school students receive their own mobile phones, often tied to a family network. Students received their first computers in high school or during the first year in college. Similarly, in the adult world, nearly all white collar employees use computers. As late as 2005, more Americans owned a computer than a mobile phone. According to the World Bank's "ICT at a Glance" report, there are 680 mobile subscribers per 1,000 Americans, compared to

762 personal computer owners per 1,000 Americans.[17] In this context, e-mail, instant messaging, and VoIP (Voice over Internet Protocol) became more widely used before text messaging. There was simply no demand for an additional, private communication space.

Yet, there have been changes over the past two and a half years. The United States is starting to become a mobile nation, and text messaging is become more popular. According to a recent survey of political word-of-mouth opinion leaders and Internet users conducted by the IPDI, text messaging is not just a tool for the young. The IPDI study, *Poli-fluentials: The New Political Kingmakers*, looked at the media consumption, technology adoption, and political activism of a group of people called the "Poli-fluentials." Most of the survey respondents who used text messaging and signed up to receive political text messages said they earned under $150,000. They are disproportionately male: around 65% of text message users and political text message sub-scribers and almost 75% of personal digital assistant (PDA) users said they were male. They also tend to be slightly more ideologically moderate (around 30%), although PDA users are also just as likely to say they are liberal (29%). Most mobile adopters interviewed in the study said they attended at least some college, and most of them are in peak career age brackets—their late forties and fifties.

Many of the political text messaging campaigns that have occurred over the past few years appeal to this population—an elite, politically active core that is likely to donate, vote, and volunteer for political organizations. People for the American Way (PFAW) was one of the earliest political organizations to tap into its mobile activists. Beginning in the summer of 2005 and continuing through 2006, PFAW asked its website visitors to sign up for its Mass Immediate Response Team (MIRT) to receive breaking text message updates about the Supreme Court nominations of John Roberts and Samuel Alito. These breaking updates rely on the immediacy of the mobile medium, lend the campaign a sense of urgency, and essentially "gift" an elite base of activists with information about the nominations before they tuned into the news or logged onto blogs. PFAW extended that sense of urgency by asking its members to take an action based on the text messages: members were asked to call their senators. PFAW received an opt-in rate of 27%, despite the fact that it only promoted its mobile response team on its website. As Justin Oberman blogged in 2006 on Personal Democracy Forum:

> This proves something. Members of PFAW are generally not the teenagers that most people in the business of text messaging services cater to. It proves that people, of any age group, can adopt the psychology behind the mobile medium much faster than anticipated.[18]

PFAW was the first in a series of political organizations and campaigns using text messaging in a similar way to push useful information and instructions to people in a controlled way, not unlike a shorter, more urgent form of e-mail. These programs have relied less on harnessing grassroots networks sending text messages and more on using mobile technology to deliver timely messages that can be customized to the recipient. Mobile Voter, a group founded in 2004, has used text messaging and real world events to register young voters over the course of several election cycles. The Mobile Voter method uses events such as concerts and shows. During the performance, the audience is told to send a text message in order to receive information about registering to vote, specific to each state. Mobile Voter sends each respondent voting reminders on election day.

During the mid-term elections in 2006, the Republican National Committee rolled out a new feature for American political parties: a website that allowed voters to find their nearest polling place. The site was mobile-accessible, which in theory meant that Republican voters had the ability to access directions to their nearest polling place on their cell phones. A candidate for governor in Michigan, Dick DeVos, used text messaging to highlight the issue of jobs in his state. The DeVos campaign asked voters to text the word "jobs" to a common short code (50555) to receive information about DeVos's platform on jobs. Respondents could sign up by text message to receive updates from the campaign.

In 2007, many of the democratic presidential candidates experimented with mobile strategies. Whether their mobile initiatives were successful or not, each new mobile tactic garnered headlines in the blogosphere and the traditional media. The Hillary Clinton campaign launched its text message campaign in May 2007. Dennis Kucinich asked his supporters to text the campaign during a video he presented during the Democratic YouTube debate. The Barack Obama campaign used its own shortcode (OBAMA/62262), the mobile equivalent of a vanity license plate, for its mobile campaign. Supporters joined by responding to an e-mail invitation or on the campaign website. The campaign also offered Obama-themed ringtones, the mobile equivalent of bumper stickers, and wallpaper. Recipients had to opt into the mobile campaign in order to receive them.[19]

The John Edwards campaign announced its mobile initiative the day that Edwards announced his candidacy on YouTube. The campaign mostly used its mobile platform to remind supporters to watch the many democratic debates. A few months later, in May 2007 the Edwards campaign became the first to launch a mobile fundraising initiative. The campaign used a tool called Mcommons to prompt supporters to donate. In one night the campaign's 13,000 mobile supporters received a text message saying, "John Edward wants 2 talk 2 you! Hit Reply. Type 'CALL' & hit Send. John will call YOU right back! OR call 202-350-9749. txt STOP 2 unsub." Recipients who sent a reply message with the word "CALL" in it soon received a phone call and message from Edwards:

> I'm calling to remind you that with just over a week before the end of the quarter the time to act is now. I'm not asking you to help us out-raise everyone else. I'm only asking you for what we need to get our message of real change out to voters in Iowa, New Hampshire, and other key states nationwide.

Supporters could "press 1" or wait on the line until they were able to connect with a phone bank that processed credit card contributions.[20]

The types of mobile initiatives developed by the Edwards, Obama, Kucinich, and Clinton campaigns provide a slicker, more controlled, top-down contrast to the other, mostly grassroots, word-of-mouth mobilization examples presented earlier in this chapter. Of course, we don't mean to imply that concentrated, carefully crafted, campaign controlled mobile initiatives cannot work or are less valuable. The ways we use mobile phones, like other forms of communication technology, is evolving. What works in, for example, Spain or China, requires some translation to succeed in the United States. For their part, American political consultants have attempted to apply lessons from many of the mobile-charged political events that have occurred across the globe to meet specific campaign and organization goals, such as fundraising or debate viewership. In other words, what began as a grassroots tool for citizen-led activism in other countries has evolved into an experimental medium for marketing candidates and causes and mobilizing an elite group of supporters in a top-down way.

Sometimes a few things get lost in translation. The world of American political consulting, which is perhaps one of the most professionalized in the world, relies on proven, repeatable results, such as fundraising dollars and voter turnout. In this environment, some of the characteristics that make mobile technology a good tool for grassroots organizing or protesting such as relying on word-of-mouth networks, make it an unreliable tool for the 2008 presidential candidates. The next few years will be a time trial and error for mobile strategies in the American political context. We anticipate that many of the big-ticket candidates will garner headlines every time that they launch a new application or mobile initiative. Perhaps more interestingly, we also anticipate that some of the best discoveries will occur in down-ticket campaigns, political non profits, and the advocacy community—environments that have nothing and everything to lose and in which real grassroots interaction can provide a tremendous benefit.

The Missing Elements

What can US organizers learn from the success of political uses of SMS abroad? Based on the success of mobile technology in other countries, the mobile medium will have the greatest effect on American politics in places where already existing networks of communication combine with a strong political momentum. In other words, just as the most successful mobile campaigns abroad occur on the grassroots level, so will the future of mobile politics in the United States.

As the history of technology use in Japan illustrates, if there is no political climate, then technology—any technology, including mobile technology—will not be political. In the United States, the use of the mobile medium by political campaigners will not be successful unless political momentum and interest around it already exists. Therefore, a mobile strategy must evolve beyond the concept of event updates and ringtone distribution. It has to be truly interactive, live, and always relevant to the fact that mobile phone users are, well, mobile. Developing an effective mobile strategy for American politics has to evolve beyond the same old "direct mail" way of doing politics. It has to incorporate the already established networks in which mobile users take part, including the social spaces and conversations of everyday life.

Mobile users are always present as well as distant, private as well as public. Therefore, mobile communications of any kind always occur in the real world and are in fact real. This is why mobile communications can be extremely powerful in politics. When developing a mobile strategy for politics, location is everything. Mobile political content consequently works best when it integrates with the mobile user's surroundings. This is what mobile communication is all about: it is a lightweight refreshment. Activities such as checking one's voice-mail messages, sending an SMS, playing a game, downloading a ringtone all occur as people step into their offices, wait online at the store, or take a mental break during a business meeting. In this sense, perhaps the most accurate metaphor is one in which mobile phones become the portable water coolers of our era. But as anyone who has ever had water-cooler conversations knows, these small moments can have great importance later.

Notes

1 Joe Trippi, *The Revolution Will Not Be Televised: Democracy, the Internet, and the Overthrow of Everything* (New York: ReganBooks, 2004); Jerome Armstrong and Markos Moulitsas Zuniga, *Crashing the Gate: Netroots, Grassroots, and the Rise of People-powered Politics* (White River Junction, VT: Chelsea Green Publishing, 2006); Dana Dunnan, *Burning at the Grassroots: Inside the Dean Machine* (New York: Pagefree Publishing, 2004); Daniel Drezner and Henry Farrell, eds, *The Political Promise of Blogging* (Ann Arbor, MI: University of Michigan Press, 2008).

2 Howard Rheingold, "Political Texting: SMS and Elections," The Feature Archives, April 12, 2004, http://www.thefeaturearchives.com/topic/Culture/Political_Texting__SMS_and_Elections.html.

3 Julie Barko Germany, *The Politics-to-Go Handbook: A Guide to Using Mobile Technology in Politics* (Washington, D.C.: George Washington University Institute for Politics, Democracy & the Internet, 2005).

4 Oliver Starr, "Mobile Communication Technology: An Overview of the Industry, Its Players and Its Disruptive Potential," in *The Politics-to-Go Handbook: A Guide to Using Mobile Technology in Politics*, ed. Julie Barko Germany (Washington, D.C.: Institute for Politics, Democracy & the Internet, 2005), 10.

5 "Quick Facts," available from the CTIA-The Wireless Association website, http://www.ctia.org.

6 Mizuko Ito and Misa Matsuda, *Personal, Portable, Pedestrian: Mobile Phones in Japanese Life* (Cambridge, MA: MIT Press, 2005).

7 Ibid.

8 Ibid.

9 "Interview with Endre Danyi," available from the Netpolitique website, http://www.netpolitique.net/php/interviews/interview24uk.php3, October 2002.

10 Howard Rheingold, *Smart Mobs: The Next Social Revolution* (Cambridge, MA: Perseus Publishing, 2002); McKenzie Wark, *A Hacker Manifesto* (Cambridge, MA: Harvard University Press, 2004).

11 Rudy de Waele, "Viral Mobile Politics," M-Trends, June 15, 2006, http://www.m-trends.org/2006/06/viral-mobile-politics.html.

12 "Catalonia Votes for More Autonomy," CBS News, June 18, 2006, http://www.cbsnews.com/stories/2006/06/18/world/main1726699.shtml.

13 "SMS Texts Energize a Chinese Protest," Asia Sentinel, June 1, 2007, http://www.asiasentinel.com/index.php?option=com_content&task=view&id=520&Itemid=31).

14 Will, "1 million Chinese Protest Chemical Plant with Text Message" *Into Mobile*, May 31, 2007. http://www.intomobile.com/2007/05/31/1-million-chinese-protest-chemical-plant-with-text-messge.html.

15 John Kennedy, "China: Liveblogging from Ground Zero," *Global Voices*, June 1, 2007, http://www.globalvoicesonline.org/2007/06/01/china-liveblogging-from-ground-zero/.

16 Paul Kedorsky, "Why We Don't Get the (Text) Message," *CNN Money*, October 2, 2006, http://money.cnn.com/magazines/business2/business2_archive/2006/08/01/8382255/index.htm.

17 "ICT at a Glance," available from the World Bank website, http://devdata.worldbank.org/ict/usa_ict.pdf.

18 Justin Oberman, "Mobile Politics USA: Stuck in First Gear," *Personal Democracy Forum*, January 30, 2006, http://www.personaldemocracy.com/node/818.

19 Justin Oberman, "A First Look at Obama on the Go," *Personal Democracy Forum*, June 22, 2007, http://www.personaldemocracy.com/node/1477.

20 Justin Oberman, "Edwards Takes a Crack at Mobile Fundraising," *Personal Democracy Forum*, June 22, 2007, http://www.personaldemocracy.com/node/1479.

21

The Modern British Campaign

From Propaganda to Political Marketing

Dominic Wring

Introduction

The marketization of politics raises profound questions about the democratic process in Britain and elsewhere. Some practitioners and theorists have welcomed this trend in the belief that it extends the principles of choice and accountability to the electoral and non-electoral arenas.[1] However from another perspective this arguably forms part of an important component of a neo-liberal ascendancy whose trajectory has encouraged the subordination of democratic politics to the economic market. It is then no coincidence that those candidates most associated with changing the way campaigns were conducted at the turn of the 1980s were the same politicians responsible for implementing the New Right agenda for government. By winning office Margaret Thatcher and Ronald Reagan defied the conventional Downsian wisdom that elections are won on the centerground; rather these conservatives, supported by a formidable alliance of corporate interests, concerned themselves with shaping their environment (which broadly equates to Andrew Gamble's politics of power) as well as influencing their market (the politics of support).[2]

The ensuing abandonment of core social democratic beliefs and objectives by those once on the center-left has led to the rebranding as "new" of everything from the party to the wider political economy. Arguably this has led to a convergence around a new consensus espousing "depoliticization" forged, in the British case, by the Thatcher governments and which has meant the major two parties share a supposedly post-ideological framework. Here there is a denial of the continuing importance of (neo-liberal) ideology, indeed it is a period of intensive ideological debate, albeit the opposition has been relegated to the margins of mainstream media and, with notable exceptions, parliamentary debate. The process by which Labour embraced neo-liberalism or, as the chief strategist Philip Gould puts it, saw the need "to concede and move on" is bound up with the marketization process that has transformed the party in policy and organizational terms.[3]

The following discussion and analysis looks at the continuities and changes in the way the parties have used marketers as agents of political change throughout their history. While advertising, public relations and market researchers have a long acknowledged role in the Conservative party it is noteworthy that the rival Labour party's intra-party democratic structures militated against the same actors' emergence as the supreme strategic authority. It is furthermore noteworthy that in what will be identified as the phases of so-called "propaganda" and "media" campaign development (see p. 285 and p. 287) there were the antecedents of the later, more centralized, presidential and capital intensive "marketing" campaign to come. The latter has been a critical factor in transforming the once federal, multifaceted British party into a more hierarchical, elitist organization.

The Modern Campaign in Context

Considerable attention has been given to accounting for how election campaigning has developed since the beginnings of mass democracy. Within this literature there is recognition that what was once a necessary activity designed to influence the wider public has also had important consequences for the party itself. This is primarily because the processes of political communication have become so much more complex and resource intensive. Furthermore there is a consensus that campaigns have evolved through three or possibly four stages of development.[4] Pippa Norris, for instance, discusses the movement through the pre-modern, modern and post-modern eras. But these terms are problematic because the "pre" period arguably understates the innovative experimentation that took place in campaigning in response to the coming of mass democracy. Furthermore the term "post-modern" implies the existence of an active electoral audience together with the abandonment of elite driven campaign narratives. If anything the investigation into the development of British electioneering discussed below reinforces the Schumpeterian view that politics has become increasingly driven by relatively few high-profile actors and, more specifically, their advisers.[5] The latter include what are now commonly referred to as spin doctors, image makers, pollsters and policy wonks; their growing ubiquity is arguably symbolic of how campaigns have evolved and become driven by professionals. Consequently it is useful to look to management theory for insights into explaining how electoral organizations change.

The classic evolutionary marketing model was devised by Robert Keith in his discussion of how the commercial strategy of food manufacturer Pillsbury's developed through what were termed the production, sales and marketing orientations.[6] Avraham Shama applied this framework to account for how American politics had changed in his insightful study of presidential campaigning.[7] The British case has been similarly examined but the terminology altered to make it more relevant to British politics.[8] Consequently the era of what can be called propaganda (rather than production-oriented) campaigning places greatest emphasis on maximizing candidate/policy exposure through interpersonal or mass communication. Here political strategists are largely dependent on their own guess and intuition although this is not to discount the pioneering use of techniques such as advertising and public relations.

The shift from propaganda to media (sales) driven campaigning was motivated by a number of factors, not least the incorporation of market research into the communications process. This enabled strategists to refine their increasingly sophisticated messages which in turn increasingly relied on advertising and public relations in order to engage a mass audience. Attention was paid to how the public received, processed and responded (or not) to different stimuli. The availability of opinion research also significantly transformed campaigning by heightening politicians' sensitivity to particular target groups of undecided "floating" voters. This together with a more consumer conscious, media-saturated environment afforded professional strategists greater influence over campaigns and simultaneously downgraded the role of the more traditional party, be this in the form of elected representatives or voluntary organizations.

The embrace of marketing-driven campaigns can not only be seen in the way modern elections are fought but also, as has been noted, in the related growth of research into this more professionally orchestrated approach to political communications. As Margaret Thatcher's marketing director Christopher Lawson saw it, his work was involved with everything "from conception to consumption."[9] Consequently ever-increasingly sophisticated forms of qualitative as well as quantitative opinion research are drawn on in order to develop policy and strategy. Modern political marketing is therefore predicated on far more than the propaganda and media eras' focus on promotion and informs every aspect of the electoral offering. Consequently concepts more readily associated with commercial management such as positioning, segmentation, targeting and branding have become an integral part of the contemporary election. That this change has come about in late twentieth-century electioneering is not least because of a wider social, cultural and economic transformation that has placed ever greater emphasis on the importance of the market, choice and consumerism. The ensuing discussion focuses on the British case and draws attention to the changes as well as some of the continuities in campaigning.

Mass Propaganda

The birth of the modern campaign dates from the Representation of the People Act 1918 which trebled the electorate and encouraged politicians to investigate the potential of mass communications. Before then electioneering had largely been conceived of in terms of canvassing, leafleting and oratory although this began to be challenged by those such as prominent advertising expert Charles Higham who, in 1912, offered his voluntary services to whichever party would appoint him their strategist. In a statement issued to the press to publicize his availability Higham argued he could make the difference between victory and defeat:

> I know that it is as easy to create votes as it is to change the breakfast food of the nation. I know that it is as simple to make half-a-million people change their minds on a political question as it is to make half-a-million people change one of the articles they have been eating for the last fifteen years—which is something I have done within the last six months.[10]

The onset of the Great War curtailed electoral activities but the experience of using propaganda during the ensuing hostilities alerted political leaders to how mass persuasion could mobilize large sections of the public.

The Conservatives, the wealthiest party, were quick to explore and exploit the possibilities of film, broadcasting and advertising.[11] Former *London Evening Standard* editor Malcolm Fraser became the first ever designated party publicist in late 1910 when he became the Tories' honorary press adviser. Initially a voluntary post, Fraser was earning a substantial £1,200 per annum by 1913 with the party spending a further £2,509 on a new Press Bureau.[12] One of the prototype spin doctor's key roles was to brief the press in advance of major speeches by leader Andrew Bonar Law and other senior figures.[13] This now familiar technique enabled the Conservatives to notify journalists in advance of their newspapers' early evening deadlines which were nearly always before the political meetings themselves. Fraser was also intimately involved in cultivating relations with newspaper proprietors and sought to encourage sympathizers to purchase major titles such as the *News of the World* and the *Sunday Times* when they came up for sale.

The Conservative publicity operation was overhauled following the appointment of Joseph Ball as publicity director in the second half of the 1920s. Ball, a former British secret service agent, had been implicated in the notorious Zinoviev Letter episode in which a forged document purporting to be from the Bolshevik government had been "leaked" and then published by the *Daily Mail* in the days running up to the 1924 general election as part of an attempt to discredit the then Labour government. Ball also had more orthodox roles and was instrumental in appointing the leading firm S.H. Benson, creators of the legendary 1930s Guinness stout ale copy, as the first ever advertising agency to work for a British party in the 1929 general election.[14] John Gilroy, the renowned artist who created the famous Guinness characters, provided many of the most memorable images for the campaign's posters. The desire to create arresting visual communication was also a motivating factor behind the setting-up of Conservative Film Association, an initiative that drew in talents such as the famed director Alexander Korda. The party used a fleet of cinema vans to display moving image propaganda that marked another notable campaign innovation.[15]

The promotion of the avuncular prime minister Stanley Baldwin along with the slogan "Safety First" ended in defeat at the 1929 election but did not stem the Conservatives' enthusiasm for professional methods. Significantly Basil Clarke's relationship with the party, which also began that year, continued through to the subsequent landslide victory of 1931. Clarke's involvement is important because he arguably more than any other consultant did most to pioneer the use of public relations in Britain in a way that resembled the work of his friend Ivy Lee in the United States.[16] By the 1935 election the party, now dominating a coalition government, had launched the National Publicity Bureau which drew together the talents of Benson's and other experts to help Joseph Ball create one of the most ambitious and expensive campaigns in history.[17] This meticulously planned effort, which ended in a landslide victory, included the identification of selected print media as well as "key constituencies" around the country and their targeting with relevant advertising material.[18]

Unlike their Conservative counterparts, Labour advocates of more professional and image-based methods of communication were marginalized within their own organization. The party, which replaced the Liberals as the main opposition to the Tories during the 1920s, was more reluctant to use finite resources on capitally intensive methods, particularly when there was a healthy activist base willing and able to promote the Labour case. Furthermore the party's traditionally federal structures meant changes, if they were agreed at all, were often incremental and limited. Arguably more fundamentally many Labour politicians were suspicious of professional advertisers and their association with what were perceived to be dubious capitalist practices. Rather these partisans believed rational instruction should and could form the basis of the party's campaigning.[19] This "educationalist" outlook was personified by the famous left-wing propagandist Robert Blatchford who spoke of the need for "making socialists" at the turn of the twentieth century. Early Labour campaigners emulated Blatchford's approach with their didactic, interpersonal methods. In doing so they eschewed what were characterized as the more emotive, shallow forms of mass persuasion they associated with the Conservatives not to mention a print and broadcast media that were perceived to be hostile to left-wing causes.[20]

The educationalist approach to campaigning was reinforced by early Labour's participatory ethos not to mention its modest finances and relative abundance of willing volunteer workers. The party did establish its own press and publicity department in 1917 but this was a modest operation led by Herbert Tracey, a former journalist, whose main duties involved responding to rather than initiating media contact. Labour's then larger, more influential organization section took the lead in running campaigns that prioritized interpersonal means of communication. There was, however, experimentation with image-based promotions courtesy of leading illustrators such as Gerard Spenser Pryse and John Armstrong who provided the party with several visually arresting posters during the first half of the twentieth century.

The experience of fighting fascism and then the largely grassroots-oriented and hugely successful 1945 general election effort strengthened educationalist opinion within the party.[21] Nevertheless there were those "persuasionalist" critics of the more didactic methods who argued that because most people were largely uninterested in politics they needed to be won over to vote rather than converted to the Labour cause. Such a view was influenced by the intellectual Graham Wallas' rejoinder to the classical scholars' conception of mass democracy as involving a deliberative electorate making informed, rational choices.[22] Rather the theorist argued emotions were the motivating factor behind much political behavior and therefore a superior way of communicating to voters would be through advertising and other primarily image-rich media.[23]

Evidently some in the party took Wallas' message seriously because they used a 1937 conference organized by Labour's prototype think tank the Fabian Society on the theme of "Selling Socialism."

The Selling Socialism event followed on from the London party's successful campaign to defend its control of the capital's municipal government. Significantly this re-election effort had, in a first for Labour politics, drawn on the help of a team of marketing experts including George Wansborough, a contributor to the Fabian conference. He and his fellow strategists had personalized the campaign around the image of the redoubtable London party leader Herbert Morrison.[24] Furthermore generous donations from wealthy supporters including John Maynard Keynes enabled them to purchase space for advertisements in best-selling newspapers.[25] The subsequent and comfortable victory did not lead to significant change at national level because of party distrust of Morrison and, more importantly, the onset of World War II. It would be over twenty years before Labour campaigning underwent a dramatic transformation that would afford professionals a decisive organizational role.

Media Campaigning

The professionalization of political campaigning intensified following World War II. Initially innovations were limited because the immediate post-war elections were called at short notice and confined to the traditional four-week period after the dissolution of parliament.[26] This altered in the late 1950s when a combination of factors conspired to effect change. Foremost amongst these was the rise of the so-called affluent society that heralded the revival of a more conspicuous consumerism after years of post-war austerity. The changing political economy was symbolized with the growth of white-collar lower-middle-class jobs and the affordability of household goods such as washing machines and televisions, the latter being popularized by the introduction of commercial broadcasting in 1955.[27] Marketing firms specializing in market research, public relations and advertising duly responded to this new highly favorable environment and extended their influence into politics.[28]

Predictably it was the Conservatives who set up the first dedicated headquarters agency responsible for monitoring voting behavior in 1948,[29] the same year they forged a durable partnership with the leading advertisers Colman Prentis Varley.[30] However, it would be nearly a decade before the new professionalism had a decisive impact on campaigning during the unusually protracted build-up to the 1959 general election.[31] The now incumbent Conservatives, anxious to move on following the Suez crisis and resignation of Prime Minister Anthony Eden, launched an ambitious initiative which used research to cultivate key target groups with more refined advertising messages. A powerful liaison committee made the strategic communication of the party's ideas a major priority.[32] Aside from using conventional polling research, leading strategist Lord Woolton took to visiting marginal seats where he undertook his own participant observation to gauge the public mood.[33]

Eden's successor Harold Macmillan proved to be a deft communicator, particularly when compared to his more studied Labour opponent Hugh Gaitskell. The experience of losing the 1959 election did, however, convince Gaitskell of the need to invest time and resources in more professional methods of campaigning. Paradoxically his sudden death in 1963 gave renewed momentum to those making the case for change because successor Harold Wilson had previously professed an educationalist disdain for what he dismissed as image politics.[34] Yet he became the first party leader and prime minister to understand how television worked and how it might be exploited for electoral gain. Wilson was also a trained economist who took a close interest in the statistics provided to him by Labour's first pollster Mark Abrams. There was also a determined effort by some in the party to encourage the use of professionals: pointedly one report discussed the coming of the "permanent campaign" two decades before the term was popularized by

Sidney Blumenthal's study of that name.[35] Abrams together with a group of sympathetic market-ing experts came to enjoy unprecedented roles of strategic influence under Wilson's leadership and were afforded considerable financial resources to do their work.[36] Inevitably more traditional educationalist minded thinkers argued the prominence and use of campaign consultants was a retrograde step that compromised the party's historic mission to emancipate society.[37]

Labour's new professionals were not necessarily instrumental in (narrowly) winning the sub-sequent 1964 general election after what had turned out to be another protracted campaign. But the party's more obviously polished image and approach to communication helped to challenge the long-held belief that interpersonal, didactic methods were preferable. Wilson's legacy was to have obviated the highly formal committee structures that previously managed campaigns by working with key headquarters officials who in turn liaised with leading figures in the marketing industries.[38] This afforded the consultants considerable influence for the duration of the thirteen-year Wilson leadership but, as will be seen, the professionals' lack of a prescribed role led to problems once the party turned in on itself in the 1970s.

The Marketization of Politics

The political turbulence of the 1970s was triggered by economic problems that originated in the previous decade and that were exacerbated by an oil crisis that wreaked havoc throughout the industrialized world. In Britain as elsewhere assorted New Right think tanks influenced by the philosophy of Frederich von Hayek and wedded to policies associated with Milton Friedman launched a formidable and ultimately successful attack on the post-war social democratic con-sensus.[39] They did so by providing support for the cerebral Conservative intellectual Keith Joseph, an influential ally of Margaret Thatcher who defeated former prime minister Edward Heath in the 1975 leadership election. Their critique of Heath's support for the consensus ultimately led to the pursuit of an ideological project characterized as eulogizing the free market and strong state.[40] With its then radical prescriptions for public policy, Thatcherism was pro-moted by a woman whose strategists defined her as a conviction politician. The instincts of the new Conservative leader did, however, set her at odds with many senior parliamentary colleagues. This factor provides a major reason why she forged particularly close working relationships with those responsible for devising the strategy to promote her agenda to transform the party not to mention the country.[41]

Party communications director Gordon Reece carefully oversaw the promotion of Thatcher first as the relatively ordinary homemaker who would solve the nation's economic woes through good housekeeping. The reality was somewhat different in that she had long been married to a millionaire, was one of the few women MPs and had pursued her own careers as a scientist and then lawyer.[42] Nevertheless this domesticity provided a useful and accessible narrative that could be promoted by Reece and others through the columns of an overwhelming majority of news-papers collectively known as the Tory press. Many media proprietors had long supported the Conservatives but the ensuing coverage was qualitatively different in its eulogizing and slavish devotion to "Maggie" Thatcher. Allied to this the party launched a major marketing effort masterminded by Saatchi & Saatchi, an idiosyncratic advertising agency headed by brothers Maurice and Charles.[43]

Saatchis' influence over strategy was considerable not least because of Thatcher's faith in Tim Bell, the agency executive who managed a party account famed for knocking out copy such as "Labour isn't Working" and "Cheer Up, They Can't Hang on Forever." Qualitative research in the guise of focus groups also identified effective ways of promoting certain manifesto commit-ments such as the proposal to sell off public housing at considerable discount to those residents who wanted to become part of the so-called "property owning democracy" but who could not otherwise afford to enter the market.[44] Campaign strategists used this as a device to drive a wedge between Labour and tenants who had previously been a traditional source of votes. In doing so this was part of a wider Saatchi-inspired initiative to portray the incumbent government as "nanny state" bureaucrats opposed to citizens' freedom of choice.

Following the Conservatives' 1979 victory, Thatcher increasingly assumed the mantel of what the official Soviet newspaper *Pravda* called the Iron Lady. Her radical policies broke with the consensus and her initial, hugely unpopular spell in office saw a sharp rise in unemployment and inner-city disturbances. The 1982 Falklands crisis, in which British forces retook the islands following an Argentine invasion, steadied the Thatcher government and enabled her strategists to promote the prime minister as an international stateswoman.[45] Critically their extensive private opinion research indicated large sections of the electorate believed the growing unemployment problem to be part of a wider global trend rather than as a consequence of government policy.[46] This fed into the carefully choreographed 1983 election campaign that ended in an even greater landslide victory for the Conservatives. Duly emboldened Thatcher embarked on her most ambitious program of economic reform that centered upon the privatization of key publicly owned utilities such as gas and electricity.

By the time of the 1987 general election Saatchi & Saatchi had become the largest advertising agency in the world. Its highly publicized work on behalf of the Conservatives had helped seal its reputation as a cutting-edge company at the heart of the service sector boom taking place in London during the decade. The firm continued to work on campaigning and promoted the "Moving Ahead" re-launch that began during the 1986 party conference.[47] Thatcher's third and final election victory only came, however, after tense and fraught rivalries had surfaced within the party hierarchy over strategy. Saatchi officials, supported by Conservative chairman Norman Tebbit, believed in emphasizing the team around the prime minister because of adverse polling suggesting she was not now an electoral asset. However, rival research from John Banks of Young and Rubicon challenged this advice by concluding that repeating something along the lines of the presidential style campaign seen in 1983 could be beneficial.

Lord Young's advocacy of John Banks' work and Thatcher's perhaps understandable reticence to accept Saatchis' recommendation created private tensions within the party's central office headquarters during the 1987 election. Famously on "wobbly Thursday," the day late in the campaign when a rogue poll indicated Labour had closed the Conservatives' once seemingly impregnable lead in the polls to 4%, the tension between Young and Tebbit boiled over into a sharp exchange of words.[48] The episode amply demonstrated how electoral marketing had become an integral aspect of political strategising, a point amplified when the party commissioned research from Ronald Reagan's pollster Richard Wirthlin, although this relationship did not survive Margaret Thatcher's ousting from office in 1990.[49]

Tensions within the Conservative hierarchy during the 1987 general election had been heightened by the Labour opposition's surprisingly upbeat and unified campaign. In both of the previous elections the party had suffered serious internal problems arising from deep-seated factional struggles that regularly exploded into a public acrimony that did not abate with the onset of the actual campaign. Both of Wilson's successors made a virtue of attacking the Conservatives' high-profile use of Saatchis & Saatchi to the dismay of some of their own professional advisers. Prior to the 1979 defeat the prime minister James Callaghan proclaimed his opposition to be sold like a consumer product: "The truth is in this election the Tories are being sold as though they were [soap powders] Daz or Omo."[50] Similarly the next Labour leader Michael Foot, himself an embodiment of the party's educationalist tradition, was more at ease using his considerable oratorical skills on a punishing meeting tour of the country. Neither Callaghan nor Foot enjoyed the close, enduring relationship that Wilson had fostered with the party's consultants. This dramatically changed with the arrival of Neil Kinnock as leader following the landslide defeat in 1983.

By the time of the 1987 general election the Labour organization had been overhauled with a team of marketing experts appointed to develop campaigning strategy. The group, known as the Shadow Communications Agency (SCA), became an integral part of Kinnock's drive to transform the party and first marginalized and then replaced longstanding consultants such as Bob Worcester, chief executive of pollsters MORI.[51] Any remaining educationalist sentiment was marginalized as the new agency's influence became all pervasive in both the 1987 and 1992 general elections and, of added importance, between these campaigns. Crucially neither of these defeats fundamentally undermined the desire of Kinnock and his successors to effectively turn Labour into a "corporate party" in the mold of the Conservatives.[52]

The reach of the SCA and its co-ordinator Philip Gould went much further than Harold Wilson's similarly convened team of advisers in that they not only promoted policy but were also responsible for collating and disseminating the opinion research on which key decisions were made. Significantly Labour recruited leading American consultants including Joe Napolitan, Robert Shrum and Mark Mellman as part of a move that underlined the leadership's determination to embrace professional methods whatever the related costs. The cumulative impact of this activity was the undermining and then abandonment of many of Labour's internal democratic procedures.[53] During the Wilson era there had always been an uneasy compromise between the various constituents within the party that that leader had carefully brokered. Initially Kinnock adopted a similar approach but once he became confident of his own position he used the party's consultants to further his agenda for policy reform. It was an important legacy bequeathed to Tony Blair.

The Blair Era

Tony Blair became Labour leader in 1994 following the sudden death of John Smith. Smith, Kinnock's immediate successor, adopted a decidedly less confrontational style and was able to capitalize on the disintegration of the Conservative government by then led by Thatcher's replacement John Major. If the terms "spin" and "spin doctor" had first entered the British political lexicon during the 1992 election, Blair's leadership and subsequent premiership ensured they became a routine part of media reporting and analysis.[54] Critically the self-styled "New" Labour project promoted itself with a revolutionary zeal that positioned the party as a major break with its past.[55] Yet in reality some of its rhetoric approach echoed the past: Wilson, for instance, had earlier used the term "New Britain" and the key Blair strategists had all been close associates of Kinnock. Although the 1997 manifesto repositioned Labour further to the right it nevertheless built on changes to policy and organization made in the aftermath of the 1987 defeat. Nor should it be overlooked that these reforms had the effect of recreating a more highly controlled party in the mold of that led by Thatcher.

Labour's use of, even devotion to, professional political communications and the subsequent landslide 1997 victory created the "Millbank myth," a reference to the supposed potency of the campaign's "war room"-styled headquarters in central London.[56] But arguably the abject performance of the incumbent Conservatives following a spectacular collapse in the value of sterling in autumn 1992 was the precipitating factor in deciding the outcome of the election five years later. Blair and his lieutenants did of course do their utmost to make this a certainty. Chief spin doctor Alastair Campbell had a ruthless reputation for briefing and bullying the media. MP Peter Mandelson, the former communications director under Kinnock, worked closely with Campbell and helped police the party. Former SCA co-ordinator Philip Gould resumed his role as Labour's strategist and made his focus group-based assessments of the public mood one of Blair's most important sources of political intelligence.

It was Gould and his colleagues who leading party MP Clare Short evidently had in mind when she criticized them as "the people in the dark" exercising a malign influence over her leader.[57] Short's admission resonated with many in her party and was subsequently directly quoted in the Conservatives' pre-election campaign that depicted a demonic Blair with the slogan "New Labour, New Danger." But the future prime minister was anything but a naive dupe of his consultants and showed himself to be a more than willing sponsor of them and their marketing methods.

Philip Gould worked closely with Stanley Greenberg, the "New" Democrat pollster who became an influential voice within Millbank.[58] Greenberg's involvement, like that of Labour's previous consultants, was purposely kept from the media because of a fear that the involvement of American consultants might provoke an adverse reaction, particularly from within the party. This was far from just a British sensibility given the presence of US professionals had proved controversial in other European countries, notably France and Sweden. Following their 1997 victory Greenberg and Gould together with James Carville set up an international political consultancy and provided their services to a range of clients throughout the world. Greenberg and Gould continued to advise Labour and played a central role in preparations for the successful 2001 general election.[59]

By 2005 Blair had brought in another American consultant, the Democratic pollster Mark Penn, to advise him on strategy at a cost of £530,372. Penn's expertise provided a by now unpopular Labour leader with particular insights into the psychological profiles of key electoral groups and fed into a campaign in which the prime minister attempted to reconnect with voters who had become disillusioned with him, notably over Iraq. The work of international consultancy also informed the development of the rival Conservative campaign. Party leader Michael Howard placed Lynton Crosby, chief strategist to his namesake the Australian premier John, in charge of the party's strategy at a cost of £441,146. Other consultants with similarly right-wing credentials involved included Republican pollster Frank Luntz, a by now familiar media commentator across a range of British media.[60]

Conclusion

The prophecy of Graham Wallas that electoral messages would be increasingly mediated through imagery and symbolism was quickly realized with the rise of mass communications. More recently Drew Westen amongst others has adopted essentially the same thesis in his explorations of contemporary political culture.[61] A century apart, both studies focus on the potency of suggestion and how it can and does shape mass democracy. Consequently since the overwhelming majority of citizens began to have the right to vote, dedicated professionals have played a role in managing campaigns and strategising. Initially those involved were former journalists turned officials and their responsibilities were largely restricted to what might be viewed as relatively pedestrian promotional work. Eventually these efforts were supplemented by the efforts of advertising, public relations and polling research specialists. By the end of the century political marketers in their various guises were exercising an enormous influence within the democratic process.

The increased power of the professional campaigner was not primarily due to developments in media and technology but, as Gerald Sussman argues, because of wider and more fundamental changes wrought by the prevailing neo-liberal orthodoxy in the 1970s and 1980s.[62] Consequently the marketization of the economy was accompanied by parallel processes within politics. These developments encouraged the rise of the management consultant be it in the commercial or democratic sphere. From a British electoral perspective this led to the further centralization of authority around leaders and their entourages consisting of largely appointed aides, strategists and consultants. The relationship between communication and power has, of course, been previously explored by the scholars who popularized the study of the political party.

Robert Michels, in his original treatise, wrote of the psychological importance of the press to leaders.[63] Similarly during the 1960s Samuel Beer wrote about the emergence of the "technocratic cadre party." During the same period Leon Epstein speculated as to how the "contagion from the right," that is the growing use of specialist professionals, would transform and undermine the traditional mass membership quasi-democratic European party organization.[64] More recently Angelo Panebianco has renewed interest in this topic by identifying and analyzing the influential role of what he termed "electoral professionals" and their preoccupation with an "opinion electorate" of floating voters.[65] But enhanced power has also brought renewed challenges and threats for the beneficiaries and it is arguably no coincidence that since the beginning of the new century each of the major party leaderships has changed. And while a formerly popular politician can be perceived to have lost their touch then so can their strategists. This was most spectacularly demonstrated with the fall of Margaret Thatcher, the leader who did most to oversee the transformation of modern British political campaigning.

Notes

1 Philip Gould, *The Unfinished Revolution: How the Modernisers Saved the Labour Party* (London: Little, Brown, 1998).
2 Anthony Downs, *An Economic Theory of Democracy* (New York: Harper and Row, 1957); Andrew Gamble, *The Free Economy and the Strong State: The Politics of Thatcherism* (Basingstoke: Macmillan, 1994).
3 Gould, *The Unfinished Revolution*.
4 Gareth Smith and John Saunders, "The Application of Marketing to British Politics," *Journal of Marketing Management* 5 (3) (1990): 295–306; David Farrell, "Campaign Strategies and Tactics," in *Comparing Democracies: Elections and Voting in Global Perspective*, ed. Lawrence LeDuc et al. (Thousand Oaks, CA: Sage, 1996), 160–83; Pippa Norris, *Electoral Change since 1945* (Oxford: Blackwell, 1997), 193–211; Jay G. Blumler and Dennis Kavanagh, "The Third Age of Political Communication: Influences and Features," *Political Communication* 16 (3) (1999): 209–30.
5 Joseph Schumpeter, *Capitalism, Socialism and Democracy* (London: Urwin, 1943).
6 Robert Keith, "The Marketing Revolution," *Journal of Marketing* (January 1960): 35–8.
7 Avraham Shama, "The Marketing of a Political Candidate," *Journal of the Academy of Marketing Sciences* 4 (1976): 764–77.
8 Dominic Wring, "Political Marketing and Organisational Development: The Case of the Labour Party in Britain," *Cambridge Research Papers in Management Studies*, 1995 series, No. 12; Dominic Wring, "Political Marketing and Party Development in Britain: A 'Secret' History," *European Journal of Marketing* 30 (10–11) (1996): 92–103.
9 Michael Cockerell, Peter Hennessy and David Walker, *Sources Close to the Prime Minister* (London: Macmillan, 1984), 198.
10 Charles Higham, "A Word to the Chief Party Whips," *The Optimist* 1 (1912): 2.
11 Richard Cockett, "The Party, Publicity and the Media," in *Conservative Century*, ed. Anthony Seldon and Stuart Ball (Oxford: Oxford University Press, 1994), 547–77.
12 John Ramsden, "The Organisation of the Conservative and Unionist Party in Britain, 1910 to 1930." Unpublished PhD dissertation, Oxford University, 1974, 232–3.
13 Malcolm Fraser, Personal Diary, Conservative Party Archive, Bodleian Library, Oxford University, 1913.
14 Timothy J. Hollins, "The Presentation of Politics: The Place of Party Publicity, Broadcasting and Film in British Politics." Unpublished PhD dissertation, Leeds University, 1981, 37.
15 Ibid.
16 Alan Clarke, "The Life and Times of Sir Basil Clarke—PR Pioneer," *Public Relations* 22 (2) (February 1969): 8–13.
17 Ralph Casey, "The National Publicity Bureau and British Party Propaganda," *Public Opinion Quarterly* (October, 1939): 623–34.
18 Joseph Ball, Personal Papers of Sir Joseph Ball, Bodleian Library, Oxford University, 1935.
19 Bernard Barker, "The Politics of Propaganda: A Study in the Theory of Educational Socialism and its

Role in the Development of a National Labour Party." Unpublished M. Phil. thesis, York University, 1972.

20 Dominic Wring, *The Politics of Marketing the Labour Party* (Basingstoke: Palgrave, 2005), 22–4.

21 Austin Mitchell, *Election 45: Reflections on the Revolution in Britain* (London: Bellew/Fabian Society, 1995).

22 Graham Wallas, *Human Nature in Politics* (London: Constable, 1908).

23 See Drew Westen, *The Political Brain: The Role of Emotion in Deciding the Fate of the Nation* (New York: Public Affairs, 2007).

24 Bernard Donoghue and George Jones, *Herbert Morrison: Portrait of a Politician* (London: Weidenfeld & Nicolson, 1973).

25 George Jones, Interview with Clem Leslie, London School of Economics archives, 1967.

26 Dominic Wring, "Power as Well as Persuasion: Political Communication and Party Development," in *Political Communication Transformed*, ed. John Bartle and Dylan Griffiths (Basingstoke: Macmillan Palgrave, 2001) 34–52.

27 Lawrence Black, *The Political Culture of the Left in Affluent Britain 1951–64* (Basingstoke: Macmillan Palgrave, 2004).

28 John Pearson and Graham Turner, The *Persuasion Industry: British Advertising and Public Relations in Action* (London: Eyre & Spottiswoode, 1965).

29 Andrew Taylor, " 'The Record of the 1950s is Irrelevant': The Conservative Party, Electoral Strategy and Opinion Research, 1945–64," *Contemporary British History* 17 (2003): 81–110.

30 Richard Rose, *Influencing Voters: A Study of Campaign Rationality* (London: Faber & Faber, 1967).

31 David Butler and Richard Rose, *The British General Election of 1959* (London: Macmillan, 1960).

32 Lord Windlesham, *Communication and Political Power* (London: Jonathan Cape, 1966).

33 Rose, *Influencing Voters*.

34 Wring, *The Politics of Marketing the Labour Party*.

35 Young Fabian Group, *The Mechanics of Victory*, February 1962; Sidney Blumenthal, *The Permanent Campaign* (New York: Simon & Schuster, 1982).

36 Windlesham, *Communication and Political Power*; Rose, *Influencing Voters*.

37 Raphael Samuel, "Dr. Abrams and the End of Politics," *New Left Review* 5 (September 1960): 2–9.

38 Wring, *The Politics of Marketing the Labour Party*.

39 Richard Cockett, *Thinking the Unthinkable: Think-Tanks and the Economic Counter-Revolution, 1931–1983* (London: Harper Collins, 1994).

40 Gamble, *The Free Economy and the Strong State*.

41 Margaret Scammell, *Designer Politics: How Elections Are Won* (New York: St Martin's Press, 1995).

42 Wendy Webster, *Not a Man to Match Her: The Marketing of a Prime Minister* (London: The Women's Press, 1990).

43 Philip Kleinman, *The Saatchi and Saatchi Story* (London: Weidenfeld and Nicolson, 1987); Nicholas J. O'Shaughnessy, *The Phenomenon of Political Marketing* (New York: St Martin's Press, 1990).

44 Robert Worcester and Paul Baines, "Two Triangulation Models in Political Marketing." Paper for the Elections on the Horizon Conference, Eccles Centre for American Studies, British Library, March, 2004.

45 Michael Cockerell, "The Marketing of Margaret," *The Listener*, June 16, 1983.

46 Scammell, *Designer Politics*, 105

47 Ibid.

48 David Butler and Dennis Kavanagh, *The British General Election of 1987* (Basingstoke: Macmillan, 1987), 107–8.

49 David Butler and Dennis Kavanagh, *The British General Election of 1992* (Basingstoke: Macmillan, 1992), 36.

50 Michael Cockerell, *Live from Number 10* (London: Faber and Faber, 1989), 248.

51 Colin Hughes and Patrick Wintour, *Labour Rebuilt: The New Model Party* (London: Fourth Estate, 1990); Eric Shaw, *The Labour Party Since 1979: Crisis and Transformation* (London: Routledge, 1994).

52 Adrian Sackman, "The Learning Curve Towards New Labour: Neil Kinnock's Corporate Party 1983–1992," *European Journal of Marketing* 30 (10/11) (1996): 147–58.

53 Shaw, *The Labour Party Since 1979*; Wring, *The Politics of Marketing the Labour Party*.

54 Nicholas Jones, *Soundbites and Spin Doctors: How Politicians Manipulate the Media—and Vice Versa* (London: Cassell, 1995); Nicholas Jones, *Sultans of Spin* (London: Victor Gollancz, 1999); Bob Franklin, *Tough on Soundbites, Tough on the Causes of Soundbites: New Labour and News Management* (London: Catalyst Trust, 1998).

55 Gould, *The Unfinished Revolution*.

56 John Bartle, Ivor Crewe and Brian Gosschalk, "Introduction," in *Political Communications: The British*

General Election of 1997, ed. Ivor Crewe, Brian Gosschalk and John Bartle (London: Frank Cass, 1998), xvii–xxiii.

57 Steve Richards, "Interview: Clare Short," *New Statesman*, August 9, 1996.

58 David Butler and Dennis Kavanagh, *The British General Election of 1997* (Basingstoke: Macmillan, 1997).

59 David Butler and Dennis Kavanagh, *The British General Election of 2002* (Basingstoke: Macmillan Palgrave, 2002).

60 David Butler and Dennis Kavanagh, *The British General Election of 2005* (Basingstoke: Macmillan Palgrave, 2006).

61 Westen, *The Political Brain*.

62 Gerald Sussman, *Global Electioneering: Campaign Consulting, Communications and Corporate Financing* (Lanham, MD: Rowman & Littlefield, 2005).

63 Robert Michels, *Political Parties: A Sociological Study of the Oligarchical Tendencies of Modern Democracies* (New York: Free Press, 1911).

64 Leon Epstein, *Political Parties in Western Democracies* (London: Pall Mall, 1967).

65 Angelo Panebianco, *Political Parties: Organization and Power* (Cambridge: Cambridge University Press, 1988).

22

German Elections and Modern Campaign Techniques

Marco Althaus

The scene is familiar. The Germans have been getting tired of the chancellor of the Christian Democratic Union (CDU). He is still respected as a reliable, experienced patriarch not fond of experimentation. But he has been in office so long even his own party tends to think he is over the hill. An old-school politician with limited charm, a stubborn conservative grandfather, few observers think he fits the modern times.

On the other side are the Social Democrats (SPD). The SPD candidate is an energetic young leader of a German state, a reform-oriented moderate appealing to middle-class and swing voter groups. A charismatic, telegenic media personality, at ease with people and in love with the camera, a cosmopolitan person with well-established international credentials—but also the target for intense attacks of negative campaigning from the right. The old guard on the left did not like him either: the candidate was once a maverick misfit, an unlikely nominee, but he scores high on electability and charisma—exactly what the constantly losing SPD needs.

The Social Democrats have—like, recently, their Labour comrades in Britain—jettisoned some ancient socialist ideas. They now market themselves as a modern, moderate, open, innovative party, market-friendly but with a social conscience. A party that calls for change but also says it will not change everything, but will do many things better.

The SPD will do anything to win, even turn to advice from Britain and America. The candidate's master strategist happens to be a Harvard-trained political scientist in touch with US labor unions. He is dispatched to London when Britons go to the polls, and then spends months in the US to take notes in a historical presidential election year, where two extraordinary candidates battle each other using the most modern campaign techniques, and change campaign history forever. What the SPD strategist sees will be applied shortly after across the Atlantic. *Der Spiegel*, the leading news magazine, will put the candidate's strategist on the cover of a post-election issue and devote a sixteen-page feature story to what they call "a political pyro-technician" unveiling all the tricks he took from the American campaign trail.

The candidate wants total personalization, American presidential style, but strategy, his sidekick insists, must be research-driven. He hands out research contracts by the dozen to have pollsters, social and statistical analysts track down the structure, motives and perceptions of the German voters. Marketing people dissect the voter as a consumer, mainly interested in health, personal progress and enjoying little luxuries, a consumer who views politics and government as a source of fear, not trust. Pollsters discover the middle-class dreams and search for access to them. They find out the voter is skeptical of the government' assertions that the economy's upturn will last. Researchers advise the candidate to avoid frontal personal attacks on the aging chancellor, and not to remind voters of ideology; instead, to force image polarization and exploit the contrast between the young, modern challenger and the grandfather figure. Unity, trust, confidence and optimism for the future must be emphasized, and the conservative opponents defined as nay-sayers trapped in yesterday's policies. To counter the chancellor's likely "experience" theme, the mass media must be steered to make sure voters and journalists understand the obvious parallels with the new American president.

The Social Democrats, once the ambassadors of dead-earnest class ideology, now train 28,000 functionaries in a modern approach. Any socialist sentimentalism is strictly forbidden. Campaign events used to end with the singing of socialist evergreens—now it is the national anthem. The candidate ends his speech with the hymn's first line, and the music sets in.

The nominating convention evolves into a coronation. Never has a post-war democratic party conference in Germany been so ridiculously celebrating one person alone, allowing him to bask in the limelight and maximize the media bonus. The party's convention colors are changed from red to blue. He injects in his speech, like the new American president has done in his nomination acceptance speech some months earlier, his executive oath of office. He closes, to the Social Democrats' disbelieving ears, with "So help me God."

The campaigners offer the voters plenty of American-style hoopla. Flags wave, rockets thunder, balloons rise up in the air, hit songs help the volunteers get rhythm. A traveling campaign revue entertains more than 100,000 voters in sixty shows titled "We are one family," while millions of color brochures are inserted in local papers, targeted to specific groups. The campaign maximizes television exposure and carefully controls the image of the candidate. His handlers behind the scenes make sure the details work for television; he wears the best suits, keeps his hands out of his pockets and never wears shirts that reflect the television lights. The SPD candidate challenges the chancellor to an American-style television debate, a duel which the old man refuses. An aggressive television strategy has all of its latest-style spots focus on the candidate, with the party hardly being mentioned.

The smiling, soft-spoken candidate with his incredible good looks storms into the hearts of middle-class women. He leads men to take a second look at modern issues: it's the economy, stupid, and the environment. Moderate and even conservative voters are appeased by the candidate's courage to stand up to the left, unquestionably a fighter and iron-willed statesman.

While the old chancellor resides in the capital or rides in a black limousine, his challenger hits the road in a creamy-yellow Mercedes-Benz convertible, the leather seats as red as the roses, gladiolus and carnations on windshield and front bumper. The candidate does not look like an opposition leader. He rides into town like live royalty.

He breaks with the tradition that the voter must come to the candidate; he makes a point of pressing the flesh every day, putting people first. While the chancellor is untouchable, he is the man the people can touch. Reaching out to the base of the moderate and conservative parties, he tours the small and medium cities. Tour sites have been selected by analysts who calculate likely swing percentages across sociodemographic target groups. An advance team makes sure ahead of time the candidate's stopover is well orchestrated locally, and a camera always finds the candidate in front of a local sight, a group of local VIPs or a cheering crowd. Learning from American examples that a candidate who accepts every bouquet and every extended hand must come hours late for the last several campaign stops, the campaign arranges for entertainment, comedy and music. In three months, the candidate travels some 25,000 miles by car, bus, train, helicopter, plane and ship, giving up to twenty-five speeches a day, touching down in five or six cities and fifteen towns and gaining direct contact to 40,000 to 50,000 people a day. Even in smaller cities where the Social Democrats count only a tiny group of sixty to eighty members, thousands turn out. The national media love the tour, but the regional and local media absolutely go crazy in their volume of coverage.[1]

Let us stop the account here. Many readers may have guessed wrong. The candidate did not go on to win the chancellory this year, and neither was the time 1998; the rivals for power were not the Social Democrats' Gerhard Schröder and CDU chancellor Helmut Kohl.

It was the summer of 1961. The American presidential campaign the SPD operatives had been following on the campaign trail was Kennedy versus Nixon, both of whom stood as models for a personalized strategy. The sitting German chancellor was aging Konrad Adenauer, eighty-five years of age and running for the fourth time. The challenger was Willy Brandt, then mayor of Berlin. His strategist was Klaus Schütz, who later became mayor of Berlin.

Brandt, the self-styled German Kennedy, seemed to have the perfect game plan. But that crumbled in ruins when the Soviets began to build the Berlin Wall in August of that year. Mayor Brandt enjoyed "front city" media hero status for a few days of the crisis and gained significantly more name identification and popularity, but then, in a Cold War game much too big for even a Berlin mayor, global players took over, including a revitalized Chancellor Adenauer. The flashy Brandt campaign remained a torso: with the Berlin crisis, Brandt canceled his planned end game tour of West Germany's big cities and dared only to fly in and out of the walled city for evening trips. Five weeks after the Berlin Wall was put up, Brandt trailed Adenauer by nine percentage points in the final count, and having won additional vote share of only a few disappointing percentage points over the election four years earlier.[2]

The 1961 Brandt episode is significant in the history of modern German campaigning because it marked the end of an era.

Coming Out of the Dark Ages

It has often been said that Germany is, or has been, a "belated nation"—late to industrialization, late to nation-building and late to democracy. Comparative historiography is always difficult, and any "belatedness" thesis carries this burden. Was Germany a late comer to modern political communications? Yes and no. Yes, because the Nazi dictatorship and post-war years meant a twenty-year-period "out of the loop" of democratic routine. No, because modern campaign techniques have a pre-1932 history and their professional development picked up steam surprisingly fast again in the 1950s which, campaign-wise, were not as sleepy in Germany as one might think.

In 1945, democratic campaigners simply returned to where they left off in early 1933, utilizing the same tactics, tools and some personnel of the pre-Nazi era. It was simple and very grassroots. Zero hour in 1945 meant no money, no members, no central headquarters and no infrastructure. Setting up a new democracy in a war-torn country then was as difficult as it is today. New parties were born (and many died), programmatic debates raged, but the style and technology of campaigning was still very much pre-war Weimar Republic: posters designed by the politicians themselves, wordy pamphlets, sound trucks, factory gate agitation and soapbox rhetoric in village inns and beer hall meetings, sometimes supported by mobile film projection units with mounted loudspeakers on an old Volkswagen Beetle, and party newspapers with limited appeal and power, most of which would not survive the 1940s and early 1950s.

The discontinuity of German culture in democratic electioneering is significant. American political historians have the pleasure of telling a continuous saga from Roosevelt's 1932 "Happy Days Are Here Again" to 1948 "Give 'em Hell, Harry" and 1952 "I like Ike." Neither depression, New Deal, World War II nor Cold War derailed biannual campaigning in the US. The same goes for the British democracy. But in Germany, for twelve years, Joseph Goebbels delegitimized and demonized political communications by using the arsenal of democracy against democracy itself.

Goebbels Campaigns, American Style

The 1920s were a time of intense party competition and parties experimenting with the instruments of the quickly developing advertising and marketing world. Yet, it is spooky to see that the most modern campaign management is found with the Nazis, which does explain to some degree the spectacular electoral success of the Nazi party between 1928 and 1932. It would be a mistake to believe that their campaigns were plump collections of terror, beerhall fights, brownshirt parades and plain demagogy. Goebbels also established a modern, research- and media-based management, integrated all best-practice instruments he could find with other parties and with commercial public relations (PR) and advertising, and took great pains to train a cadre of field executives. What's more, it is pretty clear today that Goebbels was a keen follower of the experience and theory of modern American public relations as put forward by such legends as Edward Bernays, the "Father of Spin."[3] The resulting professionalism of pre-1933 Nazi electioneering is astonishing.

Detailed campaign manuals and newsletters for communications functions were distributed, a consistent corporate design was used, a speakers' bureau kept everybody "on message." Direct mail was introduced, with model letters for target groups such as Marxists, farmers, retirees and women. Free daily campaign newspapers were delivered to millions of households in the last ten days of the election season. Some 50,000 gramophone vinyl records with speeches were distributed by mail. Sound films were shown, as the equivalent of television spots, as large-screen public viewing on major squares in most large cities. Posters and slogans were tested by researchers among test audiences. Major campaign events were spectacles orchestrated like a movie (and this was years before Leni Riefenstahl staged Nuremberg party conventions). A fleet of small airplanes was rented to have Hitler fly in to 200 events with fifteen million people. The Nazi media relations service paid much attention to working journalists at campaign events: dozens of telephone lines and special charter airplanes for couriers were made available. Local papers without correspondents were strategically courted to circumvent partisan national papers, and serviced continuously through ready-to-print news releases, articles and photos. Reading through the Nazi campaign manuals and analyses of the era must give any student of political marketing and management the creeps.[4]

It is Goebbels' modernity that haunts modern German political campaigns even today. It is safe to suggest that for the past half-century, no major campaign has gone by without some politician accusing an opponent, or some medium accusing a party or vice versa, of fiddling with the Nazi blend of commercial marketing and aggressive agitation. We should not be surprised to learn that in 1961, when Willy Brandt ran his modern campaign, quite a few Germans were less reminded of Kennedy's 1960 run than of Goebbel's campaigns thirty years earlier. Brandt himself, on the other hand, once attacked chancellor Helmut Kohl on national television for employing CDU executive director and campaign chief Heiner Geissler, "the worst rabble-rouser since Goebbels in this country."[5]

In a recent cover feature, "Hitler as a Brand," *Der Spiegel* wrote: "[Goebbels] turned the Führer into a product and was the first spin doctor. . . . Goebbels drove the art of political propaganda to perfection. Since then, any form of political inducement is suspect."[6]

In a remarkable departure from bland "Americanization" clichés entertained across the political spectrum, leftish weekly *Jungle World* commented on the widely discussed *Spiegel* feature:

> Slowly people come to the conclusion that the mediatization of politics did not begin in September 1960 when US presidential candidate Richard Nixon dueled John F. Kennedy . . . and that spin doctoring is not at all an invention of decadent Americans. . . .
>
> Political marketing can be seen as a German specialty, even though some postwar reservations against overly obvious aesthetization of the political existed.

Perhaps that is why the German electorate, in a reflex on its own susceptibility to charismatics, always demands "authenticity"—as if this ever could be real!—as a decisive criterion in judging politicians. And that is why in this country, unless something extraordinary happens, the candidate wins who is able to stage his authenticity most professionally, credibly and in a modern way.[7]

Goebbels' shadow also lingered long over political public opinion research in Germany. As propaganda minister, he had been dissatisfied with the mechanism of gauging *vox populi* through the party apparatus and looked to America, in this case the scientific method George Gallup had introduced so successfully. When journalist and sociologist Elisabeth Noelle published her 1940 doctoral dissertation "Opinion and Mass Research in the USA," having spent a year at the University of Missouri getting into Gallup's methods and the young field of media studies, Goebbels asked the twenty-four-year-old woman to be an adjutant. He wanted her to build up, for the ministry of propaganda, Germany's first public opinion research organization. Luckily she refused. Still, questions did remain over decades whether and how Germany's later most prominent political Pythia had collaborated with the Nazis and how they influenced her thinking—and, by extrapolation, many political leaders' thinking—about public opinion, particularly in election campaigns. Some, like US sociologist Leo Bogart, suggested there is a direct line from Goebbels to Noelle's theory of the "spiral of science" and "public opinion as our social skin," which interpreted the group pressure bandwagon effect and the domination of leading mass media over public opinion.[8]

Noelle's Allensbach Institute was established in 1949, the first of its kind in Germany; Noelle became polling advisor to all Christian Democratic chancellors from Adenauer to Kohl and Merkel, and she has, historically, been one of the strongest forces of polling-driven campaign strategy and its professionalization across Western Europe.

Noelle was one of a small elite of media and political people who had working knowledge of Anglo-Saxon political communications and public relations. But parties and politicians lacked the resources, and certainly, after the Nazi nightmare, the last thing Germans wanted (much less needed) was a slick political communications machinery. Post-war democracy was very grassroots, very old-fashioned, and stayed that way throughout the 1950s and the early 1960s.

Post-war Pains, Foreign Ideas and Television

The mass media system changed decidedly in post-war Germany. The Allies, through their licensing system, nailed the coffin of the old party press—which moved the most important communication channel out of the traditional party managers' hands. The once proud and high-circulation party press was not going to have a bright future: particularly the American occupation pushed for nonpartisan commercial publications of the "general advertiser" type, a model that would be greatly more successful than the old party pamphlets. This hit the Social Democrats especially hard—they had had the strongest party press in the nation and had totally relied on it for communication with their voter base.

The modern way of using PR to gain coverage and editorial support from a party-independent press—the "earned media" strategy—was a foreign idea in the mid-1940s and took root slowly. Much faster were independently minded publishers and journalists who created, by way of attractive news magazines and magazines modeled after British and American publications, an influential and totally new way of intense campaign coverage.

Radio, Goebbels' favorite outlet, was restructured on the model of the British public-service BBC. Television featured too, but much later: the advent of television as a decisive force in German politics came very late. American campaign historians mark 1952 as the year television premiered to help form a candidate's image and decide an election: "Man from Abilene,"

"Eisenhower Answers America" and "I Like Ike" spots could reach nineteen million viewers glued to their television screens during popular shows such as "I Love Lucy."[9] By contrast, in 1952 the number of television viewers in Germany was practically zero. The first post-war German television station went on air that year, but few people could afford a set.[10] By the election of 1957, only a million people could be reached, less than one-thirtieth of the West German electorate; by 1961 it was about 35%. This would grow exponentially (1964: 47%, 1970: 72%, 1974: 78%).[11] Color television, introduced in the US in 1954, arrived only in 1967. Made-for-television political events and television advertising took root only in the 1961 Adenauer/Brandt campaign and were perfected by the early 1970s.

Brandt was the first to use television as the ultimate strategic factor—it was his bad luck, or miscalculation, that television's reach was not big enough in 1961, and its role in political information, education and politainment not decisive enough, but it would be a few years later and would carry him into the chancellory. It was Brandt who, in his unsuccessful 1965 and then triumphant 1969 and 1972 campaigns continued to push for the three P's: personalization, professionalization (including outside consultants) and permanent campaigning. The SPD set up its own public opinion research shop, Infas, and its own advertising agency, ARE, and went on to set the standard for event and issue management.

In this, the SPD passed the modernization effort the Christian Democrats had undertaken in the 1950s. Adenauer had greatly invested in the government's communication staff, used ad agency input and Elisabeth Noelle-Neumann's polling, experimented with direct mail, intensified film and mobile advertising, even published comic books (a risky move, as comics were offensive to culturally conservative voters) and put to good use such gimmicks as Polaroid cameras for instant photo opportunities with local papers and party people joining the chancellor in his special trains.[12]

The CDU followed the SPD in rejuvenating its complacent headquarters, turning it into a powerhouse of highly qualified operatives, and finally found in Helmut Kohl the party chairman to let an internationally well-connected professional team of CDU managers, admakers and pollsters organize his almost-victory in 1976 and then the successful elections of 1983, 1987, 1990 and 1994. Kohl's well-oiled campaign machine would trump even the efficient SPD firing squads.

As in all democracies, social forces and historical events play a larger role than campaign managers do, but a handful of political engineers helped German parties bring out their communications potential in the 1970s—men such as Volker Riegger, Albrecht Müller, Bodo Hombach and Harry Walter with the SPD, or Peter Radunski, Coordt von Mannstein and pollster Elisabeth Noelle-Neumann with the CDU, or Klaus Golombek and Peter Schröder with the smaller, centrist Free Democratic Party (FDP). They did their work well enough to be consultants to international politicians from Eastern Europe to Latin America, and have been respected members of the international political strategy community for decades. Ever since the 1960s, German parties have trodden on the well-worn path from Europe to America to go shopping for new strategies, methods and gadgets, and study voter trends they anticipated to be meaningful for European societies as well. These campaign professionals were the second generation of modernizers. But what about the first generation?

There is hardly any big or small American campaign tactic, technique or technology that has not been experimented with in Germany—either in the parties themselves or in consultancies. It is interesting to note that the more complex techniques such as polling-based strategies, phone canvassing, attack websites and fundraising dinners made their way to Germany sooner than little simple things such as cardboard doorhangers, convention balloon showers and sign waving at rallies, which once seemed so typical American nobody would dare to introduce them. Modernization has been continually going on and tracking international and, of course, American standards, for a long time.

New Strategic Challenges After Unification

When Germany entered the 1990s, much of the old campaign hands' world had changed, of course. The stable party triad, a result of the system of proportional representation,[13] which had set the ground rules for campaigns for almost forty years was gone.

In the west, the Greens had established themselves as a major force among left-liberal urbanites and the eco-minded. Reunification increased the population from sixty to eighty million citizens and brought the post-communist Party of Democratic Socialism (PDS) into play, an odd coalition of stalwart communist functionaries and anticapitalist youth. The PDS was able to remain a potent force in the East, snatching up to almost 30% of the regional vote. In Germany's system of proportional representation, that made it hard for the other parties to ignore the postcommunists particularly because they successfully positioned themselves as the voice of the East.

Voting PDS was not a matter of ideology, it was a matter of identity for twenty million East Germans. The reconstruction of the formerly communist eastern region after the Cold War can be compared to the Reconstruction Era of the American South after the Civil War: it was costly, difficult, full of corruption and political irritation, led to tremendous party polarization, took much longer than anyone expected, and cemented the power of the very people it originally set out to remove from power. The PDS survived in a way few people had predicted after reunification. In some federal states and many localities, the PDS participated in coalition governments, and is often stronger than either the nationally leading SPD and CDU parties.

Finally in 2005, the world turned upside down: instead of dying out with the old communist cadres, the PDS managed to get out of the eastern box when it merged with a splinter party that had broken off from the SPD's western labor union wing. The new Left Party, with former SPD chief and populist Oskar Lafontaine as co-chair, now has a national base and has the potential to radically change the party system for the long term. Just a few years ago, most western party analysts saw the PDS as doomed, way out in left field when the real fight was between the SPD/Green and CDU/FDP camps. History and the voter thought otherwise.

In today's German party system, SPD and CDU can each expect nationwide vote shares between 30 and slightly over 40%, typically not being able to cover, together, more than 75%. (Back in the 1970s, it was 85–90%.) The three smaller parties (Greens, FDP and the PDS/Left Party) today win between 6 and 10% each, nationally in safe distance from the 5% knockout barrier that would keep them out of the parliament.

The multiparty system has always been one where coalition government is the norm, which means (1) party programs must be compatible with a potential coalition partner; and (2) smaller parties settle on niches rather than follow the mainstream. Having more competing parties in a differentiated system makes both communication strategies and governing more difficult. Party loyalty has long gone down where it existed in the West, and never was a stable factor in the East. Also gone—in a quite dramatic way—is the membership (measured against the population, it has halved since the early 1980s), which is also extremely thin in the East.

Also, the media system has changed dramatically after the state monopoly on television and radio, which regulated party announcements strictly, was deregulated in 1984. With the private market finally blooming in the 1990s, alleys for additional media buys by the parties opened, allowing more penetration and targeted communications. Further, the Internet, while only a side factor in 1998, has begun to leave serious marks in political communications from the 2002 elections onward.

Schröder's Way, 1998

We have seen that modernization and "Americanization" go back a long time in Germany. Yet, according to current folklore, the zero milestone mark was laid in 1998 when Gerhard Schröder toppled chancellor Helmut Kohl, who had headed the government for sixteen years, surpassing even Adenauer. The SPD campaign was personalized, media-driven, creative, energetic and emotional. Against Kohl, Schröder never played defense. The SPD effort had all the ingredients of a great, even grandiose, campaign. It had taken more than a page from the campaign playbooks of the 1997 Tony Blair and 1992 Clinton/Gore campaigns. And Schröder won.

This was no ordinary victory; for the first time, Germans voted an incumbent coalition government out of office. All other changes of government (1966, 1969 and 1982) had been based on coalition rearrangements in the Bundestag. The Social Democrats won a spectacular 40.9% of the vote, became the strongest party across all age groups except those over 60, won 212 out of 328 direct-election parliamentary seats, and beat the pants off the Christian Democrats in the eastern states. Not only did this victory bring the SPD back into power after sixteen years; it did so by forming the very first national coalition with the Green party. Today, a decade later, the euphoria around the first red/green coalition is hard to fathom, but then it was no less than a cultural shock for Germany's politics.

In a true marketing orientation, the SPD—long seen as old-fashioned and out of sync with the mainstream—remodeled its product line both in terms of policies and personalities. There was considerable strategic power in the themes the party stressed and could project through a candidate-focused campaign: change, leadership, jobs, innovation and social justice. The middle-class oriented big-tent message appealing to what the SPD campaign called "The New Center" mirrored Blair's "New Labour" and Clinton's "New Democrat" strategies. Working-class men up to forty-five years old, young male and female professionals, and the about 10% truly independent voters were among the core swing target groups. The campaign took care to accentuate the positive, but also hammered away with humor at the sitting chancellor as an outdated model.

Never had a modern German party prepared itself better and earlier for a campaign. The most prominent symbol of this had been the installation of a separate "Kampa" campaign headquarters outside of the traditional party office in then-capital city Bonn. The "Kampa" core team moved in during 1997, one year before election day—incredibly early by any standard in Europe, a continent used to short campaigns. The "Kampa" management design that came to be celebrated by the media as Germany's version of Clinton's Little Rock war room and the Millbank Towers campaign center run by New Labour's manager Peter Mandelson. Scholars, too, touted "Kampa" as the ultimate weapon that killed Kohl, the giant.

Perhaps the single most highlighted item in modern German political folklore, the Social Democratic "Kampa" was set up across the street from Kohl's CDU tower, some 250 yards away from the SPD office building, and many permanent staff moved over but kept their desks and still checked in there in the morning. This seventy-staff-headquarters was not a totally new professional organization separate from the old party hands. Quite the contrary; old hands ran it, but in a more flexible structure and with plenty of volunteers and interns fresh from college and regional party units. New fascinating units, for example, for opposition research and rebuttal, for the eastern campaign, and for special action in thirty-two marginal key seats, kindled observers' fantasies.

Eight consulting agencies were hired to bring in specialized expertise in polling and focus group research, event marketing, Internet communications, media monitoring and analysis, training, speechwriting, and of course advertising and media buying. "Kampa" was extremely service- and training-oriented, thus enabling the party base to participate in phone campaigning workshops, door-to-door canvassing optimization, candidate interview training, and the like. A hotline, a new Intranet and a fax service, audio conferences and newsletters maximized internal communications and consistency of message and visual identity.

Some innovations were direct foreign imports—for example, Blair's 1997 "pledge card" with five key promises was turned into a focus-grouped nine-point Schröder "guarantee card." But it was the creativity of events, photo ops and paid media (billboards, posters, ads, television and cinema spots) that came to be the "Kampa" handwriting, particularly with its own brand of humor to package hard-hitting negative tactics against Kohl and the CDU.

Setting up "Kampa" was smart because it fascinated capital journalists and marked the beginning of an era where the campaign itself becomes the story. Moving a "Kampa" outside of a traditional party headquarters signaled this was not the old, dusty party machine anymore. In reality, moving "Kampa" into a stand-alone building seems to have quite prosaic reasons: insiders admit that the only thing the SPD staff had wanted was to accommodate the great number of temporary campaign hands in a more communicative, war-room-like open-plan central room instead of the little quarters along typical German office corridors; for that, the managers intended to tear down a wall. The architect intervened for security reasons. Thus, they decided to use a bland neighborhood office building scheduled for demolition.

"Kampa" operations chief Matthias Machnig said to the author in March 1998: "If this is going to fly, it's going to be a legend." Indeed Machnig was a very active midwife of giving birth to a legend (and, in passing, suggesting his own genius). The "Kampa" was the beginning of a new ballyhoo based on game-scheme symbolism, setting up (seemingly) separate campaign units like sports teams going for a championship, giving them a visible home and a face, and marketing them as a brand. In the years that followed, all national parties did it, state and local parties, too. While the craze has fizzled somewhat, most such campaign units create their own merchandise, from tote bags to key rings, cigarette lighters to baseball caps—not with the party emblem or candidate name, but with the branded name of the campaign headquarters. This very public and odd self-celebration of the spinmeisters and their machinery surely began in 1998.

Forerunners and Afterthoughts

Despite "Kampa" mythology, it must be said that the SPD built successfully on its 1994 effort to be part of the 1990's era of war rooms, spin doctors and new style politainment. SPD candidate Rudolf Scharping and his team were willing to invest in an "Americanized" campaign. The party hired a former 1992 Clinton/Gore war-room deckhand (Frank Stauss, today one of Germany's leading political media masters with the Butter agency), consulted with Clinton advisors, and even organized campaign staff movie nights with *The War Room* film documentary, which turned quickly into a cult movie among young German operatives dreaming about their being as cool, tough and professional as the "Ragin' Cajun" James Carville, George Stephanopoulos and Mary Matalin. The SPD followed an issue strategy close to Clinton's, greatly improved polling and innovative advertising operations, imitated Democratic image films and—in a slacking economy and job crisis reminiscent of the 1992 Clinton vs. Bush situation—was not shy of even mimicking such Clinton campaign slogans as "jobs, jobs, jobs" which, unfortunately, translated into German billboards as a moaning "work, work, work." Candidate Scharping had the misfortune to see Kohl bounce back in the polls just in time to win it one more time.

Had Scharping's strategy worked, we can be relatively sure the 1994 SPD campaign would have been as legendary as the "Kampa." Even insiders suggest Schröder would have won no matter what, even without a "Kampa" and with a boring run-of-the-mill campaign. The time was ripe for change, the party had an able candidate. Still, "Kampa" set a new standard against which every German campaign was going to be measured against—in the understanding of many, it was a watershed.

From a political management perspective, what remain remarkable about the 1998 experience are two facts. One is that the SPD, for all its innovation, ran very much a classic twentieth-century campaign with its heavy reliance on relations with the establishment news organizations, prime-time television image making, and tight central "war-room" control. The campaign tread only cautiously into the field of paid media, direct communications and grassroots mobilization. "Kampa" was an incremental improvement, not a deep, systemic change re-designing the German campaign universe. It was a far-reaching yet only sustaining innovation, certainly an intelligent redesign of available resources and standard operating procedures. What "Kampa" was not, despite all the hype, was a disruptive innovation, a dramatic break-through toward a new operating culture. That, in all likelihood, will be brought about by the Internet.[14]

The other remarkable fact was the Christian Democrats' de facto paralysis. The Kohl machine's well-oiled professionalism of yesteryear seemed to be ineffective, despite all the media bonus (Kohl, as chancellor, always had more prime time television and more newspaper columns) and the resources invested. For example, the party bought twice as many television spots as in 1994 (559 versus 254), while the SPD only ran eighty-eight television spots. Prominent large-format print ads ate up chunks of the budget of fifty million Deutsche Marks, as did a free magazine delivered to all East German households. None of that moved any numbers. The CDU was caught off guard, despite the SPD's long and obvious preparations, and it never regained the ability to react adequately to the Schröder onslaught. Kohl had all the communica-tion resources of a large government apparatus, but in retrospect, all it did was react to SPD actions. It comes as no surprise that "rapid response" was going to be the CDU's mantra in rebuilding its political operations and choosing a new cast of consultants.

Moving Beyond "Kampa," 2002

For all its relativity, "Kampa" had a considerable impact on the other parties on national and regional levels. Four years later, when the people's mood had become sour over the red/green government parties, the co-governing Greens chose to pursue a personalization strategy centered on highly popular foreign minister Joschka Fischer. Given that the Greens once matured from an alternative, anti-establishment social movement, their total commitment to their leading candidate was a critical choice. The appeal based on personal popularity rather than on party mirrored that of their coalition partner, the SPD. The SPD, of course, opened a "Kampa 02," headed again by Matthias Machnig. The campaign team was considerably more limited in what it could do, for the campaign was effectively run out of the executive offices of the chancellory and the ministries. The driving issues, the economy and unemployment, would be completely handled by a government commission on labor market reforms and the chancellor himself. In addition, the party left rebeled against an artificial style unfit to the mood at the base, and criticized the aloofness and ineffectiveness of the campaign headquarters. Even more based on Schröder's personality and news media coverage of his leadership than in 1998, the campaign showed less creativity, the one exception being a constant humorous harassment of the chal-lenger, conservative Edmund Stoiber of Bavaria. The main line of attack was social and cultural conservatism (for example, his views on women and family values) a theme that hit home with women, the cities and East Germany.

The Christian Democrats countered with a headquarters called "Arena 02," clad in the new party color of fresh orange and full of young professionals and high-tech gear. They positioned as informal leader and personal advisor to Stoiber the former editor-in-chief of Germany's largest tabloid *Bild*—an invitation for a "Kampf der Kampas" (battle of the Kampas) between the major campaigns, a story the media loved. The CDU took pains to ensure that the journalists would discover the conservative's new-found campaigning ability at eye level with the governing Social Democrats. The postcommunist PDS, too, opened a "Kampa" lookalike in Berlin.

The centrist FDP tried to outdo everybody in both style and positioning. Encouraged by sustained regional victories, the party which had a base vote of about 6% entered on a "Project 18," suggesting it could grow into a major party, rather than filling the traditional role of securing parliamentary majorities for either CDU or SPD. The party, long considered to be the Christian Democrats' natural sidekick, asserted equidistance from both. In a corresponding bold move, party chief Guido Westerwelle even declared himself a candidate for chancellor. Such ambitions were coupled with the derring-do of the marketers. The campaign would quickly be known as "the fun campaign" which tended to play with symbols (particularly the 18), taboos and gags. For example, the campaign had video spots with porn queen Dolly Buster, Westerwelle wore a shoe with a yellow 18 on the sole to a serious television talk show, and he traveled the country in a yellow Winnebago called the Guidomobile. It was a made-for-the-media summer tour on the beaches, county fairs and city hot spots. The cheesy and satirical style did make some inroads to the young voter base the FDP coveted. However, the traditional base of the party was seriously irritated by the colorful appeals.

Moreover, the "fun campaign" saw serious problems when the destablized red/green coalition managed to turn the tables on its attackers. No campaign technique or technology did the trick, no "Kampa" invented it; policy and executive action did. A steadfast and aggressive "no" to any participation in America's Iraq invasion utilized the greatest political issue possible, war and peace. Latent anti-Americanism and pacifism helped shore up the otherwise disinterested. This became one of two decisive issues of the election, the other one being the destructive Elbe river flood that came over East Germany in the middle of the campaign. All politicians flew into the crisis zone, but this was the hour of the executive, and Chancellor Schröder proved to be a competent leader in the crisis. Schröder was on the air every day, being shown jumping out of his helicopter in rubber boots and green border patrol field jacket, making the rounds in the disaster zone, encouraging families and organizing swift aid.

At the same time seeing the FDP happy campers tour the country in their merry Guidomobile bordered on the absurd. The party parked the yellow monster, and the "fun" strategy paused; it finally collapsed when a scandal on anti-Semitic flyers and questionable fundraising practices broke.

Strategic Lessons from 2002

Germany regained confidence in its leader, and in the end the margin between the major parties was razor-thin. The difference between SPD and CDU lay at about 6,000 votes, out of 48 million cast. The red/green coalition settled in a governing majority only because of a quirky element of German election law which gave the SPD four so-called overhang mandates, and because the PDS failed at winning. Thus, Germany lived through a photo finish, including the CDU candidate declaring victory and conceding defeat a few hours later. It was very bitter for the opposition; that day, the CDU got the third-worst national election tally since 1949.

Many observers see the 2002 election result as a coincidence—a result that was not supposed to happen and hinged mainly on a last-minute swing in a particular point in time. Considerable debate has been sparked by the nonhistorical question whether the SPD could have pulled this victory a week earlier or a week later. We will never know. The CDU ranted for a long time about a "stolen election," however.

It has been widely agreed among campaign experts that the effect of the several campaigns, for all their professionalism, did not move numbers the way the Iraq war and Elbe flood did. The original SPD "Kampa" certainly had lost its mythical reputation and fought the shadow of its lost magic. Iraq and the flood were God's gift to the floundering SPD campaign, which in place of a working strategy could maximize the executive bonus and positive media exposure. Iraq was the polarizing bolt Schröder could hammer into the electorate—seriously damaging German–American diplomatic relations in the process.

The strategic lesson for the CDU campaign was that running a rationalistic, perfectionist campaign does not ensure victory. The deficit lay in flexible intelligence, room for intuition and improvisation. The very problem of "rapid response" ability was not solved by having a staff office doing twenty-four-hour monitoring and firing out online rebuttals to opposition charges.

Critics have concluded that the Stoiber campaign had locked itself into a monistic theme attacking one man (Schröder), one problem (the economy) and one message (Stoiber's competence). The logic of offense was based on a rigid frontal assault and penetration built on linear tactics. In other words, the way Stoiber pursued the showdown with Schröder with only one bullet in the revolver. It was linear, it was rational, it was perfectly planned, it was focused—just fitting with Stoiber's personal style. Strategically, it was a textbook campaign without major faults, at least for a certain situation. The problem was, once the issue arena changed, it was easy to wreak havoc with Stoiber's single-shot strategy. The campaign team seemed helpless and unable to maneuver tactically, and no exciting news, emotional events or mobilizing last-minute effects had been planned for as contingency measures. Unfortunately for their party, most in the Christian Democratic leadership refused to see anything but "events beyond our control" that took the day. The inability to deal with an unexpected scenario and Schröder actively fighting back on his own grounds was the major shortcoming of an otherwise fine and exemplary campaign.[15] The inadequacy would, in 2005, come back to haunt the CDU again.

Incremental Innovations and the Introduction of Television Debates

Conceptual and technical innovations were incremental and sparse in the 2002 campaign. The Internet did play a growing role. For the public, it was mainly used for background information dissemination, voter service (for example, on absentee mail voting) and niche playgrounds (negative campaigning found a new home in pseudo-websites and satirical sites). Internally, it helped supplement or replace traditional routes for the functionaries and the party faithful—for example, it became standard practice to put flyers of the day, campaign updates, important rebuttals, logos or advertising templates online for quick downloads.

The FDP proved to be far off on the wrong track with the "fun campaign" when the dead serious issues of war and disaster came around the corner. The illusionary "Project 18" crashed at the bottom, gathering just 7.4%. In one aspect, however, the FDP was a productive innovator: it was the first of the parties to integrate a fundraising campaign ("Bürgerfonds" or Citizen Fund) with plenty of serious as well as creative "fun" ideas. It did fall short of raising eighteen million, but helped with participatory outreach and networking, and set an unprecedented example for online communication and fundraising.

The most popular technical innovation was the television debate between Chancellor Schröder and challenger Stoiber. As in most strong multiparty systems, imitating US presidential debates as a facilitated duel between the two rivals for power is problematic because it keeps out the top candidates of the minor parties. Thus, German television had usually broadcast the so-called "Elefantenrunden," or elephants' rounds, with the chairmen of all parties represented in parliament. In addition, sitting chancellors had no incentive and no interest to give their challengers the stage for a one-on-one. Schröder was different and a confident boxer in the media arena; when Stoiber challenged him, he accepted. Nobody, certainly not Schröder himself, doubted that the telegenic, media-savvy Schröder would profit the most from a direct battle on the screen with the stiff and tense Stoiber. Schröder's image had always been that of "the media chancellor," while Stoiber's image firmly rested on a reputation to be an endlessly effective bureaucrat who often had his foot in his mouth. To pit a relaxed, charismatic camera-lover who badly needed additional votes against the austere front-runner was, simply, a no-brainer for the SPD team.

Both camps were happy to stage such a debate and ignored the howling of the other parties. The FDP even sued in court, but to no avail. However, both camps negotiated for weeks on the format and ground rules. They, the participating television stations (two public and two private networks) and an armada of journalists, political and communication scholars studied in detail all earlier US presidential debate formats and the suggestions of the US Commission on Presidential Debates. Pollsters engaged intensely in the events for pre- and post-analysis.

In the end, two rather formal debates were broadcast, both set at eighty minutes. Both had fifteen million viewers (which translates into a television market share of 45%). In the first round, the two candidates and the two co-facilitators had considerable problems with the inflexibility the pre-planning had brought—questioning, statements and rebuttals were strictly regulated in terms of seconds and order. Polls showed clearly that viewers had expected more of a slugfest. The second duel was more open, allowing more of a free-flowing debate between Schröder and Stoiber.

Nevertheless, more people saw these two television events than any other broadcast on the election; and that means that the debates were the single campaign events with the greatest one-time audience.

In the after-event viewer polls, there was no shortage of criticism, but majorities said the debates were easy to understand, interesting and well done. At least some 40% of the viewers thought they were entertaining, informative and credible. Only a quarter found them to be superficial, and only a fifth found them boring.[16]

Polls (both standard surveys and focus groups based on handheld real-time response devices) could measure no meaningful immediate movement of numbers for the parties, but otherwise, the chancellor debates were widely counted as a surprising success: quite simply, the voters like them.

On the other hand, journalists and scholars lamented about too much personalization of a party-centered election system, the danger of populism, the exclusion of three out of five parliamentary parties, and the critical effect of post-mortem media interpretation and spinning.

But the political parties and candidates have decided that democratic theory counts little when a chance to reach such a large bloc of voters is at hand, including many undecideds, late-deciders, politically less interested voters and even opponents. What's more, because of the intense media promotion and relentless post-mortem analysis and debate in the media, the core messages of a television debate reach even those who did not watch.

Conventional wisdom now has it that television debates are indeed central communication events in national—and most regional—campaigns; they will not likely change basic dynamics, but help in solidifying the support and reaching out to those not easily reached at all. All in all, they are a factor in mobilization in the last weeks of a campaign.[17]

Few doubted after the success of the 2002 that the television debates would be disposed of, and they were not. In 2005, Schröder and challenger Angela Merkel both accepted television debates without much discussion. The only practical questions left were not if, but how. This time, twenty million Germans watched. Even more polls were taken, and in no way did the rooms put up for journalists and spokespeople interpreting the debates seem any different from the original "spin alleys" of American presidential debates. Now that everybody was aware that the debate counts less than its interpretation, spinning intensified enormously.

In retrospect, the 2005 television debates were much improved. Practical experience was gained in setting up the right rules and understanding how to exploit the debates' potential. Recent empirical studies have analyzed and attempted to get rid of the many myths surrounding television debates. Among the German myths we can count the beliefs that:

- voters get more concrete information about party's goals (while in fact emotional appeals and bromides count for a lot of the talk);
- voters will be persuaded by facts (rather, they will be polarized by selected factual arguments);
- voters will be moved by the debating candidates' body language (no clear evidence here);
- voters will be moved by emotion (but even Schröder's most emotional moment in a 2005 television debate, declaring love to his wife, left viewers cold).

Researchers say today that, with those who directly watched the television debates, the most successful statements are either policy-driven hard positions or personalized platitudes that give a credible insight into where the candidate stands and comes from. So, the televised duels are neither the superficial shows the skeptics say they are, nor the highly educational information outlet their advocates praise them to be. They do have a lot of potential in terms of voter education and persuasion, more than is currently used. Still, television debates themselves will have a limited impact because viewers tend to see and hear what they want to see and hear. They do, however, change opinions about the candidates, and they do change the political knowledge of voters (but that does not mean they increase it). They do alter the criteria for election choice. But the point here is: that it is not the television debate itself that affects changes among the electorate, but the media coverage that does—particularly if there is a consonance among the press corps, that is, a trend of all weighing in on the same issues and personal performance evaluations. It has become obvious that journalists reporting the debates and their aftermath take a very different view from average voters in the polls. The impact can be considerable.[18] Generally, the findings on German television debates are not far away from the results of a much longer and deeper research tradition in the United States.

Merkel Takes a Beating—and Power, 2005

For the second time since 1949, an incumbent government was voted out of power, and for the first time, a woman was elected chancellor. The 2005 elections certainly were interesting—but for a number of different reasons. And currently German political managers have more questions than answers about that campaign year.

The main fact is that the Social Democrats, while not having the chancellory, stayed in power as an equal-size coalition partner—a feat few people in Germany would have bet upon in the campaign summer of 2005. It was a sure defeat for the SPD: all the polls said it; all the media said it; even most SPD operatives said it. But the disaster turned out to be a minor bump, and the opposition wasted a certain victory.

In any case, 2005 was not supposed to be a national election year. If any politician ever took a high-risk gamble, it was Chancellor Schröder who, when faced with a constant downslide in the polls and a major state-level election desaster for his party in May, called for a dissolution of the Bundestag. He had had more than a year until election day and a comfortable and loyal majority in parliament. True, the quick formation of the new PDS-successor, the Left Party, made reasonably dangerous trouble with its social progressivist policies, nibbling away at the labor union base and the base in the East. True also, majorities in the sixteen federal states had long turned against the Social Democrats, and cooperative legislation was no fun anymore. But to throw it all away, that instantly seemed like growing suicidal while being afraid of dying. Schröder's death wish was hard to understand even for the fiercest of his loyalists. Dissolving the parliament is probably the most unnatural act in German politics; it has happened only twice before and is made extremely difficult by constitutional design.[19]

By this daring move, the partisan world turned upside down. Schröder's government now lived on borrowed time. CDU chairwoman Angela Merkel was automatically seen as a chancellor in waiting, the Christian Democrats looked like the governing party. Unsurmountable public support was documented in all opinion surveys throughout the summer and fall.

Schröder surprised everybody. All parties had set their operational and financial sights for a campaign in late 2006. Now they had only four months to go before election day. There was simply no time to build up a "Kampa"-style campaign headquarters, go through an extensive search process to find the right consulting agencies, or order broad benchmark surveys, or build a grand orchestra of communication channels. And the party treasurers, looking over rather half-empty warchests, had to find resources to pay for the necessary, even though that meant expensive loans from the banks.

Strategic Choices

On the strategic level, the governing SPD and Greens had to make some tough decisions. For one, it was obvious that whatever the election would bring, the least likely result was a return of the red/green, Schröder/Fischer administration. This was the end, and they knew it. From now on, they would fight separately. Both parties decided on putting all their chips on one number: the personal appeal and popularity of their leaders, Schröder and Fischer. Both decided on running a classic challenger campaign, as if they were the opposition and Ms Merkel the governing chancellor. Most Christian Democrats found this desperate and laughed the threat away, but there were others who distrusted the situation: "We have to watch out that we don't get voted out of office for things we haven't even been able to do yet," said one CDU headquarters operative with incredible foresight some ten weeks before the election.[20]

Like a mirror on the government parties, the CDU chose to position itself as the non-emotional, rational force explaining concrete policy choices, including those which would hurt people. Candidate Merkel asserted she would raise the value-added tax in order to decrease non-wage labor costs. A tax hike as a campaign promise raised many eyebrows, but the candidate was convinced honesty and straight talk would be rewarded. Pollster Elisabeth Noelle-Neumann attested that for Merkel, voters attached to her an "atmosphere of sobriety and seriousness," and she would not counter the evidence.[21] The problem was that this sort of engineering was not combined with any emotional or ideological appeal, or with any attack on the ruling parties, that could mobilize the party supporters in a fight they felt would be morally right.

In order to emphasize her seriousness, Merkel offered the voter a "competence team" of party and non-party experts. The team included one star, former high court justice and Heidelberg university law professor Paul Kirchhof. A prominent man, Kirchhof was no politician, but had been part of many ideological policy battles and politicized cases on tax and budget issues. Presented as a shadow finance minister, Kirchhof not only over-shadowed all other members of Merkel's team, but became the instant focus of controversy. He had not been thoroughly prepared to participate in such a high-level campaign and took a very academic approach to presenting his own rather radical ideas on tax reform—without checking with the party program or with the leader, much less consulting with the communications team. Interviews contradicted the official party line, and from then on both Kirchhof and the CDU took constant beatings for being unfair to the average worker and socially irresponsible. Chancellor Schröder made Kirchhof his personal nemesis, dressing him down as "that professor from Heidelberg." Kirchhof, a well-meaning reformer on an incredibly complicated tax system who just happened to lack in political antennae and campaign discipline, came across as a cold-hearted technocrat unable to fathom such a thing as social justice. He was turned into a symbol for a party willing to soak the poor and make the rich richer. It was unfair, but it worked. The man who had been a star in a future cabinet became an albatross around Merkel's neck.

Kirchhof also symbolized the CDU's limited ability to balance out the conservative messages. Like Stoiber in 2002, Merkel had focused on rational solving of economic problems. Like Stoiber, Merkel found out that election campaigns can be strongly influenced and turned around by controversies driven by values. Solidarity, social justice, family, immigration and cultural identity loom large as such drivers. Much of these were not balanced out. The result: lower-middle-class voters, the less qualified and socially disadvantaged said goodbye to the Christian Democrats in large numbers.

New Tactics and Technology

On the tactical level, parties needed ideas quick. Two interconnected ideas resounded with the campaign planners who looked, among other things, to American experiences in the 2004 US presidential election. One was the growing power of the Internet and particularly the "web 2.0" social networking media and the other was grassroots mobilization. (See Chapter 23, by Emilienne Ireland on the use of the Internet in American campaigns.)

Internet functions approach serious budgets; small parties may invest as much as 10% now. For the first time, weblogs made a significant contribution to all parties' communications. Prominent politicians blogged on sophisticated sites, supported by audio and video. Instant organizations were created using web tools targeting informal opinion leaders and multipliers. Volunteering tools, dialog and participation strategies were the often heard terms of the campaign.

Another one was targeting, or micro-targeting. Direct mail, e-mail and telemarketing never got over experimental status in Germany because of the lack of adequate voter databases, tight legal restrictions on data sharing and privacy laws, and a rather prohibitive cost in postage and handling or, in the case of phone campaigns, high cost of phone lines. The cost is going down and the perceived significance of direct communications is increasing. For the first time, the FDP invested heavily in a direct mail campaign, sending millions of letters to targeted voters. Currently all parties are looking into better targeting methods but are cautious. The smaller parties with their smaller voter bases and more clearly defined voter cleavages are somewhat better off in collecting and maintaining voter files based on party affinity along certain criteria.

German eyes closely followed the "ground war" in the 2004 American election. Many would like to emulate the volunteerism that is the basis of that massive mobilization. The problem German parties have with this is not that they trust their foot soldiers less than their highly paid ad-making, spin-doctoring mercenaries responsible for the air wars and heavy artillery. The problem is that German parties traditionally have been defined as membership parties with a rigid, bureaucratic, hierarchic structure. Membership is a long-term commitment beyond paying dues and receiving a magazine subscription; members are the ones who keep a campaign operable. Without membership, or a largely inactive and elderly one, there is no ground campaign—and that is exactly the case in more and more regions, especially in East Germany. It had always been clear to German parties that personal canvasing mobilizes voters more effectively than anything else. But splendid organizational principles are worthless when no one is around for the legwork.

American-style ad hoc volunteerism, viral marketing and evolving support networks such as MeetUps thus have been foreign ideas for German parties (and for civic and charitable organizations as well). In a country that likes permanent, well-structured organizations, it is no small feat to convince parties to go beyond the membership, and redefine culturally what it means to be a "member." This is a broader, strategic question, but in 2005 the novel concept was treated as a tactical one.

Some younger Social Democrat members of the Bundestag invoked the spirit of American networking platform MoveOn.org for their own version, wirkaempfen.de (we fight), in June 2005. Based on the idea that "resignation is for cowards," the mini-campaign that had not been planned by the central party office found many supporters mainly from the state level, which snowballed the news of the platform quickly across the SPD base. The volunteer platform worked much faster than the regular party headquarters and got self-developed campaign materials and manuals out to the community before the headquarters even had any. The initiative recruited 4,000 supporters—not many, but also not bad for a spontaneous outburst that helped bridge the time until the regular campaign machine had swung into action.

The CDU tested the grassroots concept earlier and more professionally in the largest German state of North Rhine Westphalia. The "NRWin Team" would successfully contribute to an effort that brought the Christian Democrats in that state back into power after thirty-nine years. "NRWin" was a volunteer, not a membership, movement in the 128 state constituencies. Membership in the CDU was not necessary to join the campaign. It had an incentive system, "Ten for a change," which meant that anyone who had written ten e-mails or letters, had knocked on ten doors or spent ten hours manning an outdoor party table would get some special recognition, such as VIP tickets to a candidate event. Some 10,000 members would be recruited. Yet party culture made things difficult at times: for example, some existing candidate teams would not allow the "NRWin" volunteers to publicly become active and visible for their district campaigns.[22]

A grassroots network personally devoted to Angela Merkel was the idea behind "teAM Zukunft" (team future), with the AM standing for the candidate. The CDU strategic planning unit was fully aware that the 2002 election could have been won for the CDU with the smallest of additional mobilization efforts. A benchmark survey in 2004 had found that 17% of German voters would be willing to actively support a party's campaign without being a member; among these willing, some 43% tended to side with the Christian Democrats. That meant a potential of four million voters. A later workshop with representatives of the American Republicans' Victory 04 program helped in drawing a concept that was scheduled to be implemented from fall 2005 toward the expected fall 2006 election. The "teAM" was designed to include the campaign teams of all 254 constituency Bundestag candidates and presented to the media as a serious campaign innovation. When Schröder called the elections, the CDU decided to implement the program anyway faster, and immediately brought a team of thirty volunteers together to work at the "teAM" at headquarters. In four months, they would recruit 32,000 supporters for their database. Mobile units hit the road to travel to distant places, volunteers helped other volunteers write letters to the editor, call in to radio shows, get engaged in blogging, invite friends and neighbors to house parties, come in to a summer youth camp, help out with local campaign events or be a sign-waver ("Angie!", "Vote for change!") at one of fifty major rallies. The last week became virtually a round-the-clock-operation in getting out the vote, with some 1,000 events in the final 100 hours before the closing of the polls.[23]

The Polling Nightmare

The election ended in a stalemate. It was impossible for the parties to form a coalition with a larger and a smaller partner, as had been practice in most of post-war German history. All smaller parties came in strongly, and the Social and Christian Democrats were almost on par. On election night, both Schröder and Merkel claimed to be the winner and the legitimate leader to form a government. It took weeks of negotiations to settle for a CDU/SPD coalition.

The election was a disaster for the polling profession because not one institute saw it coming. Pollsters had played a great role, less for the parties, but in the media. All had predicted a Christian Democratic landslide, even in the last several days. Their projections were so far off that politicians, media and scholars severely attacked the pollsters' professionalism. The debacle showed that in 2005, pollsters have great trouble gauging real sentiments for projections when up to a third of the voters are undecided shortly before and even on election day. Analyses emphasize that voters were more, not less, distrusting of all the parties by the end of the campaign period, and a great number just did not care who won or lost. Qualitative research and target group research, the introduction of daily tracking polls and a greater combination of phone and electronic research are currently in the works to improve upon the performance of 2005.

Volatility is high and getting higher. Swing voters used to be a marginal 5 to 10% between the large, stable voting blocs. Now most analysts see them approaching half the electorate. At the same time, the relatively high standard turnout of the German electorate may also become a faint memory some day, according to the consensus among political scientists. In the past decade, turnout for national elections has typically been around 80%, at the state level usually higher than 65%. The 2005 elections, with 77.7% of the electorate voting, saw the lowest national turnout since 1949. As any campaign professionl knows, turnout is a strategic factor. Sinking turnout usually helps smaller parties gain higher vote share. Judging turnout is important in targeting: to exclude unlikely voters from campaign communications has long been an American specialty. Now even German operatives think long and hard about the concept, and look to pollsters to help them differentiate the valuable targets from the fickle non-voter.

Political strategists, for their part, conclude that even though campaigns may be long, it is the late-deciders and last-minute swing that grows as a deciding factor. To reach those important people, other people must be mobilized to move out, persuade them and bring them to the polls. That means that the "ground war" and "get-out-the-vote" drives in the last week of an election will gain a considerably higher share of future campaign budgets, and the classic "air wars" will get less. Years ago, last-minute swing seemed marginal and often more a hypothesis than a great factor to consider. This has changed. The answer, German strategists presume, often does not lie in early image advertising, or in clever spinning within the news cycle; it lies in the hands of the man or woman knocking on the door as a colleague, a neigbor or a friend, and talking about the choice. Personal communication, enhanced by technology, is the winner of the last election, and the baseline of the next elections.

The Mother's Milk

Before concluding, a final word about money is in order. Money means communication, and professional campaigning is not cheap in a large and diverse nation with many elections and many media. Germany probably has one of the more sophisticated party organizations in the world, and if counting all assets, including real estate, German parties are relatively rich. But campaign spending per voter is moderate by international standards. German parties, to varying degrees, live off public subsidies (set and limited by law), membership dues, some private donations and some other sources of income. Private donations make up about a third of the CDU budget, only 8% of the SPD, the smaller parties lie in between. Generally, the fundraising function is underdeveloped, especially as an integrated part of campaign communications. Corporations and trade associations can legally donate under certain conditions of transparency. Individual, non-corporate donations will trigger state matching funds.

According to government records, in 2005 major German parties had these budgets (in euros): Christian Democratic/Social Union: 198 million, SPD 169 million, FDP 32 million, Greens 27 million, PDS/Left Party 23 million.[24]

Government subsidies are currently set by law at a maximum of 133 million euros for all parties combined. These are divided into campaign expenditure refunds (0.84 euros for the first four million votes cast for the part, 0.70 euros for every other vote) and matching funds for membership dues and private donations (0.38 euros for every euro received).

This system ensures a relatively high independence from lobbying pressure via campaign contributions. On the other hand, it also limits the campaign communications functions. As all parties have relatively expensive offices across the country, a large part of the budget goes to permanent staff, rent and operating cost.

The parties get considerable help from the government: Proportionally allotted slots on public television and radio stations are, by law, free for party announcements during the campaign season (slots with private stations must be bought); local government citizen registers are allowed to provide parties voters lists extracted from their database for direct mail; and the parties' think tanks are wholly taxpayer-funded foundations for political adult education, research, events, publications and international outreach.[25] For example, it is usually the party foundations that finance most travel and talks with American, British and other foreign campaign professionals and party headquarters for the transfer of know-how.

In the 2005 elections, the five major national parties spent a combined sum of around 70 million euros; this was about 11 million less than in 2002. The SPD spent 25 million euros, the Conservatives budgeted 23 million, the FDP had 3.5 million, the Greens 3.8 and the Left Party/PDS 4 million at hand.[26]

In these numbers none of the permanent staff cost or state and county/city level expenditures, or private budgets or candidates are included. For example, a direct constituency Bundestag representative may spend between 20,000 and 80,000 euros for his or her district campaign, greatly depending on personal fundraising ability (again, permanent staff cost not included). Central campaign budgets reserve their largest percentages on fixed and mobile billboards and posters; the small parties typically spend up to 70–80% of their resources on these, the larger parties up to about half. Television, radio and cinema spots plus print ads and brochures supplement the advertising. Internet budgets range from 1% (major parties) to 10% (Greens). Party conventions, tours and major events are the major non-advertising budget items.

In a country of eighty-two million citizens, the campaign expenditure numbers are not impressive. German parties have so far developed no serious professional fundraising abilities; compared, for example, to German non-governmental organizations, civic organizations and charities, they are semi-professional at best and helplessly understaffed. The centralist structure of the parties adds to the problem, as most candidates will look to the party office instead of private donors to finance their campaigns. By the same token, treasurers have few incentives to help train candidates and local parties in fundraising because this would mean more independence from the central office.

Among the campaign abilities of German parties, fundraising is the least fully developed and has so far profited the least from international benchmarks and know-how transfer. Put simply: while the legal framework and technology are available, the necessary culture and experience are not there. However, the pressure is rising to find additional revenue. With sinking memberships, limited state subsidies and more party competition, the parties must invest in fundraising abilities.

In the past decade, both central and local units have begun to experiment. Candidates hold fundraising breakfasts and dinners, raffles and discos; they raise money by mail, by phone and online. Of particular interest is the potential of online fundraising. All parties have seen how giant sums are collected in US campaigns, and all have tried Internet-based donor appeals. Yet, consensus among German party operatives currently is: "It doesn't work here." This may be partly due to the fact that there are few incentive programs, donor relationship management databases or not enough transparency about what the money is needed for. Technical developments of the future may be helpful, but the problem remains that political giving, in the past, was an activity either for the rich or for the card-carrying members. Spontanous giving would be done for Greenpeace Germany, Catholic Caritas or UNICEF, but not for parties. In addition, Germans may be great shoppers at Amazon or eBay, but they still feel queasy giving their credit card number online. So the general culture is not a friendly host to fundraising.

The larger problem, however, lies in the simple notion that ad hoc volunteerism and participation is a rather novel idea. The new grassroots emphasis may change that, finally. But unless the parties open up better and more continuous financial means, they will also be unable to invest in necessary add-ons to their campaign efforts, for example deep research abilities, databases, mail and phone shops, or even targeted databases. The future lies in technology, and technology does not come cheap.

Conclusion

Among European nations, Germany has a long tradition of professional campaign management. Modernizing its practice by a search for international benchmarks and inspiration, particularly from the United States, goes back to the 1920s. The 1960s became the decade that firmly established American-pioneered polling-driven, television-centered campaign methods in West Germany. Still, some typical European characteristics always limited the "Americanization" experience: proportional representation, a multiparty system with niche parties, stable party-loyal voter blocs, highly centralized party organizations, an understanding of party membership as permanent commitment rather than ad hoc volunteering, public broadcasting and public financing—all this, and much more, gave German campaigning its specific flavor.

Much has changed since the heyday of the classic approach, and the 1990 reunification increased the speed of the turnover. To a degree few professionals expected in the 1980s, volatility has become the mark of the German electorate. In addition, it has become much more difficult to dominate any media, and the financial resources are unavailable to even attempt it. Today's German parties increasingly say "Auf Wiedersehen" to the tight controlled, mass media-based campaign concepts of the nineties, instead returning to direct personal communications and mobilization. These used to be the assets and abilities of traditional, strong party organizations. German parties realize their membership is growing older, thinner and less reliable. This brings along a redefinition of membership engagement and a new reliance on informal networks, viral marketing and ad hoc campaigning.

Notes

1 This historical account is based on "Held nach Maß," *Der Spiegel*, September 6, 1961, 28–44; Markus Stadtmüller, "Heute existiert nur noch der Bildwert: Interview mit Klaus Schütz," *Museumsmagazin Haus der Geschichte der Bundesrepublik Deutschland* 2 (2004), http://www.museumsmagazin.com/archiv/2-2004/ausstellung/part2.php; Klaus Schütz, *Logenplatz und Schleudersitz* (Frankfurt: Ullstein, 1992), 91; *Willy Brandt Biography*, Bundeskanzler Willy Brandt Stiftung foundation website, http://www.bwbs.de/bwbs_biografie/index_de.html, and Daniela Münkel, *Willy Brandt und die "Vierte Gewalt": Politik und Massenmedien in den 50er bis 70er Jahren* (Frankfurt: Campus, 2005).

2 At that time, the Bundestag had only three party groups, and Brandt broke the CDU's absolute majority. Thus theoretically, Brandt's SPD could have formed a coalition with the surprisingly successful liberal democrats of the FDP, but talks between the party leaders went nowhere. It took until 1969 before the FDP would be willing to join forces with the Social Democrats. Brandt was nominated as chancellor candidate a second time in 1965, but lost again.

3 Goebbels biographers agree that he knew books such as Gustave Le Bon's *Psychology of the Masses* (1895) and Wilfred Trotter's *Instincts of the Herd in Peace and War* (1908). He studied in detail the U.S. Committee on Public Information (Creel Committee) for the U.S. propaganda effort in World War I, being impressed by the ensuing theories of Creel operatives Walter Lippman (*Public Opinion*, 1922) and Edward Bernays (*Crystallizing Public Opinion*, 1923; *Propaganda*, 1928). In his autobiography, Bernays recalls that, in 1933, Hearst's European correspondent Karl von Weigand told him how Goebbels had shown him his propaganda library, the best Weigand had ever seen; and that Goebbels was using Bernay's *Crystallizing Public Opinion* as a basis for his destructive campaign against the Jews of Germany. Bernays himself was born Austrian, to Jewish parents, and he was a nephew of psychoanalyst Sigmund Freud. See Edward Bernays, *Biography of an Idea: Memoirs of Public Relations Counsel Edward L. Bernays* (New York: Simon and Schuster, 1965). Goebbels also utilized the writings of Friedrich Schönemann

(*The Art of Mass Influence in the United States of America*, 1926) later commercial advertising legend Emil Domitzlaff (*The Propaganda Instruments of the Idea of State*, 1932) and was in close touch with many prominent advertisers and publicity agents of his time—after all, Berlin, in the late 1920s, was Europe's New York—a city that never sleeps, full of brand managers, admakers and marketing gurus.

4 For English-language access to Nazi campaign manuals, see the excellent online *German Propaganda Archive* managed by Randall Bytwerk at Calvin College, http://www.calvin.edu/academic/cas/gpa, particularly the pamphlet *Modern Political Propaganda* (1930), http://www.calvin.edu/academic/cas/gpa/stark.htm and the campaign analysis of the 1932 elections in *Tested Methods of Political Propaganda*, http://www.calvin.edu/academic/cas/gpa/wilweg02.htm.

5 ZDF, *Bonner Runde*, spring 1985.

6 Alexander Smoltczyk, "Die Marke Hitler," *Der Spiegel*, February 2, 2005, 60–72.

7 Holm Friebe, "Merkel in Orange," *Jungle World* 26 (June 29, 2005), http://jungle-world.com/seiten/2005/26/5764.

8 Noelle has always insisted she was no part of the Nazi propaganda machine, but she did work as a newspaper journalist under tightly-controlled Nazi censorhip. She became the center of controversy while a visiting professor at the University of Chicago when sociologist Leo Bogart published "The Pollster and the Nazis" in the August 1991 issue of *Commentary*, accusing her of anti-Semitic passages in her dissertation and articles she wrote for Nazi newspapers. The accused wrote a letter of apology to the Jewish magazine, explaining that the passages served as alibi functions under the dictatorship and were not meant to be harmful. "Professor Is Criticized for Anti-Semitic Past," *New York Times*, November 28, 1991. Original article: Leo Bogart, "The Pollster and the Nazis," *Commentary* 92 (2): 47–50.

9 Museum of the Moving Image, "Introduction," *The Living Room Candidate: Presidential Campaign Commercials 1952–2004* (n.d.), http://livingroomcandidate.movingimage.us.

10 Television was technically not new, of course. Like elsewhere in Western Europe and America, Germany had experimented with television even in the 1920s. Goebbels had forced the development of television technology, and a Berlin station regularly broadcast since 1935. The 1936 Berlin Olympics were broadcast on television, as were the Nuremberg party conventions. Goebbels even intended to mass produce cheap television sets for broad distribution, a strategy that had worked brilliantly with cheap radio sets, opening up new communication channels for the Nazis. Such as television set was ready for production in 1939, but the outbreak of the war severely limited television development, and all broadcasting was shut off in 1944.

11 Daniela Münkel, *Willy Brandt und die "Vierte Gewalt"*, 145.

12 Ibid., 208–14.

13 It is an additional member system (AMS) of proportional representation. This means half the Bundestag representatives are elected from geographic constituencies, the other half proportionally from party lists. Voters have two votes, the first for the constituency candidate, the second for party. Constituencies are decided by relative majority (winner takes all). Party list representatives are drawn from regional lists until the proportional number of seats has been filled. In order to participate in the counting, small parties must either win three constituencies or more than 5% of the vote share, a threshold of exclusion.

14 The concept of disruptive innovation was put forward by Harvard scholar Clayton Christensen, *The Innovator's Dilemma: When New Technologies Cause Great Firms to Fail* (Cambridge, MA: Harvard Business School Press, 1997).

15 Elmar Wiesendahl, "Strategische Hintergründe und Konsequenzen der CDU/CSU-Niederlage bei den Bundestagswahlen 2002," *Forschungsjournal Neue Soziale Bewegungen* 16 (1) (January 2003): 72–3.

16 Ursula Dehm, "Fernsehduelle im Urteil der Zuschauer," *Media Perspektiven* 12 (2002): 600–9.

17 Karl-Rudolf Korte, "Immer wählerischere Wähler," *Frankfurter Allgemeine Zeitung*, January 20 2006.

18 Marcus Maurer and Carsten Reinemann, *Die Wirkung von TV-Duellen in politischen Kampagnen: Mythen und Fakten*, Political Communication Conference, University of Mainz, October 10, 2007, http://www.kas.de/upload/veranstaltungen/071026_maurer.pdf.

19 Chancellor Willy Brandt called elections in 1972 when the Bundestag was paralyzed by party changers, and Chancellor Helmut Kohl did it in 1982 after he had successfully ousted Helmut Schmidt. The German constitution makes it extraordinarily difficult to dissolve the parliament and instead prefers the constructive vote of no confidence, a scheme that allows the Bundestag to vote the government down on the condition that it elects a new chancellor at the same time.

20 Frank Priess, "Ein Wahlkampf der besonderen Art," *Die Politische Meinung* 431 (October 2005): 10.

21 Ibid., 12.

22 Stephan Terhorst, "Das NRWin-Team—Die Unterstützerkampagne im NRW-Landtagswahlkampf," in *In der Mitte der Kampagne: Grassroots und Mobilisierung im Bundestagswahlkampf 2005*, ed. Florian Melchert, Fabian Magerl and Mario Voigt (Berlin: Poli-c Books, 2006), 65–73.

23 Florian Melchert, Fabian Magerl and Mario Voigt, eds, *In der Mitte der Kampagne: Grassroots und Mobilisierung im Bundestagswahlkampf 2005* (Berlin: Poli-c Books, 2006).

24 Unklarheiten.de, Lars Burghard's database based on Bundestag reports, http://www.parteispenden.unklarheiten.de

25 They are Friedrich Ebert Foundation (SPD), Konrad Adenauer Foundation and Hanns Seidel Foundation (CDU/CSU), Friedrich Naumann Foundation (FDP), Heinrich Böll Foundation (Greens) and Rosa Luxemburg Foundation (Left Party).

26 Tei, "Wahlkampfetats der Pateien," *die tageszeitung*, August 10, 2005, http://www.taz.de/index.php?id=archivseite&dig=2005/08/10/a0018.

23

Falafel and Apple Pie

American Consultants, Modernization and Americanization of Electoral Campaigns in Israel

Dahlia Scheindlin and Israel Waismel-Manor[1]

Introduction

From its earliest days, Israel's electoral process has exhibited a lively, if somewhat frenetic character. With no final borders and no constitution, it is not surprising that Israel's political life is relatively unstable.

The country has held eighteen national electoral campaigns (seventeen for Parliament, and one special election for Prime Minister) and had thirty-one governments. After a period of one-party domination during the first half of its life (1948–1977), it has undergone numerous power transitions. The public tends to be highly engaged, and until the last few cycles voter turnout hovered near the 80% mark (it has declined sharply over the last three elections to roughly 63%). In short, Israel seems to relish the electoral process.

Americans have worked on Israeli campaigns early and often; since 1969, American campaign consultants have played a role, although their activity has not been contiguous. Their involvement in Israel highlights the main questions about campaigns: how and why do they professionalize? Are the changes the result of unidirectional "diffusion" of American culture?[2] Or does their presence reflect an endogenous process of modernization? Is there a combination of the two? What are the political and normative implications of these changes in general, and in Israel?

To answer these questions, we first lay out the theoretical groundwork contrasting modernization and Americanization. We then portray the changing nature of Israeli campaigns as background. Next we focus on American campaign consultants in this evolving context, starting with their earliest, low-profile days in 1969 through to the highly public, practically spectacle-style involvement from 1996 onward. Along the way we track the relevant political, institutional and structural developments in the political environment that contributed to these changes. Finally we seek to analyze the implications of the American consultants' presence and American-style campaign practices in Israeli elections.

American-Style Politics Goes Global

There is at present a lively debate over the adoption of American-style campaigning across the globe, or "new-style" campaigning.[3] This style of campaigning is usually associated with broad reliance on television advertisements and their professional production; ever-shorter spots and the use of negative advertising; targeting, segmenting and tailoring messages to the electorate; heavy reliance on polls for such targeting and strategy development (as opposed to just reporting); personalization and the declining importance of parties, policy or ideology; consultant-centered campaigns; and an ideological move toward the center by larger parties.[4]

Different frames have been developed for making sense of these changes. The most common ones are Americanization (or globalization) and modernization. While both approaches agree on what has changed, they differ significantly on how the developments came about and the role American consultants had in the process.

The term "Americanization" has been largely used as a "shorthand description of global [electioneering] trends," in which "the US is the leading exporter and role model of campaigning."[5] It is often understood to mean the diffusion of American practices.[6] Michael Barnett and Kenneth Goldstein[7] argue that the Americanization of campaign practices is driven on the one hand by the desire of American political consultants seeking foreign markets for professional and remunerative reasons,[8] and on the other hand by political actors from abroad. As the latter face increasing competitiveness of campaigns, they may seek the most updated campaign techniques that they have encountered either through institutions such as the International Association of Political Consultants or personal networks, which often leads to American models. Obviously, a "cultural match" between those countries and American culture helps;[9] in addition often newly democratizing countries that lack entrenched campaign styles and traditions are often very open to American tactics with their global image of innovation and success.

In this view, Americanization is seen as a unidirectional (one-way) cultural dissemination process.[10] This does not exclude the possibility that cultural diffusion takes other paths too (from Western to Eastern and Central Europe, for example, or a hybrid form in Latin American). However, since the United States is regarded as "the cutting edge of electioneering innovation,"[11] it is by far the most influential path of universal standardization and homogenization of campaign practices.[12]

An alternative, often competing, view is that campaign changes are mainly the result of modernization. The American style is not imported or imposed on campaigns from the outside, rather, the result of structural changes in politics, the economy, society and the media that affect campaigns in similar ways in other countries, as they did in America.[13] Because these practices originated in the US, modernization may be mistaken for Americanization, but actually the changes are endogenous.[14] In this view, the process is a non-directional convergence that independently drives all countries toward common political communication practices in a common global environment.[15]

Several forces may contribute to the modernization of campaigns. First, the decline of parties across all democratic regimes and the rise of non-allied independent and also "floating" (undecided) voters called for ever-stronger tools to mobilize those voters. Second, the rise of the electronic media and its rising cost, especially television, forced parties and candidates to hire individuals who can maximize this new medium. Last, natural competition in this environment drives all campaigns to seek the one tool that will give them the electoral edge, which was less prominent in the pre-modern era of large party machines and traditional loyalties. Hence, they either develop better practices or improvements on previous ones.[16]

So what is the Israeli story? Most of the literature on Israel adopts the view that Israeli campaigns have Americanized, not modernized. Myron Joel Aronoff takes campaign Americanization for granted and sees it as part of widespread Americanization of Israeli politics in general.[17] Others, such as Dan Caspi, while giving some credit to standardization, still views these changes as part of a "universal trend toward mutual fertilization between cultures."[18] Yet, presenting the Americanization of Israeli campaigns as a unidirectional process misses part of the story. In this chapter we illustrate what we believe to be an interplay between Americanization and modernization, as well as internal and external factors, in the changing campaigns of Israel.

The First Wave: Professionalization Prior to 1977

For the first half of statehood (1948–1977), Israeli politics was an entrenched system of patronage. Mapai, forerunner to Labor, was the largest established party and it was linked to the Histadrut, or the central labor union, through which workers also received vital services such as health care. Much like the Democratic Party during the era of party bosses in the United States, local party branches and organizations had direct contact with voters and strong, traditional party loyalties; this has been described as an era of "absolute" politics in which the parties determined the voters' political and ideological consciousness, rather than the other way around.[19]

As a result, voting behavior was notably stable for the first twenty-five years, or first eight electoral cycles: Mapai regularly won roughly one-third of the 120 Knesset seats and the General Zionists or Herut (forerunner to Likud) took between fifteen to twenty seats, creeping up through the 1960s.

Certain structural and institutional aspects served to reinforce the political status quo: radio advertising laws enacted in 1959, for example, gave free air time to parties with extra minutes for each member of Parliament (MP) represented in the outgoing Knesset—ensuring that the biggest existing parties got the largest exposure.

Two main developments contributed to a change in campaign styles. The first was an underlying shift in political electoral dynamics during the 1960s. Growing ethnic and class divisions led to increasing distrust of the establishment Labor party from a large, disenfranchised sector of the population, mainly immigrants from the Middle East and North Africa. This community began to wield its electoral clout against Mapai/Labor, which was blamed for their difficulties and was increasingly seen as elitist and corrupt. During this period the coalition of right-wing parties began gaining ground as the second largest party.

Disillusionment following the 1973 Yom Kippur war worsened the situation for Labor, bringing a deep failure on foreign affairs to its existing troubles on the domestic front. Both parties sensed that Labor was losing the traditional affinity of its voters, and altered their campaign tactics in response. Likud's 1973 campaign attacked Prime Minister Golda Meir personally for failing to foresee or prevent the war. Labor ran on the defeatist slogan: "In spite of it, Labor."

The second development was technical: the watershed caused by the introduction of Israeli television in 1967. Two years later, television entered political campaigns, ushering in an era of media politics. The parties rapidly grasped the power of this seemingly omnipotent new vehicle for reaching voters.

By all accounts the first television campaign in 1969 was predictably amateur. Relying solely on local television producers and camera crews, the ads were soporific, on-camera candidate talks that were long and smacked of lecturing.[20] In 1973 due to the trauma of the war, parties kept their budgets low and their campaigns understated,[21] and the television ads remained primitive by modern standards.

Yet parties soon realized the power of television to reach voters far beyond their traditional base.[22] Further, television led to a more populist and emotional approach, in which form is favored over content.[23]

The American Presence

As Labor began growing weaker it made greater efforts to secure its edge. In 1969, Labor member of Knesset (MK) Yossi Sarid brought the first American consultant to work on the Labor campaign, but he made little impression and no headlines. Sarid said that with no experience running campaigns, he had been told Americans could bring greater know-how, and so he sought help. "But it turned out," he said "that they didn't understand [with relation to Israeli politics]."[24] Although the 1973 elections showed the beginning of more personalized campaign strategies, there is no evidence that Americans were involved and promoting this.

By 1973 a number of endogenous processes were underway in Israel that are commonly linked to modernized campaign tactics. The major contextual ones involved the decline of organizational politics, presupposing direct contact with voters through participation in their organizations and branches, and ongoing loyalties—the main factors associated with increased need for sophisticated, modernizing campaigns.[25] Many of these changes recall those that occurred in American society and campaigns—roughly twenty years earlier.[26] Thus the impetus for modernization, or "Americanization," of Israeli campaigns began prior to any significant American presence on the campaigns themselves, and thus with little or no help from American professionals.

The Second Wave: American Involvement 1977–1996

Political Background

In 1977 a political "earthquake" rocked the country. The electoral coup shocked commentators and lawmakers alike, and ousted Labor in Israel's first transfer of political power. Likud's victory symbolized the culmination of a political "dealignment" and "realignment," in which core loyalties eroded and shifted. Since then, Likud developed a base at least as strong as Labor's had once been and the country moved to a mainly two-party system.

While many of Labor's wounds were long-term and self-inflicted, the campaign and political consultants, both American and Israeli, arguably take some credit. The 1977 election was the first in which an American consultant, David Garth, is reported to have played a significant role in the campaign.

In addition to the electoral and technical circumstances described in the first phase, three other factors created ripe conditions for the entry of American consultants and their practices.

First, in the twenty-eight years between Israel's first elections and 1977, the eligible voter population more than quadrupled due to enormous immigration (from 506,567 in 1949 to 2,236,293 in 1977).[27] Parties that once depended on grassroots organization and direct voter contact became increasingly dependent on the new mass media of television to reach them.

A second structural change was the 1979 legislation separating mayoral elections from local council elections. Mayors now ran separately from their lists, placing a new focus on the candidate-centered campaign. This contributed to an increasingly personalized campaign style set by Menachem Begin's campaign two years earlier.

The last factor is Israel's transition from a socialist to a market orientation. Up until the 1970s the biggest difference between the two countries was America's hallmark capitalist identity and Israel's traditionally socialist orientation. Labor's downfall triggered the beginning of its decline. The rise of capitalism slowly began to erode social conformism and group identities, and individualism began to grow out of an increasingly thriving consumer culture. Traditional ideologies and political loyalties gave way to fragmentation and deep social chasms. The major social institutions were progressively de-linked from the parties. Smaller group identities led to political interest voting; a civic-society approach took hold that was much less dependent on parties.[28]

Starting from its pre-state days, Israel has had an extraordinarily close relationship with the US due to America's unwavering political and financial support over the years. American culture holds a special place of envy and almost fetishistic admiration in the Israeli mind. These changes only increased the cultural affinity among the two nations.

In the period between 1973 and 1981, television became entrenched in campaigns and professional production companies were hired. Starting in 1977, major efforts and financing were put into television campaigning, which went from primitive to "professionalized and effective."[29]

Unlike 1969, television was now a core part of campaigning, and unlike 1973, sentiments—and budgets—were open to harnessing its full power.

Negative advertising became more prominent during this period as well—starting in 1973, mainly from Likud, where the campaign was assessed as having projected image at the expense of substance.[30] The trend toward negative ads gathered momentum in 1977.[31] The negative ads seemed to have begun in earnest on television, but carried over into print advertising.

By 1977 campaign advertising also took on what was considered an American tone: television spots became shorter and catchier, with music and jingles involved. This tone led some to view 1977 as a watershed marking a new era not only in politics but also in the general nature of campaigning in Israel.[32] At this time, the thirty-second television spot was considered even in the US the "most controversial" aspect of electronic communication;[33] thus American aspects of Israeli campaign developments appeared quite early—if they did not quite pre-date American consultants, it seems unlikely that they were a direct result of their influence, which began in earnest only in 1977.

Other characteristics often credited to Americanization were evident in 1977. The Likud placed enormous focus on the personality of its candidate, party leader Menachem Begin. Strategists spent considerable effort creating and filming many different facets of his "image": without his signature tie, younger than his years, a family man, a respectable figure. Alex Anski, an actor and production consultant to the campaign, concluded that "Menachem Begin was the most attractive electoral asset the party had."[34] Print ads too, often focused exclusively on the personal figure of Begin and directly attacked his rival, Shimon Peres.[35]

Many of these changes are attributed to local influences. Israeli professionals from outside politics were increasingly involved throughout the 1970s and quickly learned the transferability of their services; both Anski and the Dahaf advertising agencies worked for Labor in 1973, prior to working with Likud in 1977.[36] Local pollsters from advertising agencies and universities were hired to study the electoral market prior to the hiring of American pollsters. Some politicians were keenly aware of the need for outside professional consultants, in part to prove their own seriousness to the voters. Future president Ezer Weizman of the Likud, who ran the 1977 campaign, said:

> This is going to be a very tough and very serious election dealing with the most important things . . . I am going to recruit the best people in the country to help and advise. If we don't find those people within, we'll go out to the market . . .[37]

Anski reports that Weizman gave Eliezer Zorabin, a commercial advertising chief, total license over the daily communications, and often shifted strategy meetings to Dahaf offices rather than party headquarters. He told his staff: "They're professionals—and with all due respect, we're just amateurs."[38] With an almost Machiavellian tone, Anski reports Weizman saying:

> Let Eliezer sell and he'll sell you a car without an engine. That's his profession . . . [his people] don't care about platform-shmatform. If the platform brings votes, they'll use it. If not—they won't! . . . They can't afford to lose . . . it's their income and the measure of their professionalism . . . Eliezer is capable of doing tricks—I don't say tricks are bad, but to use tricks you need to know when and to be sure they will help. . . .[39]

Still, some felt that the influence was mainly style over substance.[40] Yet the style was radically different, and Caspi himself stated that the Zorabin–Weizman chemistry led to "far-reaching changes in campaigning methods" which became "meager in content but rich in 'easily-digestible' slogans . . ."[41] Anski reports that Zorabin pushed the introduction of debates, precisely because he knew that Israeli audiences would associate them with the prestige of American elections.[42]

Toward the end of this phase, the personalization of elections would take another leap forward. In 1992 Yitzhak Rabin introduced primaries for candidate selection to the Labor list, and Likud followed suit in 1996. With the two largest parties holding personal primaries, there was now far greater attention to the primary campaigns of individual candidates—further focusing attention on personalities rather than parties.

Early American Presence

In 1977 David Garth was involved in the Likud's campaign. Little is known about his influence; by most accounts it was minimal but probably still stronger than that of Sarid's 1969 American consultant. Many of the changes mentioned—increasing negative advertising, shorter ads and stronger focus on personality—were more prominent in the Likud's campaign, where he was involved.[43] However, some of these characteristics, such as negative advertising, had begun already in 1973 within the Likud, followed by Labor in 1977; perhaps only natural considering it was the first election when Labor finally felt the pressure of losing power.

In 1981 both the major parties hired American consultants for their campaigns and this is considered the first election in which they played a significant role. David Garth worked with the Likud again, bringing with him two then less-known pollsters from New York mayor Edward Koch's campaign: Mark Penn and Douglas Schoen. David Sawyer, a Democratic consultant who would eventually be described as a pioneer of political consulting, and one of the first Americans to export the trade, served as a consultant to the Labor Party. He was also known to use polls as a main tool for analyzing the electorate.[44] By some accounts, he was not particularly influential on the 1981 campaign.[45]

Mark Penn and Douglas Schoen claim to have introduced more concrete innovations. Their new technique of overnight polling, which they had developed during Koch's mayoral campaign, was "unheard of" at that time in Israel.[46] In addition, Peter Powell was part of Garth's team and he advised on media production. Powell observes that his own contribution was not extensive and the campaign in general was only partly influenced by the American team.[47]

By contrast, Schoen describes extensive contact with incumbent Prime Minister Begin. He recounts how over the course of the campaign, certain figures such as Ariel Sharon came to understand how polls could be used for strategic decision making; Sharon, he says, used the polls to push Begin to promise to make him defense minister if re-elected.[48] While Schoen stops short of taking credit for Begin's narrow victory that year, he believes that their involvement "helped provide one of the first examples of how American consultants could aid foreign campaigns."[49]

The American presence continued unbroken through the 1980s. Schoen and Penn were hired again in 1984 by Ezer Weizman as part of his efforts to form a new centrist party.[50] But most remained mainly behind the scenes and drew little attention.

Israeli Reactions to American Presence

Israeli politicians were reluctant to admit the Americans' influence,[51] and the political figures on the campaign expressed ongoing suspicion of their effectiveness. Nevertheless, in the years to follow, they hired them regularly and rapidly adopted their methods.

As early as 1981, there was "no question that the slickness of American-style advertising has arrived in Israel." Likud (and some of the other parties) ran ads with strong emotional content. Menachem Begin again leveraged his "emotional oratory"; Labor's ads were less so.[52] The highly personal tone employed by Begin led Peres to criticize him for "Beginization" of the elections, which was a "danger to democracy," and for creating a "cult of personality."[53]

The media immediately identified a good story and began to cover the American involvement.[54] The concept of the press covering the consultants themselves in addition to (or possibly at the expense of) the issues was noticed: at least one scholar railed against what he perceived as degradation of politics through sensationalization of its inner workings.[55] Still the notion of covering the campaign itself gathered strength and by the mid-1990s, campaign gossip became a central feature of press coverage.[56]

While Judith N. Elizur concludes that during this period (covering the 1981 and 1984 elections), the influence of the foreign consultants was limited mainly to "tactics and execution," still, by this time the television campaigns (particularly the Likud's) reflected American stylistic influence.[57] This refers to the reliance on "appearance, sound-bites, slogans and image and its 'horse-race' aspects."[58] In addition, polls were being used increasingly for strategic purposes and targeting in general was becoming a central part of campaign strategy.[59] Likud hired a polling firm to work closely with its advertising consultants. The result of the increasingly sophisticated targeting and polling, says Jonathan Mendilow, was decreasingly sophisticated messages. He believes that in 1981 and 1984, the messages became largely indistinguishable; indeed in 1984 the elections were deadlocked, leading to a coalition government and an entrenched two-party system.

By this same time, a small cadre of home-grown Israeli political consultants had established themselves—mainly advertising professionals who began developing an expertise in political campaigning. Some would go on in later decades to become kingmakers: David Fogel, Arieh Rotenberg, Eliezer Zorabin and the now-legendary Reuven Adler.

Political campaigns continued developing their own spectacle-like character, with parties commonly employing entertainment groups and celebrities to appear on their behalf; commentators continued to complain of increasingly shallow, commercial and emotional aspects.[60]

During the 1992 elections Labor ran and won its most personalized campaign yet, with a strategy focused almost exclusively on its leader Yitzhak Rabin, under the slogan "Israel is waiting for Rabin." The Likud, lacking a charismatic candidate of their own, ran a personal negative campaign, describing Rabin as someone who could not be trusted to deal with the pressure of the office, based on his nervous breakdown at the eve of the Six-Day War, when he served as commander in chief, and suggesting he had a drinking problem.

In sum, the period from 1977 to 1992 saw the most significant changes in the way elections are run in Israel. The advertising style, personalization, emotional and negative tone associated with American campaigns, together with the professionalization through the use of polls, focus groups, tailored messages and get-out-the-vote efforts were all American-style campaign innovations. Yet they were clearly driven as much by organic, endogenous modernization, local political and structural developments and Americanization alike, and it is virtually impossible to think of the electoral transformation in Israel without the interaction between them.

The Third Wave of American Involvement: 1996–Present

The 1996 elections saw the next real leap in explicit importation and influence of American practices, and personalities.

It is notoriously difficult to determine whether a campaign can take credit for electoral victory. But Benjamin Netanyahu's defeat of Shimon Peres in 1996 was a definite coup. Riding the wave of national sympathy following the trauma of the Rabin assassination in 1995, Peres was sure enough of his position to call early elections, as polls consistently showed him leading Netanyahu.[61] Only after the Israeli public had famously "gone to bed," were the final counts tallied showing a razor-thin margin favoring Netanyahu.

The election took place following the third major structural change in the Israeli voting system since the establishment of the state: the introduction of direct elections for Prime Minister. Starting in 1996, voters cast two ballots on election day, one for their party and one for Prime

Minister.[62] This cemented the campaign focus on the candidates' personality aspects, taking focus away from both parties and issues in favor of "real-time" considerations. Both major parties directed the better part of their resources towards the candidate.[63] Instead of issues, most believe that Netanyahu won his campaign on the basis of emotional, largely fear-based appeals related to terrorism,[64] and a very personality-centered campaign.

In the increasingly personalized system, Shimon Peres attempted to maintain a party-centered campaign, both in terms of its management (by party member Haim Ramon) and its message. Meanwhile, Netanyahu ran wholeheartedly on his personality, winning his nomination in a personal party primary, and ignoring the party in the campaign.[65]

In a high-profile move that was to change the way American consultants were viewed in Israeli politics, Netanyahu brought in American campaign guru Arthur Finkelstein (one of his many conservative clients was Jesse Helms of North Carolina). Already seen as mimicking American styles, Netanyahu became the quintessential "American" candidate, replete with a celebrity campaign advisor.

The strategy focused on comparing Netanyahu with Peres, highlighting Netenyahu's relative youth and his modern, "slick," global image. The effect was that Netanyahu's campaign added a past future dimension to the personality contest.

This focus on personality probably reflected an evolving American sense of individualism, materialism and consumerism now growing in Israel. Newer was inherently better, in a country eager to shed its shabby socialist image.

Some still resisted acknowledging the American influence, or its efficacy. Gadi Wolfsfeld said that since Israel is so literate, television was unlikely to influence voters much: "Unlike in America, spin doctors don't make a difference . . . here it's the events, and everything else is astrology."[66]

Although 1999 would later be seen as the classic American consultant inter-party tête-à-tête, in fact Shimon Peres had American consultants on his campaign in 1996 as well. Mark Penn and Douglas Schoen returned to Israel for the first time since their brief stint with Ezer Weizman in the 1980s. They were hired to work with Rabin in 1995; following the assassination they continued polling for Peres. But there was a sharp contrast in the relationship between Netanyahu and Finkelstein, and the one between Peres and his Americans. Although they conducted extensive polling and advising, Schoen recalls fighting an uphill battle with Peres to have their advice taken seriously.

Peres apparently believed in their strategy, but, says Schoen, was unable to convince key Israeli advisors such as campaign manager Haim Ramon to do the same. In a poignant example of the internal strife that foreigners can sometimes cause in such charged settings, Schoen recounts giving a detailed strategic presentation, after which Peres said, " 'We should do everything Schoen is saying." He then turned to Ramon and said, "But, I know you're not going to do it." Ramon shook his head and said, "That's right."[67]

The presence of Penn and Schoen had another unusual impact. Because at the time they were working for US President Bill Clinton, who openly supported Peres, they sometimes acted as a liaison between them. Schoen says that Peres tried to leverage his relationship with the wildly popular Clinton.

Penn and Schoen's presence remained discreet, and the colorful figure of Arthur Finkelstein became the star of the 1996 election. The campaign at first tried to hide his presence, fearing a backlash against over-American influence. But once the story came out, the Israeli press had a "field day."[68] This opened the door to an era of increasing media attention to American consultants.

Costas Panagopoulos argues that media attention to consultants can have important implications, such as increased public awareness of what happens behind the scenes, raising the profile of the profession and creating further demand for such services.[69] Barnett and Goldstein make the point that campaigns often recognize that the presence of a top-level consultant may earn them political capital in itself. Professional consultants may bring a level of credibility, especially given Israel's unfettered passion for America.

Although Peres lost in 1996, the American involvement with Labor seems to have turned a corner. Some of the Israeli politicians from the 1996 campaign, including Haim Ramon, would work for Ehud Barak three years later, where there was a general celebratory welcome for the three celebrity consultants. It is possible that they now accepted, and actively sought, the psychological boost of American professional legitimacy for the new candidate.[70]

In 1999 the American presence took on a new tone. The consultants were a visible and vital part of both campaigns of the two major parties. Dan Nimmo predicted in 1970 that in the future "campaigns may no longer be battles between candidates but between titans of the campaign industry working on behalf of those personalities."[71] And indeed, some viewed the campaign as a face-off between the two high-profile American rivals: controversial James Carville and the flamboyant Arthur Finkelstein. In addition to Carville, the Labor party hired Robert Shrum and Stanley Greenberg in what became affectionately known as the "dream team." This campaign would seem to have been the ultimate manifestation of Nimmo's vision of Americanization, as members of this team had been involved in the highly successful campaigns of Tony Blair in Great Britain and Gerhard Schröder in Germany.

Cultural affinity played an important role. The three Labor consultants were virtually unknown in Israel prior to 1999. But they were associated with Bill Clinton's heady victory in the 1992 American presidential elections. His consultants therefore brought an independent set of emotional associations that probably included young, strong, future-oriented and Israel-supportive, to the largely untested candidacy of Ehud Barak.

The 1999 elections can even be seen as supersaturated by Americans. Ehud Barak hired several different "streams" of pollsters, and among them Douglas Schoen, although (to Schoen's chagrin) they were not part of the official campaign. Mark Mellman, another high-level American consultant and pollster associated with Democratic politics in the US, was reported to be working for Meimad, a small, moderate Orthodox party that joined with Labor (along with Gesher) to form One Israel.[72]

By this time the American presence was fully open and drew increasing media attention. A political satire show (often significantly influential in Israel) showed the candidates debating each other while American consultants whispered in their ears.[73]

Yet in the next two elections 2001 and 2003, the American consultants were not a top story. Although 2001 was another "face-off," with Finkelstein again working for Netanyahu and Greenberg and Shrum working again for Barak, there was little new about it this time. The elections were held under the pall of the rapidly escalating al-Aqsa Intifada, which kept the tone fearful and depressed, rather than splashy or gossipy. As an unprecedented special election for Prime Minister only, some voters learned the virtues of tuning out; turnout plunged to a record low and the television ratings for the ads were at a similar nadir—only 23% on the first night, and steadily declining rating throughout the campaign,[74] although those involved in the campaign observed ruefully that the ads were particularly polished and professional.

In 2003 Ariel Sharon as head of Likud beat the diminutive former mayor of Haifa Amram Mitzna, who did not employ American consultants, in a victory largely attributed to the man who was by this time perceived as Israel's own political svengali, Reuven Adler. While Adler's political campaign experience was limited, he had been Sharon's friend and personal advisor for over two decades and Sharon trusted him immensely.[75]

By 2006, Israelis associated with the campaign for Kadima and Prime Minister Ehud Olmert, suggested that American consultants were hardly necessary anymore, because their techniques had been thoroughly internalized. This can be seen as the final triumph of Americanization.[76] Yet clearly the expertise Americans bring, perhaps simply from the great volume of campaigns they run, was still sought by others in 2006. Finkelstein shifted his services to the hard-line former Soviet immigrant Avigdor Lieberman's party. With the highly catchy campaign slogan "Nyet, nyet, Da!," for which Finkelstein's team takes credit,[77] the party moved from four seats in the outgoing Knesset to eleven in the 2006 elections. Penn and Schoen had some minimal contact with Ehud Olmert, so quietly that journalists never knew.

Amir Peretz, the Labor candidate whose initial boost following his upset victory in the primaries was fast waning, returned to the now-traditional Labor consultant Stanley Greenberg (without the rest of the 1999 "dream team"). The Peretz story highlights what seems to have become a central role of American consultants. In an early and significant blunder, he delivered a speech in embarrassingly poor, broken English, raising fears that he was not capable either as a national or international leader. Just weeks later, Greenberg's services were requested, largely at the urging of internal party political figures and despite Peretz' natural suspicion of outsiders. The political team hoped that Greenberg's presence would be viewed as a sign of professionalism and seriousness on the part of the flagging campaign. A press conference was called to announce his involvement as pollster, and his partner's role as general campaign advisor. Media commentators immediately caught this spirit: "Should Peretz be able to acquire Greenberg's services, he would be adding a definite asset to his team."[78]

It thus appeared that after the English blunder and a flurry of rumors that made his team look frivolous, the campaign sought outside legitimization. And even if their tactics had been internalized over three-odd decades of professional involvement, apparently the notion that Americans bode well for the campaign turns the consultants into a symbol in themselves.

Conclusions

In summary, American consulting in Israel over the years has followed a progressive trajectory: in the "first wave," from 1969 to 1977 elections, their presence was minimal, not visible, and considered insignificant. At the same time political, social and technology changes led to the initial campaign modernization processes from within Israel. During the "second wave," from 1977 to 1996, the cultural and national affinity for the US was conducive to their more active and influential presence, although the insider/outsider dynamic still kept their roles somewhat circumscribed and invisible to the general public.

During this time Israel's own social and electoral processes changed in ways that were conducive to American-style changes in campaigns. The rise of television, the declining importance of the large parties, and the shift to a market-oriented culture were the major hallmarks of this phase. They gave rise to a professional group of mass media and marketing experts whose skills were rapidly sought in the political realm. These changes were endogenous, but as they led to more American-style campaigns, it was logical that Israelis would seek guidance from the experts.

The 1990s brought further personalization of elections due to several changes within the electoral system (mainly party primaries in the two large parties and personal elections for Prime Minister), as well as the general waning of the large parties. This also made the political environment conducive to American techniques which themselves had evolved to a different level. Thus 1996 saw a new, far more public type of involvement in this "third wave" of American consultants, which probably some would view more in terms of a barbarian invasion.[79] In this wave, American consultants became part of the story themselves, bringing attention and legitimacy to a campaign.

With the third phase, American consultants became not just general advice-givers but actually executed work at all levels of the campaign. The trend of deep, hands-on decision-making and execution of campaign work continued through the last elections in 2006. The partial retreat in 2003 and 2006 could be either an aberration, or could actually indicate increasing internalization of American campaign lessons, making their presence less vital.

Because the conditions that created a desire or need for American consultants preceded their involvement, we do not view this as a unidirectional Americanization of campaigns. Rather, there has been an interplay of forces from inside and outside of Israel; alongside the interplay between modernization (technological, structural, institutional) and the cultural, consumer and market-driven aspects of Americanization.

Implications

The weakening of the parties across the globe, together with the rise of the individual candidate and the arrival of the mass media have professionalized campaigns in many countries. Campaigns have transformed from amateur, local affairs directed at party partisans and loyalists, to permanent marketing campaigns directed at the general electorate.[80]

Many[81] see pernicious implications of the involvement of American consultants. Mark P. Petracca thinks they contribute to less direct civic political participation. The harshest criticism is that consultants have hijacked the democratic process from the parties and have replaced it with a spectator sport,[82] leading to voter alienation and possibly lower turnout. Israeli observers too link the Americanized campaign to consumerism and populism;[83] while in general some note the increasingly manipulative aspect of campaigns.[84]

In Israel, voter turnout dropped sharply starting in 2001. But if linked to campaigns, the drop might have been expected earlier, as the American styles are now several decades old. It is likely that Israeli voters are alienated by other factors too: the salience of government corruption, despair over the peace process, disillusionment with specific politicians, and the birth of a new cohort that feels less affinity to parties in particular and politics in general.

When it comes to Americanization, it seems that a fairly normative, often one-sided and usually negative view prevails. To balance this impression, we suggest that there may be some potentially constructive aspects related to the Americanized techniques as well, regardless of who introduced them.

One such argument is that the stronger focus on personality may have led to a greater sense of accountability of politicians to voters. The party primaries, for example, could lead to greater accountability among individual list candidates.[85]

It could be that the American presence and techniques have moved Israel to the front line of modern campaigning. This is important because Israel is already in the front line of other technological developments, such as having one of the highest rates of mobile phones per capita in the world and a vibrant Internet culture—especially among young people who are significantly less likely to vote. Perhaps Israel's facility with modern campaign techniques and its symbiosis with the American example will help it harness these new tools to help engage this group. Indeed, in the US, consultants have also been seen as the opposite of their Machiavellian image. Some view them as the ones who filled the void left by the declining parties, helping candidates, and eventually the parties, re-energize campaigns and make them vital.[86]

Some might argue that prior to Americanization, consumerism and modernization, Israel's electoral system was healthier. But this indicates a longing for a mythical past, when many more Israelis cast their vote based on habit and uncritical loyalties, rather than weighing or critiquing agendas. Now candidates and parties must earn their votes. The uphill battle they face for attention can be attributed to many factors, but ought not to be reduced solely to the impact of consultants. To do so seems to evade the partial responsibility of politicians themselves for alienating voters through poor performance. Consultants may be one of the factors still able to bring voters back because, for better or for worse, it is their job to be connected to regular people and their language of communication. David A. Dulio writes:

Consultants have helped parties become more efficient and effective in assisting candidates win elections, they help candidates fight through an already cluttered field of communications by focusing their message on things potential voters care about, and they are in a position to help voters by sharpening the debate between two candidates.[87]

Will the next phase be a new "wave" of Americanization, or a global convergence of post-modern ideas flitting in multiple directions, through multiple information channels? Fortunately or not, Israelis won't have to wait too long to find out, since they rarely have the patience to wait for the official election day to run elections. There are some things even Americans can't change.

Notes

1 The names of the authors appear in alphabetical order. This chapter is in every way a collaborative enterprise.
2 Fritz Plasser, "American Campaign Techniques Worldwide," *Harvard International Journal of Press/Politics* 5 (4) (September 2000): 33–54.
3 Daniel M. Shea and Michael J. Burton, *Campaign Craft: The Strategies, Tactics, and Art of Political Campaign Management* (Westport, CT: Praeger, 2001).
4 Rachel Gibson and Andrea Römmele, "Changing Campaign Communications: A Party-Centered Theory of Professionalized Campaigning," *Harvard International Journal of Press/Politics* 6 (4) (January 2001): 31–43. James A. Thurber and Candice J. Nelson, eds, *Campaigns and Elections American Style* (Boulder, CO: Westview Press, 1995); Karen S. Johnson-Cartee and Gary A. Copeland, *Inside Political Campaigns: Theory and Practice* (Westport, CT: Praeger, 1997); Frank I. Luntz, *Candidates, Consultants, and Campaigns: The Style and Substance of American Electioneering* (New York: Basil Blackwell, 1988); David A. Dulio, *For Better or Worse? How Political Consultants are Changing Elections in the United States*, (Albany N.Y.: State University of New York Press, 2004). While not all of these authors use the term "Americanization," those who do not—such as Luntz, Shea and Johnson-Cartee and Copeland focus exclusively on the new style of campaign in America, and enumerate these factors exclusively within the American context.
5 Margaret Scammell, "The Wisdom of the War Room: U.S. Campaigning Winning Elections," research paper R-17, Harvard University: The Joan Shorenstein Center on the Press, Politics and Public Policy, 4.
6 David Swanson and Paolo Mancini, "Introduction," in *Politics, Media and Modern Democracy: An International Study of Innovations in Electoral Campaigning and their Consequences*, ed. David Swanson and Paolo Mancini (Westport, CT: Praeger, 1996).
7 Michael Barnett and Kenneth Goldstein, "Consultants Abroad: American Political Consultants And the Transformation of Democracy," paper presented at the Annual Meeting of the American Political Science Association, Boston: MA, August 29–September 1, 2002.
8 Shaun Bowler and David M. Farrell "The Internationalization of Campaign Consultancy," in *Campaign Warriors: Political Consultants in Elections*, ed. James A. Thurber and Candice J. Nelson (Washington D.C.: Brookings Institution, 2000); Fritz Plasser, "American Campaign Techniques Worldwide," *Harvard International Journal of Press/Politics* 5 (4) (September 2000): 36.
9 Plasser, "American Campaign Techniques Worldwide," 35.
10 Ibid., 34.
11 Jay G. Blumler, Dennis Kavanagh and T.J. Nossiter, "Modern Communications Versus Traditional Politics in Britain: Unstable Marriage of Convenience," in *Politics, Media and Modern Democracy: An International Study of Innovations in Electoral Campaigning and their Consequences*, ed. David Swanson and Paolo Mancini (Westport, CT: Praeger, 1996), 59.
12 Camille Elebash, "The Americanization of British Political Communications," *Journal of Advertising* 13 (3) (Fall 1984): 50–9; Plasser, "American Campaign Techniques Worldwide," 50. For an alternative perspective that views political professionalization as part of a greater process of "global economic actors, namely the translational corporate executive class, [that has] largely expropriated the political process," see Gerald Sussman and Lawrence Galizio, "The Global Reproduction of American Politics," *Political Communication* 20 (3) (2003): 309–28, 310.
13 Ralph Negrine et al., "Political Communication in the Era of Professionalisation," in *The Professionalisation of Political Communication*, ed. Ralph Negrine et al., (Chicago, IL: University of Chicago Press,

2007), 9–28; Paolo Mancini, "New Frontiers in Political Professionalism," *Political Communication* 16 (3) (July 1999): 231–45; Ralph Negrine and Stylianos Papathanassopoulos, "The 'Americanization' of Political Communication: A Critique," *Harvard International Journal of Press/Politics* 1 (2) (March 1996): 45–62.

14 Plasser, "American Campaign Techniques Worldwide," 34.

15 Richard Gunther and Anthony Mughan, *Democracy and the Media: A Comparative Perspective* (New York: Cambridge University Press, 2000); Pippa Norris, *A Virtuous Circle: Political Communication in Post-industrial Societies* (New York: Cambridge University Press, 2000); David Swanson and Paolo Mancini, "Patterns of Modern Electoral Campaigning and Their Consequences," in *Politics, Media and Modern Democracy: An International Study of Innovations in Electoral Campaigning and their Consequences*, ed. David Swanson and Paolo Mancini (Westport, CT: Praeger, 1996), 247–96; Negrine and Papathanas-sopoulos, "The 'Americanization' of Political Communication," 45–62.

16 David M. Farrell, "Campaign Strategies and Tactics," in *Comparing Democracies: Elections and Voting in Global Perspective*, ed. Lawrence LeDuc, Richard G. Niemi and Pippa Norris (Thousand Oaks, CA: Sage Publications, 1996), 160–83; Ralph Negrine et al., *The Professionalisation of Political Communication* (Chicago, IL: University of Chicago Press, 2007), 11–12; Israel Waismel-Manor, "Spinning Lessons: The Professionalization of Campaign Consultancy," PhD dissertation, Cornell University, 2005.

17 Joel Myron Aronoff, "The 'Americanization' of Israeli Politics: Political and Cultural Change," *Israel Studies* 5 (1) (Spring 2000): 92–127.

18 Dan Caspi, "American-style Electioneering in Israel: Americanisation versus Modernization," in *Politics, Media and Modern Democracy: An International Study of Innovations in Electoral Campaigning and their Consequences*, ed. David Swanson and Paolo Mancini (Westport, CT: Praeger, 1996), 173–92.

19 Yonatan Shapira, *Society Under Politicians' Power* (Tel-Aviv: Hapoalim Library, 1996). (In Hebrew.)

20 Michael Gurevitch, "Television in the Electoral Campaign: Its Audience and Function," in *The Elections in Israel: 1969*, ed. Alan Arian (Jerusalem: Academic Press, 1972), 220–37.

21 Akiva Cohen, "Radio vs. TV: The Effect of the Medium," *Journal of Communications* (Spring 1976): 26–35.

22 Gurevitch, "Television in the Electoral Campaign," 220–37.

23 Dan Caspi, "Electoral Rhetoric and Political Polarization: The Begin–Peres Debates," *European Journal of Communications* 1 (4) (December 1986): 449; Yoram Peri, *Telepopulism: Media and Politics in Israel* (Stanford, CA: Stanford University Press, 2004).

24 Yossi Sarid, telephone interview, October 10, 2007. When this consultant predicted that they would win 72 of the 120 Knesset seats Sarid threw him out. Labor eventually won only 56 seats. Sarid dismissed him so early in the campaign, that in a conversation nearly forty years later, he could not even recall his name.

25 Rachel Gibson and Andrea Römmele, "Changing Campaign Communications: A Party-centered Theory of Professionalized Campaigning," *Harvard Journal of International Press/Politics* 6(4) (January 2001): 33.

26 Some have argued that even during this period the story is one of Americanization, a "mutual fertiliza-tion between cultures" (Caspi, "Electoral Rhetoric and Political Polarization," 175). However, we found no evidence in their work or any other that supports this argument prior to 1977.

27 Knesset website, http://www.knesset.gov.il/description/eng/eng_mimshal_res.htm.

28 Yael Yishai, "Bringing Society Back In: Post-cartel Parties in Israel," *Party Politics* 7 (6) (November 2001): 667.

29 Dan Caspi and Chaim Eyal, "Professionalization Trends in Israeli Election Propaganda: 1973–1981," in *Elections in Israel, 1981*, ed. Asher Arian (Tel Aviv: Ramot, 1983).

30 Jonathan Mendilow, "Public Campaign Funding and Party System Change: The Israeli Experience," *Israel Studies Forum* 19 (Fall 2003): 115–23.

31 Judith Elizur and Elihu Katz, "The Media in the Elections of 1977," in *Israel at the Polls: The Knesset Election of 1977*, ed. Howard R. Penniman (Washington, D.C.: American Enterprise Institute for Public Policy Research, 1979), 227–54.

32 Caspi, "American-style Electioneering in Israel," 181.

33 Joe Napolitan, "Media Costs and Effects in Political Campaigns," *Annals of the American Academy of Political Science* 427 (1) (September 1976): 114–24.

34 Alex Anski, *The Selling of the Likud* (Tel-Aviv: Zmora, Bitan and Modan, 1978). (In Hebrew.)

35 "Begin's Political Campaign Ad," *Maariv*, September 5, 1977.

36 Caspi, "American-style Electioneering in Israel."

37 Anski, *The Selling of the Likud*, 30 (authors' translation).

38 Ibid., 31.

39 Ibid., 32.

40 Caspi, "American-style Electioneering in Israel," 189; Caspi and Eyal, "Professionalization Trends in Israeli Election Propaganda."

41 Caspi, "American-style Electioneering in Israel," 447–62.

42 Anski, *The Selling of the Likud*, 143.

43 Jonathan Mendilow, "Party Clustering in Multi-Party Systems: The Example of Israel 1965–1981," *American Journal of Political Science* 27 (1) (February 1983): 64–85.

44 Cited in his *New York Times* obituary, following his death in 1995. David Binder, "David H. Sawyer Dies at 59; Innovator in Political Strategy" *New York Times*, July 4, 1995.

45 Adam Nagourney, "Sound Bites Over Jerusalem," *New York Times*, April 25, 1999.

46 Douglas Schoen, *The Power of the Vote: Electing Presidents, Overthrowing Dictators, and Promoting Democracy Around the World* (New York: HarperCollins, 2007).

47 Peter Powell, telephone interview, October 9, 2007.

48 Schoen, *The Power of the Vote*.

49 Ibid.

50 Ibid.

51 David K. Shipler, "Campaign Ads Entertain Nightly," *New York Times*, June 28, 1981.

52 Ibid.

53 Tzvi Marom, "Begin is Responsible for Inciting," *Haaretz*, June 18, 1981. (In Hebrew.)

54 Judith N. Elizur, "The Role of the Media in the 1981 Knesset Elections," in *Israel at the Polls: The Knesset Elections of 1981*, ed. Howard R. Penniman and Daniel J. Elazar (Bloomington, IN: American Enterprise Institute and Indiana University Press, 1986), 206.

55 Ya'akov Tamir, "Advertisers in the Election Headquarters—Myth Versus Fact," *Migvan* (July 1981): 39–41 (In Hebrew.)

56 Akiva Cohen and Gadi Wolfsfeld, "Overcoming Adversity and Diversity: The Utility of Television in Israel," in *Political Advertising in Western Democracies: Parties and Candidates on Television*, ed. Lynda Lee Kaid and Christina Holtz-Bacha (Thousand Oaks, CA: Sage, 1995), 109–23.

57 Caspi, "American-style Electioneering in Israel."

58 Galit Marmor-Lavie and Gabriel Weimann, "Measuring Emotional Appeals in Israeli Election Campaigns," *International Journal of Public Opinion Research* 18 (3) (Autumn 2006): 318–39.

59 Mendilow, "Party Clustering in Multi-party Systems"; B. Tau and R. Navo, "An Adman in the Electoral Pan," *Otot* (1981): 12–23 (In Hebrew.)

60 Marmor-Lavie and Weimann, "Measuring Emotional Appeals in Israeli Election Campaigns."

61 Schoen notes that toward the beginning of the campaign period, Peres was routinely shown to be leading Netanyahu by a weighty seventeen–eighteen-point margin—a gap that would be considered very difficult to surmount during the space of a typical election campaign.

62 The previous single ticket ballot was reinstated in 2003.

63 Efraim Torgovnik, "Strategies under a New Electoral System: The Labor Party in the 1996 Elections," *Party Politics* 6 (1) (January 2000): 95–106.

64 Marmor-Lavie and Weimann, "Measuring Emotional Appeals in Israeli Election Campaigns."

65 Torgovnik, "Strategies under a New Electoral System." For a more detailed discussion see Peri, *Telepopulism*.

66 Joseph Berger, "He Had Pataki's Ear, Now It's Netanyahu's," *New York Times*, May 26, 1996.

67 Schoen, *The Power of the Vote*.

68 Ibid.

69 Costas Panagopoulos, "Political Consultants, Campaign Professionalization and Media Attention," *PS: Political Science and Politics* 39 (October 2006): 867–9.

70 Lee Hockstader, " 'Cajun Ragin' in a New Home: James Carville Brings American-style Politics to Israel," *Washington Post*, April 7, 1999.

71 Dan D. Nimmo, *The Political Persuaders* (Englewood Cliffs, N.J.: Prentice Hall, 1970), 50.

72 Matthew Dorf, "Israeli Campaign in the Hands of America's Top Spin Doctors," Jewish Telegraphic Agency, http://www.jewishsf.com/comtent/2/module/displaystory/story_id/11139/edition_id/213/formt/html/displaystory.html.

73 Ibid.

74 Gabriel Weimann and Gadi Wolfsfeld, "The 2001 Elections: The Election Propaganda that Made No Difference," in *The Elections in Israel 2001*, ed. Asher Arian and Michal Shamir (Jerusalem: The Israel Democracy Institute, 2002), 109.

75 Shalom Yerushalmi, "Adler Force," *Maariv*, January 19, 2001, http://www.nrg.co.il/online/archive/ART/106/569.html.

76 Brian Goldsmith, "Made in America: Israeli Politics and American Consultants," The New Republic Online, June 1, 2006, http://www.tnr.com/doc.mhtml?i=w060529&s=goldsmith060106.

77 George Birnbaum, telephone interview, November 15, 2007. George Birnbaum was part of Arthur Finkelstein's team that provided consulting, polling and strategic advising to Lieberman's campaign in 2006.

78 Attila Somfalvy, "Peretz to Meet with American Poll Guru" *YNet*, December 12, 2005. (In Hebrew.)

79 See for example, the fairly alarmist approach to Americanization in general in Uri Ram, "Citizens, Consumers and Believers: The Israeli Public Sphere between Capitalism and Fundamentalism," *Israel Studies* 3 (1) (Spring 1998): 24–44, http://muse.jhu.edu/journals/israel_studies/v003/3.1ram.html.

80 David M. Farrell, Robin Kolodny and Stephen Medvic, "Parties and Campaign Professionals in a Digital Age: Political Consultants in the United States and their Counterparts Overseas," *Harvard International Journal of Press/Politics* 6 (4) (2001): 11–30.

81 Larry J. Sabato, *The Rise of Political Consultants: New Ways of Winning Elections*, (New York: Basic Books, 1981), 7; Barnett and Goldstein, "Consultants Abroad," 25; Mark P. Petracca, "Political Consultants and Democratic Governance," *PS: Science and Politics* 22 (1) (March 1989): 11–14; Farrell, Kolodny and Medvic, "Parties and Campaign Professionals in a Digital Age," 12; Dennis W. Johnson, *No Place for Amateurs: How Political Consultants Are Reshaping American Democracy*, 2nd ed. (New York: Routledge, 2007), xvi.

82 Johnson, *No Place for Amateurs*, 18; Sabato, *The Rise of Political Consultants*.

83 Roni Shahar, *A Leader Made to Measure* (Tel-Aviv: Yediot Ahronot, 2001). (In Hebrew.); Orit Galili, *The Tele-Politicians: New Political Leadership in the West and in Israel* (Tel Aviv: Ramot-University of Tel Aviv, 2004); Yoram Peri, *Telepopulism*; Uri Ram, "Citizens, Consumers and Believers," 24–44.

84 Sam Lehman-Wilzig, "The Media Campaign: The Negative Effects of Positive Campaigning," *Israel Affairs* 4 (1) (Fall 1997): 167–86.

85 Aronoff, "The 'Americanization' of Israeli Politics."

86 Farrell, Kolodny and Medvic, "Parties and Campaign Professionals in a Digital Age," 12.

87 Dulio, *For Better or Worse*.

24

Russia

Electoral Campaigning in a "Managed Democracy"

Derek S. Hutcheson

Introduction

Since the collapse of the Soviet Union in late 1991, both the Russian political system and the political consulting market have evolved substantially. In the second decade of Russian independence, it has become almost impossible to win an election on a non-professional basis. Allied to this has been the increasing role of administrative backing in electoral campaigns, in the gray area between partisan politics and the state. As the value of political office has increased—and, in the Putin era, the numbers of elected political offices have declined—professional and well-resourced campaigns have become more important.

This chapter examines the twin phenomena of the increasing professionalization of the Russian electoral market and the increasing role of administrative resources in election campaigns. The focus is mainly on the Russian Federation, but similar phenomena to those examined can be found—sometimes in more extreme form—in other post-Soviet states.[1]

The Institutional Context

Political campaigning in Russia takes place in the context of what has been termed by some "managed democracy" (*upravlyaemaya demokratiya*), in which there is heavy influence by the political elite on the institutional framework of elections, but open competition exists within prescribed limits. The country has regular multi-candidate elections, extensive electoral legislation and a constitutional separation of executive, legislative and judicial power. Nonetheless, there are frequent criticisms that these boundaries have not been observed,[2] and it can be asked whether the country is simply "façade democracy" where "electoral institutions exist but yield no meaningful contestation for power."[3] Nonetheless, it was not until 2003, ten years after the first post-Soviet contest, that an authority-supported party won a plurality of the vote in a national parliamentary election, and Putin has made frequent pronouncements to the effect that Russian commitment to democracy is absolute.[4] However, he also makes frequent mention of the role that a democratic form of government plays in "investing functions in the state by society,"[5] and it is this more state-centered form of democracy that has embedded itself in the Russian Federation.

The political system in Russia derives from the December 1993 constitution. Institutionally, the president, who is directly elected every four years, is the lynchpin of the political system, and has a wide range of executive functions. The relatively weak Federal Assembly is a bicameral parliament: the 450-seat State Duma is also elected on a four-year cycle, while the upper Federation Council consists of two appointed representatives from each of the (currently eighty-three) subjects of the Federation. The president can dissolve the former if it fails to approve his choice of prime minister three times in a row, and his right to veto legislation requires a two-thirds majority in both chambers to be overturned. The executive functions of the state are undertaken dually by the president and the government, but State Duma deputies are proscribed by section 97.3 of the constitution from holding government office, which has traditionally limited the direct influence of parliamentary parties, and even election results, on the composition of the government.

Russia's "floating" party system has suffered throughout the post-communist period from a lack of institutionalization, with a huge volatility in the menu of parties on offer at successive elections.[6] Only two—the Communist Party of the Russian Federation and the Liberal Democratic Party of Russia—have won party list representation in all five State Duma elections held. Until recently, executive politics were relatively non-partisan, with neither Boris Yeltsin nor Vladimir Putin elected to the presidency on party platforms, and the vast majority of governors standing without party affiliation. Two clear trends have been evident through this volatility, however: programmatic parties (such as the Communist Party of the Russian Federation and the liberal Yabloko Party) have gradually imploded, and relatively ideology-free "virtual" parties, based on the twin pillars of establishment support and marketing-based campaigning, have come to the fore and been affiliated to by many of the ruling elite.

Unlike traditional dominant parties of Europe, which have first had to gain elected office from a position of opposition, Russian "parties of power" (which have differed in name from election to election) have been political structures of the entrenched establishment formed from within in an attempt to consolidate and legitimize its rule through a party façade.[7] As Table 24.1 shows, this has in recent years been achieved with some success.

In addition to their *post hoc* formation by already incumbent establishment, the "parties of power" have been pragmatic rather than dogmatic, and their identity has been defined mainly through market-oriented, media-driven television campaigns to position themselves within gaps in the electoral market (hence the Sarah Oates' description of them as "broadcast parties").[8] The "virtual" party structures have been given a public face through the presence of prominent national politicians, regional governors and numerous middle-ranking state officials to the party's regional leadership organs. This blurs the distinction between party and state organs and gives a ready structure for the recruitment of a large but loosely attached membership.[9] Vladimir Putin himself admitted when heading the party's list (as a non-party member!) in the 2007 State Duma election that United Russia "doesn't yet have stable ideological principles," but had the advantage of being "close to power" and a reliable source of support in the legislature for his policies.[10]

The Russian Political Market

The number of elections taking place in Russia has reduced in recent years. By the late 1990s there were regular executive and legislative elections taking place on rolling cycles at both national and regional levels. With the abrogation of gubernatorial elections in 2005, and the consolidation of regional legislative elections into simultaneous biannual "unified days of voting," the electoral landscape is now considerably more consolidated. Moreover, the shift in national parliamentary elections from a mixed unconnected system (with 225 single-member district and 225 party list deputies elected on a 5% threshold) to a fully party list-based system with a high 7% threshold,[11] has further consolidated the political spectrum.

333

Table 24.1. Russian "Parties of Power," State Duma Elections, 1993–2007

Year	Party Name	Leader/Position	Percentage of Party List Vote (position)	Total seats (Incl. SMDs until 2003)/450
1993	Russia's Choice	Egor Gaidar—Former Acting Prime Minister 1992	15.6 (2nd)	70
1995	Our Home is Russia	Viktor Chernomyrdin—Prime Minister 1992–1998	10.1 (3rd)	55
1999	Unity	Sergei Shoigu—Emergency Situations Minister	22.3 (2nd)	73
2003	United Russia	Boris Gryzlov—Interior Minister	37.6 (1st)	223
2007	United Russia (also Fair Russia★)	Vladimir Putin—President (Sergei Mironov—Speaker of Federation Council)	64.3 (1st) (7.7) (4th)	315 (38)

Sources: *Byulleten' Tsentral'noi Izbiratel'noi Komissii Rossiiskoi Federatsii* 1 (12) (1994), 67; V.N. Kozlov, D.B. Oreshkin and A.N. Plate, eds, *Vybory deputatov Gosudarstvennoi Dumy. 1995. Elektoral'naya statistika* (Moscow: CEC/Ves' Mir, 1996), 92, 202; V.N. Kozlov and D.B. Oreshkin, eds, *Vybory deputatov Gosudarstvennoi Dumy Federal'nogo Sobraniya Rossiiskoi Federatsii. 1999. Elektoral'naya statistika* (Moscow: CEC/Ves' Mir, 2000), 136–38, 231–33; *Rossiiskaya Gazeta*, December 20, 2003, 1; *Rossiiskaya Gazeta*, December 11, 2007, 1.

Note: ★ Fair Russia, headed by the speaker of the Federation Council, tried to carry out the difficult balancing act in 2007 of being "in opposition to the ruling liberal United Russia party but supportive of Vladimir Putin," despite the fact that the latter was heading United Russia's party list (Address of the Leader of "Fair Russia" Sergei Mironov to Voters, Interfax Press Conference, November 30, 2007, http://www.spravedlivo.ru/first_face/203.smx. Accessed December 11, 2007).

Within this institutional framework, Russia's political consulting market has developed into a multi-billion dollar indigenous industry. In the two decades since the modern era of electoral politics began in Russia, the country has to some extent mirrored the "Americanization" of worldwide political campaigning, featuring the contracting-out of electoral operations to professionally employed non-party consultants.[12] In Fritz Plasser's (with Gunda Plasser) 2002 global political consultancy survey, nearly three-fifths of top American political consultants admitted to having worked overseas; of these, some 45% of the sub-group had worked in post-communist countries. Similarly, nearly a quarter of the political consultants interviewed from Russia indicated that they had worked with US-based consultants in their most recent election campaigns, and 35% noted collaboration with West European colleagues.[13] A significant number of Russian campaign professionals have produced handbooks about the unique aspects of their work.[14] Until the recent studies by Andrew Wilson and Sarah Oates,[15] there had been relatively little analysis of this phenomenon by non-practitioners. Wilson argues that the all-encompassing "electoral technology" (*izbiratel'naya tekhnologiya*) deployed in ex-Soviet states differs from the more traditional acts of spin doctors and political consultants in the West. Whereas the former seek to propagate a particular version of real events, he argues that the fusion between politics and the state in post-Soviet politics means that it is the political framework itself that is crafted into a virtual form by consultants.[16]

The work of consultants in Russia has gradually converged then diverged from the "American" model. The development of the industry in the 1990s has been covered in detail elsewhere,[17] so it is necessary only to note at this stage that the pro-Kremlin parties' early attempts to use "marketing" focused too much on the outputs—professional-looking advertisements projecting their relatively unpopular leaders going about their duties[18]—and neglected real marketing features such as product assessment and product adjustment in the "inputs." In the latter half of the 1990s, however, the more sophisticated use of market segmentation and professional campaigning methods led to a burgeoning political consulting industry. The first high-profile campaign that used political marketing effectively was Boris Yeltsin's presidential candidacy in 1996, which identified a cleavage between Soviet nostalgists and pro-market reformers and depicted the politically beleaguered Yeltsin as the lesser of two evils.[19]

The 1996–1999 period was the "era of unlimited flights of fantasy" for Russian consultants.[20] During this period, elections were characterized by innovative campaign methods in a relatively under-regulated environment, where the creativity of the consultants was constrained mainly by their ethical codes and financial restraints. Its zenith came with the 1999–2000 electoral cycle, in which nearly half the vote in the party list section of the State Duma election was won by three movements that had hardly any infrastructure and had barely existed a few weeks before the election. Russia's leading political strategists played out a game of power politics, creating and playing these "virtual" parties off against each other as rival groups within the elite fought for control of the post-Yeltsin political era, a battle eventually won by Vladimir Putin's entourage.[21]

Throughout the 1990s, the political campaigning industry in Russia became a sophisticated indigenous one suited to the specific nuances of the country's political market.[22] The majority of companies involved in political consulting were small- to medium-sized, but a few large multi-disciplinary companies—such as "Nikkolo M," the Foundation for Effective Politics, Novokom and Image-Kontakt—established international reputations.[23] In the late 1990s there also was a mushrooming of one-man "universal" consultants, many of them academics using elections as an opportunity to derive a second income. By the early Putin era the market for the small-scale independent electoral consultant was ebbing away as the importance of access to "administrative resources" grew.[24]

The Putin era has witnessed a number of changes within the political consulting industry. First, significant legislative tightening has narrowed the market for independent consultants, as has the aforementioned reduction in the number of elections. Moreover, the new institutional focus on parties as the constituent units of election campaigns, and the stringent registration requirements on them, mean that barriers to entry are much higher and it is only through a handful of party structures that candidates stand a realistic chance of being elected.

As a result, medium-sized companies (especially Moscow-based ones), which had previously derived much of their income from single-member district and regional gubernatorial and legislative campaigns, face an increasing challenge for survival.[25] As in the United States, the leading political consultants have been diversifying beyond political campaigns into the sphere of business public relations.[26] Arguably, the increasingly corporate focus of the industry is leading to a less creative, but more professional, use of marketing.[27] The absolute level of resources put into elections has increased, however, since financial-industrial groups are now prepared to devote more resources to other regional legislative and municipal election campaigns.[28] The larger political consulting firms are in a better position to take advantage of this, with their closer links to the corridors of power and greater organizational capacity to work in various regions simultaneously on the "unified days of voting." At the other end of the scale, very narrowly specialized consultants, with low overheads, may also be able to benefit from these trends by continuing to offer particular specific services, rather than attempting to cover all aspects of a campaign.[29]

Second, there has been a professionalization of the industry per se. The late 1990s, it has been argued, was a period of a "game without rules"; more people employed within the industry now have had academic training in marketing theory and a greater sense of professional ethics.[30] It is harder than before to operate against the norms of the industry. The world of political consulting is fairly small, and the Russian Association for Links with Society (RASO) brings together most of the major actors within the industry in the capitals. The directors of the larger companies know each other and are involved in the European and international associations for political consulting. At the middle-level, employees move from company to company and sometimes into the structures of the "parties of power." Finally, the increasing proportion of business public relations undertaken by consulting companies places commercial pressures on them to operate ethically.[31]

Third, the decline in the number of electoral organizations involved has led to an increase in the amount of consulting done "in-house" by political parties. The leading parties have set up sections specifically to deal with political marketing in a more permanent manner, many of them staffed by former employees of the major independent companies.[32] This mirrors a parallel development in the world of business consulting, whereby companies are more likely to have their own public relations structures than was the case a few years ago.[33]

The move toward more "managed" campaigns has occurred in tandem with the increasing role of "administrative resources" in Russian election campaigns, a phenomenon discussed in the second half of this article. Consultants working for the "parties of power"—generally, the larger Moscow-based firms—are charged with working in partnership with a handful of business and bureaucratic structures to achieve a particular level of success, utilizing and mobilizing the administrative resources efficiently. Furthermore, whereas previously businesses tended to split their funds across a number of parties, only the "parties of power" are now in a position to deliver policy results consistently. This further strengthens their resource base and weakens that of other parties. For candidates and parties with no realistic chance of success, the consultants' task is simply to ensure a higher ranking behind the victors than would otherwise have been the case, as a well-organized campaign alone is less likely than in the past to succeed without sufficient resources.[34]

Administrative Resources and Other Political Controversies

In the "era of unlimited flights of fantasy" mentioned earlier, one of the more controversial aspects of political consulting in Russia was that so-called "dirty tricks" (gryaznaya tekhnologiya) and "black PR" (chernyi PR) manifested themselves extensively. In fact, "black PR" was more shaded than its name might suggest; it was possible for actions to be "legal but not legitimate."[35] "Black PR" and "dirty tricks" can be seen as subtypes of political technology involving the deliberate violation of acceptable moral standards to damage the reputation of an opponent.[36]

Rather than simply "digging up the dirt" and using it selectively,[37] one of the most common forms of "black PR" involved the dissemination of deliberate disinformation or "compromising material" (kompromat), usually of questionable provenance or, at best, limited veracity. As a campaign handbook to members of Vladimir Zhirinovsky's Liberal Democratic Party of Russia put it in the late 1990s, "the more unbelievable the rumor, the quicker people will believe it."[38]

"Dirty tricks" took a variety of forms. A favorite for a while was the making of phone calls in the middle of the night purporting to be from a particular candidate asking for support in the forthcoming election, the main purpose of which was to ensure that the voter would do the opposite. Other "tricks" included the issuing of false leaflets in opponents' names claiming that unpopular figures (such as oligarchs or Chechens) were backing their campaigns.[39] Another tactic that was popular in the constituency contests in the late 1990s was that of nominating tandem candidates as "doubles." For a payment of about $1,000, such "doubles" could be persuaded to be stand but play no active role in the campaign other than to have their names placed next to the real candidates' on the ballot paper.[40] Sometimes the "double" had a similar name to a real opponent's, and was nominated to confuse voters. In other cases, spurious candidates would be nominated to distract and detract from an opponent's campaign (by attacking from several sides and allowing the main candidate to remain above the fray), or to act as insurance in the event that all a candidate's real opponents were to withdraw en masse.[41] Although such phenomena still occur from time to time in Russian elections—in the 2007 State Duma election, for instance, the Yabloko Party had a (seemingly genuine) Vladimir Putin on its Stavropol regional list who was the head of the legal section of the local water company[42]—overall, these "hit and run" techniques are used less frequently than in the past. "Dirty tricks" work effectively only the first time they are used; thereafter, they are better known and easier to neutralize.[43]

Far more influential in modern Russian election campaigns is the use of "administrative resources"—the use and sometimes abuse of state offices or resources to influence the electoral process. Administrative resources are not new or even unique to Russia, and their existence has long been noted.[44] In the gubernatorial elections held between 1995 and 2005, approximately 55% of the contests were won by incumbents, with 13% won by locally prominent politicians and a further 10% by State Duma deputies.[45] If we look back to the 1999 State Duma election, we find parties on average gained roughly half as many votes again than their all-Russian averages in the regions where governors had particular affiliations.[46] However, whereas the distribution of these resources was relatively pluralist in the 1990s (and there were often candidates backed by opposing administrative resources from the regional and federal levels), the consolidation of the elite and the political system since the turn of the century means it is even more difficult than ever to run a successful campaign against an administration-backed party or candidate.

The use of administrative resources takes on many forms. Leaving aside the issue of direct electoral fraud, which is difficult to prove in anything other than isolated cases, the use of administrative resources is often legal or at least technically close to being so—although this is partly due to loopholes left in electoral legislation at the time of its passage through the legislative process. Moreover, opinion surveys do indicate that the incumbent elite is relatively popular, even without any advantage accruing from administrative structures.[47] Nonetheless, various means exist whereby the resources of the incumbent elite at the very least place parties and candidates from this group at a starting advantage.

The Institutional Framework

The institutional framework of elections affords several advantages to administration-backed parties. First, after each electoral cycle since the early 1990s, electoral legislation has been reviewed by the Central Electoral Commission and improvements passed by the State Duma. Between the 2003 and 2007 elections, however, the scope of the reforms went considerably further than that recommended by the Commission's legal experts, and also ignored some of their recommendations. The State Duma election law in particular became an instrument of political contention: between its passage into law on May 18, 2005 and the State Duma election on December 2, 2007, it was amended an impressive six times. Provisions contained within it also required the amendment of the legally superior election framework law, which itself has been amended twenty times since its passage in mid-2002.[48]

Second, the electoral reforms enacted have further closed the "cartel" by considerably narrowing the channels of entry into politics. In the 1990s a plethora of regional and national parties, movements, associations and other groups stood in Russian elections, and a significant number of deputies elected at regional and national levels were unaffiliated with any party. The change to a fully list-based public relations electoral system for elections to the State Duma no longer enables candidates to enter parliament via any route other than through inclusion on a party list that wins more than 7% of the vote. Existing Duma factions also have advantageous entry rights.[49] In order to be registered as a party in the first place it is necessary to meet stringent requirements set down by the Law on Political Parties, which has reduced the number of eligible electoral organizations from 199 to 15 between 2001 and 2007.[50] Moreover, the electoral legislation for the 2007 State Duma election favored larger party organizations: the minimum number of regional groups in a party's list was set at eighty, benefiting parties with a wide infrastructure, and the minimum percentage of the vote required for free advertising was raised from 2 to 3%; from 3 to 4% for the return of the electoral deposit; and from 5 to 7% for the distribution of seats.[51]

Third, electoral commissions can provide a useful resource base. Although there are legal quotas on the representation of different branches of power and political parties on electoral commissions, commissions can *de facto* be weighted in favor of the "party of power." At the precinct and territorial electoral commission level, it is not unusual to find that the entire commission is employed in one (usually municipal) enterprise, with each member formally representing a different part of the power structure or a political party.[52] There was also a loophole in the run-up to the 2003 State Duma election whereby United Russia was able, perfectly legally, to place up to three representatives on commissions: one from each of the State Duma factions of Fatherland–All Russia and Unity, and another from the newly registered United Russia party, which was formed between elections from an amalgamation of these two.[53]

Fourth, the state and municipally owned media provide one of the most effective mechanisms for the promotion of candidates. The ownership of the media and press in Russia is a complex web of interdependence between different holding companies, many of which are privately owned.[54] The main national television networks, however, are under direct or indirect state ownership. Some 78% of Russians claimed in a 2005 survey to watch the First Channel's evening news program, and 61% watched the other main state channel's ("Russia").[55] About a third (32%) watched local state news programs. There is evidence from past elections that voters consider the state channels to be the most important source of information, so the tone of their coverage arguably plays a role in determining attitudes toward different parties or candidates.[56] Editorially, successive waves of election media monitoring have shown that the coverage given to the "parties of power" in these state news programs has been disproportionately large and positive, and that of their main opponents usually negative or negligible.[57] In addition, each region has a municipally backed print media network that is usually the strongest in the region and delivers direct to people's postboxes.[58]

Incumbents and "Locomotives"

As in any country, incumbency affords many advantages in Russia. Although state officials are officially banned from using their office for advantage and required to take leave of absence during election campaigns in which they are participating,[59] this only applies to certain categories of state servants and it should not prevent deputies or the sitting president from "carrying out their duties to voters"—a fairly broad category of exclusion.[60] Moreover, the bureaucratic apparatus does not cease to function even if candidates themselves temporarily stand down.

Aside from the organizational support that incumbency provides, the primary campaign advantage is that it allows candidates to undertake a wide range of activities in their official capacities rather than as candidates, with commensurate publicity and resource benefits. This is not a new or even uniquely Russian phenomenon: William L. Miller's analysis of the 1987 British general election pointed to exactly the same problem, although it can be argued that the degree of direct editorial control exerted by the executive in the Russian case is considerably greater than that of the British government on the BBC.[61] Even though he did not use his allotted advertising time, Vladimir Putin still emerged with some thirty hours more television coverage than any other candidate by the end of the 2000 presidential campaign,[62] after carrying out essential acting presidential duties such as co-piloting an SU-29 fighter jet to Chechnya "without even removing his tie,"[63] and going on an opera excursion with British Prime Minister Tony Blair. During the 2004 contest he reshuffled the government in the middle of the campaign, further deflecting attention from other candidates. Yuri Luzhkov, the mayor of Moscow and a United Russia co-leader, attended the opening of a new metro station two days before the

2003 State Duma election (which coincided with the mayoral election in which he was standing for re-election).[64]

The reflected glory of association with popular incumbents can also be used to advantage. The most high-profile example of this is the handover of power from Vladimir Putin to Dmitrii Medvedev in 2008. In another such case, a routine meeting in 2003 between Putin and Valentina Matvienko, the presidential representative for the North-Eastern Federal District, was turned into a four-minute report on the main evening news bulletin in which the president called the minister of finance to organize extra funds for the region and "sincerely wished her victory" in the St Petersburg gubernatorial election.[65]

A loophole in Russian electoral legislation that allows candidates to reject legislature seats without costing their party any places in parliament allows the harnessing of incumbents' popularity for other campaigns. Since the mid-1990s, prominent politicians such as government ministers and regional governors have run as "locomotive candidates" (*parovozov*) at the top of election lists even if they have no intention of taking up the seats to which they are elected. The incumbents, who are of more interest to the public than their less well-known colleagues from further down the lists who ultimately end up as deputies in their places, front the campaign and pull their party's vote further up than would otherwise have been the case. The Central Electoral Commission has sought to remove this provision, but the parliamentary majority voted to retain it in the 2007 State Duma election law. The former head of the Commission, Aleksandr Veshnyakov, has called such electoral participants "advertisement candidates" and argued that their presence deceives voters.[66] In 2007, although the United Russia party chairman sought to refocus the parliamentary campaign as "a national referendum on Putin,"[67] neither the president nor 103 of the other 315 deputies elected from United Russia took up their seats, including the leading candidates on sixty-four of the party's eighty-three regional lists.[68]

State and Electoral Roles

The final group of advantages accruing from administrative resources involves the blurring of state and electoral roles at the administrative level. The extent of municipal control over various aspects of local life can make a difference with regard to the distribution of election material. Access to advertising spots at prominent locations—bus stops, entrances to apartment blocs, bridges and even hotel fronts—is subject not only to various financial charges (which are legitimately shown on the parties' financial accounts) but also requires municipal agreement and the necessary permissions.[69] Moreover, there is a multitude of different ways in which apparently non-political decisions can be taken at the bureaucratic level—such as the decision to close a building for a fire inspection or to investigate the legality of installed computer software—which impact on some candidates and parties more than others.

The election framework law prohibits (with the aforementioned caveats) the use of state premises and communications for electoral activity; the abuse of public transport rights; the collection of signatures during business trips; or preferential access to the state media.[70] Nonetheless, there are several legal gray areas as to how these restrictions can be enforced, and frequent suggestions that the strict delineation of state and election offices is not observed.[71] One of the key aims of the 2007 election, from the elite's point of view, was to ensure that the government's and president's course were demonstrably shown to be supported by the majority of the population, and there were numerous reports of administrative pressure being brought to bear on voters to ensure that they turned out to vote.[72] It is worth noting the very strong positive correlation between the turnout in each region and the percentage of the vote for United Russia (a significant Pearson correlation of 0.905), as seen in Figure 24.1. Despite allegations made by the opposition, this in itself does not imply that there was anything

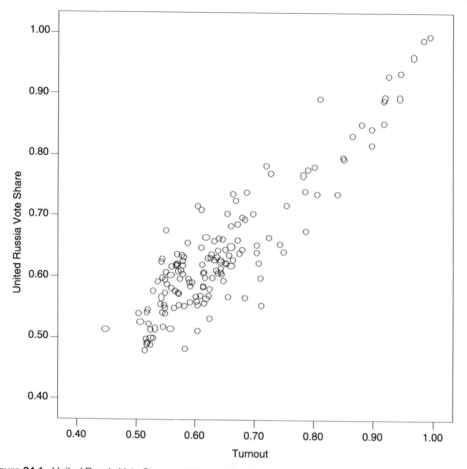

Figure 24.1. United Russia Vote Share and Turnout (by Regional Lists), 2007 State Duma Election

Source: 2007 State Duma results, as published by Central Electoral Commission, http://www.vybory.izbirkom.ru/ izbirkom.html. Accessed December 17, 2007. Fractions are as a proportion of the total electorate (turnout) and of those voting (vote share).

untoward—but given the advantages of advertising, incumbency and media coverage outlined above, it is likely that voters who would not otherwise have voted are most likely to have cast a ballot for United Russia. In a survey shortly before the election, 69% of people said that the party had been the best performer in the pre-election televised debates.[73] This achievement was all the more impressive for the fact that United Russia did not actually participate in the debates.

Conclusions

In assessing the two pillars of modern Russian elections—political consulting and administrative resources—what is the cumulative effect of each on the outcome? At a superficial level, it is difficult to quantify objectively. Few serious candidates in the single-member districts, or parties in list-based elections, would now embark upon a campaign without professional consultants involved in their campaigns. One of the leading consultants in the industry, Igor Mintusov, has jokingly stated that up to half of a consultant's honorarium is to remain quiet about what he does for the other half. At the same time, he has argued that a consultant's work can at most contribute a third of a candidate's or party's success, with the rest dependent the party or candidate and the resources available.[74]

The element of administrative resources appears to have become crucial to electoral success in recent years. Since the 1990s, their distribution has become more uni-polar. Whereas in the pre-Putin era the regional and national political elites were often working against each other, or at least had affiliations with different political forces, the institutional and political changes of the Putin era have led to a more unified elite. In view of this, it is difficult to assess whether administrative resources are necessarily more extensive than in the past, or simply more effectively channeled. Since the political course of Vladimir Putin and United Russia appear to be genuinely popular amongst Russian voters, it is also difficult to assess accurately the extent to which their electoral success is solely dependent on the use of administrative pressure and to what extent other parties would in any case be unable to compete with them.

Overall, it can be said that "managed democracy" has placed a premium on the identification of gaps in the electoral market. These have been effectively filled by specially formed "broadcast parties" or "parties of power"—administratively backed structures which rely on establishment support and effective image-making. Within the electoral and political consulting markets, greater legislative specificity combined with more restricted electoral opportunities have resulted in a concentration of the market at the top and bottom of the sector, with an increasing diversification of political marketing firms into other forms of public relations and a narrowing of political competition. In the meantime, a more sophisticated understanding of the nuances of the Russian electoral market has allowed traditional marketing techniques to be married to the specifics of the Russian electorate, and the resources afforded by incumbency to be more effectively channeled into the political process.

Notes

The author acknowledges the support of British Academy Grant SG-40918 on "Political participation, disengagement and re-engagement in post-Communist Russia and Germany" and UCD Seed Funding grant SF-149 that enabled fieldwork in Russia for the current study.

1   Andrew Wilson, *Virtual Politics* (New Haven, CT: Yale University Press, 2005).

2   See Bulletin EU 3–2004, March 17, 2004, §1.6.11; Bulletin EU 5–2005, May 12, 2005, §1.2.5; Bulletin EU 12–2005, December 15, 2005, §1.2.9; C. Malmström, "EU–Russia Relations: European Parliament Resolution on EU–Russia Relations," May 26, 2005, Session Document P6_TA(2005)0207 (2004/2170(INI)), §17 for some recent examples. OSCE/ODIHR Press Release "ODIHR Unable to Observe Russian Duma Elections," November 16, 2007, http://www.osce.org/odihr/item_1_27967.html. Accessed November 17, 2007.

3   Stephen Levitsky and Lucan Way, "The Rise of Competitive Authoritarianism," *Journal of Democracy* 13 (2): 51–65.

4   See, for example, V. Putin, "Poslanie Federal'nomu Sobraniyu Rossiiskoi Federatsii", April 3, 2001. Transcript available from Kremlin website, www.kremlin.ru/text/appears/2001/04/28514.htm; V. Putin, "Interview with the Chilean Television Channel 13 and the newspaper *El Mercurio*", November 18, 2004, Moscow. Transcript available from Kremlin website: http://www.kremlin.ru/eng/speeches/2004/11/18/2309_type82916_79637.shtml. Accessed March 18, 2006.

5   V. Putin, "Poslanie Federal'nomu Sobraniyu Rossiiskoi Federatsii," April 25, 2005, Moscow. Transcript available from Kremlin website, http://www.kremlin.ru/appears/2005/04/25/1223_type-63372type82634_87049.shtml. Accessed March 18, 2006.

6   Richard Rose, Neil Munro and Stephen White, "Voting in a Floating Party System: The 1999 Duma Election," *Europe-Asia Studies* 53 (3) (2001): 419–43.

7   Hans Overloot and Ruben Verheul, "The Party of Power in Russian Politics," *Acta Politica* 35 (2000): 123–45.

8 Sarah Oates, *Television, Democracy and Elections in Russia* (London/New York: Routledge, 2006), ch. 4.

9 Of the 1.78 million members (approximately 1.25% of the Russian population) which United Russia claimed in December 2007, approximately 150,000 worked in state organs, and 1.04 million worked in the service sector (United Russia website, http://www.edinros.ru/news.html?rid=3123#1. Accessed December 13, 2007). The real connection of members to the party can be tenuous, however: in one example witnessed by the author in 2004, members of a dance group which the party was sponsoring in Ul'yanovsk were registered en masse as party members, even though few could even remember the name of the party they were joining.

10 "Luchshe byt ne mozhet", *Kommersant'*, November 14, 2007, 1.

11 Federal Law "O vyborakh deputatov Gosudarstvennoi Dumy Federal'nogo Sobraniya Rossiiskoi Federatsii," [2007 State Duma Law] No. 51-F3, May 18, 2005, with several amendments up to July 21, 2007. Most up-to-date version available from Central Electoral Commission website, http://www.cikrf.ru/cikrf/law/2/zakon_51.jsp. Accessed December 2, 2007.

12 David M. Farrell, "Political Consultancy Overseas: The Internationalization of Campaign Consultancy," *PS: Political Science and Politics* 31 (2) (1998): 171–6; Dennis W. Johnson "The Business of Political Consulting," in *Campaign Warriors: Political Consultants in Elections*, ed. James A. Thurber and Candice J. Nelson (Washington, D.C.: Brookings Institution Press, 2000), 37–52; Fritz Plasser, "American Campaign Techniques Worldwide," *Harvard International Journal of Press/Politics* 5 (4) (2000): 33–54; Marion G. Müller "Wahlkampf à l'américan," in *Wahl-Kämpfe: Betrachtungen über ein demokratisches Ritual*, ed. Andreas Dörner and Ludgera Vogt (Frankfurt am Main: Suhrkamp, 2002), 187–210.

13 Fritz Plasser with Gunda Plasser, *Global Political Campaigning: A Worldwide Analysis of Campaign Professionals and Their Practices* (Westport, CT: Praeger, 2002), 24–34.

14 Ol'ga Berezkina, *Kak stat' deputatom ili prodat' sebya na politicheskom rynke* (St Petersburg: Izdatel'stvo Bukovskogo, 1997); G.G. Pocheptsov, *Imidzh & vybory* (Kiev: ADEF-Ukraina, 1997); V.E. Lyzlov, *Pobeda, tol'ko pobeda!* (Moscow: PAIMS, 1999); A.A. Maksimov, *"Chistye" i "gryaznye" tekhnologii vyborov: Rossiiskii opyt* (Moscow: Delo, 1999); A.M. Salmin et al., *Politicheskoe konsul'tirovanie*, special ed., *Politiya* 2 (12) (1999); L.G. Smorgunov, *Politicheskii menedzhment: elektoral'nyi protsess i tekhnologii* (St Petersburg: St Petersburg University Press, 1999); Farkhad Il'yasov, *Politicheskii marketing* (Moscow: IMA-Press, 2000); O.P. Kudinov, *Osnovy organizatsii i provedeniya izbiratel'nykh kampanii v regionakh Rossii* (Kaliningrad: Yantarnyi skaz, 2000); S.F. Lisovsky and V.A. Evstaf'ev, *Izbiratel'nye tekhnologii: istoriya, teoriya, praktika* (Moscow: RAU-Universitet, 2000); Avtandil Tsuladze, *Bol'shaya manipulyativnaya igra* (Moscow: Algoritm, 2000); V.S. Kolomiets, ed., *Izbiratel'nye tekhnologii i izbiratel'noe iskusstvo* (Moscow: ROSSPEN, 2001); Konstantin Zhukov and Aleksandr Karnyshev, *Azbuka izbiratel'noi kampanii* (Moscow: IMA-Press, 2001); Yurii Lyubashevsky, *Kak samomu proigrat' vybory v Gosudarstvennuyu Dumu: vrednye sovety kandidatam-2003* (Moscow: Russkaya Shkola PR, 2002); E. Egorova-Gantman and I. Mintusov, eds, *Politicheskoe konsul'tirovanie*, 2nd ed. (Moscow: Nikkolo M, 2002); E. Malkin and E. Suchkov, *Osnovy izbiratel'nykh tekhnologii*, 3rd ed. (Moscow: Russkaya Panorama, 2002); A.A. Miroshnichenko, *Vybory: ot zamysla do pobedy (Predvybornaya kampaniya v rossiiskom regione)* (Moscow: Tsentr, 2003); Elena Sorokina, *Kommunikatsiya v period izbiratel'noi kampanii: Keis stadis* (Moscow: Avanti, 2003); Igor' Nikolaevich Panarin, *Informatsionnaya voina: pobeda v Bashkirii* (Moscow: Gorodets, 2004); A. Sanaev, *Vybory v Rossii: Kak eto delaetsya* (Moscow: Os'-89, 2005).

15 Wilson, *Virtual Politics*; Oates, *Television, Democracy and Elections*.

16 Wilson, *Virtual Politics*, 49.

17 Derek S. Hutcheson, "How to Win Elections and Influence People: The Development of Political Consulting in Post-Communist Russia," *Journal of Political Marketing* 5 (4) (2006): 47–70; Wilson, *Virtual Politics*, 49–72.

18 Oates, *Television, Democracy and Elections*, 91–102.

19 OSCE/ODIHR, *Final Report on the Presidential Election 1996* (Moscow: OSCE, 1996); Ellen Mickiewicz, *Changing Channels: Television and The Struggle for Power in Russia*, 2nd ed. (Durham/London: Duke University Press, 1999), 167–89.

20 Sanaev, *Vybory v Rossii*, 8.

21 Tsuladze, *Bol'shaya manipulyativnaya igra*, Part 2.

22 Rustam A. Semenov and Irina V. Kolesnik, Politsovet Political Consulting Agency, interview, March 27, 2003.

23 ROMIR—*Rossiiskoe Obshchestvennoe Mnenie i Issledovanie Rynka* [Russian Public Opinion and Market Research] ranking of the leading Russian political consultancy companies, fourth wave (October 2002), http://www.romir.ru/socpolit/pr/10_2002/pr2002.htm. Accessed November 1, 2003.

24 Vyacheslav E. Lyzlov, Public Centre for Political Consulting and Electoral Technology, interview,

Moscow, April 17, 2002; Joe Napolitan and Derek Hutcheson, "Vremya universalov ukhodit," *Sovetnik* 2 (98) (2004): 23–5.

25 Igor Mintusov, "Podderzhka gubernatora—zalog uspekha na regional'nykh vyborakh," http://www.polit.ru/analytics/2007/03/09/mintusov.html. Accessed March 9, 2007.

26 Dennis W. Johnson, *No Place for Amateurs: How Political Consultants are Reshaping American Democracy*, 2nd ed. (New York/London: Routledge, 2007); Viktor Bekker, "Politkonsalting ili agitprop?", *Politicheskii Zhurnal*, 19 June 2006, http://www.nikkolom.ru/2006/10_07_06_31iarticle.htm. Accessed October 26, 2006; Maksim Kochalov, "Transformatsiya PR-rynka i PR-industrii v putinskie vremena," *Sovetnik* 1 (January 30, 2006); Igor Mintusov, Chairman of the Board of Directors, "Nikkolo-M," interview, Moscow, July 6, 2006.

27 Yurii Lubashevsky, President of the "Russian School of PR," quoted in Valeriya Filimonova, "Piarshchiki 'v zakone' ", July 27, 2005, http://www.politcom.ru/2005/prsoob38.php. Accessed October 26, 2006.

28 Mintusov interview, 2006; Mintusov, "Podderzhka gubernatora."

29 Kochalov, "Transformatsiya PR-rynka."

30 Filimonova, "Piarshchiki 'v zakone' "; Mintusov interview, 2006.

31 Sanaev, *Vybory v Rossii*, 233.

32 Mintusov interview, 2006; "Proba piara", *Kommersant'*, March 9, 2007, 3.

33 Kochalov, "Transformatsiya PR-rynka."

34 Sanaev, *Vybory v Rossii*, 7.

35 Zhukov and Karnyshev, *Azbuka izbiratel'noi kampani*; S.M. Tuchkov, "Faktory legitimnosti politicheskikh tekhnologii: 'Legitimnost' i 'legalnost' politicheskikh tekhnologii," *Vestnik Moskovoskogo Universiteta*, Series 12 (Political Science) 2 (2002), 8–14 (11).

36 Wilson, *Virtual Politics*, 70.

37 Cf. Johnson, *No Place for Amateurs*, ch. 4.

38 Liberal Democratic Party of Russia (LDPR) Central Apparatus, *Metodicheskie ukazaniya po podgotovke i provedeniyu kampanii po vyboram v Gosudarstvennuyu Dumy Federal'nogo Sobraniya Rossiiskoi Federatsii i Prezidenta RF v 1999–2000 godu* (Moscow: LDPR, 1998), 41–6.

39 Malkin and Suchkov, *Osnovy izbiratel'nykh tekhnologii*, 417–22.

40 Mintusov interview, March 28, 2003.

41 For example, Sergei Mironov, the speaker of the Federation Council, stood in the 2004 presidential election so that Putin was "not left without support", and won fewer votes than there were spoiled ballot papers (Susan B. Glasser, "Reelection Bid Requires Little Effort From Putin", *Washington Post*, February 13, 2004).

42 "Voina bilbordam", *Nezavisimaya Gazeta*, September 28, 2007, 3; "Vladimir Putin Makes Yabloko's Regional List," *The Moscow Times*, October 2, 2007, 3; Christian Lowe, "Russia's Election—A Tale of Two Putins," November 22 2007, http://uk.reuters.com/article/worldNews/idUKL2161959520071122?sp=true. Accessed December 12, 2007.

43 Andrei G. Bulychev, (then) President, European Association of Political Consultants (EAPC), interview, Moscow, March 26, 2003.

44 Marie Mendras, "How Regional Elites Preserve Their Power," *Post-Soviet Affairs* 15 (4) (1999): 295–311; S.I. Kaspe and A.I. Petrokovsky "Administrativnye i informatsionnye resursy v kontekste vyborov-99," *Politiya* 2 (16) (2000): 5–28; Vladimir Zvonovsky "Administrativnyi resurs: variant ischisleniya ob'ema," *Monitoring obshchestvennogo mneniya* 1 (45): 35–7.

45 Compiled from V.N. Kozlov, D.B. Oreshkin and A.N. Plate, eds, *Vybory glav izpolnitel'noi vlasti sub'ektov Rossiiskoi Federatsii, 1995–97: Elektoral'naya statistika* (Moscow: CEC/Ves' Mir, 1997); A. Ageeva et al., *Vybory v organy gosudarstvennoi vlasti sub'ektov Rossiiskoi Federatsii, 1997–2000: elektoralnaya statistika v 2 tomakh* (Moscow: CEC/Ves' Mir, 2001); and annual books of electoral statistics published by the Central Electoral Commission, 2002–2005.

46 Comparison results in Kozlov and Oreshkin, eds, *Vybory deputatov Gosudarstvennoi Dumy 1999*, 136–8, 231–3 and gubernatorial affiliations given in Michael McFaul, Nikolai Petrov, Andrei Ryabov and Elizabeth Reisch, *Primer on Russia's 1999 Duma Elections* (Moscow: Carnegie, 1999), 146–7.

47 Presidential and governmental trust ratings, http://www.levada.ru/prezident.html. Accessed December 13, 2007.

48 Federal Law, "Ob osnovnykh garantiyakh izbiratel'nykh prav i prava na uchastie v referendume grazhdan Rossiiskoi Federatsii" [On Fundamental Guarantees of Electoral Rights . . .], Law No. 67-F3 (June 12, 2002, with twenty amendments up to July 24, 2007). Most up-to-date version available from Central Electoral Commission website, http://www.cikrf.ru/law/2/zakon_02_67fz_n.jsp. Accessed December 2, 2007.

49 State Duma Law 2007, §39.2.

50 Marina Kholmskaya and Vladimir Tomarovsky, "Chtit' zakon", *Vybory: Zakonodatel'stvo i tekhnologii* 11 (2001): 36–9; Central Electoral Commission website, "Politicheskie partii, otvechaiyushchie trebovaniyam punkta 2 stat'i 36 Federal'nogo zakona 'O politicheskikh partiyakh' soglasno informatsii, razmeshchenoi na ofitsial'nom saite Federal'noi Registratsionnoi sluzhby po sostoyaniyu na 3 avgusta 2007 goda," http://www.cikrf.ru/elect_duma/politpart/party_tabl.jsp. Accessed December 11, 2007.

51 State Duma Law 2007, various articles.

52 Personal investigations during Precinct and Territorial Electoral Commission visits on polling days in Russian federal and regional elections, 1999 to 2004.

53 A. Novikova, *Izbiratel'nye prava grazhdan: Rossiya 2003* (Moscow: Moscow Helsinki Group, 2004), 19; OSCE/ODIHR, *Russian Federation: Elections to the State Duma, 7 December 2003. OSCE/ODIHR Election Observation Mission Report* (Warsaw: OSCE/ODIHR, 2004), 8.

54 "Rossiiskie SMI", *RBK*, April 2006, 64–5.

55 National Representative Survey conducted by Russian Research Ltd (London/Moscow) in association with the UK Economic and Social Research Council(ESRC)-funded project "Inclusion without Membership? Bringing Russia, Ukraine and Belarus closer to 'Europe' " (grant RES-00–23–0146). Fieldwork March 25, 2005 to April 20, 2005, N = 2000, question F.3. (Used by kind permission.)

56 Oates, *Television, Democracy and Elections*, 159–60.

57 Up to two weeks before polling day in 2007, United Russia had received 19.2% of coverage on the First Channel, 20.2% on the "Russia" channel, and an overwhelming 32.2% on the TV-Centre channel, affiliated with the Moscow city government. On the first two of these channels, no more than 1.9% and 3.7% was devoted respectively to any other party. In addition, 67% and 61% respectively of each channel's news coverage was devoted to Putin (who was leading the United Russia list) and the cabinet ("Vtoroi otchet o rezul'tatakh monitoringa SMI v ramkakh vyborov v Gosudarstvennuyu Dumy Rossiiskoi Federatsii 2007 (1 oktyabrya–22 noyabrya 2007)", available from the website of the Centre for Journalism in Extreme Situations, http://www.memo98.cjes.ru/?p=3&sm2=on&reports=200711. Accessed December 14, 2007).

58 Andrei Buzin, *Administrativnye izbiratel'nye tekhnologii: Moskovskaya praktika* (Moscow: Panorama, 2006), 81–92.

59 Law, "On Fundamental Guarantees of Electoral Rights . . .," §40.

60 State Duma Law 2007, §46.5; Federal Law "O vykorakh Prezidenta Rossiiskoi Federatsii" [Presidential Election Law], Law No. 19-F3 (January 10, 2003, with seven amendments up to July 24, 2007), §41.5. Most up-to-date version available from Central Electoral Commission website, http://www.cikrf.ru/law/2/zakon_19.jsp. Accessed December 2, 2007.

61 William L. Miller, *Media and Voters: The Audience, Content and Influence of Press and Television at the 1987 General Election* (Oxford: Clarendon, 1991), 66–8.

62 Benedicte Berner and Åse Grødeland, "Broadcast Media," in *Monitoring the Media Coverage of the March 2000 Presidential Elections in Russia*, ed. European Institute for the Media (Brussels/Düsseldorf: European Commission/EIM, 2000), ch. 4.

63 ORT news, 20 March 2000.

64 OSCE/ODIHR, *OSCE/ODIHR Election Observation Mission Report, 2003 State Duma*, 12.

65 First Channel evening news, September 1, 2003.

66 "Postoi 'paravoz' . . .", *Novyie Izvestiya*, October 12, 2006; "Bitva za den'gi i parovozy," *Moskovskie Novosti*, March 18, 2005.

67 "Putin ostaetsya liderom Rossii," *Rossiiskaya Gazeta*, October 17, 2007, 1.

68 Deputies of the other pro-Kremlin party, Fair Russia, swapped seven of their thirty-eight seats, and only three (of fifty-seven) Communists and two (of forty) Liberal Democrats rejected theirs (Statements of the Central Electoral Commission of the Russian Federation, Nos. 73/592–5 to 73/595–5 (December 13, 2007). Available from Central Electoral Commission website, http://www.cikrf.ru/postancik/. Accessed 13 December 2007).

69 In Moscow, the only way to place political material at building entrances is through *Gorodskaya Reklama* the Moscow government-licensed advertising agency, which has been granted a seven-year monopoly on the placing of advertisements there. As of December 2007, its prices ranged from 896 to 1,397 roubles ($36 to $57) per advertisement, and its website promised that all other unofficial advertising materials would be removed—making it impossible for parties to paste their own materials there without going through the official channels. See www.gorodreklama.ru.

70 Law, "On Fundamental Guarantees of Electoral Rights . . .", §40.

71 OSCE/ODIHR, *OSCE/ODIHR Election Observation Mission Report, 2003 State Duma*; Novikova, *Izbiratel'nye prava grazhdan*, 43–5.

72 "Gol' na vybory khitra", *Russkii Newsweek*, December 3–9, 2007, 26–8.

73 VTsIOM Press Release No. 817, November 22, 2007, http://wciom.ru/arkhiv/tematicheskii-arkhiv/item/single/9216.html. Accessed December 13, 2007.

74 "Rimas Zakarevičius, 'Mintusovas savo pergalemis Lietuvoje viešai nesigiria', *Lietuvos Rytas*, May 15, 2006. Russian version available from "Nikkolo M" website, http://www.nikkolom.ru/2006/15_05_06_1iarticle.htm. Accessed October 26, 2006.

25

Australia and the Postmodern Election Campaign

Ian Ward

Crosby–Textor is a small Australian firm with expertise in strategic communications and campaign execution. Its principals acquired and refined their skills via involvement with the conservative Liberal Party in successive Australian election campaigns. Lynton Crosby is a former Liberal national campaign director. Mark Textor remains the Liberals' chief pollster and has been intimately involved in the execution of national- and state-level Liberal election campaigns in Australia since 1996. Recently Crosby–Textor has been able to spread its wings. It advised the British Conservative Party and its leader for the May 2005 general election in that country, and then steered the Nationals' 2005 campaign in New Zealand. Crosby–Textor's capacity to ply its trade in countries other than Australia is testimony to the increasing "sameness" of campaigning in different settings which is now widely acknowledged.[1]

Electioneering in Australia closely resembles the efforts of parties and candidates to woo and win voters in Europe and North America. Since the 1960s the major Australian parties have sent employees to study firsthand campaigns in the United States and elsewhere, and then adapted those particular techniques thought useful. The national campaigns they fight to persuade voters—as campaigns elsewhere often are—are centrally controlled, capital rather than labor intensive, make extensive use of technology, and are primarily conducted through television. They commence long before the formal dissolution of parliament and the issue of election writs and are built around the qualities of party leaders rather than upon ideologically grounded policy programs. They rely upon professionals (such as Mark Textor) with specialist communications expertise in areas such as advertising, opinion polling, marketing, webpage design and ICT. Just as in Europe, Australian parties are increasingly paying attention to the local or electorate level and utilizing computerized databases, direct mail and telephone canvasing to build links between candidates and individual voters in a fashion which echoes a much earlier era of "candidates pressing flesh and working the streets."[2]

Election campaigns comprise the diverse activities undertaken by candidates and parties at the national, state and local levels in an attempt to persuade electors and secure enough votes to win public office. They require "an organized communication effort."[3] Indeed Pippa Norris suggests that campaigns are best seen as "organized efforts to inform, persuade and mobilize."[4] This particular view of election campaigns as political communication encourages a focus on the communication channels used to inform and persuade, and an appreciation that technological change over time has produced new means of wooing and winning voters and thus triggered the "modernization" of electioneering.

Paolo Mancini and David Swanson suggest that the rise of commercial television "personal-ized" politics, and thereby "radically changed the character of election campaigns."[5] Margaret Scammell cautions that "presidential-style" and personality focused campaigns predate tele-vision. Nonetheless she agrees that television was a catalyst for change. It transformed campaigning by focusing "attention on the leaders, enormously increasing the importance of the national campaign and concentrating power further in the hands of central organizations."[6] Australia well illustrates her case. By the early 1970s television had provided a new national stage. It shone a spotlight upon party leaders, greatly enhanced their importance and obliged campaign strategists to stage "pseudo-events" to win them favorable evening news coverage. It required central party organizations to employ advertising, public relations and media professionals. Moreover it required them to take control over the hitherto semi-autonomous campaigns that their state Divisions, individual candidates and party workers had conducted at the local level. In this way television, Dean Jaensch argues, triggered the first of two "virtual revolutions in the style of campaigning by political parties."[7] Thereafter Australian campaigners embraced opinion polling and other communication technologies as they emerged, and progressively developed new, more sophisticated ways of persuading and mobilizing voters. Direct mail and automated telephone canvasing involving "targeted two-way communications" with individual voters made possible by computerized databases, and the use of the Internet to mobilize and link voters, are amongst more recent examples of the inventive application of new technologies to campaigning.[8] Their use in Australia, Jaensch suggests, entailed an ongoing "second revolution" in campaigning.[9]

The Television Revolution

Other parties do stand candidates and may even secure a few Senate seats. But for more than sixty years Australian elections have chiefly been contests between the Australian Labor Party and a coalition formed by the Liberal and National parties for control of the House of Representatives and the right to form government. This contest once required the parties to mobilize armies of branch members and supporters in each electorate to conduct street corner meetings and town hall rallies, and to letter-box and door-knock on behalf of their candidates.[10] Direct contact with voters may have defined campaigning in Australia "until the 1960s,"[11] but today door-knocking and leafleting are a lesser, residual feature of Australian campaigns. The army of workers available to parties has shrunk. Party membership has declined during the past several decades.[12] Some individual candidates do still door-knock their constituencies. But the parties' campaigns no longer rely upon such forms of "greet and meet" grassroots politics. During the 2004[13] federal campaign only 2.5% of voters regularly, or even occasionally, attended election meetings or rallies. Just 8% regularly or occasionally demonstrated their support for a particular party or candidate, say, by putting up a poster or attending a meeting. Almost three-quarters (71.2%) reported having no contact of any kind with any party or candidate. Two-thirds (67.6%) reported making no attempt at all to talk with and to persuade others to vote for a particular party or candidate.[14]

Ironically the importance of campaigning is underlined by the fact that few voters now have direct contact with candidates seeking their vote. Australian Election Studies conducted since 1987 (see Figure 25.1) record the progressive erosion of party loyalty. During the 1990s there was a marked weakening in voter identification with the two parties that dominate Australian elections. As a result of this dealignment, the electorate is less firmly anchored, more volatile and contains more uncommitted or floating voters, than at any time in the recent past.[15] Since more voters are open to persuasion, carefully constructed election campaigns are more likely to decide elections. It is true that most voters (71.4% in 2001 and 75% in 2004) claim not to consider changing their vote during the period of a campaign, and that, as Table 25.1 shows, a significant

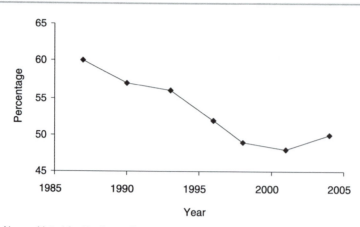

Figure 25.1. Always Voted for the Same Party

Source: Various Australian Election Studies.

Table 25.1. When Voters Made Up their Minds which Way to Vote, 1987–2004 (%)

	1987	*1990*	*1993*	*1996*	*1998*	*2001*	*2004*
A Long Time Ago	50.0	45.9	42.4	49.9	35.3	44.8	46.9
Before the Election Was Announced	23.0	10.7	13.2	12.1	13.6	13.8	14.3
When the Election Was Announced	n.a.	7.7	6.7	6.6	9.0	6.8	6.5
During the Campaign (Including on Polling Day)	26.9	35.8	37.7	31.4	42.8	34.6	32.4
On Polling Day Itself	n.a.	9.9	7.9	10.7	11.3	12.3	8.6

Source: Various Australian Election Studies.

number still report having decided for whom they will vote well before elections are announced.[16] However more than enough voters now make up their minds only after the issue of election writs to decide the outcome in finely balanced seats. Indeed one in ten voters (12.3% in 2001 and 8.6% in 2004) report delaying their final decision until polling day itself. Television is an obvious channel to use to influence them.

The Labor and coalition parties are well aware of the increased fluidity of voting patterns, and that an increasing number of voters delay their decision until the formal election campaign is underway. That Australia has compulsory voting forces their hand. The *Electoral Act* requires all registered voters to attend a polling place or submit a vote via the post. In most other jurisdictions voting is not mandated, and election campaigning is directed at identifying sympathetic voters and then insuring that they vote on polling day. Often the focus of campaigns fought in comparable democracies is upon mobilizing a base vote. Australian parties face a different challenge. It is to persuade those undecided and uncommitted voters who are required to vote, and whose eventual choice at the ballot box may well decide the outcome in key marginal electorates. In the early 1970s the parties discovered the power of television and its ability to convey a coherent, single message to a mass audience. In this respect Australian politics followed a familiar path.

In her influential analysis of the modernization of campaigning in "postindustrial democracies," Pippa Norris notes that the emergence of modern campaigning generally coincided with "the rise of television" and opinion polling. While party members and volunteers continued the "ritual of canvassing and leafleting," modern campaigns soon came to be built around television which became the "principal forum for campaign events" and the chief means of reaching voters.[17] Modern campaigns were more closely coordinated "at a central level by political leaders" and party elites who relied, not upon party officials, members and supporters, but on external consultants, pollsters and others with the skills to "conduct polls, design advertisements" and to manage photo opportunities and the other elements of "the battle to dominate the nightly television news."[18] In Australia parties turned to commercial advertising agencies and pollsters (rather than specialist political consultants). By the latter 1980s old-style machine politicians and party bureaucrats no longer ran campaigns. Control had passed to pollsters, advertising, public relations and other professionals whom Stephen Mills dubbed "the new machine men."[19]

Today television remains the parties' chief means of persuading voters despite an accelerating news cycle and that fragmentation and contraction of the free-to-air television audience caused by the emergence of rival new media. Precisely because very few voters have direct contact with candidates or are canvased by party workers, Australians are much more likely to encounter the campaign via televised news or election advertising. Ian McAllister points out that "the level of television viewing of politics is particularly high in Australia."[20] An early evening news bulletin on the top-rating national Seven network may be watched in as many as 1.5 million homes. When the same story is also carried by the Nine and Ten commercial networks and by the publicly owned ABC, it is likely to be seen by more than five million viewers (or 40% of electors).

Table 25.2 shows the use that voters made of print and broadcasting media to follow the 2004 election. Two in every three (69%) reported making "some" or a "good deal" of use of television news to follow the unfolding campaign. Not surprisingly the parties and their strategists continue to place great store on "earned media" and securing favorable television news coverage.[21] Indeed over the sequence of campaigns fought during the 1990s parties became especially adroit at managing the broadcast news media—for example by limiting their leaders' daily, carefully planned and scripted appearances before the cameras to insure that news broadcasts carry only the chosen "message of the day," and by imposing a tight veil of secrecy over the locations selected for these pre-planned appearances to prevent their disruption by demonstrators.

Televised advertising—or "paid media"—also retains a major place in Australian election campaigns. With the US, Australia is one of the few contemporary democracies to place no legislative restraint upon the purchase of broadcasting time by parties and candidates. (The only restriction is upon the broadcast of election advertising in the last forty-eight hours before polling day.) Moreover Australia has a generous public election funding scheme that underpins the campaign spending of parties and encourages them to purchase extensive broadcast time. It is true that the amounts that parties spend on advertising are miniscule in comparison to spending in US elections. For example, during the formal, six-week-long 2004 campaign the Labor and Liberal parties each spent some A\$15 million.[22] But this amount represented a sizeable portion of their overall budget. Indeed Sally Young calculates that the two major parties commit about 70% of their election budgets on television advertising. She demonstrates that between 1974 and 1998—the period for which reliable data are available[23]—their combined spending on broadcast advertising grew by 900%.[24] Often election advertising on television is negative. It is commonplace to use television spots to attack the credibility of rival party leaders.

Table 25.2. How Voters Used the Media to Follow the 2004 Campaign (%)

	Followed Campaign in Newspapers	Followed Campaign on TV	Followed Campaign on Radio
A Good Deal	15.2	28.0	14.2
Sometimes	41.7	41.0	29.9
Not Much	30.1	23.9	30.7
Never	13.0	7.1	25.2

Source: Australian Election Study, 2004.

In sharp contrast to the United States, but in common with other parliamentary democracies, Australian politics are not candidate-centered. In the case of both the Liberals and the party leader (as the prime minister or opposition leader), the central party organization and its professional advisers retain a tight control over the televised campaign and its content. The leaders of each party dominate the campaign as it is reported by television. Individual candidates for the Senate and House of Representatives seldom feature in party advertising. They very rarely receive television news coverage on the national networks. Rather their constituency-level campaigns substantially depend upon their party's wider marketing efforts and upon their party leader as its chief salesperson. Indeed Australian parties can be thought of as having a franchise business model. In effect individual candidates are franchisees whose local-level activities are both assisted and constrained by their franchise agreement with their party head office. Furthermore their prospects for success substantially depend upon their party's overarching marketing strategy and success in using television to build their franchise "brand" name.

A Second "Virtual Revolution" in Campaigning

Figure 25.2 poses something of a puzzle. While television clearly looms large within Australian election campaigns, and while the Labor and Liberal parties have spent evermore-substantial amounts on broadcast election advertising, the hold that television has over voters is declining. Free-to-air television still provides the principal window through which most Australians view election campaigns. Yet the number of voters who report closely following election news on television fell appreciably during the 1990s. Figure 25.3 appears to confirm that fewer voters now follow the televised campaign. It shows a decade-long decline in the numbers watching the televised leaders' debates, which are an institutionalised feature of Australian elections. The audience for free-to-air television has slowly declined since the 1980s under the pressure of newer, rival entertainment forms such as the VCR, PlayStations, home computers, the Internet and—after its introduction in 1995—subscription television.

At first glance it appears that the parties' investments in carefully planned "earned media" campaigns to capture favorable television news coverage may now pay a smaller dividend than previously was the case. There are no comparable Australian Election Study data measuring the attention that voters pay to televised campaign ads. However if paying "a good deal" of attention to television news coverage of an election, or watching televised debates are proxy measures, then it might also seem that the major parties are not garnering the advantage that they seek in spending much of their campaign budgets on television advertising. In fact neither of these conclusions should be drawn. Campaign strategists may have originally been drawn to television

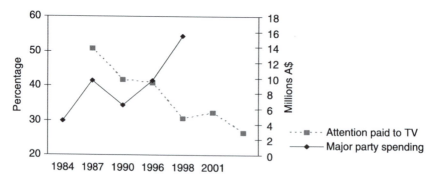

Figure 25.2. Party Spending on, and Voter Attention Paid to, TV Ads

Source: Various Australian Election Studies and Sally Young, "Spot On: The Role of Political Advertising in Australia," *Australian Journal of Political Science* 37 (1) (2002): 91.

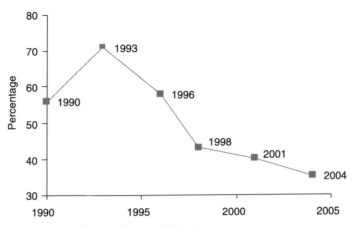

Figure 25.3. Voters Watching Televised Leaders' Debates

Source: Various Australian Election Studies.

because it enabled them to reach a mass audience but the contemporary campaigns now fought by the two major Australian parties are increasingly exercises in segmented or niche rather than mass marketing. In this respect electioneering in Australia is again following a trend that has been observed in other Western democracies.

Insofar as elections are exercises in communication, parties and candidates will be drawn to experiment with new technologies seen to offer more effective ways of influencing voters. Television is the obvious, much remarked-upon example. Far more so than the airplane, telephone, fax machine and photocopier which each had a "solid impact on their own," in the 1960s and 1970s television dramatically transformed "political campaign methodology."[25] More recently computer technologies have greatly expanded the storing, processing and transmission of information, and also begun to alter the ways in which parties and candidates communicate with voters.[26] In the lead up to the Australian 2007 election various parties experimented with YouTube and Facebook. The availability of "new communication technologies such as the Internet, direct mailing, and telephone banks" offer campaigners new tools and are seemingly changing the "mechanics of campaigning"[27] and perhaps even its very character.

Norris sees "the age of television" not as the culmination of the modernization of electioneering, but as laying the foundation for a further "*postmodern*" phase of campaigning that began to take shape in the 1980s, but which is still "under development" and "more clearly evident in some societies than in others." A defining feature of this new and still unfolding postmodern era of continual campaigning is that "professional consultants on advertising, public opinion, marketing and strategic news management" assume coequal importance with politicians. Their skills, she argues, are even more needed in a context where media have fragmented into a "complex and incoherent environment of multiple channels, outlets, and levels," and in which partisan allegiances have eroded and voting behavior is more volatile. A hallmark of postmodern campaigning is the use of new technologies that allow an interactive and highly targeted communication with voters.[28]

We have seen that Jaensch also believes that the seeds of a second "virtual revolution" in the style of campaigning were sown by the Australian parties' embrace of television as the principal means of political communication from 1972 onward. Broadcast television obliged parties to learn new tricks and to draw upon professional advice. In particular, the sheer expense of television advertising encouraged Labor and Liberal strategists to ensure that these monies were well spent, and to make increased use of opinion polling and focus group research to better target, and to confirm that their political spots had the desired impact. The pollsters and other specialist

351

advisers that the parties hired steered them toward a "positivistic, scientistic, unsentimental approach to communication and persuasion" far more reliant upon focus-group pre-tests than ideology.[29] In particular pollsters taught parties to recognize that the electorate comprised a variety of distinct segments each of which might be appealed to or "targeted" in terms of its own interests. The major Australian parties had initially embraced televised election advertising in the 1970s as a means of conducting "truly national mass campaigns" and broadcasting their campaign message into living rooms everywhere. Election ads were—and still are—used to boost a party leader's image or to attack an opponent's leadership credentials. However by the latter 1980s, parties had learned that they could use strategic polling to fine-tune and "target their TV efforts on specific groups within the national electorate." As a result their television advertising campaigns ceased to be "national effort[s] of persuasion."[30]

During the 1980s both parties learned that winning elections required a "catch-all" approach, and the election-by-election assembling of "coalitions or alliances of groups to form a majority."[31] Labor pioneered a "key marginal seats" strategy under the guidance of "opinion pollsters, focus-group interpreters, [and] direct-marketing wizards" who—along with advertising professionals—assumed an increasingly important role.[32] This involved identifying, and then appealing to the subgroups of voters likely to determine the outcome in finely balanced, marginal electorates. Television advertising was one tool used to target these subgroups. For example, ahead of the 1990 election Labor's research identified environmentally aware voters as such a critical subgroup. Consequently much of its election advertising was "suffused with a rich and relevant imagery" and, in what its advertising agency (John Singleton) later declared "the most important ad of the campaign," Labor directly appealed to "green" voters for support: "if you care about the environment . . . your preference choice must be Labor."[33] Television advertising needs to be thought of as a form of "narrowcasting" able to reach audiences with distinct characteristics. In response to competition, and in an effort to shore up its revenue base, Australian commercial free-to-air television has refined its programming strategies in order to deliver audiences with particular demographic attributes to advertisers. This in turn has allowed party strategists to direct televised campaign ads at specific interest and demographic groups. But the careful targeting of specific groups of voters now goes beyond making strategic use of the demographic profile of audiences that particular television programs may attract.

The 1996 campaign that brought the Liberals to power employed an initial thirty-second spot intended to dispel any perception, lingering from his first stint as opposition leader, that John Howard was "anti-Asian." Without spoken text, it featured a sequence of shots of the Liberal leader "chatting and laughing with a variety of Australians ranging from babies and elderly people to council workers"[34] along with a jingle with the chorus "for all of us." The specific lyric "for a better future for our families" was synchronized with a shot of an Asian family, and a smiling John Howard pictured with a young Asian male, perhaps a student. While otherwise unremarkable, this ad does illustrate how political commercials are used to target specific constituencies, even where this is not their obvious purpose. At one level this spot was clearly intended to reassure voters with an Asian background that the Liberal leader was no threat, his 1987 opposition to Asian immigration notwithstanding. But it also concluded with the line "not just for some . . . for all of us."[35] It introduced the slogan that was to become the cornerstone of the Liberal attack on the incumbent Keating Labor government as beholden to special interests, including the multicultural lobby and organized ethnic interests.[36] Thus the ad and its implication that Labor governed for special interests and not "all of us" is a particular illustration of "dog whistling" or the use of political messages that possess quite different meanings for different audience segments.

The Liberals' 1996 campaign also included a series of television spots intended to insure that it's "campaign was locally relevant, and driven through local issues."[37] These were a significant advance upon the practice both parties had pursued since the late 1970s of preparing different versions of the same ad for broadcast in individual states. They represented a new form of narrowcasting and niche marketing that both parties adopted in fighting subsequent campaigns. "Localized" ads were aired in regional Australia where the "footprint" of regional telecasters allowed the Liberals to target specific marginal seats. Each spot was predicated upon extensive research and prepared according to a standard formula. Their aim was to reduce broader themes pursued in the Liberals' national-level earned and paid media campaign to identifiable local issues—for example to translate the coalition's health policy into a concrete promise to renovate a local hospital or to paint its transport policy as the solution to a well-known local traffic bottleneck.

This same 1996 Liberal campaign is noteworthy for several other reasons. At the national level it relied upon attack ads directed at the character of the Labor leader. These marked a new development: they were distinctive, hard hitting, overwhelmingly negative and highly "personal."[38] Unflattering images of Paul Keating were shown in black and white. In some cases the "historical footage" was altered digitally for effect. Ads were quickly prepared using new non-linear video editing technology rather than film. The Liberals elected not to contract a specific advertising agency to prepare election advertising. Instead the party assembled a team of advertising specialists from different advertising agencies to produce ads "in-house" within its Melbourne campaign headquarters. This maximized the opportunity to "use valuable television dollars to [quickly and decisively] counter Labor claims."[39] It also brought the research and advertising arms of the Liberal campaign directly together (to enable a more interactive or responsive style of campaigning). It is noteworthy that the Liberals retained this same formula for subsequent campaigns, and that, prior to the 2004 campaign, Labor ended its five-year relationship with Saatchi & Saatchi to imitate this Liberal initiative, announcing that it would assemble what its national secretary described as a "virtual agency" to contest the next federal election.[40]

Database-driven, "Below-the-line" Campaigning

A journalist given rare access to the Liberal "war room" for the 1996 campaign reported that during the final weeks of the election—a campaign in which the party spent 8% of their A\$16.7 million budget on research—the Liberals assembled and analyzed some 2,000 pages of polling data each night.[41] This is a pointer to the importance of polling and to the sophistication of the tracking of voters which is pivotal to the centrally controlled campaigns fought by both major parties. Some of the Liberals' opinion research would have been directed at evaluating the impact of their television advertising. But the scale of the Liberals' polling suggests the party strategists also paid detailed attention to trends in key marginal seats and to local-level "below-the-line" campaigning that does not rely upon television.

A key marginal seat is analogous to a US "battle ground" or "swing" state. These are individual electorates with the potential to decide the election in which little separates the two major parties. They are easily identified. The Australian House of Representatives is elected using a preferential voting system that obliges voters to rank candidates in order of preference and requires the winning candidate to obtain an absolute, rather than a simple majority. It is a relatively straightforward to calculate or estimate the "two-party preferred vote" and the margin that divides the coalition and Labor parties in each seat. Moreover Australian electoral laws do not—as is the case in, say, Canada—cap the amount which candidates and parties can spend on campaigning in individual electorates. In short, the central party organizations are able to accurately identify the subset of marginal seats that they must hold or capture, and then concentrate their campaign efforts and resources on winning these. In these circumstances there is every incentive to attempt to identify and target the particular groups of undecided or uncommitted electors whose votes may prove crucial in each key marginal seat.

Norris' account of postmodern campaigning emphasizes that new technologies now allow candidates and parties to establish the direct contact with voters that characterized the much earlier era of mass parties, but via direct mail, automated telephone canvasing and other similar hi-tech methods. The "below-the-line" strategies that Australian parties have refined in key marginal seats illustrate her point. These make extensive use of persuasive direct mail and—most recently—automated telephone canvasing. Unlike television advertising, which is a relatively blunt instrument, direct mail can be precisely targeted: "the power of direct mail . . . lies in the parties' ability to send it to specific voters."[42] When supported by the extensive databases that both Australian major parties now possess, direct mail allows specific appeals to be made to a variety of subgroups of voters having particular interests.

Australian parties are no longer required to report their campaign expenditure in ways that allow calculation of the proportion they spend on particular forms of political communication. In 1996—the last election for which this data is available—the Liberal Party spent almost A$2 million (15%) and the coalition parties A$2.9 million (18%) of their overall campaign budgets on direct mail. However Sally Young points to estimates that the parties each spent some A$15 million on direct mail during the 2001 campaign,[43] which—if accurate—would suggest a recent, marked rise in the use of direct mail and a pronounced shift toward individually targeting voters, which is consistent with the parties' growing emphasis on "below-the-line" campaigning. Any recent escalation in the use of direct mail has been built on a long-established foundation.

The Labor and Liberal parties have each used direct mail since the early 1980s.[44] It quickly became an important election weapon. In the eight months prior to the 1990 poll, Labor alone mailed ten million items of direct mail—six million of these "in selected marginal seats."[45] In Australia, where the system of public election funding established in 1984 provides something of a financial buffer, direct mail has been used to persuade voters rather than to raise campaign funds. Its use is made all the easier because parties have access to, and are able to build their databases upon, the comprehensive lists of voters' names and details maintained by the Australian Electoral Commission.

The availability of these voter rolls encouraged both major parties to imitate the use of direct mail that had earned a reputation as a "silent killer" in US campaigns in the 1980s. Labor pioneered the use of direct mail using MS-DOS based database and desktop publishing software called Polfile developed in 1986 by an associated company, East West Insight. A decade later, and after a dispute about ownership of the technology, Labor switched to more user-friendly Windows-based software called Electrac, developed by Magenta Linas Software.[46] Between 1987 and 1990 the Liberals experimented with direct mail campaigning in "a small way" and without a standard "PC based software program." Following their defeat in 1990, the Liberals commissioned software for a personalized electoral roll system (PERS) and, then in 1992, replaced PERS with a nationally used system, Feedback, developed by a Queensland company, Datasearch.[47] Feedback became "fully operational just in time for the 1996 campaign." As the then Liberal campaign director remarked, it provided the Liberals with a new "capacity in every electorate to develop very close campaigning."[48]

The direct mail software packages initially used by Labor and the Liberals required considerable training, ran on expensive hardware and hence encouraged a centrally controlled campaign. Candidate mail-outs were typically prepared by, or carried out under the immediate supervision of state party headquarters or the national secretariat. However the second generation of Windows-based software was user-friendly. When it became available in the latter 1990s, computers able to run it were relatively inexpensive and widely available. As a result use of direct mail software devolved to the local level. Each party managed this in a different way. Electrac is provided to Labor candidates. The Liberals require candidates to purchase their own software.[49] There are still mechanisms in place to aggregate data in a national database, and to regularly update the Feedback software being used by Liberal candidates. Candidates are often provided with pro forma letters that can be distributed, and their use of Feedback is audited after each election. However local-level direct mail campaigns are no longer head office-controlled except in the small number of key marginals where all aspects of the party campaign are tightly controlled.

Feedback and Electrac now allow the highly targeted and individualized political communication that is a hallmark of postmodern campaigning. However, this is limited by the parties' capacity to build and maintain accurate databases. The process by which this is done is outwardly straightforward. Voter lists obtained from the Australian Electoral Commission are cross-matched with sources such as Telstra's *White Pages*. Thereafter data about the political views of individual voters is added as it comes to hand—for instance when party volunteers doorknock electorates, or when voters register issues that they are interested in by returning questionnaires distributed by candidates or by writing to, or telephoning, their local member of parliament. As it accumulates through successive federal and state campaigns, this data provides the parties with an especially valuable resource. It can be overlain with aggregate census data from the ABS Supermap geo-demographic mapping system broken down to census district level, and with similar data provided by the Australian Bureau of Statistics, say, charting unemployment levels.[50]

Maintaining databases is an ongoing, labor-intensive task. This gives an advantage to incumbents since each individual member of parliament is, at public expense, able to hire three or four electorate staff. Peter Van Onselen and Wayne Errington suggest that federal parliamentarians are better placed than their less well-resourced state counterparts, who in turn are much better positioned than challengers whose campaigns rely heavily upon often-scarce volunteer labor. They also point out that the Liberals presently enjoy a particular advantage by virtue of their occupancy of the government benches, having not only more parliamentarians and therefore staff, but also the support of the taxpayer-funded Government Members' Secretariat, which plays a key role in training Liberal parliamentarians to effectively use Feedback.[51]

A database such as Feedback can also be used for targeted telephone canvasing. Both major parties closely guard details of their campaign methodology. However until quite recently telephone canvasing in Australian campaigns appears to have been less well advanced than the use of direct mail—and less systematically used than in comparable countries such as the UK. It is noteworthy that a survey of party communication staff undertaken during 2000 by Rachel Gibson and Stephen Ward found that Labor considered telephone canvasing "quite important" but ranked this form of campaign communication well below the "most important," broadcast media. The Liberals attached more weight to telemarketing but nonetheless did not rank it as highly important.[52] Certainly Australian parties have some way to go if the litmus test of postmodern campaigning is the British Labour Party's "Operation Turnout" in which a North Shields call center with some sixty staff, in the six months ahead of the 2001 British election, regularly phoned undecided voters in selected constituencies, seeking in each instance to build an ongoing relationship with individual voters that would secure their vote.[53]

Labor employed automated telephone canvasing in selected marginal electorates early in the 2007 Australian election. But until 2004, when the Liberals flooded marginal electorates with computerized "advocacy calls" during the last days of the campaign, Australian parties had made quite rudimentary use of telemarketing. John Warhurst describes the early application of telephone canvasing in 1987 in key marginal seats to build the Polfile database.[54] Almost a decade later, during its 1996 federal campaign, the Liberals conducted a similar, more extensive, telephone campaign with the goal of building up a database encompassing about 10,000 swinging voters in each marginal seat. In some cases call centers were used. Mostly the task was left to volunteers who did not always complete their allocated number of calls. Subsequently Mark Textor said "if there are 5000 households and you connect to three quarters of them, that is a powerful technique."[55] Expecting a swing against the government, the goal of the Liberals' 1998 "localized" campaign was to "firewall" their candidates in vulnerable seats by counteracting the Labor campaign with carefully targeted messages employing local themes and issues. The tactics it used included "advocacy calling" in which commercial call centers made "hundreds of thousands" of calls to undecided voters during the last weeks of the election to remind them of their Liberal candidate's record on "cleaning up" local issues or providing "practical assistance" to the local community.[56]

In the last days of the 2001 campaign, with party pollsters finding nearly a quarter of voters in marginal seats still undecided, Labor contracted a commercial call center to conduct "telephone canvassing throughout Australia," with callers identifying themselves as telephoning on behalf of candidates and speaking from a prepared script.[57] During the forty-eight-hour broadcast media blackout at the end of the 2004 federal campaign the Liberals moved away from the use of call centers and party volunteers. Instead they turned to automated or computer-assisted dialling (with which they had only previously experimented with in state elections). They hired the Chicago-based Expedite Media firm to place calls in which voters were variously urged to listen to pre-recorded messages from the prime minister, other prominent Liberal politicians, local candidates or even candidates' wives. The technology used was able to detect answering machines and to leave an appropriate pre-recorded message. Liberal research found that "those calls had a very positive effect and people appreciated the fact that they got a direct and unfiltered message from a political leader in a new, innovative way."[58]

Although the development of database technology and computer-assisted dialling gave impetus to individually targeted telephone canvasing, neither of the Labor nor Liberal parties have been as enthusiastic about this method of campaign communication as about using direct mail to target voters. Phillippe Maarek argues that the telemarketing of politics has "evolved in different countries, according to cultural habits."[59] Australian members of parliament now enjoy sizeable postage allowances, have offices equipped to produce direct mail, have their party's software installed on their office computers and are familiar with this means of communicating with constituents. Moreover, since direct mail came first and quickly became a staple part of campaigning in the 1990s, its continued importance might also be explained by Richard Rose's dictum that the "characteristic response of campaigners to change in . . . communications technology has not been to abandon old techniques, but rather to graft on or add new techniques of electoral organisation and persuasion to traditional procedures."[60] Just as technological development made telemarketing of politics possible, the introduction caller-ID and screening devices and the rapid take-up of (unlisted) mobile phones may now limit its utility as a campaign weapon. Of course these new technologies themselves offer new possibilities for targeting voters.

During the 2001 and 2004 Australian campaigns neither major party found a use for SMS other than to link head office and candidates, or—a Liberal initiative in 2001—to inform journalists of their opponents' stumbles in the hope of securing more favorable news coverage. There is a parallel here with the parties' use of the Internet, which has yet to usher in the "new phase in political communication" often claimed for it.[61] Those who see use of the Internet and tools such as blogs as the cutting edge of campaigning in the United States lament that Australian politicians have been slow to utilize the potential of new technology for electioneering. For all its potential to push their message and "gather more specific information on their voters with opinion polls and cookies" there are still many in both parties who are skeptical about the web.[62] To date, even with the example of the innovative use of the Internet by US candidates such as Howard Dean (2004 presidential cycle) and Barack Obama (2008 presidential cycle), Australian parties have made "very modest" use of the Internet in campaigning.[63] In 2004 just 12% of respondents to the 2004 Australian Election Study survey reported using the Internet to obtain campaign information. Neither party offered more than a pedestrian official webpage from which the faithful and curious could download policies. Neither encouraged its candidates to publish their own individual websites. In the subsequent 2007 campaign both parties—especially Labor—did make much publicised use of MySpace and YouTube to post campaign commercials. However this appears to have been primarily directed at generating secondary mainstream news coverage.

There may be a number of reasons why the major Australian parties have not yet enthusiastically embraced online campaigning. There are technical barriers. Broadband in Australia is relatively slow and expensive. Other obstacles reflect Australia's distinctive political setting. Australia lacks the vibrant "blogosphere" that enlivens US politics. Parties have not found a way to harvest e-mail addresses that can be married to their key marginal seat campaigns, and Australia's public election funding scheme provides a degree of security and minimizes the incentive to exploit the web as a fundraising tool.

Conclusion

The Australian political system does have its idiosyncrasies. For example compulsory voting and public election funding arrangements in place lend Australian elections a particular character. Its three-year parliamentary term ensures that elections come quickly around, and this provides a particular impetus to continuous campaigning. Incumbency incurs the right to decide when elections are held and provides the party (or coalition) in government with a sizeable advantage—to the point where government has changed hands on just five occasions in the twenty-four federal elections held in the sixty-year period, 1944–2004. Nonetheless scholars who have investigated "Australian, Canadian, West European and Latin American election campaigns" have observed the same "universal" transformation of campaigning. Worldwide "there is plenty of evidence of an advanced degree of professionalism"[64] and Australian election campaigns are no exception. Campaigning "down under" exhibits much of the same professionalism and has much in common with electioneering in other, comparable democracies. Indeed professionals such as Crosby–Textor well experienced in running Australian campaigns have been able to find a market for their skills elsewhere.

Labor and Liberal parties still invest heavily in television. Advertising and the stage-managed appearances of their leaders before television news cameras remain pivotal to establishing a party "brand." Earned and paid media are still important elements of the parties' centrally controlled campaigns. However both Labor and the Liberals have progressively explored new ways of "narrowcasting" made possible by new—as well as adaptations of old—communication technologies. In the past decade "below-the-line" campaigning has assumed a particular importance. There is always going to be some variation in the electorate-level campaigns fought across a large continent where the 150 House of Representatives seats range in size from 30 to 2.3 million square kilometers, and where the parties judge some seats safe, others unwinnable, and a just modest number of key marginals as vital to their success. But new technologies have encouraged a further diversity. Below-the-line campaigns in key marginal seats involve the deconstruction of the parties' national campaign messages and their reassembly for consumption in specific local contexts. Opinion research has been used to understand the interests, attitudes and demographic characteristics of undecided voters. Database driven canvasing—especially but not only direct mail—has been used to re-establish a more direct and interactive contact with those voters whose ballots will make a difference. This mix of elements—a presidential-like focus on party leaders, a reliance upon pollsters, advertising specialists and other professionals, and a more localized and interactive communication with individual voters—suggests that Norris' wider thesis that campaigning is entering a new, postmodern phase provides a useful lens through which to view campaigning in Australia.

Notes

1 For example see Fritz Plasser with Gunda Plasser, *Global Political Campaigning: A Worldwide Analysis of Campaigning Professionals and their Practices* (Westport, Conn.: Praeger, 2002), esp. 15–20 and 350–1; and David Swanson and Paolo Mancini, *Politics, Media and Modern Democracy: An International Study of Innovations in Electoral Campaigning and their Consequences* (Westport, Conn.: Praeger, 1996).

2 See Andreas M. Wüst, Hermann Schmitt, Thomas Gschwend and Thomas Zittel, "Candidates in the 2005 Bundestag Election: Mode of Candidacy, Campaigning and Issues," *German Politics* 15 (4) (2006): 420–38.

3 Rüdiger Schmitt-Beck and David M. Farrell, "Studying Political Campaigns and Their Effects," in *Do Political Campaigns Matter? Campaign Effects in Elections and Referendums*, ed. David M. Farrell and Rüdiger Schmitt-Beck (London: Routledge, 2002), 3.

4 Pippa Norris, "Do Campaign Communications Matter for Civic Engagement? American Elections from Eisenhower to G.W. Bush," in *Do Political Campaigns Matter?*, ed. Farrell and Schmitt-Beck, 128. For a similar view of campaigns as communication see Robert Denton and Gary Woodward, *Political Communication in America*, 3rd ed. (Westport, CT: Praeger, 1998), 97.

5 Swanson and Mancini, *Politics, Media and Modern Democracy*, 13.

6 Margaret Scammell, *Designer Politics* (New York: St Martin's Press, 1995), 26.

7 Dean Jaensch, *Election!* (St Leonards: Allen & Unwin, 1995), 140.

8 Schmitt-Beck and Farrell, "Studying Political Campaigns," 12. Also see Wüst, Schmitt, Gschwend and Zittel, "Candidates in the 2005 Bundestag Election," 424.

9 Jaensch, *Election!*, 141–2.

10 Ian Ward, " 'Localising the National'. The Rediscovery and Reshaping of Local Campaigning in Australia," *Party Politics* 9 (5) (2003): 583–600.

11 Jaensch, *Elections!*, 140.

12 See Ian Ward, "Cartel Parties and Elections in Australia," in *Political Parties in Transition?*, ed. Ian Marsh (Annadale: Federation Press, 2003), 72–8; and Lisa Young and Patrick Weller, "Political Parties and the Party System: Challenges for Effective Governing," in *Institutions on the Edge*, ed. Michael Keating, John Wanna and Patrick Weller (Sydney: Allen & Unwin, 2000).

13 This chapter was written as the 2007 election campaign was underway but before the prime minister had announced the election day and commenced formal proceedings.

14 Australian Election Study, 2004. Canberra: Social Science Data Archives, the Australian National University, 2005, http://asda.anu.edu.au.

15 Dean Jaensch and David S. Mathieson, *A Plague on Both Your Houses: Minor Parties in Australia* (Sydney: Allen & Unwin, 1998).

16 See Ian McAllister, "Calculating or Capricious? The New Politics of Late Deciding Voters" in *Do Campaigns Matter?*, ed. David M. Farrrell and Rüdiger Schmitt-Beck (London: Routledge, 2002), 22–40.

17 Pippa Norris, *A Virtuous Circle: Political Communication in Postindustrial Societies* (New York: Cambridge University Press, 2000), 144, 160.

18 Ibid., 137–8.

19 Stephen Mills, *The New Machine Men* (Ringwood: Penguin, 1986).

20 McAllister, "Calculating or Capricious?," 35.

21 Quentin Beresford, *Parties, Policies and Persuasion* (Melbourne: Addison Wesley Longman, 1997), 28–29, 53–6.

22 Sarah Miskin and Richard Grant, "Political Advertising in Australia", *Research Brief No. 5*, Parliamentary Library of Australia (November 2004), 1.

23 As Miskin and Grant note, "the transparency of campaign-specific expenditure in Australia was lost in 1997 when a legislative change . . . removed the requirement for parties to file election returns disclosing election expenditures." Ibid., 18.

24 Sally Young, "Spot On: The Role of Political Advertising in Australia," *Australian Journal of Political Science* 37 (1) (2002): 81, 91.

25 Sig Mickelson, *From Whistle Stop to Sound Bite* (New York: Praeger, 1989), 5.

26 See Jaensch, *Elections!*, 140–1.

27 Rachel Gibson and Andrea Römmele, "Changing Campaign Communications. A Party-centred Theory of Professionalised Campaigning," *Harvard Journal of Press and Politics* 6 (4) (January 2001), 31.

28 Norris, *A Virtuous Circle*, 140–9.

29 Jay G. Blumler and Dennis Kavanagh, "The Third Age of Political Communication: Influences and Features," *Political Communication* 16 (3) (1999): 212–13.

30 Mills, *The New Machine Men*, 139.

31 Ibid.
32 John Warhurst and Andrew Parkin, "The Labor Party: Images, History and Structure," in *The Machine*, ed. John Warhurst and Andrew Parkin (Sydney: Allen & Unwin, 2000), 46. Also see Beresford, *Parties, Policies and Persuasion*, 26.
33 Clem Lloyd, "The 1990 Media Campaign," in *The Greening of Australian Politics*, ed. Clive Bean, Ian McAllister and John Warhurst (Melbourne: Longman Cheshire, 1990), 103.
34 Beresford, *Parties, Policies and Persuasion*, 50.
35 Sally Young, *The Persuaders* (Sydney: Pluto Press, 2004), 213–14.
36 Andrew Robb, "The Liberal Campaign," in *The Politics of Retribution*, ed. Clive Bean, Marian Simms, Scott Bennett and John Warhurst (Sydney: Allen and Unwin, 1997), 37–9.
37 Ibid., 39.
38 Sarah Miskin, "Campaigning in the 2004 Federal Election: Innovations and Traditions," *Research Note* No. 30, 2004–2005, Canberra: Parliamentary Library of Australia (February 2005).
39 Robb, "The Liberal Campaign," 38.
40 *The Australian*, October 31, 2003.
41 Pamela Williams, *The Victory* (Sydney: Allen & Unwin, 1997), 201.
42 Miskin, "Campaigning in the 2004 Federal Election."
43 Sally Young, "Killing Competition: Restricting Access to Political Communication Channels in Australia," *AQ: Journal of Contemporary Analysis* 75 (3) (2003): 15. It is possible that such leaked estimates include direct mail sent by incumbent parliamentarians and charged against their parliamentary postal allowance rather than party-funded mail-outs alone. If this is the case then the growth in the use of direct mail would be less dramatic.
44 See Mills, *New Machine Men*, 14, 105.
45 Frank Gruen and Michelle Grattan, *Managing Government* (Sydney: Allen & Unwin, 1993), 82.
46 See Peter Van Onselen and Wayne Errington, "Electoral Databases; Big Brother or Democracy Unbound?" *Australian Journal of Political Science* 39 (2) (2004): 352 and *The Age*, August 29, 1996.
47 Frank O'Collins, "Political and Fundraising Direct Mail," *Journal of the Australian Direct Mail Marketing Solution* 8 (3) (1992): 18–19.
48 Peter Van Onselen and Wayne Errington, "Development and Operation: Major Party Voter Databases." Paper read to the 2003 Annual Conference of the Australasian Political Studies Association (University of Tasmania, Hobart), 12, and Lynton Crosby, "The Liberal Party" in *The Paradox of Parties*, ed. Marian Simms (Sydney: Allen & Unwin. 1996), 162.
49 Van Onselen and Errington, "Electoral Databases: Big Brother or Democracy Unbound?," 355.
50 Ibid., 353.
51 Ibid., 356–7.
52 Rachel Gibson and Stephen Ward, "Virtual Campaigning: Australian Parties and the Impact of the Internet," *Australian Journal of Political Science* 37 (1) (2002): 115.
53 Paul Whiteley and Patrick Seyd, "Party Election Campaigning in Britain: The Labour Party," *Party Politics* 9 (5) (2003): 641–2.
54 John Warhurst, "The ALP Campaign," in *Australian Votes*, ed. Ian McAllister and John Warhurst (Melbourne: Longman Cheshire, 1987), 54.
55 *Weekend Australian*, October 17–18, 1998.
56 *Weekend Australian*, October 10–11, 1998.
57 *The Age*, November 7 and 9, 2001.
58 *The Age*, October 18, 2004.
59 Phillippe Maarek, *Political Marketing and Communication* (London: John Libbey, 1995), 148.
60 Richard Rose, *Influencing Voters*: A Study of Campaign Rationality (London: Faber and Faber, 1967), 14.
61 Gibson and Ward, "Virtual Campaigning," 99. Also see Peter Chen, Rachel Gibson and Karin Geiselhart, *Electronic Democracy? The Impact of New Communications Technologies on Australian Democracy*, Democratic Audi of Australia, Report No. 6 (Canberra: Australian National University, 2006).
62 Gibson and Ward, "Virtual Campaigning," 102.
63 Chen, Gibson and Geiselhart, *Electronic Democracy*, 46.
64 Plasser, *Global Political Campaigning*, 15, 350.

26

Election Campaigns in the Philippines

Louis Perron

The Philippines is often described as the loudest democracy in South-East Asia. At first glance, Philippine campaigns do indeed look like big fiestas with colorful campaign posters and singing candidates. But that's only half of the story. In reality, Philippine campaigns are a fascinating mix of traditional patronage politics and modern high-tech campaigns.

In order to comprehend Philippine campaigns, it is important to understand the country's political system, history and geography. In the 1950s, the Philippines was a more or less functioning democracy.[1] In 1965, Ferdinand Marcos was first elected president and after his re-election, he declared martial law and established an authoritarian regime. This regime collapsed in 1986 after the so-called People Power I, a popular uprising provoked by the murder of opposition leader Benigno Aquino. In a snap election, Aquino's widow Corazon succeeded Marcos.[2] A new constitution, which makes the Philippines a democratic republic following the US model, was approved. As typical in presidential systems, the head of the government, the president, is elected by direct universal suffrage for a six-year term. It is important to highlight, however, that in the Philippines the president and the vice president campaign together but—unlike in the US—are elected separately. As a result, it happened in 1992 and in 1998 that the president and the vice president were from opposing tickets. The multi-candidate system without a runoff has consigned the country to be governed by a minority president, a situation that has not helped the stabilization of the Philippine democracy.[3]

The Philippine Congress has a bicameral structure. Following the US model, it consists of a House of Representatives and a Senate. There are 219 members of the House who are elected for three-year terms in single-member constituencies. Then, there is a varying number of members elected through a party-list system, whose total cannot exceed 20% of the total number of members of Congress. The party-list seats in the House (in the present Congress there are twenty-one such seats) are thought to help represent the disadvantaged sectors of the society such as labor, the urban poor or the indigenous cultural communities.[4] As a result, each voter can cast two votes for Congress: a vote for one of the candidates in his or her district and a second vote for a party, with many voters not using their vote for the party list.

The Senate has twenty-four members who are elected for a six-year term with half of them being elected every three years. A senator can run for one re-election, then needs to wait for three years before he or she can run again for another two terms. Unlike in the US, however, Philippine senators are elected at large, which has important consequences on campaigns. Every election cycle, there are about twenty to twenty-five nationwide (senatorial) campaigns going on.

Philippine politics are personality- and candidate-centered and as a result, parties are fairly weak.[5] Similar to the situation in many Latin American countries, Philippine parties are more like electoral platforms and network organizations rather than programmatic associations of politicians with a similar political ideology. In terms of structuring the political space, the polarization around the president is in fact more important than the parties. Political players are either for or against the president; hence they belong to the administration or opposition camp.

The most basic unit of Philippine politics is the family where the wife of the candidate is often handling the campaign finances. Especially in the provinces, elections have a feudal touch where a few family clans compete against each other. This said, some of the main parties are the Christian Democratic *Lakas*, the Liberal Party (LP), the conservative Nationalist People's Coalition and the *Laban ng Demokratikong Pilipino* (LDP) (Struggle for Democratic Filipinos). *Akbayan* as well as *Bayan Muna* are leftist parties of socialist inspiration (and therefore do not compare with European social democratic labor parties). In fact, the communist party and the labor movement in general is a special case and subject of important previous research.[6] In short, the left played an important role during the People Power Revolution but then missed integration into the political system. To an important degree, the left remained an armed, revolutionary force and as a result, a mass social democratic party as there is in Europe and in some Latin American countries such as Brazil never developed. As a result, the re-distribution of wealth is not really an issue in Philippine politics the way it is in countries where such mass social democratic parties did develop.

Party switching is rampant in the Philippines. As an example, while presidential candidate Joseph Estrada won a clear victory in 1998, his allies won only about 20% of the congressional seats. Within a few weeks after the election, however, enough legislators switched so as to give Estrada a majority.[7] The weakness of the parties has an important impact on campaigns. In an environment with weak parties and a volatile public opinion, any politician with popularity and money can build a campaign organization.[8]

Logistics is a major challenge in a country that consists of more than 7,000 islands(!) and that counts eighty-eight million people. The islands are often divided into three major groups, namely Luzon, Visayas and Mindanao, but many of them are also extremely small. The national language is Tagalog, a Malay language, which is however not understood in many parts of the country. Local dialects such as Cebuano in Cebu, Visayas in Mindanao but also Ilongo, Bicolano or Ilocano are quite important. English is de facto the language of business but as far as the broader electorate is concerned, communication has to be in the local dialect. Though the Philippines was once the richest country of Asia after Japan, it is today officially classified as a developing country and one of the poorest in the region. It is still predominantly agricultural and a major source of exported labor. In recent years however, the administration of President Gloria Macapagal-Arroyo has been very successful in stabilizing the budget and attracting foreign investments. As a result, the economy has been continuously growing and the country has become a major destination of business process outsourcing.

What contributes to the description of the Philippines as the loudest democracy in South-East Asia, is the sheer amount of offices that are elected by universal suffrage. In addition to the president, the vice-president, the 250 members of Congress and the twenty-four senators, the elected powers include the governors and vice-governors of the eighty-one provinces as well as thousands of mayors and vice-mayors. Finally, the legislative power of the cities (the city councilors) and of the province (the provincial board members) are also elected by universal suffrage and at large.[9] While the Philippines is not a federal state (a transfer to a federal system has recently been debated), local elections have a long tradition in this country. As in many other countries, Philippine local government has gained in power and political importance during the past years.[10]

The quality and the consolidation of the Philippine democracy have been largely debated in previous research.[11] While democracy has been formally re-introduced after People Power I, the country has still some major problems including rampant corruption and activity of communist insurgents as well as Muslim separatists.[12] The latter one is subject of an important amount of research such as for example the studies about Islamic Mindanao offered by Thomas M. McKenna and Nathan G. Quimpo.[13] Further, previous research has also discussed the fact that the Philippine political system is still largely dominated by the elite. Many members of Congress, for example, belong to the old rich elite.[14] It is also sometimes debated to what degree the military—especially the younger generals—are devoted to democracy. Presidents since People Power I have indeed survived numerous coup attempts.[15]

Putting the Philippine democracy in comparative perspective, Mark R. Thompson concludes in a study that the Philippines is off the list of endangered democracies.[16] Other authors and observers go into the same direction and note that Philippine elections are more than episodes of vote buying.[17] Of course, the attempt of vote buying is (still) omnipresent. The simple fact that many politicians spend a third of their campaign budget on election day might be suspicious in this respect. Most Philippine voters have experienced attempts of vote buying and, of course, many voters take the offered money. But, who they really vote for on election day is another story.

While irregularities exist, the recent elections again offer several examples of underdog candidates winning against well-organized and financed political clans. In the province of Pampanga, Eduardo "Among Ed" Tongol Panlilio, a Catholic priest won an uphill fight against two well-entrenched clans. Grace M. Padaca, a former journalist and polio victim won re-election as governor of Isabela beating a powerful family clan for the second time in a row. The same holds true at the national level. During the 2007 Senate elections, two imprisoned military coup leaders made it to the winning top twelve. Pedro Laylo Jr and Carijane Dayag-Laylo come to a similar conclusion in an analysis of the 1998 presidential election.[18] Beyond the impact of family clans, regional and ethnic cleavages, the authors of this study found that the image of the main candidates had a significant impact on the vote. While their operationalization of the concept "*image*" is quite superficial (largely defined as trust and other positive personal qualities), the general conclusion (that there is more to electoral success than vote buying) is nevertheless important.

Philippine campaigners often talk about the concepts of *free market votes* and *command votes*, which are indeed helpful to comprehend Philippine elections. *Free market votes* are won through campaigning using ads, billboards, image and speeches. *Command votes*, on the other hand, are votes that local leaders deliver in exchange for patronage, pork barrel or other favors. This second kind of campaigning is often called *local machinery* in the Philippine campaign jargon. Most politicians have local leaders on their payroll. They are paid an allowance for each week of the campaign. In exchange, they wear the t-shirt of the candidate, go from fiesta to fiesta and let everybody know how great the candidate is. As television becomes more important, however, *machinery* is becoming less important. As a rule of thumb, it can be said that the more local the office a candidate is running for, and the more rural the district, the more important are the *command votes*. On the other hand, the higher the office and the more urban the district, the more important are the *free market votes*.

With regard to the consolidation of democracy, it is also important to mention that the Philippines has a vibrant civil society with thousands of non-governmental organizations that are active for the disadvantaged sectors of the society.[19] The country also has probably the freest press in the region where most television and radio stations are privately owned. The Center for Media Freedom and Responsibility (CMFR) regularly monitors the news coverage of presidential candidates.[20] For the last presidential election, when Fernando Poe Jr challenged incumbent president Gloria Macapagal-Arroyo, the CMFR study noted that there was barely an incumbency advantage or challenger disadvantage in terms of air time or news coverage. This being said, what Fritz Plasser calls *merchandizing journalism* is frequent especially at the local level.[21] The concept refers to the idea of politicians paying journalists for (positive) news coverage. Sometimes, candidates negotiate packages where candidates are offered interviews and coverage in exchange for and together with a certain amount of time buy.[22]

Religious faith is very important in Philippine culture.[23] More than 80% of Filipinos are Roman Catholic, while 5% are Muslim (who are located in Mindanao, the southern island of the country). Similar to Catholic Latin American countries such as Brazil, evangelical churches are on the rise in the Philippines. Religion and the Catholic Church in particular are important and powerful in Philippine politics. The Catholic Church firmly opposes birth control, which is one of the reasons explaining why the Philippines has one of the fastest growing populations in the world. This has important implications for the election campaigns. Since half of the voters are below the age of thirty-five, it is crucial for every candidate to court the youth. During the People Power Revolution, which ended the authoritarian regime of President Marcos, the Catholic Church played an extremely important role.[24] According to Samuel P. Huntington, Jaime Cardinal Sin may have played a more powerful role in bringing about the end of a regime than any other Catholic leader since the seventeenth century.[25] Cardinal Sin negotiated the arrangements that led to a united opposition ticket in the snap elections of February 7, 1986. He was further engaged in the election campaign and when Marcos tried to manipulate the election, Cardinal Sin used the church organization and the church radio station to mobilize the population.

This said, there are also limitations to the political influence of the church. During the 1998 presidential election campaign, the church clearly let voters know that it was opposing the election of movie actor Joseph Estrada; he still won in a landslide. Hofman makes an interesting point in this respect, comparing the influence of the church in Brazil, the Philippines and Kenya, concluding that in these cases under authoritarian rule, "the church became the primary channel of political opposition and became a surrogate of the interests of broader civil society."[26] Later when the political space opened up, the influence of the church became more selective. In all three cases, the churches were more successful in influencing constitutional reforms, a more restricted and contained process than highly partisan and politicized presidential elections, such as the election of Estrada in 1998.

In addition to the Catholic Church, there are other religious groups that play an important political role. The *El Shaddai* prayer movement and especially *Iglesia ni Cristo* (Church of Christ) are said to deliver the votes of their members in bloc.[27] In addition to the church, it is important to highlight that women played an important role in democratization in Asia.[28] Indeed, over the past decade and a half, women have led successful popular uprisings against dictators in Bangladesh, Indonesia, Pakistan and the Philippines. The female leaders were widows, wives or daughters of political martyrs and continued the cause of their male relatives. As a result, it is no surprise that women are more prominent as office-holders in the Philippines than in many other countries.[29]

Philippine election campaigns are festive occasions. During the campaign, candidates sing and dance, play jingles, bring singers and dancers to rallies, use nicknames and create colorful gimmicks. They are often described as candidate-centered popularity contests with name recognition being extremely important.[30] To understand the reason for this, it is important to highlight a unique feature of the Philippine electoral system: voters themselves have to write in the names of the candidates they select for each post.[31] This means that a voter is required to write (and remember) more than twenty names on election day. As a result, a candidate needs to appear on television and/or tour the provinces months (if not years) in advance of the election. It is therefore also no surprise that actors and other celebrities, who bring universal awareness to the table, have often been successful in Philippine elections.[32] However, it seems that in post-Estrada politics, celebrities have lost some of their appeal. During the 2007 elections, famous actor Cesar

Montano and star boxer Manny Pacquiao both lost their respective bids for Senate and Congress badly.

The 2004 presidential and senatorial election was a turning point in Philippine election campaigns. It was the first election that was held under the "Fair Election Practices Act," which allowed political television advertising. While a relatively new campaign tool in the Philippines, political ads have changed campaigns fundamentally and are now very important in Philippine campaigns.[33] During the last presidential election campaign, the main candidates spent roughly half of their campaign budget on advertising. Candidates who know how to use the new tool, can further influence an already volatile public opinion. This is exactly what happened during the 2004 and 2007 elections: candidates who were completely unknown or have already been written off had excellent results thanks to well-orchestrated and well-executed television campaigns. Other candidates, who early polls showed as winning, lost badly because they were on the air too late or with poor campaigns. Television networks are highly centralized in the Philippines and as a result, it is difficult to buy local advertising windows. Nevertheless, some members of Congress, mayors and even vice-mayors were already on the air during the 2007 campaigns. It is very likely that the trend for local candidates to go on television will further increase over the next few election cycles.

The new Fair Election Practices Act does not specifically prohibit negative advertising. Nevertheless, in view of the political culture and the multi-candidate and multi-party system, negative advertising might very easily backfire. Competitive or confrontational statements are seen as contrary to the Asian culture, which celebrates values such as harmony, politeness and respect. In order to fully comprehend Philippine campaign material, it is also important to highlight that the country is a "high-context culture" as compared to the "low-context culture" of the United States.[34] In the latter, campaigners rely on straightforward, explicit verbal messages. In the Philippines, however, where mutual respect and harmony are important cultural traits, what is said is less important than who is making a point and how things are said. In this sense, the meaning lies in the bigger environment consisting of a combination of events, relationships and images.

Other important campaign tools in addition to television—especially for local campaigns—are billboards and campaign posters.[35] In addition, the Manila Broadcasting Corp. (MBC) launched an important network of tiny radio stations with the goal of reaching every consumer and citizen at the local level.[36] With a radius of about six kilometers, these stations represent the most direct media link to communities and offer a precious opportunity to politicians.

Scholars and political observers are somehow split on the question whether the Internet plays an important role in Philippine campaigns or not. On the one hand, in a poor country such as the Philippines only a minority of the population has access to the Internet. As a result, it is an inadequate tool to reach the masses. On the other hand, it is true that the Internet played an important role during People Power II, the popular uprising that led to the ousting of President Joseph Estrada. The driving force behind the uprising was the more educated and Internet savvy elite and middle class. As many as 200 anti-Estrada websites and about 100 e-mail groups made it a multimedia revolt.[37]

Manila is often described as the text capital in the world. As a result, text messages sent via the mobile phone are an important campaign tool. During the mentioned ousting of President Joseph Estrada, more than seventy million text messages were sent during one day (compared to thirty million messages per day during Christmas break).[38] In fact, text messages are sometimes also preferred to diffuse negative and attack propaganda—often in the form of jokes. (See also, Chapter 20, by Julie Barko Germany and Justin Oberman, mobile phone technology and the Philippine elections.)

Going house to house and holding big rallies are also still quite important in Philippine campaigns. Especially as far as local offices are concerned, voters want to see and touch their candidates. In this respect, an extensive study of the Institute of Philippine Culture at the Ateneo University on how poor Filipinos make their voting choices is of particular interest.[39] The study found, for example, that the poor are very sensitive when a politician treats them as dirty or secretly sanitizes his hands after making contact.

The importance of fundraising is very important in Philippine election campaigns.[40] Similar to Thailand, the Commission of Elections "COMELEC" supervises the lawful conduct of elections. Philippine election laws are indeed quite detailed and complex. For example, campaigns are limited to a certain period of time (ninety days for nationwide and forty-five days for local elections). All campaign activities have to stop one day before the election and it is prohibited to sell alcohol on election day and the day before. While the liquor ban is strictly enforced, other rules, such as the spending limits, seem to be enforced less vigorously. Election day itself is a holiday. As a result, the Philippines generally has a high turnout with about 75 to 80% of the registered voters going to the polls.[41] Unlike, in the US, get-out-the-vote activities are less crucial for electoral success.

In East Asia—and the same holds true for the Philippines—there are few companies that specialize exclusively in political campaigning.[42] (See also Chapter 27, by Christian Schafferer, on other Asian elections systems.) There are few comparable networks such as journals, professional associations or academic programs as in the United States or in Latin America. Oftentimes, journalists, columnists, businessmen, advertising executives and/or legislative staff fulfill the role of campaign operatives and political consultants in the Philippines. The declaration of martial law was not helpful for the development of campaign skills. Luz Rimban explains in an investigative report on Philippine election campaigns that this is one of the reasons why some of today's operatives trace their roots to the revolutionary, leftist movement.[43]

To a certain degree, public opinion research companies fulfill the role of political consultants and strategists. The country has several polling companies with Social Weather Stations (SWS), Pulse Asia, Asia Research Organization (ARO), AC Nielsen and Philippine Survey and Research Center (PSRC) being the main ones. However, many candidates rely on self-made surveys that predict the respective candidate an electoral success only to be surprised when they lose on election day. As a result of the feudal structure of politics, it is often family members who play important roles of campaign operatives—even at the presidential level.[44] Oftentimes, the core group of the candidate, who makes the fundamental strategic, tactical and organizational decisions, consists largely of family members and personal friends. Allied politicians frequently fulfill the role of campaign manager such as the case of Senator Vicente Sotto III, who served as campaign manager for presidential candidate Fernando Poe, Jr, in 2004.

Philippine presidents have often hired American public relations consultants and lobbying firms to polish their personal and the country's image in the US as well as to lobby US Congress.[45] On the other side, there is also a long history of foreigners—especially Americans—coaching Philippine politicians. In 1969, Philippine President Ferdinand Marcos hired Joseph Napolitan, who had previously consulted for Presidents Kennedy and Johnson in the United States. This event marks most likely the beginning of modern international political consulting. Together with media specialist Robert Squier, Napolitan polished Marcos' image and assisted in overall campaign strategy. Since few people outside of Manila had television, radio became the most important communication tool. The campaign secured fifteen trucks, outfitted them with movie screens and projectors, and drove them from village to village.[46] When Corazon Aquino challenged President Ferdinand Marcos, American consultants were involved on both sides. While media consultant David Sawyer worked for Aquino, Marcos was represented by the firm of Black, Manafort, Stone & Kelly. Yvonne Chua, a journalist of the Philippine Center for Investigative Journalism, reports that other American political consultants such as Paul Bograd and David Sackett of the Virgina-based Tarrance Group have also worked for Philippine clients.[47]

It might indeed be helpful for a Philippine candidate to use public opinion research the way American political consultants use it, namely to develop a message and a campaign strategy. The power of message politics has long been under-estimated in Philippine politics. It was in fact presidential candidate Joseph Estrada in 1998 who pitched voters with a short but credible and appealing message. The entire campaign—one might say Estrada's entire political life—was an appeal to the masses, that he understands them, cares about them, that now is their time and that he will lift them out of poverty. It was concisely summarized in his campaign slogan "*Erap para sa mahirap*" (Erap—the nickname for Estrada—for the poor). While previous presidential candidates all belonged to the elite, Estrada tried to convey the impression that he was one with the poor. A good example for this was the day when Estrada filed his candidacy at the office of the Electoral Commission. In the Philippines, people use a *jeepney*, a sort of a small bus, as their most frequent transport vehicle. The day Estrada filed his candidacy, he drove and rode a *jeepney* himself and inside of the *jeepney* was his senatorial ticket. Further, the campaign had a clear strategy. While politicians normally tried to appeal to the ethno-geographic loyalties of Filipinos, Estrada's strategy was to target the poor nationwide. All the resources such as campaign funds and time of the candidate were allocated according to this strategy.

Since Estrada, several other candidates with an appealing message have successfully challenged frontrunners who only offered bland statements. Relying on unprofessional surveys, under-estimating the importance of the campaign message and a wrong allocation of resources are the three top reasons explaining why competitive candidates end up losing in Philippine elections. Successful Philippine candidates start early, build up the momentum of the unstoppable winner and find the right mix of *free market* and *command votes*. They have a simple but credible message, enough money to communicate the message and the discipline to implement the campaign plan.

Notes

1 Harold M. Vinacke, "Post-war Government and Politics of the Philippines," *The Journal of Politics* 9 (4) (1947): 717–30; Hirofumi Ando, "A Study of Voting Patterns in the Philippine Presidential and Senatorial Elections, 1946–1965," *Midwest Journal of Political Science* 13 (4) (1969): 567–86; Carl H. Lande, *Southern Tagalog Voting, 1946–1963: Political Behavior in a Philippine Region* (DeKalb, Ill.: Northern Illinois University, 1973).

2 Benedict J. Kerkvliet and Resil B. Mojares, *From Marcos to Aquino: Local Perspectives on Political Transition in the Philippines* (Quezon City: Ateneo de Manila University Press, 1991), 326; Teresita C. del Rosario, "Scripted Clashes: A Dramaturgical Approach to Three Uprisings in the Philippines." Unpublished PhD dissertation, Department of Sociology, Boston College, 2002, 285; R.J. May, "Elections in the Philippines 1986–1987," *Electoral Studies* 7 (1) (1988): 79–81.

3 "Political Fiesta Heats Up as Elections Near," *Inter Press Service*, April 30, 1998; "Our Senators Should Rise Above Themselves," *Business World*, October 6, 2003, 4.

4 "Opinion Party-list System is Being Abused," *Philippine Daily Inquirer*, April 4, 2001, 8.

5 Temario C. Rivera, "Transition Pathways and Democratic Consolidation in post-Marcos Philippines," *Contemporary Southeast Asia* 24 (3) (2002): 466; Steven Rood, "Elections as Complicated and Important Events in the Philippines," in *How Asia Votes*, ed. John Hsieh Fuh-sheng and David Newman (New York: Chatham House, 2002), 147–64.

6 Gregg R. Jones, *Red Revolution: Inside the Philippine Guerrilla Movement* (Boulder, CO: Westview Press, 1989); William Chapman, *Inside the Philippine Revolution* (New York: W.W. Norton, 1987), 288; Joel Rocamora, *Breaking Through: The Struggle within the Communist Party of the Philippines* (Pasig, Metro Manila: Anvil Publications, 1994), 225, 182; Patricio N. Abinales, *The Revolution Falters: The Left in Philippine Politics After 1986* (Ithaca, N.Y.: Cornell University, 1996); Patricio N. Abinales, "Filipino Communism and the Spectre of the Communist Manifesto," *Kasarinlan Philippine Quarterly of Third World Studies* 15 (1) (2000): 147–74; Patricio N. Abinales, *Love, Sex, and the Filipino Communist, or, Hinggil sa Pagpipigil ng Panggigigil* (Manila: Anvil Publications, 2004), 169; Ben Reid, *Philippine Left: Political Crisis and Social Change* (Manila and Sydney: Journal of Contemporary Asia Publishers, 2000).

7 May, "Elections in the Philippines," 673–80.

8 Carl H. Lande, "The Return of 'People Power' in the Philippines," *Journal of Democracy* 12 (2) (2001): 89.

9 For a comparison of local electoral politics in the Philippines, Thailand and Malaysia, see Jurgen Ruland, "Continuity and Change in Southeast Asia: Political Participation in Three Intermediate Cities," *Asian Survey* 30 (5) (1990): 461–80.

10 Benedict J. Kerkvliet, *Political Change in the Philippines: Studies of Local Politics Preceding Martial Law* (Honolulu: University Press of Hawaii, 1974), 261; Rood, "Elections as Complicated and Important Events in the Philippines," 161; Benedict J. Kerkvliet, *Everyday Politics in the Philippines: Class and Status Relations in a Central Luzon Village* (Berkeley, CA: University of California Press, 1990), 310; Sheila S. Coronel and Jose F. Lacaba, *Boss: Five Case Studies of Local Politics in the Philippines* (Pasig, Metro Manila: Philippine Center for Investigative Journalism, Institute for Popular Democracy, 1995), 167; Howie G. Severino and Sheila S. Coronel, *Patrimony: Six Case Studies on Local Politics and the Environment in the Philippines* (Pasig, Metro Manila: Philippine Center for Investigative Journalism, 1996), 162; Takeshi Kawanaka, *Power in a Philippine City* (Chiba: Institute of Developing Economies and Japan External Trade Organization, 2002); Takeshi Kawanaka, "The Robredo Style: Philippine Local Politics in Transition," *Kasarinlan Philippine Quarterly of Third World Studies* 13 (3) (1998): 5–36; Takeshi Kawanaka, "The State and Institutions in Philippine Local Politics," *Philippine Political Science Journal* 22 (45) (2001): 135–48; Miriam Coronel-Ferrer, "Recycled Autonomy? Enacting the New Organic Act for a Regional Autonomous Government in Southern Philippines," *Kasarinlan Philippine Quarterly of Third World Studies* 15 (2) (2000): 165–90.

11 Rivera, "Transition Pathways and Democratic Consolidation in Post-Marcos Philippines," 466; Carl H. Lande, *Leaders, Factions, and Parties; the Structure of Philippine Politics* (New Haven, CT: Southeast Asia Studies, 1965), 148; David G. Timberman, *A Changeless Land: Continuity and Change in Philippine Politics* (Armonk, N.Y.: M.E. Sharpe, Institute of Southeast Asian Studies, 1991), 433; Gabriella R. Montinola, "Parties and Accountability in the Philippines," *Journal of Democracy* 10 (2) (1999): 126–40; Jon Moran, "Patterns of Corruption and Development in East Asia," *Third World Quarterly* 20 (3) (1999): 569; Jennifer Conroy-Franco, *Campaigning for Democracy: Grassroots Citizenship Movements, Less-Than-Democratic Elections, and Regime Transition in the Philippines* (Quezon City, Philippines: Institute for Popular Democracy, 2000), 429; Rudolf Traub-Merz, "Die Philippinen nach Estrada's Sturz: Demokratie Weiter im Notstand," 2001. Available at the official website of the Friedrich Ebert Stifung, www.fes.org.ph.

12 Sheila S. Coronel, *Coups, Cults & Cannibals: Chronicles of a Troubled Decade, 1982–1992*" (Metro Manila: Anvil Publications, 1993), 246; Gregorio B. Honasan, "On Peace and Insurgency: President Estrada and the Conflict in Mindanao," *Kasarinlan Philippine Quarterly of Third World Studies* 15 (2) (2000): 237–44; Sheila S. Coronel and Cecile C.A. Balgos, *Pork and Other Perks: Corruption & Governance in the Philippines* (Pasig, Metro Manila: Philippine Center for Investigative Journalism, Evelio B. Javier Foundation, Institute for Popular Democracy, 1998), 293.

13 Thomas M. McKenna, *Muslim Rulers and Rebels: Everyday Politics and Armed Separatism in the Southern Philippines* (Berkeley, CA: University of California Press, 1998), 364; Nathan G. Quimpo, "Back to War in Mindanao: The Weaknesses of a Power-based Approach in Conflict Resolution," *Philippine Political Science Journal* 21 (44) (2000): 99–126. For a comparison of the Thai and Philippine Islamic independence movements, see Syed Serajul Islam, "The Islamic Independence Movements in Patani of Thailand and Mindanao of the Philippines," *Asian Survey* 38 (5) (1998): 441–56. For a comparison of secessionist movements in the Philippines and in Indonesia, see Rizal G. Buendia, "A Re-examination of Ethnicity and Secessionist Movements in the Philippines and Indonesia: The Moros and Acehnese," *Philippine Political Science Journal* 23 (46) (2002): 3–48.

14 Mina Roces, *Kinship Politics in Post-war Philippines: The Lopez Family 1946–2000* (Malate, Manila : De La Salle University Press, 2001), 330; Julio C. Teehankee, "Emerging Dynasties in the Post-Marcos House of Representatives," *Philippine Political Science Journal* 22 (45) (2001): 55–78; Sheila S. Coronel, *The Rulemakers: How the Wealthy and Well-born Dominate Congress* (Quezon City, Philippines: Philippine Center for Investigative Journalism, 2004), 270.

15 Raymund Jose G. Quilop, "Waltzing with the Army: from Marcos to Arroyo," *Kasarinlan Philippine Quarterly of Third World Studies* 16 (2) (2001): 91–104; Ricardo T. Jose, "The Philippine Armed Forces: Protector or Oppressor? A Historical Overview," *Kasarinlan Philippine Quarterly of Third World Studies* 16 (2) (2001): 73–90; Rosalie Arcala-Hall, "Exploring New Roles for the Philippine Military: Implications for Civilian Supremacy," *Philippine Political Science Journal* 25 (48) (2004): 107–30.

16 Mark R. Thompson, "Off the Endangered List: Philippine Democratization in Comparative Perspective," *Comparative Politics* 28 (2) (1996): 179–205.

17 Abinales, "Filipino Communism and the Spectre of the Communist Manifesto," 147–74.

18 Pedro Laylo Jr and Carijane Dayag-Laylo, "The 1998 Philippine Presidential Elections: Candidate

Images, Media Portrayals, and Vote Intention." SWS Occasional Paper, presented at the annual meeting of the American Association for Public Opinion Research in St Petersburg, Florida, 1999, 24.

19 Diana J. Mendoza, "Dependence or Self-reliance? The Philippine NGO Experience," *Philippine Political Science Journal* 19 (39–42) (1995–1998): 143–72; Gerard Clarke, *The Politics of NGOs in South-East Asia: Participation and Protest in the Philippines* (London and New York: Routledge, 1998), 299; Lisa Law and Kathy Nadeau, "Globalization, Migration and Class Struggles: NGO Mobilization for Filipino Domestic Workers," *Kasarinlan Philippine Quarterly of Third World Studies* 14 (3 & 4) (1999): 51–68; Dorothea Hilhorst, *The Real World of NGOs: Discourses, Diversity, and Development* (London and New York: Zed Books, 2003), 257.

20 Quintos, Melinda de Jesus and Luis V. Teodoro, *Citizens' Media Monitor: A Report on the Campaign and Elections Coverage in the Philippines* (Manila: Center for Media Freedom and Responsibility, 2004), 199. On the Philippine media, see also, Sheila S. Coronel, *From Loren to Marimar: The Philippine Media in the 1990s* (Quezon City, Philippines: Philippine Center for Investigative Journalism, 1999), 193.

21 Fritz Plasser with Gunda Plasser, *Global Political Campaigning: A Worldwide Analysis of Campaign Professionals and Their Practices* (Westport, CT: Praeger, 2002), 89.

22 Chay Florentino-Hofileña, *News for Sale: The Corruption and Commercialization of the Philippine Media* (Manila: Philippine Center for Investigative Journalism, 2004), 120.

23 On Philippine culture, see Paul Rodell, *Culture and Customs of the Philippines* (Westport, CT: Greenwood Press, 2002), 247.

24 "Campaigning Filipino Style," *The Investigative Reporting Magazine*, special election issue, January–June, 2004, 34–37; Thomas D. Hofman, "The Church and its Influence on Democratic Transitions: Brazil, the Philippines, and Kenya Compared," PhD dissertation at Michigan State University, Political Science Department, 1995, 453.

25 Samuel P. Huntington, *The Third Wave: Democratization in the Late Twentieth Century* (Norman, OK: University of Oklahoma Press, 1991), 84.

26 Hofman, "The Church and its Influence on Democratic Transitions," 1.

27 Grace Gorospe-Jamon, "The El Shaddai Prayer Movement: Political Socialization in a Religious Context," *Philippine Political Science Journal* 20 (43) (1999): 83–126.

28 Mark R. Thompson, "Female Leadership of Democratic Transitions in Asia," *Pacific Affairs* 75 (4) (2002): 535.

29 On the influence of women in Philippine politics, see Mina Roces, *Women, Power, and Kinship Politics: Female Power in Post-war Philippines* (Westport, CT: Praeger, 1998), 214; on Philippine gender relations, see also Leonora C. Angeles, "The Filipino Male as 'Macho-machunurin': Bringing Men and Masculinities in Gender and Development Studies," *Kasarinlan Philippine Quarterly of Third World Studies* 16 (1) (2001): 9–30.

30 Rood, "Elections as Complicated and Important Events in the Philippines"; "Campaigning Filipino Style," 34–7; "Song is the Key of Politics," *The Investigative Reporting Magazine*, special election issue, January–June, 2004, 54–60; "Political Fiesta Heats Up As Elections Nears," and "The Perpetual Campaigner," *Far Eastern Economic Review*, November 18, 1993, 26.

31 Rood, "Elections as Complicated and Important Events in the Philippines."

32 "TV—Secret Polls Weapon of Philippines' Political Lightweights," *The Straits Times*, June 10, 2001, 18; "Politics-Philippines: Actors Race For Top Billing in May Polls," *Inter Press Service*, April 30, 201; "Between Tinsel and Trapo," *The Investigative Reporting Magazine*, special election issue, January–June, 2004, 70–3.

33 "The Road to Hell is Paved with Good Intentions: The Senate and House are Rushing to Lift the Political Ad Ban," *BusinessWorld*, October 13, 2000, 30; "Who Benefited from Lifting of Political Ad Ban?," *BusinessWorld*, May 8, 2001; Ana Maria L. Tabunda, Glenda M. Gloria and Carmela S. Fonbuena, *Spin and Sell: How Political Ads Shaped the 2004 Elections* (Makati City: Foundation for Communication Initiatives and the Konrad Adenauer Foundation, 2004), 124.

34 Tabunda, Gloria and Fonbuena, *Spin and Sell*, 124

35 "Metro Common Billboards for Manila Bets," *Philippine Daily Inquirer*, February 22, 2001, 25.

36 "Tuning in to the Village Voice," *Far Eastern Economic Review*, August 29, 2002, 40.

37 "The Political Impact of the Internet," *BusinessWorld*, March 26, 2003; Emmanuel C. Lallana, Patricia Pascual and Edwin Soriano, "E-government in the Philippines: Benchmarking Against Global Best Practices," *Kasarinlan Philippine Quarterly of Third World Studies* 17 (2) (2002): 235–72; Ranjit Singh Rye, "E-governance in the Philippines: Insights for Policy-making," *Kasarinlan Philippine Quarterly of Third World Studies* 17 (2) (2002): 101–38; Divina Gracia M. Zamora-Roldan, "Bridging the Local Digital Divide: the Barangay.Net Project," *Kasarinlan Philippine Quarterly of Third World Studies* 17 (2) (2002): 293–310; Arnie C. Trinidad, "An Initial Assessment of the Philippines' Preparedness for E-learning," *Kasarinlan Philippine Quarterly of Third World Studies* 17 (2) (2002): 167–92; Sheila S. Coronel, "New

Media Played a Role in the People's Uprising," *Nieman Reports* 56 (2) (2002): 61; Sheila S. Coronel, *Investigating Estrada: Millions, Mansions, and Mistresses : A Compilation of Investigative Reports* (Metro Manila, Philippines: Philippine Center for Investigative Journalism, 2000), 185; and Sheila S. Coronel and Sigfred C. Balatan, *EDSA 2: A Nation in Revolt, a Photographic Journal* (Pasig City, Philippines: Anvil Publications, 2001), 232.

38 Quintos de Jesus and Teodoro, *Citizens' Media Monitor: A Report on the Campaign and Elections Coverage in the Philippines*, 199; Erix Ellis, "Asia Buzz: Revolution. How Text Messages Toppled Joseph Estrada," January 23, 2001, available at the *TimeAsia.com* website, www.timeasia.com. Accessed on November 22, 2007.

39 Ateneo de Manila University, Institute of Philippine Culture, *The Vote of the Poor: Modernity and Tradition in People's Views of Leadership and Election* (Quezon City: Institute of Philippine Culture, Ateneo de Manila University, 2005), 143.

40 Plasser, *Global Political Campaigning*, 176.

41 Rood, "Elections as Complicated and Important Events in the Philippines."

42 Plasser, *Global Political Campaigning*, 256; "First-world Techniques, Third-world Setting," *The Investigative Reporting Magazine*, special election issue, January–June, 2004, 14.

43 "The X-Men. The Story of Activists-turned-political Consultants," *The Investigative Reporting Magazine*, special election issue, January–June, 2004, 18–21.

44 "First-world Techniques, Third-world Setting," 12–17.

45 Malou Mangahas, "Gloria's Lobbygate? Government Splurges Millions on Multiple, Secret Lobby Contracts," The Philippine Center for Investigative Journalism, September 20, 2005, http://www.pcij.org/stories/print/2005/lobbygate.html. Accessed on November 22, 2007.

46 Dennis W. Johnson, "Going International," unpublished manuscript, George Washington University, 1999; Joseph Napolitan, *The Election Game and How to Win It* (Garden City, N.Y.: Doubleday, 1972).

47 "With a Little Help from (U.S.) Friends," *The Investigative Reporting Magazine*, special election issue, January–June, 2004, 22–7.

27

Evolution and Limitations of Modern Campaigning in East Asia

A Case Study of Taiwan

Christian Schafferer

In recent years, there has been a lively discourse on the globalization of political marketing among scholars around the world. Modern and postmodern campaigning seem to have not only become dominant forces in advanced democracies but have also made major inroads into the political domains of newly democratized polities. The global trend toward the adoption of this new media and money driven modus operandi of political campaigns seems to be unstoppable. But there still are several questions to be addressed: how effective is (post)modern campaigning? Will it be able to completely substitute pre-modern forms of electoral processes? What are the limitations of (post)modern campaigning? These questions are of great significance especially when talking about electoral campaigning in societies that have transformed from agrarian to (post)modern within a few decades. In this chapter, I would like to answer this set of questions by looking at the evolution and the current modus operandi of modern electoral campaigning in Taiwan, one of Asia's most vibrant democracies.

Evolution of Electoral Campaigning

In analytical works about the changes in electoral campaigning, the international academia usually mentions three standard models of campaigning. At different times in modern political history, each model has been the dominant modus operandi of electoral campaigning. The evolution process started with the pre-modern form of campaigning, and progressed into the modern and post-modern types.

Figure 27.1 outlines the most important characteristics of the three standard models. In Taiwan, pre-modern campaigning had dominated the electoral process until shortly after the lifting of martial law in 1987. The subsequent process of liberalization and democratization led to the adoption of several modern and postmodern forms of campaigning, as I will explain further below.

Pre-modern Campaigning in Taiwan (1935–1987)

Taiwan's experience with electoral campaigning dates back to the Japanese colonial period. In 1935, local elections were held for the first time. The right to vote was, however, restricted to wealthy male residents aged twenty-five years or older. There were several local political

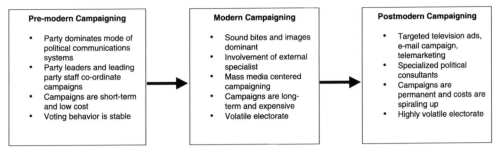

Pre-modern Campaigning	Modern Campaigning	Postmodern Campaigning
• Party dominates mode of political communications systems • Party leaders and leading party staff co-ordinate campaigns • Campaigns are short-term and low cost • Voting behavior is stable	• Sound bites and images dominant • Involvement of external specialist • Mass media centered campaigning • Campaigns are long-term and expensive • Volatile electorate	• Targeted television ads, e-mail campaign, telemarketing • Specialized political consultants • Campaigns are permanent and costs are spiraling up • Highly volatile electorate

Figure 27.1. Typical Evolution and Characteristics of Electoral Campaigning in Modern Societies

Source: Modification of Fritz Plasser with Gunda Plasser, *Global Political Campaigning: A Worldwide Analysis of Campaign Professionals and Their Practices* (Westport, Conn.: Praeger, 2002), 6.

movements that performed the functions of modern political parties. They nominated candidates and engaged in campaign activities, which were very rudimentary and included home visits, small rallies, distribution of leaflets and the spread of campaign slogans. Observed illegal activities ranged from the involvement of unauthorized campaign aides, distribution of free tickets for public transportation or exhibitions and voting without the right to vote.[1]

Nationalist Takeover and the Emergence of Machine Politics

After World War II, the Chinese Nationalist government under Chiang Kai-shek acceded control over Taiwan with the blessing of the United States. A significant part of the population could not identify with the mainland Chinese arrivals and considered the new government a foreign regime that came to Taiwan to "loot the island."[2] As to ease tensions between the Chinese Nationalists and the inhabitants of Taiwan, the Nationalists had to find a way to co-opt local elites and infiltrate Taiwan's society. Elections were functional in that attempt. The first elections at the grassroots level were held in 1946, about a year after the takeover. Taiwan's local elite was not satisfied with these rather meaningless elections and demanded full participation in the electoral processes at higher levels.[3] Growing public dissatisfaction about the new regime and its social and political policies culminated in the 2-28 Massacre, in which Nationalist Chinese troops brutally killed several thousand Taiwanese.[4]

At the end of the year, delegates to the upper house of parliament (*guomindahui*) were elected in Taiwan as well as in most parts of war-torn China. In January of the following year, elections of the members of the lower house (*lifayuan*) took place. In Taiwan, seventy-five candidates contested twenty-seven seats in the upper house, and thirteen for eight seats in the lower house. Competition and electoral campaigning was virtually non-existing.[5] A year later, the Chinese Nationalists under Chiang Kai-shek lost the civil war on the mainland and retreated to Taiwan. Between 1947 and 1949, more than 800,000 mainlanders fled to Taiwan, accounting for about 10% of the population.[6] The dramatic increase in the number of Chinese Nationalists led to further suppression of the local Taiwanese. As to prevent social and political unrest, martial law was imposed the same year. In addition, the KMT (Kuomintang or Chinese Nationalist Party) government stepped up its effort to infiltrate Taiwan's society by means of public participation in state-controlled elections and expanding the KMT party network. In 1950/1951, the first direct elections of municipality mayors and county magistrates were held, extending the scope of local direct elections.

At about the same time, the KMT launched the so-called reconstruction movement, which aimed at establishing grassroots organizations that would recruit more Taiwanese into the party and to "guide" the society at large. Within a year, the party had set up 234 local branches around the island.[7] Moreover, the KMT began to grant special rights and benefits to government employees and teachers as to build up solid votes. Workers' and farmers' associations were formed and strictly controlled by the party. The 1950s experienced a massive build-up of the KMT state-apparatus, which had a tremendous impact on the social and political transformation of the society, and of course on electoral politics. "Gentry" politics was gradually replaced by machine politics with the growing involvement of criminals in electoral activities.[8]

By the 1960s, the KMT had succeeded in establishing an electoral machine deeply rooted in Taiwan's society. Whenever there were elections, the regime would mobilize its party, local faction leaders, military and governmental networks at provincial, county and grassroots levels to guarantee the success of its candidates.[9] As a consequence, the percentage of elected non-KMT candidates decreased over the years. The most dramatic changes happened at the grassroots level. In 1946, the majority of those elected were unaffiliated, whereas a decade later two-thirds were members of the KMT. At the higher level, elections were first held in the early 1950s and the share of elected non-KMT hopefuls accounted for 20%. The share dropped by five percentage points within a decade.[10]

The KMT never intended to completely wipe out the opposition, as it was instrumental in providing legitimacy. The policy was to limit and control the activities of the opposition, instead. Opposition candidates were isolated warriors who could only challenge the KMT locally but not nationally. The formation of political parties was illegal. Those who broke the rules of the KMT were either imprisoned or executed. Until the late 1960s, electoral politics was elite politics. There was no involvement of the general public. To attract voters, the KMT's main strategy was to offer benefits to the voters and spread fear, as a retired secret police officer recalls:

> Fear and greed were the motives of the people to support the KMT regime. One may not imagine how easy it was to convince your neighbor to denounce their best friends and even their husbands and wives. We were everywhere: in factories, schools, playgrounds, restaurants, simply everywhere. I am a mainlander. I came with the others in 1949. I lost everything on the mainland. The party gave me a new identity. I did not care about others, nor did the others. Our job was to make sure that the party gained support at the polls. We faked ballots. But that was one of the harmless ways to secure votes. We would pay visits to ordinary people and inform them about whom they had to vote. Sometimes we offered money or promises. We would use other methods whenever we met resistance. I did not like it, but times were different then. They were imprisoned and often tortured. Some died. We said that they had committed suicide out of guilt. It was not only us who helped the KMT in this matter, local party cadres and especially local faction and gang leaders were also involved in these activities.[11]

The opposition, on the other hand, had very limited electoral tools, such as leaflets, slogans, magazines and government-organized speeches (see Table 27.1).

Emergence of Popular Politics

In the late 1960s and early 1970s, the KMT government faced several challenges and mapped out new strategies as to cope with them. On the international floor, the KMT government became more and more isolated. There was a dramatic decrease in the number of individual United Nations (UN) member states recognizing the legitimacy of the KMT government, which finally led to the expulsion of Chiang Kai-shek's representatives from the UN in 1971.[12] The late 1960s also brought about a change in leadership. In 1969, Chiang Kai-shek was involved in a car accident from which he never fully recovered. His son, Chiang Ching-kuo, gradually assumed control over party affairs, the military, youth organizations and the secret service. The new leadership and other policies, such as the holding of limited national elections in 1969, did not however substantially increase the people's acceptance of the KMT. On the contrary, overseas Taiwanese (allegedly with CIA backing) tried to assassinate Chiang Ching-kuo during a short

Table 27.1. Main Characteristics of Electoral Politics, 1945–1987

	Elite Politics (1945–1969)		Popular Politics (1970–1987)
	Gentry Politics (1945–1953)	Machine Politics (1954–1969)	
Agents	Local intelligentsia, mainland Chinese arrivals	Mainland Chinese arrivals, local faction leaders	KMT government apparatus, democracy activists, social movements, overseas Taiwanese organizations
Power formation and struggle	KMT vs. local intelligentsia; KMT nourishes local factions and promotes local elections	KMT vs. liberal intellectuals; local factions controlled by KMT through electoral process, society infiltrated	KMT vs. opposition; KMT vs. local faction leaders; KMT vs. social movements
Role of media	Mostly controlled by the KMT especially after 1949; a mouthpiece for KMT propaganda	Mouthpiece for KMT propaganda; engine of fear	Three terrestrial TV stations and two major newspaper networks controlled by KMT; one newspaper favorable to opposition, opposition figures publish magazines
Main campaign tools			
KMT	Vote rigging, threats, physical attacks, executions	Massive vote rigging, threats, executions, kidnapping, physical attacks, involvement of gangsters and military	Massive vote rigging until 1977, vote buying, threats, physical attacks, involvement of gangsters and military, nomination of attractive and young Taiwanese party cadres
Opposition	Speeches, leaflets, magazines	Speeches, leaflets, magazines; some successful attempts to organize across electoral districts	Public speeches, rallies, street demonstrations, verbal attacks on incumbents, appeals to people's compassion, campaign slogans, populist rhetoric, books, magazines, leaflets, fundraising banquets, nationwide election activities

stay in the United States. The failed assassination attempt and the growing legitimacy crisis were instrumental in Chiang Ching-kuo's subsequent efforts to initiate several policy reforms.

The KMT leadership intended to use the reforms as a means to increase the KMT's legitimacy to rule Taiwan, while expanding the authority of the party itself. The first goal was achieved by recruiting more talented Taiwanese into the party. To obtain the latter objective, Chiang Ching-kuo tried to minimize the power of the local factions. At that time, about 60% of KMT-nominated candidates running in elections at provincial and county levels were affiliated with a local faction. Chiang's plan was to replace factional candidates with party cadres, which would have increased the party's authority.[13]

Although the reform helped the KMT to stabilize its position in the beginning, the reforms failed to extend the party's authority in the long run. To a substantial degree, the policies were ill fated because Taiwan's electoral politics of the 1970s was no longer elite politics. Taiwan had already entered the period of popular politics. In the past, the KMT had to fight against localized powerbrokers, but in the 1970s the party increasingly had to deal with the power of the people, that is the growing demand for mass participation in the electoral process (see Table 27.1).

The KMT government's economic, social and educational policies brought about several societal changes, such as rising labor problems, urbanization and a growing, politically more demanding, middle class. The KMT failed to respond appropriately to the changing environment.

It made every effort to discourage socially concerned politicians (or scholars) from running for office and tried to diffuse criticism. The government, for instance, implemented "reform" programs to meet with the growing discontent of factory workers. The Teacher Chang counseling program, for example, aimed at training college students to become volunteer counselors to workers. Their mission was not to solve conflicts but to emphasize that workers had to adjust to factory life.[14] Candidates of the opposition took advantage of the KMT's ignorance and soon social problems and the government's failure to deal with them became a central theme among the new opposition. The time appeared to be ripe to address social issues and mingle them with political ones. Most of the opposition candidates were hardly interested in socialism, rather they tried to explore the power of the people, as one activist noted:

> A person with only a little capital and some education and earthy knack for speech-making can ride the wave of popular resentment against the regime in elections. Though the population generally appears cowed and quiescent, there is admiration and secret support for those who dare to step forward.[15]

It was the time when populism entered Taiwan's electoral campaigns. Using Margaret Canovan's typology, it was politicians' populism, a "broad, non-ideological coalition-building that draws on the unificatory appeal of 'the people.' "[16] The most successful populist at that time certainly was Hsu Hsin-liang, who was elected to the Provincial Assembly in 1972 under the KMT banner. He was a very ambitious young politician who sought to reach out to the masses. In his constituency, Taoyuan County, he spent hours talking with people from different walks of life. The farmers loved him and said that he was one of them. The business community loved him and said that he was one of them. Wherever he gave a speech, he would make sure to mention the problems of the ordinary people, the *laobaixing*.[17] In 1976, Hsu began to prepare for his participation in the 1977 county magistrate election. The KMT did not nominate him: Hsu appeared to be too progressive, especially when it came to political management.

Notwithstanding, Hsu contested the election as an independent and worked out a campaign strategy that made the KMT understand that the period of elite politics was over. His electoral strategy made use of conventional campaign tools, such as books, leaflets and public speeches. But what was different was the successful attempt to integrate ordinary citizens in his campaign. His campaign headquarters, a huge tent, attracted large crowds of people who would donate all types of foods and drinks, and spend hours there talking about life and politics. The KMT tried to counter Hsu's campaign strategy by applying its traditional campaign techniques, such as vote rigging and buying, but massive protests against the rigged result (known as the Chungli Incident) forced the KMT leadership to accept the victory of Hsu Hsin-liang.[18]

In retrospect, Hsu Hsin-liang's political management style not only influenced future electoral campaigns but also showed the KMT that the involvement of massive vote rigging in the electoral process no longer guaranteed the party's success at the polls. Chan Pi-Hsiang, a former KMT activist involved in vote buying and vote rigging, noted in her book *Vote Buying: A Confession* that with the Chungli Incident the application of systematic and widespread vote rigging became obsolete.[19]

The 1977 local elections were a success for the candidates of the opposition. They brought about the highest number of non-KMT provincial assembly members, chief executives of counties and provincial municipalities. At least fourteen of the twenty-one independent assembly members were genuine opposition figures, eight of whom were the highest vote getters in their constituencies. Moreover, four out of twenty chief executives of Taiwan's twenty counties and provincial municipalities were anti-KMT activists. In thirteen counties and provincial municipalities the number of votes cast for candidates of the opposition almost equaled the KMT votes, which took the party by surprise and can be seen as some evidence that the KMT's reform policies initiated earlier that decade failed to materialize.[20] This unprecedented electoral success gave the opposition confidence to challenge the KMT's ban on political parties.

In the past, opposition candidates could not form coalitions, nor could they run on a common platform. They were isolated warriors. Any attempt to break these rules ended in unfortunate accidents. The campaigns for the 1978 parliamentary elections (National Assembly and Legislative Yuan) were groundbreaking. Several opposition leaders, such as Huang Hsin-chieh and Shih Ming-teh, jointly founded a special electoral campaign committee (*dangwai zhuxuan tuan*). The aim of the committee was to maximize the support of the opposition candidates and to co-ordinate campaign activities throughout the island. Well-known opposition figures, such as independent legislator Huang Hsin-chieh, toured the island in a united effort to canvass votes. The committee also organized a series of fundraising banquets, something new in Taiwan's electoral campaigns. (Opposition candidate Chang Chun-hong was the first politician in the country to hold fundraising banquets during his electoral campaign in 1973.) Another invention was the use of a common logo printed on all the various campaign materials.[21]

In general, the electoral campaign environment appeared to be much freer than in previous elections. Opposition candidates were even allowed to make public the committee's common platform. US president Jimmy Carter's decision to recognize the regime in Beijing and de-recognize Taipei as the only legitimate government of China just a few days before the election was a shock to the KMT government, and elections were postponed indefinitely. (In December 1980 the elections finally took place.)

A year after the postponed elections, the opposition founded the *Formosa Magazine*. Although the application of regular publication was nothing uncommon among opposition figures, the *Formosa Magazine* was different in many ways. It was more than just an ordinary publication dealing with social, economic and political problems; its branch offices soon developed into community help centers, where ordinary people could get advice on legal, social and economic issues. It more and more became a fully-fledged political party in disguise.[22] Being aware of the magazine's true (political) function, the KMT regime staged the so-called Kaoshiung Incident to obtain legitimacy for the imprisonment of the magazine's leaders. The imprisonment of the opposition activists helped to shape new electoral campaigning techniques, such as the utilization of the people's compassion. In the 1970s, a number of opposition candidates made emotional appeals as to win support at the polls.

The Kaoshiung Incident turned the people's compassion into one of the most frequently applied electoral tools in local and national elections of the 1980s. A year after the incident, for example, the relatives of the imprisoned democracy activists participated in national elections. Whenever there was a campaign activity, there was little need to give lengthy speeches. The candidates only had to play the popular song *Hope You'll be Back Soon* (*wang ni zao gui*) and people would feel sympathetic enough to cast their votes for the relatives of the imprisoned activists. Another group of opposition activists, riding the wave of the people's compassion, comprised the defense lawyers of the indicted activists of the Kaoshiung Incident. Among the most prominent were You Ching, Chen Shui-bian, Hsieh Chang-ting, Su Chen-chang, Chiang Peng-chian and Chang Chun-hsiung. All of them won elections consecutively; most of them were the highest vote getters in their constituencies. Their campaign strategy was to present themselves as the defenders of human rights. It was because of their willingness to defend the Formosa activists that the electorate was convinced about their honesty and commitment to democracy. Their popularity was beyond description. No matter where they went to give speeches, tens of thousands of people would cheer enthusiastically.[23]

The 1970s marked the beginning of a new era in electoral campaigning. Elite politics dominated the postwar years and was gradually replaced by popular politics. Hsu Hsin-liang's successful populist appeal to the masses confirmed the waning of pure elite politics. In the 1980s, public participation in the electoral processes increased drastically, especially in the form of social movements. There were at least eight major social movements promoting the interests of consumers, environmentalists, laborers, women, aborigines, farmers, students and teachers. Even though some of these movements emerged earlier than the 1980s, they all gained considerable political significance in that decade. Moreover, they succeeded in determining election issues and thus the political agenda of the regime. In the 1983 national election campaign, consumer protection emerged as the issue. Three years later, "environmental protection was the issue raised by almost every candidate."[24] Opposition candidates benefited from the increase in social protests and the rising power of the movements. They were instrumental in enlarging popular support in constituencies previously controlled by the KMT, such as the functional parliamentary seats for labor organizations.

Modern Campaigning

The lifting of the martial law decree in 1987 and the subsequent political liberalization led to an over-politicized society.[25] There was great enthusiasm and it looked as if all of a sudden everyone wanted to be a politician and have his or her own political party. Consequently, political competition increased. Both the KMT and the DPP (Democratic Progressive Party), Taiwan's largest and first true opposition party, had to adjust themselves to the new environment as to survive. This search for new concepts paved the way for a new era of electoral campaigning, namely the era of commodification politics, that is, the encroachment of political marketing into spheres previously subjugated by conventional wisdom. Conventional campaigning (pre-modern campaigning) is merely the art of attracting voters by intuition, whereas modern campaigning is science in action.[26] Despite the fact that it was the opposition that had sophisticated electoral campaigning and successfully applied a number of new campaign techniques, the idea to apply professional marketing management concepts to the domain of electoral campaigning first came from the ruling KMT.

A year after the lifting of martial law, a group of liberal intellectuals stressed the need for a modernization of the KMT through the application of modern political marketing (management) concepts. One of the most outspoken supporters of such reforms was John Kuan, a senior party official. John Kuan described the changing political and social environment of the late 1980s with the following words:

> During the past four decades, our society has undergone three major changes in development. In the 1950s and early 1960s, political forces predominated. From the 1960s on, economic forces had the upper hand. Now we are entering a third stage where social forces are predominant. People are better educated and more resourceful today. They are more concerned with social issues such as environmental protection, law enforcement, and public health measures. Moreover, they are ready to act if necessary to make their voices heard.[27]

Kuan viewed those changes as a challenge not as a threat to the existence of the KMT, and contradicted the conservative forces in the party, who considered the above-mentioned trends symptoms of social disorder. Between April 1988 and October 1989, Kuan delivered a number of speeches at party meetings highlighting the urgency of a modernization of the KMT so it could adapt to the changing political and social environment. He believed that the problems the KMT faced were the consequences of the new social forces, the failure of the KMT to react timely to the changing environment and the subsequent growth of the opposition movement. Kuan noted that the KMT was confronted with several worrisome trends, such as a worsening party image, a steep decline in the membership recruitment rate since 1986 and disillusioned supporters, especially at the grassroots level.

He outlined three key strategies that should help to overcome these difficulties:

1 *The application of scientific methods (keijihua).* Kuan acknowledged that the KMT had lost track of a considerable part of its 2.4 million members. In the past, the party could rely on teachers, government employees, military personnel and high-school students to mobilize support for the party, but in the mid-1980s "about 75% of the party groups were not reasonably active and about 80% of the total had not held party meetings on time."[28] A related shortcoming was the party's failure to analyze the wishes of its members and the general public.

Kuan argued that the application of modern technology was inevitable in the attempt to boost the party's performance and to prevent the party's collapse. Under this new paradigm, the KMT should set up a computerized database containing all sorts of information about its members, and apply modern survey techniques in formulating electoral strategies. "From now on, we must strive to adopt scientific concepts and methodology, and apply them to the party's democratization and build-up of its competitiveness."[29]

2 *The sophistication of entrepreneurship (qiyehua).* Kuan compared the KMT with the American company Procter & Gamble. Both "companies," he believed, harbored similarities. Both had a long history, the KMT a history of ninety-four years and P&G one of 150 years, and both had developed a strong and vigorous entrepreneurial culture, "which perpetuates its functions and prosperity."[30] He also noted that during the martial law period the party had enjoyed a virtual monopoly on political resources. The party had merely functioned as a mechanism for "the internal distribution of power," whereas "today the party is confronted with political competition."[31] Kuan called for a sophistication of the KMT's entrepreneurship, that is, the application of professional marketing techniques, as to cope with the changing environment.

> In this open, competitive and market-conscious society, consumers can pick and choose from among many commodities. Rational consumers will always choose those commodities that are of good quality with reasonable prices. We must not forget that we are entering the age of marketing. In a market-driven age, producers must take whatever measures are necessary to produce attractive commodities. Everywhere we turn today, we run into the "SP" acronym for sales promotion. For a political party, its platform and candidates can be considered products. Voters can be considered consumers. The question is how do we make our party platform and candidates attractive to the voters. In this age of enlightenment, voters know their personal preferences. They are autonomous and independent. Under these circumstances, our primary job is to design comprehensive plans for promoting and advertising our party platform and our candidates during non-election times as well as at election time.[32]

3 *Democratization of the party (minzhuhua).* Kuan described the KMT as a revolutionary party, that is, a political party that originates outside conventional democratic institutions, such as the electoral and legislative process. According to Kuan, outside factors, such as social injustices and wars, form a revolutionary party. Revolutionary parties can thus be referred to as "outside parties" (*waizao de zhengdang*).[33] He spoke of the necessity to transform the KMT from a revolutionary party into a democratic party, to "institutionalize" (*zhiduhua*) the KMT. Institutionalization here meant to make the KMT part of the new political environment so that a new party, a democratic one, is formed by "internal factors," that is, by electoral processes. Kuan believed that such transformation was crucial because the KMT as a revolutionary party could not persist to exist in a democratic environment.

In the past, the KMT was virtually the only political power and monopolized social resources. Over that long period, through government service and training a large number of elites became accustomed to enjoying a monopoly on political power. At present, however, the KMT is unable to continue monopolizing political power. Rather, it must live in a competitive world.[34]

The KMT should, thus, change from "a political monopolist to a political competitor," or in other words "abandon its position as a monopolistic power distributor and play the role of a social mobilizer."[35]

According to Kuan, the institutionalization process required a streamlining of the party apparatus, an increase in intra-party competition and a substantial buildup of highly trained party cadres. Kuan acknowledged that KMT's party apparatus at that time was too difficult to maintain in a competing environment. Greater emphasis had to be put on the efficiency of party organs, especially the party cadres who had "sufficient knowledge to maintain the status quo but lack[ed] enough expertise to deal with a changing society."[36] Party cadres should thus receive professional training and attain the necessary professional skills to mobilize the people. They should become the sales managers of a new modernized KMT. Any party cadre "must know how to sell his product to the customers."[37]

Moreover, Kuan believed that the KMT had to encourage intra-party competition as to survive in the new competitive environment:

> Because the KMT has monopolized social resources and enjoyed such great power, members have been dependent on the party so much that it weakens their morale when forced to face outside challenges. The sometimes demoralizing effects of these challenges stems from KMT institutions and past elections, when mere nomination by the party used to be equal to winning. In dealing with this changing society and its challenges, party members and candidates must learn to be less dependent on the party. Only by combination of members, efforts, and party support can success be achieved and the party's power base grow stronger. The party will become increasingly weaker with each round of elections if its members continue to compete only for the limited resources of the party.[38]

Kuan argued that the KMT party leadership ought to empower lower-ranking officials and integrate the opinion of grassroots supporters in the party's decision-making process. Since the mid-1980s, membership recruitment rate had plummeted. Apart from other contributing factors, the party leadership's ignorance of grassroots supporters certainly was a major one, as Kuan himself acknowledged.[39] In the past, only the top leadership had the right to make policy decisions. The opinion of lower-ranking party officials, grassroots supporters or experts was simply ignored, especially when electoral issues, such as party nominations, were discussed. Kuan saw in the holding of transparent party primaries a way out of the crisis. He fiercely defended the introduction of transparent selection processes and frequently listed four major reasons why they were an indispensable part of the KMT's modernization efforts:[40]

1 Party primaries allow members at all levels to fully express their opinion. This active participation in the party's decision-making progress creates a sense of identification and loyalty to the party, which enhances the party's mobilization capabilities.
2 Party primaries help to polish the party's image and assist the electorate to better evaluate hopefuls. Party primaries are marketing activities that aim at educating the electorate about candidates' real potentials. They should assist the electorate to better distinguish between those contestants with "proper democratic attitudes" and those who "have no concrete political opinions."[41] Kuan believed that politicians of the opposition comprised the latter type of candidates, whereas those of the KMT made up the group of candidates with "proper democratic attitudes."[42] Party primaries should prove to the electorate that the KMT is really democratic.
3 Party primaries strengthen the party "because they strengthen the ability of our candidates to compete."[43] Kuan argued that primaries would force candidates to appeal to grassroots supporters, which would be instrumental in the party's effort to secure future electoral success: "If they can win the support of party members they will be more likely to win the people's votes."[44]
4 Party primaries create unity in the party, since they allow for transparency (fairness) in the nomination process. In the past, the nomination process was kept secret and excluded

ordinary party members, which caused disharmony and lowered the morale of grassroots supporters.

Toward a New Political Marketing Management Model

Kuan's approach was revolutionary in the way that it tried to put an end to the KMT's conventional campaign strategies and instead incorporated scientific methods of political management into the party. From the point of marketing management theory, the KMT of the past clung to the selling concept, whereas Kuan's party reforms aimed at the application of a more expedient management form, namely the marketing concept.

The selling concept if applied to the political domain holds that the electorate is apathetic and unwilling to support a political party "unless it undertakes a large-scale selling and promotion effort," as Gary Armstrong, Philip Kotler and Geoffrey da Silva note about its usage in the conventional business domain.[45] The concept is usually practiced in transactions that involve unsought goods—those that ordinary consumers do not normally want to buy, such as insurance and encyclopedias. Politicians, party memberships and votes can be considered unsought goods, especially during periods of authoritarianism. The selling concept requires the establishment of well-designed sales networks and aggressive sales methods as to obtain the company's objectives.

Kuan questioned the appropriateness of the selling concept in a democratizing environment. The political domain should no longer be considered to be a mere pool of unsought goods. As Kuan observed, the electorate at the late 1980s was better educated, more concerned about social issues and well prepared to take to the streets as to get their voices heard.[46] The KMT, therefore, had to listen to people's wishes and design its policies (products) accordingly. With Kuan's reform the KMT changed its political management philosophy. The party no longer intended to act as a provider of unsought goods. It believed exactly what marketing management gurus define as the marketing concept, namely, that "achieving organizational goals depends on knowing the needs and wants of target markets and delivering the desired satisfactions better than the competitors do."[47] Under this concept, the KMT had to alter its focus, means and goals (see

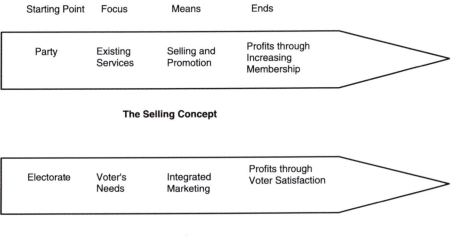

Figure 27.2. Political Marketing Management Concepts

Source: Adapted from Gary Armstrong, Philip Kotler and Geoffrey da Silva, *Marketing: An Asian Perspective* (New York: Pearson, Prentice Hall, 2005), 21.

Figure 27.2). The new management concept required the party to shift its focus from itself to the wishes of the people. Profits through voter satisfaction was the new maxim.

But was the reform really necessary? A former senior party member argued that the reforms were inevitable given the tremendous social and political changes that had occurred in the 1980s:

> The KMT was a revolutionary party. But where was the revolution? Most of the Mainlanders, who had fought against the Communists on the mainland, had either passed away or given up the idea of unification. They did not care about the revolution; what they cared about was where the future source of income would be. Would the KMT continue to pay their bills? The KMT at the time was ideologically bankrupt. The party had to go shopping for ideas. Kuan and his fellows were highly educated intellectuals. Their ideas were promising. The party had to give in.[48]

Even though the new political management concept appeared to be promising, not all party members were favorable to it. This same party official continued:

> Of course there was opposition from the old guard, especially from those of Mainland origin who despised [Chairman] Lee Teng-hui. Party primaries, adjust party policies to the wishes of the people, and utilize scientific methods: These all were phrases they did not like. Some say because the new concept contradicted their Confucian culture, but that was not the real reason. They were frightened to death by the new concept. Why? Because the new concept was expected to turn the KMT into a Taiwanese party without fat pension plans for the retired Mainland Chinese party cadres. And who knows, maybe one day they would have to stand trial to defend the injustices of the past. Uncertainties create fear and resistance.[49]

The modernization of the KMT mostly benefited the mainstream faction led by Chairman Lee Teng-hui. Critics argue that Lee was supportive of the modernization processes just because they were instrumental in minimizing the power of the non-mainstream faction. As a former senior KMT election aide stated: "The KMT since Lee Teng-hui has used the people's wishes to exterminate enemies. The party has become a full-service wholesaler exactly because of this required function."[50]

Whatever his true motives were, Lee was very susceptible to the wishes of the ordinary people. The growing public demand for a variety of political reforms, such as direct presidential elections, met considerable resistance among the non-mainstream faction of the KMT. Lee used public opinion to force most of his outspoken critics out of the party. His populist leadership style made him popular with the electorate. Even those voters who strongly disliked the KMT supported him. With the use of the people's power, Lee pushed through constitutional reforms mandating direct presidential elections. Lee's popularity seemed to be unbreakable and there was little doubt among political analysts that he would win the first direct presidential election that was scheduled to take place in March 1996. The so-called Lee Teng-hui complex dominated the political sphere of the early and mid-1990s.

The Perils of the New Campaign Paradigm

It did not take long and the adoption of consumer-oriented marketing strategies sparked off a serious debate about the perils of modern political management concepts. Several scholars were concerned that the KMT's new management philosophy would undermine democratic institutions and eventually lead to a new dictatorship. Members of the local academia, such as Wang Chen-huan and Chian Yong-hsiang, publicly criticized the commodification of politics.[51]

Huang Kuang-guo, professor of psychology at National Taiwan University, elaborated on Wang and Qian's observations in his popular book, *About Populism and the End of Taiwan*.[52] Huang branded Lee a populist who would in the end bring about the collapse of the country. He asserted that most people misunderstood the true meaning of liberal democracy. In a liberal democracy, he argued, the government should protect the rights of the individuals. The rules and regulations concerning the question of how to protect those rights should be obtained through a democratic process. In his view, the government should guarantee the execution of those rules and regulations. Elections should only be part of the democratic process, not the ultimate goal. Huang believed that in Taiwan elections were viewed as the core value of democracy, which he thought was a misconception that would finally lead to populist authoritarianism and the end of the rule of law and social justice. Huang cited several examples illustrating how commodification politics had already trivialized politics and cultivated mob rule. For these reasons, Huang and other conservative mainstream scholars favored elite politics over popular politics, and were outspoken opponents of commodification politics.

At the late 1980s and early 1990s, there were indeed several candidates who trivialized politics and heavily relied on the involvement of the mass media, celebrity politics and variety shows. The Labor Party is a good example of what Huang and other scholars would describe as the perils of commodification politics. Socialist intellectuals and labor activists under the leadership of former DPP legislator Wang Yi-hsiung founded the party in 1987. At the end of the 1980s, labor disputes were on the rise and Wang Yi-hsiung thought that a party representing the interests of Taiwan's 3.4 million industrial laborers would have a political future in democratizing Taiwan.

From the beginning, Wang assumed that listening to the hearts of Taiwan's workers and utilizing the mass media would lead him and his party to election victories. Some socialist intellectuals could not identify with Wang's approach and left to found their own party. The 1989 parliamentary election was the first national election after the lifting of martial law. Wang Yi-hsiung had great expectations and his party nominated candidates in eight constituencies. Wang himself ran in the industrial city of Kaoshiung. The party, however, garnered only about 1% of the total votes cast, and none of the hopefuls was elected.

In 1992, the party took part in elections for the last time. Hope was vested in artist Hsu Hsiao-tan, who contested in the city of Kaoshiung. The party adopted a rather different way of attracting voters in that election campaign: the candidate, Hsu Hsiao-tan, undressed publicly on various occasions and promised an *open* campaign. She also challenged her rival female candidate (KMT) with the size of her nipples. The party's strategy almost worked: Hsu Hsiao-tan succeeded in getting 32,349 votes and would have needed another 108 votes to be elected. It was not only the Labor Party that tried to attract votes by entertaining the electorate.[53]

Moreover, the KMT and its candidates were increasingly engaged in event marketing. Well-known singers, entertainers and even strippers were invited to perform during election rallies. Such events known as *gewuxiu* become very popular at the beginning of the 1990s.[54] The trivialization of politics was often the issue of critical debates among liberal intellectuals and was highlighted in the movie *The Candidates* by movie producer Hsu Li-kong.[55]

As to the DPP, the largest opposition party, the lifting of martial law not only brought about positive developments. The party experienced unprecedented difficulties in mobilizing voters. During the martial law period, any political activity was severely restricted or even illegal, and thus was something out of the ordinary. Whenever a politician of the opposition camp appeared at a public place, openly attacking the government, 30,000 to 50,000 people would show up to listen. After the lifting of martial law, things changed. Whenever a candidate could attract a crowd of 200 people, he or she was said to be fortunate. A speech attacking the ruling KMT suddenly was not enough to have tens of thousands cheer enthusiastically.[56] The opposition adjusted itself to the changing environment by either holding a series of smaller events or by creating political stunts. Both of these new approaches became common at the end of the 1980s. Any election rally had to be dramatic, mysterious and something out of the ordinary as to attract the masses.[57]

Telemarketing and Mass Media Advertising

Apart from the variety show character of electoral campaigns (see Table 27.2), the involvement of modern technology in the electoral process was a further observable trend. Computerized tele-marketing was one of the new electoral tools used by a growing number of candidates in the early 1990s.[58]

The utilization of the mass media as a campaign tool was legalized in 1989, when candidates could place advertisements in newspapers and magazines. In 1991, legislation allowed for a limited number of political ads to be aired on Taiwan's three terrestrial television stations. In 1994, regulations were relaxed. Since then, political ads have paradoxically only been limited in parliamentary elections. The election law states that only publicly funded ads may be aired during the official campaign period of ten days.

In general, political ads are common in Taiwan's media. In recent years, there has been a trend toward permanent advertising campaigns. Not surprisingly, expenditures have risen dramatically since the early 1990s, especially in presidential election campaigns. Estimates suggest that the total market value of political advertisements amounted to about NT$4 billion in the last presidential election. Although the effective advertising expenditure was estimated by experts to be only one-tenth of the market value, the number is still impressive.[59]

Underground Radio

In the early 1990s, opposition figures attempted to break the KMT monopoly on the island's broadcast media by illegally setting up their own televison and radio stations. Soon, underground radio stations and later cable television networks became an important and new campaign tool. The most popular and most influential radio station at that time was Hsu Rong-chi's *Voice of Taiwan*, which went on air in November 1993. Hsu's radio station was the first equipped with powerful transmitters and could be received in most parts of Taipei. His *Voice of Taiwan* soon became an inspiring example all over the island. Hsu himself hosted most of the programs that focused on various social and political problems. *Voice of Taiwan* as well as other stations became popular because the common people could (by calling in) publicly and anonymously air their grievances against the ruling KMT.[60]

Underground radio stations have since then been an important campaign tool of the DPP, especially in southern Taiwan, where farmers are used to listening to underground radio stations while working in the fields. The influence of underground ration stations on the voting behavior of farmers is still substantial. In the 2008 presidential election campaign, the KMT, thus, bought airtime on radio stations in the South as to compete with the popular pro–DPP underground stations.[61]

Cable Television and Political Talk Shows

Cable television was a further way to counter the terrestrial network's pro-government election coverage. At the end of February 1990, DPP supporters launched the first political cable network, Democratic Cable TV (*zhonghe minzhu youxian dianshitai*) in Taipei County. In October, other networks were set up around the island.[62] By the end of 1993, fifty-four cable systems labeled themselves as Democratic Cable TV.[63] Cable television had a profound influence on election campaign strategies. It was cable television that first aired debates between candidates and call-in talk shows with politicians, which gave opposition candidates the opportunity to get the attention of the electorate. For the DPP, cable television took party leaders from the streets turning "street politics" into "media politics." Cable television, especially the call-in programs, funda-mentally changed the DPP's campaign style. These changes included: (1) to be brief and to the point; (2) to modify the party's campaigning emphasis from negative personal attacks to issues and credentials; and (3) to reposition the party as a "rational" party rather than street protesters by softening the gestures and expressions of its members appearing on television.[64]

Until 1993, cable television was illegal. The legalization brought about even more cable television stations and networks. At the end of the decade, over 80% of Taiwan's households had cable television. Since then, cable television has played an important role in the marketing mix of political parties and candidates. A number of networks air political talk shows. The main characteristics of such television programs are that (1) the moderator and his/her guests are in most cases the same people; (2) there is a lack of discussion between the participants; (3) they unanimously attack either the KMT or the DPP; (4) their audiences tend to be the same group of voters who belong to the same political camp as the participants. In short, there is no such thing as an objective political talk show. Nevertheless, cable television is very powerful because it influences the agenda setting of other television stations and the print media.

Product Placement

In general, there has been a tendency toward permanent media campaigning in recent years. Political advertisement wars are only part of the picture, though. Probably more effective is the airing of entire campaign rallies, being a guest at popular entertainment programs and/or obtaining favorable news coverage.[65] As to ensure co-operation, companies affiliated with political parties or government agencies offer lucrative advertising revenues to media outlets in return. This political advertising in disguise (product placement) has become the issue of numerous confrontations between all political parties. Each side accuses the other of abusing the media for campaign purposes.

Professional Consultants

In Taiwan, the campaign consultancy industry emerged in the early 1990s. One of the first campaign professionals was Wu Hsiang-hui. Like other campaign professionals, Wu had previously been involved in electoral campaign work for opposition candidates during the martial law period. In 1991, he founded the Good Morning Political Marketing Corporation. Since then,

Table 27.2. New Trends in Campaigning during Period of Commodification Politics

1989–2000	*2000–2008*
Variety shows (*gewuxiu*) since 1989	Mobile phone texting since 2000
Stunt politics 1989–1997★	Placement marketing since 2000
Computerized telemarketing since 1989	Blogging since 2005
Underground terrestrial TV 1989★	
Print media advertising since 1989	
TV advertising since 1991	
Illegal cable TV 1990–1993★	
Underground radio since 1992★	
Call-in political talk shows since 1992	
Professional consultancy since 1991	
Cable TV since 1993	
TV debates between candidates since 1993	
Polling since 1994	
Internet since 1996	
Campaign merchandise since 1998	

Note: ★ Only applied by non-KMT candidates.

candidates of all political camps have hired him to design electoral campaigns. During the first ten years of operation he had successfully advised over forty hopefuls. Although the industry has grown over the years, the number of campaign professionals who make a living out of campaigns is limited: "probably not more than a few dozen," according to a senior campaign professional.[66]

Opinion Polls

In Taiwan, opinion polling became an electoral tool in 1994. Since then, its application in the electoral process has only been restricted in presidential elections: individuals, political parties and organizations are prohibited from releasing opinion polls ten days before election day. Mass media may neither cite newly released nor previously released outcomes of opinion polls during this period. Apart from that blackout time, opinion polls are abundantly used to influence voting behavior. Most opinion polls are either fake or unprofessionally conducted. The media are biased and often misinterpret poll results or use unreliable data. The majority of newspaper articles and television news analyses reveal a fundamental misunderstanding of what "margin of error" means. Inaccurate poll reporting has become a serious problem in Taiwan and has already led to several disputes after media-declared winners lost elections. Local analysts claim that the abundant misuse of opinion polling reached a high in the 2000 presidential election.[67] Four years later, faked and misinterpreted opinion polls contributed to social unrest, when incumbent president Chen Shui-bian officially won the election with a margin of 0.3% of the vote and the media, nevertheless, proclaimed rival candidate Lien Chan as the winner, since he had 'led' in opinion polls.

Moreover, candidates frequently use opinion polls conducted by major cable news networks, such as TVBS, to manipulate voting behavior. When opinion polls show that the candidate is right behind the highest vote getters in his or her constituency (multi-member under SNTV), that candidate is likely to place a newspaper ad quoting the poll and urging the electorate not to let him or her down. Opinion polls may also suggest that the rival candidate lags behind. In such a situation, the candidate is likely to urge the electorate to give up supporting the rival candidate since he or she obviously has no chance whatsoever to win the election.

The Internet as a Campaign Tool

In the first direct election of the provincial governor in 1994, the three main hopefuls used a bulletin board system (BBS) to communicate with the electorate. BBS allowed computer users to dial into the system over a phone line and, with the help of a terminal program, to view and exchange messages. At the early 1990s, BBS was widely used and highly popular in Taiwan, especially among the younger generation. In the mid-1990s, however, its popularity faded as the World Wide Web became popular. Prior to the 1995 parliamentary election, the three major political parties, the KMT, the DPP and the NP (New Party), set up party websites. During the election campaign, however, the Internet was hardly used. In total, only seven candidates made use of the new media.[68]

The first time the Internet was more seriously used in electoral campaigns dates back to the 1996 presidential election. The election was a watershed in Taiwan's political development, since it was the first time that the president of the island-state was directly elected by people. All four presidential candidates and their running mates had their own websites. Peng Ming-min and his running mate Hsieh Chang-ting of the DPP, Taiwan's largest opposition party, were the first to set up their campaign websites. The site contained extensive information on the candidates' personal backgrounds and political visions. Independent candidate Chen Lu-an and his running mate Wang Ching-feng had their website designed by volunteers. It was similar to Peng's website but less professional. Independent candidate Lin Hsiang-kang and his running mate first had an

English website designed and maintained by an overseas supporter residing in the United States. It was hoped that the website could help promote Lin among the overseas community. Three months before the election, a Chinese website was set up. Lin and his running mate expected the website to counter the pro-government mainstream media. The campaign team of the ruling KMT was the last to set up a website. The site was designed and maintained by students. Unlike the websites of the other candidates, the target group of this website was young people.[69]

In the 1996 elections, websites of candidates were more considered a must-have item, rather than an effective campaign tool. Since then, the involvement of the Internet in electoral campaigning has increased. The impact of websites run by politicians and political parties on campaigning has been limited, though. One of the rare exceptions is incumbent president Chen Shui-bain's campaign website, abian.net, which was extremely popular with the electorate. The website offered a large variety of functions ranging from downloading video clips to online shopping of campaign merchandise. Chen's website was set up in 1998 in the run-up to the Taipei mayoral election and soon developed into the most popular website of a politician.

In 1998, Chen's rival candidate was Ma Ying-jeou, who was extremely popular among female voters who found him "charming and handsome." Nevertheless, Chen's website outperformed Ma's in terms of visitors. A few days before the election, about 140,000 people had visited Ma's site and almost 400,000 that of Chen Shui-bian.[70] Chen's website was permanent rather than temporary. His campaign team wanted to create a stable and long-term relationship with the Internet community. The website constantly improved and became an important campaign tool in the 2000 presidential race.

Apart from the politicians' websites, online mock voting, popularity ratings and special election websites have become popular. Major media networks, such as TVBS, usually set up special websites containing all sorts of information regarding upcoming elections, such as profiles of candidates and opinion polls.

In the 2005 mayoral and county magistrate elections, several candidates set up their own blogs. A year later, several candidates running in the parliamentary election used the free Internet encyclopedia Wikipedia as a campaign tool by modifying their entries as to receive more favorable media reporting. An increasing number of politicians have also incorporated YouTube into their Internet campaign strategies. Nevertheless, Web 2.0 applications are in general still underutilized in Taiwanese electoral campaigns.

Structure of Campaign Organizations

Figure 27.3 shows the typical structure of a candidate's electoral campaign organization. The size of the official campaign team depends on the type of election and the financial capabilities of the candidate. At the core of the team are the candidate, the campaign manager (zongganshi) and his or her assistants. They are the major decision-makers. Under their office, there are several key divisions responsible for different tasks.

The survey division, for example, uses opinion poll data and computer-assisted calling systems to find out the strengths and weaknesses of the candidate and his/her rivals. The division also engages in telemarketing activities and more recently in the utilization of the text messaging function of mobile phone operators for campaign purposes. In the 2004 presidential election, for example, the campaign team of the KMT candidate extensively used text messaging to convey campaign messages to the electorate and urge them to join the candidate's election activities.

The media relations division is in charge of drafting press releases, organizing press conferences and establishing/utilizing private relationships with journalists. The propaganda division is responsible for designing and producing campaign literature, posters, advertisements and campaign merchandise. External advertising agencies or advisors usually support the division. The

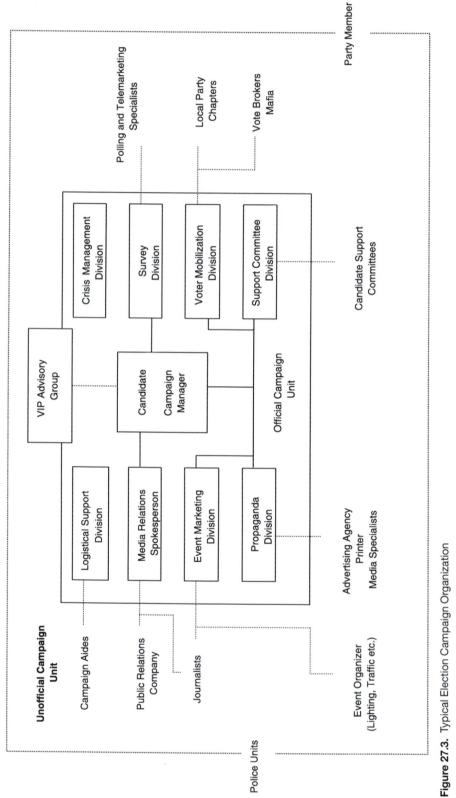

Figure 27.3. Typical Election Campaign Organization

Source: Based on Chian-wu Chiu, *Shei shuo xuanju un shifu [Who Says Elections Have No Master?]* (Taipei: Bluelime, 2007), 52.

campaign event division organizes electoral activities, such as rallies, visits to traditional markets and campaign speeches. The candidate support committee division has to co-ordinate and supervise the activities of the various support committees that may exist outside the official campaign unit.

A very important campaign function is the vote mobilization division. It plans vote buying activities. In Taiwan, vote buying emerged in the 1950s when businessmen entered electoral politics and gradually replaced the local gentry. In the 1980s, electoral competition intensified and most candidates had little to offer except money to convince voters to support them. In the 1990s, vote buying became commonplace, with price tags ranging from NT$500 (US$16) to NT$2,000 (US$67). "This was particularly true of the KMT, whose candidates rarely campaigned on their good image or on ideology," as political scientist Tien Hung-mao notes in his works on Taiwanese politics.[71]

The voter mobilization division has to recruit vote brokers, the so-called *tiau-a-ka*. Chin Kuo-lin, a leading expert on organized crime involvement in Taiwanese politics, claims that "anybody who can persuade about twenty people to vote for a particular candidate is a potential *tiau-a-ka*."[72] The big *tiau-a-ka*, the vote wholesalers, however, are usually local politicians, underworld figures, head of interest groups, influential business people and other individuals with high social status.[73] In practice, the candidate directly or through the voter mobilization division solicits wholesalers, who use their connections to recruit smaller voter brokers, the vote captains. Each of these vote captains has to deliver between fifty and a hundred votes. They have to submit a list of possible target voters to the wholesaler who will hand it over to the campaign unit, where names are keyed into a computerized database. All names are cross-checked as to make sure that bribes are only once distributed to each target voter.[74]

Vote buying is still common in Taiwan, especially in rural areas and smaller cities. Although several local election experts believe that the impact of vote buying on the electoral process has decreased since the late 1990s, those involved in electioneering at grassroots level doubt that vote buying is "just a lubricant," as renowned political scientist Chu Yun-han noted during a post–election discussion in 1998.[75]

Another important part of the campaign unit is the VIP advisory group (*darenwu guwentuan*), which typically consists of well-known and respected local personalities, such as leading politicians, and members of the business community and academia. They serve as advisors to the candidate and publicly endorse the candidate.

Involvement of the Underworld

The growing electoral competition after the lifting of martial law and the inability of the KMT to cope effectively with the changing environment has substantially increased the involvement of underworld figures in politics.[76] Even ranking KMT members in the party's Taipei headquarters admit quite frankly that criminal records do not matter in the selection of candidates and that the KMT fully supports underground figures as long as they help the party to defend constituencies against the DPP.[77] Local political analysts estimate that in the 1970s, about 10% of city and county councilors had gang backgrounds. A decade later, the figure increased to 40% and in the 1990s, approximately half of the councilors belonged to the underworld.[78] Moreover, over 60% of Taiwan's major crime syndicates had publicly elected officials at all administrative levels, including the parliament.[79]

There are several reasons why underworld figures have succeeded in winning elections despite the fact that they are criminals. Political scientist Chao Yung-mao, a leading expert on local politics, stated that they are popular because they help the community in a better and more efficient way than other politicians. They (1) help the supporter to find a job; (2) try to help to solve personal problems of the supporter (for example, make sure that a husband who hits his wife would be beaten up); (3) they put sentiment above the law; and (4) they are very aggressive in improving the streets and temples in the supporter's neighborhood.[80]

Underworld figures who do not run in elections themselves have several other functions in the electoral process:[81]

1 They help the candidate to establish a vote base, and ensure that the candidate's constituency is his or her turf and recruit vote-brokers.

2 They work as bodyguards for the candidate and they will make sure that the audience applauds when the candidate delivers a speech.

3 They will make sure that the voters who were bribed to vote for their candidate did, indeed, do so. If not, they will make sure that the bribe is returned in full.

The significant influence and role of underworld figures in electoral campaigning (especially in rural areas) cannot be denied, even today.[82]

Limits of Modern Campaigning

How modern or postmodern are Taiwanese electoral campaigns today? In the first part of this analysis, I have outlined the main characteristics of the overall electoral process in the immediate postwar years. State-controlled elections during the martial law period transformed gentry politics into machine politics and contributed to the growing involvement of the underworld in the electoral process. Social, economic and political changes in the late 1970s and early 1980s brought about the involvement of the general public in politics. Electoral campaigns became more competitive and campaign strategies diversified. Using Fritz Plasser's typology of standard campaign models (see Figure 27.1), Taiwan's electoral campaigns were still pre-modern at that time.

The lifting of the martial law decree in 1987 even more intensified electoral competition, which in turn forced the opposition as well as the ruling KMT to adopt new methods of campaigning. As I mentioned earlier, the opposition relied on stirring the people's emotions and the utilization of illegal radio and TV stations to increase its popularity in the early 1990s. The KMT, on the other hand, responded by adopting two different approaches: the first called for a shift toward more professional campaigning and the second approach sophisticated conventional campaign methods, such as the mass mobilization of the electorate through vote brokers and underworld figures. The first approach was the official one and was proposed by senior party figures, such as John Kuan, who wanted the KMT to apply modern and highly sophisticated marketing techniques as to deal with the changing environment. Although the new approach boosted the popularity of Chairman Lee Teng-hui, the majority of ranking KMT members distrusted the modern form of campaigning because they saw their own power waning. Consequently, John Kuan lost the internal strife within a couple of years and the KMT had to rely more than ever on traditional forms of campaigning, such as vote buying and the involvement of underworld figures.

At the end of the 1990s, the KMT was again confronted with internal rifts over the nomination of the party's presidential candidate. Finally, Song Chu-yu, former provincial governor, could not obtain the party's endorsement and contested the election as an independent candidate. The move hit the KMT hard since Song had a very strong support base, especially in the South, where the KMT traditionally had less support. Song practically overnight robbed a substantial number of the KMT's vote brokers and other influential grassroots "campaign aides." The consequences were a foregone conclusion rather than a surprise. Although the KMT engaged in cost-intensive advertising wars, hired specialists and reportedly applied modern survey techniques, their presidential candidate received by far fewer votes than the DPP candidate and Song Chu-yu. The KMT felt so bitterly what it meant to fight a war without having the ability to utilize traditional forms of campaigning. Its defeat in the 2000 presidential election was a major and devastating setback for the party. Losing the election meant losing even more power and money. In the 1990s, the KMT still was one of the richest (if not even the richest) parties in the world, but the defeat in the year 2000 cut it off from substantial future revenues.

No matter how sophisticated electoral strategies may appear to be, the truth is that the KMT has never left the stage of pre-modern campaigning. As a senior KMT official observed:

> They never intended to adopt something like modern campaigning. They never believed that the party could rely on modern campaigning. Why should they? Vote buying had always worked in the past. . . . In Taipei, perhaps, media campaigning and images are important to win elections. Mob involvement is low there. But in most other areas, I would say, the party headquarters does not like to waste money on sophisticated campaigning. . . . Anyhow, what is the purpose of hiring campaign specialists and conducting surveys? The party leadership does not care about what experts say. They rely on their own sources, mostly friends and relatives.
>
> Take the last two presidential elections as an example. The campaign manager had little to say. It was mostly his [the presidential candidate's] daughter and other relatives who made decisions on how to run the campaign and what issues we should emphasize. . . . I would say that the DPP is much more professional. The party leaders respect the decisions of lower-ranking officials. Their strategies make more sense. They have real issues, so they can set up long-term marketing plans. The KMT is a loose organization of different groups with different ideas. . . . Modern campaigning is just one layer of campaigning. It is to attract the 30%-unaffiliated voters that possibly won't take bribes. Nowadays, election results are very close and if we can get some of these votes in addition to the ones we bought than we will succeed at the polls.[83]

Another example highlighting the limited impact of modern campaigning is the 2005 National Assembly election. In that election, delegates to the National Assembly were for the first time elected based on a party-list proportional representation system. Unlike other elections, the voter had to select a party and not a candidate. Consequently, individual candidates did not engage in campaigning at all, grassroots campaign activities were non-existent, and political parties engaged in media-oriented campaigning only. Unsurprisingly, voter turned dropped to a historic low of 23%. (Voter turnout in parliamentary elections usually is above 60% and in presidential elections above 80%.)

It is, thus, safe to say that the current mode of campaigning in Taiwan is a dual process of campaigning, that is the utilization of modern and postmodern campaign techniques in combination with traditional forms. Applying Plasser's typology (Figure 27.1), it is, however, debatable whether Taiwan's mode of campaigning is pre-modern with modern and postmodern features or vice versa.

Conclusion

In this chapter, I have tried to give the reader a picture of the evolution of modern campaigning in Taiwan and its limits. A further interesting question is how far the Taiwan case is representative for other polities in the region. In East Asia we have four democracies (Taiwan, South Korea, Mongolia and Japan) and two authoritarian regimes (China and North Korea). If we look at the other three democracies of the region, each has a distinct form of electoral campaigning, but none could be described as a polity that clearly fits into one of the three standard campaign models. There are tendencies toward postmodernity, though.[84]

Political theorists have frequently stated that the application of postmodern campaigning faces certain limitations that usually arise from the institutional, legal and socio-political background of the transforming polity. I believe, however, that the most crucial factor determining the growth of postmodern campaigning lies in the answer to the question whether previous campaign techniques have lost in effectiveness or not. In Taiwan, legal and institutional barriers are very rare, but still postmodern campaigning has neither outperformed nor entirely replaced traditional forms of campaigning. What limits the scope of postmodern campaigning is the affirmative answer to the question whether traditional forms of campaigning are still effective or not. In Taiwan, traditional campaign methods are still effective and it is this fact that limits the adoption of postmodern campaigning. From this perspective, this chapter is not only representative for East Asia, but for all transitional societies.

Notes

1 Tzi-long Cheng, *Jingxuan chuanbo yu taiwan shehui [Electoral Campaigning and Taiwan's Society]* (Taipei: Yang-Chih, 2004), 10.
2 Peng Ming-min, *A Taste of Freedom: Memoirs of a Formosan Independence Leader*, 3rd ed. (Taipei: Taiwan Publishing, 2005), 61.
3 John Leighton Stuart, "Memorandum on the Situation in Tawain, 1947," http://www.taiwandocuments.org/228_01.htm. Accessed February 20, 2002.
4 Yan-Xian Li, Zhen-long Yang and Yan-xian Zhang, eds, *Report on the Responsibility for the 228 Massacre [ererba shijian zeren guishu yanjiu baogao]* (Zhonghe: 228 Memorial Foundation, 2006).
5 Central Election Commission, *Republic of China Election History [Zhonghua minguo xuanjushi]* (Taipei: Central Election Commission, 1986).
6 Tao-yi Liu, *Why Abolish the Province? Self-criticism and Adjustments of Administrative Areas [Wei shen ma yao fei sheng? Wo guo xing zheng qü de jian tao yü tiao cheng]* (Taipei: Central Library Publication, 1997), 101.
7 Teh-fu Huang, "Elections and the Evolution of the Kuomintang," in *Political Change in Taiwan*, ed. Cheng Tun-jen and Stephan Haggard (Boulder, CO: Rienner, 1992), 114.
8 Chia-shu Huang and Rui Cheng, *Taiwan zhengzhi yu xuanju wenhua [Taiwan Politics and Election Culture]* (Taipei: Boy Young, 1991), 16.
9 Huang and Cheng, *Taiwan Politics*, 18.
10 Author's own calculation based on data provided by the Central Election Commission, Taipei.
11 Interview with retired secret police officer, June 2005.
12 Evan Luard, "China and the United Nations," *International Affairs* 47 (4) (1971): 729–35.
13 Ming-tong Chen, "Local Factions and Elections in Taiwan's Democratization," in *Taiwan's Electoral Politics and Democratic Transition: Riding the Third Wave*, ed. Charles Chi-Hsiang, Robert A. Scalapino, and Hung-mao Tien (New York: M.E. Sharpe, 1997), 179.
14 Lin-ta Ai, *Jidang! Taiwan fandui yundong zongpipan [Muckraker! An Overall Critique of the Opposition Movement in Taiwan]* (Taipei: Chianwei, 1997), 107.
15 Ibid., 119.
16 Margaret Canovan, *Populism* (New York: Harcourt Brace Jovanovich, 1981), 13.
17 Ai, *Muckraker*, 117.
18 New Taiwan Cultural Foundation, *Meiyou dangming de dang: meilidao zhengtuan de fazhan [The Party Without Name: The Development of Formosa]* (Taipei: Shibao Wenhua, 1998), 11–16.
19 Pi-Hsiang Chan, *Maipiao chanhui lu [Vote Buying: A Confession]* (Taipei: Shangyezhoukan, 1999).
20 Jia-long Lin, "Taiwan difang xuanju yu guomindang zhengquan de shichanghua" [Taiwan's Local Elections and the Marketization of KMT's Political Power], in *Liangan jiceng xuanju yu zhengzhi shehui bianqian [Grassroots Elections, Political and Social Changes in China and Taiwan]*, ed. Chen Ming-Tong and Cheng Yong-nian (Taipei: Yuandan, 1998), 236.
21 New Taiwan Cultural Foundation, *Lishi de ningjie: 1977–79 taiwan minzhu dongyun xiangshi [A Pictorial History of Taiwan's Opposition Movements 1977–79]* (Taipei: Shibao Wenhua, 1999), 21–3, 63–5.
22 Ai, *Muckraker*, 148–58.
23 Yong-cheng Chang, *Xuan zhan zaoshi [Electoral Warfare]* (Taipei: Shichanchihuitsongshu, 1992), 185–92; Huang and Cheng, *Taiwan Politics*, 150.

24 Mao-gui Chang, *She hui yun dong yu zheng zhi zhuan hua [Social Movements and Political Change]* (Taipei: Institute for National Policy Research, 1994), 57.

25 Yung-mao Chao, *Taiwan di fang zheng zhi de bian qian yu te zhi [Changes in Taiwan Local Politics]* (Taipei: Han Lu, 1998), 248–63.

26 Philip Kotler, *Marketing for Nonprofit Organizations* (Englewood Cliffs, N.J.: Prentice-Hall, 1982), 461–2.

27 John Kuan, *The Modernisation of the Kuomintang: Observations and Expectations* (Taipei: Democracy Foundation, 1992), 17.

28 Ibid., 29.

29 Ibid., 15.

30 Ibid., 49.

31 Ibid., 18.

32 Ibid., 15.

33 Chong Kuan, *Jintian bu zuo mingtian houhui [If We Do Not Do it Today, We Will Regret Tomorrow]* (Taipei: Democracy Foundation, 1991), 91.

34 Kuan, *The Modernisation of the Kuomintang*, 60.

35 Ibid., 60.

36 Ibid., 60.

37 Ibid., 38.

38 Ibid., 61.

39 Ibid., 81.

40 Ibid., 81–82.

41 Ibid., 82.

42 Ibid., 82.

43 Ibid., 82.

44 Ibid., 82.

45 Gary Armstrong, Philip Kotler and Geoffrey da Silva, *Marketing: An Asian Perspective* (New York: Pearson, Prentice Hall, 2005), 19.

46 Kuan, *The Modernisation of the Kuomintang*, 17.

47 Armstrong, Kotler and da Silva, *Marketing*, 20.

48 Interview with former senior KMT member, June 2006.

49 Ibid.

50 Interview with former senior KMT election aide, April 2006

51 Chen-huan Wang and Yong-hsiang Chian, "Yuxiang xinguojia? Mincuiweiquan zhuyi de xingcheng yu minzhuwenti" ["March Towards a New Nation State? The Rise of Populist Authoritarianism in Taiwan and its Implication for Democracy"], *Taiwan: A Radical Quarterly in Social Studies* 20 (August 1995): 17–55.

52 Kuang-guo Huang, *Mincuiwangtailun [About Populism and the End of Taiwan]* (Taipei: Shangchou, 1995).

53 Christian Schafferer, "Political Parties and Electoral Politics in Taiwan," in *Understanding Modern East Asian Politics*, ed. Christian Schafferer (New York: Nova Science, 2005), 125.

54 Huang and Cheng, *Taiwan Politics*, 145–7.

55 For more on the DPP's response: Christian Schafferer, "Electoral Campaigning in Taiwan," in *Election Campaigning in East and Southeast Asia*, ed. Christian Schafferer (Aldershot: Ashgate, 2006), 46–7.

56 Chang, *Electoral Warfare*, 212.

57 See Christian Schafferer, *Election Campaigning in East and Southeast Asia* (Aldershot: Ashgate), 40.

58 Tzi-long Cheng, *Jingxuan wenxuan celue [Electoral Propaganda]*, 4th ed. (Taipei: Yuanliu, 2001), 135.

59 Data provided by Rainmaker and XKM, Taipei.

60 Chao-ru Chen, *Call in!! dixia diantai taiwan xin chuanbo wenhua de zhenhan yu misi [Call in!! Underground Radio: Taiwan's New Broadcasting Culture]* (Taipei: Richen, 1994); Song-ting Lu, *Taiwan zhi sheng [Voice of Taiwan]* (Chonghe: Tatsun, 1994).

61 Qing-feng Tong, "Lüse dianbo weichao mayingjiu lanying bushu fangong" ["Green Waves attack Ma Ying-yeou: Blue Camp Fights Back"], *Yazhou Zhoukan*, September 9, 2007.

62 Tian-yuan Wang, *Taiwan xinwen chuanboshi [The Evolution of Mass Communication in Taiwan]* (Taipei: Yatai, 2002), 574–5.

63 Peilin Chiu and Silvia M. Chan-Olmsted, "The Impact of Cable Television on Political Campaigns in Taiwan," *Gazette* 61 (6) (1999): 494.

64 Sisy Chen cited in Chiu and Chan-Olmsted, "The Impact of Cable Television," 502.

65 Tian-bin Wang, *Xinwen ziyou [Freedom of the Press]* (Taipei: Yatai, 2005), 376–80.

66 Interview with a senior campaign professional, March 2006.

67 Huang and Cheng, *Taiwan Politics*, 218–31.

68 Po-Chong Chuang, *Wanglu Xuanzhan [Internet Campaigning in Taiwan]* (Taipei: Miluo, 2007), 38–40.

69 Yun Peng, *Xin meijie yu zhengzhi: lilun yu shizheng [New Media and Politics: Theorie and Practice]* (Taipei: Wunan, Taipei, 201), 332.

70 Ibid., 356.

71 Hung-mao Tien, "Elections and Taiwan's Democratic Development," in *Taiwan's Electoral Politics and Democratic Transition: Riding the Third Wave*, ed. Charles Chi-Hsiang, Robert A. Scalapino, and Hung-mao Tien (New York: M.E. Sharpe, 1997), 19.

72 Kuo-lin Chen, *Heijin [Black Gold]* (Taipei: Shangzhou, 2004), 211.

73 Ibid.

74 Ibid., 210.

75 Interviews with former local KMT and DPP campaign managers and aides, May–June 2006.

76 Chen, *Black Gold*, 188.

77 Ibid., 196–97.

78 Ibid., 117.

79 Ibid., 119.

80 Chao Yung-mao cited in Chen, *Black Gold*, 208.

81 Chen, *Black Gold*, 190.

82 Interviews with former local KMT and DPP campaign managers and aides, May–June 2006

83 Interview with senior KMT official, March 2007.

84 Christian Schafferer, "Is There an Asian Style of Electoral Campaigning?" in *Election Campaigning in East and Southeast Asia*, ed. Christian Schafferer (Aldershot: Ashgate, 2006), 103–40.

28

Mexico's 2000 Presidential Election

Long Transition or a Sudden Political Marketing Triumph?

Eduardo Robledo Rincón

> There are words that bewitch. When listening to their sound, when conjugating or declining them, we immediately fall under the spell of an invisible cage which transports us to its territories without allowing any truce. The imagination runs wild. Reason weakens. A single word can cause short-sightedness, blindness. Democracy is one of those words.
>
> (Federico Reyes Heroles)[1]

Vicente Fox did not create Mexican democracy. Rather, democracy is a consequence of the great political, economic, and social transitions that Mexico experienced between 1977 and 2000. Fox's victory in the 2000 elections, which ended the seventy years of government by the same party, the Institutional Revolutionary Party (PRI), was not just a product of political marketing, the work of his private political strategists, Fox's performance, or all the mistakes his opponent made. His triumph and the peaceful rise of his presidency was, above all, a consequence of a long process of democratization. To focus only on the defeat of PRI and the victory of PAN (National Action Party) hides the deep transitions that Mexico had been experiencing years before.

The 2000 elections brought an enormous political change. Mexico went from a hegemonic party system to a multi-party, balanced one; from having elections with little or no competition, to experiencing true competitive elections. Vicente Fox was not the one who started this change. Fox, no doubt, initiated party change in the presidency. His triumph constituted a fundamental act; nevertheless, it was possible because previous norms, institutions, party systems, and forces were at work. Mario Ojeda Gomez, a Mexican political analyst, once said, "When Fox appeared, the table was already set for a new companion to join them."[2]

The international experience suggested that the Mexican transformation would follow in one of two ways: a transition controlled by an old regime, or a violent change like the one expected by one of the most powerful union leaders, Fidel Velázquez:[3] "We arrived at gun point, and only at gun point shall we leave." But it happened otherwise. The political transformation in Mexico was characterized by a deep respect for the electoral results. "A smooth transition" some said. The electoral journey beginning on July 2, 2000, was calm, without the typical charge of electoral fraud. Vicente Fox and his party (PAN) were able to celebrate their victory across the country, without the ruling party trying to change its course.[4]

The transition toward democracy in Mexico does not culminate in just one date. It is a historical period. It is not an idea, nor a preconceived program; it is not the project of a group, or a party, or candidate; it does not have a privileged main actor or a unique person; it is not a date, a situation, a struggle, an episode, let alone an electoral campaign, no matter how important this is. The transition is the sum of all the above and much more. Its background is one of a modern society that no longer fits into the political frame of a hegemonic party.

Things were going well on July 2, 2000; and the results were more like a confirmation. This chapter explores how successive phenomena, installed in Mexico years ago, gave birth to a major political change and an irresistible expansion of democracy in Mexico. Those phenomena include: political parties with increasing power, greater competition, abundant voters, and a change in state power within municipal and local governments.

Characterization of the Mexican Political System (1929–2000)

The PRI and the Mexican Political System

The Institutional Revolutionary Party, from which fourteen presidents ruled in Mexico from 1929 all the way to 2000,[5] was founded in 1929 under the name of the Revolutionary National Party by its main leader Plutarco Elías Calles. The goal of the party was to overcome the military factionalism, which divided Mexico in two, and handle the constant conflicts among the members of a heterogeneous "revolutionary family," which turned each election into an armed confrontation. The idea, according to Calles, was to substitute individuals for institutions; but in practice, he established himself as the one and only leader, the power behind the presidential chair. It was Lázaro Cárdenas, president from 1934 to 1940, who gave the system its true form and content. Cárdenas organized all forces who had contributed to the Revolution—peasants, workers, middle class, and soldiers—in cooperation within the party. The alliances of the social classes strengthened along with the state and its party; through them the nation, its goals, independency, and wellbeing were strengthened. Cárdenas passed on a political system *sui generis* where the main pieces were the president and the party, both for the service of a national state which would enhance Mexico by saving it from both internal anarchy and external pressure, making it possible for the country to impose its own independent goals.

Carlos Fuentes has pointed out that:

> Cárdenas proceeded then to establish the new conditions for the Mexican presidency: all the power for Caesar, but only during a period of nine years. Caesar could success himself, but he had the right—like Augustus—to designate his successor. So, he chose the Dolphin, given the power of the Party over the electoral system, he would unfortunately be the new Caesar, and would also execute his complete power only during six years, respecting the rule of no re-election, and designating his own successor. *And so on, ad infinitum.*[6]

There are a lot of descriptions on the Mexican political system that prevailed during most of the twentieth century. But none is absolute. Daniel Cosío Villegas, scholar of modern Mexico, defined the post-revolutionary Mexican political system: "[I]t is about an absolute six-year monarchy, hereditary by transversal lineage."[7] The Revolution Party was considered by most foreign analysts and observers as the "only party," "official," or "dominating". Robert Scott, in *Mexican Government in Transition*, points out that "it is adequate to say that Mexico has an only party system, as it is right to state that the US has a two-party system."[8] The Frenchman Jacques Lambert also classifies PRI as an "official party," and adds the qualifying term "privileged."[9] Pablo González Casanova characterizes national elections as an "electoral ceremony."[10] In 1990, Octavio Paz, the recipient of the Nobel Prize in Literature, described the regime:

> The invention of the Revolutionary National Party, which today we know as the Institutional Revolutionary Party, was a great act of political imagination. It gave the country the chance to avoid falling into a revolutionary Caesarism, and at the same time to escape from the civil war, and the military uprisings. . . . We did not live in a dictatorship, but a political monopoly of one party, afterwards turned into a "political class."[11]

The distinctions for this regime were, according to Juan Linz, the restriction of political competence, the lack of effective devices of institutional moderation, the purpose of social demobilization, and the absence of a complete ideology.[12]

The greatest success of the system was the political stability, and social peace. While Latin America gave in to a dictatorship and anarchy, and democracy was defeated again and again by the military power, Mexico kept a constitutional continuity and an economic development. However, despite all its synthetic ability, the Revolution Party never gave up on centralism, and absolute domination of the electoral political area. The system began showing its own limits; the party was unable to transform itself at the speed required by the society. The structures or central pieces that explained and held the stability of the political life in Mexico, the presidency, and the "dominating official party," constituted, respectively, a power without counterweight that determined the basic course of the public life, and an effective instrument, but without independence. The system was not totalitarian, but it was not democratic; it was a political system with a physiognomy of its own. Jesús Silva-Herzog Márquez, writes:

> It is like the duck-billed platypus, the portrait of the Mexican regime turns out to be a creature full of "buts." It is authoritarian but civil; not competitive, but with periodical elections; hyper-presidential but with a great institutional continuity; with a revolutionary hegemonic party but without a narrow ideology; corporate but inclusive.[13]

When the year 2000 arrived, the PRI no longer appealed to most citizens, who were not able to participate in politics. They thought of the political system as something strange, not something they owned, so they felt more and more frustrated, and disenchanted by their situation and the one of the country.

Eventual Conquering by the Power of Opposition

The mechanics for political change in Mexico, according to a theory developed by José Woldemberg,[14] affirm the eventual democratization of the country: pluralistic and different parties participated in authentic elections, competing for legislative and executive position, promoting reform, seeking rights, security, and prerogatives. The parties, thus strengthened, participated again on new elections, where they gained more and more places, and launched a new cycle of demands and electoral reforms. For Woldemberg, Mexican politics could not have been understood for the last twenty-five years "if this process which strengthened the parties and is found in each electoral reform an attack for a new phase of change is not recognized."[15]

Thus it is possible to assure that the transition was developed "from the sides to the center, and from the bottom to the top"[16] in what Woldemberg calls a "slow colonization of the national state" by different parties. The Mexican transition cannot be understood from the perspective of only one election: it is the store of hundreds of processes that ended up pluralizing the state and to that extent they were eroding the authoritarianism practiced by the hegemonic party. Rafael Aranda, who studied the context of the 2000 electoral revolution, was one of the first analysts who departed from the preconceived ideas about the political transition in Mexico. According to him, the scope and impact of the electoral competition in the municipal area in Mexico, have not been perceived and identified clearly, due to the force and emotion of the debate about the transition process towards democracy, and the alternation within the Presidency of the Republic.[17]

This is the first hypothesis. The electoral competition in Mexico started on the urban municipalities, and on the systems from the municipal parties to expand afterwards to a national level. Data support this. In 1977, from 2,435 municipalities, only four were ruled by other parties different from the PRI. In 1988, they were already thirty-nine. Before July 2, 2000 they were 583, including the most populated and thriving of the country. The election day on the year 2000, the PRI had lost eleven of the thirty-one state governments,[18] or provinces of the country, apart from the Federal District. These states represented 37% of the total population.

The Opposition at a Local Level

A more detailed approach shows that from the 236 more urbanized municipalities, where 60% of the population is concentrated, 70% of them had already experienced the electoral change of power between 1988 and 2000. Figure 28.1 shows that the municipal elections by each three-year period and the percentage of urban municipalities where alternation is shown. The democratic advance at a municipal level is undeniable.[19]

The urban municipalities present a higher level of development; these are populations where the most informed and critical people live. This means that they are also the most sophisticated in electoral matters. The advances made by parties other than the PRI within the municipal dimension proves that the party alternation started at least twelve years before 2000.

The PRI began losing governmental places locally, and the "opposition" during those twelve years (1988–2000) considerably increased its voters. This means that, even if they did not win positions of public power, they became more competitive against the PRI during elections.

Figure 28.2 shows the group of voters among all opposing parties, for local and federal elections. It can be observed that since 1988, the opposition already had 35% to 58% of the votes, within the local elections. And for federal legislators it increased from 38% to 62%.

The decided increase of votes for the opposition parties eventually weakened the electoral control of the PRI. Elections became more and more competitive, and what was once an exception, turned into something commonplace for the citizens.

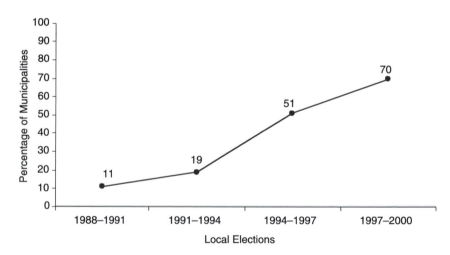

Figure 28.1. Percentage of Urban Municipalities where an Electoral Alternation Took Place between 1988 and 2000

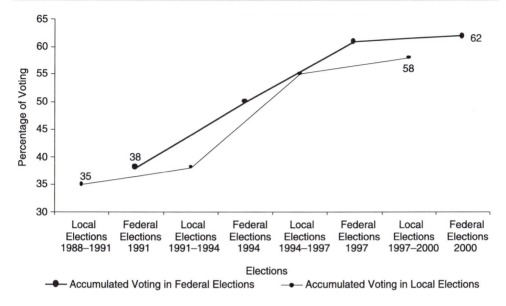

Figure 28.2. Accumulated Voting of Opposition Parties to the PRI

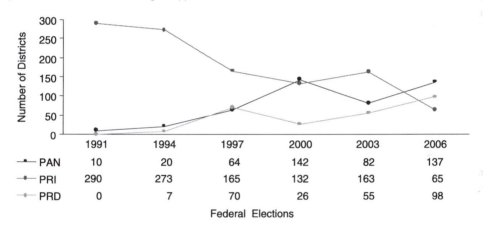

Federal Elections	1991	1994	1997	2000	2003	2006
PAN	10	20	64	142	82	137
PRI	290	273	165	132	163	65
PRD	0	7	70	26	55	98

Figure 28.3. Electoral Districts (Counties) Won by Political Party

On this tendency, the PAN, the opposition party which gained the most, shows an increase rate of 56.8% in the local elections between 1988 and 2000; and 121.5% for federal elections during the same period of time.

The Opposition Arrived at the Congress

The opposition conquest was not only an expression within the local governments; it was also a significant impact on the legislative power and on the national level. Mexico is divided into 300 *uninominal* districts, representing 60% of the House of Representatives; the other 40% corresponds to the *plurinominal* lists represented by the political parties.

Figure 28.3 shows the districts in which each political party won the elections from 1991 to 2006 (the most recent federal election).

This shows that the PRI comes from winning 290 out of 300 districts in 1991, to sixty-five districts during 2006. For 2000, the PAN would add ten more districts than the PRI; this had a great impact on the House of Representatives.

Figure 28.4 shows the percentage of PRI representatives, and the one for the added opposition, out of the six legislative sessions for the House of Representatives from 1991 until today.

Figure 28.4 is convincing. The decrease suffered by the PRI representatives is noticeable, from 64% to 21% during all the previously mentioned periods. By the elections held in July, the PRI had already lost. In 1997, the majority was no longer occupied by this party, which limited the president, Ernesto Zedillo (PRI), from approving laws since such approval required 50% plus one of the votes. Now it became necessary to negotiate with the opposition legislators in order to make any reforms.

The loss of the complete majority within the House represented the first federal body conquered by the opposition. The hegemonic party was forced to coexist with a regime based on new rules: "the winner does not win them all, but the loser does not lose them all either." States and municipalities, as well as the legislative power, all became places held by the opposition. They began conquering them slowly, but it became an utter reality in 2000 with the presidential change of power. In short, the elections carried out on July 2, 2000 represented an electoral mechanical change that had already been experienced in Mexico in other governmental areas.

Political and Electoral Reforms

Woldemberg has argued that the changes in political matters in Mexico have been "systematic and permanent," and the "neuralgic episodes" for the political parties have been focused on electoral matters and Congress:

> What would be a proper composition for the Congress to represent and reflect the real political forces in Mexico? How were they to protect the political rights of the citizens and parties? Which authority could turn out to be reliable for arbitrating an increasingly intense competition? Which are the mechanisms that will allow the disappearance of the electoral fraud for good?[20]

During the elections of 1976, José López Portillo became the only adversary. When he became president the regime called for political reform that led the way to the development of organized opposition and for its assistance in the electoral area.

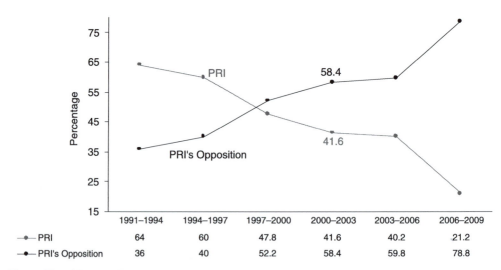

	1991–1994	1994–1997	1997–2000	2000–2003	2003–2006	2006–2009
PRI	64	60	47.8	41.6	40.2	21.2
PRI's Opposition	36	40	52.2	58.4	59.8	78.8

Figure 28.4. Members Percentage within the House of Representatives

In 1977, there were five pillars of reform: the parties were declared as "entities created for the public interest" and the parties' judicial entities were recognized, as well as their importance in the composition of state organs. The electoral competition is now open through a "conditioned registration" of the most important political forces of the Mexican opposition, which until then had been left out. The expansion of the Congress is now completed, as well as the introduction of the plurinominal representation. The new formula had 300 majority representatives and more than 100 coming from proportional representation. A more intense pluralism was added to the House of Representatives, along with a sufficient amount of incentives for the parties to develop campaigns at a national level, searching for all the votes they could get for the plurinominal bag. For the first time, the state accepts the obligation of granting resources for supporting all political parties. They, in turn, acquired prerogatives with the media, as well as with funding.[21]

Constitutional changes promoted by President López Portillo were considered as the first true political reform of the modern Mexico. This began by restating pluralism and vowing to resolve all political conflicts and contradictions in a more civilized way. This reform was stated on the Federal Law for Political Organizations and Electoral Procedures, known as the LOPPE.

The reform resulted in the integration of all types of ideologies and adversaries, some of which used to be sealed off from electoral matters. Parties expanded and created new alternatives, or strengthened the already existing ones. In certain regions of the country the elections began showing symptoms of competitiveness, even real electoral dispute.

Later, these reforms would deepen the changes and set precedent: independence for the electoral mechanisms regarding the executive, rules for a fair and equal competition, and democratization of the federal district. These changes were critical since the most important subjects of the electoral process were the citizens who focused their political activities on the elections. The elections of 1997 were crucial, since the loss of the majority by the PRI inside the House of Representatives made the way for a balance among parties. This event was stressed by the free and critical presence of the media, two ingredients of modern democratic composition.

In 1996, another political reform modified the rules of the electoral game with transcendental consequences: most important in terms of electoral institutions was the autonomy and, indeed, true citizenship of the Federal Electoral Institution (IFE). It is important because autonomy was granted in the context of mistrust, but most of all, the guarantees and resources for strengthening this autonomy were given by the political regime itself. The IFE has been acknowledged by Mexicans as one of the must trustworthy institutions for electoral matters in 2000.

Figure 28.5 shows the levels of public satisfaction in the conduct of the 2000 presidential campaign. These levels of satisfaction are comparable to other institutions such as the church and the army.

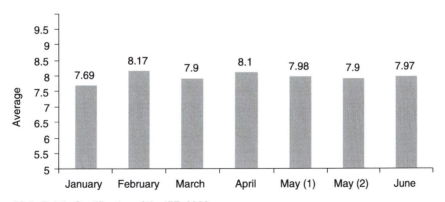

Figure 28.5. Public Qualification of the IFE, 2000

The IFE was to be composed of advisors ratified by the Congress. Most of them came from important universities and had academic credentials that validated their participation. Along with the high level of credentials of the advisers and the autonomy of the IFE would come a strong advertising campaign that enhanced both its image and prestige.[22]

The IFE was one of the main characters acting in the presidential elections of 2000. It would be impossible to explain the conditions in which the change in government took place without the support of this body.

The 2000 Elections and PRI Succession

For seventy years, the presidential succession in Mexico has consisted of the ritualizing of the power held by one party alone. As his last prerogative, the soon-to-retire president had the absolute right to chose his successor, and impose his choice on society. For the elections of 2000 these rules changed. The PRI was the only party that pushed for competition, and organized an internal election for determining its candidate. Vicente Fox, getting ahead of his time, and with an important economic investment, had already inhibited any attempt of competition toward the inner part of the PAN. Cuauhtémoc Cárdenas competed for the third time with a candidateship that was understood as an historical right. Thus the only party uncertain about its candidate for president was the PRI. A debate was held between the four pre-candidates (Francisco Labastida, Roberto Madrazo, Manuel Bartlett, and Humberto Roque Villanueva), the internal rules and mechanisms were established for the elections, and open voting was held in November 1999. Ten million votes decided that the candidate for the PRI would be Francisco Labastida Ochoa.

This internal party competition had its risks. The prickliness of the exchange among the main adversaries for the PRI candidateship, Francisco Labastida and Roberto Madrazo, ratified the legitimacy of the internal competition, but at the same time divided the activists. Table 28.1 shows the results of a survey performed on the presidential elections of 2000. It cross-tabulates their vote in the November 1999 PRI election with the constitutional elections on July 2, 2000.

The data show that 14% of those who voted for Francisco Labastida during the PRI election voted for Fox during the constitutional election. Most importantly, 51.6% who voted for Roberto Madrazo during the PRI elections voted for Fox during the constitutional elections. For Manuel Barlett and Humberto Roque percentages are greater than 55% and 72%, respectively.[23]

After the internal elections the PRI had a weakened political performance that could not keep the unity of its electoral base. An important percentage of PRI sympathizers, most of all those who voted for Roberto Madrazo and the other losing candidates, changed their vote in favor of the PAN. It is about a powerful argument that explains the defeat of the PRI; after the internal elections, the winner could not bring together the preferences of its activists and sympa-

Table 28.1. PRI Elections Cross-tabulated with the Constitutional Elections

		Vote for President (Constitutional Election)*					Total
		Fox	Labastida	Cárdenas	Camacho	Rincon	
Primary Voters of	Labastida	14.1	79.6	5.4	0.4	0.5	100
the PRI (No. 99)	Madrazo	51.6	32.4	14.2	0.5	1.4	100
	Bartlett	55.1	34.7	10.2	0.0	0.0	100
	Roque	72.0	20.0	8.0	0.0	0.0	100

Note: * Only those who voted in the primary of the PRI.

thizers. The negative campaigns among the pre-candidates Labastida and Madrazo, polarized all preferences within the same party. Consequently, there was a split in the vote of those who would traditionally have voted for the PRI.

The experiment of the first PRI elections strengthened Labastida in terms of public opinion, but he paid a high price. The PRI's traditional and effective electoral machinery, based on its ability to form political alliances and to distribute power among its members, was not able to process the results of its internal election without direct designations or favoritisms. Consequently, Labastida faced his adversaries without external political alliances. The environmentalist party *Partido Verde Ecologista de México*, the fourth electoral force, after failing to negotiate with the PRI, decided to ally with Fox, forming the *Alianza por el Cambio*.

The 2000 Elections and the Fox Phenomenon

The elections of July 2, 2000 represent an electoral mechanical change already experienced by Mexico in other representative and governmental areas. The candidate for the *Alianza por el Cambio* Vicente Fox won by a clear majority of votes: nearly sixteen million votes and 42.52% of the total votes cast. His victory was undeniable, clean, without precedents, acknowledged, and immediately accepted by his main adversaries, the PRI. His victory was accepted by the then current president and by the electoral authority. It is possible to understand this: civilized, democratic change. We only need take history into consideration, the learning of the masses, and the complex political process in Mexico during the last twenty years.

Figure 28.6 shows the preferences of probable voters in the 2000 election, between Vicente Fox (PAN), Francisco Labastida (PRI), and Cuauhtémoc Cárdenas (Partido de la Revolucion Democratica (Party of Democratic Revolution), PRD) during the pre-election period.[24]

As we can see, on November 1999, after the first PRI elections, Labastida had a twenty-one point advantage over Vicente Fox. Four months later, between March and April 2000, Fox would catch up and make it a horse race, and toward the end the advantage for PAN and Fox varied from four to nine points.

Scholars have focused on three elements that determine electoral performance in democracies: political communication, party organization, and political negotiation. It is possible to explain the Mexican elections of 2000 by using one of these elements, political speech.

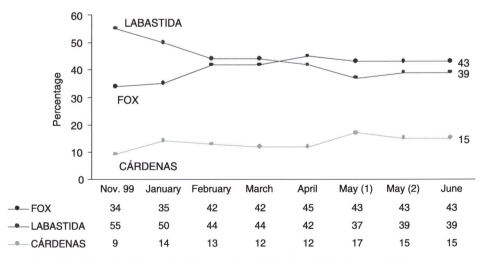

	Nov. 99	January	February	March	April	May (1)	May (2)	June
—•— FOX	34	35	42	42	45	43	43	43
—•— LABASTIDA	55	50	44	44	42	37	39	39
—•— CÁRDENAS	9	14	13	12	12	17	15	15

Figure 28.6. Intention to Vote by Likely Voters Relating to Presidential Preference, 2000

Political Communication, Image Evaluation, Message, and Candidate Proposal for the Presidency of 2000

On the verge of the new millennium, the political and electoral times had changed in Mexico. Three years before the July 2, 2002 election, when PAN's status as principal opposition party was in danger, Guanajuato governor Vicente Fox started his campaign for the presidency, with the increasing support by economic groups who saw him as a second bet for the presidential elections. International tours and excessive advertising, under a well-directed marketing strategy made his candidacy nearly unstoppable. For two years, 1998–1999, Fox was at the top of the electoral preferences.

His speeches were disciplined and this paid off in the end. He knew how to seize the moment, the millennium spirit, the idea of renewal, the need for "change." He spoke to the citizens' weariness with the PRI. "Change" was build more upon resentfulness than upon hope; it was a positive vote "yes to the change" supported by another negative "Stop the PRI." The seven decades of history, of accomplishments and failures, as well as the work of very useful institutions, lay on the table, were criticized by candidate Fox and the voters responded positively.

In the two presidential debates, on April 25 and May 26, voters identified Vicente Fox as the clear winner. Among the six candidates in the April debate, Fox was preferred by 43.9%, while Labastida was second with 14.3%. In the May debate, Fox was preferred 46.8% to second place Labastida's 19.1%. Fox was considered as the most capable, honest, and closer to the people, while Francisco Labastida was perceived as the most experienced one.

Conclusions

The relevance of July 2, 2000 election focuses on the capacity of the institutions that were able to start the process of alternation toward the presidency on a normal environment. That day, and what happened afterwards, left very positive results, and important precedents for the consolidation of a genuinely democratic tradition: the performance of the president under norms characteristic of the governor and the acknowledgment of the result by the other candidates and preceded by appropriate and reliable accounts by the media.

The odd thing about the results of July 2 was the existence for the first time of a different vote, and this generated an extraordinary political balance. The PAN and its coalition triumphed, for the first time; the PRI was in the federal chambers and the PRD won the government of the federal district. In the future, history will place these elections as a milestone for the Mexican political regime and surely, a democratic normalcy that needs no more explanations or analysis. The change of power between parties produced on July 2 was more of a compliment to society than to the parties or their candidates.

Society made several things clear by its vote: first, that the change of government among the parties did not need to exclude the executive power. Second, it made very clear that the new political dynamics would be more than just the result of the victory of a single party, but an agreement produced by all with a designated place within public power. Third, that the new political arrangement defined in the ballot box is to become a solution for most of the country's problems, not to be a problem itself.

Democracy is generous with those who are defeated and very demanding with those who win. The first one admits its defeat and understands the new situation by adding his or her presence. Time will provide the loser the benefit of the doubt. The winner, in contrast, has to meet the country's expectations. For Vicente Fox the strong words said on his campaign turn into an inconvenient dead weight increased as time went by. Facing the inexperience of the new government, society was very patient, but not that patient. The immeasurable hope brought along by the change of government soon became an immeasurable disappointment. The reforms that Mexico needed never came with the self-named "different government." The unprecedented opportunity to shape a great democratic consensus was stopped by obstacles such as the lack of vision and greatness, both from the executive power and the political class in general.[25]

In Mexico the democratic culture has not been yet deepened into the society, and the wishing for popular candidates covers not only the already known collective subconscious, but also the elite interests that long to return to power. Political scientist Robert Dahl has pointed out:

> During the twentieth century, democratic countries were never out of critics who easily stated that democracy was at stake, doomed, even. Well, it might have been, at times, in great danger. But it was not doomed after all. The pessimists as we would later see were far too willing to give up on democracy. Breaking down their dark predictions, the experience showed that once the democratic institutions were firmly established in a country, they turned out to be strong and sound.[26]

In this sense, it is the responsibility of those who believe in democracy to preserve the advances and transformations that reached Mexico with such delay.

Notes

1 Federico Reyes Heroles, *Memorial del mañana* (México, Distrito Federal: Taurus, 1999) 35.

2 Mario Ojeda Gómez, *México antes y después de la alternancia política: Un testimonio* (México, Distrito Federal: El Colegio de México, Centro de Estudios Internacionales, 2005), 29

3 Fidel Velázquez Sánchez (1900–1997) was the preeminent Mexican union leader of the twentieth century. In 1936 he was one of the original founders, along with Vicente Lombardo Toledano, of the Confederation of Mexican Workers (CTM), the national labor federation most closely associated with the ruling party, the PRI. He replaced Lombardo as the leader of the CTM in 1941, then expelled him from it in 1948. He led the CTM until his death in 1997.

4 Julia Preston and Samuel Dillon, *Opening Mexico: The Making of a Democracy* (New York: Farrar, Straus & Giroux, 2004).

5 Emilio Portes Gil (1928–1930), Pascual Ortiz Rubio (1930–1933), Abelardo L. Rodríguez (1932–1934), Lázaro Cárdenas del Rio (1934–1940), Manuel Ávila Camacho (1940–1946), Miguel Alemán Valdez (1946–1952), Adolfo Ruiz Cortines (1952–1958), Adolfo López Mateos (1958–1964), Gustavo Díaz Ordaz (1964–1970), Luís Echeverría Álvarez (1970–1976), José López Portillo (1976–1982), Miguel de la Madrid Hurtado (1982–1988), Carlos Salinas de Gortari (1988–1994), Ernesto Zedillo Ponce de León (1994–2000).

6 Carlos Fuentes, *Nuevo Tiempo Mexicano* (México, Distrito Federal: 1994), 69.

7 Daniel Cosio Villegas, *La sucesión presidencial* (México, Distrito Federal: Joaquín Mortiz, 1975)

8 Robert Scott, *Mexican Government in Transition* (Urbana, Ill.: University of Illinois Press, 1959).

9 Jacques Lambert, *América Latina, estructuras sociales e Instituciones Políticas* (Barcelona, Editorial Ariel, 1968).

10 Pablo González Casanova, *La democracia en México* (México, Distrito Federal: Editorial Era, 1967).

11 Octavio Paz, *El ogro filantrópico* (Barcelona: Seix Barral, 1979), 128.

12 Juan Linz, *La quiebra de las democracias* (México, Distrito Federal: Consejo Nacional para la Cultura y las Artes y Alianza Editorial Mexicana, 1990).

13 Jesús Silva-Herzog Márquez, *El antiguo régimen y la transición en México* (México, Distrito Federal, Planeta/Joaquín Mortiz, 1999).

14 Ricardo Becerra, Pedro Salazar, and José Woldemberg, *La mecánica del cambio político en México, Elecciones, partidos y reformas* (México, Distrito Federal: Ediciones Cal y Arena, 2000).

15 Ibid., 16.

16 Ibid., 61.

17 Rafael Aranda Vollmer, *Poliarquías Urbanas: competencia electoral en las ciudades y zonas metropolitanas de México* (México, Distrito Federal, Ed. Porrua e IFE, 2004), 135.

18 Including Baja California, Guanajuato, Nuevo León, Jalisco, San Luis Potosí, Aguascalientes and Querétaro, ruled by PAN, and Distrito Federal, Baja California Sur and Zacatecas, by PRD.

19 Vollmer, *Poliarquías Urbanas*, 105.

20 Becerra, Salazar, and Woldemberg, *La mecánica del cambio político en México*, 29.
21 Octavio Rodríguez Araujo, *La reforma política y los partidos en México* (México, Distrito Federal: Siglo XXI Editores, 1979).
22 Data from the national surveys held by Reforma (2000).
23 Reforma's exit poll of the July 2000 election.
24 Alejandro Moreno, *El Votante Mexicano: Democracia, actitudes políticas y conducta electoral* (México, Distrito Federal, FCE, 2003), 143.
25 Lorenzo Meyer, *El Espejismo Democrático, de la euforia del cambio a la continuidad* (México, Distrito Federal: Editorial Océano, 2007), 24.
26 Robert Dahl, *La democracia, una guía para los ciudadanos* (Buenos Aires: Taurus, 1998), 212.

.

Part 4

Lobbying, Advocacy, and Political Persuasion

29

The Creation of the US Lobbying Industry

Conor McGrath and Phil Harris

Introduction

A recent article asserts that "political scientists know precious little about the contours of interest group politics in the United States before the 1960s."[1] Although no definitive history of lobbying has been produced—and indeed, none may be possible, given that no systematic archive exists of records kept by early lobbyists—it is nevertheless possible to trace some outlines of the industry's early development. We certainly lack many wide-ranging empirical studies of historical lobbying and it is true that few theoretical models are tested other than in contemporary settings, but we can draw upon a wealth of anecdotal and journalistic information about the activities of lobbyists prior to the modern era. What is most striking from such an overview is the extent to which some of the tactics and techniques used by the industry's pioneers, and the debates over their legitimacy, are familiar to today's observers of the lobbying scene.

Confusion surrounds even the origins of the words "lobbying" and "lobbyist." While "lobby" as a noun, denoting the halls of a legislature in which elected officials may meet with non-members, can be traced back to the seventeenth century, its use as a verb ("to lobby") began in the second half of the nineteenth century according to the *Oxford English Dictionary*. The OED supplies quotes from the period: "Lobbying [is] buying votes with money in the lobbies of the Hall of Congress" (1864); and "The arrangements of the committee system have produced and sustain the class of professional 'lobbyists' who make it their business to 'see' members" (1888).[2] An early journalistic account of lobbying dates the use of the term "lobby-agent" to 1829, and asserts that by 1832 "lobbyist" was a well-recognized term in Washington.[3] Certainly, it is apparent that by 1847, these terms had been in usage for some time, as one writer discussed "the *third house*, or lobby, which is always so potent in giving direction to American legislation."[4] The second edition of *Webster's Dictionary* that same year defined "lobby-member" as "a person who frequents the lobby of a house of legislation."[5] Yet another source suggests that the word "lobby" was first used to denote those seeking to influence legislation in 1808—which, if true, means that we have been using it for 200 years.[6] Deanna Gelak (a former president of the American League of Lobbyists) has traced the word "lobbying" to an article in the April 1, 1820, edition of the *New Hampshire Sentinel*:

> Other letters from Washington affirm, that members of the Senate, when the compromise question was to be taken in the House, were not only "lobbying about the Representatives' Chamber," but

were active in endeavoring to intimidate certain weak representatives by insulting threats to dissolve the Union.[7]

A search (in September 2007) on Google News for "lobbying" produced 791 newspaper articles using the term before 1850; a similar search for "lobbyist" revealed 555 results before 1869.[8]

Whenever "lobbying" or "lobbyist" first appeared in common usage, however, the terms have always had pejorative overtones. As early as 1846, one article on politics in Louisiana thundered: "Lobby influences are too strong to be resisted. Intimidation is too easily effected upon the weak nerves of members. Good dinners, fetes and soirees change votes in twenty-four hours irresistibly."[9] In the early 1860s, a businessman who was seeking to have a bill passed by the state legislature in Pennsylvania soon became acquainted with what was described to him as the "Third House" and which

> consisted of old ex-members of either House or Senate, broken-down politicians, professional borers, and other vagrants who had made themselves familiar with the *modus operandi* of legislation, and who negotiated for the votes of members on terms to be agreed upon by the contracting parties—in short, these were the Lobby members of the Legislature—a portion of mankind which I had never heard mentioned in terms other than contempt and disgust. Was I then to become familiar with these leeches—these genteel loafers, who, having no apparent business, yet manage to live at the best hotels, drink the best of wines, and go home at the end of the session with more money than any of the *honest* members?[10]

An 1869 magazine article defined the professional lobbyist as "a man whom everybody suspects; who is generally during one half of the year without honest means of livelihood; and whose employment by those who have bills before a legislature is only resorted to as a disagreeable necessity."[11] Four years later, a book on the infamous *Credit Mobilier* scandal suggested that a company president uses a professional lobbyist "as the huntsman uses his hound, to run down the game."[12] According to an 1888 political dictionary, "*Lobby, The*, is a term applied collectively to men that make a business of corruptly influencing legislators. The individuals are called lobbyists."[13] Lobbyists, according to one journalist, "may be peddlers of personal influence, paid propagandists or amateurs promoting causes in which they sincerely believe. These are the pressure boys."[14]

And, in truth, it has to be acknowledged that while many early lobbyists were extremely talented and personable men with a tremendous range of experience in public life, they were in addition masterful manipulators of the political system. Thurlow Weed—who dominated the Washington lobbying scene in the 1850s and worked on behalf of wool mills, railroad companies, banks, land speculators and so on despite having been a noted liberal reformer as a journalist and state representative in New York in the 1830s—was known as "the Lucifer of the Lobby."[15] Weed got his start as a lobbyist in 1823 when he was hired by the town of Rochester, N.Y., for $300 to persuade the state legislature to grant the town a bank charter. Despite the fact that, "so little confidence was felt in Mr. Weed's appointment, as he was only a journeyman printer, that a majority of the committee [which hired him] declined to pay over the money contributed to defray the expenses of the agent," Weed's mission was successful and he "returned to Rochester with the bank charter in his pocket, like a conquering hero, and was very cordially received on his return."[16]

The next great fixer was Sam Ward—known as the "King of the Lobby" for two decades following the Civil War. Ward once boasted of having been paid $5,000 to prevent a particular congressman from attending a committee meeting, which he achieved by the expedient of stealing the member's boots![17] Ward wrote in 1875 that, "I quite agree that the profession of lobbying is not commendable"[18]; he was wrong, though, on two counts—lobbying is not a profession in 2008 in the same way as medicine and law are, and it certainly was not in 1875; and it is (at least, can be) a commendable industry and activity. Ward was on firmer ground that same year when he testified before the House of Representatives Ways and Means Committee: "I am not ashamed—I do not say I am proud, but I am not ashamed—of the occupation. It is a very useful one."[19] In her memoir of Ward, his niece suggests that "Sam Ward was above all else perhaps a profound psychologist and much of his success as a manipulator of legislation at the Capitol was due to his deep insight into the character of men."[20]

Constitutional Underpinnings

It has been noted (for example, by Burdette Loomis[21]) that it is a truism to suggest that America's founding fathers could scarcely have devised a system of government more congenial to lobbyists. Such an observation, though, is commonplace precisely because there is much truth in it. The structure of US government—with its separation of powers, checks and balances, and federalism—insures that interest groups are able to utilize multiple entry points to the policy-making process. In his famous *Federalist Paper No. 10*, James Madison noted the inevitability of what he termed "factions"—essentially interest groups such as farmers and merchants—and asserted that the proposed Constitution would control factions. In reality, as we see every day, the United States in some ways now resembles a government of interest groups, by interest groups, for interest groups: Woodrow Wilson (the only American president to have been a political science professor, and whose own scholarship dealt with lobbying) declared in a 1912 campaign speech that "[t]he government of the United States is a foster child of the special interests."[22]

The development of lobbying in the United States has been immeasurably assisted and sustained by the American predilection toward collective (and self-interested) action. Writing in 1835, Alexis de Tocqueville noted the prevalence of "associations" in American political culture:

> As soon as several of the inhabitants of the United States have taken up an opinion or a feeling which they wish to promote in the world, they look out for mutual assistance; and as soon as they have found each other out, they combine.[23]

(It is worth recalling that in de Tocqueville's native land, a variety of laws were in force between 1791 and 1901 that severely limited freedom of association, or what legislation termed "intermediary interests" coming between the individual and the state;[24] it perhaps should not be altogether surprising that to this day France is less accepting of open and transparent lobbying than America.)

The Bill of Rights has always been central to lobbying in America: the First Amendment states that: "Congress shall make no law . . . abridging the freedom of speech . . . or the right of the people peaceably to assemble, and to petition the Government for a redress of grievances." These liberties are in a real sense the lifeblood of lobbying—Loomis regards them as providing "a constitutional cornerstone for the practice of lobbying."[25] As Madison wrote: "Liberty is to faction what air is to fire."[26] Expressing the most common defense of her role, one lobbyist wrote in her autobiography that "[a]nyone who wants Congress to do anything has a right to say so, to bring it to that body's attention. It is part of free speech. It is the right of petition."[27] A current lawyer-lobbyist has told one of the authors that because of the low regard in which both lawyers and lobbyists are held by the public, he prefers to describe himself as "a First Amendment practitioner."

The Organization of Interests

While it is true to say that "[n]obody knows who was the first American lobbyist or what interest he represented,"[28] lobbying certainly pre-dated US independence. Loomis suggests that

> [s]teeped in their knowledge of legislative politics from state assemblies and the Continental Congress, the framers of the Constitution had ample first-hand experience of the pressures that particular interests, like farmers, merchants, and churches, could place upon them. They appreciated both the virtues of petition and the unseemly potential for corrupt bargains between legislators and even loosely organized interests.[29]

The delegates to the Constitutional Convention were routinely lobbied—sometimes through discussion, often through copious hospitality—on behalf of interests such as merchants and landowners who had a stake in the deliberations. The delegates decided not to publish a record of their proceedings, for fear that such openness would inevitably cause them to be subjected to the daily harangues of those wanting to insinuate their self-interests to the debates. Indeed, it has been posited in a 1913 book hotly contested ever since that the Constitution itself represents, at least partially, a compromise between the economic and commercial interests of the Founding Fathers.[30] One writer asserts that passage of the 1789 Tariff Act witnessed "the beginning of definite pressure tactics upon Congress" and highlighted the Philadelphia Society for the Promotion of National Industry, founded by Alexander Hamilton around 1800, as the "first business lobby formed for the purpose of influencing legislatures on behalf of a powerful faction."[31] Certainly, the early years of the Senate saw numerous petitions presented by groups such as merchants, veterans, chambers of commerce and even state legislatures, all lobbying for or against specific legislation.[32]

The lobbying industry entered a period of rapid expansion in the wake of the 1861–1865 Civil War, as America expanded physically westwards and as urbanization, industrialization and immigration took root. This led to a growth in the number of large voluntary associations, which in turn encouraged both the development of national parties and electoral competition, and the role of mass-member interests in policy-making. We do not have much very systematic or rigorous data on the number of interest groups in the early years of the industry, although some anecdotal information is available. By 1852, lobbying was so prevalent that James Buchanan (later to become president) asserted:

> The host of contractors, speculators, stockjobbers, and lobby members which haunt the halls of Congress . . . on any and every pretext to get their arms into the public treasury are sufficient to alarm every friend of his country. Their progress must be arrested.[33]

According to one estimate from 1870, in addition to more or less legitimate lobbyists who deluged members of Congress with pamphlets setting out the merits of their arguments, there were then also

> fifty lobbies every winter, in Washington, pushing for objects obviously beyond the constitutional power of Congress. . . . Nearly all of them fail, as a matter of course; but not until they have tempted, warped, perverted, corrupted, men who, but for such projects, would leave Washington as innocent as they came to it.[34]

During the 1876–1877 congressional session, it was estimated by a railroad operator that one of his rivals alone had (ultimately unsuccessfully) hired 200 lobbyists.[35]

The volume of lobbying escalated over time, and an analysis of appearances by interest groups before congressional committees indicates that 216 groups testified for the first time between 1890 and 1899, and that 622 groups did so between 1900 and 1909.[36] By 1929, one study suggested that there were around 500 groups whose main function was to lobby Congress,[37] while another observer counted 300 "effective lobbies."[38] By the end of the 1950s, most accounts agree that there were around 1,000 lobbyists in Washington; the number of individuals listed in the *Washington Representatives* directory has risen from 4,000 in 1977 to over 18,000 in 2007.

Moreover, not only was lobbying an established fact of political life even in the first years of the independent United States, but it also settled down quite quickly into forms of organization that remain very familiar today. As today, individual corporations were prolific lobbyists even 200 years ago. Lawyers dominated the industry from its beginnings. Business associations had long existed and occasionally intervened in public policy (for instance, efforts by the New York Bakers' Guild in 1741 to influence a city ordinance on the price of bread),[39] but they began to develop in numbers and strength during the Civil War period as industries such as the railroads and iron manufacturers became major national concerns. Indeed, a study of the influence of one railroad company in New Jersey in the post Civil War period went so far as to assert:

> It soon came to be recognized as the power behind the throne in the control of all the affairs of the Commonwealth. . . . Such a thing as a candidate announcing his opposition to the railroad company and surviving the election was almost unheard of in state politics. . . . The legislation proposed for the people was all scrutinized at the company's offices in Trenton and allowed to go through if the company was favorable or indifferent, but its disapproval doomed it to certain defeat. . . . There was never a more complete master anywhere of the destinies of a state than was this monster monopoly of the affairs of New Jersey.[40]

The early years of the twentieth century witnessed another period of marked expansion by business associations, with the establishment of the Chamber of Commerce and the rise of the National Association of Manufacturers as a potent lobbying force. Trade unions also existed in particular industries and in local areas prior to the Civil War but again began to develop mass memberships and political power in the post Civil War era, alongside America's national economic growth. Single-interest groups (for causes such as the abolition of slavery, female emancipation, veterans' welfare, and prohibition) sprung up across the country. The last three decades of the nineteenth century witnessed a fundamental shift in the American political landscape, at the heart of which were interest groups: interests became increasingly formalized and organized; they developed mass and national memberships; they adopted more explicitly political roles, and structured themselves around the achievement of political goals; they insinuated their money and memberships into electoral politics to a greater extent than before; new federal and state agencies were created as a result of group demands, thus offering groups new and permanent linkages into the policy-making process; groups took their demands to the mass media to a greater extent than before; and to some degree they supplanted the political parties by offering citizens new outlets for political participation and mobilization.[41]

Early Lobbying Tactics and Techniques

While much of what a nineteenth-century lobbyist might do would be not dissimilar to the activities of a current inhabitant of K Street, there were certainly lobbying practices common then that would not be considered ethical today (though that is not to say that such activities are wholly unknown even in the modern age). One member of Congress was expelled and three others resigned in the late 1850s after they were discovered to have fixed a sliding scale of prices in return for their votes—a system that brings to mind the "menu" devised by Randy Cunningham (a California Republican congressman) that indicated what level of payment would be required for him to secure government military contracts for clients; he was sentenced in 2006 to over eight years in prison. Many lobbyists in the mid-nineteenth century organized gambling houses, in which politicians were always welcome.[42] Should they run up losses they could ill afford to repay, legislators would find it impossible to vote against the interests of the lobbyist holding their chits. Alternatively, the "thin subterfuge of allowing an amenable Congressman to win at poker"[43] would serve the lobbyist's needs equally well.

One of the most senior of the current Washington lobbyists has suggested to the authors that there are "three legs of the lobbying stool—direct contact with Capitol Hill, building coalitions, and public outreach." These are indeed the staple elements of a lobbying strategy, and have been for some time. Today's lobbyists may engage in each of the activities in a somewhat more sophisticated manner than their predecessors, but nevertheless early lobbyists were aware of the potential of all three tactics.

The first of these—direct contact and communication with elected officials and their staff—can be based upon access to decision-makers or upon expertise and knowledge of policy issues. The first approach is clearly very relationship-driven, and has always been the source of periodic outrage as it tends to rely upon personal contact to the exclusion of any professional skills. So, for instance, the lavish entertaining of politicians by "good ole boy" lobbyists that is often summed up as "booze, broads and beefsteaks" has come to epitomize access-based lobbying. The most consummate and prolific diner of politicians was Sam Ward, a noted gourmet. Much of his lobbying was based around Welcher's restaurant in Washington:

> A Congressman, for example, might drop in and from a side table Sam Ward would be seen to rise and go to greet the new arrival with a beaming welcome; he would find a table for the Congressman, and stand chatting for a few minutes, perhaps to recommend the best on the bill of fare that day. Then he would bow pleasantly and retire to his own unobtrusive seat. But by some mysterious concatenation, the Congressman might find seated opposite him, after a while, a man with whom he particularly wished to talk in some neutral and irreproachable setting. One thing would lead to another and the conversation might drift into serious discussion of a mutual problem, legislative or personal. Sam Ward, meanwhile, would appear to be oblivious of the happy encounter, absorbed in his coffee and meditations; yet perhaps he had been paid precisely to bring those two men together in an apparently accidental manner.[44]

Bribery was rampant at times (though in fairness we must note that by no means all lobbyists resorted to this—Sam Ward, for instance, is never believed to have offered outright bribes);[45] slightly more discreet was the common practice by which lobbyists would give lavish gifts to the wives of politicians as a way of cementing friendships with the wives and thereby move lobbying messages from back rooms to boudoirs.[46] Alexander Hay, a lobbyist for the Colt gun company "kept more attractive bait in the persons of three charming ladies who were professionally known as Spiritualists . . . [who were] very active in 'moving with the members' of Congress."[47] According to an 1873 account, sex was a common lobbying tool. Outwardly respectable women would cultivate increasingly intimate friendships with congressmen, progressing from seemingly casual meetings to lunches in hotels, at which point

> the party adjourn to the private parlor to more wine, to cards, to flash music, to general chaff, and to such commerce of charms against votes as can be struck between a drunken, conscienceless man and a wily, willing woman. In any single "first-class" hotel in Washington, at any time during mid-session, at least half a dozen of these lobbyesses are thus at work at once, each one roping in her dozen or ten of wild-cat Congressmen. The lever of lust is used to pry up more Legislators to the sticking-point than money itself avails to seduce.[48]

This may not yet have been entirely eradicated: Paula Parkinson, an agricultural lobbyist who went on to pose nude in *Playboy*, admitted in 1981 that she had slept with eight members of Congress; she escorted three legislators on a golf trip to Florida, after which all three voted against a piece of legislation opposed by Parkinson's employer.[49] However, the more explicitly venal lobbyist-legislator interactions have certainly declined as they are increasingly regulated in terms of the amounts and kinds of hospitality that may be accepted (and also because they were not always terribly effective[50]), but are still not wholly unknown—in 2006, a lobbyist, Jack Abramoff was sentenced to almost six years in prison for corruption and fraud; he gave many politicians free meals at a DC restaurant he owned, spent over $1 million a year on hosting politicians in skyboxes at sporting arenas, and funded golfing trips to Scotland for legislators.

Contacting policy-makers on the basis that the lobbyist has detailed knowledge and expertise of a particular issue is less contentious. It is this approach that characterizes the common rationale that lobbying acts as a bridge between the governed and the government, across which data and analysis can flow in order to insure that policy decisions are better informed. As early as the 1820s, Friedrich List (a lobbyist for the Pennsylvania Society for the Encouragement of Manufactures and the Mechanic Arts) was proposing that "the friends of domestic industry should meet annually to prepare the necessary legislation for Congress after discussing the measures and gathering the facts." As James Deakin notes: "This forward-looking idea was the precursor of the comprehensive legislative programs now prepared every year or two by the large business associations and labor organizations."[51]

In truth, legislators themselves have long appreciated the value of the detailed information and analysis that lobbyists can provide: good lobbyists are able to explain complex policy alternatives in a comprehensible manner, and to point out the likely effects of each option. This was as true 200 years ago (when politicians had no or only a small number of staffers to undertake policy research and legislative drafting) as it is today (when despite having large staffs, politicians are called upon to wrestle with ever larger and more intricate public policy issues). In a discussion of lobbying during the 1870s, Thompson argues that many prominent lobbyists of the day, "to the greatest extent possible, could be relied upon to be informed thoroughly about the issues in the cases they accepted. Legislators . . . [knew] that they could count on the substantive accuracy of what they were told."[52]

Grassroots lobbying—essentially, involving citizens in a lobbying campaign so that they indirectly influence politicians on behalf of the interest group that they support or are members of—has long been a staple of the lobbying industry. One analysis of lobbying during the 1870s notes the use of grassroots campaigns in which constituents "wrote letters, sometimes from prescribed texts; signed petitions, frequently appended to standardized, printed forms; confronted their own congressmen personally"[53]; among the organizations employing grassroots tactics to good effect during this period were the American Medical Association, the temperance movement and veterans' groups. Indeed, as we shall see, grassroots lobbying was the cause of the first congressional regulation of lobbying in 1875. Elisabeth S. Clemens argues that an emphasis by interest groups on mobilizing and harnessing their members in grassroots campaigns represented an important shift in the lobbying industry: "What was novel in the late nineteenth century was the intent *and* organizational technologies to link 'lobbying' to significant numbers of voters who would be guided by associational ties rather than partisan loyalty."[54] The less attractive side of grassroots campaigns—today referred to as "astroturf" lobbying (to denote its fundamental artificiality) is also of long-standing. In 1935, power companies were discovered to have unsuccessfully campaigned against the Public Utility Holding Company bill by means of flooding Congress with telegrams—up to 4,000 an hour—using the names of people (without their knowledge) taken from phone directories; thus, "the great flood of protest, supposedly spontaneous from a citizenry suddenly aroused to the socialistic dangers of the New Deal, was in reality a wholly false and malicious propaganda drive by the utilities."[55]

413

Another key lobbying tactic often employed today is that of coalition-building, whereby groups with a common interest in a particular policy outcome will co-operate together to work for its advancement. Joint advocacy campaigns allow organizations to both pool resources for the sake of efficiency and at the same time maximize effectiveness through enhanced credibility; this is particularly true when coalitions are forged between groups not generally regarded as natural allies. A current Washington lobbyist has suggested to one of the authors that "non-traditional allies are the most sought after currency because non-traditional alliances demonstrate broad based support." Lobbyists have always known this to be true. During the first Congress, a campaign against frontier Indian wars was undertaken by both those who were philosophically opposed to war and those land speculators for whom war interfered with business: "These men were strange bedfellows . . . but they were powerful allies nonetheless."[56] In 1792, William Hull, a lobbyist for Virginia veterans of the Continental army, wrote to other organizations representing veterans, proposing a coalition to lobby for passage of a compensation bill in Congress.[57] Despite these very early examples, though, it is striking from accounts of nineteenth-century lobbying that coalitions are mentioned much less than either direct advocacy or grassroots campaigns. On the other hand, the appearance of trade associations in this period indicates that interest groups were keenly aware of the basic value of collaboration on policy issues where possible.

Lobbying has always been intimately connected with the electoral process: indeed the National Labor Union went so far as to set up the National Labor Reform Party in 1872 to pursue elected office; and the Farmers Alliance established the Populist Party whose candidate carried four states in the 1892 presidential election. A 1913 investigation by the House of Representatives into the activities of the National Association of Manufacturers revealed, among much else, that the organization had spent significant amounts of money during congressional election campaigns to support candidates whose views tallied with its interests and to defeat those who disagreed with the association. Similarly, one of the explicit aims of the Anti-Saloon League during the congressional elections of the 1910s was to help get elected a higher proportion of "dry" congressmen who would vote for prohibition. In his classic work, David B. Truman notes a number of ways in which interest groups may attempt to influence the electoral process: by publicizing to their members and supporters the views and records of candidates; by formally endorsing specific candidates; by providing direct or indirect funding to a candidate's campaign; and by enlisting its membership in get-out-the-vote efforts to mobilize electors on behalf of a candidate.[58] All are routinely undertaken by interest groups, and indeed have been for more than a century: for all the attention that financial contributions from groups to candidates has always received in the media, it is quite likely that the other forms of assistance are more valuable to candidates.

Regulation and Reform Initiatives

What may well have been the first reform related to lobbying in America was certainly one of the most unusual. A group of land speculators in 1795 persuaded the Georgia legislature to pass a bill, which was then signed by the governor, authorizing the sale of almost fifty million acres of land for $500,000, or around one cent per acre. The lobbying mounted by the businessmen included bribery on a scale probably never seen before or since (rather breathtakingly, even by the standards of the day, all but one member of the state legislature reportedly accepted bribes).[59] However, when the public realized the extent of the corruption, every sitting member of the Georgia House and Senate was defeated at the next election, and bizarrely the incoming lawmakers passed an act that imposed a $1,000 fine on any subsequent legislator who publicly made reference to the original law.

An early legal challenge to the lobbying industry came in 1855 in New York in which the judge ruled that lobbying contracts were not enforceable by courts: "It is against the genius and policy of our government that her legislative and executive officers shall be surrounded by swarms of hired retainers of the claimants upon public bounty or justice."[60] A similar case in 1874 ended up being argued before the US Supreme Court, *Trist v. Child*. Linus Child was a lobbyist hired by N.P. Trist to advance Trist's claim for payment by the Congress of a bill submitted by Trist over thirty years earlier relating to services he had provided the United States during negotiations over the Treaty of Guadalupe Hidalgo. Child succeeded in persuading the Congress to pay Trist several thousand dollars, but Trist then declined to pay Child his 25% fee. When the case ended up in the Supreme Court, the Court acknowledged that Child had pursued Trist's claim without resort to bribery or corruption, but found against him on the grounds that lobbying was illegitimate and against the interests of public policy. In his decision, Justice Noah H. Swayne argued:

> If any of the great corporations of the country were to hire adventurers who make market of themselves in this way, to procure the passage of a general law with a view to the promotion of their private interests, the moral sense of every right-minded man would instinctively denounce the employer and employed as steeped in corruption and the employment as infamous.[61]

On the heels of this Supreme Court judgment came the first federal regulation of lobbying when the US House of Representatives passed a resolution in May 1875 (which remained in force only for the rest of the forty-fourth Congress) requiring "agents" representing the interests of companies before the House to register their names with the clerk of the House and prohibiting anyone not so registered from appearing before a House committee. The resolution's sponsor, George Frisbie Hoar (Republican-Massachusetts), noted that his interest in the subject arose from his chairmanship of the House Judiciary Committee. During its consideration of a bill, "[f]our persons, coming from different parts of the country, coming from cities and neighborhoods which the different members of the committee come from, have accosted the different members of the committee in regard to that particular measure."[62] Grassroots lobbying continues to work in much the same manner.

While we regard the "revolving door" (whereby former politicians and officials go on to lucrative lobbying positions) as constituting a particular ethical problem, even that is by no means a new phenomenon. As early as 1897, one senator proposed that former senators should not be permitted privileged access to the floor of the chamber if they were there to lobby former colleagues on behalf of private clients.[63] In an indication of how established the lobbying industry had become by 1935, Hugo L. Black (then a senator and later a Supreme Court justice) asserted:

> Contrary to tradition, against the public morals, and hostile to good government, the lobby has reached such a position of power that it threatens government itself. Its size, its power, its capacity for evil; its greed, trickery, deception and fraud condemn it to the death it deserves.[64]

As we know, lobbying flourished in the second half of the twentieth century, despite periodic efforts to regulate it more effectively. Federal regulatory initiatives lagged behind those of the states—the first major piece of congressional legislation was the 1946 Regulation of Lobbying Act, while thirty-two states had passed lobbying laws by 1927 and Georgia had gone so far as to declare lobbying illegal as early as 1877.[65]

Conclusion

As an industry—simply in terms of its sheer size and scope—lobbying today is vastly different from its early days; it is much more visible, undertaken on a more professional basis, involves much more money and has become in some senses an institutionalized component of government and policy-making. It developed exponentially in the post World War II period, prompted by a variety of factors: economic and industrial expansion in the 1950s and 1960s; changes within the party system and electoral competition; institutional reforms of the workings of state and federal legislatures and executives; technological advances in communication; and social movements such as in civil rights, consumer protection and environmentalism. All these, and other issues, have impacted upon the lobbying industry we see today.

But it is a mistake—albeit one that many observers of lobbying are guilty of—to dismiss the historical development and evolution of lobbying. Mark P. Petracca suggests that "the essential structure of the interest group system is much as it was at the beginning of the 'modern' system of interest representation back in 1946."[66] Another close observer of lobbying notes that "some of the lobbying techniques of the Gilded Age were not unlike those of today, with speeches supplied, analyses prepared, opposition arguments suggested, personal contacts with key members, appearances before committees, and grassroots campaigns generated by lobbyists."[67] Indeed, it is possible to go further and assert that the landscape of lobbying today would not be unrecognizable to a lobbyist of the early nineteenth century. Writing in 1938, an academic and politician suggested that "[t]he old lobby, then, used only two methods that are no longer common, corrupt practices and the entertainment of legislators."[68]

Lobbying techniques and practices have evolved over time, to be sure; but nothing being undertaken along K Street today was unknown to the pioneers of lobbying. As institutional frameworks have been reformed, the attractiveness of particular lobbying targets has varied. Lobbying operates within a context of governmental structures, so it is natural that as those structures and processes have changed so too does the focus of lobbying efforts. Woodrow Wilson, for instance, laid much of the blame for lobbyists' influence in his day on the congressional committee system: "He argued that whereas business lobbies could not buy up or otherwise control the entire membership of Congress . . . they could arrange to keep members of small committees in their vest pockets."[69] Even within committees, as more meetings began to be held in public, the scope for back-stage deals by lobbyists was reduced by greater transparency.[70]

Lobbyists scarcely enjoy more favorable public perceptions today than they have ever done: one academic has written: "Today, as a century ago, lobbyists commonly are regarded as premier symbols of corruption, as attractive scapegoats to whom blame can be ascribed for any problems in the body politic."[71] An 1858 newspaper article opined:

> The Legislative Lobby, which is getting to be the governing power in this country, has also a language of its own. It discards all such plain speaking as requires the harsh terms of *bribery* and *corruption* to be applied to its performances, and invents euphuisms of a more delicate and inoffensive sound.[72]

Just as in today's lobbying world, it is possible for perhaps 95% of lobbyists to operate professionally and ethically yet for public attention to focus solely on the 5% who fail to meet the industry's standards, so too can we find some evidence that in the nineteenth century some observers were conscious that not all lobbyists were reprehensible. We noted earlier, for instance, that his contemporaries never suggested that Sam Ward engaged in bribery. Writing in 1897, one journalist contrasted "professional lobbyists" who work "openly" and perform a "legitimate and valuable service to employers" with the "special lobby" of "unregistered lobbyists" or "political manipulators and placeholders of high standing" who act as "the go-between for the petitioners and the corrupt members"; he also asserted that "[i]t is to be observed in every instance of scandalous lobbying . . . that it is not the professional lobby which costs the most money or which exerts the most influence."[73] ·

So, some of the specifics of the lobbying industry have changed over time, but the fundamentals have remained remarkably stable. Nineteenth-century lobbyists undertook grassroots campaigns, built coalitions and communicated directly with policy-makers—all of which are the essentials of lobbying today. Debate about the legitimacy of lobbying has persisted in very similar forms. It is curious that lobbying is regarded with distaste by so many Americans when at the same time most voters are members of at least one large interest group (churches; labor unions; professional associations; groups for consumers, veterans, the elderly and so on) and are thus themselves represented by lobbyists in Washington, D.C., and in the fifty state capitols. It may be that if lobbyists paid a greater attention to the history of their industry, they would take from its past the current need to grasp the challenge of professionalization—establishing an inclusive and substantial professional body, an increasing emphasis on explaining the function and merits of lobbying to the public, creating rigorous codes of conduct, supporting purposeful university education and in-career training for lobbyists and so on.[74] If that agenda is taken up and advanced by lobbyists today, the lessons of lobbying's past can be learnt from and built upon to the benefit of its future development and evolution.

Notes

1 Daniel J. Tichenor and Richard A. Harris, "The Development of Interest Group Politics in America: Beyond the Conceits of Modern Times," *Annual Review of Political Science* 8 (2005): 253.

2 Organisation for Economic Co-operation and Development, "Lobbying: Key Policy Issues," Public Governance Committee, GOV/PGC/ETH(2006)6, January 4, 2006, 4.

3 Karl Schriftgiesser, *The Lobbyists: The Art and Business of Influencing Lawmakers* (Boston, MA: Little, Brown, 1951), 5.

4 John McKrum, "The True Functions of Government," *The Commercial Review* 4 (1) (September 1847): 103.

5 Graham Wootton, *Pressure Groups in Britain, 1720–1970* (Hamden, CT: Archon, 1975), 4.

6 "Lobbyist", from the World Wide Words website, http://www.worldwidewords.org/qa/qa-lob2.htm. Accessed September 3, 2007.

7 "Lobbying," from the C-SPAN website, http://cspan.org. Accessed October 3, 2007.

8 See Google News Archive Search website, http://news.google.com/archivesearch?hl=en. Accessed September 5, 2007.

9 Anonymous, "Louisiana," *The Commercial Review* 1 (5) (May 1846): 430.

10 Anonymous, "Is There Anything In It?," *The Continental Monthly* 3 (6) (June 1863): 690.

11 Quoted in Margaret Susan Thompson, *The "Spider Web": Congress and Lobbying in the Age of Grant* (Ithaca, N.Y.: Cornell University Press, 1985), 53–4.

12 Edward Winslow Martin, *Behind the Scenes in Washington: Being a Complete and Graphic Account of the Credit Mobilier Investigation* (Philadelphia, PA: Continental Publishing Co. and National Publishing Co., 1873), 220.

13 Everit Brown and Albert Strauss, *A Dictionary of American Politics: Comprising Accounts of Political Parties, Measures and Men* (New York: A.L. Burt, 1888), 253.

14 Kenneth G. Crawford, *The Pressure Boys: The Inside Story of Lobbying in America* (New York: Julian Messner, 1939), ix.

15 James Deakin, *The Lobbyists* (Washington, D.C.: Public Affairs Press, 1966), 60.

16 Hudson C. Tanner, *"The Lobby" and Public Men From Thurlow Weed's Time* (Albany, N.Y.: George MacDonald, 1888), 9–10 and 13–14.

17 Deakin, *The Lobbyists*, 63.

18 Sam Ward, quoted in Lately Thomas, *Sam Ward: "King of the Lobby"* (Boston, MA: Houghton Mifflin, 1965), 375.

19 Ibid., 370.

20 Maud Howe Elliott, *Uncle Sam Ward and His Circle* (New York: Macmillan, 1938), 502–3.

21 Burdett Loomis, "From the Framing to the Fifties: Lobbying in Constitutional and Historical Contexts," *Extensions* (Fall 2006): 1, http://www.ou.edu/special/albertctr/extensions/fall2006/Loomis.pdf. Accessed September 5, 2007.

22 Woodrow Wilson, quoted in Schriftgiesser, *The Lobbyists*, 35.

23 Alexis de Tocqueville, *Democracy in America*, Vol. 2, ed. Phillips Bradley (New York: Alfred A. Knopf, 1976), 109.

24 Graham Wootton, *Interest Groups: Policy and Politics in America* (Englewood Cliffs, N.J.: Prentice-Hall, 1985), 43–4.

25 Loomis, "From the Framing to the Fifties," 1.

26 James Madison, Alexander Hamilton and James Jay, *The Federalist Papers*, ed. Issac Kramnick (London: Penguin, 1987), 123.

27 Olga Moore, *I'll Meet You in the Lobby* (Philadelphia, PA: J.B. Lippincott, 1949), 14.

28 Schriftgiesser, *The Lobbyists*, 3.

29 Loomis, "From the Framing to the Fifties," 1.

30 Charles A. Beard, *An Economic Interpretation of the Constitution of the United States* (New York: Macmillan, 1913).

31 Schriftgiesser, *The Lobbyists*, 6.

32 Cited by Senator Robert C. Byrd in his September 28, 1987 speech on "Lobbyists," http://senate.gov/legislative/common/briefing/Byrd_History_Lobbying.htm. Accessed September 24, 2007.

33 James Buchanan, quoted in Schriftgiesser, *The Lobbyists*, 7.

34 James Parton, "The Pressure Upon Congress," *The Atlantic Monthly* 25 (148) (February 1870): 156.

35 Cited by Byrd on "Lobbyists."

36 Tichenor and Harris, "The Development of Interest Group Politics in America," 256.

37 Pendleton Herring, *Group Representation Before Congress* (New York: Russell & Russell, 1929), 276–83.

38 Oliver McKee, "Lobbying for Good or Evil," *North American Review* 227 (April 1929): 350.

39 Harmon Zeigler, *Interest Groups in American Society* (Englewood Cliffs, N.J.: Prentice-Hall, 1964), 94.

40 William E. Sackett, *Modern Battles of Trenton: Volume One* (Trenton, N.J.: J.L. Murphy, 1895), 17.

41 Elisabeth S. Clemens, *The People's Lobby: Organizational Innovation and the Rise of Interest Group Politics in the United States, 1890–1925* (Chicago, IL: University of Chicago Press, 1997).

42 Herring, *Group Representation Before Congress*, 32–3.

43 Crawford, *The Pressure Boys*, 40.

44 Thomas, *Sam Ward*, 344–5.

45 Ibid., 339–40.

46 Martin, *Behind the Scenes in Washington*, 222.

47 Schriftgiesser, *The Lobbyists*, 10.

48 Martin, *Behind the Scenes in Washington*, 231. Also see Herring, *Group Representation Before Congress*, 36–7.

49 Ronald Kessler, *Inside Congress: The Shocking Scandals, Corruption, and Abuse of Power Behind the Scenes on Capitol Hill* (New York: Pocket Books, 1998), 98–9.

50 Herring, *Group Representation Before Congress*, 40.

51 Deakin, *The Lobbyists*, 57–8.

52 Thompson, *The "Spider Web"*, 171.

53 Ibid., 159.

54 Clemens, *The People's Lobby*, 85.

55 Schriftgiesser, *The Lobbyists*, 71.

56 Gerard Clarfield, "Protecting the Frontiers: Defense Policy and the Tariff Question in the First Washington Administration," *The William and Mary Quarterly* 32 (3) (July 1975): 446.

57 Cited by Byrd on "Lobbyists."

58 David B. Truman, *The Governmental Process: Political Interests and Public Opinion* (New York: Alfred A. Knopf, 1951), 304–14.

59 David Goldsmith Loth, *Public Plunder: A History of Graft in America* (New York: Carrick and Evans, 1938).

60 Quoted in Truman, *The Governmental Process*, 4.

61 Justice Noah H. Swayne, quoted in Schriftgiesser, *The Lobbyists*, 17.

62 George Frisbie Hoar, quoted in Schriftgiesser, *The Lobbyists*, 18.

63 Herring, *Group Representation Before Congress*, 55.

64 Hugo Black, quoted in Zeigler, *Interest Groups*, 34.

65 James K. Pollock, "The Regulation of Lobbying," *American Political Science Review* 21 (2) (May 1927): 336–7.

66 Mark P. Petracca, "Introduction," in *The Politics of Interests: Interest Groups Transformed*, ed. Mark P. Petracca (Boulder, CO: Westview Press, 1992), xix.

67 Byrd on "Lobbyists."

68 Dayton David McKean, *Pressures on the Legislature of New Jersey* (New York: Columbia University Press, 1938), 192.

69 Crawford, *The Pressure Boys*, 42–3.
70 Herring, *Group Representation Before Congress*, 41–2.
71 Thompson, *The "Spider Web,"* 53.
72 "The Language of the Lobby," *New York Times*, May 29, 1858, 4.
73 Raymond L. Bridgman, "The Lobby," *New England Magazine* 22 (2) (April 1897): 151–60.
74 Conor McGrath, "Towards a Lobbying Profession: Developing the Industry's Reputation, Education and Representation," *Journal of Public Affairs* 5 (2) (May 2005): 124–35.

30

Best Practices in Online Advocacy for Associations, Nonprofits, and Corporations

Brad Fitch

By the time you read this, most of what is written in this chapter might be outdated. It is probably unwise to use a technology perfected in the fifteenth century (printing) to explain a constantly evolving technology of the twenty-first century (the Internet). Authors, industry experts, and researchers frequently try to nail down global conclusions about the Internet, only to find that, before the ink is dry, some new upstart has rewritten the rulebook and forced us to rethink our assumptions about communications.

Over the course of one morning three disparate e-mails arrived in my inbox, all portending potential implications to the online advocacy industry. I felt the world was changing so rapidly that I could not adapt quickly enough. I sent an e-mail out to colleagues: "Would everyone please stop innovating for just a week so I can catch up?" This is perhaps the first and most important rule of understanding online advocacy: it may always be in a state of transition.

Unlike the advent of other communications media, such as radio and television, there are few defining "before" and "after" moments that lend themselves to thoughtful comparison. Franklin D. Roosevelt gave us "fireside chats," and the power of radio and how to use a broadcast medium to persuade the public was defined. John F. Kennedy beat Richard M. Nixon in a televised debate, and we learned that the power of personality and communications skills are significantly amplified in a visual medium.

It used to be that communications professionals measured changes in years in how one uses a medium. With the Internet, we measure change in weeks, sometimes days. This means, by definition, any analyst must be extremely flexible, open to change at any minute, and ready to re-evaluate basic assumptions.

With that enormous disclaimer as an introduction, we can still take a snapshot of the world of online advocacy today. We can look back on the last decade of its existence, identify successful online advocacy efforts, and categorize strategies, tactics, and tools. I will touch on examples in the real world of online public affairs advocacy, refer to research connected to practical advocacy campaigns intended to influence policy, and offer guidance for influencing governmental decision-making. Further, I will refer to examples and relevant trends from political campaigns, but will not examine that topic in depth, as it is a much different animal than work conducted by associations, nonprofits, and corporations to influence policy-makers.

To understand the basic principles of successful online advocacy, it is important first to understand what it is not. There is great deal of activity conducted on the Internet in the name of advocacy; however, the perpetrators of this activity sometimes have little interest in actually changing legislative or regulatory outcomes. For example, many organizations use petitions to "send a message to Washington." However, research suggests that online petitions are routinely ignored by policy-makers,[1] and some are even silent on who the petition is delivered to and whether it is actually delivered. Invitations to sign up are either tactical efforts by organizers to identify potential advocates who may be willing to engage in genuine advocacy efforts or, unfortunately, the efforts of data mining enterprises seeking potential donors in order to sell as lists. Regrettably, some advocacy campaigns are more about the self-preservation of the campaign organizer than the enactment of real change.

Advocacy is not just about producing numbers. Many association grassroots managers pride themselves on the number of identical e-mails sent to Capitol Hill, reinforcing the group's message. However, these types of communications are far less persuasive than a fewer number of individually crafted communications.[2] Online advocacy is not about pleasing the boss, or producing reports alleging impact. Online advocacy is about effectively influencing policy outcomes that make a genuine difference in people's lives.

Finally, online advocacy is not just about technology. Clearly the tools now available to advocates have changed the rules of the game significantly in the last decade, and the potential for attracting new advocates is extraordinary. But in the end, it is not about the box with buttons—it is about citizens, and the power they use to "petition their government for a redress of grievances."[3] We can make a computer or website do just about anything. But getting doctors to call their congressman about an intrusive new regulation, or convincing a mother of three to attend a town hall meeting on education—that's hard. Yet it is precisely that human interaction that is required in successful online advocacy efforts. The policy-maker must believe there is a passionate person behind whatever communication is delivered. And it is the job of the online advocacy organizer to act as a promoter and conduit for that relationship between the governing class and the governed.

Defining Goals and Understanding the Audience

Even though we are using a twenty-first-century technology, the age-old basics of communications strategy still apply. At the beginning of an advocacy effort, you ask yourself: (1) Who is our audience? (2) What message will work? (3) What paths, communications vehicles, or strategies will work best with our audience? (4) How will we judge success?

Understanding your audience is a fundamental first step, as different demographic groups react differently to entreaties for advocacy. Usually professional organizers have a keen understanding of their audience, since they themselves may be members of the same group, association, or company. In addition to appreciating their interests, one must never lose sight of what the *audience* wants to get out of the advocacy relationship. Groups often focus on their own advocacy goals, as they should, but if the advocate does not find the online user experience satisfying, then you have lost them for future campaigns.

When assessing audience it is also important to consider that different people are likely to be at different stages of the advocacy and technology "adoption curve." This is especially important if the appeal crosses generations. For example, savvy users of technology are prepared for a "take action" page on the front of a website. New or slow adopters of the technology or message may be interested in links or background on your issue.

In the development of an advocacy message, whether it is a one-time blast e-mail requesting a call to a state legislator or the overall theme of an entire website, one must consider three factors in order to connect the issue to your audience: *values*, *desires*, and *needs*.

Any communications message must connect to the audience's *values*. People associate with those organizations and campaigns that they believe advance their own view of the world. When your website speaks to someone by appealing to their values you have built a lasting bond that can be tapped almost indefinitely. The National Rifle Association (NRA) has demonstrated on countless occasions that it can mobilize a small army of supporters in nearly every rural district to instill a politician with the fear of losing an election. NRA messages rarely articulate something as specific as this: "The right to possess armor-piercing bullets and ammo magazines containing 50 rounds is a basic constitutional right." Rather, they connect with the broader values of their members by connecting their message to patriotism, the US Constitution, and historic American ideals related to individual freedoms.

Another powerful appeal to audiences is based on *desires* or wants. Appealing to an individual's aspirations is often the best way to motivate advocacy. The advocacy group Moveon.org's anti-Iraq War effort not only played off their members' values, but also built upon the supporters' hopes and desires to end the war. Often organizers will present a vision for advocacy targets: imagine a world with universal health care, or no estate taxes. This strategy is not new: 1928 presidential candidate Herbert Hoover combined both the needs and desires of voters by using the slogan: "A chicken in every pot and a car in every garage." The first component appealed to his audience's basic need for food, and the second element appealed to the audience's aspiration for a symbol of wealth.

Messages that connect to the recipient's *needs* also have the potential to motivate action. Associations built around industries often can tap into the needs of employers, businesses, or professionals for government support or subsidies—or supporters' interest in reducing government regulation. Every year Congress seeks ways to squeeze more money out of the Medicare system. Every year Congress examines reducing the reimbursement amounts it pays doctors for treating patients receiving Medicare. And every year doctors mount campaigns suggesting that if Medicare payments were lowered they would seriously consider dropping Medicare patients from their rolls. This is a direct government-hits-pocketbook issue, and online pleas of this type often evoke a response.

It is also important for online organizers to appreciate that traditional views of political activists are shifting, and yesterday's profiles may not apply. W. Lance Bennett has put forward the concept of the Dutiful Citizen of the past and the Actualizing Citizen of the present.[4] According to Bennett, the Dutiful Citizen feels an obligation to participate in government, views voting as the core democratic act, learns about issues and government from mass media, and joins organizations that use one-way communications (such as direct mail) to mobilize supports.

But Bennett argues that, in a digital age, an Actualizing Citizen is emerging. This individual has a diminished sense of government obligation and a higher sense of individual purpose. To Actualizing Citizens, voting is less meaningful, and their personal sense of civic involvement is defined by consumerism (such as avoiding environmentally unfriendly products or companies), community volunteering, or transnational activism. They mistrust politicians and the mainstream media and prefer loose networks, often established through friends or peer relationships and thin social ties maintained through interactive online communities. A casual reader might conclude that Bennett is simply talking about older people (Dutiful Citizens) and younger people (Actualizing Citizens). But that would be too simplistic a view, and fails to appreciate the extraordinary amount of time that all people spend online at work, during which they are susceptible to advocacy messages. According to surveys, 73% of all Americans consider themselves "Internet users," including 71% of adults 50 to 64 years of age.[5] People of all ages are redefining their views and relationship with government and advocacy organizations. If trends continue, all Americans will become in some way Actualizing Citizens, less connected to traditional organizations and more open to rapid involvement through peer networks and online advocacy efforts.

After identifying an appropriate message, determine which strategies or communications pathways are most appropriate to reach the audience. Prior to the Internet, this choice was limited to a few options: print, radio, television, direct mail, advertising, or public relations—or some other "off-line" approach. In the online world new strategies and opportunities abound. Do we use Google Adwords or YouTube? How do bloggers fit into our strategy? Can we build partnerships with other websites to share audience lists or message stickers?

Before mapping an online strategy, first appreciate that online and off-line strategies cannot be separated. In fact, the most effective advocacy strategies integrate online and off-line activities. By understanding the strengths and weaknesses of off-line and online advocacy strategies, you maximize the impact of all media.

Off-line media still have the potential of reaching the broadest possible audience. For example, television ads presented during the Super Bowl get people's attention. Off-line news media carry more credibility than online-only news media, and therefore are more likely to spur action. However, off-line media are extremely expensive, whether used through paid (advertising) or free (public relations) media efforts. Off-line media is often difficult to precisely target, which means that much of your investment is wasted on an audience for whom the message is not intended.

In contrast, online media are relatively low in cost. Moreover, launching online advocacy efforts is comparatively easy and extremely fast. You think it up at 9 a.m., write and design it at 10 a.m., and launch it by 11 a.m. Online advocacy also offers an unparalleled degree of involvement by the advocate. Off-line media is a strict sender-to-receiver communication process. However, don't be wedded to the sender-to-receiver model when using online communications—it can be an ongoing dialogue and relationship. The more interaction, the greater the likelihood the advocate will stay engaged.

On the downside, online advocacy offers almost zero stealth. You might be able to sneak a direct mail piece to advocates under the radar of opponents, but almost anything done online can be traced back to the originator. Also, it can be hard to communicate with emotional precision and intensity. E-mails received by members of Congress are often the result of a one-click advocacy campaign. In such a case there is no way for the elected official to gauge how strongly the sender may feel about the issue. How does a member of Congress distinguish between someone who feels so passionately about the issue that they are willing to give money to the member of Congress's political opponent, compared to someone who just said, "eh, OK," and hits click and send. Each communication—from the legislator's perspective—is identical.

Ideally, organizers can create a perfect strategic balance between online and off-line media to garner the greatest impact. Finally, organizers also must develop relevant metrics to measure that impact. One expects that the ultimate metric is change in the targeted policy, the public position of a legislator altered, or a bill passed by a legislature. The most sophisticated lobbying organizations always keep these goals in their sights. This kind of discipline creates a clarity of purpose that pervades an organization and influences both the tactics and the work ethic of those charged with achieving the goal. While it is helpful to establish milestones, such as number of messages generated or calls placed, these should not replace definitive legislative, regulatory, or policy progress or outcomes.

Leaders, Enemies, Quests, and Battles

While issues can excite an audience and motivate them to take action, human beings are still generally hardwired to follow other human beings. Movements are at their best when a single individual embodies the values and goals of the audience. Martin Luther King, Jr, Mahatma Gandhi, and Dwight D. Eisenhower all mobilized people to act based in part on their leadership, charisma, personality, media skills, and management abilities.

The creator of Senator John McCain's 2000 presidential site, Max Fose, was once asked how others could recreate the incredible success the site experienced in the early days of the campaign. The site raised millions of dollars and registered thousands of volunteers in a matter of weeks after McCain's surprise victory in the New Hampshire primary. Others wanted to emulate the model. When asked how they did it, he answered, "Easy. First you start with a US Senator who will take on big tobacco, sponsor campaign finance reform legislation, propose a line-item veto, and was held prisoner of war in Vietnam for seven years. Then you build a website." Fose's point was clear: people didn't come to the website to visit the website, they were interested in helping a man they wanted to be president. The fastest computer and greatest website can only accelerate and enhance a message, they cannot create it. Do not expect technology by itself to generate interest in your mission. Start with your core beliefs and those shared values with a logical target audience, and build from there. In 2003–2004, former Vermont governor Howard Dean, running for the Democratic presidential nomination, created a similar stir with a plain-spoken campaign that brilliantly used every Internet tool available (and invented a few new ones) to build excitement about his campaign. But as the Dean campaign demonstrated, "excitement" does not necessarily translate into practical results. Both the McCain and Dean examples do, however, show that advocacy campaigns that can be connected to a single leader have an increased chance of garnering support.

It is often more challenging to associate advocacy efforts with an individual leader in the nonprofit, association, and corporate community. Yet when they do find leaders, the results can be extraordinary. In 2002 and 2003, the anti-Iraq War effort got a significant boost when it found a leader: Cindy Sheehan, a mother whose son was killed in Iraq. Unlike the off-line environment, online tools allow leaders to connect with followers in extraordinarily personal ways—and successful campaigns employ these strategies. Organizations can set up online chats, send personalized e-mail, create video messages, and stage webinars combining phone conference calls and online presentations.

Similarly, campaigns that fixate on an audience's perceived common enemy are more likely to garner involvement than those that do not. Again, this is not a new phenomenon to the art of persuasion. Senators in Ancient Rome raised armies based on the perceived threat of their city-state neighbor Carthage; American progressives in the early twentieth century focused on monopolies to spark the union movement; Senator Joseph McCarthy in the 1950s used the specter of communists infiltrating the US government to spread his message.

Left-of-center groups raised millions in their campaign coffers by pillorying President George W. Bush and Vice President Dick Cheney during their administration. In these cases the attacks are tied to specific online actions: send a message to a legislator; join an organization; or make a donation. The online message evokes an emotional response, "I want to do something to stop him." And the organization tees up a cafeteria menu of options to take advantage of that fear or rage.

Yet many advocacy efforts are not "campaigns" in the colloquial sense, in that there are not two diametrically opposed camps pitted against one another. At any one moment there may be thousands of organized online efforts by associations, nonprofits, and corporations directed to the Congress, but only a small percentage of them pit two defined groups against each other in the effort to win over public opinion. While the examples of titanic battles garner most of the off-line and online media coverage, most organizations online advocacy efforts resemble *quests*, not battles. They experience no organized opposition, no maligning attacks misrepresenting their record or trashing their accomplishments. Instead, they face hurdles, obstacles in their path to achieving the holy grails of their advocacy goals.

For example, Big Cat Rescue is a small nonprofit seeking to prohibit the ownership and sale of tigers and cheetahs in the US by individuals. The nonprofit's leaders were moved by stories of private individuals *buying* tigers as pets (no kidding), then realizing that they probably made a big mistake. The slightly mauled owners end up selling the big cats to brokers who later kill the animals and sell their parts in the Asian market. Big Cat Rescue's challenge is to overcome apathy, not some organized opposition such as the "National Association of Idiots Who Think That Tigers Would Be Good Pets."

In essence, many online campaigns are just seeking to get on the congressional agenda and to get *attention*, in order to allow their government relations professionals (lobbyists) to close the deal. For example, every year hundreds of organizations representing people who have diseases descend upon the halls of Capitol Hill, lobbying lawmakers for more research funding. There is not a contrasting lobbying group engaged in a similar effort with online action alerts saying, "Don't spend money to cure cancer." While there may be groups advocating lower spending overall, the two camps are not on the same battlefield. This means that online organizers' greatest challenge is to generate energy and attention. It is sometimes harder to engage advocates without an enemy. In cases where the only real opponent is apathy, groups must demonstrate the value of action and the consequences of inaction.

Advocate Audience: Finding Activists and Keeping Them Engaged

Most associations, nonprofits, and corporations start with some kind of list—members, donors, employees, or company retirees. The group does not need to be asked permission or to "opt-in" to receive an advocacy e-mail from an organization they belong to. By joining the organization, they have made an overt act to start a relationship. Individuals should always be given the opportunity to opt-out of the online relationship at any time. Yet as long as an organization serves the advocate's needs, the bond should stay firm.

If your organization detects that a supporter has taken action, you've hit gold. Individuals who take online action related to policy are some of the most influential people in a community, according to the authors of "Poli-Influentials: The New Political Kingmakers."[6] These individuals are more likely to vote in elections, contribute to a campaign, speak out at public forum, and write a letter to the editor. Nurture these activists; cajole them; fawn over them, because they are the key to legislative and regulatory success. These individuals will be instrumental—if not the determining factor—in the outcome of any significant policy debate. Their care and feeding is the highest priority in any organization that seeks to engage in online advocacy.

It is important that strategy, tactics, and message be guided by advocacy professionals who understand the subtle differences in online and off-line advocacy. And it is equally important that these efforts *not* be guided by senior managers and executives who are not connected to either the audience or the online world. I've had more than one glum grassroots organizer tell me, "We don't invest a lot in online advocacy. My boss doesn't use e-mail much and he doesn't think our supporters will respond to e-mail campaigns." I confess my reply is sarcastic. "Yea, he's probably right. This e-mail thing is probably just a passing fad."

In addition to considering association members, nonprofit donors, and company employees as potential advocates, organizations should think creatively about other sources of advocate lists. In 2007 a major chemical company found itself in the political wilderness after the 2006 election that resulted in a Democratic takeover of both the House of Representatives and the Senate. With a solid employee base in Texas, this company lost major champions in the House Majority Leader, Tom DeLay (Republican-Texas) who resigned his seat, and chairman of the House Energy and Commerce Committee, Joe Barton (Republican-Texas), who lost his chairmanship. This presented a dilemma for a company that, from an advocacy perspective, had all or most of its eggs in the Texas basket.

Then it occurred to grassroots organizers: "We spend hundreds of millions of dollars on vendors, buying everything from plastic to pencils. They are tied to our future as well." The company starting building lists of companies that had *connections* and a stake in their financial future in order to prepare for future campaigns. Since they had a business relationship with these companies, there was no need to create an "opt-in" campaign. The company realized it had an instant network of potential advocates. The lesson is to think creatively about your organization's relationship. Partnerships and alliances can be slightly transient in the online world (in advocacy, just like dating), but that doesn't mean those relationships are not powerful.

Searching for lists can be as simple as contacting a list-broker and buying names. But this is a very tricky (and potentially expensive) strategy. One of the most successful organizations in the area of list development is Care2, which boasts seven million members focused on left-of-center issues from health care to environmental protection. Other non-partisan efforts to cultivate lists have not had nearly the success. Real-world examples to date suggest that, in order to find and build lists of adequate size, they must be built around communities with similar political sensibilities. Organizers should not to be parochial in their thinking, and conclude that they can only get a good list of potential environmental advocates from an environmental list-building operation. For example, it is quite likely that fervent environmentalists also might support expanding health care access to low-income families.

While organizers absolutely should obey laws governing spam e-mail, we have to recognize that asking a citizen to get involved in advocacy is not the same thing as trying to sell them Viagra. As the US Supreme Court has ruled, there are fundamental ethical and legal differences between political speech and commercial speech. And while there is no case law testing online advocacy outreach, common sense and some research suggest that potential advocates *desire* information to help them be more effective. Information on pending legislation or regulations, if correctly targeted to interest groups, likely would be welcome and could result in a long-term online advocacy relationship. According to a national poll commissioned by the Congressional Management Foundation, 84% of Internet users who contacted Congress in the last five years were asked to do so by a third party group.[7]

In building and growing a list of advocates, an essential component is *viral marketing*. Organizers should use any tool to encourage advocacy message recipients to recruit more supporters. A unique capability of the Internet, in contrast to other media, is the ability of individuals to easily perpetuate an advocate's or marketer's message. This has earned the unfortunate term "viral marketing." Nearly all online advocacy tools include a "Tell a Friend" feature, whereby the advocacy organizer allows message recipients to become recruiters for the cause. These features usually are simple buttons that open up new web pages, allowing the recipient to submit friends' e-mail addresses so that they will receive a similar message. The most effective recruiter of advocates is not a grassroots organizer; it's the organizer's supporters. People are much more likely to respond to a plea from a friend than an association leader they've never met. In early 2007 the National Kidney Foundation began an effort to expand its online advocacy, and viral marketing was a key component. It made a "Tell-a-Friend" feature prominent in its campaign effort. Of those messages that were forwarded by advocates to friends, 93% of the recipients signed up to join the campaign.[8]

With a solid list of advocates, what strategy should be employed to keep them engaged? Below are several strategies to consider.

1 *Inform/educate.* Advocates usually want an intellectual underpinning before they act. Emotional appeals are more effective for spurring action, but people still want to know a little about what they are talking about when they interact with a policy-maker online. Statistics, testimonials, and other educational tools are powerfully persuasive and tend to keep a supporter in the camp of the committed.

2 *Shape emerging policy.* One of the overlooked opportunities to influence legislative and regulatory outcomes is before a bill or regulation has actually been written. As each new

Congress, state legislature, president, or governor takes office, they will come to the job with some broad concepts but with few specifics about their proposals. (Political history shows us that if they had specifics attached to their proposals, they probably wouldn't have won the election.) Launching campaigns with *specific* recommendations for the legislative or regulatory drafting process can have a powerful impact. Moreover, once politicians have staked out a position, it is extremely difficult to get them to change their mind. By striking when the policy is still forming, you have the opportunity to win the game before the other team has even gotten to the playing field.

3   *Advance or block initiatives.* Online campaigns are very effective at adding support to or undercutting support from policy initiatives. Because online campaigns can be employed rapidly, advocates can quickly see results in added cosponsors to legislation, public opposition to a chief executive's proposal, or support for a federal or state regulation.

4   *Alert or warn.* Advocates rely on the organizations they join to alert them of potential policy actions that will either help or hurt their common cause. This is especially important when action is pending in a legislative committee, which often works outside the scrutiny of local media because the outcomes usually don't have widespread impact. This is where online alerts that encourage e-mail or phone outreach to policy-makers can make the difference. Legislative action and announcements can be unusually fast—a congressional committee can announce its intentions to amend pending legislation on Tuesday and vote on amendments on Thursday. This means that online action is the only way to influence legislative outcomes at the committee level.

5   *Influence undecided's through off-line activity.* In-person contact with legislators is always more influential than online advocacy. But online tools can be invaluable in making that off-line interaction occur. In 2007 the American Farm Bureau Federation faced a legislative challenge—the renewal of the Farm Bureau, which occurs every five years. By purchasing a database of upcoming congressional town hall meetings, they were able to motivate their farmers to attend these meetings in order to influence policy-makers in their home districts. Similarly, in 2003 the Win Without War campaign sent e-mails to millions of supporters opposed to the congressional resolution authorizing the use of military force against Saddam Hussein. However, instead of asking people to send e-mails, they asked activists to phone US Senate offices. The resulting deluge of this "virtual march" on Washington shut down the entire US Senate phone system for a day.

6   *Update on outcome.* Once legislative or regulation decisions have been made, it is vital for organizers to keep their supporters updated through online communications. Updating advocacy sections of websites, sending out e-mails with final regulatory language, and linking supporters to actual vote counts are all crucial to keeping the advocate engaged.

7   *Encouraging thank yous.* Members of Congress almost never get thanked for their efforts, which makes those infrequent expressions of gratitude from supporters so much more influential. These kinds of good-will efforts stick in legislators' minds, which is extremely helpful when the next advocacy campaign arises.

Tools of the Trade

Any communications craft has basic tools of the trade. Public affairs press secretaries have press releases, op-ed pieces, and radio actualities. The Internet has spawned an entire new genre of communications tools, and continues to generate new tools every few months. Below is a rough inventory of tools available to online advocates.

E-Newsletters

The most basic communications tool of online advocates is the e-newsletter. Advocates say they crave objective information about what is going on in government.[9] But most people are busy and don't want to spend the time poking around complicated and disorganized government websites. Creating regular, easy-to-read communications for your advocates is a great way to maintain their interest in the topic. Important note: Slave over the writing. There are many weak government relations e-newsletters that don't get read. Make sure your text appeals to your membership and speaks to their values, needs, and desires.

Advocacy Messages

The staple of online advocacy is the "action alert," or blast e-mail message, to advocates asking them to take some action, e-mail, call, or visit a legislator. Because this type of communications vehicle has evolved so rapidly, there is a lot of variance in style and effectiveness of these messages. Below is a list of proven methods for advocacy messages.

1 *Communicate immediacy.* Make sure advocates know that their involvement is crucial *now*. Time-sensitive issues are much more likely to elicit a response.
2 *Encourage personalization.* According to a 2005 survey of congressional staff, personalized e-mail messages are ten times more effective than bulk messages with identical content. Encourage your membership to tell their story.[10]
3 *Keep it short.* E-mail is a short-hand medium, whether it be the message sent to the advocate, or the messages advocates sent to legislators. Unless the recipient is very closely aligned to your group, 100 words or less should do the trick.
4 *Offer additional information.* People expect links in e-mails. Maybe the advocate wants to feel more educated about the issue before he or she takes action. Provide more information, but *always* include the opportunity to take action on those background pages.
5 *Offer multiple avenues of advocacy.* For the same reasons as fundraisers offer the opportunity to give $25 or $100, you should offer advocates the option of calling, e-mailing, writing, or attending a town hall meeting.
6 *Track and evaluate results.* Internet advocacy offers organizations the opportunity to track and evaluate campaigns in a way that off-line media, such as direct mail, do not. Use evaluation tools to test messages; determine which words work better than others in subject lines; assess optimum times to reach your membership; and analyze campaigns based on content and issues. These types of evaluation methods not only help refine strategy, they look very good to boards of directors and demonstrate that advocacy efforts are making a difference.

Blogs

No chapter on online advocacy would be complete without a discussion of blogs. The mainstream media (or as blogs refer to them, the "lame-stream media") is atwitter with commentary about their impact and role in the political process. After close intensive study of this phenomenon over the last few years I have come to only one clear conclusion about blogs: They are very good at getting people fired. This is sometimes called a "blog swarm." Dan Rather got canned from his anchor position at CBS Nightly News in large part due to the research conducted by blog writers who discovered that a story Rather did on President George W. Bush's National Guard service during the Vietnam War was based on false evidence. Similarly, bloggers could claim partial credit for Senator Joe Lieberman's primary defeat in the 2006 Connecticut Democratic primary.

Bloggers can promote stories that otherwise would go unnoticed by mainstream media, and therefore influence policy. In late 2006 Talking Points blogger Josh Marshall was the only writer talking about the unusual firing of several US attorneys. The subsequent firestorm ultimately led to the resignation of Attorney General Alberto Gonzalez. (It should be noted that Attorney General Gonzalez's mediocre performances before congressional committees were a contributing factor in his downfall.) Some cheered about Dan Rather losing his anchorman job, Joe Lieberman losing the Democratic nomination in Connecticut (to a Senate seat he later won as an Independent) and Alberto Gonzalez's removal from his cabinet position. And some say this demonstrates the power of blogs—but beyond these high-profile examples there have been few other cases of blogs' impact on public policy outcomes. This may be due in part to the fact that many of the best read blogs have not initiated advocacy campaigns. If a major blog site, such as Daily Kos or Instapundit, tries to marshal readers into advocacy, and they followed, this would be a turning point in the role of blogs in the political process.

Research suggests that the staff of policy-makers read political blogs, and therefore one can deduce that information is either passed onto lawmakers or somehow influences the policy process.[11] Yet this category of influence is similar to staff reading a weekly news magazine or daily newspaper's op-ed piece. Moreover, there is little evidence that organizations benefit from starting their own blogs, since they would have little readership. This does not mean that blogs can be ignored. But they are an evolving phenomenon, and online advocates should approach them in the same way they approach unstable material that could explode at any moment—cautiously and with some kind of protective gear in place.

Petitions and Polls

Advocates want a diverse menu of ways to get involved in policy process. Some want to fly to Washington and bang on a senator's desk—others want to simply add their name to a list. It is important to give supporters a variety of ways to voice their opinions on an issue and feel involvement. However, these opportunities to contribute opinions should be conducted in an ethical fashion. Too many organizations commit a form of "communications fraud" on both the sender and receiver of the communication. Organizers asking for online "signatures" know that they cannot deliver those signatures to a policy-maker. Or organizations will ask supporters for "signatures," transforming those "signatures" into full-blown e-mails with text the organizer inserts. Petitions and polls must have clear policies on how the data will be used and what will result from the individual's participation.

Personal Calculators

The Internet allows each visitor to your website to have a unique experience, even if it's only the order in which they review pages on your site. One way to make a personal plea to an advocate is to calculate exactly what the impact of a policy will be on his or her life. For example, the Environmental Working Group, which is trying to reduce the levels of mercury in tuna, has a simple calculator on its website. Visitors plug in their weight and it reports how much tuna you can eat before you exceed the FDA recommendations for mercury in food. This is a persuasive way to convince a person that the policy affects the advocate in a personal way. (Note: If you ask for someone's personal information—like one's weight—it's a good idea to have a very explicit privacy policy that indicates the data won't be stored or shared.)

Video

We are watching the emergence of a transformative and powerful component in advocacy: video. The 2006 election and the CNN–YouTube 2008 presidential debate demonstrated that video offers an opportunity for advocates to articulate a powerful message using simple technology available to millions of Americans. Some advocates have begun sending their video messages to Congress and state legislatures, creating a new tool in the advocacy arsenal.

Cynics ask, "Will legislators and staff actually watch advocate videos?" My reply is yes. First, it is a novel delivery system, and people like checking out new technology. Second, it will take only ONE congressman who ignores the plea of a kid who's got an incurable disease to generate a "watch everything" policy in every legislator's office.

Moreover, unlike an in-person constituent visit—which currently is the most effective way to influence lawmakers—video has the quality of *permanence*. After the constituent has left the office, the visit is over. However, a video can live for days or weeks on YouTube and in re-broadcasts on television stations. (If you doubt this, just ask former senators George Allen (Republican-Virginia) and Conrad Burns (Republican-Montana) who both owe part of their defeats in 2006 to ubiquitous YouTube videos.)

Individual Stories

Legislators, staff, and the media continue to implore advocacy groups to supply them with individual stories of citizens explaining how public policy will impact them. And yet, ironically, there is an extraordinary dearth of personal narratives whenever a major public policy matter is considered. There are large, national data points about billions of dollars and millions of people, but those facts and figures lack the names and faces of actual people affected by the debated policy.

For example, during the debate in 2007 over the reauthorization of the State Children's Health Insurance Plan (SCHIP), Democrats railed against President Bush's opposition and talked about the millions of children who would not have health insurance as a result of the president's position. However, could you find any of those children on legislators' websites? Could you hear any of their stories in podcasts? In a few cases legislators had some kids at press conferences, but there was no systemic effort to demonstrate the impact of the legislation on real people.

In 2005 Congressman George Miller (Democrat-California) actually did collect individual stories to highlight the potential problems of under-funded pensions. The Democratic staff of the House Education and Labor Committee opened their website for comments from workers of United Airlines, which was facing a pension failure, and collected more than 2,000 individual stories. Organizations have extraordinary credibility with their membership or supporters to collect this kind of information, tapping into the imagery, logo, and slogans that will connect with visitors. Using branded websites that have credibility or connections to membership groups to collect personal stories is one of the greatest untapped tools of online advocacy.

Text Messaging

Political organizers have been waiting for the text messaging craze to find a home in the advocacy community. Sometimes called "Smart Mob"[12] or "Flash Mob," advocates send messages to advocates urging them to take action. Most of the best practice examples of "mobile advocacy" have occurred in Europe, Africa, and Asia. (See, for example, Chapter 20 by Julie Barko Germany and Justin Oberman.) In the US political campaigns have sought to take advantage of this new tool, urging supporters to rallies for and against their candidate. However we've yet to see a concrete example of text messaging used in advocacy to affect legislation or a regulation. This is another emerging tool that could have a significant impact given the right set of circumstances.

Policy-Maker Audience: Content, Delivery Mechanisms

There are too many myths and not enough research on what exactly motivates legislators. The most extensive survey of Congress on this topic was released by the Congressional Management Foundation in 2005 based on survey answers from more than 350 staff members from 200 offices in the House of Representatives and the Senate.[13] The results debunked one of the myths that exist about advocacy—the efficacy of e-mail. The survey indicated that it was the *content* that influenced legislators, not the *delivery vehicle* in which the content was delivered. A significant majority of staff respondents, 64%, said that personally written e-mail messages would have "some" or "a lot" of influence on an undecided lawmaker (see Figure 30.1).

In focus groups, interviews, and surveys of congressional staff the overwhelming message is, "add personal content to the communication." Many organizers create one-click advocacy campaigns. These campaigns merely ask the supporter to click and send a message, which requires about ten seconds. Legislators and their staff understand the ease with which a message can be sent and place a value on the message equal to the amount of time and effort that went in to its crafting and transmission. Therefore, form communications campaigns (e-mail, postcard, fax) are devalued by legislators. While some count the input, they are viewed like polls, and do not convey the writer's passion for the cause.

In contrast, any communication that the advocate has individualized is considered more valuable and is much more likely to be integrated into the policy decision-making process. This mentality of lawmakers and staff permeates the correspondence triage that exists in every legislative operation. In the late 1990s a senior US Senate staffer who oversaw the mail operation in the office had a "stamped and signed" policy with regards to postcards. He instructed his mail-

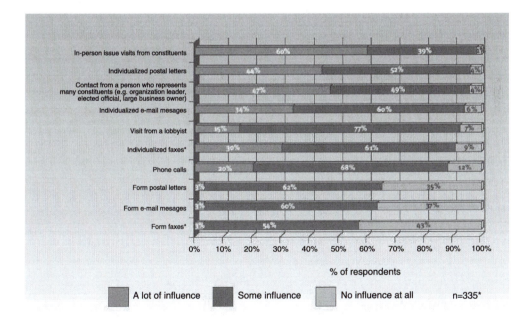

Figure 30.1. Responses from Congressional Staffers on Effectiveness of Persuasion Techniques

Source: Permission to reprint from the Congressional Management Foundation. Brad Fitch and Kathy Goldschmidt, *Communicating with Congress: How Capitol Hill is Coping with the Surge in Citizen Advocacy* (Washington, D.C.: Congressional Management Foundation, 2005).

Note: * The question regarding faxes was asked only of House correspondence staff and Senate office managers. N = 209.

431

handling and data-entry staff to separate out those postcards which were not stamped and signed. The logic behind this classification was that if constituents had neither signed their name to the cause nor invested 13 cents for postage (meaning, the advocate's organization had pre-paid the postage) then the constituents did not have a significant investment in the issue. Research suggests that this logic is flawed, and that those sending communications to lawmakers are more likely to get involved in campaigns, motivate others to advocacy, and speak out in public.[14]

Conclusion

As students, experts, and practitioners go forth into the online world of advocacy, be guided by the prophetic words of the 1960s band, Buffalo Springfield: "There's something happenin' here. What it is ain't exactly clear." Recognize that a profound and historic communications transformation is underway and never may be fully complete. Acknowledge that the old ways of "engineering consent" as defined 100 years ago by the father of public relations, Edward Bernays, are being replaced by a new medium, language, and strategy. And be aware that the constantly shifting topography defining communicators' world requires us to integrate new data and trends on a daily basis. Never be certain of anything, and always be open to the idea that some quirky new tool, feature, or website can rock your world.

Notes

1 Brad Fitch and Kathy Goldschmidt, *Communicating with Congress: How Capitol Hill is Coping with the Surge in Citizen Advocacy* (Washington, D.C.: Congressional Management Foundation, 2005).

2 Ibid.

3 United States Constitution, First Amendment.

4 W. Lance Bennett, "Changing Citizenship in the Digital Age," OECD/INDIRE conference on Millennial Learners, March 5–6, 2007.

5 Mary Madden, "Internet Penetration and Impact," Pew Internet and American Life survey, April 26, 2006.

6 *Poli-Influentials: The New Political Kingmakers* (Washington, D.C.: George Washington University Institute for Politics, Democracy and the Internet, 2007).

7 Kathy Goldschmidt and Leslie Ochreiter, *Communications with Congress: How the Internet has Changed Citizen Engagement* (Washington, D.C.: Congressional Management Foundation, 2008).

8 Interview with Jayne Mardock, National Kidney Foundation, November 16, 2007.

9 Congressional Management Foundation, Focus Group Research, October 2002.

10 Fitch and Goldschmidt, *Communicating with Congress*.

11 T. Neil Sroka, *Understanding the Political Influence of Blogs* (Washington, D.C.: George Washington University, Institute for Politics Democracy and the Internet).

12 Howard Rheingold, *Smart Mobs: The Next Social Revolution* (New York: Perseus Publishing, 2002).

13 Fitch and Goldschmidt, *Communicating with Congress*.

14 *Poli-Influentials*.

31

Building Constituencies for Advocacy in the United States and Other Democracies

Edward A. Grefe

In the late 1920s, Sigmund Romberg and Oscar Hammerstein II wrote a song entitled "Stout Hearted Men" for the Broadway show, and a subsequent movie for really late-night movie fans, *The New Moon*. The sentiment of the lyric still resonates regardless of the gender of those who lead political movements today. Following the intro, the melody asserts:

> Give me some men
> Who are stout-hearted men
> Who will fight for the right they adore.
> Start me with ten
> Who are stout-hearted men
> And I'll soon give you ten thousand more

Most major political movements start with fewer than ten, often only one or two stout-hearted persons who have a passionate belief in either their cause or their candidacy. History shows that with a cadre of true believers one can build a movement. This chapter describes how this is accomplished.

Those who build constituencies of volunteers and activists to support a cause or candidate are called grassroots organizers. Those who become engaged are referred to as grassroots activists, the cadre of true believers. The number of such activists, even if an organizer does the very best job possible, rarely reaches more than 5% of the electorate. However, that 5% is essential. That number, seemingly small, is needed to give authenticity to the effort. It shows that a committed group truly cares.

Few political campaigns are won or lost by greater than 5%. The same is true with public policies when they are fought out in the legislative or regulatory arena. Thus, an organized group of 5% of the community has a major effect on the outcome of political campaigns and in shaping public policies. That fact is certainly true in the US today and is becoming an increasingly factor in democracies around the world.

Grassroots constituencies are the same powerful messengers in the political process as those in the non-political arena who tell their neighbors—"this is really a great movie, or this is the best place to buy a pizza, or don't buy a car from this place," and so forth. In a nation of volunteers, word of mouth from a credible source is still key, perhaps more today as the Internet becomes the new way for individuals to reach one another. High-tech may be trendy but person-to-person contact, what is often referred to as "high touch," produces the heat that fuels political movements, political action, and shifts in public policy.

There has been a re-emerging recognition of the importance of grassroots participation to affect substantive change in the body politic. Emphasis on grassroots and building a constituent base began to fade in the mid-twentieth century as broadcast media became viewed as either the *principal* or the *only* way to move the body politic. Its re-emergence is due to the success of recent political campaigns that stressed traditional grassroots techniques buttressed by such new technologies as micro-targeting and the new media spawned by the Internet.

To build a constituency it helps to understand the political arena in which one is operating. This is especially true when one is about to build a constituency that will advocate for the outcome desired by a few stout-hearted leaders. For cognizance of the political arena requires a conscious appreciation of a fact seldom discussed but essential for one to launch a political effort, namely, that in the United States we have three *distinct* but *inseparable* political arenas:

1 a specific fixed-timetable *election* campaign to elect an individual or settle an issue that has been presented to the electorate through either the referendum or initiative process;
2 an organized *lobbying* campaign that is often—but not always—of specific duration to support or oppose a legislative or regulatory proposal; and,
3 a *community advocacy* campaign that will probably be waged over many years to build public acceptance for a change to be popularly held by the majority.

Historically, the three arenas operated only in US politics. Legislative and regulatory campaigns in other democracies were an almost unknown phenomenon. Now, even in parliamentary-based democracies this phenomenon is growing as people demand to be listened to between elections. This chapter first presents community advocacy in the context of US politics and later presents ideas for organizing constituencies in other democracies.

Each of the three arenas is *inseparable* from the other two as they each influence and interact with one another; but they are *distinct* in several important ways:

1 the time period of each: from fixed to indefinite to indeterminate;
2 the outcome: from win–lose to multiple outcomes to possible win–win; and,
3 the impact that the time period and the outcome have both on building a constituency and sustaining the active support of that constituency: from an engaged and enthusiastic group working around the clock because there is a clear timetable to a situation in which the enthusiasm of a group of volunteers can wane as they suffer the fatigue of battles within what they come to understand may be a protracted war.

Elections

As he worked to build the Republican Party in Illinois, Abraham Lincoln spelled out most accurately what it is we should do and how to do it in his instructions to volunteer leaders:

> To divide their county into small districts, and to appoint in each a subcommittee, whose duty it shall be to make a perfect list of all the voters in their respective districts, and to ascertain with certainty for whom they will vote.

In an electoral effort there is a definitive beginning, middle, and date certain for the campaign's conclusion. In the United States there is usually a clear winner. The system is based almost entirely on a "winner takes all" accounting and in most elections the winner is the person with the most votes even if the total number of votes cast for the winner amounts only to a plurality. A few states insist on the winner having a majority, and have provisions for run-off elections when only a plurality occurs in an initial contest, but those states and localities are the exception.

The outcome described another way is that the candidate or the issue either wins or loses. There is no coming in second as in parliamentary systems in which those coming in second or even lower get some share of the political power based on their position on the list submitted by their political party. The uniquely US phenomenon of fixed dates for elections, that is, dates certain for elections from now until infinity, makes organizing people toward the fixed deadline relatively easier to do, certainly in comparison to building a constituency for a change in public policy.

Volunteers in a political campaign can be asked to undertake specific tasks and to do so according to specific timetables with the tasks being not only measurable but also clear targets that can become incentives. Progress can be charted. Growth can be readily seen. Political campaigns can be calculated on a tote board much like a day at the ponies. The media—and most people—look at the ebb and flow of the effort and view it as a horse race especially as polls show progress or decline. This notion of a fixed time period looms large in the organizer's tool chest because of the certainty of both the date upon most elections will occur[1] and therefore the time between now and then when activities need to take place.

Traditionally, the electorate was looked at in terms of a proclivity to vote and to do so along fairly predictable voting patterns. That proclivity meant that a district or precinct could be analyzed in terms of its total population in this manner:

- total eligible voters: usually a significant number;
- total registered voters: again often a sizeable number but far less than eligible;
- actual voters for this office: usually a varying number depending on the office with far greater numbers often voting for the top of the ticket and the number of votes cast declining per precinct as the office sought dropped further to the bottom of the list; and, if needed
- actual voters for a specific election: the die-hard, dependable political "junkies" and activists, often defined as those who show up to vote in a primary for a local school board election versus those who only voted in a general election and perhaps only in presidential election years.

Today, few campaigns have the luxury of time, the money, or the manpower to conduct voter registration drives. That is the work of political parties and issue-based organizations. Some political strategists even suggest that a campaign that bases its strategy on finding the eligible unregistered voters is a campaign about to implode. The focus today is definitely on those who vote even if they have not been consistent in their voting turnout or in voting for all candidates or propositions.

The plan to build a constituency for a political campaign is usually divided into three stages:

- phase one: solidify base; focus on those with us and leaning our way;
- phase two: add to the base; focus on undecided and those leaning against;
- phase three: return to base to get-out-the-vote (GOTV).

An initial analysis is done as to how a precinct might vote given previous voting patterns. The precincts are then weighed in terms of their historical proclivity. That research is able to generate information about five categories of voters:

- those with the candidate/your side in the issue/ballot measure;
- those leaning toward the candidate/proposition;
- those undecided;
- those leaning against the candidate/proposition;
- those opposed to candidate/your position on the issue/ballot measure.[2]

The basic principle for building constituencies for political campaigns has always been: "Go pick cherries where the cherries grow." That concept has been true for years. But, precinct analysis has changed over the years. Lincoln's advice to make a perfect list of voters and determine their preference is still the goal. But discerning where one can pick one's "cherries," for much of the last half of the twentieth century and today is far more sophisticated. "Cherry-picking" for voters was once based on party preference and past precinct analysis. With polling data such analysis was next based on *targeting*. Today campaign organizers use *micro-targeting*. The difference between the two is based on having primarily or only *demographic* data and the ability today to have a more robust analysis with the addition of *psychographic* data as well.

When political parties ruled[3] and determined who their candidates would be, about all that was needed to project the outcome of an election was party affiliation about those in a specific precinct in a specific election. Today, party identification is only one factor and usually just the starting point. As the party role declines and candidates, with consultants who specialize in organizing campaigns, create their own personal organizations, new tools have emerged. These tools include new polling techniques and computers able to provide more sophisticated ways of targeting. Building potential constituencies can now be based on a link to the candidate that may supersede any link to a particular political party. Campaigns to elect a candidate or promote an issue seek to identify voters who will be for them, rather than for a particular party.

Building a constituency often starts with a client's address book. That book contains names of people on the candidate's holiday card list or people who had gone to school with the client or who were members of the same place of worship or voluntary organization in the community. The goal is to find people who like the candidate regardless of the issues, people who trust the candidate and are willing to become publicly identified with the candidate. That group usually represents what is called the "family," people who had some attachment to the candidate.[4]

Ideally, in that list are one or more persons of some substance who will step forward and head up the fundraising effort and possibly one or two among them who are good at organizing who will head up a portion of the voter identification and GOTV efforts, and host their neighbors at campaign/fundraising events in their homes. Hopefully, among them will be one or more whose position in the community clearly identifies them as "influentials,"[5] people with some stature in the community who command respect when they add their name to a cause or candidate.

Beyond the initial group, the family, a list of potential friends is developed. Early computer programs enabled an organizer to evaluate potential friends in the various precincts with new data often supplied by polls. This includes:

- those who share the same *general* philosophy: conservative to liberal;
- those who share the same view on a specific topic: pro-life, pro-choice;
- those who share a *general* economic interest: a business view/union view;
- those with a specific economic interest: paving contractors looking for contracts;
- those who truly *hate* the opponent: a group that may seek out your campaign and one dealt with gingerly at best, and always at arm's length.[6]

Organizers move beyond the traditional sorting based on either existing voter registration or previous voting patterns. By cross-referencing past voting behavior with the characteristics noted above, new priority precincts can be determined based on whether voters in that precinct could be considered either *for* a candidate or cause or *against* the opponent. The identification voters might feel between themselves and the candidate or issue began to emerge. This accelerated the trend away from pure party identification to real and potential voting patterns that seemed to blur the traditional lines between parties.

For example, polling firms developed ways to enable voters to place themselves, their view of each political party, and the candidate for office on a spectrum of "1" (extremely conservative) to "7" (extremely liberal). People might see themselves as 3.6 on the scale, a candidate as 3.6, and the candidate's party as 2.4. That means the candidate could be separated from the party and reaching out to "switch" voters—those who would "switch" from their normal proclivity to vote for candidates of one party if they sensed a kinship with a candidate who they believed more accurately reflected their own views regardless of party affiliation.[7]

This has led to the use of a technique know as a "push" poll.[8] Used legitimately, a "push" poll can identify a potential ally based on factors beyond party affiliation or that party's traditional stance on an issue. People are asked questions based on facts a campaign believes relevant to determine whether those facts would cause a person to "switch" because of some new fact presented by the caller. If the facts being tested are genuine and one is testing merely for their saliency, the polling technique is legitimate and may be called "hard ball." (See Chapter 1, by Dennis W. Johnson, for further discussion of push polls.)

However, the fact that there can be only one winner tempts some campaigns to practice "spitball" techniques rather than be honest. Such campaigns use polling techniques as a guise to inject outright lies that are designed to build on the fear or "hate" felt by some to either get them to switch their vote, or to not vote at all.

Today there is a view that building one's base among those with, and leaning toward the candidate, can only be supplemented by reaching out to those leaning against and getting them to switch. The notion is that at the end of the day, the only people candidates want coming to the polls are those they are certain will vote for them and the added view that time is too short to try to convince the undecided since undecided can mean one of three things, none of them good so far as voter certainty:

- undecided as to whether or not to register;
- undecided as to whether or not to vote; or
- undecided as to whether or not to vote for your candidate or cause.

Another innovation of the late twentieth century is the expansion of psychographic or lifestyle data to do even more sophisticated *micro-targeting*. Today instead of conceding a precinct that normally votes "blue," those managing "red" seek out the few potential "red" voters in each "blue" precinct, and vice versa, based on hundreds of variables including not only polling data on selected social issues, but also such information as the magazines they subscribe to, where they shop, organizations they belong to, and a host of other variables.[9]

From the simple proclivity to vote one way or another, to simple demographics data, to the addition of sophisticated psychographic or lifestyle and philosophic views, all these factors make building a constituency a more complex and more expensive process. But the process is still one in which organizers build a constituency via the "*multiplier*" effect of identifying, recruiting, training, and motivating one's "family" of true believers, then challenging them to reach out to others in their community.

The difference today is that at one time, volunteers knew only that the "stranger" whose door they were knocking on had a proclivity to vote and possibly an interest in voting for a candidate versus the volunteers today who arrive at someone's door armed with a PDA in hand indicating how the prospect feels on specific issues. This enables volunteers to deliver the right message to the right household. Organizers can also use the information to make certain that each volunteer is, in addition, the right messenger for that prospect.

The Internet does have value as a tool. It can enable one to identify supporters. It can communicate with supporters instantaneously. Its effectiveness is enhanced when the identification of supporters includes a way to bring them together to "press the flesh" and "put a name to a face" via "meet-ups." That said, the Internet is definitely not, as some enthusiasts believe, the equivalent of the Second Coming for politics. (Further on the Internet and campaigns, see Chapter 13 by Emilienne Ireland.)

The emerging mythology that over-simplifies the Internet as having become, or on the threshold of becoming, the ultimate key to grassroots organizing is just that: a myth. That is because the ultimate challenge to the success of using the Internet is its seeming inability to become a forum for achieving collaboration. On the contrary, like successful direct mail fundraising appeals, the Internet presents a forum not for debate but for diatribe. Its appeal is to the extremists who want to scream at each other, often in obscenities, and hide behind the veil of anonymity.[10] *Analog man*, a known person who could be reasoned with, has been replaced by *digital man*, a hidden force able to throw bombs and destroy lives seemingly with impunity.

The Internet is a nice tool, an important ingredient to be added to the communications process. It works well in a political campaign when the goal is to find only one's supporters and get them to the polls. But ultimately it can never replace the human element of one person reaching out to another. That remains the essence of building a collaborative process in which good governance can occur, a need that will remain until humans become machines. Today, it is still all about Lincoln's admonition to build a perfect list and ascertain for whom a person will vote; then getting that person to the voting booth on election day.

Lobbying Proposed Laws/Regulations

Legislative and regulatory battles have slightly different characteristics. To begin, the timeline is not as precise as a political campaign. There are hundreds of thousands of bills and regulatory proposals at the federal, state, county, and municipal level in any given year. Tracking that activity is a business all its own, compartmentalized by those bills and regulations that affect one industry, or one mega-issue, or one portion of an industry's or non-profit organization's agenda. Few proposed laws advance beyond being introduced to make a political point for the sponsor. Regulatory proposals usually move forward and may or may not lend themselves to grassroots action requiring the building of a constituency.

Hearings on a proposed law may or may not be scheduled. Hearings may advance the proposal and action may be required by interested parties. But the decision to build an organization to voice one position or another on the proposed law or regulation can depend on other factors. At the outset there are three possible ways to proceed if action is required.

The first way is to allow a single individual, such as a volunteer or paid lobbyist, to handle the situation entirely. That decision is often affected by the realization that the proposal is too technical or seemingly so irrelevant to large numbers of people that little public notice will be given the proposal—not only by the public at large but also by the media. Roughly 90% of all proposals fall into this category. If public and media interest is nil or desultory, the lobbyist may be able to handle the proposal successfully.

If the issue is important but so complex that its importance is difficult if not impossible to explain in a bumper sticker or simple slogan there may be a need to move beyond having a single individual and create a group to support or oppose the proposal.[11] A decision is then made as to whether a large group is needed, which is referred to as *grassroots*, or if a select few should make the effort. The mobilization of a select few is known as *grasstops*.

The decision to identify and mobilize the grasstops or grassroots, like the campaign for a candidate or issue, requires establishing an organization. There are several reasons for establishing a campaign issue organization. The issue group enables those with a clear vested interest to engage others. The others become third-party surrogates for those whose vested interest in the outcome makes them potentially suspicious as biased.

The new organization is created for one purpose: to advance or defeat one issue. Often these organizations are led by a board composed of individuals who are viewed by the media, the public, and elected officials as being objective. The group's existence allows people not associated with the primary sponsoring and funding organization, as employees of a corporation or members of an association, to become "members" of this single issue organization. The creation of the single issue organization allows the sponsoring organization to continue to focus on multiple issues. Single issue organizations created properly acknowledge publicly the role of their founders and funders. Some single issue organizations choose to conceal the identity of their true founders or funders. Such organizations are referred to as "Astroturf," or phony "grass."

Grasstops differs from "grassroots," which usually refers to the mass of people. Grasstops groups are comprised almost entirely by a select group referred to as "the influentials." Influentials may include genuine *stakeholders*, people who have a vested interest in the outcome, but influentials can also refer to others chosen for primarily because (1) they have a position of respect and/or visibility within the community, may understand the proposal's impact, and are willing to support those with a vested interest; and/or (2), they are well known to the legislators who will vote on the proposal. The prime reason for being recruited to be a member of the grasstops group is that the prospect is a donor and/or prominent politically in the legislator's district.

Those elected to other political offices count among this group. It includes individuals who head local organizations, the chamber of commerce, a union, a garden club, the Rotary Club, an alumni group, a parent–teacher organization. By virtue of having been chosen by their peers they are automatically seen as influentials in the community.

Grasstops can also include those who have been appointed to run a local for-profit or not-for-profit organization, a bank president, the head of a local charity, the leader of a church, synagogue, or mosque. It includes those who have become publicly involved in the community, they may have written a letter or made a speech. They may be one of Malcolm Gladwell's "salesmen," "mavens," or "connectors" or one of David Riesman's "inside-dopesters."[12] They are clearly one of Jon Berry and Ed Keller's "influentials."[13] They are people others turn to as trusted fonts of wisdom who add third party credibility to bolster one's position on the outcome of the issue.

Another reason to organize the grasstops versus the grassroots has to do with the uncertainty of the possible outcomes of the proposal. The grassroots promotes a simple message and a straightforward timetable: "Get involved today because an action will be taken this week and tell your legislator to vote . . . ['yes' or 'no']." Legislative proposals and sometimes regulatory proposals are often more nuanced. In contrast to a win–lose outcome for a political campaign, a legislative, and sometime a regulatory, battle can potentially have five outcomes:

1 A win—a "green" light solution for the winner.
2 A loss—a "red" light for the loser.
3 A compromise—a "yellow" light solution destined to re-arise if one of the parties ultimately feels the compromise was not fair.
4 A delay—a decision to postpone any decision repeatedly—perhaps a "double-blinking" yellow light scenario.
5 An entirely new proposal acceptable to both sides not in the sense that both sides gave up something as in the compromise, but a proposal in which both sides feel they won something important without appearing to give up anything, a "blue" light solution.

With five outcome potentials the challenge for the organizer of a legislative or regulatory battle is both timing and often message. Not always is there a fixed date as to when a vote will be called when legislation is first introduced.[14] There are votes in both subcommittees and full committees, and votes on the floor on the proposal itself plus various amendments. When the issue is clear and the date of the vote clear, the message can be clear, our group supports or opposes the proposal, so act today!

The decision to organize grasstops versus grassroots is affected by the twin challenges, the timing of when to ask people to get involved and the message to be delivered. With grasstops, the number involved in smaller. The depth of understanding may be greater. The attention paid to the issue is often more current.

When the outcome is neither a clear "red" nor a clear "green" light one, there can be difficulty with building a true grassroots effort, one that reaches out to Mr/Ms Joe or Sally Six-pack who tend to be more comfortable knowing what they oppose or support than to any nuanced situation. It is easier to get someone to say, for example, "I am for/against smoking in a restaurant" than to say "I think we should have separate sections for smokers and non-smokers," the latter statement more easily understood and argued by a clear stakeholder such as the owner of a restaurant or a tavern.

When the decision is made to build a large grassroots organization other factors must also be considered. To begin, the organizer needs to appreciate that the essence of grassroots is one-on-one communications. In the context of any political effort this means a candidate or the campaign reaching out to individuals one-on-one to seek their support and to recruit their participation. The connection is direct between the volunteer and the candidate or cause.

With a legislative or regulatory grassroots effort there are slightly different needs and motivations. The goal initially is to build a relationship on two levels. First, between the organization building the grassroots network and the volunteer; and next, between the volunteer and the legislator or regulator the organization is trying to influence and/or the community at large. The initial trust and rationale for involvement in the process is dependent on the link between the prospective volunteer and the organization not between the volunteer and the decision-maker. Thus, there are different, and sometimes conflicting, values for achieving participation whether the volunteer is part of a for-profit or a non-profit organization.

One value of a successful grassroots program is two-way communications. That works more easily in a political campaign as the smart candidate seeks the involvement of a volunteer by "listening" to the volunteer. Employing listening skills is often more easily achieved between well-run non-profit organizations and their volunteers because volunteers usually come with a predisposition to advocate based on their own interest. It is a challenge among most for-profit organizations.

The initial goal then is to create and build a relationship first with the organization. Within the for-profit corporate and association world there is often a need to first determine whether those most affected by a decision:

1 have any knowledge of the issue or proposals to change public policy, or the impact of such changes not only on the organization, but also on the workers and the community in which the organization exists;
2 have any idea of how to express their support or opposition to proposals; or
3 with whom to communicate their views.

It is not that potential volunteers are unwilling to become involved if asked, it is usually because they lack information on a proposal's impact, what to do, and when. The reason is that the education on issues among for-profit ventures is usually between none and zero, that is, until a crisis arises. Beyond that, many of those asking for political participation from among those who work for them are usually not accustomed to listening to their people, but are far more comfortable giving orders than joining in a dialogue.[15]

Building a relationship between an organization and a group of potential volunteers begins among those who are most affected by any change in public policy. But where an advocate for a non-profit organization may already have an emotional attachment to an issue, those who are employed by a for-profit organization may not initially have that same attachment. The strength of the relationship will be determined, in part, by the commitment an organization makes to build a program of outreach to its constituent groups. But, it will also be determined, in part, by how each individual assesses the relevance of the issue to themselves, their families, and their communities.

At the outset of this process of building a grassroots organization, the initial group to organize is that group which has or should share an *emotional* attachment to the issue. Because they have an emotional attachment they are referred to as "family." In a for-profit organization this group usually includes employees, retirees, and their spouses. The connection with the issue should be more than a paycheck. In well-run organizations that feeling is based on being treated with respect, enjoying working for the company, and other considerations often reported in employee surveys as having more impact on one's decision to work somewhere.

In the non-profit world those emotionally connected usually includes those who have expressed interest by virtue of joining via a membership, either with dues or on a subscription basis, or on the basis of a contribution. Contributions can be of three kinds: time, talent, or treasure, and treasure can be hard currency or the most precious of all gifts, the use of one's name as publicly supporting the non-profit's cause. A term used to describe these people instead of "family" is "saints."

In the for-profit world there is a second category that includes stockholders, vendors, and possibly customers. They are described as "friends." They stand slightly apart from employees and retirees in one critical way. They share only an *economic* interest in our issue. "Friends" will stay with us unless or until a better option presents itself. If given a stronger economic incentive for deserting, they're gone. Those who are emotionally committed will hang in there. The non-profit world rarely has advocates whose only rationale for involvement is financial.

"Family" or "friends" or "saints" represent at most 10% of the electorate. The next category—"strangers" or "savables"—represents as much as 80% of the electorate. Organizing this group is essential not only because it is the largest, but also because, as such, it represents the balance of power. The nation is governed from the middle even if elections are won at the margins. Hence the endorsement or participation by the "strangers" or "savables" is proof that people without a vested interest in the outcome can be supportive.

One reason for calling them "strangers" is that they start with little or no interest or knowledge in the issue being contested. They often best reflect the person asked by the pollster, "Which is worse—ignorance or apathy?" who responds, "I don't know and I don't care." The challenge to the grassroots organizer, especially in community advocacy but often as well in legislative and political battles, is to convince these people that they should know and they should care.

Customers, along with influentials in the community, may also fall into a third group. Generally, they often have little or no idea that an issue affecting the organization also affects them. That they know nothing means that they are a "stranger," at least initially in terms of the issue. They must be educated and given a reason for joining the effort because they share an *intellectual* attachment to the issue. That means they will become supporters because they "buy into" the rightness of the argument and they agree with the specified course of action. Another term for "strangers" is the "savables."

Whether or not an attempt is made to reach out to the "strangers" or "savables" depends on a number of factors. In a legislative or regulatory effort such an outreach to the general community may not be necessary. Organizing family and friends, the saints, and the influentials in the community, may achieve all that is needed in order to influence a legislator. That determination can depend on a number of factors, the timing of the issue, the budget, the intensity level of debate surrounding the issue, and the level of government.[16]

The approach to the "strangers" or "savables" is done in a manner similar to the approach made in political campaigns: one-on-one. The organizer uses the "multiplier" effect noted earlier to build upon strength from those who support the group as family and friends to those who are not involved. Figure 31.1 shows both the relative strength of the various groups as the battle is launched. The only sure way to build a constituency that includes strangers or the newly converted "savables" is to build a foundation with those who care and then grow the group by reaching out through the committed volunteers to the uninvolved.

Foes, or "sinners," fall into the final category. This group holds as passionately to their view as the family/saints hold to their side of the issue. Understanding the foes and creating a countervailing force, one that balances the scales between the advocates of two sides of an issue, is part of the goal.

The ultimate rationale of grassroots is quite simple. It is to demonstrate to the legislator or regulator that a position is supported by an equal, if not greater, number of people in the community. By so doing, legislators or regulators can be assured that by taking your side they have chosen the prudent course to follow.[17]

Community Advocacy

The third arena that is discrete, but inseparable, is community advocacy. It is the ultimate lynchpin under-girding how society governs itself. It reflects the way in which communities view change—accepting or resisting based on many factors. Usually the goal is monumental and takes years to accomplish. Community advocacy campaigns can last decades if not centuries before the desired outcome is achieved. They require enormous perseverance.

Victories are often miniscule. Volunteers can become easily discouraged. They may begin with one or two "stout-hearted" types who cry "ouch," who are then heard by others who agree that the pain must stop however one defines that pain or identifies its cause. Those who begin a movement may or may not be able to carry it forward alone. They are usually led by non-profit or non-governmental organizations.

Examples of the impact of a community advocacy campaign include changing community attitudes toward who is permitted to vote or community acceptance of new or different lifestyles.

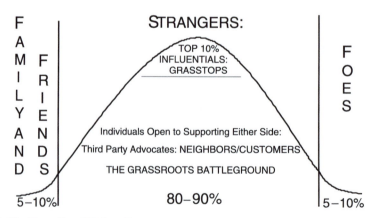

Figure 31.1. The Strengths of Various Groups

It may include acceptance of the notion that children have rights, that "pressing '1' for English" is appropriate in a bilingual society, that nuclear power is acceptable as a viable energy source, that wearing seat belts makes sense and is not some imposition on personal rights, that animals have rights that supersede any notion that they exist only for the pleasure of humans, that "caveat emptor" is not an acceptable warning to consumers, that one's ownership of land is anything more than stewardship, or that women have rights equal to men in *all* areas of life.

Often those seeking redress are challenging the status quo, and possibly those in charge, to change existing mores and/or open the process so that change can occur. Some would argue that this is accomplished via laws and political campaigns. But campaigns, laws, and regulations represent mere process. Community advocacy requires a change in minds. To pass a law that someone of color can live anywhere means nothing if a white person is unwilling to live next door to a black person. Many individuals still refuse to wear seat belts. Passing laws requiring all measurements be done using the metric system was meaningless since people were unwilling to let go of standard US measurements and learn something new. Despite efforts to implement the change from the use of fahrenheit and miles to celsius and kilometers, the public was unwilling to abide by federal law. With community advocacy the ideal goal is a win–win outcome: the changes sought are adapted by the community at large, new mores are accepted.

The process of building community advocacy is similar in many ways to building a political or lobbying campaign. Starting from a source of strength, those who are known and trusted, and building out to those whose help may be needed. If approached one-on-one, hopefully those who represent the core and those who can assist will respond in a positive way and become active in the grassroots effort to shape both public opinion and a new public policy.

The process of building community advocacy is different in two major ways from building a political or lobbying campaign. First, evoking change in community attitudes requires addressing people's *fear of change*, especially of the unknown. Second, finding a way to *bridge* from that fear to the new way of looking at things that makes sense to those who have resisted, either because they begin to see that it is the right thing to do and/or because they need give up nothing, and are in no way truly inhibited.

The first challenge is fear, that very powerful impediment to change so often fermented during political and legislative/regulatory battles. In community advocacy efforts this fear is often reinforced by the tendency of most people to "go along and get along." This is especially true if people hold the current majority views or believe that they will prosper under the current system. The perpetrators of fear, truly brilliant tacticians who pawn themselves off as strategists, succeed by building a political effort that appeals to the reptilian portion of the brain that has but one response function, "flight or fight."

The message reinforces the majoritarian view of how life is and should be. It is a message that focuses on a human tendency to "not rock the boat"; "life's too short," "what's wrong with the way things are?," "that's the way it has always been," and "that's politics" are among the many phrases heard frequently for either one's reticence or resistance to change. Add to these and others the show-stopper: "Yes, we should change, but not now." The speaker really means not ever, but hyperbole being a well-honed practice finds refuge in the alleged support the speaker will offer at "the right time," a time generally meaning either, "after I'm no longer in charge," or "after I'm dead."

Alexis de Tocqueville warned the United States in the 1830s that the single greatest impediment to its success as a democracy would be the inclination toward majoritarianism. Were de Tocqueville writing today, he might have described majoritarianism by using the following seven examples of confrontations between those who resist change and those who seek change within the US body politic:

1   The economic "haves" do not willingly give power to the economic "have-nots."
2   The Caucasian community does not willingly give power to the non-Caucasian.
3   Men do not willingly give power to women.
4   English-speaking people do not willingly give power to non-English speakers.
5   Christians do not willingly give power to non-Christians.
6   Straight people do not willingly give power to gays.
7   Persons without physical or mental challenges do not willingly give power to those with special needs.[18]

However, the author Saul D. Alinsky[19] argues that society is not divided simply between the "haves" and the "have-nots," but rather there exists a third group—the "have-a-little-want-mores." The third group exists in all seven confrontational situations, becoming ultimately the balance of power that can repel change or embrace change. Those who are seeking power need to appeal to and win over this middle group. The most powerful argument is often "fairness," as the center may be moved to action if it senses not simply unfairness, but stridency in its strategy and bullying in its tactics.

Overcoming the fear prompting resistance to change often requires one or more "champions," individuals who can rally others to the cause. In legislative and regulatory battles a champion is at least one member of the legislature or regulatory board who will carry the fight internally. Such individuals are in a power position and thus able to do battle from the inside. In a political campaign the champion is the candidate. In a referendum or initiative the champion may be selected or self-select, but the individual is part of a movement that has a pre-ordained end date. Such individuals, unlike those for a community advocacy cause, may not be committed to a multi-year effort.

Champions in community advocacy efforts often become champions by virtue of their single-minded determination to change what they believe to be an injustice. They may gain fame because of their actions, and the acknowledgment of their role may or may not be achieved in their lifetime. These individuals have charisma and either own or are able to gain access to a podium that commands community attention. They keep volunteers committed when otherwise the results would cause spirits to flag. They are keys to the "bridging" process by which a community begins to embrace the new paradigm.[20]

That person may be a Martin Luther King, Jr, for the civil rights movement or a Ralph Nader for the consumer movement. Jody Williams won the Nobel Peace Prize and is credited as being the moving force behind the global effort to ban land mines, but some contend her effort really expanded and gained momentum once she had a champion, Princess Diana.

Candice Lightner is credited with being the moving force that sparked a whole new attitude toward drinking and driving. Before Mothers Against Drunk Driving (MADD) came on the scene, the prevailing view in the community was to blame the drink. Today we blame the drinkers and hold them accountable for their actions. The anti-tobacco movement had many champions, but an early one, John Banzhaf III, is given a lot of credit for challenging the industry initially. Today it is rare for people to smoke in public in the United States, a change in public behavior that has evolved over some fifty years.

There are challenges to change. The first is to have a plan to *reform* the system. A plan that calls for revolution is doomed to failure. A true radical according to Alinsky and others is someone who wants the system to work equally well for all, to reform the way things currently work.

Others who have labored in this field offer an equally compelling first step, to link the call for reform to a challenge that those in charge (1) live by the same rules they impose on others and (2) enforce the rules equally. In both instances the organizers are hopeful that the media will follow its traditional role "to comfort the afflicted and afflict the comforted."

In the United States, attitudes also shift like a pendulum from right to left, and then back again, every decade or so.[21] As these shifts occur, an opportunity is often created to fuel the momentum for changes in community attitudes advocated by a multitude of different groups. The Vietnam war helped cause such a shift in the 1960s, which presented an opportunity to advance the cause of civil rights, the rights of women, environmental rights, and consumer rights. The aftermath of the Iraq war may contribute to a similar shift today propelling the agendas of those who seek other changes in community attitudes.

When one person shouts, "ouch," and is moved to action, the first step is to identify others who share the emotional attachment to the issue. For example, when a few courageous individuals were first willing to share their experience of being sexually abused by priests and nuns in the Roman Catholic Church, it was only by reaching out to one another and hearing one another's stories that the abused came to realize they collectively shared an even greater indignity. Each thought their abuser had been dealt with and each was led to believe by the bishops they spoke to that their experience was unique. They only learned by coming together that the entire hierarchy of the Church knew of the problem, was involved in a conspiracy to cover up the abuse, and pretended it never existed except in isolation. This information fueled the establishment of a national organization of victims ready to reach beyond the Church to demand accountability. In this particular example, the victims of abuse who are leading what is becoming a global movement are not simply "family," but truly "saints" and the opposing Church hierarchy the "sinners."

Wining over the "savables," called in another context the "strangers," requires both a lot of work and time. Solid research is essential. Telling the actual, that is, non-embellished, truth is equally essential.[22] In politics there is an old adage, you get one chance to lie, never a second. Building a network of allies that will be patient and seek change gradually with measured goals that can be used both to continue to rally one's own troops and as evidence to those who resist by saying, "wait," that the wait is over for that stage and time to move on toward the next stage.

Incrementalism is often useful to those in charge and may be acceptable at times. But the pace of change can be frustrating to those who seek reform. Changes in community attitudes can take years. These changes may result in efforts to enact laws and regulations, and be the subject of political campaigns, but such laws, regulations, and candidates ultimately succeed because there is a change in community attitudes, what is referred to as the *authorizing environment*.[23]

When change does occur, members of a community begin to think differently about a subject, be it drinking and driving or smoking anywhere anytime, or acceptance of those who speak different languages, lead different lifestyles, are physically challenged, or see the role of religion in their lives differently than the majority. Ideally this change is a win–win for the community.

Years ago a cartoon in the *New Yorker* showed a man grabbing his coat as he was intent on rushing to leave an office saying to all in earshot, "I must hurry. I am their leader and they have left." This cartoon succinctly captures the challenge to community advocacy efforts. For the effort to get leaders to move is based on their fear that doing anything will cost them their leadership role. Or as one author puts it if politicians have their finger to the wind to test public opinion, the role of the community advocate is to become someone who changes the direction of the wind.[24] That is the ultimate challenge and goal of any group seeking to change the prevailing view of the community in the United States. To some extent the same is true in other democracies as well.

Democracies Around the World

At the outset, it is essential to realize that building constituent support by an organization for its side of an issue is emerging albeit slowly and with much resistance in many parts of the world. There is evidence, however, that grassroots mobilization works in some situations.

For example, Canadians have long embraced the concept of voter feedback between citizens of a riding, the Canadian equivalent of a US congressional or state legislative district, and their elected member of either the national parliament or provincial parliament. A former Canadian external affairs minister said that not only did grassroots work in Canada, it was often the *only* way to bring pressure upon the government when an ill-advised policy is being considered. Many corporations and associations in Canada have adopted grassroots efforts as a tool in their lobbying arsenal.

Australia has also embraced grassroots advocacy. In the early 1980s, the Australian Soft Drink Association put together a grassroots program to oppose mandatory deposits on every bottle or can of soft drink sold. The campaign included linking employees to their parliamentary districts in much the same way employees are linked to their legislative districts in the United States. The goal was to get those members of parliament who were in swing districts to carry the message to their leadership in Canberra that this issue had detrimental impact on jobs. Success was achieved.

Grassroots efforts in Britain are emerging as a viable tool in some situations. Generally, the careers of members of parliament depend on voting in line with parties: they must follow the instructions of the Party "whip." There are some "free votes," or votes on issues where the political party makes no judgment, on which grassroots campaigns in the UK have the most impact. But even on proposals based on party platforms grassroots efforts can have some impact if only to delay or slightly amend the measure or its effectiveness.

One such example is the recent battle over whether to permit the continuation of fox hunting with hounds. Two well-resourced coalitions of pressure groups had been fighting over the issue of fox hunting for years. One faction supported the status quo. Its position was supported by the Conservative Party when that party was in power. When Labour came to power there was a move to ban fox hunting. A major grassroots effort, however, succeeded in delaying Labour's attempt. A group of grassroots activists organized as Countryside Alliance and mobilized its members. A defining moment in the campaign came when the Alliance brought an estimated 400,000 supporters to London.

London was brought to a standstill as "ordinary country folk" came to protest about the intentions of a Government apparently made up of left-wing intellectual urbanites. This outpouring of real grassroots opposition left Labour in a quandary and looking for cover. Labour temporarily abandoned its effort.

Differences do exist between the way grassroots impacts decisions made in the United States and in other democratic nations. Timing, outcome, and impact may vary as well as other differences. Outside of the US the timing of grassroots efforts must be done earlier. It is not possible to wait until just before a vote is taken. Party discipline means that the party caucus will decide and once that decision is made in caucus the likelihood of passage is essentially inevitable. That means grassroots effort must be organized *pre-caucus*, or before the government has decided to proceed with its plan. The goal is to have backbenchers advocating one's position during the deliberations in caucus.

The outcome is also different. The design of the US political process, be it for campaigns or legislative initiatives, is confrontational. Compromise may occur but the system is designed so the issues are constantly under review and rarely settled. The parliamentary systems, reflecting their countries' political cultures, seek an outcome that is truly *collaborative* rather than confrontational. If the party in power has misread the collaborative process, the "out" party will regain a majority.

In the United States, building a collaborative effort in the political campaign or legislative and regulatory tussle is secondary to the "no holds barred" approach. Collaboration seems almost "Un-American." But even in the United States, success in community advocacy requires collaboration. The process of getting legislative bodies or decision-makers around the world to take action begins by asking some of the same questions one asks in the United States. These include:

- Whose ox is being gored? Who beyond our company is being hurt financially?
- Who will make the decision?
- What is the process they follow to make a decision?
- Who can reach the decision-makers? Whose counsel might the decision-makers seek? Who do they trust? Why do they trust them?
- What message will sway the open-minded decision-maker?
- How do those affected make their views known? How can a coalition be formed?
- What can each member of the coalition do?
- What realistically can be accomplished in terms of killing the proposition, amending it, or having it delayed?
- How might an adverse decision affect the community?
- How is the community alerted to the adverse consequences?
- How do individual people make known their displeasure with any proposal?
- How can that collective displeasure be channeled to the decision-makers?
- How is media involvement built?
- Is the proposal responding to a "real" or "perceived" need and, if the latter, how is the need presented as a case to the media, the coalition, and the grassroots component so they will rally to the defense?
- In short, how is a grassroots program developed or "a fire built"?

The great secret in building any grassroots effort has been stated: *listening* to potential supporters. One obstacle grassroots efforts have around the world is the fact that elected officials resist listening to their constituents between elections. In the United States, elected officials are somewhat more attentive because they must create their own majority coalition of supporters, often separate from any party effort. In other democracies party discipline says that the party wins or loses together, not as individuals. Thus, a misreading of public opinion may have no consequence to the elected individual, and perhaps only to the party or the governing process itself.

A recent example is the referendum defeat in The Netherlands of ratification of the European Constitution. Members of the both the Dutch parliament and the European Parliament appeared out of contact with any voters and immune from public pressure when they were stunned that the measure was defeated. Dutch people when polled said that no one had ever asked them how they felt about decisions made in Brussels. No grassroots effort in support of the Constitution was initiated. Grassroots efforts in the case would have accomplished the twin goals of any grassroots effort—educating the constituents and providing a forum for *listening* to all views. (For a discussion of grassroots activity at the European Union, see Chapter 34 by Marco Althaus.)

An example of a grassroots effort that educated but did not provide a forum for listening is the PRI party effort recently in the State of Mexico. In an effort to win an election, the party conducted a grassroots that included an excellent educational effort. But by the admission of party leaders their plan did not include providing forums for potential supporters to voice their views. This ultimately led to the party's defeat.

As these examples illustrate grassroots effort as an organizing tool has not fully emerged in many democracies outside the United States. But as issues move about the world at warp speed and more people gain access via the Internet to new ideas, the elected politicians are finding more and more that they are more like the person in the *New Yorker* cartoon, a leader whose people have left. It is prompting many, especially those among the out party, to seek advice on how to build a more powerful link between themselves and the voters.

Grassroots organizing, enabling those with a view to come together and then to reach out to educate and listen to others, is central to the process of good governance. Should these concepts be adapted globally that adaptation may well represent the most important export of the democratic experiment known as the United States.

If done properly, with local buy-in from the bottom-up and adapted to local customs, as opposed to being forced upon people as in Iraq or other forms of US-led proselytizing, such activism may well be worth yet another Nobel Peace Prize.[25] That would be nice.

Notes

1 Even the uncertainty around primary dates for determining delegates to presidential nominating conventions and some other U.S. elections is an aberration, easily dealt with, versus the unpredictability of even a general election date in most parliamentary systems.

2 Efforts to convert those who oppose the candidate or issue are rarely successful and considered a waste of time, money, and talent.

3 Party rule ended some believe following the 1962 and subsequent Supreme Court decisions known collectively as "one man one vote" especially when coupled with those laws and decisions that outlawed patronage. Many believe the demise of the political party as an entity that organized constituencies, funded candidacies, and determined "via smoke-filled rooms" who the candidates would be, led to the rise of the modern political consultant as "hired gun" who may work for many candidates but for only one candidate in one specific election. Today, candidates must fund their own campaigns and create their own corps of volunteers.

4 Democratic consultants have reported that Bill Clinton had friends from Arkansas who went door-to-door in other states. Al Gore did not have such a corps of volunteers from Tennessee validating his effort.

5 In an issue campaign such "influentials" are recruited to chair the committee that either supports or opposes the proposition, and who they, in turn, know become targets for early recruitment.

6 I was first introduced to this example of a hate-based campaign early in my career while engaged as a consultant in 1970 to J. Glenn Beall, a Republican candidate for the U.S. Senate in Maryland. It was obvious that winning would be a challenge in a "blue" 3-to-1 Democratic state. However, Beall won, even as statewide all the Democratic candidates won, a fact attributed in part to the existence of a group of some 12,000 voters called Committee Against Tydings (CAT), the incumbent Joseph D. Tydings. CAT despised Tydings for his anti-gun stance. No contact between the Beall campaign and CAT ever occurred.

7 "Switch" voters were distinguished from "swing" voters, the latter prepared to swing from one party to another based on circumstances in which anger was felt across the board and one party in power at many levels would be swept out of power by the challenging party, a phenomenon not as frequent as "switch" voting.

8 Dennis W. Johnson states that "under the guise of a legitimate poll, anonymous telephone callers feed damaging or misleading information about a candidate, attempting to persuade or change the opinion of the contacted voter." Dennis W. Johnson, *No Place for Amateurs: How Political Consultants are Reshaping American Democracy*, 2nd ed. (New York: Routledge, 2007), 158.

9 The Republican strategist Karl Rove has said that as many as 225 variables may be cross-tabulated in order to target a specific household as being approachable to either "switch" and/or to turn out to decrease the normal margin of "blue" votes by which a precinct is carried.

10 The Internet as a political communications tool contributes, in this author's opinion, to the divisiveness in the United States, supporting Putnam's thesis that as a nation we are increasingly "bowling alone." Robert D. Putnam, *Bowling Alone: The Collapse and Revival of American Community* (New York: Simon and Schuster, 2001).

11 It has been said that Franklin D. Roosevelt would tell lobbyists on some issues: "You have convinced me. Now go out and force me." He meant build a fire of support among those who might vote for him.

12 Gladwell's *The Tipping Point* follows by some fifty years David Riesman's *The Lonely Crowd* which also noted the unique role some play to influence others and move information within society. Malcolm Gladwell, *The Tipping Point: How Little Things Can Make a Big Difference* (Boston, MA: Back Bay Books, 2002); David Riesman, *The Lonely Crowd: A Study of the Changing American Character* (New York: Doubleday Anchor, 1953).

13 Jon Berry and Ed Keller, *The Influentials: One American in Ten Tells the Other Nine How to Vote, Where to Eat, and What to Buy* (New York: The Free Press, 2003).

14 There is more clarity for regulatory proposals because the regulatory body when publishing the proposal is legally bound to establish a specific time for comment.

15 This may change with the Internet. In *The Naked Corporation*, Tapscott and Ticoll note that as Internet access can lay bare an organization, they admonish all: "If you are going to be naked [due to possible

internal transgressions being made public by disgruntled employees] you'd better be buff." Don Tapscott and David Ticoll, *The Naked Corporation: How the Age of Transparency will Revolutionize Business* (New York: Free Press, 2003).

16 To sway a U.S. senator or member of Congress may require a huge effort, while to sway a member of a state legislature may only require a small effort, and even fewer contacts with a city or county official.

17 In more candid moments some former legislators have admitted that if they have to choose between doing what is right and what will get them re-elected, they will chose the latter. The grassroots effort is designed to assure legislators that they can achieve both goals, much as Roosevelt suggested.

18 Some would add an emerging eighth: Some humans do not willing acknowledge the right of animals to be treated with dignity.

19 See Saul D. Alinksy, *Rules for Radicals* (New York: Vintage, 1989) and Saul D. Alinsky, *Reveille for Radicals* (New York: Vintage, 1989).

20 Champions often have major detractors who do something stupid in their opposition, thereby bolstering the image and impact of the champion. For example, when General Motors was exposed for having attempted to smear Ralph Nader when Nader revealed the company's questionable auto safety practices, Nader's consumer effort gained widespread support.

21 See Arthur M. Schlesinger, Jr, *The Cycles of American History* (Boston, MA: Houghton Mifflin, 1986).

22 For example, the agenda of the pro-choice movement was set back when one of its spokesperson minimized the actual number of late-term abortions.

23 See Edward A. Grefe and Martin Linsky, *The New Corporate Activism: Harnessing the Power of Grassroots Tactics for Your Organization* (New York: McGraw-Hill, 1995).

24 See Jim Wallis, *God's Politics: Why the Right Gets It Wrong and the Left Doesn't Get It* (New York: HarperOne, 2005).

25 The one given for the global grassroots effort to ban land mines was the first.

32

Political Consultants, Interest Groups and Issue Advocacy Work

A Lasting Relationship

Douglas A. Lathrop

Over the past three decades, political consultants have proven themselves to be opportunistic and resourceful innovators responsible for introducing focus groups and "astroturf" campaigning into mainstream politics. During that time, the profession evolved from its basic origins with the Madison Avenue advertising executives who moonlighted as campaign operatives and the handful of academics determined to put their empirical knowledge to use into a specialized, professional workforce numbering in the tens of thousands. One of the reasons for the rapid growth of political consulting has been the willingness of practitioners to probe new territory and take advantage of political change.

Nowhere is this more evident than in the world of issue advocacy. Since the early 1990s political consultants have put talents honed in candidate campaigns to use in managing issue strategies on behalf of interest groups. In fact, issue advocacy work has become a mainstay in the industry illustrated by the amount of money committed to it in recent years. According to an analysis conducted by the Annenberg Public Policy Center of the University of Pennsylvania, during the 108th Congress (2003–2005) interest groups spent $404 million on issue advertising with many of those millions finding their way to political consultants.[1] Perhaps more telling is the peer recognition of issue advocacy work demonstrated by the number of American Association of Political Consultants "Pollie" awards given to consultants who specialize in issue advertising (twenty in 2006 compared to four in 1996).[2] It is no surprise that consultants would occupy a lucrative perch within the cottage industry of issue advocacy. After all, they possess the necessary skills and experience coveted by interest groups seeking to influence public discourse.

Today's consultants can provide every service required to run an issue advocacy campaign, ranging from detailed, poll-tested strategic advice to finely tuned wordsmithing and evocative advertising. The robust market for political consultants is a clear sign that they have successfully adapted their practices and business model to the needs of interests groups. Indeed, the influence of consultants on issue advocacy activities transcends their presence. Today, many interest groups subscribe to the notion that on high-profile issues a good "inside" strategy, comprised of face-to-face lobbying and elite contact, should be complemented by an equally worthy "outside" strategy.[3] Thus, the campaign ethic exemplified by political consultants has been embraced by interest groups and it is evident in the tactics they use. The belief in the power of mass marketing, polling and focus groups is so strong, in fact, that some interest groups have gone so far as to eliminate the contract middleman completely and have created permanent positions for campaign operatives within their organizations.[4]

This chapter will endeavor to answer three important questions raised by the burgeoning relationship between consultants and issue advocacy. The first is why consultants have migrated from their traditional work with candidates to issue advocacy. Political consultants were undoubtedly attracted by the money, but why did interest groups, beginning in the 1990s seek out the counsel of political consultants? What changes in the political realm helped cement the link between interest groups and consultants? The second question explores their effectiveness. Some skeptics suggest that the presence of political consultants at the heart of issue advocacy campaigns is more the function of clever self-promotion on their part than documented impact. Are consultant-inspired issue campaigns an effective way to influence public policy? Finally, accepting the fact that political consultants have ingratiated themselves into issue advocacy what are the larger implications for the legislative process and governance in general?

From a legislative process perspective, the introduction of campaign tactics into public policy debates forces us to confront normative questions about the nature of governing versus campaign. What political consultants bring to issue advocacy is a win or lose mentality shaped by the zero-sum game of political elections. A campaign is a high stakes conflict in which there is a decisive outcome; it is not a collaborative ongoing exercise like lawmaking. Do the inclinations of consultants to simplify the policy process into a contest defined by winners and losers have a distorting and potentially harmful effect on the exchanges necessary to pass laws in a system where today's enemy could be tomorrow's ally? There are also legitimate concerns about the role political consultants' play in tipping the balance of power further in favor of moneyed interests. One need not be an adherent of political scientist E.E. Schattschneider to suspect that multi-million dollar issue advocacy campaigns can amplify the already loud voice of a well-heeled interest group often to the disadvantage of the unorganized.[5]

Before delving into these questions, several basic definitions are in order. Despite the catch-all phrase, political consulting is a varied and segmented profession. Under the rubric of political consulting there are media experts, pollsters, demographers and an assortment of marketing gurus. They can provide to a candidate or an interest group a complete playbook from a macro strategic level down to the words and phrases used in a print campaign. When I use the terms political consultant and political consulting in this chapter it will be with the broadest possible meaning. Second, we need to articulate what we mean by issue advocacy. Issue advocacy can be defined as conducting a campaign in order to influence the course of public policy. It can take many different forms including, but not limited to, television advertising, grassroots activity and other forms of electronic and print outreach. In the context of this discussion it includes issue advertising in all mediums, but also the background research that goes into creating a final campaign, namely polling, focus group testing and the like. In most cases, the final print or television ad is the product of months of research conducted behind the scenes. That work is almost as important to shaping the terms of the debate as the ad itself. There is no single point of contact with respect to political consulting and issue advocacy; they are entwined from the start to the finish.

Change and Opportunity—Political Consultants Move into Issue Advocacy

In 2000, American University professor James A. Thurber conducted a survey of over 200 political consultants in an attempt to bring more rigor to the study of the profession and to create a rough taxonomy.[6] One of the many interesting details to emerge was the large number of consultants who had eschewed candidate work and operated almost exclusively in the policy realm. The reasons they offered were manifold, ranging from better pay and more job stability to a greater sense of personal accomplishment. Yet, political consultants desire to do more work with interest groups has to be matched with opportunity. Issue-based political consulting has flourished because of a confluence of factors: the rise of television and mass media politics; politicians' corresponding belief in the power and persuasiveness of advertising and mass media outreach; and, unrelated to the first two, new legal restrictions on candidate campaign spending that has inadvertently channeled money toward issue advocacy.

The story of political communication in America during the last half-century is largely the tale of how technology has changed the way we engage in politics. Inventions such as the television and the Internet have had a profound impact on the way information is disseminated and understood. Political communications scholars continue to wrestle with weighty issues stemming from the changes wrought by technology on our political system, but it is an accepted theory in the discipline that the medium through which politics is conducted has a direct effect on the underlying message.[7] Mass media politics shapes and binds the ways in which the public perceives the political process and how politicians, in turn, communicate with their constituents. The sheer size of our country and the clipped pace of our lifestyle practically dictates the ways in which people receive their political information. Effective communication through television and the Internet requires an understanding of how they change and filter a message. The state of affairs provides a partial explanation for interest groups' willingness to spend millions of dollars on advertising. In their view, advertising and issue promotion do a variety of important tasks such as defining terms, curtailing or setting agendas, raising the profile of a viewpoint, generating free media and encouraging public support.[8]

Pursuing an "outside" lobbying strategy through a mass communications medium such as television and the Internet, or even investing in something smaller such as a print or direct mail campaign, requires interest groups to build a compelling narrative.[9] Here is where the political consultant provides the most added value. Political consultants are hired to build an effective media strategy from the ground up: from poll testing phrases and reference points to storyboarding the ads and finally to providing strategic advice about the roll out and the subsequent capture of free media exposure. Interest groups, even large well-funded groups, rarely have the internal expertise or capacity to coordinate an "outside" lobbying plan.

In a legislative setting it can work this way. Let us say that a group of life insurance companies is promoting a bill that would provide preferential tax treatment to annuity products that they sell.[10] The bill itself is complicated and the topic is esoteric so garnering support on Capitol Hill is a challenge. To aid the on-the-ground lobbying effort the insurance companies pool their money and hire an outside consultant to "brand" the issue and build a media campaign designed to foster broader awareness of the bill. The first action the consultants take is to drop the stultifying terminology used by the companies to describe the bill and replace it with phrases that ordinary citizens can understand. Instead of providing capital gains treatment for annuity payouts, the legislation is recast as a way to give people a "paycheck for life." Until then the most impressive and relevant feature of the legislation—that it will provide a way for individuals to safely supplement a pension or Social Security with a steady stream of income—was obscured by confusing language.

Once the new brand is established, the next step is promotion. Since this is a relatively low-profile issue, the focus is on print ads with a corresponding website to share more information. Both the ads and the website communicate an accessible narrative that describes the benefits of a paycheck for life for older Americans while simultaneously downplaying the role of the insurance industry. For the companies, the consultants have provided a touchstone phrase and a storyline that they can parrot in all of their subsequent lobbying visits. While the fate of the legislation will not likely be determined by the new marketing plan, it is clear that contracting an "outside" lobbying strategy was a valuable exercise.

Interest groups are not given to spending money without a good reason. They invest in issue advocacy to bolster their traditional lobbying efforts because they believe it works. Undoubtedly some of the faith in the power of ads and focus groups is based on high-profile anecdotal examples, like the "Harry and Louise" marketing campaign on the Clinton health care proposal. Yet, political science literature provides further explanation at a theoretical level for the influence of issue advocacy on the mindset of legislators. In the *Logic of Congressional Action*, R. Douglas Arnold, building on seminal work conducted by David Mayhew and Richard F. Fenno, Jr, argues that risk averse members of Congress are always concerned with latent opinions of inattentive publics.[11] Arnold maintains that these obscured and unfocused sentiments can surface quickly and with great effect. Capable legislators endeavor to anticipate public opinion and respond accordingly. Issue advocacy in this context is simply another way for interest groups to activate the public and to have them serve as another voice in the lobbying effort.

Although there is some debate whether the use of political consultants to stimulate a public response can alter the trajectory of legislation on a consistent basis, it is an established fact that a vigorous public reaction will gain legislators' attention. From the legislators' point of view, the dynamic is so simple to understand it is almost intuitive. The "Harry and Louise" ads used to defeat the Clinton health care reform effort are a good example of the feedback loop created by an effective issue advocacy. Even though the ads were seen in a small portion of the country, they were re-broadcast in news stories and did an excellent job in crystallizing latent doubts and the nascent hostility toward big government.[12] As the message promoted by the ads began to resonate with the general public, representatives took stock. According to interest group scholars Darrell M. West and Burdett A. Loomis,

> the reason it [issue advertising] works is simple. Constituents have a high degree of credibility that no Washington lobbyist can match. They are not hired guns, they have not sold their soul for special interests, and they reflect the concerns of ordinary citizens.[13]

Interestingly, an issue advocacy campaign does not need to move public opinion to be effective, it merely has to leave the impression with elite decision-makers that it has.

The triumph of mass media politics explains in part why interest groups would seek out the service of political consultants, but the astonishing growth in issue advocacy is not simply a matter of choice. Changes in campaign finance laws have prompted groups to put their money into issue advocacy by curtailing and in some cases eliminating other options. For decades, good government groups and public interest lobbies such as Public Citizen and Common Cause have urged the Congress to restrict what they deem to be the corrosive influence of money in politics. Since the early 1970s until the passage of the Bipartisan Campaign Finance Reform Act (BCRA) in 2002, campaign finance reformers and their allies in Congress made incremental progress in limiting the roles money can play in politics. However, the overarching ambition of reformers has been constrained by judicial decisions intended to protect freedom of speech. The land-mark Supreme Court decision *Buckley v. Valeo* (1976) created two spheres of political speech: unregulated issue advocacy and regulated express advocacy.[14] The court essentially stated that it was permissible for the government to restrict political advertising that featured candidates but that efforts to curb issue oriented advertising or outreach amounted to an unconstitutional breach of the First Amendment. The predictable outcome of the bifurcation was a gradual migration of interest group funding toward unregulated issue advocacy. By the mid-1990s interest groups had blurred the distinction between issue advocacy and express advocacy to the point that reformers sought further legislation to remedy the problem. The BCRA widened the category of impermissible communications and created a proximity trigger that prevents campaign advertising that refer to federal candidates within a sixty-day period before a general election or thirty days before a primary. However, perhaps owing to their losing experience in the courts, reformers left out of the BCRA a large and growing component of spending: true issue advocacy. All interest groups retain the right to spend unlimited funds on issue ads and communications provided they do not mention candidates. The allowance for true issue advocacy has diverted funds that may at one time have been used to challenge sitting members of Congress and are instead used to pressure them on specific topics.

The Effectiveness of Political Consultants in Issue Advocacy

The legend of "Harry and Louise" aside, it is difficult, if not impossible, to attribute the success or failure of a policy to an issue advocacy campaign. However, it is not as hard to find cases where, on the margins, issue advocacy succeeded in influencing the outcome of a policy fight. Two examples, the battle to repeal the estate tax and President George W. Bush's ambitious plan to alter the structure of Social Security, present situations where political consultants at the behest of interest groups were a notable addition.

The crusade to repeal the estate tax is an illustrative example of how political consultants and the tactics they pioneered can impact public policy debates. Through clever marketing, "grass-tops" campaigning and rhetorical flourish, a small number of interest groups were able to frame the debate and even redefine the issue to their advantage.[15] Advocates for repeal worked with Republican wordsmith and pollster Frank I. Luntz to build a narrative that had broad based appeal but little resemblance to reality. The result was an overwhelming bipartisan vote to repeal a tax that the Treasury Department claims affects less than 1% of tax filers.[16] According to the critics, the effort to repeal the estate tax was the quintessential case of form triumphing over substance.

During the late 1990s a small group of wealthy families formed an alliance of convenience with the small business lobby around the idea of repealing the estate tax. For wealthy families and individuals, the reason was self-evident. Billionaires such as the Gallos family, the California vintners, and the Mars family, famous for making M&Ms and other candies, were loath to see their businesses disrupted by the estate tax. These families maintained personal control over their financial empires, but the cost of the estate tax would probably mean that the companies would have to become shareholder-owned C corporations in order to stay viable. Even though most small businesses avoided paying the tax, small business owners also had to budget for the potential liability. Small businesses and family farmers resented the costs of estate planning and felt that the tax was a serious threat to continuing a business to the next generation.[17] Although the Republican-led Congress was ideologically disposed to reform the estate tax, outright repeal was seen by many insiders as a steep challenge. The enormous cost of full repeal and its relatively small audience had kept the Republicans from passing legislation.

Supporters understood that the easiest way to secure a spot on the congressional agenda was to generate the impression of widespread grassroots support. Through phone calls, letters and face-to-face meetings interest groups such as the National Federation of Independent Businesses (NFIB), the American Farm Bureau Federation, and the National Cattlemen's Association made estate tax repeal a high-profile issue. Meanwhile, the umbrella lobbying group, The Family Business Estate Tax Coalition, looked to construct a readily shared storyline. For this they turned to Frank I. Luntz, the coauthor of the Republican Party's famous mission statement the "Contract with America." Luntz used focus groups to discern the best way to sell repeal. According to his research, support for repeal peaked when the issue was recast as the death tax. Calling it the death tax, while technically inaccurate, was an inspirational choice and enabled proponents to capitalize on a boost in negativity ratings that followed from pairing the tax with the death of a loved one. The print campaign that followed built on the theme with the tag line "because death shouldn't be a taxable event." The imagery of a wake being disrupted by a visit from the Internal Revenue Service generated a visceral reaction. In addition, his research indicated that repeal groups should highlight the emotional stories of potential tax victims. They had to, in effect, erase the image of the plutocrats such as the Gettys or the Rockefellers and replace it with ma and pa farmer who just wanted to pass the family plot along to their children.

Following his advice and the counsel of other strategists, the groups mined their membership lists for families that fitted the contrived profile. The result was a consistent and persuasive storyline with real people at its core that helped redefine the estate tax debate. The rebranding of the estate tax into the death tax was so compelling and so complete that groups opposed to repeal were forced to confront the truth that clever marketing and powerful narratives were too much for data-driven facts. Shortly after the Congress voted to repeal the estate tax, opponents, proving that imitation is the sincerest form of flattery, reorganized around stronger marketing strategy. While it was too late for them to defeat the vote, the new lobbying pitch incorporated its own symbolism based on the notorious behavior of some the scions of America's wealthiest families instead of dry tax statistics.[18]

Another example of the power of well-crafted issue advocacy affecting the policy process is found in the opposition to President Bush's Social Security reform. In that case liberal interest groups operating outside the official channels of legislative power successfully turned back the president by imposing their terms and vocabulary on the debate. They deliberately crafted words and phrases intended to engender doubt and apprehension among the general public. Supporters of the president's plan were caught flatfooted in the public relations battle and before the year was out had to admit defeat.

The seeds that germinated into President Bush's Social Security reform plan were planted years earlier by scholars working in conservative think tanks. In places such as the Heritage Foundation and the Cato Institute, ideological hostility to the New Deal program was married to a growing concern that the program was on a fiscally unsustainable path. President Bush recognized the long-term challenges that faced Social Security and wanted to use a reform plan as an opportunity to promote his ownership agenda. In 2001, he appointed a blue ribbon commission to explore solutions to Social Security's fiscal problems. The commission, however, was not given an open-ended charter. According to the executive order that created the panel, it had to adhere to certain restrictions. Current recipients and those near retirement, for example, could not see benefit reductions under any reform proposal. He also mandated that the panel produce a plan that would embrace the controversial idea of creating individual accounts within Social Security.[19] The president not only wanted to address the solvency crisis facing the seventy-year-old pension program, but also he wanted to refashion it so that it retained its insurance value whilst looking more like a 401(k) plan.

President Bush's desire to incorporate the conservative values of individual ownership and responsibility into Social Security drew immediate protest from seniors groups such as the AARP and from liberal policy groups who believed that private Social Security accounts would erode the social compact that had been a hallmark of the program. The individual accounts stipulation spawned a vigorous policy debate among academics and high-level government officials about the nature of Social Security and the needs for its future. While economists were sparring over the questions about the rate of return and the wisdom of investing in stock portfolios, partisans were organizing an aggressive campaign to halt the effort before it could be considered.

In an attempt to undermine the president's agenda, a host of progressive groups came together under the umbrella of Americans United to Protect Social Security. In short order they built an impressive machine comprised of grassroots activism, press outreach, mass media advertising, websites and direct mail in a concerted effort to redefine the president's plan. The group worked with veteran Democratic campaign strategists to come up with a lobbying playbook that would lead to legislative victory. They seized upon the term "privatization" as a way to stoke public fears and challenge the president's intentions regarding Social Security. During 2005, Americans United to Protect Social Security succeeded in shifting the ground under the policy debate and kept the president's allies on the defensive. Although the group claimed to be representing the authentic majority opinion of the populace, there is little doubt that their relentless campaign acted upon the latent and unfocussed concerns over the health of Social Security. The president's plan to ultimately resolve the financial problems became, instead, seen as a threat to its existence.

Much to the dismay of the president, privatization became a synonym for dismantling Social Security.[20] As the media and grassroots campaign picked up steam during the spring of 2005, members of Congress began to hear hostile comments from their constituents. Members, who were unhappy with the process that led to the plan, took their cues from the voters and quietly backed away from the president. By the end of the year, the plan was shelved and talk about reform had all but died down.

As both cases demonstrate, the partnership between interest groups and political consultants is a potent combination. Judging by the outcome, one can conclude that professionally developed issue advocacy can have a significant impact on public policy. It is important to remember, however, that issue advocacy work is not done in a vacuum. While successful issue advocacy can help define the terms of debate and help set the agenda by foreclosing some options and enhancing others, its overall impact is tempered by its subservient role within a larger lobbying strategy. Issue advocacy is almost always used as a complement to a traditional "insider" strategy.

Impact on Policymaking

Skeptics will continue to doubt the influence of political consultants on policy outcomes despite evidence that shows otherwise. Such skeptics maintain that campaign tactics and issue advocacy are just one component of a larger lobbying strategy. However, dwelling on deterministic questions is a distraction from the larger issue. The important question is not whether political consultants can be identified as the weight that tipped an issue from success to failure or vice versa, but, rather, what does their presence mean to governing? How have they, through actions or inspiration, affected public policy debates? It is a subtler, more value-laden query to be sure, but one that links the phenomenon of political consultant crafted issue advocacy with broader questions about governance.

The issue advocacy work championed by political consultants presents three serious implications for governing. First, critics contend that much of the issue advocacy work done by political consultants is propaganda with barely a passing relationship to facts. In practice, it is used to distort policy proposals and, at its worst, to deliberately spread falsehoods. A second concern is that campaigning and governing are not the same and to the extent that governing takes on the trappings of a campaign and becomes harder to distinguish from campaigning, it diminishes the right and proper role of compromise and bipartisanship. Finally there is the question of elite bias, or more precisely, wealth bias. Broad issue advocacy campaigns employing campaign professionals are expensive and thus beyond the reach of average citizens or poorly funded public interest lobbies. Compare, for example, the resource advantage owned by the financial service lobby pushing for bankruptcy reform against that of the consumer interest lobbies that were opposed. In these cases, political consultants help the wealthy redefine issues and set agendas.

For some scholars paid issue advocacy in all its forms is akin to propaganda and, like propaganda, in the wrong hands it is a malevolent force trying to misrepresent and obscure an issue. The prejudice is easy to understand if harder to defend. Scholars who study issue advocacy see the attempts to sell a viewpoint and manufacture public opinion as an affront to authentic democratic activity where citizens and politicians engage in an unmediated exchange. Efforts by interest groups to overwhelm some voices and foreclose policy options are seen by scholars and outside observers as an abuse of power.[21] The problem with this criticism is that it is one-sided and begins with the premise that all issue advocacy work is an attempt to mislead the public, not educate it.

It can be argued that issue advocacy work, biased as it is, serves an important purpose by highlighting problems that would otherwise go unnoticed. In fact, some laudable policy changes have occurred as a result of increased public awareness brought on by issue advocacy work. A case in point is the dolphin safe tuna mandate that benefited from work done by a host of animal rights and environmental groups. Other examples include the campaigns to raise the profile of public health problems such as breast cancer or autism. Nevertheless, dividing issue advocacy work into "good" and "bad" categories is an entirely subjective exercise that implies a normative assessment of policy outcomes. Pursuing that line of reasoning is a rabbit hole with no end in sight. Indeed, scholars are correct to apply critical judgment to paid issue advocacy. The current research has been deficient. In its zeal to demonstrate how pervasive paid advocacy is, such research has lost sight of what the problems are.

Implicit in the description of paid issue advocacy as propaganda is a sense that it is artificial and that, although it purports to represent the popular will, it really represents the opinions of a few powerful interests. Effective issue advocacy, such as the estate tax repeal effort, cloaks itself in populism to maximize its impression on legislators. Members of Congress expect to be lobbied on issues, they expect to hear disparate points of view on complicated policy matters and they expect their constituents to harbor strong feelings and weigh in with them. In this respect, professional crafted issue advocacy that leads to public contact is simply part of the important feedback loop that connects a legislator with his or her constituents.[22] There is, however, a major caveat to that description. Not all forms of public pressure are qualitatively equal. There is a difference between engineered activism guided from the top and the real thing. Interest groups that are essentially renting the credibility of the public at large should not be confused with an authentic and spontaneous reaction.

To address the next concern one has to subscribe to the idea that there are important differences between governing and campaigning and, more precisely, that there *should* be differences. The advent of the "permanent campaign" is a phenomenon that has been lamented by scholars and political pundits for a variety of reasons. To be clear, we are not talking about the protean version of campaigning-as-governing that is practiced by the president through his use of the bully pulpit. His ability to rally the public or pressure lawmakers by using his office is a power that is associated with his role as the head of state. What we are talking about is the gradual erosion of the boundary that used to differentiate behaviors associated with a campaign and those associated with governing. I am not, of course, suggesting that a firewall has historically existed between campaigning and governing, but I am saying that rules and customs that manage interactions in a campaign setting are much different than customs that guide behavior in governing.

How do political consultants and issue advocacy fit into this paradigm? The answer is simple: professionally crafted issue advocacy at its most effective can transform a policy debate from a principled conflict over ideals conducted with an eye toward compromise to a pitched rhetorical battle where for one party to win the other party must lose. The struggle over the future of Social Security is an example of the deleterious impact campaign-style issue advocacy can have on public policy. In that case, interest groups successfully derailed consideration of reform before legislators had a chance to evaluate and deliberate on its merits or shortcomings. Issue advocacy simplifies complex problems to poll tested phrases and snappy campaign slogans and while there will always be room for rhetoric in policy debates it is not beneficial to the legislative process to have serious matters exclusively defined by the most superficial and provocative means.

Issue advocacy campaigns, even those that are conducted on a small or limited scale, are beyond the reach of the disorganized and the poorly funded. Recent surveys buttress the claim that issue advocacy is the domain of the wealthy. According to a study conducted by the Annenberg School of Public Policy at the University of Pennsylvania, during the 108th Congress (2003–2005) spending on issue advertising was tilted toward business/corporate interests by a five-to-one margin.[23] The absolute dollar gap that exists between wealthy business groups and citizen- or cause-oriented groups raises concerns about elite bias in the policy sector. Devotees of Schattschneider's trenchant critique of American-style pluralism note that one of the enduring failures of our system is that interest group activities are dominated by the economically advantaged. The employment of expensive political consultants to develop and implement expensive issue advocacy campaigns is a clear reflection of that dynamic. In the cacophony of interest group politics, those with large financial reserves (for example, the drug industry or organized labor) can use their money to rise above the din and effectively drown out other voices. The ability of moneyed interests to tell a compelling story and spread it around to as many people as are willing to listen does not ensure that they will always win the argument.

Interest group theory is not that deterministic. If it were, then big tobacco would have had nothing to fear from poorly funded anti-smoking advocates. Yet, the imbalance cited by Schattschneider fifty years ago remains a valid criticism and concern. The pattern is exemplified by the estate tax repeal where a small group of deep-pocketed actors set the tone and terms of a policy debate to their benefit. It would be an exaggeration to attribute the legislative outcome to a marketing campaign, but even repeal opponents acknowledged the power of recasting the issue into a populist cause.

Conclusion

The expanding market for issue advocacy work will ensure that professional political consultants will play a role in public policy debates from hereon. In fact, if the current trend holds, the field of political consultants who specialize in issue work could eventually surpass the numbers who work with candidates. At the very least, the book of business provided by interest groups is sure to play a larger role in the financial health of political consulting firms.

The boom in issue advocacy consulting work would be a notable curiosity were it not for the implications it has for public policy. Further encroachment of campaign tactics into governing is a troubling trend and one that is unfortunately being exacerbated by interest groups. Politicians in both parties pay lip-service to the idea of finding common ground and of working in a respectful way to find compromise, but that effort is seriously undermined when policy debates become captured in a zero-sum campaign. The future of Social Security, for instance, is a problem that cannot be resolved without the explicit cooperation of both political parties. Cooperation becomes more tenuous if proxies for the elected officials are setting the tone of the debate and manipulating public opinion through inflammatory and divisive issue advocacy work. In a democratic society there will always be a certain amount of rhetorical posturing and symbolic gesturing. Paid issue advocacy, however, has raised the stakes.

It is tempting to suggest at this point that political consulting has reached an evolutionary plateau. Consultants have moved successfully beyond the temporary, cyclical world of candidate-centered campaigns into the virtually limitless realm of public policy. However, that reasoning goes against the history and nature of political consultants. Moreover, it discounts the possibility of further change in how political discourse is conducted. So that begs the question, what is next for political consulting and policymaking?

I believe part of the answer lies in what Wal-Mart has chosen to do. After years of bearing the brunt of daily attacks from labor unions and other progressive advocates, Wal-Mart has joined the public relations battle by constituting a permanent campaign "war room" at its corporate headquarters in Bentonville, Arkansas. The unit, known as "action alley," is staffed by experienced political operatives from both parties with expertise in all forms of campaign work. The job of the in-house political consultants is to promote Wal-Mart, respond to threats and claims, and pressure the opposition through negative campaigning.[24] Wal-Mart's decision to essentially absorb the permanent campaign into its corporate culture may not be a step other companies are willing or able to take. It is conceivable, however, that other well-heeled interests will see the benefit of employing a stable of campaign operatives within their organization to shape and sway public opinion. This could lead to a political arms race where groups stockpile political advisors to ensure they have the capability to engage in issue advocacy at a moment's notice.

Even if the Wal-Mart experience turns out to be a curiosity and not a glimpse into the future, it is clear that the stage is set for a long and lasting partnership between political consultants and interest groups. The incentives for interest groups to employ an issue advocacy approach as part of a lobbying strategy are strong. Meanwhile, consultants are attracted to the work for obvious financial reasons. What the relationship means in the long term for the legislative process is hard to say. If the assessment of the situation is that the marriage of political consultants and issue advocacy is, on balance, a threat to bipartisanship or the ability of legislators to work on high-profile complicated problems such as Social Security, the question is what can be done about it? The answer, unfortunately, appears to be not much.

The corrosive effects unfettered issue advocacy has on deliberation, legislative cooperation and compromise pale in comparison to the harm that would be done to the broader citizens' rights to petition their government by implementing controls on interest group activity. Furthermore, as the campaign finance laws have shown, efforts to clamp down on objectionable behavior simply lead to the exploitation of another outlet. Possibly the best (that is, least intrusive) ways to limit the bad outcomes are to expose the groups' activities through disclosure and to educate citizens and legislators alike so that they are able to discern media hype from useable information. In truth this admittedly narrow inquiry just scratches the surface of a broader philosophical question of how responsive should our government be to the actions and pleadings of interest groups.

Notes

1 Erika Falk, Erin Grizard and Gordon McDonald, "Legislative Issue Advertising in the 108th Congress," *The Annenberg Public Policy Center Report Series*, 47: 3.
2 "Pollie Award Winners." The American Association of Political Consultants, http://www.theaapc.org/content/pollieawards/pastwinners/pastwinners.asp.
3 Ken Kollman, *Outside Lobbying: Public Opinion & Interest Group Strategies* (Princeton, N.J.: Princeton University Press, 1998).
4 Jeffery Goldberg, "Selling Wal-Mart," *The New Yorker*, April 2, 2007, 23–30.
5 Elite bias and the use of political consultants is covered thoroughly by Darrell West and Burdett Loomis, *The Sound of Money: How Political Interests Get What They Want* (New York: W.W. Norton, 1998).
6 James Thurber and Candace Nelson, eds, *Campaign Warriors: The Role of Political Consultants in Elections* (Washington, D.C.: The Brookings Institution, 2000).
7 Robert Denton and Gary Woodward, *Political Communications in America*, 2nd ed. (New York: Praeger Publishing, 1990).
8 Falk et al., "Legislative Issue Advertising in the 108th Congress," 8.
9 Kollman, *Outside Lobbying*. See also Robert Friedenberg, *Communications Consultants in Political Campaigns* (Westport, CT: Praeger Publishers, 1997), 165.
10 During the 109th Congress the author worked for Congresswoman Nancy Johnson (Republican-Connecticut) and the annuity legislation described here is a real example of a political consultancy working on behalf of an interest group.
11 R. Douglas Arnold, *The Logic of Congressional Action* (New Haven: Yale University Press, 1990).
12 Darrell West, Diane Heath and Chris Goodwin, "Harry and Louise Go to Washington: Political Advertising and Health Care Reform," *Journal of Health Politics, Policy and Law* 21 (1996): 40.
13 West and Loomis, *The Sound of Money*, 61.
14 Trevor Potter and Kirk Jowers, "Speech Governed by Federal Elections Laws," in *The New Campaign Finance Source Book*, ed. Thomas Mann and Anthony Corrado (Washington, D.C.: The Brookings Institution, 2005), 205.
15 Lizette Alvarez, "In 2 Parties' War of Words, Shibboleths Emerge as Clear Winner," *The New York Times*, April 27, 2001, A5.

16 Martha Britton Eller, "Which Estates are Affected by the Federal Estate Tax?: An Examination of the Filing Population for the Year-of-Death 2001," IRS SOI Bulletin, http://www.irs.gov/taxstats/indtaxstats/article/0,,id=96442,00.html#5.

17 For an insightful take on the politics of the estate tax see Michael J. Graetz and Ian Shapiro, *Death by a Thousand Cuts: The Fight over Taxing Inherited Wealth* (Princeton, N.J.: Princeton University Press, 2005). Graetz and Shapiro, both professors at Yale University, offer a fascinating look at the quiet yet powerful influence wielded by some of America's most private wealthy families.

18 David Cay Johnston, "A Boon for the Richest in Estate Tax Repeal," *New York Times*, June 7, 2006, C8.

19 Richard W. Stevenson, "Social Security Panel Faces Challenges," *New York Times*, May 3, 2001, A13.

20 Glen Justice, "Groups that Clashed During the Campaign Are Facing Off Again," *New York Times*, April 13, 2005, A3.

21 See Nicholas O'Shaughnessy, *The Phenomenon of Political Marketing* (New York: St Martin's Press, 1990); and Kathleen Hall Jamieson, *Everything You Think You Know about Politics and Why You're Wrong* (New York: Basic Books, 2000), and Thomas Mann and Norman Ornstein, eds, *The Permanent Campaign and Its Future* (Washington, D.C.: The Brookings Institution, 2000).

22 Lawrence Grossman, *The Electronic Republic: Reshaping Democracy in the Information Age* (New York: Viking Press, 1995), 3–4.

23 Falk et al., "Legislative Issue Advertising in the 108th Congress," 52.

24 Goldberg, "The Selling of Wal-Mart," 26.

33

Military and Defense Lobbying

A Case Study

Julius W. Hobson, Jr

> In development since 1994, the Crusader weighed sixty tons and would be too heavy for the Army to transport in a timely manner. Moreover, the Crusader was designed to fight a heavy land battle, more likely during the Cold War than the 21st Century. Rather than continuing a system with questionable future relevance, the President reallocated the Crusader's funds to more advanced technologies including precision guided artillery weapons. The President's Crusader decision, endorsed by the Congress, represents a real step towards transformation.[1]

This statement in President George W. Bush's fiscal year (FY) 2004 budget proposal was the final word on the demise of the Crusader artillery system.

Lobbying is a process for influencing public and governmental policy. It involves the advocacy, either by individuals, groups, corporations, organizations, or associations, or a coalition of some or all of these, of a policy point of view.

Lobbyists seek to influence public policymakers for several reasons. They seek to gain benefits or relief that may be unavailable in the private sector; an economic advantage over others; relief or advantage up the government ladder based upon success or failure at another level of government; to create beneficial programs; or, to resolve public problems that only governments can adequately handle due to size, cost, or complexity.

This chapter describes a case study of a lobbying effort to preserve the Crusader artillery system. National security contractors have the advantage of being members of the big business culture, as well as manufacturers of weapons that guarantee national security. These contractors, as well as any other interest entity, trade in both information and influence. These are the normal elements in the government relations process. The Congress, Pentagon, and contractors form the "iron triangle" that has been discussed so often.[2]

Those seeking to influence the process included the private sector, as well as the government (Department of the Army), in opposition to a policy decision made by the President and the Secretary of Defense. In the end, everyone but the Army won. Here is what happened.

Crusader's History

American field artillery can trace its history to November 1775, when Henry Knox was appointed Chief of the Continental Artillery. The Marine Corps Field Artillery, along with the

10th Marines, was formed in April 1914. In each major war or conflict—War of 1812, Mexican War, Civil War, World Wars I and II, Korea, Vietnam—artillery played a major role in close indirect fire support for ground troops.

In an army, artillery has responsibility for big, long-range weapons, formerly known as cannons. In a battle, artillery's role is to provide fire support for the infantry, armor, and other units. Indirect fire systems fire artillery projectiles over a distance. These can be missiles, rockets, or bombs. Indirect fire can cause casualties to troops, inhibit mobility, suppress or neutralize weapon systems, damage equipment and installations, and demoralize the enemy. Napoleon was the first commander since the introduction of gunpowder artillery to understand the true killing power of the cannon, saying that "God fights on the side with the best artillery." Historian John Norris argues that Napoleon's use of artillery in some battles may have inflicted over 50% of the battle casualties suffered by opposing armies.[3]

It has been argued that artillery, historically, has caused more combat deaths, in initial rounds, through indirect fire than by any other means. Hence, artillery has been called the "King of Battle." Artillery fire can destroy an enemy using high-explosive (HE) or concrete-piercing (CP) shells. Destruction does require a large expenditure of ammunition, but it can neutralize the enemy. Artillery can suppress the ability of an enemy to perform its function, but it works only during the firing sequence, which requires a low expenditure of ammunition.

Besides the US Army, the US Marines also have their own field artillery. However, the Marines have their own fixed-wing "air force" which is dedicated to providing air support for ground troops. The Army's "air force" consists of only helicopters—but no fixed-wing aircraft. This is the result of an agreement between the services when the Department of Defense was created. Thus, the Army has a historically greater dependency on artillery because it has sole control of its usage.

During the 1991 Gulf War, the Army discovered that its 1960s vintage, manual loading 155 mm self-propelled Paladin howitzer could not keep up with the Bradley Fighting Vehicle or the M1 Abrams Main Battle Tank. The Abrams could move up to fifty miles per hour, much faster than the twenty-five to thirty miles per hour capability of M109 artillery batteries that were powered by diesel engines. To make up for this deficiency, field commanders leapfrogged artillery battalions and supply elements, a solution that ultimately reduced fire support, since only half the artillery pieces could fire while the other half raced forward. The 155 mm Paladin, which was scheduled to be fielded shortly after the Gulf War, was believed to be only a temporary solution. Of the three combat arms (Field Artillery, Infantry, and Armor), the Field Artillery had the least modern systems. The Crusader was designated as the replacement artillery system.

The Crusader artillery system consisted of a self-propelled howitzer, a tracked resupply module and the wheeled resupply system. The forty-ton system carried a payload of forty-eight rounds and fires up to twelve rounds per minute. Crusader was designed to travel across country at speeds of up to forty-eight kilometers per hour, with highway speeds of seventy-eight kilometers per hour. The design called for 32% less ammunition per target, 38% less support and 15% less peace time costs. The system was to be operated by six soldiers.

Live fire trials of the Crusader began in February 2000 at the Yuma Proving Grounds in Arizona. In November 2000, the system achieved a rate of 10.4 rounds per minute. Crusader successfully completed its Preliminary Design Review in November 2001. The first versions of the system were scheduled for 2006 and the system was to begin service in 2008. Crusader was to be able to deliver fifteen tons of ammunition, in a six-battery unit, in less than five minutes.

United Defense Industries (UDI), a subsidiary of the Carlyle Group, became the prime contractor for research and development of the Crusader. UDI was also the lead contractor for the Bradley Fighting Vehicle. The major subcontractors for mobility and resupply were General Dynamics Armament Systems (Burlington, Vermont), General Dynamics Land Systems (Muskegon and Sterling Heights, Michigan), and Lynx Real-Time Systems (California).

Honeywell, Raytheon, and General Dynamics were the major software subcontractors. Ultimately there were more than 100 developers of and suppliers to the Crusader program. Together they employed thousands of people and were located in twenty-seven states and the District of Columbia. Key among these states were Michigan, home of then Senate Armed Services Committee Chairman Carl Levin (Democrat-Michigan), and Massachusetts, home of Committee Member Edward Kennedy (Democrat-Massachusetts). Also included was Minnesota, home to Senators Paul Wellstone and Mark Dayton, both Democrats.

UDI, headquartered in Arlington, Virginia, considered itself "a leader in the design, development and production of combat vehicles, artillery, naval guns, missile launchers and precision munitions used by the US Department of Defense and allies worldwide."

Secretary of Defense Donald Rumsfeld announced on May 8, 2002, his decision to cancel Crusader. President Bush sent Congress a letter containing a budget amendment on May 29, requesting reallocation of Crusader's $475.6 million for research and development to support transformation of the Army by accelerating development of the Army's Future Combat System/ Indirect Fires program, the Excalibur 155 mm precision projectile, as well as other artillery systems.[4] The Excalibur is the next generation family of projectiles for the Army and US Marine Corps artillery. It is a 155 mm precision guided artillery round with extended range. Excalibur will contain the latest Global Positioning System/Internal Measurement Unit (GPS/IMU) technology to deliver a variety of lethal payloads on target up to fifty kilometers in range. Raytheon is the prime contractor for Excalibur.

Lobbying to Save Crusader

Established in 2001, the Crusader Industrial Alliance (also known as Team Crusader or TC), was a coalition of nationwide contractors and subcontractors involved in the artillery system's design and development. According to its charter, the Alliance was intended to "inform and educate the American public and national policymakers." The Alliance sought to advance the Crusader program through communications, legislative alerts, and relevant articles. The Alliance hosted Washington, D.C. briefings and events designed to enable contractors to meet with members of Congress "to discuss the importance of the Crusader program and the artillery industrial base." The Alliance also provided tours to facilities for members of Congress and their staff. The leadership of the Alliance consisted of representatives of Honeywell Aerospace, General Dynamics Land Systems, and United Defense, and employed four full-time staff.

When the Secretary announced his intention to cancel Crusader, the United Defense and the Alliance immediately stepped up their lobbying efforts.

UDI made the rounds of the K Street lobbying corridor to hire lobbyists willing to seek support from members of Congress on their behalf. Several big name Republican lobbyists turned UDI down flat. Earlier, UDI signed Barbour Griffith & Rogers, which has very strong Republican ties. A principal in Barbour Griffith is Haley Barbour, a former Republican National Committee Chairman. *Roll Call* reported that under Administration pressure, the firm ended the contract. The paper confirmed with UDI that Barbour Griffith had agreed to represent UDI on May 13, but reversed its decision two days later. The White House also confirmed that there had been conversations with Barbour Griffith, but denied any pressure to drop the contract.[5] Losing Barbour Griffith would be a severe blow to UDI's attempts to save Crusader.

UDI also talked to Quinn Gillespie & Associates, another strong Republican Party strategy and lobbying firm, but it declined the contract after talking to Administration officials and Capitol Hill sources.

Eventually, the company did hire Stuart E. Eizenstat, a former official in the Carter and Clinton administrations and a partner at Covington & Burling. UDI also talked to Cassidy &

Associates and Greenberg Traurig. Patton Boggs, which was on retainer to UDI, did virtually no work on Crusader.

Powell Tate was retained by United Defense to provide communications and lobbying support. Powell Tate specializes in preparing and implementing communications strategic plans as a means of impacting the governmental decision-making process. Its services include message development, coalition development and management, editorial services, grassroots organizing, and advocacy advertising.

To begin their campaign, UDI produced a statement supporting Crusader signed by several retired Army four-star generals—Barry McCaffrey, the White House National Drug Policy Director from 1995–2001; David Maddox, a former Commander in Chief of the US Army in Europe; and Joe Reeder, a former Undersecretary of the Army—signed a statement in support of Crusader. The statement attacked Rumsfeld for his decision to cancel the system. Then it held a press conference to spotlight three defense experts supporting Crusader. They included retired General John Tilelli, who commanded the First Calvary Division during Operations Desert Shield and Desert Storm and was later Commander in Chief for Korea; Philip Coyle, who served as Director of Operational Test and Evaluation in the Department of Defense from 1994 to 2001; and, Dr Peter Cherry, Vice President of Altarum, a non-profit research institute.[6]

McCaffrey also penned a column in the *Armed Forces Journal International*, after being retained by the Carlyle Group, the eleventh largest US defense contractor. He noted that not "a single, confirmed official of the Office of the Secretary of Defense has visited the Crusader team—neither the technicians with the enormously successful live-fire prototype in Yuma, Arizona, nor those at the systems-integration laboratories in Minneapolis, Minnesota."[7]

The Alliance produced Internet materials in defense of Crusader. A "Crusader Myths and Facts" sheet to refute Rumsfeld's criticisms. For example, one myth alleged that Crusader was a Cold War relic design, while the fact sheet claimed that Crusader was conceived in 1994, well after the end of the Cold War, and that it would be a smart gun.[8] Full-page color ads were produced for publication in the *National Journal, CQ Weekly, Roll Call, The Hill*, and several daily newspapers.

Part of any public relations lobbying campaign requires friendly, as well as opposition, research. Most importantly, opposition research seeks to find statements or actions that are contrary to currently stated positions by policymakers or opponents. The Alliance public relations effort also produced a list of quotes (copyrighted by United Defense) from key policymakers, including Senators Daniel Inouye (Democrat-Hawaii), Don Nickles (Republican-Oklahoma), and James Inhofe (Republican-Oklahoma); Representative J.C. Watts (Republican-Oklahoma); and Department of Defense Comptroller Don Zakheim. One of the "quotable quotes" came from Deputy Secretary of Defense Paul Wolfowitz, who when testifying before the Senate Subcommittee on Defense Appropriations, stated, "I'm not one of those people who think I can bet the farm on not needing artillery ten years from now. And I think this [Crusader] is the best artillery system available."[9] This was an excellent attempt to turn a key decision-maker's previous statement against his revised policy position.

The public relations campaign included press releases at each stage of the process. A May 1, 2002 press release praised the House Armed Services Committee for retaining Crusader at $475 million. It quoted Representative Watts as saying the "Crusader program clearly retains the full confidence of the . . . Committee."[10] A "clipping service" reproduced statements, such as a floor statement by Senator Paul Wellstone (Democrat-Minnesota), whose state was home to more than a handful of Crusader jobs.[11]

The Carlyle Group, which was created in 1987, is "a private global investment firm that originates, structures and acts as lead equity investor in management-led buyouts, strategic minority equity investments, equity private placements, consolidations and buildups, and growth capital financings." Its mission is to become the "premier global private equity firm and to generate extraordinary returns while maintaining [its] good name and the good name of [its] partners." The firm has been led by former Defense Secretary Frank C. Carlucci, a former Princeton University classmate of Defense Secretary Rumsfeld. In November 2002, Carlyle announced that Louis V. Gerstner, Jr, former Chairman of IBM, would become its new Chairman, succeeding Carlucci.[12] The key Carlyle players include former Secretary of State James A. Baker III; former Office of Management and Budget Director Richard Darman; former British Prime Minister John Major; former President George H.W. Bush; former SEC Chairman Arthur Levitt, William E. Conway, Jr, former Chief Financial Officer of MCI Communications Corp; and former Carter administration Domestic Policy Adviser and Carlyle Co-founder David M. Rubenstein.

In a profile, the *Washington Post* noted that since acquiring United Defense in October 1997 for about "$173 million in cash and $700 million in borrowed funds, Carlyle has reaped more than $400 million in dividends and capital gains from this acquisition."[13] United was the prime contractor for the Bradley Fighting Vehicle, the M109 self-propelled artillery system, and the Navy's Mk 45 DDX destroyer gun system. Given that the M109 and Bradley were completing production cycles, Carlyle's survey of United suggested the company stood to lose more than $1 million in 1996 and 1997. But Carlyle was looking at the lucrative Crusader contract worth over $1.1 billion as a very strong asset. Crusader was already under attack by critics for its size and weight. The *Washington Post* noted that following Carlyle's takeover, United "appointed three outside directors to its board; two of them were former top Army generals, J.H. Binford Peay III, the just retired Commander-in-Chief of Central Command, and John M. Shalikashvili, the retired former Chairman of the Joint Chiefs of Staff."[14]

According to *CQ Weekly*, less than 10% of Carlyle's investments are in defense-related companies. It quoted Richard L. Aboulafia, senior analyst with the Teal Group, a defense business forecasting firm, as saying:

> [T]he one virtue that Carlyle has is a feel for the political climate, so they also have a feel for what is a bankable asset . . . The closer you get to perfect intelligence about future revenue streams, the better you are. And they're a lot closer than other people.[15]

This ability to obtain intelligence was underscored when it was revealed that United Defense was warned that the Crusader was due to be canceled. Peay sent a fax to Army Vice Chief of Staff General John M. Keane on April 30, more that seven hours before Deputy Defense Secretary Paul Wolfowitz told Army Secretary Thomas White. According to the *Washington Post*, Peay told Keane that UDI was "prepared to assist the Army by any means that seem appropriate in reversing this decision."[16] The advance information enabled the Army to commence a congressional lobbying campaign. UDI's intelligence was immediately passed to members of Congress prior to the Army's official notification of Crusader's cancelation. In fact, the office of Senator James M. Inhofe (Republican-Oklahoma) contacted the White House requesting information on the Crusader decision.

According to the Center for Responsive Politics, UDI spent $1.26 million lobbying the Congress in 2000, while the Carlyle Group spent $1.38 million. The *Washington Post* reported that United spent more than $1 million a year from 1998 to 2001, on lobbying both for the Crusader and the Bradley Fighting Vehicle upgrade. In 1999 and 2000, United paid former Representative Marvin Leath (Democrat-Texas) in lobbying fees. Leath, who died in 2000, spent ten years in Congress, serving on the Armed Services Committee. Meanwhile, United hired other firms, including Verner, Liipfert, Bernhard, McPherson & Hand, at a price of $140,000. The firm used former Senator Dan Coats (Republican-Indiana), a former Senior Member of the Senate Armed Services Committee, and Coats' former Legislative Assistant, R. O'Brien, to handle defense authorization and appropriations bills. Finally, United paid $30,000 in 2000 to Ervin Technical Associates, a lobbying firm, after former House Defense Appropriations Subcommittee Chairman Joseph M. McDade (Republican-Pennsylvania) became the firm's Board Chairman.[17]

As word of the Department of Defense's decision to cancel Crusader spread, United Defense took a hit in the markets. On May 2, 2002, Credit Suisse First Boston analyst Pierre Chao, cut his rating on UDI shares to "hold" from "buy." Chao noted that Crusader was such a large portion of UDI's future revenues and thus felt investors needed to prepare for greater volatility and uncertainty in the near future. While Crusader had strong Congressional backing, Chao believed the Department of Defense's decision would stand. As a result, UDI shares declined 15%.[18]

Army Lobbying for Crusader

The Army desperately wanted to retain the Crusader as the Paladin replacement for force replacement. It was Army Chief of Staff General Eric Shinseki who, upon taking office, first ordered that the original Crusader be reduced in size. But Crusader stood out as a weapons system ripe for the kill under the Army's transformation program. Initially, Rumsfeld caved under political pressure and the system was included in the President's FY 2003 budget proposal.

However, President Bush continued to mention Crusader as a transformation target. The White House Chief of Staff told Rumsfeld to prepare the necessary briefing and if the system should be canceled, the White House would concur. Department of Defense Undersecretary for Acquisition, Technology, and Logistics Edward Aldridge prepared a memorandum that concluded the reconfigured Crusader program should continue. *InsideDefense* reported that the memorandum stated:

> [T]he transforming Army has a need for massive, continuous, all-weather and mobile firepower within the battle area. While short-range tactical missiles and close air support can contribute, they cannot substitute for the flexibility, 24-hour presence, sustained lethality and close support of mobile cannon artillery.[19]

But Aldridge never got an opportunity to brief President Bush. On April 30, "Aldridge and Deputy Defense Secretary Paul Wolfowitz told Army Secretary White that Rumsfeld was again considering termination of the Crusader."[20]

White was given thirty days to prepare a defense. Surprised Army leaders felt they could win in Congress and prepared for an all-out lobbying effort. An Army legislative liaison prepared talking points to convince legislators to save Crusader. Rumsfeld was accused of putting soldiers at risk for the sake of budget cutting and that he chose Crusader because he could not kill more expensive programs, such as the F-22 and the Marines' troubled V-22 Osprey. The document argued that the Army had been living with inferior artillery systems since the end of World War II and that the forty-year-old Paladin was an inferior system. It further suggested that Rumsfeld's decisions would return to the Carter administration's "hollow Army." This was clearly the Army's indictment of Rumsfeld.

The Army's talking points document surfaced on Capitol Hill and Rumsfeld immediately seized the opportunity to assert his authority. Boyer points out that the Department of Defense "portrayed the Army memo as rank insubordination, a defiance of civilian authority over the military, and White ordered an investigation by the Army's Inspector General."[21]

As required by the previous year's defense authorization bill (S. 2514, 107th Congress), Shinseki submitted a report to the Congress, which identified requirements for organic, indirect fires, and possible options to replace the canceled Crusader. He took another swing at Rumsfeld, stating that the Army supported the Secretary's proposals to accelerate the Army's precision fire initiatives. This acceleration of programs alone would not fully meet the operational requirement of organic indirect fires by 2008. He further said capabilities

> that would have been provided by Crusader (revolutionary cockpit design, enhanced robotics, autonomous fire control system with inherent sensor to shooter capabilities, higher sustained rates of fire, extended range, increased lethality, and improved mobility to match maneuver forces) are required to meet organic indirect fire support requirements no later than FY08.[22]

Shinseki argued that the Army could not fully employ objective force operational concepts without the above capabilities. In other words, the Army could be weakened and soldiers lives would be at risk without these capabilities.

The report also suggested that canceling the Crusader would increase future costs to field an appropriate artillery system. Most of the increased costs for replacing Crusader would come from deploying a lighter version of the forty-ton artillery system by the 2008 date, which was when Crusader was supposed to be ready. Also due in that year are a number of very expensive Department of Defense weapons systems, including the Air Force's $200 million F-22 air superiority fighter and the Joint Strike Fighter. The Pentagon simply may not have enough funds to deploy everything. The *Wall Street Journal* reported that some of Rumsfeld's staff was pressing the Army to delay Crusader's replacement until the middle of the next decade and simply upgrade the Paladin. Other staffers argued that rockets and heavy mortars, along with air support, could replace artillery pieces and eliminate the need for a Crusader replacement. Army officials continued to maintain, however, that there was no substitute for precise munitions.[23]

Following the Secretary's decision, the National Taxpayers Union President John Berthoud sent a letter to Rumsfeld praising him for making the decision. Berthoud cited a statement by General Tommy Franks, Head of Central Command, that Crusader would not have aided the war on terror in Afhganistan, stating when

> a senior commander in the war on terror expresses concerns over whether Crusader would have made a difference in his combat theater, taxpayers may be forgiven for wondering whether Congress should commit an additional $9.6 billion to find out which side's predictions will prove accurate.[24]

Congressional Response

As often happens when money may impact a state or Congressional district, the affected members of Congress rally to protect their interests. Senators Don Nickles, James Inhofe, and Mark Dayton, along with Representative J.C. Watts, Chairman of the House Republican Conference, began lobbying other members of Congress on behalf of Crusader.

Using data provided by UDI, the lawmakers pointed out that about 2,200 jobs in twenty-four states would be affected by cancelation of Crusader. This did not include jobs that would be lost in Oklahoma, the proposed site Crusader assembly, and located in Watt's congressional district.

Dayton wrote a letter to the editor, arguing that Crusader was worth over 800 direct contract jobs in Minnesota, as well as approximately 1,200 subcontract jobs. He questioned the Rumsfeld's decision, pointing out that Minnesota citizens were "working hard on Crusader for the sake of their country."[25]

House of Representatives

When the House Armed Services Committee reported its version of the National Defense Authorization Act for FY 2003 (H.R. 4546), it sustained continuation of Crusader. In its report, the Committee expressed concern that the Department of Defense had not fully acknowledged Crusader's potential. It forbade the Department of Defense from making any changes in the Crusader program pending completion of the Army's Milestone B Analysis of Alternatives (AOA). The Committee further required the Army Secretary to report the completed analysis to Congress by April 2003.[26]

On June 24, the House Appropriations Committee reported its Defense Appropriations bill (H.R. 5010). As reported, the legislation terminated the Crusader. In its place, the bill appropriated $648 million for work in FY 2003 on a new artillery system, $173 million more than Bush initially requested for Crusader before deciding to terminate the system. The bill also required the Department of Defense to retain the technologies developed after already spending $2 billion on Crusader. This provision had the effect of retaining UDI as the contractor since it was the lead contractor on Crusader. The Committee did not take a separate vote on Crusader. Crusader defenders on the Appropriations Committee, such as Representative Martin Olav Sabo (Democrat-Minnesota) had to bow to White House veto pressure and accept the compromise. Sabo issued a press statement the same day announcing the plan to save Crusader technologies and jobs. In fact, claimed to be "instrumental in brokering the compromise."[27]

US Senate

In April 2002, Senators Inhofe and Daniel Akaka (Democrat-Hawaii) convened the first meeting of the Senate Army Caucus to discuss issues related to Army transformation, as well as ongoing antiterrorist activities. The guest speaker was Army Chief of Staff General Eric Shinseki. The Crusader was among the topics discussed. Inhofe first suggested creation of a Senate Army Caucus during a Senate Armed Services Air Land Subcommittee hearing the previous month.

Meanwhile, Rumsfeld hosted breakfasts for Senate Armed Services Committee members, meeting with John McCain (Republican-Arizona), Jon Kyl (Republican-Arizona), Jeff Sessions (Republican-Alabama), Jack Reed (Democrat-Rhode Island), Edward Kennedy (Democrat-Massachusetts), Mark Dayton (Democrat-Minnesota), Ben Nelson (Democrat-Nebraska), and John Warner (Republican-Virginia), the Committee Chairman.

The Armed Services Committee, by a bipartisan vote of 17-8, reported its version of the National Defense Authorization Bill for FY 2003 (S. 2514). The Committee approved the President's initial FY 2003 budget request of $475.6 million for Crusader. The Committee's report noted that during its markup of the bill, the Secretary "suddenly" announced the decision to terminate Crusader.[28] In its press release following the markup, the Committee took note of the decision to terminate Crusader and pledged to review the matter with the Secretary and the Army Chief of Staff prior to Senate floor debate on the bill.

On May 16, 2002, the Senate Armed Services Committee held a hearing concerning the Crusader, a day after voting to report its version of the Defense Authorization Bill. Though several Senators expressed concerns about the process leading to the decision to cancel Crusader, including Senator Inhofe, Rumsfeld and his staff handled the hearing expertly. Rumsfeld argued that precision-guided systems are important. He pointed out that in Afghanistan, US Special Forces on the ground called in long-range bombers to provide tactical close air support, something that had not been done before. Further Rumsfeld noted that precision strikes "reduced the number of friendly fire incidents, as well as incidents of civilian collateral damage."[29] In addition, precision fire meant fewer projectiles utilized. Rumsfeld also presented the argument that Crusader could be replaced by accelerating the development of satellite-guided artillery shells, such as Excalibur munitions and the guided multiple launch system. He argued that such indirect fire systems as the High Mobility Artillery Rocket System could more easily be transported in C-130 aircraft. Almost in anticipation of the eventual compromise over Crusader, Rumsfeld also stated:

In short, the decision to recommend that we skip Crusader is one that emphasizes accelerating a shift to precision munitions of all indirect fire systems—cannon as well as rocket, Marine Corps as well as Army. Our recommendation is not to abandon the technologies already developed by the Crusader program. In fact, it would ensure that the key pieces of Crusader technology are maintained for use in both the Army's Future Combat System and possibly in the Advanced Gun System that the Navy is developing for its future surface combatants.[30]

Senators McCain and Sessions backed Rumsfeld in the hearing. As the battle raged on, newspaper columnist Robert Novak suggested that Congress would not likely preserve Crusader over the objections of the President, "but the battle is now over whether Army infantrymen will enter combat without traditional artillery cover."[31]

During full Senate consideration of the Defense Authorization Bill, S. 2514, Senator Carl Levin (Democrat-Michigan), Armed Services Committee Chairman, offered an amendment to transfer the $475.6 million that the Department of Defense requested for Crusader into a separate account for the Army's future combat system line. The amendment was adopted 96–3. Voting against the amendment were Senators Hillary Clinton (Democrat-New York), Charles Schumer (Democrat-New York), and George Voinovich (Republican-Ohio).[32] The amendment also required the Army Chief of Staff and the Secretary of Defense to submit a report on future uses of these funds. Senator John Warner successfully offered a second degree amendment that permitted the Secretary to notify Congress about how he proposed to spend the funds, after a thirty-day delay, rather than go through the formal reprogramming process. Following the Senate vote, the Crusader Alliance issued a press statement praising the Senate for taking the right course, and it further argued that during the debate, "Senators expressed a strong consensus that the Army needs a new, technologically advanced mobile artillery system."[33]

The Senate's version of the FY 2003 Department of Defense Appropriations Bill (H.R. 5010) included a provision terminating Crusader. In its "Statement of Administration Policy," the Office of Management and Budget, though concerned about several provisions in the bill, nevertheless praised the Appropriations Committee for supporting the "President's decision to terminate the Crusader artillery program in favor of more transformational efforts to improve the Army's indirect fire capabilities."[34]

Final Congressional Action

The FY 2003 Defense Appropriations Bill conference report provided for $368.5 million in funds for the Non-Line of Sight (NLOS) Cannon. This amount was $173 million above the Administration's request. The conferees directed that the additional funding be utilized to "integrate cannon technologies with a suitable platform and munitions to ensure that this NLOS Cannon can be delivered in the 2008 time-frame."[35]

When the dust settled, Crusader was finished. The Defense Authorization Bill conference report adopted the Secretary's decision to terminate Crusader. The House receded to the Senate with an amendment that simply required the Department of Defense to implement a program to leading to fielding a self-propelled Future Combat Systems (FCS) NLOS for the Army by FY 2008. The ultimate victory for UDI was contained in language directing the Department of Defense to take maximum advantage "of technology developed through other programs, such as the composite armored vehicle, Crusader, and the joint United States–United Kingdom Future Scout and Cavalry System."[36]

Why Crusader Failed to Survive

A number of factors contributed to Crusader's demise. First, in March 2000, the Congressional Budget Office (CBO) released a report, which listed Crusader as a cancelation option. CBO suggested procurement of German PzH 2000 self-propelled howitzer previously identified by the US General Accounting Office (GAO), saving the Army $6.7 billion over ten years.[37]

Second, a GAO report noted that Crusader's critical technologies would not be mature enough, based upon Army plans, for product development because the technologies had not been tested in an appropriate operational environment. GAO stated that achieving higher technology would reduce the risk of costly schedule delays. The Army was redesigning Crusader to reduce individual vehicle weight from sixty tons to about forty tons so that the two-vehicle system could be deployed on a C-17 aircraft, but GAO found that the deployability advantage gained did not appear significant. Further GAO stated that an "Army analysis conducted at our request shows that the reduction in the Crusader system's weight would only decrease the number of C-17 flights needed to transport two complete systems and support equipment from five flights to four flights."[38] GAO also recommended that the Army mature its Crusader technologies and that it assess the projected capabilities and fielding schedules prior to beginning product development. The Department of Defense did not agree with GAO's recommendation on technologies. Of note, at the time of the GAO report, the Crusader program had spent $1.7 billion of the planned $11 billion for research, development, and procurement.

Crusader acquired a number of prominent opponents. In January 2002, the Center for Defense Information Military Reform Project released a report concerning military transformation that recommended cancelation of the Crusader. The report argued that neither the C-5 nor the C-17 were able to carry a complete Crusader system. The report criticized the total program cost, as well as the price per two-vehicle unit—$23 million.[39] CDI senior analyst Christopher Hellman was quoted as saying he thought the Crusader was a ripe candidate for termination, especially if one "looked at the rhetoric of the Bush administration as far as mobility and deployability, it didn't seem as if it was a useful model for the future."[40]

Moreover, Crusader was a weapon system conceived and designed, at the end of the Cold War, for combat in Europe. Its ability to fire GPS guided projectiles a long distance and moving at great speed, was seen as indispensable to the Army. However, the first Iraq War, plus the Bosnia conflict, showed there was no need for such a weapon system when speed, agility, light-weight, and maneuverability are key. Crusader stood out like a modern-day dinosaur. Rather than adjust, the Army's military leaders chose to stand fast.

Third, the Army's relations with the Secretary Rumsfeld were less than stellar. The US Army, as an organization, is too big and slow. It's relevance has become less important due to both new warfighting technology and politics. Rumsfeld was heavily involved in planning of the Afghanistan War, which virtually ruled out conventional ground forces. Instead, the Department of Defense relied on a combination of air and special operations forces, as well as the Afghan Northern Alliance. Among Army forces deployed were the 101st Air Assault (Airborne).

Fourth, one author has written that the high point of the military lobby activities comes when the service Chiefs and their aides appear before the committees to answer questions. As is standard lobbying practice, some of the questions are planted in advance to allow a Chief to provide "personal opinion" answers. This allows them to sidestep any charges they are in conflict with either the Secretary of Defense or the President.[41] Army Chief of Staff Eric Shinseki, a former armor officer, failed at this process. Furthermore, Rumsfeld undermined Shinseki in a very public manner. While visiting Fort Leavenworth, Kansas, to speak to several officers in April 2001, Shinseki learned of a *Washington Post* article announcing his own replacement as Army Chief of Staff, fifteen months prior to his scheduled retirement. Rumsfeld let it be known that his choice was Deputy Army Chief of Staff John Keane, who had previously commanded the

101st Airborne Division (Keane subsequently decided to retire to spend more time with his family). Thus, Shinseki became an instant lame duck. Clearly, Rumsfeld had so little confidence in Army generals, he recalled Peter J. Schoomaker from retirement to become the Army's 35th Chief of Staff.

Meanwhile, Army Secretary White came under fire for his continued support for Crusader. Rumsfeld and White House spokesman Ari Fleischer (on behalf of Bush) both expressed confidence in White. But his tenure remained in doubt. Not only did White, a former Enron executive, lack support in the Pentagon, he also faced the wrath of Senators Levin and Warner for not fully revealing the extent of his Enron holdings. In a story broadcast May 10, CNN reported that Rumsfeld was very angry with White for allowing the talking point document defending Crusader to go to Capitol Hill.[42]

Aside from the Crusader controversy, White was under investigation by the FBI and the Securities and Exchange Commission over whether his contacts with former Enron colleagues may have violated any laws or rules. The Department of Defense Inspector General was probing his use of a military jet to conduct personal business. *Time* magazine reported that one month after the Crusader decision, Rumsfeld's staff let it be known that White was "one more mistake away from losing his job."[43] White ultimately lost his job when the Office of the Secretary of Defense announced his resignation on April 25, 2003. The announced departure caught White's staff and the Army generals by surprise. Two days later, it was reported that Rumsfeld had actually fired White.[44]

Shinseki lost a number of battles over Army weapons programs. Rumsfeld almost immediately took action to make the Army work harder to re-create itself. Besides killing Crusader, he cut the Army's Comanche helicopter program by almost half.

Shinseki's only victory, in collaboration with White, was saving Stryker, a lightly armored personnel carrier, capable of carrying eleven men in remote areas at speeds of more than fifty miles per hour. Six brigades, at a cost of $1.5 billion each, would be equipped with 309 Stryker vehicles. The President's FY 2004 budget proposed cutting the number to four and it further calls for a reassessment of the Army's plans to field the final two units. The Army launched a public relations and bureaucratic campaign designed to break "its string of losing battles with Rumsfeld."[45]

Fifth, Pentagon generals and admirals have grown use to capturing their civilian overseers. The building's military leaders easily controlled their civilian superiors by wining and dining them, along with surface obedience. The generals and admirals do not enjoy having civilian superiors, even though the Constitution makes it very clear that the military is subservient to the President and Secretary of Defense.

Challenging the Joint Chiefs of Staff became a Rumsfeld habit, if not simply sport. The *Washington Times* reported that Rumsfeld issued a single page memorandum challenging the necessity for numerous reports on force structure, personnel, missions, pay, and benefits. The paper quoted the memorandum as criticizing reports and documents that "the Joint Staff, the Chairman and the Vice Chairman seemed to think they have to put out on vision, strategies and all that stuff."[46] The article did make the point that Congress often mandates such reports.

Rumsfeld's management style was new to the Pentagon's military leaders. Serving a second time as Department of Defense Secretary gave him a leg up on the normally new appointee. During the Bush presidency, Rumsfeld has continuously challenged the nation's top generals in military areas long ceded to them based upon their long military service. He has operated under the firm constitutional belief that civilians should control the defense establishment. Rumsfeld came into office thinking the Pentagon had become too risk-adverse and independent.

Bush appointed three service secretaries recruited from the private sector in order to bring strong business practices to the Pentagon. In a profile of his management style, the *Washington*

Post quoted an anonymous source as saying the Joint Chiefs Chairman worked as staff to the Secretary. It noted that Rumsfeld was working to strip the Joint Staff of a series of offices. These included legislative liaison, legal counsel, and public affairs, all of which gave the military leadership autonomy and more importantly, direct pipelines to the Congress and media.[47]

During a Department of Defense news briefing, Rumsfeld was asked about his tendency to "ride roughshod over your military leadership."[48] He responded stating he had received unsatisfactory work from civilian and military personnel since he became Secretary and that he had returned items as much as six or seven times before accepting a final product. Rumsfeld reminded reporters that the "Constitution calls for civilian control of this department. And I'm a civilian."[49] In reporting on these statements the *Washington Times* noted that Rumsfeld's management style has endeared him with the rank and file, but offends those with whom he has regular contact. It noted that Rumsfeld has "chastised officials at briefings for not writing or speaking in what he considers clear English."[50]

In a series on the President's cabinet, the *National Journal* awarded Rumsfeld a grade of B+, largely for his method of managing the Pentagon and his relationship with the Congress. "With Rummy, Mr. Outside Outshines Mr. Inside," the author comparing Rumsfeld's management style to former secretary Robert McNamara. Like McNamara, Rumsfeld's influence within the Bush administration is strong, especially after he won budget battles with Office of Management and Budget Director Mitch Daniels and helped advance Bush's strong public support following the September 11th terrorist attacks.[51]

Former Army officer and author Stephen K. Scroggs has concluded that the Army fails in its legislative liaison and lobbying efforts in several ways. He notes that the other services see that flag officers with key global assignments, are brought back to the Pentagon for occasional meetings with Members of Congress and their staffs in order to share their professional experiences.

The military services have strong lobbying and pressure opportunities. They can produce extensive public relations campaigns and maintain powerful direct contacts with members of Congress through their legislative liaison officers. But the Army's work on Capitol Hill is viewed as "less sophisticated and attuned to the interests of the congress audience that the Army is targeting."[52] Members of Congress look to the legislative liaison activity of the services as a legitimate lobbying activity. After all, lobbyists serve as librarians of knowledge. Scroggs also noted that when it comes to the services' representational activities on Capitol Hill, the "Army is viewed as the least effective in conducting this representational activity and supporting it with the service's more valuable agency resources."[53]

Scroggs' descriptions of ineffective Army lobbying activity certainly suggested the failed overall lobbying effort to save Crusader. Army leaders were "particularly steamed at how Rumsfeld and Wolfowitz killed the system, keeping the Army in the dark about what was happening until Congress was ready to vote on the fiscal 2003 budget."[54]

At a time when the Air Force, Navy, and Marines are looking forward to fielding such high-profile, high-cost, weapons systems as the F-22 Raptor, Joint Strike Fighter, F/A-18/E-F Super Hornet and construction of a new Nimitz class aircraft carrier, the Army continues to lose out in the Pentagon–Congressional defense budget struggle. During the Senate Armed Services hearing on Crusader, Joseph Lieberman (Democrat-Connecticut) summed it all up when he pointed out the Army was attempting to complete its transformation by 2008. Congress had not given the Army sufficient funds to complete the transformation. Lieberman said,

> even as in this year the Army's overall budget has increased significantly, by $9.9 billion, and procurement funds increased by 13%, that even with that increase, the Army has found it necessary to cancel another 18 programs, cancellation which has been sustained, incidentally, by our subcommittee and now the full committee, including termination of certain programs that the committee restored last year at the Army's urging.[55]

He also noted that General Shinseki had submitted a list of unfunded requirements totaling an additional $9.5 billion, notwithstanding the $9.9 billion increase.

Sixth, on May 10, 2002, the Army announced the results of the Inspector General's investigation of the "unauthorized" release of talking points to Congress. The investigation revealed that after learning from Paul Wolfowitz about the preliminary decision to terminate Crusader, Army Secretary Thomas White directed his staff to respond to inquiries about the Crusader. White stated that the Army continued to support the Crusader program, as provided for in the President's FY 2003 defense budget. Major General Joe G. Taylor, the Army's Chief, Office of Legislative Liaison (OCLL), directed his staff to prepare talking points to reflect White's guidance. According to the Army, "a staff officer in OCLL drafted talking points that deviated significantly from the Secretary's general direction . . . The talking points contained inappropriate, inaccurate and offensive language, and did not represent the Army's views."[56] The Army claimed that the talking points had not been reviewed by the Chief, OCLL. On May 1, the talking points were distributed to certain members of Congress and their staffs by Kenneth A. Steadman, Principal Deputy, OCLL.

The Inspector General's report absolved Army Secretary White for direct responsibility for the talking points. It concluded, however, that OCLL did not have appropriate procedures for ensuring that talking point documents are prepared appropriately and approved prior to release. The same day the Inspector General's report was released, Steadman, a political appointee, resigned. The talking points were an amateur effort that damaged the overall Army objective of saving Crusader.

Seventh, UDI followed the usual defense contractor practice of spreading work for sub-contractors around the country, especially in key congressional districts and states. This has become standard procedure.[57] When weapons systems have been in trouble, this geographic subcontract distribution has been a saving grace.[58] On August 9, 2002, when the Pentagon announced the termination of Crusader, UDI announced receipt of a new contract with the Army to transition most of the more than two dozen cutting edge technologies developed, during the Crusader work, for a lighter, more deployable NLOS Cannon. While a recent author charges that Carlyle, and its UDI subsidiary did something shady,[59] Kenneth R. Mayer is closer to the truth of defense contracting.[60] Carlyle simply adjusted to the political terrain, where the Army could not, and made the best of the situation.

Lobbying Lesson

A great deal of lobbying is based upon the ability to build trust between the lobbyist and the staff and members of Congress. This trust takes time. The Crusader lobbying effort is an example of a number of lobbying successes and failures.

For example, Scroggs makes a strong point that Army legislative liaison personnel are often passed over for promotions and commands, resulting in early retirement. This is important because members and staffs view these individuals as sources of information "in their subsequent assignments in and out of Washington at increasing higher and more important levels."[61]

This problem was compounded by a situation in which the Army and its Secretary were overruled within the Department of Defense by the Secretary. The Army Secretary allowed talking points strongly contrary to the decision of the Secretary to be circulated in Congress. In his weakened position, White could not withstand the onslaught. An Army civilian lobbyist lost his job. White temporarily held on to his. The Army Chief of Staff made a number of efforts to save Crusader, both within the Department of Defense and in the Congress. In the end, he was not only outmaneuvered on Crusader, but also embarrassed by Rumsfeld's decision to name his successor long before his term was up. Thus the top Army civilian and service leaders were shown to have no substantial influence either within or without the Department of Defense.

The final blow for the Army came when Rumsfeld decided to name Air Force Secretary James G. Roche as the new Army Secretary. Roche, a retired Navy Captain, previously served as the Democratic Staff Director for the Senate Armed Services Committee and as a Senior Executive at Northrop Grumman Corp for sixteen years.[62] Then in March 2004, Roche asked that his nomination be withdrawn due to fallout from the Air Force Academy sexual assault scandal. Less than six months prior to the 2004 elections, the White House prepared to nominate another candidate. All the time, the Army Undersecretary continued to serve as Acting Army Secretary.

James G. Burton has made a strong point that contentious issues create friction on a daily basis in the Pentagon. The bureaucratic battles occur without bloodshed. There are no gracious losers. He goes further in stating:

> Winning the battle is sometimes more important than the subject at hand, and this leads to all kinds of dirty games. The players of these games are truly masters at winning, no matter how underhandedly. Machiavelli himself would be considered a rank amateur in many of these contests.[63]

In highly adversarial lobbying situations, associations, organizations, or corporations often quickly recognize when a situation may not be winnable and thus require compromise. The weakness of both the Army Secretary and Chief of Staff, plus the strong opposition of both the President and the Department of Defense Secretary made it obvious that Crusader was doomed. The advocates, namely UDI and Carlyle, abandoned Crusader in favor of a future contract to develop a different artillery system.

Thus, UDI and Carlyle took the next step which was to seek a compromise with which all sides can live and which preserved UDI's bottom line. When UDI recognized that it could not save Crusader over the opposition of Rumsfeld and Bush, it quickly struck a deal with the Department of Defense and the Congress that won it an exclusive contract to utilize its acquired Crusader technology for a contract to develop a smaller artillery system. Congressional staff and defense lobbyists James Ervin, Ervin Technical Associates, and Towsend Van Fleet, Van Fleet-Meredith Group, are said to have played key roles.[64]

Congress, in its constitutional and historical role, is a mediating institution. It is the place in the national government where competing interests, foreseen by James Madison, could battle without bloodshed over the public interest. Like UDI and Carlyle, members of Congress, even those with specific constituent interests, realized that Crusader was not a defensible weapons system and could not survive opposition from both the President and the Secretary. Congress did what any legislative institution would do, it compromised. In the end, everyone got something that allowed victory to be claimed. The institutional loser was the Army. The individual losers were General Shinseki and Army Secretary White. The winners—the Carlyle Group, UDI, and the Secretary of Defense.

Notes

1 *Fiscal Year 2004 Budget of the U.S. Government*, February 3, 2003, 79.
2 Gordon David, *The Iron Triangle: The Politics of Defense Contracting* (New York: Council on Economic Priorities, 1981).
3 John Norris, *Artillery: A History* (Stroud: Sutton Publishing, 2000), 112.
4 Letter from President George W. Bush to House Speaker J. Dennis Hastert, May 29, 2002.
5 "Barbour Drops Crusader Contract," *Roll Call*, May 20, 2002.
6 "Defense Experts Say Ground Forces Need Crusader: Question Unproven Alternatives," Team Crusader Internet Press Release, June 6, 2002.

7 General Barry R. McCaffrey, USA-Ret., "Challenges to U.S. National Security: Crusader Essential to High-Intensity Combat," *Armed Forces Journal International* (June 2002).

8 "Crusader Myths and Facts," Team Crusader Internet Press Release, June 7, 2002, 1.

9 "Quotable Quotes: Support for the Crusader Advanced Artillery System," June 6, 2002.

10 "Watts Hails Armed Services Committee Passage of Defense Authorization Bill—Army's Crusader Program Strengthened Significantly," Press Release from the Crusader Industrial Alliance, www.crusaderalliance.com/press/pressrelease-05-01-02.php, May 1, 2002.

11 Crusader Industrial Alliance, Clipping Service, "Floor Statement by Senator Paul Wellstone," www.crusaderalliance.com/press/wellstone.php, June 19, 2002.

12 "Gerstner to Be Chairman of Carlyle Group," *New York Times*, November 22, 2002, C3.

13 "Crusader a Boon to Carlyle Group Even if Pentagon Scraps Project," *Washington Post*, May 14, 2002, A03.

14 "Crusader a Boon," A03.

15 "Carlyle's Political Heavyweights Bring Insight, Draw Criticism," *CQ Weekly*, March 9, 2002, 626.

16 "Developer Was Warned on Crusader," *Washington Post*, May 31, 2002, A04.

17 "Developer Was Warned on Crusader."

18 "CSFB Pulls Plug On United Defense," Susan Lerner, CBS, MarketWatch.com, May 2, 2002.

19 "Aldridge Wrote January Memo to Convince Bush Of Crusader's Worth," *InsideDefense* 14 (21), May 27, 2002, available at www.teamcrusader.com/briefing/briefing_insidedefense.

20 "A Different War: Is the Army becoming Irrelevant?," *The New Yorker*, July 1, 2002, 66.

21 "A Different War," 66.

22 "Chief of Staff, Army Report on Indirect Fire (Section 214, S. 2514, 107th Congress," United States Army Chief of Staff, July 25, 2002, 16.

23 "Army Says Canceling Crusader Would Lead to Greater Expenses," *Wall Street Journal*, August 6, 2002, A6.

24 NTU Letter, June 5, 2002, 1.

25 "Crusader is More than Political Pork," *St Paul Pioneer Press*, May 27, 2002.

26 U.S. House of Representatives, "Bob Stump National Defense Authorization Act for Fiscal Year 2003," House Report 107–436, May 3, 2002, 144.

27 Representative Martin Olav Sabo (Democrat-Minnesota), Press Release, June 24, 2002.

28 US Senate, "National Defense Authorization Act for Fiscal Year 2003," Senate Report 107–51, May 15, 2003, 242.

29 Testimony by Secretary of Defense Donald H. Rumsfeld on Crusader Artillery System before the Senate Armed Services Committee (transcript), www.defenselink.mil/speeches/2002, May 16, 2002, 6.

30 Rumsfeld testimony, 8.

31 "Battle of the Crusader," *Washington Post*, May 27, 2002, A23.

32 Senate Roll Call #158 (Levin Amendment No. 3899, as amended, to S. 2514), June 19, 2002.

33 Crusader Alliance Press Release, "United Defense Welcomes Senate Crusader Vote," June 20, 2002, 1.

34 Statement of Administration Policy, "H.R. 5010—Department of Defense Appropriations Bill, FY 2003" (Senate), July 31, 2002, 1.

35 U.S. House of Representatives, "Department of Defense Appropriations Act, 2003," (Conference Report), House Report 107–732, October 9, 2002, 256.

36 U.S. House of Representatives, "National Defense Authorization Act for Fiscal Year 2003" (Conference Report), House Report 107–772, November 12, 2002, 561.

37 Congressional Budget Office, *Budget Options for National Defense*, March 2000, 49. In July 2004, the GAO was renamed the Government Accountability Office.

38 "Defense Acquisitions: Steps to Improve the Crusader Program's Investment Decisions," U.S. GAO, February 25, 2002, 2.

39 "U.S. Military Transformation: Not Just More Spending, But Better Spending," Center for Defense Information, www.cdi.org/mrp/transformation-pr.cfm, January 31, 2002.

40 "The Crusader Program's Tale of Survival", *CQ Weekly*, March 9, 2002, 624.

41 Jack Raymond, *Power at the Pentagon* (New York: Harper & Row, 1964), 203.

42 "The Debate over the Crusader," Cable News Network, May 10, 2002, www.globalsecurity.org/org/news/2002/020510-crusader1.htm.

43 "Pentagon Warlord: Donald Rumsfeld's Secret Plan to Defeat Saddam Relies on Special Forces, High-Tech Weaponry and a Defense Secretary Involved in Every Detail," *Time*, January 27, 2003, 29.

44 "Rumsfeld Fired Army Civilian Chief after Rocky Tenure," *Washington Times*, April 27, 2003, A3.

45 "Army Holds Its Ground in Battle With Rumsfeld," *Los Angeles Times*, November 29, 2002.

46 "Rumsfeld Criticizes Top Staff," *Washington Times*, January 24, 2003, A-1.

47 "Rumsfeld's Style, Goals Strain Ties In Pentagon," *Washington Post*, October 16, 2002, A01.

48 U.S. Department of Defense News Transcript, www.defenselink.mil/news/Jan2003/t01292003_t0129sd.html, January 29, 2003, 16.

49 Defense Department News Transcript, 17.

50 "Rumsfeld Makes No Apology for Style," *Washington Times*, January 30, 2003, A-1.

51 "With Rummy, Mr. Outside Outshines Mr. Inside," *National Journal*, January 24, 2003.

52 Stephen K. Scroggs, *Army Relations with Congress: Thick Armor, Dull Sword, Slow Horse* (Westport, CT.: Praeger, 2000), 81.

53 Scroggs, *Army Relations with Congress*, 215.

54 *Washington Post*, October 16, 2002, A01.

55 *Washington Post*, October 16, 2002, 18.

56 "Army Announces Results of Investigation into Crusader 'Talking Points,' " U.S. Army News Release (R–02–023), May 10, 2002.

57 Ann Markusen, Peter Hall, Scott Campbell, and Sabina Deitrick, *The Rise of the Gunbelt: The Military Remapping of Industrial America* (New York: Oxford, 1991).

58 See Orr Kelly, *King of the Killing Zone: The Story of the M-1, America's Super Tank* (New York: Norton, 1989); and Nick Kotz, *Wild Blue Yonder: Money, Politics, and the B-1 Bomber* (New York: Pantheon, 1988.)

59 Dan Briody, *The Iron Triangle: Inside the Secret World of the Carlyle Group* (Hoboken, N.J.: Wiley, 2003).

60 Kenneth R. Mayer, *The Political Economy of Defense Contracting* (New Haven, CT: Yale University Press, 1991).

61 Scroggs, *Army Relations with Congress*, 101.

62 "Air Force's Roche Picked to Head Army," *Washington Post*, May 2, 2003, A29.

63 James G. Burton, *The Pentagon Wars: Reformers Challenge the Old Guard* (Annapolis, MD: Naval Institute Press, 1993), 65.

64 "On a Crusade," *Influence*, December 11, 2002, 5.

34

Discovering Our (Corporate) Grassroots

European Advocacy 2.0

Marco Althaus

"That's not the way we do it here" or "That doesn't work here" are the unnerving comments political consultants dread to hear whenever they fly in to a new place. The European Union (EU) is such a place, and particularly American lobbying and advocacy specialists are prone to get an earful whenever they dare to suggest modern-day legislative strategies and hard-nosed pressure campaign tactics that have become the staple in the United States both at the federal and state level.

Coalition-building? Advocacy campaigns? Grassroots? Grasstops? Lobby days, fly-ins, Capitol steps picketing, orchestrated constituent mail, patch-through phone campaigns, corporate employee "civic action networks," "voter education" advertising and election-year get-out-the-vote (GOTV) mobilization based on viral marketing and web 2.0 techniques?

Until recently, most pan-European strategists would have none of that. It seemed to fit neither the resources nor the culture. The supranational structure of the EU, different languages, and the absence of a common European people or public have made grassroots lobbying, if not unfeasible in the EU, at least not worth the cost in the past.[1]

Until recently, most returning American political professionals would tell baffled colleagues that Brussels is a place where only elite lobbying counts, parties and elections are irrelevant to the lobbyist's trade, political money is mainly invested in gourmet cuisine expense accounts, Lobbying Disclosures Act (LDA)-style registration and disclosure is unknown, news media-driven debates and public opinion polls are fringe phenomena for lobbying work, and citizens are far-away abstract entities because constituents have no clue what Brussels does or who their representatives are, anyway.

Consensus politics, they would iterate, gives cover to unintelligible policy-making, and the lack of adversarial party competition contributes to the phenomenon of a perfect insider game. The confederated Euro-interest groups do not help at this point either, as they have more incentives to play institutional politics rather than engage their members in polarizing advocacy campaigns; even the lobby sector seems "over-institutionalized."[2]

Brussels, the American political traveler would report, is the place where organizing pressure or using anti-big-government rhetoric will quickly turn the perceived aggressor into the village pariah. In Washington, one can make a career being anti-Washington; in Brussels, no one can be anti-Brussels. Therefore, the quintessential Brussels advocate must be anything but a Washington political warrior: the Brussels advocate must be a soft-spoken, multi-cultural, multi-tongued polite diplomat, the servant of consensus and constructive consultation, a friendly policy coordinator and connoisseur of knowledge for the myriad of expert groups and "comitology" system. A person who can serve reliable evidence, legal arguments and scientific data to policy-makers, an unbiased supplier of robust facts. The job description means, always be part of the solution (even if you don't like it), and never of the problem.

No political hellraisers need apply. That's Brussels. Or it used to be.

All Wonks, No Hacks in Brussels

American Democratic operative Bruce Reed once pointed out that when one strips away the job titles and party labels, one will find two kinds of people in a capital city: political hacks and policy wonks. Washington depends, like all European capitals, on a balance of the two tribes. "A president," said Reed about his country, "must know the real problems on Americans' minds. For that he needs hacks. But ultimately, he needs policies that will actually solve those problems. For that he needs wonks."[3]

By that standard, Brussels has long been almost uninhabitable for political hacks of any sort. The European capital is so wonkish it is hard to find anyone being driven by pure ideology or partisanship. Those who love the adrenaline rush of an election campaign's seventy-two-hour end run, those who love the rhetorical fireworks of parliamentary partisanship, those who love to spin the headlines and thrive on televised brawls between the left and the right will be found in London, Rome, Berlin or Warsaw, but not in Brussels.

Even the political consultancies and lobby shops have long been filled with PhDs or alumni with a master's degree from the Brugge College of Europe, and other propeller-heads. These are just the right people to hobnob with the elite and highly intellectual cadre of EU civil servants, few of whom ever leave their well-respected, well-paid Golden Cage through a revolving door to work on a campaign or earn a living in the lobby.

Brussels has neither the glamour nor the perspiration of the boxing arena of national capitals; Brussels is the quintessential policy apparatus. Even if it should be true that good policy makes good politics, the point is that for a long time, few in Brussels cared what good politics is. European elections since 1979 have been largely run on a national basis on national issues, with parties not taking the trouble to explain to voters much about the complex EU machinery or its output. And the turnout among voters has been low. Nobody seemed to know how to rally and mobilize Europeans for or against anything on the Brussels agenda. Reed says about Washington political hacks that the only results they understand are polling. But public opinion polls, a necessary daily diet for most European national politics, are hardly discussed over coffee in Brussels.

The Changing Arena of European Politics

But Brussels is changing. Hacks may unpack their suitcases. Once a policy wonk's dream city, Brussels slowly but surely becomes more of a political town. Communications and campaign strategies grow in importance. Public affairs management takes a larger perspective now, including more interaction with more stakeholders, and doing so in a more public way. We could, and should, talk about a new chapter in European advocacy—not a totally new, but revised and more democratic version.

As these days anything digital is in vogue, let us propose "European Advocacy 2.0" as a term. European observers in the know will note "Public Affairs 2.0" is already the name of a weblog published by the public affairs team of the Fleishman Hillard agency in Brussels,[4] and the term has been spread by the Berlin/Brussels consultancy Plato,[5] in both cases describing the digital toolbox of information management, social networks and participatory approaches.

"European Advocacy 2.0" has indeed much to do with the Internet, albeit the shift from "1.0" to "2.0" is not a technical one. It is about opportunities for public participation, membership engagement, coalitions, mobilizing employees and other stakeholders, and opportunities to change policy by doing so. Moreover, it is about a pressing need to find strategic approaches interlocking Brussels and national efforts in pan-European campaigns with pan-European teams.

My argument here is supply-sided: more opportunities for people-powered advocacy already increase the demand, and will continue to do so. Learning from non-governmental organizations (NGOs), labor unions and farmers, industry trade associations and corporations recognize the change in context of their lobbying, and have begun to invest in developing more communications and mobilization capabilities, happily served by political consultants.

It's Not Yet "Brussels, D.C." But . . .

It is still true that the EU capital city is not the "Brussels, D.C." that some have presented as a parallel universe to American politics. Seen constitutionally (even though we have no constitution), our European polity is still "a shifting compromise between the supranational 'community method' and various forms of intergovernmentalism." This also means that, despite the high profile of business lobbies, the most lobbying that is going on in Brussels is member states and governmental sub-units lobbying each other.[6]

Cultural, social, economic and political divisions run much deeper than they seem for the non-European. In a Europe of twenty-seven nations there are now twenty-seven forms of public affairs—plus one, that is, working the EU institutions. It would be ludicrous to assume that any one person could professionally handle all systems (it would have been a doubtful proposition even for the EU-15 before enlargement in 2004), or even know them in any detail. They do not converge easily into one handy model, a fact that Brussels lobbyists wake up to every day—the EU capital scene is not a melting pot of political cultures but rather a tossed salad, and the approach and style that works with a Commission eurocrat from Finland may be bad advice for the lobbyist sitting down with a Romanian Member of the European Parliament (MEP).

In some of these twenty-eight variations, public communications, campaigns, coalitions and indeed full-fledged American-style grassroots advocacy concepts have a greater chance of implementation than they have in others. Arguably the British have a civic society base, pluralistic advocacy tradition and campaigning practice that comes closest to that of the US, but any diverse, competitive democracy in Europe has the potential for more mobilization and participation as "outside" forces to supplement "inside" lobbying strategies.

The last thirty years have seen such strategies in Western Europe, occasionally with the help of US expertise. For example, Washington grassroots consultant Edward A. Grefe tells the story of how an American multinational company in 1976 asked him to help its French subsidiary to build public support for the company's position on a proposed law before the French National Assembly.[7] This should come as no surprise as many communication agencies are parts of American-led networks and, specifically, US election campaign styles have been shopped for and adapted by West Europeans even half a century ago, and know-how transfer was organized officially with the 1969 founding of the International Association of Political Consultants. However, grassroots techniques were always thought to be fit only for the truly political wars of the national and regional level, not at the European level.

It has not gone unnoticed in EU member states that Brussels today can and will drive the legislative agenda for most national policy-makers, and few policy arenas are excluded. In some fields, half of national laws are predetermined, in others—such as environmental regulation—we find almost all is done at the supranational level. National governments have considerable freedom to fiddle with the details, but implement the laws they must, and any divergence from the mainstream implementation in other states may be subject to administrative review by the

Commission's agencies or judicial review by the European Court of Justice. True, the EU is more a confederacy than a federal state, which makes lobbying cumbersome and public, outside-oriented lobbying strategies difficult. But an EU member state cannot ignore Community legislation, regulation, standards and guidelines any more than a US state can ignore federal laws, regulation, standards and guidelines. Thus, national policy-makers feel the impact.

While the national politics and publicly perceived policy priorities differ greatly, central policy content is usually pre-determined by Brussels. Many national politicians are still in denial that this is so. But most have long realized that today's member of a parliament will mostly see bills that turn EU directives into national legislation, and the general direction of policy has been set years earlier. So national policy-makers who take no interest in the EU will usually arrive too late for a meaningful date with destiny. Lobbyists at the national level are usually the ones who urge national players to act early and influence whatever process goes on in Brussels.

In most cases, the people who follow the lobbyists' call are members of the executive branches, not the elected parliamentarians. The ministries much better understand what goes on in Brussels, and they have the institutional means to act via the Council and the Permanent Representatives. The political circles in national parliaments and parties, by contrast, long engaged in agitated melancholia over their loss of power.

Yet more realistic and particularly younger politicians, it seems, these days stop whining and yammering, and step aboard the EU public affairs train. They do not really have a choice. They know that currently national publics and parliaments cannot follow the moves of their ministers in Council horse-trading and log-rolling.

Public affairs strategies, therefore, are more and more integrated, working both the national and the Brussels beat at the same time. Pan-European teams are formed, as some Brussels offices can be quite blind without their national radar.

Indeed, Brussels and national capitals work like communicating pipes. Multi-layer lobbying is a current catchword describing the need for advocates to be present at the top as well as the bottom, and often at the same time.

But that, of course, depends on the issue. Sometimes Brussels-based sector specialists can go it alone, sometimes they can only go to work with the backdrop of a complementary public awareness or pressure campaign.

According to Brussels WeberShandwick former CEO John Russel:

> The broader and the more important the issue, the bigger is the need for Europe-wide campaigns. For instance, if a client is only concerned with a specific minor technical detail in a legislative proposal, the help of a sector specialist will most likely be sufficient. However, for broad and fundamental issues such as animal testing for cosmetics or the advertising ban for tobacco, for example, issues which also have emotional aspects to them, a grass-roots campaign will increase the awareness and the pressure, and provide fertile ground for the sector specialists targeted lobbying effort.[8]

The New Coalitions Game

Coalition-building is a concept that does not necessarily involve a grassroots effort, but many grassroots efforts depend on successful coalition-building. The involvement of a greater number of participants, the outreach to various European, national and regional networks a coalition allows helps a lot to enhance legitimacy.

Coalition-building is, of course, by necessity an art long practiced in Brussels. No wonder: the EU never had, for any issue, majorities built into the structure. Every bill, every initiative, every dossier must find a majority of its own. Finding not only channels and access but partners to form a representative, cross-European voice was the *conditio sine qua non* of Brussels lobbying.

The understanding of what coalition-building entails changes in Brussels. Traditionally, this was the natural field of trade associations—the larger, the better and the more legitimacy with EU institutions. The key point here is that in the past, these alliances rested on their representativity alone, and that is why they followed a big-is-beautiful philosophy. More and more coalitions do not claim to be as representative of a larger universe of interests; and even if they claim to be representative, it is credibility and unity that count. In addition, it is less a sectoral and more an issues management approach.

Thus, a new kind of actor has stepped onto the scene: relatively small alliances (often called "platforms") led by a handful of companies and groups, concentrating on single issues. When their job is done, they just disappear. Sometimes they are gone before we have barely noticed them. But many are geared toward external communications, following the example of NGO coalitions, and move into much visibility. Such platforms can take various forms. According to a typology proposed by Daniel Guéguen, there are five:[9]

- Public/private partnership platforms: the most common type, often financed by the Commission to foster dialogue with civil society. Lobbying does not always describe what such a platform does—because this type is often vast and large, it is less bent on action than on discussion. An example is the Commission-financed "EU Platform for Action on Diet, Physical Activity and Health" uniting food industry, retailers, advertisers, consumer associations, health NGOs, scientists and experts on obesity. Corporate members often join to decrease the risk of regulatory action, to show they are willing to talk and be a responsible member of such a forum. By contrast, other public/private partnership platforms are much more specific and unite complementary, rather than adversary, members willing to lobby the EU institutions—and the EU Commission helps them do that. This often happens in research, development and technology fields. This is, in a way, the European version of the American "iron triangle."
- "Shop window" platforms are primarily information outlets and take care of the public image of a sector, often as the extended public relations arm of established trade or umbrella associations. For example: the European Food Information Council, composed of big agri-food multinationals (such as Coca-Cola, Ferrero, Danone, Kraft, Masterfoods, Pepsico, Unilever).
- "Counter balance" platforms are established by smaller players to counter the weight of a dominant lobby organization. Instead of forming a full-fledged association, they use a platform concept to challenge the giant's hegemony. For example: the European Initiative for Sustainable Development in Agriculture, an assortment of national associations to counter farming heavyweight COPA-COGECA.
- Industrial platforms: companies and related research and development institutes like to promote technologies. For examples: Mobile and Wireless Communications Technology Platform (Ericsson, Siemens, Nokia, Motorola, France Telecom and Vodafone, plus universities) or the European Robotics Platform (Acrobat, Philips, Bosch, Thales, Sagem Defence & Security, Mitsubishi Electric Neuronics, plus universities).
- Platforms created as ad hoc lobbying tools are practical answers to difficult advocacy tasks where European associations do not have the structure, flexibility, expertise or will to act. For example: the Platform for Ingredients in Europe (a voice for companies such as ADM, Bunge, Cargill, Danisco, Roquette, Tate & Lyle, and others) to work on food ingredients regulation.

In addition to platforms, the preference for sector alliances sometimes gives way to "horizontal" or "transversal" coalitions—those that bring together even adversaries, for example, producers, consumers and environmentalists across the whole spectrum of a product's value chain. What such alliances offer to EU institutions may be pre-negotiated compromise solutions rather than opposition politics.[10]

The key point here is that NGOs, consumer groups and labor unions have something to offer to corporate players looking for partners. Previously such organizations were perceived as good only on pressure and communications, but lacking in technical competence, that is, the wonk side of governing and lobbying where the expertise of economists, engineers, scientists, lawyers and public policy analysts is needed. But while many NGOs are still small and best in the field of media relations, others have large offices filled with specialists. Some, like the World Wide Fund for Nature (WWF) European Office, have some thirty staff available, huge compared to most corporate offices in Brussels. They have the technical expertise, they have the access, they have the standing, they have the allies and they have the resources to follow through on any commitment to the EU institutions—including, of course, a pan-European network at the grassroots. They can use it, and have used it, in partnerships with industry.

Some corporations have begun to recognize that and, despite some critical distance, are willing to build constructive relationships with NGOs, labor unions and consumer groups in their policy arena. This offers the opportunity to break the segregation of interests and explore possible points of convergence. This is also a chance to be more pro-active in advocacy and avoid some ugly confrontations, or at least reduce some risks of escalation. It allows for changing lobbying strategies from opposition to proposition.[11]

Putting the Public Back into Public Affairs

The old truism that public affairs often means non-public relations has been nowhere truer than in Brussels. But these days the public comes back in. Public opinion begins to play a more significant role. Remarkably the Commission under President Jose Manuel Barroso is more attuned to *vox populi*, turning more and more to popular decisions and policies cheered by the media back home.

Barroso's Commission is quite clear about its intent to win back support from citizens for the 2009 European elections. One could say that the Commission, once the palladium of remote eurocracy which did not care whether citizens understood or liked what Brussels did, now bends over backwards to push participatory democracy—even to the dislike of some member states.

The Commission does it because of the institutional crisis that had been triggered by the French and Dutch "nos" to the Constitution draft. In the Fall 2005, the Commission began to talk about a "Plan D"—for democracy, dialogue and debate—in the run-up to the 2009 elections (elections that tend to have a very low turnout). A 2006 White Paper on European Communication Policy Strengthening EU civics education in schools is only one point. Among the more direct measures are plans to develop a network of "European public spaces" at EU representations in the member states, setting up "citizen consultation" procedures, stakeholder dialogues and citizen conference series, installing a "citizens' agenda" into the Commission's work program, and heavy investments in the Internet, including such stunts as an EUtube channel on YouTube, and commissioners operating their own daily blogs.

Citizen distrust of the EU and lack of interest may be disturbing, but the actual picture, as both the official Eurobarometer and private polls show, is much more differentiated. While people certainly feel they are poorly informed about the EU, do not understand the way it works and talk about it less often than they talk about national or local issues, there is more confidence in Europe than one would think.

One recent EU-wide Penn Schoen Berland poll commissioned by the *European Voice* found that people trust the EU (37%) more than their own governments (22%), and this is more so in the new member states (49% versus 11%).

People believe the EU should be involved in areas such as the environment (86%), food safety (82%), energy (78%), trade (73%), health (72%)—a lot more than in competition policy (54%), tax (49%) and culture (47%). Some 79% of respondents also believed the EU is strongly influenced by business, while NGOs are seen as less influential.

Pollster Mark Penn saw opportunities

> to convince some groups—like women with children—who typically are not hostile to the EU but at present believe it is not relevant to their lives. To better engage with such citizens, the data shows that the EU needs to transform itself into a body which is seen as open and transparent about its workings, with an agenda of policies which reflect the priorities of its people and where the benefits that EU membership brings are clear.[12]

This is exactly the strategy of the Commission, and it has implications for policy. The volume of legislation and regulation is going up, not down, and the tendency to engage in social engineering and nanny governing, so long as some sort of popular demand is perceived, is very observable in Brussels.

It is thus no coincidence that the most emotionally charged issues, such as personal safety, climate policy, environmental and consumer protection (for example, food labeling, obesity, tobacco advertising) get so much attention in Brussels, as these issues are more easily reported and get more column inches back home (EU correspondents still have a hard time convincing their news editors to make room for their stories).

The commissioners, once very aloof guardians of the EU treaties, seem to enjoy the new-found popularity and focus on (sometimes dramatized) decisions and initiatives people can actually understand—and like. The Commission also invests a lot more money in communications nationally. It is quite unclear whether that will work, given that member state governments have the habit of taking credit for popular policies and pointing fingers at Brussels whenever people get angry (the "Brussels blame game" so often criticized by the Commission).

Windows of Populist Opportunity

The first to take note and profit from change were NGOs, particularly environmental campaigners who began in the 1990s to run transnational advocacy campaigns to put pressure on European decision-makers. It is the NGOs that are able to force emotional, more political issues onto the EU agenda. Today, many NGOs are well equipped for "European Advocacy 2.0," not competing with business, labor and government interests via inside access and expertise, but via public pressure and exposure.

The NGOs took advantage of the growing awareness of the democratic deficit of the EU setup of institutions, a setup seen as being inaccessible to the ordinary citizen and lacking legitimacy. This issue came up in all treaty stages of the European integration process. The EU is crawling toward the principle of participatory democracy, with its institutions, most notably the Commission, taking a decidedly more populist stance. This populism translates into anti-big business, anti-monopoly, pro-consumer policies.

The Commission, being the guardian of the European idea, accepts that it has a responsibility for more democratic governance. A new vice president for communication and relations with civil society was installed. Rules on access to documents have been strengthened, dialogue forums, new procedures for open stakeholder consultations offer broad access to groups of all sorts that can claim European representativity—principles that were also included in the Constitution draft.

The civil dialogue—a public symbol of which is the Commission's CONECCS online database of civil society actors and web-based stakeholder consultation—is basically an open door policy to NGOs. Current plans include installing civil society "contact points" at the

Commission's offices to improve even more NGO access to information and documents from EU institutions.

Further, the Commission also engages heavily in financing NGOs, even helping to set them up. The EU Commission spends well over a billion euros a year to enable NGOs to participate in Brussels. A lot of NGOs in Brussels are in a gray area: many are government-interested NGOs (GINGOs for short), quasi-governmental NGOs (QUANGOs) or government-organized NGOs (GONGOs).[13]

It should be noted that these EU-financed NGOs openly advertise on the websites and brochures that one of their major roles is to "lobby" the EU institutions and run campaigns to supplement that lobbying; and informally, in the various Directorates General of the Commission staff are quite open that their idea is to set up counter-lobby groups that are able to mobilize support for their policy proposals, or against some other Directorates' General proposals or other lobby organization's demands. They lobby the European Parliament (EP), they lobby the national representatives, and they operate membership organizations and effective media relations, sometimes even miniature policy think tanks. This goes not only for Brussels but for the national and regional level, too. In effect, most Directorates General finance a political arm by friendly dependent NGOs.

One place where NGO presence and influence is felt strongly is the European Parliament. When NGOs joined the lobbying scene, they also changed the culture of interest representation before the Parliament in Brussels and Strasbourg. They not only stood up as experts but also made clear the connection to constituencies and public opinion. They brought in journalists to get more attention, orchestrated publicity stunts, marches and rallies, started letter-writing, fax and e-mail campaigns. It did not take long for industry associations, corporate coalitions and the consultancies that work for them to match the NGO campaign activities with campaigns of their own.

Parliament Rising

Once reason is that today's MEP is a lot more in the focus of the Brussels lobbyists than he or she used to be, and unlike the Commission and Council actors, the MEP is an elected person with a political mandate. EU treaties have significantly strengthened the Parliament's role in legislation. Most relevant legislation gets passed via the co-decision procedure, a sharp knife the members of the body have learned to handle.

While it is still true that the best influence a lobbyist has is early, meaning at the creation of a Commission proposal (the executive branch is the only EU institution with the privilege to introduce new legislation), the days are past when the Parliament rubber-stamped all bills.

Once known as "the Parliament that can't say no," elected legislators now teach bureaucrats lessons in the school of hard knocks. They can, because unlike in the usual European constellation, there is no majority party or party coalition that must protect the government. The Commission and Council of Ministers now routinely expect plenty of amendments and a necessity for long conference committee negotiations. Arrogance backfires immediately, and unpopular measures get bogged or even shot down. We have even seen Commission proposals die in an EP committee—something unheard of just a few years ago.

This means, of course, that lobbyists have to re-think the traditional wisdom that if you cannot influence an initiative before the Commission puts it out, you cannot influence it at all (unless you have a national government blocking it in the Council). Now lobbyists increasingly turn to Parliament committees to make it happen; that makes lobbying so much more political.

MEPs think about being re-nominated and re-elected, and they are accountable to many more people and groups than the civil servants are. Out of enlightened self-interest, they pay more attention to the consent of the governed. And not a few of them will delight in the chance to grow a profile as a red-tape fighter.

It used to be that European national parties sent their past-their-glory-days political retirees to the EP. But that is changing, too, as young career-minded politicans realize an EP mandate gets less television time but also means less party control and more actual influence over governing 400 million people. Legislative activism and increasing powers of the EP increase side by side.

Looking into the future of European parliamentarism, it is highly unlikely that the EP will tolerate much longer not to have the right to introduce legislation. Once that barrier falls, as it eventually will, lobbyists will swarm over the Parliament in massive numbers. They will have great chances to succeed, as the EP has a great disadvantage in staff power.

Yes, currently it is still better to be present at the creation of a draft and to influence the legislative embryo. Because the Parliament does not have the right of introducing legislation, the Commission, always open to outside input, is the place to focus on. Their core 6,000 policy-makers—a ridiculously small number compared to national European or the US federal government—are the most important phone numbers to have on file. But even today, if a bill can be painted as an unpopular error, chances are it will be changed once it's out of the Commission's hands. Or even stopped dead.

Recently, even the ultimate underground fortress of bureaucracy and insider lobbying, the comitology process, was razed by reformer shock troops. The committee system where national implementation of EU acts is overseen now gives Parliament opportunities to oppose and block executive action if it exceeds implementing powers given by the primary legislation, if it is incompatible with the aim or content of the primary instrument, or if it is in conflict with the principles of subsidiarity or proportionality.

Challenges to the Old Club Consensus

But it is not just the Parliament. Among national member governments, the old club benign pressure for consensus is history, and many a romp has been registered at the Council of Ministers, too.

Confrontations at the Justus Lipsius building are likely to rise with a great number of EU members and a cumbersome qualified-majority-voting procedure. It's easier now to play veto poker, and the new EU member states are not shy of a fight. "You forgot Poland," once a Bushism, is now a Brussels running gag.

What drives them? Usually, national politics and opinion dynamics. National governments pay a lot more attention to EU-related public opinion, as some learned the hard way that people do pay attention to what their governments are doing in Brussels. It's risky to assume they don't. The 2008 and 2005 EU Constitution referenda debacles and various issue fights have made clear to politicians, organizations and media that national and EU policy-making is intertwined in most policy arenas. Lobbyists learn to mobilize public opinion, members and sympathizers to a cause to pressure policy-makers at home so to handle change in Brussels.

In summary, what a lobbyist can do now in Brussels is alter policy and even kill bills by using genuine political tools—showing that the majority is not behind it, that it is unpopular and that anyone who dares to stare down the people will be trampled into the ground. Brussels is indeed getting more political and more public. Consensus gives way to controversy and competition. Not always, of course, but more often now than in the past.

From Elite Lobbying to Popular Advocacy

Still, some European public affairs practitioners may fail to recognize that "political and social change is rendering its traditional approach to lobbying redundant. The key change is the growing importance of public opinion," as one observer warned back in 2002.

The extraordinary rise in the power of NGOs and single issue groups may signal the advent of a different approach: Emotional appeals, pressure campaigns, using both media and direct communication to set the political agenda, reinforced by the internet, could be the wave of the future, aligned with companies' brand strategies and shifting away from traditional elite lobbying toward NGO-style campaigning and mobilization of public support.

For the business players in particular, it has become risky to see politics as extraneous and public protest as a nuisance, and seek to minimize regulation only on an ad hoc basis, disregarding the broader political and social context. They, too, must accept that policy change can spring from grassroots sentiment rather than the wonky elites. EU Consultant Simon Titley asserts:

> Unless the [public affairs] industry changes, it risks being downgraded to a low-margin tactical delivery service. . . . In terms of skills, practitioners can no longer rely on elite lobbying as a tactic, but will have to develop complementary skills in stakeholder relations and coalition building, grassroots and Internet campaigning, media relations, and Internet-based intelligence gathering/ analysis. They must be prepared to mix and match these skills and not rely on any single tactic. They must learn how to balance rational arguments with emotionally appealing messages. They will also need to develop the agility to respond to rapid day-to-day change, as the Internet increases the speed at which issues develop. . . .
>
> Corporations will also change. The manufacturing of public consent for company operations will become an integral part of corporate strategy, and (by aiming to keep issues out of the formal political arena) will be intended to pre-empt lobbying as much as to support lobbying. Political campaign techniques will become an integral part of branding and marketing campaigns. In-house public affairs staff will find themselves marginalised or redundant unless they have already forged strong relationships with their colleagues in strategic planning and brand management. Corporations' public affairs campaigns will learn not only from pressure groups but also from the latest marketing techniques. . . . Political intelligence work will be transformed, with an emphasis on adding value through analysis and interpretation, and the early detection of emerging political issues before they enter the formal political process.[14]

In 2002, this prophecy still seemed a bit far off. But much has changed since then: the number of EU members almost doubled; the competition of lobbying forces in Brussels is fierce; the constitutional effort was derailed; half the national governments changed party colors; media take a lot more note of what goes on at the EU; and Internet-based campaigns have grown up to be a serious force in politics and society. The list of change factors is long.

All of this sets the stage for a new era of more populist politicking, more citizen participation and more lobbying based on outsider, grassroots pressure strategies.

Two Mini-Case Examples

We now turn to two recent mini-cases to track the grassroots element in Brussels. Both involve initiatives of small and medium sized enterprises (SMEs) organizing to stop and alter EU legislation. In the first case, SMEs moved alongside large multinational corporate players and their associations, and confronted NGOs; in the second, SMEs stood in clear opposition to large corporations and formed an effective coalition with NGOs. Both examples started in Germany because the country was severely affected, but both were quickly turned into pan-European advocacy coalitions with grassroots outreach across the continent.

Mini-case 1: Mobilizing Chemical Industry Grassroots[15]

It took seven years to be written into law and triggered the biggest, loudest, most complex and bitter European policy battle in decades: REACH. The acronym stands for Registration,

Evaluation, Authorisation and Restriction of Chemicals and was written into law as regulation 2006/1907 in December 2006, becoming effective in June 2007. Industry players from all continents were involved in the controversy, as well as governments from the US to China, and this piece of law will impact them for decades to come. It all started in 1999 when the Commission began work on future chemicals policy. The 2001 White Paper and 2003 consultation process generated a bill that enraged industry; meanwhile, environmental NGOs cheered REACH loudly as the most progressive measure in decades.

First, the policy background: the regulation states that all chemicals produced or imported at a volume of at least one ton a year are subject to health and safety testing and must be registered with a newly created European Chemicals Agency. The regime applies to all, not just new, chemicals, including 30,000 substances already in regular use in various industries. In addition, it pressed for the substitution of substances suspected to be unsafe—a move supposed to increase innovation. The prospect of compliance was not so unnerving for big chemical conglomerates but for downstream users and smaller manufacturers across many industries. For some it meant only trouble, while for others costs and red tape were expected to jeopardize the very existence of companies. REACH turned into a survival issue for SMEs.

The industrial SME lobby is a highly fragmented, conservative and slow-moving one. European SMEs tend to rely solely on their trade and umbrella associations. Few hire consultants to represent them; almost none have their own offices in Brussels to influence policy-making directly. SMEs are also more engaged with their national and trade-specific industry groups than the big umbrella eurogroups that tend to be dominated by industry heavyweights (such as Germany's BDI industrial and VCI chemical federation, the CEFIC chemical industry eurogroup, or BusinessEurope).

As the battle of many lobby organizations heated up, the Commission proposal was amended many times. The legislation was softened, then rewritten into a strict regime. Commission, Parliament and Council settled for a long period of intense conferencing (the "trilogue"). During the REACH debates, environmental and consumer organizations had their heyday both among the elites and in the media. They campaigned massively and very professionally for the Commission bill. In coalitions of their own, they concerted their efforts and succeeded in making a seemingly odd and complicated topic a widely reported media subject no politician could ignore. Public relations stunts made even the lamest pay attention, for example when NGOs blood-tested MEPs, listed the chemicals they found and attacked the chemical industry for irresponsible contamination of everyday consumer products. The groups were able to push all the emotional hot buttons and tugged the media along.

By contrast, corporate EU and national lobbying had changed considerably. First it aimed at open dialogue, then opened fire via the media, then returned to a low-profile strategy avoiding the arena of public opinion and sticking to influence decision-makers behind the scenes. Associations followed a matter-of-fact, legal and scientific, almost clinical course that was no match for NGO campaigns aiming directly at public opinion power. It was a case of wonks versus hacks, and because the decision was now with the Parliament, environmental and consumer protection advocates weighed in successfully with their popular power.

SMEs and their specialist trade organizations began to feel that what the large umbrella associations and the big chemicals did in Brussels was inadequate to their needs and insensitive to the threats on survival. Until 2003, they had been reluctant to raise objections and publicize expected problems, fearing backlash from customers and business stakeholders.

This feeling was widespread across Europe, but not all national business organizations tracked the issue and educated their members at the same intensity. In Germany, which has a strong SME industrial base and an active network of associations, REACH was clearly at the top of the agenda. One broad-based federation of manufacturers, TEGEWA of Frankfurt, moved to act in 2004. TEGEWA is a collective organization of manufacturers of textile, paper, leather and fur auxiliaries, surfactants, polymers, cosmetic raw materials, pharmaceutical excipients and allied specialist chemistry; it is also a sub-group of the powerful VCI, the German chemical industry association.

When the sub-group began to explore whether it could start a European advocacy campaign of its own, VCI officers bristled at the idea—their strategy in Brussels was different. After arguments went back and forth seemingly not always in the best of taste, they finally settled on the proposition that an outreach and media effort unconnected to VCI could be constructive; VCI could help coordinate but was unwilling to be the platform for such advocacy.

TEGEWA member companies began to organize. As they wanted to raise an objection with Parliament and Council, they called it "Aktion Einspruch," or Objection! initiative (this legal term could easily be translated into all European languages). For all the attention it got, this German SME initiative needed allies in other countries to really have an impact on Brussels and not allowing REACH supporters to point to some "odd man out" kind of national industry position mirroring some strange German angst. In two years, it would grow into an alliance of 400 supporting manufacturing enterprises from fifteen EU member states and (non-EU member) Switzerland. Most coalition partners were based in Britain, Spain, Belgium, Italy, Poland and the Czech Republic. In these countries, the campaign installed "National Focal Points"—regional campaign coordinators volunteered by one or two SMEs. A supranational steering committee, assisted by the coalition's permanent Brussels/Berlin secretariat run by a consultancy, helped ensure a one-voice policy.

Objection!'s strategic message was based on proving authoritatively why and how SMEs were directly affected, particularly in the constituencies of MEPs, but also national governments influential in the Council. In addition, public opinion was to be agitated to counter NGO dominance in media relevant to decision-makers—that is, in regional papers as much as in national opinion leaders and the Brussels community media. While doing that, the campaign signaled it was not about fundamentalist opposition to a harmonized EU chemicals policy. Central talking points included seeing REACH generate a serious loss of manufacturing jobs without considerable benefit for environmental and consumer protection, a high bureaucratic and financial burden, and a likely strong increase of chemicals imported from outside the EU with less strict controls.

Most campaign materials were produced in three languages (English, French and German). Ready-to-use support packages for actively participating SMEs included checklists, address lists, talking points, templates for ads, letters, speeches, articles and project plans. The campaign rested on the idea that companies would communicate directly with both national and European decision-makers. They had to be enabled to organize a regional event with their representatives or run an intelligent letter writing mini-campaign. For all the little practical questions in setting up their part of the campaign business, the secretariat's hotline was always available by phone and e-mail. A DVD with the full toolbox and a video trailer in five languages was sent out to all supporters. A series of ads and posters, and a traveling exhibition could be utilized for event preparation. Within a time frame of six months, the member companies collected 33,000 signatures. They were presented—close to the first reading—to the Parliament's vice president, Dagmar Roth-Behrendt, in a public event in Brussels showcasing a stage full of empty chairs to symbolize threatened jobs in the EU. When the first reading came, Objection! business campaigners stood shoulder to shoulder with their opposition from the environmentalist camp at the entrances to the Strasbourg plenary hall, competing for last-minute access to pitch their views. While the legislative process went on, a series of Brussels events had SME managers from many EU countries flown in to make their case.

The two-year campaign can be summarized with some numbers. The kickoff in Berlin began with 1,000 business people, labor union leaders and chemical workers forming, with red umbrellas, the word· "Einspruch" (objection) in front of the Reichstag building and the

Brandenburg Gate, mainly aimed at getting the attention of the German government—which it did, as the Chancellor Schröder's chief of staff spontaneously invited demonstrators in and German MPs came out to see what went on. Eleven events in Brussels, Berlin and various regions were set up, and fifty-eight high-level political talks introduced. Six times letters and faxes with invitations to MEPs in Brussels and Strasbourg were sent, as were eighteen e-mails to MEPs, eighteen e-mails and nine policy newsletters to supporters. Twenty news releases and various advertisements in lead media were produced, as was a bilingual website. A total of 33,000 signatures were collected in a petition drive. It should be noted that the campaign only had a budget for one year; when the legislative process dragged on, supporters extended its mission for another year—which also meant extended fundraising, for the 400 members had to make individual pledges to finance the effort.

Did it reach its objectives? Partly. The REACH compromise that the institutions finally settled on was complex and had many parents. Objection! did its part and was a visible and audible advocate, sometimes the only industry group to clearly counter Greenpeace and other groups. The key point is that the brand name of the campaign mattered less than the direct lobbying of regional representatives by companies (managers and labor) in their constituencies. It was enough to plant the seed of doubt. This certainly helped turn the issue around—Parliament majorities swung clearly in a less environmentalist direction.

Mini-case 2: Software Patents—Mobilizing the IT Community[16]

Quite a different story is the fight over computer-implemented inventions (CIIs) in 2003–2005. Politics makes strange bedfellows, but sometimes the strangest coalition is the most effective. Here, an alliance ranged from conservative high street entrepreneurs to new-economy techie corporations, from the open source programming community to university researchers and the anti-globalization activists of Attac.[17] In a remarkable coordinated effort they did what is extremely difficult to do: completely stop and kill an EU directive already under consideration in the EP.

The software patent opponents succeeded against intense pro-patent lobbying. They succeeded against the combined political power of the Commission, almost all EU member governments except Spain, all Parliament groups except the Greens, the European Patent Office, the national patent judiciaries and patent lawyers all over the continent. Pro-patent groups included umbrella groups such as the European Information, Communications and Consumer Electronics Industry Technology Association, the IT Services Association, the Computing Technology Industry Association, the Business Software Alliance (BSA), the Association for Competitive Technology and Europe's biggest employer organization UNICE/Business Europe. National associations also lobbied heavily for it, as did companies such as Microsoft, SAP, Nokia, Ericsson, Philips, IBM, Siemens, Bosch, Oracle, Alcatel. All of these Goliaths defended the Commission proposal. But SMEs and an assortment of free-software activist NGOs had David's good fortune. And they killed the giants' effort through a grassroots effort alone.

The policy background: CII is an issue of intellectual property, a field of much legislative activity. Today, ideas and innovation drive company value, particularly in the industries earning their money with information technology (IT). To protect ideas and innovation, the EU uses a portfolio of legal instruments, among these patents. As a matter of principle, however, software "as such" cannot be patented in Europe (however, it can in America). The European Patent Convention of 1973 excluded computer programs from patents. Why? Because programs are mathematical expressions of scientific truth, and are thus unpatentable. Patents should be limited to machinery. Unlike hardware, software would be protected like this book: by copyright laws, which are more flexible and less costly to handle. In fact, while patents are often said to protect independent inventors and SMEs, there is great skepticism among this group because of many patent infringement lawsuits brought about by large corporations with an army of patent lawyers.

The problem with CII lies in the merging of technologies. Many inventions are implemented by computers which, of course, run only when programmed with software. Automobiles have anti-lock braking systems (ABS) run by software; cell phones, washing machines and medical resonance imaging all depend on software as well. It is plausible that industries with such complex products want patent protection on competitive world markets. But that is only half the story.

While patent advocates stress the matter of concern is CIIs, its opponents talk about software patents: They say the proponents are trying to patent the software itself, rather than the technical solution it came to. The consequence is, they assert, that everyday simple processes on the Internet, in e-commerce and multimedia applications could be patented: the MP3 data compression method, the progress bar, GIF and JPEG graphics formats, image previews, plugins, online one-click-shopping baskets, search engines, user interfaces and so on. The point is that "trivial" patents, unlike copyright laws, would impede software development and could carry a high risk of making programmers and IT companies liable to patent fees and costly patent litigation.

All of this made CII a complex legal issue, especially because the US followed a pro-patent philosophy. While the law lacked clarity, European patent offices already granted tens of thousands of CII patents that, according to the critics, are illegal and could be tested in court. The legal framework was diffuse.[18]

The Commission proposed a CII directive in 2002. Once introduced in the EP, the Commission was surprised by a flood of amendments. But the Council of Ministers, next in line of the procedure, ignored practically all of them and returned the bill for a parliamentary vote. This was an all-out provocation. The media began to cover the power game intensely. The Spanish, Dutch and German parliaments voted on anti-patent resolutions, the latter two even reversing their own governments' position. Instead of promoting the Commission pro-patent bill as an innovation-friendly law, the patentability of software was attacked as a barrier to innovation and a threat to SMEs. The atmosphere heated up. Grassroots visits and letter campaigns, already strong, poured in. Opponents staged demonstrations in Brussels and around European capitals with T-shirts and banners screaming "Power to the Parliament!," even "All Power to the Parliament," or "Ministers: Respect the Parliament Decision!"

With even a constitutional crisis in the air, majorities on the various sub-issues were so incalculable that all leaders decided to drop the Commission bill like a hot brick. In July 2005, the EP voted down a last compromise bill with 648 out of 680 votes. Brussels hardly ever saw such drama. "The Parliament that couldn't say no" had shown it could.

But one could not explain the drama without understanding grassroots lobbying as applied in this case. Mobilizing against the CII directive built on three strategic advantages: an uncommon coalition; a tech-savvy community well-connected and well-informed via online networks and online media; and sympathies among national and European policy-makers for the open source movement (for example, Linux and OpenOffice as alternatives to Windows products). The campaign against CII would polarize between SMEs and multinational corporations, between free and commercial software development, between Europe and the US Software. Patents were defined as a survival issue for a dynamic and innovative IT sector of the economy.

The driver behind this campaign was Germany's IT-based service economy. These mostly young companies were not an active part of the big business and industry federations (for example, Germany's powerful Bitkom) which had promoted the CII directive. Some companies had been talking about the developing Brussels issue in SME associations such as Germany's Bundesverband Mittelständische Wirtschaft (BVMW); some had done so in Internet forums or in trade fair conferences. Three groups would become the leaders:

- Foundation for a Free Information Infrastructure (FFII), headquartered in Munich but registered in twenty EU countries with a very heterogeneous membership of students, professors, research and development professionals, freelance programmers and IT companies. FFII is a member of the SME association in Brussels, Confédération Européene des Associations de Petites et Moyenne Entreprises (CEA-PME). Software patents had always been on the agenda. FFII had the most political experience, already had a part-time one-person Brussels presence (a desk in the corner of the CEA-PME office). However, the solo lobbyist could not be fully financed by FFII, so some Swedish and Norwegian IT firms footed the bill. It was the most international body of the three, but had fewer true business credentials; It was seen as a network of highly knowledgeable computer experts.
- The ad hoc campaign platform No Software Patents. This was a coalition of medium-sized companies such as Swedish database vendor MySQL, Norwegian browser firm Opera ASA and a range of German companies: Internet provider 1&1, German Linux service company Red Hat, e-mail provider GMX, customer relationship service company CSB-System and software companies Materna and CAS. They were joined by American–Israeli venture capitalists Benchmark Capital (eBay's first investor) and Swiss firm Index Ventures (who had, for example, helped start up the Internet telephone firm Skype). It was international by design, offered information online in seventeen languages, and concentrated on building mass letter writing and international publicity for the lobbying effort.
- Patentfrei (patent free), an intiative of SMEs first established in Hamburg. Patentfrei quickly snowballed into an organization of regional chapters covering most of West Germany. It did not take private individuals as members. Some 700 SMEs joined. It officially partnered with the small business association BVMW and the computer science professional association BVSI. Patentfrei stayed a German national coalition and focused on putting pressure on the large German delegation in their home constituencies.

FFII, No Software Patents and Patentfrei had very different organizations, goals and campaign styles. They competed for attention and support, sometimes walked over each other and never formed an official alliance. Still, they often coordinated their moves and helped each other out; for all three, it was important to be in touch with established associations such as BVMW and its European counterpart CEA-PME.

FFII worked like a typical NGO, with a strong open common of chats, wikis and mailserv lists. Some of these were private, such as the list "europarl-help" which was a channel to aid staffers of sympathetic MEPs with instant expert knowledge and for drafting up critical questions to confront Commissioners and industry lobbyists with. FFII is neither a campaign or lobby organization in the strict sense, nor a true business association; in fact, it partly overlaps with web activist clubs and even Attac. That network could stage demonstrations, media events and various guerrilla actions, all of which it did. But learning that Brussels targets had a particular interest in hearing from business people rather than computer experts, FFII took care to emphasize its business credentials and bring in entrepreneurs and employers. It started an online campaign platform "Economic Majority" and positioned itself as the voice of the European independent IT industry.

The problem with FFII seemed to be that (1) actual, visible companies did not play a leading role, and (2) the potential for escalating media coverage was underutilized by the expert community. No Software Patents meant to address these problems by charging ahead with populism and polarized messages to get media and politicians to pay attention. It found the perfect kickoff when FFII warnings over the Brussels patent controversy made the mayor of Munich stop the prestigious project of moving the city administration completely from Windows to Linux. This was not a local technical decision but carried great symbolic power for all software companies selling to the public sector. After all, Microsoft chief Steve Ballmer had traveled to Munich to talk the mayor out of it, creating international headlines. Now the mayor began to attack Brussels for an ill-fated legal assault on open source software. International media picked up the story after No Software Patents helped make it public, and the European debate on CII picked up steam. Showing that the CII directive could have an impact on government operations was significant. Other much publicized highlights were an open letter by Linux inventor Linus Torvalds against the CII directive, and the surprising no vote of the Polish government in the Council of Ministers—a spontaneously established Swiss website, thankpoland.info, got 30,000 software patent opponents to sign a petition that was later physically welcomed in Warsaw in an official ceremony with the government.

All three organizations invested heavily in motivating business managers and owners to get in touch with their MEPs, national or even regional representatives—in visits, by mail, e-mail or phone. Fly-ins to Brussels events were arranged, MEPs were won as co-sponsors, businesspeople were contacted on conferences and industry get-togethers such as the world's largest computer fair, CeBIT. Offices helped identify the right targets and provide background information on them. Lobbying guides, letter templates, parliamentary calendars and other tools were published online, and action alerts sent out regularly to mobilize the IT community. Demonstrations in some ten European cities helped get national and regional media coverage. Software program-mers picketed in jailbird uniforms, others would sing songs such as "Killing my software with patents" or simulated a "patent minefield." Some of this creative action was more the world of Attac than of business activists, but the marches and picketing did not quite look like a lefty walkabout: banners demanded "Protect the software industry!" or "Software patents risk Europe's competitiveness." Media-wise, the campaigns, particularly No Software Patents, were able to get intense coverage in both general media and the IT trade press, most of which is online, moves fast and is often, via RSS, syndicated to thousands of European websites. The FFII also initiated several "net strikes," which means the (voluntary) blackening of company and institutional homepages with campaign logos and activating messages as an alternative entry.

This is just a sample of the many campaign activities. It is interesting to see that no campaign showed significant professionalism in planning and organizing the grassroots tactics; the three organizations were quite experimental in what they did. None had hired a communications consultancy to help with anything or transfer in American grassroots know-how; the individuals and SMEs involved did everything on their own. Some of it was high quality work, some not; and in any case, an unprecedented, organic and interesting blend of NGO, business association and company lobbying was created. It showcased the hidden power of online networks, which are, for obvious reasons, very strong and borderless in the IT community. Activating the grassroots was possible because many SMEs did believe the patent issue was a threat to their livelihood, and fighting against the biggest in the business seemed to motivate and politicize many. The compli-cated patent issue became the subject of a planned emotionalization, making out clear enemies: eurocracy, patent lawyers, big business, monopolies and particularly Microsoft.

Microsoft, of course, was only one of many corporate players, but it did have a special interest in this legislation. It also tried to intensify the pro-patent advocacy when the issue seemed to slip away in disaster. The most difficult problem was the growing perception among decision-makers that CII would be bad for SMEs. To confront this, a "Campaign for Creativity" (C4C) was started in May 2004, financed by Microsoft, SAP and the CompTIA association, and ran until summer 2005. As the name suggests, the campaign was not about legal and industrial arguments. While its allies fought the CII battle in the style of high-tech sobriety, the C4C campaign came along colorfully, playfully and with a butterfly as a logo. Patents were to be presented as a device for protecting creative people and any form of intellectual property. Instead of putting forward testimonials from programmers and IT experts, the campaign was to appeal to artists, musicians, product designers, photographers and just about anyone with a stake in intellectual property. The issue's borders were redrawn to include product piracy, bootleg copies, license theft, design forgery, brand and copy rights all of a sudden were introduced into the debate (few of which really had anything to do with the CII problem). The campaign also organized e-mail and letter-writing campaigns and in June 2005 staged a demonstration of its own with 250 activists in front of the EP, flying banners like "Yes to the EU directive" or "Patents Protect Innovations."

The campaign had an interesting and legitimate approach but came relatively late, and it had serious problems proving its legitimacy. The C4C was not transparent about who was behind it. It became quickly known that it was run by CampbellGentry, which had lobbied Brussels intensely in 1999 for pharmaceutical client SmithKlineBeecham to win the biopatent directive. The agency, so it was told, had even then organized letter writing from patient groups to MEPs and on the day of the vote had brought in to the Parliament wheel-chaired patients wearing T-shirts "Patents for Life!" Despite being obviously unsuccessful, the C4C campaign provoked so many questions it was an easy target for those who saw only a manipulative "astroturf" campaign. Some months later, watchdog groups declared the campaign the winner of Brussels' least-coveted, satirical annual "Worst EU Lobbying Award"—"nominated as a fake NGO brilliantly disguising corporate demands as grassroots concerns."[19]

Conclusion

Europe is not what it used to be. The old elite club in Brussels has been opening up, and new players have begun to play a different ball game. Old structural problems remain, of lacking resources, culture, public opinion saliency and democratic legitimacy. Still, the European arena has undergone real change. Some of it favors new coalition-building, populism and participation. As the examples show, business is beginning to understand that it can mobilize policy support or political opposition as much as NGOs can—or even better.

Currently, grassroots advocacy is only experimental in the corporate realm and the wide range of SME oriented associations. What goes on is learning by doing. More strategists than ever understand that European public affairs begins with an integration of national and supranational efforts. More find it plausible that the multiplying number of countries, citizens and organized interests now involved in EU policy-making opens up many new avenues of campaigning and outsider lobbying. Corporate advocates discover they can show convincingly that business is people, too. In this age of growing transparency and distrust of business, that is a good practical idea.

Does all of this automatically lead to transforming Brussels into a Babel of populist democracy? Most likely not. However, depending on the issue and situation, the European level is open for alternative pressure, more political and more public strategies. Grassroots advocacy may still be a stranger to Brussels. But it has moved in and is here to stay.

Notes

1   Andreas Geiger, *EU Lobbying Handbook: A Guide to Modern Participation in Brussels* (Berlin: Helios Media, 2006), 123.
2   Justin Greenwood as quoted in European Citizen Action Service, *The European Commission and Consultation of NGO* (Brussels: European Citizen Action Service, November 2004), ww.ecas.org/file_uploads/743.doc.
3   "Hacks come to Washington because anywhere else they'd be bored to death. Wonks come here because nowhere else could we bore so many to death. These divisions extend far beyond the hack havens of political campaigns and consulting firms and the wonk ghettos of think tanks on Dupont Circle. Some journalists are wonks, but most are hacks. Some columnists are hacks, but most are wonks. All members of Congress pass themselves off as wonks, but many got elected as hacks. Lobbyists are

hacks who make money pretending to be wonks. The *Washington Monthly*, *The New Republic*, and the entire political blogosphere consist largely of wonks pretending to be hacks. 'The Hotline' is for hacks; *National Journal* is for wonks. 'The West Wing' is for wonks; 'K Street' was for hacks." Bruce Reed, "Bush's War Against Wonks," *Washington Monthly* (March 2004), http://www. washingtonmonthly.com/features/2004/0403.reed.html.

4 Fleishman Hillard, Public Affairs 2.0 weblog, http://pagoesdigital.wordpress.com.

5 Tina Kunath and Sebastian Schwarz, "Informations management: Public Affairs 2.0—Digitales Monitoring," *Public Affairs Manager* 2 (1): 74–80.

6 Thomas Spencer, "The External Environment of Public Affairs in the European Union and the United Kingdom: Public Policy Process and Institutions," in *The Handbook of Public Affairs*, ed. Phil Harris and Craig S. Fleisher (London: Sage, 2005), 72.

7 Edward A. Grefe, "Global Grassroots is a Reality," in *Winning at the Grassroots*, ed. Tony Kramer and Wes Pedersen (Washington, D.C.: Public Affairs Council, 2000), 265–75.

8 John Russell, interview with EurActiv, September 29, 2003, http://www.euractiv.com/en/pa/john-russell-ceo-weber-shandwick-adamson-brussels/article-117408.

9 Daniel Guéguen, *European Lobbying* (Brussels: Europolitics, 2007), 132.

10 Ibid., 136.

11 Ibid., 137.

12 European Voice, *EU Citizens Want One European Parliament Seat in Brussels*, Press Release, May 30, 2006, http://www.bmbrussels.be/pdf/PR_EU-widesurvey30May.pdf and for fill report tables, see, http://www.bmbrussels.be/pdf/SurveyEUcitizensResults.pdf.

13 Rinus van Schendelen, *Machiavelli in Brussels: The Art of Lobbying the EU* (Amsterdam: Amsterdam University Press, 2005), 39.

14 Simon Titley, "How Political Change Will Transform the EU Public Affairs Industry," *Journal of Public Affairs* 3 (1) (2002): 83.

15 This account is based on Dominik Meier, Erhardt Fiebiger, Alex Föller, "Einspruch—Ein Aktionsbündnis mobilisiert den Mittelstand," in *Kampagne! 3 Neue Strategien im Grassroots Lobbying für Unternehmen und Verbände*, ed. Marco Althaus (Münster and Berlin: Lit), 346–82.

16 This account is based on Marco Althaus, "Mittelstandskoalitionen gegen EU-Softwarepatente," in *Kampagne! 3 Neue Strategien im Grassroots Lobbying für Unternehmen und Verbände*, ed. Marco Althaus (Münster and Berlin: Lit), 230–78.

17 Attac (Association for the Taxation of Financial Transactions for the Aid of Citizens) is a global activist organization, founded in 1998, whose slogan is "the world is not for sale."

18 There had been a similar problem with biotechnology in the 1990s, solved by a biopatent directive in 1998, heavily lobbied for by the pharmaceuticals bent on winning venture capital for the young industry; investors wanted patents as a collateral.

19 Corporate Europe Observatory, "Worst EU Lobbying Award 2005," http://www.worstlobby.eu/2005/intro.html.

Part 5

Political Parties, Political Management, and Democracy

35

Campaign Consultants and Political Parties Today

Maik Bohne, Alicia Kolar Prevost, and James A. Thurber

The rise of political consultants represents one of the most important changes to electoral politics worldwide,[1] but in no other country have consultants been as central to political campaigning and issue advocacy as in the United States. Here, they are at the core of professionalized electioneering; their number is growing and their services have become increasingly specialized. Each year, at least 50,000 campaigns for local, state, and federal office employ political consultants, offering everything from polling, fundraising, strategic advice about allocating campaign resources to developing a campaign theme and message, to legal advice about campaign finance law.[2] In the 2006 House and Senate races, the average number of paid consultants per campaign was 2.2, and sixty-seven campaigns had four consultants or more.[3] Electioneering services offered by consultants today encompass an impressive array of technologies: survey research, predictive turnout models to enhance targeting efforts, Internet advertising, campaign blogs, and computer-assisted phone calls, to name a few. Political consultants are such an important part of campaigns at all levels—from small town mayors to presidential candidates—that some scholars even see a shift from candidate-centered to consultant-centered campaigns.[4]

Occasionally, the consultant has been almost as well known as the candidate: think of James Carville in the 1992 Clinton campaign or Karl Rove in the 2004 Bush campaign. President Clinton was so concerned about the role of consultants in the 1996 campaign that he said: "I don't want to read about you in the press. I'm sick and tired of consultants getting famous at my expense."[5] But in most cases, the celebrity political consultant is the exception. Most consultants remain unknown to the voters and shrouded in mystery. Without a public role or a good understanding of their motivations, consultants were blamed for excessive negativity in campaigns and for caring more about making a profit than the health of the political system. Among political scientists, consultants were blamed for "aiding and abetting" the decline of the major political parties.[6]

Recent scholarship on political consultants has dispelled some of these myths, and a new view of political consultants has emerged in the academic literature.[7] In this chapter we review the political science literature on political consultants, and show that consensus has been reached on the question of whether consultants and political parties are adversaries (they are not). (See also, Chapter 4, by Stephen C. Craig, on political science and political management.) Using a database of consulting firms in the 2006 congressional elections, interviews with principals in those firms, and the most extensive survey of political consultants to date (conducted by the Improving Campaign Conduct project in 1999 and 2002) we find that not only are consultants and parties allies, but that they are important electoral partners in a modern partisan campaign network who rely on each other for vital services and funding. The eight surveys conducted from 1999 to 2004, updated with the in-depth 2007 interviews, allow us to describe the partisan world of the campaign consulting industry today.

Literature Review

Although political consultants have been in the electoral arena since the 1930s, scholars were slow to give attention to these new "campaign wizards."[8] Initial works explored whether consultants came from public relations backgrounds,[9] but it was not until an explosion in the creation of consulting businesses starting in the 1970s that scholars began to evaluate the impact of consultants on elections and democracy. Early studies were critical of the rise of this new class of campaign professionals that seemed to be transforming American electoral politics.[10] An uneasiness and controversy was associated with political consultants, since their appearance in the electoral arena coincided with the breakthrough of a new style of campaigning, sometimes extremely negative, which focused intensively on the selling of individual candidates via television and using market and survey research. In this regard, the "new experts of politics"[11] were perceived as causing the deterioration of the health of American campaigning and democracy by stressing images over substance, introducing negative campaigning into US politics, and raising the costs of elections.[12] (See also, Chapter 1, by Dennis W. Johnson on some of the historical aspects of campaign consulting.)

However, at the center of the charges issued against political consultants was their contribution to the decline of political parties in the United States. This *adversarial view* of the party–consultant relationship depicted consultants as marketing specialists who were exclusively focused on the success of individual candidates and not committed to any overarching political ideology or party goals. Consultants were perceived as supplanting the formal party structure by monopolizing services that the parties once could offer themselves. Larry J. Sabato wrote: "While certainly not initiating the party's decline, they have nonetheless aided and abetted the slide, sometimes with malicious afterthought."[13]

More recent studies, however, have shown a different picture. Beginning with Frank I. Luntz who pointed out that professional consultants have strengthened party organizations by supporting their revitalization,[14] scholars began to see parties and consultants increasingly as electoral partners. This *allied view* shows consultants and political parties working together to achieve common goals.[15] It became apparent that consultants are partisan actors who work almost exclusively for the Democrat or the Republican community and who were often socialized inside the party network.[16] Moreover, political parties and consultants seemed to benefit from each other by developing a distinct division of labor. Consultants manage campaign tasks, such as direct mail, polling, and media production, which parties do not have the capacity to offer. Meanwhile, parties use their economy-of-scale advantage to perform voter mobilization, fundraising, and opposition research services.[17]

Definition of Political Consultants

Anyone can be considered a campaign or political consultant. There is no license or officially required qualification other than the test of hard knocks or experience that confers the title of "campaign consultant" to someone. We define a professional campaign consultant as a paid professional who is engaged primarily in the provision of services or strategic advice to candidates, their campaigns, political parties, or other organizations helping to elect or defeat candidates, or in initiative or referendum campaigns. Political consultants are also often engaged in issue and advocacy campaigns—lobbying—but that activity is not discussed in this chapter.

Campaign consultants and their firms are involved in a variety of services such as strategic advice, polling, media production, direct mail, fundraising, opposition research, field operations, and increasingly the use of the Internet in campaigning (see Table 35.1). They are well educated, ideologically moderate, and politically experienced professionals.[18] In addition to their work for candidates, political parties, party allied interest groups, and 527 groups, campaign consultants might also work for unions, business groups, and a variety of other clients, especially during the off-years when political campaigns alone might not be enough to cover the firm's expenses, including consultants' salaries.

Consultants and Political Parties—A Network of Cooperation and Trust

To fully understand political consultants today means to understand the partisan environment in which they are working. Our surveys and interviews show that political consultants are deeply divided along partisan lines and are an essential part of a wider partisan campaign network. This network is based on common philosophies, goals, and mutual trust, but also on symbiotic cooperation and business relations. As we will show empirically, the relationship between parties and consultants is stronger today than ever before.

Political Consultants—Professionalism Joins Partisanship

In theory, political consultants can be agents to multiple principals.[19] They appear to be a modern form of medieval journeymen who get hired for a short period of time to do a highly skilled job before moving on to the next construction (or campaign) site. Due to this professional, short-term focus on helping individual candidates or organizations to win their campaigns, they would not be expected to subscribe to a more abstract common partisan cause or to develop long-term partisan loyalties.

Table 35.1. Professional Campaign Firms by Services Delivered, 2006–2007

Service Provided	Number of Firms
Strategic Advice/General Consulting	71
Media	
Media Buying	115
Media Consultants	78
Polling	76
Direct Mail	155
Opposition Research	6
Fundraising	38
Field and GOTV	
Grassroots Organizing	47
Petition and Signature Gathering	5
Targeting	14
Telephone and Direct Contact	28
Voter Files and Mailing Lists	33

Source: Dennis W. Johnson, *No Place For Amateurs: How Political Consultants are Reshaping American Democracy*, 2nd ed. (New York: Routledge, 2007), 241; and "Consultants' Score Card 2006," *Campaigns and Elections* (March 2007).

However, recent research on political consultants has refuted this assumption. An analysis of the socialization and career paths of consultants shows that they are far from being apolitical public relations professionals who are only motivated by the thrill of political campaigning or the prospect of making money or gaining political power. Indeed, the most overwhelming reason which consultants cite for entering the business of political consulting is their "political beliefs or ideology" (see Table 35.2). More than 60% cited an ideological or partisan reason for becoming a professional consultant.

Recent in-depth interviews with thirty-five national Democratic and Republican consultants who were actively involved in the 2006 congressional elections support this finding. Most entered the campaign arena driven by well-defined ideological beliefs and a strong affinity to one party. Many started as campaign volunteers or interns at the local level, then worked their way up inside the campaign hierarchy to the state or national level. Becoming a top consultant can thus be seen as an endpoint of a strenuous career ascension after working in various campaign jobs over several election cycles. Although it is far from mandatory to complete this climb inside the formal party apparatus, the career paths of consultants include work for a variety of different actors inside the wider party network: candidates, members of Congress, state and national party committees, party-allied interest groups, and think tanks.

Thus, working for a formal party organization is only one of many ways to work one's way up the campaign hierarchy, but it is a very common and important one. As Robin Kolodny found in a study in which she surveyed 125 general consultants, 40.8% had a previous employment experience at a party committee before becoming a political consultant.[20] James A. Thurber, Candice J. Nelson, and David A. Dulio also found that the most common past experience or training cited by professional consultants was working for a national, state, or local party organization.[21] Consultants interviewed in our 2007 study also emphasize this view. It is not mandatory for consultants to have prior working experience at state or national party committees, but party employment, particularly in leading positions inside political, field, research, or communications divisions, offers campaign staffers an important path to advance their careers for several reasons. First, party committees offer a valuable opportunity to work on a wide variety of races at the same time. They provide young campaign professionals with insights into crucial, highly competitive campaigns in different parts of the country. Once staffers have been through this quick-paced ordeal, they gained a mark of approval that is very valuable for consulting firms that look to employ young talent. Second, working at party committees also offers networking opportunities with party candidates, party leadership, and other experienced consultants, and thus with future clients or employers. As Randy Kammerdiener, consultant at Majority Strategies, one of the top Republican direct mail firms, describes it:

Table 35.2. The Motivations of Political Consultants for Getting into the Business

Your Political Beliefs or Ideology	53.5%
To Help Your Party be the Majority Party in Government	7.5%
The Thrill of the Competition	18.7%
The Money You Could Earn	11.2%
The Power and Influence that Come with the Job	4.5%
Other	4.7%
Total (N)	**493**

Source: David Dulio, *For Better or Worse: How Political Consultants Are Changing Elections in the United States* (Albany, N.Y.: State University of New York Press, 2004), 56.

Note: Full question wording (multiple responses were not allowed): "Thinking back to when you first became active in political campaigns in a paid capacity, what would you describe as your main motivation for becoming a professional consultant?"

It is a such a valuable on-the-job training that you get. And the other part of it is the relationships, the people that you meet, the network. In effect, you are creating your own future client network if you come up through the party.[22]

Especially on the Republican side, today's top consultants spent their formative campaign years at the party committees. Dan Hazelwood, president of Creative Targeted Communications; Glen Bolger, president of Public Opinion Strategies; Ed Goeas and Dave Sackett, partners at the Tarrance Group; Linda DiVall, president of American Viewpoint; Rick Reed and Paul Curcio, partners at Stevens, Reed, Curcio & Potholm or Scott Howell, president of Scott Howell & Company, are just a few examples. Third, it is a way for the party and their candidates to test the expertise, business savvy, and loyalty of people who want to become professional consultants.

Whether or not political consultants have worked for party committees, they are partisans who are segregated into Democratic and Republican communities. In the early days of the consulting business, mainly in the 1960s and 1970s, it was more common to switch party sides or work for both parties,[23] but when the national political environment grew more polarized, working for candidates on both sides of the aisle became almost impossible and impracticable. Studies by Kolodny and Logan, Thurber and Nelson, and Dulio[24] have stressed this partisan divide among political consultants. New data from our 2007 study confirm these findings. Our database of 324 consultants and their clients in the 2006 congressional elections show that with the exception of two firms, every consulting firm worked exclusively for either Democratic or Republican candidates.[25] The exceptions were the Republican polling firm Public Opinion Strategies, which was employed by Connecticut Senator Joe Lieberman after he decided to run as an Independent in the general election; and Glover Park Group, a Democratic media firm run by several former Clinton administration officials, that crossed party lines to work for Republican Congressman Mike Ferguson (New Jersey). These were unique circumstances. As veteran Democratic pollster Geoff Garin puts it:

> There are some consultants who still can cross over to a minor degree, but it doesn't happen very frequently. Politics have changed. The battle lines between the two parties are firmly drawn. . . . All the consultants I work with certainly believe in what they are doing. They didn't flip a coin and ended up as Democrats.[26]

Political consultants live in partioned partisan worlds that rarely allow them to step over to the other side. There are basically three reasons for this. One is the above-mentioned philosophical affinity of most consultants with one party or the other. Most consultants are in fact partisan professionals with ideological leanings and a distinctive Manichean view of the campaign world. Dave Sackett, partner at the Tarrance Group, one of the top Republican polling firms, reveals these partisan underpinnings in the consulting community:

> While we [Republican consultants] may define the party differently and while we may believe that there are different priorities that the party should have, at the end of the day, we want to elect as many Republicans to office at every level as possible and defeat as many Democrats at every level as possible. . . . This firm exists to do one thing and that is to elect as many Republicans as possible and to defeat as many Democrats as possible.[27]

Part of this close alignment with the party is that consultants see their work for individual candidates as an important contribution to the overarching party goal of winning a majority in Congress or in state legislatures. They may not always agree with the party committees over how to reach that objective, for example, when they see their candidate's cautiously developed campaign agenda shaken up by hard-hitting party independent expenditure ads. But in general, party committees and consultants form a professional party campaign caste that has the same pragmatic, candidate-centered approach to elections: as witnessed in the 2006 congressional elections, the ultimate goal for both is to help their party candidates win, even though this sometimes means that one has to support a candidate who does not share essential parts of the party agenda.[28]

A second reason for the segregation of the consultant world into two partisan camps is trust. Consultants who give strategic advice handle very sensitive information. Consequently, the relationship between candidates and consultants reaches beyond a normal business tie with a non-strategic vendor. Campaigns are political wars; they are intensive times of success and crisis, of ups and downs. Thus, candidates need personnel that have an ultimate loyalty to them and to the party. They need staff who are expected not to reveal crucial information to the other party or candidates once the campaign is over.[29] Third and consequently, limiting the share to half of the campaign market is the only business model that works for consultants. They fare economically better by staying on one party side as opposed to offering their services to all candidates in the market. Paul Curcio, partner at the Republican media firm Stevens, Reed, Curcio & Potholm stresses this point: "We are limited to half of the market, yes, but this 50% would probably go down to 10% if we started to dabble, because candidates would say: 'We can't trust you!' "[30]

As a result, it is extremely rare for consultants to switch sides. The most famous of party switchers surely is Dick Morris who has a colorful history of working for Republicans and Democrats, particularly for President Bill Clinton. Other examples are Mark McKinnon and Matthew Dowd who had worked for Democratic candidates in Texas before joining the presidential campaign of George W. Bush. John Weaver switched from being John McCain's political director in 2000 to work as a Democratic consultant to eventually rejoin the McCain campaign in 2006.[31] What it means to switch party sides in this business is symbolized by the case of Katie Cook, a former Republican direct mail fundraiser who joined the presidential campaign of Howard Dean in 2003. Cook said in an interview that on the day the Federal Election Commission (FEC) report came out, which showed that she had done fundraising work for Howard Dean, the Republican National Committee told her that she would never work for them again. As a result of her switch, Cook had to give up all her Republican clients and is now trying to integrate herself into her new Democratic Party network.[32]

Political Parties and Consultants—A Close Electoral Partnership

Early studies on the role of consultants in American elections portrayed the relationship between political parties and political consultants as adversarial and even hostile. They assumed a zero-sum game in which one electoral actor replaced the other.[33] However, more recent studies have found that parties and consultants do not regard themselves as competitors in election campaigns, but as helpful partners. Both found their place inside the campaign nexus; both have special selling points to offer and form a close, complementary electoral partnership that is based on a sophisticated division of labor. Two surveys of political consultants and party elites by the Center for Congressional and Presidential Studies (CCPS) at American University in 1999 and 2002 show the consultants and party elites' assessments of their roles in providing electioneering services to candidates (see Table 35.3).

Consultants and party elites fully agree that some electioneering tasks and services for individual candidates are better provided by consultants than by the parties themselves, namely polling, media, and direct mail services. The degree of sophistication needed to perform these specialized tasks is so high in modern election campaigns that parties opted not to directly provide them to individual candidates. In times of candidate-centered campaigning, it would be almost impossible for party committees, especially for congressional campaign committees, which have to be responsible for thirty to sixty competitive races, to offer these professionalized

Table 35.3. Consultants' and Party Elites' Assessments of whether Consultants have Replaced Parties in Providing Electioneering Services to Candidates

Service	Consultants		Party Elites, 2002	
	1999	2002	State	National
Strategic Advice	3.51	3.50	2.46	2.47
Media	3.49	3.50	3.04	3.00
Polling	3.42	3.31	3.14	3.20
Direct Mail	3.31	3.35	2.85	2.73
Opposition Research	3.07	3.05	2.48	2.20
Fundraising	2.91	2.94	2.41	2.13
Field and GOTV	2.65	2.60	1.78	1.67
Total (N)	**487**	**199**	**93**	**15**

Source: David A. Dulio and Candice J. Nelson, *Vital Signs: Perspectives on the Health of American Campaigning* (Washington, D.C.: Brookings Institution Press, 2005), 39.

Note: The question asked was: "Thinking specifically now, please tell me whether you strongly agree, somewhat agree, somewhat disagree, or strongly disagree that political consultants have largely taken the place of political parties in providing each of these services. Mean rankings are based on a scale in which 4 = strongly agree, 3 = somewhat agree, 2 = somewhat disagree, and 1 = strongly disagree."

and individualized day-to-day services for every single race. With the passing of the Bipartisan Campaign Reform Act (BCRA),[34] which imposes a stricter ban on message coordination between party committees and candidate campaigns, it would even be more complex to provide this kind of wholesale party campaign service. Consultants are simply more capable of giving candidates individual attention as well as offering them the customized services they are looking for.

However, the CCPS surveys show that consultants and party elites see party organizations performing valuable campaign tasks in elections. What parties seem to offer best is manpower, money, and information. First, party organizations can make use of their economy-of-scale advantage in field and get-out-the vote (GOTV) operations. They are still the best equipped to provide the resources for extensive ground operations. Second, their monetary help for candidates is valued. This fundraising assistance focuses mostly on sending party leaders into districts to do fundraising events, brokering political action committee (PAC) money to targeted races, and creating what insiders call "buzz" around a certain race by releasing official lists of candidates in competitive races to the donor community. Third, parties function as an important information resource center. This information can come in the form of opposition research, but it increasingly consists of voter file and micro-targeting services. Over the course of the last election cycles, both parties put much more emphasis on creating common databases that can be offered to campaigns and consultants to improve their voter targeting information and efforts. The Republican National Committee (RNC) with its centralized database *Voter Vault* is now the key provider of mirco-targeting information used by consultants and campaign staff on the Republican side.[35] The Democratic Party is currently trying to catch up with the RNC by creating its own *VoteBuilder*.[36] (See Chapter 36, by Peter N. Ubertaccio on micro-targeting.)

This general division of labor between consultants and parties is described by Chris Cooper, one of the top Democratic direct mail consultants and partner at MSHC:

> When it comes to paid communications, consultants drive that bus because that is what we do for a living. It is a very specialized field: polling, media, direct mail, Internet. And this communication side of the campaign is around 70% of the budget. The party will take the lead more in candidate recruitment, fundraising, GOTV and lining up all the political pieces that need to be lined up.[37]

Interestingly, Table 35.3 shows that consultants and party elites have different perceptions on their role in providing strategic advice to candidates. Conflicts of responsibilities can occur in this area between consultants and party committees. Consultants are the day-to-day advisers to candidates, but as shown in the 2006 cycle, party committees are not willing to give up their counseling role and will sometimes apply a more intensive hands-on approach in advising their candidates on strategy and message. Democratic Congressional Campaign Committee (DCCC) chairman Rahm Emanuel (Illinois) and Democratic Senatorial Campaign Committee chairman Charles Schumer (New York), in particular, took a hand in trying to push candidates in certain strategic directions, which occasionally led to frictions with the campaigns and their consultants.[38]

Another crucial campaign activity parties are involved in, and which has become increasingly important, is advertising and agenda setting in competitive states and races. Although the BCRA banned parties from spending soft money on advertisement and grassroots activities, it allowed them to make hard-money expenditures independently of the candidate campaign. Consequently, the party campaign committees have turned in recent campaign cycles to this kind of electioneering (usually in the form of television ads), which they provide in support of a candidate but that cannot be coordinated with the candidate's campaign.[39] (See also, Chapter 12, by Anthony Gierzynski, on the BCRA and campaign finance.) In the 2006 congressional election cycle alone the six party committees spent $223 million in independent expenditures (IE),[40] 17% of their total expenditures. In some competitive districts party committees invested more in IE than the candidate campaigns spent overall.[41]

Importantly, however, party committees do not offer most of these valuable campaign services to candidates (GOTV, fundraising, voter targeting, and IE) themselves. Instead of performing their "own" crucial campaign tasks in-house, they choose to outsource a large part of them to their professional army of campaign consultants.[42] Thus, although party committees have a significant body of staffers during the height of a campaign, many of the electioneering tasks parties perform are in fact being done or at least guided by consultants.

The bulk of the work professional political consultants handled for the party organizations came in the form of IE, which are fertile ground for them. Since IE campaigns have to follow awkwardly strict non-coordination rules, party's IE operations have to be placed behind a firewall generally outside of the party headquarters.[43] These outsourced IE campaigns usually have a small overhead of six to eight staffers who set rough guidelines for themes and messages, and approve the ads or mailings as soon as they have been produced. The crucial part of the work, however, is done by political consultants who have leeway to decide on message strategy as well as the content of the advertisements. The DCCC IE operation is a good example of how today's IE operations are run. It set up six separate IE teams who were each made up of a pollster, a media consultant, and a direct mail consultant. These teams were respectively managed by one IE staffer who oversaw the operation, but they operated independently to a considerable degree.[44]

In the 2006 congressional elections parties also employed consultants to guide and execute their voter targeting and field operations. The RNC hired TargetPoint Consulting to run and refine its micro-targeting efforts. Both the RNC and the NRCC (National Republican Congressional Committee) spent more than $13 million on the telemarketing firm FLS Phones, which handled the bulk of their phone campaigns. At the DCCC field veteran Michael Whouley, founder and partner at the marketing and grassroots communications firm Dewey Square Group, oversaw the development and implementation of more than forty customized field plans for most of the competitive House races.[45] To implement these field plans, the DCCC spent $366,000 in consulting fees to four different grassroots consulting firms, namely Grassroots Campaigns, Grassroots Solutions, Field Works, and Hildebrand Tewes. Party committees additionally spent significant amounts of money on pollsters, fundraising consultants, and voter file experts.[46] Through IE and other party work consultants today not only have a lucrative source of income, but also they have become an essential part of modern party organizations. They not only function as crucial vendors that implement party strategy, but also they help to craft and shape party message, strategy, and tactics.

It is, however, only a small group of top consultants that is hired by party organizations. This elite is largely made up of the same consultants who handle most of the work for candidates in competitive districts. Notably, 90% of firms that we identified as key polling, media, and direct mail firms in the 2006 congressional elections (because they have worked for a considerable number of candidate campaigns in competitive races)[47] were also employed by one or several national party committees. Thus, a limited circle of consultants seems to exist that helps shaping key messages and strategy in races that are electorally most important: districts and states that decide which party will win the majority. Dan Hazelwood describes it for the Republican Party:

> There is definitely an elite group that knows each other, we are all friends and competitors. We socialize together and when we work together, we know what other people's styles are. . . . A lot of the people who are part of that elite group view themselves as, "We are the party strategists". I mean, there is the party leadership which we are not, but we are a force that gets sent in somewhere to solve a bad situation.[48]

One of the reasons for the existence of such an elite group of top consultants that works for party organizations and in the most competitive races is that party committees actively recommend preferred consultants to their candidates.[49] Data from the 2002 survey show that large majorities of party elites considered engaging in such an activity. The 2007 interviews support this finding. Party elites reported keeping an informal list of consultants that they primarily provide to less experienced challengers who need help in putting skilled campaign teams together. However, party committees will usually not force candidates to employ one particular consultant who they think would be the best fit for the race, but they will usually give them several consulting firms to choose from.

The number of consultants suggested to candidates varies, it mostly depends on the competitiveness of the race, the style and philosophy of party committee chairs and their senior staffs. For instance, in the 2005–2006 cycle, the NRCC only recommended a small slate comprised primarily of three pollsters, three media firms, and three direct mail firms.[50] To make it clear: being recommended by party committees is only one way for consultants to acquire clients,[51] but the willingness of parties to make sure that candidates in competitive races have the right consultant infrastructure in place shows the close electoral partnership between political consultants and party organizations in US elections.

Summary

Campaign consultants and political parties form a close electoral partnership that is based on a shared political ideology, mutual trust, reciprocity, and built from close working relations developed over the course of sometimes several campaigns. Our findings suggest that political consultants are campaign professionals with strong partisan backgrounds, closely allied to either the Democratic or the Republican campaign community. In contrast to party committees, which have high turnovers of chairs and staff, consultants can be seen as the most stable keepers of campaign knowledge and expertise inside their respective party. Campaign consultants have helped keep American parties strong, but in a way that has changed the structure of parties by stressing a fluid, non-hierarchical, and loosely coupled network structure. Political consultants play an essential part in this new party network that will continue to evolve and adapt to the realities of modern campaigns.[52]

Notes

1 David M. Farrell, Robin Kolodny, and Stephen Medvic, "Parties and Campaign Professionals in a Digital Age: Political Consultants in the United States and Their Counterparts Overseas," *Harvard International Journal of Press/Politics* 6 (4) (2001): 11–30; Fritz Plasser with Gunda Plasser, *Global Political Campaigning: A Worldwide Analysis of Campaign Professionals And Their Practices* (Westport, CT: Praeger, 2002).

2 Dennis W. Johnson, *No Place for Amateurs: How Political Consultants are Reshaping American Democracy*, 2nd ed. (New York: Routledge, 2007).

3 According to data collected by *National Journal's Hotline* database of political consultants.

4 Daniel M. Shea and Michael J. Burton, *Campaign Craft: The Strategies, Tactics, and Art of Political Campaign Management*, 2nd ed. (Westport, CT: Praeger, 2001), 9ff.

5 Johnson, *No Place for Amateurs*, 3.

6 Larry J. Sabato, *The Rise of Political Consultants: New Ways of Winning Elections* (New York: Basic Books, 1981), 286.

7 James A. Thurber and Candice J. Nelson, eds, *Campaign Warriors: The Role of Political Consultants in Elections* (Washington, D.C.: Brookings Institution Press, 2000).

8 Ibid., 5.

9 Stanley Kelley, Jr, *Professional Public Relations and Political Power* (Baltimore, MD: Johns Hopkins University Press, 1956); Dan Nimmo, *The Political Persuaders: The Techniques of Modern Election Campaigns* (Englewood Cliffs, N.J.: Prentice-Hall, 1970).

10 Robert Agranoff, *The New Style in Election Campaigns* (Boston, MA: Holbrook Press, 1972); David Broder, *The Party's Over: The Failure of Politics in America* (New York: Harper & Row, 1972); Mark P. Petracca "Political Consultants and Democratic Governance," in *PS: Political Science and Politics* 22 (1) (March 1989): 11–14; Sabato, *The Rise of Political Consultants*.

11 Agranoff, *The New Style in Election Campaigns*, 15.

12 Petracca, "Political Consultants," 11–15.

13 Sabato, *The Rise of Political Consultants*, 286.

14 Frank I. Luntz, *Candidates, Consultants, and Campaigns: The Style and Substance of American Electioneering* (New York: Basil Blackwell, 1988).

15 David A. Dulio and James A. Thurber, "The Symbiotic Relationship Between Political Parties and Political Consultants: Partners Past, Present and Future," in *The State of the Parties: The Changing Role of Contemporary American Parties*, ed. John C. Green and Rick Farmer, 4th ed. (Lanham, MD: Rowman & Littlefield), 214–27; David A. Dulio, *For Better or Worse: How Political Consultants Are Changing Elections in the United States* (Albany N.Y.: State University of New York Press), 101–33.

16 Robin Kolodny and Andrea Logan, "Political Consultants and the Extension of Party Goals," *PS: Political Science and Politics* 31 (2) (June 1998): 155–9; Robin Kolodny, "Electoral Partnerships: Political Consultants and Political Parties," in *Campaign Warriors: The Role of Political Consultants in Elections*, ed. James A. Thurber and Candice J. Nelson (Washington, D.C.: Brookings Institution Press, 2000), 110–33; Dulio, *For Better or Worse*, 101–33.

17 David A. Dulio and Candice J. Nelson, *Vital Signs. Perspectives on the Health of American Campaigning* (Washington, D.C.: Brookings Institution Press, 2005), 25–51; David A. Dulio and Sam Garrett, "Organizational Strength and Campaign Professionalism in State Parties," *The State of the Parties: The Changing Role of Contemporary American Parties*," ed. John C. Green and Daniel J, Coffey, 5th ed. (Lanham, MD: Rowman & Littlefield, 2007), 199–217.

18 James A. Thurber, Candice J. Nelson, and David A. Dulio "Portrait of Campaign Consultants," in *Campaign Warriors: The Role of Political Consultants in Elections*, ed. James A. Thurber and Candice J. Nelson (Washington, D.C.: Brookings Institution Press, 2000), 13.

19 David B. Magleby, Kelly D. Patterson, and James A. Thurber, "Campaign Consultants and Responsible Party Government," in *Responsible Partisanship? The Evolution of American Political Parties Since 1950*, ed. John C. Green and Paul S. Herrnson (Lawrence, KS: University Press of Kansas), 101–23.

20 Kolodny and Logan, "Political Consultants," 156.

21 Thurber, Nelson, and Dulio, "Portrait of Campaign Consultants," 13.

22 Telephone interview with Randy Kammerdiener, Majority Strategies, June 19, 2007.

23 Based on interviews with Geoff Garin, president of Garin-Hart-Yang Research Group, July 31, 2007 and Paul Curcio, partner at Stevens, Reed, Curcio & Potholm, September 19, 2007.

24 Kolodny and Logan, "Political Consultants," 156; Thurber and Nelson, *Campaign Warriors*; Dulio, *For Better or Worse*.

25 The findings are based on a dataset of consultants who worked on House and Senate races in the 2006

congressional elections. To create this database we blended the two most comprehensive datasets on hired consultants generated every cycle by (1) "Campaigns & Elections" magazine ("Winner&Loser Record 2006") and (2) *National Journal's* "Hotline." Due to the fact that Senate candidates Joe Lieberman and Bernie Sanders caucus with Senate Democrats we counted them as Democratic candidates, although they ran as Independents.

26 Garin interview.
27 Interview with Dave Sackett, the Tarrance Group, April 24, 2007.
28 Neftali Bendavid, *The Thumpin'. How Rahm Emanuel and the Democrats Learned to Be Ruthless and Ended the Republican Revolution* (Chicago, IL: Doubleday, 2007); "After Hackett's Close Call, Iraq War Veterans are in Demand," *Roll Call*, August 8, 2005, 12; "The Democrats' Field of Dreams," *National Journal*, April 30, 2005, 23. "Emanuel is the Embodiment of a Jolt for Democrats," *CQ Weekly*, March 27, 2006, 820–1; "In a Pivotal Year, GOP Plans to Get Personal," *Washington Post*, September 10, 2006, A01; Associated Press, "Millions Spend on Political Ads and Most of Them Negative," October 31, 2006, 2.
29 Based on interviews conducted with thirty-five political consultants from March to September 2007.
30 Curcio interview.
31 "McCain Hires 'Best Bricklayer'," *Washington Post*, March 19, 2006, A05.
32 Based on interview with Katie Cook, President of Directline Politics, April 11, 2007; see also "Switching Sides. The Political Conversion of a Direct Mail Guru," *Campaigns & Elections*, April 4, 2006, 21–2.
33 Sabato, *The Rise of Political Consultants*, 3ff. Petracca, "Political Consultants," 11–15.
34 "Bipartisan Campaign Finance Reform Act of 2002," http://www.fec.gov/pages/bcra/bcra_update.shtml.
35 Peter Ubertaccio, "Machine Politics for the Twenty-First Century? Multilevel Marketing and Party Organizations", in *The State of the Parties: The Changing Role of Contemporary American Politics*, ed. John C. Green and Daniel J. Coffey (Lanham, MD: Rowman & Littlefield), 173–84.
36 "DNC Holds National Training as it Rolls Out New Voter File," *The Hill*, August 15, 2007, http://thehill.com/campaign-2008/dnc-holds-national-training-as-it-rolls-out-new-voter-file-2007-08-15.html.
37 Interview with Chris Cooper, partner at MSHC Partners, April 24, 2007.
38 Dulio, *For Better or Worse*, 126; Bendavid, *The Thumpin'*, 69–79, 157–69, 181; "Emanuel is the Embodiment of a Jolt for Democrats", 820–1; "Schumer Attack: Chuck Calls 06 all About Bush," *New York Observer*, July 3, 2006, A1.
39 David B. Magleby and Kelly D. Patterson, *War Games: Issues and Resources in the Battle for Control of Congress*, a report funded by the Pew Charitable Trusts, 2007, 24.
40 "Party Financial Activity Summarized for the 2006 Election Cycle," http://www.fec.gov/press/press2007/partyfinal2006/20070307party.shtml.
41 Data available from Campaign Finance Institute website, http://www.cfinst.org/pr/pdf/06-PostElec-Table3.pdf.
42 Robin Kolodny and David A. Dulio, "Political Party Adaption in US Congressional Campaigns: Why Political Parties Use Coordinated Expenditures to Hire Political Consultants," *Party Politics* 9 (6) (November 2003): 729–46.
43 "Bipartisan Campaign Finance Reform Act of 2002," http://www.fec.gov/pages/bcra/bcra_update.shtml.
44 Based on interviews with DCCC IE staff and Cooper.
45 The Dewey Square Group is a Democratic powerhouse when it comes to grassroots campaigning. Michael Whouley worked on writing and implementing the DCCC field plans with Dave Barnhart who is at Dewey Square Group's office in Washington, D.C. Karin Johansen who was the executive director of the DCCC in 2006, now works for Dewey Square. DSCC Political Director Guy Cecil (now National Field Director for Hillary Clinton) held a position at the firm prior to his employment at the Democratic Senatorial Campaign Committee.
46 Party expenditure data available from Center for Responsive Politics website, http://www.opensecrets.org.
47 We included the Republican National Committee (RNC), Democratic National Committee (DNC), National Republican Congressional Committee (NRCC), Democratic Congressional Campaign Committee (DCCC), National Republican Senatorial Committee (NRSC), Democratic Senatorial Campaign Committee (DSCC), Republican Governors Association (RGA), and the Democratic Governors Association (DGA).
48 Interview with Dan Hazelwood, president of Targeted Creative Communications, September 13, 2007.
49 Paul S. Herrnson, *Party Campaigning in the 1980s. Have the National Parties Made a Comeback as Key Players in Congressional Elections?* (Cambridge, MA: Harvard University Press, 1988); Dulio, *For Better or Worse*, 115, Dulio and Nelson, *Vital Signs*, 49–50.

507

50 Based on interviews with NRCC staff and Paul Curcio.
51 There are two main ways of finding clients: one is to search websites and databases such as *National Journal's* Hotline to find out what candidates are thinking about running and to pitch them. The second way is to tap into one's own personal network with other consultants as well as members of Congress or state legislatures to get recommended to or employed by a candidate.
52 Mildred A. Schwartz, *The Party Network. The Robust Organization of Illinois Republicans* (Madison, WI: University of Wisconsin Press, 1989); Jonathan H. Bernstein, "The Expanded Party in American Politics." PhD dissertation, University of California, Berkeley, 1999; Jonathan H. Bernstein and Casey B.K. Dominguez, "Candidates and Candidacies in the Expanded Party," *P.S. Political Science and Politics* 36 (2) (April 2003): 165–9; Seth Masket, "The Emergence of Unofficial Party Organizations in California," *Spectrum: The Journal of State Politics* 75 (3) (Fall 2002); John B. Bibby and Brian A. Schaffner, *Politics, Parties, and Elections in America*, 6th ed. (Belmont, MA: Thomson-Wadsworth, 2007).

36

Network Marketing and American Political Parties

Peter N. Ubertaccio

The arrival of mass-based democracy in the 1830s, with the concomitant formal organization of political parties, created the first popular attempts to market candidates and ideas to the general population. Figuring out how to make politics and political campaigns appealing to common voters led to torch-light parades, events featuring candidate speeches and hard cider, and sloganeering such as "Tippecanoe and Tyler, too!" In the late twentieth and early twenty-first centuries, as political campaigns became more sophisticated, political marketing has taken on greater significance. Network marketing and micro-targeting are the tools *du jour* and they have the potential of changing the face of party politics.

Network Marketing in American Political History

Network marketing firms are those that rely on multi-level techniques—direct selling of products or services through person-to-person contacts or social occasions, such as the home parties made famous by Tupperware. In 2006, more than fifteen million Americans involved in network marketing firms as direct representatives were responsible for more than $32 billion in sales.[1]

These firms are built around personal relationships and social networks. A direct representative of a network marketing firm recruits from their "network" of family, friends, and co-workers. Online social and professional networking sites such as Facebook, Linkedin, and MySpace are modern phenomena that have built on the successes of traditional network marketing firms. These online networks take a person's network into the stratosphere by linking the user with any other person whose interests, education, aspirations, or thoughts qualify as a networking possibility. Network marketing firms and tactics are somewhat more targeted but there is always a push to find new representatives and increase the circle of one's contacts. Dale Buss followed one network marketer in Wisconsin, Mary Adashek, and wrote that "as Adashek climbs the ladder of success, she actually is doing a lot more than selling kitchen implements and enlarging the family budget: she's building her own micro-enterprise while promoting a business opportunity for other women."[2] It is the concept of a micro-enterprise that appeals to campaigns and party organizations.

To a large extent, informal networks of supporters and activists have always been central to the success of candidates and political parties. Relationships formed by class and education helped fuel a politics of "personal factionalism" in the early history of the republic.[3] Breaking the back of this politics became a goal that helped fuel the organization of political parties in the 1830s and the politics of patronage, a network of job seekers, party regulars, and party leaders that followed. The latter network was built strongly on personal and political networking. Voters were attracted to these organizations for reasons sometimes beyond the electoral. James Reichley has noted that voters gravitated to these new organizations and their events for social and emotional reasons, even spiritual ones.[4]

Network marketing, as such, was not on the minds of early party pioneers. Network marketing companies emerged in the United States in the mid- to late twentieth century and their success and growth was fueled by the desire of their adherents both to achieve financial success and to tap into a social network. While the former is difficult for political parties to replace, they have tried mightily to provide incentives for volunteers, activists, and political recruiters. The latter, however, can prove a strong motivating factor for people to enter into party activities and stay there.

One of the best-known names in network marketing, also know as multi-level marketing, is Amway, the parent company of which is Alticor, formerly headed by Dick De Vos Jr, the 2006 Republican candidate for governor in Michigan. De Vos' father, Richard De Vos, founded Amway in 1959 and it had 2004 sales in excess of $6.2 billion. The De Vos family has long had an affiliation with Republican politics and Dick DeVos' wife was the former chair of the Michigan Republican Party. De Vos' entry into formal party politics is due in large measure to the experience gained by running a large network marketing firm.

Amway's sales plan is compelling for political parties. According to the company's website:

> It allows you to build your business through retailing products and sponsoring other people who, in turn, can retail products and offer the business opportunity to others. By passing your sales and marketing knowledge to your developing team, you not only build your own business network but also enable others to build one of their own.[5]

Network marketing emphasizes a team approach to profit-making and business organization. Kleeneze, a major British network marketing firm, explains the approach this way:

> By introducing (sponsoring) other people into the business, you are entitled to extra profits, based on the turnover of your group. This is the network marketing side of the business and the higher your group turnover, the more money you will make. Believe it or not there are people earning over £10,000 per month via this method.[6]

Similarly, Tupperware describes its team-driven approach as:

> As your recruits build you become an Associate Manager, hosting an average of five Demonstrations per week. On top of your Demonstrator rewards you will receive monthly bonuses for your team achieving sales targets, and for your first six months we support you with our New Manager Development Program.[7]

Entrepreneur.com published an article on the success of network marketing that makes clear the utility of this approach to party politics. The key components are:

1   Mentorship: "Practice what they teach. [To succeed,] you need to be willing to listen and learn from mentors . . . Whatever [your mentor] did to become successful, it's very duplicatible, but you have to be willing to listen and be taught and follow those systems."
2   Hierarchy: "The higher-ups. It can be called various things, but the general term is the 'upline,' meaning the people above you. How supportive are they? Do they call you? Do

they help you put a plan in place? Are they as committed to your success as they are to their own? You should be able to relate to [the people in your upline] and be able to call them at any time to say 'I need some help.' "

3   Recruitment: "Take up the lead with your downline. There's a term in the network marketing industry called 'orphans'—when somebody is brought in and then the person who brought them in is just so busy bringing in other people that they don't spend the time to teach and train [the new person]. You should be prepared to spend at least thirty days helping a new person come into the industry—training them, supporting them and holding their hand until they feel confident to be able to go off on their own. . . . This is really about long-term relationship building. It's not about just bringing people into the business and just moving forward. It's about working with these people and helping them to develop relationships."[8]

These tactics have been part and parcel of precinct building and successful party building for some time, but as network marketing emerged in the twenty-first century as a multi-billion dollar, technologically savvy enterprise, the major parties were forced to closely study their efforts. The success of network marketing firms is due in no small measure to their pitch. An analysis in the alternative online magazine *EnergyGrid* declared:

> The reason why network marketing (multi-level marketing) can work so well is that people are much more likely to fall for a sales pitch from a friend or relative, or a stranger in a home setting, than they are from a stranger in a shop or market, or an advert in a paper, magazine or on the Internet.[9]

Political Parties Adapt Network Marketing Techniques

Since the dawn of the television era, marketing techniques have become formal elements of campaign strategy. Selling a candidate has been a staple of American political campaigns since before the "new Nixon" of 1968. This general style of marketing, however, is not the type of networking favored by contemporary multi-level marketing firms.

By the late 1970s, network marketing principles had entered political parties through the use of direct mail. Targeted mail was widely credited with rebuilding the Republican National Committee (RNC) in the aftermath of Watergate. Bruce I. Newman refers to the technique as "relationship marketing." This is an "orientation that views the consumer with long-term perspective." As such it is "implemented in the commercial marketplace by customizing products, personalizing promotional appeals, creating flexible pricing policies, and going direct to the consumer."[10]

Direct mail targets a much more narrow subset of the population and makes a personal appeal for donations, campaign assistance, and/or votes. Hedrick Smith quoted the head of a direct response firm in Atlanta, Georgia, in *The Power Game*:

> The nice thing about direct mail is I can hit you in your home and make the pitch directly to you and tell you exactly what you want to hear and that I don't want other people to know I said to you.[11]

This type of personal appeal has been aided by technology. Voter segmentation and data processing have allowed campaigns and political parties to micro-target populations of voters with direct mail and, increasingly, direct outreach. This was achieved most effectively by the Republican Party in the 2002 and 2004 elections.

The Republicans instituted the "Seventy-Two-Hour Task Force" in 2002 in order to keep their 2000 campaign mistakes from happening again. Then, Republican Party predictions that nearly twenty million evangelical voters would turn out for Bush proved to be off by about four million. The closeness of the 2000 race was reason enough for the Republican Party to ensure a greater get-out-the-vote (GOTV) drive in 2002 and 2004. This seventy-two-hour project was designed to increase the number of Republican voters by contacting them seventy-two hours before the polls opened on election day. In its implementation, the Seventy-Two-Hour Task Force drew heavily on network marketing techniques to create a new organizational level of activism, the grassroots network, complete with "upline" and "downline" participants, who could more effectively reach prospective voters and increase turnout.

Dan Balz described these efforts as "a throwback that both Democrats and Republicans have rediscovered as an antidote to television ads."[12] But this "throwback" was applied with modern marketing techniques. For example, the RNC ran experiments to test the claims of network marketing firms. According to Garance Franke-Ruta and Harold Meyerson, in 2002, as an experiment, "four volunteers were pitted against a professional telemarketing firm, each with an identical script and separate lists of voter names. The four volunteers got almost 5% more people to the polls than the pros."[13] As Ken Mehlman noted:

> The most important thing you can do in politics is give someone a personal contact from a credible source. Not just a personal contact from a paid person on the ground, but someone in their church, their gun club or the PTA.[14]

Volunteers were recruited by national, state, local, and collegiate party organizations at rallies, meetings, and through the Internet. The new downline recruits were assigned to precincts in which they would network. All such volunteers reported to a RNC marshal who would organize them into units of two or three individuals. Each unit was assigned a specific task: operating phone banks, canvasing precincts, and assisting with campaign rallies. The training involved in this approach was rigorous, often occurring over period of months and often targeted at specific goals of expanding the Republican Party coalition and registering new voters.

Harnessing network marketing techniques was the brainchild of Karl Rove and Blaise Hazelwood at the RNC. Hazelwood was quite aware of the fact that network marketing tactics applied older concepts of party organizations to the modern era of marketing campaigns. As Balz pointed out soon after the 2002 elections:

> In some ways, Hazelwood was a natural to oversee the 72-Hour Project. . . . She began door-to-door canvassing as a 10-year-old in Arizona when her father was running for precinct committeeman, and she learned firsthand the value of human contact, meticulous organization and volunteer muscle in political campaigns.[15]

GOTV drives were not the only traditional party activities updated by network marketing. A new type of patronage has infiltrated these organizations. In his analysis of the role of money in Colorado's seventh district race of 2002, Daniel A. Smith documented the use of campaign "volunteers" recruited through state and national party organizations:

> Aided by a $250,000 soft money contribution from the RNC, the state party's ninety-six hour program paid "volunteers" $200 for their efforts and included 114 Oral Roberts University students bused in from Oklahoma. During literature drops, the students were seen talking on cellular telephones provided by the party and driving cars courtesy of a John Elway dealership. The NRCC also spent $14,559 in hard money to target Latinos in a late surge of "robo-calls" starring [Democratic candidate] Feeley's legislative and lobbying record.[16]

Republican Bob Beauprez won the district by 121 votes. Smith credits the victory to the coordinated campaign plan of the national party organizations and its financial backing and adds the concern that "the parties' outside money contributed to the widening disconnect between the constituents residing in the district and the candidates who tirelessly campaigned to represent them."[17]

Other less selective incentives were employed as well, such as receiving a signed picture of the president or tickets to Bush reelection events. The *Washington Post* reported that "[t]ickets to Bush events, distributed by the Republican Party, go only to those who volunteer or donate to the party or, in some cases, sign an endorsement of the GOP ticket and provide names and addresses."[18] Viewed from the lens of network marketing, this practice was a way in which to reward "downline" workers with a tangible benefit for their organizational prowess.

Matt Bai's analysis of network marketing tactics in the 2004 Ohio presidential campaign illustrates the degree to which parties have mastered the techniques of network marketing. Campaign manager Ken Mehlman was one of the preeminent architects of what was referred to as "the Plan." Local parties and campaign organizations were to work in consultation with the national party and Bush campaign to set goals for the volunteer aspect of the reelection effort. Said Mehlman:

> The lessons of reality TV are that people are into participatory activities . . . They want to have influence over a decision that's made. They don't want to just sit and passively absorb. They want to be involved, and a political program ought to recognize that.[19]

The Republican effort to coordinate the activity of thousands of volunteers and use them to target voters is a new twist on traditional party mobilization. Bruce Newman's study of political marketing details the transition of an older "party concept" of campaign strategy where patronage and a "lifetime of party affiliation" play a crucial role in a candidate's success, to a "marketing concept" of strategy. In the latter, "strategy originates from the voter and begins by breaking down the electorate into distinct and separate segments of voters." Using the techniques of political consultants, once segmentation has been achieved, "the candidate creates an image for himself and uses that to position himself. The strategy is then executed through information channels based on the results of marketing research and polling."[20]

The party approach to Newman's candidate-centered strategy broadens the techniques to include party and national campaign organizations. Where Smith sees a worrisome trend of interference and disconnect, Bai sees the layers of party and campaign organizations working together in a consultative fashion:

> Rove and Mehlman gleaned a critical lesson from the 2002 Congressional and 2003 gubernatorial elections . . . the way to build a grass-roots movement is to get one volunteer to recruit several other volunteers, and so on, so that the organization is constantly growing, feeding off itself.[21]

The process of mobilizing voters in the 2004 Republican campaign was left in the hands of local volunteers, called Bush Team Leaders. Bai was introduced to Todd Hanks, the Delaware County, Ohio Bush campaign chair. Bush won Delaware County with 66% of the vote in 2000, so it was a solidly Republican county where Bush needed to win big to offset expected Democratic gains in the urban areas of the state. In order to keep Ohio in the Republican Party fold, Hanks was committed to maximizing the Republican vote. As a "downline" participant, Todd Hanks was recruited and kept in the organization in the same way someone is recruited and kept in a network marketing company. Despite his strong political preference for Bush, "Hanks readily admitted that his ultimate goal is to rise through the ranks of local and even state politics," wrote Bai. "For Hanks, the Bush campaign offers a chance to recruit a 'downline' of new volunteers who will, ideally, remain loyal to him in future campaigns—including his own."[22] Old-style patronage-based machine has thus been replaced by the pyramid goals of network marketing organizations.

The organizational capacity of network marketing exceeds in sheer numbers the limited scope of the consultant-driven candidate organizations from which it grew. The traditional party organizations of the early twentieth century, with their dependence on party bosses, local autonomy and patronage, gave way in the 1970s and 1980s to new candidate-centered organizations separated from the normal party structure. These candidate-centered entities were dominated by a professional staff of consultants and pollsters and only tangentially related to their party organizations, which had become large funnelers of money to candidates. The Richard Daleys of an earlier era gave way to the James Carvilles of modern electoral politics. The tried-and-true methods of these traditional organizations were pushed aside by the new communication techniques. In the late twentieth century, "[t]he campaign's theme and message are communicated through television and radio commercials, through direct mail pieces, and increasingly through campaign websites," Dennis W. Johnson has written. "Those communications are developed and honed through the use of sophisticated research analyses, especially survey research, focus groups, and dial meter sessions."[23] In an important sense, network marketing merges old-fashioned grassroots methods with sophisticated modern messages.

Developing the Bush "Brand" 2002–2004

The approach of the Republican campaign in 2002 had three prongs. The first was financial and Bush used the summer months to raise record amounts of money for Republican candidates while focusing on GOTV drives and defending the record of his party during the fall months leading up to the election. This financial effort was by all accounts quite successful.

The second was to use Bush's leadership to unite the Republican Party. The "Bush leadership," specifically his wartime record post 9/11, was the focal point of the strategy. In the spring of 2002, a Republican Party pollster called this development the "Bush brand." The branding was in part a product of "Bush's sky-high approval ratings" that have had the effect of extending his popularity far "longer than normal, making him the GOP symbol." Having a "product" to "sell" is, of course, critical to any marketing technique, and it is especially for network marketing where the personal contact of the "sales force" is on the line. Wrapping a presidency in the cloak of party is both unusual by contemporary standards and fraught with political uncertainty. In this regard, Bush's involvement in the party was not dissimilar to his predecessors, but was more intense and comprehensive. The terrorist attacks of 2001 had the same effect on the polity as the Great Depression in the 1930s, creating a wave of public support for the president that allowed him to reverse the historical course and demonstrate the strength of a strong executive as party leader. In any event, the Bush "brand" was essential to the success of the network marketing techniques. Unlike most of its predecessors, the Bush White House took an active, if at times behind the scenes, role in promoting particularly strong Republican Party candidates in state primary elections.

Once the financial and leadership elements were in place, the third prong was organizational, the implementation of network marketing techniques in the party and campaign. The key organizational units in battleground states became the living room of "upline" managers and "downline" recruits. "The big thing that brings them [campaign volunteers] all together is viral activity," claimed Ken Mehlmen.[24] Because the goal of this vibrant grassroots organization was to reach as many voters as possible during the final seventy-two hours of the campaign and get them to the polls, human interaction and organization of efforts was at a premium.

When Bush entered the general election campaign, he became the best "upline" salesman for the "brand." He was relentless in these efforts, visiting forty states and over 100 congressional districts on behalf of Republican candidates in 2002. During the last five days of the 2002 campaign, Bush participated in seventeen key candidate events. The *Washington Post* reported that

> the work paid big dividends on Election Day, when a surge of Republican voters in states such as Florida, Georgia, North Carolina and Missouri overwhelmed the Democrats and turned what many had called one of the most competitive midterm campaigns in history into a substantial Republican victory.[25]

The Republican Party won 73% of the seventeen key races where Bush had personally campaigned, some by a margin of just 1% of the vote. The relatively low turnout in the 2002 election assuredly assisted the Republican Party, particularly because the turnout of Republican Party voters increased 4% nationally over turnout in 1998.

The success of the 2002 campaign provided the evidence Republican Party leaders needed of the effectiveness of not only Bush as party leader but also the network marketing of parties. Indeed, by 2004, Bush's efforts as party leader bore fruit because of the organizational network marketing techniques on the ground. According to Bush's chief strategist Matthew Dowd:

> [W]e were able to win some close races that we probably wouldn't have won unless we had learned from what we had learned in 2000 through the 72-Hour Task Force and done some things. I mean, we put a lot of stuff in place in Georgia, where we had some surprising victories in the senate and the governor's race. We put some stuff in place in Minnesota, where [former Vice President Walter] Mondale was supposed to win and ended up losing to Sen. [Norm] Coleman. Missouri. So there were some spots that we did some stuff that I think we pulled some races out. We had good candidates, but also, we had such good tactics. But having a president with a 60%, 59% job approval helps.[26]

The Republicans faced a similar strategic problem at the 2004 campaign and set out to implement network marketing techniques on an even larger scale. The 2004 election also presented the Bush campaign with a greater challenge than its 2002 efforts on behalf of congressional candidates. The president's public approval rating dipped to 41% in May as concerns over the war in Iraq and the nation's economy mounted and Democrats had a high degree of unity in their preference to have Bush removed from power. Bush would have to rely strongly on his own base, rather than winning over Independents or Democrats and that reliance would focus on particular states, such as Ohio. It was in that state that network marketing was most crucial. Evidence of the heightened emphasis on network marketing is found in a series of PowerPoint presentations put together by Karl Rove. According to Byron York, the Rove presentation was "unintentionally made available" to Democratic strategists at the outset of the campaign. In fact, knowledge of this document was a major inspiration for the grassroots innovations among Democrats in 2004, including Americans Coming Together.[27]

The document uses the language of network marketing from key phrases such as "Back to People Power" and "The results were conclusive–It Works!" It also borrows heavily from network marketing techniques:

> "If you need votes from a constituency, go after them in a serious and targeted way."
> "Don't wait for outside groups to turnout voters, do it yourself."
> "Customize mail and phone programs to individual voters and their concerns."
> "Make all voter contact motivational, visually appealing."
> "Fight for this vote like you mean it."
> "Devote resources."

The Republican Party "Plan" in 2004 developed grassroots organizations in all fifty states, but with special emphasis on sixteen "battleground states," using the lessons of 2002 and the Seventy-Two-Hour Task Force. The top of the "upline" managers was at the campaign head-quarters in Arlington, Virginia, followed by regional coordinators and state-level coordinators; these three levels were paid campaign officials. Beneath the state-level coordinators were the "downline" managers and participants—county, city, and precinct officials—who were volunteers. By election day, this cooperative operation had more than one million volunteers nationwide, a party machine for the modern era.

The Ohio version of this organization was described as follows:

> To conduct the ground war, the Republican Party constructed an extraordinary grassroots organization that reached into every region of the state. Based on roughly 150 field staff and involving some 12,000 local party officials, it recruited more than 85,000 volunteers. The overall effort also included a full-time registration coordinator, fifty field personnel dedicated to registration, and ten coordinators working with churches. These activists were recruited from social and political networks and the Bush website, which generated six different kinds of "team leaders." The success of these efforts relied on detailed information about voters, clear goals, and a high degree of accountability for results.[28]

According to the Plan, "The first thing is to determine where the most important voting blocs/coalitions are that need to be penetrated and maximizing in order to achieve victory. It is important to prioritize to be effective." This was followed by the movement to "target coalition groups on issues that they care about and that will motivate them to vote. Some of these groups include; social conservatives, agriculture, Catholics, Sportsmen, etc. Targeting these groups can increase Republican turnout 4%."

The final element was to draft a county-wide plan of action:

> Now all that is needed is to put all the information gathered in one plan and one timeline. This is critical. A plan lets everyone know what is expected of them and the timeline allows volunteers to plan ahead and save the dates on their calendars.

This effort was similar in design to the Meet-Up phenomenon of the 2004 election, used to great effect early in the campaign by the Howard Dean campaign. But network marketing techniques advanced by the Republican Party promised greater results and organizational clarity.

The "upline" managers set specific goals for the "downline" participants, including recruiting volunteers, organizing campaign events, registering and contacting voters. Participants at every level of the organization were held accountable for meeting these goals. Just as importantly, the Bush campaign provided highly targeted messages for the volunteers to deliver. This "micro-targeting" was produced by extensive and sophisticated research. As Dan Balz and Mike Allen reported:

> [T]he Bush operation sniffed out potential voters with precision-guided accuracy, particularly in fast-growing counties beyond the first ring of suburbs of major cities. The campaign used computer models and demographic files to locate probable GOP voters. Once those people were identified, the RNC sought to register them, and the campaign used phone calls, mail and front-porch visits—all with a message emphasizing the issues about which they cared most—to encourage them to turn out for Bush.[29]

The net result of the network marketing techniques was greater attention to the grassroots and more viral activity among potential Bush voters in 2004. According to state senator Jane Earll of

Erie County, Pennsylvania, compared to past campaigns, "[t]here are more campaign people around, more coordination, more ground troops and grass-roots organizing."[30]

After the 2004 election, RNC chair Ed Gillespie e-mailed his followers with the good news:

> 1.2 million volunteers made over 15 million contacts, knocking on doors and making calls in the 72 hours before the polls closed. 7.2 million e-activists were contacting their family, friends, co-workers. The RNC registered 3.4 million new voters, enlisted 1.4 million Team Leaders, and contacted—on a person to person basis—30 million Americans in the months leading up to and including Election Day, and in the final 72 hours we met 129% of our door-knocking goal; and met 120% of our phone-calling goal.[31]

Of course, President Bush was deeply involved in the 2004 campaign and the Republicans lavished extensive resources on television advertising and other high-tech activities. However, the grassroots operation made a critical difference, such as tipping Ohio into the Republican column and delivering the presidency to Bush. A good example is the case of Todd Hanks, the Bush Team Leader in Delaware County, Ohio described by Matt Bai: although Bush won the county by the same percentage 66% as in 2000, the actual number of Bush voters increased dramatically due to the expanded turnout. The *Columbus Dispatch* reported that Democratic counties saw turnout increase in some places up to 24% over 2000, Bush counties exceeded those numbers: "Delaware County led the way with a 43% voter increase over 2000, followed by Warren with 34%, Union with 31% and Pickaway with 26%."[32]

Republican consultant Barry Bennet explained the focus on traditional GOP voters:

> They live in counties that are so Republican that their vote never really mattered before . . . We just went in and maximized our vote. We called, mailed, knocked on doors and they came out.[33]

Many observers were impressed by these results, which suggested a historical comparison. The *Los Angeles Times* reported:

> [I]n some ways the technologically-driven outreach is a throwback to the days of the urban political machines, when ward heelers knew how to get out the vote in their part of the big city. After decades of less efficient direct mail and cold calls, the technology has evolved to the point that millions of residents living in battleground states are getting as much personal attention as a 1940s Democrat did in Chicago.[34]

Along the same lines, Bai commented: "To watch [the Bush volunteers] recruit new voters and volunteers in exurban town houses, cajoling one neighbor at a time, is to imagine how it might have looked to see the Democratic ward bosses organize their tenements in the days of Tammany Hall."[35]

The 2006 Defeat: Network Marketing in Retreat

Given their successes in 2002 and 2004, against historic odds, the Republican Party's network marketing plan received significant media attention in the months and weeks leading up to the 2006 midterm elections, as well as in their immediate aftermath. Coverage focused primarily on the ability of the Republican Party's turnout apparatus to stave off impending defeat. The election was portrayed as a battle between an energetic Democratic Party, highly motivated to oust an increasingly unpopular Republican majority, and a Republican Party possessing mechanics that, in consecutive elections, had proven capable of giving their candidates a critical edge. Ultimately, an overwhelming Democratic victory that resulted in gaining control of both the

House and Senate led some to point to the failure of Republican mobilization techniques. However, while both of these initial assumptions regarding the 2006 midterm were largely accurate, hindsight has shown that framing the contest as such is an oversimplification that misses some crucial developments specific to this election.

Initially, the match up between Democratic motivation and Republican professionalism was indeed an intriguing one. Robin Toner highlighted these apparent discrepancies in what were perceived as the two party's individual advantages going into the election. She stressed the continuing relevance of the seventy-two-hour project to the Republicans in 2006 as well as the supreme confidence placed in it by many of the party's elite. Indeed, in an election where a sour national mood driven by an unpopular war in Iraq and a litany of high-profile Republican scandals was mounting against the Republican Party, many saw their voter outreach program as the biggest reason to remain hopeful going into the election. The ability of Republican strategists to target nearly every potential Republican voter through comprehensive computer databases and micro-targeting and deliver an individually tailored message was considered an adequate compensation for a relatively unmotivated base. Party strategist Tom Cole described the 2006 midterms as "a race where professionalism has to make up for enthusiasm."[36]

Certainly, the mastermind behind the seventy-two-hour project, Karl Rove, maintained unfaltering confidence in the ability of these strategies to pull through in crucial battleground states. Rove widely dismissed overwhelming polling that suggested the possibility of a Democratic landslide and even predicted outright victory, citing his own "metrics" or figures on voter outreach as proof that Republicans would prevail on election day. Such optimism seemed to buoy some Republican officials in the weeks leading up to the election, but even Ken Mehlman was less than enthusiastic about the Seventy-Two-Hour Task Force's prospects for success in the midst of such a hostile atmosphere. While Rove and other top Republican strategists were firmly entrenched in "specs" and "metrics," Mehlman had a much more comprehensive view of the political realities surrounding the election and he recognized these realities as sharply turning against the Republican Party despite the party machine's best efforts.

This became indicative of a hard reality regarding the Seventy-Two-Hour Task Force and network marketing principles in general that would become apparent in 2006, namely that it could not be expected to be fully effective in the event that the Republican base was simply unmotivated to vote. The Republican Party remained committed to the same strategies that had launched them to victory in 2002 and 2004 and was looking to build upon those successes in 2006. According to the National Journal, in the months prior to the midterm election the Republican Party had established a goal of adding roughly 2.2 million downline supporters to augment its 170 million member strong Voter Vault database. On top of this were efforts to register over 400,000 new votes and recruit 2,000 more GOTV coordinators along with thousands of precinct captains and roughly 100,000 new volunteers.[37] The Republican Party had also planned to invest roughly $26 million in its grassroots, GOTV efforts. Thus, the mechanics in terms of manpower and financial backing were in place to run a Republican Party mobilization campaign that was at very least on par with the once vastly superior Republican efforts fielded in the previous two elections.

However, the Republican Party formula for success in 2002 and 2004 did not work in 2006 and in the process damaged the seventy-two-hour project's prospects for widespread success. As opposed to previous elections, in 2006 Republicans could no longer rely on the "Bush brand" as a driving force for network marketing initiatives. The steep decline in public approval for the president left the Seventy-Two-Hour Task Force without the symbol of powerful executive leadership it had enjoyed during the height of its success. Indeed, whereas in 2002 and 2004 Bush was one of the Seventy-Two-Hour Task Force's biggest assets, in 2006 Bush's presence became detrimental to Republican Party campaign efforts. This could be witnessed in attempts on the part of many Republican candidates to distance themselves from Bush as well as the limited amount of states that Bush was able to campaign in relative to 2002 and 2004. Furthermore, Bush's ability to rely on support from core Republican Party voters and the Seventy-Two-Hour Task Force's ability to mobilize these votes in large numbers was undermined by a marked decline in Republican enthusiasm. Polls before the 2006 election showed Republican candidates receiving between 75 and 80% of Republican support, at least ten points below average. In addition, fewer voters were identifying as Republican in the weeks leading up to the election and many Independents cited the war in Iraq as their major concern. Given the fact that the success of previous Seventy-Two-Hour Task Force initiatives were largely contingent upon the sense of connection and viral activity fostered between Republican Party strategists, grassroots volunteers, and potential voters, a demoralized Republican base seriously limited the potential of 2006 turnout operations. These factors led realistic Republican officials to temper their hopes for their turnout programs as many believed: "It won't work if the base is unmotivated."[38]

On the other hand, the Democrats enjoyed the distinct advantage of a highly energized base of support. Many polls conducted prior to the election found that nearly 50% of Democrats were more excited about voting in the 2006 midterms than in past elections, compared with merely 33% of Republicans. Voter intensity is a critical element to midterm elections that generally receive less attention and enthusiasm. The intensity gap between Democrats and Republicans was summed up by one Democratic pollster: "There's been a consistent pattern for the better part of a year that Democrats are pretty focused on what they're voting for and what they're voting against, while Republican voters are feeling ambivalent on both fronts."[39] However, in the aftermath of the election it appears that the narrowing of a different gap between Democrats and Republicans may go even farther in explaining the extent of the Democratic victory.

The disparity between the marketing and mobilization techniques of the Democrats and Republicans has been widely cited as a major contributing factor to Republican victories in 2002 and 2004. The above framing of the 2006 contest as a bout between the Democrat's energy versus the Republican's machine implies a continuation of vast superiority on the part of Republicans. While the Democrats were indeed well behind the Republicans in terms of microtargeting and voter databases leading up to 2006, and there initially existed internal dissension among top Democratic strategists, post election analysis demonstrates that the once formidable Republican advantage was nearly nullified in 2006. Prior to the election Michael McDonald, a Brookings Institution expert on voter turnout, said: "The Republicans have about a four-year head start on where the Democrats are now. The good news for the Democrats: You can catch up pretty quickly."[40] Democrats were able to prove the wisdom of that statement by crafting their own sophisticated voter outreach programs, programs capable of competing with the seventy-two-hour project outright, almost completely under the radar.

After two elections characterized by falling victim to the seventy-two-hour project's inherent superiority to their own efforts, the Democrats were able to achieve success through a concerted effort on the part of the party, as well as labor and interest groups, to match Republican sophistication in voter outreach. Perhaps most critical to such an effort was the fact that, for the first time, the Democratic Party explicitly addressed Republican superiority with financial resources. According to the *National Journal*, Democratic Congressional Campaign Committee (DCCC) chairman Rahm Emanuel and Democratic Senate Campaign Committee (DSCC) chairman Charles Schumer placed the seventy-two-hour project firmly within their gaze and incorporated its capabilities into their campaign strategies over a year before the 2006 midterm elections. While dissention between Emanuel and Schumer and Howard Dean was well documented, Democratic strategic leadership was eventually able to coalesce around the need for a better funded GOTV effort.

The increased commitment to voter outreach helped open the possibility that combined Democratic efforts would actually be able to exceed those of their Republican rivals. This was aided by an assertive fundraising campaign on the part of Democrats that allowed them to enter into the final weeks of the campaign with nearly as much money as the Republicans. Prior to the election, the totals projected from the DSCC, the DCCC, and the Democratic National Committee (DNC) were expected to eclipse the $30 million budgeted for the seventy-two-hour program. The DNC alone had budgeted around $12 million for voter outreach programs, setting a new high for a midterm election. Through the DNC, Emanuel allocated more than $250,000 to the development of customized GOTV efforts in thirty-three competitive districts.

Increased funds for voter turnout helped the Democrats to bridge a crucial gap in micro-targeting in the 2006 election. Stephen Weismann, associate director for policy at the non-partisan Campaign Finance Institute, stated:

> The big trend is micro-targeting, and that was used by Democratic-oriented groups to supplement their knowledge. Before, they just used polls and sent a lot of mail. [This time] they were trying to get more precise. Republicans were in this area first, but Democrats are catching up.[41]

Micro-targeting and the use of sophisticated Internet databases were a crucial facet of the successful implementation of multi-level marketing strategies by the Republican Party in 2002 and 2004. In fact, the seventy-two-hour project was essentially fueled by the information contained within the Republican database or the "Voter Vault." A massive collection of voter data, Voter Vault contained a wealth of information pertaining to individual voter biases, habits, and points of view and was accessible to Republican Party volunteers and organizers as well as the party leadership. As such, Voter Vault existed simultaneously as a means to monitor and organize party activity within the seventy-two-hour project framework as well as a source of practically limitless data on potential voters. This voter data allowed the Republican Party to tailor specific messages to meet the preferences and persuasions of potential voters as well as deliver them with precision.

While evidence does not suggest that the Democrats attempted to engage in the specifically multi-level marketing aspects of the seventy-two-hour project (that is, the means by which the Republicans recruited and managed the volunteer network which utilized micro-targeting to GOTV), it clearly points to the adoption of similar micro-targeting efforts. For example, in Montana and Missouri, the Democratic Party explicitly focused on micro-targeting as a campaign strategy by developing sophisticated, up-to-date voter lists. In the case of Missouri, such a database was utilized to invite selected voters to a series of events with the Democratic Senate candidate Claire McCaskill's mother who was said to demonstrate problems with the Republican Party's Medicare drug benefit. Montana Democrats utilized their voter database to target less certain voters and urge them to cast early ballots.

Organized labor and other liberal interest groups were also able to come together to give the Democrats an increased boost in grassroots capabilities. The 2006 election marked a distinct turnaround for such groups as their efforts proved superior to similar programs on the part of business and conservative interests. The *National Journal* noted:

> After two previous election cycles in which conservative and business interests deployed superior get-out-the-vote efforts, labor, human-rights, environmental, pro-choice, and other left-leaning groups won the ground game on election day, helping Democrats to take back the House and Senate.[42]

Labor specifically was able to participate in the 2006 election in record numbers. According to the *Washington Post*, labor was able to contact 13.4 million voters as well as supplying 187,000 volunteers to Democratic GOTV efforts.[43] This reversal was accomplished by way of improved coordination between like-minded liberal groups, but most importantly through an increased sophistication of GOTV efforts. Once again, this included the adoption of the same micro-targeting strategies and technologies that had been utilized by Republican Party groups. Given the well-documented unhappiness with the Republican establishment that was concurrently energizing Democrats and demoralizing Republicans, the Democrat's new-found capability to micro-target in highly contested states such as Michigan, Ohio, and Pennsylvania provided them with a critical advantage.

These strides in GOTV technology allowed Democrats to largely nullify any vast disparities in voter contact in highly contested races. However, 2006 provided evidence of another important fact behind the Republican's vaunted turnout machine. Shocking Democratic upsets in both of New Hampshire's House districts proved to be case studies of the extent to which the seventy-two-hour project framework exists as a comprehensive strategy. While the Republican's faith in the seventy-two-hour project was never in question leading up to the election, New Hampshire highlights the fact that despite a commitment on the part of the national party, not all Republicans could have expected to benefit from a multi-level marketing approach to voter turnout.

Indeed, conducting voter turnout within the seventy-two-hour project framework remains resource intensive in terms of both financial backing and volunteer support. The Democrats' need for a revamped fundraising effort to begin to compete with Republican Party GOTV efforts is a clear indication of this fact. Furthermore, the time needed to establish the infrastructure and volunteer army necessary for the seventy-two-hour project was in itself considerable. Given this, Republican seats that were initially considered safe did not receive an investment of resources from the national party that would allow them to conduct the same sophisticated turnout strategies as their more highly contested counterparts. In an election in which anti-Republican sentiment struck many districts suddenly and without advanced warning, many Republicans were left without sufficient time or resources for advanced GOTV operations.

New Hampshire witnessed this phenomenon as both incumbent Republicans had enjoyed a history of popularity and relatively easy reelections. Neither was afforded more than a couple of weeks before polls indicated any real sense of danger. In New Hampshire's second district Republican Charles Bass received little attention from the national party and subsequently struggled to organize a coherent GOTV strategy in the face of mounting support for his well-funded opponent, Paul Hodes. Jeb Bradley, the Republican incumbent in the first district was taken by surprise by the grassroots campaign of challenger Carol Shea-Porter. Neither Republican race witnessed any vestige of the seventy-two-hour project strategies that were thought capable of carrying Republican candidates across the finish lines.

These races highlight the focused nature of seventy-two-hour project initiatives. The cost in time, money, and manpower required to execute these strategies is simply too great to be used in races that are not foreseen as competitive. Furthermore, it has been established that the Republican Party is not capable of bringing the seventy-two-hour project to bear upon races that only become competitive at the last minute. Rather, sophisticated GOTV initiatives generally remain isolated to those races that are initially established as being critical to the overall party strategy at the outset of an election.

Conclusions

The Republican application of network marketing techniques to party organization paid off with party victories in 2002 and 2004. Significantly, however, Republican Party affiliation in the electorate has not changed since the 2000 election of Bush, hovering around 31% of the population, with Democrats declining from 36% to 33%.[44] Network marketing has thus not served to increase the number of Americans who are members of the Republican Party, nor could it stave off defeat in 2006. But the processes are in place to maximize their GOTV role for both parties in the future. If the Republicans and Democrats continue to fund marketing operations, they hold out the possibility of providing the organizational apparatus necessary for a sustained increase in turnout.

The unique role played by Bush and the use of network marketing in 2002 and 2004 suggests that however fleeting the Bush "brand" is in the early part of the new century, a new model of presidential–party interaction and the multi-level marketing of such may transform party organizations. Bush's efforts as party leader and the integration of national Republican themes to local party organizations and campaigns is a remarkable turnaround for a party that had witnessed three electoral landslides at the presidential level under Eisenhower, Nixon, and Reagan, but watched its fortunes founder in other races. Network marketing techniques, combined with the technological advances of both parties, may help reverse the trend of declining party organizations as they solidify their positions in the twenty-first century.

Notes

1 "Direct Selling by the Numbers—Calendar Year 2006," www.dsa.org.
2 Dale D. Buss, "A Direct Route for Customers," *Nation's Business* 85 (9) (September 1997): 46.
3 Richard Hofstadter, *The Idea of a Party System: The Rise of Legitimate Opposition in the United States* (Berkeley, CA: University of California Press, 1969).
4 James Reichley, *The Life of the Parties: A History of American Political Parties* (New York: The Free Press, 1992).
5 "The Amway Sales Plan," www.amway.com.
6 "Team Building—the Power of Network Marketing," www.kleeneze2003.co.uk.
7 "Career Path," www.tuppercare.com/au.
8 Devlin Smith, "7 Tips for Network Marketing Success," http://www.entrepreneur.com. Accessed May 5, 2005.
9 "Techniques of Persuasion in MLM or Network Marketing Companies," www.energygrid.com.
10 Bruce I. Newman, *The Marketing of the President: Political Marketing as Campaign Strategy* (Thousand Oaks, CA: Sage Publications, 1994), 47.
11 Hedrick Smith, *The Power Game: How Washington Works* (New York: Ballantine Books, 1988), 148.
12 Dan Balz, "Getting the Votes—And the Kudos," *Washington Post*, January 1, 2003, 1.
13 Garance Franke-Ruta and Harold Meyerson, "The GOP Deploys," *American Prospect Online*, http://www.prospect.org. Accessed February 1, 2004.
14 Morton Kondracke, "Registration Wars in Ohio, Florida Produce a Draw," *Roll Call* 28 (October 2004).
15 Balz, "Getting the Votes."
16 Daniel Smith, "String Attached: Outside Money in Colorado's Seventh District," in *The Last Hurrah? Soft Money and Issue Advocacy in the 2002 Congressional Elections*, ed. David Magleby and J. Quin Monson (Washington, D.C.: Brookings Institution Press, 2004), 198.
17 Ibid.
18 Dan Eggen, "Policing is Aggressive at Bush Events," *Washington Post*, October 28, 2004.
19 Matt Bai, "The Multilevel Marketing of the President," *New York Times Magazine*, January 1, 2003, 45–6.
20 Newman, *The Marketing of the President*, 38.
21 Bai, "The Multilevel Marketing of the President," 47.
22 Ibid., 68.
23 Dennis W. Johnson, *No Place for Amateurs: How Political Consultants are Reshaping American Democracy* (New York: Routledge, 2001), 13.
24 Bai, "The Multilevel Marketing of the President," 47.
25 Balz, "Getting the Vote," 17.
26 Matthew Dowd, "Interview with PBS Frontline's *Karl Rove: The Architect*, www.pbs.org/wgbh/pages/frontline/shows/architect. Accessed September 5, 2005.
27 Byron York, "The Vast Left Win Conspiracy," www.randomhouse.com/crown/crownforum/vlwc. Accessed September 5, 2005.
28 Stephen T. Mockabee, Michael Margolis, Stephen Brooks, Rick Farmer, and John C. Green, "The Battle for Ohio: The 2004 Presidential Campaign," in *Dancing without Partners: How Candidates, Parties, and*

Interest Groups Interact in the Presidential Campaign, ed. David B. Magleby, J. Quin Monson, and Kelly D. Patterson (Lanham, MD: Rowman & Littlefield), 135.

29 Dan Balz and Mike Allen, "Four More Years Attributed to Rove's Strategy," *Washington Post*, November 7, 2004, 1.

30 Tom Raum, "Bush Makes Gains in Battleground States," *Las Vegas Sun*, September 14, 2004, 1.

31 Pauline East, "Notes from the Campaign Chair," RWLC Blog, www.rwlc.net. Accessed October 4, 2004.

32 Joe Hallett and Jonathan Riskind, "Ohio Results Defy Conventional Wisdom," *The Columbus Dispatch*, November 4, 2004, 1.

33 Ibid.

34 Joseph Menn, "The Race for the White House," *Los Angeles Times* October 28, 2004, 1.

35 Bai, "The Multilevel Marketing of the President," 126.

36 Robin Toner, "Democrats Have an Intensity, But G.O.P. Has Its Machine" *New York Times*, October 15, 2006, 1.

37 Marc Ambinder, "Know Thy Voter," The Hotline, http://news.nationaljournal.com/articles/0915hotline.htm.

38 Ibid.

39 Toner, "Democrats Have Intensity."

40 Liz Sidoti, "Dems Facing Proven GOP Turnout Machine," Democratic Underground October 14, 2006, http://www.democraticunderground.com/discuss/duboard.php?az=view_all&address=102×2562521.

41 Bara Vaida and Neil Munro, "Reversal of Fortunes", *National Journal*, November 11, 2006.

42 Ibid.

43 Dale Rusakoff, "Labor to Push Agenda in Congress It Helped Elect," *Washington Post*, December 8, 2006, 13.

44 Harris Interactive, *The Harris Poll* No. 19, www.harrisinteractive.com. Accessed March 9, 2005.

37

Managing a Market-orientation in Government

Examples from Tony Blair and Helen Clark

Jennifer Lees-Marshment

One of the basic principles of marketing is that organizations should be responsive to market demand; in other words, be market-oriented. Political marketing is no different. Political party leaders or candidates who want to win control of government often try to be, or at least appear to be, in touch with the public; making significant use of public opinion research and strategic consultants. Tony Blair in the UK won a landslide election in 1997 with his New Labour design arguably because of his ability to convey market-oriented behavior. However in government Blair faced challenges in maintaining his responsive image, as have other leaders who copied his strategies, such as the prime minister of New Zealand, Helen Clark. This chapter will explore what leaders can do to maintain or re-gain a market-orientation, by examining tools and techniques used by Blair and Clark in their later terms of office. The focus will be empirical, because although there is a significant body of commercial marketing literature addressing the nature, antecedents and strategies for implementing and no doubt maintaining a market-orientation, political marketing literature has not as yet addressed this issue, but we can learn from practice and consider these examples when developing new theoretical frameworks in further research.[1]

A Market-orientation in Politics

A market-orientation in politics can be defined in numerous ways, and not surprisingly given the literature on this within the business marketing sphere, there are already different opinions and attempts to explain what this means. A number of scholars have dealt with this area, using different terms (customer-centric, consumer-led, market-oriented, marketing-orientated, voter-responsive) and different models (for example, Bruce I. Newman: candidate and campaign theories; Jennifer Lees-Marshment: market-oriented party framework; Patrick Butler and Neil Collins: positioning by niche parties; and Robert P. Ormrod: extended political market-orientation model)[2] which have in turn attracted further debate as to their practical utility as well as democratic consequences. All are rooted in the traditions of two disciplines: in political science, the Downsian model of rational-choice; and in marketing, Philip Kotler and Sidney J. Levy's initial statement that marketing can be broadened beyond commerce to all organizations.[3]

Within political marketing, there are two sets of models. One focuses on the principles of marketing applied to communication, such as Dominic Wring on the marketing of campaigns and Claire E. Robinson on the market-orientation of political advertising.[4] The others focus on the marketing of the candidate or party as a whole, including the product, not just how it is sold, such as the aforementioned Newman model derived for the US candidate-based system and Lees-Marshment's model of the marketing of the whole party within the UK two-party majoritarian electoral system. What the second group of models all share is the principle inherent from the business marketing literature and rational-choice political science literature that in order to gain power, political leaders need to be market-oriented. They also all draw on the basic principle that a market-orientation involves the politician or party being:

- in touch with ordinary voter concerns;
- interested in public views;
- responsive to what the public are concerned about;
- able to demonstrate this in the way they behave (not just how they sell themselves).

Models of political marketing add to these essential concepts further specifics, such as what politicians can do to be market-oriented including:

- conduct market intelligence to understand public opinion; and
- develop policies and positions that respond to public concerns.

This kind of behavior is distinctive from seeing marketing as being about selling; it is more concerned with the product. However the nature of the political product itself is variable and complex. Lees-Marshment[5] noted how in UK politics this translated into everything encompassing political party behavior, at all levels, such as:

- Leadership: powers, image, character, appeal, relationship with the rest of the party organization, and with the media.
- Members of Parliament (MPs) (existing or candidates).
- Membership: powers, recruitment, loyalty and behavior.
- Staff: researchers, professionals, advisers etc.—their role, influence, office powers, and relationship with other parts of the party organization.
- Symbols: name, logo and anthem.
- Constitution: formal, official rules.
- Activities: party conferences, rallies and meetings.
- Policies: those proposed for when in office and those enacted once in office.

How the public perceive the product is also another factor to consider: as Kotler and Levy said, "everything about an organization talks."[6] Jenny Lloyd's[7] marketing literature-led analogy of the political product conveys this by adding further components such as the investment a voter has in the product:

1 *Services offering*: this includes not just the policy, but "appropriate management skills and expertise" to implement them.
2 *Representation*: how the party is communicated, or represented, including controlled and uncontrolled communication.
3 *Accommodation*: parties need to understand and respond to the needs of the electorate; encourage participation at all levels; and demonstrate this by politicians at all levels being seen as accessible and open.
4 *Investment*: parties/candidates need to deliver a return on the voter's investment; this varies depending on how much investment or stake a voter has in the MP or party. In business, this is about the price of a good, but in politics this involves membership subscription or

donation, their time and energy spent helping the candidate, or expected/actual financial benefit/loss from party/government policies: "electors expect to see a return, either tangible or intangible."

5 *Outcome*: this is about delivery of election promises; in politics often there is more talk about a potential product, then only in government can it be delivered.

Clearly the political party product, however defined, is a complex and evolving being. A market-orientation is about trying to ensure the product satisfies market demands in order to achieve your goals—so to win an election. It is not just about doing what everyone (as the market can be segmented) wants (as it involves needs as well). Each section of the market (including not just voters and members but stakeholders,[8] the media, think tanks and environmental factors) evaluates the product differently. Beyond the specific product, the overall image, or brand, of the party can affect whether the public perceives the political leader to be in touch.

Not surprisingly, a full model of a market-orientation therefore remains a complex process and under debate; but, while acknowledged, this is not the focus of this chapter.[9] The question here is, given the basic principle, how can leaders in government remain market-oriented and the focus is to examine recent empirical examples that can provide a guide both to further academic research and current practice as to how to manage a market-orientation. First, though, there are a number of forces against maintaining a market-orientation in government that we should consider.

The Forces Against Managing a Market-orientation in Government

It has been suggested that the market-oriented party concept is only suitable for opposition rather than government.[10] Government is busy business. Leaders become separated from public quite easily; they gain information and advice from a whole new sector, the civil service or bureaucracy. As Mike Munro, Clark's chief press secretary from 1999–2005, noted when interviewed, "coming into government is just so different because suddenly you have support structures all around you, you've got so much more advice, you've got so much more expertise."[11] Leaders also enjoy the feeling of having won, rather than trying to win, an election. They also gain experience, knowledge, power, and with this, can grow arrogant. As Alastair Campbell, Blair's chief press secretary, observed when interviewed, Westminster operates "in a political bubble" and you "need to step outside the bubble and get back with the public" but "it's very hard" to stay in touch. Another Labour party staff member noted that you "become more detached from the party . . . caught up in government machine" and while governments develop a "maturity of being in office" you "need to also balance this with the need to be fresh."[12] Leaders can forget to respond to market intelligence; their advisors can become deferential and unable to challenge them in office as they did in opposition; and they become separated from the party apparatus because they are supported by government bureaucracy.

There is also an unpredictability to governing, with issues such as war and economic turbulence coming onto the agenda without leaders asking for it. Mike Munro noted how

> a large element of government ends up being crisis management. That's just the nature of government really. You're fighting fires almost every day. Things go wrong, hospitals botch up operations, schools shut down, crime waves occur, weather events come along and smash up infrastructure or whatever so you spend a lot of time reacting and responding.

They learn much more about the realities and constraints of government than in opposition.

In other words, most of the conditions in government work against fostering a market-orientation. At the same time, the desire for the public to see tangible delivery and a difference grows. This is despite delivery being a slow process in government. The forces for the public perception of the leader's market-orientation to decline are also in place.

Managing a market-orientation over time is essential to the long-term success of political marketing, but there are clearly many obstacles to overcome. There has been little academic research into this, as the focus remains more on pre-election and campaign behavior. Darren G. Lilleker and Jennifer Lees-Marshment did begin to suggest strategies that a government might employ to maintain a market-orientation,[13] such as:

- Collect market intelligence both internally and externally; disseminate it; and be seen to be discussing and at least considering feedback; and to discuss current and potential future party behavior.
- Ensure space and time to think about product design/development for the next election. Future product design over time may require initially held policies to be reneged on in response to new results from market intelligence or changed circumstances in the economy or government finances.
- Pay attention to the need to adjust the product—both the pre-electoral design policies and that for the next election, taking into account achievability in government given any changed circumstances, but also the need to gain acceptance internally, respond to developments in the competition and possibly target new markets of support. Support analysis may lead to new target markets related to the reality of governing, related to not just product design, but communication efforts—for example targeting campaign effort in seats where an MP/Minister is particularly effective at delivery or has a special skill that the party/government needs to ensure they stay in power.
- Carry out careful party management in the continued implementation of the product, with effective leadership to ensure party unity and smooth governing but without suffocating internal debate which would damage internal market intelligence results. If policy is to be changed, this in particular needs careful internal management.
- Communicate the existing and future design, both internally and externally, incorporating the need to communicate delivery to gain credit for success in this area. Communication is also important if the previously promised design needs to be changed in any way due to changed circumstances.

Undoubtedly, further theorizing could be conducted, adapting commercial marketing literature on the measurement, development, implementation and maintenance of a market-orientation.[14] However, given that solutions have been developed by leaders in government, the rest of the chapter will focus on empirical examples drawn from Tony Blair, UK Labour prime minister from 1997 to 2007; and Helen Clark, New Zealand Labour prime minister from 1999 onwards.[15] Both Blair and Clark were successful in adopting market-oriented strategies to win elections;[16] and then struggled to remain market-oriented in government.

UK Labour Government: Tony Blair

Tony Blair was successful in adopting a market-orientation in 1997, and largely, in maintaining it through to his second election in 2001.[17] After this period, it became much harder. There are several points to note with this case.

527

Maintaining a Market-orientation in Government is not Easy

In Blair's case a market-orientation declined during his second term, 2001–2005, largely due to unpopular policies on university education fees, foundation hospitals and the Iraq war but also a change in attitude by Blair. Alastair Campbell felt he was always able to offer objective, critical advice but he left Downing Street in 2003 and with it Blair lost a good advisor who could help keep him in touch. The realities of being in government, and being "the" leader also hit Blair over time. In his resignation speech in May 2007 Blair observed:

> My duty was to put the country first. . . . But what I had to learn as Prime Minister is what putting the country first really meant. . . . They advise you to listen to the people, but they don't always agree. In opposition you listen. . . . But in government you have to give answers.

Towards the end of his leadership, Blair reflected on a change in his own style over time, commenting on the BBC *Politics Show* April 15 2007:

> I'm not a different human being from what I was ten years ago, but I'm a different type of politician and in the last few years I've tried to do what I really think is right, take difficult decisions on behalf of the country, that I think are in the country's long-term interests.

However the Labour team involved effective advisors and strategists who learned from their Conservative predecessors that to erode research departments and let policy/product development grind to a halt (as in Thatcher's case) or hide the results of market intelligence from the leader (as they did with John Major) would cause problems.

Continuing Market Intelligence is Essential to Maintaining—or Recovering—a Market-orientation

Labour were successful in continuing to conduct market intelligence throughout their time in power, and this alerted them to problems in the second term and ensured there was a chance to do something about it while Blair was still in office. As Phillip Gould, Blair's strategist said, "we never, ever took the electorate for granted; we were always vigilant."[18] In 2001–2005 for example, the Labour Party continued to obtain formal intelligence from ICM and Stan Greenberg/Mark Penn. The research findings indicated that the public felt Labour was out of touch mid-term and alerted key party figures to the need to respond more proactively to the issue of the Iraq war. Matt Carter, who was Labour's general secretary, recalled how

> in the period before 2005, the numbers show that. . . . there was an issue to do with trust, that people felt that the Prime Minister lost the public's respect and that Tony Blair had somehow moved away from the agenda that they had elected him on.[19]

Then the government responded.

Hold a Listening Exercise

Labour launched "The Big Conversation" in 2003 to get back in touch. This was an extensive range of events that facilitated positive, reflective and constructive discussion—a different mode of market intelligence to focus groups and polls—as a "way of engaging the public beyond the party."[20] It attracted over 40,000 direct submissions; and involved 80 cabinet, 100 ministers, 200 MPs, as well as trade unions and organizations such as OXFAM, Boots, RSPB. The format encouraged more mature discussion: a government minister commented that "it was amazing—two hours with sixty people and no one had a go at me."[21] It identified key public priorities, some of which made their way into the 2005 manifesto and campaign. Such a method can be used by other politicians: Hillary Clinton used it before getting into power during her senate campaign, and during her bid for presidential nomination with "Let the Conversation Begin" but it is perhaps something to be continued in office. However such listening exercises come with caveats: governments need to make sure they are genuine in some way and have a feedback loop. "The Big Conversation" existed only for a limited time and it was criticized for not reporting back to the public, and just being a public relations exercise.[22] After 2005 Labour re-launched it as a more ongoing process called "Let's Talk," but under Gordon Brown this was replaced with more emphasis on Citizens' Juries.

Just Conducting Market Intelligence is not Enough—it Needs to be Responded to

Another lesson from this case is that despite conducting the formal and informal intelligence, Labour and in particular Blair did not always seem to respond to it. Three of the top priorities identified by "The Big Conversation" were largely ignored in policy-making, including council tax that emerged as a key issue—and a weakness for Labour—in the actual campaign. Interviews with staff during this time suggested that market intelligence was viewed more as a tool as part of a sales than a market-oriented strategy. Market intelligence was used more to "inform the way something was presented than the actual policy" and to help design "phraseology" to influence perception; they could not "think of a major policy position that has been taken on the basis of whether it is popular publicly."[23] With regard to the top up fee policy, polls noted this policy might be unpopular, but polls were used to make the "framework to present that policy in"; if the party had listened to the polls they would most probably not have pursued that policy.[24] Furthermore, Blair seemed reluctant to involve even cabinet colleagues in formulating new policies for 2005 and a third term, although he was persuaded to take department's five-year plans to the full cabinet in late 2004.[25] This, together with the style of leadership during 2001–2005, suggested that the party therefore seemed to be heading for a sales-orientation. However the return of Alastair Campbell with his magic-gut instinct, along with other key party advisors, managed to pull it back for the 2005 campaign.

Reconnecting in the 2005 Election Campaign

Election campaigns are not always the best examples of market-oriented principles in action, but Labour's 2005 campaign was. It responded to market intelligence effectively. Tony Blair was a clear weakness in the Labour product and in response Team Labour was born: senior figures launched the manifesto, and ran the last press conference of the campaign. Brown and Blair were together in a special party election broadcast, giving key speeches and photo opportunities, again offsetting perceived weaknesses in their relationship. Blair himself was dealt with very carefully. He appeared on non-political television, such as the popular daytime program *Richard and Judy*, and *Ant and Dec's Saturday Night Takeaway*, a mainstream Saturday evening program.

On the sensitive issue of the Iraq war, the party also responded to the research showing that not only was the public concerned about Blair's actual questionable decision, he appeared to dismiss voters' concerns, thus undermining his market-oriented image. As Matt Carter explained:

> [I]t was like a block on people's minds. Until that issue had been engaged in and discussed and their views and concerns had been heard, I don't think they were willing to listen to the other issues that were at stake. Part of the campaign that Labour conducted was to let people know . . . we listened to those concerns, that we had acted and would continue to act on those concerns. And only through that insight that we were engaging and listening and participating that they would then be willing to talk about how to take the country forward.[26]

In order to do this, Labour put Blair in positions to take criticism from ordinary people over coffee in shopping malls so he was then seen to suffer and accept voters' discontent, later referred to as the *masochism* strategy. He also explained that as leader he had to make a decision at that time, something people could sympathize with as a dilemma for anyone in that situation. Carter noted that

> taking the Prime Minister to studios after studios and putting him in front of live audiences that could engage and talk with him and put their concerns . . . helped to show that the Prime Minister had not moved off the key agendas that he had been elected on.

Upon winning power and returning to Downing Street, Blair declared outside Downing Street "I've listened and I've learned," trying to show he didn't take the third election victory for granted. This shows how a market-orientation can be regained even after a difficult period.

Blair's Exit Strategy: a Happier Goodbye Helps the Next Leader

The other tool Blair's managers used was to try to re-gain some of Blair's popularity after winning again in 2005 with soft or non-political media appearances to help make the whole Labour brand more positive. A memo from Philip Gould and other advisors called "Reconnecting with the public—a new relationship with the media" in early 2006, leaked in the *Daily Mirror* September 2006, suggested appearances on *Blue Peter*, *Songs of Praise* and Chris Evans' radio show.[27] Downing Street's own website had visual and audio recordings of Blair's interview with Chris Evans, on *Blue Peter*, and a series of films showing what it was like to be prime minister.[28] He even appeared in a comedy sketch for Comic Relief with stroppy teenager Lauren, better known as comedy actress Catherine Tate, displaying scarily impressive acting skills while proving entertaining and appealing to the public. It makes you question the sincerity of his other more politically inclined performances!

Gould noted how "Tony's leaving made him more popular and lifted people's appreciation of the government" and played some part in aiding Brown to attract a positive public standing when he took over.[29] This could be a lesson for any would-be successor—make sure you boost the appeal of your predecessor first.

There are therefore a number of examples we can see from Blair's time in office that other leaders could learn from. Indeed, they already are—Helen Clark in New Zealand is a prime example.

New Zealand Labour Government: Helen Clark

Helen Clark won power in New Zealand in 1999 with a strategy modeled on Blair in the UK.[30] Like Blair she too struggled to maintain a market-orientation over time, only just winning her third election in 2005, and facing a more effective competitor in the National Party under the leadership of John Key since 2006. We can therefore see similar problems, but also other solutions with this case in both the 2005 election and behavior in the third term leading up to the 2008 election.

Avoid Moving from Market-oriented to Product-oriented Communication

Communication often reflects behavior, and Clark's election broadcasts over the three elections in 1999, 2001 and 2005 show a move away from responsive communication. As Robinson noted, over the space of six years, Labour's opening night leadership message has gone from being target-voter oriented with a message of empathy and caring for ordinary Kiwis, to being more detached and product-oriented, focused on selling the inspirational virtues of its leader irrespective of the needs of voters.[31]

Robinson's theory argues that parties need to demonstrate "in their advertising messages both core voter maintenance strategies and an improvement in their value offerings," with two particularly relevant points for incumbents:

- show ability to sense and respond to voters' needs and care about satisfying voters in the long-term; and
- demonstrate you are offering something new in policy and/or leadership.

In 1999, Clark took part in a party election broadcast where she was pictured listening to voters. In 2005 she was instead featured telling the "camera" why New Zealand was good, rather than listening to voters share their concerns—more of a product than a market-oriented approach. Steve Maherey, a key minister in Clark's government, concluded of the 2005 election: "Labour stuck to its values, refused to change its policies and thereby secured a historic third term"—suggesting a degree of rigidity and complacency.[32]

Clark's government, like Blair's, has continued to produce new policy. For example, in June 2007 Labour launched three major policies—the Kiwi saver (a new pension scheme), extension of the Working for Families welfare benefits program, and government funding of twenty hours of child care for three and four year olds.[33] This could still be criticized for not fitting Robinson's market-oriented communication criteria, however, just because Clark tells voters her policies are good does not mean that voters will think they are. As of June 2007, the New Zealand Labour website[34] and government website[35] remained very stark and formal in comparison with UK Labour Party and Number 10 website. However July saw video being introduced, and also appear on the Beehive site (the official website of the government of New Zealand),[36] so developments may be on their way. Clark could still benefit though from careful communication similar to that surrounding Blair's exit—it may stop her from needing to exit herself!

Leaders in Power Increasingly Sell Elite-determined Policy Rather than Respond to Voter Opinion in its Design

Helen Clark is not so much of a liability as Blair given she was against the Iraq war and New Zealand terms are only three years. She has also been a more effective party manager than Blair,[37] enjoyed positive perceptions of capability as a leader by Kiwi voters, and been successful in seeking and obtaining cross-party coalition needed to run a government in New Zealand pro-portional representation electoral system. However signs of a decline in market-oriented behavior are nonetheless evident. Like Blair's, her chief press secretary Mike Munro resigned after two terms and Clark therefore lost a significant source of support and arguably criticism. Although Labour won in 2005, studies showed that pre-election, National was the party closest to voters' views on the most important problem facing New Zealand, and the party closest to voters' views on particularly important issues.[38]

During her third term, the government has also become more introspective and less responsive to underlying public concerns. While Labour did engage in post-election analysis after the near-loss in 2005, it is always difficult for leaders to be self-reflective and honest about the weaknesses of their team. Clark did however attempt to create governmental market intelligence and policy discussion, instructing public servants to create new ideas for the third and fourth term, although Clark did not follow these through. "Labour: Sustainable New Zealand" became the idea for a key theme, but unfortunately this has not resonated with media or public.[39] As of half-way through the parliamentary period, the government, and its leader, has been unable to refresh itself with a clear strategy that would inform the product to be offered to voters at the next election.

Develop a Clearer Strategy not Reliant on Opposition Weakness

The 2005 was a close election. It was so close that explanations for why either party won/lost are unclear—there are various factors that created it. One is that the National Party under a new leader Don Brash responded to certain discontent amongst middle-class voters on issues such as taxes and attracted unexpected support. Labour responded only at the last minute, suggesting they had taken their victory and the opposition weakness for granted. Their responses were effective however. Labour sought to get a quick marketing hit by offering a better deal on student loans to Kiwi students, pledging that interest would be waived on loans whether they were working in New Zealand or abroad (previously payments were deferred but only if they lived outside the country). In another bid to secure support, Labour sent letters to owners of state-owned homes, particularly in South Auckland where there were many potential Labour voters who might otherwise not turn out, with a mock eviction notice, arguing if National won tenants would be forced out of their homes. They sent these notices in the last weeks of the campaign. Not surprisingly turnout—and Labour votes—went up in that area and helped to secure victory.

These quick marketing fixes helped them win—but the result was so close other leaders would be unwise to rely on them. Furthermore, Labour's overall approach was overtly responsive to National, suggesting a lack of a clear strategy, and failing to instil the feeling of a market-oriented government in public opinion. More work was needed in the third term if Clark was to have a good chance of winning the next election in 2008.

Refreshing the Team Refreshes the Leader

Clark did however develop a more responsive approach in 2006 by addressing the usual problem governments face in looking stale and old once they have been in power several terms. Unlike Blair, Clark decided not to leave, but clearly realized the need to inject fresh blood into the party to counteract the disadvantages of her own longevity. In her 2007 conference speech she said:

> Our party is in the midst of a major program of renewal and recruitment. . . . My message from the 2005 election on has been that we must make room for new people and new ideas so we can continue to offer the very best leadership for New Zealand. Many new Labour MPs will be elected next year, and we will say goodbye to retiring members who have made an incredible contribution to our party, to our government, and to New Zealand.[40]

Clark announced reshuffles of her senior team in November 2007, with the aim of rejuvenating it, including resignations of scandal-embroiled ministers. At the party conference in mid-November Labour publicized the retirement of older MPs alongside new candidates for office.

Responding in Policy Terms

The other sign of responsiveness is that at the party conference in November 2007, Clark finally announced that the party would look at reducing tax, responding to the popularity of the opposition leader's stance on tax and aspiration. Tax was an area of weakness for Labour because higher tax rates kicked in at relatively low salary levels, especially compared to rising house prices in the biggest city Auckland (where 25% of the national population lives), hitting the professional middle classes who could not benefit from working family packages designed to target very low income families. In 2005 when National, drawing on its own ideology as well as responding to this market discontent, launched plans to cut income tax, it enjoyed a sudden rise in polled support in a TV3 poll at the end of August 2005. Labour needed to find an appropriate response, especially given there were no financial reasons against this as Labour had seen successive surpluses in recent years.

Clark could have developed an innovative, center-left way to spend such surpluses, such as investing in public transport in the biggest city to help commuters and the environment, linked to a theme of sustainability and investing in infrastructure. Instead, in November 2007, she copied the opposition and announced tax cuts would be forthcoming. The difficulty for Labour is making this genuine. They are not traditionally a tax-cutting party. Clark argued that officials had been against tax cuts previously because the rising surpluses were one-offs and unsustainable. Now the officials had changed their advice, she could act differently.

All of this was open to the criticism again of being overtly responsive to the opposition. Strategists talk more of political marketing techniques as opposed to strategy, such as opposition research, get-the-vote-out, and selling government policies. Their desire to campaign effectively was clear, but the focus was on fighting the opposition rather than responding to the public. However Clark may yet learn from Blair, and also Brown, and appeal more convincingly to the middle ground of voters unsatisfied with the government performance overall but not yet convinced by opposition leader John Key. The government has also looked to the UK to borrow policies from Brown's government, such as housing affordability policies, which also respond to market dissatisfaction.

The overall sense from the Clark case, therefore, is that she faced similar problems to Blair, but also, used various tools to regain a market-orientation. Political marketing is possible in government, even if it does not seem as straightforward as in opposition.

Conclusion

While we argue parties/leaders need to be market-oriented and responsive to voters, in practice there are many difficulties with managing a leader's image, behavior, and a party's behavior to insure it fits in with a market-orientation and can be maintained over time and especially in government. Factors hindering maintenance of a market-orientation in government include:

1   loss of critical, objective, advisors with that gut feel—such as Alastair Campbell;
2   realities and constraints of government, including unpredictability;
3   increasing knowledge, experience and information amongst leaders, encouraging feelings of invincibility, arrogance and superiority;
4   weak opposition, which encourages and facilities complacency as victory can be achieved without being overtly responsive;
5   difficulty and slow pace of delivery in government.

However it would be too early to write off marketing in governments—they can be managed in a way to help maintain a market-orientation, and the Blair and Clark cases provide examples of how to do this. We can learn a number of generic points from both of these case studies that could be applicable to any government around the world. Tools helping maintenance or re-gaining of a market-orientation in government include:

1   continued market intelligence;
2   listening or consultation exercises to get back in touch;
3   refreshing the overall team;

4 use of public-friendly, non political communication;

5 acknowledgment of public concern with leaders' difficult, unpopular decisions or issues;

6 development of new strategy for future terms; and insuring there is the space and time to think about product design/development for the next election;

7 learning from mistakes.

One additional point is the performance of the opposition. Had Clark and Blair both faced a more effective opposition earlier this might have helped stop a decline of their market-oriented behavior; commercial marketing literature suggests that competition is a factor in maintaining a market-orientation.[41]

All leaders can consider ways to manage a market-orientation in office. Even President Bush, not known for his responsiveness to polls, knew to visit the scene of the California fires in October 2007 immediately after losing popularity for not visiting New Orleans after Hurricane Katrina. No doubt new research into this area could also further develop our understanding of this complex, yet vital, aspect of political management. Such work could analyze a greater range of governments; interview advisors, strategists and leaders, or look at the marketing literature for theoretical frameworks on how businesses have maintained a customer- or market-focus. In the meantime world leaders and their advisors would do well to learn lessons from previous practice.[42]

Notes

1 Interviews conducted from 2006 onwards that are quoted in this chapter were funded by Auckland University new staff grant and departmental PBRF funds.

2 Bruce I. Newman, *The Marketing of the President: Political Marketing as Campaign Strategy* (Thousand Oaks, CA: Sage Publications, 1994); Bruce I. Newman, *The Mass Marketing of Politics: Democracy in an Age of Manufactured Images* (Thousand Oaks, CA: Sage Publications, 1999); Patrick Butler and Neil Collins, "Strategic Analysis in Political Markets," *European Journal of Marketing* 30: 10–11 (1996): 32–44; Jennifer Lees-Marshment, *Political Marketing and British Political Parties* (Manchester: Manchester University Press, 2001); and Robert P. Ormrod, "A Conceptual Model of Political Market Orientation," in *Current Issues in Political Marketing*, ed. Jennifer Lees-Marshment and Walter Wymer (Binghampton, N.Y.: Haworth Press, 2005), 47–64.

3 Anthony Downs, *An Economic Theory of Democracy* (New York: Harper and Row, 1957); and P. Kotler and S. Levy, "Broadening the Concept of Marketing," *Journal of Marketing* 33 (1) (January 1969): 10–15.

4 Dominic Wring, "Reconciling Marketing with Political Science: Theories of Political Marketing," in *Proceedings of the 1997 Academy of Marketing Conference* (Manchester: Manchester Metropolitan University, 1997); Dominic Wring, "Conceptualising Political Marketing: a Framework for Election-campaign Analysis," in *The Idea of Political Marketing*, ed. Nicholas J. O'Shaughnessy and Stephan C. M. Henneberg (New York: Praeger, 2002), 171–86; Dominic Wring, "The Labour Campaign" in *Britain Votes 2005*, ed. Pippa Norris and Christopher Wlezien (Oxford: Oxford University Press, 2005), 56–68; and Claire E. Robinson, "Advertising and the Market Orientation of Political Parties Contesting the 1999 and 2002 New Zealand General Election Campaigns", PhD dissertation, Massey University, Palmerston North; Claire E. Robinson, "Images of the 2005 Campaign," in *The Baubles of Office: The New Zealand General Election of 2005*, ed. Stephen Levine and Nigel S. Roberts (Wellington: Victoria University Press, 2007), 182–3.

5 Lees-Marshment, *Political Marketing and British Political Parties*, 27.

6 Kotler and Levy, "Broadening the Concept of Marketing."

7 Jenny Lloyd, "Square Peg, Round Hole?: Can Marketing-based Concepts such as the 'Product' and the 'Marketing Mix' Have a Useful Role in the Political Arena?" in *Current Issues in Political Marketing*, ed. Jennifer Lees-Marshment and Walter Wymer (Binghampton, N.Y.: Haworth Press, 2005).

8 A. Hughes and S. Dann, "Political Marketing and Stakeholders," Australian and New Zealand Marketing Academy Conference, QUT, December 4–6, 2006.

9 For a more thorough literature review see Margaret Scammell, "Political Marketing: Lessons for Political Science," *Political Studies* 47 (4) (1999): 718–39 and for a critique see Robert

P. Ormrod, "A Critique of the Lees-Marshment Market-oriented Party Model," *Politics* May 26 (2) (2006): 110–18.

10 Darren Lilleker and Jennifer Lees-Marshment, eds, *Political Marketing: A Comparative Perspective* (Manchester: Manchester University Press, 2005).

11 Mike Munro, Prime Minister's chief press secretary 1999–2005, New Zealand, interviewed by author, November 2006.

12 Senior Labour Party staff interviewed by author in 2004.

13 Lilleker and Lees-Marshment, *Political Marketing*, 225–6.

14 Such literature includes R. Deshpandé, *Developing a Market Orientation* (Thousand Oaks, CA: Sage, 1999); B.J. Jaworski, and A.K. Kohli, "Market Orientation: Antecedents and Consequences," *Journal of Marketing* 57 (3) (1993): 1–17; A. Kohli, and B.J. Jaworski, "Market Orientation: The Construct, Research Propositions and Managerial Implications," *Journal of Marketing* 54 (2) (April 1990): 1–18. The broader management literature may also offer relevant concepts, as well as public sector marketing or local government marketing literature.

15 Clark remains prime minister at time of writing in November 2007. She is expected to contest the 2008 election and so be leader for at least nine years, over three terms, winning previous elections in 1999, 2001 and 2005.

16 Lees-Marshment, *Political Marketing and British Political Parties* and Chris Rudd, "Marketing the Message or the Messenger? The New Zealand Labour Party, 1990–2003," in *Political Marketing*, ed. Darren Lilleker and Jennifer Lees-Marshment (Manchester: Manchester University Press, 2005).

17 See Jennifer Lees-Marshment, *Political Marketing and British Political Parties*, 2nd ed. (Manchester: Manchester University Press, 2008), for detail.

18 Phillip Gould, "Labour Strategy," in *Political Communications: The General Election Campaign of 2001*, ed. J. Bartle, S. Atkinson and R. Mortimore (London: Frank Cass, 2002), 61.

19 Matt Carter, former general secretary of the Labour Party, current managing director of London PSB company, interviewed by author, September 2007.

20 Kamlesh Karia, Labour Party political development manager, interviewed by author in 2004.

21 Internal Labour Party Document, 2004.

22 See Dominic Wring, "The Labour Campaign," 60, for example.

23 Senior Labour Party staff interviewed by author.

24 Senior Labour Party staff interviewed by author.

25 David Butler and Dennis Kavanagh, *The British General Election of 2005* (Basingstoke: Palgrave Macmillan, 2005), 25.

26 Carter interviewed by author.

27 "Leaked Memo Maps out Blair's Exit Strategy," *Daily Telegraph*, September 5, 2006.

28 See the official website of 10 Downing Street, http://www.pm.gov.uk/output/Page3054.asp. Accessed 19 April, 2007.

29 Lord Phillip Gould, interviewed by author, September, 2007.

30 Rudd, "Marketing the Message or the Messenger?"

31 Robinson, "Images of the 2005 Campaign," 185.

32 Steve Maharey, "Labour—An Historic Third Term," in *The Baubles of Office: The New Zealand General Election of 2005*, ed. Stephen Levine and Nigel S. Roberts (Wellington: Victoria University Press, 2007), 104.

33 See the official website of the New Zealand Labour Party, http://labour.org.nz/news/latest_labour_news/news070701b/index.html. Accessed July 12, 2007.

34 Ibid.

35 Official website of the prime minister of New Zealand, http://www.primeminister.govt.nz/. Accessed July 12, 2007.

36 See the official website of the government of New Zealand, http://www.beehive.govt.nz/HomepageFeature.aspx?id=42. Accessed July 12, 2007.

37 Jennifer Lees-Marshment, "Political Marketing," in *New Zealand Government and Politics*, 4th ed., ed. Raymond Miller (Oxford: Oxford University Press, 2006).

38 "The 2005 Victoria University of Wellington Pre-election Survey," in *The Baubles of Office: The New Zealand General Election of 2005*, ed. Stephen Levine and Nigel S. Roberts (Wellington: Victoria University Press, 2007), 377.

39 Colin James, New Zealand journalist, relayed this to me in informal discussions. I would like to thank Colin for his comments and engagement with political marketing research.

40 The official Labour Party website, http://www.labour.org.nz/news/hot_topics/Speech_to_Labour_Party_conference/index.html. Accessed November 13, 2007.

41 See for example Stanley F. Slater and John C. Narver, "Does Competitive Environment Moderate the

Market Orientation-Performance Relationship?" *Journal of Marketing* 58 (1) (January 1994): 46–55 and is a natural effect of party competition. Other literature discusses a learning orientation, innovation culture and organizational structures all contributing to the ability of an organization to maintain a market-orientation—see for example John C. Narver, Stanley F. Slater and Brian Tietje "Creating a Market Orientation," *Journal of Market-focused Management* 2 (3) (1998): 241–55; William E. Baker and James M. Sinkula, "Market Orientation, Learning Orientation and Product Innovation: Delving into the Organization's Black Box," *Journal of Market-focused Management* 5 (1) (2002): 5–23.

42 For example, the *European Journal of Marketing* recently published a special issue on trust, including what happens when trust is violated. It focused on commercial organizations, but lessons from this work could be adapted to politics. See for example Sijun Wang and Lenard C. Huff, "Explaining Buyers' Responses to Sellers' Violation of Trust," *European Journal of Marketing* 41 (9/10) (2007): 1033–52; or Richard Elliott and Natalia Yannopoulou, "The Nature of Trust in Brands: A Psychosocial Model," *European Journal of Marketing* 41 (9/10) (2007): 988–98.

38

Machiavellian Marketing

Justifying the Ends and Means in Modern Politics

Phil Harris, Conor McGrath, and Irene Harris

In the end each nation is no more than a flock of timid and hardworking animals with each government as its shepherd.[1]

Introduction: Niccolo Machiavelli, Old Nick and Machiavellianism

Niccolo Machiavelli is used here as a guide to some of the key issues facing modern government and we apply his insights to the effective management and development of civic society: political marketing, good governance, lobbying, ethics and effective communication with the consumer are all issues developed from an understanding of Machiavelli's thought.

> Machiavellian: a follower of the teachings of Niccolo Machiavelli (d.1527), of Florence, author of *Il Principe*, which advocates the principle that any political means, no matter how unscrupulous, are justifiable, which strengthen the central government of State.[2]

> Crafty, subtle person, who sacrifices moral scruples to the attainment of power, or furtherance of his ends.[3]

In recent times Machiavelli has been looked at with more clarity and less emotion by such management writers as Antony Jay, Michael Shea, Roger Fisher, Elizabeth Kopelman and Andrea Kupfer Schneider and has even been referred to as the first real marketer. In marketing communications the use of Machiavellian tactics have more recently become associated with spin doctoring, issues management and power politics, resulting in works such as those by Alistair McAlpine, Edward Pearce, Patrick Curry, Phil Harris, Andrew Lock and Patricia Rees.[4]

Niccolo Machiavelli was born in 1469 in Florence of an old citizen family and his name has become a byword for perfidy within political life since he wrote in 1513 his treatise on how to rule, *Il Principe*.[5] His other works are often regarded as a major contribution to management, marketing and understanding power. Machiavelli wrote *The Discourses on Livy*, which Antony Jay has likened to a guide book for the modern manager.

> If one wishes a Sect or a Republic to live long. It is necessary to draw it back often toward its beginning.[6]

Upon this, one has to remark that men ought either to be well treated or crushed, because they can avenge themselves of lighter injuries, of more serious ones they cannot; therefore the injury that is to be done to a man ought to be such a kind that one does not stand in fear of revenge.[7]

Having come to freedom, a corrupt people can with the greatest difficulty maintain itself free.[8]

Benefits should be granted a little at a time, so that they may be the better enjoyed.[9]

But one thing consoles me: when something involves a number of people, no one person in particular can be blamed.[10]

One change leaves the way open for the introduction of others.[11]

In 1512 Machiavelli was dismissed from office with the fall of the Florentine Republic, suffered imprisonment and torture before retiring to his farm in San Castriano, where he wrote his major works. All but one of Machiavelli's works (*The Art of War*) were not published until after his death in 1527. Twenty-five years later all his books were proscribed and banned by the Catholic Church. Old Nick and Machiavellianism are born.

But what is the reality of Machiavellian thought and its influence and relevance for government? We begin by examining the place of the state in Machiavelli's thought, followed by a discussion of the concepts of "*Virtu*" and "*Fortuna*" which are central to Machiavelli's cyclical theory of history and government. By bringing all these together it is hoped to demonstrate that Machiavelli was not amoral, and that the maxim that the end justifies the means attributed to him is inaccurate.

Liberty and the Role of the State

Many political philosophers have based their theories on the assumption that the individual is more important than the state and indeed most people living in democracies would agree with them. Machiavelli on the other hand felt that such an idea was too simplistic and impractical.

While John Locke argued that Liberty, "tis plain, consists in a power to do or not to do; to do or to forbear doing as we will,"[12] Machiavelli would have pointed out that such liberty is contingent upon the state being free from external domination, and internal instability. Therefore the first priority of the state is to secure its own liberty, so as to secure the liberty of its own citizens. To this end the state may use whatever means necessary: for when the safety of one's country wholly depends on the decision to be taken, no attention should be paid to either justice or injustice, to kindness or cruelty, or to its being praiseworthy or ignominious. On the contrary, "that alternative should be wholeheartedly adopted which will save the life and preserve the freedom of one's country."[13] If, as Aristotle says, the purpose of the state is to secure the good life,[14] should the state not take the necessary means to insure it can carry out that function?

This may sound like a pretext for fascism, but, as we show later, Machiavelli strictly limits the use of these necessary means. We may not, quite understandably, be entirely comfortable with Machiavelli's methods, but we cannot condemn the end: after all, the end is nothing more than self-determination, an idea accepted today as a fundamental principle of international law and good governance.

Virtu and Fortuna

Virtu and *Fortuna* are terms that recur throughout Machiavelli's works, and they underlie his recommendations for good government. *Virtu* has no straightforward, direct English translation. It has been described as vitality, or energy and courage[15] and the idea of a tremendous force of will and inner strength that enables one to overcome the most recalcitrant opposition and perilous adversity.[16] In addition, *virtu* is a quality that may be found in states as well as individuals. This civic *virtu* is compounded of many ingredients: a balanced constitution; sound military organization; intelligently planned expansion; respect for religion and the laws; and above all liberty.[17]

Fortuna is a simpler concept: not surprisingly, it is essentially fortune. Machiavelli believes that circumstances, chance or fortune can act as a restrictive force on our actions, but it need not determine our fate. In *The Prince*, fortune is compared to a river: the river will be calm at times, but will flood and cause damage at others. However the flooding can be prevented simply by taking the precaution of building dykes and embankments.

Overcoming fortune requires *virtu*; the virtuous man (or woman) will know how to act, as fortune requires. Success awaits the man whose actions are in accordance with the times and failure the man whose actions are out of harmony with them.[18]

The Cyclical Theory of History and Government

As the times change, so the fortunes of states change: it may be observed that provinces, amid the vicissitudes to which they are subject, pass from order into confusion, and afterward recur to a state of order again.[19] As *virtu* should be able to cope with these vicissitudes, the changes can also be attributed to the degeneration of *virtu* into corruption on the part of both individuals and the populace as a whole.

Machiavelli's advocacy of acting in harmony with the times, combined with his view of the role of the state, result in the prescriptions for different types of government at different times, which are set out in *The Prince* and *The Discourses*. Essentially, Machiavelli believes in the need for two types of government: rule by the individual or a prince (a principality), which is necessary during a time of civic corruption; and rule by the people (a republic) during a time of stability.

We may begin by examining a period of corruption and instability in the state. During such times Machiavelli believes that existing laws and institutions need radical change to return the state to order, and the only way to bring about these changes is to place a single person in charge of the state: the Prince. For rarely, if ever, does it happen that a state, whether it be a republic or a kingdom, is either well ordered at the outset or radically transformed *vis-à-vis* its old institutions unless this be done by one person.[20]

Machiavelli would fully agree with Aristotle's assertion that man is the worst of all animals when divorced from law and justice,[21] and for that reason he sees the job of the Prince as the establishment of the rule of law. The Prince may act in whatever way may be necessary to establish stability (and certainly Machiavelli suggests many ruthless and draconian measures), but it is for that particular purpose only that he may use such measures, and no other. Contrary to the popular perception, at no point does Machiavelli support tyranny (that is, rule by one person in his own interest). For example he declares that a prince who does what he likes is a lunatic,[22] that tyranny cannot please the good, and license is offensive to the wise.[23]

The Prince's role is an interim one: effectively his job is to put himself out of a job. For when the proper laws and institutions are established, and the *virtu* of the populace has been restored, the populace will be fit to govern itself, having good laws for its basis and good regulations for carrying them into effect, "[the state] needs not . . . the *virtu* of one man for its maintenance."[24]

The state becomes a republic, the type of government that Machiavelli feels is best because alike in goodness and glory the populace is far superior.[25]

Machiavelli, however, believes that men are never content with what they have; their ambition will cause corruption to spread, and the state will return to the beginning of the cycle again. Thus the state constantly undergoes changes as corruption and *virtu* dominate in turn.

As can be seen, Machiavelli's theories are very broad. The choice of government is reduced to principality or republic, and even then he never fully explains what course the government should take in terms of a legislative program. There is much talk of good laws and institutions but he does not elaborate further making it difficult to conceive of a typical Machiavellian system.

Morality

Machiavelli's methods are more often than not described as amoral. This is at best over-simplistic, and at worst incorrect. It is over-simplistic in the sense that Machiavelli advocated behavior that we might consider amoral only in limited circumstances, that is, when the liberty of the state was threatened. In effect he was supporting the granting of what we would now call emergency powers to the government, except the sort of actions permitted in those times were more appropriate to volatile and violent sixteenth-century Italy than to comparatively stable twenty-first-century liberal democracies.

Machiavelli never suggested that amoral actions should be the norm. He believed that man should always act in a way appropriate to the times, and this rule applied to morality. It is simply not practical to take the moral line always, for anyone who sets out to play the part of the virtuous man on all occasions is bound to come to grief among so many who are not virtuous.[26] But as a general rule, the Prince should seem to be merciful, true to his word, humane, honest and religious, and he really should have those qualities.[27] So when possible the prince should act morally.

It must be accepted, therefore, that to label Machiavelli amoral would be a generalization and a distortion; by far the larger proportion of his work encourages actions, which are, by our standards, moral. We could push the analysis a step further and say that Machiavelli simply cannot be classified on the basis of our conception of morality, as our moral absolutism is simplistic. A useful perspective is that of Sheldon S. Wolin,[28] whose interpretation is that, for Machiavelli, there were two levels of morality or ethics: public and private. The moral worth of one was not inherently superior to the other, but if a conflict arose between the two then the one, which would produce the most practical result, should take precedence. In practice this meant, if necessary, taking action that was publicly moral (that is, designed to secure the liberty of the state) at the short-term expense of private morality.

This produced a situation not where the end justified the means, but where the end dictated means of a type that rendered both the wholly good man and the wholly evil man superfluous.[29] Circumstances periodically require that the government acts in ways that, to Machiavelli, will be publicly moral, but privately immoral: so how, under our conception of morality, do we classify such actions? To say they are amoral is merely a deft way of avoiding the issue! Clearly, then, morality is a redundant concept in the characterization of Machiavelli.

Our intention has not been to agree or disagree with any of Machiavelli's theories; it has been solely to attempt to clarify the character and meaning of his work, and hopefully to show that he was not Machiavellian. Machiavelli's work was exclusively for application in the public sphere; he was not concerned with private relations. The role of the government was to secure the stability, liberty and self-determination of the state. Whether the state was a principality or a republic, the ruler was never to act in his own interest; tyranny and corruption were despised and viewed as being entirely contrary to the interests of the state.

Fortune was such that it was believed that the state would inevitably become corrupt at times, and on those occasions a single ruler with great *virtu* would be needed to rebuild the legal system and the institutions of normal government. When this framework was in place, republican government could take over and rule would be in accordance with public and private morality.

Machiavelli would not have supported a general maxim "that the end justifies the means"; he believed that one particular end (liberty) dictated the means. He was not amoral and unscrupulous: he simply believed that our morality was dangerously dogmatic, impractical and irresponsible. For these reasons it must be concluded that the Machiavellian image of Machiavelli is nothing more than a gross distortion of somebody who observed power at first hand and suggested how it really worked. His insight leads one to understand the workings of good government and the tools/philosophies that are necessary to achieve this.

The Emergence of Political Marketing

Only relatively recently has any significant research begun to address the interface between politics and marketing, with Nicholas J. O'Shaughnessy's work, *The Phenomenon of Political Marketing*,[30] though this tends to be grounded primarily in the earlier political communication and political science literature rather than have a strong marketing and management science base. Bruce I. Newman, Newman and Jagdish N. Sheth, Patrick Butler and Neil Collins, Dominic Wring, Phil Harris and Andrew Lock[31] and a growing number of others have begun to explore this difficulty and have applied marketing theory to explore consumer behavioral aspects of polling and other tools.

However, this research is limited, as it tends to concentrate on the marketing issues associated with electoral politics, image, voter behavior, promotion and some aspects of party management, especially media management or what has come to be known as "spin doctoring." It does not comment on commercial lobbying as it focuses on the marketing of politicians for elections and tends to concentrate on specific observable marketing tools, which are being used within the political arena. In fact until recently most writings in the area called political marketing have concentrated on electoral and political communications and have not looked at the management of pressure on the legislative process as part of marketing. Nevertheless, it does supply a useful starting point from which to develop a conceptual analysis of where marketing and politics meet and there is growing evidence beginning to be published by L. Andrews, Harris and Lock and S. Harrison[32] that campaigning techniques are being directly adopted from the political electoral arena and being used to influence the business environment for strategic corporate advantage.

Political scientists have a long tradition of writing in the psephological area, especially that relating to elections, party strategy, imaging of politicians and polling techniques. The Nuffield series of election studies carried out by David Butler and others are well known and have been extensively added to by others, and the most recent have begun to show a particular marketing emphasis: Nicholas Jones, Brian McNair, Dennis Kavanagh, Margaret Scammell and Philippe J. Maarek.[33]

The first text (Jones) is rather journalistic, not surprisingly given the author is the political correspondent of the BBC, but does give some invaluable insights into modern party management and manipulation of the media, based upon first hand experiences during the 1980s and 1990s. McNair gives a sound modern commentary on the use of all political campaigning techniques in both elections and pressure group campaigning in the UK. This is rather useful, as it is one of the few works that attempts to do this. Kavanagh in his work calls upon his knowledge of elections from the various Nuffield Election Studies; however, the text focuses very heavily on particular campaign techniques and is very communications orientated. Scammell in her argument can be criticized for similar reasons as the work focuses on image building in British

541

electoral campaigning throughout the 1980s and 1990s, particularly Margaret Thatcher, although it does give a good historic commentary on the US origins of what has come to be called political marketing. The last two authors (Scammell and Maarek) are well-known political scientists, but it must be argued that their understanding of the philosophical debates, theoretical underpinnings and breadth of marketing techniques and their use is still developing. Thus, although the texts by their respective titles and chapter headings would appear to embrace a managed marketing approach, they in fact only highlight one or two electoral techniques and, as in so much of the research, concentrate on the market communication aspects of politics.

Scammell[34] has attempted to address this shortfall in her most recent work and shows a considerable appreciation of how marketing theory has been broadening into service and "not for profit" sectors. The development of appropriate political marketing models is one of the prime areas of current research. She suggests that the marketing concept appears to be the key to understanding political marketing. She further argues that one of the most fruitful paradigms is that of "relationship marketing," which developed from research of service sectors in Scandinavia.[35] Originating from a services marketing perspective in the 1980s, relationship marketing offers valuable insights into political lobbying. As one text puts it: "In its earliest guise, relationship marketing focused simply on the development and cultivation of longer-term profitable and mutually beneficial relationships between an organization and a defined customer group."[36] An illustration of how this can apply to lobbying is given by a Washington consultant who specializes in grassroots programs, when he told one of the authors:

> Many people do mass grass roots organizing where huge numbers of people will contact their member of Congress. Staffers are very good at judging the level of personal commitment which is involved in a grass roots communication. The most effective method is to find one person with a strong interest in the issue from a member of Congress' own district. Now you are into grass roots based on developing relationships between the members and the constituents, rather than based on how many people deliver a message. The number one tension in relationship based grass roots is ensuring that the central message is consistent in every congressional office while allowing each person the freedom to tell their personal story and local statistics, but always ending up asking for the same thing. But this approach is more long-term, allows messages to be crafted to maximum effect with each individual legislator, and makes the most effective use of the people who are the key strength of the grass roots campaign.

Harris also notes this connection between relationships and lobbying when he argues that, "the strategic use of lobbying . . . is very much a marketing focused activity, which is part of the development of relationship and in particular political marketing."[37]

A Swedish academic argues that, "the prime focus of [relationship marketing] is on the *individual*, on the segment of one. It's one-to-one marketing."[38] Again, this fits neatly with lobbying, in which most direct advocacy is characterized by personal and individual approaches between a lobbyist and a policy maker. Relationship marketing holds that a personal relationship between a seller and a customer is of key importance. In order to achieve that, the seller must have direct access to the customer, just as a lobbyist prizes personal access to a policy maker above almost all else. As a Washington consultant put it to one of the authors: "Lobbying in particular is very relationship driven." Another Brussels lobbyist has suggested that "[t]here are three important things to know about lobbying: contacts, contacts, contacts."[39] Or as K. Moloney expresses it: "It is a sine qua non of all lobbying that there be contact with public decision-makers. . . . The provision of access results in the ability of the group for whom the lobbyist works to make its case to a decision-maker."[40]

It is imperative to the lobbyist not only that he or she can establish a direct and personal relationship with a policy maker, but that this relationship can then be maintained over time.

While much historical work on marketing tended to view marketing as involving an immediate sale or satisfaction, relationship marketing goes far beyond a "one-shot deal": it is concerned with protecting and nurturing the personal seller–customer relationship on a sustained and ongoing basis. Similarly, in lobbying, most of the literature suggests that lobbyists spend the vast majority of their time and effort working with their known supporters (in an effect to reinforce pre-existing views) rather than attempting to convert people who disagree with them. One American study asserted:

> In many instances, effective lobbying consists not so much of persuading congressmen to espouse an alien point of view, but rather identifying members who are already friendly to the general proposition and providing them with enough material to serve as a rationale for voting the way they would have voted in the first place. . . . In sheer volume it probably surpasses every other technique for getting bills passed.[41]

Most recently a growing research interest in the area has begun to emerge reflecting renewed interest and this has led to increased conference activity and collaborative research that is beginning to appear as publications.[42] Maarek[43] has set out in a practical way the fundamentals of what he terms political marketing, outlining the complete range of techniques available for marketing politicians and communicating political messages for the use of practitioners and researchers. He even attempts to give practical advice in what is the nearest publication in the area to a text on how political marketing and communication can be managed. The text is very much a manual on how to run effective campaigns using a number of marketing techniques, however, like the other works in this area it concentrates on communications. A similar high quality manual has been produced for political campaign (election) managers by Michael Shea[44] aimed at the US political consultant market.

A more recent article outlining the main criticisms made of current political marketing research agrees that the field has been, "overly focused on one aspect of marketing theory (that is, communication) as part of an election campaign. Political campaigns and political marketing activities are often exclusively defined through their communication content and the media vehicles employed."[45] A similar point has been made by another academic:

> Pure concentration on campaigning or marketing techniques will only take us so far. While such a locus of study is a good place to go, we must be careful not to rest there too long and miss the broader (if longer) journey to apply marketing to all areas of politics.[46]

Even the small amount of political marketing literature on lobbying tends to focus on the recruitment and retention of members and the provision of benefits to members by interest groups.[47] Very little research has been undertaken to date on how (political) marketing theory can explain or illustrate the representation of interests by lobbyists, or their policy-influencing activities.

Machiavelli and Marketing

Machiavelli, in *Il Principe*, set down the reflections and lessons he had learned from the reality of having been the second most senior civil servant in the short lived Florentine Republic in this period of turbulent Italian history. He had observed, facilitated and administered government decision making at first hand and wanted to pass best practice and reflection on to others. The short text gives realistic advice to aspiring princes and leaders of organizations and consequently it is not difficult therefore to draw parallels with the modern day. Where *Il Principe* and its doctrines interest the authors is as a starting point to view and observe the growth of lobbying and campaigning pressure group activity as part of modern marketing.

The Functions of Lobbying

Although lobbying was viewed as an alien concept in the UK by many until explicit recognition of its more overt forms by Lord Nolan,[48] the use of lobbying within the political system has been a common phenomenon ever since the birth of politics itself. However public policy is formulated there will always be a tendency for those affected to influence the outcome. Indeed what emerges from Machiavelli's *Il Principe* is that it is one of the first guides to the emerging realities of the government process and shows the role that influence and pressure play in state decision making. The key problem for Machiavelli was that past failures resulting from lack of strategic planning and well-thought-out policies had escalated into crisis situations resulting in the whole of Renaissance Italy being engulfed in war. *Il Principe* is therefore a treatise on how the effective use of power and influences could have avoided such disasters. Parallels of the situations and problems Machiavelli described are still obvious in modern organizations.

Public affairs—the organizational practice encompassed at the intersection of management, communication and politics—is by now a major facet of the work of any large organization. Often regarded as primarily involving the external projection of the organization (particularly in terms of lobbying and public relations), it is in fact at least as much to do with representing the views of stakeholders back into the organization's thinking and strategizing. Thus, much of a lobbyist's work today mirrors the type of activities routinely undertaken by other, more explicitly commercial, divisions within an organization. Just as no product is launched on the market without extensive thought regarding potential sales and profitability, no lobbying campaign should be undertaken until a rigorous and systematic issues management review has been undertaken. In a large part, this sort of process derives from the collective experience of business in the marketing of products.

An American issues management firm has devised a very useful process by which organizations can undertake their public affairs in a proactive manner.[49] The first stage is to anticipate issues and establish priorities—this involves tracking trends across the whole area of the organization's activity to determine which are likely to become significant in the short-term, medium-term and long-term. So for instance, most in-house public affairs executives will spend a day or two at the beginning of each year trying to predict the issues that will form a major part of their workload in the coming year and then reviewing their prioritization each quarter.

Second, it is important to analyze the issues rigorously—how would particular policy changes impact upon the organization's operations? What is the external climate of opinion on the issue? In management terms, this may take the form of a SWOT (Strengths, Weaknesses, Opportunities, Threats) or PEST (Political, Economic, Social, Technological) analysis.

This leads to a third stage, which is to recommend an organizational position on the issue. In other words, the formulation of corporate policy and objectives. It is always bad practice to start approaching policy makers without having already formed a clear and coherent judgment about the issue. This stage can require a tremendous amount of research, consultation, drafting and redrafting before a statement can be produced that satisfies all the needs and concerns of the organization.

Public affairs is about communicating effectively with key publics, except that in public affairs the publics tend to be concentrated in the political and administrative worlds. Therefore, you have to identify publics/opinion leaders who can help advance your position. This means determining which people will be involved in making decisions about the issue, and which advisers will most influence them; those people or groups that are likely to support your organization's view and those that will oppose it, because much of public affairs is about building coalitions of support that can work together in a common cause; and, of course, reaching a view about which members of the various publics identified should be most heavily targeted as a way of securing your organization's goals.

Finally, the authors of this system point to the importance of being able to identify desired behaviors of publics/opinion leaders—after all, you have to have a clear idea of how people could help you, not only because you have to ask them for that help but also because many other consequences (future objectives, budgets, tactics) flow from it. In addition, it is through setting detailed objectives in this manner that one is able to evaluate the extent to which the campaign was actually effective.

It is immediately obvious that much of this process as applied to lobbying would be quite familiar to a commercial marketer—identifying and forecasting trends, setting objectives, communicating with key audiences, targeting messages, influencing behavior, evaluation. According to Charles S. Mack:

> Marketing, politics, and lobbying share a common characteristic, the need to persuade in order to sell. Whether the sale be that of a product or service, a candidate, or a public policy, each of the three fields has become ever more sophisticated in its sales approach. Marketing, spurred by economic incentive, generally has taken the lead in technical innovation. Politics and lobbying have borrowed many of these innovations freely.[50]

Shaping the external environment by influencing government through lobbying activities or corporate campaigning is now typical of strategic marketing management practice, whether it be for business, public or not-for-profit sectors. The relevance of such activities stems of course from the fact that there is hardly an item of legislation passed through the UK parliament which does not in some way encroach upon business interests or impinge on organizational goals. The proposal to tax audio tapes[51] for example would have affected a variety of organizations including educationalists and charities such as the Royal National Institute for the Blind (RNIB), not to mention a large number of consumers of blank tapes, and discreet organizing via a commercial lobbyist company funded by the European Japanese Electronic Manufacturers Association resulted in the proposals being substantially amended. Changing the wording of a proposal or the insertion of a special exception in regulations can be worth millions of pounds to commercial organizations and be crucial to the survival of non-profit organizations' activities.

Former Chief Secretary to the Treasury in John Major's government, Michael Portillo, observed that political lobbyists are "as necessary to the political process as a thoroughly efficient sewage system is to any city."[52] This might be seen as a backhanded compliment given that lobbyists have been described by some as unethical and against the public interest. There are two competing views on the legitimacy of lobbying. There is the view that lobbyists abuse the democratic system for their own selfish interests and that the growth in the industry, particularly in the use of political consultants, requires the imposition of greater controls over lobbying activities. The alternative position is that lobbying is genuinely an intrinsic part of the democratic process because it can create a counter balance to potentially ill informed or badly thought out policy decisions. Moreover, in reality it can be argued that government liaison is necessary because the government, like the ruler in Machiavelli's *Il Principe*, cannot operate in a vacuum, but depends on others for information and advice. After all the nub of political and marketing is having information and as Jordan[53] argues, members of parliament are only as good as the information they receive. The same applies to politicians and civil servants in Whitehall and their role in policy making and other parts of the legislative, executive and judicial process.

An American writer described lobbying in terms of its relationship to marketing thus:

> Organizing support for a position on an issue is similar to planning a marketing campaign. Selling the policy issue in the government marketplace is parallel to selling a product or service. It is

essential to plan, package, and present the issue to convince the decision maker, often a legislator or a government policymaker. The most cost-effective technique is to show the numbers of supporters (and voters) on your side.[54]

In a similar vein, a British lobbyist pointed out the similarities between marketing and lobbying:

[L]obbying can sometimes be seen as a specialist form of marketing communications, often engaged with similar concerns, measurements and promotional campaigns, contributing directly to business performance. Knowledge of the political market, understanding the relevance of one's product or service, determining how to promote the product or service as meeting the needs of government or helping to meet its needs, demonstrating value for money and ability to meet targets for availability (product, promotion, pricing and place) are directly relevant skills.[55]

And some lobbyists themselves recognize the connection here—for instance, David Rehr, then president of the National Beer Wholesalers Association in America, has said that he sees a direct connection between marketing and lobbying: "We are marketing and selling a product . . . a bill or a regulation, or something that we want from the government, or something that we want the government not to do to us."[56]

Growth of Lobbying

Lobbying has grown considerably in the past fifteen years in the UK, which was outlined in the factors discussed earlier. Precise information on the current scale of activity is hard to come by, the first Nolan Report notwithstanding, due to the difficulty of choosing what to measure and the general discretion in the way in which lobbying has to be conducted. However, there is substantial evidence of its dramatic increase.[57] The growth of corporate lobbying and campaigning is a response to the complexities of modern business society caused by more pervasive government and increased need for competitiveness in a global market by companies. Harris and Lock[58] reported estimates that expenditure on commercial political lobbying, both in-house and by independent lobbyists, in the UK was between 200 and 300 million pounds and that over 4,000 people were directly employed in this activity. It was also estimated that expenditure at European Union (EU) level was at least one order of magnitude greater than at national level. Recent evidence suggests that political lobbying in the EU is worth over £3 billion.[59]

The Devonport Naval Dockyard Campaign—A Case Study in Lobbying

This campaign won the Institute of Public Relations "Silver Sword of Excellence Award" for the most effective public affairs campaign in 1993, for Rowland Sallingsbury Casey (RSC). A government affairs company (part of the old Saatchi Group), RSC was appointed by Devonport Management Limited (DML) to coordinate the political campaign for the Ministry of Defence (MOD) Trident Nuclear Submarine Refitting Contract. The contract was worth £5 billion and would ensure a future for the winning dockyard and safeguard thousands of jobs. "For Devonport it meant 5,200 jobs in the yard, 20,000 regional jobs and £540 million in annual regional income."[60]

RSC quickly found out through contact with politicians, officials and journalists that it was behind its competitor Rosyth in gaining the contract. Rosyth had its key supporters in strategic positions in government and parliament, which was giving it a major advantage. The Defence Secretary, Malcolm Rifkind, was a Scot, while the South West had no voice in Cabinet. The Scottish Secretary, Ian Lang, was a public and strong supporter of Rosyth. Not surprisingly Scots Tories backed this position, which was in turn supported by all Labour MPs in Scotland. Gordon

Brown, the Shadow Chancellor, was very much to the fore of the Rosyth campaign as MP for Dunfermline East, which included the Naval Yard.

This position was changed by a very effective campaign, which made the center of its strategy three key points:

1 Devonport as the right strategic location for Trident.
2 The DML bid as the best value to the Royal Navy and the taxpayer.
3 Trident in Plymouth as essential to the South West region's economic, and the government's political, health.

To achieve this, an aggressive lobbying and media campaign was organized which would organize the community, workforce, MPs, business community and media. It was intended to show the MOD specialists and political advisers, Cabinet ministers and parliamentarians, the strategic, economic and political case for Trident in Devonport. Consequently RSC worked with DML and produced the following during the campaign:

- lobbying material and literature;
- a detailed media audit to work out who was sympathetic and who was not;
- personal briefings for relevant MPs, civil servants, political advisers throughout the summer of 1992;
- lobbying at party conferences and Westminster;
- a 20,000 signature petition;
- amended proposals for the contract to make them more innovative;
- increased local media awareness;
- trained staff to deal with various media and influencers;
- reviews of political events to see how they could be used to the advantage of the campaign;
- regular monitoring of progress.

In 1993 DML won the contract. Looking critically at the DML campaign, it can be seen that RSC's involvement broadened the approach from purely procurement issues. RSC provided a critical edge of political awareness, which before then DML had missed. It is also useful to remember that the 1992 general election brought significant Liberal Democrat gains in the Tory dominated South West and fear of the impact of losing the Devonport contract clearly could have tipped the decision in the South West's favor. However, this needed pointing out to many people. See L. Andrews[61] for full details and background to case.

Business Situations in Which Lobbying Plays a Role

Over the last forty years, a decided trend is evident whereby government increasingly involves itself in business decisions, in a number of ways: this "shift from market to political decisions"[62] has vastly expanded the scope of lobbying. So, for instance, the lobbying industry in the UK mushroomed during the mid-1980s, at the same time as the Thatcher government was privatizing major companies and liberalizing much of the rest of the economy. Equally, though, during periods of increased regulation lobbyists will profit. In essence, any government decision will stimulate lobbying activity as organizations seek to benefit or protect themselves from the decision. It is impossible for business to ignore government, and there is always a near-direct correlation between the extent to which an industry is directly affected by government—through regulation, for instance—and the amount of lobbying it will undertake: car manufacturers, tobacco and alcohol companies, energy utilities and the medical profession will always be near the top of any list of lobbying activity. We propose below a taxonomy of situations in which government is involved and postulate the relative importance of lobbying in influencing outcomes.

1   *Government as purchaser or allocator.*

   a   Winner takes all on a number of situations, there is only one contract or opportunity to be bid for. A recent example is Camelot's successful bid to run the National Lottery. Television franchises, the Channel Tunnel consortium and certain military contracts have similar characteristics. Price is rarely the sole criterion. The public decision is usually very visible and lobbying is rife.

   b   Large, infrequent contracts: defence and large public works contracts are typical of this category. Increasingly failure to obtain such contracts threatens the very existence of the company or a strategic business unit with a visible and politically delicate impact on employment. The situation of ABB's railway works interests is one example. Again lobbying plays an important role.

   c   Regularly supplied items apart from highly specialized items, these are usually supplied through standard purchasing procedures, notably by competitive tender. These procedures leave little scope for lobbying, except insofar as it may be necessary to qualify a supplier to be included in the approved list or to pass any other pretender hurdles.

   d   Those situations whereby government is the main customer for a given product, and thus uses its position to set prices directly or indirectly. For example, the National Health Service offers the only market for those drugs which the UK government determines can be supplied solely by a doctor's prescription. If the Department of Health directs doctors not to prescribe particular medicines, their manufacturers will have no market for those products. If a drug is allowed to be used, the government fixes maximum profit margins that each manufacturer is allowed to make, with any profit in excess of a set limit being repaid to the government. Lobbying is thus vital here in two regards: first, to ensure that a given drug can be used by doctors, and second, to facilitate an optimal payment mechanism.

2   *Government as legislator and framer of regulations.* Legislation on matters such as product safety, trademarks and intellectual property, and fair trading are obvious targets for business lobbying to insure that legitimate interests are protected. However, it is easily forgotten that a great deal of matters that affect specific businesses are enacted through regulations under enabling legislation. Visible examples are vehicle construction and use regulations, and regulations affecting food and agriculture. Lobbying is important here to ensure that regulations are sensibly framed and represent an appropriate balance of business and other pressure group interests.

3   *Government as initiator of action.* There are a number of explicit circumstances in which the relevant secretary of state initiates action by a quango (quasi-autonomous non-government agency) or similar body. The most familiar case is the Monopolies and Mergers Commission. In other examples, where a quango can initiate action itself, the government of the day exerts some influence in terms of matters that are taken up and is frequently the final arbiter in terms of action upon the recommendations it receives. Lobbying in terms of provision of information as well as persuasive communication play an important role in shaping the progress of events.

4   *Government and European legislation and regulation.* In Europe with the increasing influence of European directives and regulations upon product markets, proper representation of manufacturers' and marketers' interests have become critical in those areas which the EU is seeking to regulate. As well as direct lobbying of Commission officials and MEPs and representation through pan-European business bodies, support from one's own national

government through civil servants and the Council of Ministers is critical to success on significant issues. In these instances, lobbying at both national and EU level is an essential activity.

5   *Government as decision maker.* There are a range of other situations where the government has de facto or de jure powers to take decisions which affect business. While the example is not directly a marketing one, the recent controversy over the decision to permit Shell to sink the Brent Spar platform in the Atlantic is a good illustration, both of convincing government of the correctness of a course of action, and also of a failure of a broader public relations campaign against a more well-organized, but less well-funded opponent.

6   *Government as employer.* As the largest single employer in any country, government clearly plays a substantial role in the workings of the labor market and thus affects every other organization. Government will, for instance, determine whether a minimum wage should operate and if so then at what level, set employment protection and health/safety at work guidelines, and exercise a significant function in the labor relations field generally. All these are areas which directly impact upon all employers, and are matters on which organizations may need to lobby.

Future Directions

We have recently conducted research with members of both UK houses of parliament and Whitehall officials and what clearly emerges is that organizations can be seriously disadvantaged if they are not providing information to support their long-term business positions or counter their national and international corporate competitors by providing information to relevant bodies. This may well sound very logical, but the reality is that a number of interests and companies do not know how or do not understand the various UK and EU government processes and their ability to develop policy and regulations which impact upon them and the markets in which they operate. This puts them at a serious disadvantage.

If we are to rely on our guide Machiavelli, we would take from him five things:

1   His appreciation of *realpolitik* and getting things done and observing reality.
2   The importance of lobbying, and he would recognize this as more important in the twenty-first century.
3   The importance of influence and being able to exert pressure to gain competitive advantage.
4   The importance of being able to manage the political process, being able to predict election results and being able to exert influence in campaigns to achieve just political ends.
5   The use of Machiavellian marketing.

Modern Machiavellian Marketing

Increasingly, to be able to compete means being able to exert pressure on government to gain competitive edge. A well-argued case, which has been outlined before, is that it has been suggested that a number of German and French car manufacturers successfully lobbied the EU for them to adopt catalytic converters as their preferred vehicle emissions measures. This became compulsory legislation, to the advantage of Mercedes, Audi, VW and Peugeot and others. At a stroke this wiped out one billion pounds worth of investment by Ford in lean burn engine technology and half a million pounds worth of investment by Austin Rover, also developing this technology. Both Ford and Austin Rover deemed this technology to be a lot cleaner than just using catalytic converters. They had opted to go for a higher specification system rather than the intermediate catalytic converters. Once the legislation was enacted across the EU, Ford lost its billion pound investment in research and development and had to reinvest in catalytic converters to catch up. Austin Rover, as a result of this policy, lost its investment, could never catch up and went bankrupt. BMW now owns Austin Rover.

The second example is that Philip Morris is probably spending in the order of at least £50 million a year in Brussels trying to stop national states and the EU bringing in similar measure for compensation to meet health care risks of cancer infected tobacco smokers. The money is being used to delay legislation, which leads to compulsory care and compensation for sufferers. In the United States, it is now almost mandatory for many to get care for tobacco related diseases. By delaying the legislation Philip Morris benefits financially.

Other areas where one can exert pressure to lobby for advantage are:

- Packaging that may use only particular materials across Europe to meet specifications. Clearly this disadvantages its competitive edge to certain processes and companies.
- Broadcasting. As broadcasting internationalizes the granting of licences or privatization of public broadcasting can give strategic advantages. Look at Murdoch or Time Warner.
- Health. Delays in environmental protection, tobacco legislation or alcohol abuse have an effect both on the health care industry and certain businesses.
- Travel/Ecology. Restricting travel and tourism may benefit the ecology or may just mean that if you have the money then you can go there.
- Resources. Clearly, the allocation of fossil fuels, emissions and scarce resources and their availability also impact on competitive edge. Reliable and renewable electricity can give competitive advantage. Erratic and hazardous energy systems can lead to decline. People do not shop in Chernobyl any more.

The Rise of Regulation

Lobbying has grown as a result of business and non-governmental organizations (NGOs) wishing to influence government regulatory policy. As government has sold its ownership of control of various sectors of the economy utilities, broadcasting and other ventures, so it has tried to shape the direction of these now private companies or organizations and their interests through regulation.

In fact the last part of the twentieth century and early part of the twenty-first has seen government at every level develop the regulator and regulation. To influence that regulation leads to strategic gain for the organization. If you can shape the market to your advantage then you win and lobbying is about shaping that regulation so that it suits you and your interests. A number of core graphs can be used to indicate graphically how one exerts pressure. Figure 38.1 is called the Machiavellian graph and shows that each time government increases regulation, lobbying public affairs activity increases to shape that regulation.

This can also be graphically shown in a 2 × 2 matrix which is here called the Machiavellian matrix (see Figure 38.2): the more government regulatory policy, the higher the level of lobbying, thus intense activity.

We can see this being developed further if we look at the ways in which business, lobbying and policies can be used to influence government in the following model of influencing decision making at the national and transnational government levels (see Figure 38.3).

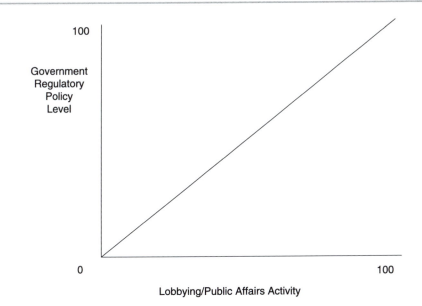

Figure 38.1. The Machiavellian Graph

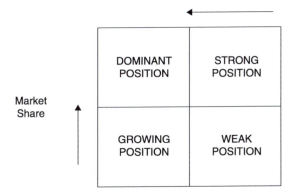

Figure 38.2. The Machiavellian Marketing Matrix: The Isotropic Relationship Between Market Share and Levels of Political Lobbying: The Maintenance of a Dominant or Monopolistic Position in a Market Sector Through Political Lobbying

Conclusion

Machiavelli provides a useful guide to exploring government and where to exert influence. There has been a growth in lobbying because as government has withdrawn from its role of being owner in the economy it has attempted to regulate and set the business environment for companies to operate in. However, the more competitive companies and NGOs influence that regulation to their own competitive advantage. There are currently 28,000 NGOs registered in Brussels explicitly just to influence EU policy. Why might that be?

Lobbying is part of modern political communication. As politicians become increasingly isolated and short of quality information, effective lobbying fills up that vacuum and allows good decision making (and of course sometimes bad decision making). Globalization is meaning that

551

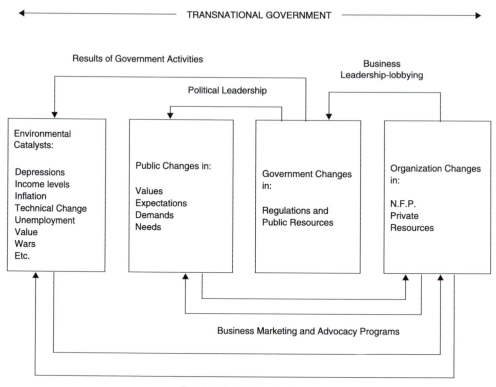

Figure 38.3. The Role of Political Lobbying as a Feature of Political Marketing Communication with Government: A Model

to gain competitive edge transnationally, lobbying is used to influence the EU, the World Trade Organization (WTO), North American Free Trade Agreement (NAFTA) and so forth.

Another trend is, of course, accountability, and lobbying has to be seen to be accountable like government and be of a high ethical standard and have its interests declared. As society has higher demands, so it will want its voices heard and society will become more consumer driven and government will have to become more responsive to consumer needs. Perhaps consumer needs in Bulgaria would be better roads, better health care, better education, rather than some of the things that politicians in the past have wanted. Consumers need to lobby for that quality of life and for resources to be spent on priority areas. All that we can say is that we can be sure of one thing that as government increasingly develops a regulatory society, so lobbying will grow and the only way to counter this is that if your voice is to be heard "all armed prophets win, and unarmed ones fall."[63]

Notes

1 Alexis de Tocqueville, *Democracy in America*, trans. George Lawrence (New York: Harper Collins, 2000), 692.
2 Phil Harris, "Commentary—Machiavelli, Political Marketing and Reinventing Government," *European Journal of Marketing* 35(9/10) (2001): 1136.
3 *Universal English Dictionary* (London: Longman).
4 Antony Jay, *Management and Machiavelli* (London: Hodder and Stoughton, 1967); Michael Shea, *Influence: How to Make the System Work for You: A Handbook for the Modern Machiavelli* (London: Century,

1998); Roger Fisher, Elizabeth Kopelman and Andrea Kupfer Schneider, *Beyond Machiavelli: Tools for Coping with Conflict* (Cambridge, MA: Harvard University Press, 1994); Alistair McAlpine, *The Servant: A New Machiavelli* (London: Faber and Faber, 1992); Edward Pearce, *Machiavelli's Children* (London: Victor Gollancz, 1993); Patrick Curry, *Machiavelli for Beginners* (Cambridge: Icon Books, 1995); Phil Harris, Andrew Lock and Patricia Rees, *Machiavelli, Marketing and Management* (London: Routledge, 2000).

5 Niccolo Machiavelli, *The Prince*, trans. G. Bull (London: Penguin, 1961).

6 Niccolo Machiavelli, *The Discourses* (London: Penguin, 1983).

7 Niccolo Machiavelli, *The Prince* (London: Everyman, 1992).

8 Machiavelli, *The Discourses* (London: Penguin, 1983).

9 Machiavelli, *The Prince*, Everyman edition.

10 Niccolo Machiavelli, *Mandragola* (New York: The Macaulay Company, 1927).

11 Machiavelli, *The Prince*, Everyman edition.

12 John Locke, *An Essay Concerning Human Understanding*, ed. Peter Nidditch (Oxford: Oxford University Press, 1975), 270.

13 Machiavelli, *The Discourses*, 515.

14 Aristotle, *The Politics* (London: Penguin, 1961), 59.

15 John P. Plamenatz, *Man and Society* (London: Longman, 1970).

16 N. Wood, "Introduction in Niccolo Machiavelli," *The Art of War* (New York: De Capo Press, 1965), 16.

17 Sudney Anglo, *Machiavelli: A Dissection* (London: The Camelot Press, 1960), 102.

18 Machiavelli, *The Prince*, Everyman edition, 99.

19 Niccolo Machiavelli, *The Florentine History* (New York: Harper & Row Publishers, 1960), 204.

20 Machiavelli, *The Discourses*, 132.

21 Aristotle, *The Politics*, 62.

22 Machiavelli, *The Discourses*, 257.

23 Machiavelli, *The Florentine History*, 158.

24 Ibid.

25 Machiavelli, *The Discourses*, 256.

26 Machiavelli, *The Prince*, Everyman edition, 67.

27 Ibid., 75.

28 Sheldon S. Wolin, *Politics and Vision* (Boston, MA: Little, Brown, 1960).

29 Ibid., 208.

30 Nicholas J. O'Shaughnessy, *The Phenomenon of Political Marketing* (New York: St Martin's Press, 1990).

31 Bruce I. Newman, *The Marketing of the President: Political Marketing as Campaign Strategy* (Thousand Oaks, CA: Sage Publications, 1994); Bruce I. Newman, ed., *The Handbook of Political Marketing* (Thousand Oaks, CA: Sage Publications, 1999); Bruce I. Newman and Jagdish N. Sheth, *A Theory of Political Choice Behavior* (New York: Praeger, 1987); Patrick Butler and Neil Collins, "Marketing Public Sector Services: Concepts and Characteristics," *Journal of Marketing Management* 11 (1–3) (1994): 83–96; Dominic Wring, "Reconciling Marketing with Political Science: Theories of Political Marketing," *Journal of Marketing Management* 13 (7) (1997): 651–64; Phil Harris and Andrew Lock, "Machiavellian Marketing: The Development of Corporate Lobbying in the UK," *Journal of Marketing Management* 9/10 (1996): 313–28.

32 L. Andrews, "The Relationship of Political Marketing to Political Lobbying: An Examination of the Devonport Campaign for the Trident Refitting Contract," *European Journal of Marketing* (Special edition on Political Marketing edited by Phil Harris) 10/11 (1996): 30; Harris and Lock, "Machiavellian Marketing"; S. Harrison, "Lobbying: Shouts and Whispers: The Campaign For and Against Price Maintenance," *European Journal of Marketing* 34 (1–2) (2000): 207–22.

33 Nicholas Jones, *Soundbites and Spin Doctors: How Politicians Manipulate the Media and Vice Versa* (London: Cassell, 1995); Brian McNair, *An Introduction to Political Communication* (London: Routledge, 1995); Dennis Kavanagh, *Election Campaigning: The New Marketing of Politics* (Oxford: Blackwell, 1995); Margaret Scammell, *Designer Politics: How Elections are Won* (New York: St Martin's Press, 1995); and Philippe J. Maarek, *Political Marketing and Communication* (London: John Libbey, 1995).

34 Margaret Scammell, "Political Marketing: Lessons for Political Science," *Political Studies* 47 (1999): 718–39.

35 Christian Grönroos, "Quo Vadis, Marketing? Toward a Relationship Marketing Paradigm," *Journal of Marketing Management* 10 (5) (1994): 347–61.

36 Helen Peck, Adrian Payne, Martin Christopher and Moira Clark, *Relationship Marketing: Strategy and Implementation* (Oxford: Elsevier Butterworth-Heinemann, 1999), 3–4.

37 Phil Harris, "Lobbying and Public Affairs in the UK: The Relationship to Political Marketing," unpublished PhD thesis, Manchester Metropolitan University, 1999, 254, www.phil-harris.com.

553

38 Evert Gummesson, *Total Relationship Marketing: Rethinking Marketing Management—From 4Ps to 30Rs* (Oxford: Butterworth-Heinemann, 1999), 6.
39 Cited in C.S. Thomas and R.J. Hrebenar, "Comparing Lobbying Across Liberal Democracies: Problems, Approaches and Initial Findings," paper presented at the annual conference of the 2000 American Political Science Association, 34.
40 K. Moloney, "Government and Lobbying Activities," in *Public Relations: Principles and Practice*, ed. Philip J. Kitchen (London: Thompson Learning, 2000), 175.
41 Austin H. Kiplinger and Knight A. Kiplinger, *Washington Now* (New York: Harper & Row, 1975), 207.
42 Newman, ed., *The Handbook of Political Marketing*.
43 Maarek, *Political Marketing and Communication*.
44 Shea, *Influence*.
45 Stephan C.M. Henneberg, "The Views of an *Advocatus Dei*: Political Marketing and its Critics," *Journal of Public Affairs* 4 (3) (2004): 235.
46 Jennifer Lees-Marshment, "Political Marketing: How to Reach that Pot of Gold," *Journal of Political Marketing* 2 (1) (2003): 29.
47 See G. Jordan and William A. Maloney, *The Protest Business? Mobilizing Campaign Groups* (Manchester: Manchester University Press, 1997). Also Grant Jordan and William A. Maloney, *Democracy and Interest Groups: Enhancing Participation?* (London: Palgrave Macmillan, 2007).
48 "Standards in Public Life," First Report of the Committee on Standards in Public Life, chairman Lord Nolan, vol. 1 (London: HMSO, May 1995).
49 Cited in Jon White and Laura Mazur, *Strategic Communications Management: Making Public Relations Work* (Reading, MA: Addison-Wesley, 1994).
50 Charles S. Mack, *Business, Politics, and the Practice of Government Relations* (Westport, CT: Quorum Books, 1997), 4–5.
51 Harris and Lock, "Machiavellian Marketing."
52 Michael Portillo cited in *Marketing* (London), (September 29, 1994).
53 G. Jordan, "Insider Lobbying: The British Version," *Political Studies* 37 (1989): 107–13.
54 E.A. Fraser, "Coalitions," in *The Public Affairs Handbook*, ed. Joseph S. Nagelschmidt (New York: Amacom, 1982), 195.
55 Andrews, "The Relationship of Political Marketing to Political Lobbying," 79.
56 Cited in Conor McGrath, "Family Businesses Distributing America's Beverage: Managing Government Relations in the National Beer Wholesalers Association," *Journal of Public Affairs* 3 (3) (2003): 215.
57 Jordan, "Insider Lobbying"; S. Attack, *The Directory of Public Affairs and Government Relation* (London: Berkeley International Recruitment Consultants, 1990); Harris and Lock, "Machiavellian Marketing."
58 Harris and Lock, "Machiavellian Marketing."
59 Source is author's informant.
60 IPR Sword of Excellence Awards, 1994.
61 Andrews, "The Relationship of Political Marketing to Political Lobbying."
62 Harrison W. Fox and Martin Schnitzer, *Doing Business in Washington: How to Win Friends and Influence Government* (New York: Free Press, 1981), 4.
63 Niccolo Machiavelli, *The Prince*, trans. Alan H. Gilbert, in *Machiavelli: The Chief Works and Others*, 5th ed., vol. 1 (Durham, N.C.: Duke University Press, 1989), 26.

39

Ethics in Campaigns and Public Affairs

Candice J. Nelson

Introduction

Cash in the freezer of a Congressman's Capitol Hill office. Two million dollars in bribes. A 2008 presidential candidate returns $850,000 raised for the campaign by an indicted felon. Is this ethics in campaigns and public affairs? Does this contribute to democracy in the United States?

This chapter will examine ethics in campaigns and public affairs at the beginning of the twenty-first century. As this chapter was being written, the United States Congress enacted legislation that was billed as a major ethics reform bill. Yet the ink on the President's signature was barely dry when reports began to surface of behavior not covered in the bill, raising questions of how significant the reform actually was. Ethical questions face candidates as they run for office and officeholders when they are elected to office. While there are some practices that are illegal, and more with the ethics bill signed into law by President Bush in September 2007, a number of ethical questions that confront candidates and lawmakers are not so clear-cut. They are, as two colleagues and I have described elsewhere, "shades of gray."[1]

From Congressional Scandals to Congressional Reform

A series of scandals, primarily involving Republican members of Congress, set the stage for an environment favorable to Democratic candidates in the 2006 congressional elections. The Republicans' problems began in November 2005, when California Republican Congressman Randy (Duke) Cunningham admitted to taking more than $2 million in bribes from defense contractors.[2] Their problems continued into early 2006, when former Republican lobbyist Jack Abramoff was sentenced to five years in prison after he plead guilty to charges of conspiracy to bribe public officials (along with charges of tax evasion and fraud).[3] Congressman Robert Ney, caught up in the Abramoff scandal, plead guilty to corruption charges in October 2006. Ney admitted to using his position in Congress to benefit lobbyists in return for campaign contributions, meals, travel, and tickets to sporting events.[4] Republicans were further demoralized in the fall of 2006 when Republican Congressman Mark Foley unexpectedly resigned his Florida House seat after reports surfaced that he had engaged in inappropriate contact with a House male page.[5]

While Republicans faced the brunt of ethics scandals in the 109th Congress (2005–2006), one Democratic member showed that Democrats in the House were not immune from scandal. Representative William Jefferson from Louisiana was under investigation in 2006 for allegations of bribery. In May 2006 federal agents searched Congressman Jefferson's Capitol Hill office, admitting at the time that a search of his home in 2005 had turned up $90,000 in cash stored in his home freezer.[6] Thirteen months later, in June 2007, Congressman Jefferson was indicted on sixteen counts of bribery, racketeering, obstruction of justice, and money laundering.[7]

When the Democrats took control of both the House and Senate following the 2006 elections, both House Speaker Nancy Pelosi and Senate Majority Leader Harry Reid promised to enact legislation to correct the "culture of corruption" that they described as pervading Capitol Hill under Republican rule. At the very start of the 110th Congress, in January 2007, both houses of Congress passed rules to place stricter regulations on congressional travel and gifts. The new rules prohibited House members and their staffs from accepting meals or gifts of any amount from lobbyists or organizations that "retain or employ" lobbyists.[8] The rules also provided much tougher restrictions on travel, requiring that, beginning March 1, 2007, House members

> cannot accept travel funded by lobbyists or organizations that retain or hire lobbyists, except for one-day/one-night trips to specific sites, where there is "de minimis" lobbyist involvement, may not travel with a lobbyist present on any segment of the trip . . ., and cannot pay for non-commercial, non-charter jet air travel from personal or campaign funds, or use their official allowance.[9]

The rules were written to allow House members to continue to travel to give speeches and participate in forums, but to outlaw "junkets" where lobbyists had opportunities to try to influence members on the golf course or the ski slope.

On January 18, 2007, the Senate passed legislation to enact gift and travel restrictions similar to the changes in the House. The Senate bill also included provisions that addressed lobbying activities. However, because the Senate decided to put its changes into legislation, rather than change Senate rules, as the House had done, the changes to Senate rules would not take effect until the legislation passed the House and was signed into law by the President, something that didn't happen until nine months later.

During the spring of 2007 the House worked to craft ethics reform legislation to address the issues raised in the Senate bill. In late May a bill passed the House, and, after a summer of negotiation between House and Senate leaders, the Honest Leadership and Open Government Act of 2007 passed the House and Senate just before the August recesses, as congressional leaders had promised. President Bush signed the legislation into law on September 14, 2007.

Provisions of the Legislation

The legislation upheld the gift ban in the Senate legislation and House rules passed in January 2007. Members of Congress and their staffs may not accept gifts in any amounts from lobbyists or organizations that employ lobbyists. The legislation also increased the number of reporting periods for lobbyists to disclose their lobbying activity. Lobbyists must now file quarterly reports; in the past biannual reports were required. Also, the legislation requires that such reports be filed electronically in a way that is available on the Internet.

The House and Senate enacted slightly different rules for charter plane travel for members and House candidates and senators and Senate candidates. Members of Congress and congressional candidates are prohibited, under the legislation, from accepting any travel on private planes. Senators and Senate candidates may accept such travel, but must pay charter rates when traveling on private planes.

The rules for lobbying by former House and Senate members and their staffs also differ for Senators and members of Congress. Under the legislation former Senators are prohibited from lobbying Congress for two years after they leave office; House members and senior Senate and House staffers must wait only one year after leaving office before lobbying Congress.

Rules for lobbying Congress by congressional spouses are also slightly different for the House and Senate. In the House, lobbyist spouses are prohibited from contacting their spouse's staff. The same provision holds in the Senate, but with an exemption for spouses who were registered lobbyists one year before they were married or one year before the Senator was elected.

One of the most widely discussed provisions of the legislation was the reform of "earmarks." Legislators use earmarks to provide federal funds for projects, usually for their own congressional district or state. According to the Congressional Research Service, "from 1994 to 2005 the number of earmarks more than tripled, while their cost shot up from $30 billion to $47 billion."[10] What made the practice particularly controversial was that members of Congress could insert earmarks into legislation without identifying themselves with the project, thus minimizing transparency. The Honest Leadership and Open Government Act requires that Senators and members of Congress identify their earmarks two days prior to a vote and also confirm that neither the member nor their family members have any financial interest in the project receiving the earmark.

The legislation also addressed one aspect of campaign financing, namely, the practice of "bundling." Bundling occurs when an individual collects campaign contributions from a number of contributors, and then the individual gives the "bundled" contributions to a candidate for office, thereby getting credit for raising the money for the candidate. While bundling itself was not prohibited by the legislation, the legislation aims to make such practices more transparent. Members of Congress must disclose the names of lobbyists who raise $15,000 or more for the member within a six-month period. The legislation also prohibits members of Congress from attending receptions in their honor at the national party conventions, unless the member is the presidential or vice presidential nominee.

Finally, the legislation prohibits Senators from putting anonymous "holds" on legislation. Any Senator who places a hold on legislation must now do so in writing.

Enforcement of the Legislation

Democratic members of Congress were quick to hail the Honest Leadership and Open Government Act as a significant reform of lobbying practices. House Speaker Nancy Pelosi described the legislation as "momentous" and "historic."[11] Senate Majority Leader Harry Reid called the legislation "the most sweeping lobbying and ethics reform in the history of the country."[12] Congressman Rahm Emanuel (Democrat-Illinois), the Chairman of the House Democratic Caucus, declared that "lobbying laws and rules have been collecting particles and dirt for thirty years, and this is the most comprehensive scrub they've gotten."[13] Even Fred Wertheimer, the president of Democracy 21 and a thirty-six-year advocate for ethics and campaign finance reform, described the legislation as "big-time fundamental reforms."[14]

Yet despite the promise surrounding the passage of the ethics reform legislation, the ink was barely dry when questions of enforcement of the law began to be raised. Much of the responsibility for the enforcement of the new law lies with the House and Senate ethics committees. Shortly after the legislation was passed Kenneth Gross, an ethics lawyer, stated that "this law will put a significant new burden on the ethics committees and the public disclosure offices in the House and Senate. They have to do more than sticking the reports in a filing cabinet."[15] Gross went on to comment that "without a way to manage disclosure information the enforcement process will be weakened at its base."[16]

Monitoring disclosure of lobbying and bundling practices is one responsibility of the ethics committees; a second is preapproval of congressional travel. Craig Holman, legislative representative for Public Citizen, a government watchdog group, stated that such a rule "is just one brand-new rule that would overwhelm the existing ethics committees."[17] Holman also raised questions about the requirement that lobbying reports be available on the Internet. "Who's supposed to be in charge of this centralized database?" Holman asked.[18] Melanie Sloan, head of Citizens for Responsibility and Ethics in Washington, also questioned how effective the enforcement of the legislation would be:

> The bill puts more onerous reporting on lobbyists, but the House and Senate don't have new responsibilities—except to keep hold of all of this . . . So many concerns raised by the Abramoff scandals were enforcement issues. There is no change to that here.[19]

Not only have questions been raised about the ability of Congress to enforce the new ethics rules, efforts to circumvent those rules began before the bill even became law. One of the most notable efforts comes from those who try to get around the new provision requiring the disclosure of earmarks. For example, a provision in the legislation allows committee chairs, or other primary sponsors of legislation, to include special projects in legislation without identifying such projects as earmarks. In March, when questioned about a $35 million allocation in a spending bill, Congressman David Obey (Democrat-Wisconsin), Chairman of the House Appropriations Committee, denied that the allocation was an earmark. "An earmark is something that is requested by an individual member. This item was not requested by an individual member; it was put in the bill by me."[20] Another way in which members of Congress have attempted to get around the earmark provisions is to ask executive branch agencies, either through congressional hearings or letters to the agencies, to direct funds to specific programs in congressional districts.[21] For example, in February Congressman Emanuel sent a letter to the Department of Energy requesting "support and assistance in securing $500,000 for Children's Memorial Hospital in Chicago and $750,000 for the Illinois Institute of Technology."[22] While in the past such requests would commonly be known as earmarks, Congressman Emanuel stated that "letter-writing is not an earmark."[23]

As members of Congress attempt to redefine how to get money to pet projects while still staying within the confines of the new ethics rules, government watchdog groups have pointed out the slight of hand. Ellen Miller of the Sunlight Foundation commented that "going to agencies outside the congressional process avoids any measure of transparency or accountability. Earmarks remain and are just called by a different name."[24] Steve Ellis, vice president of Taxpayers for Common Sense, commented that "they are trying to change the whole vernacular so that earmarks aren't earmarks anymore."[25]

Finding new and creative ways to get money to special projects in members' districts is just one way in which the actual implementation of the new ethics laws is challenged. The interpretation of the restrictions on meals and gifts is another area which has seen some malleability. For example, while members of Congress cannot accept meals from lobbyists, the restriction does not apply to fundraising events. Jeffrey Birnbaum, a *Washington Post* reporter and the author of *The Lobbyists*, noted that this loophole created "the following perversity: Lobbyists will not be able to pick up a check for a member of Congress unless they also hand the lawmakers a check to help their reelections."[26] Another example of circumventing the meals and gifts ban was seen in October 2007, during the Hispanic Caucus Institute and Congressional Black Caucus Foundation galas in Washington, D.C. Corporations and lobbyists purchased tickets for the galas, tickets that cost up to $2,500 apiece, and then donated the tickets back to the Hispanic Caucus Institute and Congressional Black Caucus Foundation, along with a list of members of Congress that the corporations and lobbyists wanted invited to the galas.[27]

As the above examples suggest, implementing the new ethics rules will be a challenge, and whether the "culture of corruption" will actually change remains to be seen. In the months following the enactment of the law the House and Senate ethics committees received more than 1,000 requests from lobbyists and congressional staffers seeking guidance in interpreting the new law.[28] The successful implementation of the law will depend on the willingness of members of Congress to give their ethics committees the resources to oversee and enforce the law and the willingness of members of Congress to translate the spirit of the law into practice. The early months following the enactment of the law suggest little success on both counts.

Ethics in Electoral Campaigns

Ethical questions in electoral campaigns come in a variety of forms: the amount of money it costs to run for political office in the United States and the sources of that money, the negative campaign ads that are a part of most campaigns, and the role of political consultants and the means they will use to elect candidates are all often raised as issues in discussions of campaign ethics.

At the start of the 2008 presidential election the expectation was that to be competitive a candidate would have to raise $100 million in 2007. In September 2007, after the third quarter Federal Election Commission (FEC) filing period, two candidates, Senators Hillary Clinton (Democrat-New York) and Barack Obama (Democrat-Illinois), seemed to be on track to reach that goal, each having raised approximately $75 million. Their opponents for the Democratic nomination, and the Republican candidates for the nomination, were not close to that goal. It seems likely that the 2008 presidential election will be the most expensive in the history of the United States, despite legislation passed in 2002 to attempt to change campaign financing of federal elections. The Bipartisan Campaign Finance Act (BCRA) was enacted to address two main problems that had developed in federal elections: soft money and issue advocacy. (See also Chapter 12, by Anthony Gierzynski, on campaign financing.)

When the Federal Election Campaign Act (FECA) was enacted in 1971 and amended in 1974, limits were established on the amount of money individuals, political parties, and political action committees could contribute to candidates for federal office, and on the amount of money individuals and political action committees could contribute to political parties. As a result of a series of FEC advisory opinions in the 1980s, individuals, corporations, labor unions, and others were allowed to contribute unlimited additional amounts to political parties. These contributions, known as soft money (compared to the contribution limits established by the FECA, which were referred to as hard money), undermined the limits in the FECA, and by the 2000 election had become an important source of funding for the national political parties. The BCRA prohibited the national political parties from accepting soft money, and prohibited candidates for federal office from raising soft money.

As soft money was becoming an integral part of the campaign landscape in the 1990s, so were so called "issue ads." Issue ads in the modern era began in 1993, when the Health Insurance Association of America ran a series of ads, entitled "Harry and Louise," criticizing the Clinton administration's health reform proposals. In 1996, the political parties began running "issue ads" on behalf of their candidates, ads that looked very much like actual candidate ads. Such advertisements could be run, and paid for with soft money, because they did not contain words advocating express electioneering.[29] The BCRA required that any political ad run by a political party or interest group within thirty days of a primary election or sixty days of a general election that mentioned a candidate for federal office had to be paid for with hard money.

These two main provisions of the BCRA were designed to remove soft money from federal elections and to recognize that issue ads were in fact ads designed to influence the outcome of elections. However, as with ethics reform in Congress, soft money was not entirely removed from federal elections. In the 2004 election there developed a new way for individuals and groups to run advertisements aimed to influence the outcome of the election, ads funded by soft money. The Internal Revenue Service classifies all political organizations as 527 organizations, named after the portion of the tax code that regulates these organizations' tax status. During the 2004 elections a group of Democratic activists, fearful that the Democratic nominee for President would not be able to compete financially with President George W. Bush's presidential campaign, formed several groups to raise money and run ads in support of the Democratic nominee. The most well known of the organizations, which were called "527s," were the Media Fund and ACT (Americans Coming Together). Republican-leaning 527s were also formed during the summer of 2004; the best known of the Republican 527s was Swift Boat Veterans for Truth. Despite BCRA, soft money found its way back into federal elections, though, at least in 2004 and 2006, not in the same amounts as in the pre-BCRA elections.

The FECA of 1971, and its 1974 amendments, not only established contribution limits for federal elections, it also established partial public funding of the pre-nomination phase of presidential elections and public funding of the nominating conventions and, if a general election candidate so chose, full public funding of the general election. The primary purpose of partial public funding during the primaries and caucuses was to allow candidates with limited financial resources but demonstrated political support (as seen by their winning a proportion of the vote in primaries and caucuses), to be financially competitive in seeking the nomination. The purpose of public funding in the general election was to allow candidates to seek the presidency unencumbered by the demands of special interests and special interest money. While the system put in place for the 1976 elections worked well for two decades, by the 2000 presidential elections it began to crumble, and almost completely disappeared by the 2008 presidential elections.

In the 2000 pre-nomination phase of the campaign George W. Bush announced that he would not accept partial public funding. Bush again did not accept partial public funding for his re-election campaign in 2004, nor did his Democratic rival, Senator John Kerry. (Former Vermont governor Howard Dean, who lead in the polls for much of the summer and fall before the primaries and caucuses occurred, also did not accept partial public funding.) By the 2008 election, only a handful of second-tier candidates accepted partial public funding, largely because they had nowhere near the financial resources of the frontrunners senators Barack Obama and Hillary Clinton for the Democratic nomination and former Massachusetts governor Mitt Romney and former New York City mayor Rudy Giuliani for the Republican nomination.

With partial public funding largely removed from the pre-nomination phase of the presidential elections and questions being raised about whether the major party nominees would accept public funding for the general election, the opportunities exist for private interests to once again play a role in presidential elections. Nowhere is this more obvious than in the funding of the 2008 nominating conventions. The host committees for the Democratic and Republican conventions have been soliciting corporate sponsorship of the conventions, with the promise of access to policymakers and candidates for office. For example, solicitations for sponsorship of the Democratic convention promise that "as a corporate sponsor, you will be invited to exclusive forums and special events where you will interact with our state's and the nation's government and business leaders."[30] Financial sponsorship levels at the Republican Convention range from $5 million to $50,000; financial sponsorship levels at the Democratic Convention range from $1 million to $52,800. For $5 million, sponsors are assured of a "private reception with Minnesota Governor Tim Pawlenty, Senator Norm Coleman, the mayors of Minneapolis, St. Paul and Bloomington, and a private dinner and golfing with the Republican leadership."[31] This access to lawmakers is being promised despite the fact that the ethics reform legislation prohibits members of Congress from attending lobbyist-sponsored parties in their honor at the party conventions.

One provision of BCRA was a requirement that candidates for federal office state in any campaign advertisement sponsored by their campaign "I'm [candidate name] and I approve this message." This provision, known as "stand by your ad," was put in the legislation to reduce negative advertisement. The argument was that candidates would be less likely to say negative things about their opponents if they had to state their name and that they approved of the negative ad. However, in practice the language has had no effect on either the number or tone of negative ads.

The broader question is the effect of negative ads on voters' perceptions of candidates, voters' knowledge of candidates' positions on issues, and voter turnout. Political scientists Steven Ansolabehere and Shanto Iyengar argue that negative ads decrease turnout in elections.[32] While the Ansolabehere and Iyengar study received quite a bit of attention when it was first published in 1995, other, more recent studies have found that negative advertising does not adversely affect turnout in elections, and some studies find that negative ads may slightly increase turnout.[33]

Apart from the effect of negative ads on turnout, voters and journalists widely decry the use of negative ads during elections. Yet, studies have shown that there is actually more information in negative, or contrast, ads than in positive ads. Kathleen Hall Jamieson and her colleagues examined the content of ads that aired in presidential elections from 1952 to 1996, and found that both attack ads and contrast ads (ads in which candidates both present their views on issues and critique the views of their opponents) "offered more policy information to the electorate than the so-called positive ads."[34] In a more recent study political scientist John Geer argues that "negativity provides a chance for those competing for power to make a case for why they should be given power and it gives those in power the chance to show the risks associated with the other side."[35]

The creators of campaign ads, media consultants, and political consultants more generally, are often cited as contributing to questionable ethical practices in campaigns. While there are examples of political consultants who have clearly crossed ethical lines, most political consultants have a clear delineation in their minds as to what is ethical and what is not. In a seven-year study of political consultants two colleagues and I conducted three surveys of political consultants, and in each survey we asked a series of questions about specific ethical practices. We found that some practices, such as making statements that are factually untrue, political consultants found unethical, and some practices, such as contrasting a candidate's stand on issues with that of his/her opponent, consultants found completely ethical. There were other practices, such as the use of "push polls,"[36] which some consultants found acceptable, some found questionable, and some found unethical.[37] However, we found that the proportion of consultants that found various practices acceptable, questionable, and unacceptable was remarkably stable over the course of the three surveys. From these findings we concluded that while political consultants may differ in their views of the ethics of various campaign practices, they have thought about campaign practices, and know where they stand. While there may be instances of questionable behavior, it is not the case that political consultants will do whatever is necessary to win.

Conclusions

Questions about ethical practices in campaigns and in government will continue, even with reform legislation. Part of this is because there is no distinct line that defines one behavior as ethical and another as not ethical. For example, the ethics legislation enacted by Congress in 2007 requires former Senators to wait two years before they can lobby their former colleagues. Senate gym privileges were removed, and former Senators are no longer allowed on the Senate floor. Yet when former Senator Conrad Burns, now working for a lobbying firm, joined his former colleagues at their weekly lunch shortly after the ethics legislation was signed into law, there was no violation of the ethics law.[38] Senator Jim DeMint, organizer of the weekly luncheons, stated that "there's no lobbying that ever goes on."[39] However, even if there was no lobbying, would it benefit a former Senator and current lobbyist to listen to his former colleagues discuss legislation and policy agendas? Probably.[40]

This chapter has provided numerous examples of attempts to circumvent the ethics legislation passed in 2007. As more provisions of the law take effect in 2008, the implementation of the law will likely face more questions and problems. Part of the problem is the efforts of candidates and members of Congress to test and push what is permissible; part of the problem is the lack of resources to effectively enforce the laws. Questions were raised earlier in this chapter about the ability of the House and Senate ethics committees to command the resources necessary to enforce the provisions of the ethics legislation. Similar questions are raised about the enforcement capabilities of the FEC, the agency responsible for overseeing campaign finance laws. The FEC has six commissioners, equally divided between Democrats and Republicans. Historically, when major cases come before the Commission that might adversely affect one party or the other, the Commission splits three-to-three, essentially not making a decision. For example, when the Republican National Committee asked the Commission to rule on the legality of the actions of the Media Fund and ACT in the spring of 2004, the FEC declined to render a decision during the 2004 presidential election.

Ethical questions have been a part of US campaigns and policymaking almost since the founding of the country. Legislation has changed the way candidates campaign and policymakers govern, but ethical questions have persisted. It is likely that such questions will continue during the elections of 2008, 2010, and 2012, and the Congresses and administrations that follow those elections.

Notes

1 Candice J. Nelson, David A. Dulio, and Stephen K. Medvic, eds, *Shades of Gray: Perspectives on Campaign Ethics* (Washington, D.C.: Brookings Institution Press, 2002).
2 "Congressman Resigns After Bribery Plea," *CNN*, hppt://www.cnn.com/2005/POLITICS/11/28/Cunningham/. Accessed October 6, 2007.
3 Susan Schmidt, James V. Grimaldi, and R. Jeffrey Smith, "Investigating Abramoff—Special Report," *Washington Post*, February 5, 2006.
4 Susan Schmidt and James V. Grimaldi, "Ney Pleads Guilty to Corruption Charges," *Washington Post*, October 1, 1006.
5 Charles Babington and Jonathan Weisman, "Rep. Foley Quits in Page Scandal," *Washington Post*, September 2, 2006.
6 "Affidavit: $90,000 found in Congressman's Freezer," *CNN*, http://www.cnn.com/2006/POLITICS/05/21/jefferson.search/index. Accessed October 7, 2007.
7 "Congressman William Jefferson Indicted on Bribery Charges," *FOXNews.com*, http://www.foxnews.com/printer_friendly_story/0,3566,277774,00. Accessed October 7, 2007.
8 "House Imposes New Ethics Rules," *OMB Watch* 8 (1), January 9, 2007, http://www.ombwatch.org/article/articleview/3672/1/474. Accessed October 6, 2007.
9 Ibid.
10 Danielle Knight, "Loading the Pork Train," *U.S. News and World Report*, May 29, 2006.
11 Jonathan Weisman, "House Votes 411–8 to Pass Ethics Overhaul," *Washington Post*, August 1, 2007, A1.
12 Elizabeth Williamson, "Draining the 'Swamp' Is Not Easy," *Washington Post*, August 7, 2007, A11.
13 Elizabeth Williamson, "Lawmakers Agree on New Ethics Rules," *Washington Post*, July 28, 2007, A4.
14 Wesiman, "House Votes 411–8 to Pass Ethics Overhaul," A9.
15 Williamson, "Draining the 'Swamp' Is Not Easy," A11.
16 Ibid.
17 Ibid.
18 Ibid.
19 Ibid.
20 John Soloman and Jeffrey H. Birnbaum, "Pet Projects Veil Is Only Partly Lifted: Lawmakers Find Other Paths to Special-Interest Funding," *Washington Post*, September 9, 207, A5.

21 Ibid.
22 Ibid.
23 Ibid.
24 Ibid.
25 Ibid.
26 Jeffrey Birnbaum, "Congressman, It's (Still) on Us: the Ethics Law's Many Loopholes," *Washington Post*, August 14, 2007, A11.
27 Elizabeth Williamson, "Getting Around the Rules on Lobbying," *Washington Post*, October 14, 2007, A1, A5.
28 Ibid.
29 In a footnote in *Buckley v. Valeo*, the Supreme Court ruled that only advertising that contained so called "magic words," such as "vote for," "vote against," "support," or "oppose," was electioneering advertising. *Buckley v. Valeo*, 424 U.S. 1, 12–59 (1976).
30 Jeffrey H. Birnbaum, "Convention Party Favors Include Face Time," *The Washington Post*, August 14, 2007, D2.
31 Ibid.
32 Stephen Ansolabehere and Shanto Iyengar, *Going Negative: How Political Advertisements Shrink and Polarize the Electorate* (New York: Free Press, 1995).
33 Richard R. Lau and Lee Sigelman, "Effectiveness of Negative Political Advertising," in *Crowded Airwaves: Campaign Advertising in Elections*, ed. James A. Thurber, Candice J. Nelson, and David A. Dulio (Washington, D.C.: Brookings Institution Press, 2000), 32.
34 Kathleen Hall Jamieson, Paul Waldman, and Susan Sherr, "Eliminate the Negative? Categories of Analysis for Political Advertisements," in *Crowded Airwaves: Campaign Advertising in Elections*, ed. James A. Thurber, Candice J. Nelson, and David A. Dulio (Washington, D.C.: Brookings Institution Press, 2000), 58.
35 John G. Geer, *In Defense of Negativity: Attack Ads in Presidential Campaigns* (Chicago, IL: University of Chicago Press, 2006), 162.
36 Push polls are not actually polls at all, but rather a telemarketing technique that gives false or misleading information to potential voters, with the purpose of "pushing" them away from voting for the candidate that is the target of the push poll.
37 David A. Dulio and Candice J. Nelson, *Vital Signs: Perspectives on the Health of American Campaigning*, (Washington, D.C.: Brookings Institution Press, 2005), 130.
38 Mary Ann Akers and Paul Kane, "In the Loop," *Washington Post*, October 4, 2007, A23.
39 Ibid.
40 Ibid.

40

Winning Over a Cynical Public

The Debate Over Stem Cell Research and Other
Biotechnologies

Bonnie Stabile and Susan J. Tolchin

Introduction

Over time, Americans have traditionally been distrustful of government, and disdainful of authority in general.[1] Their attitudes toward government, which range from healthy skepticism to scathing cynicism, are often credited with maintaining a healthy democracy by acting as a mechanism for keeping politicians and policymakers honest.[2] At times, the cynicism of citizens is seen as a threat to the political process, leading to apathy, antagonism or even "a decaying of the social and political order."[3] Since the 1970s studies have shown that cynicism is on the rise,[4] paralleling a "long-term slide in public confidence in the core institutions of representative democracy."[5] And while some scholars maintain that "robust predictors of trust or confidence" are elusive, they acknowledge "a contemporary zeitgeist of suspicion and cynicism,"[6] a veritable "epidemic" of cynicism blamed for the "deterioration of public discourse."[7]

The political realm is by no means the only sphere in which public cynicism is evident. Confidence in the fields of media, science, education, medicine, the military and religion declined steadily in the late twentieth century,[8] and shows no signs of abating. Despite the steady decline, the public appears to express the greatest confidence in medicine, with the scientific community running a close second.[9] Perhaps this reflects Americans' optimistic disposition toward the future,[10] with the vast majority of Americans, fully 86%, believing that there will be more opportunities for the next generation due to advances in science and technology.[11] Public confidence in the leadership of the scientific community, tracked for over three decades by the General Social Survey, consistently surpasses that expressed toward other institutions, including the Supreme Court, major companies and the executive branch of government.[12] The esteem in which citizens regard both government and scientific enterprise are particularly relevant at the beginning of the twenty-first century, as rapid advances in science and technology increasingly call for government to address issues of public policy in which ever more complex scientific issues are implicated.

Despite an atmosphere of demonstrated enthusiasm for science and technology—91% of Americans agree that science and technology are making their lives healthier, easier and more comfortable[13]—it has been lamented by some since the 1970s that perhaps the "golden age" of science and technology has passed.[14] Though the scientific community has been held in high regard relative to other institutions, it has not been immune to public distrust. The era of political turmoil and social unrest that led to increased public wariness and scrutiny of authority in all quarters also cast aspersions on the institutions and individuals associated with science and technology.

A recent headline asked, "Can science win back the public trust?"[15] This was followed by an article speculating that a general skepticism existed toward the fact that scientific advances would be used for the good of humanity as a whole.[16] Well aware that its reputation is at risk, many members of the scientific community as well as their supporters have expressed the desire to burnish their image. This chapter will consider the extent to which public cynicism has infected the scientific and political communities, especially at points where they intersect with each other. It will also consider how they might join forces to gain public trust by forging effective policy solutions. As science has become increasingly politicized, and policy has become more infused with scientific data and methodology, political actors may benefit from the rationality of science in advancing agendas in the public interest. Scientists, in turn, may find their work more effectively employed in the public sphere by engaging in activities associated with political persuasion. In this way, both communities may achieve greater success in winning over an increasingly cynical public.

The Meaning of Public Cynicism

A cynic has been variously defined as one who "attributes all actions to selfish motives,"[17] and "a sneering fault finder" given to expressions of sarcasm."[18] As a formal school of thought, "Cynicism" originated in ancient Greece, and was founded by Antisthenes, a follower of Socrates.[19] Like their modern namesakes, the first cynics disparaged cherished conventions and institutions, particularly religion and government, while the "privileged and powerful" were primary targets of their scorn.[20] Scholars concerned with social and political theory have equated cynicism with a low level of trust, and "a pervasive 'disbelief in the possibility of good' in dealing with others,"[21] particularly those in the public sphere. Though indicators of declining trust in government often prompt fears that rising cynicism will eat away at the foundation of our political system, Seymour Martin Lipset and William Schneider reassuringly conclude that what they refer to as "the confidence gap" has "never amounted to a full-scale legitimacy crisis."[22] In other words, cynicism has coexisted with democracy since antiquity without yet precipitating its downfall.

While the degree to which public cynicism has taken hold and the extent of its effects are debatable, two broad truths are taken as a given by most who study it: (1) the public has become increasingly cynical since the mid-1960s; and (2) public cynicism is potentially detrimental to the political process. In *Political Ideology: Why the American Common Man Believes What He Does*, Robert Lane noted in 1962 that the subjects of his study, when they thought of the role of government in their lives at all, saw it as a source of "benefits and protections."[23] Such attitudes were forged in a "golden era," when government was perceived as having saved the country from the Great Depression and won a World War.[24] In contrast, when Marc J. Hetherington considered the question of political trust thirty years later, he concluded that the government was regarded "as producing scandal, waste, and unacceptable intrusions on people's personal lives."[25] In a Harvard commencement address in 1994, Vice President Al Gore, Jr, recalled that when he was a college freshman at Harvard in 1965, over 60% of the public believed that government "generally tries to do the right thing."[26] But by the time of his twenty-fifth reunion, only 10% of the populace held that view. Among people of all political persuasions, the percentage of citizens believing that "government favors the rich and powerful" had risen from 29% to 80% during that same time period.[27] The seeds of discontent sown during the 1960s race riots, campus protests and the violence of the Vietnam War only became more deeply entrenched in the aftermath of the Watergate scandal,[28] creating a deficit of public trust that would persist for decades, if not indefinitely.

Addressing the Johns Hopkins University's class of 1999, Senator John McCain (Republican-Arizona) exhorted the assembled graduates to put forth their best efforts to defeat a threat he deemed as dangerous as any war or depression: the "pervasive public cynicism that is debilitating our democracy."[29] Calling the defeat of cynicism "a new patriotic challenge for a new century," McCain warned that when citizens "come to believe that government is so dysfunctional or corrupt that it no longer" supports "our constitutional purposes" that "basic civil consensus will deteriorate to the point that our culture might fragment beyond recognition."[30] While academics tend to be more circumspect in their assessment of the consequences of cynicism for society than are politicians, they nonetheless deem it a subject worthy of consideration. High levels of cynicism and low levels of trust are often associated with voter apathy, the weakening of civil society and the inability of the government to implement effective policy.

The causes and effects of public dissatisfaction with government can be seen as self-reinforcing. Hetherington, for instance, points out that declining political trust leads to negative evaluations of "the incumbent president and Congress as a political institution."[31] A cynical public makes it harder for government to get things done, while the reverse is true as well: a government that doesn't get things done gets a cynical public. Arthur H. Miller's seminal article on political cynicism, "Political Issues and Trust in Government: 1964–1970," chronicles the beginnings of the downslide toward disillusionment. According to Jack Citrin, Miller calls to mind "the language of the corporation balance-sheet," by suggesting that political elites "produce" policies that attract both the trust of satisfied citizens as well as the cynicism of those not well served or satisfied by those policies.[32] Indeed, "policy-related discontent is a source of political cynicism."[33]

Miller defines political cynicism as "the degree of negative affect toward the government" and describes it as the endpoint of a dimension running from high trust to high distrust, with cynicism occupying the highest form of distrust.[34] Viewing cynicism as a matter of degree, rather than as an absolute negative for the political process, can soften cataclysmic predictions about its effects on society and make it seem less of a threat to democratic ideals. In making the point that cynicism is an intrinsic characteristic of the American identity, some scholars have referenced James Madison's contention in the *Federalist Papers* that a balance of power must be created in the Constitution, an assertion based on "a certain degree of skepticism about human nature" that lies at the foundation of our representative democracy.[35] Indeed Timothy E. Cook and Paul Gronke argue that low levels of trust are not necessarily the harbingers of "cynicism and alienation" that they are often interpreted to be, but are instead a reflection of public *skepticism*, a mere reluctance to give political authorities the benefit of the doubt.[36] Evan Berman notes that the literature "makes a distinction between ardent cynicism and its milder forms" and says that while ardent cynicism "is usually linked to ideological beliefs that are highly critical of government," its milder expressions are both less critical of government and "more open to influence by reason."[37] This milder form of cynicism might also usefully be described as skepticism.

Modern skepticism has been said to be "embodied in the scientific method."[38] It involves data, testing and evidence. Skeptics refrain from judging a policy, as scientists do with theory, until sufficient evidence has been provided to convince them of its merits; cynics, who do not make up their minds on the basis of evidence, are apt to dismiss policy proposals out of hand, based on their presupposition of ill will or incompetence on the part of policymakers. And while skeptics, like scientists, can be persuaded by facts, they understand all facts to be "provisional and subject to challenge."[39] With policy, as with scientific theory, newly discovered facts can override previously held paradigms: in other words, there are no sacred idols and skeptics must remain open to the possibility of change. While many Americans may certainly be described as cynics, the American psyche may be more accurately described as skeptical. Some commentators label all Americans "Missourians," who deserve the reputation of their fellow citizens in the "show-me-state."[40] This does not make them hardened cynics, rather doubters, who are not convinced of the trustworthiness of government or the soundness of a proposed course of action without proof or the reassurance of safeguards.

Finally, in addition to its nuances of meaning as an adjective describing the chronically doubting or suspicious, some consideration must be given to a newer usage of the word cynical, as a descriptor "no longer applying to the suspicious but to the suspect."[41] In this usage, it is not the disposition of a particular individual or population that is characterized, but instead the motivation for particular actions. It implies willful misrepresentation, insincerity or intentional manipulation. For example, efforts by advocates of federally funded embryonic stem cell research to allow scientists access to leftover IVF embryos were called "a cynical political tactic" by Wesley Smith, a senior fellow at the Discovery Institute, who believed their real motive was to garner public support for "unlimited human biotechnological research."[42]

Policy Dissatisfaction as a Cause of Public Cynicism

Miller's study showed that public discontent in his day arose partly "out of dissatisfaction with the policy alternatives . . . offered as solutions to contemporary problems."[43] Problems then most prominent on the public agenda, which Miller included for consideration when gauging policy preferences and public cynicism, included racial issues and the Vietnam War. In the age of biotechnology, some anticipated advances might have the potential to fundamentally transform society. Much public concern is focused on continuing the progress of scientific and technological advancement, while insuring the ability of government to formulate policies that will guide rapid change, and safeguard the public at the same time. Therefore, public cynicism as it relates to science and biotechnology, broadly defined, will be the focus of consideration here.

Tom Abate, a reporter with the *San Francisco Chronicle*, wonders if "the explosion of knowledge and accelerating pace of innovation" we are experiencing might just "push the possibilities" of biotech developments "past the breaking point."[44] Specifically, he claims that public suspicion of the US regulatory system has created a situation rendering government inadequate to the task of controlling such advancements as cloning, genetic engineering of plants, animals and people, and many other possibilities previously confined to the world of science fiction. Though Abate recognizes Americans' "implicit faith in technology" as well as the impressive track record of improvements to "life spans and prosperity," he also notes that there is public cynicism regarding the government's role in such advancement, and its ability to rein in potentially errant technologies. "Even a perfect regulatory system" would have a hard time keeping up with the increasing rapidity and complexity of scientific and technological developments, "and we know our system isn't perfect."[45]

Just how imperfect our regulatory system is has been evident in two areas of oversight in recent years: (1) the case of hormone replacement therapy (HRT) for menopausal women; and (2) the case of tainted pet food and other products from China. In the former instance millions of women discovered that they had unwittingly increased their risk of breast cancer, strokes, heart attacks and blood clots as a result of using HRT. In the pet food case, over 14,000 pets became sick after eating tainted food, leading to at least sixteen animal deaths and the recall of over sixty million packages of pet food.[46] These two disparate scenarios share one important fact in common: they occurred due to a lapse in government oversight, specifically oversight by the US Food and Drug Administration (FDA). According to its mission statement, the FDA is responsible for

protecting the public health by assuring the safety, efficacy, and security of human and veterinary drugs, biological products, medical devices, our nation's food supply . . . [and] . . . for advancing the public health by helping to speed innovations that make medicines and foods more effective, safer, and more affordable; and helping the public get the accurate, science-based information they need to use medicines and foods to improve their health.

If in the routine conduct of its mission such egregious episodes occur with any regularity, it is easy to see how public cynicism could develop in response. Since the public's expectation is that the government will insure that food, medicine and therapies made available to them will be safe, repeated instances in which the government fails to adequately protect them are likely to result in diminished public trust. Traditionally, the FDA resources have not been equal to the mission of the agency; budgets and personnel have decreased over the past few decades as each president joined the bandwagon toward the rush to deregulate. Indeed, the public has shown surprise—before cynicism—at the well-known fact that the FDA has been forced to rely almost exclusively on drug companies to conduct their own research on the very drugs they plan to market.

Hormone Replacement Therapy

Pharmaceuticals are just one facet of the biotech revolution, which, it is hoped, will lead to advances that will lengthen and enhance lives. The prospect of some biotech advancements, such as genetic engineering of people, animals and crops, is sufficient cause for misgivings. But beyond curing disease, drugs are sought to improve athletic ability, sexual prowess, wakefulness, youthfulness and cognitive capacity. HRT, a combination treatment of estrogen and progesterone, was approved by the FDA in 1986 for the treatment of osteoporosis (the weakening and loss of bone mass most commonly occurring in post-menopausal women), and was first used to treat other physical symptoms of menopause, like hot flashes, in the 1930s.[47] In the 1960s, a book called *Feminine Forever*, by Robert Wilson, helped to popularize the notion that HRT would keep women young, vital, sexually vibrant and wrinkle-free by replacing the hormones lost during the natural process of menopause. The thinking of the medical community at that time was that women could simply replace the hormones no longer made by their own bodies as they aged, much as diabetics take insulin to replace what their bodies fail to produce.[48] Maintaining estrogen levels was also believed to prevent heart disease, and even help women hold on to their husbands, according to some proponents of HRT. By 2002, "about 30% of women older than fifty took estrogen regularly,"[49] representing about six million women in the United States.[50]

Trusting both science and the medical community, and relying upon implicit government assurance of safe and effective medications, women hoping to forestall aging and prevent disease took HRT willingly and without undue concern. But, much to their dismay, the National Institutes of Health (NIH) announced in 2002 that a Women's Health Initiative (WHI) study was being halted because it was discovered, three years before any results were even expected, that the risks of HRT outweighed any purported benefits.[51] Specifically it was shown that women taking HRT experienced "a 26% increase in breast cancer, a 41% increase in strokes, and a 200% increase in the rates of blood clots in legs and lungs."[52] While red flags had been raised on previous occasions about potential health risks to women taking hormones, none were well heeded until after the 2002 study findings were announced, when, doctors estimate, half of all women who were taking hormones stopped taking them.[53] A dramatic 15% drop in the breast cancer rate supported the link between HRT and adverse health effects within eighteen months of the announcement of the study's results.[54] Researchers are careful to point out that a correlation between the cessation of hormone therapy by millions of women and the rapid subsequent reduction in anticipated breast cancer cases could not be proven. In the words of one researcher carefully maintaining an air of scientific skepticism, "epidemiology can never prove causality."[55] But according to Donald A. Berry of M.D. Anderson Cancer Center in Houston, lead investigator of the follow up study, there is strong evidence to suggest that HRT is the "smoking gun."[56] Susan Love, noted expert on breast cancer and women's health, agrees that the drop of

14,000 anticipated cases of breast cancer is attributable to the cessation of HRT by so many women.[57] And no alternative explanation has been offered for the first decline in the breast cancer rate seen in almost fifty years.

Nancy Worcester, professor of Women's Studies at the University of Wisconsin-Madison, has asked what women's response to this news has been—whether they have felt a sense of outrage, for instance, either personal or political.[58] While Worcester favors priming women for political action in response to the failure of government and the medical community to protect them from significant health risks, one possible answer to the question could be that women's response has been to adopt an air of political cynicism. After all, in the case of HRT the government clearly failed to produce a policy to protect the public, an eventuality that is usually associated with a diminishment in public trust. Studies probing the issue of public cynicism often focus on questions of citizens' perceptions of government, such as whether they believe government services are meeting their needs;[59] whether government is run "for the benefit of all"; or is controlled by "a few big interests looking out for themselves."[60]

In the case of HRT, and in the realm of biotechnology generally, some of the biggest of those "big interests" are, of course, pharmaceutical manufacturers. Those who decry the "medicalization" of menopause are quick to point to drug company profits as the motive behind the promotion of HRT for many uses beyond the two for which they have FDA approval. For decades women were encouraged by their physicians to take HRT for a variety of "off label" uses, despite a dearth of scientific studies supporting the efficacy of HRT for these purposes.[61] Physicians, many persuaded by pharmaceutical company perks and PowerPoint presentations extolling the purported virtues of HRT, formed the front line in dispensing it. Some, funded by companies such as Wyeth, the makers of Premarin, a combination of estrogen and progestin, helped to make it the most prescribed drug in the United States in the 1990s,[62] and perhaps the most prescribed drug of all time. After the WHI study was halted by the NIH, it was revealed to the *New York Times* that the book *Feminine Forever* had been funded by Premarin's parent company.[63] In 2001 alone, Premarin garnered over $2 billion in sales for Wyeth.[64]

Despite evidence that drug companies and physicians had oversold HRT there has been no overwhelming public outcry condemning them for it. In fact, many seem reticent to believe the bad, but scientifically supported, news that hormones are not the elixir of youth that had been hoped for. While half of those taking HRT—some three million women in the United States alone—renounced it upon hearing of the NIH's recommendation, another three million women did not reject the drug. As Fran Visco, president of the National Breast Cancer Coalition, remarked in subsequent years "doctors kept prescribing and women kept taking."[65] Many women have steadfastly maintained that their quality of life is greatly enhanced by taking hormones. Some, with dramatically diminished bone density, or what they describe as debilitating hot flashes and night sweats, continued taking the medication. Still others, convinced that taking hormones allowed them to keep playing a good game of tennis or maintain a healthy libido, felt the same. One woman, a patient of Dr Wulf Utian of the North American Menopause Society, who had been taking hormones for thirty years, captured the reaction of some long-time HRT users to the WHI study when she declared, "Why would I come off it? I'd rather be dead."[66]

In striving to protect the health and well-being of the public, while keeping it adequately informed, government regulators also serve to protect the health of democracy, by maintaining public trust and forestalling public cynicism. In so doing they encountered various forces that shaped the success of their efforts. These included: (1) the strength and influence of industry groups with a product on the market, and profits to be made; (2) public demand for particular products, regardless of associated risk; and (3) varying interpretations of scientific findings regarding the safety and health implications of using certain products. One reason for differing interpretations of scientific findings may have involved deliberate efforts on the part of stakeholders to present facts in a manner most favorable to their positions. Another was strong public sentiment regarding a product's merits or disadvantages. Finally, a lack of familiarity with, or even a mere difference of opinion in interpreting, scientific results might also have been responsible for a lack of consensus when choosing a course of action. How is the public to understand the implications of such findings when making personal decisions regarding health, or supporting more broadly applicable policy measures? In order for the public to exercise healthy skepticism and eschew corrosive cynicism, further education in discerning the import of scientific results seems in order.

Tainted Pet Food, and Beyond

While most would not consider the safety of the pet food supply in the United States to be on par with women's health as a public health concern, problems in maintaining the purity and soundness of pet food nonetheless highlight an increasingly important concern facing government regulators: the impact of globalization. In March 2007 the FDA learned that certain pet foods, which were found to contain contaminated vegetable protein imported from China, were "sickening and killing cats and dogs." After receiving more than 14,000 reports of sick pets, the FDA banned imports of wheat gluten from China, which is commonly used by pet food manufacturers in the US. The problem was traced to the presence of melamine, a substance derived from coal and used to make plastics and fertilizer. Supplementing animal feed with a powdered form of scrap melamine makes the feed appear to be richer in protein due to its high nitrogen content, and bolsters profits by bulking it up with cheap, non-nutritive filler. It is illegal to use melamine as an ingredient for any food in the US, whether for human or animal consumption. But the substance is not easily detectable in imported feed. As the manager of a small animal feed operation in Zhangqiu, China, explained, melamine can be dyed to match the color of whatever type of feedstock it is being added to.[67]

The president of the Humane Society of the United States, Wayne Pacelle, noted that the 2007 pet food crisis served to shake consumer confidence in industry's adherence to safety standards.[68] Some, such as Bruce Friedrich, vice president of People for the Ethical Treatment of Animals (PETA), have long questioned the FDA's commitment to its mission to insure the purity and safety of pet food. He says that the agency doesn't do any actual inspections of either pet food or the plants where it is processed.[69] Instead, says Friedrich, the FDA relegates this responsibility to the Association of American Feed Control Officials (AAFCO), which has no regulatory authority.[70] This would be concern enough if ingredients in the feed came exclusively from within US borders, but the increasing presence in all foods of ingredients from abroad, where food safety standards may vary vastly from US standards, seems to raise the threat level considerably. Just one offending source, as the pet food crisis demonstrates, can have far reaching consequences. Tainted wheat gluten from a single Chinese company found its way into over 100 brands of pet food,[71] made by at least seven companies, and necessitated the recall of more than sixty million cans of dog and cat food.[72]

Endangering the lives of beloved pets and interrupting the flow of commerce are enough to inspire a crisis in public confidence, but things could be worse. It is not far fetched to extrapolate from these circumstances, and imagine a scenario in which human health is similarly put at risk. The US has thus far been spared any such large-scale calamity. But other nations have not been as fortunate, and there have been several close calls with contaminated Chinese goods in the US. In May 2007, Chinese toothpaste containing diethylene glycol, a cheap, and poisonous, industrial grade substitute for glycerin, was found to have been widely distributed to institutions such as hospitals and prisons throughout the country. The FDA subsequently advised that all Chinese-made toothpaste be discarded, not just the 900,000 or so tubes known to be tainted.[73] The offending ingredient—diethylene glycol—was the same substance from the same country of origin that had been responsible for the deaths of 100 people in Panama in 2006, when it was mixed into 260,000 bottles of cold medicine.[74] A decade earlier, dozens of Haitian children died when the cheap glycerin substitute imported from China was used in fever medicine there.[75]

Effective regulation is critical both to averting disaster and to nurturing public trust. The Chinese government sought to restore the confidence of the international community in the safety of its exports through a series of measures in 2007. In April it banned the use of melamine in food products, though denied the substance had been the cause of pet deaths in the US.[76] In June it announced the development of a five-year plan to improve food and drug safety standards, including stepped up efforts at monitoring and inspecting exports.[77] In July the Chinese government revoked the licenses of two biotechnology companies and a glycerin factory that they said had been responsible for tainted pet food, cold medicine and toothpaste ingredients.[78] And, in a dramatic and disturbing move that same month, the government also took the draconian measure of executing Zheng Xiaoyu, founder and former director of China's State Food and Drug Administration, for accepting bribes from drug companies. The corrupt regulatory system that Zheng oversaw put the health of untold numbers of Chinese citizens and members of the world community at risk. During his tenure, the agency approved over 150,000 applications for new drugs (compared with a mere 1,100 or so approved by the US FDA during the same time period), at least six of which were proven to be fake.[79]

Until the Chinese government establishes a credible track record of producing and exporting more consistently safe products, companies and countries with whom they do business must implement safeguards of their own. The toymaker Mattel, for instance, has established stringent internal procedures to insure the safety of its Chinese-made products, including analyzing and testing both raw materials and finished products alike. After the recent spate of problems with Chinese goods and materials, companies wishing to reap the substantial cost benefits of manufacturing in China must "figure out how to do business [t]here, without risking their reputation, consumer trust, or customer's lives."[80] Nations concerned with public health and the uninterrupted flow of commerce should also redouble their efforts in the face of such acute foreign threats. Yet the US FDA is said to have the ability to inspect only about 1% of all food imports.[81] The US Consumer Products Safety Commission has even less enforcement power. In light of current crises, these agencies are inadequate to their mission of protecting the public, particularly given the rapid expansion of the globalized economy. Consumers who have lost faith in a product or the company that sells it will take their business elsewhere. Citizens who have lost faith in the country's commitment to protecting their health and well-being may become cynical and detached from the democratic process, a condition detrimental to the health of the nation as a whole.

Stem Cells and Cynicism

Concern with public cynicism since the 1960s has focused on pressing policy issues and biotechnology is no exception. The threat of political cynicism looms in any instance in which public expectations fail to be met by government, or are handled in such a way as to leave a substantial portion of the public dissatisfied. Crafting policy solutions can be a messy and complex process, and with the increasing ethical, moral and scientific complexity of some issues on the policy agenda in the early twenty-first century, they become even more so. The potential of biotechnology to offer enhancements as well as cures, as well as its ability to alter nature (both human and natural) renders the responsibility of lawmakers and regulators profoundly important, and particularly difficult. As in the case of existing pharmaceuticals and products, newer technologies will raise concerns for regulators regarding industry influence, consumer demand, the interpretation of scientific data and the impact of globalization. Examining the case of stem cell technology will illustrate and expand upon some of these themes. While various attempts at stem cell policymaking have encountered the type of policy impasse that can create fertile conditions

571

for public cynicism, they have also presented circumstances that offer hope that such cynicism can be offset by healthy skepticism and the spirit of scientific inquiry.

According to Marc J. Hetherington and John D. Nugent, distrustful voters are more likely to favor devolution to the states for decision making on individual policy issues.[82] Where stem cell research is concerned, a smattering of states have been at the forefront of policymaking, perhaps because the federal government has failed to reach a broadly satisfactory policy resolution. President George W. Bush twice vetoed a Stem Cell Research Enhancement Act, initially in 2005, and then again in 2007. This act proposed to loosen the terms of his August 2001 executive order limiting funding of research on stem cell lines to those in existence prior to the date of his declaration. Those lines are considered to be inadequate in number and quality by stem cell researchers. President Bush has said that he made his decision to disallow the use of excess embryos from fertility clinics for stem cell research based on his view that every embryo represents a potential human life. But because he has not addressed the fact that "modern fertility procedures," which he has praised, "create and destroy many embryos for each baby they bring into the world," his position has been viewed as morally inconsistent, and his executive order seen by some as the calculated decision of a political cynic.[83] His suppression of stem cell research satisfies constituents who see it as a pro-life issue, but frustrates proponents who are motivated by the desire to find cures, support scientific endeavors and keep the US competitive both scientifically and economically.

Ironically, excluding stem cell research from federal funding also excludes it from federal oversight, and makes it more likely that decisions regarding the conduct of the research will be made within a corporate, rather than a public, context. In the case of HRT, some took the view that pharmaceutical company profits might be driving research agendas and exerting undue influence in defining the medical and public debates regarding its use. Similar concerns apply in the developing field of stem cell research. The prospect of stem cell therapies has generated much bioethical discussion, but most such discussion has focused on public policy options and overlooked the point that in the face of rapid scientific advancement, legislatures often lag behind laboratories. A public that has yet to reach consensus regarding the proper conduct of stem cell research has by default ceded authority to corporate decision making,[84] whereas public authority in the form of regulation can serve to guide corporate conduct.

Overly high expectations regarding the curative potential of stem cell research on the part of potential patients sets the stage for two distinct forms of cynicism. The first is the possibility of cynically exploiting patients in ill-advised clinical trials that may constitute unethical experimentation rather than innovative treatment.[85] Roop Gurashani, a neurosurgeon writing in the *Indian Journal of Medical Ethics*, recounts the case of a quadriplegic patient who became convinced, based on information gleaned from the Internet, that stem cell transplants could cure him. When confronted with the fact that no reputable hospital or surgeon would offer him such a "treatment," he eventually planned a trip to China, where he would presumably be offered the transplant he sought. HRT patients demonstrated similar reluctance to relinquish the hope that hormones might offer an alternative to aging, despite evidence to the contrary. Their willingness to assume any risk associated with HRT in pursuit of hoped-for benefits parallels that of many patients with a plethora of conditions thought to one day be curable through stem cell therapies. In far more desperate circumstances, these patients are more than willing to offer themselves as fodder for experimentation and assume the substantial risk of accepting "treatment" before scientific consensus has been reached or government guidelines and safeguards have been established for their use. And in many cases patients are willing and able to travel abroad in pursuit of such alternative treatments, since purported stem cell therapies cannot be administered to patients in the US without FDA approval.

While "willy-nilly plugging stem cells into people" before human trials are scientifically justified is ill advised from the point of view of patient health, it is also considered by reputable researchers to be a threat to the emerging stem cell field. David Beck, head of the Coriell Institute for Medical Research in Camden, New Jersey, believes that at this stage of the game, work in animals will offer better data regarding what approaches may ultimately have the greatest therapeutic potential in humans.[86] According to Beck, "it is hype, not science, that is being used to justify human trials, and overly high expectations could breed cynicism that would set the field back."

Charges of cynicism are lobbed from all sides of the stem cell debate by opponents who simply cannot fathom any alternative explanation for opinions or actions diametrically opposed to their own positions on the issue. When scientists use the term "somatic cell nuclear transfer" (SCNT) instead of the more colloquial "therapeutic cloning," a controversial facet of stem cell research, opponents of the research cry "foul." To them such words are "obfuscating" rather than more scientifically accurate, and are cynically employed "to sow confusion in the minds of the American people."[87] Opponents of embryonic stem cell research also hold the cynical view that scientists and the media are suppressing success stories about adult stem cell therapies because they believe that using embryonic stem cells for research would somehow support the abortion industry.[88] In fact, most scientists support the pursuit of both adult and embryonic stem cell research. But there exists wide consensus in the scientific community that the pluripotent nature of embryonic stem cells, which are currently believed to have the potential to develop into any type of body cell, gives them greater therapeutic potential. David T. Scadden, professor of medicine at Harvard Medical School and co-director of the Harvard Stem Cell Institute, has said that it would be "unwise to ignore the potential" of either adult or embryonic stem cells, and that "studying them side by side offers the greatest potential to rapidly generate new therapies."[89]

In some instances the politicization of stem cell research has perhaps deservedly either led to accusations of cynical intent or engendered cynical responses. When Ron Reagan, younger son of the late president, spoke at the Democratic National Convention in July 2004 to tout the benefits of stem cell research, his over-stated endorsement of the science's potential led to charges that his appearance was a "cynical strategy" to garner votes for the Kerry campaign.[90] Worse, he was accused of cynically exploiting his father's name and cruelly raising the hopes of the afflicted by making purely theoretical therapies seem imminent.[91] In another instance, Elizabeth Blackburn remarked, upon her removal from the President's Council on Bioethics, that the "healthy skepticism of scientists has turned to cynicism" and despair that scientific research "was being manipulated for political ends."[92] Blackburn, a molecular biologist, and William May, another dismissed member of the council, were suspected to have been removed because they voted against a ban or moratorium on therapeutic cloning that had been championed by the council's chairman, and Bush appointee, Leon Kass. Blackburn charged that the President's Council on Bioethics, and the administration at large, had created a climate where scientists "must fear that descriptions of their research will be misrepresented and misused by their government to advance political ends" and that advisory bodies were being stacked not with experts per se, but with like-minded thinkers supporting the party line.

Similar to other enterprises in the twenty-first century, science is conducted on a global scale. Political wrangling and uncertainty over the fate of stem cell research in the US made the likelihood of significant breakthroughs in the field coming from abroad much greater. When Hwang Woo Suk of Seoul National University claimed to have cloned human embryos and derived embryonic stem cell lines from them, it certainly appeared to be the case that US researchers had been left on the sidelines of an exciting discovery. But in December 2005 it was revealed that evidence of the groundbreaking accomplishment had actually been fabricated. Scientists such as John Gearhart, a stem cell researcher at Johns Hopkins Medical Institutions, immediately anticipated a swell in political cynicism in response to the news.[93] Laurie Zoloth, director of bioethics at Northwestern University's Center for Genetic Medicine described what happened in South Korea as "a body blow to ethics and a setback to public trust."[94] Hwang Woo Suk, who had achieved rock-star status in his native Korea, resigned from his university post.

Despite fears that the scientific community would be "seriously damaged by phony stem cell claims" the scandal brought to light some reasons why there should be more government funding for such research rather than less.[95] Sean Tipton of the Coalition for the Advancement of Medical Research remarked that "if you don't allow the best American scientists to do the best—and that means research with thorough oversight—research, you force it overseas and into the private sector, and this is the result."[96] Federal funding of the research, Tipton added, would involve the NIH, the "strongest research oversight system in the world." In the new world economy, controversial research is apt to be pursued beyond America's borders if not within them. Ironically, federal government bans can lead to a wild-West atmosphere for such research. Only government funding and its attendant oversight capabilities can insure sufficient regulation to create a climate of public trust.

Science, Skepticism and Reason to Hope

While many scholars despaired that the fraud perpetrated upon the scientific community in the South Korean stem cell case and its aftermath would damage public trust in the institution of science, at least one scientist surmised that any setback would be temporary. Lawrence Goldstein, a professor of cellular and molecular medicine at the University of California in San Diego, pointed out that it would be "hard to perpetuate a lie for very long in the scientific community because mostly we are born skeptics."[97] Any deception, he noted, is "pretty readily identifiable by other scientists looking at the data." If scientific research cannot be replicated, other scientists will look for flaws well before the general public becomes privy to discoveries.

A certain degree of cynicism is perhaps inevitably a part of the political fray. Some have called it "the most powerful force in American politics."[98] Indeed in its most ardent form, cynicism is linked to strong ideological beliefs that characterize much politically charged dialogue in the United States. But in the more mundane process through which policy eventually gets made, milder expressions of cynicism are more likely to come into play. These, according to Evan Berman, are more heavily dependent on facts, and open to the influence of reason. This milder form of cynicism is akin to skepticism, the *modus operandus* of science.

Early efforts at stem cell policy making in the states focused on whether or not to allow therapeutic cloning research, or to ban it along with reproductive cloning, which all states agreed should be prohibited. By the end of 2005, fourteen states had established cloning laws. Research has shown that in states where university scientists stepped forward to participate in educating the public, the language of the policy debate was more rational and neutral. In these states— California, Connecticut, Massachusetts, Missouri, New Jersey and Rhode Island—the policy debate focused on whether supporting therapeutic cloning research would support the state economy and promote the eventual discovery of cures for a variety of diseases. In states where there was no university support for therapeutic cloning research, and where no economic benefit to the state was perceived to be associated with the pursuit of such research—Arizona, Arkansas, Indiana, Iowa, Michigan, North Dakota and South Dakota—the policy debate took on more moralistic tones, and was characterized by ardent cynicism and science fiction inspired alarmism.[99]

States opting to regulate rather than ban so-called cloning research held public hearings and informational meetings, where data and evidence were examined. Skeptical citizens weighing the option of allowing the research were "open to the influence of reason." And in allowing SCNT they established guidelines for its oversight by regulatory and advisory bodies. In banning states, on the other hand, dialogue was limited and more ideologically charged. Opponents distrustful of the motives of scientists and cynical about the ability of government to properly steward and contain the potential of a new scientific discovery dismissed it out of hand.

Although empirical studies rarely make the distinction between cynicism and skepticism, it is a distinction worth noting. Seen as two ends of the same spectrum, the former stance may well be a detriment to democracy, while the latter may serve it quite well. By employing rational inquiry, checking facts and requiring adherence to established standards, both government and scientific institutions can successfully nurture public trust, and succeed in winning over what might otherwise become an increasingly cynical public.

Notes

1 Seymour Martin Lipset, *American Exceptionalism* (New York: W.W. Norton and Company, 1965), 21.

2 Arthur H. Miller, "Political Issues and Trust in Government: 1964–1970," *The American Political Science Review* 68 (3) (September 1974): 951–72.

3 Ibid.

4 Virginia A. Chanley, Thomas J. Rudolph and Wendy M. Rahn, "The Origins and Consequences of Public Trust in Government: A Time Series Analysis," *Public Opinion Quarterly* 64 (3) (Fall 2000): 239.

5 Pippa Norris, *A Virtuous Circle: Political Communications in Post-Industrial Societies* (New York: Cambridge University Press, 2000), ch. 11: "Cares Less? Cynical Media, Cynical Public?"

6 Timothy E. Cook and Paul Gronke, "The Skeptical American: Revisiting the Meanings of Trust in Government and Confidence in Institutions" *The Journal of Politics* 67 (3) (August 2005): 784.

7 David S. Broder, "War on Cynicism; Politicians and the Media Badly Need a Dialogue about the Deterioration of Public Discourse," *Washington Post*, July 6, 1994, A19.

8 Allan Mazur, "Commentary: Opinion Poll Measurement of American Confidence in Science," *Science, Technology & Human Values* 6 (36) (Summer 1981): 17.

9 Ibid., 17–18.

10 Lipset, *American Exceptionalism*, 51–2.

11 National Science Foundation, *Science and Engineering Indicators 2006*, http://www.nsf.gov/statistics/seind06/front/about.htm.

12 Ibid.

13 Ibid.

14 Todd R. LaPorte and Daniel Metlay, "Technology Observed: Attitudes of a Wary Public," *Science* 188 (11) (April 1975): 121.

15 Anna Wagstaff, "Can Science Win Back Public Trust?" *Cancer World* (January/February 2006): 32–6.

16 Ibid., 32.

17 *The Merriam-Webster Dictionary* (Springfield, MA: Merriam-Webster, Inc., 2004), 178.

18 James W. Dean, Pamela Brandes and Ravi Dharwadkar, "Organizational Cynicism," *Academy of Management Review* 23 (1998): 342.

19 Ibid.

20 Ibid.

21 Evan Berman, "Dealing with Cynical Citizens," *Public Administration Review* 57 (2) (March/April 1997): 105.

22 Seymour Martin Lipset and William Schneider, "The Confidence Gap During the Reagan Years, 1981–1987," *Political Science Quarterly* 102 (Spring 1987): 22, cited in Joseph A. Cappella and Kathleen Hall Jamieson, "New Frames, Political Cynicism, and Media Cynicism," *Annals of the American Academy of Political and Social Science* 546 (July 1996): 73.

23 Robert E. Lane, *Political Ideology: Why the Common Man Believes What He Does* (New York: The Free Press, 1962), cited in Marc J. Hetherington, "The Political Relevance of Political Trust," *American Political Science Review* 92 (4) (December 1998): 791.

24 Bill Schneider, "Cynicism Didn't Start With Watergate," *All Politics*, June 17, 1997, http://www.cnn.com/ALLPOLITICS/1997/gen/resources/watergate/trust.schneider/.

25 Hetherington, "The Political Relevance of Political Trust," 791.

26 Al Gore, "Remarks as Delivered by Vice President Al Gore, Harvard Commencement Day, Harvard University," June 9, 1994, http://clinton3.nara.gov/WH/EOP/OVP/speeches/harvard.html.

27 Ibid.

28 Schneider, "Cynicism Didn't Start With Watergate."

29 John McCain, "Commencement Address to the Johns Hopkins University Class of 1999," May 27, 1999, http://www.jhu/news/commence99/mccainsp.html.

30 Ibid.

31 Hetherington, "The Political Relevance of Political Trust," 791.
32 Jack Citrin, "Comment: The Political Relevance of Trust in Government," *The American Political Science Review* 68 (3) (September 1974): 973–88.
33 Ibid.
34 Miller, "Political Issues and Trust in Government," 952.
35 Gore, "Remarks as Delivered by Vice President Al Gore," and Ray Sheehan, "Ethical Perspectives," *Office of Ethics Newsletter*, U.S. Department of Agriculture, 4 (July 2003): 1–2.
36 Cook and Gronke, "The Skeptical American," 785.
37 Berman, "Dealing with Cynical Citizens," 106.
38 "What is a Skeptic?" *Skeptic* 13 (1) (Spring 2006): 5.
39 Ibid.
40 Ibid., and Cook and Gronke, "The Skeptical American," 800.
41 Dot Wordsworth, "Mind Your Language (Use of the Word Cynical)," *Spectator*, September 15, 2001, 26.
42 Wesley J. Smith, "Misguidelines: The National Academy of Sciences is Pursuing an 'Anything Goes' Approach to Biotechnological Research," *The Weekly Standard*, May 4, 2005, http://www.discovery.org/scripts/viewDB/index.php?command=view&id=2549.
43 Miller, "Political Issues and Trust in Government," 970.
44 Tom Abate, "Biotech Pushing the Possibilities Past the Breaking Point: Society Will Soon Need to Decide When to Stop," *San Francisco Chronicle*, February 5, 2001, B1.
45 Ibid.
46 David Barbosa and Alexei Barrionuevo, "Filler in Animal Feed is Open Secret in China," *New York Times*, April 30, 2007.
47 Boston Women's Health Book Collective, *Our Bodies, Ourselves: Menopause* (New York: Simon & Schuster, 2006), 100.
48 Gina Kolata, "Reversing Trend, Big Drop is Seen in Breast Cancer," *New York Times*, December 16, 2006.
49 "Hot Flash: No Relief in Sight," *USA Today*, December 20, 2006, 19A.
50 Nancy Worcester, "Hormone Replacement Therapy (HRT): Getting to the Heart of the Politics of Women's Health?" *NWSA Journal* 16 (3) (Fall 2004): 56.
51 Ibid.
52 Ibid.
53 Marilynn Marchione, "Dramatic Decline in Breast Cancer," *StarTribune.com*, December 14, 2006, http://www.startribune.com/1244/story/875958.html.
54 Gina Kolata, "Sharp Drop in Rates of Breast Cancer Holds," *New York Times*, April 19, 2007.
55 Gina Kolata, "Reversing Trend, Big Drop is Seen in Breast Cancer."
56 Ibid.
57 Susan Love, "Breaking Down Breast Cancer Findings," video of ABC News appearance, December 16, 2006, http://abcnews.go.com/GMA/OnCall/story?id=2731775.
58 Worcester, "Hormone Replacement Therapy (HRT)," 56.
59 Berman, "Dealing with Cynical Citizens," 106.
60 Miller, "Political Issues and Trust in Government," 956.
61 Boston Women's Health Book Collective, *Our Bodies, Ourselves: Menopause*, 105.
62 "Bombshell: Major Premarin Trial Halted," available from the website of Dr. Joseph Mercola, http://www.mercola.com/display/router.aspx?docid=26533.
63 Sarah Boseley, "The Truth about HRT," *Guardian*, June 6, 2007, http://www.guardian.co.uk/print/0,,329981614-103691,00.html.
64 Ibid.
65 Fran Visco, "Decrease in Breast Cancer," letter to the editor, *New York Times*, December 26, 2006.
66 Gina Kolata, "Many Taking Hormone Pills Now Face a Difficult Choice," *New York Times*, July 15, 2002.
67 David Barbosa and Alexei Barrionuevo, "Filler in Animal Feed is Open Secret in China," *New York Times*, April 30, 2007.
68 Andrew Bridges, "Pet Food Recall Expanded; Industrial Chemical Found in Second Ingredient," *Associated Press Online*, April 19, 2007, http://mutex.gmu.edu:2083/universe/printdoc.
69 Kristina Dell, "Unraveling the Pet-Food Mystery," *Time*, April 5, 2007, http://www.time.com/time/nation/article/0,8599.160743,00.html.
70 Ibid.
71 Ibid.
72 Bridges, "Pet Food Recall Expanded."
73 Walt Bogdanich, "Wider Sale Is Seen for Toothpaste Tainted in China," *New York Times*, June 28, 2007.

74 Ibid.

75 Walt Bogdanich, "FDA Tracked Poisoned Drugs, but Trail Went Cold in China," *New York Times*, June 28, 2007.

76 "China Bans Melamine, Rejects Pet Food Link," *CBS News*, April 26, 2007, http://www.cbsnews.com/stories/2007/04/26/health.

77 "China's Food Safety," *The Economist*, June 12, 2007, http://www.economist.com/agenda/displaystory.cfm?story_id=9325404.

78 David Barboza and Walt Bogdanich, "China Shuts 3 Companies Over Safety of Products," *New York Times*, July 21, 2007.

79 David Barboza, "A Chinese Reformer Betrays His Cause and Pays," *New York Times*, July 13, 2007.

80 David Barboza and Louise Story, "Toymaking in China, Mattel's Way," *New York Times*, July 26, 2007.

81 "China Bans Melamine, Rejects Pet Food Link," *CBS News*, April 26, 2007.

82 Marc J. Hetherington and John D. Nugent, "Explaining Public Support for Devolution: The Role of Political Trust," in *What is it About Government that Americans Dislike?*, ed. John R. Hibbing and Elizabeth Theiss-Morse (Cambridge: Cambridge University Press, 2001), 134–51, cited in Chanley, Rudolph and Rahn, "The Origins and Consequences of Public Trust in Government," 239.

83 Michael Kinsley, "Taking Bush Personally," *Slate*, October 23, 2003, http://www.slate.com/id/2090244.

84 Chris MacDonald, "Stem Cell Ethics and the Forgotten Corporate Context," *American Journal of Bioethics* (Winter 2002): 54.

85 Roop Gurashani, "Therapeutic Innovation or Cynical Exploitation?" *Indian Journal of Medical Ethics* 4 (October–December 2006), http://www.ijme.in/144cs133.html.

86 Monya Baker, "Stem Cell Therapy or Snake Oil?" *Nature Biotechnology* 23 (12) (December 2005): 1467.

87 Wesley J. Smith, "None Dare Call It Cloning," *Center for Bioethics and Culture Newsletter*, August 13, 2004, http://www.discovery.org/scripts/viewDB/index.php?command=view&id=2158.

88 S.T. Karnick, "Cures That Don't Kill," *The American Spectator*, December 2, 2004, http://www.spectator.org/util/print.asp?art_id=7457.

89 David T. Scadden, "Current Human Clinical Applications Using Adult Stem Cells." *International Society for Stem Cell Research* website, August 14, 2006, http://www.isscr.org/public/curent_sc.htm.

90 Steven Milloy, "Ron Reagan Wrong on Stem Cells," *FOXNews.com*, July 16, 2004, http://www.foxnews.com/printer_friendly_story/0,3566,125873,00.html.

91 Michael Fumento, "Cynical and Cruel; Ron Reagan's DNC speech Was Exploitation—of His Father and of Science," *National Review Online*, July 29, 2004, http://www.nationalreview.com/comment/fumento200407291243.asp.

92 Elizabeth Blackburn, "Bioethics and the Political Distortion of Biomedical Science," *The New England Journal of Medicine* 350 (April 1, 2004): 1379–80.

93 Rick Weiss, "Stem Cell Field Rocked by Scam of Star Scientist; Scandal in South Korea Could Jeopardize U.S. Research Projects," *San Francisco Chronicle*, December 24, 2005, A1.

94 Edward W. Lempinen, "Stem Cell Experts Assess the Impact of Hwang Fraud on Research, Public Trust," News Archives, American Association for the Advancement of Science, 18 February, 2006, http://www.aaas.org/news/releases/2006/0218stemcell.shtml.

95 "Scientific Community Seriously Damaged by Phony Stem Cell Claims," *Culture and Cosmos* 3 (22) (January 4, 2006), http://www.culture-of-life.org/?Control=ArticleMaster&aid=1158.

96 Weiss, "Stem Cell Field Rocked by Scam of Star Scientist."

97 Edward W. Lempinen, "Stem Cell Experts Assess the Impact of Hwang Fraud on Research, Public Trust."

98 Bill Schneider, "Cynicism Didn't Start With Watergate."

99 Bonnie Stabile, "Balancing Morality and Economy: The Case of State Human Cloning Policies," unpublished doctoral dissertation, George Mason University, May 2006.

About the Editor and Contributors

Editor

Dennis W. Johnson is professor of political management at the George Washington University, Washington, D.C. He is author of a number of works on government, politics, campaigns, and public policy, including *No Place for Amateurs: How Political Consultants are Reshaping American Democracy*, 2nd edn (2007), *Congress Online: Bridging the Gap between Citizens and their Legislators* (2004), and *Laws that Shaped America* (forthcoming). He is editor of *2008 Presidential Election: Strategy, Tactics, New voices, New Techniques* (forthcoming) and author of *Campaigning in the Twenty-first Century: A Whole New Ballgame* (with Gary Nordlinger, forthcoming). His current research interests include political consulting, new media and online communications policy, and the history of public policy.

Contributors

Marco Althaus is visiting professor of social sciences at Wildau University of Applied Sciences near Berlin, Germany. He has been academic director of the German Institute for Public Affairs (DIPA) in Berlin since 2004, where he coordinates executive education for corporate and association managers. He has published numerous books and articles on campaigns and public affairs management. Previously he was director of communications for the Social Democratic Party's media holding company in Berlin. He is an alumnus of George Washington University's Graduate School of Political Management.

Kathleen Barr has served as the communications and research director for Young Voter Strategies, a non-partisan, non-profit organization based at the George Washington University's Graduate School of Political Management, where she coordinated media outreach for a nationwide program that registered more than 500,000 eighteen- to thirty-year-old voters and helped increase young voter turnout in 2006. Currently, she is the director of political outreach at Rock the Vote, a non-partisan organization dedicated to building the political power of the Millennial Generation.

Steven E. Billet is the director of the Masters in Legislative Affairs and the Graduate Certificate program in PAC management at the George Washington University's Graduate School of

Political Management. His current research and teaching interests include campaign finance, PAC management, international lobbying, and lobbying in the European Union. For twenty years prior to joining the George Washington University, he worked as an advocate for AT&T, managing its political action committee, and establishing and managing its public affairs office for Europe, Africa, and the Middle East.

Maik Bohne is a PhD candidate in political science at the University of Göttingen, Germany. He was a research fellow at the Center for Congressional and the Presidential Studies at American University, Washington, D.C., from February to September 2007. His doctoral dissertation focuses on the structure, shape, and activities of party networks (party organizations, political consultants, party-connected interest groups) in the 2006 US congressional elections.

Colton C. Campbell is associate professor in the Department of Strategy and Policy at the National War College, Washington, D.C. He has published several books on Congress and American politics and has served in the House of Representatives as a congressional aide, an analyst in American national government at the Congressional Research Service, an associate professor of political science at Florida International University, and as an American Political Science Association Congressional Fellow. His current interests include Congress, campaigns and elections, and civil–military relations.

Stephen C. Craig is professor and chair of the Political Science Department at the University of Florida, as well as director of the university's Graduate Program in Political Campaigning. He is author of *The Malevolent Leaders: Popular Discontent in America* (1993), editor of *Broken Contract? Changing Relationships between Citizens and Their Government in the United States* (1996), and *The Electoral Challenge: Theory Meets Practice* (2006), and co-editor of several other books dealing with aspects of contemporary public opinion and political behavior in the United States. He also has published numerous articles in the *American Political Science Review, American Journal of Political Science, Journal of Politics, Public Opinion Quarterly*, and other professional journals.

Wojciech Cwalina is professor in the Department of Marketing Psychology at the Warsaw School of Social Psychology in Poland. He is guest author (with Andrzej Falkowski) of *Television Political Advertising and Political Marketing* (2000), and numerous articles and book chapters and is member of editorial board of the *Journal of Political Marketing*. He was awarded the Domestic Grant for Young Beneficiaries by the Foundation for Polish Science. His research specialties include political marketing psychology and analysis of media coverage and he is marketing specialist and media advisor in Polish political campaigns.

David A. Dulio is associate professor of political science at Oakland University, Rochester, Michigan. He is the author or editor of five books on campaigns and elections, including *Vital Signs: Perspectives on the Health of American Campaigning* (with Candice J. Nelson, 2005), *The Mechanics of State Legislative Campaigns* (with John S. Klemanski, 2006), and *For Better or Worse? How Political Consultants are Changing Elections in the United States* (2004). He also served as an American Political Science Association Congressional Fellow in the office of former US Representative J. C. Watts, Jr (Republican-Oklahoma).

Andrzej Falkowski is a professor of psychology and marketing, and head of the Department of Marketing Psychology at the Warsaw School of Social Psychology in Poland. His research specialty is cognitive psychology, including consumer behavior, marketing, and political advertising. He has been a Fulbright Scholar at the University of Michigan. His publications include *Television and Politics in Evolving European Democracies* (with Wojciech Cwalina) and

A Cross-cultural Theory of Voter Behavior (with Cwalina and Bruce I. Newman, 2007). He is advisory editor of the *Handbook of Political Marketing*, and editorial board member of the *Journal of Political Marketing*.

Ronald A. Faucheux has taught courses in campaign management and strategy, running for office, and the history of US presidential elections at the Graduate School of Political Management at the George Washington University since 1993. Elected three times to the Louisiana House of Representatives as one of its youngest members, he has advised 116 candidate and issue campaigns as a political consultant. Formerly the editor and publisher of *Campaigns & Elections* magazine, he also served as a US Senate chief of staff. He is the author or editor of numerous books on politics, including *Running for Office* (2002), *Winning Elections* (2003), *Campaign Battle Lines* (with P.S. Herrnson, 2002) and *The Debate Book* (2003).

Peter Fenn is the head of Fenn Communications Group, a leading media organization that has worked on campaigns from president to mayor, as well as representing *Fortune 500* companies, trade associations, and advocacy groups. Prior to forming Fenn Communications, he served on the staff of the Senate Intelligence Committee, was a top aide to Senator Frank Church (Democrat-Idaho), and was the first executive director of Democrats for the 80s, a political action committee founded by Pamela Harriman. He is also an adjunct professor at the Graduate School of Political Management of the George Washington University.

Brad Fitch is the chief executive officer and co-founder of Knowlegis, a government relations data and online tools company. He is the author of *Media Relations Handbook for Agencies, Associations, Nonprofits, and Congress* (2004), editor of *Setting Course: A Congressional Management Guide* (2002, 2004), co-author of "Communicating with Congress: How Capitol Hill is Coping with the Surge in Citizen Advocacy" (2005), and author of *Citizen's Handbook for Influencing Elected Officials* (forthcoming). He is an adjunct associate professor of communications at American University and worked on Capitol Hill for thirteen years.

Julie Barko Germany is director of the Institute for Politics, Democracy & the Internet (IPDI) at the George Washington University. She is the principal author and editor of several IPDI publications, including *The Politics-to-Go-Handbook: A Guide to Using Mobile Technology in Politics* (2006), *Constituent Relationship Management: The New Little Black Book of Politics* (2006), and *Person-to-Person-to-Person: Harnessing the Political Power of Online Social Networks and User-Generated Content* (2005).

Anthony Gierzynski is an associate professor of political science at the University of Vermont. His research focuses on elections, parties, campaign finance, and the media. He is author of *Money Rules: Financing Elections in America* (2000) and *Legislative Party Campaign Committees in the American States* (1992) as well as a number of journal articles and book chapters. He is currently working on a book on electoral reform.

Edward A. Grefe is credited by the Public Affairs Council as the "inventor of corporate grassroots." In his forty-year career he has been involved in over 200 political campaigns. He has been teaching grassroots and issue advocacy at the George Washington University's Graduate School of Political Management since 1995. He has written *Fighting to Win: Business Political Power* (1981) and *The New Corporate Activism* (with Martin Linsky, 1995) and numerous articles and chapters in his subject areas. He has been a lecturer and political consultant in numerous countries including Australia, Canada, Mexico, Venezuela, the Netherlands, France, Indonesia, Austria, Germany, Costa Rica, and Ecuador.

Michael G. Hagen is associate professor of political science and director of the Institute for Public Affairs at Temple University. His current research focuses on the conduct and consequences of campaigns and elections in the United States. He is co-author of *The 2000 Presidential Election and the Foundations of Party Politics* (with Richard Johnston and Kathleen Hall Jamieson, 2004) and *Race and Inequality: A Study in American Values* (with Paul M. Sniderman, 1985). He has previously been on the faculties of Rutgers University, the University of Pennsylvania, and Harvard University.

Irene Harris works on a number of accreditation and research projects at the University of Otago, Dunedin, New Zealand. Her teaching and research interests include management development, management learning, academic staff development, and government interventions in training, education, and development. Before becoming an academic she was a senior civil servant with the Department of Employment in the UK. She holds a Business Studies degree, a Master's in Management Learning, and a Postgraduate Diploma in Education. She is a member of the Chartered Institute of Personnel and Development (UK) and a Fellow of the Higher Education Academy (UK).

Phil Harris is professor of marketing at the University of Otago, Dunedin, New Zealand and international research director of the European Centre for Public Affairs. He is joint founding editor of the *Journal of Public Affairs* and has published extensively over 150 publications in the area of communications, lobbying, political marketing, public affairs, relationship marketing, and international trade. His latest book is *The Handbook of Public Affairs* (with Craig Fleisher, 2005), *European Business and Marketing* (with Frank Macdonald, 2004), and *Machiavelli, Marketing and Management* (2000). He is the author of the forthcoming *Dictionary of Marketing* and editor-in-chief of the advanced marketing series by Sage Publications.

Stephan C. Henneberg is senior lecturer in marketing at the University of Manchester Business School, United Kingdom. His current research interests are in the areas of strategic marketing, relational marketing, consumer behavior, and social and political marketing. He publishes regularly on political marketing and has organized several international academic conferences. He is co-editor of *The Idea of Political Marketing* (with Nicholas O'Shaughnessy, 2002).

Paul S. Herrnson is founding director of the Center for American Politics and Citizenship and a professor in the Department of Government and Politics at the University of Maryland. He has published several books, including *Congressional Elections: Campaigning at Home and in Washington* (5th edn, 2007), *The Financiers of Congressional Elections* (with P.L. Francia, J.C. Green, and L.W. Powell, 2003), *War Stories from Capitol Hill* (with C.C. Campbell, 2003), and *Voting Technology: The Not-so-Simple Act of Casting a Ballot* (with R.G. Niemi, M.J. Hanmer, and B.B. Bederson, 2008). He has served as an American Political Science Association Congressional Fellow, and he has received several teaching awards, including a Distinguished-Scholar Teacher Award from the University of Maryland.

Julius W. Hobson, Jr is senior policy advisor at Powell Goldstein, LLP, Washington, D.C., where he lobbies on a range of issues including health care, banking and securities, appropriations, budget, and taxes. He previously managed congressional affairs for the American Medical Association, the District of Columbia government, and Howard University. He has served as a staffer in both the US House of Representatives and the US Senate, and was an elected school board member in the District of Columbia. He teaches courses on lobbying at the Graduate School of Political Management, George Washington University.

Derek S. Hutcheson is a lecturer in comparative politics and head of subject in European Studies at University College Dublin, Ireland. His research interests include comparative electoral politics, including political campaigning; political transition in post-communist states; the quality of democracy; and political participation. He is the author of *Political Parties in the Russian Regions* (2003) and co-editor of *The Quality of Democracy in Post-Communist Europe* (2006).

Emilienne Ireland is the president of CampaignAdvantage.com, a firm that provides strategic websites, fundraising, and online communications services for candidates and causes. Her publications include *Winning Campaigns Online* (2001), and contributions to *Online Fundraising Primer* (2004) and *Politics-To-Go* (2005). She was named a "Rising Star of American Politics" in 2002 by *Campaigns & Elections*, and her firm has won numerous Pollie and other top industry awards, including the 2007 Golden Dot for Best Local Campaign Website nationwide.

Lynda Lee Kaid is professor of telecommunication at the University of Florida. Her research specialties include political advertising and news coverage of political events. A Fulbright Scholar, she has also done work on political television in international contexts. She is the author/editor of more than twenty-five books, including *The Encyclopedia of Political Communication* (2008), *The Handbook of Political Communication Research* (2004), *The Sage Handbook of Political Advertising* (with Christina Holtz-Bacha, 2006), and *Videostyle in Presidential Campaigns* (with Anne Johnston, 2001).

Robin Kolodny is associate professor of political science at Temple University. Her current research is on the role political consultants play in party politics. She is the author of *Pursuing Majorities: Congressional Campaign Committees in American Politics* (1998) as well as articles and book chapters on political parties in Congress, in elections, and in comparative perspective. She has served as an American Political Science Association Congressional Fellow in 1995 and is a member of the Academic Advisory Board of the Campaign Finance Institute in Washington, D.C.

Douglas A. Lathrop is director of tax policy in the government affairs department of EDS, a global *Fortune 100* information technology company. In that capacity he is responsible for representing EDS tax policy interests before the US Congress and federal agencies. Prior to joining EDS, he spent six years working on Capitol Hill for two senior members of the House Ways and Means Committee. He is author of *The Campaign Continues: How Political Consultants and Campaign Tactics Affect Public Policy* (2003) and is on the legislative affairs adjunct faculty of George Washington University.

Jennifer Lees-Marshment is senior lecturer at the University of Auckland, New Zealand. Her previous work focused on UK politics and broadening the concept of political marketing from selling to the design of political products. She is author of *Political Marketing and British Political Parties* (2nd edn, 2008) and *The Political Marketing Revolution* (2004). She co-edited *Political Marketing in Comparative Perspective* (with D.G. Lilleker, 2005) and is presently working on a second comparative collection, an introductory political marketing book.

Günther Lengauer is the head of the Research Department of MediaWatch, Institute for Media Analysis, in Innsbruck, Austria. He is a research fellow at the Political Science Department, University of Innsbruck, where he received his doctorate and was a Fulbright Fellow at the University of Illinois at Chicago and earned a Master's degree in Communication.

Conor McGrath is an independent scholar and deputy editor of the *Journal of Public Affairs*, and was lecturer in political lobbying and public affairs at the University of Ulster in Northern

Ireland from 1999 to 2006. His recent publications include *Lobbying in Washington, London and Brussels* (2005). He is editing a three-volume collection on *Interest Groups and Lobbying* (forthcoming). His current areas of research include legislators with prior lobbying experience, lobbying and political marketing, and public perceptions of lobbying.

Stephen K. Medvic is associate professor of government at Franklin & Marshall College, Lancaster, Pennsylvania. His research and teaching interests include campaigns and elections, political parties, the media and politics, and public opinion. In addition to numerous academic articles and book chapters, he is the author of *Political Consultants in US Congressional Elections* (2001), co-editor of *Shades of Gray: Perspectives on Campaign Ethics* (2002), and an associate editor of the *Guide to Political Campaigns in America* (2005).

Candice J. Nelson is associate professor and chair of the Department of Government at American University. She is the co-author of *Vital Signs: Perspectives on the Health of American Campaigning* (with David A. Dulio, 2005), *The Myth of the Independent Voter* (with B.E. Keith, D.B. Magleby, E. Orr, M. C. Westlye, and R. E. Wolfinger (1992), and *The Money Chase: Congressional Campaign Finance Reform* (with David B. Magleby, 1990), and co-editor of *Campaigns and Elections American Style* (with James A. Thurber, 1995), *Shades of Gray: Perspectives on Campaign Ethics* (with David A. Dulio and Stephen K. Medvic, 2002), *Campaign Warriors: Political Consultants in Election* (with James A. Thurber, 2000), and *Crowded Airwaves: Campaign Advertising in Elections* (with James A. Thurber and David A. Dulio, 2000).

Bruce I. Newman is professor of marketing at DePaul University, Chicago, and editor-in-chief of the *Journal of Political Marketing*. He was a William Evans Visiting Fellow at the University of Otago, New Zealand, in 2006, and a visiting scholar at the Institute of Government at the University of California Berkeley and the Department of Political Science at Stanford University. He is the author of *The Marketing of the President* (1994) and several other books, as well as articles that have appeared in both scholarly journals and the popular press. He lectures around the world on the subject of political marketing and has served as an advisor to the Clinton White House on communication strategy from 1995–1996.

Justin Oberman consults in the new media space. He is the founder of Digitisms and the founder and editor of the popular mobile technology weblog MOpocket.com. He has a BA from Brandeis University, a Master's degree in Philosophy from the Graduate Faculty at the New School, and two or three start-up ideas written on napkins in his back pocket.

Nicholas J. O'Shaughnessy is professor of marketing and communication at Queen Mary, University of London and is Quondam Fellow of Hughes Hall, Cambridge University. Previously he was director of the Centre for Research in Consumer and Social Marketing at Brunel University Business School, and he is the author of a number of books and journal articles on marketing and political marketing. His most recent book is *Politics and Propaganda: Weapons of Mass Seduction* (2006).

Louis Perron combines research and practice in the field of political campaigns. As a political consultant, his company Perron Campaigns has worked for more than twenty-five campaigns in various countries at the local and national level. As part of his research work, he earned a Master's degree at the Graduate School of Political Management, the George Washington University. In addition, he conducted a research project at the University of Zurich, Switzerland, comparing election campaigns in Europe, Asia, Latin America, and the United States.

Fritz Plasser is professor of political science and dean of the Faculty of Political Science and Sociology at the University of Innsbruck in Austria. In recent years he was Fahrenkopf-Mannatt

Visiting Professor at the Graduate School of Political Management at the George Washington University and Shorenstein Fellow at the John F. Kennedy School of Government at Harvard University. He has been author, co-author, or editor of thirty-four books and has published widely on campaigns, elections, and political consultancy from a comparative perspective. His book *Global Political Campaigning* (2002, with Gunda Plasser) has been translated into four languages.

Alicia Kolar Prevost is a PhD candidate in political science at American University, Washington, D.C., and a research fellow at the Center for Congressional and Presidential Studies. Her current research interests include electoral reforms, voting behavior, and the presidential nominating system. She is a Truman Scholar and holds a BA from the University of Michigan and MPP from Harvard University.

Eduardo Robledo Rincón is a prominent Mexican politician and political consultant. He is the founder and chief executive officer of Re: Gerencia del Poder, a political consulting firm specializing in political strategies, corporate public relations, and public politics. He has been a legislator and governor of Chiapas, and was ambassador of Mexico to Argentina and secretary of state in agrarian reform during the administration of Ernesto Zedillo. He has published several books and is a regular collaborator in *Reforma* and other important newspapers.

Mark J. Rozell is professor of public policy at George Mason University, Fairfax, Virginia. He is the author of numerous studies on the intersection of religion and politics. His latest books are *Religion and the Presidency* and *Religion and the Bush Presidency* (both co-edited with Gleaves Whitney, 2007). He has lectured extensively in the United States and abroad on religion and politics and on the American political system more generally.

Christian Schafferer is associate professor of international trade at the Overseas Chinese Institute of Technology and has recently been a visiting professor at the Department of Political Science, Meiji University, Japan. His research interests embrace East Asian politics and the globalization of political marketing. During the last ten years, he has personally interviewed over three hundred campaign specialists in Taiwan, Japan, South Korea, and Thailand. He has authored numerous articles and books. His latest books and edited volumes include *The Power of the Ballot Box: Political Development and Election Campaigning in Taiwan* (2003), *Understanding Modern East Asian Politics* (2005), and *Electoral Campaigning in East and Southeast Asia* (2006).

Dahlia Scheindlin is a public opinion researcher and international political consultant who has advised political campaigns in ten different countries. She has conducted research and strategic consulting for three national election Labor campaigns in Israel for prime ministerial candidates and has conducted extensive public opinion research on Israeli attitudes for non-governmental projects related mainly to politics, the conflict, and internal social issues. She has worked on national campaigns extensively in Eastern Europe and the Balkans in newly democratizing countries and has also conducted research on EU accession and other public affairs projects. She is also currently a doctoral student in political science at Tel Aviv University.

Bonnie Stabile is an adjunct professor in the School of Public Policy and the Department of Public and International Affairs at George Mason University, Fairfax, Virginia. Her research on human cloning policies has been published in the *Social Science Quarterly* and *Politics and the Life Sciences*. Her work has been presented at numerous conferences, including those sponsored by the Alden March Bioethics Institute of Albany Medical College, the Science and Democracy

585

Network of Harvard's Kennedy School of Government, and the Cambridge-MIT Institute in Cambridge, UK.

James A. Thurber is distinguished professor of government and director of the Center for Congressional and Presidential Studies at American University, Washington, D.C. He was the principal investigator of a seven-year grant from the Pew Charitable Trusts to the Campaign Management Institute to study campaign conduct. He is author and co-author of numerous books and more than seventy-five articles and chapters on Congress, congressional–presidential relations, congressional budgeting, congressional reform, interest groups and lobbying, and campaigns and elections.

Susan J. Tolchin is university professor in the School of Public Policy at George Mason University, Fairfax, Virginia. She has written *The Angry American: How Voter Rage is Changing the Nation*, 2nd ed., 1998). With Martin Tolchin, she has co-authored seven books, most recently *A World Ignited: How Apostles of Ethnic, Religious and Racial Hatred Torch the Globe* (2006). She served on the board of the National Academy of Public Administration. In 1997, she received the Marshall Dimock Award from the American Society for Public Administration and in 1998, the Trachtenberg Award for Research from the George Washington University.

Terri L. Towner is an assistant professor of political science at Oakland University, Rochester, Michigan. She specializes in American political behavior and public opinion. Towner's recent publications focus on media coverage of elections and political institutions, and the politics of race, class, and culture.

Brian C. Tringali is a partner in the Tarrance Group, one of the most respected and successful Republican survey research and strategy teams in America and is an adjunct professor at Graduate School of Political Management, George Washington University. During the historic 1994 elections when Republicans took over Congress for the first time in forty years, he was the pollster for the Republican *Contract with America*. His clients include Republican governors, senators and members of Congress, as well as some of the largest corporations in the world.

Peter N. Ubertaccio is director of the Joseph W. Martin Institute for Law and Society and associate professor of political science at Stonehill College in Easton, Massachusetts. His specialties are the American Presidency, American political history, politics and law, and political parties. A recent article, "Wilson's Failure: Roots of Contention about the Meaning of a Science of Politics," (with Brian Cook) was published in the *American Political Science Review* in November 2006. His recent interests in political marketing and party organizations have led to a study of the Republican Party's network marketing activities since the 2000 election. He is working on a book on political parties and network marketing tactics.

Israel Waismel-Manor is an assistant professor at the School of Political Sciences at the University of Haifa. He has published in journals such as *PS* and the *Journal of Communication*. His current work on American political behavior won awards from the Russell Sage Foundation, the Commission for the Voting Rights Research Initiative at the University of California-Berkeley, and from TESS: Time-Sharing Experiments in the Social Sciences.

Ian Ward is a reader in politics at the University of Queensland, Brisbane, Australia. His research and teaching interests are in Australian politics and political communication. His recent publications include essays on Australian political parties and cartel party theory, lobbying as political communication, and on the absence of a thriving blogosphere in Australia. He has written extensively on the subject of Australian elections.

Dominic Wring is senior lecturer in communication and media studies at Loughborough University in the UK. He is author of *The Politics of Marketing the Labour Party* (2005) and co-editor of *Political Communications: the British General Election Campaign of 2005* (2007). Currently he chairs the International Political Science Association's Research Committee for Political Communication and is associate editor for Europe of the *Journal of Political Marketing*.

References

Aarts, Kees, Andre Blais, and Herman Schmitt, eds. *Political Leaders and Democratic Elections.* Oxford: Oxford University Press, forthcoming.

Abinales, Patricio N. "Filipino Communism and the Spectre of the Communist Manifesto." *Kasarinlan Philippine Quarterly of Third World Studies* 15 (1) (2000): 147–74.

——. *Love, Sex, and the Filipino Communist, or, Hinggil sa Pagpipigil ng Panggigigil.* Manila: Anvil Publications, 2004.

——. *The Revolution Falters: The Left in Philippine Politics After 1986.* Ithaca, N.Y.: Cornell University Press, 1996.

Agranoff, Robert. *The Management of Election Campaigns.* Boston, MA: Holbrook, 1976.

——. *The New Style in Election Campaigns.* Boston, MA: Holbrook Press, 1972.

Ageeva, A. et al. *Vybory v organy gosudarstvennoi vlasti sub'ektov Rossiiskoi Federatsii, 1997–2000: elektoralnaya statistika v 2 tomakh.* Moscow: CEC/Ves' Mir, 2001.

Ailes, Roger and Jon Kraushar. *You Are the Message.* New York: Bantam Doubleday, 1995.

Ai, Lin-ta. *Jidang! Taiwan fandui yundong zongpipan [Muckraker! An Overall Critique of the Opposition Movement in Taiwan].* Taipei: Chianwei, 1997.

Aldrich, John H. *Why Parties? The Origin and Transformation of Political Parties in America.* Chicago, IL: University of Chicago Press, 1995.

Alinsky, Saul D. *Reveille for Radicals.* New York: Vintage, 1989.

——. *Rules for Radicals.* New York: Vintage, 1989.

Althaus, Marco. "Mittelstandskoalitionen gegen EU-Softwarepatente." In *Kampagne! 3 Neue Strategien im Grassroots Lobbying für Unternehmen und Verbände,* edited by Marco Althaus, 230–78. Münster and Berlin: Lit.

Althaus, Scott L. "Information Effects in Collective Preferences." *American Political Science Review* 92 (September 1998): 545–58.

Alvarez, R. Michael. *Information and Elections.* Ann Arbor, MI: University of Michigan Press, 1997.

Anderson, Walt. *Campaigns: Cases in Conflict.* Pacific Palisades, CA: Goodyear Publishing Company, 1970.

Ando, Hirofumi. "A Study of Voting Patterns in the Philippine Presidential and Senatorial Elections, 1946–1965." *Midwest Journal of Political Science* 13 (4) (1969): 567–86.

Andrews, L. "The Relationship of Political Marketing to Political Lobbying: An Examination of the Devonport Campaign for the Trident Refitting Contract." *European Journal of Marketing* 10/11 (1996): 68–91.

Angeles, Leonora C. "The Filipino Male as 'Macho-machunurin': Bringing Men and Masculinities in Gender and Development Studies." *Kasarinlan Philippine Quarterly of Third World Studies* 16 (1) (2001): 9–30.

Anglo, Sydney. *Machiavelli: A Dissection.* London: The Camelot Press, 1960.

Ansell, Jeff. "Picking a Media Trainer." In *Winning Elections: Political Campaign Management, Strategy and Tactics,* edited by R. Faucheux, 462–3. New York: M. Evans and Co.

Anski, Alex. *The Selling of the Likud.* Tel-Aviv: Zmora, Bitan and Modan, 1978. (In Hebrew.)

Ansolabehere, Stephen and Shanto Iyengar. *Going Negative: How Political Advertisements Shrink and Polarize the Electorate*. New York: Free Press, 1995.

——. "Riding the Wave and Claiming Ownership Over Issues: The Joint Effects of Advertising and News Coverage in Campaigns." *Public Opinion Quarterly* 58 (Fall 1994): 335–57.

Ansolabehere, Stephen, Shanto Iyengar, Adam Simon, and Nicholas Valentino. "Does Attack Advertising Demobilize the Electorate?" *American Political Science Review* 88 (December 1994): 829–38.

Araujo, Octavio Rodríguez. *La reforma política y los partidos en México*. México, Distrito Federal: Siglo XXI Editores, 1979.

Arcala-Hall, Rosalie. "Exploring New Roles for the Philippine Military: Implications for Civilian Supremacy." *Philippine Political Science Journal* 25 (48) (2004): 107–30.

Arceneaux, Kevin. "Do Campaigns Help Voters Learn? A Cross-national Analysis." *British Journal of Political Science* 36 (1) (January 2006): 159–73.

Aristotle. *The Politics*. London: Penguin, 1961.

Armstrong, Gary, Philip Kotler, and Geoffrey da Silva. *Marketing: An Asian Perspective*. New York: Pearson, Prentice Hall, 2005.

Armstrong, Jerome and Markos Moulitsas Zúniga, *Crashing the Gate: Netroots, Grassroots, and the Rise of People-Powered Politics*. White River Junction, VT: Chelsea Green Publishing, 2006.

Arnold, R. Douglas. *The Logic of Congressional Action*. New Haven: Yale University Press, 1990.

Aronoff, Joel Myron. "The 'Americanization' of Israeli Politics: Political and Cultural Change." *Israel Studies* 5 (1) (Spring 2000): 92–127.

Ateneo de Manila University, Institute of Philippine Culture. *The Vote of the Poor: Modernity and Tradition in People's Views of Leadership and Election*. Quezon City: Institute of Philippine Culture, Ateneo de Manila University, 2005.

Atkin, Charles K., Lawrence Bowen, Oguz B. Nayman, and Kenneth G. Sheinkopf. "Quality Versus Quantity in Televised Political Ads." *Public Opinion Quarterly* 37 (1973): 209–24.

Attack, S. *The Directory of Public Affairs and Government Relation*. London: Berkeley International Recruitment Consultants, 1990.

Austin, Reginald and Maja Tjernström, eds. *Funding of Political Parties and Election Campaigns*. Stockholm: International IDEA, 2003.

Babbie, Earl R. *The Practice of Social Research*. Second edition. Belmont, CA: Wadsworth Publishing Company, 1979.

Baines, Paul R. "Voter Segmentation and Candidate Positioning." In *Handbook of Political Marketing*, edited by Bruce I. Newman, 405–8. Thousand Oaks, CA: Sage, 1999.

Baines, Paul and John Egan. "Marketing and Political Campaigning: Mutually Exclusive or Exclusively Mutual?" *Qualitative Market Research* 4 (1) (2001): 25–34.

Baines, Paul R., Phil Harris and Barbara R. Lewis. "The Political Marketing Planning Process: Improving Image and Message in Strategic Target Areas." *Marketing Intelligence & Planning* 20 (1) (2002): 6–14.

Baines, Paul R., Robert M. Worcester, David Jarrett, and Roger Mortimore. "Market Segmentation and Product Differentiation in Political Campaigns: A Technical Feature Perspective." *Journal of Marketing Management* 19 (1–2) (2003): 225–49.

——. "Product Attribute-Based Voter Segmentation and Resource Advantage Theory." *Journal of Marketing Management* 21 (9) (2005): 1079–115.

Baker, Monya. "Stem Cell Therapy or Snake Oil?" Nature Biotechnology 23 (12) (December 2005): 1467–9.

Baker, William E. and James M. Sinkula. "Market Orientation, Learning Orientation and Product Innovation: Delving into the Organization's Black Box." *Journal of Market-focused Management* 5 (1) (2002): 5–23.

Bannon, D.P. "Relationship Marketing and the Political Process." *Journal of Political Marketing* 4 (2) (2005): 85–102.

Barber, B.R., K. Mattson, and J. Peterson. *The State of "Electronically Enhanced Democracy": A Survey of the Internet*. New Brunswick, N.J.: The Walt Whitman Center or the Culture and Politics of Democracy, 1997.

Bartels, Larry M. "Messages Received: The Political Impact of Media Exposure." *American Political Science Review* 87 (2) (June 1993): 267–85.

——. "Resource Allocation in a Presidential Campaign." *Journal of Politics* 47 (August 1985): 928–36.

——. "Uninformed Votes: Information Effects in Presidential Elections." *American Journal of Political Science* 40 (February 1996): 194–230.

Bartle, J. and D. Griffiths. "Social-psychological, Economic and Marketing Models of Voting Behaviour Compared." In *The Idea of Political Marketing*, edited by N.J. O'Shaughnessy and S.C. Henneberg, 19–37. Westport, CT: Praeger, 2002.

Bartle, John, Ivor Crewe, and Brian Gosschalk. "Introduction." In *Political Communications: The British General Election of 1997*, edited by Ivor Crewe, Brian Gosschalk, and John Bartle, xvii–xxiii. London: Frank Cass, 1998.

Basil, Michael, Caroline Schooler, and Byron Reeves. "Positive and Negative Political Advertising: Effectiveness of Ads and Perceptions of Candidates." In *Television and Political Advertising*, edited by F. Biocca, 245–62. Hillsdale, N.J.: Lawrence Erlbaum, 1991.

Bass, Harold F., Jr "Partisan Rules, 1946–1996." In *Partisan Approaches to Postwar American Politics*, ed. Byron E. Shafer, 220–70. New York: Chatham House Publishers, 1998.

Bauer, Hans H., Frank Huber, and Andreas Herrmann. "Political Marketing: An Information-Economic Analysis." *European Journal of Marketing* 30 (10/11) (1996): 152–65.

Beard, Charles A. *An Economic Interpretation of the Constitution of the United States*. New York: Macmillan, 1913.

Becerra, Ricardo, Pedro Salazar, and José Woldemberg. *La mecánica del cambio político en México, Elecciones, partidos y reformas*. México, Distrito Federal: Ediciones Cal y Arena, 2000.

Begala, Paul and James Carville. *Take It Back: A Battle Plan for Democratic Victory*. New York: Simon & Schuster, 2006.

Beltran, Ulises. "The Combined Effect of Advertising and News Coverage in the Mexican Presidential Campaign of 2000." *Political Communication* 24 (1) (2007): 37–64.

Bendavid, Neftali. *The Thumpin'. How Rahm Emanuel and the Democrats Learned to Be Ruthless and Ended the Republican Revolution*. Chicago, IL: Doubleday, 2007.

Beniger, James R. *The Control Revolution: Technological and Economic Origins of the Information Society*. Cambridge, MA: Harvard University Press, 1986.

Bennett, W. Lance. *News: The Politics of Illusion*. Seventh edition. London: Pearson Longman, 2006. (Third edition, 1996.)

Bennett, W. Lance and Robert M. Entman. "Mediated Politics: An Introduction." In *Mediated Politics: Communication in the Future of Democracy* edited by W.L. Bennett and R.M. Entman, 1–32. Cambridge, MA: Cambridge University Press, 2001.

Benoit, William L. *Accounts, Excuses, and Apologies: A Theory of Image Restoration Strategies*. Albany, N.Y.: State University of New York Press, 1995.

—— *Communication in Political Campaigns*. New York: Peter Lang, 2007.

——. "Political Party Affiliation and Presidential Campaign Discourse." *Communication Quarterly* 52 (2004): 81–97.

Benoit, William and Pamela Benoit. "The Virtual Campaign: Presidential Primary Websites in Campaign 2000." *American Communications Journal* 3 (3) (2000).

Benoit, William L. and Glenn J. Hansen. "Issue Adaptation of Presidential Television Spots and Debates to Primary and General Audiences." *Communication Research Reports* 19 (2002): 138–45.

Benoit, William L., Glenn J. Hansen, and Rebecca M. Verser. "A Meta-Analysis of the Effects of Viewing U. S. Presidential Debates." *Communication Monographs* 70 (December 2003): 335–50.

Berelson, Bernard, Paul Lazarsfeld, and William McPhee. *Voting: A Study of Opinion Formation in a Presidential Campaign*. Chicago, IL: University of Chicago Press, 1954.

Beresford, Quentin. *Parties, Policies and Persuasion*. Melbourne: Addison Wesley Longman, 1997.

Berezkina, Ol'ga. *Kak stat' deputatom ili prodat' sebya na politicheskom rynke*. St Petersburg: Izdatel'stvo Bukovskogo, 1997.

Berg, Bruce L. *Quantitative Research Methods for the Social Sciences*. Second edition. Needham Heights, MA: Allyn & Bacon, 1995.

Bergan, Daniel E. et al. "Grassroots Mobilization and Voter Turnout." *Public Opinion Quarterly* 69 (5) (2005): 760–77.

Bergo, Sandy. *Campaign Consultants: The Price of Democracy*. Washington, D.C.: Center for Public Integrity, 2006.

Berman, Evan. "Dealing with Cynical Citizens." *Public Administration Review* 57 (2) (March/April 1997): 105.

Bernays, Edward. *Biography of an Idea: Memoirs of Public Relations Counsel Edward L. Bernays*. New York: Simon and Schuster, 1965.

Berner, Benedicte and Åse Grødeland. "Broadcast Media." In *Monitoring the Media Coverage of the March 2000 Presidential Elections in Russia*, edited by the European Institute for the Media. Brussels/Düsseldorf: European Commission/EIM, 2000.

Bernstein, Jonathan H. and Casey B.K. Dominguez. "Candidates and Candidacies in the Expanded Party." *P.S. Political Science and Politics* 36 (2) (April 2003): 165–9.

Berry, Jon and Ed Keller. *The Influentials: One American in Ten Tells the Other Nine How to Vote, Where to Eat, and What to Buy*. New York: The Free Press, 2003.

Berry, Leonard L. "Services—Marketing Is Different." *Business* 30 (3) (1980): 24–9.

Bibby, John. "Party Networks: National-State Integration, Allied Groups, and Issue Activists." In *The State of the Parties: The Changing Role of Contemporary American Parties*. Third edition, edited by John C. Green and Daniel M. Shea. Lanham, MD: Rowman & Littlefield, 1999.

Bibby, John B. and Brian A. Schaffner. *Politics, Parties, and Elections in America*. Sixth edition. Belmont, MA: Thomson-Wadsworth, 2007.

Biddle, Larry. "Fund-Raising: Hitting Home Runs On and Off the Internet." In *Mousepads, Shoe Leather, and Hope*, edited by Zephyr Teachout and Thomas Streeter, Boulder, CO: Paradigm Publishers, 2007, 166–78.

Bimber, Bruce. *Information and American Democracy: Technology in the Evolution of Political Power*. New York: Cambridge University Press, 2003.

Bimber, Bruce and Richard Davis. *Campaigning Online: The Internet in U.S. Elections*. New York: Oxford University Press, 2003.

Frank Biocca, ed. *Television and Political Advertising*. Volume 1. Hillsdale, N.J.: Lawrence Erlbaum, 1991.

Black, Lawrence. *The Political Culture of the Left in Affluent Britain 1951–64*. Basingstoke: Macmillan Palgrave, 2004.

Blackburn, Elizabeth. "Bioethics and the Political Distortion of Biomedical Science." *The New England Journal of Medicine* 350 (April 1, 2004): 1379–80.

Blumenthal, Sidney. *The Permanent Campaign*. New York: Simon and Schuster, 1982.

Blumler, Jay G. and Michael Gurevitch. " 'Americanization' Reconsidered: U.K.–U.S. Campaign Communication Comparisons Across Time." In *Mediated Politics*, edited by W.L. Bennett and R.M. Entman, 380–403. Cambridge: Cambridge University Press, 2001.

Blumler, Jay G. and Dennis Kavanagh. "The Third Age of Political Communication: Influences and Features." *Political Communication* 16 (3) (1999): 209–30.

Blumler, Jay G., Dennis Kavanagh, and T.J. Nossiter. "Modern Communications Versus Traditional Politics in Britain: Unstable Marriage of Convenience." In *Politics, Media and Modern Democracy*, edited by David Swanson and Paolo Mancini, 49–72. Westport, CT: Praeger, 1996.

Bogart, Leo. "The Pollster and the Nazis." *Commentary* 92 (2): 47–50.

Bormann, Ernest G. "The Eagleton Affair: A Fantasy Theme Analysis." *Quarterly Journal of Speech*, 59 (1973): 143–59.

——. "Fantasy and Rhetorical Vision: The Rhetorical Criticism of Social Reality." *Quarterly Journal of Speech* 58 (1972): 396–407.

Boston Women's Health Book Collective. *Our Bodies, Ourselves: Menopause*. New York: Simon & Schuster, 2006.

Bowler, Shaun and David M. Farrell. "The Internationalization of Campaign Consultancy." In *Campaign Warriors. Political Consultants in Elections*, edited by James A. Thurber and Candice J. Nelson, 153–74. Washington D.C.: Brookings Institution Press, 2000.

Bowman, Karlyn. "Polling to Campaign and to Govern." In *The Permanent Campaign and Its Future*, edited by Norman J. Ornstein and Thomas E. Mann, 54–74. Washington, D.C.: American Enterprise Institute and The Brookings Institution, 2000.

Brader, Ted. "Striking a Responsive Chord: How Political Ads Motivate and Persuade Voters by Appealing to Emotions." *American Journal of Political Science* 49 (2005): 388–405.

Brasher, Holly. "Capitalizing on Contention: Issue Agendas in U.S. Senate Campaigns." *Political Communication* 20 (October 2003): 453–71.

Brians, Craig L. and Martin P. Wattenberg. "Campaign Issue Knowledge and Salience: Comparing Reception From TV Commercials, TV News, and Newspapers." *American Journal of Political Science* 40 (1996): 172–93.

Bridgman, Raymond L. "The Lobby." *New England Magazine* 22 (2) (April 1897): 151–60.

Briody, Dan. *The Iron Triangle: Inside the Secret World of the Carlyle Group*. Hoboken, N.J.: John G. Wiley, 2003.

Brock, David. *The Republican Noise Machine*. New York: Crown Publishing, 2004.

Broder, David S. *Democracy Derailed: Initiative Campaigns and the Power of Money*. New York: Harcourt, 2000.

——. *The Party's Over. The Failure of Politics in America*. New York: Harper & Row, 1972.

Brooks, Deborah Jordan. "The Resilient Voter: Moving Toward Closure in the Debate over Negative Campaigning and Turnout." *Journal of Politics* 68 (August 2006): 684–96.

Brown, Everit and Albert Strauss. *A Dictionary of American Politics: Comprising Accounts of Political Parties, Measures and Men*. New York: A.L. Burt, 1888.

Buckley, William F. Jr *God and Man at Yale: The Superstitions of "Academic Freedom."* New York: Gateway Editions, 1978, 1951.

Buendia, Rizal G. "An Examination of Ethnicity and Secessionist Movements in the Philippines and Indonesia: The Moros and Acehnese." *Philippine Political Science Journal* 23 (46) (2002): 3–48.

Burton, James G. *The Pentagon Wars: Reformers Challenge the Old Guard*. Annapolis, MD: Naval Institute Press, 1993.

Burton, Michael John and Daniel M. Shea. *Campaign Mode: Strategic Vision in Congressional Elections*. Lanham, MD: Rowman & Littlefield, 2003.

——. "Campaign Strategy." In *The Electoral Challenge*, edited by S.C. Craig, 22–38. Washington, D.C.: CQ Books, 2006.

Buss, Dale D. "A Direct Route for Customers." *Nation's Business* 85 (9) (September 1997): 46–51.

Butler, David and Dennis Kavanagh. *The British General Election of 1987*. Basingstoke: Macmillan, 1987.

——. *The British General Election of 1992*. Basingstoke: Macmillan, 1992.

——. *The British General Election of 1997*. Basingstoke: Macmillan, 1997.

——. *The British General Election of 2002*. Basingstoke: Macmillan Palgrave, 2002.

——. *The British General Election of 2005*. Basingstoke: Macmillan Palgrave, 2006.

Butler, David and Austin Ranney, eds. *Electioneering. A Comparative Study of Continuity and Change*. Oxford: Oxford University Press, 1992.

Butler, David and Richard Rose. *The British General Election of 1959*. London: Macmillan, 1960.

Butler, Patrick and Neil Collins. "A Conceptual Framework for Political Marketing." In *Handbook of Political Marketing*, edited by Bruce I. Newman, 55–72. Thousand Oaks, CA: Sage, 1999.

——. "Marketing Public Sector Services: Concepts and Characteristics." *Journal of Marketing Management* 11 (1–3) (1994): 83–96.

——. "Political Marketing: Structure and Process." *European Journal of Marketing* 28 (1) (1994): 19–34.

——. "Strategic Analysis in Political Markets." *European Journal of Marketing* 30: 10–11(1996): 32–44.

Buzin, Andrei. *Administrativnye izbiratel'nye tekhnologii: Moskovskaya praktika*. Moscow: Panorama, 2006.

Campbell, Angus, Philip E. Converse, Warren E. Miller, and Donald E. Stokes. *The American Voter*. New York: John Wiley and Sons, 1960.

Campbell, James E. *The American Campaign: U.S. Presidential Campaigns and the National Vote*. College Station, TX: Texas A&M University Press, 2000.

——. "When Have Presidential Campaigns Decided Election Outcomes?" *American Politics Research* 29 (5) (September 2001): 437–60.

Campbell, Karlyn Kohrs and Kathleen Hall Jamieson. *Deeds Done in Words: Presidential Rhetoric and the Genre of Governance*. Chicago, IL: University of Chicago Press, 1990.

Canovan, Margaret. *Populism*. New York: Harcourt Brace Jovanovich, 1981.

Cappella, Joseph N. and Kathleen Hall Jamieson. "New Frames, Political Cynicism, and Media Cynicism." *Annals of the American Academy of Political and Social Science* 546 (July 1996): 71–84.

——. *Spiral of Cynicism: The Press and the Public Good*. New York: Oxford University Press, 1997.

Carothers, Thomas. *Confronting the Weakest Link. Aiding Political Parties in New Democracies*. Washington D.C.: Carnegie Endowment for International Peace, 2006.

Casanova, Pablo González. *La democracia en México*. México: Distrito Federal: Editorial Era, 1967.

Casey, R. "The National Publicity Bureau and British Party Propaganda." *Public Opinion Quarterly* (October 1939): 623–34.

Caspi, Dan. "American-style Electioneering in Israel: Americanisation versus Modernization." In *Politics, Media and Modern Democracy*, edited by D.L. Swanson and P. Mancini, 173–92. Westport, CT: Praeger, 1966.

——. "Electoral Rhetoric and Political Polarization: The Begin–Peres Debates." *European Journal of Communications* 1 (4) (December 1986): 447–62.

Caspi, Dan and Chaim Eyal. "Professionalization Trends in Israeli Election Propaganda: 1973–1981." In *Elections in Israel, 1981*, edited by Asher Arian. Tel Aviv: Ramot, 1983.

Caspi, Dan and Baruch Leshem. "From Electoral Propaganda to Political Advertising in Israel." In *The Sage Handbook of Political Advertising*, edited by L.L. Kaid and C. Holtz-Bacha, 109–28. Thousand Oaks, CA: Sage, 2006.

Central Election Commission. *Republic of China Election History [Zhonghua minguo xuanjushi]*. Taipei: Central Election Commission, 1986.

Chaffee, Steven, ed. *Political Communication*. Beverly Hills, CA: Sage Publications, 1975.

—— "Presidential Debates: Are They Helpful to Voters?" *Communication Monographs* 45 (1978): 330–46.

Chaffee, Stephen and Rajiv N. Rimal. "Time of Vote Decision and Openness to Persuasion." In *Political Persuasion and Attitude Change*, edited by Diana C. Mutz, Paul M. Sniderman, and Richard A. Brody, 267–92. Ann Arbor, MI: University of Michigan Press, 1996.

Chan, Pi-Hsiang. *Maipiao chanhui lu [Vote Buying: A Confession]*. Taipei, MI: Shangyezhoukan, 1999.

Chang, Chingching and Jacqueline C. Bush Hitchon. "When Does Gender Count? Further Insights into Gender Schematic Processing for Female Candidates' Political Advertisements." *Sex Roles* 51 (2004): 197–208.

Chang, Mao-gui, *She hui yun dong yu zheng zhi zhuan hua [Social Movements and Political Change]*. Taipei: Institute for National Policy Research, 1994.

Chang, Yong-cheng. *Xuan zhan zaoshi [Electoral Warfare]*. Taipei: Shichanchihuitsongshu, 1992.

Chanley, Virginia A., Thomas J. Rudolph, and Wendy M. Rahn. "The Origins and Consequences of Public Trust in Government: A Time Series Analysis." *Public Opinion Quarterly* 64 (3) (Fall 2000): 239–56.

Chao, Yung-mao. *Taiwan di fang zheng zhi de bian qian yu te zhi [Changes in Taiwan Local Politics]*. Taipei: Han Lu, 1998.

Chapman, William. *Inside the Philippine Revolution*. New York: W.W. Norton, 1987.

Chen, Chao-ru. *Call in!! dixia diantai taiwan xin chuanbo wenhua de zhenhan yu misi [Call in!! Underground Radio: Taiwan's New Broadcasting Culture]*. Taipei: Richen, 1994.

Chen, Kuo-lin. *Heijin [Black Gold]*. Taipei: Shangzhou, 2004.

Chen, Ming-tong. "Local Factions and Elections in Taiwan's Democratization." In *Taiwan's Electoral Politics and Democratic Transition: Riding the Third Wave*, edited by Charles Chi-Hsiang, Robert A. Scalapino, and Hung-mao Tien. New York: M.E. Sharpe, 1997.

Chen, Peter, Rachel Gibson, and Karin Geiselhart. *Electronic Democracy? The Impact of New Communications Technologies on Australian Democracy*. Democratic Audi of Australia, Report No. 6. Canberra: Australian National University, 2006.

Cheng, Tzi-long. *Jingxuan chuanbo yu taiwan shehui [Electoral Campaigning and Taiwan's Society]*. Taipei: Yang-Chih, 2004.

———. *Jingxuan wenxuan celue [Electoral Propaganda]*. Fourth edition. Taipei: Yuanliu, 2001.

Chernatony, Leslie de and Jon White. "New Labour: A Study of the Creation, Development and Demise of Political Brand." *Journal of Political Marketing* 1 (2/3) (2002): 45–52.

Chiu, Chian-wu. *Shei shuo xuanju wu shifu [Who Says Elections Have No Master?]*. Taipei: Bluelime, 2007.

Chiu, Peilin and Sylvia M. Chan-Olmsted. "The Impact of Cable Television on Political Campaigns in Taiwan." *Gazette* 61 (6) (1999): 491–509.

Christensen, Clayton. *The Innovator's Dilemma: When New Technologies Cause Great Firms to Fail*. Cambridge, MA: Harvard Business School Press, 1997.

Chuang, Po-Chong. *Wanglu Xuanzhan [Internet Campaigning in Taiwan]*. Taipei: Miluo, 2007.

Citrin, Jack. "Comment: The Political Relevance of Trust in Government." *The American Political Science Review* 68 (3) (September 1974): 973–88.

Clarfield, Gerard. "Protecting the Frontiers: Defense Policy and the Tariff Question in the First Washington Administration." *The William and Mary Quarterly* 32 (3) (July 1975): 443–64.

Clarke, A. "The Life and Times of Sir Basil Clarke—PR Pioneer." *Public Relations* 22 (2) (February 1969): 8–13.

Clarke, Gerard. *The Politics of NGOs in South-East Asia: Participation and Protest in the Philippines*. London/New York: Routledge, 1998.

Clemens, Elisabeth S. *The People's Lobby: Organizational Innovation and the Rise of Interest Group Politics in the United States, 1890–1925*. Chicago, IL: University of Chicago Press, 1997.

Clinton, Joshua D. and John S. Lapinski. " 'Targeted' Advertising and Voter Turnout: An Experimental Study of the 2000 Presidential Election." *Journal of Politics* 66 (February 2004): 69–96.

Cockerell, Michael. *Live from Number 10*. London: Faber and Faber, 1989.

Cockerell, Michael, Peter Hennessy, and David Walker. *Sources Close to the Prime Minister*. London: Macmillan, 1984.

Cockett, Richard. "The Party, Publicity and the Media." In *Conservative Century*, edited by Anthony Seldon and Stuart Ball, 547–77. Oxford: Oxford University Press, 1994.

———. *Thinking the Unthinkable: Think-tanks and the Economic Counter-revolution, 1931–1983*. London: Harper Collins, 1994.

Cohen, Akiva. "Radio vs. TV: The Effect of the Medium." *Journal of Communications* (Spring 1976): 26–35.

Cohen, Akiva and Gadi Wolfsfeld. "Overcoming Adversity and Diversity: The Utility of Television in Israel." In *Political Advertising in Western Democracies*, edited by L.L. Kaid and C. Holtz-Bacha, 109–23. Thousand Oaks, CA: Sage, 1995.

Coleman, Stephen. *Televised Election Debates. International Perspectives*. Houndmills: Palgrave Macmillan, 2000.

Collins, Neil and Patrick Butler. "Market Analysis for Political Parties." In *The Idea of Political Marketing*, edited by N.J. O'Shaughnessy and S.C.M. Henneberg, 1–17. Westport, CT: Prager Press, 2002.

———. "When Marketing Models Clash with Democracy." *Journal of Public Affairs* 3 (1) (2003): 52–62.

Conroy-Franco, Jennifer. *Campaigning for Democracy: Grassroots Citizenship Movements, Less-than-democratic Elections, and Regime Transition in the Philippines*. Quezon City, Philippines: Institute for Popular Democracy, 2000.

Conway, M. Margaret. "The Use of Polls in Congressional, State, and Local Elections." *Annals of the American Academy of Political and Social Science* 472 (1984): 97–105.

Cook, Corey. "The Permanence of the 'Permanent Campaign': George W. Bush's Public Presidency." *Presidential Studies Quarterly* 32 (4) (December 2002): 753–64.

Cook, Timothy E. and Paul Gronke. "The Skeptical American: Revisiting the Meanings of Trust in Government and Confidence in Institutions." *The Journal of Politics* 67 (3) (August 2005): 748–803.

Cooper-Chen, Anne. "Televised International News in Five Countries: Thoroughness, Insularity and Agenda Capacity." *International Communication Bulletin* 24 (1–2) (1989): 4–8.

Coronel, Sheila S. *Coups, Cults & Cannibals: Chronicles of a Troubled Decade, 1982–1992.* Metro Manila: Anvil Publications, 1993.

——. *From Loren to Marimar: The Philippine Media in the 1990s.* Quezon City, Philippines: Philippine Center for Investigative Journalism, 1999.

——. *Investigating Estrada: Millions, Mansions, and Mistresses: A Compilation of Investigative Reports.* Metro Manila, Philippines: Philippine Center for Investigative Journalism, 2000.

Coronel, Sheila S. "New Media Played a Role in the People's Uprising." *Nieman Reports* 56 (2) (2002).

——. *The Rulemakers: How the Wealthy and Well-born Dominate Congress.* Quezon City, Philippines: Philippine Center for Investigative Journalism, 2004.

Coronel, Sheila S. and Cecile C.A. Balgos. *Pork and Other Perks: Corruption & Governance in the Philippines.* Pasig, Metro Manila: Philippine Center for Investigative Journalism, Evelio B. Javier Foundation, Institute for Popular Democracy, 1998.

Coronel, Sheila S. and Sigfred C. Balatan. *EDSA 2: A Nation in Revolt, a Photographic Journal.* Pasig City, Philippines: Anvil Publications, 2001.

Coronel, Sheila S. and Jose F. Lacaba. *Boss: Five Case Studies of Local Politics in the Philippines.* Pasig, Metro Manila: Philippine Center for Investigative Journalism, Institute for Popular Democracy, 1995.

Coronel-Ferrer, Miriam. "Recycled Autonomy? Enacting the New Organic Act for a Regional Autonomous Government in Southern Philippines." *Kasarinlan Philippine Quarterly of Third World Studies* 15 (2) (2000): 165–90.

Corrado, Anthony. "Party Finance in the Wake of BCRA: An Overview." In *The Election after Reform,* edited by M.J. Malbin. Lanham, MD: Rowman & Littlefield, 2006.

——. "Running Backward: The Congressional Money Chase." In *The Permanent Campaign and its Future,* edited by N.J. Ornstein and T.E. Mann, 75–107. Washington, D.C.: American Enterprise Institute and the Brookings Institution, 2000.

Council of State Governments. *The Book of the States, 2000–2001.* Volume 31. Lexington, KY: Council of State Governments, 2000.

Craig, Douglas B. *Fireside Politics: Radio and Political Culture in the United States, 1920–1940.* Baltimore, MD: The Johns Hopkins University Press, 2000.

Craig, Stephen C.. ed. *The Electoral Challenge: Theory Meets Practice.* Washington, D.C.: CQ Books, 2006.

Craig, Stephen C., James G. Kane, and Jason Gainous. "Issue-related Learning in a Gubernatorial Campaign: A Panel Study." *Political Communication* 22 (October–December 2005): 483–503.

Crawford, Alan. *Thunder on the Right.* New York: Pantheon Books, 1980.

Crawford, Craig. *Attack The Messenger.* New York: Rowman & Littlefield, 2005.

Crawford, Kenneth G. *The Pressure Boys: The Inside Story of Lobbying in America.* New York: Julian Messner, 1939.

Crosby, Lynton. "The Liberal Party." In *The Paradox of Parties,* edited by Marian Simms, 160–5. Sydney: Allen & Unwin, 1996.

Cundy, Donald T. "Political Commercials and Candidate Image: The Effects Can Be Substantial." In *New Perspectives on Political Advertising,* edited by L.L. Kaid, D.D. Nimmo, and K.R. Sanders, 210–34. Carbondale, IL: Southern Illinois University Press, 1986.

Curry, Patrick. *Machiavelli for Beginners.* Cambridge: Icon Books, 1995.

Cwalina, Wojciech and Andrzej Falkowski. "Cultural Context of the Perceptual Fit of Political Parties' Campaign Slogans: A Polish Case." In *Political Marketing: Cultural Issues and Current Trends,* edited by Kostas Gouliamos, Antonis Theocharous, Bruce I. Newman, and Stephan C.M. Henneberg. Binghamton, N.Y.: Haworth Press, 2008.

——. *Marketing Polityczny: Persepektywa Psychologiczna* [*Political Marketing: A Psychological Perspective*]. Gdansk, Poland: GWP, 2005.

Cwalina, Wojciech, Andrzej Falkowski, and Lynda Lee Kaid. "Role of Advertising in Forming the Image of Politicians: Comparative Analysis of Poland, France, and Germany." *Media Psychology* 2 (2) (2000): 119–46.

Cwalina, Wojciech, Andrzej Falkowski, and Bruce I. Newman. *A Cross-cultural Theory of Voter Behavior.* Binghamton, N.Y.: Haworth Press, 2007.

Cwalina, Wojciech, Andrzej Falkowski, Bruce I. Newman, and Dejan Verčič. "Models of Voter Behavior in Traditional and Evolving Democracies: Comparative Analysis of Poland, Slovenia, and U.S." *Journal of Political Marketing* 3 (2) (2004): 7–30.

Dahl, Robert. *La democracia, una guía para los ciudadanos.* Buenos Aires: Taurus, 1998.

Dalager, Jon K. "Voters, Issues, and Elections: Are the Candidates' Messages Getting Through?" *Journal of Politics* 58 (May 1996): 486–515.

Damore, David F. "Candidate Strategy and the Decision to Go Negative." *Political Research Quarterly* 55 (September 2002): 669–85.

———. "The Dynamics of Issue Ownership in Presidential Campaigns." *Political Research Quarterly* 57 (September 2004): 391–7.

———. "Issue Convergence in Presidential Campaigns." *Political Behavior* 27 (March 2005): 71–97.

David, Gordon. *The Iron Triangle: The Politics of Defense Contracting.* New York: Council on Economic Priorities, 1981.

Davidson, Roger H., Walter J. Oleszek, and Francis E. Lee. *Congress and Its Members.* Eleventh edition. Washington, D.C.: CQ Press, 2008.

Davies, John Philip and Bruce I. Newman, eds. *Winning Elections with Political Marketing.* Binghamton, N.Y.: Haworth Press, 2006.

Davis, Richard. *The Web of Politics: The Internet's Impact on the American Political System.* New York: Oxford University Press, 1999.

Day, George S. "What Does It Mean to Be Market-Driven?" *Business Strategy Review,* 9 (1) (1998): 1–14.

Deacon, David, Dominic Wring, Michael Billing, John Downey, Peter Golding, and Davidson Scott. *Reporting the 2005 U.K. General Election.* Loughborough University: Communication Research Centre, August 2005.

Deakin, James. *The Lobbyists.* Washington, D.C.: Public Affairs Press, 1966.

Dean, James W., Pamela Brandes, and Ravi Dharwadkar. "Organizational Cynicism." *Academy of Management Review* 23 (1998): 341–52.

Dehm, Ursula. "Fernsehduelle im Urteil der Zuschauer." *Media Perspektiven* 12 (2002): 600–9.

Delli Carpini, Michael X. "In Search of the Informed Citizen: What American Know About Politics and Why it Matters." The Pew Charitable Trust. Paper presented at the *Transformation of Civic Life* Conference, Nashville, Tennessee, 1999

Denmark, David, Ian Ward, and Clive Bean. "Election Campaigns and Television News Coverage: The Case of the 2001 Australian Election." *Australian Journal of Political Science* 42 (1) (2007): 89–109.

Denton, Robert and Gary Woodward. *Political Communications in America.* Third edition. Westport, CT: Praeger Publishing, 1998. (Second edition, 1990.)

Dermody, J. and R. Scullion. "Delusion of Grandeur? Marketing's Contribution to 'Meaningful' Western Political Consumption." *European Journal of Marketing* 35 (9/10) (2001): 1085–98.

Deshpandé, R. *Developing a Market Orientation.* Thousand Oaks, CA: Sage Publications, 1999.

Devlin, L. Patrick. "Contrasts in Presidential Campaign Commercials of 2004." *American Behavioral Scientist* 49 (2005): 279–313.

Diamond, Edwin and Stephen Bates. *The Spot: The Rise of Political Advertising on Television,* 3rd ed. Cambridge, MA: MIT Press, 1992.

Dinkin, Robert J. *Campaigning in America: A History of Election Practices.* Westport, CT: Greenwood Press, 1989.

Dionne, Jr, E.J. *Why Americans Hate Politics.* New York: Simon & Schuster, 1991.

Dolny, Michael. "Right, Center Think Tanks Still Most Quoted." *Fairness and Accuracy in Reporting Extra!* (May/June 2005): 1–3.

Donoghue, B. and G. Jones, *Herbert Morrison: Portrait of a Politician.* London: Weidenfeld & Nicolson, 1973.

Donsbach, Wolfgang. "Drehbücher und Inszenierungen. Die Union in der Defensive." In *Kampa. Meinungsklima und Medienwirkung im Bundestagswahlkampf 1998,* edited by Elisabeth Noelle-Neumann, Hans-Matthias Kepplinger, and Wolfgang Donsbach, 141–80. Freiburg: Alber, 1999.

Douglas, Mary. *Natural Symbols.* New York: Pantheon Books, 1982.

Downey, Sharon D. "The Evolution of the Rhetorical Genre of Apologia." *Western Journal of Communication* 57 (1993): 42–64.

Downs, Anthony. *An Economic Theory of Democracy.* New York: Harper and Row, 1957.

Drezner, Daniel and Henry Farrell, eds. *The Political Promise of Blogging.* Ann Arbor, MI: University of Michigan Press, 2008.

Druckman, James N., Lawrence R. Jacobs, and Eric Ostermeier. "Candidate Strategies to Prime Issues and Image." *Journal of Politics* 66 (November 2004): 1180–202.

Dudley, Robert L. and Alan R. Gitelson. *American Elections: The Rules Matter.* New York: Longman Publishers, 2002.

Dulio, David A. *For Better or Worse? How Political Consultants are Changing Elections in the United States.* Albany, N.Y.: State University of New York Press, 2004.

——. "Party Crashers? The Relationship between Political Consultants and Political Parties." In *Handbook of Party Politics*, edited by R.S. Katz and W. Crotty, 348–58. Thousand Oaks, CA: Sage Publications, 2006.

Dulio, David A. and Sam Garrett. "Organizational Strength and Campaign Professionalism in State Parties." In *The State of the Parties*, edited J.C. Green and D.J. Coffey, 199–217. Lanham, MD: Rowman & Littlefield, 2007.

Dulio, David A. and Candice J. Nelson. *Vital Signs: Perspectives on the Health of American Campaigning.* Washington, D.C.: Brookings Institution Press, 2005.

Dulio, David A. and Erin O'Brien. "Campaigning with the Internet: The View from Below." In *Campaigns and Elections American Style*. Second edition, edited by J.A. Thurber and C.J. Nelson, 173–94. Boulder, CO: Westview, 2004.

Dulio, David A. and James A. Thurber. "The Symbiotic Relationship Between Political Parties and Political Consultants: Partners Past, Present and Future." In *The State of the Parties*, edited by J.C. Green and R. Farmer, 214–27. Lanham, MD: Rowman & Littlefield, 2003.

Dunnan, Dana. *Burning at the Grassroots: Inside the Dean Machine.* New York: Pagefree Publishing, 2004.

Edwards, Lee. *The Conservative Revolution.* New York: The Free Press, 1999.

Egan, John. "Political Marketing: Lessons from the Mainstream." *Journal of Marketing Management* 15 (6) (1999): 498–502.

Egorova-Gantman, E. and I. Mintusov, eds. *Politicheskoe konsul'tirovanie.* Second edition Moscow: Nikkolo M, 2002.

Elebash, Camille. "The Americanization of British Political Communications." *Journal of Advertising* 13 (3) (Fall 1984): 50–9

"Election 2000 Special: Al Gore and George Bush's Not-So-Excellent Adventure." *PS: Political Science and Politics* 34 (1) (March 2001): 8–44.

Elliott, Maud Howe. *Uncle Sam Ward and His Circle.* New York: Macmillan, 1938.

Elliott, Richard and Natalia Yannopoulou. "The Nature of Trust in Brands: A Psychosocial Model." *European Journal of Marketing* 41 (9/10) (2007): 988–98.

Ellis, Richard J. *Democratic Delusions: The Initiative Process in America.* Lawrence, KS: University Press of Kansas, 2002.

Elizur, Judith N. "The Role of the Media in the 1981 Knesset Elections." In *Israel at the Polls: The Knesset Elections of 1981*, edited by Howard R. Penniman and Daniel J. Elazar 227–34. Bloomington, IN: American Enterprise Institute and Indiana University Press, 1986.

Elizur, Judith N. and Elihu Katz. "The Media in the Elections of 1977." In *Israel at the Polls: The Knesset Election of 1977*, edited by Howard R. Penniman, 227–54. Washington, D.C.: American Enterprise Institute for Public Policy Research, 1979.

Entman, Robert. "Framing: Towards Clarification of a Fractured Paradigm." *Journal of Communication* 43 (1993): 52.

Epstein, Leon. *Political Parties in Western Democracies.* London: Pall Mall, 1967.

Espindola, Roberto. "Professionalized Campaigning in Latin America." *Journal of Political Marketing* 1 (4) (2002): 65–81.

Esser, Frank and Paul D'Angelo. "Framing the Press and Publicity Process in U.S., British, and German General Election Campaigns: A Comparative Study of Metacoverage." *Harvard International Journal of Press/Politics* 11 (3) (2006): 44–66.

Esser, F. and B. Spanier. "News Management as News: How Media Politics Leads to Metacoverage." *Journal of Political Marketing* 4 (4) (2005): 27–58.

Esser, Frank, Carsten Reinemann, and David Fan. "Spin Doctors in the United States, Great Britain, and Germany: Metacommunication about Media Manipulation." *International Harvard Journal of Press/Politics* 6 (1) (2001): 16–45.

Ewen, Stuart. *PR! A Social History of Spin.* New York: Basic Books, 1996.

Exley, Zack. "An Organizer's View of the Internet Campaign." In *Mousepads, Shoe Leather, and Hope*, edited by Z. Teachout and T. Streeter 212–19. Boulder, CO: Paradigm Publishers, 2007.

Falk, Erika, Erin Grizard and Gordon McDonald. "Legislative Issue Advertising in the 108th Congress." *The Annenberg Public Policy Center Report Series*, 47, 3.

Falkowski, Andrzej and Wojciech Cwalina. "Methodology of Constructing Effective Political Advertising: An Empirical Study of the Polish Presidential Election in 1995." In *Handbook of Political Marketing*, edited by Bruce I. Newman, 283–304. Thousand Oaks, CA: Sage, 1999.

Fallon, Richard H. Jr "Making Sense of Overbreadth." *Yale Law Journal* 100 (1991): 853–908.

Farber, David and Jeff Roche. *The Conservative Sixties.* New York: Peter Lang Publishing, Inc., 2003.

Farnsworth, Stephen J. and S. Robert Lichter. *The Nightly News Nightmare: Television's Coverage of U.S. Presidential Elections, 1988–2004*. Second edition. Lanham, MD: Rowman & Littlefield, 2006.

Farrell, David. "Campaign Modernization and the West European Party." *Political Parties in the New Europe: Political and Analytical Challenges*, edited by Richard Luther and Ferdinand Müller-Rommel, 63–83. Oxford: Oxford University Press, 2002.

Farrell, David. "Campaign Strategies and Tactics." In *Comparing Democracies: Elections and Voting in Global Perspective*, edited by Lawrence LeDuc et al., 160–83. Thousand Oaks, CA: Sage, 1996.

Farrell, David M. "Political Parties in a Changing Campaign Environment." In *Handbook of Political Parties*, edited by Richard S. Katz and William J. Crotty, 122–33. Thousand Oaks, CA: Sage Publications, 2006.

——. "Political Consultancy Overseas: The Internationalization of Campaign Consultancy." *PS: Political Science and Politics* 31 (2) (1998): 171–6.

——. "Political Parties in a Changing Campaign Environment." In *Handbook of Party Politics*, edited by R.S. Katz and W.J. Crotty, 122–33. Thousand Oaks, CA: Sage Publications, 2006.

Farrell, David and Paul Webb. "Political Parties as Campaign Organizations." In *Parties without Partisans: Political Change in Advanced Industrial Democracies*, edited by Russell J. Dalton and Martin Wattenberg, 102–28. Oxford: Oxford University Press, 2000.

Farrell, David M. and Martin Wortmann. "Parties Strategies in the Electoral Market: Political Marketing in West Germany, Britain and Ireland." *European Journal of Political Research* 15 (1987): 297–318.

Farrell, David, Robin Kolodny and Stephen Medvic. "Parties and Campaign Professionals in a Digital Age: Political Consultants in the United States and Their Counterparts Overseas." *Harvard International Journal of Press/Politics* 6 (4) (2001): 11–30.

Faucheux, Ronald A. *Running for Office: The Strategies, Techniques and Messages Modern Political Candidates Need to Win Elections*. New York: M. Evans and Co., 2002.

Faucheux, Ronald A., ed. *The Debate Book*. Washington, D.C.: Campaigns & Elections Publishing Co., 2002.

——. "What Voters Think About Political Debates: Key Findings from a Nationwide Voter Poll." *Campaign and Elections* 23 (2002): 22–4ff.

——, ed. *Winning Elections: Political Campaign Management, Strategy and Tactics*. New York: M. Evans and Co., 2003.

Faucheux, Ronald A. and Paul S. Herrnson. *The Good Fight: How Political Candidates Struggle to Win Elections Without Losing Their Souls*. Washington, D.C.: Campaigns & Elections, 2000.

Federal Election Commission. *Guide for Corporations and Labor Organizations*. Washington, D.C.: Government Printing Office, 2007.

Feigenbaum, Lee et al. "The Semantic Web: How the Internet is Getting Smarter." *Scientific American* 297 (6) (December 2007): 90–7.

Fenno, Richard F., Jr *Home Style: House Members in Their Districts*. Boston, MA: Little, Brown, 1978.

Finer, Lawrence and Stanley Henshaw. "Abortion Incidence and Services in the United States in 2000." *Perspectives on Sexual and Reproductive Health* 35 (1) (2003): 6–15.

Finkel, Steven E. "Reexamining the 'Minimal Effects' Model in Recent Presidential Campaigns." *Journal of Politics* 55 (1) (February 1993): 1–21.

Finkel, Steven E. and George G. Geer. "A Spot Check: Casting Doubt on the Demobilizing Effect of Attack Advertising." *American Journal of Political Science* 42 (1998): 573–95.

Fiorina, Morris P. *Congress: Keystone of the Washington Establishment*. Second edition. New Haven, CT: Yale University Press, 1989.

Fiorina, Morris P. with Samuel J. Abrams and Jeremy C. Pope. *Culture War? The Myth of a Polarized America*. New York: Pearson Longman, 2004.

Fisher, Roger, Elizabeth Kopelman, and Andrea Kupfer Schneider. *Beyond Machiavelli: Tools for Coping with Conflict*. Cambridge, MA: Harvard University Press, 1994.

Fitch, Brad and Kathy Goldschmidt. *Communicating with Congress: How Capitol Hill is Coping with the Surge in Citizen Advocacy*. Washington, D.C.: Congressional Management Foundation, 2005.

Flipse, Scott. "Below the Belt Politics." In *The Conservative Sixties*, edited by David Farber and Jeff Roche, 127–41. New York: Peter Lang Publishing, Inc., 2003.

Florentino-Hofileña, Chay. *News for Sale: The Corruption and Commercialization of the Philippine Media*. Manila: Philippine Center for Investigative Journalism, 2004.

Foot, Kirsten A. and Steven M. Schneider. *Web Campaigning*. Cambridge, MA: The MIT Press, 2006.

Fox, Harrison W. and Martin Schnitzer. *Doing Business in Washington: How to Win Friends and Influence Government*. New York: Free Press, 1981.

Francia, Peter L. et al. *The Financiers of Congressional Elections*. New York: Columbia University Press, 2003.

Franklin, Bob. *Packaging Politics*. London: Edward Arnold, 1994.

——. *Tough on Soundbites, Tough on the Causes of Soundbites: New Labour and News Management*. London: Catalyst Trust, 1998.

597

Franz, Michael M. and Travis N. Ridout. "Does Political Advertising Persuade?" *Political Behavior* 29 (4) (December 2007): 465–91.

Franz, Michael M. et al. *Campaign Advertising and American Democracy*. Philadelphia, PA: Temple University Press, 2008.

Fraser, E.A. "Coalitions." In *The Public Affairs Handbook*, edited by Joseph S. Nagelschmidt, 192–9. New York: Amacom, 1982.

Freedman, Paul and Kenneth Goldstein. "Measuring Media Exposure and the Effects of Negative Campaign Ads." *American Journal of Political Science* 43 (1999): 1189–208.

Freedman, Paul, Michael Franz, and Kenneth Goldstein. "Campaign Advertising and Democratic Citizenship." *American Journal of Political Science* 48 (October 2004): 723–41.

Friedenberg, Robert. *Communications Consultants in Political Campaigns*. Westport, CT: Praeger Publishers, 1997.

Fuentes, Carlos. *Nuevo Tiempo Mexicano*. México, Distrito Federal: 1994.

Galbraith, John Kenneth. *The Affluent Society*. New York: Houghton Mifflin, 1958.

Galili, Orit. *The Tele-politicians: New Political Leadership in the West and in Israel*. Tel Aviv: Ramot-University of Tel Aviv, 2004.

Gamble, Andrew. *The Free Economy and the Strong State: The Politics of Thatcherism*. Basingstoke: Macmillan, 1994.

Gamson, William A. and Andre Modigliani. "The Changing Culture of Affirmative Action." *Research in Political Sociology* 3 (1987): 137–77.

Garramone, Gina M. "Effects of Negative Political Advertising: The Roles of Sponsor and Rebuttal." *Journal of Broadcasting & Electronic Media* 29 (1985): 147–59.

——. "Voter Responses to Negative Political Ads." *Journalism Quarterly* 61 (1984): 250–9.

Garramone, Gina M. and Sandra J. Smith. "Reactions to Advertising: Clarifying Sponsor Effects." *Journalism Quarterly* 61 (1984): 771–5.

Geiger, Andreas. *EU Lobbying Handbook: A Guide to Modern Participation in Brussels*. Berlin: Helios Media, 2006.

Gelman, Andrew and Gary King. "Why Are American Presidential Election Campaign Polls So Variable When Votes Are So Predictable?" *British Journal of Political Science* 23 (4) (October 1993): 409–51.

Geer, John G. "Assessing Attack Advertising: A Silver Lining." In *Campaign Reform*, edited by L.M. Bartels and L. Vavreck, 62–78. Ann Arbor, MI: University of Michigan Press, 2000.

——. *In Defense of Negativity: Attack Ads in Presidential Campaigns*. Chicago, IL: University of Chicago Press, 2006.

Geer, John G. and James H. Geer. "Remembering Attack Ads: An Experimental Investigation of Radio." *Political Behavior* 25 (March 2003): 69–95.

Geer, John and Richard R. Lau. "Filling in the Blanks: A New Method for Estimating Campaign Effects." *British Journal of Political Science* 36 (April 2006): 269–90.

Genz, Andreas, Klaus Schoenbach, and Holli A. Semetko. " 'Amerikanisierung?' Politik in den Fernsehnachrichten während der Bundestagswahlkämpfe 1990–1998." In *Wahlen und Wähler: Analysen aus Anlass der Bundestagswahl 1998*, edited by Hans-Dieter Klingemann and Max Kaase, 401–13. Wiesbaden: Westdeutscher Verlag, 2001.

Gerber, Alan S., Donald P. Green, and Ron Shachar. "Voting May Be Habit-forming: Evidence from a Randomized Field Experiment." *American Journal of Political Science* 47 (July 2003): 540–50.

Germany, Julie Barko. *The Politics-to-Go Handbook: A Guide to Using Mobile Technology in Politics*. Washington, D.C.: George Washington University Institute for Politics, Democracy & the Internet, 2005.

Gershtenson, Joseph. "Mobilization Strategies of the Democrats and Republicans, 1956–2000." *Political Research Quarterly* 56 (September 2003): 293–308.

Gertzog, Irwin W. "The Electoral Consequences of a Local Party Organization's Registration Campaign." *Polity* 3 (Winter 1970): 247–64.

Gibson, Rachel and Andrea Römmele. "Changing Campaign Communications. A Party-centred Theory of Professionalised Campaigning." *Harvard Journal of Press and Politics*, 6 (4) (January 2001): 31–43.

Gibson, Rachel and Stephen Ward. "Virtual Campaigning: Australian Parties and the Impact of the Internet." *Australian Journal of Political Science* 37 (1) (2002): 99–130.

Gierzynski, Anthony. "Gubernatorial and State Legislative Elections." In *Financing the 2000 Election*, edited by David Magleby, 188–212. Washington, D.C.: Brookings Institution Press, 2002.

——. *Money Rules: Financing Elections in America*. Boulder, CO: Westview Press, 2000.

Gimpel, James G., Karen M. Kaufmann, and Shanna Pearson-Merkowitz. "Battleground States versus Blackout States: The Behavioral Implications of Modern Presidential Campaigns." *Journal of Politics* 69 (August 2007): 786–97.

Gladwell, Malcolm. *The Tipping Point: How Little Things Can Make a Big Difference*. Boston, MA: Back Bay Books, 2002.

Glick, Henry R. *Courts, Politics and Justice*. New York: McGraw Hill, 1993.

Godin, Seth. *Permission Marketing: Turning Strangers into Friends and Friends into Customers*. New York: Simon and Schuster, 1999.

Goldstein, Kenneth and Paul Freedman. "Campaign Advertising and Voter Turnout: New Evidence for a Stimulation Effect." *Journal of Politics* 64 (August 2002): 721–40.

Goldstein, Kenneth and Patricia Strach, eds. *The Medium and the Message. Television Advertising and American Elections*. Upper Saddle River, N.J.: Prentice Hall, 2004.

Gómez, Mario Ojeda. *México antes y después de la alternancia política: Un testimonio*. México, Distrito Federal: El Colegio de México, Centro de Estudios Internacionales, 2005.

Goodman, Paul. "The First American Party System." In *The American Party Systems: Stages of Political Development*, edited by William Nisbet Chambers and Walter Dean Burnham, 56–89. New York: Oxford University Press, 1967.

Gordon, Stacy B. Gordon. *Campaign Contributions and Legislative Voting: A New Approach*. New York: Routledge, 2005.

Gorospe-Jamon, Grace. "The El Shaddai Prayer Movement: Political Socialization in a Religious Context." *Philippine Political Science Journal* 20 (43) (1999): 83–126.

Gottfried, Paul and Thomas Fleming. *The Conservative Movement*. Boston, MA: Twayne Publishers, 1988.

Gould, Philip. "Labour Strategy." In *Political Communications: The General Election Campaign of 2001*, edited by J. Bartle, S. Atkinson, and R. Mortimore, 57–68. London: Frank Cass, 2002.

——. *The Unfinished Revolution: How the Modernisers Saved the Labour Party*. London: Little, Brown, 1998.

Graber, Doris. "Press and Television as Opinion Resources in Presidential Campaigns," *Public Opinion Quarterly* 40 (1976): 285–303.

Graetz, Michael J. and Ian Shapiro. *Death by a Thousand Cuts: The Fight over Taxing Inherited Wealth*. Princeton N.J.: Princeton University Press, 2005.

Green, Donald P. and Alan S. Gerber. *Get Out the Vote! How to Increase Voter Turnout*. Washington, D.C.: Brookings Institution Press, 2004.

Green, John C. "Money and Elections." In *The Electoral Challenge*, edited by S.C. Craig, 58–78. Washington, D.C.: CQ Books, 2006.

Green, John C., Mark J. Rozell, and Clyde Wilcox, eds. *The Christian Right in American Politics: Marching to the Millenium*. Washington, D.C.: Georgetown University Press, 2004.

——, eds. *Prayers in the Precincts: The Christian Right in the 1998 Elections*. Washington, D.C.: Georgetown University Press, 2000.

——, eds. *The Values Campaign? The Christian Right and the 2004 Elections*. Washington, D.C.: Georgetown University Press, 2005.

Greenberg, Stanley B. *The Two Americas: America's Current Political Deadlock and How to Break It*. New York: St Martin's Press, 2004.

Grefe, Edward A. "Global Grassroots is a Reality." In *Winning at the Grassroots*, edited by Tony Kramer and Wes Pedersen, 265–75. Washington, D.C.: Public Affairs Council, 2000.

Grefe, Edward A. and Martin Linsky. *The New Corporate Activism: Harnessing the Power of Grassroots Tactics for Your Organization*. New York: McGraw-Hill, 1995.

Grönroos, Christian. "From Marketing Mix to Relationship Marketing: Towards a Paradigm Shift in Marketing." *Management Decision* 32 (2) (1994): 4–20.

——. "Marketing Services: The Case of a Missing Product." *Journal of Business & Industrial Marketing* 13 (4/5) (1998): 322–38.

——. "Quo Vadis, Marketing? Toward a Relationship Marketing Paradigm." *Journal of Marketing Management* 10 (5) (1994): 347–61.

Grossman, Lawrence. *The Electronic Republic: Reshaping Democracy in the Information Age*. New York: Viking Press, 1995.

Gruen, Frank and Michelle Grattan. *Managing Government*. Sydney: Allen & Unwin, 1993.

Guéguén, Daniel. *European Lobbying*. Brussels: Europolitics, 2007.

Gummesson, Evert. *Total Relationship Marketing: Rethinking Marketing Management—From 4Ps to 30Rs*. Oxford: Butterworth-Heinemann, 1999.

Gunther, Richard and Anthony Mughan. *Democracy and the Media: A Comparative Perspective*. New York: Cambridge University Press, 2000.

Gurashani, Roop. "Therapeutic Innovation or Cynical Exploitation?" *Indian Journal of Medical Ethics* 4 (October–December 2006): 133–4.

Gurevitch, Michael. "Television in the Electoral Campaign: Its Audience and Function." In *The Elections in Israel: 1969*, edited by Alan Arian, 220–37. Jerusalem: Academic Press, 1972.

Gurian, Paul-Henri. "Resource Allocation Strategies in Presidential Nomination Campaigns." *American Journal of Political Science* 30 (November 1986): 802–21.

Gurian, Paul-Henri and Audrey A. Haynes. "Campaign Strategy in Presidential Primaries, 1976–88." *American Journal of Political Science* 37 (February 1993): 335–41.

Hacker, Jacob S. and Paul Pierson. *Off Center: The Republican Revolution and the Erosion of American Democracy.* New Haven: Yale University Press, 2005.

Hagel, John III and Marc Singer. *Net Worth.* Cambridge, MA: Harvard Business School, 1999.

Hagen, Michael G. and Richard Johnston. "Conventions and Campaign Dynamics." In *Rewiring Politics: Presidential Nominating Conventions in the Media Age,* edited by Costas Panagopoulos. Baton Rouge, LA: Louisiana University Press, 2007.

Hale, Jon F., Jeffrey C. Fox, and Rick Farmer. "Negative Advertisements in U.S. Senate Campaigns: The Influence of Campaign Context." *Social Science Quarterly* 77 (June 1996): 329–43.

Hall, Melinda Gann and Chris W. Bonneau. "Does Quality Matter? Challengers in State Supreme Court Elections." *American Journal of Political Science* 50 (1) (January 2006): 20–33.

Hall, Richard L. and Frank W. Wayman. "Buying Time: Moneyed Interests and the Mobilization Bias in Congressional Elections." *American Political Science Review* 84 (1990): 797–820.

Hallin, Daniel C. "Sound Bite News: Television Coverage of Elections, 1968–1988," *Journal of Communication* 42 (1992): 5–24.

Hallin, Daniel C. and Paolo Mancini. *Comparing Media Systems: Three Models of Media and Politics.* Cambridge: Cambridge University Press, 2004.

Hamilton, William. "Political Polling: From the Beginning to the Center." In *Campaigns and Elections American Style,* edited by James A. Thurber and Candice J. Nelson, 161–80. Boulder, CO: Westview Press, 1995.

Harris, Louis. "Polls and Politics in the United States." *Public Opinion Quarterly* 27 (1963): 3–8.

Harris, Phil. "Commentary—Machiavelli, Political Marketing and Reinventing Government." *European Journal of Marketing* 35 (9/10) (2001): 1136–54.

——. "To Spin or not to Spin that is the Question: The Emergence of Modern Political Marketing." *Marketing Review* 2 (1) (2001): 35–53.

Harris, Phil and Andrew Lock. "Machiavellian Marketing: The Development of Corporate Lobbying in the UK." *Journal of Marketing Management* 9/10 (1996): 313–28.

Harris, Phil, Andrew Lock, and Patricia Rees. *Machiavelli, Marketing and Management.* London: Routledge, 2000.

Harrison, S. "Lobbying: Shouts and Whispers: The Campaign For and Against Price Maintenance." *European Journal of Marketing* 34 (1–2) (2000): 207–22.

Haskell, John. *Direct Democracy or Representative Government: Dispelling the Populist Myth.* Boulder, CO: Westview Press, 2001.

Hayek, Friedrich von. *Road to Serfdom.* New York: Routledge, 2006, 1944.

Hayes, Bernadette C. and Ian McAllister. "Marketing Politics to Voters: Late Deciders in the 1992 British Election." *European Journal of Marketing* 30 (10/11) (1996): 127–39.

Hayes, Danny. "Candidate Qualities through a Partisan Lens: A Theory of Trait Ownership." *American Journal of Political Science* 49 (October 2005): 908–23.

Heard, Alexander. *The Cost of Democracy.* Chapel Hill, N.C.: University of North Carolina Press, 1960.

Heclo, Hugh. "Campaigning and Governing: A Conspectus." In *The Permanent Campaign and its Future,* edited by N.J. Ornstein and T.E. Mann, 1–37. Washington, D.C.: American Enterprise Institute and the Brookings Institution, 2000.

Henneberg, Stephan C.M. *Generic Functions of Political Marketing.* Bath: University of Bath School of Management Working Paper Series 19, 2003.

——. "Leading or Following? A Theoretical Analysis of Political Marketing Postures." *Journal of Political Marketing* 5 (3) (2006): 29–46.

——. "The Views of an *Advocatus Dei*: Political Marketing and its Critics." *Journal of Public Affairs* 4 (3) (2004): 225–43.

——. "Understanding Political Marketing." In *The Idea of Political Marketing,* edited by N.J. O'Shaughnessy and S.C.M. Henneberg, 93–170. Westport, CT: Praeger Press, 2002.

Heroles, Federico Reyes. *Memorial del mañana.* México, Distrito Federal: Taurus, 1999.

Herr, J. Paul. "The Impact of Campaign Appearances in the 1996 Election." *Journal of Politics* 64 (August 2002): 904–13.

Herring, Pendleton. *Group Representation Before Congress.* New York: Russell & Russell, 1929.

Herrnson, Paul S. "Campaign Professionalism and Fundraising in Congressional Elections," *Journal of Politics* 54 (1992): 859–70.

——. *Congressional Elections: Campaigning at Home and in Washington.* Fourth edition. Washington, D.C.: CQ Press, 2004.

——, ed. *Guide to Political Campaigns in America*. Washington D.C.: CQ Press, 2005.

——. "Hired Guns and House Races: Campaign Professionals in House Elections." In *Campaign Warriors*, edited by J.A. Thurber and C.J. Nelson, 65–90. Washington, D.C.: The Brookings Institution, 2000.

——. *Party Campaigning in the 1980s. Have the National Parties Made a Comeback as Key Players in Congressional Elections?* Cambridge, MA: Harvard University Press, 1988.

——. "The Evolution of Political Campaigns." In *Guide to Political Campaigns in America*, edited by P.S. Herrnson, 19–36. Washington, D.C.: CQ Press, 2005.

——. *The Campaign Assessment and Candidate Outreach Project*. College Park, MD: University of Maryland, 2001.

——. *The 2002 Congressional Campaign Study*. College Park, MD: University of Maryland, 2002.

Herrnson, Paul S. and Jennifer C. Lucas. "The Fairer Sex? Gender and Negative Campaigning in U.S. Elections." *American Politics Research* 34 (January 2006): 69–94.

Hershey, Marjorie. "Campaigns, Elections and the Media." In *Encyclopedia of Media and Politics*, edited by Todd M. Shaefer and Thomas A. Birkland, 34–7. Washington, D.C.: CQ Press, 2007.

Hess, Stephen. "The Press and the Permanent Campaign," in *The Permanent Campaign and Its Future*, edited by N.J. Ornstein and T.E. Mann, 38–53. Washington, D.C.: American Enterprise Institute and the Brookings Institution, 2000.

Hetherington, Marc J. "Resurgent Mass Partisanship. The Role of Elite Polarization." *The American Political Science Review* 95 (3) (September 2001): 619–31.

——. "The Political Relevance of Political Trust." *American Political Science Review* 92 (4) (December 1998): 791–808.

Hetherington, Marc J. and John D. Nugent. "Explaining Public Support for Devolution: The Role of Political Trust." In *What is it About Government that Americans Dislike?*, edited by John R. Hibbing and Elizabeth Theiss-Morse, 134–51. Cambridge: Cambridge University Press, 2001.

Higham, Charles. "A Word to the Chief Party Whips." *The Optimist* 1 (1912): 2.

Hilhorst, Dorothea. *The Real World of NGOs: Discourses, Diversity, and Development*. London/New York: Zed Books, 2003.

Hill, David and Seth C. McGee. "The Electoral College, Mobilization, and Turnout in the 2000 Presidential Election." *American Politics Research* 33 (September 2005): 700–25.

Hills, Stecey Barlow and Shikhar Sarin. "From Market Driving to Market Driven: An Alternative Paradigm for Marketing in High Technology Industries." *Journal of Marketing Theory and Practice* 11 (3) (2003): 13–24.

Hillygus, D. Sunshine. "Campaign Effects and the Dynamics of Turnout Intention in Election 2000." *Journal of Politics* 67 (February 2005): 50–68.

Hillygus, D. Sunshine and Simon Jackman. "Voter Decision Making in Election 2000: Campaign Effects, Partisan Activation, and the Clinton Legacy." *American Journal of Political Science* 47 (4) (October 2003): 583–96.

Hoffman, Donna R. and Alison D. Howard. *Addressing the State of the Union: The Evolution and Impact of the President's Big Speech*. Boulder, CO: Lynne Rienner Publishers, 2006.

Hofstadter, Richard. *The Idea of a Party System: The Rise of Legitimate Opposition in the United States*. Berkeley, CA: University of California Press, 1969.

Hogan, Robert E. and Keith E. Hamm. "Variations in District-level Campaign Spending in State Legislatures." In *Campaign Finance in State Legislative Elections*, edited by Joel A. Thompson and Gary F. Moncrief, 59–79. Washington, D.C.: CQ Press, 1998.

Holbrook, Allyson L. et al. "Attitudes toward Presidential Candidates and Political Parties: Initial Optimism, Inertial First Impressions, and a Focus on Flaws." *American Journal of Political Science* 45 (October 2001): 930–50.

Holbrook, Thomas M. *Do Campaigns Matter?* Thousand Oaks, CA: Sage, 1996.

——. "Do Campaigns Really Matter?" in *The Electoral Challenge*, edited by S.C. Craig, 1–21. Washington, D.C.: CQ Books, 2006.

——. "Presidential Campaigns and the Knowledge Gap." *Political Communication* 19 (October–December 2002): 437–54.

Holbrook, Thomas M. and Scott D. McClurg. "The Mobilization of Core Supporters: Campaigns, Turnout, and Electoral Composition in United States Presidential Elections." *American Journal of Political Science* 49 (4) (October 2005): 689–703.

Holian, David B. "He's Stealing My Issues: Clinton's Crime Rhetoric and the Dynamics of Issue Ownership." *Political Behavior* 26 (June 2004): 95–124.

——. "Trust the Party Line: Issue Ownership and Presidential Approval From Reagan to Clinton." *American Politics Research* 34 (November 2006): 777–802.

Holman, Craig and Luke P. McLoughlin. *Buying Time 2000: Television Advertising in the 2000 Federal Elections*. New York: Brennan Center for Justice at New York University School of Law, 2001.

Holtz-Bacha, Christina and Eva Maria Lessinger. "Wie die Lustlosigkeit Konterkariert Wurde: Fernsehwhahlwerbung 2005." In *Die Massenmedien im Wahlkampf: Die Bundestagswahl 2005*, edited by Christina Holtz-Bacha, 164–82. Wiesbaden: VS Verlag, 2006.

Honasan, Gregorio B. "On Peace and Insurgency: President Estrada and the Conflict in Mindanao." *Kasarinlan Philippine Quarterly of Third World Studies* 15 (2) (2000): 237–44.

Howard, Philip N. *New Media Campaigns and the Managed Citizen*. New York: Cambridge University Press, 2006.

Huang, Chia-shu and Rui Cheng. *Taiwan zhengzhi yu xuanju wenhua [Taiwan Politics and Election Culture]*. Taipei: Boy Young, 1991.

Huang, Kuang-guo. *Mincuiwangtailun [About Populism and the End of Taiwan]*. Taipei: Shangchou, 1995.

Huang, Teh-fu. "Elections and the Evolution of the Kuomintang." In *Political Change in Taiwan*, edited by Cheng Tun-jen and Stephan Haggard. Boulder, CO: Rienner, 1992.

Huber, Gregory A. and Kevin Arceneaux. "Identifying the Persuasive Effects of Presidential Advertising." *American Journal of Political Science* 51 (4) (October 2007): 957–77.

Hughes, Colin and Patrick Wintour. *Labour Rebuilt: The New Model Party*. London: Fourth Estate, 1990.

Huntington, Samuel P. *The Third Wave: Democratization in the Late Twentieth Century*. Norman, OK: University of Oklahoma Press, 1991.

Hutcheson, Derek S. "How to Win Elections and Influence People: The Development of Political Consulting in Post-Communist Russia." *Journal of Political Marketing* 5 (4) (2006): 47–70.

Il'yasov, Farkhad. *Politicheskii marketing*. Moscow: IMA-Press, 2000.

Ireland, Emilienne. "Secrets of Successful Online Fundraising: Tips for Increasing Donations." *Campaigns & Elections* 22 (6) (August 2001).

Ireland, Emilienne and Phil Tajitsu Nash. "Campaign 2000: Parties Vie for Internet Dominance." *Campaigns and Elections* 20 (9) (1999): 62–5.

——. *Winning Campaigns Online*. Second edition. Bethesda, MD: Science Writers Press, 2001.

Islam, Syed Serajul. "The Islamic Independence Movements in Patani of Thailand and Mindanao of the Philippines." *Asian Survey* 38 (5) (1998): 441–56.

Ito, Mizuko and Misa Matsuda. *Personal, Portable, Pedestrian: Mobile Phones in Japanese Life*. Cambridge, MA: MIT Press, 2005.

Iyengar, Shanto and Adam F. Simon. "New Perspectives and Evidence on Political Communication and Campaign Effects." *Annual Review of Psychology* 51 (2000): 149–69.

Jackson, Brooks and Kathleen Hall Jamieson. *unSpun: Finding Facts in a World of Disinformation*. New York: Random House, 2007.

Jacobs, Lawrence R. and Robert Y. Shapiro. "Issues, Candidate Image, and Priming: The Use of Private Polls in Kennedy's 1960 Presidential Campaign." *American Political Science Review* 88 (September 1994): 527–40.

——. *Politicians Don't Pander: Political Manipulation and the Loss of Democratic Responsiveness*. Chicago, IL: University of Chicago Press, 2000.

Jacobson, Gary C. "The First Congressional Elections after BCRA." In *The Election after Reform: Money, Politics, and the Bipartisan Campaign Reform Act*, edited by Michael Malbin 185–203. Lanham, MD: Rowman & Littlefield Publishers, 2005.

——. *The Politics of Congressional Elections*. Sixth edition. New York: Longman, 2004.

Jacobson, Gary C. and Michael Dimock. "Checking Out: The Effects of Bank Overdrafts on the 1992 House Election." *American Journal of Political Science* 38 (1994): 601–24.

Jaffe, Joseph. *Life After the Thirty-Second Spot: Energize Your Brand with a Bold Mix of Alternatives to Traditional Advertising*. Hoboken, N.J.: John Wiley, 2005.

Jaensch, Dean. *Election!* St Leonards: Allen & Unwin, 1995.

Jaensch, Dean and David S. Mathieson. *A Plague on Both Your Houses: Minor Parties in Australia*. Sydney: Allen & Unwin, 1998.

Jamieson, Kathleen Hall. *Dirty Politics*. New York, Oxford University Press, 1992.

——. *Everything You Think You Know about Politics and Why You're Wrong*. New York: Basic Books, 2000.

——. *Packaging the Presidency: A History and Criticism of Presidential Campaign Advertising*. New York: Oxford University Press, 1984. (Second edition, 1992.)

Jamieson, Kathleen Hall, Paul Waldman, and Susan Sherr. "Eliminate the Negative? Categories of Analysis for Political Advertisements." In *Crowded Airwaves*, edited by J.A. Thurber, C.J. Nelson and D.A. Dulio, 44–64. Washington, D.C.: Brookings Institution Press, 2000.

Jasperson, Amy E. and David P. Fan. "An Aggregate Examination of the Backlash Effect in Political Advertising: The Case of the 1996 U.S. Senate Race in Minnesota." *Journal of Advertising* 31 (2002): 1–12.

Javits, Jacob K. "How I Used a Poll in Campaigning for Congress." *Public Opinion Quarterly* 11 (1947): 222–6.

Jaworski, B.J. and A.K. Kohli. "Market Orientation: Antecedents and Consequences." *Journal of Marketing* 57 (3) (1993): 1–17.

Jay, Antony. *Management and Machiavelli.* London: Hodder and Stoughton, 1967.

Johnson, Dennis W. "The Business of Political Consulting." In *Campaign Warriors*, edited by J.A. Thurber and C.J. Nelson, 37–52. Washington, D.C.: Brookings Institution Press, 2000.

——. "Campaigning and the Internet." In *The Electoral Challenge*, edited by S.C. Craig, 121–42. Washington, D.C.: CQ Books, 2006.

——. *Congress Online: Bridging the Gap Between Citizens and Their Representatives.* New York: Routledge, 2004.

——. "Connecting with Constituents." In *Congress and the Internet*, edited by James A. Thurber and Colton Campbell, 123–32. Englewood Cliffs, N.J.: Prentice-Hall, 2003.

——. "First Hurdles: The Evolution of the Pre-primary and Primary Stages of American Presidential Elections." In *Winning Elections with Political Marketing*, edited by J.P. Davies and B.I. Newman, 177–210. Binghampton, N.Y.: Haworth Press, 2006.

——. *No Place for Amateurs. How Political Consultants Are Reshaping American Democracy.* Second edition. New York: Routledge, 2007. (First edition, 2001.)

——. "Perspectives on Political Consulting." *Journal of Political Marketing* 1 (1) (2002): 7–21.

Johnson, Richard M. "Market Segmentation: A Strategic Management Tool." *Journal of Marketing Research* 8 (1) (1971): 13–19.

Johnson-Cartee, Karen S. and Gary A. Copeland. *Inside Political Campaigns: Theory and Practice.* Westport, CT: Praeger, 1997.

Johnston, Richard, Michael G. Hagen, and Kathleen Hall Jamieson. *The 2000 Presidential Election and the Foundations of Party Politics.* Cambridge: Cambridge University Press, 2004.

Johnston, Ronald J., Charles J. Pattie, and J. Graham Allsopp. *A Nation Dividing? The Electoral Map of Great Britain 1979–1987.* London: Longman, 1988.

——. "Southern Voters' Reaction to Negative Political Ads in 1986 Election." *Journalism Quarterly*, 66 (1989): 888–93, 986.

Jones, Charles O. "Campaigning to Govern: The Clinton Style." In *The Clinton Presidency: First Appraisals*, edited by Colin Campbell and Bert A. Rockman. Chatham, N.J.: Chatham House Publishers, 1996.

——. "Preparing to Govern in 2001: Lessons from the Clinton Presidency." In *The Permanent Campaign and its Future*, edited by N.J. Ornstein and T.E. Mann, 185–218. American Enterprise Institute and the Brookings Institution, 2000.

Jones, Gregg R. *Red Revolution: Inside the Philippine Guerrilla Movement.* Boulder, CO: Westview Press, 1989.

Jones, Jeffrey M. "Does Bringing Out the Candidate Bring Out the Votes? The Effects of Nominee Campaigning in Presidential Elections." *American Politics Quarterly* 26 (October 1998): 395–419.

Jones, Nicholas. *Soundbites and Spin Doctors: How Politicians Manipulate the Media and Vice Versa.* London: Cassell, 1995.

——. *Sultans of Spin.* London: Victor Gollancz, 1999.

Jordan, G. "Insider Lobbying: The British Version." *Political Studies* 37 (1989): 107–13.

Jordan, Grant and William A. Maloney. *Democracy and Interest Groups: Enhancing Participation?* London: Palgrave Macmillan, 2007.

——. *The Protest Business? Mobilizing Campaign Groups.* Manchester: Manchester University Press, 1997.

Jose, Ricardo T. "The Philippine Armed Forces: Protector or Oppressor? A Historical Overview." *Kasarinlan Philippine Quarterly of Third World Studies* 16 (2) (2001): 73–90.

Judis, John B. *The Paradox of American Democracy.* New York: Routledge, 2000.

Judis, John B. and Ruy Teixeira. *The Emerging Democratic Majority.* New York: Scribner, 2002.

Just, Marion, Ann Cigler, and Lori Wallach. "Thirty Seconds or Thirty Minutes: What Viewers Learn from Spot Advertisements and Candidate Debates." *Journal of Communication* 40 (Summer 1990): 120–33.

Just, Marion, Anne Crigler, Dean Alger, et al. *Crosstalk: Citizens, Candidates, and the Media in a Presidential Campaign.* Chicago, IL: University of Chicago Press, 1996.

Kahn, Kim Fridkin and John G. Geer. "Creating Impressions: An Experimental Investigation of Political Advertising on Television." *Political Behavior* 16 (1994): 93–116.

Kahn, Kim Fridkin and Patrick J. Kenney. "Do Negative Campaigns Mobilize or Suppress Turnout? Clarifying the Relationship between Negativity and Participation." *American Political Science Review* 93 (1999): 877–89.

——. *No Holds Barred: Negativity in U.S. Senate Campaigns.* Upper Saddle River, N.J.: Pearson Prentice Hall, 2004.

——. *The Spectacle of U.S. Senate Campaigns.* Princeton, N.J.: Princeton University Press, 1999.

Kahn, Kim Fridkin et al. "Capturing the Power of a Campaign Event: The 2004 Presidential Debate in Tempe." *Journal of Politics* 69 (August 2007): 776–7.

Kaid, Lynda Lee. "Political Advertising." In *The Electoral Challenge*, edited by S.C. Craig, 79–96. Washington, D.C.: CQ Books, 2006.

——. "Political Advertising." In *The Handbook of Political Communication Research*, edited by L.L. Kaid, 155–202. Mahwah, N.J.: Lawrence Erlbaum, 2004.

——. "Political Advertising and Information Seeking: Comparing Exposure via Conventional and Internet Channels." *Advertising Age* 31 (1) (2002): 27–36.

——. "Political Advertising in the United States." In *The Sage Handbook of Political Advertising*, edited by L.L. Kaid and C. Holtz-Bacha, 37–64. Thousand Oaks, CA: Sage, 2006.

——, ed. *Television and Politics in Evolving European Democracies.* Commack, N.Y.: Nova Biomedical, 1999.

——. "The Effects of Television Broadcasts on Perceptions of Political Candidates in the United States and France." In *Mediated Politics in Two Cultures: Presidential Campaigning in the United States and France*, edited by Lynda Lee Kaid, Jacques Gerstlé, and Keith R. Sanders, 247–60. New York: Praeger, 1991.

Kaid, Lynda Lee and John Boydston. "An Experimental Study of the Effectiveness of Negative Political Advertisements." *Communication Quarterly* 35 (1987): 193–201.

Kaid, Lynda Lee and Mike Chanslor. "The Effects of Political Advertising on Candidate Images." In *Presidential Candidate Images*, edited by Kenneth L. Hacker, 133–50. Westport, CT: Praeger, 2004.

Kaid, Lynda Lee and Daniela V. Dimitrova. "The Television Advertising Battleground in the 2004 Presidential Election." *Journalism Studies* 6 (2005): 165–75.

Kaid, Lynda Lee and Christina Holtz-Bacha, eds. *Political Advertising in Western Democracies. Parties and Candidates on Television.* Thousand Oaks, CA: Sage, 1995.

——, eds. *The Sage Handbook of Political Advertising.* Thousand Oaks, CA: Sage, 2006.

——. "Political Advertising in International Comparison." In *The Sage Handbook of Political Advertising*, edited by L.L. Kaid and C. Holtz-Bacha, 3–14. Thousand Oaks, CA: Sage, 2006.

——. "Television Advertising and Democratic Systems Around the World: A Comparison of Videostyle Content and Effects." In *The Sage Handbook of Political Advertising*, edited by L.L. Kaid and C. Holtz-Bacha, 445–57. Thousand Oaks, CA: Sage, 2006.

Kaid, Lynda Lee and Anne Johnston. *Videostyle in Presidential Campaigns: Style and Content of Televised Political Advertising.* Westport, CT: Praeger, 2001.

Kaid, Lynda Lee and Keith R. Sanders. "Political Television Commercials: An Experimental Study of the Type and Length." *Communication Research* 5 (1978): 57–70.

Kaid, Lynda Lee and John C. Tedesco. "Tracking Voter Reactions to Television Advertising." In *The Electronic Election*, edited by L.L. Kaid and D.G. Bystrom, 236–46. Mahwah, N.J.: Lawrence Erlbaum, 1999.

Kaid, Lynda Lee, Mike Chanslor, and Mark Hovind. "The Influence of Program and Commercial Type on Political Advertising Effectiveness." *Journal of Broadcasting & Electronic Media* 36 (1992): 303–20.

Kaid, Lynda Lee, Mitchell S. McKinney, and John C. Tedesco. *Civic Dialogue in the 1996 Presidential Campaign: Candidate, Media, and Public Voices.* Cresskill, N.J.: Hampton Press, 2000.

Kaplan, Noah, David K. Park, and Travis N. Ridout. "Dialogue in American Political Campaigns? An Examination of Issue Convergence in Candidate Television Advertising." *American Journal of Political Science* 50 (July 2006): 724–36.

Kaspe, S.I. and A.I. Petrokovsky. "Administrativnye i informatsionnye resursy v kontekste vyborov-99." *Politiya* 2 (16) (2000): 5–28.

Kavanagh, Dennis. *Election Campaigning: The New Marketing of Politics.* Oxford: Blackwell, 1995.

——. "Speaking Truth to Power? Pollsters as Campaign Advisors." *European Journal of Marketing* 30 (10/11) (1996): 104–13.

Kawanaka, Takeshi. *Power in a Philippine City.* Chiba: Institute of Developing Economies and Japan External Trade Organization, 2002.

——. "The Robredo Style: Philippine Local Politics in Transition." *Kasarinlan Philippine Quarterly of Third World Studies* 13 (3) (1998): 5–36.

——. "The State and Institutions in Philippine Local Politics." *Philippine Political Science Journal* 22 (45) (2001): 135–48.

Kearsey, Anthony and Richard J. Varey. "Managerialist Thinking on Marketing for Public Services." *Public Money & Management* 18 (2) (January–March 1998): 51–61.

Keith, Robert. "The Marketing Revolution," *Journal of Marketing* (January 1960): 35.

Keller, Kevin Lane. "Building Customer-based Brand Equity: A Blueprint for Creating Strong Brands." *Marketing Management* 28 (1) (2001): 35–41.

Kelley, Stanley, Jr. *Professional Public Relations and Political Power.* Baltimore, MD: The Johns Hopkins University Press, 1956.

Kelly, Orr. *King of the Killing Zone: The Story of the M-1, America's Super Tank.* New York, Norton, 1989.

Kennedy, George A. *A New History of Classical Rhetoric.* Princeton, N.J.: Princeton University Press, 1994.

Kennedy, Robert R. *Crimes Against Nature.* New York: Harper Perennial, 2005.

Kerbel, Matthew. *Edited for Television: CNN, ABC, and American Presidential Elections.* Second edition. Boulder, CO: Westview Press, 1998.

Kerkvliet, Benedict J. *Everyday Politics in the Philippines: Class and Status Relations in a Central Luzon Village.* Berkeley, CA: University of California Press, 1990.

——. *Political Change in the Philippines: Studies of Local Politics Preceding Martial Law.* Honolulu: University Press of Hawaii, 1974.

Kerkvliet, Benedict J. and Resil B. Mojares, *From Marcos to Aquino: Local Perspectives on Political Transition in the Philippines.* Quezon City: Ateneo de Manila University Press, 1991.

Kessler, Ronald. *Inside Congress: The Shocking Scandals, Corruption, and Abuse of Power Behind the Scenes on Capitol Hill.* New York: Pocket Books, 1998.

Key, V.O., Jr. *Politics, Parties, and Pressure Groups.* Fifth edition. New York: Ty Crowell Company, 1964.

Kholmskaya, Marina and Vladimir Tomarovsky. "Chtit' zakon." *Vybory: Zakonodatel'stvo i tekhnologii* 11 (2001): 36–9.

Klapper, Joseph. *The Effects of Mass Communication.* New York: Free Press, 1960.

Kleinman, Philip. *The Saatchi and Saatchi Story.* London: Weidenfeld and Nicolson, 1987.

Klemperer, Victor. *The Language of the Third Reich.* London: Athlone Press, 2000.

King, Anthony. *Running Scared: Why America's Politicians Campaign Too Much and Govern Too Little.* New York: Free Press, 1997.

Kiplinger, Austin H. and Knight A. Kiplinger. *Washington Now.* New York: Harper & Row, 1975.

Kirk, Russell. *The Conservative Mind: From Burke to Eliot.* Fourth edition. New York: Equinox Books, 1973, 1953.

Kochalov, Maksim. "Transformatsiya PR-rynka i PR-industrii v putinskie vremena." *Sovetnik* 1 (January 30, 2006).

Kohli, Ajay K. and Bernard J. Jaworski. "Market Orientation: The Construct, Research Propositions, and Managerial Implications." *Journal of Marketing* 54 (2) (April 1990): 1–18.

Kollman, Ken. *Outside Lobbying: Public Opinion & Interest Group Strategies.* Princeton, N.J.: Princeton University Press, 1998.

Kolodny, Robin. "Electoral Partnerships: Political Consultants and Political Parties." In *Campaign Warriors,* edited by J.A. Thurber and C.J. Nelson, 110–32. Washington, D.C.: The Brookings Institution, 2000.

Kolodny, Robin and David A. Dulio. "Political Party Adaption in US Congressional Campaigns: Why Political Parties Use Coordinated Expenditures to Hire Political Consultants." *Party Politics* 9 (6) (November 2003): 729–46.

Kolodny, Robin and Diana Dwyre. "A New Rule Book: Party Money after BCRA." In *Financing the 2004 Election,* edited by David B. Magleby, Anthony Corrado, and Kelly D. Patterson, 183–207. Washington, D.C.: Brookings Institution Press, 2006.

Kolodny, Robin and Andrea Logan. "Political Consultants and the Extension of Party Goals." *PS: Political Science and Politics* 31 (2) (1988): 155–9.

Kolodny, Robin, Sandra Suárez, and Justin Gollob. "Why Context Matters: The Pennsylvania Thirteenth Congressional District Race." In *Electing Congress: New Rules for an Old Game,* edited by David B. Magleby, J. Quin Monson and Kelly D. Patterson, 123–46. Upper Saddle River, N.J.: Prentice-Hall, 2007.

Kolodny, Robin, Sandra Suárez, and Kyle Kreider. "The 2000 Pennsylvania Thirteenth Congressional District Race." In *Election Advocacy: Soft Money and Issue Advocacy in the 2000 Congressional Elections,* edited by David B. Magleby, 57–60. Provo, UT: Center for the Study of Elections and Democracy, Brigham Young University, 2001.

Kolodny, Robin, Sandra Suárez, and Michael Rodríguez. "Pennsylvania Thirteenth District." *Outside Money: Soft Money and Issue Ads in Competitive 1998 Congressional Elections,* edited by David B. Magleby and M. Holt, 165–75. Provo, UT: Center for the Study of Elections and Democracy, Brigham Young University, 2001.

Kolomiets, V.S., ed. *Izbiratel'nye tekhnologii i izbiratel'noe iskusstvo.* Moscow: ROSSPEN, 2001.

Kotler, Philip. *Marketing for Nonprofit Organizations.* Englewood Cliffs, N.J.: Prentice-Hall, 1982.

——. "Overview of Political Candidate Marketing." *Advances in Consumer Research* 2 (1975): 761–9.

Kotler, Philip and Alan Andreasen. *Strategic Marketing for Nonprofit Organizations.* Englewood Cliffs, N.J.: Prentice-Hall, 1991.

Kotler, Philip and Neil Kotler. "Political Marketing: Generating Effective Candidates, Campaigns, and Causes." In *The Handbook of Political Marketing,* edited by B.I. Newman, 3–18. Thousand Oaks, CA: Sage Publications, 1999.

Kotler, Philip and S. Levy. "Broadening the Concept of Marketing." *Journal of Marketing* 33 (1) (January 1969): 10–15.

Kotz, Nick. *Wild Blue Yonder: Money, Politics, and the B-1 Bomber.* New York: Pantheon, 1988.

Kozlov, V.N. and D.B. Oreshkin, eds. *Vybory deputatov Gosudarstvennoi Dumy Federal'nogo Sobraniya Rossiiskoi Federatsii. 1999. Elektoral'naya statistika.* Moscow: CEC/Ves' Mir, 2000.

Kozlov, V.N., D.B. Oreshkin, and A.N. Plate, eds. *Vybory deputatov Gosudarstvennoi Dumy. 1995. Elektoral'naya statistika.* Moscow: CEC/Ves' Mir, 1996.

——. *Vybory glav izpolnitel'noi vlasti sub"ektov Rossiiskoi Federatsii, 1995–97: Elektoral'naya statistika.* Moscow: CEC/Ves' Mir, 1997.

Krasno, Jonathan and Kenneth Goldstein. "The Facts About Television Advertising and the McCain-Feingold Bill." *PS: Political Science and Politics* 35 (2) (2002): 207–12.

Krastev, Iwan. "Democracy's Doubles." *Journal of Democracy* 17 (2) (2006): 52–62.

Kraus, Sidney, ed. *The Great Debates: Background, Perspective, Effects.* Bloomington, IN: Indiana University Press, 1962.

Krehely, Jeff, Meaghan House and Emily Kernan. *Axis of Ideology, National Committee for Responsive Philanthropy,* 2004.

Kuan, Chong. *Jintian bu zuo mingtian houhui [If We Do Not Do it Today, We Will Regret Tomorrow].* Taipei: Democracy Foundation, 1991.

Kuan, John. *The Modernisation of the Kuomintang: Observations and Expectations.* Taipei: Democracy Foundation, 1992.

Kudinov, O.P. *Osnovy organizatsii i provedeniya izbiratel'nykh kampanii v regionakh Rossii.* Kaliningrad: Yantarnyi skaz, 2000.

Kunath, Tina and Sebastian Schwarz. "Informationsmanagement: Public Affairs 2.0—Digitales Monitoring." *Public Affairs Manager* 2 (1): 74–80.

Lallana, Emmanuel C., Patricia Pascual, and Edwin Soriano. "E-government in the Philippines: Benchmarking Against Global Best Practices." *Kasarinlan Philippine Quarterly of Third World Studies* 17 (2) (2002): 235–72.

Lambert, Jacques. *América Latina, estructuras sociales e Instituciones Políticas.* Barcelona, Editorial Ariel, 1968.

Lande, Carl H. *Leaders, Factions, and Parties; the Structure of Philippine Politics.* New Haven: Southeast Asia Studies, 1965.

——. *Southern Tagalog Voting, 1946–1963: Political Behavior in a Philippine Region.* DeKalb, IL: Northern Illinois University, 1973.

——. "The Return of 'People Power' in the Philippines." *Journal of Democracy* 12 (2) (2001): 88–102.

Lane, Robert E. *Political Ideology: Why the Common Man Believes What He Does.* New York: The Free Press, 1962.

Lang, Annie. "Emotion, Formal Features, and Memory for Televised Political Advertisements." In *Television and Political Advertising,* edited by F. Biocca, 221–43. Hillsdale, N.J.: Lawrence Erlbaum, 1991.

Langbein, Laura I. and Mark A. Lotwis. "The Political Efficacy of Lobbying and Money: Gun Control in the U.S. House, 1986." *Legislative Studies Quarterly* 15 (August 1990): 413–40.

LaPorte, Todd R. and Daniel Metlay. "Technology Observed: Attitudes of a Wary Public." *Science* 188 (11) (April 1975): 121.

Lau, Richard R. "Two Explanations for Negativity Effects in Political Behavior." *American Journal of Political Science* 29 (February 1985): 119–38.

Lau, Richard R. and Gerald M. Pomper. "Effects of Negative Campaigning on Turnout in U.S. Senate Elections." *Journal of Politics* 63 (August 2001): 804–19.

——. *Negative Campaigning: An Analysis of U.S. Senate Elections.* Lanham, MD: Rowman & Littlefield, 2004.

Lau, Richard R. and David P. Redlawsk. "Voting Correctly." *American Political Science Review* 91 (September 1997): 585–98.

Lau, Richard R. and Lee Sigelman. "Effectiveness of Negative Political Advertising." In *Crowded Airwaves,* edited by J.A. Thurber, C.J. Nelson, and D.A. Dulio, 10–43. Washington, D.C.: Brookings Institution Press, 2000.

Lau, Richard R., Lee Sigelman, Caroline Heldman, and Paul Babbitt. "The Effects of Negative Political Advertisements: A Meta-analytic Assessment." *American Political Science Review* 93 (1999): 851–75.

Law, Lisa and Kathy Nadeau. "Globalization, Migration and Class Struggles: NGO Mobilization for Filipino Domestic Workers." *Kasarinlan Philippine Quarterly of Third World Studies* 14 (3 & 4) (1999): 51–68.

Lazarsfeld, Paul F., Bernard Berelson, and Hazel Gaudet. *The People's Choice: How the Voter Makes Up His Mind in a Presidential Campaign.* New York: Duell, Sloan, and Pearce, 1944.

Lees-Marshment, Jennifer. "Political Marketing." In *New Zealand Government and Politics,* edited by Raymond Miller. Fourth edition. Oxford: Oxford University Press, 2006.

——. *Political Marketing and British Political Parties.* Manchester: Manchester University Press, 2001. (Second edition, 2008.)

——. "Political Marketing: How to Reach That Pot of Gold." *Journal of Political Marketing* 2 (1) (2003): 1–32.

——. "The Product, Sales and Market-oriented Party: How Labour Learnt to Market the Product, Not Just the Presentation." *European Journal of Marketing* 35 (9/10) (2001): 1074–84.

Lehman-Wilzig, Sam. "The Media Campaign: The Negative Effects of Positive Campaigning." *Israel Affairs* 4 (1) (Fall 1997): 167–86.

Lemert, James B., Wayne Wanta, and Tien-Tsung Lee. "Party Identification and Negative Advertising in a U.S. Senate Election." *Journal of Communication* 49 (1999): 123–34.

Lengauer, Günther. *Postmoderne Nachrichtenlogik. Redaktionelle Politikvermittlung in medienzentrierten Demokratien.* Wiesbaden: VS Verlag, 2007.

Levinson, Jay Conrad. *Guerilla Marketing Weapons.* New York: Penguin Books, 1990.

Levitsky, Stephen and Lucan Way. "The Rise of Competitive Authoritarianism." *Journal of Democracy* 13 (2): 51–65.

Li, Yan-Xian, Zhen-long Yang, and Yan-xian Zhang eds., *Report on the Responsibility for the 228 Massacre [ererba shijian zeren guishu yanjiu baogao].* Zhonghe: 228 Memorial Foundation, 2006.

Liberal Democratic Party of Russia (LDPR) Central Apparatus. *Metodicheskie ukazaniya po podgotovke i provedeniyu kampanii po vyboram v Gosudarstvennuyu Dumy Federal'nogo Sobraniya Rossiiskoi Federatsii i Prezidenta RF v 1999–2000 godu.* Moscow: LDPR, 1998.

Lichter, S. Robert and Richard E. Noyes. *Good Intentions Make Bad News.* Lanham, MD: Rowman & Littlefield, 1995.

Lichter, S. Robert, Richard E. Noyes, and Lynda Lee Kaid. "No News or Negative News: How the Networks Nixed the '96 Campaign." In *The Electronic Election*, edited by L.L. Kaid and Bystrom, 3–13. Mahwah, N.J.: Lawrence Erlbaum, 1999.

Lilleker, Darren G. and Jennifer Lees-Marshment, eds. *Political Marketing. A Comparative Perspective.* Manchester: Manchester University Press, 2005.

Lin, Jia-long. "Taiwan difang xuanju yu guomindang zhengquan de shichanghua" [Taiwan's Local Elections and the Marketization of KMT's Political Power]. In *Liangan jiceng xuanju yu zhengzhi shehui bianqian [Grassroots Elections, Political and Social Changes in China and Taiwan]*, edited by Chen Ming-Tong and Cheng Yong-nian. Taipei: Yuandan, 1998.

Lindberg, Steffan I. *Democracy and Elections in Africa.* Princeton, N.J.: Princeton University Press, 2006.

Linz, Juan. *La quiebra de las democracias.* México, Distrito Federal: Consejo Nacional para la Cultura y las Artes y Alianza Editorial Mexicana, 1990.

Lipset, Symour Martin. *American Exceptionalism.* New York: W.W. Norton and Company, 1965.

Lipset, Seymour Martin and William Schneider. "The Confidence Gap During the Reagan Years, 1981–1987." *Political Science Quarterly* 102 (Spring 1987): 1–23.

Lisovsky, S.F. and V.A. Evstaf'ev. *Izbiratel'nye tekhnologii: istoriya, teoriya, praktika.* Moscow: RAU-Universitet, 2000.

Liu, Tao-yi. *Why Abolish the Province? Self-criticism and Adjustments of Administrative Areas [Wei shen ma yao fei sheng? Wo guo xing zheng qü de jian tao yü tiao cheng].* Taipei: Central Library Publication, 1997.

Lloyd, Clem. "The 1990 Media Campaign." In *The Greening of Australian Politics*, edited by Clive Bean, Ian McAllister, and John Warhurst, 92–113. Melbourne: Longman Cheshire, 1990.

Lloyd, Jenny. "Square Peg, Round Hole? Can Marketing-based Concepts Such as 'Product' and the 'Marketing Mix' Have a Useful Role in the Political Arena?" In *Current Issues in Political Marketing*, edited by Walter W. Wymer Jr and Jennifer Lees-Marshment, 27–46. Binghamton, N.Y.: Haworth Press, 2005.

Lock, Andrew and Phil Harris. "Political Marketing—*Vive la Différence!*" *European Journal of Marketing* 30 (10/11) (1996): 14–16.

Locke, John. *An Essay Concerning Human Understanding*, edited by Peter Nidditch. Oxford: Oxford University Press, 1975.

Loth, David Goldsmith. *Public Plunder: A History of Graft in America.* New York: Carrick and Evans, 1938.

Lozano, Jose-Carlos. "Political Advertising in Mexico." In *The Sage Handbook of Political Advertising*, edited by L.L. Kaid and C. Holtz-Bacha, 259–68. Thousand Oaks, CA: Sage, 2006.

Lu, Song-ting. *Taiwan zhi sheng [Voice of Taiwan].* Chonghe: Tatsun, 1994.

Luard, Evan. "China and the United Nations." *International Affairs* 47 (4) (1971): 729–35.

Luntz, Frank I. *Candidates, Consultants, and Campaigns: The Style and Substance of American Electioneering.* New York: Basil Blackwell, 1988.

Lyubashevsky, Yurii. *Kak samomu proigrat' vybory v Gosudarstvennuyu Dumu: vrednye sovety kandidatam-2003.* Moscow: Russkaya Shkola PR, 2002.

Lyzlov, V.E. *Pobeda, tol'ko pobeda!* Moscow: PAIMS, 1999.

Maarek, Philippe J. *Political Marketing and Communication.* London: John Libbey, 1995.

McAlpine, Alistair. *The Servant: A New Machiavelli.* London, Faber and Faber, 1992.

McAllister, Ian. "Calculating or Capricious? The New Politics of Late Deciding Voters." In *Do Campaigns Matter?*, edited by David Farrrell and Rüdiger Schmitt-Beck, 22–40. London: Routledge, 2001.

——. "The Personalization of Politics." In *The Oxford Handbook of Political Behavior*, edited by Russell J. Dalton and Hans-Dieter Klingemann, 571–88. Oxford: Oxford Handbook of Political Behavior, 2007.

McCaffrey, General Barry R. USA-Ret. "Challenges to U.S. National Security: Crusader Essential to High-Intensity Combat." *Armed Forces Journal International* (June 2002).

McCombs, Maxwell and Donald Shaw. "The Agenda-Setting Function of the Mass Media." *Public Opinion Quarterly* 36 (1972): 176–87.

McCurry, Michael. "Mass Media Politics: Historic Perspective." In *Winning Elections: Political Campaign Management, Strategy and Tactics*, edited by Ronald A. Faucheux, 470–4. New York: M. Evans and Co., 2003.

MacDonald, Chris. "Stem Cell Ethics and the Forgotten Corporate Context." *American Journal of Bioethics* (Winter 2002): 54–6.

McFaul, Michael, Nikolai Petrov, Andrei Ryabov, and Elizabeth Reisch. *Primer on Russia's 1999 Duma Elections*. Moscow: Carnegie, 1999.

McGrath, Conor. "Family Businesses Distributing America's Beverage: Managing Government Relations in the National Beer Wholesalers Association." *Journal of Public Affairs* 3 (3) (2003): 212–24.

——. "Towards a Lobbying Profession: Developing the Industry's Reputation, Education and Representation." *Journal of Public Affairs* 5 (2) (May 2005): 124–35.

Machiavelli, Niccolo. *Florentine History*. New York: Harper & Row Publishers, 1960.

——. *Mandragola*. New York: The Macaulay Company, 1927.

——. *The Discourses*. London: Penguin, 1983.

——. *The Prince*, trans. G. Bull. London: Penguin, 1961.

——. *The Prince*. London: Everyman, 1992.

——. *The Prince*, trans. Alan H. Gilbert. In *Machiavelli: The Chief Works and Others*. Fifth edition. Volume 1. Durham, N.C.: Duke University Press, 1989.

Mack, Charles S. *Business, Politics, and the Practice of Government Relations*. Westport, CT: Quorum Books, 1997.

McKean, Dayton David. *Pressures on the Legislature of New Jersey*. New York: Columbia University Press, 1938.

McKee, Oliver. "Lobbying for Good or Evil." *North American Review* 227 (April 1929).

McKenna, Thomas M. *Muslim Rulers and Rebels: Everyday Politics and Armed Separatism in the Southern Philippines*. Berkeley, CA: University of California Press, 1998.

McKinney, Mitchell S. and Diana B. Carlin. "Political Campaign Debates." In *The Handbook of Political Communication Research*, edited by L.L. Kaid, 203–34. Mahwah, N.J.: Lawrence Erlbaum, 2004.

McKrum, John. "The True Functions of Government." *The Commercial Review* 4 (1) (September 1847): 95–106.

McNair, Brian. *An Introduction to Political Communication*. London: Routledge, 1995.

McWilliams, Cary. "Government by Whitaker and Baxter: The Triumph of Chrome-Plated Publicity." *The Nation*, April 14, 21, May 5, 1951.

Madison, James, Alexander Hamilton, and James Jay. *The Federalist Papers*, edited by Issac Kramnick. London: Penguin, 1987.

Magleby, David B., ed. *The Other Campaign: Soft Money and Issue Advocacy in the 2000 Congressional Elections*. Lanham, MD: Rowman & Littlefield, 2002.

Magleby, David B., Kelly D. Patterson, and James A. Thurber. "Campaign Consultants and Responsible Party Government." In *Responsible Partisanship? The Evolution of American Political Parties Since 1950*, edited by John C. Green and Paul S. Herrnson, 101–23. Lawrence, KS: University Press of Kansas.

Magleby, David B., J. Quin Monson, and Kelly D. Patterson, eds. *Electing Congress: New Rules for an Old Game*. Upper Saddle River, N.J.: Prentice-Hall, 2007.

Maharey, Steve. "Labour—An Historic Third Term." In *The Baubles of Office: The New Zealand General Election of 2005*, edited by Stephen Levine and Nigel S Roberts, 97–104. Wellington: Victoria University Press, 2007.

Maisel, L. Sandy. *Parties and Elections in America: The Electoral Process*. Third edition. Lanham, MD: Rowman & Littlefield, 1999.

Maisel, L. Sandy, Cherie Maestas, and Walter J. Stone. "The Party Role in Congressional Competition." In *The Parties Respond: Changes in American Parties and Campaigns*, edited by L. Sandy Maisel. Fourth edition, 121–38. Boulder, CO: Westview Press, 2002.

Maksimov, A.A. *"Chistye" i "gryaznye" tekhnologii vyborov: Rossiiskii opyt*. Moscow: Delo, 1999.

Malbin, Michael J., ed. *The Election after Reform: Money, Politics, and the Bipartisan Campaign Reform Act*. Lanham, MD: Rowman & Littlefield, 2006.

Malkin, E. and E. Suchkov. *Osnovy izbiratel'nykh tekhnologii*. Third edition. Moscow: Russkaya Panorama, 2002.

Maltese, John Anthony. *Spin Control: The White House Office of Communications and the Management of Presidential News*. Chapel Hill, N.C.: University of North Carolina Press, 1992.

Mancini, Paolo. "New Frontiers in Political Professionalism." *Political Communication* 16 (3) (July 1999): 231–45.

Mann, Thomas and Anthony Corrado, eds. *The New Campaign Finance Source Book*. Washington, D.C.: The Brookings Institution, 2005.

Mann, Thomas and Norman Ornstein, eds. *The Permanent Campaign and Its Future*. Washington, D.C.: The Brookings Institution, 2000.

Mapes, Mary. *Truth and Duty*. New York: St Martin's Press, 2005.

Marcus, George E. and Michael B. MacKuen. "Anxiety, Enthusiasm, and the Vote: The Emotional Underpinnings of Learning and Involvement during Presidential Campaigns." *American Political Science Review* 87 (September 1993): 672–85.

Markusen, Ann, Peter Hall, Scott Campbell, and Sabina Deitrick. *The Rise of the Gunbelt: The Military Remapping of Industrial America*. New York, Oxford, 1991.

Marland, Alex. "Marketing Political Soap: A Political Marketing View of Selling Candidates Like Soap, of Electioneering as a Ritual, and of Electoral Military Analogies." *Journal of Public Affairs* 3 (2) (2003): 103–115.

Marmor-Lavie, Galit and Gabriel Weimann. "Measuring Emotional Appeals in Israeli Election Campaigns." *International Journal of Public Opinion Research* 18 (3) (Autumn 2006): 318–39.

Márquez, Jesús Silva-Herzog. *El antiguo régimen y la transición en México*. México, Distrito Federal: Planeta/Joaquín Mortiz, 1999.

Martel, Myles. *Political Campaign Debates: Images, Strategies, Tactics*. New York: Longman, 1983.

Martin, Edward Winslow. *Behind the Scenes in Washington: Being a Complete and Graphic Account of the Credit Mobilier Investigation*. Philadelphia, PA: Continental Publishing Co. and National Publishing Co., 1873.

Martin, Paul S. "Inside the Black Box of Negative Campaign Effects: Three Reasons Why Negative Campaigns Mobilize." *Political Psychology* 25 (August 2004): 545–62.

Martinez-Pandiani. "La Irrupcion del Marketing Politico en las Campanas Electorales de America Latina." *Contributiones* XVII (2) (2000): 69–102.

Masket, Seth. "The Emergence of Unofficial Party Organizations in California." *Spectrum: The Journal of State Politics* 75 (3) (Fall 2002).

May, R.J. "Elections in the Philippines 1986–1987." *Electoral Studies* 7 (1) (1988): 79–81.

Mayer, Kenneth R. *The Political Economy of Defense Contracting*. New Haven, CT: Yale University Press, 1991.

Mayer, William G. "In Defense of Negative Campaigning." *Political Science Quarterly* 111 (Fall 1996): 450.

——. "The Swing Voter in American Presidential Elections." *American Politics Research* 35 (3) (May 2007): 358–88.

Mayer, William G. and Andrew E. Busch. *The Frontloading Problem in Presidential Nominations*. Washington, D.C.: Brookings Institution Press, 2004.

Mayhew, David. *Congress: The Electoral Connection*. New Haven, CT: Yale University Press, 1974.

Mazur, Allan. "Commentary: Opinion Poll Measurement of American Confidence in Science." *Science, Technology & Human Values* 6 (36) (Summer 1981): 106–15.

Mazzoleni, Gianpietro. "TV Political Advertising in Italy: When Politicians are Afraid." In *The Sage Handbook of Political Advertising*, edited by L.L. Kaid and C. Holtz-Bacha, 241–57. Thousand Oaks, CA: Sage, 2006.

Mazzoleni, Gianpietro and Winfried Schulz. " 'Mediatization' of Politics: A Challenge for Democracy?" *Political Communication* 16 (1999): 247–61.

Medvic, Stephen K. "Campaign Organization and Political Consultants." In *Guide to Political Campaigns in America*, edited by P.S. Herrnson, 162–75. Washington, D.C.: CQ Press, 2005.

——. *Political Consultants in U.S. Congressional Elections*. Columbus: Ohio State University Press, 2001.

——. "Professional Political Consultants: An Operational Definition." *Politics* 23 (2003): 119–27.

——. "Professionalization in Congressional Campaigns." In *Campaign Warriors*, edited by J.A. Thurber and C.J. Nelson, 91–109. Washington, D.C.: The Brookings Institution, 2000.

——. "Understanding Campaign Strategy: 'Deliberate Priming' and the Role of Professional Political Consultants." *Journal of Political Marketing* 5 (1/2) (2006): 18–19.

Medvic, Stephen K. and David A. Dulio. "The Permanent Campaign in the White House: Evidence from the Clinton Administration." *White House Studies* 4 (3) (2004): 301–17.

Medvic, Stephen and Silvo Lenart. "The Influence of Political Consultants in the 1992 Congressional Elections." *Legislative Studies Quarterly* 22 (February 1997): 61–77.

Meier, Dominik, Erhardt Fiebiger, and Alex Föller, "Einspruch—Ein Aktionsbündnis mobilisiert den Mittelstand." In *Kampagne! 3 Neue Strategien im Grassroots Lobbying für Unternehmen und Verbände*, edited by Marco Althaus, 346–82. Münster and Berlin: Lit.

Meirick, Patrick. "Cognitive Responses to Negative and Comparative Political Advertising." *Journal of Advertising* XXXI (2002): 49–62.

Melchert, Florian, Fabian Magerl, and Mario Voigt, eds. *In der Mitte der Kampagne: Grassroots und Mobilisierung im Bundestagswahlkampf* 2005. Berlin: Poli-c Books, 2006.

Mende Fernandez, Maria Belen. *Campanas Electorales. La Modernizacion en Latinoamerica*. Mexico City: Editorial Trillas, 2003.

Mendelsohn, Harold and Irving Crespi. *Polls, Television, and the New Politics*. Scranton, PA: Chandler Publishing Company, 1970.

Mendilow, Jonathan. "Party Clustering in Multi-Party Systems: The Example of Israel 1965–1981." *American Journal of Political Science* 27 (1) (February 1983): 64–85.

——. "Public Campaign Funding and Party System Change: The Israeli Experience." *Israel Studies Forum* 19 (Fall 2003): 115–23.

Mendoza, Daniel J. "Dependence or Self-reliance? The Philippine NGO Experience." *Philippine Political Science Journal* 19 (39–42) (1995–1998): 143–172.

Mendras, Marie. "How Regional Elites Preserve Their Power." *Post-Soviet Affairs* 15 (4) (1999): 295–311.

Menefee-Libey, David. *The Triumph of Campaign-centered Politics*. New York: Chatham House, 2000.

Merritt, S. "Negative Political Advertising." *Journal of Advertising* 13 (1984): 27–38.

Meyer, Frank S. *In Defense of Freedom: A Conservative Credo*. Chicago, IL: H. Regnery Co., 1962.

Meyer, Lorenzo. *El Espejismo Democrático, de la euforia del cambio a la continuidad*. México, Distrito Federal: Editorial Océano, 2007.

Michels, Robert. *Political Parties: A Sociological Study of the Oligarchical Tendencies of Modern Democracies*. New York: Free Press, 1911.

Mickelson, Sig. *From Whistle Stop to Sound Bite*. New York: Praeger, 1989.

Mickiewicz, Ellen. *Changing Channels: Television and the Struggle for Power in Russia*. Second edition. Durham, N.C./London: Duke University Press, 1999.

Micklethwait, John and Adrian Wooldridge, *The Right Nation*. New York: Penguin Books, 2004.

Miller, Arthur H. "Political Issues and Trust in Government: 1964–1970." *The American Political Science Review* 68 (3) (September 1974): 951–72.

Miller, William L. *Media and Voters: The Audience, Content and Influence of Press and Television at the 1987 General Election*. Oxford: Clarendon, 1991.

Mills, Stephen. *The New Machine Men*. Ringwood: Penguin, 1986.

Miroshnichenko, A.A. *Vybory: ot zamysla do pobedy (Predvybornaya kampaniya v rossiiskom regione)*. Moscow: Tsentr, 2003.

Miskin, Sarah. "Campaigning in the 2004 Federal Election: Innovations and Traditions." *Research Note* No. 30, 2004–2005 (February 2005). Canberra: Parliamentary Library of Australia.

Miskin, Sarah and Richard Grant. "Political Advertising in Australia." *Research Brief No. 5*, Parliamentary Library of Australia, November 2004.

Mitchell, A. *Election '45: Reflections on the Revolution in Britain*. London: Bellew/Fabian Society, 1995.

Mitchell, Greg. *The Campaign of the Century: Upton Sinclair's Race for Governor of California and the Birth of Media Politics*. New York: Random House, 1992.

Mockabee, Stephen T., Michael Margolis, Stephen Brooks, Rick Farmer, and John C. Green. "The Battle for Ohio: The 2004 Presidential Campaign." In *Dancing without Partners*, edited by D.B. Magleby, J.Q. Monson, and K.D. Patterson, 135–62. Lanham, MD: Rowman & Littlefield, 2006.

Moen, Matthew. "The Changing Nature of Christian Right Activism." In *Sojourners in the Wilderness*, edited by C. Smidt and J. Penning, 21–40. Lanham, MD: Rowman & Littlefield, 1997.

Moloney, K. "Government and Lobbying Activities." In *Public Relations: Principles and Practice*, edited by Philip J. Kitchen, 84–101. London: Thompson Learning, 2000.

Moncrief, Gary. "Candidate Spending in State Legislative Races." In *Campaign Finance in State Legislative Elections*, edited by Joel A. Thompson and Gary F. Moncrief, 37–58. Washington, D.C.: CQ Press, 1998.

Monson, J. Quin and Stephanie Perry Curtis. "Appendix B—Methodology." In *eSymposium: The Noncandidate Campaign: Soft Money and Issue Advocacy in the 2002 Congressional Elections*. Washington, D.C.: American Political Science Association, 2003.

Montinola, Gabriela R. "Parties and Accountability in the Philippines." *Journal of Democracy* 10 (2) (1999): 126–40.

Moore, David W. *The Superpollsters: How They Measure and Manipulate Public Opinion in America*. New York: Four Walls Eight Windows, 1995.

Moore, Olga. *I'll Meet You in the Lobby*. Philadelphia, PA: J.B. Lippincott, 1949.

Moran, Jon. "Patterns of Corruption and Development in East Asia." *Third World Quarterly* 20 (3) (1999): 567–89.

Moreno, Alejandro. *El Votante Mexicano: Democracia, actitudes políticas y conducta electoral.* México, Distrito Federal: FCE, 2003.

Morris, Dick. The *New Prince: Machiavelli Updated for the Twenty-first Century.* Los Angeles, CA: Renaissance Books, 1999.

Müller, Marion G. "Wahlkampf à l'américan." In *Wahl-Kämpfe: Betrachtungen über ein demokratisches Ritual,* edited by Andreas Dörner and Ludgera Vogt, 187–210. Frankfurt am Main: Suhrkamp, 2002.

Münkel, Daniela. *Willy Brandt und die "Vierte Gewalt": Politik und Massenmedien in den 50er bis 70er Jahren.* Frankfurt: Campus, 2005.

Murray, Peter. *Winning from Within.* Washington, D.C.: Center for Progressive Leadership, 2006.

Murray, Shoon Kathleen. "Private Polls and Presidential Policymaking: Reagan as a Facilitator of Change." *Public Opinion Quarterly* 70 (4) (2006): 477–98.

Murray, Shoon Kathleen and Peter Howard. "Variation in White House Polling Operations: Carter to Clinton." *Public Opinion Quarterly* 66 (4) (2002): 527–58.

Napolitan, Joe. "Media Costs and Effects in Political Campaigns." *Annals of the American Academy of Political Science* 427 (1) (September 1976): 114–24.

———. *The Election Game and How to Win It.* Garden City, N.Y.: Doubleday, 1972.

Napolitan, Joe and Derek Hutcheson. "Vremya universalov ukhodit." *Sovetnik* 2 (98) (2004): 23–5.

Narver, John C. and Stanley F. Slater. "The Effect of a Market Orientation on Business Profitability." *Journal of Marketing* 54 (4): 20–35.

Narver, John C., Stanley F. Slater, and Brian Tietje. "Creating a Market Orientation." *Journal of Market-focused Management* 2 (3) (1998): 241–55.

Nassmacher, Karl-Heinz, ed. *Foundations for Democracy: Approaches to Comparative Political Finance.* Baden-Baden.: Nomos, 2001.

National Party Conventions 1831–2004. Washington, D.C.: CQ Press, 2005.

Negrine, Ralph and Stylianos Papathanassopoulos. "The 'Americanization' of Political Communication: A Critique." *Harvard International Journal of Press/Politics* 1 (2) (March 1996): 45–62.

Negrine, Ralph et al., eds. *The Professionalisation of Political Communication.* Chicago, IL: University of Chicago Press, 2007.

Nelson, Candice J., David A. Dulio, and Stephen K. Medvic, eds. *Shades of Gray: Perspectives on Campaign Ethics.* Washington, D.C.: Brookings Institution Press, 2002.

Nelson, Candice J., James A. Thurber, and David A. Dulio. "Portrait of Campaign Consultants." In *Campaign Warriors: Political Consultants in Elections,* edited by James A. Thurber and Candice J. Nelson, 10–36. Washington, D.C.: Brookings Institution Press, 2000.

Negrine, Ralph et al. "Political Communication in the Era of Professionalisation." In *The Professionalisation of Political Communication,* edited Ralph Negrine et al., 9–28. Chicago, IL: University of Chicago Press, 2007.

Nesbitt-Larking, Paul and Jonathan Rose. "Political Advertising in Canada." In *Lights, Camera, Campaign!,* edited by David A. Schultz, 273–99. New York: B&T, 2004.

Nesson, Charles and David Marglin. "The Day the Internet Met the First Amendment." *Harvard Journal of Law and Technology* 10 (1996): 113–35.

Newhagen, John E. and Byron Reeves. "Emotion and Memory Responses for Negative Political Advertising: A Study of Television Commercials Used in the 1988 Presidential Election." In *Television and Political Advertising,* edited by F. Biocca, 197–220. Hillsdale, N.J.: Lawrence Erlbaum, 1991.

Newman, Bruce I. "A Predictive Model of Voter Behavior: The Repositioning of Bill Clinton." In *Handbook of Political Marketing,* edited by Bruce I. Newman, 259–82. Thousand Oaks, CA: Sage, 1999.

———. "Image-manufacturing in the USA: Recent U.S. Presidential Elections and Beyond." *European Journal of Marketing* 35 (9) (2001): 966–70.

———, ed. *The Handbook of Political Marketing.* Thousand Oaks, CA: Sage Publications, 1999.

———. *The Marketing of the President: Political Marketing as Campaign Strategy.* Thousand Oaks, CA: Sage Publications, 1994.

———. *The Mass Marketing of Politics: Democracy in an Age of Manufactured Images.* Thousand Oaks, CA: Sage Publications, 1999.

Newman, Bruce I. and Jagdish N. Sheth. "A Model of Primary Voter Behavior." *Journal of Consumer Research* 12 (2) (1985): 178–87.

———. *A Theory of Political Choice Behavior.* New York: Praeger, 1987.

New Taiwan Cultural Foundation. *Lishi de ningjie: 1977–79 taiwan minzhu dongyun xiangshi [A Pictorial History of Taiwan's Opposition Movements 1977–79].* Taipei: Shibao Wenhua, 1999.

———. *Meiyou dangming de dang: meilidao zhengtuan de fazhan [The Party Without Name: The Development of Formosa]*. Taipei: Shibao Wenhua, 1998.

Newton, Jim. *Justice for All: Earl Warren and the Nation He Made*. New York: Riverhead Books, 2006.

Nickerson, David W. "Quality is Job One: Professional and Volunteer Voter Mobilization Calls." *American Journal of Political Science* 51 (April 2007): 269–82.

———. "Volunteer Phone Calls Can Increase Turnout: Evidence from Eight Field Experiments." *American Politics Research* 34 (May 2006): 271–92.

Nickerson, David W., Ryan D. Friedrichs, and David C. King. "Partisan Mobilization Campaigns in the Field: Results from a Statewide Turnout Experiment in Michigan." *Political Research Quarterly* 59 (March 2006): 85–97.

Niffenegger, Philip B. "Strategies for Success from the Political Marketers." *Journal of Services Marketing* 2 (3) (1988): 15–21.

Nimmo, Dan. "The Permanent Campaign: Marketing as a Governing Tool." In *Handbook of Political Marketing*, edited by Bruce I. Newman, 73–86. Thousand Oaks, CA: Sage, 1999.

———. *The Political Persuaders: The Techniques of Modern Election Campaigns*. Englewood Cliffs, N.J.: Prentice-Hall, 1970.

Nimmo, Dan and James E. Combs. *Mediated Political Realities*. Second edition. New York: Longman, 1990.

Nimmo, Dan and Keith R. Sanders. *Handbook of Political Communication*. Beverly Hills, CA: Sage Publications, 1981.

Niven, David. "The Limits of Mobilization: Turnout Evidence from State House Primaries." *Political Behavior* 23 (December 2001): 335–50.

———. "The Mobilization Calendar: The Time-Dependent Effects of Personal Contact on Turnout." *American Politics Research* 30 (May 2002): 307–22.

———. "The Mobilization Solution? Face-to-Face Contact and Voter Turnout in a Municipal Election." *Journal of Politics* 66 (August 2004): 868–84.

Nivola, Pietro S. and David W. Brady, eds. *Red and Blue Nation? Characteristics and Causes of America's Polarized Politics*. Washington, D.C.: Brookings Institution Press, 2006.

Nord, Lars W. "Still the Middle Way: A Study of Political Communication Practices in Swedish Election Campaigns." *Harvard International Journal of Press/Politics* 11 (1) (2006): 64–76.

Norris, John. *Artillery: A History*. Stroud: Sutton Publishing, 2000.

Norris, Pippa. *A Virtuous Circle: Political Communication in Postindustrial Societies*. New York: Cambridge University Press, 2000.

———. "Campaign Communications." In *Comparing Democracies 2*, edited by L. LeDuc, R.G. Niemi, and P. Norris, 127–47. Thousand Oaks, CA: Sage Publications, 2002.

———. "Do Campaign Communications Matter for Civic Engagement? American Elections from Eisenhower to G.W. Bush." In *Do Political Campaigns Matter?*, edited by D.M. Farrell and R. Schmitt-Beck, 127–44. London: Routledge, 2002.

———. *Electoral Change since 1945*. Oxford: Blackwell, 1997.

———. *Electoral Engineering. Voting Rules and Political Behavior*. New York: Cambridge University Press, 2004.

Novikova, A. *Izbiratel'nye prava grazhdan: Rossiya 2003*. Moscow: Moscow Helsinki Group, 2004.

Novotny, Patrick. "From Polis to Agora: The Marketing of Political Consultants." *Harvard International Journal of Press/Politics* 5 (3) (2000): 12–26.

Oates, Sarah. "A Spiral of Post-Soviet Cynicism: The First Decade of Political Advertising in Russia." In *The Sage Handbook of Political Advertising*, edited by L.L. Kaid and C. Holtz-Bacha, 309–24. Thousand Oaks, CA: Sage, 2006.

———. *Television, Democracy and Elections in Russia*. London/New York: RoutledgeCurzon, 2006.

Oates, Sarah and Laura Roselle. "State-Controlled and Commercial Television Channels. Russian Elections and TV News: Comparison of Campaign News." *Harvard International Journal of Press/Politics* 5 (2) (2000): 30–51.

O'Cass, Aron. "Political Marketing." *European Journal of Marketing* 35 (9/10) (2001): 1003–25.

———. "Political Marketing and the Marketing Concept." *European Journal of Marketing* 30 (10/11) (1996): 45–61.

———. "The Internal–External Orientation of a Political Party: Social Implications of Political Party Marketing Orientation." *Journal of Public Affairs* 1 (2) (2001): 136–52.

O'Collins, Frank. "Political and Fundraising Direct Mail." *Journal of the Australian Direct Mail Marketing Solution* 8 (3) (1992): 18–19.

Oldfield, Duane M. *The Right and the Righteous: The Christian Right Confronts the Republican Party*. Lanham— MD: Rowman & Littlefield, 1996.

Ormrod, Robert P. "A Conceptual Model of Political Market Orientation." In *Current Issues in Political*

Marketing, edited by Jennifer Lees-Marshment and Walter Wymer, 47–64. Binghampton, N.Y.: Haworth Press, 2005.

——. "A Critique of the Lees-Marshment Market-oriented Party Model." *Politics*, 26 (2) (2006): 110–18.

Ornstein, Norman J. and Thomas E. Mann, eds. *The Permanent Campaign and its Future*. Washington, D.C.: American Enterprise Institute and the Brookings Institution, 2000.

Ornstein, Norman J., Thomas E. Mann, and Michael J. Malbin. *Vital Statistics on Congress, 1997–1998*. Washington, D.C.: Congressional Quarterly Press, 1998.

OSCE/ODIHR. *Final Report on the Presidential Election 1996*. Moscow: OSCE, 1996.

——. *Russian Federation: Elections to the State Duma, 7 December 2003. OSCE/ODIHR Election Observation Mission Report*. Warsaw: OSCE/ODIHR, 2004.

O'Shaughnessy, Nicholas J. "America's Political Market." *European Journal of Marketing* 21 (4) (1987): 60–6.

——. "High Priesthood, Low Priestcraft: The Role of Political Consultants." *European Journal of Marketing* 24 (2) (1990): 7–23.

——. *Politics and Propaganda: Weapons of Mass Seduction*. Manchester: University of Manchester Press, 2004.

——. *The Phenomenon of Political Marketing*. New York: St Martin's Press, 1990.

——. "Towards an Ethical Framework for Political Marketing." *Psychology & Marketing* 19 (12) (2002): 1092–3.

Overloot, Hans and Ruben Verheul. "The Party of Power in Russian Politics." *Acta Politica* 35 (2000): 123–45.

Panagopoulos, Costas. "Political Consultants, Campaign Professionalization and Media Attention." *PS: Political Science and Politics* 39 (October 2006): 867–9.

Panarin, Igor' Nikolaevich. *Informatsionnaya voina: pobeda v Bashkirii*. Moscow: Gorodets, 2004.

Panebianco, Angelo. *Political Parties: Organization and Power*. Cambridge: Cambridge University Press, 1988.

Parton, James. "The Pressure Upon Congress." *The Atlantic Monthly* 25 (148) (February 1870): 156.

Patterson, James T. *Grand Expectations*. New York: Oxford University Press, 1996.

Patterson, Thomas E. *Doing Well and Doing Good: How Soft News and Critical Journalism are Shrinking the News Audience and Weakening Democracy—and What News Outlets Can Do About It*. Cambridge, MA: Joan Shorenstein Center on the Press, Politics and Public Policy, Harvard University, 2000.

——. *The Mass Media Election: How Americans Choose their President*. New York: Praeger, 1980.

——. *Out of Order*. New York: Knopf, 1993.

Patterson, Thomas E. and Robert D. McClure. *The Unseeing Eye: The Myth of Television Power in National Politics*. New York: G.P. Putnam's Sons, 1976.

Paz, Octavio. *El ogro filantrópico*. Barcelona: Seix Barral, 1979.

Pearce, Edward. *Machiavelli's Children*. London, Victor Gollancz, 1993.

Pearson, John and Graham Turner. *The Persuasion Industry: British Advertising and Public Relations in Action*. London: Eyre & Spottiswoode, 1965.

Peck, Helen, Adrian Payne, Martin Christopher, and Moira Clark. *Relationship Marketing: Strategy and Implementation*. Oxford: Elsevier Butterworth-Heinemann, 1999.

Peng, Ming-min. *A Taste of Freedom: Memoirs of a Formosan Independence Leader*. Third edition. Taipei: Taiwan Publishing, 2005.

Peng, Yun. *Xin meijie yu zhengzhi: lilun yu shizheng [New Media and Politics: Theories and Practice]*. Taipei: Wunan, Taipei, 2001.

Pennington, N. and Hastie, R. "A Theory of Explanation-based Decision Making." In *Decision Making in Action: Models and Methods*, edited by C. Klein et al., 188–204. Norwood N.J.: Ablex, 1993.

Peri, Yoram. *Telepopulism: Media and Politics in Israel*. Stanford, CA: Stanford University Press, 2004.

Perron, Louis. "Internationale Wahlkampfberatung." In *Handbuch Politikberatung*, edited by S. Falk et al., 300–14. Wiesbaden: VS Verlag, 2006.

Perry, James M. *The New Politics: The Expanding Technology of Political Manipulation*. New York: Clarkson N. Potter, Inc., 1968.

Peterson, David A.M. and Paul A. Djupe, "When Primary Campaigns Go Negative: The Determinants of Campaign Negativity." *Political Research Quarterly* 58 (March 2005): 45–54.

Petracca, Mark P. "Introduction." In *The Politics of Interests: Interest Groups Transformed*, edited by Mark P. Petracca. Boulder, CO: Westview Press, 1992.

——. "Political Consultants and Democratic Governance." *PS: Science and Politics* 22 (1) (March 1989): 11–14.

——, ed. *The Politics of Interests: Interest Groups Transformed*. Boulder, CO: Westview Press, 1992.

Petrocik, John R. "Issue Ownership in Presidential Elections, with a 1980 Case Study." *American Journal of Political Science* 40 (August 1996): 826.

Petrocik, John R., William L. Benoit, and Glenn J. Hansen. "Issue Ownership and Presidential Campaigning, 1952–2000." *Political Science Quarterly* 118 (Winter 2003): 599–626.

Pfau, Michael and Michael Burgoon. "Inoculation in Political Campaign Communication." *Human Communication Research* 15 (1988): 91–111.

——. "The Efficacy of Issue and Character Attack Message Strategies in Political Campaign Communication." *Communication Research Reports* 2 (1989): 52–61.

Pfau, Michael and Henry C. Kenski. *Attack Politics: Strategy and Defense*. New York: Praeger Publishers, 1990.

Pfau, Michael, Roxanne Parrott, and Bridget Lindquist. "An Expectancy Theory Explanation of the Effectiveness of Political Attack Television Spots: A Case Study." *Journal of Applied Communication Research* 20 (1992): 235–53.

Pfau, Michael et al. "Issue-advocacy Versus Candidate Advertising: Effects on Candidate Preferences and Democratic Process." *Journal of Communication* 52 (2002): 301–15.

Pfetsch, Barbara. "Political Communication Culture in the United States and Germany." *Harvard International Journal of Press/Politics* 6 (1) (2001): 46–67.

Pinkleton, Bruce E. "Effects of Print Political Comparative Advertising on Political Decision-making and Participation." *Journal of Communication* 48 (1998): 24–36.

——. "The Effects of Negative Comparative Political Advertising on Candidate Evaluations and Advertising Evaluations: An Exploration." *Journal of Advertising* XXVI (1997): 19–29.

Pinto-Duschinsky, Michael. "Financing Politics: A Global View." *Journal of Democracy* 13 (4) (2006): 69–86.

Pitchell, Robert J. "The Influence of Professional Campaign Management Firms in Partisan Elections in California." *Western Political Quarterly* 11 (1958): 278–300.

Pitney, John J., Jr *The Art of Political Warfare*. Norman, Okla.: University of Oklahoma Press, 2000.

Plamenatz, John P. *Man and Society*. London: Longman, 1970.

Plasser, Fritz. "American Campaign Techniques Worldwide." *Harvard International Journal of Press/Politics* 5 (4) (2000): 33–54.

——. "Par et Impar: Wahlkommunikation in den USA und Europa im Vergleich." In *Medien und Kommunikationsforschung im Vergleich*, edited by Juergen Wilke et al. Wiesbaden: VS Verlag, 2008.

——. "Parties' Diminishing Relevance for Campaign Professionals." *Harvard International Journal of Press/Politics* 6 (4) (2001): 44–59.

——. "Political Consultant." In *The Oxford International Encyclopedia of Communication*, edited by Wolfgang Donsbach. Oxford: Oxford University Press, 2008.

——. "Selbstverständnis strategischer Politikberater." In *Handbuch Politikberatung*, edited by S. Falk et al., 343–53. Wiesbaden: VS Verlag, 2006.

Plasser, Fritz with Gunda Plasser. *Global Political Campaigning: A Worldwide Analysis of Campaign Professionals and Their Practices*. Westport, CT: Praeger, 2002.

Plasser, Fritz, Christian Scheucher, and Christian Senft. "Is There a European Style of Political Marketing?" In *The Handbook of Political Marketing*, edited by Newman, 89–112. Thousand Oaks, CA: Sage Publications, 1999.

Pocheptsov, G.G. *Imidzh & vybory*. Kiev: ADEF-Ukraina, 1997.

Poen, Monte M. *Harry S. Truman Versus the Medical Lobby: The Genesis of Medicare*. Columbia, MO: University of Missouri Press, 1979.

Pollock, James K. "The Regulation of Lobbying." *American Political Science Review* 21 (2) (May 1927): 336–7.

Polsby, Nelson W. and Aaron Wildavsky. *Presidential Elections: Strategies and Structures of American Politics*. Twelfth edition. Lanham, MD: Rowman & Littlefield, 2008.

Pomper, Gerald M. "The Presidential Election: The Ills of American Politics After 9/11." In *The Election of 2004*, edited by Michael Nelson, 42–68. Washington, D.C.: CQ Press, 2005.

Popkin, Samuel L. *The Reasoning Voter: Communication and Persuasion in Presidential Campaigns*. Chicago, IL: University of Chicago Press, 1991.

Porto, Mauro, P. "Framing Controversies: Television and the 2002 Presidential Election in Brazil." *Political Communication* 24 (1) (2007): 19–36.

——. "Political Advertising and Democracy in Brazil." In *The Sage Handbook of Political Advertising*, edited by L.L. Kaid and C. Holtz-Bacha, 129–44. Thousand Oaks, CA: Sage, 2006.

——. "Trends in Brazilian Election News Coverage." Paper presented at the Annual Conference of the International Communication Association (ICA), San Francisco, May 2007.

Postelnicu, Monica, Justin D. Martin, and Kristen D. Landreville. "The Role of Campaign Web Sites in Promoting Candidates and Attracting Campaign Resources." In *The Internet Election: Perspectives on the Web in Campaign 2004*, edited by Andrew Paul Willliams and John C. Tedesco, 99–110. Lanham, MD: Rowman & Littlefield, 2006.

Potter, Trevor and Kirk Jowers. "Speech Governed by Federal Elections Laws." In *The New Campaign Finance Source Book*, edited by Thomas Mann and Anthony Corrado, 5–20. Washington, D.C.: The Brookings Institution, 2005.

Preston, Julia and Samuel Dillon. *Opening Mexico: The Making of a Democracy*. New York: Farrar, Straus & Giroux, 2004.

Priess, Frank. "Ein Wahlkampf der besonderen Art." *Die Politische Meinung* 431 (October 2005): 10.

Priess, Frank and Fernando Tuesta Soldevilla, eds. *Campanas Electorales y Medios de Communicacion en America Latina*. 2 vols. Buenos Aires: Editorial Trillas, 1999.

Putnam, Robert D. *Bowling Alone: The Collapse and Revival of American Community*. New York: Simon and Schuster, 2001.

Quilop, Raymund Jose G. "Waltzing with the Army: From Marcos to Arroyo." *Kasarinlan Philippine Quarterly of Third World Studies* 16 (2) (2001): 91–104.

Quimpo, Nathan G. "Back to War in Mindanao: The Weaknesses of a Power-based Approach in Conflict Resolution." *Philippine Political Science Journal* 21 (44) (2000): 99–126.

Quintos de Jesus, Melinda and Luis V. Teodoro. *Citizens' Media Monitor: A Report on the Campaign and Elections Coverage in the Philippines*. Manila: Center for Media Freedom and Responsibility, 2004.

Rademacher, Eric W. and Alfred J. Tuchfarber. "Preelection Polling and Political Campaigns." In *Handbook of Political Marketing*, edited by Bruce I. Newman, 197–221. Thousand Oaks, CA: Sage, 1999.

Rahat, Gideon and Tamir Sheafer. "The Personalization(s) of Politics: Israel, 1949–2003." *Political Communication* 24 (1) (2007): 65–80.

Ram, Uri. "Citizens, Consumers and Believers: The Israeli Public Sphere between Capitalism and Fundamentalism." *Israel Studies* 3 (1) (Spring 1998): 24–44.

Rampton, Sheldon and John Stauber. *Banana Republicans*. New York: Penguin Group, 2004.

——. *Weapons of Mass Deception: The Uses of Propaganda in Bush's War on Iraq*. New York: Tarcher/Penguin, 2003.

Rapoport, Ronald, Kelly L. Metcalf, and John Hartman. "Candidate Traits and Voter Inferences: An Experiental Study." *Journal of Politics* 51 (4) (November 1989): 917–32.

Raymond, Jack. *Power at the Pentagon*. New York: Harper & Row, 1964.

Reeves, Peter, Leslie de Chernatony, and Marylyn Carrigan. "Building a Political Brand: Ideology or Voter-driven Strategy." *Brand Management* 13 (6) (2006): 424–5.

Reichley, A James. *The Life of the Parties: A History of American Political Parties*. New York: The Free Press, 1992.

Reid, Ben. *Philippine Left: Political Crisis and Social Change*. Manila/Sydney: Journal of Contemporary Asia Publishers, 2000.

Resnick, D. "Politics on the Internet: The Normalization of Cyberspace." In *The Politics of Cyberspace*, edited by C. Toulouse and T. Luke, 48–68. New York: Routledge, 1998.

Reynolds, Andrew et al., eds. *Electoral System Design: The New International IDEA Handbook*. Stockholm: IDEA, 2005.

Rheingold, Howard. *Smart Mobs: The Next Social Revolution*. Cambridge, MA: Perseus Publishing, 2002.

Rich, Andrew. *War of Ideas*. Stanford, CA: Stanford Social Innovation Review, 2005.

Riesman, David, *The Lonely Crowd: A Study of the Changing American Character*. New York: Doubleday Anchor, 1953.

Ritter, Kurt and Martin J. Medhurst, eds. *Presidential Speechwriting: From the New Deal to the Reagan Revolution and Beyond*. College Station, TX: Texas A&M University Press, 2003.

Rivera, Temario C. "Transition Pathways and Democratic Consolidation in Post-Marcos Philippines." *Contemporary Southeast Asia* 24 (3) (2002): 466–83.

Robb, Andrew. "The Liberal Campaign." In *The Politics of Retribution*, edited by Clive Bean, Marian Simms, Scott Bennett, and John Warhurst. Sydney: Allen and Unwin, 1997.

——. "Images of the 2005 Campaign." In *The Baubles of Office: The New Zealand General Election of 2005*, edited by Stephen Levine and Nigel S. Roberts, 180–96. Wellington: Victoria University Press, 2007.

Rocamora, Joe. *Breaking Through: The Struggle within the Communist Party of the Philippines*. Pasig, Metro Manila: Anvil, 1994.

Roces, Mina. *Kinship Politics in Post-war Philippines: The Lopez Family 1946–2000*. Malate, Manila : De La Salle University Press, 2001.

——. *Women, Power, and Kinship Politics: Female Power in Post-war Philippines*. Westport, CT: Praeger, 1998.

Roddy, Brian L. and Gina M. Garramone. "Appeals and Strategies of Negative Political Advertising," *Journal of Broadcasting & Electronic Media* 32 (1988): 415–27.

Rodell, Paul. *Culture and Customs of the Philippines*. Westport, CT: Greenwood Press, 2002.

Rood, Stephen. "Elections as Complicated and Important Events in the Philippines." In *How Asia Votes*, edited by John Hsieh Fuh-sheng and David Newman, 147–64. New York: Chatham House, 2002.

Rose, Richard. *Influencing Voters: A Study of Campaign Rationality*. London: Faber & Faber, 1967.

Rose, Richard, Neil Munro, and Stephen White. "Voting in a Floating Party System: The 1999 Duma Election." *Europe-Asia Studies* 53 (3) (2001): 419–43.

Rosenbloom, David L. *The Election Men: Professional Campaign Managers and American Democracy*. New York: Quandrangle Books, 1973.

Rothschild, Michael. "Political Advertising: A Neglected Policy Issue in Marketing." *Journal of Marketing Research* 15 (1978): 58–71.

Rothschild, Michael T. and Michael L. Ray. "Involvement and Political Advertising Effect: An Exploratory Experiment." *Communication Research* 1 (1974): 264–85.

Rozell, Mark J. "Growing Up Politically: The New Politics of the New Christian Right." In *Sojourners in the Wilderness*, edited by C. Smidt and J. Penning, 235–48. Lanham, MD: Rowman & Littlefield, 1997.

Rozell, Mark J. and Clyde Wilcox. *God at the Grassroots: The Christian Right in the 1994 Elections*. Lanham— MD: Rowman & Littlefield, 1995.

——, eds. *God at the Grassroots 1996: The Christian Right in American Elections*. Lanham, MD: Rowman & Littlefield, 1997.

——, eds. *Second Coming: The New Christian Right in Virginia Politics*. Baltimore, MD: Johns Hopkins University Press, 1996.

Rozell, Mark J., Clyde Wilcox, and John C. Green, "Religious Constituencies and Support for the Christian Right in the 1990s." *Social Science Quarterly* (December 1998): 815–20.

Rudd, Chris. "Marketing the Message or the Messenger? The New Zealand Labour Party, 1990–2003." In *Political Marketing*, edited by D.G. Lilleker and J. Lees-Marshment 79–96. Manchester: Manchester University Press, 2005.

Ruland, Jurgen. "Continuity and Change in Southeast Asia: Political Participation in Three Intermediate Cities." *Asian Survey* 30 (5) (1990): 461–80.

Rye, Ranjit Singh. "E-governance in the Philippines: Insights for Policy-making." *Kasarinlan Philippine Quarterly of Third World Studies* 17 (2) (2002): 101–38.

Sabato, Larry J. *The Rise of Political Consultants: New Ways of Winning Elections*. New York: Basic Books, 1981.

Sackett, William E. *Modern Battles of Trenton: Volume One*. Trenton, N.J.: J.L. Murphy, 1895.

Sackman, A. "The Learning Curve Towards New Labour: Neil Kinnock's Corporate Party 1983–1992." *European Journal of Marketing* 30 (10/11) (1996): 147–58.

Saletan, William. *Bearing Right*. Berkeley, CA: University of California Press, 2003.

Salmin, A.M., ed. *Politicheskoe konsul'tirovanie*. Special edition. *Politiya* 2 (12) (1999).

Samuel, R. "Dr. Abrams and the End of Politics." *New Left Review* 5 (September 1960): 2–9.

Sanaev, A. *Vybory v Rossii: Kak eto delaetsya*. Moscow: Os'-89, 2005.

Scammell, Margaret. *Designer Politics: Political Marketing and Communication*. New York: St Martin's Press, 1995.

——. "Political Marketing: Lessons for Political Science." *Political Studies* 47 (4) (1999): 718–39.

——. "The Wisdom of the War Room: U.S. Campaigning Winning Elections." Research paper R-17. Harvard University: The Joan Shorenstein Center on the Press, Politics and Public Policy.

Schafferer, Christian, ed. *Election Campaigning in East and Southeast Asia: Globalization of Political Marketing*. Aldershot: Ashgate, 2006.

——. "Electoral Campaigning in Taiwan." In *Election Campaigning in East and Southeast Asia*, edited by C. Schafferer, 29–54. Aldershot: Ashgate, 2006.

——. "Is There an Asian Style of Electoral Campaigning?" In *Election Campaigning in East and Southeast Asia*, edited by C. Schafferer, 103–40. Aldershot: Ashgate, 2006.

——. "Political Parties and Electoral Politics in Taiwan." In *Understanding Modern East Asian Politics*, edited by Christian Schafferer. New York: Nova Science, 2005.

Schattschneider, E.E. *The Semi-Sovereign People: A Realist's View of Democracy in America*. New York: Holt, Rinehart, and Winston, 1960.

Schenck-Hamlin, William J., David E. Procter, and Deborah J. Rumsey. "The Influence of Negative Advertising Frames on Political and Politician Accountability." *Human Communication Research* 26 (2000): 53–74.

Schendelen, Rinus van. *Machiavelli in Brussels: The Art of Lobbying the EU*. Amsterdam: Amsterdam University Press, 2005.

Scheufele, Dietram A. "Framing as a Theory of Media Effects." *Journal of Communication* 49 (1999): 103–22.

Schlesinger, Arthur M., Jr. *The Cycles of American History*. Boston, MA: Houghton Mifflin, 1986.

Schmitt-Beck, Rüdiger. "New Modes of Campaigning." In *The Oxford Handbook of Political Behavior*, edited by R.J. Dalton and H.-D.Klingemann, 744–64. Oxford: Oxford University Press, 2007.

Schmitt-Beck, Rüdiger and David M. Farrell. "Studying Political Campaigns and Their Effects." In *Do Political Campaigns Matter?*, edited by D.M. Farrell and R. Schmitt-Beck, 1–21. London: Routledge, 2002.

Schoen, Douglas E. *The Power of the Vote: Electing Presidents, Overthrowing Dictators, and Promoting Democracy Around the World.* New York: HarperCollins, 2007.

Schrag, Peter. *Paradise Lost: California's Experience, America's Future.* New York: The New Press, 1998.

Schriftgiesser, Karl. *The Lobbyists: The Art and Business of Influencing Lawmakers.* Boston, MA: Little, Brown, 1951.

Schudson, Michael. "Social Origins of Press Cynicism in Portraying Politics." *American Behavioral Scientist* 42 (6) (1999): 998–1008.

Schulz, Winfried. "Wahlkampf unter Vielkanalbedingungen." *Media Perspektiven* 8 (1998): 378–91.

Schulz, Winfried and Reinmar Zeh. "Changing Campaign Coverage of German Television. A Comparison of Five Elections 1990–2005." Paper presented at the Annual Conference of the International Communication Association (ICA), San Francisco, May 2007.

Schumpeter, Joseph. *Capitalism, Socialism and Democracy.* London: Urwin, 1943.

Schütz, Klaus. *Logenplatz und Schleudersitz.* Frankfurt: Ullstein, 1992.

Schwartz, Mildred A. *The Party Network: The Robust Organization of Illinois Republicans.* Madison, WI: University of Wisconsin Press, 1989.

Schwartz, Tony. *The Responsive Chord.* New York: Anchor Press/Doubleday, 1973.

Schwartzman, Edward. *Campaign Craftsmanship.* New York: Universe Books, 1972.

Scott, Robert. *Mexican Government in Transition.* Urbana, IL: University of Illinois Press, 1959.

Scroggs, Stephen K. *Army Relations with Congress: Thick Armor, Dull Sword, Slow Horse.* Westport, CT: Praeger, 2000.

Searls, Doc and David Weinberger. "Markets Are Conversations." In *The ClueTrain Manifesto: The End of Business as Usual,* edited by C. Locke, R. Levine, D. Searls, and D. Weinberger. Cambridge, MA: Perseus Publishing, 2000.

Sellers, Patrick J. "Strategy and Background in Congressional Campaigns." *American Political Science Review* 92 (March 1998): 159–71.

Selnow, Gary W. *High-tech Campaigns: Computer Technology in Political Communication.* Westport, CT: Praeger, 1994.

Semetko, Holli A. "Political Balance on Television: Campaigns in the United States, Britain and Germany." *Harvard International Journal of Press/Politics* 1 (1) (1996): 51–71.

Semetko, Holli A. et al. *The Formation of Campaign Agendas: A Comparative Analysis of Party and Media Roles in Recent American and British Elections.* Hillsdale, N.J.: Erlbaum, 1991.

Severino, Howie G. and Sheila S. Coronel. *Patrimony: Six Case Studies on Local Politics and the Environment in the Philippines.* Pasig, Metro Manila: Philippine Center for Investigative Journalism, 1996.

Shahar, Roni. *A Leader Made to Measure.* Tel-Aviv: Yediot Ahronot, 2001. (In Hebrew.)

Shama, Avraham. "Applications of Marketing Concepts to Candidate Marketing." *Advances in Consumer Research* 2 (1) (1975): 793–801.

——. "The Marketing of a Political Candidate." *Journal of the Academy of Marketing Sciences* 4 (1976): 764–77.

Shapira, Yonatan. *Society Under Politicians' Power.* Tel-Aviv: Hapoalim Library, 1996. (In Hebrew.)

Shaw, Catherine. *The Campaign Manager: Running and Winning Local Elections.* Third edition. Boulder, CO: Westview, 2004.

Shaw, Daron R. "A Study of Presidential Campaign Event Effects from 1952 to 1992." *Journal of Politics* 61 (May 1999): 387–422.

——. "The Effect of TV Ads and Candidate Appearances on Statewide Presidential Votes, 1988–96." *American Political Science Review* 93 (June 1999): 345–61.

——. "The Methods behind the Madness: Presidential Electoral College Strategies, 1988–1996." *Journal of Politics* 61 (November 1999): 893–913.

Shaw, Daron R. and Brian E. Roberts. "Campaign Events, the Media and the Prospects of Victory: The 1992 and 1996 U.S. Presidential Elections." *British Journal of Political Science* 30 (2) (April 2000): 262.

Shaw, Eric. *The Labour Party Since 1979: Crisis and Transformation.* London, Routledge, 1994.

Shea, Daniel M. and Michael John Burton. *Campaign Craft: The Strategies, Tactics, and Art of Political Campaign Management.* Third edition. Westport, CT: Praeger, 2006. (Second edition, 2001.)

Shea, Michael. *Influence: How to Make the System Work for You: A Handbook for the Modern Machiavelli.* London: Century, 1998.

Shen, Fuyuan and H. Denis Wu. "Effects of Soft-money Issue Advertisements on Candidate Evaluations and Voting Preference: An Exploration," *Mass Communication & Society* 5 (2002): 295–410.

Shiv, B. and A. Fredorikhin. "Heart and Mind in Conflict: the Interplay of Affect and Cognition in Consumer Decision Making." *Journal of Consumer Research* 26 (1999): 278–92.

Sides, John. "The Consequences of Campaign Agendas." *American Politics Research* 35 (July 2007): 465–88.
——. "The Origins of Campaign Agendas." *British Journal of Political Science* 36 (July 2006): 407–36.

Sigelman, Lee and Emmett H. Buell, Jr. "Avoidance or Engagement? Issue Convergence in U.S. Presidential Campaigns, 1960–2000." *American Journal of Political Science* 48 (October 2004): 650–61.

——. "You Take the High Road and I'll Take the Low Road? The Interplay of Attack Strategies and Tactics in Presidential Campaigns." *Journal of Politics* 65 (May 2003): 518–31.

Sigelman, Lee and Mark Kugler. "Why Is Research on the Effects of Negative Campaigning so Inconclusive? Understanding Citizens' Perceptions of Negativity." *Journal of Politics* 65 (February 2003): 142–60.

Silberman, Michael. "The Meetup Story." In *Mousepads, Shoe Leather, and Hope*, edited by Z. Teachout and T. Streeter, 110–29. Boulder, CO: Paradigm Publishers, 2007.

Simon, Adam F. *The Winning Message: Candidate Behavior, Campaign Discourse, and Democracy*. Cambridge: Cambridge University Press, 2002.

Skaperdas, Stergios and Bernard Grofman. "Modeling Negative Campaigning." *American Political Science Review* 89 (March 1995): 49–61.

Skillen, Daphne. "Russia." In *The Media and Elections*, edited by Bernd-Peter Lange and David Ward, 123–43. Mahwah, N.J.: Erlbaum, 2004.

Slater, Stanley F. and John C. Narver. "Customer-led and Market-oriented: Let's not Confuse the Two." *Strategic Management Journal* 19 (1998): 1001–6.

——. "Does Competitive Environment Moderate the Market Orientation-Performance Relationship?" *Journal of Marketing* 58 (1) (January 1994): 46–55.

——. "Market-oriented is More than Being Customer-led." *Strategic Management Journal* 20 (1999): 1165–8.

Smith, Daniel. "String Attached: Outside Money in Colorado's Seventh District." In *The Last Hurrah? Soft Money and Issue Advocacy in the 2002 Congressional Elections*, edited by David Magleby and J. Quin Monson, 191–207. Washington, D.C.: Brookings Institution Press, 2004.

Smith, Gareth. "Positioning Political Parties: The 2005 UK General Election." *Journal of Marketing Management* 21 (9) (2005): 1139–44.

——. "The 2001 General Election: Factors Influencing the Brand Image of Political Parties and their Leaders." *Journal of Marketing Management* 17 (2001): 989–1006.

Smith, Gareth and John Saunders. "The Application of Marketing to British Politics." *Journal of Marketing Management* 5 (3) (1990): 295–306.

Smith, Hedrick. *The Power Game: How Washington Works*. New York: Ballantine Books, 1988.

Smorgunov, L.G. *Politicheskii menedzhment: elektoral'nyi protsess i tekhnologii*. St Petersburg: St Petersburg University Press, 1999.

Smyth, Regina. *Candidate Strategies and Electoral Competition in the Russian Federation. Democracy without Foundation*. New York: Cambridge University Press, 2006.

Sonner, Brenda S. "The Effectiveness of Negative Political Advertising: A Case Study." *Journal of Advertising Research* 38 (1998): 37–42.

Sorensen, Theodore C. *Kennedy*. New York: Harper & Row, 1965.

Sorokina, Elena. *Kommunikatsiya v period izbiratel'noi kampanii: Keis stadis*. Moscow: Avanti, 2003.

Spencer, Thomas. "The External Environment of Public Affairs in the European Union and the United Kingdom: Public Policy Process and Institutions." In *The Handbook of Public Affairs*, edited by Phil Harris and Craig S. Fleisher. London: Sage, 2005.

Spiliotes, Constantine J. and Lynn Vavreck. "Campaign Advertising: Paritsan Convergence or Divergence?" *Journal of Politics* 64 (February 2002): 249–61.

Sroka, T. Neil. *Understanding the Political Influence of Blogs*. Washington, D.C.: George Washington University, Institute for Politics Democracy & the Internet.

Starr, Oliver. "Mobile Communication Technology: An Overview of the Industry, Its Players and Its Disruptive Potential." In *The Politics-to-Go Handbook: A Guide to Using Mobile Technology in Politics*. Washington, DC: Institute for Politics, Democracy & the Internet, 2005.

Starr, Paul. "What Happened to Health Care Reform?" *The American Prospect* 20 (Winter 1995): 20–31.

Stewart, Julianne. "Political Advertising in Australia and New Zealand." In *The Sage Handbook of Political Advertising*, edited by L.L. Kaid and C. Holtz-Bacha, 269–84. Thousand Oaks, CA: Sage, 2006.

Stevens, Daniel. "Separate and Unequal Effects: Information, Political Sophistication and Negative Advertising." *Political Research Quarterly* 58 (September 2005): 413–26.

Straubhaar, Joseph et al. "What Makes News: Western, Socialist, and Third-World Television Newscasts Compared in Eight Countries." In *Mass Media Effects Across Cultures*, edited by Felipe Korzenny and Stella Ting-Toomey, 89–109. Newbury Park, CA: Sage, 1992.

Street, John. *Politics and Technology*. New York: The Guilford Press, 1992.

Sulkin, Tracy and Jillian Evans. "Dynamics of Diffusion: Aggregate Patterns in Congressional Campaign Agendas." *American Politics Research* 34 (July 2006): 505–34.

Surlin, Stuart H. and Thomas F. Gordon. "Selective Exposure and Retention of Political Advertising." *Journal of Advertising* 5 (1976): 32–44.

Sussmann, Gerald. *Global Electioneering. Campaign Consulting, Communications, and Corporate Financing.* Lanham, MD: Rowman & Littlefield, 2005.

Sussman, Gerald and Lawrence Galizio. "The Global Reproduction of American Politics." *Political Communication* 20 (3) (2003): 309–28.

Swanson, David and Paolo Mancini. "Introduction." In *Politics, Media and Modern Democracy: An International Study of Innovations in Electoral Campaigning*, eds. David Swanson and Paolo Mancini, 1–26. Westport, CT: Praeger, 1996.

——. "Patterns of Modern Electoral Campaigning and Their Consequences." In *Politics, Media and Modern Democracy: An International Study of Innovations in Electoral Campaigning and their Consequences*, edited by David Swanson and Paolo Mancini, 247–96. Westport, CT: Praeger, 1996.

——, eds. *Politics, Media, and Modern Democracy: An International Study of Innovations in Electoral Campaigning and their Consequences.* Westport, CT: Praeger, 1996.

Tabunda, Ana Maria L., Glenda M. Gloria, and Carmela S. Fonbuena. *Spin and Sell: How Political Ads Shaped the 2004 Elections.* Makati City: Foundation for Communication Initiatives and the Konrad Adenauer Foundation, 2004.

Tak, Jinyoung. "Political Advertising in Japan, South Korea, and Taiwan." In *The Sage Handbook of Political Advertising*, edited by Lynda Lee Kaid and Christina Holtz-Bacha, 285–305. Thousand Oaks, CA: Sage, 2006.

Tanner, Hudson C. *"The Lobby" and Public Men From Thurlow Weed's Time.* Albany, N.Y.: George MacDonald, 1888.

Tapscott, Don and David Ticoll. *The Naked Corporation: How the Age of Transparency will Revolutionize Business.* New York: Free Press, 2003.

Tau, B. and R. Navo. "An Adman in the Electoral Pan." *Otot* (1981): 12–23. (In Hebrew.)

Taylor, A. " 'The Record of the 1950s is Irrelevant': The Conservative Party, Electoral Strategy and Opinion Research, 1945–64." *Contemporary British History* 17 (2003): 81–110.

Taylor, Paul. *Gouging Democracy: How the Television Industry Profiteered on Campaign 2000.* Washington, D.C.: Alliance for Better Campaigns, 2001.

Teachout, Zephyr and Thomas Streeter, eds. *Mousepads, Shoe Leather, and Hope: Lessons from the Howard Dean Campaign for the Future of Internet Politics.* Boulder, CO: Paradigm Publishers, 2007.

Tedesco, John C. "Changing the Channel: Use of the Internet for Communicating about Politics." In *The Handbook of Political Communication Research*, edited by L.L. Kaid, 507–32. Mahwah, N.J.: Lawrence Erlbaum, 2004.

——. "Televised Political Advertising Effects: Evaluating Responses During the 2000 Robb–Allen Senatorial Election." *Journal of Advertising* 31 (1992): 37–48.

Tedesco, John C. and Lynda Lee Kaid. "Style and Effects of the Bush and Gore Spots." In *The Millennium Election*, edited by L.L. Kaid et al., 5–16. Lanham, MD: Rowman & Littlefield, 2003.

Teehankee, Julio C. "Emerging Dynasties in the Post-Marcos House of Representatives." *Philippine Political Science Journal* 22 (45) (2001): 55–78.

Tenpas, Kathryn Dunn. "The American Presidency: Surviving and Thriving amidst the Permanent Campaign." In *The Permanent Campaign and its Future*, edited by N.J. Ornstein and T.E. Mann, 108–33. Washington, D.C.: American Enterprise Institute and the Brookings Institution, 2000.

Tenpas, Kathryn D. and James McCann. "Testing the Permanence of the Permanent Campaign: An Analysis of Presidential Polling Expenditures, 1977–2002." *Public Opinion Quarterly* 71 (3) (2007): 349–66.

Terhorst, Stephan. "Das NRWin-Team—Die Unterstützerkampagne im NRW-Landtagswahlkampf." In *In der Mitte der Kampagne: Grassroots und Mobilisierung im Bundestagswahlkampf 2005*, edited by Florian Melchert, Fabian Magerl, and Mario Voigt, 65–73. Berlin: Poli-c Books, 2006.

Theilmann, John and Allen Wilhite. "Campaign Tactics and the Decision to Attack." *Journal of Politics* 60 (November 1998): 1050–62.

Thomas, Evan and *Newsweek* staff. *Election 2004.* New York: Public Affairs, 2004.

Thomas, Lately. *Sam Ward: "King of the Lobby."* Boston, MA: Houghton Mifflin, 1965.

Thompson, Margaret Susan. *The "Spider Web": Congress and Lobbying in the Age of Grant.* Ithaca, N.Y.: Cornell University Press, 1985.

Thompson, Mark R. "Female Leadership of Democratic Transitions in Asia." *Pacific Affairs* 75 (4) (2002): 535–55.

——. "Off the Endangered List: Philippine Democratization in Comparative Perspective." *Comparative Politics* 28 (2) (1996): 179–205.

Thorson, Esther, William G. Christ, and Clarke Caywood. "Effects of Issue-image Strategies, Attack and Support Appeals, Music, and Visual Content in Political Commercials." *Journal of Broadcasting & Electronic Media* 35 (1991): 465–86.

———. "Selling Candidates Like Tubes of Toothpaste: Is the Comparison Apt?" In *Television and Political Advertising*, edited by F. Biocca, 145–72. Hillsdale, N.J.: Lawrence Erlbaum, 1991.

Thurber, James. A. and Candice. J. Nelson, eds. *Campaigns and Elections American Style*. Boulder, CO: Westview Press, 1995.

———, eds. *Campaign Warriors: The Role of Political Consultants in Elections*. Washington, D.C.: The Brookings Institution, 2000.

Thurber, James A., Candice J. Nelson, and David A. Dulio. *Crowded Airwaves: Campaign Advertising in Elections*. Washington, D.C.: Brookings Institution Press, 2000.

———. "Portrait of Campaign Consultants." In *Campaign Warriors: The Role of Political Consultants in Elections*, edited by J.A. Thurber and C.J. Nelson, 10–36. Washington, D.C.: Brookings Institution Press, 2000.

Tichenor, Daniel J. and Richard A. Harris. "The Development of Interest Group Politics in America: Beyond the Conceits of Modern Times." *Annual Review of Political Science* 8 (2005): 253.

Tien, Hung-mao. "Elections and Taiwan's Democratic Development." In *Taiwan's Electoral Politics and Democratic Transition: Riding the Third Wave*, edited by Charles Chi-Hsiang, Robert A. Scalapino, and Hung-mao Tien. New York: M. E. Sharpe, 1997.

Timberman, David G. *A Changeless Land: Continuity and Change in Philippine Politics*. Armonk, N.Y.: M.E. Sharpe, Institute of Southeast Asian Studies, 1991.

Tinkham, Spencer F. and Ruth Ann Weaver Lariscy. "A Diagnostic Approach to Assessing the Impact of Negative Political Television Commercials." *Journal of Broadcasting & Electronic Media* 37 (1993): 377–400.

Titley, Simon. "How Political Change Will Transform the EU Public Affairs Industry." *Journal of Public Affairs* 3 (1) (2002): 83–9.

Tocqueville, Alexis de. *Democracy in America*, trans. George Lawrence. New York: Harper Collins, 2000. (1976 edition, edited by Phillips Bradley, New York: Alfred A. Knopf.)

Torgovnik, Efraim. "Strategies under a New Electoral System: The Labor Party in the 1996 Elections." *Party Politics* 6 (1) (January 2000): 95–106.

Trent, Judith and Robert Friedenberg. *Political Campaign Communication: Principles and Practices*. Sixth edition. Lanham, MD: Rowman & Littlefield, 2007.

Trinidad, Arnie C. "An Initial Assessment of the Philippines' Preparedness for E-learning." *Kasarinlan Philippine Quarterly of Third World Studies* 17 (2) (2002): 167–92.

Trippi, Joe. *The Revolution Will Not Be Televised: Democracy, the Internet, and the Overthrow of Everything*. New York: ReganBooks, 2004.

Troy, Gill. *See How They Ran: The Changing Role of the Presidential Candidate*. New York: The Free Press, 1991.

Truman, David B. *The Governmental Process: Political Interests and Public Opinion*. New York: Alfred A. Knopf, 1951.

Tsuladze, Avrandil. *Bol'shaya manipulyativnaya igra*. Moscow: Algoritm, 2000.

Tuchkov, S.M. "Faktory legitimnosti politicheskikh tekhnologii: 'Legitimnost'' i 'legalnost' politicheskikh tekhnologii." *Vestnik Moskovoskogo Universiteta*, Series 12 (Political Science) 2 (2002): 8–14.

Ubertaccio, Peter. "Machine Politics for the Twenty-first Century? Multilevel Marketing and Party Organizations." In *The State of the Parties. The Changing Role of Contemporary American Politics*, edited by J.C. Green and D.J. Coffey, 173–84. Lanham, MD: Rowman & Littlefield, 2007.

Valentino, Nicholas A., Vincent L. Hutchings, and Dmitri Williams. "The Impact of Political Advertising on Knowledge, Internet Information Seeking, and Candidate Preference." *Journal of Communication* 54 (2004): 337–54.

Valenzuela, Sebastián and Maxwell McCombs. "Agenda-setting effects on vote choice: Evidence from the 2006 Mexican election." Paper presented at the Conference of the International Communication Association, San Francisco, May 2007.

Van Noy, Carolyn M. "The City of Seattle and Campaign Finance Reform: A Case Study." *Public Integrity* II (IV) (Fall 2000): 303–16.

Van Onselen, Peter and Wayne Errington. "Electoral Databases; Big Brother or Democracy Unbound?" *Australian Journal of Political Science* 39 (2) (2004): 349–66 and *The Age*, August 29, 1996.

Vargo, S.L. and R.F. Lusch. "Evolving to a New Dominant Logic for Marketing." *Journal of Marketing* 68 (1) (2004): 1–17.

Vavreck, Lynn. "How Does it All 'Turnout'? Exposure to Attack Advertising, Campaign Interest, and Participation in American Presidential Elections." In *Campaign Reform*, edited by L.M. Bartels and L. Vavreck, 79–105. Ann Arbor, MI: University of Michigan Press, 2000.

Verba, Sidney, Kay Lehman Schlozman, and Henry E. Brady. *Voice and Equality: Civic Voluntarism in American Politics*. Cambridge, MA: Harvard University Press, 1995.

Villegas, Daniel Cosio. *La sucesión presidencial*. México, Distrito Federal: Joaquín Mortiz, 1975.

Vinacke, Harold M. "Post-war Government and Politics of the Philippines." *The Journal of Politics* 9 (4) (1947): 717–30.

Vollmer, Rafael Aranda. *Poliarquías Urbanas: competencia electoral en las ciudades y zonas metropolitanas de México*. México, Distrito Federal: Ed. Porrua e IFE, 2004.

Waisboard, Silvio. "Practicas y Precios del Proselitismo Presidential: Apuntes Sobre Medios y Campanas Electorales en America Latina y Estados Unidos." *Contribuciones* 2 (1997): 159–82.

Wald, Kenneth. *Religion and Politics in the United States*. Fourth edition. Lanham, MD: Rowman & Littlefield, 2003.

Wallas, Graham. *Human Nature in Politics*. London: Constable, 1908.

Wallis, Jim. *God's Politics: Why the Right Gets It Wrong and the Left Doesn't Get It*. New York: HarperOne, 2005.

Wang, Chen-huan and Yong-hsiang Chian. "Yuxiang xinguojia? Mincuiweiquan zhuyi de xingcheng yu minzhuwenti" ["March Towards a New Nation State? The Rise of Populist Authoritarianism in Taiwan and its Implication for Democracy"]. *Taiwan: A Radical Quarterly in Social Studies* 20 (August 1995): 17–55.

Wang, Sijun and Lenard C. Huff. "Explaining Buyers' Responses to Sellers' Violation of Trust." *European Journal of Marketing* 41 (9/10) (2007): 1033–52.

Wang, Tian-yuan. *Taiwan xinwen chuanboshi [The Evolution of Mass Communication in Taiwan]*. Taipei: Yatai, 2002.

Wang, Tian-bin. *Xinwen ziyou [Freedom of the Press]*. Taipei: Yatai, 2005.

Ward, Ian. "Cartel Parties and Elections in Australia." In *Political Parties in Transition?*, edited by Ian Marsh. Annadale: Federation Press, 2003.

——. " 'Localising the National:' The Rediscovery and Reshaping of Local Campaigning in Australia." *Party Politics* 9 (5) (2003): 583–600.

Ware, Alan. *The Breakdown of Democratic Party Organization, 1940–1980*. Oxford: Clarendon Press, 1988.

Ware, B.L. and Wil A. Linkugel. "They Spoke in Defense of Themselves: On the Generic Criticism of Apologia." *Quarterly Journal of Speech* 59 (1973): 273–83.

Warhurst, John. "The ALP Campaign." In *Australian Votes*, edited by Ian McAllister and John Warhurst. Melbourne: Longman Cheshire, 1987.

Warhurst, John and Andrew Parkin. "The Labor Party: Images, History and Structure." In *The Machine*, edited by John Warhurst and Andrew Parkin. Sydney: Allen & Unwin, 2000.

Wark, McKenzie. *A Hacker Manifesto*. Cambridge, MA: Harvard University Press, 2004.

Warren, Donald. *Radio Priest: Charles Coughlin, the Father of Hate Radio*. New York: The Free Press, 1996.

Wattenberg, Martin P. and Craig L. Brians. "Negative Campaign Advertising: Demobilizer or Mobilizer?" *American Political Science Review* 93 (1999): 891–9.

Weaver, David, Maxwell McCombs, and Donald L. Shaw. "Agenda-Setting Research: Issues, Attributes, and Influences." In *The Handbook of Political Communication Research*, edited by L.L. Kaid, 257–82. Mahwah, N.J.: Lawrence Erlbaum, 2004.

Webb, Paul and Robin Kolodny. "Professional Staff in Political Parties." In *Handbook of Party Politics*, edited by R.S. Katz and W.J. Crotty, 337–47. Thousand Oaks, CA: Sage Publications, 2006.

Webster, Wendy. *Not a Man to Match Her: The Marketing of a Prime Minister*. London: The Women's Press, 1990.

Weimann, Gabriel and Gadi Wolfsfeld. "The 2001 Elections: The Election Propaganda that Made No Difference." In *The Elections in Israel 2001*, edited by Asher Arian and Michal Shamir. Jerusalem: The Israel Democracy Institute, 2002.

Weissman, Steve and Ruth Hassan. "527 Groups and BCRA." In *The Election after Reform: Money, Politics, and the Bipartisan Campaign Reform Act*, edited by Michael Malbin. Lanham, MD: Rowman & Littlefield Publishers, 2005.

West, Darrell M. *Air Wars. Television Advertising in Election Campaigns, 1952–2004*. Fourth edition. Washington D.C.: CQ Press, 2005.

West, Darrell, Diane Heath, and Chris Goodwin. "Harry and Louise Go to Washington: Political Advertising and Health Care Reform." *Journal of Health Politics, Policy and Law* 21 (1996): 35–68.

West, Darrell and Burdett Loomis. *The Sound of Money: How Political Interests Get What They Want*. New York: W.W. Norton, 1998.

Westen, Drew. *The Political Brain: The Role of Emotion in Deciding the Fate of the Nation*. New York: Public Affairs, 2007.

621

White, Jon and Laura Mazur. *Strategic Communications Management: Making Public Relations Work*. Reading, MA: Addison-Wesley, 1994.

Whiteley, Paul and Patrick Seyd. "Party Election Campaigning in Britain: the Labour Party." *Party Politics* 9 (5) (2003): 641–2.

Wielhouwer, Peter W. "Grassroots Mobilization." In *The Electoral Challenge*, edited by S.C. Craig, 163–82. Washington, D.C.: CQ Books, 2006.

Wielhouwer, Peter W. and Brad Lockerbie. "Party Contacting and Political Participation, 1952–90." *American Journal of Political Science* 38 (February 1994): 211–29.

Wiesendahl, Elmar. "Strategische Hintergründe und Konsequenzen der CDU/CSU-Niederlage bei den Bundestagswahlen 2002." *Forschungsjournal Neue Soziale Bewegungen* 16 (1) (January 2003): 72–3.

Wilcox, Clyde. *God's Warriors: The Christian Right in 20th Century America*. Baltimore, MD: Johns Hopkins University Press, 1992.

Wilcox, Clyde and Carin Larson, *Onward Christian Soldiers: Religious Right in American Politics*. Third edition. Boulder, CO: Westview Press, 2006.

Wilcox, Clyde, Rachel Goldberg, and Ted G. Jelen. "Full Pews, Musical Pulpits: The Christian Right at the Turn of the Millenium." *The Public Perspective* (May/June 2000): 36–9.

Wilcox, Clyde, Mark J. Rozell, and John C. Green. "The Meaning of the March: A Direction for Future Research." In *The Christian Right in American Politics*, edited by J.C. Green, M.J. Rozell, and C. Wilcox, 277–80. Washington, D.C.: Georgetown University Press, 2004.

Wilcox, Clyde, Mark J. Rozell, and Roland Gunn, "Religious Coalitions in the New Christian Right." *Social Science Quarterly* 77 (September 1996): 543–58.

Wilke, Juergen and Carsten Reinemann. "Do the Candidates Matter? Long-term Trends of Campaign Coverage—A Study of the German Press since 1949." *European Journal of Communication* 16 (3) (2001): 291–314.

Williams, Pamela. *The Victory*. Sydney: Allen & Unwin, 1997.

Wilson, Andrew. *Virtual Politics*. New Haven, CT: Yale University Press, 2005.

Wilson, Douglas L. *Lincoln's Sword: The Presidency and the Power of Words*. New York: Knopf, 2006.

Wind, Yoram. "Issues and Advances in Segmentation Research." *Journal of Marketing Research* 15 (3) (1978): 317–37.

Windlesham, Lord. *Communication and Political Power*. London: Jonathan Cape, 1966.

Witko, Christopher. "Explaining Increases in the Stringency of State Campaign Finance Regulation, 1993–2002." *State Politics and Policy Quarterly* 7 (4) (Winter 2007): 369–93.

Wlezien, Christopher and Robert S. Erikson. "The Timeline of Presidential Election Campaigns." *Journal of Politics* 64 (4) (November 2002): 969–93.

Wolak, Jennifer. "The Consequences of Presidential Battleground Strategies for Citizen Engagement." *Political Research Quarterly* 59 (September 2006): 353–61.

Wolin, Sheldon S. *Politics and Vision*. Boston, MA: Little, Brown, 1960.

Wood, N. "Introduction in Niccolo Machiavelli." In *The Art of War*, iii–xxv. New York: De Capo Press, 1965.

Woodward, Bob. *The Agenda: Inside the Clinton White House*. New York: Simon & Schuster, 1994.

Wootton, Graham. *Interest Groups: Policy and Politics in America*. Englewood Cliffs, N.J.: Prentice-Hall, 1985.

——. *Pressure Groups in Britain, 1720–1970*. Hamden, CT: Archon, 1975.

Worcester, Nancy. "Hormone Replacement Therapy (HRT): Getting to the Heart of the Politics of Women's Health?" *NWSA Journal* 16 (3) (Fall 2004): 56–69.

Wring, Dominic. "Conceptualising Political Marketing: A Framework for Election-Campaign-Analysis." In *The Idea of Political Marketing*, edited by N.J. O'Shaughnessy and S.C.M. Henneberg, 171–85. New York: Praeger, 2002.

Wring, Dominic. "Political Marketing and Organisational Development: the Case of the Labour Party in Britain." *Cambridge Research Papers in Management Studies*, 1995 series, No.12.

——. "Political Marketing and Party Development in Britain: A 'Secret' History." *European Journal of Marketing* 30 (10–11) (1996): 92–103.

——. "Power as Well as Persuasion: Political Communication and Party Development." In *Political Communication Transformed*, edited by John Bartle and Dylan Griffiths, 34–52, Basingstoke: Macmillan-Palgrave, 2001.

——. "Reconciling Marketing with Political Science: Theories of Political Marketing." In *Proceedings of the 1997 Academy of Marketing Conference*. Manchester Metropolitan University, 1997.

——. "Reconciling Marketing with Political Science: Theories of Political Marketing." *Journal of Marketing Management* 13 (7) (1997): 651–63.

——. "The Labour Campaign." In *Britain Votes 2005*, edited by Pippa Norris and Christopher Wlezien, 56–68. Oxford: Oxford University Press, 2005.

——. *The Politics of Marketing the Labour Party*. Basingstoke: Palgrave, 2005.

Wüst, Andreas M. et al. "Candidates in the 2005 Bundestag Election: Mode of Candidacy, Campaigning and Issues." *German Politics* 15 (4) (2006): 420–38.

Yishai, Yael. "Bringing Society Back In: Post-cartel Parties in Israel." *Party Politics* 7 (6) (November 2001): 667–87.

Yorke, D.A. and Sean A. Meehan. "ACORN in the Political Marketplace." *European Journal of Marketing* 20 (8) (1986): 63–76.

Young, Lisa and Patrick Weller. "Political Parties and the Party System: Challenges for Effective Governing." In *Institutions on the Edge*, edited by Michael Keating, John Wanna, and Patrick Weller, 156–77. Sydney: Allen & Unwin, 2000.

Young, Sally. "Spot On: The Role of Political Advertising in Australia." *Australian Journal of Political Science* 37 (1) (2002): 81–98.

——. *The Persuaders*. Sydney: Pluto Press, 2004.

Young Fabian Group. *The Mechanics of Victory*, February 1962.

Young, Sally. "Killing Competition: Restricting Access to Political Communication Channels in Australia." *AQ: Journal of Contemporary Analysis* 75 (3) (2003): 9–15.

Zamora-Roldan, Divina Gracia M. "Bridging the Local Digital Divide: The Barangay.Net Project." *Kasarinlan Philippine Quarterly of Third World Studies* 17 (2) (2002): 293–310.

Zeigler, Harmon. *Interest Groups in American Society*. Englewood Cliffs, N.J.: Prentice-Hall, 1964.

Zhukov, Konstantin and Aleksandr Karnyshev, *Azbuka izbiratelnoi kampanii*. Moscow: IMA-Press, 2001.

Zisk, Betty H. *Money, Media and the Grass Roots: State Ballot Issues and the Electoral Process*. Newbury Park, CA: Sage Publications, 1987.

Zvonovsky, Vladimir. "Administrativnyi resurs: variant ischisleniya obema." *Monitoring obshchestvennogo mneniya* 1 (45): 35–7.

Index